HARVARD GUIDE TO

AMERICAN

HISTORY

Oscar Handlin

Arthur Meier Schlesinger

Samuel Eliot Morison

Frederick Merk

Arthur Meier Schlesinger, Jr.

Paul Herman Buck

THE BELKNAP PRESS

of HARVARD UNIVERSITY PRESS

CAMBRIDGE · MASSACHUSETTS · 1966

Copyright 1954 by the President and Fellows of Harvard College

Fifth Printing

Distributed in Great Britain by
Oxford University Press, London

Designed by Burton J. Jones, Jr.

Printed in the United States of America

Library of Congress Catalog Card Number 53–5066

TO THE MEMORY OF

EDWARD CHANNING

ALBERT BUSHNELL HART

FREDERICK JACKSON TURNER

WHO BLAZED THE WAY

PREFACE

The development of scientific history and the spread of formal historical instruction in the closing decades of the nineteenth century created the need for a manual that would introduce readers to the evolving methods and growing literature of the historical discipline. In 1896, Albert Bushnell Hart and Edward Channing prepared such a guide, drawing upon their experience in teaching at Harvard and presenting a concise and lucid introduction to American history down to 1865. The popularity of this guide led to a revision in 1912 in which Hart and Channing were joined by Frederick Jackson Turner, who had recently arrived from the University of Wisconsin. Channing, Hart, and Turner's *Guide to the Study and Reading of American History* brought the subject down to 1910 and remained a standard reference volume for many years. Several generations of students and scholars have testified to its continuing usefulness; and it still retains an essential position on the desk of historians.

The *Guide* in its second form was never revised. The first world war, the pressure of other duties, and the ultimate dissolution of the triumvirate by retirement and death prevented that. Some twenty years ago the publisher's stock of the volume was exhausted and the book went out of print. Since then there has been a continuous demand within the profession for a new work to replace the old. That demand led to the sponsorship of this volume under the direction of the Department of History of Harvard University.

The four decades since the publication of the Channing, Hart, and Turner manual have seen enormous changes in the character of American historical writing. The output of the past forty years has been depressingly abundant. The shelf of the American Historical Association's *Writings in American History* is evidence of the volume and variety of scholarship in the American field. The editors' task was therefore not so much one of simple compilation as of rigorous selection among the items most useful for present-day needs. Furthermore, the subject itself has spread in directions scarcely foreseen four decades ago; and that spread has created an obligation to make room for such new interests as social and intellectual history. Finally, the audience has changed. Channing, Hart, and Turner addressed readers who were just beginning to know their own past, who worked in universities or lived in communities with inadequate libraries, and who had no other reference tools at hand. The present editors have attempted to devise a manual useful to readers who have been through schools and colleges in which American history was well taught, who have available the resources of numerous excellent libraries, and who find special bibliographies at their finger tips in almost every monograph.

In general, the editors have attempted to construe American history in its widest sense, and to find' a place in the *Guide* for both the old and new areas of historical studies. They have attempted to assimilate the findings of recent scholarship, and yet to remember that in many cases older books still retain their value — sometimes even more value than the newer ones. Finally, the editors have attempted to maintain a balance between useful sections of general works available in all libraries, and learned monographs that will interest few except the specialist. References are as specific as is likely to be helpful. With occasional exceptions, December 31, 1950 has been the terminal date for publications.

In executing these tasks we realize we have often been compelled to work in fields in which many of our colleagues in the profession are far more expert. In spite of ready assistance from many specialists, a work of this scope is certain to contain errors of omission and commission. We will be grateful if these are called to our attention for correction in later editions.

As to the general scope of the work a paragraph may be quoted from the preface to the first edition: "The immense mass of rich material on American history cannot be condensed into a single volume; and doubtless much has been omitted that ought to go in, or inserted that might well be left out. . . . However, the plan of the work does not admit of complete bibliographical information on any topic. It has been our endeavor to select out of the available material that likely to be most immediately useful to the searcher into political, social, constitutional, and economic history. For the antiquarian and the genealogist we have not been able to provide. We have, however, noted as many as possible of the more elaborate bibliographies, to serve as guides to more complete information."

This volume is addressed to the intelligent general reader, to the student, and to the scholar. For the first named, it will supply a thorough guide to the great body of literature of our country's past, and, for the student, a manual unlocking the methods and resources of American history. We hope also it may speed the scholar on his way. It will not, of course, take the place of the scholar's own investigations, but as a reference tool it may simplify his problems. Its selectivity, in this sense, will be an asset rather than a liability.

Our arrangement in its main outlines follows that of Channing, Hart, and Turner. The work falls into two main divisions. Chapters I–V consist of sixty-six essays dealing with the methods, resources, and materials of American history. These essays bring the reader and student the current techniques and sources of American history. To each of the essays is appended a list of relevant works for further investigation.

The second large division, Chapters V–XXX, consists of detailed reading lists arranged with reference to historical periods. Each is prefaced with a summary that outlines the topics treated, then proceeds to cite general and special works, as well as sources, maps, and relevant bibliographies. Wherever useful, references are to pages and chapters. Citations are to the best work and best edition — generally, though not always, the latest — for the purpose specified.

Works cited in this volume are given their full title and relevant bibliographical information only once, generally at the point of first mention. However, the *Guide* is fully indexed, and the reference to the full citation can always be located through the index. In the first eight chapters we have supplied complete bibliographical data. In the remainder of the volume necessities of space have forced us to abbreviate titles and data of publication.

In a few respects space limitations have led us to depart from the practice of the older guide. After the first citation of a work, we have omitted the initials of authors, except in cases in which, like Adams, Jones, and Smith, omission would be confusing. In cases of articles and passages from books, we have supplied the first but not the terminal pages, on the supposition that, told where to begin, most readers will themselves know where to stop. For similar reasons, we have not used the word *passim*, which is to be taken for granted where no page or chapter references are given.

We have not found it possible, or desirable, to impose absolute uniformity of concept and style on the various sections of the work. We have necessarily been guided by the state of the literature — which accounts for the fact that some sections have a higher proportion of articles and monographs than others; and that in the contemporary period it was not useful to draw as sharp a line between primary and secondary works as elsewhere.

Abbreviations are set forth in a table (p. xxiii). All bibliographical data supplied by the editors are enclosed in square brackets [ ].

The editors take joint responsibility for the whole work; but Oscar Handlin was especially interested in §§ 1, 4, 7, 8, 10, 16, 44–48, 54–57, 60–62, 150–188, 226–244, and coördinated the work of the various collaborators; A. M. Schlesinger was especially interested in §§ 2, 9, 11, 14, 15, 17, 18, 49–53, 58–59, 63–66, 189–225; S. E. Morison was especially interested in §§ 3, 12, 13, 26–32, 48, 54–56, 67–122; Frederick Merk was especially interested in §§ 14, 19–25, 33–43, 123–151; A. M. Schlesinger, Jr., was especially interested in §§ 5, 6, 245–277; and P. H. Buck shared the burdens of planning and criticism.

In the long course of preparation, we have profited by assistance from many sources. The project was made possible in part by gifts of friends of the Department, including Messrs. Robert W. Bliss, Stewart Mitchell, J. Duncan Phillips, Henry L. Shattuck, and the late Allyn Bailey Forbes, Francis Russell Hart, and Charles H. Taylor, Jr.; and in part by a grant from Harvard University. It could not have been carried to completion without the resources of the superb Harvard College Library, to the staff of which we are obliged for many helpful acts.

Our colleagues in the University provided never failing coöperation. We are particularly grateful to R. G. Albion, J. O. Brew, Otto Gombosi, C. H. Haring, W. L. Langer, K. B. Murdock, D. E. Owen, F. M. Palmer, Erwin Raisz, Alfred Tozzer, and A. P. Usher.

We are also grateful for the advice and assistance of numerous scholars outside the University. We must particularly acknowledge the aid of Ray A. Billington, Donald Born, Lyman H. Butterfield and the staff of the Institute of Early American History and Culture, Lawrence V. Coleman, J. H. Easterby, H. Bruce Fant, E. James Ferguson, Dumas Malone, Donald H. Mugridge, Charles R. Ritcheson, Albert B. Saye, R. H. Shryock, H. M. Silver, Culver H. Smith, Richard P. Sonderegger, and John K. Wright.

We profited from the help as research assistants of Ralph S. Bates, Francis G. Collier, William A. Davis, Sidney James, Jr., James R. Leiby, Robert A. Feer, and Judah Rubinstein.

W. E. Spaulding and H. B. McCurdy supplied the editors with useful technical assistance.

The very difficult manuscript was prepared by Elizabeth F. Hoxie, Antha E. Card, Julie Jeppson, Jean Juihn, Edith Caudill, Sue Gardner, Esther L. Andersen, and Marian S. Adams. Martha Rowland, Cynthia Ross, Dorothy Dean, Mary E. Beck, and Nancy Parkes aided in preparation of the index.

The final editorial preparation of copy profited from the skill of Katharine Strelsky. We are grateful also to the editorial staff of the Harvard University Press for the solution of many vexing problems.

Finally, through the whole course of compiling and publishing this volume, we have drawn heavily upon the devotion and ability of Mary F. Handlin.

We have undertaken this arduous task out of a sense of gratitude to the high achievement of American historians in bringing Americans a comprehension of our past. We hope, as we complete this volume, that it may stimulate higher achievement in the future. The *Guide* will best have served its purpose if it is quickly outdated by the writings of those who use it.

Oscar Handlin
Arthur Meier Schlesinger
Samuel Eliot Morison
Frederick Merk
Arthur Meier Schlesinger, Jr.
Paul Herman Buck

August 31, 1953

CONTENTS

4 AIDS TO HISTORICAL RESEARCH 105

5 HISTORICAL SOURCES 118

PART III

Colonial History and the Revolution, 1492–1788

6 FROM PREHISTORIC TIMES TO 1600 249

PART V

The Rise of Modern America, 1865–1900

19   LIQUIDATION OF THE CIVIL WAR, 1865–1880   401

20   ECONOMIC REVOLUTION, 1865–1880   410

21   NATIONAL POLITICS AND ECONOMIC TRENDS, 1880–1900   421

PART VI

America in the Twentieth Century

CONTENTS

ABBREVIATIONS

Ac.	Academy	Eve.	Evening
Ag.	Agriculture, Agricultural	esp.	especially
Am.	American	et al.	*et alii* (and others)
Antiq.	Antiquarian	Ex.	Executive
App.	Appendix	Feb.	February
Apps.	Appendices	Fla.	Florida
Arch.	Archeological, Archeology	Fol.	Folio
Ariz.	Arizona	Ga.	Georgia
Ark.	Arkansas	Geneal.	Genealogical
Assoc.	Association	Geog.	Geography, Geographies, Geographer
Atl.	Atlantic		
Balt.	Baltimore	Geol.	Geological
Bibliog.	Bibliographical	H.	House
Biog.	Biographical	Hist.	History, Historical
Biol.	Biology, Biological	Ia.	Iowa
Bk.	Book	*ibid.*	*ibidem* (in the same place)
Bull.	Bulletin	Ida.	Idaho
Bur.	Bureau	Ill.	Illinois
Bus.	Business	Ind.	Indiana
Calif.	California	Inst.	Institute
Cath.	Catholic	Int.	International
ch.	Chapter	intro.	Introduction
chs.	Chapters	Jan.	January
Chi.	Chicago	Jour.	Journal
Cin.	Cincinnati	Kan.	Kansas
Civ.	Civilization	La.	Louisiana
Cleve.	Cleveland	lect.	Lecture
Col.	Colonial	Mag.	Magazine
Coll.	Collections	Mar.	March
Colo.	Coloraᴅo	Mass.	Massachusetts
Comm.	Committee	Md.	Maryland
comp.	Compiler	Me.	Maine
Cong.	Congress	Med.	Medicine
Conn.	Connecticut	Mex.	Mexico
contribs.	contributions	Mich.	Michigan
Coun.	Council	Minn.	Minnesota
Dela.	Delaware	Misc.	Miscellaneous
Dept.	Department	Miss.	Mississippi
Doc.	Documents	Mo.	Missouri
Econ.	Economics	Mon.	Monday
ed.	Editor, Edition	MS.	Manuscript
eds.	Editors	N.	New
Educ.	Education	n.d.	no date
e.g.	*exempli gratia* (for example)	N.H.	New Hampshire
Eng.	England	N.J.	New Jersey

N.M.	New Mexico	sci.	science
n.p.	no place	sect.	section
N.Y.	New York	Sen.	Senate
Neb.	Nebraska	ser.	series
No. Car.	North Carolina	Sess.	Session
Okla.	Oklahoma	So. Car.	South Carolina
Ore.	Oregon	Soc.	Society, Social
p.	page	Sociol.	Sociology
Penn.	Pennsylvania	Stat.	Statistics, Statistical
Phila.	Philadelphia	Sun.	Sunday
Philos.	Philosophical	Suppl.	Supplement
Pitt.	Pittsburgh	Supt.	Superintendent
pl.	plate	surv.	survey
Pol.	political	Theol.	Theological
pp.	pages	tr.	translator
Proc.	Proceedings	trans.	transactions
Psych.	Psychological	transl.	translation, translated
pt., pts.	Part, parts	Univ.	University
Publ.	Publications	U.S.	United States
Quar.	Quarterly	Va.	Virginia
r.	revised	vol., vols.	volume, volumes
R.I.	Rhode Island	Vt.	Vermont
res.	research	W. Va.	West Virginia
Rev.	Review	Wash.	Washington
Sat.	Saturday	Wisc.	Wisconsin
Scand.	Scandinavian	W.P.A.	Works Progress Administration

CORRECTIONS

Page 568   *delete* Carson, W. C., *Early Graduate Educ.*, 213

Page 664   *delete* Shoepf, J. D., Travels in Confed., 309

PART I

Status, Methods, and Presentation

Chapter One

THE NATURE OF HISTORY

1. HISTORY OF AMERICAN HISTORY

History was the first American literature. From the start, European settlers in the New World took pains to set down accounts of their experiences, eager from a variety of motives to acquaint the people at home with the fate of their enterprises. Christopher Columbus' "Letter" telling the story of his first voyage opened the series; Peter Martyr and Oviedo followed; and after them came a continuous line of other writers.

In seventeenth-century Virginia practical considerations moved the more literate settlers to take up their pens and compose contemporary history. Promoters eager to attract newcomers and to convince potential investors wrote glowing accounts of the plantations. John Smith and others mingled descriptions of the country with narratives of travels and with history in the narrower sense. They also on occasion mingled hopes with realities and fiction with fact.

The same considerations were not lacking in the thoughts of the New England writers who also wished to stimulate immigration and investment. But an additional motive made the Puritans prolific historians. For them, the drama of history was dictated by Almighty God; and in that drama their own settlements occupied a peculiarly significant place. Their coming to America was part of a divine plan; its consequences were incalculable. Their migration "afforded a singular prospect of churches erected in an *American* corner of the world, on purpose to express and pursue the Protestant Reformation." To write the history of that migration was therefore of the highest importance; it was the means of conveying to the whole world the glad tidings of its future redemption. Among the many Puritans who accepted what they regarded as a divine mandate to write the history of New England were Governors Bradford and Winthrop, and Edward Johnson of the *Wonder-Working Providence*.

Seventeenth-century American history, whether in the North or in the South, by Anglican or Puritan or Quaker, rested on the assumption that providential forces operated directly on the events of history. As a result these writings were discontinuous and disjointed and often adopted the unusual, the abnormal, or the picturesque as the measure of significance.

Early in the eighteenth century a new view altered the nature of historical

3

writing. The Enlightenment made familiar a conception of natural law operating
in a universe of ordered occurrences. The events of the past were not each the
product of a particular providence, but links in a continuous chain. Even those
Americans who, like Jonathan Edwards, still thought a general providence shaped
the ends of history, nevertheless believed also that immediate things were "wound
up and settled in their everlasting state." Within human history there was regularity and law.

Eighteenth-century histories, in the case of the newer English colonies, were
still somewhat promotional in nature. But most of them were more concerned
with the effort to uncover illustrations of general laws and to describe the influence
on society of the natural environment. Laboring toward those objectives, though
imperfectly, the writers of this period took pains to assemble their materials from
documentary sources and approached, if they did not realize, an ideal of scientific
objectivity. Since they emphasized secular rather than religious concerns and
attempted to be judicious and impartial, these authors, in a sense, laid the foundations for modern American historiography. The sources available to them limited
them to writing the histories of particular colonies. Among the more important
works of the period were Beverley's Virginia, Hutchinson's Massachusetts Bay,
Smith's Pennsylvania, Jones's New York, and Colden's history of the Five Nations.

In terms of historical method, the Revolution marked no break with the eighteenth century. The writers of the years after Independence and, indeed, those
of the first half of the nineteenth century, continued along the lines already fixed
in the late colonial period. But a new spirit now animated their work. Like the
practitioners of other literary genres, the historians of the new nation took it as
their mission to express the ideals of the Republic; affirmation of the virtues and
the glorious destiny of the United States was the central theme of their writings.
What Barlow's Columbiad attempted to say in verse, Washington Irving and the
other literary figures who followed him in occasional excursions into history or
biography took up in prose. The favorite subjects were the men and events of
the American Revolution and its antecedents. The history of the Revolution by
Mercy Warren and the biographies of Washington by Weems and Marshall, at
different intellectual levels, illustrated the tone and spirit of the writing of these
years.

The climax of these trends came in the works of George Bancroft. A Jacksonian
intellectual who devoted a good part of his time, between 1834 and 1882, to
the composition of a monumental history of the origins of the American people
down to the period of the making of the Constitution, Bancroft embodied the
best qualities of the historiography of his age. More than his predecessors of the
eighteenth century, he reached out to foreign countries for sources of American
history; but like them, he believed that "God is visible in History," and that a
divine providence guides the affairs of men. Like the eighteenth-century historians
also he believed in the continuity of the immediate events of history. Progress
as a process was part of a larger plan, and the direction of progress was, in the
long run, determined; but the specific incidents of the process followed each other
in a natural sequence.

In describing the process of history, Bancroft and his contemporaries, of
whom perhaps the best was John G. Palfrey, the historian of New England, were
able to adhere mostly to a strictly chronological exposition. From this point of

view it was necessary, in most cases, only to set forth the events of the past in the order in which they occurred. Working in a milieu that gave a high value to the qualities of literary presentation, Bancroft, along with Prescott and Motley in other fields, created a style of history that reached a relatively large audience; and even Hildreth, who disagreed with Bancroft's assumptions, followed the same narrative form. The limitations to such writings were an excessive preoccupation with politics, a simple view of motivation, and a mechanical conception of causation. Francis Parkman, with a strong sense of drama, succeeded in breaking through a purely narrative exposition and, through his power of expression, achieved a more illuminating analysis of the events he described.

The narrative style reached its high point in the third quarter of the nineteenth century in the writings of Parkman. But it has continued to supply a medium for some American historians down to our own day. It has given shape to most biographical writing and, in the 1880's and 1890's, had to its credit such substantial achievements as the "American Statesmen" series. Among the more successful later narrative historians were James Ford Rhodes, Theodore Roosevelt, and James Schouler, who, after the turn of the new century, still defined history as the record "of consecutive public events."

While the writers of narrative histories took for granted many problems of organization and interpretation, they nevertheless continued to emphasize the necessity of scientific method. They were persistent accumulators of documents and publishers of source materials; they worked with both old and new historical societies (§ 4); and the many town and state histories that emerged in these years show the effects of their influence (§ 62). Perhaps the greatest achievement of the period, from this point of view, was the editing by Justin Winsor of the *Narrative and Critical History*, a monument to meticulous scholarship that will always be useful.

In the last decades of the nineteenth century, fresh impulses began to transform the writing of American history. Until then history had not been a profession, but the avocation of gentlemanly scholars and litterateurs; only a few, beginning with Jared Sparks, had ever taught the subject in universities. Now history found a recognized place, of growing consequence, as one of the rigorous disciplines in college curricula. There was no clear turning point. Herbert Baxter Adams established his seminar at Johns Hopkins in 1876, almost at the same time that Henry Adams began to teach at Harvard and Charles Kendall Adams at Michigan, and shortly before Hermann E. von Holst came from Germany to lecture at Johns Hopkins, Cornell, and Chicago. From these various sources, and through young men who studied across the Atlantic, American historians acquired a new sense of the professional scientific potentialities of their craft. Shortly this became the dominant viewpoint.

The primary contribution of the scientific historians was not the notion of objectivity. That was already an ideal in the eighteenth century; as an actuality, it was never fully to be attained. The more significant achievements of these scholars sprang rather from their attitude toward facts and from their concern with the technique of handling them. Early writers, fixing their attention on the large canvas of history, had often been casual in matters of detail. In the interests of what they knew was the larger truth, they were sometimes willing to sacrifice literal verity, as when Bancroft urged the engraver to remove the warts from

Franklin's nose or when Jared Sparks took the liberty of improving the grammar of Washington's letters. To the scientific historian the fact was absolutely intractable; whatever flights of fancy his interpretation might take, he must be scrupulous in accuracy of detail. This change in attitude was a major contribution.

With the heightened respect for factual accuracy came a new preoccupation with the methods of critical analysis and verification of data. Graduate schools set themselves the task of training specialists; their seminars were workshops in which the requisite skills were taught. The form of writing shifted from the loose discursive narrative to the heavily footnoted monograph. Henry Adams and Edward Channing, and later Herbert L. Osgood, Charles M. Andrews, and Ellis P. Oberholtzer still responded to the impulse to compose longer works; but even these partook of some monographic qualities. And more generally the historians of these generations, in their more extended efforts, preferred the collaborative series, like the "American Nation" (edited by Albert Bushnell Hart), in which a galaxy of professional specialists pooled their talents.

Greatly influenced by contemporary currents of European historical scholarship, Americans devoted the larger part of their energies to description of the development of institutions. An institution they regarded as a form of social action, primarily one that was defined by law, that had a continuity and an inner development of its own. The evolutionary speculation of the period strengthened these interests; viewed, as it were, as species, institutions could be interpreted as following each a determined evolutionary path of its own. Among the more prominent writers whose works reflected the influence of such assumptions were John Fiske, Hermann E. von Holst, George L. Beer, Herbert L. Osgood, and Charles M. Andrews. Because of their desire to discover the roots or germs of institutions, these authors tended to focus their research in the colonial period. But they did not necessarily deal only with political subjects. The institutional approach was also applied to other fields — to systems of production, for instance, as in the Carnegie Institution's economic histories.

Almost from the start, moreover, some scholars sought a more comprehensive synthesis. Emphasizing still the scientific nature of their work, they nevertheless strove to widen the framework within which the institutional historians told their story. In the quest for such a synthesis a number of leading hypotheses as to the nature of the American past were stimulating. Frederick Jackson Turner's theses as to the influence of the frontier and of sections thus challenged a generation of students whose monographs contributed a fund of useful information about, and insight into, the nature of American development. But more important than Turner's own theories or than the specific points made by his followers was the attention his work called to the limitations of the older institutional histories. By directing the efforts of historians to the discovery of connections between politics and economics, between culture and physiography, Turner helped to reveal that institutions did not simply evolve within their own set patterns, that external forces could decisively influence their course (§ 19). That endowed history with a fresh richness and complexity.

Early in the new century the influence of Turner coalesced with another which emanated from the exponents of the "New History." At Columbia University, James Harvey Robinson and Charles A. Beard induced their students to regard history as more than past politics, to treat as well the development of ideas, of social forms, and of the economy. Gradually these scholars, and Carl Becker at Cornell, were groping toward the conception that the proper subject of history was the whole life of a people.

Even in the nineteenth century there had been a continuing interest in the materials of social history. Local historians had generally found room for some consideration of popular ways of life; and the emergence of interest in American antiques had also increased popular interest in the historical context of these objects. Some of the narrative historians — John Bach McMaster, James Schouler, and Edward Eggleston, for instance — had also dealt with these materials. But their approach had tended to be antiquarian. Too often they failed to ask the appropriate questions and, useful as their work had been, it lacked consistency of theme or of interpretation.

After the First World War, American social historians received the assistance of the developing social sciences: government, economics, sociology, and anthropology (§ 2); and began to treat their data, not simply as curiosities, but as revelations of patterns of behavior that extended through the whole life of a society. "The History of American Life" series thus treated the literature, the art, the religion, the economy, and the government of the United States, at various periods, as parts of an integral whole; and a growing number of monographs have added steadily to the knowledge of many neglected fields.

The search for a synthesizing principle also led in other and less fruitful directions. The Marxist interpretation never attracted any considerable support; but the Populist movement brought prominence to an old strain in American political thought that treated the past as the story of a running conflict between diverse economic interests, most often between the mercantile and the agrarian. Sometimes this conception was joined to that of sectionalism derived from Turner. It received notable expression in Charles A. Beard's works on the Constitution and on Jeffersonian democracy, and in his *Rise of American Civilization*, and also in Vernon L. Parrington's *Main Currents in American Thought*.

Significantly, the problems of historical knowledge did not seriously trouble American scholars. It is true that Beard and Becker showed some concern with the questions of epistemology raised by philosophers; but consideration of such matters was largely confined to occasional papers and addresses. In the same way the problems of cycles, of progress, and of race occasionally troubled historians but rarely affected the history that they wrote. The pragmatic temperament with which they approached the subject, the disciplined methods with which they treated it, and the consciousness of a tradition of historical writing that reached back to the earliest colonial settlements, have set the terms within which their most productive efforts have continued to come.

For general secondary treatments, see: W. T. Hutchinson, ed., *Marcus W. Jernegan Essays in American Historiography* (Chi., 1937); J. F. Jameson, *The History of Historical Writing in America* (Boston, 1891); and Michael Kraus, *A History of American History* (N.Y., 1937). On particular aspects, see: Perry Miller, *The New England Mind: The Seventeenth Century* (N.Y., 1939), ch. xvi; K. B. Murdock, *Literature and Theology in Colonial New England* (Cambridge, 1949); J. S. Bassett, *Middle Group of American Historians* (N.Y., 1917); W. S. Holt, "The Idea of Scientific History in America," *Jour. of the Hist. of Ideas*, I (1940), 352; Fulmer Mood, "Development of Frederick Jackson Turner as a Historical Thinker," Col. Soc. of Mass., *Publ.*, XXXIV (1939), 283; S. E. Morison, "Edward Channing," Mass. Hist. Soc., *Proc.*, LXIV (1931), 250; R. H. Shryock, "American Historiography," Am. Philos. Soc., *Proc.*, LXXXVII (1943), 35;

John Higham, "The Rise of American Intellectual History," *Am. Hist. Rev.*, LVI (1951), 453. See also § 5 and the biographies of particular historians (§ 56).

2. HISTORY AND OTHER FIELDS OF KNOWLEDGE

History is a method, a particular way, of studying the record of human experience (§ 6). It is also a body of information. In both respects it is basic to each and every other branch of learning. There is a history of biology, of economics, of medicine, of religion, of architecture, of letters. The best of such treatises utilize not only the professional historian's technique of ascertaining facts, but also his knowledge of the time-and-place setting in which the particular events occurred.

The subject of history, however, is a debtor as well as a creditor in its relations to other disciplines. The professional historian, however much he may try, can hardly be expert in all the phases of human thought and activity that constitute either the present or the past of society. His toolbox must contain a variety of implements, many of them fashioned by craftsmen in other fields of inquiry.

History, as one of the social sciences, naturally lays heavy tribute on economics, political science, cultural anthropology, sociology, law, statistics, and psychology, and seeks to use the special insights which these subjects derive from their intensive study of selected aspects of human behavior. Statistics, for example, enables the historian to deal with masses of data more intelligibly and to correct judgments based upon random individual instances (§ 7). Psychology, it may be observed, not only guides him in probing the inner workings of men's minds in other times, but it should also equip him to lay bare his own mental processes, and so help to ward off those unconscious biases that may otherwise warp his interpretation of events.

But history is not merely a social science; it is also one of the humanities. In the hands of a Parkman or a Becker, historical writing becomes a department of belles-lettres (§ 12); and even those who lag behind these masters of style have constant recourse to the fruits of humanistic scholarship. Thanks to the archaeologists, for example, the pre-Columbian history of the New World has been pushed back many centuries. For later times the historian may lean on the specialized knowledge of literary scholars or the writers on the fine arts; he may also glean much from the trends of human thought revealed by students of philosophy. He may even benefit from scholars who delve into linguistic study. Thus the word usages and verbal inventions recorded in Sir William A. Craigie and J. R. Hulbert's *Dictionary of American English on Historical Principles* (4 vols., Chi., 1938–44) incidentally reveal many of the factors and conditions that have differentiated American civilization from its Anglo-Saxon base.

The relation of history to biography is inescapable. Despite the emphasis which present-day historians justly place on impersonal forces, history is, after all, a narrative of human beings. Man is necessarily the agency through which impersonal forces act, and he may even modify or redirect them. In this sense Emerson spoke truly in saying, "There is properly no history, only biography." The increasing attention of biographers to men and women in nonpolitical spheres has greatly enriched the historian's view of the past, and more of such work should be done. Only less important has been the mounting number of portrayals of secondary political figures. Such individuals often typify the public life of an age better than the more conspicuous personages.

Finally, history draws heavily on the subject matter of the natural and applied sciences. The light which geography throws upon physiography, climate, and soil resources is fundamental to an understanding of many aspects of American development (§ 19). In a different fashion, a knowledge of the succession of labor-saving and distance-shortening inventions supplies an important key to the past. Less attention has been paid to the impact on American history of scientific agriculture, mineralogy, oceanography, industrial chemistry, medical science, and the like; but these too will in time assume their rightful place as handmaids of the historian. The practical utilization of atomic energy in the last few years shows dramatically how profoundly applications of theoretical science can affect human fortunes.

In Emerson's words, man's power through the ages has consisted "in the multitude of his affinities, in the fact that his life is intertwined with the whole chain of organic and inorganic being." A recognition of the importance and complexity of these affinities has led the American Historical Association to band with national organizations in the other social sciences in the Social Science Research Council, and has further impelled it to join with them and the main associations of humanistic scholars in the American Council of Learned Societies. For many years history and the related social sciences have also constituted a special section of the American Association for the Advancement of Science.

The following discussions treat in fuller detail the ties of history with other branches of study: H. E. Barnes, *The New History and the Social Studies* (N.Y., 1926); Norman Foerster, ed., *The Reinterpretation of American Literature* (N.Y., 1928); Wilson Gee, ed., *Research in the Social Sciences, Its Fundamental Methods and Objectives* (N.Y., 1929); E. C. Hayes, ed., *Recent Developments in the Social Sciences* (Phila., 1927); A. B. Hulbert, "The Increasing Debt of History to Science," Am. Antiq. Soc., *Proc.*, XXIX (1919), 29; C. H. Hull, "The Service of Statistics to History," Am. Stat. Assoc., *Publ.*, XIV (1914), 30; W. E. Lingelbach, ed., *Approaches to American Social History* (N.Y., 1937); W. F. Ogburn and Alexander Goldenweiser, eds., *The Social Sciences and Their Interrelations* (Boston, 1927); J. H. Robinson, *The New History* (N.Y., 1912); Gaetano Salvemini, *Historian and Scientist* (Cambridge, 1939); George Sarton, *The History of Science and the New Humanism* (N.Y., 1931); A. M. Schlesinger, "An American Historian Looks at Science and Technology," *Isis*, XXXVI (1946), 162; W. F. G. Swann, *et al.*, *Essays on Research in the Social Sciences* (Wash., 1931).

3. THE HISTORIAN AND THE PUBLIC

Historians have a peculiar relation to the public, since they are at the same time the creators, the guardians, and the revisers of tradition. More than any other class of writers or teachers they influence, through their access to the youthful mind, a people's conception of its past. As such they have perhaps more influence on events and on the shaping of the future than they modestly admit. Consequently a historian has a grave responsibility; and he should not shirk it, but endeavor to increase his influence.

Historians are not, of course, the sole creators of tradition. In times of popular movements and rapid events a tradition is created by orators, poets, politicians, clergymen, and actual participants. The historian's part comes when the excitement dies down and he endeavors to reconcile, clarify, and weave into a connected narrative the confusing happenings of the past. The nearer that a historian lives to the events he describes, and the more intimate his participation in them, the closer his narrative is apt to be to the popular tradition. As examples we may cite Cotton Mather's *Magnalia Christi Americana* (§ 90), Mercy Warren's *History of the . . . American Revolution* (Boston, 1805), Henry Wilson's *History of the Rise and Fall of the Slave Power in America* (Boston, 1872–77), Jefferson Davis' *The Rise and Fall of the Confederate Government* (N.Y., 1881) and Henry Cabot Lodge's *War with Spain* (N.Y., 1899). These works confirmed and hardened a popular tradition. School histories were compiled from them, and the rising generation was thus brought up to what its elders believed to be the correct and patriotic point of view.

The march of time is merciless to orthodox views. For one thing, important facts known only to insiders when or shortly after they occur gradually become public, partly through candid memoirs and autobiographies, but mostly through the work of historians who go to the sources and dig out the facts. Secondly, it is easier to see the true relation of events in perspective, just as we can grasp the lay of the land more easily from an airplane than from a treetop. Finally, fashions both in writing and in interpreting history change, sometimes very rapidly. Charles A. Beard, for instance, brought forth an economic interpretation of American history in 1912. He made it seem significant what sort of property the framers of the Federal Constitution held; and now we all wish to know about the business affairs of statesmen and the dominant economic interests of the sections that they represent. Others, less successfully, have attempted psychological interpretations. Still others, very successfully, have aroused public interest in social history. Almost all these new points of view are illuminating; the danger lies in supposing that any single one explains everything.

New facts, fresh viewpoints, and a lengthened perspective lead to the writing of new histories, which may ignore or describe as untrue popular tradition. This may offend national, sectional, racial, or party pride; and the new historian is likely to be denounced as a Tory, radical, reactionary, fellow traveler, subversive, or whatever the unpopular label happens to be at the time. His book is then apt to be excluded from public schools and libraries. The book may be merely sensational and soon forgotten. It may be worthless as history and yet represent a current trend in public opinion, and consequently have some value as a document in the history of thought. But a really sound and scholarly piece of work that upsets accepted theories will first be accepted by historians and other educated people who are capable of following the argument and are not afraid of the truth. These spread the new interpretation; and after a number of years — generally not less than twenty — it trickles into school histories and so modifies the popular tradition.

For instance, about a half-century ago, United States history from 1815 to the Civil War, as taught in the North and West, turned about slavery; and the Democrats were the villains in this drama. Whigs like Daniel Webster who compromised with the "Slave Power" were treated as renegades; Stephen A. Douglas was a rascal. The South, of course, never accepted this tradition; but not until a series of books by such men as Woodrow Wilson and Frederick J. Turner showed how many other important topics besides slavery had been discussed during the period, and how vital the Compromise of 1850 was for preserving the

Union, did school histories in the North break away from *Uncle Tom's Cabin*. Before the process was complete, along came the Beards, who told us that the Compromise of 1850 involved a sordid and successful effort of "Wall Street" to unload Texas bonds. Economic determinists naturally seized upon this as the outstanding feature of the Compromise, snatching from the godlike Daniel's brow his recently recovered laurels. Now we have come full circle: a younger historian has denounced the pussyfooting of his immediate predecessors on the slavery question, and has even revived the use of that invidious old phrase, "The Slave Power."

Another good instance of changing interpretation is that of Christopher Columbus. For centuries everyone believed that Columbus was seeking the Orient by sailing west, and that the one object of his voyage was to make contact with the Indies. At the opening of this century Henry Vignaud challenged the tradition and, in a series of provocative and scholarly volumes, attempted to prove that Columbus had no interest in the Orient; that he was seeking a new continent, and that his supposed discovery of India was an afterthought supported by a conspiracy of silence and the mutilation of documents. This revised view of Columbus was so cogently presented that almost every writer on American history for thirty years thought it was correct. It was only after pursuing independent research on Columbus that S. E. Morison found the Vignaud thesis to be built on nothing but hypotheses and, in his *Admiral of the Ocean Sea*, returned to the same view of the Discoverer's objects and motives as the classic one of Washington Irving.

So far we are assuming that the historian is a free agent attempting to tell the truth. Of course, none of us is completely free. Our unconscious prejudices of section, religion and the like are always jogging our elbows. But these subjective pressures, which none of us can wholly escape, are very different from the external pressures that in many countries today constrain scholars to teach and write in support of the views of their political masters. Nothing so crude as that has been attempted in England or the United States; but even in the freest countries, timid souls among historians suffer a constant fear of authorities or of public opinion, while occasional crusades by pressure groups tempt them to suppress what they believe to be true, or to state what they know to be false.

The public is the historian's client, not his sovereign. His professional as well as his patriotic duty is to tell the truth in such measure as his faculties enable him to grasp it. He must be as honest, accurate, and objective as is humanly possible. He should bring everything to the test of fact, and make no statement that he suspects to be unsound merely because it is popular, traditional, provocative, or what some current fad makes the people inclined to hear and believe. But he should also maintain balance, common sense, and "a decent respect for the opinions of mankind." He is not to assume that tradition is necessarily false; or that everyone who treated his subject before was either fool or knave. Mere cleverness is a poor substitute for sound knowledge. Popular feelings should not be unnecessarily lacerated nor heroes needlessly insulted. In almost every legend — even those of Pocahontas, the Pilgrim Fathers, and the Mecklenburg Declaration of Independence — there is some element of truth; and the historical crusader who wishes to rescue his holy land from the domination of error had best begin by conceding a few virtues to the enemy. The mass murder of historical characters by the "debunker" of the 1920's did little hurt to the characters, but great harm to the profession, since, although very few of the "debunkers" were academic historians, the historians as a group were nevertheless blamed. If the reviser of history wishes to reach the great public, he must use discretion. A historian who displays anger at the stupidity or inaccuracy of his predecessors injures his cause. "What prevents us from telling the truth with a smile?" remarked Horace almost two thousand years ago. What, indeed?

There are other means than the written word by which a historian may reach the people. Celebrations of historic anniversaries by meetings, pageants, and broadcasts reach thousands who never read history after they leave school. The historian will serve the public as well as his profession if he accepts (within reasonable limits) such opportunities as come his way to deliver centennial and founders' day speeches, address clubs, lodges, and patriotic societies, and provide data for pageants and broadcasts on anniversaries. At such times it has been customary to call on politicians, clergymen, professional orators, artists — anyone but historians — because the public wishes to be amused rather than instructed. If historians as a whole were less solemn, they would be more frequently invited to hold forth on these occasions; and such occasions may often be improved to present to the public in an attractive and even humorous way some historical truth or viewpoint of which it is not yet apprised. Manner is often more important than matter. A dull, lugubrious presentation overcrowded with facts, or a "smart aleck" attack on popular beliefs will repel the audience and defeat the speaker's ends. The historian has no obligation to be clever or dull, but he had better be interesting! He should speak graciously, without condescension. If there is one thing a popular audience dislikes more than pedantry, it is to be treated condescendingly.

If the historian has no talent or opportunity for public speaking, there are many other ways in which he can serve the public. Every American historian should maintain, outside his main interest, a sideline of local history. There are very many historical societies — state, county, city, and town — in the United States (§ 4). The history teacher should join the nearest one, help keep it going, wake it up if it is moribund, read papers, and get others to do so. If there is no local society, let him interest leading citizens in founding one and so stir up pride in the regional history. Perhaps he can help others to organize the dramatic talent of the community in getting up a pageant or other celebration of an important historical event. He can photograph or make measured drawings of historic buildings and arouse public interest in their preservation. He can urge that tablets or markers be put on historic spots and (what is even more important) see that the inscriptions are readable and correct. Historians should coöperate with patriotic and ancestral societies such as the Colonial Dames, Daughters of the American Revolution, and Daughters of the Confederacy instead of regarding them (however strong the provocation) as natural enemies. These ladies are to some extent interested in history or they would not belong to these organizations. Often they take an exclusive, personal or family view of history; but they are willing to listen to historical truth if it is reasonably presented, and it is a mistake to ignore or slight them.

In these and many other ways that will occur to active and vigorous historians, they can make themselves "solid" in their community, a force for enlightenment, and, at the same time, a power for the enrichment of American history.

4. HISTORICAL SOCIETIES

The learned societies of Europe, expanding their activities through the seventeenth and eighteenth centuries, often found history a worthwhile subject of encouragement. It was quite natural, therefore, that the American Philosophical Society, modeled after those across the Atlantic, should, from its founding in 1743, propose to take history as one of the several fields of its concern.

While the quest for general knowledge was still the ideal end of such associations, there had also emerged in Europe, in the eighteenth century, particular organizations of antiquarians and historians who gave more specialized attention to the past. The Academy of Inscriptions in France, the Royal Academy of History in Spain, the Royal Danish Society, and the Society of Antiquarians of London were undoubtedly familiar, by name at least, to the Americans who, in the aftermath of the Revolution, felt moved by a sense of patriotic dedication to preserve and arrange the materials that would tell the story of their country. A group of such men organized the Massachusetts Historical Society in 1791 and these in turn were imitated by like-minded citizens in other states in the next few decades.

The early societies were restrictive; they drew together by coöption a limited membership. They took all history as their province, although they were perforce likely to concentrate upon North America. And their conception of history was broad, or vague, enough to include natural history and even geology. They did, however, mark out the activities that continued to preoccupy their successors to our own times. They established collections of books and objects that illustrated the past; and they published, in volumes of proceedings, papers by their members on a variety of historical subjects.

Toward the middle of the nineteenth century a fresh impulse added a large number of new societies. Interest in local history had long led Americans to devote their time to study of the places in which they lived. But that interest now grew much stronger, partly out of a consciousness of the significance of local events, partly out of the desire to establish genealogical connections, a desire strong in a people much on the move, in a society extremely mobile. The preoccupation with local history developed to such a degree that by the time of the Civil War almost every state had at least one society devoted to its study; and Americans thereafter continued to show marked interest in the subject.

In the last two decades of the nineteenth century two additional forces stimulated the development of historical societies in the United States. In the first place substantial groups, moved by pride in ancestry, began to devote themselves to study of the achievements of their progenitors. The associations in which these enthusiasts gathered were sometimes local, but more generally were national and based on common ancestry. Among such societies were several to celebrate the first immigrants from England; but there were also a large number devoted to the history of other nationalities. In general these associations tended to stress the colonial antecedents of each group, seeking to justify its place in American society by searching out its traces as far back in the history of the continent as possible. These societies were at first restrictive in intention and often laid down hereditary qualifications for membership. Their work was sometimes characterized by an invidious group pride. After the opening of the twentieth century, however, they gradually recognized that their own heritage could be shared; and more recently they have given themselves over to the serious study and the accumulation of materials relevant to the history of the whole American society.

In the second place, the example of Europe stimulated the growth of historical societies toward the end of the nineteenth century; in the Old World new associations drew together professional scholars devoted to the scientific study of the past. With the development of departments of history in American universities, academic interest developed rapidly and led to the creation by a charter of the Congress of the American Historical Association in 1884. As time went on and as the discipline itself became more specialized, groups of historians organized still other societies devoted to the study of special subjects, societies in which the professional historian could enter a profitable partnership with others concerned with particular phases of the past.

By the end of the century also, academic historians had begun to penetrate into the older societies which, under their influence, were transformed into more effective instruments of scholarship. In Michigan, C. H. van Tyne; in Illinois, C. W. Alvord; in Minnesota, S. J. Buck; and in Wisconsin the notable succession, L. C. Draper, R. G. Thwaites, M. M. Quaife, and Joseph Schafer, built up the holdings of the libraries, edited the publications critically, and zealously labored to assist research, with notable success.

The result was a steady rise in the number of learned societies. By 1936, well over five hundred in the United States were listed by the American Association for State and Local History; a decade later there were well over eight hundred, in addition to a large number of unaffiliated societies. The number of participating members grew correspondingly.

The earliest societies were supported by dues and by occasional contributions from their members. From gifts many built up substantial endowments with incomes adequate to maintain their collections and their activities. But from an early date the historical societies also profited by the assistance of governments which regarded these labors within the scope of public educational interest. The federal government gives the American Historical Association space in the Library of Congress and prints the annual report of the organization. Some states have made grants for individual projects; others have supplied societies with quarters in public buildings; and still others have established fruitful relationships between the societies and the state archives, library, or university.

At the present there is little uniformity among the numerous historical societies actively at work in the United States. Almost all issue publications of some sort (§ 50). Most have libraries. They vary widely in the extent of their activities and in the nature of their organization, but whatever the form they take they serve as means of bringing together scholars and of making available facilities for their investigations and also of relating those investigations to the public. Therein lies their strength.

See: J. F. Jameson, *History of Historical Societies* (Savannah, [1914]); L. W. Dunlap, *American Historical Societies 1790–1860* (Madison, 1944); *Historical Societies in the United States and Canada: A Handbook* (Wash. 1944; earlier eds., 1926 and 1936); R. G. Thwaites, "Bibliographical Activities of Historical Societies of the United States," Bibliog. Soc. of Am., *Papers*, I (1906–07), 140; A. P. C. Griffin, *Bibliography of American Historical Societies* (§ 34); B. L. Heilbron, "How to Organize a Local Historical Society," Am. Assoc. for State and Local Hist., *Bull.*, I (1944), 227; E. B.

Greene, "Our Pioneer Historical Societies," Ind. Hist. Soc., *Publ.*, X (1931), 83; R. G. Thwaites, "State-Supported Historical Societies and Their Functions," Am. Hist. Assoc., *Report*, 1897, 61; R. G. Thwaites, *et al.*, "Report of Committee on Methods of Organization and Work on the Part of State and Local Historical Societies," Am. Hist. Assoc., *Report*, 1905, I, 249; H. H. Bellot, "Some Aspects of the Recent History of American Historiography," Royal Hist. Soc., *Trans.*, Fourth Ser., XXVIII (1946), 138; H. L. Carson, *History of the Historical Society of Pennsylvania* (Phila., 1940).

5. THEORIES OF HISTORICAL INTERPRETATION

The historian, in his attempt to reconstruct the past, is confronted with a mass of materials with which he must somehow come to terms. He cannot simply reproduce these materials in all their chaos and confusion. Instead, through arrangement, selection, and generalization, he must discern some order within them. To do so requires a series of choices, conscious or unconscious. This process of choice is the subjective element inherent in the historian's duty of analyis and synthesis. If the statesman cannot escape history, the historian cannot escape himself and his prepossessions.

While the "facts" of history, moreover, can to a considerable measure be proven "right" or "wrong," historical interpretations are far less determinate. Dealing with a multitude of facts at a high level of abstraction, interpretations can be proven "right" or "wrong" only within narrow limits. This is not only because the past itself, gone beyond recall, is no longer available for checking purposes. If a time machine were available to carry the historian back through the past at will, he would confront, on stepping off the machine, the very problems of interpretation he thought he had left behind.

As a consequence, theories of interpretation are peculiarly dependent on the needs and values of the age which produces them. In the most primitive stages, historical interpretation was absorbed into the myth-making compulsions of the early tribes. In the Middle Ages, under the influence of Augustine's *De Civitate Dei*, history was pressed into the service of the Christian faith. Successive theories of historical interpretation over the last thousand years have reflected the ever quickening pace of social and intellectual change.

The last great historical watershed came in the eighteenth century. The revolutionary new intellectual world involved, among other things, new conceptions of history. The Enlightenment liberated history from theology, encouraged the idea of the disinterested pursuit of knowledge as an end in itself, and developed techniques for the critical use of historical materials. It thus established the study of the past for its own sake as an independent field. The romanticism of the early nineteenth century added a sympathetic concern with the inwardness of the past. These were fruitful years of historical meditation and scholarship. This experience, when generalized in the middle of the nineteenth century by Hegel in the realm of philosophy of history and by Ranke in the realm of historical practice, laid the foundations for modern historical theory.

In the years since Hegel and Ranke, approaches to historical interpretation have been at several levels. For purposes of convenience, they can be grouped as follows: (1) interpretations assuming a plurality of separate civilizations and dealing with the reasons for their cyclical rise and decline, such as those of Toynbee and Spengler; (2) interpretations setting forth, in systematic rules, the general principles of continuous historical change applicable to all civilizations, such as those of Hegel and Marx; (3) interpretations, such as F. J. Turner's frontier thesis, which emphasize neglected factors in the historical development of a civilization, without claiming that those factors explain its whole development; (4) interpretations which deny the need for interpretation, asserting that objectivity is an attainable ideal, that the facts "speak for themselves," and that history is ultimately "scientific" (Ranke, though not a member of this school, was its hero); (5) interpretations (such as those of Croce, Collingwood, and Beard) which assert that objectivity is an unattainable ideal and rest on the frank belief that all history is contemporary history; (6) interpretations which concede that perfect objectivity is unattainable but remain hostile to rigid or dogmatic historical theories. (This school is pragmatic and pluralistic, assuming always multiplicity of causation, and prepared to use *ad hoc* whatever general theories may illuminate a particular point.) The first three types deal with concrete historical interpretation; the last three turn upon the problem of historical knowledge. There is no escape from this confusion of categories. The philosophy of history deals with problems that are methodological as well as substantive, with every age asserting its own particular interests and emphases.

Interpretations of the first type — universal cyclical histories — have not much affected the writing of American history. Such theories are not particularly useful for detailed historical inquiry, and the buoyancy of the American spirit and the faith in American "exceptionalism" have made it difficult for historians to identify American history with patterns of inexorable decay.

Interpretations of the second type — systematic doctrines of continuous historical change — have profoundly influenced the writing of American history, though they have found few dogmatic exponents among American historians. Hegel, the dominant figure in the school, provided the major nineteenth-century statement of the idealist attitude. He saw in human striving the reflection of the transcendental "idea" fulfilling itself through the three dialectic stages of thesis, antithesis, and synthesis. At any given time, in Hegel's view, the discrepancy between ideas and social conditions reacts upon the social conditions; and as ideas bring conditions up to their level, new ideas arise, and out of the ideas new conditions — until history reaches its ultimate fulfillment (which Hegel, in a burst of anticlimax, located in the Prussian state). The historian must not only record the events; he must, by penetrating through the events to the thoughts beyond them, establish the higher logic of history. In this sense, history is rational, though not in the sense that all human behavior is rational.

Hegelian idealism in its central thrust had a broad and deep impact on American theories of historical interpretation. Not only did many leading American historians drink in idealism at its source in Germany, but by the latter part of the nineteenth century Hegelianism was the official academic philosophy in the United States. While the dialectic receded to the background, the Hegelian conception of the supremacy of the "idea" dominated American historical writing, displacing the naïve views which interpreted history in terms of providential intervention or of the achievements of great men. Thus for George Bancroft, who had heard Hegel lecture at Berlin, the ideas of freedom and democracy were primary historical forces, urging the American people forever on to make material reality an ever closer approximation of the ideal. For historians writing after the Civil War — H.

von Holst and J. W. Burgess, for example — the idea of the Union was the great propelling force in American progress.

In later decades, however, the idealistic conception of history lost its influence, partly because it did not prove an especially usable instrument for the investigation of concrete episodes, partly because it omitted or obscured so much obviously essential in social change. In the meantime, Karl Marx in Europe had inverted the Hegelian system (or, as he said, stood Hegel on his feet), retaining and strengthening the dialectic, but making it now the engine of a materialistic rather than an idealistic interpretation. The prevailing ideas in any historical epoch, Marx argued, as well as the prevailing forms of social organization, were determined by its method of economic production and exchange. So long as the means of production remained in private hands, every society was divided between exploiting and exploited, ruling and oppressed classes; and each class society constituted a thesis, whose existence provoked the inevitable antithesis in the shape of a class rising in revolt. For Marx the dialectical process had finally reduced the warring societies to two — the bourgeoisie and the proletariat; and the triumph of the working class would produce the climactic synthesis — a classless society, emancipating the world forever from all exploitation and class struggle.

Marx did not invent the economic interpretation, or even the class interpretation of history. The British empiricist tradition of Hobbes and Locke had long directed attention at the material factors in historical change; James Madison had provided, in the tenth *Federalist* paper, a classic statement of the role of economic interests; and historians in the Federalist tradition, like Richard Hildreth, had acute insights into the relationship between political and economic forces. As Marx himself wrote, "The honour does not belong to me for having discovered the existence either of classes in modern society or of the struggle between the classes. Bourgeois historians long before me expounded the historical development of this class struggle." "To limit Marxism to the teaching of the class struggle," Lenin added, "means to curtail Marxism. . . . A Marxist is one who *extends* the acceptance of the class struggle to the acceptance of the *dictatorship of the proletariat.*"

Nevertheless, by providing a systematic formulation of the economic interpretation of history and by charging that formulation with messianic zeal, Marx made it increasingly difficult for American historians to ignore the role of economic factors. Few Americans attempted a doctrinaire application of Marxist ideas (and even in this category, it should be noted, a wide variation was possible, as between the social-democratic approach of Simons and Oneal, the Trotskyite approach of Calverton, and the Stalinist approach of Foner and Aptheker). But many were affected directly by Marx, and even more, like Beard, were stimulated by the new interest in economic factors to revive the early insights of Madison and Hildreth.

The American atmosphere, however, with its concrete and practical preoccupations, has been uncongenial to monolithic theories. As a consequence, it has generally tended to convert dogmatic interpretations of historical change into partial and provisional ones, theses into hypotheses. It has tended to reduce interpretations of the second type — general theories of social change — to interpretations of the third type — special theories spotlighting special factors. Thus, the attempt to apply the principle of economic interpretation to American history at once raised two separate and limited problems: the question, on the one hand, of the influence of man-made economic systems, and, on the other, of the natural physical and geographical setting. Writers like Beard and Josephson were chiefly concerned with the first problem. But the American development was so plainly dependent in so many crucial respects on space, climate, geology, and natural resources that, beginning with the work of N. S. Shaler, a fruitful line of inquiry focused on physiographical factors, leading toward a geographical interpretation of history. The most notable special theory of the American development, the frontier theory of F. J. Turner, applied economic and geographical interpretations to the problem of the westward movement of American society.

For Turner, the process of opening up and subduing an ever receding frontier gave a unique cast to American history. "The existence of an area of free land, its continuous recession, and the advance of American settlement westward," he wrote in 1893, "explain American development." (Later he would agree that these factors do not explain *all* American development and would admit the need for an urban reinterpretation of American history.) He drew special attention to the struggle between frontier and tidewater and to the role of sections, and he portrayed American democracy as "fundamentally the outcome of the experience of the American people in dealing with the West," not the product of a theorist's dream, but rising "stark and strong and full of life, from the American forest."

Though some of Turner's claims for his theory were unguarded, and some of his followers applied it all too mechanically, his own practice was modest and tentative. The result of his work was to place American history in an illuminating new perspective. For a generation the frontier theory dominated the imagination and directed the energies of a large group of American historians. Indeed, its compelling, almost poetic vision of the uniqueness of the American development gave it a better chance than any other theory of triumphing over the anti-theoretical disposition of the American mind.

But the Turner theory had to make its terms with American pragmatism and even more, in the period of its first formulation, with the increasing belief in "scientific history," the fourth type of historical interpretation. Science itself never enjoyed such prestige as in the last quarter of the nineteenth century; history, like literature and art, accepted the goal of the exact transcription of external reality, conceiving itself capable of an objectivity which, in the long run, would guarantee it results approaching certainty.

The scientific historians tended to scorn excessive concern about historical interpretation as wanton encouragement of unnecessary subtleties. History, they contended, was an accumulation of facts, like science itself. As a series of experiments ultimately led to scientific generalizations, so a series of monographs ultimately led to historical generalizations. In the meantime, the historian, consecrated to the ideal of objectivity, flying Ranke's standard of *wie es eigentlich gewesen*, should devote himself to the infinitely scrupulous collection and verification of facts. As Albert J. Beveridge put it, "Facts when justly arranged interpret themselves."

For the scientific historians, history had a determinate structure accessible to the patient and objective scholar; objectivity could be achieved through the rigorous suppression of personal opinion and the systematic exercise of detachment and industry. James F. Rhodes said characteristically that his aim had been "to get rid so far as possible of all preconceived notions and theories"; once this was achieved, the prize was presumably almost certain. "Scientific" history thus gave historians a passionate sense of vocation — a conviction that the dedicated life of research and analysis, if the temptations of theory and prejudice were sternly rebuffed, would lead in the end to definitive results. The first effect was to professionalize the historical field and to improve markedly the standards and techniques of research. The very concern with monographic studies implied far stricter canons of criticism and exactitude. Impressionism and even generalization began to fall under the professional ban.

Yet for all its bracing effects on history as a discipline, "scientific" history rested on premises which seemed increasingly naïve and unsatisfactory in the early years of the twentieth century. The conviction that historians could easily divest themselves of all prepossessions could pass only in a relatively stable age, when prepossessions were not widely questioned — though even then the claims of Rhodes might have provoked skepticism. "Scientific" history, moreover, rested on a false analogy with science, if not on a misunderstanding of scientific method. For the scientist, the adoption of a hypothesis might well be a neutral act, though even the scientist could never escape altogether the egocentric predicament; for the historian, this act instantly reopened the Pandora's box of subjectivism which it had been the whole aim of scientific history to shut. And science itself, as in the new physics, revealed an ultimate indeterminacy in fundamental assumptions and came increasingly to abandon the positivistic professions with which historians continued to credit it.

The intellectual "revolt against formalism" brought the premises of scientific history under withering fire. The attack on Ranke, led by Robinson and Beard was, at first, essentially a protest against the narrowness of the political conception of history and against the refusal to face the full obligations of historical explanation. But, as political and social upheavals after 1914 hastened the trend toward relativism, the reconsideration of the premises of "scientific" history became more drastic and devastating.

This process of criticism eventually led Beard to dismiss the whole ideal of objectivity as "that noble dream." In developing his views, he drew heavily on the writings of Croce and Mannheim. Croce's powerful restatement of Hegelian idealism argued that all history was contemporaneous; it existed only in the mind of the historian and then only insofar as historical evidence thrust it into the historian's mind. The historian's impulse, moreover, was artistic and not scientific. But Beard carried Croce's idealism, as well as Mannheim's sociological relativism, to brutally extreme conclusions. If historical objectivity were unattainable, he said, then there was little point in trying to attain it; if subjective interpretation were inescapable, then that interpretation might as well be in accord with the personal interests and values of the historian. He thereupon advised historians to make basic value commitments as "an act of faith"; for his part, this meant a commitment as to the direction of social change, which he conceived to be toward a "collectivist democracy."

For most American historians, the Beard thesis — the fifth in the categories of historical interpretation — seemed a leap from the frying pan into the fire. Even Beard in his practice only intermittently acted upon it. Yet the critique of "scientific" history seemed conclusive. The debate placed historians in a dilemma. Somewhere between the naïve positivism of those who felt that historical interpretation could be definitive and the naïve relativism of those who felt that, since it could not be definitive, it might as well be entirely subjective, it was essential to carve out an area for history. Fortunately the resolution of this dilemma corresponded to the pragmatic instinct of the American mind.

Most American historians today operate from the sixth type of interpretation. They agree with the relativists that interpretation is inescapable; they agree with the scientific historians, however, that objectivity, even if unattainable, must stand as the historian's ideal. Accordingly, they forswear all single-valued or dogmatic theories of history and subject theory itself to the perpetual countercheck of facts. If facts are no longer held to speak for themselves, still historians must speak through them; and the interpretations which can hold in suspension the largest number of diverse facts are those most likely to do justice to the total complexity of a past which can never be fully recovered.

Historical analysis has never had so many weapons in its arsenal as today. American history has been enriched by the growing tendency to interpret the evolution of the United States within the context of the whole of Western culture and also by the development of special theories in history and in related disciplines such as economics, sociology, and social psychology (§ 2). Recent years, indeed, have been rich in new insights casting brilliant light on tangled problems of the past: the theories of Mosca and Pareto on the circulation of political élites, of Michels on bureaucracy, of Freud, Fromm, and Riesman on individual and social psychology, of Keynes on the nature of capitalism, of Lenin and Schumpeter on imperialism, of Schumpeter on entrepreneurial innovation, of Turner on the influence of the frontier, of Weber and Tawney on the sociology of religion, of Mahan on the influence of sea power, of Butterfield on the significance of lost causes, of Sumner on the persistence of folk customs, of Veblen on the meaning of the machine process, of Whitehead on the role of science, and others touching many crucial areas of human and social change. But these are not dogmas; they are hypotheses, to be discarded when they do not do their job. Objectivity must survive as a value, if no longer as an imminent achievement. Above all, in the judgment of this pragmatic and pluralistic school, theories of historical interpretation are to be used by men, and not men by theories.

For a discussion of general issues, see: M. E. Curti, *et al., Theory and Practice in Historical Study: A Report of the Committee on Historiography* (N.Y., Social Sci. Res. Coun., *Bull.* 54, 1946); Raymond Aron, *Introduction à la philosophie de l'histoire: Essai sur les limites de l'objectivité historique* (Paris, 1938); Carl Becker, *Everyman His Own Historian* (N.Y., 1935); M. R. Cohen, *The Meaning of Human History* (La Salle, 1947); R. G. Collingwood, *The Idea of History* (Oxford, 1946); Sidney Hook, *The Hero in History* (N.Y., 1943); G. J. Renier, *History: Its Purpose and Method* (Boston, 1950); Patrick Gardiner, *The Nature of Historical Explanation* (Oxford, 1952).

For universal histories, see: M. H. Fisch and T. G. Bergin, eds., *The New Science of Giambattista Vico* (Ithaca, 1948): Oswald Spengler, *The Decline of the West* (2 vols., N.Y., 1926–28); A. J. Toynbee, *A Study of History* (6 vols., London, 1934–39). For penetrating comments from the Christian viewpoints, see: Reinhold Niebuhr, *Faith and History* (N.Y., 1949); and Karl Löwith, *Meaning in History: The Theological Implications of the Philosophy of History* (Chi., 1949).

The fundamental idealistic work is G. W. F. Hegel, *Lectures on the Philosophy of History* (Berlin, 1837, tr. by E. S. Haldane and F. H. Simson, 3 vols., London, 1892–96). For an exposition of the Hegelian approach to history, see: J. G. Droysen, *Outline of the Principles of History* (Boston, 1893); for trenchant criticism, Karl Popper, *The Open Society and Its Enemies* (Princeton, 1950), 199–273. For American historical writing on Hegelian premises, see: the historical works of George Bancroft and J. W.

Burgess; also E. D. Adams, *The Power of Ideals in American History* (New Haven, 1913); J. H. Denison, *Emotional Currents in American History* (N.Y., 1932). For Marx, see: Karl Marx and Friedrich Engels, *The Communist Manifesto* (London, 1848; N.Y., 1933); also Marx's preface to *A Contribution to the Critique of Political Economy* (1854, tr. by I. N. Stone, N.Y., 1904); this and other writings of Marx may be conveniently consulted in Émile Burns, ed., *A Handbook of Marxism* (N.Y., 1935). The best book on Marx is Isaiah Berlin, *Karl Marx* (London, 1939). The standard work on Marx's philosophy of history is M. M. Bober, *Karl Marx's Interpretation of History* (2 ed., Cambridge, 1948). See also: Sidney Hook, *Towards Understanding Karl Marx* (N.Y., 1933), and *From Hegel to Marx* (N.Y., 1950). For criticism from a Marxist viewpoint, see: G. V. Plekhanov, *Essays in Historical Materialism* (N.Y., 1940); and his *Fundamental Problems of Marxism* (N.Y., 1930); for critical evaluation, Popper, *Open Society*, 274–297, and J. A. Schumpeter, *Capitalism, Socialism and Democracy* (r. ed., N.Y., 1947), 1–58. For the economic interpretation in general, see: E. R. A. Seligman, *The Economic Interpretation of History* (r. ed., N.Y., 1922); Henri Sée, *The Economic Interpretation of History* (N.Y., 1929).

The following works touch on the frontier theory and its antecedents. For physiographic factors, see: N. S. Shaler, *Nature and Man in America* (N.Y., 1891); E. C. Semple, *American History and Its Geographic Conditions* (Boston, 1903); A. P. Brigham, *Geographic Influences in American History* (Boston, 1903); W. W. Atwood, *The Physiographic Provinces of North America* (Boston, 1940); and R. H. Brown, *Historical Geography of the United States* (N.Y., 1948). For the Turner theory, see: Turner, *Frontier in American History*, and *Significance of Sections in American History*. The literature on the Turner theory is varied and extensive. For a bibliography of items to 1935, see: E. E. Edwards, *References on the Significance of the Frontier in American History* (Dept. of Ag., Bibliog. Contributions, No. 25, Wash., 1935). A convenient sampling of opinions is to be found in G. R. Taylor, ed., *The Turner Thesis Concerning the Role of the Frontier in American History* (Boston, 1949). For critical views, see: Richard Hofstadter, "Turner and the Frontier Myth," *Am. Scholar*, XVIII (1949), 433; Murray Kane, "Some Considerations of the Frontier Concept of Frederick Jackson Turner," *Miss. Valley Hist. Rev.*, XXVII (1940), 379; J. C. Malin, "The Turner-Mackinder Space Concept of History," *Essays on Historiography* (Lawrence, Kansas, 1946); G. W. Pierson, "The Frontier and Frontiersmen of Turner's Essays," *Penn. Mag. of Hist. and Biog.*, LXIV (1940), 449; idem, "The Frontier and American Institutions," *New Eng. Quar.*, XV (1942), 224; and B. F. Wright, "Political Institutions and the Frontier," in D. R. Fox, ed., *Sources of Culture in the Middle West* (N.Y., 1934).

The great source of inspiration for scientific history was Leopold von Ranke, *Zur Kritik neurer Geschichtschreiber* (Berlin, 1824). See also: Auguste Comte, *Positive Philosophy* (tr. by H. Martineau, 2 vols., London, 1853); and H. T. Buckle, *History of Civilization in England* (2 vols., London, 1857–61). For scientific history in America, see: Holt, "Idea of Scientific History." For a general discussion, see: Salvemini, *Historian and Scientist* (§ 2).

The manifesto of the New History movement was Robinson, *The New History*. See also: Benedetto Croce, *History: Its Theory and Practice* (N.Y., 1920); Karl Mannheim, *Ideology and Utopia* (London, 1946); C. A. Beard, "Written History as an Act of Faith," *Am. Hist. Rev.*, XXXIX (1934), 219; idem, "That Noble Dream," *Am. Hist. Rev.*, XLI (1935), 74; idem, *The Nature of the Social Sciences* (N.Y., 1934); idem, *The Discussion of Human Affairs* (N.Y., 1936). For an able critique of relativism, see: M. H. Mandelbaum, *The Problem of Historical Knowledge* (N.Y., 1938). For a discriminating account of the "new history," see: White, *Social Thought in America*, chs. iv, xiv.

The following are special theories of interest to the student of American history: Herbert Butterfield, *The Whig Interpretation of History* (London, 1931); A. A. Brill, ed., *The Basic Writings of Sigmund Freud* (N.Y., 1938); Erich Fromm, *Escape from Freedom* (N.Y., 1941); J. M. Keynes, *The General Theory of Employment, Interest and Money* (London, 1936); V. I. Lenin, *Imperialism* (N.Y., 1917); A. T. Mahan, *The Influence of Sea Power upon History, 1660–1783* (Boston, 1890); Roberto Michels, *Political Parties* (Glencoe, 1949); Gaetano Mosca, *The Ruling Class* (Arthur Livingston, ed., N.Y., 1939); Vilfredo Pareto, *The Mind and Society* (Arthur Livingston, ed., N.Y., 1935); David Riesman, *The Lonely Crowd* (N.Y., 1950); J. A. Schumpeter, *The Theory of Economic Development* (Cambridge, 1934); *idem, Imperialism and Social Classes* (P. M. Sweezy, ed., N.Y., 1951); George Sorel, *Reflections on Violence* (Glencoe, 1950); W. G. Sumner, *Folkways* (Boston, 1906); R. H. Tawney, *Religion and the Rise of Capitalism* (N.Y., 1926); Thorstein Veblen, *What Veblen Taught* (W. C. Mitchell, ed., N.Y., 1936); Max Weber, *The Protestant Ethic and the Spirit of Capitalism* (London, 1930); H. H. Gerth and C. W. Mills, eds., *From Max Weber: Essays in Sociology* (N.Y., 1946); A. N. Whitehead, *Science and the Modern World* (N.Y., 1925).

6. PRINCIPLES OF HISTORICAL CRITICISM

The historian cannot, any more than any other mortal, escape the egocentric predicament: everything he perceives is mediated through his own perceptions. Yet, the fact that perfect objectivity is unattainable does not relieve the historian of the duty of striving for it. He is thus committed, above all else, to the rigorous and unrelenting scrutiny of historical evidence. This commitment distinguishes his trade from that of the novelist, the propagandist, the prophet. Evidence is the only means by which to establish a historical fact; facts are the bricks out of which the structure of historical interpretation is erected. If there are not enough of them, the structure will collapse.

Historical research deals with two general categories of sources: primary and secondary. Primary sources are firsthand testimony about a historical event; secondary sources are descriptions of the event derived from and based on primary sources. The primary source represents the view of the eye-witness, the secondary source the view of the journalist or the scholar, who comes along later and tries to reconstruct the story. The line between the two categories is often indistinct. A single document may be a primary source for one purpose and a secondary source for another. A book like Robert E. Sherwood's *Roosevelt and Hopkins* (N.Y., 1948), for example, is a primary source on some matters and a secondary source on others; or a book on current American economic policy, written from outside the government, might be a secondary source so far as policy-making is concerned but a primary source for the study of public opinion.

The sources available to the historian are primarily, but not exclusively, documents; sources may also take the form of museum materials (§ 17), pictures (§ 18), sound recordings (§ 66), and newsreel films (§ 18). But, whatever the character of the source, its critical examination is the historian's first obligation. This critical examination involves three procedures: (1) the authentication of the physical remains, or *external criticism*; (2) the analysis of contents, or *internal criticism*; and (3) the *evaluation* of the resulting data as *evidence*.

The purpose of external criticism is to assess the genuineness of documents or of other physical survivals. It seeks, first, to expose counterfeits, and then to establish positive identifications of origin. For the American historian, the techniques of external criticism are less essential than they are for the ancient or medieval student, who survives by his skill in the esoteric arts of paleography, epigraphy, sphragistics, and diplomatics. Yet it may occasionally be useful for a student of American history to know that there are tests which can reliably determine the age of paper, ink, or binding so that unscrupulous dealers or scholars fanatically bent on proving their points will not intimidate him by a display of fading manuscripts, spidery handwriting, and crumbling bindings. The inquiries of the Committee on the Horn Papers provide useful examples.

The purpose of internal criticism is to detect inconsistencies, errors, or false-hoods through analysis of the text of a document or through inspection of the contents of nondocumentary sources. Handbooks and manuals have made various attempts to codify the principles of internal criticism. But abstract propositions decide concrete cases no more often in history than in law; and most codes come down to recommendations for vigilance, skepticism, and common sense.

Internal criticism is indispensable, of course, in assessing evidential value. But, in a stricter sense, internal criticism is most useful for the historian when confronted by pseudonymous, anonymous, or spurious texts. In these cases, espe-cially when no original manuscript survives, the historian must comb the text for clues which will betray and trap the unknown author. The most celebrated anon-ymous document in American history is perhaps "The Diary of a Public Man," published in the *North American Review* in 1879; the researches of F. M. Ander-son into its authorship present a spectacular exercise in internal criticism. The close analysis of texts too may uncover anachronisms and inconsistencies which expose a paper as false; the *Atlantic Monthly's* Lincoln letter which spoke blithely of forty sections in a township and depicted emigrants moving to Kansas in 1834 inevitably provoked the skepticism of experts. The investigations by the Commit-tee on the Horn Papers display a patient and scrupulous use of internal criticism.

The climax of the critical process is the evaluation of the evidence produced by research and validated by the techniques of external and internal criticism. The historian must not permit himself to be satisfied by the mere accumulation of "evidence." He must relentlessly subject himself to the question: what is this "evidence" evidence of?

Certain general remarks may be made about the reliability of types of ma-terials. Official reports vary in reliability according to time and source. United States census reports, for example, are more valuable for some years than for others (§§ 7, 44). Political speeches and documents must be considered in terms of the immediate political context. Personal documents — diaries and letters — must be subject to the usual discounts of private bias, hope, or anxiety; many, indeed, were written, consciously or subconsciously, for the historical record. Reminiscences are ordinarily exercises in retrospective justification; histories gen-erally reflect the values and preoccupations of the historian; and fiction — is fiction (§ 64). Collected editions of letters depend in value on the prevailing state of the editorial technique; Jared Sparks's edition of Washington's letters, for example, is worth considerably less than Julian Boyd's of Jefferson's (§§ 54, 55). Newspapers bend sharply to the breezes of political partisanship, editorial com-petition, and countinghouse control (§ 53). There is no form of historical evidence in which the historian must not labor to winnow the facts from the embellish-ments.

How is the historian to approach specific problems of evaluation? As a first step, it may often be useful to attempt the imaginative leap into the shoes of the witness. In making this leap, the historian must first consider what the *words* of the testimony meant for the witness. This is not so simple as it sounds. The process of construction, Mr. Justice Frankfurter has observed, "is not an exercise in logic or dialectic: The aids of formal reasoning are not irrelevant; they may simply be inadequate." The problem is that context creates and alters meaning — that mere "common sense" or logic may omit much which is below the surface of words and yet an indispensable part of them.

"Property" thus meant one thing to John Locke, another to the American Liberty League; "democracy" one thing to Fisher Ames, another to Woodrow Wilson, and quite another to Joseph Stalin. The history of the developing meaning of the word "corporation" is a history of American economic life. Moreover, men in the past, like men in the present, were given to irony, satire, epigram, literary flourish, overstatement, understatement, and the whole human range of nuance, inflection, and exaggeration.

Once satisfied that he understands what the witness is saying, the historian must then consider whether the witness was in a position to know what he was talking about; then whether, if the witness was in that position, he had the skill and competence to observe accurately; then whether, if he knew the facts, he would be inclined to represent them fairly, or whether circumstances — emotional, intellectual, political — might incline him to emphasize some aspects of an episode and minimize others. Many motives, worthy and unworthy, deflect or distort observation: national patriotism, class conditioning, political partisanship, religious faith, moral principle, love, hate, and survival.

Because the witness is not available for cross-examination, the historian may be compelled to make a rough evaluation of his general character; the words of a Henry L. Stimson, for example, would presumably command greater respect than those of a General James Wilkinson. Yet the historian must guard equally against the logical fallacy of confusing the origin of a story with its value: the chronic liar may bear true witness on a particular occasion, and the high-minded man may get hopelessly muddled. Even the high-minded man is, after all, prey to the normal gamut of human emotions. Students who know well how hasty and careless their own letters are, or how premeditated their diaries may be, must resist the temptation to accept statements in the letters and diaries of others as exact and dispassionate simply because the writers have been dead for a hundred years. The witness's age, moreover, may be a factor: too many historians have been seduced by the confident but faulty recollections of men misrecalling events in which they had participated forty years earlier. We all know, or should know, how treacherous an instrument memory is, how much it is at the mercy of our overriding desire to show ourselves in the best possible light. Nor is the distinction between primary and secondary sources very helpful in these cases. The firsthand witness is as subject to the winds of passion as the man who comes along later.

Then too there is the problem of the myth-making propensity of man. Poetic fancy often drifts into acceptance as historical fact: how many apt stories must be ascribed in last analysis to that talented Italian raconteur, Ben Trovato! Nor can the historian forget that, beyond myths, there are hoaxes. H. L. Mencken's bathtub story will not down, for all its inventor's valiant attempts to kill it: in 1948 President Truman, answering the critics of his new White House balcony, recalled that Mrs. Millard Fillmore had been "almost lynched" when she installed a bathtub. And the egregious fictions of A. C. Buell's *Paul Jones* (N.Y., 1900) keep creeping into subsequent popular biographies. It is all too easy to poison the bloodstream of history.

Once the historian has completed his imaginative leap and has plucked the flower of fact out of the nettle of embellishment, he can proceed to the next and more conclusive test — that is, the search for independent corroboration. Like treason in the Constitution, a historical fact ideally should rest "on the testimony of two witnesses to some overt act, or on confession in open court." But sometimes, alas, there is but a single witness; or, if there are two, and of equal competence and probity, their versions may be in head-on collision. Charles Evans Hughes told his biographer that he had recommended Robert H. Jackson as chief justice of the Supreme Court; President Truman's firm recollection is that Hughes recommended Fred M. Vinson; no documentary evidence survives: how to solve the insoluble conflict?

A judge and jury, indeed, would go mad if they had to decide cases on evidence which will often seem more than satisfactory to the historian. But there is no escape; the historian, if he is to interpret at all, will try and convict on evidence which a court would throw out as circumstantial or hearsay. The victims of the historical process have to seek their compensation in the fact that history provides them with a far more flexible appellate procedure. The historian's sentences are in a continuous condition of review; few of his verdicts are ever final.

The classical works on historical method are: Ernst Bernheim, *Lehrbuch der historischen Methode und der Geschichtsphilosophie* (6 ed, Leipzig, 1908); C. V. Langlois and Charles Seignobos, *Introduction aux études historiques* (Paris, 1898; G. G. Berry, tr., N.Y., 1925); Wilhelm Bauer, *Einführung in das Studium Geschichte* (2 ed., Tübingen, 1928). Other useful works include: C. G. Crump, *History and Historical Research* (London, 1928); F. M. Fling, *Outline of Historical Method* (Lincoln, 1899); for the Catholic viewpoint, G. J. Garraghan, *A Guide to Historical Method* (J. Delanglez, ed., N.Y., 1946); Louis Gottschalk, *Understanding History* (N.Y., 1950); Sherman Kent, *Writing History* (N.Y., 1941); Allan Nevins, *The Gateway to History* (N.Y., 1938); Renier, *History*; J. M. Vincent, *Historical Research* (N.Y., 1911). Of special interest to American historians is H. C. Hockett, *Introduction to Research in American History* (2 ed., N.Y., 1950).

H. B. George, *Historical Evidence* (Oxford, 1909) is a sensible survey. For modern techniques of external criticism, see: G. J. Lacey, "Questioned Documents," *Am. Archivist*, IX–X (1946), 267; also, C. H. Hart, "Frauds in Historical Portraiture," Am. Hist. Assoc., *Report*, 1913, I, 85. Of special usefulness for American historians is Allen Johnson, *The Historian and Historical Evidence* (N.Y., 1926). For specific examples of criticism, F. M. Anderson, *The Mystery of "A Public Man"* (Minneapolis, 1948); A. P. Middleton and Douglass Adair, "The Mystery of the Horn Papers," *William and Mary Quar.*, IV (1947), 409; H. L. Mencken, "Hymn to the Truth," *Prejudices: Sixth Series* (N.Y., 1927), 194; and the series of Social Science Research Council studies, *Critiques of Research in the Social Sciences*, especially F. A. Shannon, "An Appraisal of Walter Prescott Webb's *The Great Plains*" (N.Y., 1940).

C. B. Williams and A. H. Stevenson, *A Research Manual* (N.Y., 1940), Appendix A; Louis Kaplan, *Research Materials in the Social Sciences* (Madison, 1939); and William Rose, ed., *An Outline of Modern Knowledge* (N.Y., 1931) contain bibliographies of method.

7. STATISTICS AND HISTORY

The accumulation and the study of statistics developed in the early modern period out of the desire of legislators and administrators for information as they dealt with the concrete problems of state. This was thus a form of applied political science, a character that has clung to statistics throughout its development.

In the late seventeenth and early eighteenth centuries, however, John Graunt and William Petty, among others, made an effort to convert the study into a quantitative science susceptible of greater abstraction. There was still considerable emphasis on practical utility, as the term "political arithmetic" indicated; but there was also an aspiration to develop a theoretical approach to the nature of numerical groupings. Through most of the nineteenth century the major emphasis was, however, on the accumulation of data, largely directed toward practical ends. Improvements in technique therefore aimed primarily at making the material gathered as exhaustive and as wide in coverage as possible.

A decisive shift came in the last quarter of the nineteenth century, when geneticists dealing with subjects that involved very large numbers began to work out sampling techniques with the aid of the calculus of probability. From their studies emerged the devices through which statistics developed reliable measurements of distribution and the means of establishing correlations from which causal connections might be drawn. In several of the social sciences, notably in economics and psychology, there was a parallel trend.

Historians have not been influenced by the development of statistics to the same degree as have other social scientists. Preoccupied with the uniqueness of events rather than with their relationship to a theoretical pattern, historians have generally used statistics as illustrations to lend concreteness to their arguments or narratives. Their quantitative measurements have therefore usually been simple. With the aid of time series, changes in the size of groups can be demonstrated at successive chronological intervals. With the aid of distribution series, the dispersal or concentration of the members of a group can be shown at any given moment.

In presenting such data historians have generally been content to use simple tabular forms. They thus frequently neglect the possibility of making the most convincing presentation of their material. Even simple tables call for decisions, as to what should go in the rows and what in the columns, or as to whether there should be a complete or incomplete cross classification. Graphic devices are too often neglected because the historian cannot make a choice among the various available forms; line curves, bar and band charts, pie diagrams, statistical maps, and pictographs may each be effective when their uses are understood. The same is true of the index numbers or representative figures designed to measure trends and to eliminate as many short-term variables as possible. Finally, historians are all too ready to use loose, common-sense terminology when more refined concepts would assist them in expressing themselves. They would often find it helpful, for instance, to discriminate among the various types of averages and to use mode, median, and mean, as well.

Although they rarely go beyond these simple descriptive measurements in their own work, historians need a more general knowledge of statistical theory to assimilate in their thinking the conclusions of the other social scientists. Since economists and sociologists, armed with statistics, may arrive at generalizations that impinge upon his own field of interests, the historian must be able to check their results, if not in a detailed technical manner, at least in terms of coherence and logical validity.

Two particular aspects of statistical theory touch upon the subject matter of history. In the first place, there are well-developed means of determining by quantitative measurement the nature of trends in time, for distinguishing among changes that are secular, cyclical, seasonal, or merely the products of chance variations. Such judgments form the basis of much of business-cycle theory. There are also comparable measurements for determining tendencies to centrality and dispersion, for measuring variations and deviations from a central tendency, and for establishing trend relationships between two or more variables or between related frequency distributions. The complex formulae through which statisticians express such findings may involve generalizations, or reorganizations of data, of substantial importance to the historian. All sampling procedures, increasingly significant in the accumulation of contemporary statistical information (§ 8), thus rest on such assumptions.

Even theory, however, is limited by the accuracy of the observed data upon which it rests. Oskar Morgenstern's thoughtful essay *On the Accuracy of Economic Observations* (Princeton, 1950), has demonstrated that. But the historian is particularly circumscribed in this respect. He cannot experiment, cannot, under most circumstances, gather his material at first hand; for the universe with which he deals has disappeared. He is perforce compelled to depend on intermediaries. He finds it necessary, therefore, to examine with care the validity and reliability of the measurements he uses, as other social scientists do. But in addition, he must consider the source of his information of paramount importance.

These considerations are particularly important in the early periods of American history, before the organization of the present state and federal governments. A substantial fund of quantitative data for the colonial era is scattered through the reports of officials, through the administrative records of English and provincial authorities, through tax lists, parish records, and the like. Such material, uncertain as to origin, must be treated with discrimination. Nevertheless, used with care it may yield a wide variety of significant information. See, e.g.: E. B. Greene and V. D. Harrington, *American Population before the Federal Census of 1790* (N.Y., 1932); S. H. Sutherland, *Population Distribution in Colonial America* (N.Y., 1936).

Fortunately the fund of statistical data has grown rapidly, particularly in the last century. As earlier, much of the accumulation has been by agencies of government, and the development of techniques of collection and analysis has reflected the expansion of the role of government in society. This is particularly true of the federal government, the publications of which have a general importance, are best classified, and are most readily available.

A number of general guides will introduce the student to these sources. Those by A. M. Boyd and E. S. Brown listed below classify material by agency of issue; those by Hirshberg and Melinat and by Schmeckebier, by subjects (§ 41). See also: §§ 42–47.

The earliest statistical work of the federal government sprang out of the customs and census services. Duties on foreign imports were long the main source of federal revenue, and reports on them were compiled by the Treasury Department. Figures on foreign commerce and navigation became increasingly detailed and broader in scope, particularly after the creation of the Bureau of Foreign and Domestic Commerce. These materials are supplemented, especially after 1875, by records of internal commerce and finance.

The census was originally taken by United States marshals under the direction of the State Department, for purposes of fixing Congressional representation. It listed white males over and under age sixteen, white females, other free persons, and slaves. To population figures were added, in 1810, manufactures; in 1820, occupations; in 1840, mines, agriculture, commerce, illiteracy, insanity, and pensioners; in 1850, libraries, newspapers and periodicals, and criminals. The machinery and techniques of enumeration were not equal to these ambitious programs, and the results were correspondingly open to error. Not until 1830 were uniform printed schedules introduced. The census of 1850 was the first to aspire to scientific accuracy. The raw data then were compiled and classified in a central office in the new Interior Department. But not until 1880 was there centralized control of supervisors and enumerators; the census for that year was tabulated in twenty-four volumes, five times as many as in any previous census. Machine tabulation was introduced in 1890, and in 1902 a permanent Census Bureau with its own staff was created. The Bureau broke up the decennial census by enumerations at more frequent intervals, such as the biennial census of manufactures. In 1906 a religious census was added, and in 1940 sampling techniques made their appearance in the census.

Regulatory bureaus established to deal with specific problems — agriculture, immigration, labor, conservation, public health, to name a few — include statistical information in their reports. Independent commissions, like the Interstate Commerce Commission, release statistics gathered in the course of investigation and regulation. The Federal Reserve Board and Banks similarly collect data on finance.

Apart from such official statistics accumulated in the routine administration of government, there is also a useful body of data gathered as the result of special *ad hoc* inquiries. Congress, through its committees; administrative agencies; and the courts have all conducted such inquiries from time to time. The results of these investigations are valuable because they probe topical and controversial questions; on the other hand, they are correspondingly subject to bias.

Beginning in 1878, *The Statistical Abstract of the United States,* issued annually by various agencies, has contained general statistics on practically every subject for which data are collected by governmental (and certain other) agencies. Besides annual figures, it includes the most recent statistics collected at longer intervals. In 1949 the Bureau of the Census issued a supplement, *Historical Statistics of the United States, 1789–1945,* a convenient compendium and collation of statistical materials, together with valuable notes on sources and their use.

State and municipal materials vary considerably in nomenclature, quantity, and quality. Early in the nineteenth century most states had registration laws that supplied them with information on births, marriages, and deaths. Local, like federal, governments faced problems of taxation and representation that called for statistical data. The city and state agencies were the first to feel pressure for information as the changing currents of political thought stressed their police and reform functions; they needed data on public carriers, public health, education, industry, and the conditions of labor. The earliest statistics in these fields must be sought in state rather than in national sources. In addition, Massachusetts, New York, and Michigan for a time had more comprehensive censuses than the federal one. State agencies also served as the training ground for many statisticians who later commanded the federal government's expanding statistical apparatus. Thus the Massachusetts Bureau of Labor Statistics, organized in 1869, earliest of many similar state bureaus, provided Carroll D. Wright with the experience he used in organizing the national department. The general bibliographies of state documents are helpful in locating and assessing material. See especially the works of Bowker, Childs, and Hasse listed below (§§ 42, 43).

Privately collected statistics must meet only private standards, and vary accordingly. Most useful are special and continuing inquiries of industrial and commercial organizations into production and exchange. The American Iron and Steel Institute has long gathered such information. Stock-exchange records begin early and are reliable. Such material may be available in periodic reports or in trade journals, like *Iron Age* or the *Publishers' Weekly*, or through the business sections of newspapers. Chambers of commerce and boards of trade often gather and publish data. Private manuals, like Moody's and Standard and Poor, and periodicals of general business interest, like *Barron's*, conveniently draw together statistical information gathered elsewhere. Farmer, labor, and professional organizations compile and publish data; the American Medical Association, for example, keeps track of the number, distribution, and education of its members. Occasional advertising agencies like J. Walter Thompson have compiled studies that touch on the problems of population and marketing. Insurance companies are often useful sources for data on fires, floods, and theft, as well as on mortality, health, and population. Early and late, reformers gathered the "facts" to prove their case, argued in behalf of abolition, prohibition, suffrage, education, or eugenics. Handled with care, their work may be useful.

Of a different order are fact-books or almanacs, often associated with newspapers. The *Tribune Almanac*, the *World Almanac*, and the *Information Please Almanac* are the modern versions of the compilations of Tench Coxe, Pelatiah Webster, and Adam Seybert, as well as of registers like Niles and Hazard. In addition many early gazetteers were repositories of miscellaneous information (§§ 22, 24, 49).

In a special class is the American Statistical Association. Founded in emulation of the English society in 1838–39 by a group of Boston professional men led by Lemuel Shattuck, it early focused its interest on technical problems. Particularly useful was its criticism of the census of 1840. After 1880, it attracted a national constituency in the universities and in government service. Its *Journal* (1888–   ) and other publications include miscellaneous statistics and discussions of high quality which are themselves of considerable historical interest. A selective cumulative index covers its publications through 1939.

More specialized statistical research organizations have recently entered the field. The National Bureau of Economic Research, the National Industrial Conference Board, and the Brookings Institution have sponsored investigations into areas the government was slow to consider: for instance, the determination of national income, of employment, of the labor force, and of productivity.

For the history of statistics, see: F. S. Baldwin, "Statistics in the Service of the Municipality," Am. Stat. Assoc., *Quar. Publ.*, XIV (1914), 103; J. A. Hill, "Historical Value of the Census Records," Am. Hist. Assoc., *Report*, 1908, I, 197; W. S. Holt, *The Bureau of the Census* (Wash., 1929); C. H. Hull, "Service of Statistics to History," in John Koren, ed., *The History of Statistics, Their Development and Progress in Many Countries* (N.Y., 1918); F. F. Stephan, "The History of the Uses of Modern Sampling Procedures," Am. Stat. Assoc., *Journal*, XLIII (1948), 12; C. D. Wright, "Address," Am. Stat. Assoc., *Quar. Publ.*, LXXXI (1908), 1; C. D. Wright and W. C. Hunt, *The History and Growth of the United States Census* (Wash., 1900).

For statistical theory and manuals of method, see: M. M. Blair, *Elementary Statistics*

(N.Y., 1944); T. L. Kelley, *Fundamentals of Statistics* (Cambridge, 1947); M. G. Kendall, "On the Future of Statistics," Royal Stat. Soc., *Journal*, CV (1942), 69; Simon Kuznets, Lillian Epstein, and Elizabeth Jenks, *National Income and Its Composition, 1919–1938* (2 vols., N.Y., 1941); R. F. Martin, *National Income in the United States, 1799–1938* (N.Y., [1939]); A. M. Mood, *Introduction to the Theory of Statistics* (N.Y., 1950); W. A. Neiswanger, *Elementary Statistical Methods* (N.Y., 1943); S. A. Rice, *et al.*, *Next Steps in the Development of Social Statistics* (Ann Arbor, 1933); S. A. Rice, ed., *Statistics in Social Studies* (Phila., 1930); Mortimer Spiegelman, "Construction of the State and Regional Life Tables," Actuarial Soc. of Am., *Trans.*, XLIX (1948), 303; W. F. Willcox, *Studies in American Demography* (Ithaca, 1940).

Guides to statistical sources include: E. S. Brown, *Manual of Government Publications. United States and Foreign* (N.Y., 1950); J. B. Childs, *Government Document Bibliography in the United States and Elsewhere* (3 ed., Wash., 1942); H. J. Dubester, *Catalog of United States Census Publications 1790–1945* (Wash., 1950); H. J. Dubester, *State Censuses: An Annotated Bibliography of Censuses of Population Taken After the Year 1790 by States and Territories of the United States* (Wash., 1948); Florence Du Bois, *Guide to the Statistics of Social Welfare in New York City* (N.Y., 1930); M. B. Givens and Ernestine Wilke, *Guide to Statistical Series Relating to Wages in the United States* (Ann Arbor, 1933); P. M. Hauser and W. R. Leonard, *Government Statistics for Business Use* (N.Y., 1946); J. H. Parmelee, "Public Service Statistics," Am. Stat. Assoc., *Quar. Publ.*, XIV (1915), 489; E. J. Reece, *State Documents for Library Use* (Urbana, 1915); S. A. Rice, "Co-Ordination of Federal Statistical Programs," *Am. Jour. of Sociol.*, L (1944), 22 ff.; L. F. Schmeckebier, *Statistical Work of the National Government* (Balt., 1925); I. B. Taeuber, *General Censuses and Vital Statistics in the Americas* (Wash., 1943); United States Bureau of the Budget, *Federal Statistical Directory* (8 ed., Wash., 1944); J. K. Wilcox, ed., *Manual on the Use of State Publications* (Chi., 1940); W. F. Willcox, *Introduction to the Vital Statistics of the United States, 1900 to 1930* (Wash., 1933).

See also: R. R. Bowker, *State Publications*; A. M. Boyd, *United States Government Publications*; A. R. Hasse, *Index to Economic Materials*; Hirshberg and Melinat, *Subject Guide* (§§ 41, 42).

8. HISTORY AND CONTEMPORARY SOCIAL RESEARCH

As the range of their interests has broadened, historians have increasingly drawn upon diverse bodies of material. Once they became involved with subjects other than the political and diplomatic, they found it necessary to use types of social observation that originated from outside the documents of government. At the start of the nineteenth century, the most important descriptions of social life were contained in incidental comments in letters and travel accounts. These grew more abundant as the century advanced (§ 48). But they soon were supplemented by more coherent and more organized bodies of information.

By the middle of the century, philanthropic individuals were accumulating data on the health and welfare of the population. Guided by the assumption that the incidence of disease was influenced by social factors, they also gathered information on the surrounding environment. Occasional great outbreaks, such as the cholera epidemic of 1849, gave a dramatic incentive to these efforts. But the day-to-day concerns of physicians and philanthropists also produced a valuable body of reports. Furthermore, such doctors as Lemuel Shattuck extended the range of their investigations to other aspects of American life; they and other humanitarian reformers made surveys of housing conditions, of immigration, and of the conditions of labor.

The emergence of the organized study of social science toward the end of the century increased the emphasis upon the importance of gathering such material. Under the influence of Lester Ward, social scientists felt the compulsion to make their studies practical and to apply their generalizations to the real conditions of the societies in which they lived. To that end they were disposed to regard the city as a "social laboratory" susceptible of study and capable of yielding generalizations that could be applied to improve society.

In the 1890's, sociologists undertook a variety of examinations of the conditions of life in American cities, modeled to some degree after those of London by Charles Booth. Often, like Robert A. Woods's volumes on Boston, these were produced by settlement houses and by philanthropic organizations dedicated to improving the condition of the poor. Others, like Kate Claghorn's work on New York, embodied investigations of the status of various minority groups. Still others, like the Pittsburgh Survey or the De Forest and Veiller tenement-house investigation, were the outcome of particular violent disorders or of pressing social tensions. Mostly they dealt with the large cities, although smaller towns like Lawrence and Minneapolis, Kansas, and Springfield, Illinois, also received attention. Common to all was the emphasis upon such problems as intemperance, housing, and the malfunctioning of institutions like the family or the church. With the appearance of community funds and the pressure for more scientific and more efficient philanthropy, such studies became more frequent; and they constitute a valuable body of historical information.

Such investigations preëmpted the field until the 1920's. They then began to give way in importance to projects undertaken by social scientists who had no direct concern with ameliorating social conditions and who, instead, viewed the survey as a means for gathering data for abstract generalizations. Back in the first decade of the twentieth century, the studies of J. M. Gillette and C. J. Bushnell had demonstrated how maps and statistical tables could serve as analytical devices toward that end (§ 22). Under the influences of the sociologists F. H. Giddings, R. E. Parks, and C. J. Galpin, a large number of studies were directed at examining the American community in its ecological context, rural and urban. Although such works put greater emphasis on generalization and on the theoretical implications of their data, they were still primarily empirical in approach. Like the older social surveys, they stressed the concrete nature of the material and made it possible for the reader to differentiate between the generalizations of the scientist and the observations of the investigator. In such books as those by Williams, Sims, Wilson, Ware, Wirth, Zorbaugh, and Frazier, the historian will discover much usable data, whether he accepts the theory or not.

In the last twenty years, sociologists and social anthropologists have pushed the community survey to still newer uses. They have accumulated a considerable body of significant material, much of it dealing with attitudes and habits not earlier studied in detail. But the historians who wish to incorporate that data in their own work must do so with a clear consciousness of the means by which it was gathered and the purposes it was intended to serve.

The most recent investigators have decisively subordinated their empirical findings to theoretical considerations. Among these scholars, some have been moved by the desire to use the survey as a means of developing a general theory of social-structural stratification. They therefore approach the community with the intention of analyzing its general divisions into classes. *Middletown* by R. S. and H. M. Lynd was a pioneer effort, but Lloyd Warner's "Yankee City Series" has gone much further since. Another group of investigators, often taking as their points of departure the sociology of Durkheim and Tönnies, have attempted to develop typological theories through the survey. Their objectives are generalizations as to the types of personality and of character structure found in the community; Whyte's *Street Corner Society* and Riesman's *Lonely Crowd* are notable examples. Unlike the ecological works of the earlier part of the century, these surveys shift their interest away from the specific place and the concrete data and focus it on the generalization. At the same time they center their interest on the theoretical steps by which they arrive at their conclusions, and, in presentation at least, minimize the importance of their direct observations.

These tendencies complicate the problems of historians who wish to draw upon such data. Increasingly, for instance, these works have been disposed to assume the appearance of generality by obscuring the identity of the place described. In *Middletown*, in *Deep South*, in the "Yankee City Series," and in *Plainville*, the authors draw their data from specific places, but insist they are dealing with kinds of communities, so that the species in general assumes more importance than the individual town or city.

The justification for this practice, that anonymity is the condition for securing the desired information, is hardly impressive; earlier works encountered no difficulty on this score. In any case the practice diminishes the utility of these books to historians. The peculiarity of the subject disappears and the reader has no means of checking upon the reliability of the data. In particular instances scholars who have ventured beyond the information supplied in these studies have discovered that considerable liberty had been taken with the material and that it had been distorted.

The shift in interest has also altered the techniques of the community study. Although the old formal questionnaire is still used for limited purposes, recent years have seen a growing inclination to use less formal means of securing information. The open-ended interview, a directed conversation without defined questions and responses, often uncovers valuable insight not available in any other fashion; but it also lends an impressionistic quality to the data that limits its utility. Lloyd Warner has carried this technique to altogether unjustified extremes, in the use of "fictive" personalities or characters invented to embody supposed social qualities. Perhaps the historian's safest course is to regard these observations as he would the descriptions of a traveler. Doubtful in their reliability as to particulars, these works may nevertheless contain useful general information and the reflections of thoughtful observers.

The students of the community early encountered the problem of describing the attitudes of the groups with which they dealt. In the last twenty years they have had the assistance of a new body of techniques for measuring attitudes quantitatively by means of public-opinion polls. These developments have been stimulated by the commercial utility of market analysis, the estimate of the tastes and preferences of consumers. These polls have also been of service to such agencies of the government as the Department of Agriculture. Finally, the confused political conditions of the 1930's put a premium on the ability to forecast political events.

All polls rest on some sampling theory. Their procedures have become progressively defined as sampling has developed since its rough beginnings in the nineteenth century. Down to 1936 the most important poll was that of the *Literary Digest*, based on a large number of mail interrogations from a list of automobile registrants and telephone subscribers. Since then a smaller but more carefully selected and weighted sample has furnished the basis for the polls of George Gallup (American Institute of Public Opinion), of Elmo Roper, and others. Furthermore, the pollers have been able both to extend the area of their investigations from simple political preferences to the analysis of a wide range of social attitudes, and to examine intensively such particular groups as soldiers and factory workers. These data are available, and are potentially useful to the cautious and critical historian. Much of this material is conveniently assembled in Hadley Cantril's *Public Opinion* (Princeton, 1950).

The exaggerated claims of the poller that he has introduced a "fourth stage" of democracy have discredited him in the eyes of many social scientists and have sometimes obscured the real value of such data. While no poll can itself prove or disprove a historical interpretation, many polls can add new types of evidence and illustrative material.

Clearly a liberal discount must be made of the claim that polls can reliably predict the outcome of elections. The failure of the polls in 1948 showed that; and the results of 1936 and 1944 hardly less so (Daniel Katz and Hadley Cantril, "Public Opinion Polls," *Sociometry*, I [1937], 155; Benson, Young, and Syze, "Polling Lessons"). Using, as they do, a national sample of three thousand or less, the polls cannot expect to avoid errors of 3 or 4 per cent; and that margin in a presidential election may easily be decisive.

Other technical considerations may diminish the reliability of the polls. The preconceptions that entered into construction of the sample, the phrasing of the text of the questions, the variability of the responses, the bias of the interviewers and of the auspices under which the poll is executed, and the nature of the rapport with the respondents can seriously affect the results.

More general factors that shape the reliability of this material arise out of the inherent ambiguity of the situation of the poll itself and out of uncertainty of the pollers as to what it is they are measuring. The situation is ambiguous because the subject is confronted with the unusual demand that he predict his own future actions or analyze his own attitudes. The responses may be inaccurate since the respondents may themselves be incapable of forecasting or understanding their actions. The large percentage of "no answers" in all polls may be the product of lack of knowledge or of apathy, or of an unwillingness to answer, and may substantially distort the conclusions. Finally, there is a large margin of indefiniteness as to the meaning of "public opinion" and of "attitudes." Does a summing up of individual answers without weighting for intensity give a reliable picture of a whole? Can respondents be treated simply as parts of a homogeneous "public," rather than as members of a variety of groups? If the sampling does take account of such groupings, is not the actual poll redundant? The pollers themselves are aware of the gravity of these questions; historians cannot afford to be less so.

For general problems of community and attitude research, see: Nathan Glazer, " 'The American Soldier' as Science," *Commentary*, VIII (1949), 487; Oscar Handlin, review of "Yankee City Series," *New Eng. Quar.*, XV (1942), 554, XVIII (1945), 523, *Jour. of*

Econ. Hist., VII (1947), 275; S. M. Harrison, *The Social Survey* (N.Y., 1931); Tom Harrisson, "What is Public Opinion?," *Pol. Quar.*, XI (1940), 368; A. B. Hollingshead, "Community Research: Development and Present Condition," *Am. Sociol. Rev.*, XIII (1948), 136; P. F. Lazarsfeld, "Obligations of the 1950 Pollster to the 1984 Historian," *Public Opinion Quar.*, XIV (1950), 617; P. F. Lazarsfeld and Marjorie Fiske, "The 'Panel' as a New Tool for Measuring Opinion," *Public Opinion Quar.*, II (1938), 596; R. K. Merton, *et al.*, *Continuities in Social Research* (Glencoe, 1950); C. W. Mills, review, *Am. Sociol. Rev.*, VII (1942), 263; A. M. Schlesinger, Jr., review of "The American Soldier," *Partisan Rev.*, XVI (1949), 521; S. A. Stouffer, *et al.*, *The American Soldier* (2 vols., Princeton, 1949); C. C. Taylor, "Techniques of Community Study and Analysis as Applied to Modern Civilized Societies," in Ralph Linton, ed., *Science of Man in the World Crisis* (N.Y., 1945), 416.

For examples of social surveys of various types, see: F. W. Blackmar and E. W. Burgess, *Lawrence Social Survey* (Topeka, 1917); C. E. Buckingham, *et al.*, *Sanitary Condition of Boston* (Boston, 1875); R. W. De Forest and Lawrence Veiller, *The Tenement House Problem* (N.Y., 1903); H. P. Douglass, *The Springfield Church Survey: A Study of Organized Religion with Its Social Background* (N.Y., [1926]); Eaton and Harrison, *Bibliography of Social Surveys* (§ 35); M. C. Elmer, *The Minneapolis Survey* (Topeka, 1918); J. H. Griscom, *Sanitary Condition of the Laboring Population of New York* (N.Y., 1845); S. M. Harrison, *Springfield Survey* (10 vols., N.Y., 1916–20); S. M. Harrison and Allen Eaton, *Welfare Problems in New York City Which Have Been Studied and Reported Upon during the Period from 1915 through 1925* (N.Y., 1926); P. U. Kellog, ed., *Pittsburgh Survey* (6 vols., N.Y., 1909–14); K. H. Claghorn, "Foreign Immigrant in New York City," U.S. Industrial Commission, *Reports*, XV (1900–02), 449; P. S. Peirce, *Social Surveys of Three Rural Townships in Iowa* (Iowa City, 1917); "Report of the Committee of Internal Health on the Asiatic Cholera," *Boston City Doc.* (1849), No. 66; "Report of the Theodore Roosevelt Commission on Country Life," 60 Cong., 2 Sess., *Sen. Doc.*, No. 705; G. P. Warber, *Social and Economic Survey of a Community in Northeastern Minnesota* (Minneapolis, 1915); R. A. Woods, ed., *Americans in Process; a Settlement Study by Residents and Associates of the South End House* (Boston, 1902); R. A. Woods, ed., *The City Wilderness; a Settlement Study; by Residents and Associates of the South End House* (Boston, 1898).

Among community surveys emphasizing ecology are: Nels Anderson, *The Hobo* (Chi., 1923); Albert Blumenthal, *Small Town Stuff* (Chi., 1932); C. J. Bushnell, "Some Social Aspects of the Chicago Stock Yards," *Am. Jour. of Sociol.*, VII (1901), 145, 433; I. B. Cohen, *et al.*, *Economic and Social Survey of Botetourt County* (Charlottesville, 1942); E. F. Frazier, *The Negro Family in Chicago* (Chi., 1932); C. J. Galpin, *Social Anatomy of an Agricultural Community* (Madison, 1915); J. M. Gillette, "The Culture Agencies of a Typical Manufacturing Group: South Chicago," *Am. Jour. of Sociol.*, VII (1901), 91, 188; L. T. Kohler, *Neosho, Missouri under the Impact of Army Camp Construction* (Columbia, 1944); R. D. McKenzie, *The Neighborhood: A Study of Local Life in the City of Columbus, Ohio* (Chi., 1923); N. L. Sims, *A Hoosier Village* (N.Y., 1912); F. M. Thrasher, *The Gang* (Chi., 1927); J. E. Voss, *Summer Resort: An Ecological Analysis of a Satellite Community* (Phila., 1941); J. M. Williams, *An American Town* (N.Y., 1906); W. H. Wilson, *Quaker Hill* (n.p., 1907); C. F. Ware, *Greenwich Village* (Boston, 1935); Louis Wirth, *The Ghetto* (Chi., 1928); H. W. Zorbaugh, *The Gold Coast and the Slum* (Chi., 1929).

Community surveys emphasizing social stratification include: Allison Davis, B. B. Gardner, and M. R. Gardner, *Deep South* (Chi., 1941); John Dollard, *Caste and Class in a Southern Town* (New Haven, 1937); St. C. Drake and H. R. Cayton, *Black Metropolis* (N.Y., 1945); R. S. and H. M. Lynd, *Middletown* (N.Y., [1929]); *idem*, *Middletown in Transition* (N.Y., 1937); W. L. Warner, "Yankee City Series" (4 vols., New Haven, 1941–47).

Community surveys emphasizing typologies include: E. H. Bell, *Sublette, Kansas* (Wash., 1942); W. M. Kollmorgan, *The Old Order Amish of Lancaster County, Pennsylvania* (Wash., 1942); Olen Leonard and C. P. Loomis, *El Cerrito, New Mexico* (Wash., 1941); Kenneth Macleish and Kimball Young, *Landaff, New Hampshire* (Wash., 1942); E. O. Moe and C. C. Taylor, *Irwin, Iowa* (Wash., 1942); James West (pseud. of

Carl Withers), *Plainville, U.S.A.* (N.Y., 1945); Waller Wynne, *Harmony, Georgia* (Wash., 1943); W. F. Whyte, *Street Corner Society* (Chi., 1943).

Among the more useful works on the public opinion poll are: Albert Blankenship, *Consumer and Opinion Research* (N.Y., 1943); Herbert Blumer, "Public Opinion and Public Opinion Polling," *Am. Sociol. Rev.*, XIII (1948), 542; Hadley Cantril, *Gauging Public Opinion* (Princeton, 1947); S. C. Dodd, "The Washington Public Opinion Laboratory," *Public Opinion Quar.*, XII (1948), 118; George Gallup, *A Guide to Public Opinion Polls* (Princeton, 1944); George Gallup and S. F. Rae, *The Pulse of Democracy, the Public Opinion Poll and How it Works* (N.Y., 1940); Herbert Goldhamer, "Public Opinion and Personality," *Am. Jour. of Sociol.*, LV (1950), 346; Herbert Hyman, "Problems in the Collection of Opinion — Research Data," *Am. Jour. of Sociol.*, LV (1950), 362; Arthur Kornhauser, "Public Opinion and Social Class," *Am. Jour. of Sociol.*, LV (1950), 333; G. A. Lundberg, *Social Research* (N.Y., 1942), ch. viii; R. K. Merton and P. K. Hall, "Election Polling Forecasts and Public Images of Social Science," *Public Opinion Quar.*, XIII (1949), 185.

The more important critical and defensive works on polling are: E. G. Benson, C. C. Young, and C. A. Syze, "Polling Lessons from the 1944 Election," *Public Opinion Quar.*, IX (1945), 467; Ernest Borneman, "The Public Opinion Myth," *Harper's*, CXCV (1947), 30; W. E. Deming, "On Errors in Surveys," *Am. Sociol. Rev.*, IX (1944), 359; S. de Grazia, review, *Am. Jour. of Sociol.*, LV (1950), 415; A. M. Lee, "Sociological Theory in Public Opinion and Attitude Studies," *Am. Jour. Sociol.*, XII (1947), 312; Frederick Mosteller, *et al.*, *Pre-Election Polls of 1948* (N.Y., [1949]); "The Opinion Polls and the 1948 U.S. Presidential Election: A Symposium," *Intl. Jour. of Opinion and Attitude Res.*, II (1948–49), 453, III (1949), 1, 157; Lindsay Rogers, *The Pollsters* (N.Y., 1949); C. M. Sparrow, "Measurement and Social Science," *Voyages and Cargoes* (Charlottesville, 1947), 150; "Hearings [on the Gallup Poll] before the Committee to Investigate Campaign Expenditures," 78 Cong., 2 Sess., *H. Res.*, 551, pt. 12.

Chapter Two

RESEARCH AND WRITING

9. OPPORTUNITIES FOR RESEARCH

An inquiry some years ago by M. W. Jernegan into the "Productivity of Doctors of Philosophy in History" (*Am. Hist. Rev.*, XXXIII [1927], 1) indicated that only about one in four holders of the degree had kept up an active interest in research and writing after completing their doctoral dissertations. According to a later study by W. B. Hesseltine and Louis Kaplan of "Doctors of Philosophy in History" (*ibid.*, XLVII [1942], 795), the proportion in the next decade rose to one out of two or better. Even this showing — if we may assume that the estimate is not overoptimistic — does not speak very well for a degree that is designed in major part to train its recipients for continuing contributions to knowledge. Among the reasons discovered by Professor Jernegan for this disappointing record four stand out: heavy teaching and administrative loads; salaries too meager to permit of travel to essential library centers; the uncertainty of finding an outlet for publication; and the dearth of local source materials.

The individual scholar can do little to surmount the first two of these obstacles, though he may sometimes be able to procure financial aid for research projects from outside agencies (§ 14). The third difficulty, that of a medium of publication, actually bears less heavily upon the student of American history than upon the American student of the history of other countries. In both cases treatises of book length may go begging whatever their merit, but the student of United States history can always resort to the many national, regional, state, and local historical journals, provided he is willing to present his material in the form of articles (§ 50). Extremely important contributions have been made in this way, as the essays and articles of J. Franklin Jameson, Frederick Jackson Turner, Carl L. Becker, and others have shown. Some subjects are best handled in this manner. Nearly any can be.

The complaint as to the lack of local sources oftentimes means merely that the scholar has not been making the most of his opportunities. As Thoreau once observed, "None is so poor that he need sit on a pumpkin." Obviously many pieces of investigation can be pursued only at a distance, but other possibilities lie richly at hand if the student is sufficiently resourceful. It is only on the basis of a multiplicity of local and regional "case studies" that an adequate insight into our diversified national culture will ever be arrived at. A minute examination of the transformation of a village along the Erie Canal may lend new significance to the role which that historic waterway played in American development. Delving into small-town newspaper files may not only illuminate the attitude of the particular community toward local and national situations, but may also evidence the preoccupations and points of view of a host of similar communities. The primary records necessary for inquiries like these are usually available, if not in public depositories, then in private hands (§§ 4, 46). For helpful suggestions, see: D. D. Parker, *Local History, How to Gather It, Write It, and Publish It* (B. E. Josephson, ed., Social Science Research Council, N.Y., 1944), chs. i–vi; M. W. Schlegel, "Writing Local History Articles," Am. Assoc. for State and Local Hist., *Bull.*, II (1949), 47.

Undoubtedly a further impediment to scholarly productivity, even where the conditions are otherwise favorable, is the difficulty of hitting upon a suitable topic for investigation. The student wishes to avoid hackneyed and overworked subjects, yet does not know where more rewarding opportunities lie. Some years ago two different conferences of American historians addressed themselves in part to this question. Their conclusions appear in *Historical Scholarship in America: Needs and Opportunities* (N.Y., 1932), a report by a Committee of the American Historical Association on the Planning of Research. The topics which they listed as "profitable but somewhat neglected" (with more detailed suggestions as to the possibilities under most of the headings) may still be so described in spite of the work that has been done on some of the subjects since then:

1. Urban life and urbanization as factors in American civilization.
2. The role of rural life and institutions.
3. History of ethnic relations and of acculturation.
4. Interstate migration of people and institutions.
5. The changing fortunes of the family.
6. History of patriotism and nationalizing tendencies.
7. Legal history.
8. Administrative history and institutions.
9. The development of business and of business enterprise.
10. The social impact of technological changes.
11. The history of leisure.
12. Shifting standards of public and private morality.
13. Changing religious folkways.
14. History of book publishing and of reading habits.
15. Formation and operation of public opinion.
16. The life history of individual newspapers.
17. Social conditions and forces as reflected and affected by literature.
18. Social conditions and forces as reflected and affected by education.
19. Social conditions and forces as reflected and affected by the arts (painting, sculpture, music, the theater, the graphic arts, and photography).
20. History of science and pseudoscience.
21. History of intellectual attitudes (such as the national trait of optimism).
22. The international movement of ideas and cultural institutions to and from America.

More recently a committee of the Mississippi Valley Historical Association published the results of a similar survey under the title, "Projects in American History and Culture," *Miss. Valley Hist. Rev.*, XXXI (1945), 499. Besides reiterating and amplifying many of the proposals of the earlier report, it offered some additional ones, notably syntheses of particular periods, studies of American humor, and more thorough research into public-land policy, agriculture, conservation, transportation, mining, logging, and lumbering.

Specialists in different phases or periods of American history have offered further and usually more explicit suggestions.

See particularly: H. K. Beale, "On Rewriting Reconstruction History," *Am. Hist. Rev.*, XLV (1939–40), 807; S. F. Bemis, "Fields for Research in Diplomatic History to 1900," *ibid.*, XXXVI (1930), 68; T. C. Cochran, "Problems and Challenges in Business History Research with Special Reference to Entrepreneurial History," Bus. Hist. Soc., *Bull.*, XXIV (1950), 113, and "Social History of the Corporation," in C. F. Ware, ed., *The Cultural Approach to History* (N.Y., 1940), 168; D. A. Dondore, "Points of Contact between History and Literature in the Mississippi Valley," *Miss. Valley Hist. Rev.*, XI (1924), 227; E. E. Edwards, "Agricultural History as a Field of Research," Canadian Hist. Assoc., *Report for 1941*, 15; Robert Fortenbaugh, "Religious History as a Field for Study and Research," *Social Sci.*, III (1928), 151; G. S. Gibb, "The Pre-Industrial Revolution in America: a Field for Local Research," Bus. Hist. Soc., *Bull.*, XX (1946), 103; M. L. Hansen, "Immigration as a Field for Historical Research," in his *Immigrant in American History* (Cambridge, 1940), 191; R. M. Hower, "Problems and Opportunities in the Field of Business History," Bus. Hist. Soc., *Bull.*, XV (1941), 17; Henrietta M. Larson, "Problems and Challenges in Business History Research with Special Reference to Business Administration," *ibid.*, XXIV (1950), 120; R. W. Leopold, "The Mississippi Valley and Foreign Policy, 1890–1941," *Miss. Valley Hist. Rev.*, XXXVII (1951), 625; A. E. Martin, "Research in State History: Its Problems and Opportunities," *Ohio Arch. and Hist. Quar.*, XL (1931), 565; Allan Nevins, "Some Neglected Aspects of Frontier Life," *Ind. Hist. Bull.*, VI (1929), extra no. 2, 113; C. W. Ramsdell, "Some Problems in Writing the History of the Confederacy," *Jour. Southern Hist.*, II (1936), 133; J. G. Randall, "Has the Lincoln Theme Been Exhausted?" *Am. Hist. Rev.*, XLI (1935), 270; R. R. Russel, "A Revaluation of the Period before the Civil War: Railroads," *Miss. Valley Hist. Rev.*, XV (1928), 341; L. B. Schmidt, "The History of Agriculture as a Field of Research," *Ag. Hist.*, XIV (1940), 117; R. H. Shryock, "Medical Sources and the Social Historian," *Am. Hist. Rev.*, XLI (1936), 458, and "The Historian Looks at Medicine," Inst. of Hist. of Med., *Bull.*, V (1937–38), 887, and "Promising Fields," *Penn. Mag. of Hist. and Biog.*, LXXIII (1949), 191; F. B. Simkins, "New Viewpoints of Southern Reconstruction," *Jour. Southern Hist.*, V (1939), 49; J. R. Starr, "Some Gaps in the History of the Northwest," *Minn. Hist.*, IX (1928), 109; B. F. Wright, "Research in American Political Theory," *Am. Pol. Sci. Rev.*, XXXVIII (1944), 733; Southern Hist. Assoc., Committee of Ten, "Research Possibilities in Southern History," *Jour. Southern Hist.*, XVI (1950), 52.

As a ready means of keeping informed of current trends of investigation at the graduate-student level and of avoiding unnecessary duplication of subjects, consult the *List of Doctoral Dissertations in History Now in Progress at American Universities*, initiated in 1902 for annual publication by the Carnegie Institution of Washington and now issued biennially by the American Historical Association.

10. METHODS OF NOTE-TAKING

Historians in the past have used a wide variety of methods for accumulating and arranging the data that will be the basis of their narrative accounts. The essential requisite of a successful system of note-taking is that it permit the organization of the factual material in forms in which it may readily be used, ordered, and reordered in accord with the writer's needs. Any system is suitable to the degree that it relieves the historian of dependence upon his memory and enables him to draw, when he wishes, upon a store of verifiable facts.

The nineteenth-century historians were rather limited in this respect. Often the difficulty of rearranging their information compelled them to write from a single body of records — diplomatic or governmental documents, correspondence, or newspapers — and frequently the internal organization of their narrative reflected the organization, often arbitrary, of the sources from which they worked. Some scholars, like George Bancroft, first filled their notebooks with abstracts or transcriptions, then drew upon those as best they could while they wrote. Even the most careful could not guard against errors of quotation and citation. Others worked directly from books with notes only to guide them to the relevant pages; they were therefore restricted to what they possessed or could borrow. At least one historian, in a period of lower publishing costs, made a practice of tearing what he needed out of his journals and books as a preliminary to the task of composition.

More recently the development of filing devices has eased the labors of the historian. Each research worker before long discovers the type of equipment most appropriate to his needs. Index cards of various sizes (3×5, 4×6, 5×8) are available. Where the magnitude of a task makes these bulky, paper slips may be substituted. In any case the actual process of note-taking is one of isolating references to facts, principles, or ideas which can then be arranged along the line of the writer's own argument. Success depends upon the ability to discern the significant information, to abstract it as concisely and economically as possible, and to transcribe it accurately and in such form as will allow easy checking.

There are occasional conditions under which the usual methods of note-taking are not feasible. If the sources are out of reach or are contained in libraries difficult of access, it may be profitable to make use of the mechanical devices that aid note-taking. Manuscripts no longer need be copied by hand; and historians are not now, as Prescott and Parkman were, dependent upon the slow, laborious, and uncertain services of copyists. Mechanical developments have cheapened the process, speeded it, and eliminated the possibility of error in transcription (§ 31).

When the source consists of a large number of items in sequence, the most useful device is microfilming, by which a photographic copy is made on 35-mm. film, generally one page or one sheet to a frame. This process is inexpensive, expeditious, and produces a compact copy. On the other hand it calls for the use of a special reading device. When material to be copied is scattered or is small in quantity, it is better to depend upon photostats. Photostats developed by a photographic process are relatively expensive but produce excellent facsimiles, easily read, and capable of being preserved and filed. Photostats produced by contact devices such as the "Contoura" are low in cost and have the advantage of using equipment that can easily be transported. On the other hand, the copies that result are often not of high order and can sometimes be read only with difficulty. None of these devices absolves the historian of the necessity of digesting and assimilating the material he uses. But, properly applied, they can relieve him of some of the drudgery of his task.

See also: § 31; H. C. Hockett, *Introduction to Research,* 46; E. W. Dow, *Principles of a Note System for Historical Studies* (N.Y., 1924).

11. THE MECHANICS OF CITATION

A scrutiny of historical publications will disclose variations of usage as to forms of citation. A uniform practice would be desirable; but in a field of learning so highly individualistic it is hardly likely to be attained. It is much more important that the system, whatever one be chosen, should conform to scholarly standards. Such standards require that it be consistent with itself, and that the citations supply the essential information in a manner readily intelligible to others. It is the reader's convenience, not the author's, that should be consulted.

The plan of citation used by the *Harvard Guide* is an inheritance from the earlier editions of the work and, because of the multiplicity of references and the necessity for economizing space, makes a special merit of conciseness and simplicity. Many publishers, learned-society editors, graduate schools, and departments of history have their own specifications, one of the most comprehensive compilations being the *Manual of Style* (11 ed., Chi., 1949) of the University of Chicago Press. *The MLA Style Sheet*, compiled by W. R. Parker of the Modern Language Association of America with the coöperation of seventy-eight learned periodicals in that and other fields and of thirty-three university presses, may be found in *PMLA*, the Association's official organ, LXVI (April, 1951), 3; it is also obtainable in separate form. It governs the usage of forty-six journals, including the *American Historical Review* and the *Journal of the History of Ideas*. Legal citations often pose special problems. The style preferred by scholars in that field is set forth in *A Uniform System of Citation* (8 ed., Cambridge, 1949), sponsored by the *Law Reviews* of Columbia, Harvard, the University of Pennsylvania, and Yale. The following succinct directions, based upon a pamphlet of the Harvard Department of History, embody the underlying principles common to most systems of historical reference.

GENERAL

Manuscripts must be typed double-spaced on bond paper on but one side of the sheet, which should be 8½ by 11 inches in size. Italics are indicated by underlining the appropriate words. In order to ensure consistent practice as to spelling and hyphenation, use the same dictionary throughout. The most recent edition of *Webster's New International Dictionary* is standard in the United States. For the approved spelling of place names, consult "A Pronouncing Gazetteer or Geographical Dictionary of the World" in the appendix of *Webster's*. For publishing procedures, see: § 15.

FOOTNOTES

A footnote must accompany each important statement of fact, each quotation, each citation of statistics, and every conclusion borrowed from another writer. When the matter in any paragraph comes from several sources, one footnote may contain all these references. Content footnotes are permissible to discuss or amplify points in a manner and to an extent inappropriate in the text. Footnotes should be single-spaced and be numbered consecutively by chapters.

The first footnote citation of a work must supply the full name of the author (though initials may be used for the given names), the exact title as found on the title page (unless it is excessively long), the edition (if later than the first), the city named first as the place of publication, the date of publication (preferably the latest copyright date of the copy in question), and the pertinent volume and inclusive page references, according to the following form:

Asher Crosby Hinds, *Precedents of the House of Representatives of the United States Congress* (Washington, 1907), III, 81–82.

(This is the simplest form of reference, and the one generally preferred. If the citation is that of a volume or an article in a composite work, the relevant information should be given in accordance with the forms suggested later under "Formal Bibliography.")

Subsequent citations of the same work should be shortened so as to give merely the author's surname and the key word (or words) of the title, thus:

Hinds, *Precedents*, III, 104–109.

Students, however, may prefer a more formal style of reference and, at any rate, should be familiar with it. According to this practice, if a book is cited in successive footnotes and no titles of other works intervene, the later references should make use of the Latin abbreviation *ibid.* (from *ibidem*, "in the same place"), thus:

Ibid., IV, 61–78.

If a work is cited frequently but other titles intervene, the later references should make use of the Latin abbreviation *op. cit.* (from *opere citato*, "in the work cited"), thus:

Hinds, *op. cit.*, VI, 141–142.

In the case of a similarly repeated citation of a magazine article or other contribution to a composite publication, the Latin abbreviation *loc. cit.* (from *loco citato*, "in the place cited") should be employed instead of *op. cit.*

None of the foregoing abbreviations or shortened forms of citation should be used to refer to a book or article that is cited only in a preceding chapter.

In a footnote mentioning two or more authorities the various items should be connected by semicolons, thus:

Hinds, *Precedents*, III, 96; James Bryce, *The American Commonwealth* (London, 1888), I, 130–132.

Exact page citations must be given wherever possible. In exceptional cases, however, an author may desire to indicate generally that his material comes from a particular page and the pages following. Then the abbreviation ff. (not italicized) should be employed, thus:

Hinds, *Precedents*, I, 81 ff.

If the author wishes to indicate that the material is derived from scattered parts of a work, the Latin expression *passim* ("here and there") is convenient.

In the case of quotations, footnotes should always cite the actual work consulted. If a passage is copied not from the original source but as quoted by some other person, the footnote should follow this form:

Letter from Francis Lieber, Columbia, S. C., to Dorothea L. Dix, Nov. 5, 1846, quoted by Francis Tiffany, *Life of Dorothea Lynde Dix* (Boston, 1890), 149.

References to judicial decisions follow a special form, and do not require a citation of the inclusive pages, thus:

De Lima *v*. Bidwell, 182 U.S., 1.

If it is desired to make comparison in a footnote with a statement in some other work, the Latin expression cf. (abbreviated from *confer*, "compare," but usually not italicized) may be employed. If comparison is made with some statement appearing in the author's own pages, the expression cf. may be used in connection with *ante* ("before") or *post* ("later"). Thus: Cf. *ante*, 21. A simpler and wholly acceptable alternative is: See earlier, 21.

QUOTATIONS

All quotations should be plainly so indicated, should be made with scrupulous accuracy, and should, if possible, be verified from the first source. Omissions within a quotation are permissible provided the sense is not distorted, and must be indicated by three periods or omission marks, thus . . . ; when the final words of a sentence are omitted, four periods must be used instead of three. Editorial comment within a quotation must be enclosed in brackets, not parentheses. Example: "That for each said district there shall be appointed by the President [of the United States] a provost-marshal, . . . who shall be under the direction and subject to the orders of a provost-marshal-general, . . . whose office shall be at the seat of government . . . ."

In quoting phrases or short passages, quotation marks must be used, as the foregoing example indicates. Longer quotations (commonly of fifty words or more) should be single-spaced in the typescript and set in from both margins of the page. In the case of such inset passages, no quotation marks should be used except as they may appear in the original.

Passages in foreign languages should be in English translation when used in the text. When important to do so, the original wording should be reproduced in a footnote.

APPENDIX

An author may on occasion desire to develop an aspect of his subject more fully than would be suitable either in the main narrative or in a footnote. In such case he should use the device of an appendix, which should be placed at the end of the study just before the formal bibliography. Reference to this supplementary material should be made at the appropriate point or points in the treatise proper.

FORMAL BIBLIOGRAPHY

A formal bibliography of all the essential materials used by the author comes at the conclusion of the study. "Primary Sources" must always be separated from "Secondary Works." If the number of titles is large, further subdivisions under these main headings are desirable, thus: "Manuscripts," "Pamphlets," "Public Documents," "Newspapers and Periodicals," and "Writings of Statesmen." Under each subheading the items must be arranged alphabetically by author. Unlike the practice in footnotes, the surnames should appear first. If the work is anonymous, the first important word of the title determines its place in the alphabetical list.

Each bibliographical reference must contain the author's full name (though initials may be used for the given names), the exact title of the work as found on the title page (unless it is excessively long), the edition (if later than the first), the number of volumes (if in a set), the city named first as the place of publication, and the year of publication (preferably the latest copyright date of the copy used). Certain variations from this practice are illustrated in the examples given below. Evaluative comments should accompany every important title, except that in some cases a critical introduction to the entire bibliography may be preferable.

The following examples do *not* present a scheme of classification for the bibliography. They illustrate different styles of citation according to the nature or form of the reference and without regard to whether it is a primary source or secondary authority.

1. When an Entire Volume is Cited

Adams, Samuel, *The Writings of Samuel Adams.* Henry Alonzo Cushing, ed. 4 vols. N.Y., 1904–1908.

Andrews, Charles McLean, *Colonial Self-Government, 1652–1689* (Albert Bushnell Hart, ed., *The American Nation: a History,* V). N.Y., 1904.

Frankfurter, Felix, and James M. Landis, *The Business of the Supreme Court, a Study of the Federal Judicial System.* N.Y., 1928.

The Interest of the Merchants and Manufacturers of Great Britain in the Present Contest with the Colonies Stated and Considered. London, 1774.

Locke, David Ross (Petroleum V. Nasby, *pseud.*), *The Nasby Papers.* Indianapolis, 1864.

Nasby, Petroleum V. See Locke, David Ross.

Strong, Josiah, *Our Country, Its Possible Future and Its Present Crisis.* Rev. ed. N.Y. 1891.

Tocqueville, Alexis de, *Democracy in America.* Henry Reeve, tr. 2 vols. N.Y., 1862.

2. When Part of a Composite Publication is Cited

Eggleston, Edward, "The New History," American Historical Association, *Annual Report for the Year 1900,* I, 35–47.

Shotwell, James Thomson, "History," *Encyclopaedia Britannica* (11th ed.), XIII, 527–533.

Turner, Frederick J., "The Colonization of the West, 1820–1830," *American Historical Review,* XI (1905–1906), 303–327.

3. When a Newspaper is Cited

The New York Herald, 1868–1878.

The Ohio State Journal (Columbus, Ohio), April 1–20, 1900.

4. When a Public Document is Cited

"Certain Illegal Tonnage Duties," *House Report,* 48 Cong., 2 sess., no. 467 (March 10, 1880), 1–16. (The serial number may be included if desired.)

(Where the material consulted is scattered through a number of volumes, the series as a whole may be cited.)

Malloy, William M., comp., *Treaties, Conventions, International Acts, Protocols and Agreements between the United States of America and Other Powers, 1776–1909.* 2 vols. Washington, 1910.

5. When a Manuscript is Cited

References to unprinted material obviously can follow no rigid form, but, in every case, they should include the name of the author (when ascertainable), the number of volumes if more than one, the inclusive dates, and the place of deposit. Do not italicize the titles of manuscripts and manuscript collections. Example:

> Boston Committee of Correspondence, Minutes of the Committee of Correspondence, November, 1772–December, 1774. 13 vols., mostly in the handwriting of William Cooper. In the George Bancroft Collection, New York Public Library.

INDEX

Every historical monograph or larger work when printed should have a full index. Subjects should be included as well as names. If a given item is followed by two or more page numbers, sufficient explanatory comment should be inserted to enable the reader to find readily the particular reference he desires. For expert guidance in these matters, consult B. E. Josephson, "Indexing," *Am. Archivist*, X (1947), 133.

12. HISTORY AS A LITERARY ART

Exploring American history has been a very absorbing and exciting business now for three quarters of a century. Thousands of graduate students have produced thousands of monographs on every aspect of the history of the Americas. But the American reading public for the most part is blissfully ignorant of this vast output. When John Citizen feels the urge to read history, he goes to the novels of Kenneth Roberts or Margaret Mitchell, not to the histories of Professor this or Doctor that. Why?

Because American historians, in their eagerness to present facts and their laudable anxiety to tell the truth, have neglected the literary aspects of their craft. They have forgotten that there is an art of writing history.

Even the earliest colonial historians like Bradford and Beverley knew that; they put conscious art into their narratives. And the historians of our classical period, Prescott and Motley, Irving and Bancroft, Parkman and Fiske, were great literary craftsmen. Their many-volumed works sold in sufficient quantities to give them handsome returns; even today they are widely read. But the first generation of seminar-trained historians, educated in Germany or by teachers trained there, imagined that history would tell itself, provided one were honest, thorough, and painstaking. Some of them went so far as to regard history as pure science and to assert that writers thereof had no more business trying to be "literary" than did writers of statistical reports or performers of scientific experiments. Professors warned their pupils against "fine writing." And in this flight of history from literature the public got left behind. American history became a bore to the reader and a drug on the market; even historians with something to say and the talent for saying it (Henry Adams, for instance) could not sell their books. The most popular American histories of the period 1890–1905 were those of John Fiske, a philosopher who had no historical training but wrote with life and movement.

Theodore Roosevelt in his presidential address before the American Historical Association in 1912 made a ringing plea to the young historian to do better:

> He must ever remember that while the worst offense of which he can be guilty is to write vividly and inaccurately, yet that unless he writes vividly he cannot write truthfully; for no amount of dull, painstaking detail will sum up the whole truth unless the genius is there to paint the truth.

Theodore Roosevelt's trumpet call fell largely on deaf ears, at least in the academic historical profession. A whole generation has passed without producing more than a very few great works on American history. Plenty of good books, valuable books, and new interpretations and explorations of the past; but none with fire in the eye, none to make a young man want to fight for his country in war or live to make it a better country in peace. There has been a sort of chain reaction of dullness. Professors who have risen to positions of eminence by writing dull, solid, valuable monographs that nobody reads outside the profession, teach graduate students to write dull, solid, valuable monographs like theirs; the road to academic security is that of writing dull, solid, valuable monographs. And so the young men who have a gift for good writing either leave the historical field for something more exciting, or write more dull, solid, valuable monographs. The few professional historians who have had a popular following or appeal during the last thirty years either started their careers as journalists or broke loose young from academic trammels.

The tremendous plowing up of the past by well-trained scholars is all to the good. Scholars know more about America's past than ever; they are opening new furrows and finding new artifacts, from aboriginal arrowheads to early twentieth-century hub caps. But they are heaping up pay dirt for others. Journalists, novelists, and free-lance writers are the ones that extract the gold; and they deserve every ounce they get because they write histories that people care to read. What we wish to see is a few more Ph.D.'s in history winning book-of-the-month adoptions and reaping a harvest of dividends.

There are no special rules for writing history; any good manual of rhetoric or teacher of composition will supply the rules for writing English. But what terrible stuff passes for English in Ph.D. dissertations, monographs, and articles in the historical reviews! Long, involved sentences that one has to read two or three times in order to grasp the meaning; poverty in vocabulary, ineptness of expression, weakness in paragraph structure, constant misuse of words and, of late, the introduction of pseudoscientific and psychological jargon. There is no fundamental cure for this except better teaching of English in our schools and by all teachers, *whatever their other subjects.* If historical writing is infinitely better in France than in America, and far better in the British Isles than in America, it is because every French and British teacher of history drills his pupils in their mother tongue, requiring a constant stream of essays and reports, and criticizing written work not only as history but as literature. The American university teacher who gives honor grades to students who have not yet learned to write English, for industrious compilations of facts or feats of memory, is wanting in professional pride or competency.

Of course what we should all like to attain in writing history is style, "the last acquirement of the educated mind; . . . the ultimate morality of mind."

Unfortunately, there is no royal road to style. It cannot be attained by mere industry; it can never be achieved through imitation, although it may be promoted by example. Reading the greatest literary artists among historians will help; but what was acceptable style in 1850 might seem turgid today. We can still read Macaulay with admiration and pleasure, we can still learn paragraph structure and other things from Macaulay, but anyone who tried to imitate Macaulay today would be a pompous ass. The writer of history had better not work consciously to develop a style but concentrate on day-by-day improvement in craftsmanship. Then perhaps he may find some day that his industry, which left readers cold, is carried to a large popular audience by something that the critics call style.

A few hints as to literary craftsmanship may be useful to budding historians. First and foremost, *get writing*! Young scholars generally wish to secure the last fact before writing anything, just as General McClellan refused to advance until the last mule was shod. But there is the "indispensablest beauty in knowing how to get done," said Carlyle. In every research there comes a point, which you should recognize like a call of conscience, when you must get down to writing. And when you once are writing, go on writing as long as you can; there will be plenty of time later to shove in the footnotes or return to the library for extra information. Above all, *start* writing. Nothing is more pathetic than the historian who from graduate school on is promising to write a magnum opus but never completes his research and dies without anything to show for a lifetime's work.

Dictation is usually fatal to good historical writing. Write out your first draft in longhand or, if you compose easily on the typewriter, type it out yourself, revise with pencil or pen, and have it retyped clean. Don't stop to consult notes for every clause or sentence; it is better to get what you have to say in your mind and dash it off; then return to your notes and compose your next few pages or paragraphs. After a little experience you may find that you think best with your fingers on the typewriter keys or your fountain pen poised over the paper. For some, the mere writing of a few words seems to point up vague thoughts and make jumbled facts array themselves in neat order. Whichever method you choose, composing before you write or as you write, do not return to your raw material or verify facts and quotations or insert footnotes until you have written a substantial amount, an amount that will increase with practice. It is significant that two of our greatest American historians, Prescott and Parkman, were nearly blind during a good part of their active careers. They had to have the sources read to them and turn the matter over and over in their minds before they could give anything out.

Now, the purpose of this quick, warm synthesis between research, thinking, and writing is to attain the three prime qualities of historical composition — clarity, vigor, and objectivity. You must think about your facts, analyze your material, and decide exactly what you mean before you can write it so that the average reader will understand. Do not fall into the fallacy of supposing that "facts speak for themselves." Most of the facts that you excavate from the archives, like all relics of past human activity, are dumb things; it is for you to make them speak by proper selection, arrangement, and emphasis. Dump your entire collection of facts on paper, and the result will be unreadable if not incomprehensible.

So, too, with vigor. If your whole paragraph or chapter is but a hypothesis, say so at the beginning, but do not bore and confuse the reader with numerous "buts," "excepts," "perhapses," "howevers" and "possiblys." Use direct rather than indirect statements, the active rather than the passive voice, and make every sentence and paragraph an organic whole. Above all, if you are writing historical narrative, make it move. Do not take time out in the middle of a political or military campaign to introduce special developments or literary trends, as Mc-Master did to the confusion of his readers. Place those admittedly important matters in a chapter or chapters by themselves so that your reader's attention will not be lost by constant interruption.

That brings us to the third essential quality — objectivity. Keep the reader constantly in mind. You are not writing history for yourself or for the professors who (you may imagine) know more about it than you do. Assume that you are writing for intelligent people who know nothing about your particular subject but whom you wish to convince of its interest and significance. The late Senator Beveridge was once asked why his *Life of John Marshall*, despite its great length and scholarly apparatus, was so popular. He replied, "The trouble with you professors of history is that you write for each other. I write for people almost completely ignorant of American history, as I was when I began my research."

Social history puts a greater strain on literary expression and the sense of balance than any other kind. Hitherto the novelists have been very much better at writing it than the historians. The latter need to improve their human perception as well as their literary style if they expect to be the teachers of social history that, for instance, Marcel Proust was and Conrad Richter is. Historians notably lack the talent at description which novelists have developed to a high degree; Prescott had it, of course, and Parkman; but few American historians now living can describe a scene, an event, or a natural setting in such a way that the reader can see it. The reason is largely that the writer cannot see it himself; he sits in a library and writes instead of going about by whatever means of transportation is available, and finding out for himself what historic sites look like today. Then, too, some social historians forget that history is a *story* that moves; they divorce their subject altogether from the main stream of history, giving it no context and no time. The American historian of architecture, education, labor, medicine, or any other social subject, should have a sense of chronology and make history move.

Now for a few practical details. Even if the work you are writing does not call for footnotes, keep them in your copy until the last draft, for they will enable you to check up on your facts, statements, and quotations. And since accuracy is a prime virtue of the historian, this checking must be done, either by the author or by someone else. You will be surprised by the mistakes that creep in between a first rough draft and a final typed copy. And, the better you write, the more critics will enjoy finding misquotations and inaccuracies.

The matter of handling quotations seems to be a difficult one for young historians. There is nothing that adds so much to the charm and effectiveness of a history as good quotations from the sources, especially if the period be somewhat remote. Note how effectively this was done in Professor McIlwain's presidential address before the American Historical Association (*Am. Hist. Rev.*, XLII [1937], 207). But there is nothing so disgusting to the reader as long, tedious, broken quotations in small print, especially those in which, to make sense, the author has to interpolate words in square brackets. Young writers are prone to use quotations in places where their own words would be better, and to incorporate in the text source excerpts that belong in footnotes or appendices. Avoid ending chapters with quotations, and never close your book with one. Above all, do not be afraid to revise and rewrite. Reading aloud is a good test — historians' wives have to stand a lot of that!

Undoubtedly the writer of history can enrich his mind and broaden his literary experience as well as better his craftsmanship, by his choice of leisure reading. If he is so fortunate as to have had a classical education, no time will be better spent in making him an effective historian than in reading Latin and Greek authors. Both these ancient languages are such superb instruments of thought that a knowledge of them cures slipshod English and helps one to attain a clear, muscular style. All our greatest historical stylists — notably Prescott, Parkman, Fiske and Frederick J. Turner — had a classical education and read the ancient historians in the original before they approached American history.

If you have little Latin and less Greek and feel unable to spare the time and effort to add them to your stock of tools, read the ancient classics in the best literary translations, such as North's Plutarch, Rawlinson's Herodotus, John J. Chapman's Sophocles, Gilbert Murray's Euripides and, above all, Jowett's or Livingstone's Thucydides. Through them you will gain the content and spirit of the ancient classics which will break down your provincialism, refresh your spirit, and give you a better philosophical insight into the ways of mankind than most of such works as the new science of psychology has brought forth. Moreover, you will be acquiring the same background as many of the great Americans of past generations, thus aiding your understanding of them

The reading of English classics will tend in the same direction, and will also be a painless and unconscious means of improving your literary style. Almost every English or American writer of distinction is indebted to Shakespeare and the English Bible. The Authorized Version is not only the great source book of spiritual experience of English-speaking peoples, it is a treasury of plain, pungent words and muscular phrases, beautiful in themselves and with long associations, that we are apt to replace by smooth words lacking in "punch," or by hackneyed or involved phrases. Of course much of the biblical phraseology is obsolete, and there are other literary quarries for historians. You can find many appropriate words, phrases, similes, and epigrams in American authors such as Mark Twain, Emerson, and Thoreau.

What of imagination in history? A historian or biographer has restrictions unknown to a novelist. He has no right to override facts by his own imagination. If he is writing on a remote or obscure subject on which very few facts are available, his imagination may legitimately weave them into a pattern. But to be honest he must make clear what is fact and what is hypothesis. The quality of imagination, if properly restrained by the conditions of historical discipline, is of great assistance in enabling one to discover problems to be solved, to grasp the significance of facts, to form hypotheses, to discern causes in their first beginnings and, above all, to relate the past creatively to the present. There are many opportunities in historical narrative for bold, imaginative expressions. "A complete statement in the imaginative form of an important truth arrests attention," wrote Emerson, "and is repeated and remembered." Imagination used in this way invests an otherwise pedestrian narrative with vivid and exciting qualities.

Finally, the historian should have frequent recourse to the book of life. The richer his personal experience, the wider his human contacts, the more likely he is to effect a living contact with his audience. In writing, similes drawn from the current experience of this mechanical age rather than those rifled from the literary baggage of past eras are the ones that will go home to his reader. The great historians, with few exceptions, are those who have not merely studied, but lived; and whose studies have ranged over a much wider field than the period or subject of which they write. Veterans of the wars, who have seen man at his best and his worst, can read man's doings in the past with far greater understanding than if they had spent these years in sheltered academic shades.

To young men especially, we say (as the poet Chapman said to the young Elizabethan), "Be free, all worthy spirits, and stretch yourselves!" Bring all your knowledge of life to bear on everything that you write. Never let yourself bog down in pedantry and detail. Bring History, the most humane and noble form of letters, back to the proud position she once held; knowing that your words, if they be read and remembered, will enter into the stream of life, and perhaps move men to thought and action centuries hence, as do those of Thucydides after more than two thousand years.

A fuller treatment of the theme of § 12 will be found in S. E. Morison's pamphlet of the same title published by the Old South Association, Old South Meeting House, Boston, Mass. See also, J. J. Jusserand, *et al.*, *The Writing of History* (N.Y., 1926); Theodore Roosevelt, "History as Literature," *Am. Hist. Rev.*, XVIII (1913), 473.

13. BOOK REVIEWING

The day when he is first asked to write a formal book review marks an epoch in the young scholar's life. If the invitation comes from the *American Historical Review* or from one of the regional historical quarterlies, he regards it as an accolade hardly less important than the Ph.D. How is he to go about it? The following suggestions to reviewers, written by J. Franklin Jameson for the *American Historical Review*, and later adopted by the editor of the *Mississippi Valley Historical Review*, are excellent to start with:

1. Reviews of Books are addressed to an audience more special than that of the body-articles, consisting, in the case of each book, of those particularly interested in its special subject. While reviews consisting of minute criticisms are to be deprecated, it is hoped that reviewers will not hesitate to write for the special student rather than for the general reader, with a scientific rather than a literary intention, and with definiteness and precision in both praise and dispraise.

2. It is desired that the review of a book shall be such as will convey to the reader a clear and comprehensive notion of its nature, of its contents, of its merits, of its place in the literature of the subject, and of the amount of its positive contribution to knowledge. The Editors do not favor that type of review which deals with only a part of a book, or makes the book merely a text for a digressive essay. The interests of readers require that the pages headed "Reviews of Books" be filled with reviews in the literal sense; for original contributions, however brief, another place is reserved.

3. It is hoped that the reviewer will take pains, first of all, to apprehend the author's conception of the nature and intent of his book and to criticize it with a due regard to its species and purpose. It should, however, be remembered that the review is intended for the information and assistance of readers, and not for the satisfaction of the author of the book. Sympathy, courtesy, a sense of attachment, readiness to make allowance for a different point of view, should not therefore withhold the reviewer from the straightforward

expression of adverse judgment sincerely entertained; otherwise, the *Review* cannot fulfill the important function of upholding a high standard of historical writing.

4. Reviewers are asked to take great pains to be exact in their quotations.

In the third section, the editor places his finger on the chief vice of historical reviewers — softness. Young men fear to pull to pieces the work of an old hand that deserves it, lest they make enemies or be considered too uppish; older men are too kind to deprecate a young historian's maiden effort; colleagues hesitate to speak ill of one another. In consequence, far too many reviews are weakly amiable.

The wise editor will not give a book for review to the author's colleague, teacher, pupil, close friend, or bitter rival. It should always be possible to find an expert in the special field outside these relationships; and anyone so related should decline to review the book. The professional audience wants of a book review a critical appraisal by a man who knows the subject as well as, or better than, the author, and whose opinion will not be distorted by prejudice. Very few professional journals pay reviewers. The copy of the book itself, and the consciousness of having performed a service for fellow historians, are the reviewer's only rewards.

In order to test an author's accuracy, the reviewer should check some of his references and quotations. Symptomatic inaccuracies or misquotations revealing prejudice should be noticed, and a few examples may be quoted; but a review is no place for a list of errata.

The general scope of the work should be indicated; but do not attempt to reproduce the table of contents. Quotations may be made as examples of the author's approach or style; the sources that he used should be indicated, important omissions noted, and the conclusions summarized. If a textbook is under review, the amount of space allotted to different periods or branches may well be noted as an indication of the author's set of values. The quality of the maps and index, if any (or absence of them if, as is often the case, they are wanting), should be noted. Remarks about paper, presswork, format, and binding are out of place unless there is something extraordinary about them.

Reviewing in nonprofessional periodicals is a different matter. Every young historian would do well to establish relations with a newspaper in his vicinity that has a book column, and to try his hand with some of the histories and historical biographies that are sent to the editor for review. After filling several columns of newspaper type with his reviews, he may send some of the best of them to the literary editor of a weekly such as *The Saturday Review of Literature*, the *New York Times Book Review*, or the *New York Herald-Tribune Book Review*. A historian can perform a real service by reviewing for these publications, or for newspapers that are widely read; and he should be paid for doing it.

In reviewing for newspapers, general periodicals, and literary weeklies, many of the *American Historical Review* suggestions do not apply. The main questions that the reader of these journals wants answered are: "What is the book about?" "Can I read it with pleasure or profit?" "Is it the truth?" and "Does it upset any of the accepted theories taught us in school or college?" Occasionally a new work may give the reviewer an opportunity to expose a fresh trend or development among professional historians with which the public is not yet acquainted, and thus pave the way for a favorable reception of other works of the new school.

Professional reviewers in general periodicals should expose dishonest, inaccurate, and slipshod work, especially if so charmingly presented as to conceal its shortcomings from the public. But the test of honesty, accuracy, and neatness should be the book itself, and not the author's methods. Young men trained in seminars are apt to overvalue method and underrate achievement; to assume that any book without copious footnotes and a thick bibliography is superficial and, conversely, that any book which makes the right methodological gestures is thorough and sound. A literary artist can sometimes write better and truer history without conventional methods or manuscript sources than historians can do with the most laborious and scientific methods. Praise should be given where praise is due, but puff and gush are out of place in a general, as in a historical, periodical. The reviewer should not hesitate to say, "This is an exceedingly erudite and important work, but addressed to the specialist rather than the general reader"; or, "This biography of so-and-so is inferior to the two earlier books on him, and there was no real reason for publishing it." If the enormous potential market for history among the intelligent American public is to be developed, historians must serve as discriminating guides.

See also: Carl Becker, "The Reviewing of Historical Books," Am. Hist. Assoc., *Report*, 1912, 130. *The Book Review Digest* (1904–   ) is a convenient guide; § 38.

14. FINANCIAL AIDS FOR RESEARCH

Subsidies for research and study in the field of American history are available both for beginners in course of training and for more mature scholars. It is customary for Graduate Schools to offer scholarships, fellowships, and assistantships to outstanding students. Such awards sometimes provide specifically for travel to distant archives in the United States or abroad. The relevant information can be obtained from the official catalogues of the institutions. Many universities also administer special funds open to faculty members with historical projects. These subventions may make it possible to finance trips or leaves of absence for work elsewhere.

Outside agencies add considerably to such resources. The Social Science Research Council grants predoctoral and postdoctoral fellowships to qualified applicants who wish to acquire more advanced training than the usual Ph.D. program affords. It also gives grants-in-aid (including expenses of clerical help, travel, microfilming, and similar services) to established scholars for research projects. The American Council of Learned Societies sponsors predoctoral and postdoctoral fellowships for those who desire to broaden their knowledge by study in fields outside their special interests. The American Association of University Women provides fellowships at both stages for women to pursue investigations and, in the case of mature scholars, to take time off also for uninterrupted writing. The American Philosophical Society offers grants-in-aid for ripe scholars. The John Simon Guggenheim Memorial Foundation similarly awards research fellowships.

Among other agencies with programs of financial assistance are the Henry E. Huntington Library, San Marino, Calif.; the Institute of Early American History and Culture, Williamsburg, Va.; the Newberry Library, Chicago; the General Society of Colonial Wars, New York City; and the Pennsylvania Historical and

Museum Commission, Harrisburg. S. N. Feingold, *Scholarships, Fellowships and Loans* (revised ed., 1951), is a general guide to the available opportunities. It lists under each of the agencies the stipends, qualifications for applicants, and fields of interest. In some cases no field is indicated, but help is given to candidates on such bases as religious affiliation, kinship to veterans of the World Wars, place of residence, and membership in fraternal organizations.

Opportunities for study and research in designated foreign countries are offered by the State Department under the Fulbright Act of 1944 and like programs. These awards are available at both predoctoral and postdoctoral levels. A work of reference for intending applicants is UNESCO, *Study Abroad, International Handbook of Fellowships, Scholarships and Educational Exchange* (Paris, 1948–), which appears in annual revisions.

For completed studies the American Historical Association administers two awards: the annual Albert J. Beveridge Memorial Fellowship of $1,000 for the best original historical manuscript concerned with the United States, Canada, or Latin America (this award also provides for publication); and the biennial John H. Dunning Prize of about $100 for a monograph on a subject in American history. Out of its Carnegie Revolving Fund the Association also finances the publication of scholarly treatises which make distinct contributions to historical knowledge in any field. For encouraging research in the history of the South, the United Daughters of the Confederacy confer a prize of $1,000 biennially. In addition, publishers occasionally offer prizes for American history manuscripts, and some state historical societies have funds for this purpose. Published works may also compete for the annual Pulitzer Prizes in American history and biography of $500 each; the two annual Frederic Bancroft Prizes in American history of $2,000 each; and the two quinquennial Loubat Prizes, $1,000 and $400 respectively, in American history and related fields. The Pulitzer, Bancroft, and Loubat awards are administered by Columbia University.

15. ARRANGING FOR BOOK PUBLICATION

Historical writings find their way into book form in three ways. They may be printed privately, be issued by university presses, or be put out by commercial publishers. In the first instance the author shoulders the entire expense, and the arrangement usually has the further drawback of devolving upon him the task of finding purchasers for the volume. Because of these disadvantages he would generally do better, other means failing, to carve up his work into articles suitable for publication in historical journals (§ 50). University presses, as nonprofit concerns devoted primarily to the advancement of scholarship, are naturally more receptive than commercial publishers to treatises of restricted appeal and slow sale. In cases, however, where the probable financial return will not meet the actual costs of manufacture and distribution, these presses may require a subsidy of some sort, whether from special publication funds or grants, or from the author himself. Their practice in regard to royalties differs so widely that any attempt to summarize is useless.

Most historical volumes, however, carry the imprint of commercial publishers. The terms of publication may vary even in the case of the same company, being governed by such considerations as the author's subject, the type of audience addressed, and the prospect of profits. Under most contracts the author must not only supply the typescript, but also the copy for any maps and other illustrations. He must further agree to exempt the publisher from legal liability for libelous matter or for any infringement of another's copyright. The author must secure written permission for the reproduction of any copyrighted material, whether text matter or illustrations.

Publishers as a rule have their own stylebooks with which the author should acquaint himself before the manuscript is in its final form. It is important that the typescript be letter-perfect and legible, and, if possible, in final form (including paragraphing, punctuation, hyphenation, capitalization, and other such typographical details), because the contract limits the alterations that the author can make in proof at the company's expense. Carelessly prepared copy is a bad investment for a writer. Manuscripts submitted for typesetting should always be the ribbon copy, not a carbon; typed double-spaced, with margins at least one inch around the page. Paper with a waxed surface, although easily erased, may take the editor's ink badly and may smear during the course of the editor's and printer's handling.

Royalties are based either on the retail selling price (list price) of the book, or on the price at which it is sold to bookstores (the net or wholesale price). If the latter, the author's royalty should be correspondingly higher. Whatever the basis of calculation, the rate offered by reputable companies agrees roughly with their expectation of how well the book will sell. Despite some diversity of practice, certain arrangements with authors are fairly standard.

Broadly speaking, a historical manuscript falls into one of four categories from a publisher's point of view. First, it may be so highly specialized as to preclude a large sale, in which case the author may be asked to subsidize its publication. His royalty then varies ordinarily with the proportion of his financial contribution. Secondly, the work may be suitable for reference reading in college and public libraries, as well as make some appeal to a wider audience. In this instance the company commonly assumes the full cost of publication and grants a royalty of at least 10 per cent on the list price. Thirdly, the work may definitely be one to interest the general public, in which case the company not only bears the publication charges, but pays a royalty of from 10 to 15 per cent on the list price, often in accordance with a sliding scale as sales increase. Lastly, if the manuscript is designed as a college textbook, the publisher issues it at his own expense, and, as in the preceding instance, provides a royalty of from 10 to 15 per cent, usually on a sliding scale. Rates of royalty for textbooks in the elementary and secondary schools average less than for college texts.

This schedule is only a broad guide to which special circumstances may warrant exceptions. It need hardly be said that the financial terms are not the only factor a writer should consider in choosing a publisher. Important also are the company's general reputation, its record in marketing books of a similar character, and its enthusiasm for the particular manuscript. In order to foster relations of mutual good will between author and publisher, the former should have the clearest possible understanding of a contract before signing it. Among other things he should note how the royalty is to be reckoned and when it is to be paid. Finally, he should give as scrupulous regard to his own commitments to the publisher as to the publisher's commitments to him. For a detailed discussion emphasizing the legal aspects of book contracts, see Philip Wittenberg, *The Protection and Marketing of Literary Property* (N.Y., 1937), ch. xi.

The rising cost of manufacturing books has necessitated numerous changes in modes of producing scholarly works destined for limited distribution. Some publishers have discarded the common methods of typesetting and printing for much less costly ways of reproduction. The methods used vary greatly, depending in part upon the availability of typewriters (and machines resembling them) equipped with type faces approximating the appearance of traditional (metal) types, and designed for the specific purpose of cutting the cost of "typesetting." The work of such machines is reproduced photomechanically in different ways. The terms lithoprinting, planographing, and similar expressions designate these substitute methods. For succinct accounts of near-print processes, see Parker, *Local History*, ch. xi; and H. M. Silver, "New Methods of Printing and Reproducing Scholarly Materials," *Am. Documentation*, II (1951), 54.

PART II

Materials and Tools

Chapter Three

THE MATERIALS OF HISTORY

16. GREAT HISTORICAL LIBRARIES

Although books made their way to the American colonies from the very first years of settlement, it was not until well in the nineteenth century that libraries became effective instruments for historical research. Libraries of sorts could, it is true, be found much earlier. But even by the end of the eighteenth century, these belonged either to exceptional individuals or to colleges. In the largest cities there were, in addition, subscription societies that supplied books and journals to their members. All these libraries were small; their collections were uneven; and they were poorly housed and arranged, ever subject to the risk of loss by fire.

After 1820 new interests stimulated the development of libraries. In some towns, mechanics' institutes collected books for the education of their members and of apprentices; and after the middle of the century some municipalities began to emulate the example of the Boston Public Library established in 1854. Such expansion aimed at making books more popular and more available to the mass of people. Commendable as this was in itself, it did not add much to the resources available to scholars.

Not until the last quarter of the nineteenth century did libraries accept as part of their responsibilities the task of assembling the books and manuscripts essential to historical research. Then the example of the English universities and, even more, of such German universities as Göttingen stirred up a feverish activity in the United States that produced an impressive array of great storehouses of learning. Progress since the 1870's has been rapid; numerous libraries now devote themselves to furnishing students with the services necessary for study and research.

History — and particularly American history — has always been a prominent interest of libraries in this country. The largest ones are also the richest in their holdings of works on American history. Furthermore, scores of smaller ones contain valuable collections in many special fields.

The Library of Congress is perhaps the greatest research library in the United States. Established in 1800, it suffered from fires in 1814, in 1825, and in 1851, and did not play an important role until the end of the century. In 1870 it acquired the right to copies of every book copyrighted in the United States. Its period of great growth began in 1899 when Herbert Putnam became librarian.

Under his determined efforts the library built its magnificent collections. In 1950 it contained an estimated 28,685,000 items, including three and one-half million books as well as pamphlets, bound newspapers, microfilms, manuscripts, and phonograph records. In addition, it held almost three million unbound parts of serials. Among its notable collections are a million and a half maps and atlases, files of state and federal documents, of photographs and of plans of early American buildings, and the manuscripts of many of the Presidents and other public figures. It also has extensive series of reproductions of materials for American history in European libraries and archives (§ 47). The national union catalogue, maintained by the library, lists some 12,000,000 volumes in 700 libraries throughout the country, while its own printed catalogue of books (1942–46) and union-card catalogues in strategically located institutions offer useful guides to its own collections (§§ 35, 36). See also: Lucy Salamanca, *Fortress of Freedom: The Story of the Library of Congress* (Phila., 1942); D. C. Mearns, "Story Up to Now," *Annual Report of the Librarian of Congress for the Year Ending June 30, 1946,* 13; W. D. Johnston, *History of the Library of Congress* (Wash., 1904); N. A. Roberts, *Library of Congress in Relation to Research* (Wash., 1939).

The Harvard College Library was established in 1638, two years after the founding of the university. It is thus the oldest library in the United States and only a little younger than the Bodleian in England. All but about four hundred of the five thousand volumes in the old library were destroyed by fire in 1764. Reëstablished, the library grew slowly thereafter, by 1875 containing some 150,000 volumes. Toward the end of the century, it expanded even more rapidly than did other university libraries. It now possesses some 5,400,000 books and pamphlets, and is especially rich in the general literature of American history. Its collection of maps, charts, and newspapers started with the acquisition of the library of the German scholar Ebeling, who died in 1817, and has been added to steadily since. Its manuscript resources include the papers of prominent alumni like Charles Sumner and materials gathered by scholars like Jared Sparks. In addition to the main collection there are important special libraries, including the unparalleled law-school library of 700,000 volumes, the Baker Library of business history and economics with 207,000 volumes, the Andover Theological Library of over 200,000 volumes, and the Littauer Library of Public Administration with 166,000 volumes. ("Harvard College Library 1638–1938," *Harvard Library Notes,* XXIX [1939], 207.)

The New York Public Library was organized in 1895 by consolidation of the Astor and Lenox libraries and of the Tilden Trust. Under the leadership of J. S. Billings it quickly assembled a splendid collection strong in American history. The library has a reference catalogue outstanding in the extent to which subjects are indexed. Among its more important holdings of books and manuscripts dealing with American history are the Lenox, Bancroft, Ford, Emmett, and Myers collections. It has some 100,000 prints, many relevant to American history, and large newspaper, map, and music sections strong in Americana. Among other notable holdings are the Robinson genealogy collection, the business records of many New York City firms, the Gompers labor collection, the Henry George collection, the Berg collection of American literature, and the Arents collection on tobacco. (H. M. Lydenberg, *History of the New York Public Library* [N.Y., 1923].)

Historical societies have always regarded the maintenance of libraries as among their functions (§ 4). Many now possess outstanding accumulations of material for American history. The Massachusetts Historical Society, founded in Boston in 1791, specializes in the history of Massachusetts and early New England and houses the most important collection of American manuscripts outside the Library of Congress. It holds the Dowse and Waterston libraries, many colonial newspapers, Civil War materials, valuable American portraits, coins, and maps, as well as important groups of manuscripts, including the Adams, Winthrop, Pickering, and Parkman collections, and Jefferson's private papers. The New York Historical Society has an excellent collection of Americana. The Historical Society of Pennsylvania in Philadelphia has almost 4,000,000 items of Americana, including collections of colonial laws, of Pennsylvania newspapers, of French Americana, and of pamphlets and manuscripts on the formation and adoption of the American Constitution. The American Antiquarian Society at Worcester, Massachusetts, has the largest collection of American newspapers printed before 1820 and the best collection of American state, county, and local histories. The American Philosophical Society in Philadelphia holds significant collections on the history of science in America as well as on the American Revolution. The State Historical Society of Wisconsin includes a collection on socialism and the labor movement, together with the Thwaites and Draper collection of Americana. Many other societies have more specialized collections. Thus the Essex Institute at Salem has concentrated on the records of New England settlement and seafaring, the McCormick Historical Association (Chi.) on agriculture, the American Geographical Society (N.Y.) on maps and atlases, the Minnesota Historical Society (St. Paul) on the Scandinavians in the United States, the New England Historic Genealogical Society (Boston) on family records and printed genealogies, and the others generally on the districts in which they are situated.

All the great universities possess collections on American history for research purposes. Many have focused on special fields. The William L. Clements Library of the University of Michigan holds a striking collection of materials on colonial and Revolutionary history. Yale University has the magnificent W. R. Coe collection of western Americana, as well as notable sections on the history of religion and on the World War and the peace conference (1914–19). The Columbia University Library is strong in law, politics, government, and the history of education, and thanks to the oral-history project, possesses a series of recorded interviews with prominent Americans. Among the important research holdings of the Princeton University Library are the Grenville Kane Early Americana, the Rollins Western Americana, the Pierson Civil War, and the Woodrow Wilson, collections. The University of Pennsylvania Library holds the Curtis collection of Franklin imprints, the Carey collection on early economic history, and the Biddle Law Library. The University of Chicago Library owns large collections on the Civil War. The University of North Carolina and the University of Virginia are rich in Southern History. Duke University Library has a noteworthy accumulation of material on the history of the South and also the archives of the Socialist Party of America. Stanford University possesses good files of colonial and early American newspapers as well as the Hoover Library on War, Revolution, and Peace. At the University of California is the Hubert Howe Bancroft Collection of original Western materials. Other university libraries, such as those of Cornell, California,

Texas, and Louisiana, emphasize the history of their own regions. The Catholic University of America, Georgetown University, and the University of Notre Dame are the best on the history of Catholicism, while Haverford College has a fine collection on the history of the Quakers. Other special holdings include those of Brown University on Lincoln and of The Johns Hopkins on slavery, trade unions, and medicine.

Some of the private libraries still serve a significant function. The Boston Athenaeum (1807) is strong in the entire field of Americana, has the bulk of George Washington's private library and a remarkable collection of Confederate imprints. The John Carter Brown Library (Providence) has the best collection of European imprints on the discovery and exploration of the Western Hemisphere. The Library Company of Philadelphia is strong in materials on the Revolutionary period, on internal improvements, and on the westward movement. The John Crerar Library in Chicago owns collections on American labor, on social and economic subjects, and on science and technology. The Newberry Library in Chicago has almost 700,000 books, maps, and manuscripts emphasizing the era of discovery, American Revolution, slavery, the Civil War, Indians, the cultural history of the Middle West, and railroad developments. The Henry E. Huntington Library at San Marino, California, has a splendid collection on the history of literature, on the seventeenth and eighteenth century in England and America, and on California.

Though the public libraries have turned their energies mostly toward service of the public rather than of scholars, some have valuable historical collections. The Boston Public Library, for example, has a fine statistical collection, a strong section on patent history, the John Adams and Prince libraries, and an extensive holding of general Americana. The Detroit Public Library possesses the Burton historical collection on the history of the old Northwest and on the westward movement. The state libraries of New York, Massachusetts, and Connecticut own extensive accumulations of public documents, pamphlets, and related materials. A good brief survey of library resources, by regions, may be found in Spiller, *Literary History* (§ 61), III, 3.

Many specialized libraries possess unique collections. Thus the Army Medical Library has the greatest store of books in the world on the history of medicine and public health. In addition there are hundreds of libraries more specialized still, sponsored by schools, societies, newspapers, banks, insurance companies, and trade associations. Nor should the research student forget the possibilities of the great libraries in England — the British Museum, the Bodleian at Oxford, the Cambridge University Library, the John Rylands Library in Manchester, as well as their counterparts on the Continent (§ 47).

The usefulness to the scholar of these institutions has been greatly increased by the development of services that help relieve him of the burden of travel. An extensive interlibrary-loan system will bring books to any part of the country from almost any library (with the notable exception of the New York Public Library). Many libraries make available to students microfilm copies of their valuable holdings. Some 25,000 films in 197 American institutions are recorded in the Philadelphia Bibliographical Center's *Union List of Microfilms* (Ann Arbor, 1951). University Microfilms of Ann Arbor will supply a copy of any work in the University of Michigan Library; and the more important libraries throughout the country provide facilities for microfilming and photoduplication at low cost. Details and prices may be found in *Directory of Microfilm Services in the United States and Canada* (N.Y., 1947), published by the Special Libraries Association.

LIBRARY HISTORIES AND GUIDES

American Library Directory. 19 ed. N.Y., 1951.

C. E. Babcock, *Latin American Libraries*. Wash., 1935.

T. D. Barker, *Libraries of the South; a Report on Developments, 1900–1935*. Chi., 1936.

Bibliographical Planning Committee of Philadelphia, *Philadelphia Libraries and Their Holdings*. Phila., 1941.

Bibliographical Planning Committee of Philadelphia, *Philadelphia Libraries, a Survey of Facilities, Needs and Opportunities*. Phila., 1942.

Margaret Burton, *Famous Libraries of the World*. London, 1937.

S. H. Ditzion, *Arsenals of a Democratic Culture; a Social History of the American Public Library Movement in New England and the Middle States 1850–1900*. Chi., 1947.

R. B. Downs, *American Library Resources: A Bibliographical Guide*. Chi., 1951.

R. B. Downs, *Resources of New York City Libraries*. Chi., 1942.

S. S. Green, *Public Library Movement in the United States, 1853–1893*. Boston, 1913.

D. S. Hill, *Libraries of Washington*. Chi., 1936.

John Crerar Library, *The John Crerar Library 1895–1944; an Historical Report*. Chi., 1945.

Émile Leroy, *Guide pratique des bibliothèques de Paris*. Paris, 1937.

Fritz Milkau and Georg Leyh, *Handbuch der Bibliothekswissenschaft*. Vol. III. Leipzig, 1940. Ch. vi by Albert Predeek has been translated by L. S. Thompson as *History of Libraries in Great Britain and North America*. Chi., 1947.

L. C. Powell, "Resources of Western Libraries for Research in History," *Pacific Hist. Rev.*, XI (1942), 263.

Hans Praesent, *Minerva-Handbücher. Die Bibliotheken*. 3 vols. Berlin, 1927–34.

E. A. Savage, *The Libraries of Bermuda, the Bahamas, the British West Indies, British Guiana, British Honduras, Puerto Rico, and the American Virgin Islands*. London, 1934.

J. H. Shera, *Foundations of the Public Library; Origins of the Public Library Movement in New England, 1629–1855*. Chi., 1949.

Louis Shorea, *Origins of the American College Library 1638–1800*. Nashville, 1934.

Gladys Spencer, *Chicago Public Library*. Chi., 1943.

UNESCO, *Répertoire des bibliothèques de France*. 2 vols. Paris, 1950–51.

U.S. Bureau of Education, *Public Libraries in the United States of America; Their History, Condition, and Management*. Wash., 1904.

John Van Male, *Resources of Pacific Northwest Libraries, a Survey of Facilities for Study and Research*. Seattle, 1943.

R. L. Vormelker, ed., *Special Library Resources*. 4 vols. N.Y., 1941–47.

L. R. Wilson, *et al.*, *Libraries of the Southeast, a Report of the Southeastern States Cooperative Library Survey 1946–1947*. Chapel Hill, 1949.

L. R. Wilson and M. F. Tauber, *University Library*. Chi., 1945.

L. C. Wroth, *First Century of the John Carter Brown Library; A History with a Guide to Its Collections*. Providence, 1946.

17. NONDOCUMENTARY SOURCES

The documentary sources of American history are so voluminous that it is easy to overlook the data afforded by physical survivals and objects of material culture. Yet such vestiges of the past may be quite as revealing as written records. Historical students who have never themselves examined the location of Jamestown, Virginia, are not likely to perceive its advantages as well as disadvantages as a place of settlement. Failure to visit a battle site may lead to egregious misunderstanding of crucial field actions. Chroniclers of the westward movement write with more confidence if they have traversed Cumberland Gap, followed the Oregon Trail, or crossed Death Valley. By the same token, the social historian may blunder if he has not sought out the visible evidence of how people formerly lived. Reminders of once prevalent ways of life meet the eye in virtually any locality: residential sections changing over into business districts; old-fashioned dwellings standing cheek by jowl with newer ones; perhaps an abandoned canal bed, a lichen-covered stone fence, or a rotting covered bridge.

A rapidly increasing number of history-conscious communities have housed indoor relics in museums. Many hundreds of these institutions exist in the United States, including those devoted to art, science, transportation, agriculture, and other specialties — all shedding light on the development of American civilization. Though the older museums are sometimes mere storehouses of miscellaneous items, the modern conception is to arrange the exhibits so as to present a visual transcript of a facet of life at a given time and place: thus, a colonial kitchen, an early nineteenth-century schoolroom, or the interior of a wagon factory in the 1880's. When the genuine historical accessories are not available, an alternative plan is to construct dioramas of miniature models. It is hardly necessary to observe that the staffs of present-day museums must be as well grounded in American history and as exacting in their standards of scholarship as the writers of learned monographs.

A still more personalized type of museum is that represented by historic houses. The number open to the public has grown from one in 1850 to approximately a thousand today, strewn through all parts of the country. In some places organizations such as the Association for the Preservation of Virginia Antiquities, the Society for the Preservation of New England Antiquities, and the National Society of Colonial Dames have been responsible; elsewhere local initiative sufficed. The wide range of these undertakings is illustrated in the case of one state by such instances as the Fraunces Tavern, the Edgar Allan Poe cottage, and the Theodore Roosevelt house in New York City, General Knox's headquarters at New Windsor, the Philip Schuyler mansion in Albany, the John Brown house at North Elba, and the Ulysses S. Grant cottage at Mt. McGregor. Such preservations serve not only as memorials of particular individuals, but also as mute witnesses to changing standards in architecture, interior furnishings, and household appliances.

Even museums not avowedly "historical" should interest the student of America's past. Thus, the great art museums of New York City, Boston, and Philadelphia afford a running commentary on the progress of the fine arts in the United States and at the same time offer some of the best American period rooms. The Museum of Natural History in New York presents rich material on Indian life. The United States National Museum in Washington touches upon multifold aspects of America's social history, including costumes, furniture, patent-office models of inventions, and industrial apparatus. Two of the best institutions devoted exclusively to technological exhibits are the Museums of Science and Industry in New York and Chicago. Among numerous other specialized collections important for the historian are the Museum of New Mexico, Santa Fe, notable for its models of prehistoric villages, ancient artifacts, and products of modern Indian handicraft; the Peabody Museum, Salem, Massachusetts, featuring rare fabrics and other articles secured in the Far Eastern trade, and ship models; the Bucks County Historical Society, Doylestown, Pennsylvania, containing tools and utensils in use before 1820; the Confederate Museum, Richmond, Virginia; the Museum of Historic Pioneer Relics, Shasta, California; the Studebaker Museum of Transportation, South Bend, Indiana, the exhibits of which illustrate the evolution of American wheeled vehicles; and the National Baseball Hall of Fame and Museum, Cooperstown, New York.

A significant recent development is the open-air, multiple-unit museum after the manner of the Scandinavian countries. One example of the rapidly mounting number is Colonial Williamsburg in Virginia, a painstaking and elaborate reconstruction of the famous eighteenth-century capital both indoors and out. Another is at Luther College, Decorah, Iowa, where have been gathered appropriately furnished cabins and houses of Norwegian-American settlers. A third instance, less unified in plan, is Greenfield Village at Dearborn, Michigan. Here are to be found some two hundred and fifty structures, including an early village post office, a pioneer Michigan tavern, a tintype studio, a livery stable, a grist mill, and Edison's original laboratory at Menlo Park, New Jersey. Still another example of such museums may be found at Sturbridge, Massachusetts, where an attempt is made to preserve a New England village of the early nineteenth century.

A different sort of outdoor display is provided by the national monuments, military parks, and certain other reserves administered by the National Park Service of the Department of the Interior. Scattered in all parts of the country, these tracts contain not only natural wonders, but also historical landmarks such as aboriginal ruins, battle sites, obsolete fortifications, and the like. In addition, the Park Service has preserved type dwellings representative of nearly every important period of American history. Similar memorials are maintained by most of the state governments and by a growing number of municipalities.

The bibliographical chapters of *A History of American Life* (A. M. Schlesinger and D. R. Fox, eds.) contain sections on "Physical Survivals." More extensive bibliographies include E. E. Edwards, comp., *References on Agricultural Museums* (U.S. Dept. of Ag., Bibliog. Contribs., No. 29, Wash., 1936), and R. C. Smith, comp., *A Bibliography of Museums and Museum Work* (Wash., 1928). The following references are useful both for historical scholars and for museum workers:

Am. Assoc. of Museums, *Handbook of American Museums*. Wash., 1932. — An annotated list of American and Canadian museums.
L. V. Coleman, *College and University Museums*. Wash., 1942.
L. V. Coleman, *Company Museums*. Wash., 1943.
L. V. Coleman, *Historic House Museums*. Wash., 1933.
L. V. Coleman, *The Museum in America*. 3 vols. Wash., 1939.
J. C. Fitzpatrick, ed., *Some Historic Houses, Their Builders and Their Places in History*. N.Y., 1939.
National Park Service, *Historical Handbooks*. Wash., 1949– . — A continuing series describing historical properties belonging to the federal government.
Walter Pach, *The Art Museum in America, Its History and Achievement*. N.Y., 1948.
A. C. Parker, *A Manual for History Museums*. N.Y., 1935. — Practical suggestions.
Society for the Preservation of New England Antiquities, *Bull*. Boston, 1910–1919.
Society for the Preservation of New England Antiquities, *Old-Time New England*. Boston, 1920– . — A quarterly periodical.
A. P. Stauffer and C. W. Porter, "The National Park Service Program of Conservation for Areas and Structures of National Historical Significance," *Miss. Valley Hist. Rev.*, XXX (1943), 25.

18. PICTORIAL RECORDS

As an aid to recapturing the living past, pictorial materials appear at last to be assuming the importance they deserve after long neglect by professional historians. These materials are of many kinds. Imaginative delineations are least trustworthy historically because of the possibility that the artist, however unintentionally, may have distorted the truth. A classic example is John Trumbull's painting, "The Signing of the Declaration of Independence" (1794), which, though faithfully reproducing the likenesses of the individual participants, misrepresents them as having all attached their signatures at one time. In any event, it is better to consult the originals of paintings or drawings than the engravings, which may have been executed with considerable license. Nonetheless, portraits, photographs, and other graphic representations often provide data in regard to dress, artifacts, and everyday living — the retail traffic of life — that escaped the written records and may even have eluded museum collectors.

Caricatures and cartoons are of value not only for the light they cast upon shifting conceptions of humor, but also because they may incidentally tell much about social customs and political conditions. Such sketches, moreover, besides registering feelings and attitudes of the time, sometimes helped to create them. A notable example is Thomas Nast's pictorial crusade in *Harper's Weekly*, 1869–72, against the infamous Tweed Ring in New York City. Another is the partisan warfare waged by the two outstanding illustrated humor weeklies of the late nineteenth and early twentieth centuries: *Puck*, which aimed its shafts at the Republicans, and *Judge*, which sniped away at the Democrats. Bernhard Gillam's trenchant series in *Puck* depicting James G. Blaine as "The Tattooed Man" went far to discredit the Republican standard-bearer in 1884 as a man with a checkered and corrupt Congressional record. Such instances have been frequent in American political history.

The most recent type of pictorial material is the motion picture. Two varieties possess particular importance for the historian. One consists of news shots, newsreels, and documentary films, which image actual events and people. In the Library of Congress collection factual movies go back as far as 1897. Such sources on occasion may supply irrefutable historical evidence. Thus, when Japanese air bombers sank the neutral United States gunboat *Panay* on December 12, 1937, during the Sino-Japanese war, a Universal newsreel proved that, contrary to Tokyo's allegations, American flags were plainly exhibited on the vessel.

Fictional films, the second general category, vary greatly in historical value. Those which, while telling a story, give it a more or less realistic setting are the most remunerative. To consider some actual instances, one may thus gain indirect knowledge at particular periods of the lot of Polish-American tobacco growers, of labor troubles in the coal fields, of prison discipline, and of race bigotry. Pictures of this kind, though dealing with the contemporary scene, become material for the historian when, with the lapse of time, they describe conditions that once existed. Unfortunately, screen plays avowedly treating historical events are generally less veracious than the better historical novels (§ 63). For a protest on this score by MacKinlay Kantor, an accomplished historical novelist, see the *New York Times*, May 26, 1940, sect. 2.

Certain institutions have established great cinematic collections. In addition to the Library of Congress, the National Archives in Washington and the Museum of Modern Art in New York lead in preserving such sources. The last named also maintains a card index of important films produced since 1889. The Library of Congress has published *Motion Pictures, 1912–39* (Wash., 1952), giving information on more than 50,000 films of all varieties. A supplementary volume is to follow for the period 1940–49. The United States Office of Education has published *3440 Government Films* (Wash., 1951), a descriptive catalogue of motion pictures, filmstrips, and lantern slides available for public use in federal agencies, and *A Directory of 2002 16mm Film Libraries* (Wash., 1951), a national list of depositories with brief notes on the holdings of each. W. H. Hartley, *Selected Films for American History and Problems* (N.Y., 1940); Teaching Film Custodians, *Films for Classroom Use* (N.Y., 1950); and Seerley Reid, comp., *Motion Pictures on Democracy* (Wash., 1950), are handbooks designed particularly for teachers.

Whatever their nature, pictorial records have to be subjected to the same critical scrutiny as any other body of primary material (§ 6). When pictures are used in a scholarly work, their source and date should always be given with any needful remarks as to historical authenticity. For an example of this procedure, consult the notes on illustrations prefacing the volumes of *A History of American Life*. Among periodicals valuable for illustrations are *Gleason's Pictorial Drawing-Room Companion, Harper's Weekly,* and *Frank Leslie's Illustrated Newspaper* in the nineteenth century, and *Life* and *Look* in the twentieth century (§ 52). The news-distributing agencies such as the Associated Press and the United Press maintain files of their pictures. In the 1930's the Works Projects Administration compiled check lists of American portraits in the states of New Jersey, Connecticut, Rhode Island, Massachusetts, Maine, and New Hampshire; copies are available at the Library of Congress among other places. The following list itemizes some of the more important published pictorial collections along with a few other books unusually rich in such material.

INCLUSIVE COMPILATIONS

J. T. Adams, ed., *Album of American History.* 5 vols. N.Y., 1944–49. — From colonial times to the present.

G. W. Bonté and S. E. Forman, eds., *America Marches Past.* N.Y., 1936. — From colonial times to publication date.

Roger Butterfield, *The American Past.* N.Y., 1947. — From 1776 to publication date.

Holger Cahill, ed., *American Folk Art, the Art of the Common Man, 1750–1900.* N.Y., [1932].

A. C. Collins, ed., *The Story of America in Pictures.* Garden City, 1940. — From colonial times to publication date.

M. B. Davidson, ed., *Life in America.* 2 vols. Boston, 1951. — From colonial times to the present.

C. W. Dreppard, *Early American Prints.* N.Y., 1930. — From colonial times to the Civil War.

Dunbar, *A History of Travel in America.* — § 61.

H. L. and W. L. Ehrich, eds., *One Hundred Early American Paintings.* N.Y., 1918. — From 1750 to 1850.

R. H. Gabriel, ed., *The Pageant of America.* 15 vols. New Haven, 1926–29. — From colonial times to publication date.

C. P. Horning, ed., *Handbook of Early American Advertising Art.* N.Y., 1947. — Through the 1890's.

Milton Kaplan, ed., *Presidents on Parade.* N.Y., 1948. — From the beginning to the present.

Library of Congress, *An Album of American Battle Art, 1755–1918.* Wash., 1947.

Stefan Lorant, ed., *The Presidency.* N.Y., 1951. — From the beginning to the present.

William Murrell, *A History of American Graphic Humor.* 2 vols. N.Y., 1933–38. — From colonial times to publication date.

Allan Nevins, ed., *A Century of Political Cartoons.* N.Y., 1944. — The nineteenth century.

John Robinson and G. F. Dow, eds., *The Sailing Ships of New England, 1607–1907.* 3 vols. Salem, 1922–28.

Agnes Rogers and F. L. Allen, eds., *The American Procession: American Life since 1860 in Photographs.* N.Y., 1933.

I. N. P. Stokes and D. C. Haskell, comps., *American Historical Prints, Early Views of American Cities, Etc.* N.Y., 1932. — Through 1849.

John Walker and Macgill James, eds., *Great American Paintings from Smibert to Bellows, 1729–1924.* London, 1943.

H. B. Wehle, *American Miniatures, 1730–1850.* Garden City, 1927.

COLONIAL PERIOD

R. G. Adams, *Pilgrims, Indians and Patriots.* Boston, 1928. — Illustrated with cuts from old books.

F. W. Bayley, *Five Colonial Artists of New England.* Boston, 1929. — Badger, Blackburn, Copley, Feke, and Smibert.

Philip Hendy, ed., *Loan Exhibition of One Hundred Colonial Portraits.* Boston, 1930.

NATIONAL PERIOD TO 1900

C. L. Bartholomew (Bart, *pseud.*), *Cartoons of the Spanish-American War.* Minneapolis, 1899. — From the *Minneapolis Journal.*

Brentano's, *American Caricatures Pertaining to the Civil War.* N.Y., 1918. — Covers 1856–72.

Lamont Buchanan, ed., *A Pictorial History of the Confederacy.* N.Y., 1951.

Homer Davenport, *Cartoons.* N.Y., 1898. — From the *New York Journal.*

A. B. Frost, *Sports and Games in the Open.* N.Y., 1899.

A. B. Frost, *A Book of Drawings.* N.Y., 1904.

C. D. Gibson, *Drawings.* N.Y., 1894.

C. D. Gibson, *Sketches and Cartoons.* N.Y., 1898.

C. D. Gibson, *The Americans.* N.Y., 1900. — From *Life.*

E. W. Kemble, *Comical Coons.* N.Y., 1898.

E. W. Kemble, *Kemble's Sketch Book.* N.Y., 1899.

Joseph Keppler, *Selection of Cartoons from Puck.* H. C. Bunner, ed. N.Y., 1893.

J. A. Kouwenhoven, ed., *Adventures of America, 1857–1900.* N.Y., 1938. — Illustrations from *Harper's Weekly.*

Henry Lewis, *Das Illustrirte Mississippithal* (1857). — § 48.

J. B. Longacre and James Herring, comps., *The National Portrait Gallery of Distinguished Americans.* 4 vols. Phila., 1834–39. — Leaders in politics, industry, literature, and the arts.

Stefan Lorant, ed., *Lincoln, His Life in Photographs.* N.Y., 1941.

A. B. Maurice and F. T. Cooper, *The History of the Nineteenth Century in Caricature.* N.Y., 1904. — Includes many American cartoons.

Roy Meredith, ed., *Mr. Lincoln's Camera Man, Mathew B. Brady.* N.Y., 1946.

Roy Meredith, ed., *Mr. Lincoln's Contemporaries,* N.Y., 1951. — Brady photographs.

F. T. Miller, ed., *Portrait Life of Abraham Lincoln.* Springfield, Mass., 1910.

F. T. Miller, ed., *The Photographic History of the Civil War.* 10 vols. N.Y., 1911–12. — Brady photographs.

M. S. Morgan, ed., *The American Civil War Cartoons of Matt Morgan and Other English Artists.* London, 1874.

Charles Nelan, *Cartoons of Our War with Spain*. N.Y., [1898]. — From the *New York Herald*.

F. B. Opper, *The Tariff Question*. N.Y., 1888. — From *Puck*.

Paine, *Nast* (§ 56).

Bellamy Partridge and Otto Bettmann, *As We Were, Family Life in America, 1850–1900*. N.Y., 1946.

Peters, *Currier & Ives*. — A profusely illustrated history of the firm (§ 56).

Nathaniel Pousette-Dart, comp., *Winslow Homer*. N.Y., 1923.

Frederic Remington, *Drawings*. N.Y., 1897.

Frederic Remington, *Remington's Frontier Sketches*. Chi., 1898.

Agnes Rogers, ed., *Abraham Lincoln, a Biography in Pictures*. Boston, 1939.

C. M. Stow, ed., *Best Fifty Currier & Ives Lithographs, Large Folio Size*. N.Y., 1933. — Also issued in a small folio size, N.Y., 1934.

A. J. Volck, *Confederate War Etchings*. N.p., n.d.

A. J. Volck, *Sketches from the Civil War in North America*. London, 1863.

TWENTIETH CENTURY

H. G. Alsberg, ed., *America Fights the Depression, a Photographic Record of the CWA*. N.Y., 1934.

F. G. Attwood, *Attwood's Pictures: an Artist's History of the Last Ten Years*. N.Y., 1910. — From *Life*.

George Bellows, *Memorial Exhibition of the Work of George Bellows*. N.Y., 1925.

Daniel Blum, ed., *A Pictorial History of the American Theater*. N.Y., 1951. — From 1900.

Erskine Caldwell and Margaret Bourke-White, *Say! Is This the U.S.A.?* N.Y., 1941. — Scenes of the Great Depression.

Oscar Cesare, *One Hundred Cartoons*. Boston, 1916. — From the *New York Sun* and *Harper's Weekly*.

Otho Cushing, *The Teddyssey*. N.Y., 1907. — Theodore Roosevelt as pictured by the artist in *Life*.

J. N. Darling (Ding, *pseud.*), *Cartoon Book*. Title varies slightly. 2 vols. Des Moines, 1909–22. — From the *Des Moines Register*.

Walker Evans, *American Photographs*. N.Y., 1938. — Scenes of the Great Depression.

Raymond Gros, ed., *T. R. in Cartoon*. Akron, 1910.

W. S. Hall, ed., *Eyes on America*. N.Y., 1939. — Over 200 recent paintings.

G. J. Hecht, ed., *The War in Cartoons*. N.Y., 1919. — World War I as pictured by twenty-seven cartoonists.

Herbert Johnson, *Cartoons*. Phila., 1936. — From the *Saturday Evening Post*.

Camillus Kessler, *At the Bottom of the Ladder*. Phila., 1926. — Cartoons from the *New York Globe*.

Rollin Kirby, *Highlights; a Cartoon History of the Nineteen Twenties*. H. B. Hoffman, ed. N.Y., 1931. — From the *New York World*.

Dorothea Lange and P. S. Taylor, *An American Exodus*. N.Y., 1939. — Scenes of the Great Depression.

Stefan Lorant, ed., *FDR, a Pictorial Biography*. N.Y., 1950.

J. T. McCutcheon, *Cartoons*. Chi., 1903.

J. T. McCutcheon, *Congressman Pumphrey, the People's Friend*. Chi., 1907.

J. T. McCutcheon, *T. R. in Cartoons*. Chi., 1910. — From the *Chicago Tribune*.

F. J. Mackey and M. W. Jernegan, eds., *Forward — March: the Photographic Record of America in the World War and the Post War Social Upheaval*. 2 vols. Chi., 1935. — World War I.

Archibald MacLeish, ed., *Land of the Free*. N.Y., 1938. — Scenes of the Great Depression.

Bill Mauldin, *Up Front*. N.Y., 1945. — Cartoons of World War II from *Stars and Stripes*.

Wright Morris, *The Inhabitants*. N.Y., 1946. — Photographs of ways of folk living.

Joseph Pennell, *Pictures of the Panama Canal*. 5 ed. Phila., 1913.

Boardman Robinson, *Cartoons on the War*. N.Y., 1915. — Drawings of World War I from *Harper's Weekly* and the *New York Tribune*.

Agnes Rogers, ed., *Women Are Here to Stay*. N.Y., 1949.

Agnes Rogers and F. L. Allen, *I Remember Distinctly, a Family Album of the American People, 1918–1941.* N.Y., 1947.

W. A. Rogers, *America's Black and White Book.* N.Y., 1917.

W. A. Rogers, *A World Worth While.* N.Y., 1922. — From the *New York Herald.*

Albert Shaw, ed., *A Cartoon History of Roosevelt's Career.* N.Y., 1910. — Theodore Roosevelt.

Laurence Stallings, ed., *The First World War, a Photographic History.* N.Y., 1933.

A. B. Tourtellot and others, eds., *Life's Picture History of World War II.* N.Y., 1950. — Photographs and paintings.

U.S. Department of the Army, Office of Military History, *Pictorial Record.* 3 vols. Wash., 1951. — Photographs of World War II operations in (1) Mediterranean and adjacent areas, (2) Europe and adjacent areas, and (3) Pacific theater.

Don Wharton, ed., *The Roosevelt Omnibus.* N.Y., 1934. — Franklin D. Roosevelt in photographs and cartoons.

Art Young, *This 1928 Campaign in Cartoons.* N.Y., 1928.

Art Young, *The Best of Art Young.* N.Y., 1936. — From the *Masses, Liberator, Collier's,* etc.

19. MAPS AND HISTORY

To the historian maps are eloquent documents. They constitute a common language used by men of different races and tongues to express the relationship of their society — its needs, ideas, and growth — to a geographic environment. As sources for the study of the history of the western world in modern times maps are well-nigh indispensable.

Their impact is especially clear in the field of geographic exploration. Explorers from the time of the discovery of the New World to our own day have relied upon maps to guide their journeys. Christopher Columbus formed his concepts of the unknown sea he proposed to sail from a series of charts which the ancient geographer Ptolemy was believed to have drawn and which Cardinal d'Ailly reinterpreted. After Columbus, maps and atlases, flowing in a steady stream from the printing presses of Europe, served to guide explorers and to illustrate to present-day students of history the gradual growth of geographic knowledge. Some information appearing on these maps was the work of sheer fancy; it was not for that reason less important in producing historical results. The mythical Strait of Anian, a supposed passage to the Orient through the newly discovered continent of America, persisted on maps in one form or another for centuries, teasing the imagination of governments and explorers, and influencing successive exploring expeditions and measures of state policy. The great survey by Captain George Vancouver of the Northwest Coast of North America at the end of the eighteenth century was motivated still by the hope of finding such a strait.

In the field of diplomacy maps have had a similar importance. They have furnished to diplomats basic information for boundary and other settlements. The foreign offices of modern governments have found maps of such usefulness that they have created libraries of them for current use, often of considerable size, and have kept in close touch, as special need has arisen, with the larger map collections. Not only correct, but incorrect, information on early maps of North America, has shaped American history. The charting of a vast wilderness led almost inevitably to errors, and these, in diplomacy, to boundary disputes. Thus the inaccuracies of the John Mitchell map of North America of 1775, the map relied on by the negotiators of the peace of 1782, produced such results as the Northwest boundary gap, the Maine boundary controversy, and the "Battle of the Maps." In the Oregon negotiation of 1818, American diplomats, relying on British maps which exhibited a mythical "Caledonia River," set the stage for later difficulties of boundary settlement.

In the field of economic development maps have had a like significance. They have been instruments shaping development and, in the process, have been themselves reshaped. In the fur trade, which was an early economic interest of Europeans in North America, maps guided traders, traders redrew maps. The Hudson's Bay Company provided the information which gave distinction to the North American maps of the great London cartographer, Aaron Arrowsmith. The North West Company maintained on its payroll, as geographer, David Thompson, one of the greatest of American explorers and surveyors. In the field of transportation the surveys made of railroad routes to the Pacific in the 1850's were formative of policy and are now the materials of the historian. The nautical charts issued by the Coast and Geodetic Survey, the aeronautical charts issued by the several agencies of the federal government, the soil maps and the climate maps of bureaus of the Department of Agriculture, the topographic maps of the Geological Survey, the maps of river systems executed by the Corps of Engineers, these, and scores of other varieties of maps put forth by the federal government have been the basis of economic planning and action, and have become prime documents to later students.

An ever widening range of data of social nature has appeared on maps, such as vital statistics, ethnic groupings, local option regarding alcoholic beverages, the incidence of disease, church affiliation, illiteracy, education, woman suffrage, tenancy prevalence, and distribution of wealth. Such maps are often the tools of social planning, whether urban, regional, or national, and are of corresponding value to the historian.

In warfare, maps and charts have been traditionally important. They have been relied on by military headquarters and by armies and navies for fighting battles and for planning the logistics of campaigns. With the advent of the airplane and the development of air reconnaissance and strategic bombing, the range and variety of military mapping has been vastly expanded. Among the major mapping agencies of the federal government are at present the several branches of the military service.

The manifold relationships of cartography to history are discussed in the general works listed in § 20. See also Colton Storm, "Maps as Historical Documents," *Publisher's Weekly*, CXLVI (1944), 2060.

Among the more important depositories of the map collections in the United States are the following:

Library of Congress, Wash., D.C.
National Archives, Wash., D.C.
Army Map Service, Wash., D.C.
Hydrographic Office, Wash., D.C.
American Geographical Society, N.Y.C.
New York Public Library, N.Y.C.
Hispanic Society of America, N.Y.C.
Yale University Library, New Haven, Conn.

John Carter Brown Library, Providence, R.I.
Harvard University Library, Cambridge, Mass.
William L. Clements Library, Ann Arbor, Mich.
Newberry Library, Chi., Ill.
State Historical Society of Wisconsin Library, Madison, Wisc.
University of California Library, Berkeley, Calif.
Henry E. Huntington Library, San Marino, Calif.
University of North Carolina Library, Chapel Hill, No. Car.
Canadian Archives, Ottawa, Canada.

20. GENERAL GUIDES AND MAPS

The maps, manuscript and printed, of North America that have appeared since the voyages of Columbus are a vast quantity. An even greater quantity of cartographic sources has appeared. Together these would form a bewildering maze were it not for the existence of guides to show the way through. The guides comprise works of two types: general works covering world cartography, and regional and special works covering the United States.

Of the general guides the most useful are the following:

L. A. Brown, *The Story of Maps.* Boston, 1949. — Includes a classified bibliography of cartographic literature.
Erwin Raisz, *General Cartography.* R. ed. N.Y., 1948.
R. V. Tooley, *Maps and Map-Makers.* London, 1949.
J. K. Wright, *Aids to Geographical Research.* R. ed. N.Y., 1947. — A discussion of the tools of map research.
Walter Thiele, *Official Map Publications.* Chi., 1938. — This work, in chs. vii–ix, summarizes the mapping of the North American continent from the sixteenth to the nineteenth centuries as associated with discovery and surveying, with helpful bibliographical footnotes.
British Museum Catalogue of Maps. 2 vols. London, 1883–84. — A catalogue of one of the great map collections of the world.

Of the special guides and aids relating to American cartography, the following are of particular value:

P. L. Phillips, *A List of Maps of America in the Library of Congress.* Wash., 1901.
P. L. Phillips, *A List of Geographical Atlases in the Library of Congress.* 4 vols. Wash., 1909–20.
C. E. LeGear, *United States Atlases.* Wash., 1950. — This is a listing of atlases of the United States under captions such as agriculture, boundaries, canals, climate, coal, commerce, forests, history, industries, railroads, roads, statistics, states, counties, and cities.
C. O. Paullin, *Atlas of the Historical Geography of the United States.* Wash., 1932. — The front matter contains useful bibliographical discussions of special topics and map sources.

In the writings of Justin Winsor (see § 21) are valuable footnote references to the cartographic literature of America.

Paullin's *Atlas* is the most elaborate of the one-volume historical atlases of the United States. Among other school atlases of American history are:

C. L. Lord and E. H. Lord, *Historical Atlas of the United States.* N.Y., 1944.
J. T. Adams, *Atlas of American History.* N.Y., 1943.

Harper's Atlas of American History. N.Y., [1920]. — A series of maps excerpted from the *American Nation* series.

W. R. Shepherd, *Historical Atlas.* N.Y., 1911. — A general atlas containing 24 maps connected with United States history, and still one of the most useful of the school atlases.

Tripod stands of American history maps, or alternatively, roller sets of maps in cases, may be purchased from the commercial map-publishing houses. The first of the stands listed below, contains in addition to American history maps, other social-studies maps. The second and older set consists entirely of American history maps.

E. D. Morrison and Erwin Raisz, *Social Studies Maps.* 44 x 30 inches. Modern School Supply Company, Goshen, Ind.

A. B. Hart and H. E. Bolton, *Basic American History Maps.* 44 x 32 inches. Denoyer-Geppert, Chicago.

21. HISTORICAL SOURCES FOR MAPS OF THE UNITED STATES

The advance by periods of geographic knowledge of America may be traced in the following lists:

PRE-COLUMBIAN AND COLUMBIAN PERIOD

C. R. Beazley, *Dawn of Modern Geography.* 3 vols. London, 1897–1906. — Contains many reproductions of maps.

J. K. Wright, *Geographical Lore of the Time of the Crusades.* N.Y., 1925.

E. L. Stevenson, *Geography of Claudius Ptolemy.* N.Y., 1932.

Pierre d'Ailly, *Imago Mundi.* Edmond Buron, ed. 3 vols. Paris, [1930–31]. — Includes marginal notes of Columbus.

L. C. Jane, ed., *Select Documents Illustrating the Four Voyages of Columbus* (Hakluyt Society Works, 2 ser., LXV, LXX). London, 1930–33.

E. G. Ravenstein, *Martin Behaim, His Life and His Globe.* London, 1908.

E. L. Stevenson, *Atlas of Portolan Charts.* N.Y., 1911.

A. E. Nordenskiöld, *Facsimile Atlas.* Stockholm, 1889.

Henry Harrisse, *Discovery of North America.* London, 1892. — Includes descriptions of 250 maps or globes before 1536.

SIXTEENTH AND SEVENTEENTH CENTURY MAP MAKERS AND MAPS

The earliest map extant which depicts any part of the North American continent is the world map (1500) of Juan de la Cosa. A good account of it is G. E. Nunn, *Mappemonde of Juan de la Cosa: a Critical Investigation of its Date* (Jenkintown, 1934). The next two centuries may be traced through:

E. L. Stevenson, *Maps Illustrating Early Discovery and Exploration in America, 1502–30.* New Brunswick, N.J., 1903.

Stokes, *Iconography of Manhattan Island* (§ 62). — Much wider in scope than its title.

Frederik Muller and Company, *Remarkable Maps of the XVth, XVIth, and XVIIth Centuries Reproduced in Their Original Size.* Amsterdam, 1894–97.

F. C. Wieder, *Monumenta Cartographica; Reproductions of Unique and Rare Maps, Plans and Views.* 5 vols. The Hague, 1925–33.

E. F. Jomard, *Les Monuments de la géographie.* Paris, 1842–62.

G. E. Nunn, *The Geographical Conceptions of Columbus.* N.Y., 1924.

G. E. Nunn, *Origin of the Strait of Anian Concept.* Phila., 1929.

For the contributions made by explorers of this period to the geographic and cartographic knowledge of the New World, see works relating to them below (§§ 56, 70, 72, 75, 76, 78) under such names as Cabot, Cartier, John Smith, Champlain, De Soto, Coronado, Nicollet, Marquette, Joliet, La Salle. A concise account of these explorations is J. B. Brebner, *Explorers of North America, 1492–1806* (London, 1933). See also: Edward Heawood, *History of Geographical Discovery in the Seventeenth and Eighteenth Centuries* (Cambridge, Eng., 1912); L. J. Burpee, *Search for the Western Sea* (R. ed. Toronto, 1935); F. W. Hodge and T. H. Lewis, eds., *Spanish Explorers in the Southern United States, 1528–1553* (N.Y., 1907); H. E. Bolton, ed., *Spanish Exploration in the Southwest, 1542–1706* (N.Y., 1916). A good account of the Spanish voyages to the Northwest Coast, with map reproductions, is H. R. Wagner, *Spanish Voyages to the Northwest Coast of America in the Sixteenth Century* (San Francisco, 1929).

A selection of reproductions of maps of this period is in Paullin's *Atlas*. See also: L. J. Burpee, *Historical Atlas of Canada* (Toronto, 1927); and references in §§ 79–100.

EIGHTEENTH AND NINETEENTH CENTURY MAPS AND MAP MAKERS

P. L. Phillips, ed., *The Lowery Collection. A Descriptive List of Maps of Spanish Possessions within the Present Limits of the United States, 1502–1820.* Wash., 1912.

H. R. Wagner, *Cartography of the Northwest Coast of America to the Year 1800.* 2 vols. Berkeley, 1937.

L. C. Karpinski, *Bibliography of the Printed Maps of Michigan, 1804–1880.* Lansing, 1931. — An outstanding regional bibliography much wider than its title.

Facsimiles of maps of this period appear in the following collections:

A. B. Hulbert, *Crown Collection of Photographs of American Maps.* 5 vols. Cleve., 1904–08. — A second series, in 3 vols. (1910), relates to Canada. A third series (n.d.), of 250 plates, relates primarily to individual American colonies. The same author has issued two further series on western trails in blue print.

L. C. Karpinski, *Manuscript Maps, Prior to 1800, Relating to America* (n.p., 1927). — 986 photographic facsimiles, made from the originals in various libraries and archives in Paris, Spain, and Portugal. To be found in a number of subscribing American libraries, including the Library of Congress, Clements Library, and Huntington Library.

Famous individual maps and atlases of the period include: John Mitchell, *Map of the British and French Dominions in North America* (London, 1755); Lewis Evans, *General Map of the Middle British Colonies in America* (Phila., 1755); Aaron Arrowsmith, *A Map Exhibiting All the Discoveries in the Interior of North America* (London, 1795, reissued repeatedly with additions and corrections). Well-known American publishers of maps and atlases of this period are Mathew Carey, John Melish, Jedidiah Morse and H. S. Tanner. Their works are listed in Phillips (see § 20).

The contributions to geographic knowledge made in this period by explorers may be traced in the references in §§ 71–8, 164 under such names as Verendrye, Escalante, Vancouver, Mackenzie, Lewis and Clark, Pike, Thompson, Ashley, Smith. Important collections of journals of explorers are R. G. Thwaites, ed., *Early Western Travels, 1748–1846* (§ 48); *idem, Original Journals of the Lewis and Clark Expedition* (8 vols. N.Y., 1904–05); *idem, Jesuit Relations* (§ 48). Documents relating to the fur trade and biographies of the traders are valuable sources for the study of cartography. An important twelve-volume collection of Hudson's Bay Company documents appears in the *Publications* of The Champlain Society (Toronto, 1938–49). An earlier publication of the same society that deals with one of the major figures in the exploration and surveying of western America is: *David Thompson's Narrative of His Explorations in Western America, 1784–1812* (J. B. Tyrrell, ed., Toronto, 1916). Another volume (1934) is devoted to *Documents Relating to the North West Company* (W. S. Wallace, ed., Toronto, 1934). The Hudson's Bay Record Society now makes its own publication of Hudson's Bay Company records. See also: Washington Irving, *Astoria* and *Captain Bonneville* (2 vols. N.Y. [1895]);

Stuart, *Discovery of the Oregon Trail* (§ 48); and G. L. Nute, ed., "Calendar of the American Fur Company's Papers, 1831–1849," Am. Hist. Assoc., *Report*, 1944, II, III.

Government surveys are important sources of geographic and cartographic information concerning the West. In the decade of the 1850's, army surveying expeditions traversed the trans-Missouri region seeking a suitable railroad route to the Pacific. Their reports, published in fourteen volumes, are in 33 Cong., 1 Sess., *H. Ex. Doc.*, No. 129, and 33 Cong., 2 Sess., *Sen. Ex. Doc.*, No. 78. After the Civil War four well-known surveying and mapping expeditions were sent to the West — the Hayden, King, Powell, and Wheeler expeditions (1867–79). Their reports, published in the Congressional documents, are catalogued and indexed in U.S. Geol. Survey, *Bull.*, 222 (1904). These surveys followed no standard pattern or method. In some areas they overlapped. In 1879, as a means of future uniformity, Congress created the United States Geological Survey (§ 22).

BOUNDARIES AND BOUNDARY CONTROVERSIES

For the colonial period, boundaries and boundary controversies may be studied in such of the standard early atlases as Henry Popple, *Map of the British Empire in America* (London, 1733); and Thomas Jefferys, *American Atlas* (London, 1778). In the works of Justin Winsor, and especially in his *Narrative and Critical History of America* (8 vols., Boston, 1884–89) will be found map reproductions and valuable discussions of boundary problems. For the northern boundary, see: Burpee, *Historical Atlas of Canada*. See also: the collections of map facsimiles listed above.

The sources for the boundary claims of the colonies are found in the various patents and charters, English, Spanish, Portuguese, French, Dutch, Swedish, and Russian. The principal English patents have been collected in B. P. Poore, ed., *Federal and State Constitutions, Colonial Charters, . . . of the United States* (2 vols., r. ed., Wash., 1878); and are reëdited in Thorpe's edition (§ 46). Many of the Dutch and Swedish documents are to be found in O'Callaghan, *Documentary History of New York* (§ 46); the French grants of Louisiana are in Gayarré, *History of Louisiana*. Canadian documents may be found through the index, published at Ottawa in 1909, to the archives of Canada. See also: colonial records (§§ 46, 47), and the decisions of the Privy Council. Imperfect translations and texts are common, so that the student should keep as near as possible to the originals.

For the texts of treaties of partition and delimitation among the European nations since 1492 the best collections are:

F. G. Davenport, *European Treaties Bearing on the History of the United States* (§ 57).
— Covers the years to 1715. A fourth volume, edited by C. O. Paullin (Wash., 1937), continues the series to 1815.
Recueil des traitez de paix, de trève, . . . et d'autre actes publics. 4 vols. Amsterdam, 1700.
George Chalmers, *Collection of Treaties between Great Britain and Other Powers.* 2 vols. London, 1790.
Jean Dumont, *Corps universel diplomatique du droit des gens.* 8 vols. Amsterdam, 1726–31. — Extended by the supplements of Jean Barbeyrac and Jean Rousset de Missy. 5 vols. Amsterdam, 1739.
Guillaume de Garden, *Histoire générale des traités de paix.* 15 vols. Paris, 1848–87.
A General Collection of Treatys. 4 vols. London, 1732.
C. G. Koch, *Abrégé de l'histoire des traités de paix.* 4 vols. Basle, 1796–97.
Friedrich Schoell, *Histoire abrégée des traités de paix.* 15 vols. Paris, 1817–18. — This is Koch's work recast and continued.
Karl von Martens and Ferdinand de Cussy, *Traités, Conventions et autres Actes Diplomatiques.* 7 vols. Leipzig, 1846–57.
G. F. de Martens, *et al.*, *Recueil de traités des puissances et états de l'Europe* (1761–   ). Göttingen, Leipzig, and Greifswald, 1817–   . — A continuing series, now numbering over a hundred volumes. After vol. VIII the title becomes *Nouveau Recueil*, and other changes appear in titles of later volumes.

For the boundaries and boundary controversies of the national period the *Atlas* of Paullin is useful. One series of its plates (91–96) and a corresponding section of the text (pp. 52–72) are devoted entirely to boundary controversies since 1776. Useful maps appear in such texts as Bailey, *Diplomatic History* and Bemis, *Diplomatic History*. Illustrative maps of boundary problems are to be found in the general histories of the United States (§§ 59, 60), and in the "American Nation" series; also in the monographs relating to particular boundary controversies listed in Bemis and Griffin, *Guide to Diplomatic History* (§ 35). See also: the school atlases listed in § 20. One of the primary mapping agencies of the federal government is the International Boundary Commission of the State Department.

The texts of boundary settlements to which the United States was a party are in the official volumes, Malloy, Redmond, and Treworth, *Treaties, Conventions,* and Miller, *Treaties and Other International Acts* (all in § 45).

Detailed accounts of boundary negotiations and settlements are to be found in Moore, *International Arbitrations* (§ 45), and in Bemis, *American Secretaries of State.* See also the references above.

For the evolution of state and territorial boundaries, illustrative maps will be found in two series in the *Atlas* of Paullin, plates 60–66 and 97–101. Texts for these maps are on pp. 43–45 and 72–87. Since internal boundaries are normally defined by acts of Congress, the source materials for them will be found in *Statutes at Large* (§ 45). They are, sometimes, found in presidential proclamations, for which see Richardson, *Messages and Papers* (§ 45). Controversies between states have almost always been subjects for investigation by Congress, and in such cases they are described in the *Congressional Documents*; or they have given rise to suits before the Supreme Court of the United States, the decisions of which are recorded in the *Reports* of the Court (§ 45).

The history of state boundaries is conveniently summarized in E. M. Douglas, "Boundaries, Areas, Geographic Centers and Altitudes of the United States and the Several States," U.S. Geol. Survey, *Bull.*, No. 817 (1930). Discussions of individual boundaries will be found under the topical readings in Parts Three, Four, and Five, below.

22. PHYSIOGRAPHIC MAPS

Physical maps of the United States are issued by various departments and bureaus of the federal government. The Geological Survey in the Department of the Interior, which is the major federal mapping service, has been engaged for many years in producing a detailed topographic or relief map of the United States. The scale of the map, published in segments, or quadrangles, varies with the sheets. The older sheets are usually on a scale of an inch to a mile or an inch to two miles. The recent sheets, based on airplane photography, are double this scale or more. Approximately half the area of the United States has been mapped. Guidance in the use of these sheets is given in R. D. Salisbury and W. W. Atwood, *Interpretation of Topographic Maps* (U. S. Geol. Survey, *Professional Paper*, No. 60 [1908]), in a revised guide under the same title by R. D. Salisbury and A. C. Trowbridge (N.Y., 1940), and in W. M. Davis, C. F. King, and G. L. Collie, *Report on Governmental Maps for Use in Schools* (N.Y., 1894). The Geological Survey has issued useful single-sheet maps, among them a *United States Relief Map* and a *United States Contour Map* in shades of brown. Other Interior Department agencies which issue maps are the Bureau of Land Management (formerly General Land Office) and the Bureau of Reclamation.

In the Department of Agriculture, the Soil Survey produces section maps on the scale of an inch to a mile and also in larger scale. It has covered about half the area of the United States. Other agencies in this Department issuing maps are the Bureau of Agricultural Economics, the Forest Service, and the Soil Conservation Service.

In the Commerce Department, the Coast and Geodetic Survey, one of the major federal mapping agencies, issues nautical and also aeronautical charts.

Its nautical sheets cover the coastal waters of the United States in detail. Its aeronautical charts, on a scale of eight miles to an inch, give the largest complete coverage for the United States of any of the government sheet maps. Other important mapping services in the Commerce Department are the Bureau of the Census and the Bureau of Public Roads.

In the Defense Department the chief mapping services are the Corps of Engineers, the Lake Survey Offices, and the Hydrographic Office.

The mapping services of the federal government are described, as of 1938, in Thiele, *Official Map Publications*, chs. x, xi. They are also described, as later reorganized, in brief form, in *The American Year Book*, 1950, 222. The Map Information Office of the U. S. Geological Survey issues each year a summary of the year's accomplishments of all the important federal mapping services. The work of the state geological surveys is described, *ibid.*, 235.

A valuable study of the impact of physical geography on the economic development of the United States is J. R. Smith and M. O. Phillips, *North America* (r. ed., N.Y., 1940). An older but still useful work of like character is Isaiah Bowman, *Forest Physiography* (N.Y., 1911). These two works are regional in their approach. A bibliography by W. L. G. Joerg of the regional geographies of North America is in *Geog. Rev.*, XXVI (1936), 640. For single regions or groups of regions detailed studies are available, such as R. B. Vance, *Human Geography of the South* (Chapel Hill, 1935), Webb, *Great Plains*, and J. C. Malin, *Grassland of North America* (Lawrence, Kans., 1947). A bibliography of the regional physiographic studies is contained in Wright, *Aids to Geographical Research*, 157.

WALL MAPS

Wall maps exhibiting the physical geography of the United States are published in a variety of forms. Especially useful are the landform maps, of which the following are examples:

Erwin Raisz, *Landforms of the United States*, 47x31 inches. Cambridge.
A. K. Lobeck, *Physiographic Diagram of the United States*, 62x44 inches. A. J. Nystrom and Company, Chi.

Less valuable for their maps than for their text are N. M. Fenneman, "Physiographic Divisions of the United States," Assoc. Am. Geographers, *Annals*, VI (1916), 19, and J. W. Powell, *Physiographic Regions of the United States* (Wash., [1895]). A relief map in striking new form is *Aero Plastic Relief Map of the United States*, 64x40 inches, Aero Service Corporation, Phila. Relief maps are published by the leading commercial map publishing companies of the United States, whose catalogues describe their virtues.

23. ECONOMIC AND POLITICAL MAPS

Population Maps. Maps illustrating the spread of population during the colonial period are found in H. R. Friis, "Distribution of Population, 1625–1790," *Geog. Rev.*, XXX (1940), 463. This is a series of ten maps exhibiting population distribution by the dot method. It was reissued with added maps and a valuable bibliography by the American Geographical Society as *Mimeographed Publ.*, No. 3 (1940). Less accurate maps for the colonial period are found in such general histories as Avery and Channing. For the national period, series of maps showing distribution of population at ten-year intervals are found in the United States Census for 1880 and for 1890, both under the title, *Population*, Pt. 1, and also in the Census *Atlas* for 1900. For maps of the expansion of New England population, see L. K. Mathews, *Expansion of New England* (Boston, 1909). For the retreat of the Indian frontier, see C. C. Royce, "Indian Land Cessions in the United States," Bureau of Am. Ethnology, *Annual Report* (1899). For the advance of the Negro, see Paullin, *Atlas*, plates 67, 68.

Agricultural Development. Maps illustrating the physical basis of American agriculture will be found in the valuable Dept. of Ag., *Atlas of American Agriculture* (O. E. Baker, ed., Wash., 1936). This includes sections on land relief, climate, soils, and natural vegetation. Each section contains a useful bibliography. A section illustrating the history of the cotton crop, intended for the *Atlas*, but actually published only in advance sheets, is Dept. of Ag., *Atlas of American Agriculture, Part V, Cotton* (Wash., 1918). Maps illustrating the historical spread of crops other than cotton will be found scattered through the *Yearbook* of the Department of Agriculture, especially for the years 1921 to 1925 inclusive, and through the Department's *Graphic Summary*. For maps illustrating the growth of farm tenancy, see Dept. of Ag., *Miscellaneous Publ.*, No. 261. A useful series of desk maps on agricultural subjects is published by the Bureau of Agricultural Economics. Outstanding examples are: F. J. Marschner, *Major Land Uses in the United States* (Wash., 1950); *Regionalized Types of Farming in the United States* (Wash., n. d.); *Rural Cultural Regions in the United States* (Wash., 1940); *Land Use Adjustment Areas* (Wash., 1940).

Railroad Transportation. Maps illustrating the growth of the American railroad net are in F. W. Hewes and Henry Gannett, eds., *Scribner's Statistical Atlas* (N.Y., 1885). Pioneer maps illustrating this development were issued annually from 1853 to the Civil War by H. V. Poor, the pioneer American railroad cartographer. Corrections of these maps for the pre-Civil War years for the Old Northwest are in F. L. Paxson, "Early Railways of the Old Northwest," Wisc. Ac. Sci., *Trans.*, XVII (1911–13), 243.

Geography of Politics. Maps of national elections are valuable aids to historical analysis. They are found in such monographs as O. G. Libby, *Geographical Distribution of the Vote . . . on the . . . Constitution* (Madison, 1894), A. C. Cole, *Whig Party in the South* (Wash., 1913), and F. J. Turner, *United States, 1830–1850* (N.Y., 1935). The maps in Turner are a highly suggestive correlation of physiography, crops, politics, and social conditions. In the Paullin *Atlas* is a series of maps (plates 102–111) depicting every presidential election from the first to 1928. E. E. Robinson has a more accurate series in his *Presidential Vote, 1896–1932* (Stanford University, Calif., 1934), carried forward by supplements to 1940. In the Paullin *Atlas* a valuable map series of votes on Congressional measures of importance appears (plates 112–122), and another of votes on American reforms (plates 123–132).

24. GAZETTEERS AND OTHER FORMS OF TRAVEL GUIDES

Gazetteers are compilations in which are gathered the names of localities in a given state, nation, or wider area, arranged in alphabetical order. For each locality listed is given its location and population, and, for the more important places, descriptive matter such as transportation facilities, trade, industry, building developments, and intellectual or educational facilities. A well-known work of this character, which has been in circulation in the United States in various editions since 1855, is Lippincott's, reissued in revised form as *Columbia Lippincott Gazetteer of the World* (L. E. Seltzer, ed., N.Y., 1952).

Gazetteers of past periods are of value to historians for information as to names that have disappeared from the map, local populations that have dwindled or grown, transportation facilities that were once of importance, or industries that have decayed or flourished. Sometimes they give details of routes of travel or rates of fare or fugitive information of other sorts difficult to find elsewhere. A selected list of gazetteers containing information such as this is given below. With the gazetteers are listed other forms of travel guides, described in their titles as directories or registers or travel guides.

William Amphlett, *The Emigrant's Directory to the Western States of North America.* London, 1819.
Appletons' Companion Hand-Book of Travel to the United States and British Provinces. N.Y., 1861.
Daniel Blowe, *Geographical, Historical, Commercial, and Agricultural View of the United States.* London, 1820.
S. R. Brown, *The Western Gazetteer, or Emigrant's Directory,* Auburn, N.Y., 1817.
J. R. Browne, *Resources of the Pacific Slope.* N.Y., 1869.
William Cobbett, *The Emigrant's Guide; in Ten Letters, Addressed to the Tax-Payers of England.* London, 1829.
A. J. Coolidge and J. B. Mansfield, *History and Description of New England, General and Local.* Boston, 1859. — Vol. I, Maine, N.H., and Vt.; no more published.
Samuel Cumings, *The Western Pilot, Containing Charts of the Ohio River, and of the Mississippi.* Cin., 1825. — Frequent r. eds., 1829–54.
E. A. Curley, *Nebraska, Its Advantages, Resources and Drawbacks,* N.Y., 1875.
Dakota: Department of Immigration, *Resources of Dakota.* Pierre, 1887. — Other editions.
Edmund Dana, *Description of the Bounty Lands in the State of Illinois.* Cin., 1819. Contains also the principal roads and routes, by land and water, in the United States, from New Brunswick to the Pacific.
Edmund Dana, *Geographical Sketches on the Western Country: Designed for Emigrants and Settlers.* Cin., 1819. — Contains also a list of the public roads from Eastport to the Missouri River.
William Darby, *The Emigrants' Guide to the Western and Southwestern States and Territories.* N.Y., 1818.
William Darby, *Geographical Description of the State of Louisiana.* Phila., 1816.
G. M. Davison, *The Traveller's Guide through the Middle and Northern States and the Provinces of Canada.* 8 ed. Saratoga, 1840. — Early eds. (1825–1830) were called *The Fashionable Tour.*
[John Disturnell], *A Trip through the Lakes of North America . . . . A Complete Guide for the Pleasure Traveler and Emigrant.* N.Y., 1857.
[John Disturnell], *The Western Traveller; Embracing the Canal and Railroad Routes, from Albany to Troy, to Buffalo and Niagara Falls.* N.Y., 1844.
[Theodore Dwight], *The Northern Traveller and Northern Tour.* 5 ed. N.Y., [1834]. — Earlier eds., 1825–31.
The Emigrants' Guide; or, Pocket Geography of the Western States and Territories. Cin., 1818.
R. S. Fisher, *A New and Complete Statistical Gazetteer of the United States of America.* N.Y., 1853.
Timothy Flint, *History and Geography of the Mississippi Valley.* 3 ed. Cin., 1833. — Earlier eds., 1828–32.

John Hayward, *Gazetteer of the United States of America*. Hartford, 1853. — Hayward also compiled *The New England Gazetteer* (Boston, 1839) and gazetteers of Massachusetts, New Hampshire, and Vermont.

Samuel Hazard, ed., *Hazard's United States Commercial and Statistical Register*. 6 vols. Phila., 1840–42.

Daniel Hewett, *The American Traveller*. Wash., 1825.

J. S. Hittell, *Resources of California*. 6 ed. San Francisco, 1874.

C. C. Hutchinson, *Resources of Kansas*. Topeka, 1871.

Indiana Gazetteer, or Topographical Dictionary. Indianapolis, 1833, 1849.

A. D. Jones, *Illinois and the West*. Boston, 1838. — Especially good on pioneer conditions.

John Melish, *Geographical Description of the United States*. N.Y., 1826. Earlier eds., 1816–22. Some of the material was published in 1815 as Pt. 1 of *The Traveller's Directory* (below).

John Melish, *Information and Advice to Emigrants to the United States*. Phila., 1819.

John Melish, *The Traveller's Directory through the United States*. 5 ed. Phila., 1819. — Earlier eds., 1815–18; enlarged ed. called *A Statistical View of the United States*, N.Y., 1825. The second part of the work is *A Description of the Roads in the United States* (Phila., 1814).

[S. A. Mitchell], *An Accompaniment to Mitchell's Reference and Distance Map of the United States*. Phila., 1834.

[S. A. Mitchell], *Illinois in 1837*. Phila., 1837.

Montana: Bureau of Agriculture, *The Treasure State: Montana and Its Magnificent Resources*. Helena, 1899.

Jedidiah Morse, *The American Gazetteer*. Boston, 1797. 2 and 3 eds., r. and enlarged, 1804, 1810.

Jedidiah Morse, *The American Geography*. Elizabethtown, 1789.

New Empires in the Northwest. ("Library of Tribune Extras," I, No. 8), N.Y., 1889.

Oregon: Immigration Board, *Pacific Northwest: Information for Settlers and Others*. N.Y., 1883. — Various later eds.

J. M. Peck, *A Guide for Emigrants, Containing Sketches of Illinois, Missouri*. Boston, 1831.

J. M. Peck, *A New Guide for Emigrants to the West*. Boston, 1837.

Joseph Scott, *Geographical Dictionary of the United States of North America*. Phila. 1805.

Joseph Scott, *United States Gazetteer*. Phila., 1795.

Ernest Seyd, *California and Its Resources*. London, 1858.

Joshua Shaw, *United States Directory for the Use of Travellers and Merchants, Giving an Account of the Principal Establishments, of Business and Pleasure, Throughout the Union*. Phila., [1822].

J. C. Smith, *Western Tourist and Emigrant's Guide*. N.Y., 1840.

H. G. Spafford, *Pocket Guide for the Tourist and Traveller along the Line of the Canals and the Interior Commerce of the State of New York*. N.Y., 1824.

[O. G. Steele], *Steele's Western Guide Book and Emigrant's Directory*. 11 ed. Buffalo, 1839. — 1 ed., 1832.

H. S. Tanner, *The American Traveller; or Guide through the United States*. 8 ed. Phila., 1842.

H. S. Tanner, *The Central Traveller, or Tourist's Guide through the States of Pennsylvania, New Jersey, Delaware, Maryland*, etc. 2 ed. N.Y., 1844.

H. S. Tanner, *Geographical, Historical, and Statistical View of the Central or Middle United States*. Phila., 1841.

George Temple, *The American Tourist's Pocket Companion; or a Guide to the Springs, and Trip to the Lakes*. N.Y., 1812.

D. B. Warden, *Statistical, Political, and Historical Account of the United States of North America*. 3 vols. Edinburgh, 1819.

H. J. Winser, *The Great Northwest; a Guide Book and Itinerary*. N.Y., 1883.

A few state gazetteers are listed above. Others, compiled by Henry Gannett, may be found in the Bulletins of the United States Geological Survey for the following states and territories: Colorado, Connecticut, Delaware, Indian Territory (Oklahoma), Kansas, Maryland, Massachusetts, New Jersey, Puerto Rico,

Rhode Island, Texas, Utah, Virginia, and West Virginia. These *Bulletins* also contain geographic dictionaries of Connecticut, Massachusetts, New Jersey, and Rhode Island. The same authority has produced another work useful to historians. *The Mountains of the United States* (Compiled in 1910–12 and published by the Board of Surveys and Maps, Wash., 1929) lists mountains, ranges, hills, and similar physiographic units drawn from official topographic maps, and locates and describes them.

25. PLACE NAMES

Place names are valuable sources of historical information. They tell of Indian tribes that once occupied the land, of the preoccupations and nationalist aspirations of explorers and fur traders, the location of forts, the activities of land speculators, the sectional or foreign origins of early settlers, the impression made by the landscape on first comers, the national moods and fashions of different eras, and much else of national and local interest. Historical works describing the origins and changes in place names and the different forms of the same names which have been in use are an important part of the national literature. A brief popular account is *Names on the Land*, by G. R. Stewart (N.Y., 1945).

The best guide to this literature is R. B. Sealock and P. A. Seely, *Bibliography of Place Name Literature, United States, Canada, Alaska, and Newfoundland* (Chi., 1948). This work contains sections on each of the American states, as well as a general section on the United States. It contains also (pp. 30–36) a brief list of gazetteers, supplementing the list above (§ 24), which are sources of information regarding place names.

The U. S. Geographic Board, created in 1890 to establish uniform nomenclature and orthography in the executive departments and especially on maps issued by the various federal departments, has published reports helpful to the historian. The *Sixth Report* (1933) of decisions regarding place names reached in the years 1890–1932 is especially useful. This *Report* is supplemented annually by the printed decisions of the Board.

The early history of place names may most conveniently be traced through publications of the Post Office Department. Between 1803 and 1874, it issued, at irregular intervals and under various titles, a series of directories. Since 1874 it has prepared *The United States Official Postal Guide*, revised annually, and accompanied by current Post Route state maps and large-scale county maps.

26. GUIDES TO MANUSCRIPT MATERIALS

A great majority of the existing materials of American History are still in manuscript form; and, despite the destruction that is continually going on, the daily deposit constantly increases the bulk. Every student of American History who becomes a researcher, librarian, archivist, or editor, comes into contact with some of these manuscripts.

These vast historical accumulations may be divided roughly into "Archives" and "Manuscript Collections." An archive is organic; a collection is inorganic and fortuitous.

An archive consists of the manuscript accumulation, over a period of years, of a government department, institution, business, family, or individual. Archives are merely back files; current files are future archives. (The term "Records" often used instead of "Archives," especially by business firms, is misleading, since historical records include everything that has survived from the past: manuscript and printed material, monuments, inscriptions, buildings, artifacts, sculpture, and the graphic arts.)

A collection consists of the manuscripts brought together by an individual, library, or other institution through gift or purchase (occasionally also by theft); it may include documents as far apart as an Egyptian papyrus and an autograph letter of President Truman. Collections may include archives or portions of archives that have left their original location, as well as manuscripts brought together for their autograph or intrinsic value. Private collections should be, and sometimes are, left to libraries on the owner's death; more often they are thrown onto the market and broken up. But it must be admitted that dealers in rare manuscripts, by finding a market for historical documents, aid greatly in their preservation.

Every historian engaged in research wishes to know the manuscript sources for his subject. Every library or institution that collects manuscripts, every governmental unit that maintains an archivist, should put out a printed guide to what it has; but few have done so. This *Guide* does not have room for references to the manuscript sources for various periods and aspects. It can only refer students to the more important printed guides to manuscript collections, and to some of those for archives. Others will be found below in the accounts of public records, federal, state, colonial, and foreign (§§ 45, 46, 47).

GENERAL AND TOPICAL GUIDES

W. H. Allison, comp., *Inventory of Unpublished Material for American Religious History in Protestant Church Archives and Other Repositories.* Wash., 1910.

Archives and Libraries. Papers Presented at the 1939 Conference of the American Library Association. Chi., 1939.

H. P. Beers, comp., *Bibliographies in American History* (§ 34), 84.

H. P. Beers, comp., "The Papers of the British Commanders in Chief in North America," *Military Affairs*, XIII (1949), 79.

S. F. Bemis and G. G. Griffin, eds., *Guide to Diplomatic History* (§ 21), 855.

R. A. Billington, comp., "Guides to American History Manuscript Collections in Libraries of the United States," *Miss. Valley Hist. Rev.*, XXXVIII (1951), 467.

E. C. Burnett, "A List of Printed Guides to . . . Repositories of Historical Manuscripts," Am. Hist. Assoc., *Report*, 1896, I, 481.

J. G. DeR. Hamilton, "Three Centuries of Southern Records," *Jour. Southern Hist.*, X (1944), 3.

H. M. Larson, *Guide to Business History* (§ 35), 21, 988.

Manuscripts in Public and Private Collections in the United States. Wash., 1924. — A check list published by the Library of Congress.

T. F. O'Connor, "Catholic Archives of the United States," *Catholic Hist. Rev.*, XXXI (1946), 414.

C. S. Peterson, comp., *American-Scandinavian Diplomatic Relations.* [Balt.], 1948. — A calendar.

Buford Rowland, "The Papers of the Presidents," *Am. Archivist*, XIII (1950), 195.

Justin Winsor, *Narrative and Critical History* (§ 21), VIII, 413.

Other helpful references will be found in the annual volumes of *Writings on American History* (§ 34), in accounts of accessions in the historical journals and in *Am. Archivist*, and in the publications of individual libraries (§ 16).

Use should also be made of the publications of the Historical Records Survey which prepared inventories of collections in every state and in many cases listed private collections and church archives, early American imprints and portraits, as well as public archives. The most comprehensive list of the completed Surveys is S. B. Child and D. P. Holmes, *Bibliography of Research Projects Reports: Check List of Historical Records Survey Publications* (W.P.A. Technical Series Research and Records Bibliog. No. 7, Wash., 1943). Some of the unpublished materials may be traced in M. E. Colby, *Final Report on Disposition of Unpublished Materials of the W.P.A. Writers Program* [Wash., 1943].

GUIDES TO MANUSCRIPTS IN WASHINGTON, D.C.

The latest guides to the contents of the National Archives Building, the most important depository of archival or other manuscript material in the United States, are: *Guide to the Records in the National Archives* (Wash., 1948) which includes everything received to June, 1947; and *Your Government's Records in the National Archives* (Wash., 1950), a much briefer list than the above.

Accessions are described in the annual *Report* of the Archivist of the United States (1936–   ) and in a quarterly, *National Archives Accessions* (1940–   ). In addition the Archives has prepared a number of preliminary inventories, enumerated below, that give more detailed information on a number of departments and agencies. Those already published follow:

1. War Industries Board. 1941.
2. Council of National Defense, 1916–1921. 1942.
3. Headquarters Offices of the Food Administration. 1943.
4. War Labor Policies Board. 1943.
5. National War Labor Board. 1943.
6. Bureau of Medicine and Surgery. 1948.
7. Federal Trade Commission. 1948.
8. Chemical Warfare Service. 1948.
9. Office of the Paymaster General. 1948.
10. Bureau of Yards and Docks. 1948.
11. Civilian Conservation Corps. 1948.
12. Senate Committee on Appropriations: Subcommittee on Inquiry in re Transfer of Employees, 1942. 1948.
13. Naval Establishments Created Overseas During World War II. 1948.
14. United States Direct Tax Commission for the District of South Carolina. 1948.
15. War Production Board. 1948.
16. United States Secret Service. 1949.
17. Adjutant General's Office. 1949.
18. Forest Service. 1949.
19. Board of Investigation and Research — Transportation. 1949.
20. Maritime Labor Board. 1949.
21. Office of the United States Counsel for the Prosecution of Axis Criminality. 1949.
22. General Land Office (Land-Entry Papers). 1949.
23. United States Senate. 1950.
24. United States War Ballot Commission. 1951.
25. Office of War Mobilization and Reconversion. 1951.
26. Bureau of Aeronautics. 1951.
27. Selective Service System, 1940–47. 1951.
28. Retraining and Reemployment Administration. 1951.
29. Foreign Economic Administration. 1951.
30. War Shipping Administration. 1951.
31. Petroleum Administration for War. 1951.
32. Accounting Department of the Office of Price Administration. 1951.
33. Bureau of Ordnance. 1951.
34. Solid Fuels Administration for War. 1951.

The following special lists are also useful:

List of Climatological Records in the National Archives. 1942.

Records of the Bureau of Insular Affairs Relating to the Philippine Islands, 1898–1935; a List of Selected Files. Kenneth Munden, comp. 1942.

Records of the Bureau of Insular Affairs Relating to the United States Military Government of Cuba, 1898–1902, and the United States Provisional Government of Cuba, 1906–1909; a List of Selected Files. Kenneth Munden, comp. 1943.

Records of the Bureau of Insular Affairs Relating to Puerto Rico, 1898–1934; a List of Selected Files. Kenneth Munden and Milton Greenbaum, comps. 1943.

List of Records of the Bureau of Insular Affairs Relating to the Dominican Customs Receivership, 1905–1940. Kenneth Munden, comp. 1943.

List of Documents Concerning the Negotiation of Ratified Indian Treaties, 1801–1869. J. H. Martin, comp. 1949.

List of Documents Relating to Special Agents of the Department of State, 1789–1906. Natalia Summers, comp. 1951.

Population Schedules, 1800–1870; Volume Index to Counties and Major Cities. 1951.

In addition, some forty *Reference Information Circulars* analyze records in the Archives on such subjects as transportation and small business. Records of World War I have been described in the *Handbook of Federal World War Agencies and Their Records, 1917–1921* (Wash., 1943) and those of World War II in the two-volume guide, *Federal Records of World War II* (Wash., 1950–51).

Nonofficial guides to materials in the National Archives include: G. A. Lee, "General Records of the United States Department of Agriculture in the National Archives," *Ag. Hist.*, XIX (1945), 242; Paul Lewinson, *Guide to Documents in the National Archives for Negro Studies* (Wash., 1947); J. R. Masterson, "Records of the Washington Superintendency of Indian Affairs, 1853–1874," *Pacific Northwest Quar.*, XXXVII (1946), 31. See also: § 45.

The extensive manuscript collections of the Library of Congress may be traced through the following guides: *Handbook of Manuscripts in the Library of Congress* (Wash., 1918); C. W. Garrison, "List of Manuscript Collections in the Library of Congress to July, 1931," Am. Hist. Assoc., *Report*, 1930, I, 123; C. P. Powell, "List of Manuscript Collections Received in the Library of Congress, July, 1931 to July, 1938," *ibid.*, 1937, I, 113; *Annual Report of the Librarian of Congress* (1938–42); *Quarterly Journal of Current Acquisitions* (1943–   ).

GUIDES TO AMERICAN COLLECTIONS OUTSIDE WASHINGTON

The following is a list of guides to the more important collections in the rest of the country, arranged by the state in which they are located. Information on new accessions and current changes in these collections will generally be found in the regular reports of their custodians or of the appropriate historical societies (§§ 4, 50).

Arkansas

D. T. Herndon, "Arkansas History Commission," Ark. Hist. Assoc., *Publ.*, IV (1917), 272.

California

O. C. Coy, *Guide to the County Archives of California.* Sacramento, 1919.

N. B. Cuthbert, *American Manuscript Collections in the Huntington Library for the History of the Seventeenth and Eighteenth Centuries.* San Marino, 1941.

G. P. Hammond, "Manuscript Collections in the Bancroft Library," *Am. Archives*, XII (1950), 15.

Historical Records Survey, *Guide to Depositories of Manuscript Collections in the United States: California.* Los Angeles, 1941.

"Huntington Library Collections," Huntington Library, *Bull.*, I (1931), 33.

Connecticut

A. C. Bates, "Report on the Public Archives of Connecticut," Am. Hist. Assoc., *Report*, 1900, II, 26.

Z. J. Powers, "American Historical Manuscripts in the Historical Manuscripts Room," *Yale University Library Gazette*, XIV (1939), 1.

Select List of Manuscripts in the Connecticut State Library. Hartford, 1920.

M. C. Withington, comp., *A Catalogue of Manuscripts. . . . Western Americana . . . Yale University Library*. New Haven, 1952.

Delaware

Calendar of Records in the Custody of the Public Archives Commission of the State of Delaware. Dover, 1935.

Florida

Historical Records Survey, *Guide to Depositories . . . Florida*. Jacksonville, 1940.

Hawaii

Board of Commissioners of Public Archives, *Report*, 1926–28.

Illinois

P. M. Angle, *Survey of Manuscript Collections, University of Chicago Libraries*. [Chi.], 1944.

R. L. Butler, *A Check List of Manuscripts in the Edward A. Ayer Collection*. Chi., 1937.

Historical Records Survey, *Guide to Depositories . . . Illinois*. Chi., 1940.

E. C. Jackson and Carolyn Curtis, *Guide to the Burlington Archives in the Newberry Library, 1851–1901*. Chi., 1949.

"The McCormick Historical Association," Bus. Hist. Soc., *Bull.*, X (1936), 76.

"Materials for Historical Research Afforded by the University of Illinois," University of Ill., *Bull.*, XX (1922).

C. C. Mohr, *Guide to the Illinois Central Archives in the Newberry Library*. Chi., 1951.

C. B. Pike, "Chicago Historical Society," Bus. Hist. Soc., *Bull.*, VIII (1934), 37.

G. B. Utley, "Source Material for the Study of American History in the Libraries of Chicago," Bibliog. Soc. of Am., *Papers*, XVI (1922), 17.

Indiana

C. B. Coleman, "Indiana Archives," *Am. Archivist*, I (1938), 201. — An older account by J. A. Woodburn is in Am. Hist. Assoc., *Report*, 1900, II, 37.

M. C. Stoler, "Indiana Historical Society Manuscript Collections," *Ind. Mag. of Hist.* XXX (1934), 267.

M. C. Stoler, "Manuscript Accessions — Indiana State Library," *ibid.*, XXIX (1933), 44.

M. C. Stoler, "Manuscripts in Indiana State Library," *ibid.*, XXVII (1931), 236.

Iowa

Historical Records Survey, *Guide to Depositories . . . Iowa*. Des Moines, 1940.

Louisiana

Historical Records Survey, *Guide to Depositories . . . Louisiana*. University, La., 1941. — Also in *La. Hist. Quar.*, XXIV (1941), 305.

W. R. Hogan, ed., *Guide to the Manuscript Collections in the Department of Archives, Louisiana State University*. University, La., 1940.

Maine

E. A. Ring, ed., *A Reference List of Manuscripts Relating to the History of Maine*. 3 vols. University of Maine, *Studies*, 2 ser., No. 45 (1938).

Maryland

Catalogue of Archival Material, Hall of Records, State of Maryland. [Annapolis, 1942].

Massachusetts

Howard Corning, "The Essex Institute of Salem," Bus. Hist. Soc., *Bull.*, V (1933), 1.

M. R. Cusick, *List of Business Manuscripts in Baker Library*. Boston, 1932.

A. M. Davis, "Report on the Public Archives of Massachusetts," Am. Hist. Assoc., *Report*, 1900, II, 47.

A Guide to the Resources of the American Antiquarian Society. Worcester, 1937.

Handbook of the Massachusetts Historical Society, 1791–1948. Boston, 1949.

"Historical Index of the Pickering Papers," Mass. Hist. Soc., *Coll.*, 6 ser., VIII (1895).

Historical Records Survey, *A Description of the Manuscript Collections in the Massachusetts Diocesan Library*. Boston, 1939.

Historical Records Survey, *Guide to Depositories . . . Massachusetts*. Boston, 1939.

Historical Records Survey, *Guide to the Manuscript Collections in the Worcester Historical Society*. Boston, 1941.

"Manuscript Records of the French and Indian War in the Library of the Society," Am. Antiq. Soc., *Trans. and Coll.*, XI (1909).

C. K. Shipton, "The American Antiquarian Society," *William and Mary Quar.*, 3 ser., II (1945), 164.

Justin Winsor, *Calendar of the Jared Sparks Manuscripts in Harvard College Library*. Cambridge, 1889.

Justin Winsor, *Calendar of the Arthur Lee Manuscripts*. Cambridge, 1882.

Michigan

C. M. Burton, "The Burton Historical Collection of the Public Library, Detroit," Bibliog. Soc. of Am., *Papers*, XVI (1922), 10.

Historical Records Survey, *Guide to Depositories . . . Michigan*. Detroit, 1940.

Historical Records Survey, *Guide to the Manuscript Collections in Michigan*. 2 vols. Detroit, 1941–42.

H. H. Peckham, *Guide to the Manuscript Collections in the William L. Clements Library*. Ann Arbor, 1942.

Minnesota

Historical Records Survey, *Guide to Depositories . . . Minnesota*. St. Paul, 1941.

G. L. Nute and G. W. Ackermann, *Guide to the Personal Papers in the Manuscript Collections of the Minnesota Historical Society*. St. Paul, 1935.

Mississippi

"An Official Guide to the Historical Materials in the Mississippi Department of Archives and History," *Report*, 1911–12, App. 43.

Missouri

Historical Records Survey, *Guide to Depositories . . . Missouri*. St. Louis, 1940.

"Western Historical Manuscripts Collection," University of Missouri Library, *Bull.*, No. 5 (1949).

Nebraska

Historical Records Survey, *Guide to Depositories . . . Nebraska*. Lincoln, 1940.

New Hampshire

Historical Records Survey, *Guide to Depositories . . . New Hampshire*. Manchester, 1940.

New Jersey

Historical Records Survey, *Calendar of the New Jersey State Library Manuscript Collection*. Newark, 1939.

Historical Records Survey, *Guide to Depositories . . . New Jersey*. Newark, 1941.

New York

"Annotated List of the Principal Manuscripts in the New York State Library," New York State Library, *Bull.*, History, No. 3 (1899), 209. — Other accounts are in the *Sixty-Fourth Annual Report* (1881), 11 and the *Ninety-Fourth Annual Report* (1911), 7 of the New York State Library.

R. E. Day, comp., *Calendar of the Sir William Johnson Manuscripts in the New York State Library.* Albany, 1909.

E. B. Greene and R. B. Morris, *A Guide to the Principal Sources for Early American History in the City of New York* (§ 35), pt. 2.

Historical Records Survey, *Guide to Depositories . . . New York City.* N.Y., 1941.

Historical Records Survey, *Guide to Depositories . . . New York State.* Albany, 1941. — Five supplements have appeared in *N.Y. Hist.*, XXIV (1943), 265, 417, 560, XXV (1944), 64, 226.

"Manuscript Collections in the New York Public Library," New York Public Library, *Bull.*, V (1901), 306. — A supplement was printed *ibid.*, XIX (1915), 149.

"Manuscript Sources for the History of Central and Western New York in the New York Public Library," *N.Y. Hist.*, XIX (1938), 53.

H. L. Osgood, "Report on the Public Archives of New York," Am. Hist. Assoc., *Report*, 1900, II, 67.

"Our Special Collections," University of Rochester, *Bull.*, IV (1949), 45.

"Rough List of Manuscripts in the Library," Buffalo Hist. Soc., *Publ.*, XIV (1910), 421.

E. F. Rowse, "Archives of New York," *Am. Archivist*, IV (1941), 267.

Survey of the Manuscript Collections in the New York Historical Society. N.Y., 1941.

North Carolina

J. S. Bassett, "Report on the Public Archives of North Carolina," Am. Hist. Assoc., *Report*, 1900, II, 251.

D. L. Corbitt, ed., *Calendars of Manuscript Collections . . . of the North Carolina Historical Commission.* Raleigh, 1926.

Historical Records Survey, *Guide to Depositories . . . North Carolina.* Raleigh, 1940.

Historical Records Survey, *Guide to the Manuscript Collections in the Archives of the North Carolina Historical Commission.* Raleigh, 1942.

Historical Records Survey, *Guide to the Manuscripts in the Southern Historical Collection of the University of North Carolina.* Chapel Hill, 1941.

N. M. Tilley and N. L. Goodwin, *Guide to the Manuscript Collections in the Duke University Library.* Durham, 1947.

Ohio

E. J. Benton, "The Western Reserve Historical Society," *Ohio State Arch. and Hist. Quar.*, LIV (1945), 96.

"Catalogue of Manuscript Collections at the Library of the Ohio State Archaeological and Historical Society," *ibid.*, LV (1946), 44.

Hortense Foglesong, "The Charles G. Slack Collection of Manuscripts, Marietta College," Ohio Valley Hist. Assoc., *Report*, II (1909), 20.

An Index and List of the Letters and Papers of Rutherford Birchard Hayes . . . with Notes on Other Source Material at the Hayes Memorial Library. Columbus, 1933.

W. D. Overman, "Ohio Archives," *Am. Archivist*, V (1942), 36.

Oregon

Historical Records Survey, *Guide to Depositories . . . Oregon-Washington.* Portland, 1940.

Historical Records Survey, *Guide to the Manuscript Collections of the Oregon Historical Society.* Portland, 1940.

D. O. Johansen, "The Simeon G. Reed Collection," *Pacific Northwest Quar.*, XXVII (1936), 54.

Pennsylvania

H. V. Ames, "Report on the Public Archives of Pennsylvania," Am. Hist. Assoc., *Report*, 1900, II, 267.

E. M. Braderman and B. S. Levin, "Pennsylvania and Her Archives," *Penn. Hist.*, VIII (1941), 59.

E. S. Brinton and Hiram Doty, *Guide to the Swarthmore College Peace Collection.* Swarthmore, 1947.

I. M. Hays, *Calendar of the Papers of Benjamin Franklin in the Library of the American Philosophical Society.* 5 vols. Phila., 1908.

R. H. Heindel, "Historical Manuscripts in the Academy of Natural Sciences, Philadelphia," *Penn. Hist.*, V (1938), 30.

Historical Records Survey, *Guide to Depositories . . . Pennsylvania.* Harrisburg, 1939.

Inventory of the Manuscript and Miscellaneous Collections of the Historical Society of Western Pennsylvania. Pittsburgh, 1933.

B. S. Levin, ed., *Guide to the Manuscript Collections of the Historical Society of Pennsylvania.* 2 ed. Phila., 1949. — Revised from the Historical Records Survey of 1940.

W. E. Lingelbach, "The Library of the American Philosophical Society," *William and Mary Quar.*, 3 ser., III (1946), 48.

"List of Manuscripts," Geneal. Soc. of Penn., *Publ.*, VI (1917), 309.

Primary Source Materials on Western Life . . . at the Presbyterian Historical Society. Phila., 1948.

J. B. Turner, "A Catalogue of Manuscript Records in the Possession of the Presbyterian Historical Society," Presbyterian Hist. Soc., *Jour.*, VIII (1915), 13.

A. R. Wentz, "Collections of the Lutheran Historical Society," *Penn. Hist.*, III (1936), 66.

South Carolina

H. G. McCormack, "A Provisional Guide to Manuscripts in the South Carolina Historical Society," *So. Car. Hist. and Geneal. Mag.*, XLV (1944), III, 172; XLVI (1945), 49, 104, 171, 214; XLVII (1946), 53, 171; XLVIII (1947), 45, 177.

R. H. Woody, "Public Records of South Carolina," *Am. Archivist*, II (1939), 244.

Tennessee

Historical Records Survey, *Guide to Depositories . . . Tennessee.* Nashville, 1940.

Historical Records Survey, *Guide to Collections of Manuscripts in Tennessee.* Nashville, 1941.

Texas

"The Eugene C. Barker Texas History Center," University of Texas, *Library Chronicle*, IV (1950), 3.

Harriet Smither, "Archives of Texas," *Am. Archivist*, III (1940), 187.

W. A. Whatley, "The Historical Manuscript Collections of the University of Texas," *Texas Hist. Teachers' Bull.*, IX (1920), 19.

Virginia

Catalogue of the Manuscripts in the Collection of the Virginia Historical Society. Richmond, 1901.

"Historical Manuscripts in the Library of the College of William and Mary," *William and Mary Quar.*, 2 ser., XX (1940), 388.

E. G. Swem, "A List of Manuscripts Recently Deposited in the Virginia State Library," Virginia State Library, *Bull.*, VII (1914), 3.

Washington

See: Oregon.

Wisconsin

Historical Records Survey, *Guide to Depositories . . . Wisconsin.* Madison, 1941.

O. G. Libby, "Report on the Public Archives of Wisconsin," Am. Hist. Assoc., *Report*, 1900, II, 294.

A. E. Smith, *Guide to the Manuscripts of the Wisconsin Historical Society.* Madison, 1944.

R. G. Thwaites, *Descriptive List of Manuscript Collections of the State Historical Society of Wisconsin; Together with Reports on Other Collections . . . in Adjacent States.* Madison, 1906.

M. C. Weaks, *Calendar of Kentucky Papers of Draper Collection.* Madison, 1925.

L. M. Homsher, *University Archives and Western Historical Manuscripts Collection. University of Wyoming.* Laramie, 1949.

GUIDES TO FOREIGN MANUSCRIPTS

So far we have mentioned only manuscript materials on American history located in the United States. There are also valuable sources located in foreign countries. In a few instances, sections of foreign archives have been transferred bodily to the United States. R. G. Adams's Calendar of the Sir Henry Clinton Manuscripts in the W. L. Clements Library, *Headquarters Papers of the British Army in North America during the . . . American Revolution* (Ann Arbor, 1926), lists one of the most important. Furthermore, during the last forty years, the Library of Congress by a systematic effort has obtained typewritten, microfilm, and photostatic copies of the most important manuscripts in European archives, particularly those in the Public Records Office, London. The latest list of its possessions is G. G. Griffin, *A Guide to Manuscripts Relating to American History in British Depositories Reproduced for the Division of Manuscripts* (Wash., 1946). Later accessions are listed in the Library's *Quarterly Journal of Current Acquisitions.*

Among other lists of transcriptions are:

R. A. Humphrey, "War-born Microfilm Holdings of the Department of State," *Jour. of Modern Hist.*, XX (1948), 133.

W. G. Leland, "Report on Transcription of Documents from French Archives," Librarian of Congress, *Report*, 1921, 179.

M. J. Pease, *Guide to Manuscript Materials Relating to Western History in Foreign Depositories Reproduced for the Illinois Historical Survey.* Urbana, 1950.

J. A. Robertson, *List of Documents in Spanish Archives Relating to the History of the United States, . . . Printed or in American Libraries* (Wash., 1910).

The bulk of such manuscript material, however, remains in foreign depositories. General guides to the archives will be found in § 47. The Carnegie Institution of Washington has published an important series of guides to those manuscripts that relate particularly to American history in foreign archives and libraries. These and a few similar guides follow below:

C. M. Andrews, *Guide to the Materials for American History, to 1783, in the Public Record Office of Great Britain.* 2 vols. Wash., 1912–14.

C. M. Andrews and F. G. Davenport, *Guide to the Manuscript Materials for the History of the United States to 1783, in the British Museum, in Minor London Archives, and in the Libraries of Oxford and Cambridge.* Wash., 1908.

H. C. Bell, *et al., Guide to British West Indian Archive Materials in London and in the Islands, for the History of the United States.* Wash., 1926.

H. E. Bolton, *Guide to Materials for the History of the United States in the Principal Archives of Mexico.* Wash., 1913.

C. E. Chapman, *Catalogue of Materials in the Archivo General de Indias for the History of the Pacific Coast and the American Southwest.* Berkeley, 1919.

A. B. Faust, *Guide to the Materials for American History in Swiss and Austrian Archives.* Wash., 1916.

C. R. Fish, *Guide to the Materials for American History in Roman and Other Italian Archives.* Wash., 1911.

F. A. Golder, *Guide to Materials for American History in Russian Archives.* 2 vols. 1917–37.

R. R. Hill, *Descriptive Catalogue of the Documents Relating to the History of the United States in the Papeles procedentes de Cuba. Deposited in . . . Seville.* Wash., 1916.

J. F. Jameson, ed., "Guide to the Items Relating to American History in the Reports of the English Historical Manuscripts Commission," Am. Hist. Assoc., *Reports*, 1898, 611. — Addenda to 1927 are in the *Cambridge History of the British Empire*, I, 837 (§ 77).

M. D. Learned, *Guide to the Manuscript Materials Relating to American History in the German State Archives*. Wash., 1912.

W. G. Leland and J. J. Meng, *Guide to Materials for American History in the Libraries and Archives of Paris*. 2 vols. Wash., 1932–43. — Two more volumes remain to be published.

D. M. Matteson, *List of Manuscripts Concerning American History Preserved in European Libraries*. Wash., 1925.

D. W. Parker, *Guide to the Materials for United States History in Canadian Archives*. Wash., 1913.

C. O. Paullin and F. L. Paxson, *Guide to the Materials in London Archives for the History of the United States since 1783*. Wash., 1914.

Julian Paz, *Catálogo de manuscritos de América existentes en la Biblioteca Nacional*. Madrid, 1933.

L. M. Pérez, *Guide to the Materials for American History in Cuban Archives*. Wash., 1907.

Report on American Manuscripts in the Royal Institution of Great Britain. 4 vols. London, 1904–09. — Many of these have since been transferred to American repositories.

[Milton Rubicam], ed., "Materials in Foreign Archives for Writing Pennsylvania History," *Pennsylvanian*, II (1944–45), 17.

W. R. Shepherd, *Guide to the Materials for the History of the United States in Spanish Archives*. Wash., 1907.

All these guides and catalogues give the student leads only; there is no substitute for visiting a likely repository, for using its shelf lists, and for enlisting the aid of a librarian or archivist to find what may be relevant.

Important as manuscript materials are, there is no magic in a manuscript source as such; the collector's values differ from the historian's. A collector may pay $30,000 for a document signed by Button Gwinnett; the historian would much rather have the deposition of some village Hampden containing crossroads gossip of 1776. A printed document, if fully and correctly printed, is as useful to an historian as the original manuscript.

27. THE HANDLING, CARE, AND PRESERVATION OF MANUSCRIPTS

These matters are for the most part in the hands of professional librarians and archivists, who need no instruction from historians. Among the useful discussions of the subject are A. E. Minogue, "The Repair and Preservation of Records," *Bull. of the National Archives*, No. 5 (1943); and R. B. Haselden, *Scientific Aids for the Study of Manuscripts* (Oxford, 1935).

A brief résumé of the methods of handling manuscripts may be of use to historical students. For, not infrequently, a historical researcher is admitted to some untouched private or public archive, or as secretary of a historical society is presented with a collection which has never been disturbed and which requires a certain amount of processing before historical data can be extracted from it.

Down to the middle of the nineteenth century, letters and other documents were generally preserved in dockets; that is, they were folded up and tied or wrapped in bundles of more or less uniform size. Gradually the modern system of vertical filing came in, and most private and public archives of recent years will be found in filing cases in the exact order that they were left by a filing clerk. Often, however, the investigator will discover manuscripts all jumbled together in trunks, chests, and bundles, torn, eaten by mice and insects, damaged by mold, dust, or heat. Collections, on the other hand, are generally left in good order by the collector, who paid good money for them.

In the classification and arrangement of archives, two leading principles — one negative and the other positive — should almost invariably be followed. The negative one is: never catalogue or arrange manuscripts as if they were books, that is, alphabetically by author or signer and subject. The positive one is what professional archivists call *respect des fonds*, "the method of classifying archives according to which each document is placed in the collection, and in the series of that collection to which it belonged when that collection was a living organism" (V. H. Paltsits, quoting Dr. S. Muller, Fz. of Utrecht, Am. Hist. Assoc., *Report*, 1912, 260).

In most cases, *respect des fonds* will require that the documents be left in the order in which they were found; just as they were filed by the department, firm, family, or individual to whom they belonged. But if the documents have been hopelessly jumbled, or if the task is to reassemble a dispersed, scattered, and imperfect archive from various sources, it will probably be better to arrange the manuscripts in chronological order. Common sense must determine the decision, of course; a continuous diary, for instance, should not be broken up and filed with letters of the same date; account books and loose accounts may profitably be placed in a separate file from letters.

Manuscripts found in folded dockets should first be opened and laid out flat, and all pins, clips, and rubber bands should be removed. (Methods of cleaning and removing stains are discussed by Miss Minogue in "The Repair and Preservation of Records," p. 24.) In almost every docket or collection of manuscripts, some will be more or less damaged. Amateur attempts at repair by transparent mending tape or other means should be entered on with great caution. It will be better not to mend a document that is legible. Safe library tapes with gum arabic or neutral glues, and transparent gummed muslin may be obtained at library supply houses; but plastic tape sometimes contains chemicals that rot paper. Thousands of manuscripts in the Massachusetts Archives were ruined by members of a WPA project covering them with cellophane tape.

Crumbling or torn manuscripts should be processed either by *silking* or *lamination.* The former, which means to cover documents with a fine gauze called crepeline, or Japanese tissue, is practiced in most important libraries and public archives, where advice may be sought for the names of private firms who can do it for individuals. Lamination means covering both sides of the document with a sheet of transparent cellulose acetate foil, or cellulose acetate-butyrate sheeting, and subjecting it to heat and pressure in a hydraulic press. This is the process used in the National Archives. (See: A. E. Kimberly and B. W. Scribner, "Summary Report of National Bureau of Standards Research on Preservation of Records," National Bureau of Standards, *Misc. Publ.*, MI54 [1937].) Lamination requires such expensive apparatus as to be too costly for individuals or for most historical societies; but it is hoped that the less expensive lamination machine developed by W. J. Barrow of the Virginia State Library may be acquired by a number of institutions so as to be of service locally. The fear has been expressed that lamination will in the long run damage manuscripts. Most of the authorities are now satisfied that it will not do so, but some are still skeptical of it, and believe silking to be the only safe process. (See: B. W. Scribner, "Comparison of Accelerated Aging of Record Papers with Normal Aging for Eight Years," National Bureau of Standards, *Jour. of Research*, XXIII [1939], 405.)

After the manuscripts have been assembled they may be filed or preserved in a number of ways. The simplest is merely to lay them in manila folders and to place the folders in cardboard, buckram, or steel filing boxes, properly labeled. Both boxes and documents should be numbered to facilitate reference. But documents that are likely to have much handling, or that are written on modern wood-pulp paper, or that will be used in places where readers cannot be watched by the librarian, had better be mounted with transparent linen hinges on sheets of rag paper of uniform size, and numbered. These sheets should then be bound into books. The loose-filing system is used at the New York Public Library; the more expensive bound system at the Library of Congress.

28. CALENDARING AND INDEXING MANUSCRIPTS

A calendar, in diplomatics, is a list of documents in *chronological* order. If the list is in any other order, it is not a calendar but an index or catalogue (§ 11).

The individual researcher, or librarian of a historical society, as he opens up and arranges manuscripts, should make at least a brief calendar of them. As each document is opened, list a few particulars about it on a slip or standard 3" × 5" library card, one to each document; the cards can then be arranged in chronological order. Write on the top line of the card, a heading and the date, followed by a brief digest of the contents. You may add a "code" abbreviation such as ALS (autograph letter signed), DS (document signed). For ready reference the card entries, after being arranged chronologically, should be typewritten on 8½" × 11" or larger paper, and those sheets bound. It saves researchers time and spares the manuscripts from unnecessary handling to have such a calendar ready for consultation. Any printed volume of documents should have a calendar at the beginning, like a table of contents. Good examples are the Boyd edition of the *Papers of Thomas Jefferson* (§ 55), and the *Winthrop Papers* (§ 55) published by the Massachusetts Historical Society.

A more extended sort of calendar is common to British and Canadian official publications, such as the *Calendar of State Papers, Colonial and West Indies*, the *Reports* of the Historical Manuscripts Commission, and the *Reports* of the Canadian Archives. In this form of calendar, a digest of each document is printed and the more important and interesting parts are quoted. Thus a large part of the expense of printing the documents in full is saved, yet the meat of them is rendered available to students. As Americans are such inveterate indexers, arrangers, and bibliographers, it seems strange that they have seldom used this cheap but excellent method of presenting the heart of a manuscript collection or archive to the public. Of course the preparation of this sort of calendar requires much more intelligence than the other sort, or even than printing *in extenso*. See also: R. L. Poole, *et al.*, "Report on Editing Historical Documents," University of London, Institute of Hist. Research, *Bull.*, I (1923), 6; M. L. Radoff, "Guide to Practical Calendaring," *Am. Archivist*, XI (1948), 123, 203.

29. DECIPHERING: ELEMENTARY PALEOGRAPHY

The first requisite for deciphering manuscripts is a knowledge of the language in which they are written. Unless a student is willing to undergo the preliminary discipline of learning to read a foreign language — or, for that matter, Elizabethan English — he had better keep clear of manuscript sources save those in his own language of the last three centuries.

Once the language is mastered, deciphering is comparatively easy; for there are handbooks of paleography from which one may learn the forms of letters, contractions, and abbreviations used in all the western languages. Once these forms are learned, only practice is needed to make the reading of all but the most illegible manuscripts as easy as print.

The following manuals will be useful to students of American history:

Andrew Wright, *Court-Hand Restored, or The Student's Assistant in Reading Old Deeds, Charters, Records.* 10 ed. Corrected by C. T. Martin. London, 1912. — Excellent for Latin and English medieval documents, with numerous examples, tables of contractions and diacritical marks, Latin glossary, and alphabets, sufficient to carry the student through the seventeenth century.

Hilary Jenkinson, *The Later Court Hands in England, from the Fifteenth to the Seventeenth Century.* Cambridge, Eng., 1927. — Accompanied by a portfolio of 44 plates. The various alphabets and examples in this comprehensive work supply all forms of letters found in English manuscripts relating to, or emanating from, the colonies in the sixteenth and seventeenth centuries.

C. K. Bolton, "Colonial Handwriting," *Essex Antiquarian,* I (1897), 175. — Reproduces the alphabets used in early New England, Virginia, and Maryland. Most of the letters are given in the facsimiles in § 32.

Maurice Prou, *Manuel de paléographie latine et française.* 4 ed. Paris, 1924. — Accompanied by a portfolio of 24 plates, and the best for French and Papal documents.

Jesús Muñoz y Rivero, *Manual de paleografía diplomática española de los siglos xvi al xvii.* 2 ed. Madrid, 1917. Agustín Millares Carlo, *Tratado de paleografía española.* 2 ed. Madrid, 1932. — These volumes are the best for Spanish and Portuguese documents.

On the identification of handwriting, see: M. A. Benjamin, *Autographs.* N.Y., 1946.

30. DATING OF MANUSCRIPTS

In studying, arranging, and calendaring documents, you will find many that are undated. Endeavor to date these either from their position in the collection (provided the order has been undisturbed) or from internal evidence, such as the events and persons that are mentioned or the persons who sign the document. Even an approximate date is better than none. The best book on problems of dating, including tables for regnal years and law terms, is J. J. Bond, *Handy-Book of Rules and Tables for Verifying Dates* (London, 1889).

Unfortunately, the date written on a document is not always conclusive. Letter writers are apt to write the date of the old year by mistake after the first of January. And there is the problem of Old Style and New Style, and of numbered months.

Old Style (commonly abbreviated O.S.) means the Julian Calendar. Pope

Gregory XIII decreed New Style (N.S.) or the Gregorian Calendar, by a bull of February 24, 1582. It went into effect in Spain and parts of Italy in the fall of that year, the calendar jumping from October 4 to October 15. France and the Dutch provinces of Holland and Zeeland adopted it before the end of 1582, Catholic Germany in 1584; but there were no more adoptions in countries that are important for early American history until the last decade of the seventeenth century, when Protestant Germany, Switzerland, and the Scandinavian countries went New Style.

England held out until 1752. By act of 24 George II, c. 23, the next day after September 2, 1752, was September 14 in Great Britain and all British colonies. The Russian branch of the Orthodox or Greek Church has not changed to this day; and those countries where the Orthodox was the established church adopted New Style for civil purposes comparatively recently. Bulgaria went New Style on April 1/14, 1916; Russia on February 1/14, 1918; Yugoslavia and Rumania in 1919; Greece on October 1/14, 1923.

A further complication is the date of the New Year. In England from the twelfth century to 1752, and in most other countries using the Julian Calendar, the New Year began on March 25. All dates between January 1 and March 24 inclusive belonged to the old year. About 1670 it began to be customary to hyphenate the old and new years between January 1 and March 24 in some such manner as this:

March 14, 1732/33

3 February 1689–90

January 26, $17\frac{03}{04}$.

March was reckoned the first month of the year, which made February the twelfth. This must be kept in mind, since Puritan and Quaker prejudice against using "pagan" names for months impelled members of those sects to number them, placing the month number second. Here are a few examples:

12. 12. 12   means 12 February 1612/13

7. 1 mº 1654 means 7 March 1654/55

21 iv 72   means 21 June 1672

In American history one often has to translate one calendar into another. Down to 1582 *everyone* was using the Julian Calendar; but in tracing the course of discoverers one often has to know the date by the Gregorian Calendar in order to calculate a phase of the moon or to check data in sea journals. When dealing with international events, or using French, Spanish, or Dutch sources for English colonial history, one must remember that two different calendars are in force down to September 3/14, 1752, when the English colonies went New Style, and the Julian Calendar has to be reckoned with in Alaskan history, and in Russo-American and Hellenic-American relations, almost to the present day.

CONVERSION TABLE

for turning dates in the Julian Calendar (O.S.) into those of the Gregorian Calendar (N.S.)
(All dates are inclusive)

From 1 March $\frac{1399}{1400}$ to 29 February $\frac{1499}{1500}$ add   9 days.

"   1 March $\frac{1499}{1500}$ to 18 February $\frac{1699}{1700}$ add 10 days.

" 19 February $\frac{1699}{1700}$ to 17 February 1800 add 11 days.

" 18 February 1800 to 16 February 1900 add 12 days.

" 17 February 1900 to 28 February 2100 add 13 days.

When dating documents or events, historians should use the current style of the country or colony with which they are dealing. If they are concerned with two countries (as in an Anglo-Spanish war) they may either reduce all their dates to one style or give double dates consistently. The first method is difficult, but easier for the reader.

In the early nineteenth century it was customary for antiquarians to translate all Old Style dates into New Style dates. This made trouble because the pedants were not always bright enough to add the right factor. Thus, although the "Landing of the Pilgrims" at Plymouth took place December 11, 1620, Old Style, when the day began to be celebrated in the eighteenth century, the date December 22 was chosen. It should have been December 21 if changed, but why not celebrate December 11? Persons whose lives spanned the change of style generally added eleven days to their birthdays. Thus Washington, born February 11, 1732, celebrated his birthday on February 22 after 1752.

The rule now is that, unless you have to deal with dates in both styles, leave them as you find them. An exception may be made of the number of the year, before 1752. Either state the year as if January 1 were New Year's Day; or, better, give both years to avoid misunderstanding. Thus, the Charter of Massachusetts Bay is dated "the Fourth Day of March, in the Fourth yeare of Charles I." A contemporary would have called this 4 March 1628. The historian should either call it 4 March 1629; or, if he wishes to leave no room for doubt, 4 March 1628/29. Toward the close of the seventeenth century, English writers began to consider the new year as beginning January 1. Hence the historian must be careful not to step up the date when it has already been done.

In printing or transcribing a manuscript, *never* step up, alter, or translate a date. Print it exactly as written, explaining it if necessary, in square brackets or a footnote. Thus, if the date is between January 1 and March 24, and the manuscript gives only the old year, the double date or the new year may be added in square brackets thus:

James Town, 22 February 1618 [1619]
Salem, 18. 1. 1652 [18 March 1652/53]
Philadelphia, January 1, 1699 [1700]
15 Jany. 1671 [1672]

If the month is numbered the whole date may be repeated in square brackets.

31. THE COPYING OF MANUSCRIPTS

The cheapest and most accurate methods of copying manuscripts are by photostat and by photography on a 35-mm. film. All large repositories of manuscripts have a photostat machine, or employ a commercial photographer, and furnish both negative and positive photostats at a regular tariff. Some repositories and many individual researchers are provided with a miniature camera which takes photographs of manuscript or printed pages at a few cents a page. The film has an advantage over the photostat of taking up very little space, but it requires a projector for ready and frequent use. (See also: § 10.)

The average student using a manuscript collection, and finding only here and there a sentence or passage of interest to him, will prefer to copy what he wants in longhand or on his typewriter, using the same sorts of cards or slips that he employs for all his notes. In copying he should take care to place a heading of his own on each card or slip, and to give an exact reference to the source, together with the date if it does not appear in the matter copied. The transcript should be made literally and exactly, with all abbreviations, contractions, misspellings, and the like, just as in the original. For, whatever system may be used in printing manuscripts (and the decision may not rest with the copyist), an exact copy in one's notes is indispensable.

The making of transcripts on a typewriter for another person or for an institution that is collecting transcripts presents special problems which have been well stated by G. L. Nute in *Copying Manuscripts: Rules Worked Out by the Minnesota Historical Society* (St. Paul, Minn., n.d.). These may be condensed as follows:

In the first place, the standard keyboard of a typewriter owned by anyone who does much copying of manuscripts should be altered by replacing some of the symbols and fractions infrequently used with [ ], §, £, and the straight tilde —. For French, the three accents and the cedilla; for German, the umlaut; and for Spanish, the curved tilde ~ and the reversed question mark are also desirable.

The transcriber should supply for each document:

1. A descriptive heading, such as:
   John C. Calhoun to Henry Clay
   Minutes of Discussions, National Security Board
   Ledger of Jones, Peters & Co.
   Deed of Pecos Ranch from Martin Rodriguez to John Doe
2. The date, if it does not appear at the head of the document.
3. The "code," which includes a reference to the source, and a conventional abbreviation indicating the sort of document it is. The abbreviations most commonly used are:

A.L.S. Autograph Letter Signed (a letter in the writer's own hand, with his signature)
C.   Copy (with addition of "At." if attested; "S." if signed, and "Cb." if a carbon copy)
Df.   Draft (rough copy of a letter, kept by the writer)
D.S. Document Signed (for any sort of document not a letter that has one or more signatures)
L.P.C. Letter-press Copy (copy on thin paper made in one of the oldfashioned letter-presses)

L.S.   Letter Signed (a letter not in the writer's hand, but with his signature)

After the heading and the code, proceed with the body of the document according to the directions for the literal method of printing, as in § 32.

32. THE EDITING AND PRINTING OF MANUSCRIPTS

Almost every historical student will confront the problem of preparing manuscripts for printing, either separately, or in the body of a book or an article, or as part of a series. No uniform and satisfactory set of rules appropriate for printing documents on American history has yet been published. E. G. Bourne's "Suggestions for the Printing of Documents Relating to American History," Am. Hist. Assoc., *Report*, 1905, I, 44, are not satisfactory and are not now followed by the *American Historical Review*. Poole, "Report on Editing Historical Documents," Inst. of Hist. Research, *Bull.*, I, 6, is, however, excellent.

The following pages are an attempt to set forth general principles of editing American documents. But no set of rules can cover every case, and each editor will have to use a certain flexibility and much common sense. The one rule always to be observed is that of consistency. State a method in the preface or preliminary note, and stick to it!

Difficulties arise from the fact that printing is unable to reproduce a longhand manuscript exactly. Before the invention of printing, and for three centuries thereafter, writers used a large number of abbreviations, signs, and contractions. Renaissance printers cast type to represent these characters, in the attempt to make their books resemble manuscripts. *Bibliotheca Americana. Catalogue of the John Carter Brown Library* (§ 34) employs over a hundred specially cast characters and diacritical signs in order to reproduce early book titles exactly; and the editors of the *Rolls Series* of English medieval documents were almost as lavish.

Earlier American editors such as Peter Force and Jared Sparks took excessive liberties in printing manuscripts. They cared little for consistency, and even attempted to improve the text. As a reaction from these practices, later editors resorted to meticulous accuracy. In official publications for which expense was no object, such as Shurtleff, *Records of the Governor and Company of the Massachusetts Bay* (§ 46), the manuscript text was followed as closely as type allowed, and some thirty characters were cast to represent seventeenth-century forms of the ampersand, crossed *b's, d's, h's, l's*, three differently tailed *p's*, tailed *c's, m's, n's*, and *q's. U's* and *v's* were printed as written, and canceled type was used for erased words. This sort of reproduction is proper for very important documents such as charters, or drafts of the Declaration of Independence. It is very well for de luxe printing, but far too expensive for the ordinary publication.

The methods by which manuscripts of American history are usually printed today may be reduced to three: the *Literal*, the *Expanded*, and the *Modernized*. In addition there is one that we might call the *Garbled* or *Bowdlerized*, which should be avoided.

I. DIRECTIONS THAT APPLY TO ALL THREE METHODS

1. Supply a heading (§ 31), and print it in a different type from the text. State the source of every document unless it is one of a collection in the same repository, which may be explained in the preface. The provenance should be

printed right under the heading, or given as a footnote to the heading, together with a reference to any earlier printing of the document. Code letters such as A.L.S. are generally of no interest to readers, and may be omitted when printing.

2. The address of a letter should be printed either in *italics* under the heading, or at the end. The date line, even if found at the end in the original, may be printed at the head, so long as the practice is consistent. Anything significant in the endorsements — and they often are the only clue to the identity of the writer — may be printed at the end with the word [*Endorsed*] preceding them. The salutation ("MY DEAR SMITH," or "WORSHIPFUL SIR") should be in SMALL CAPITALS.

3. All matter interpolated in the text by the editor should be printed in *italics* and enclosed in square brackets. Thus [*torn*], [*blotted*], [*illeg.*] take the places of a word or words lost by mutilation, defacement, or illegibility. Another means of dealing with illegibility is to insert within square brackets approximately as many asterisks or short dashes as there are illegible letters. If a lost word can be inferred with reasonable certainty from the context, it should be printed in Roman type within square brackets; the same should be done with part of a long word, but if only one to four letters are missing, brackets are unnecessary and pedantic. A mere conjecture, as distinct from a certain inference, can be followed by the question mark and placed within square brackets. Thus, if the edge of a Civil War letter is torn, leaving at the end two words "Stonewall Jack", the editor should print "Stonewall Jackson" because it could be nothing else. But, if a letter of 1788 says, "I do not share your opinion of the Con[*blotted*]," the editor had better print "Con[stitution ?]" because it might be "Congress" or "Convention." If the greater part of any edge or a large corner is torn off, print what exists, line for line, leaving the torn part blank. Very doubtful or alternate readings had better be placed in a footnote.

4. Every omission made by the editor within a sentence should be indicated by suspension points, thus, . . . , preserving the punctuation, if any, that occurs before the omission. If a whole paragraph or a line or more of poetry is omitted, insert a line of points or of asterisks.

5. Place in square brackets the number of each new page of a long manuscript at the point where it begins, in order to facilitate comparison with the original. Place [*sic*] after a very strange spelling or mistake of the original writer, which the reader might suppose to be a printer's error; but use *sic* sparingly; it is a tiresome interpolation. One may correct, without notice, obvious slips of the writer's pen such as "an an hour ago."

6. Blank spaces in the manuscript, where the writer intended to insert a word and did not, should be represented by a blank space in the printed text, or by "[*blank*]."

7. Interlineations are to be brought down into the line of text at the place indicated by the writer; canceled passages are omitted unless they contain something of particular interest, when they may be inserted in a footnote. In court and similar records, where marginal glosses have been written in by the clerk for his convenience in reference, these may either be omitted, or used as subheadings to save expense.

8. All words underlined should be printed in *italics*; words underlined twice in SMALL CAPITALS. Words strongly emphasized by being written in larger letters

than the rest may be printed in LARGE CAPITALS or boldface type. Signatures may be printed in LARGE AND SMALL CAPITALS, if desired. The initial *ff*, which is only an old form of the capital F, should be printed F. The long-tailed *s* (ſ) should be represented by the modern lower-case *s*, never by *f*.

9. In reprinting a document it is better to prepare a fresh text from the manuscript or photostat; for if an earlier printed edition is used as the basis, one is apt to repeat some of the former editor's errors, or maybe add others of one's own.

II. SPECIAL DIRECTIONS FOR THE LITERAL METHOD

1. Follow the manuscript absolutely in spelling, capitalization, and punctuation. Exceptions: in very illiterate manuscripts, where little or no punctuation is used, a minimum necessary to understand the text may be supplied; and in documents where the writer begins practically every word with a capital, the editor may use his discretion. In either case, the practice followed should be stated in a preliminary note.

2. Superior letters are printed as such, in smaller point; for instance, y^e, *Cap*^{t}, *Co*^{t}. But the period or colon usually found under superior letters may be omitted.

3. The tilde should be reproduced either as a straight or curved line, according to the text, over the letter or letters where it occurs.

4. All contractions and abbreviations should be printed exactly as written *within the limitations of available type.* If a supply of differently tailed *p*'s is to be had, they should be used; but it is better to expand tailed *p*'s into *per-*, *pro-*, and *pre-*, than to use a single type of tailed *p* to represent two or three different ones.

5. Remember that every diacritical mark (commonly called "wiggle") represented, in the scribe's mind, one or more letters. If the limitations of type forbid the use of these marks, the omitted letters *must* be supplied by the editor. For instance:

> *aɕ̃* should be printed *acres*, not *acs*;
> *ſre* should be printed *lettre*, not *lre* or *letter*;
> *mannᵒ* should be printed *manner*, not *mann*

Manuscript abbreviations for *-es*, *-us*, *-que* and the like should be spelled out. There is no need for special type to represent obsolete forms of the ampersand or of individual letters.

On the other hand, the writer's use of *u* and *v*, *i* and *j* should be followed through all vagaries. In the seventeenth century it was usual to begin a word with a *v*, but to place *u* in the middle, no matter whether *u* or *v* was meant. Thus: *vse*, *riuer.* The same character was commonly used for capital I and capital J. Small *i* was often used for *j* ("whom God hath ioyned"). Follow all this exactly. A long-tailed *i*, which may be represented in print by *j*, is often used for the final *i* on a Roman numeral ending with 7 or 8, such as xxviij. Follow this usage if you wish; but as this apparent *j* is really an *i*, it may, consistent with this method, be printed *i*. Some scribes used the long-tailed *i* almost exclusively; in that case, print it *i*, just as you represent the long-tailed *s* (ſ) by *s*.

III. SPECIAL DIRECTIONS FOR THE EXPANDED METHOD

A very good set of directions for this method is set forth by Boyd, in his edition of *The Papers of Thomas Jefferson*, I, xxv (§ 55). These differ in certain particulars, noted below, from the practice preferred by the editors of the *Harvard Guide*.

1. Follow the spelling, capitalization, and punctuation as in II, 1; but always capitalize the first word and put a period at the end of the sentence no matter what the writer does.

2. In general, spell out all abbreviations except those still used today (like *Mr., U.S., H.M.S.*), and those of months, proper names, and titles (*Dec., Tho:, Jno:, Fr., H.E.*, for examples). A reason for *not* expanding such abbreviations is the doubt of their meaning. *Fr.* may mean Francis or Frances; *Jno.*, John or Jonathan; *H.E.*, may stand for His Excellency or His Eminence. Almost every other type of manuscript abbreviation should be expanded as follows:

a. Expand all *th* abbreviations such as y^e, y^t, y^m, y^n, to *the, that, them, then*. For this apparent *y* is really a debased form of the early English letter þ (thorn).

b. Bring superior letters down to the line of text. In so doing, supply the letter or letters omitted in the manuscript, *provided they are in the middle of the word*, but not otherwise. Thus, w^{ch}, Co^rt, Mo^{th} are printed: which, Court, Month; but Capt, m^o, s^h are printed: *Capt., mo., sh.* If the abbreviation is still obscure after superior letters are brought down and a point added, the additional letters may be supplied in square brackets; e.g., m^o might be rendered *mo[nth]* if desired; y^r w^{or} as *Your wor[ship]*. Note that y^r may mean either your or their; y^{ow} is an eccentric form for *you* and may be so printed.

c. The tilde, except in Spanish words, is replaced by the letter or letters it represents. *Hañmond*, print *Hammond; accõn*, print *accion* or action; it is often uncertain whether $\tilde{c}$ means *ci* or *ti*.

d. Tailed *p's* are expanded and all diacritical marks rendered by the corresponding letters, as under the Literal Method. Boyd, however, retains the contraction ℓ for *per-, pre-*, and *pro-*.

e. The ampersand in all its forms is printed *and*; and &c becomes *etc.* whether the writer uses the full stop or not. Exception: preserve the ampersand in names of firms and companies, as Texas & Pacific R. R., A. Brown & Co.

3. Standardize monetary and weight and measure abbreviations. Thus, "25^{li} 7^s 3^d" may be rendered "25*li* 7*s* 3*d*" or "£25 7*s* 3*d*." Points after monetary abbreviations are superfluous. Odd crossed capital L's should all be printed £; odd dollar signs in the early days of the republic should all be printed $, but need not necessarily be placed before the sum. The sign # in French documents, which means *livres tournois*, should be printed *l.t.* Similarly, decide what abbreviations you will use for pounds, grams, millimeters, and yards, and be consistent. But Boyd retains all monetary, weight, and measure designations as written.

4. As regards *u* and *v*, *i* and *j*, there are two schools of thought. The first, which is preferable, points out that the *v* in *vp*, for instance, is not really a *v*, but an optional form of *u*; and the *u* in *liue* is really a kind of *v*. Consequently modern forms should be used if the expanded method is to be followed. The other school insists that these letters should be printed exactly as they are, on the principle of respecting spelling.

5. Certain editors always begin a proper name with a capital, and even stand-

ardize the spelling of them to help identification. This practice is undesirable. An apparently erratic spelling of a proper name may be a clue to its pronunciation; and "Roger cook" in an early document may mean a cook whose given name is *Roger*, not Roger Cook.

6. Some editors begin every new sentence with a capital letter, even if the writer does not. This is unobjectionable if it is clear where the writer intended a new sentence to begin; but often it is not clear. Punctuation in all manuscripts before the nineteenth century is highly irregular; and if you once start replacing dashes by commas, semicolons, or periods, as the sense may seem to warrant, you are asking for trouble. Note the example from one of Washington's letters, below.

IV. THE MODERNIZED METHOD

This method may properly be used in an English translation from another language, or to make an early document, chronicle, or narrative intelligible to the average reader who is put off by obsolete spelling and erratic punctuation. The texts of recent editions of Shakespeare, Dryden, and the King James Bible have been established by this method.

1. Modernize the spelling, capitalization, and punctuation, but pay scrupulous respect to the language; do not attempt to improve the writer's grammar, syntax, or choice of words, or you will be called a bowdlerizer. Where the original writer has obviously omitted a word like *not*, or, for instance, has written *east* when you know he means *west*, the editor may add or correct a word; but he should place it within square brackets. Paragraphs and sentences that are too long may be broken up.

2. Expand all abbreviations as in III above, excepting only such as are in common use today.

3. In translations, the translator should endeavor to use such words and phrases as will best convey the meaning of the original, and not aim at literary elegance.

V. ILLUSTRATIONS

We shall now give facsimiles of a few examples of the different methods, and comment upon them.

A. A Passage from William Bradford, *Plimmoth Plantation*

1. Part of fol. 53 of the original manuscript.

2. Same passage as printed in the Commonwealth of Massachusetts edition (Boston, 1897), 107, supposedly by the Literal Method but not altogether consistent. Note following:

a. Line 1: The paragraphing is correct, as the previous line stopped before the margin. Writers did not commonly indent paragraphs until the eighteenth century. The centered periods around "15" and other arabic numerals should have been printed as written, as in (3). The italics are unnecessary for the underlined words because inspection of the manuscript shows that the underlining was not done by Bradford but by a later reader. The colon after *Desem*[r] is unnecessary, and misplaced.

b. Lines 2 and 3: *u* and *v* are modernized, while superior letters are retained.

c. Line 8: the tilde is over the wrong letter, and the comma after *them* is omitted.

3. Same passage as printed in Massachusetts Historical Society edition (Boston, 1912), I, 177, ed. by W. C. Ford. A modified but not consistent Expanded Method.

Line 1: The square brackets in the month might have been, and the colon should have been, omitted. Use of italics more consistent than in 1 but unnecessary, as explained above.

4. Same passage as printed in Morison edition (N.Y., 1952), 72. Modernized Method. All spellings are corrected, and abbreviations spelled out.

a. Line 1: *th* added to *15*.

b. Line 4: *afterwards* made one word.

c. Line 6: position of comma altered.

5. The following is a sample of the garbled or bowdlerized method, the same quotation "Rendered into Modern English" by Harold Paget (1920), 73:

". . . came within two leagues of it, but had to bear up again. On the 16th day the wind came fair, and they arrived safe in the harbour. Afterwards they took a better view of the place, . . ."

A. William Bradford, Plimmoth Plantation

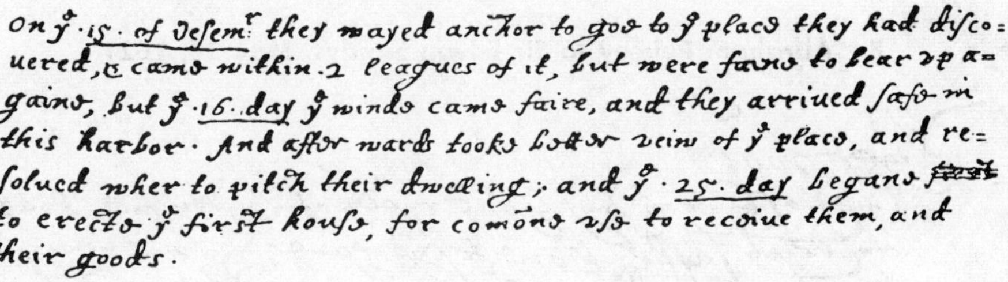

[handwritten facsimile:]

On ỹ· 15· of Desemᵣ they wayed anchor to goe to ỹ placᵈ they had disco=
uered, & camᵈ within·2· leagues of it, but were faine to bear vp a-
gaine, but ỹ·16·day ỹ winde camᵈ faire, and they arriued safᵈ in
this harbor· And after wardᵈ tookᵈ beter vein of ỹ placᵈ, and re=
solued wher to pitch their dweling; and ỹ·25·day begane first
to erecte ỹ first house, for comõnᵈ vſᵈ to recoiue them, and
their goods·

1. Bradford Ms., p. 53

On yᵉ 15. *of Desemʳ:* they wayed anchor to goe to
yᵉ place they had discovered, & came within 2. leagues
of it, but were faine to bear up againe; but yᵉ 16.
day yᵉ winde came faire, and they arrived safe in this
harbor. And after wards tooke better view of yᵉ
place, and resolved wher to pitch their dwelling;
and yᵉ 25. *day* begane to erecte yᵉ first house for
com̅one use to receive them and their goods.

2. Bradford, Commonwealth ed., p. 107

On the *·15· of Desem[be]r:*[3] they wayed anchor to goe to the place
they had discovered, and came within ·2· leagues of it, but were
faine to bear up againe; but the *·16· day* the winde came faire, and
they arrived safe in this harbor.[4] And after wards tooke better
view of the place, and resolved wher to pitch their dwelling; and
the *·25· day*[5] begane to erecte the first house for commone use to
receive them and their goods.[6]

Bradford, Ford ed., I, 177

(d)

On the 15th of December they weighed anchor to go to the
place they had discovered, and came within two leagues of it,
but were fain to bear up again; but the 16th day, the wind came
fair, and they arrived safe in this harbor. And afterwards took
better view of the place, and resolved where to pitch their dwelling; and the 25th day began to erect the first house for common
use to receive them and their goods.

Bradford, S. E. Morison ed., p. 72

B. Abraham Peirsey to Sir Edwin Sandys, May 24, 1621

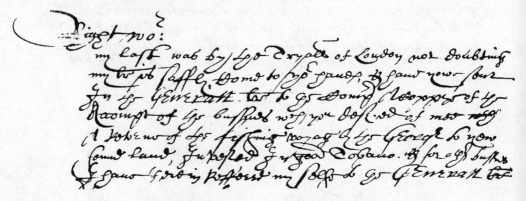

1. Ferrar Papers, Magdalene College, Cambridge — List of Recs., No. 248

Right Wo[r]

my last was by the Tryall of London not doubting my łr is saffly
Come to yo[r] hande, & haue nowe sent In the Generall łr to the
Comp̄ A Coppye of the Accompt of the bussnes w[ch] you desyred of mee
wth A Retorne of the fishing voyag by the George to new found land
Invested In good Tobacco. & for oth[r] bussnes I haue there in Refferrd my
selfe to the Generall łr beeing sorrye the Country is not pvyded of any

2. Records of Virginia Company, III, 454

Right Wo[r] :

My last was by the Tryall of London not doubting my l[re]
is saffly come to yo[r] hands, & have yours but in the General l[re]
to the Comp[a] a coppye of the Accomp[t] of the business—which
you desired of me wth a —— of the fishing voyage by the George
to new foundland —— in good Tobaccoe for the business I have
therein proffered my self to the Generall l[re] beeing sorry the

3. Virginia Magazine of History and Biography, X (1902-03), 418

B. Abraham Piersey to Sir Edwin Sandys, May 24, 1621

1. The original, in the Ferrar Mss., Magdalene College, Cambridge.

2. A very fine example of the Literal Method, with special type, as printed in S. M. Kingsbury, ed., *Records of the Virginia Company* (§ 46), III, 454. But note following:
a. Salutation: to Wo*r* the letters [shipful] might have been added.
b. Line 2: there is no cross on the *l* of this *lr*, although there is on the next.
c. Line 3: printers lacking special characters would be content to print the fourth word *handes*.
d. Line 4: first word, fourth letter, a *p* with a rising tail should have been used, not *p* with a tilde. The *u* in *you* is superior.

3. A good example of garbling, from *Va. Mag. of Hist*, X (1902–03), 418. The editor uses a long dash for words he cannot decipher, misreads others, spells some in the modern way but leaves others as is.

C. George Washington to Joseph Reed, Middlebrook, 28 March 1779

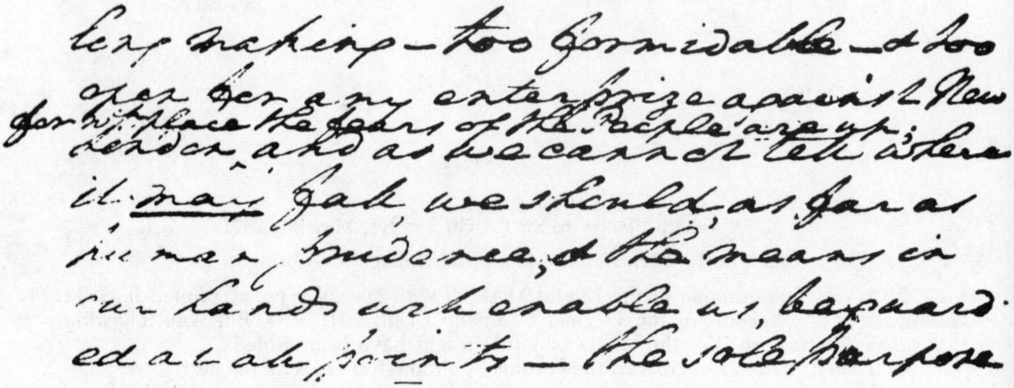

[handwritten manuscript text]

1. George Washington Mss., Library of Congress

preparations have been too long making, too formidable, and too open, for any enterprise against New
London, for wch. place the fears of the people are up,
and, as we cannot tell where it may fall, we should,
as far as human prudence and the means in our
hands will enable us, be guarded at all points.   The

Writings of George Washington (W. C. Ford, ed., 1890), VII (1778-79), 386

long making, too formidable, and too open for any enterprize
against New London for wch place the fears of the People are
up; and as we cannot tell where it *may* fall, we should, as far
as human prudence, and the means in our hands will enable
us, be guarded at all points; the sole purpose therefore of this

Writings of Washington (Fitzpatrick, ed., 1936), 307

C. George Washington to Joseph Reed, Middlebrook, March 28, 1779

An autograph draft of a letter by George Washington, a more modern example, is the sort of document with which American historians generally deal, and offers few difficulties.

1. Original, in Library of Congress.

2. Printed version in W. C. Ford, *Writings of Washington* (N.Y., 1890), VII, 386, which follows no particular method. Note following:
   a. Lines 1 and 6: No good reason for replacing the dashes by commas and a period.
   b. Line 2: the spelling of *enterprize* has been corrected.
   c. Line 3: since this editor always prints *&* as *and*, it would be consistent to expand *wch* to *which*; and the semicolon after *up* has been replaced by a comma. *People* should have a capital *P*.
   d. Line 4: *may*, underlined by Washington, should have been printed in italics.
   e. Line 5: a comma has been omitted.

3. Printed version in J. C. Fitzpatrick, *Writings of George Washington*, XIV, 307 (§ 55). Good example of Expanded Method.
   a. Lines 1 and 2: the same inconsistency between treatment of *&* and *wch* as in 2c.
   b. Line 5: Washington's dash has been replaced by a semicolon, as this editor thinks he did not intend to end a sentence there.

Jared Sparks, the first to print this letter, in his *Writings of George Washington* (Boston, 1834), VI, 209, improved the General's English by expanding "for wch" to "concerning which," and changing "the fears . . . are up" to "the fears . . . are awake." He doubtless thought "for" was the wrong preposition and that "up" was vulgar.

VI. CHOICE OF METHOD

Whether the Literal, Expanded, or Modernized Method should be used depends partly on the kind of document in question, but mainly on practical considerations, especially on the purpose of the publication. In printing English, Spanish, or French documents of the sixteenth and seventeenth centuries that are full of contractions or abbreviations, and where expense is no object, the Literal Method is preferable in a publication destined for scholarly readers only. The Expanded Method is much easier to read and cheaper to print, since monotype and linotype operators find it difficult to deal with superior letters, diacritical marks, or special symbols. The young student will be put off by texts such as A2, B2, and B3 above, but he can read A3 and A4 readily enough. For the student A3 is better than A4 because the wording, spelling, and punctuation of the original give it a certain flavor. For a translation, or for a new edition of some classic such as the Virginia "Lament for Mr. Nathaniel Bacon," or the poetry of Edward Taylor, the Modernized Method is best. It is particularly unfortunate to print y^e as *ye* since the general reader will imagine that it is to be read and pronounced as *ye* instead of as *the*.

For extracts and quotations from documents incorporated in a secondary work, the Expanded Method is far preferable to the literal, since the latter clashes unnecessarily with a modern text and makes readers pause to puzzle over odd spellings and abbreviations. Historians are apt to be careless and inconsistent about this. Nor is it good style to interpolate an explanation within a quotation as in the following example, where the abbreviation for *Christian* should either have been spelled out or explained in a footnote:

. . . and peculiarly need the Candour of my Xtn. [= Christian] friends (W. C. Bronson, *History of Brown University* [Providence, 1914], 92).

Every printed document or quotation from a document should be compared word for word with the original, or with a microfilm or photographic copy. And whoever prints historical documents might well make his motto:

Accuracy without Pedantry.
Consistency first, last, and always.

Chapter Four

AIDS TO HISTORICAL RESEARCH

33. BIBLIOGRAPHY OF BIBLIOGRAPHIES

The printed materials of American history comprise all the extant works of American presses, from the earliest to the latest, together with much of the rest of the world's published product. This is an embarrassment of riches, a vast body of books, pamphlets, broadsheets, maps, periodicals, and newspapers; and so swiftly does it multiply that to keep abreast of the growth in even a portion of the field taxes the time of the specialist. The student would find the accumulation a wilderness, wherein he would be lost were it not for the fact that guides are available to direct him through it in the form of bibliographies, finding devices, and indexes. These guides are the Baedekers of American historical study.

A student entering upon a research program should proceed first to find the best of these guides. This is not as simplè a task as it might seem. The guide literature includes the aids to all fields of knowledge, since history concerns itelf with all the interests and activities of man, and in all fields the guide literature is large and growing.

The search for guides will be lightened by the fact that works, describing the latest and best of them in the various fields, may be found — the general bibliographies of bibliographies. An inspection of one or more such bibliographies should come early in any research program.

The following works are especially useful for general purposes:

C. M. Winchell, ed., *Guide to Reference Books.* 7 ed. Chi., 1951. — This is a new edition of a standard work (I. G. Mudge, *Guide to Reference Books* [6 ed., Chi., 1936]). It arranges its entries topically. A critical estimate is given of each entry. Sections are devoted to general bibliographical works and to such research tools as guides to libraries, to periodicals and newspapers, and to dictionaries and encyclopedias.

Theodore Besterman, ed., *World Bibliography of Bibliographies.* 3 vols. 2 ed. London, 1947–49. — Entries are arranged alphabetically according to topic. The work lists 63,776 bibliographies. Indexed.

Dorothy Charles and Bea Joseph, eds., *Bibliographic Index, 1937–1942.* N.Y., 1945. — This work is carried to 1946 by a supplementary volume. It is brought to date by monthly issues which are cumulated in annual volumes. Entries are arranged topically.

Bibliographies devoted to history include:

G. M. Dutcher, *et al.*, eds., *Guide to Historical Literature.* N.Y., 1949. — This divides the world into geographic areas, such as Great Britain and the United States. It lists

105

the bibliographies, periodicals, and government publications of each area. Within chapters for each area are sections devoted to various aspects of its history, such as diplomacy, economic life, and religion; also chapters devoted to great eras and trends, such as Christianity and the Middle Ages. Evaluations of the bibliographies by experts are given.

E. M. Coulter and Melanie Gerstenfeld, eds., *Historical Bibliographies*. Berkeley, 1935.

Pierre Caron and Marc Jaryc, eds., *World List of Historical Periodicals*. Oxford, 1939.

34. BIBLIOGRAPHIES OF AMERICAN HISTORY

H. P. Beers, ed., *Bibliographies in American History*. 2 ed. N.Y., 1942. — This is the standard work. It devotes sections to general aids, and to bibliographies of the colonial, Revolutionary, Confederation, and national periods. There are also sections on subject bibliographies, such as those for economic, constitutional, diplomatic, social, cultural, and scientific history. Each of the states is also covered bibliographically. The scope of each work cited is given, but without critical comment.

Writings on American History, 1902– . Princeton, N.Y., New Haven, and Wash., 1904–52. — For the year 1902, compiled by E. C. Richardson and A. E. Morse; 1903, by A. C. McLaughlin, *et al.*, 1904 and 1905, never issued; 1906–32 by G. G. Griffin; 1933–40 by G. G. Griffin, *et al.*; 1941–47 never issued; 1948 by J. R. Masterson. Since 1918, issued as part of the Am. Hist. Assoc., *Report*. Indexed annually. A cumulative index covering the years 1906–40 has been prepared and will be published by the Am. Hist. Assoc. This series contains annually a classified list of all books and important articles on American history that have appeared in the year. It covers not only the writings on the history of the United States, but in addition until 1940, also those on British North America, and until 1936 those on Latin America.

A. P. C. Griffin, ed., "Bibliography of American Historical Societies," Am. Hist. Assoc., *Report*, 1905, II. — A useful key that analyzes and indexes each volume of the publications of American and Canadian historical societies down to 1905.

J. N. Larned, ed., *Literature of American History. A Bibliographical Guide*. Boston, 1902. — A very serviceable book, excellent in analysis, choice of titles, execution, and index. Brief signed evaluations are given of about 4,000 books. Supplements for 1900–04 by P. P. Wells separately in 1902; in the Am. Library Assoc., *Annotated Titles of Books on English and American History* (1904); and in *A. L. A. Booklist*, Feb., 1906.

M. B. Stillwell, *Incunabula and Americana, 1450–1800*. N.Y., 1931. — This contains a comprehensive list of bibliographies of Americana.

John Carter Brown Library, *Bibliotheca Americana, Catalogue of the . . . Library*. 3 vols. Providence, 1919–31. — A catalogue, chronologically arranged, of an important collection of Americana printed before the nineteenth century. The volumes thus far issued cover the period to 1674.

35. BIBLIOGRAPHIES OF SPECIAL SUBJECTS

The literature of bibliographies of special subjects is large and growing. It includes bibliographies of areas and eras of American history, prepared under the auspices of such organizations as the Library of Congress Division of Bibliography, the several departments and bureaus of the federal government, the American Library Association, the New York Public Library, and commercial publishers. The following list will suggest the type and range of the formal special-topic and special-area bibliographies.

Agriculture   E. E. Edwards, ed., *Bibliography of the History of Agriculture in the United States*. Wash., 1930.

Biography   E. H. O'Neill, ed., *Biography by Americans, 1658–1936*. Phila., 1939. — A subject bibliography. See also: § 56.

Business	H. M. Larson, ed., *Guide to Business History*. Cambridge, 1948.
Canada	M. V. Higgins, ed., *Bibliography of Canadian Bibliographies*. Montreal, 1930.
	Gustave Lanctot, *L'Oeuvre de la France en Amérique du Nord. Bibliographie selective et critique*. Montreal, 1951.
	Royal Empire Soc. (London), Library, *Subject Catalogue of the Library: Vol. III, Dominion of Canada and Its Provinces, the Dominion of Newfoundland, the West Indies, and Colonial America*. London, 1932. — The fullest bibliography of Canadian history.
	F. M. Staton and Marie Tremaine, eds., *Bibliography of Canadiana*. Toronto, 1934. — Covers the period 1534–1867.
	Marie Tremaine, *Bibliography of Canadian Imprints 1751–1800*. Toronto, 1952.
Colonial Period	E. B. Greene and R. B. Morris, eds., *Guide to the Principal Sources for Early American History (1600–1800) in the City of New York*. N.Y., 1929.
Crime	A. F. Kuhlman, ed., *Guide to Material on Crime and Criminal Justice*. N.Y., 1929. — Prepared by the Comm. on Survey of Res. on Crime. Social Sci. Res. Coun.
	J. T. Sellin and J. P. Shalloo, eds., *A Bibliographical Manual for the Student of Criminology*. Phila., 1935.
Diplomatic History	S. F. Bemis and G. G. Griffin, eds., *Guide to the Diplomatic History of the United States, 1775–1921*. Wash., 1935.
Federal Judiciary	Library of Congress, *List of Works Relating to the Supreme Court of the United States*. Wash., 1909. — A valuable list.
Frontier	R. W. G. Vail, ed., *Voice of the Old Frontier*. Phila., 1949. — A bibliography of North American frontier literature, 1542–1800.
Free Speech	Theodore Schroeder, ed., *Free Speech Bibliography*. N.Y., 1922.
Geology	J. M. Nickles, ed., *Geologic Literature on North America, 1785–1918*. 2 vols. Wash., 1923–24. — This work is carried forward by other publications of the Geological Survey to 1943.
Germans	Emil Meynen, *Bibliography on German Settlements in Colonial North America*. Leipzig, 1937.
Indians	F. W. Hodge, ed., *Handbook of American Indians North of Mexico*. 2 vols. Wash., 1907–10. — Contains a subject and an author list of authorities, the former embodied in the articles.
	U.S. Bureau of Am. Ethnology, *List of Publications of the Bureau of American Ethnology with Index to Authors and Titles*. Wash., 1937.
	H. F. DePuy, ed., *Bibliography of the English Colonial Treaties with the American Indians, Including a Synopsis of Each Treaty*. N.Y., 1917.
Industry	A. G. S. Josephson, ed., *List of Books on the History of Industry and Industrial Arts*. Chi., 1915.
Journalism	C. L. Cannon, ed., *Journalism; a Bibliography*. N.Y., 1924.
	E. H. Ford, *Bibliography of Books and Annotated Articles on the History of Journalism in the United States*. Minneapolis, 1939.
Land Use	D. C. Culver, ed., *Land Utilization: a Bibliography*. Berkeley, 1935.
	L. O. Bercaw, *et al.*, eds., *Bibliography on Land Settlement* (U.S. Dept. of Ag., *Misc. Publ.*, No. 172 [1934]).
Law	Lawrence Keitt, ed., *Annotated Bibliography of Bibliographies of Statutory Materials of the United States*. Cambridge, 1934. — Lists bibliographies of the states and the United States.
Literature	R. E. Spiller, *et al.*, *Literary History of the United States*, vol. III.
Medicine	U.S. Surgeon-General's Office, Library, *Index Catalogue*, 4 ser. Wash., 1880–[1948]. — This catalogue, of one of the largest medical libraries in the world, is a notable bibliography of the subject of medicine.

Navy	R. W. Neeser, *Statistical and Chronological History of the United States Navy, 1775–1907.* 2 vols. N.Y., 1909. — Vol. I consists of a comprehensive bibliography.
Negro	M. N. Work, ed., *Bibliography of the Negro in Africa and America.* N.Y., 1928.
Pacific Northwest	C. W. Smith, ed., *Pacific Northwest Americana.* Portland, Ore., 1950.
Political Parties	A. B. Claflin, ed., *Political Parties in the United States, 1800–1914.* N.Y., 1915.
Political Science	Laverne Burchfield, ed., *Student's Guide to Materials in Political Science.* N.Y., 1935.
Propaganda	B. L. Smith, *et al.*, eds., *Propaganda, Communication, and Public Opinion; a Comprehensive Reference Guide.* Princeton, 1946.
Public Administration	Sarah Greer, ed., *Bibliography of Public Administration.* N.Y., 1933. Sarah Greer, ed., *Bibliography of Civil Service and Personnel Administration.* N.Y., 1935. W. B. Munro, ed., *Bibliography of Municipal Government in the United States.* Cambridge, 1915.
Religious History	P. G. Mode, ed., *Source Book and Bibliographical Guide for American Church History.* Menasha, Wisc., 1921. H. S. Bender, ed., *Two Centuries of American Mennonite Literature; a Bibliography . . . 1727–1928.* Goshen, Ind., 1929. N.Y. Public Library, *List of Works in the . . . Library Relating to the Mormons.* N.Y., 1909.
Science	E. J. Crane and A. M. Patterson, eds., *Guide to the Literature of Chemistry.* N.Y., 1927. Max Meisel, ed., *Bibliography of American Natural History . . . 1769–1865.* 3 vols., N.Y., 1924–29.
Social Sciences	Allen Eaton and S. M. Harrison, *Bibliography of Social Surveys.* N.Y., 1930. B. M. Headicar and Clifford Fuller, eds., *London Bibliography of the Social Sciences.* 4 vols. London, 1931–32. — Supplements, 1934, 1937.
Tariff	U.S. Tariff Commission, *The Tariff: a Bibliography.* Wash., 1934.
Transportation	M. E. Pellett, ed., *Water Transportation; a Bibliography, Guide and Union Catalogue.* N.Y., 1931.

For individual topics in American history, bibliographical aids can be found which are often more helpful than those provided in formal bibliographies. Especially useful are the card catalogues, provided they are subject catalogues, of research libraries. Similarly helpful are the bibliographical lists appended to special monographs or to individual volumes in the comprehensive collaborative works (§§ 59, 61). The *Dictionary of American Biography* (§ 56), the *Dictionary of American History* (§ 58), and the encyclopedias listed in § 58 generally provide bibliographical aids at the end of each of their sketches. The footnote references and critical essays on authorities in Justin Winsor, *Narrative and Critical History*, are still of value.

Catalogues of special collections and of special libraries are useful bibliographical aids. A comprehensive work listing the special collections and libraries in the United States and Canada is Vormelker's *Special Library Resources* (§ 16), a four-volume directory and account of the special collections and libraries of the United States and Canada. The collections listed are described in detail in many cases in the printed catalogues of the libraries possessing them. The "Union Catalog" of the Library of Congress (§ 37) has an "Index to Special Collections in the United States and Canada," arranged by locality and by subject, which contains helpful descriptions of individual collections, giving numbers of volumes, pamphlets, and manuscript material wherever possible, comparisons with similar collections elsewhere, and the existence or otherwise of published catalogues and lists of the collections.

36. BIBLIOGRAPHIES OF CURRENT BOOKS

For current books bibliographical guides are published in a variety of forms. Especially useful for books printed in the English language is the *Cumulative Book Index* (N.Y.). This is a subject index of current titles, and it is also an author and title index. Published since 1898, it appears monthly, and is cumulated semiannually and annually to form the annual supplement to the *United States Catalog* (§ 38).

For books printed in foreign languages, in addition to those in the English language, a valuable guide is the *Library of Congress Subject Catalogue*, of which the initial set of volumes appeared in 1948. This is a catalogue, arranged alphabetically by subject, of the cards prepared for publication by the Library of Congress in or since 1945. It is a continuing work, published in three quarterly issues with an annual cumulation. The British Museum, *Subject Index of Books*, a similar work, at present extends to 1940.

Weekly lists of new books appear in the *Publishers' Weekly* and in less inclusive form in the literary supplements of some of the large metropolitan newspapers, such as the *New York Times Book Review*.

37. AIDS FOR LOCATING BOOKS AND PAMPHLETS

A study of bibliographies is the beginning of research. From it emerges a mere collection of titles of such books, pamphlets, articles, and maps as are promising. The next step is to locate the actual volumes. This will be a matter of no great difficulty if the works are common and a good research library is at hand. But it may happen that important items are rare or are unavailable in a local library. The student should know the means by which their location can be traced. A book traced to a distant library can sometimes be borrowed through an interlibrary loan. Or a pamphlet or an article in a periodical, located in a distant collection, can be reproduced by photostat or microfilm. The finding devices for books, pamphlets and nonofficial reports are listed below. Those for periodicals are given in § 39; for newspapers in § 53.

Joseph Sabin, *et al.*, eds., *Bibliotheca Americana. A Dictionary of Books Relating to America, from its Discovery to the Present Time.* 29 vols. N.Y. and Portland, Me., 1868–1936. — Begun by Joseph Sabin, continued by Wilberforce Eames, and completed by R. W. G. Vail. In its late volumes the scope of this monumental work was narrowed, the term "present time" being considerably restricted. See: XXIX, ix–xi.

Charles Evans, ed., *American Bibliography: a Chronological Dictionary of All Books, Pamphlets and Periodical Publications Printed in the United States . . . 1639 . . . 1820.* 12 vols. Chi., 1903–34. — The last volume comes to 1799. This is an important list of early American publications. Each volume has three indexes: author, subject, and printer and publisher.

A. W. Pollard and G. R. Redgrave, eds., *Short-Title Catalogue of Books Printed in England, Scotland and Ireland, and of English Books Printed Abroad, 1475–1640.* London, 1926.

D. G. Wing, *Short-Title Catalogue of Books Printed in England, Scotland, Ireland, Wales, and British North America and of English Books Printed in Other Countries, 1641–1700.* 3 vols. N.Y., 1945–51. — Each entry carries one or more "locations" libraries, where copies may be found.

A Catalog of Books Represented by Library of Congress Printed Cards Issued to July 31, 1942. 167 vols. Ann Arbor, 1942–46. — This is the printed edition of the author card catalogue of the Library of Congress. A 42-volume supplement appeared in 1948; and this is now a continuing project. Annual author catalogues have appeared since 1948, and subject catalogues since 1950.

An even more comprehensive finding aid is the "Union Catalog" of the Library of Congress. This lists by author, or by title if the work is anonymous, not only the holdings of the Library of Congress but of some 800 other North American libraries. Since 1932 it has been enlarged by the addition of the titles of some of the greatest of the European libraries and it may well become a world union catalogue. Each card carries one or more "locations" libraries, where the book may be found. The services of the "Union Catalog" are extended free to persons who write regarding the location of books to the Library of Congress. For an account of this service and directions as to applying for it, see: *The Union Catalog of the Library of Congress* (Wash., 1942); also R. B. Downs, ed., *Union Catalogs* (1942).

The British Museum Catalogue of Printed Books 1881–1900. 58 vols. Ann Arbor, 1946. — Reproduced from the printed catalogue of the Museum (London, 1881–1900). The supplement (London, 1900–05) was also reproduced (10 vols., Ann Arbor, 1950). These works are the British equivalent of the *Library of Congress Catalog of Printed Cards.*

British Museum General Catalogue of Printed Books. 47 vols. London, 1931–51. — A new edition, in process, of the above. The volumes thus far issued reach through the letters "DANT."

Current pamphlets are often not promptly collected or catalogued by libraries. A convenient guide to such material is: Vertical File Service Catalog, 1932– N.Y., 1935–

38. MISCELLANEOUS AIDS

Students preparing dissertations or manuscripts for publication frequently need to verify bibliographical information about books not readily accessible. Sabin and Evans are standard works for the period they cover, and the *Library of Congress Catalog of Printed Cards* or the British Museum equivalent will serve for other periods. See also:

American Catalogue of Books, 1876–1910. N.Y., 1880–1911.

United States Catalog; Books in Print, 1899. Minneapolis, 1900. — This work is carried by supplements and new editions to 1928. It is continued from that point by the Cumulative Book Index (§ 36).

Reviews of current history books will be readily found in the professional history journals (§ 50); also in journals in political science, economics, law, and other fields. Particularly helpful is the *United States Quarterly Book Review* (1945–), published by the Library of Congress. Reviews will also be found in the literary supplements of the metropolitan newspapers. In abbreviated form they are reproduced in the *Book Review Digest* (N.Y., 1905–   ), a monthly publication with semiannual and annual cumulations. Cumulative indexes appear in the volumes for 1926, 1931, 1941, and 1946. Additional aids include:

Microfilm Abstracts (Ann Arbor, 1938–   ), and Unesco, *List of Current Abstracting and Indexing Services* (The Hague, 1949).

39. INDEXES TO PERIODICALS

Indexes to periodicals fall into two classifications, those to general, and those to special, periodicals. Indexes of the first type of greatest use to the historian are:

Poole's Index to Periodical Literature, 1802–81. R. ed. Boston, 1891. — Supplements, Jan. 1, 1882 — Jan. 1, 1907. (Boston, [1887–1908]). This pioneer index is by subjects only and is limited to American and English periodicals.
Reader's Guide to Periodical Literature. N.Y., 1900–   . — Issued monthly and cumulated in an annual volume. The number of periodicals indexed has steadily increased. In 1903 it absorbed the *Cumulative Index* and in 1911 the field of the *Annual Library Index.*
International Index to Periodicals. N.Y., 1907–   . — Similar in character to *Readers' Guide,* but covers more scholarly journals, including some foreign-language journals. Prior to 1920 it appeared under the title *Readers' Guide Supplement.*
Annual Magazine Subject Index. Boston, 1908–   . — Covers by subject American and British periodicals largely historical and includes state historical society journals. A large number of periodicals included have been indexed from their first issue, the oldest going back to 1876.
Canadian Periodical Index. Windsor and Toronto, 1928–48. — A subject and author index issued quarterly. Superseded in 1948 by *Canadian Index* (Ottawa).
An unpublished index to early American periodical literature covering 351 periodicals of the years 1728–1870 — a W. P. A. project — is housed at New York University. In 1940 a mimeographed list of the periodicals covered was issued.

The indexes to periodicals of special interest are so numerous that they can be listed only by example in the more important fields. Indexes to particular journals are mentioned in § 50.

Agriculture	*Agricultural Index.* 1916–48. N.Y., 1919–49. — A subject index to agricultural periodicals and bulletins, brought to date by annual and triennial cumulations.
	U.S. Office of Experiment Stations, *General Index to Experiment Station Record, 1889–1929.* Wash., 1903–32. — Serves as an index to agricultural periodical literature.
Art	*Art Index.* 1929– . N.Y., 1933– . — A subject and author index, issued monthly and in annual and triennial cumulations.
Biography	*Biography Index* (Bea Joseph and C. W. Squires, eds.). N.Y., 1946– — This work is carried forward by quarterly and annual cumulations to date. It is an index to biographical material in magazines and books.
Engineering	*Engineering Index.* 1884– . N.Y., 1907– . — An alphabetical subject index to engineering and technical periodicals, kept to date by annual cumulations.
Industrial Arts	*Industrial Arts Index.* 1913– . N.Y., 1913– . — A subject index to engineering, trade, and business periodicals, books, and pamphlets, kept to date by monthly issues and annual cumulations.
Law	*An Index to Legal Periodical Literature.* (L. A. Jones and F. E. Chipman, eds.) 5 vols. Boston, 1888–1933. — The first volume covers the period 1791–1886. The succeeding volumes cover the period 1887–1932. This is a subject index (and a brief author index) to American, English, Canadian,

and British colonial legal periodicals. Vols. IV–V are practically a consolidation of vols. I–XXV of the annual *Index to Legal Periodicals.*

Index to Legal Periodicals. 1908– . N.Y., 1909– . — This is a quarterly, with an annual cumulation, and, since 1926, a triennial cumulation.

A number of legal journals have issued cumulative indexes: *Columbia Law Review* (1–10); *Harvard Law Review* (1–40); *Michigan Law Review* (1–10); *Yale Law Journal* (1–38).

Century Edition of the American Digest, 1658–1896. 50 vols. St. Paul, 1897–1904. — This is a complete digest of all reported American legal cases from the earliest to 1896. In L, 1864–2763, appears a descriptive-word index for the 50 volumes. The *Digest* is carried from 1897 to 1925 by successive decennial editions, and it is brought to date by the *Current Digest.* Descriptive-word indexes of the successive decennial editions appear in the following years: 1924, 1940, and 1950.

Medical Science *Index Medicus; a . . . Classified Record of the Current Medical Literature of the World.* Boston and Wash., 1879–1927. — An index of periodicals and of books. Suspended 1899–1900 during which time its place was taken by the French *Bibliographia Medica* (Paris, 1899–1900).

Quarterly Cumulative Index Medicus. Chi., 1927– . — The successor to the *Index Medicus.* A practically complete index to the journal literature of the field. Issued quarterly and cumulated semiannually and annually.

Mining W. R. Crane, ed., *Index of Mining Engineering Literature.* 2 vols. N.Y., 1909–12. — An index to periodicals, society transactions, and some government reports from about 1877 to 1912.

Religion E. C. Richardson, ed., *Alphabetical Subject Index and Index Encyclopaedia to Periodical Articles on Religion, 1890–1899.* 2 vols. N.Y., 1907–11.

Science Royal Society of London, *Catalogue of Scientific Papers, 1800–1900.* London and Cambridge, Eng., 1867–1925. — A monumental author index of scientific periodicals and transactions.

A useful guide to cumulative indexes to individual periodicals is D. C. Haskell, *Checklist of Cumulative Indexes to Periodicals in the New York Public Library* (N.Y., 1942).

40. FINDING AIDS FOR PERIODICALS

Files of the older periodicals and periodicals of restricted interest are often obtainable only in the larger libraries and in special collections. It is important to know, therefore, where the more nearly complete sets may be consulted. This information is given in Gregory, *Union List of Serials in Libraries of the United States and Canada* (§ 52), in which the periodical holdings of more than 200 United States and Canadian libraries are listed. In this list it was possible to cover only the more important libraries. For certain localities and regions there exist local union lists. Convenient bibliographies of these local lists may be found in the work mentioned, pp. 3053–59.

For a directory of periodicals published in the United States and Canada, see: § 50. For newspapers, see: § 53.

41. GUIDES TO FEDERAL DOCUMENTS

The United States government publishes its official documents in two great categories, the Congressional, and the departmental. The Congressional is the lesser of the two in bulk. It includes all documents originating in Congress which Congress orders printed. Also it includes many documents which, though originating elsewhere than in Congress, are ordered to be printed in the Congressional series. In the series are the journals of the House and the Senate, also the reports and documents of House and Senate committees. Until 1874, the debates were printed unofficially, thereafter in the *Congressional Record* (§ 45). The *Record* and the earlier series are indexed by individual volumes.

The departmental publications, which are far greater in bulk than the Congressional, consist of reports of executive departments and bureaus, bulletins, circulars, and miscellaneous documents. The reports of decisions handed down by the federal judiciary, like the debates of Congress, were printed under private auspices until 1923. They are indexed year by year.

Guides of two types unlock the documents of the federal government. One is the general descriptive account of the federal system of documents which provides an historical survey of the output of the various Congresses, departments and bureaus of the government. The most useful works of the sort are:

A. M. Boyd, ed., *United States Government Publications: Sources of Information for Librarians.* 3 ed. R. by R. E. Rips. N.Y., 1949. — This is, in many ways, the most useful as well as the most recent of the general guides to the federal documents. It is organized according to source of issue of the documents rather than according to subject-content. Its sections deal with such topics as the publications of Congress, federal courts, executive departments, and independent establishments. The index serves as a subject guide.
H. S. Hirshberg and C. H. Melinat, eds., *Subject Guide to United States Government Publications.* Chi., 1947. — The arrangement is by subject.
J. L. McCamy, *Government Publications for the Citizen.* N.Y., 1949.
L. F. Schmeckebier, ed., *Government Publications and Their Use.* R. ed. Wash., 1939. — This work describes the guide-and-index literature and its limitations, explains systems of numbering documents, and makes its point of emphasis the utilization of government publications.

The second group of guides to the federal documents consists of checklists, catalogues and indexes prepared ordinarily by branches of the government. These cover, taking them altogether, practically all the government publications, Congressional and departmental, from 1774 to date. In quality those prepared since 1895 are much superior to those prepared earlier. The most important of the series are the following:

B. P. Poore, ed., *Descriptive Catalogue of the Government Publications of the United States, 1774–1881.* Wash., 1885. — A useful guide which gives brief abstracts of the documents it lists. Must be used with care as its listings are very incomplete, especially for departmental publications. The index is very defective.
P. L. Ford, ed., *Some Materials for a Bibliography of the Official Publications of the Continental Congress, 1774–89.* Boston, 1890. — A private work which corrects and supplements Poore for its period. At the end of the *Journals of the Continental Congress* (§ 45) for each year appear an index and bibliographical notes.
A. W. Greely, ed., *Public Documents of the First Fourteen Congresses, 1789–1817* (56 Cong., 1 Sess., Sen. Doc., No. 428). — A good descriptive list. A supplement to it is published in Am. Hist. Assoc., *Report,* 1903, I, 343.
Superintendent of Documents, *Tables of and Annotated Index to the Congressional Series of United States Public Documents (1817–1893).* Wash., 1902. — A good selective index to the more important documents and reports in the congressional series. Covers only about 50,000 of the 96,875 numbered documents and reports appearing in this series from 1817 to 1893. A student wishing to find all the government publications on a particular subject in this series should use in addition to the *Tables and Index,* Poore, and Ames. The "tables" in the volume are now superseded by the more complete *Checklist of United States Public Documents* (below).

J. G. Ames, ed., *Comprehensive Index to the Publications of the United States Government, 1881–1893*. Wash., 1905. — A good index covering both Congressional and departmental series for its period. Its listing of departmental documents is, however, incomplete.

M. A. Hartwell, ed., *Checklist of United States Public Documents, 1789–1909. Congressional: to the Close of the Sixtieth Congress; Departmental: to End of Calendar Year 1909*. 3 ed. Wash., 1911. — This work, issued by the Superintendent of Documents, is an approximately complete checklist (not a catalogue) of all public documents in the period of the volume. A knowledge of its contents and how to use it is fundamental in the study of United States government publications. Especially useful are its lists of publications of departments and bureaus. Gives serial numbers for congressional documents.

Most of the works in this list, after B. F. Poore, are supplements and corrections to Poore. For the period since Poore, the following works are essential.

Superintendent of Documents, *Catalogue of the Public Documents . . . 1893–1940*. Wash., 1896– . — A minute index in the form of a dictionary-catalogue. Covers the congressional and departmental publications. Commonly cited as the *Document Catalogue*. It is a continuation of the *Comprehensive Index*. Each Congress is covered by one volume except the 54 Congress which has two. Prior to the 70 Congress the *Document Catalogue* listed only the printed government publications, but later it included the more important processed works as well. This series was discontinued with the end of the year 1940.

Superintendent of Documents, *United States Government Publications Monthly Catalogue*. Wash., 1895– . — This work, which until 1939 bore the title, *Monthly Catalogue*, lists all current printed (and from 1936 on, important processed) congressional and departmental publications. An annual index is issued at the end of the calendar year.

Superintendent of Documents, *Selected United States Government Publications*. Wash., 1928– . — This is a semimonthly advertising list of government publications. It is sent free on request. Its entries are arranged by title.

Congressional hearings on bills of public interest or on issues of public policy before committees of either house of Congress constitute a rapidly growing and an increasingly important source of historical materials. They have not ordinarily been printed by order of Congress, and those printed prior to 1938 were not normally distributed to depository libraries. Only since 1938 have depository libraries been entitled to receive all printed Congressional hearings. An incomplete list of the published hearings before 1910 is found in the *Checklist of United States Public Documents, 1789–1909*, under committee publications.

The first of a new series planned to cover the major committees of the two houses prior to 1923 is: Library of Congress, Legislative Reference Service, *Checklist of Hearings before Congressional Committees through the Sixty-seventh Congress: Part I, House Committee on Agriculture* (Wash., 1941).

Of the indexes to congressional hearings the most useful are:

E. M. Shumaker, comp., *Index of Congressional Committee Hearings in the Library of the U. S. House of Representatives Prior to January 3, 1943*. Wash., 1944. — This work is carried by a *Supplemental Index* to Jan. 3, 1947.

J. D. Preston, *et al.*, eds., *Index of Congressional Committee Hearings (Not Confidential in Character) Prior to January 3, 1935 in the Senate Library*. Wash., 1935. — This work is carried by a *Supplement* to Jan. 3, 1941.

Individual departments, bureaus, and independent establishments issue guides to their own publications that are supplementary to the general guides listed above. These special guides are likely to be more minute in their analysis or more convenient in their arrangement of material than is possible in the general guides. Examples are:

Department of Agriculture, *General Index of the Agricultural Reports of the Patent Office . . . 1837 to 1861; and of the Department of Agriculture . . . 1862 to 1876*. Wash., 1879. — This work is carried forward by a series of indexes to the *Publications* of the Department of Agriculture from 1862 to 1940. For the period since 1942 the Department of Agriculture Library has published a monthly *Bibliography of Agriculture*, with an annual index.

H. J. Dubester, ed., *Catalog of United States Census Publications* (§ 7) is currently continued by an annual publication of the Bureau of the Census entitled, *Census Publications Catalog and Subject Guide*.

W. M. Johnson, ed., *United States Department of Commerce Publications*. Wash., 1952.

U. S. Department of State, *General Index to the Published Volumes of the Diplomatic Correspondence and Foreign Relations of the United States 1861-99*. Wash., 1902.

Other departmental and bureau guides and indexes will be found listed in Boyd and Rips, mentioned above. Important guides of a different type are:

A. R. Hasse, ed., *Index to United States Documents Relating to Foreign Affairs, 1828-1861*. 3 vols. Wash., 1914-1921.

J. K. Wilcox, *Official War Publications Guide to State, Federal and Canadian Publications*. 9 vols. Berkeley, 1941-45.

The statutes of the federal government are unlocked by an index, prepared under the direction of the Library of Congress.

M. G. Beaman and A. K. McNamara, eds., *Index Analysis of the Federal Statutes (General and Permanent Law), 1789-1873*. 2 vols. Wash., 1908-11.

W. H. McClenon and W. C. Gilbert, eds., *Index to the Federal Statutes, 1874-1931*. Wash., 1933.

Presidential executive orders are indexed by C. L. Lord, *List and Index of Presidential Executive Orders 1789-1941*. Newark, N.J., 1943.

Foreign government documents are important sources of material for American history. In most American libraries they are found in broken sets only. Information as to what holdings individual libraries have is, therefore, essential to the student of American history. Such information is given in:

Gregory, *List of the Serial Publications of Foreign Governments, 1815-1931*. — This indicates the holdings of 85 American libraries of foreign government documents. See also: § 47.

42. GUIDES TO STATE DOCUMENTS

The published documents of the American states are a rich and relatively unused source of data for students of American history. Their value grows with the expansion of state activity. Unfortunately there are no collections of printed state documents that are even approximately complete. Some states lack full sets of even their own printed documents, an indication of the confusion that has attended the printing and housing of state publications. The best collections are those in the Library of Congress, the University of North Carolina Library, the Massachusetts State Library, the New York State Library, the New York Public Library, and the library of the State Historical Society of Wisconsin.

The guides to the use of state documents are of two types, those which cover the documents of the states collectively and those which cover the documents of individual states or groups of states.

Of those which are in the first category the more important are:

R. R. Bowker, ed., *State Publications; a Provisional List of the Official Publications of the Several States of the United States from Their Organization*. 4 pts. N.Y., 1899-1908. — This is a checklist of state publications to 1900. It is incomplete, although painstakingly compiled, owing to lack of coöperation from some states. Moreover, it lists the documents of the states only from the date of their organization as states. It is now superseded in part by the following works:

G. E. MacDonald, ed., *Check-List of Session Laws*. N.Y., 1936. A supplement by F. H. Pollack, appeared Boston, 1941.

G. E. MacDonald, ed., *Check-List of Statutes*. Providence, 1937. This work includes revisions, compilations, digests, codes, and indexes of state statutes.

G. E. MacDonald, ed., *Check-List of Legislative Journals*. Providence, 1938.

The three above works fill gaps in Bowker and carry the record down to the date of their publication. Amplifications of the scope of Bowker are the following works which undertake to assemble a complete list of the legislative records and of the "collected documents" of the states in their colonial, territorial, and state periods.

W. S. Jenkins, ed., *Supplement Check List of Legislative Journals*. Boston, 1943.

W. S. Jenkins, ed., *Collected Public Documents of the States; a Check List*. Boston, 1947.

For the period since 1910 the following checklist is standard:

Library of Congress, Division of Documents, *Monthly List of State Publications*. Wash., 1910– . — This is a record of all state publications currently received by the Library of Congress. The Library of Congress wishes to make it an exhaustive list but has been hampered by the lack of coöperation from some. states. This monthly list is not cumulated, which impairs its value as a bibliographical tool.

Other lists of state documents that are of value to the historian are:

L. W. Morse, "Historical Outline and Bibliography of Attorneys General Reports and Opinions," *Law Library Journal*, XXX (1937), 39. — This is a bibliography by states of reports and opinions of state attorneys general from the beginning through 1936.

University of Chicago Libraries, *Official Publications Relating to American State Constitutional Conventions*. Chi., 1936. — The materials are grouped by state. Under each state the colonial, provincial, and territorial materials come first, followed by materials for the period of statehood.

A. H. Shearer, ed., *List of Documentary Material Relating to State Constitutional Conventions 1776–1912*. Chi., 1915.

C. C. Soule, *Lawyer's Reference Manual of Law Books and Citations*. Boston, 1883. — This is the standard bibliography of the court reports of the state and federal courts to 1883. It is brought to date in Hicks, *Materials and Methods of Legal Research* (§ 47), and in F. A. Eldean, *How to Find the Law* (r. by C. B. Putnam, St. Paul, 1949), 522.

U.S. Office of Experiment Stations, *List of Bulletins of the* [State] *Agricultural Experiment Stations in the United States from Their Establishment to the End of 1920* (U.S. Dept. of Ag., *Dept. Bull.*, No. 1199 [1924]). — Lists which carry this guide forward can be found under the caption "Bulletins" in the indexes to the publications of the United States Department of Agriculture mentioned in § 41.

State documents are indexed in the following works:

New York State Library, *Bulletin: Legislation*, Nos. 1–39 (Albany, 1891–1908). — An annual index to the legislation of the states (predecessor to the *State Law Index*).

Library of Congress, *State Law Index: An Index and Digest to the Legislation of the States of the United States . . . 1925*. Wash., 1929– . — An annual subject index to the general state laws. The volume for 1934 includes a list of all court cases found in law digests interpreting the laws. The latest volume of this work extends it through 1947–48.

U.S. Bureau of Labor, *Index of All Reports Issued by Bureaus of Labor Statistics in the United States Prior to . . . 1902*. Wash., 1902.

For individual states there are checklists and indexes to published documents too numerous to be mentioned here. Accounts of them will be found in J. K. Wilcox, *Manual on the Use of State Publications* (Chi., 1940), 75. This work is brought forward to 1948 by Gwendolyn Lloyd, "State Document Bibliography," *Library Quar.*, XVIII (1948), 192. A more extensive, but older list is Keitt, *Annotated Bibliography* (§ 35).

A valuable set of indexes to printed documents of particular states which deserves special mention is A. R. Hasse, *Index of Economic Material in Documents of the States of the United States* (Carnegie Institution, *Publ.*, No. 85, 13 pts. Wash., 1907–22). These indexes cover the period to 1904. A broad interpretation is given in them to the term "economic material." The states covered are California, Delaware, Illinois, Kentucky, Maine, Massachusetts, New Hampshire, New Jersey, New York, Ohio, Pennsylvania, Rhode Island, Vermont.

43. GUIDES TO LOCAL GOVERNMENT DOCUMENTS

Local government documents are covered by guides the most important of which are the following:

J. G. Hodgson, ed., *Official Publications of American Counties: a Union List*. Fort Collins, 1937. — A checklist that indicates the holdings of 184 American libraries.

A. D. Manvel, ed., *Checklist of Basic Municipal Documents* (Census Bureau, *State and Local Government Special Studies*, No. 27). Wash., 1948.

Other guides for particular states are listed in the bibliographies mentioned above. See also: § 46.

Chapter Five

HISTORICAL SOURCES

44. THE VALUE OF PUBLIC DOCUMENTS FOR THE HISTORIAN

Public documents are among the most abundant and most useful sources of information available to the historian. Material of this nature exists for the discovery and earliest settlement of the Americas, and both the quantity and the scope of it increase through the centuries.

In general, the reliability of these documents springs from the fact that they are public and are used in the regular course of official business. Often they are published promptly and even those that remain in manuscript form are open to scholars and other citizens. There is therefore little likelihood of falsification or forgery. The precautions the historian must take in using these materials are of another order: he must examine them in their context, determine if they are what they purport to be, and use them for what they are (§ 6).

The largest fund of public records consists of those which arise from the normal administrative procedures of various government agencies. These records have a high degree of reliability since they are kept for the information of the officials who use them in the usual processes of their work. Nevertheless even such records must be scrutinized with care. Sometimes the responsible officials may lack the technical means of assuring accuracy. Thus, the colonial governors who sent home statistics of population were only passing on informed guesses. Furthermore the data may not always be what it is labeled: there are times when an estimate of imports is only an estimate of imports on which a duty was paid or when the volume of immigration is only the volume of immigration by sea through certain ports. The scholar would have to take account of what goods were smuggled or of what newcomers entered by land. Nevertheless these administrative documents ordinarily bear on their face clear indications of their origins and purposes and the historian can use them with confidence.

Official records also contain a variety of texts, including the correspondence of executives, the statutes of legislatures, and the decisions of courts. In the modern period these are almost always edited and printed with care and need little in the way of verification. But the accuracy of the text is, of course, no guarantee of the accuracy of the facts cited in it or of the logic of the arguments it contains.

This is even more true of the records of the deliberations of various legislative and executive bodies. The *Congressional Record* will reveal what a senator said, or would like to have said, but the historian must himself determine how much weight to give the utterance. In some cases, moreover, the official record is less informative than other sources. The diaries of members, for instance, are the most useful sources of information as to what happens in cabinet meetings.

In the last half-century official records have come to comprise still another category of material. Both the administrative agencies and the legislative arms of government have come to depend upon fact-finding inquiries to pursue their work. The result has been a large number of investigations into every branch of life with which the government is concerned. These investigations have as their prime objective the accumulation of data upon the basis of which action may be taken. Such data have also a substantial historical value. Yet the very purposes for which these inquiries are undertaken may distort their factual findings as well as their conclusions. Being closely related to specific political proposals, these investigations often suffer from the bias of the investigators as well as from inaccuracies of technique and from faults of procedure. These studies must therefore be also used with caution; but so used, they contain exceedingly valuable information.

Public documents are generally arranged for the convenience of the officials who use them. Historians may usually find their way to them through a knowledge of the general administrative organization of the government. But there is a special category of documents that enter regularly into the work of lawyers and which are arranged primarily for ease of citation in legal arguments. These materials have a distinctive form of their own. They may be divided into four general categories: laws, reports of cases, legal dictionaries, and periodicals. Laws are found in the annual reports of the legislatures which enact them or in the periodic revisions and codifications. Cases are reported for all modern courts and those reports are often revised, edited, and abstracted topically. Dictionaries and abridgments arrange both statute and case law by subjects. And legal periodicals provide guides to current legislation and decisions as well as comments upon them. A useful handbook to such sources is F. C. Hicks, *Materials and Methods of Legal Research* (3 ed., Rochester, 1942).

See also, in general: E. S. Brown, *Manual of Government Publications;* J. B. Childs, *Government Document Bibliography;* A. F. Kuhlman, ed., *Public Documents. Their Selection, Distribution, Cataloguing, Reproduction and Preservation* (Chi., 1935); J. K. Wilcox, "New Guides and Aids to Public Documents Use, 1945–1948," *Special Libraries,* XL (1949), 409; and §§ 41–43.

45. FEDERAL PUBLIC RECORDS

Until 1934 each federal department was the custodian of its own records. In that year Congress created the National Archives and charged it with the responsibility for accumulating, appraising, destroying or preserving, and storing all archives or records belonging to the government of the United States. No affirmative requirement for record-keeping existed in the federal government, however, until President Truman's Executive Order 9784 of September 25, 1946. The statutory basis for the administration of these records was finally established in the Federal Records Act of 1950. By that year the Archives had gathered some 875,000 cubic feet of material, including documents, phonograph records, maps, photographs, and motion picture films. With relatively minor restrictions, these are available for the use of scholars.

The material in the Archives may be traced in a general way in the guides listed above (§ 26). But the most profitable exploitation of these federal records depends upon the use of the preliminary check lists and finding aids prepared for each record group and kept up to date in the Archives reading rooms.

The Archives makes its materials available in its reading rooms; but it is also ready to supply microfilm or photostat copies of particular documents and series to scholars. It has published a *List of File Microcopies in the National Archives* (Wash., 1950) through which sources on 3,500 rolls of microfilm may be located. Positive prints of those rolls are available for sale.

The Archives houses the records of the central federal agencies. Large stores of material remain dispersed, however, in local depositories. These include the records of courts, customhouses, hospitals, and every other type of federal institution. The Division of Professional and Service Projects of the W.P.A. prepared a valuable *Inventory of Federal Archives in the States*, of which well over 150 volumes have appeared in multigraphed form. The inventory consists of seventeen series, series I being a general description of the project and the succeeding series dealing with each of the departments and agencies of the government. Within each series individual volumes treat each state. These volumes are all listed in the Child and Holmes *Bibliography* cited above, § 26. The depositories of guides still in manuscript may be traced through lists available in the National Archives and the Library of Congress.

The fund of documents in print matches that in manuscript. By the Constitution each of the houses of Congress was charged with keeping a journal and making a record of receipts and expenditures. For a long time the congressional documents were the most important single medium through which federal documents were issued. But each of the executive departments and the judiciary quickly evolved publication series of their own. Today an enormous mass of material emanates from the Government Printing Office. No single complete list of these materials exists, the most comprehensive, Hartwell's *Checklist* (§ 41), extending only to 1909.

T. C. Merritt, *United States Government as a Publisher* (Chicago, 1943), discusses the problem in general; and a number of useful indexes and catalogues (§ 41) assist the student attempting to locate particular publications. The Government has been liberal in making these documents available in depositories in every state. A list of such depositories will be found in *Annual Report of the Public Printer, 1947*, 213; and also in the guides of Schmeckebier (p. 439), and Boyd and Rips (p. 29).

The list which follows includes only the most important and the most frequently cited collections of documents. It starts with a section for the period up to 1789 when the records were not yet differentiated by departments. The sections that follow are organized according to the branches of the Government within which the documents originate.

RECORDS OF THE FEDERAL GOVERNMENT BEFORE 1789

Peter Force, ed., *American Archives . . . a Documentary History of . . . the North American Colonies.* 4 ser. 6 vols. (March 7, 1774 to Aug. 21, 1776); 5 ser. 3 vols. (May 3, 1776 to December 31, 1776). Wash., 1837–53. No more published.

W. C. Ford, *et al.*, eds., *Journals of the Continental Congress, 1774–1789.* 34 vols. Wash., 1904–37.

Francis Wharton, ed., *Revolutionary Diplomatic Correspondence.* 6 vols. Wash., 1889.
Department of State, Bureau of Rolls and Library, *Documentary History of the Constitution of the United States.* 5 vols. Wash., 1894–1905.
Jonathan Elliot, ed., *Debates in the Several State Conventions on the Adoption of the Federal Constitution, . . . Together with the Journal of the Federal Convention [and Other Papers].* 2 ed. 5 vols. Phila., 1861.
Max Farrand, ed., *Records of the Federal Convention of 1787.* 4 vols. New Haven, 1911–37.
C. C. Tansill, ed., *Documents Illustrative of the Formation of the Union of the American States* (69 Cong., 1 Sess., H. Doc., No. 398).
The Constitution of the United States of America (Annotated) Annotations of Cases Decided by the Supreme Court of the United States to January 1, 1938. (74 Cong., 2 Sess., Sen. Doc., No. 232).

FEDERAL STATUTES

The Congress has produced two types of documents: the laws which are the products of its deliberations, and the records of the proceedings by which it arrives at decisions. Federal statutes are well arranged and helpfully indexed.

Statutes at Large. Issued at the close of each session of Congress or for each calendar year.
Statutes at Large of the United States of America, 1789–1873. 17 vols. Boston, 1850–73. [Little, Brown edition]
United States Statutes at Large Containing the Laws and Concurrent Resolutions Enacted during the . . . Session of the . . . Congress . . . , and Proclamations, Treaties, and International Agreements other than Treaties. 43 Congress–date. Vol. XVIII–date. Wash., 1874– . [State Department edition.]
Revised Statutes of the United States . . . Embracing the Statutes . . . General and Permanent in Their Nature, in Force on December 1st, 1873. 2 ed. Wash., 1878.
Supplement to the Revised Statutes of the United States, Embracing the Statutes, General and Permanent in Their Nature, Passed after the Revised Statutes. 2 ed., 2 vols. Wash., 1900–01.
United States Code 1946 Edition Containing the General and Permanent Laws of the United States in Force on January 2, 1947. 5 vols. Wash., 1948. Four supplements have been published 1947–51.

Indexes to federal laws may be found in the volumes of Beaman and Mc-Namara and of McClenon and Gilbert (§ 41), as well as in the older *Synoptical Index to Laws and Treaties of the United States, March 7, 1789–March 3, 1851* (Boston, 1852).

CONGRESSIONAL DOCUMENTS

The remaining congressional documents may be divided into three categories: the journals give an account of the actions of each house; the *Annals* and its successors supply a record of debates; and the various series of reports and documents contain materials supplied to Congress by its own committees and by the executive officers of government. A more detailed account of the contents of these documents may be found in Boyd and Rips, *Government Publications*, 52.

The debates of Congress prior to 1874 were printed by private publishing houses. There was no systematic contemporaneous reporting of the debates of the first seventeen Congresses or of the first session of the eighteenth; but the *Annals* provide a kind of record, "compiled from authentic materials," of Congressional debates from 1789 to 1824. From 1824 to 1837 the debates were reported and published as *Register of Debates in Congress*. The next series, the *Congressional Globe*, began in 1833; until the end of the first session of the twenty-fifth Congress, both the *Register* and the *Globe* reported the proceedings. From 1837 to 1873 the *Globe* provides the only continuous report. The *Congressional Record* was thereafter published by the government. Speeches delivered in Congress are often edited and rewritten before incorporation in the *Record*; and sometimes speeches are printed there which were never delivered on the floor. In certain cases, thus, newspapers furnish a more exact version of the actual proceedings than does the *Record*.

Journal of the House of Representatives of the United States. Annual volumes since 1789. Phila. and Wash.
Journal of the Senate of the United States. Annual volumes since 1789. Phila. and Wash.
Journal of the Executive Proceedings of the Senate of the United States, 1789–1905. 90 vols. Wash., 1828–48. — Contains nominations to office and treaties omitted from the public journals.

o   o   o

[Annals of Congress.] *Debates and Proceedings in the Congress of the United States, 1789–1824.* 42 vols. Wash., 1834–56.
[Congressional Debates.] *Register of Debates in Congress, 1825–1837.* 29 vols. Wash., 1825–37.
Congressional Globe, Containing the Debates and Proceedings, 1833–73. 109 vols. Wash., 1834–73.
Congressional Record, Containing the Proceedings and Debates, 1873–   . Wash., 1873–   .

o   o   o

American State Papers: Documents, Legislative and Executive. 38 vols. Wash., 1832–1861. Covers the first through the twenty-fifth Congresses, 1789–1838.
Senate Documents, 1817–1849.
State Papers, 1817–1830. Made up of House documents.
Executive Documents, 1830–47. Made up largely of House documents.
Senate Executive Documents, 1847–95.
Senate Miscellaneous Documents, 1847–76.
Senate Reports, 1847–   .
House Executive Documents, 1847–95.
House Miscellaneous Documents, 1847–76.
House Reports, 1819–   .
Senate Documents, 1876–   .
House Documents, 1876–   .

REPORTS OF JUDICIAL DECISIONS

The most important judicial documents are the decisions of the various courts. The verdicts of the Supreme Court were reported almost at once. Until 1874 these were issued under the name of the official court reporter. Thereafter they bore the title *United States Reports*, and are usually cited that way.

A. J. Dallas, *Reports of Cases in the Courts of the United States, and Pennsylvania, 1790–1800.* 3 vols. — Numerous editions.
William Cranch, *Reports of Cases Argued and Adjudged in the Supreme Court of the United States, 1801–1815.* 9 vols. Wash., 1804–17.
Henry Wheaton, *Reports of Cases Argued and Adjudged in the Supreme Court, 1816–1827.* 12 vols. Phila., 1816–27.
Richard Peters, Jr., *Reports of Cases Argued and Adjudged in the Supreme Court, 1828–1842.* 17 vols. Phila., 1828–43.

B. C. Howard, *Reports of Cases Argued and Adjudged in the Supreme Court, 1843–1861.* 24 vols. Phila., 1843–61.

J. S. Black, *Reports of Cases Argued and Determined in the Supreme Court, 1861–1862.* 2 vols. Wash., [1862–63].

J. W. Wallace, *Cases Argued and Adjudged in the Supreme Court, 1863–1874.* 23 vols. Wash., 1864–76.

United States Reports, Supreme Court, 1875– . W. T. Otto, J. C. B. Davis, C. H. Butler, Ernest Knaebel, and Walter Wyatt, reporters. 251 vols. Boston, N.Y., and Wash., 1876– . These volumes are numbered 91–341, continuously with the earlier series.

These reports have often been digested and abridged. The best such compilation, *United States Supreme Court Digest 1754–* (16 vols., St. Paul, 1944–45), is kept current by cumulative supplements.

The decisions of the lower (circuit and district) courts may be found in the following sources:

Federal Cases, 1789–1879. 31 vols.
Federal Reporter, 1880–1924. 300 vols.
Federal Reporter, 1924– . 2 ser. 122 vols.
Federal Supplement, 1932– . 40 vols.
Court of Claims Reports, 1863– . 117 vols.

On occasion the historian may wish to consult the other documents in a particular case. These are preserved in the libraries and in the clerks' offices of the various courts. However, in recent years, appeal papers have generally been printed and deposited also in the Library of Congress.

GENERAL EXECUTIVE DOCUMENTS

Documents emanating from the executive departments have grown steadily in bulk and in importance. Below are listed the more significant series.

Code of Federal Regulations of the United States of America Having General Applicability and Legal Effect in Force June 1, 1938. 17 vols. Wash., 1939. — Supplemented by *Federal Register* (daily, except Sun. and Mon.), Mar. 14, 1936– ; and also by annual and quinquennial supplements.

J. D. Richardson, ed., *Compilation of the Messages and Papers of the Presidents, 1789–1897.* 10 vols. (53 Cong., 2 Sess., *H. Misc. Doc.*, No. 210, pts. 1–10). Wash., 1907. — See also: by individual presidents, § 55; and also § 57.

Presidential Executive Orders. Compiled by the W. P. A. Historical Records Survey. 2 vols. N.Y., [1944].

In addition, each executive department and agency issues a large number of annual reports, technical manuals, and periodical bulletins. These may be located through the various guides and indexes (§ 41).

FEDERAL RECORDS RELATING TO FOREIGN AFFAIRS

G. H. Hackworth, ed., *Digest of International Law.* 8 vols. Wash., 1940–44. Covers the period since 1906.

M. O. Hudson, ed., *International Legislation, a Collection of the Texts of Multipartite International Instruments of General Interest.* 4 vols. Wash., 1931. Deals particularly with the period, 1919–29.

W. M. Malloy, C. F. Redmond, and E. J. Treworth, eds., *Treaties, Conventions, International Acts, Protocols, and Agreements between the United States and Other Powers. 1776–1937.* 4 vols. Wash., 1910–38.

W. R. Manning, ed., *Diplomatic Correspondence of the United States. Canadian Relations 1784–1860.* 4 vols. Wash., 1940–45.

W. R. Manning, ed., *Diplomatic Correspondence of the United States Concerning the Independence of the Latin-American Nations.* 3 vols., N.Y., 1925.

W. R. Manning, ed., *Diplomatic Correspondence of the United States Inter-American Affairs 1831–1860.* 12 vols., Wash., 1932–39.

H. R. Marraro, ed., *Diplomatic Relations between the United States and the Kingdom of the Two Sicilies.* 2 vols., N.Y., 1951–52.

Hunter Miller, ed., *Treaties and Other International Acts of the United States of America, 1776–1863.* 8 vols., Wash., 1931–48.

J. B. Moore, ed., *Digest of International Law, as Embodied in Diplomatic Discussions, Treaties, and Other International Agreements, International Awards, the Decisions of Municipal Courts, and the Writings of Jurists, and Especially in Documents, Published and Unpublished, Issued by Presidents and Secretaries of State of the United States, the Opinions of the Attorneys General, and the Decisions of Courts, Federal, and State.* 8 vols., Wash., 1906.

J. B. Moore, ed., *History and Digest of the International Arbitrations to Which the United States Has Been a Party.* 6 vols., Wash., 1898.

J. B. Moore, ed., *International Adjudications, Ancient and Modern: History and Documents.* 8 vols., N.Y., 1929–36.

J. B. Scott, ed., *Diplomatic Correspondence between the United States and Germany August 1, 1914–April 6, 1917.* N.Y., 1918.

J. B. Scott, ed., *Treaties for the Advancement of Peace between the United States and Other Powers Negotiated by the Honorable William J. Bryan, Secretary of State of the United States.* N.Y., 1920.

L. F. Stock, *Consular Relations between the United States and the Papal States.* Wash., 1945.

L. F. Stock, *United States Ministers to the Papal States . . . 1848–1868.* Wash., 1933.

The above compilations contain diplomatic material systematically arranged. The documents published directly by the Department of State include the following series, all published in Washington, in the year mentioned:

Papers Relating to the Foreign Relations of the United States, 1861– . — In 1952 the series had reached the volumes for 1935. Supplements include the Lansing Papers, 1914–20 (2 vols.), diplomatic correspondence relating to the World War, 1914–18 (9 vols.), relations with Russia, 1918–19 (4 vols.), relations with Japan, 1931–41 (2 vols.), the Paris Peace Conference, 1919 (13 vols.), and the Soviet Union, 1933–39. There are indexes for the series, 1861–99 (Wash., 1902) and 1900–18 (Wash., 1941).

Arbitration Series, 1929– .

Commercial Policy Series, 1934– .

Conference Series, 1929–47. 105 nos. Wash., 1929–47.

Department and Foreign Service Series, 1948– .

Economic Cooperation Series, 1948– .

European and British Commonwealth Series, 1948– .

European Series, 1930–47. 29 nos. Wash., 1930–47.

Executive Agreement Series, 1929–46. 506 nos. Wash., 1929–46.

Far Eastern Series, 1932– .

General Foreign Policy Series, 1948– .

Immigration Series, 1936– .

Inter-American Series, 1929– .

International Information and Cultural Series, 1948– .

International Organization and Conference Series, 1948– .

Latin American Series, 1929–37. 15 nos. Wash., 1929–37.

Map Series, 1932– .

Near Eastern Series, 1931– .

Passport Series, 1929– .

Russian Series, 1919. Wash., 1919.

Treaties and Other International Acts Series, 1946– .
Treaty Series, 1908–46. 505 nos. Wash., 1908–46. — There is an index for the series to
    July 1, 1931 (Wash., 1932).
List of Treaties Submitted to the Senate, 1789–1934. Wash., 1935.
United States Relations with China . . . 1944–1949. [Wash., 1949].

MISCELLANEOUS COLLECTIONS

C. E. Carter, ed., *The Territorial Papers of the United States.* 18 vols. Wash., 1934–52.
Journal of the Congress of the Confederate States of America. 3 vols. Wash., 1904–05.
C. J. Kappler, ed., *Indian Affairs: Laws and Treaties.* 2 vols. Wash., 1904.
Library of Congress. *Naval Records of the American Revolution 1775–1788.* Wash.,
    1906. A calendar.
Naval Records and Library Office. *Naval Documents Related to Quasi-War Between the
    United States and France. 1797–1801.* 7 vols. Wash., 1935–38.
Naval Records and Library Office. *Naval Documents Related to the United States Wars
    with the Barbary Powers. 1785–1807.* 7 vols. Wash., 1939–44.
Richard Rush, *et al.,* eds., *Official Records of the Union and Confederate Navies in the
    War of the Rebellion.* 30 vols. Wash., 1894–1914. — Published by Naval War
    Records Office.
E. F. Hall, *et al.,* eds., *Official Opinions of the Attorneys-General of the United States.
    1791–1948.* 40 vols. Wash., 1852–1949.
R. N. Scott, *et al.,* eds., *War of the Rebellion: a Compilation of the Official Records of
    the Union and Confederate Armies.* 130 vols. Wash., 1880–1901.

46. COLONIAL, STATE, AND LOCAL PUBLIC RECORDS

State and local records parallel those of the federal government. Since these
jurisdictions were, for long periods, concerned with more phases of life than the
national government, their functioning produced a large body of records which
can reveal significant information to the historian.

Down to the Revolution the records of the colonies were divided among the
colonial capitals, the local county seats, and the center of imperial government
in London. By and large, the documents have remained where they were
originally lodged, although many of the records in English depositories have
been transcribed or printed and are available in the United States.

After the Revolution each state government, in its own fashion, accumulated
its own fund of documents. Most were slow, however, to take adequate precautions to preserve such materials. By the Civil War the increase in interest in
historical studies led to the formation of central archival establishments in some
of the states. But throughout the nineteenth century all such efforts were hap-
hazard. Many records did not survive the occasional transfer of the capital from
city to city; others were victims of fire; and still others fell into private hands
or into the possession of libraries or historical societies. Only in the last fifty
years have state administrators seen the wisdom of housing these documents
properly and of making them readily available to scholars.

There is still no central guide to American state and local archives, although
there are descriptions of particular collections. The contents of the state archives
must be traced through the reports of various state commissions, archivists, state
historians, state societies, and periodicals such as *Am. Archivist* (1938–). The
more important guides are cited, by states, in § 26. See also: L. J. Cappon,
"Directory of State Archival Agencies," *ibid.,* X (1947), 269; E. A. Davis,

"Archival Development in the Lower Mississippi Valley," *ibid.*, III (1940), 42;
"Public Archives Commission," Am. Hist. Assoc., *Report*, 1900, II; A. R. Hasse,
"Materials for a Bibliography of the Public Archives of the Thirteen Original
States," *ibid.*, 1906, II, 239.

Some of the states early began to publish their official documents. As the
nineteenth century reached its mid-point these publications became ever larger
in quantity. Almost all the legislatures and executive departments of each of the
states put forth in growing abundance bulletins and reports in a manner comparable to their federal counterparts. Unlike the federal government moreover,
the states were also given to frequent review of their organic constitutions at
conventions. The records of the debates and proceedings at these meetings are
important sources of political and intellectual history. A number of helpful guides
provide an over-all view of the character of these materials (§§ 42, 43).

But there is enormous variation among the states in the character and quality
of their publications; and few have held to any consistent program. Their documents fall into several general categories. Many have published the journals of
their legislatures. Records of legislative debates are, however, less usual; for
many periods and places the historian must consult the newspapers to know what
happened in the legislatures. A more consistent record of printing has been
maintained with regard to the statutes. Most states publish the laws enacted at
each session and prepare, as well, occasional compilations or codes. With the
exception of Arizona, Delaware, Georgia, Idaho, and Oklahoma each state has
also issued series of executive and administrative documents that parallel the
Congressional documents. Most of the states provide for publication of the
decisions of their highest court of appeals. (See: Hicks, *Materials*, ch. viii.)
Finally, most of the states have put forth a good deal of material on their constitutional conventions. All these may be traced through Bowker's guide for the
years up to 1908 and through the monthly checklist of state publications issued
by the Library of Congress since 1909 (§ 42).

The most important general collection of early state records is that prepared
by the Library of Congress and the University of North Carolina. This collection
preserves on microfilm the equivalent of two and a half million pages of early
colonial and state records. The 160,000 feet of film are available to scholars, and
particular reels may be purchased from the Photoduplication Division of the
Library of Congress. The project has drawn together the surviving records of
legislative proceedings, statutes, constitutional data, and administrative documents, together with some local and judicial material. The terminal date is not
the same for every state or for every class of materials. L. A. Hamrick has
published *A Guide to the Microfilm Collection of Early State Records* (Wash.,
1950; supplemented by W. S. Jenkins, Wash., 1951). In addition, a few large
works, like Carter's *Territorial Papers*, cover several states. The most important
of these is F. N. Thorpe, *Federal and State Constitutions, Colonial Charters, and
Other Organic Laws* (7 vols., Wash., 1909). For the more recent period the
Council of State Governments, a joint agency, has been publishing *The Book of
the States* (Chi., 1935–), a helpful biennial compilation of official material
relevant to state problems.

County records are varied and dispersed. Many are still disorganized and
unsystematized. The Historical Records Survey made a valiant effort to give

some order to these collections through an inventory of the archives. By August 1, 1940, inventories for some three hundred counties had appeared, about one-tenth of the total number of counties in the United States. Other inventories, in various stages of preparation, were left on file in local offices. These supply a brief history of the county and essays on its government and records; they describe facilities for using the archives and give chronological and subject entries on the collections.

The historian will find it somewhat easier to manage the official publications of counties. Hodgson's guide (§. 43) is a helpful tool in using these sources.

By contrast, there are few guides to the records and publications of American municipalities, each of which has abundant documentary materials in print and in manuscript. These constitute a largely untapped source of information. The only useful checklist is that of Manvel, § 43.

In addition to the records published by colonial, state, and local authorities in the course of their regular administrative operations, there have been sporadic efforts, private and governmental, to put into print earlier series of documents. Sponsored by states, towns, and historical societies, these ventures have made useful bodies of material widely available. Such operations vary widely in extent from place to place; but almost everywhere, they have been confined to the period up to 1820. In some cases such publications appear in separate series, but often they will be found in the collections of the state historical societies (§§ 4, 50). A good deal of source material is also often found in state and local histories (§ 62).

The following list enters, by states, the most important published series of colonial, state, and local records. In each case, the state publications precede the local publications. No reference is made to laws which may readily be traced through indexes, except where the particular edition cited has historic value; and there are only general references to collected public documents and to the proceedings of constitutional conventions, for which good checklists exist. Under each state, the years in which constitutional conventions were held are given, as well as the years of the earliest legislative journals. These records may then be traced through the checklists cited in § 42.

Alabama

There are journals of the General Assembly as a territory and as a state (1818–   ) as well as accounts of the constitutional conventions of 1819, 1861, 1865, 1867, 1875, and 1901.

Alaska

The journals of both houses of the territorial legislature and the governors' reports are the most important published sources.

Arizona

There are legislative journals (1864–   ) and minutes of the constitutional conventions of 1860, 1891, 1893, and 1910.

Arkansas

Legislative journals begin in 1818; and there were conventions in 1836, 1861, 1864, 1868, 1874, and 1918.

California

Legislative journals go back to 1849; and there were conventions in 1849 and 1878. See also: Coy, *Guide to the County Archives* (§ 26); and J. F. Davis, ed., *An Index to the Laws of the State, 1850–1907* (Sacramento, 1911). San Francisco and Los Angeles published municipal document series.

Colorado

The legislative journals go back to 1861; and there is material on the convention of 1875.

Connecticut

The legislative journals go back to 1708; and there are publications on the convention of 1818 and 1902. In addition the following series of public records have been published:

Acts and Laws of His Majesty's Colony of Connecticut in New England. New London, editions of 1715 and 1769, with supplements to 1779.

Acts and Laws of the State of Connecticut, in America. New London, 1784, with supplements to 1794.

The General Laws and Liberties of Connecticut Colonie. Cambridge, 1673. — Reprinted, Hartford, 1865.

C. J. Hoadly, ed., *New Haven Colonial Records [1638–1665].* 2 vols. Hartford, 1857–58.

C. J. Hoadly and L. W. Labaree, eds., *Public Records of the State of Connecticut (1776–1796).* 8 vols. Hartford, 1894–1951.

J. H. Trumbull and C. J. Hoadly, eds., *Public Records of the Colony of Connecticut (1636–1776).* 15 vols. Hartford, 1850–90.

There are good files of the current publications of Connecticut municipalities including journals of various common councils and municipal registers of New Haven, Hartford, and other towns. In addition the following series of older records have been published:

F. B. Dexter, ed., *Ancient Town Records, New Haven Town Records, 1649–1684.* 2 vols. New Haven, 1917–19.

J. T. Farrell, ed., *The Superior Court Diary of William Samuel Johnston, 1772–1773.* Wash., 1942.

N. O. Phillips, ed., *Town Records of Derby, Connecticut, 1655–1710.* Derby, 1901.

Delaware

There are legislative journals as far back as 1739; and records of conventions of 1776, 1791, 1831, 1852, and 1896. The reports of state officers include those of the state auditor. In addition the following older records have been published:

Delaware Archives. 5 vols. Wilmington, 1911.

Amandus Johnson, ed., *The Instruction of Johan Printz for Governor of New Sweden.* Phila., 1930.

"Minutes of the Council of the Delaware State, from 1776 to 1792," Delaware Hist. Soc., *Papers,* VI (1887).

H. C. Reed, *et al.,* eds., *Minutes of House of Representatives of the Government of the Counties of New Castle, Kent and Sussex upon Delaware (1765–70).* Dover, 1931.

Records of the Court of New Castle on Delaware, 1676–1681. Lancaster, 1904.

District of Columbia

The public records of the District of Columbia are found in the Congressional Documents (§ 45) and in the published annual reports of the commissioners for the district.

Florida

The legislative materials were not published before 1831. The journals for earlier years must be sought in newspapers. There are printed records for the conventions of 1838, 1861, 1865, 1868, and 1885; also printed series of records for the State Comptroller, Attorney General, Secretary of State, and for the State Treasurer; the *Minutes* of the Board of Trustees of the Internal Improvement Fund are published also. The publications of the Florida State Historical Society (§ 50) contain some material of use, as do the following collections:

J. T. Connor, ed., *Colonial Records of Spanish Florida, 1570–1580.* 2 vols. Deland, 1925–30.

Manuel Serrano y Sanz, ed., *Documentos historicos de la Florida y la Luisiana.* Madrid, 1912.

Georgia

The first legislative journals are in 1769. There are records of the conventions of 1788, 1789, 1798, 1833, 1839, 1850, 1861, 1865, 1867–8, 1877; also reports by the Comptroller General and by the various municipalities. Collections of documents include:

A. D. Candler, ed., *Colonial Records of the State of Georgia (1732–1782).* 26 vols. Atlanta, 1904–16.

A. D. Candler, ed., *Confederate Records of Georgia (1860–1868).* 6 vols. Atlanta, 1909– .

A. D. Candler, ed., *Revolutionary Records of Georgia (1769–84).* 3 vols. Atlanta, 1908.

G. G. Davidson, ed., *Early Records of Georgia, Wilkes County.* 2 vols. Macon, 1932.

C. C. Jones, ed., *Acts Passed by the General Assembly of the Colony of Georgia, 1755 to 1774.* Wormsloe, 1881.

John Perceval, First Earl of Egmont, *Journal of the Transactions of the Trustees for Establishing the Colony of Georgia in America.* [Wormsloe], 1886. — Also in Candler, *Colonial Records,* V.   [See also p. 544.]

Hawaii

There are records of the territorial legislature and of the governor.

Idaho

Legislative records begin in 1863; the constitutional convention was in 1866; and the reports of the Secretary of State are useful.

Illinois

Current records include the journals of Senate and House, an annual bluebook, the reports of Directors of Departments (1918 ff.), the governors' messages, and the reports of the Public Utilities Commission, and the Public Welfare Department. Legislative journals go back to 1812 and there are reports of the conventions of 1818, 1847, 1862, and 1867. Carter's *Territorial Papers* contains earlier records, as does F. S. Philbrick, ed., *Laws of Illinois Territory, 1809–1818* (1950).

Among the local materials are the proceedings of the Cook County Commissioners, of the Chicago Council, and the reports of the Chicago Sanitary District. Various cities have also published municipal codes.

Indiana

The legislative journals begin in 1805 and there are materials on the constitutional conventions of 1816 and 1850. Current reports include those of the Attorney General, the Auditor, the Bureau of Statistics (1879–1916), and *The Indiana Yearbook* (1917–50); in addition there are documentary journals (1835–1912). Carter's *Territorial Papers* includes information on the earlier period, as does Gayle Thornbrough and Dorothy Riker, *Journals of the General Assembly of Indiana Territory, 1805–1815* (Indianapolis, 1950); and F. S. Philbrick, *Laws of Indiana Territory* (1930).   [See also p. 544.]

Iowa

Legislative journals begin in 1838 and have documentary series appended. The state publishes an official register as well as the messages of the Governors. There is material on the constitutional conventions in 1844, 1846, and 1857. There are annual reports on agriculture, the Auditor's Department, labor, and the State Planning Board. State censuses appeared in 1885, 1895, and 1905. See also:

B. F. Shambaugh, ed., *Documentary Material Relating to the History of Iowa.* Iowa City, 1897–1900.

B. F. Shambaugh, ed., *Executive Journal of Iowa, 1838–1841, Governor Robert Lucas.* Iowa City, 1906.

B. F. Shambaugh, ed., *Messages and Proclamations of the Governors of Iowa.* 7 vols. (1836–1901). Iowa City, 1903–05.

Kansas

In addition to the legislative journals, which begin in 1855, there are series of public documents and reports on agriculture, the bank commission, and by the labor bureau and public officials. The Official Roster of Kansas was issued, 1854–1925; Secretary of State issues directory currently. There is material on the constitutional conventions of 1855, 1857, 1858, and 1859.

Kentucky

Legislative journals begin in 1792. There is material on the conventions of 1793, 1799, 1849, 1861, and 1890. In addition to the documents, the auditors' reports are helpful.

Louisiana

Legislative journals go back to 1806 (for the territory of Orleans to 1804). There is material on the conventions of 1812, 1844, 1852, 1861, 1864, 1867, 1879, 1893, and 1913. The governors' messages are published in series. The following collections and documents are also helpful:

Civil Code of the State of Louisiana. [New Orleans], 1825.

D. A. O'Reilly, *Ordonnances* (1769). — In French, in Appendix to C. E. A. Gayarré, *Histoire de la Louisiane* (2 vols., New Orleans, 1846); in English, in B. F. French, *Historical Collections of Louisiana* (N.Y., 1846–53), V, 254–88, and in *American State Papers*, folio edition, *Miscellaneous*, I, 363. O'Reilly's *Regulations* of 1770 in regard to land grants are also printed in English in the two sources last named, and in *American State Papers, Public Lands*, V, 729.

[Buckingham Smith, ed.], *Coleccion de varios documentos para la historia de la Florida y tierras adyacentes.* London, [1857].

J. M. White, ed., *A New Collection of Laws, Charters . . . of Great Britain, France and Spain Relating to the Concessions of Lands.* 2 vols. Phila., 1839.

See also: Florida.

Maine

Legislative journals begin in 1820. Conventions were held in 1816, 1819, and 1875. The state publishes helpful series, the *Legislative Record*, public documents, *Maine Register, Agriculture of Maine*, industrial and labor statistics, (1887–   ). The following collections also are useful:

Province and Court Records of Maine. 3 vols. Portland, 1928–47. — From 1636 to 1692. *York Deeds* (1642–1726). 11 vols. Portland, 1887–96.

William Willis, *et al.*, eds., *Documentary History of the State of Maine.* Me. Hist. Soc., *Coll.*, 2 ser. 24 vols. Portland, 1869–1916.

Maryland

The legislative journals go back to 1722. Conventions were held in 1776, 1850, 1864, and 1867. The state published legislative documents until 1921, a manual, reports of the Bureau of Statistics and Information (1884–1915). Baltimore municipal reports are extensive and include a municipal journal until 1932.

In addition the following collections and documents are helpful:

Acts of Assembly Passed in the Province of Maryland from 1692 to 1715. London, 1723.
Archives of Maryland. W. H. Browne, *et al.*, eds., 65 vols. Baltimore, 1883–1952.
Elizabeth Hartsook and Gust Skordas, *Land Office and Prerogative Court Records of Colonial Maryland.* [Annapolis, 1946].
William Kilty, ed., *Laws of Maryland, (1692–1799).* 2 vols. Annapolis, 1799–1800.
Virgil Maxcy, ed., *Laws of Maryland, With the Charter, the Bill of Rights, etc. (1704–1809).* 3 vols. Baltimore, 1811.

Massachusetts

Legislative journals go back to 1689. There is material on the constitutional conventions in 1778, 1779, 1820, 1853, and 1917. The state publishes currently a manual for the General Court, a legislative and an executive document series, its acts and resolves, the Governor's addresses, and reports on banks, state charities, education, insurance, labor (1870–   ), health (1870–   ), and railroads (1832–   ). There were state censuses every ten years between 1855 and 1915.

Boston has its own series of city-council minutes, a city record (1909–   ), city documents (1842–   ), published tax lists, and school-committee reports (1857–   ), as well as old municipal records.

The important collections of documents include:

Acts and Laws of the Commonwealth of Massachusetts (1780–1797). Boston, 1781–96. — Reprinted, 9 vols. Boston, 1890–96; Supplement (1780–1784), ed. by E. M. Bacon, 1896.

Acts and Resolves, Public and Private, of the Province of the Massachusetts Bay. (1692–1786). 21 vols. Boston, 1869–1922.

Book of the General Lawes and Libertyes Concerning the Inhabitants of the Massachusets. Cambridge, 1660. — Reprinted in facsimile, with supplements to 1672, in W. H. Whitmore, *Colonial Laws of Massachusetts*. Boston, 1889.

Alden Bradford, ed., *Speeches of the Governors of Massachusetts from 1765 to 1775; and the Answers of the House of Representatives, with Their Resolutions*. Boston, 1818.

The General Laws and Liberties of the Massachusetts Colony: Revised and Reprinted. By Order of the General Court Holden at Boston, May 15th, 1672. Edward Rawson, Secr. Cambridge, 1672. — Reprinted in facsimile, with supplements through 1686, in Whitmore, *Colonial Laws of Massachusetts*.

Thomas Hutchinson, ed., *Collection of Original Papers Relative to the History of the Colony of Massachusetts-Bay*. Boston, 1769. — Reprinted, 2 vols., Albany, 1865.

Journals of the House of Representatives of Massachusetts, 1715–1749. 25 vols. Boston, 1919–50.

William Lincoln, *Journals of Each Provincial Congress of Massachusetts in 1774 and 1775 . . . and Other Documents*. Boston, 1838.

Records of the Court of Assistants of the Colony of Massachusetts Bay, 1630–1692. 3 vols. Boston, 1901–28.

N. B. Shurtleff, *et al.*, eds., *Records of the Colony of New Plymouth in New England (1620–1692)*. 12 vols. Boston, 1855–61.

N. B. Shurtleff, ed., *Records of the Governor and Company of the Massachusetts Bay in New England (1628–86)*. 5 vols. Boston, 1853–54.

W. H. Whitmore, ed., *Bibliographical Sketch of the Laws of the Massachusetts Colony from 1630 to 1686*. Boston, 1890.

Local records include:

Abstract and Index of the Records of the Inferiour Court of Pleas (Suffolk County Court). Held at Boston 1680–1698. Boston, 1940.

S. A. Bates, ed., *Records of the Town of Braintree, 1640 to 1793*. Randolph, Mass., 1886.

Catalogue of Records and Files in the Office of the Clerk of the Supreme Judicial Court for the County of Suffolk. Boston, 1890.

W. A. Davis, ed., *The Old Records of the Town of Fitchburgh, Massachusetts*. 8 vols. Fitchburg, 1898–1913.

D. G. Hill, ed., [*Dedham Records, 1635–1845*. 5 vols.]. Dedham, 1886–99.

F. B. Hough, ed., *Papers Relating to the Island of Nantucket*. Albany, 1856.

Muddy River and Brookline Records, 1634–1838. "By the Inhabitants of Brookline in Town Meeting," 1875.

H. S. Nourse, ed., *Early Records of Lancaster, 1643–1725*. Lancaster, 1884. — *Military Annals of Lancaster, 1740–1865*. Lancaster, 1889. — *Supplement* (to both), Lancaster, 1900.

M. F. Peirce, *Town of Weston, Records (1746–1826)*. 2 vols. Boston, 1893–94.

The Probate Records of Essex County, 1635–1681. 3 vols. Salem, 1916–20.

The Proprietors' Records of the Town of Mendon. Boston, 1899.

Records and Files of the Quarterly Courts of Essex County, Massachusetts. 1656–1683. 8 vols. Salem, 1912–21.

"Records of the Suffolk County Court 1671–1680," Colonial Society of Massachusetts, *Coll.*, XXIX, XXX (1933).

Records of the Town of Plymouth (1636–1783). 3 vols. Plymouth, 1889–1903.

The Register Book of the Lands and Houses in the "New Towne" and the Town of Cambridge. Cambridge, 1896.

Reports of the Record Commissioners of the City of Boston. 39 vols. Boston, 1876–1909.
F. P. Rice, ed., *Worcester Town Records* . . . [1722–1848]. 7 vols. Worcester, 1879–95.
Suffolk Deeds. Libri I–XIV (1629–97). Boston, 1880–1906.
W. P. Upham, "Town Records of Salem, 1634–1659," Essex Inst., *Hist. Coll.*, 2 ser., I (1869).
Watertown Historical Society, *Watertown Records (1634–1829).* 8 vols. Watertown, 1894–1939.

Michigan

Legislative journals begin in 1824 and there were constitutional conventions in 1835. 1836, 1850, 1867, 1873, and 1907. Current state publications include the *Michigan Manual*, the journals of the Senate and House, reports of Directors of Departments, and the Governors' messages. Local series include the annual reports and journals of the common councils of municipalities like Detroit.
Among the collections of older documents are:

W. W. Blume, ed., *Transactions of the Supreme Court of the Territory of Michigan, 1805–1836.* 6 vols. Ann Arbor, 1935–40.
G. N. Fuller, *Messages of the Governors of Michigan, 1824–1927.* 4 vols. Lansing, 1925–27.
Transcriptions of the Municipal Archives of Michigan, 1901–1908. 2 vols. Detroit, 1940–41.   [See also p. 544.]

Minnesota

There are records of the constitutional convention of 1857. Current records include the legislative manual, House and Senate Journals, and executive documents. Local records include the proceedings of councils and annual municipal reports of cities like Minneapolis.

Mississippi

There is material on the constitutional conventions of 1817, 1832, 1851, 1861, 1865, 1868, and 1890. Legislative journals go back to 1803; and current publications include the *Mississippi Official and Statistical Register*; and a bluebook. Collections of older documents are:

Dunbar Rowland and A. G. Sanders, eds., *Mississippi Provincial Archives: French Dominion. 1729–1740.* 3 vols. Jackson, 1927–32.
Dunbar Rowland, ed., *Mississippi Provincial Archives: English Dominion. 1763–1766.* Nashville, 1911.
Dunbar Rowland, ed., *Mississippi Territorial Archives, 1798–1803.* Nashville, 1905.

Missouri

The legislative journals begin in 1820 (earlier reports must be sought in newspapers). There is material on the constitutional conventions of 1820, 1845, 1861 (3), 1862, 1863, 1865, and 1875. Current publications include an official manual; reports of departments in appendices to the House and Senate journals; reports of the state auditor. Statistics of labor have been published since 1880, separately until 1907, then in *Resources of Missouri*, and after 1917, in *Missouri Redbook*. Local documents include the St. Louis mayors' messages and accompanying documents. Older collections are:

Louis Houck, ed., *Spanish Regime in Missouri: a Collection of Papers and Documents.* 2 vols. Chi., 1909.
Buel Leopard and F. C. Shoemaker, eds., *Messages and Proclamations of the Governors of the State of Missouri.* 16 vols. Columbia, 1922–51.

Montana

Legislative journals begin in 1864 and there is material on the conventions held in 1866, 1884, and 1889. The most important reports are those on agriculture.

Nebraska

Legislative journals go back to 1855; there is material on the conventions of 1860, 1864, 1866, 1871, 1875, and 1919–20; and current publications include the *Nebraska Blue Book*, as well as public documents and reports on railways, agriculture, and labor and industry. *The Messages and Proclamations of the Governors of Nebraska (1854–1941)* have been collected in 4 volumes ([Lincoln], 1941–42).

Nevada

There is material on the convention held in 1864. Legislative journals go back to 1861 and documents are regularly printed in the appendices of the journals.

New Hampshire

Legislative journals go back to 1744. There are records of the constitutional conventions of 1775, 1778, 1781, 1791, 1850, 1876, 1889, 1902, and 1912. In addition to the usual documents, the state also publishes series of department and county reports. The collections of older documents include:

Nathaniel Bouton, *et al.*, eds., *Documents and Records Relating to the Province [Towns and State] of New Hampshire* (1623–1800). 40 vols. Concord, 1867–1943. — Commonly cited as *New Hampshire Provincial* (or *State*) *Papers*.
Concord Town Records, 1732–1820. Concord, 1894.
F. W. Hackett, ed., *Portsmouth Records, 1645–1656*. Portsmouth, 1886.

[See also p. 544.]

New Jersey

Legislative journals begin in 1710. Materials exist for the conventions of 1776 and 1844. Published series include a legislative *Manual* and documents, and reports on banks, the treasury, local governments, public utilities, and statistics of labor. The more important collections are:

Samuel Allinson, ed., *Acts of the General Assembly of the Province of New Jersey, 1702–1776.* Burlington, 1776.
Calendar of the State Library Manuscript Collection. Newark, 1939.
P. W. Edsall, ed., *Journal of the Courts of Common Right and Chancery of East New Jersey, 1683–1702.* Phila., 1937.
John Hood, ed., *Index . . . of Laws of New Jersey between . . . 1663 and 1903.* Camden, 1905.
Journal and Votes of the House of Representatives of the Province of Nova Cesarea of New Jersey. Jersey City, 1872.
Journal of the Procedure of the Governor and Council of the Province of East New Jersey from and after the First Day of December Anno Domini 1682. Jersey City, 1872.
Aaron Leaming and Jacob Spicer, *Grants, Concessions, and Original Constitutions of the Province of New Jersey (1664–1682).* Phila., [1752]. — Reprinted, Somerville, N.J., 1881.
Minutes of the Board of Proprietors of the Eastern Division of New Jersey from 1685 to 1705. Perth Amboy, 1949.
Minutes of the Council of Safety of the State of New Jersey, 1777–1778. Jersey City, 1872.
Minutes of the Provincial Congress and the Council of Safety of the State of New Jersey, 1774–1776. Trenton, 1879.
William Paterson, ed., *Laws of the State of New Jersey (1703–1798).* New Brunswick, 1800.
H. C. Reed and G. J. Miller, eds., *Burlington Court Book, a Record of Quaker Jurisprudence in West New Jersey, 1680–1709.* Wash., 1944.
George Scot, *Model of the Government of the Province of East New Jersey.* Edinburgh 1685. — Reprinted in W. A. Whitehead, *East Jersey under the Proprietary Governments.* [N.Y.], 1846.
W. A. Whitehead, *et al.*, eds., *Archives of the State of New Jersey. 1631–1800.* 30 vols Newark, etc., 1880–1906.

Peter Wilson, comp., *Acts of the General Assembly of the State of New Jersey (1776-1783)*. Trenton, 1784.

New Mexico

Legislative journals go back to 1851. There are materials on the conventions of 1850, 1889, and 1910. Published series include the governors' reports and a *Blue Book*. See also: R. E. Twitchell, *Spanish Archives of New Mexico*, 2 vols. Cedar Rapids, 1914.

New York

Legislative journals begin in 1695. Materials are available on the conventions of 1776, 1801, 1821, 1846, 1867, 1894, 1915, and 1938; and also on the constitutional commissions of 1872 and 1890.

Important series include the legislative documents, the reports of *ad hoc* commissions on special topics, legislative manuals (1840-), a *Red Book*, governors' messages, reports on banking, charities, insurance, labor statistics, and railroads.

Extensive local series include the proceedings of common councils and municipal documents. New York City's *City Record* (daily) goes back to 1873.

Useful documentary collections are:

Acts of Assembly Passed in the Province of New York from 1691 to 1718. London, 1719.

Colonial Laws of New York from the Year 1664 to the Revolution. 5 vols. Albany, 1894–96.

E. T. Corwin, ed., *Ecclesiastical Records of the State of New York*. 7 vols. Albany, 1901–16.

Hugh Hastings, ed., *Military Minutes of the Council of Appointment of the State of New York, 1783–1821*. 4 vols. Albany, 1901.

Journal of the Legislative Council of the Colony of New York (1691–1775). 2 vols. Albany, 1861.

Journal of the Votes and Proceedings of the General Assembly of the Colony of New York (1691–1765). 2 vols. N.Y., 1746–66.

Journals of the Provincial Congress, Provincial Convention, etc., of the State of New York (1775–1777). 2 vols. Albany, 1842. — The journals are also printed, in part, in O'Callaghan and Fernow, *Documents* (below) v. 15.

Laws of New York from 1691 to 1773. N.Y., 1774.

Laws of the State of New York (1777–1801). 5 vols. Albany, 1886–87.

C. Z. Lincoln, ed., *Messages from the Governors . . . 1863 . . . 1906*. 11 vols. Albany, 1909.

N. Y. State Library, Calendar of Council Minutes 1668–1783. Albany, 1902.

E. B. O'Callaghan, ed., *Documentary History of the State of New York*. 4 vols. Albany, 1849–51.

E. B. O'Callaghan and Berthold Fernow, eds., *Documents Relative to the Colonial History of the State of New York*. 15 vols. Albany, 1856–87. — Vol. XI, General Index; Vol. XV, State Archives.

E. B. O'Callaghan, *Laws and Ordinances of New Netherland, 1638–1674*. Albany, 1868.

V. H. Paltsits, ed., *Minutes of the Executive Council of the Province of New York,* [with] *Collateral and Illustrative Documents. 1668–1673*. 2 vols. Albany, 1910.

Revised Statutes of the State of New York. 3 vols. Albany, 1829.

Second Annual Report of the State Historian of the State of New York. 2 vols. Albany, 1896–97.

W. P. Van Ness and John Woodworth, eds., *Laws of the State of New York (1784–1813)*. 2 vols. Albany, 1813.

Local collections include:

J. W. Case, ed., *Southold (L.I.) Town Records*. 2 vols. Printed by order of the towns of Southold and Riverhead. [1882–84].

Berthold Fernow, ed., *Minutes of the Orphanmasters of New Amsterdam 1655–1663*. N.Y., 1902.

Berthold Fernow, ed., *Records of New Amsterdam (1653–1674)*. 7 vols. N.Y., 1897.

J. C. Frost, ed., *Records of the Town of Jamaica, Long Island, New York*. 3 vols. Brooklyn, 1914.

Minutes of the Common Council of the City of New York 1675–1776. 8 vols. N.Y., 1905.

Minutes of the Common Council of the City of New York, 1784–1831. 21 vols. N.Y., 1917–30.

R. B. Morris, ed., *Select Cases of the Mayor's Court of New York City, 1674–1784.* Wash., 1935.

Joel Munsell, *Annals of Albany (1609–1858).* 10 vols. Albany, 1850–59.

Oyster Bay Town Records, 1653–1763. 6 vols. N.Y., 1916–31.

Jonathan Pearson, *Early Records of the City and County of Albany and Colony of Rensselaerswyck.* 4 vols. Albany, 1916.

Records of the Town of Brookhaven, New York, 1798–1886. 2 vols. N.Y., 1888–93.

Records of the Town of East-Hampton, Long Island. 5 vols. Sag-Harbor, 1887–1905.

Records of the Towns of North and South Hempstead, Long Island, New York. 8 vols. Jamaica, 1896–1904.

C. R. Street, ed., *Huntington Town Records including Babylon, Long Island, New York, 1653–1873.* 3 vols. Huntington, L.I., 1887–89.

Transcriptions of Early Town Records of New York: Minutes of the Town Courts of Newtown, 1656–1734. 3 vols. N.Y., 1940–41.

A. J. F. Van Laer, ed., *Minutes of the Court of Albany, Rensselaerswyck and Schenectady, 1688–1673.* 3 vols. Albany, 1926–32.

A. J. F. Van Laer, ed., *Van Rensselaer Bowier Manuscripts.* Albany, 1908.

[See also p. 544.]

North Carolina

The legislative journals begin in 1749. There are materials on the constitutional conventions of 1835, 1861, 1865, 1868, and 1875, on the Congress of 1776, and on the constitutional commission of 1913. Series include legislative documents and a manual; among the reports are those on labor statistics (1887–   ).

Important publications are:

Walter Clark, ed., *State Records of North Carolina, 1777–1790.* 16 vols. Winston and Goldsboro, 1895–1905.

C. C. Crittenden and Dan Lacy, eds., *The Historical Records of North Carolina. The County Records.* 3 vols. Raleigh, 1938–39.

W. L. Saunders, ed., *Colonial Records of North Carolina (1662–1776).* 10 vols. Raleigh, 1886–90.

S. B. Weeks, ed., *Index to the Colonial and State Records of North Carolina.* 3 vols. Goldsboro, 1909.

North Dakota

Legislative journals of Dakota Territory begin in 1862, of North Dakota in 1889. Materials exist for the convention held in 1889.

Ohio

Legislative journals begin in 1803; there are materials on the conventions of 1802, 1850, 1873, and 1912. Reports include those of the State Board of Agriculture (1845–   ), on labor statistics (1877–   ), and of the commissioner of statistics (1857–   ). The municipalities publish annual reports. Cleveland has a *City Record* (1914–   ), Columbus, a *City Bulletin* (1916–   ), and Toledo, a *City Journal* (1916–   ). See also:

Annals of Cleveland, *Court Record Series. Cuyahoga County. 1837–1877.* 10 vols. Cleveland, 1939.

Oklahoma

Legislative journals begin in 1890 as do collections of Session Laws and Statutes of Oklahoma Territory and Oklahoma State; governors' reports a year later. Materials exist for the convention held 1906–7. Other reports include those of the Departments and Boards, Supreme Court, and Criminal Court. There are materials on Indian constitutions, land allotments, and final rolls.

Oregon

Legislative journals begin in 1841 with the Provisional government; there are materials for the convention of 1857. Annual series include a *Blue Book*, governors' messages and accompanying documents. There are biennial reports by the secretary of state. The mayors of municipalities deliver annual messages and reports.   [See also p. 544.]

Pennsylvania

Legislative journals begin in 1724. There are materials on the conventions of 1776, 1789, 1837, and 1872; and in addition, on the quasi-constitutional conference in 1776 and on the Council of Censors (1783–84).

Annual series include the governors' messages and reports on agriculture (1854–), banking, factories (1890–), public charities (1870–), the state treasury, and internal affairs. A useful compilation of official material may be found in *Smull's Legislative Handbook* (continued as *Pennsylvania State Manual*). An industrial directory has been published since 1913 and a monthly bulletin of the Department of Labor and Industry since 1914. The municipalities put forth journals of their common councils, municipal records, annual reports, and mayors' messages.

Collection of older documents include:

[*Colonial Records of Pennsylvania, 1683–1790.*] 16 vols. Phila., 1852–53. — *General Index*. Phila., 1860.

Staughton George, *et al.*, eds., *Charter to William Penn and Laws of the Province of Pennsylvania Passed between 1682 and 1700 Preceded by Duke of Yorke's Book of Laws (1676–1682)*. Harrisburg, 1879.

Samuel Hazard, *et al.*, eds., *Pennsylvania Archives* (1664–). 9 ser., 138 vols. Phila. and Harrisburg, 1852–1949. — Index by H. E. Eddy. Harrisburg, 1949.

J. T. Mitchell and Henry Flanders, eds., *Statutes at Large of Pennsylvania from 1682 to 1801*. Harrisburg, 1896–1908.

Votes and Proceedings of the House of Representatives of the Province of Pennsylvania (1682–1776). 6 vols. Phila., 1752–76.

Rhode Island

Legislative journals go back to 1728. There is material on the conventions of 1824, 1834, 1840 (2), and 1842; and also on the commission in 1898 to revise the constitution. Annual series include a manual, governors' messages, documents, and industrial statistics (1887–). The municipalities publish documents and manuals.

Important collections are:

Acts and Laws of His Majesty's Colony of Rhode-Island and Providence-Plantations in New England. Newport, 1745, 1764, and 1767. — All editions are imperfect.

J. R. Bartlett, ed., *Records of the Colony of Rhode Island and Providence Plantations in New England (1636–1792)*. 10 vols. Providence, 1856–65.

G. S. Kimball, ed., *Correspondence of the Colonial Governors of Rhode Island, 1723–1775*. 2 vols. Boston, 1902–03.

Rhode Island Court Records, 1647–1670. 2 vols. Providence, 1920–22.

Rhode Island Land Evidences, 1648–1696. Providence, 1921.

J. J. Smith, ed., *Civil and Military List of Rhode Island (1647–1850)*. 3 vols. Providence, 1900–07.

D. S. Towle, ed., *Records of the Vice-Admiralty Court of Rhode Island 1716–1752*. Wash., 1936.

o   o   o

R. L. Bowen, ed., *Index to the Early Records of the Town of Providence*. Providence, [1949].

Early Records of the Town of Portsmouth (1639–1697). Providence, 1901.

Early Records of the Town of Warwick. Providence, 1926.

W. C. Pelkly, ed., *Early Records of the Town of Providence*. 21 vols. Providence, 1892–1915.

Records of the Town of Plymouth, 1636–1783. 3 vols. Plymouth, 1889–1903.

South Carolina

Legislative journals begin in 1671; and there are materials on the conventions of 1790, 1832, 1852, 1860, 1865, 1868, and 1895, as well as on the Provincial Congress of 1775 and 1776. Series include a legislative manual and reports of the General Assembly. Charleston publishes a *Year-book*. Collections include:

Joseph Brevard, ed., *Alphabetical Digest of the Public Statute Law of South Carolina* 3 vols. Charleston, 1814.

Thomas Cooper and D. J. McCord, eds., *Statutes at Large of South Carolina*. 10 vols. Columbia, 1836–41.

J. H. Easterby, ed., *Colonial Records of South Carolina*. (*1736–1742*). 3 vols. Columbia, 1951–53.

A. K. Gregorie and J. N. Frierson, eds., *Records of the Court of Chancery of South Carolina, 1671–1779*. Wash., 1950.

J. F. Grimké, ed., *Public Laws of the State of South Carolina* (*1694–1790*). Phila., 1790.

A. S. Salley, ed., *Commissions and Instructions from the Lords Proprietors of Carolina to Public Officials of South Carolina, 1685–1715*. Columbia, 1916.

A. S. Salley, ed., *Documents Relating to the History of South Carolina during the Revolutionary War*. Columbia, 1908.

A. S. Salley, ed., *Journal of His Majesty's Council for South Carolina May 29, 1721–June 10, 1721*. Atlanta, 1930.

A. S. Salley, ed., *Journal of the Commissioners of the Indian Trade of South Carolina, September 20, 1710–April 12, 1715*. Columbia, 1926.

A. S. Salley, ed., *Journal of the Commissioners of the Navy of South Carolina . . . 1776 . . . 1780*. 2 vols. Columbia, 1912–13.

A. S. Salley, ed., *Journal of the Commons House of Assembly of South Carolina* (*1692–1726/7*). 19 vols. Columbia, 1907–46.

A. S. Salley, ed., *Journal of the Convention of South Carolina Which Ratified the Constitution of the United States May 23, 1788*. Atlanta, 1928.

A. S. Salley, ed., *Journal of the Grand Council of South Carolina*. Columbia, 1907.

A. S. Salley, ed., *Records in the British Public Record Office Relating to South Carolina 1663–1710*. 5 vols. Columbia, 1928–47.

A. S. Salley, ed., *Records of the Secretary of the Province and the Register of the Province of South Carolina, 1671–1675*. Columbia, 1944.

A. S. Salley, ed., *South Carolina Treasury. Accounts Audited of Revolutionary Claims against South Carolina*. 3 vols. Columbia, 1935–43.

A. S. Salley, ed., *South Carolina Troops in Confederate Service*. 3 vols. Columbia, 1913–30.

A. S. Salley, ed., *Stub Entries to Indents Issued in Payment of Claims Against South Carolina*. 9 vols. Columbia, 1910–39.

A. S. Salley, ed., *Warrants for Lands in South Carolina, 1672–1711*. 3 vols. Columbia, 1910–15.

South Carolina Legislative Times; Being the Debates and Proceedings in the South Carolina Legislature at the Session Commencing November 1855. Columbia, 1856.

Nicholas Trott, ed., *Laws of the Province of South Carolina before 1734*. 2 vols. Charleston, 1736.

P. C. J. Weston, ed., *Documents Connected with the History of South Carolina*. London, 1856.

* * *

Digest of the Ordinance of the City Council of Charleston . . . 1783–1818. Charleston, 1818.

A. S. Salley, ed., *Minutes of the Vestry of St. Helena's Parish, South Carolina, 1726–1812*. Columbia, 1919.

A. S. Salley, ed., *Minutes of the Vestry of St. Matthew's Parish, South Carolina, 1767–1838*. Columbia, 1939.

A. S. Salley, ed., *Register of St. Philip's Parish, Charles Town, South Carolina, 1720–1810*. 2 vols. Charleston, 1904–27.

South Dakota

Legislative journals for the Dakota Territory begin in 1862, for the state of South Dakota in 1890. There are materials on the conventions of 1883, 1885, and 1889.

Tennessee

Legislative journals begin in 1794; there are materials on the conventions of 1796, 1834, and 1870. Series include governors' messages and a *Blue Book*. Documents are published in the appendices to the House and Senate journals.

Texas

Legislative journals begin in 1835. There are materials on the conventions of 1832, 1835, 1836, 1845, 1861, 1866, 1868, and 1875. Various collections of documents that draw materials from the Spanish colonial, the Mexican, the Republican, and the state periods include:

E. D. Adams, ed., *British Diplomatic Correspondence Concerning the Republic of Texas, 1838–1846.* Austin, [1918].

Austin, *Papers* (§ 54).

W. C. Binkley, ed., *Official Correspondence of the Texan Revolution, 1835–1836.* 2 vols. N.Y., [1936].

G. P. Garrison, ed., "Diplomatic Correspondence of the Republic of Texas," Am. Hist. Assoc., *Report,* 1907–08, II.

O. C. Hartley, ed., *Digest of the Laws of Texas.* Phila., 1850.

J. P. Kimball, ed., *Laws and Decrees of the State of Coahuila and Texas (1824–1835).* Houston, 1839.

[Sinclair Moreland], ed., *Governors' Messages, Coke to Ross . . . 1874–1891.* Austin, 1916.

Harriet Smither, ed., *Journals of the Fourth Congress of the Republic of Texas, 1839–1840.* 3 vols. Austin, [1931].

Harriet Smither, ed., *Journals of the Sixth Congress, 1841–42.* Austin, 1940.

E. W. Winkler, ed., *Journal of the Secession Convention of Texas, 1861.* [Austin], 1912.

E. W. Winkler, ed., "Secret Journals of the Senate, Republic of Texas, 1836–1845," Texas Library and Historical Commission, *First Biennial Report, 1909–1911.*

Utah

Legislative journals begin in 1851; and there is material on the conventions of 1850, 1856, 1862, 1872, 1882, 1887, and 1895.

Vermont

Legislative journals begin in 1784. Material exists for the conventions of 1777, 1814, 1822, 1828, 1836, 1843, 1850, 1857, and 1870; for the Council of Censors which met in 1785, 1792, 1799, 1806, 1813, 1820, 1827, 1834–35, 1841–42, 1848–49, 1855–56, 1862, and 1869 and for a constitutional commission which met in 1908. Series include a legislative directory, the collected *Reports of State Officers,* public and legislative documents, *Walton's Vermont Register* (1803–   ), later known as *Vermont Register* and *Vermont Yearbook,* and a survey of agriculture (1872–   ). Collections include:

William Slade, ed., *Vermont State Papers: Being a Collection of Records and Documents.* Middlebury, 1823.

E. P. Walton, ed., *Records of the Council of Safety and Governor and Council of the State of Vermont, 1775–1836.* 8 vols. Montpelier, 1873–80.   [See also p. 544.]

Virginia

Legislative journals go back to 1619. There is material on the conventions of 1774, 1775, 1776, 1829, 1850, 1861, 1864, 1867, and 1901. Current series include *Annual Reports of the Officers, Boards and Institutions of the Commonwealth of Virginia,* last issued in 1948, and additional legislative documents.

Virginia is rich in collections of earlier public documents. Among the more important are:

R. T. Barton, ed., *Virginia Colonial Decisions . . . Reports by Sir John Randolph and by Edward Barradall of Decisions of the General Court of Virginia, 1728–1741.* 2 vols. Boston, 1909.

H. J. Eckenrode, ed., *Fifth Annual Report of the Library Board, Calendar of Legislative Petitions Arranged by Counties Accomac-Bedford.* Richmond, 1908. — From the Revolution on.

W. W. Hening, ed., *The Statutes at Large Being a Collection of All the Laws of Virginia (1619–1792).* 13 vols. Richmond, 1809–1823.

S. M. Kingsbury, ed., *Records of the Virginia Company of London: the Court Book, from the Manuscript in the Library of Congress.* 4 vols. Wash., 1906–35.

H. R. McIlwaine and W. L. Hall, eds., *Executive Journals of the Council of Colonial Virginia, 1680–1754.* 5 vols. Richmond, 1925–45.

H. R. McIlwaine, ed., *Journals of the Council of the State of Virginia, 1776–1781.* 2 vols. Richmond, 1931–32.

H. R. McIlwaine and J. P. Kennedy, eds., *Journals of the House of Burgesses of Virginia (1619–1776)*. 13 vols. Richmond, 1905–15.

H. R. McIlwaine, *Minutes of the Council and General Court of Colonial Virginia, 1622–1632, 1670–1676.* Richmond, 1924.

H. R. McIlwaine, ed., *Official Letters of the Governors of the State of Virginia*. 3 vols. Richmond, 1926–29.

W. P. Palmer, *et al.*, eds., *Calendar of Virginia State Papers and Other Manuscripts . . . Preserved . . . at Richmond (1652–1869)*. 11 vols. Richmond, 1875–93.

Report of the Committee of Revisors Appointed by the General Assembly of Virginia in 1776. Richmond, 1784.

Virginia Colonial Abstracts, 1652–1820. 34 vols. Richmond, 1937–49, 1952– .

T. H. Wynne and W. S. Gilman, eds., *Colonial Records of Virginia [1619–1680].* Richmond, 1874.

✸ ✸ ✸

L. C. Bell, ed., *Cumberland Parish, Lunenburg County, Virginia, 1746–1816, Vestry Book, 1746–1816.* Richmond, [1912].

Lyman Chalkley, ed., *Chronicles of the Scotch-Irish Settlement in Virginia Extracted from the Original Court Records of Augusta County 1745–1800.* 3 vols. Rosslyn, 1912.

C. G. Chamberlayne, ed., *Vestry Book of St. Paul's Parish, Hanover County, Virginia, 1706–86.* Richmond, 1940.

W. A. Crozier, ed., *Virginia County Records.* 11 vols. N.Y., [1905–13].

Washington

Legislative journals begin in 1854; legislative manuals in 1889; and there is material on the conventions of 1878 and 1889. Series include *Public Documents,* and the reports of the Labor Bureau (1903–).

West Virginia

Legislative journals begin in 1863; and there is material on the conventions of 1861, 1863, and 1872. Series include *Public Documents,* the *Legislative Handbook and Manual* (*Blue Book* after 1935) and reports of the State Board of Control (1910–).

Wisconsin

Legislative journals begin in 1836; and there is material on the conventions of 1846 and 1847. The state currently publishes journals of the Senate and Assembly with documents in appendices, as well as the annual governors' messages with accompanying documents, a legislative manual (1861–) and statistical series (1883–). Among the collections are:

Check List of the Journals and Public Documents of Wisconsin. Published by the Wisconsin Free Library Commission. Madison, 1903. — Supplemented by a list published in 1918 by the State Historical Society, and monthly thereafter.

Index to Governors' Messages, Prepared by the Wisconsin Historical Records Survey, Madison, 1941.

Wisconsin Territorial Papers, County Series. Madison, 1941–42. — Volumes have been published for Crawford, Iowa, and St. Croix counties.

Wyoming

Legislative journals begin in 1869; and there is material on the convention held in 1889.

47. FOREIGN PUBLIC RECORDS CONTAINING AMERICAN HISTORICAL MATERIAL

The historian of the United States often has occasion to turn to the records of foreign governments. For the long period when the American people were colonists, dependent upon European administrators, the records of these officials are of obvious importance. But even in the era of national independence, the student of diplomacy, of trade, of immigration, and of economic and social history will find it necessary to turn to documents and other sources emanating from other governments.

All the powers with which the United States had contact have extensive archival systems. Until the twentieth century the most important for American history are those of Great Britain, France, Spain, and Canada. For particular aspects of American history, the scholar will turn also to the collections of the other European powers and of Latin America. The guides that describe the contents of these collections of special interest to American historians are listed in § 26. More general guides are included below under each country.

In order to make European archival materials available to Americans there have been extensive efforts to transcribe, photograph, reprint, and abstract the main bodies of information relative to the history of the United States. Often this was done under the sponsorship of states and state historical societies. In the nineteenth century, Brodhead, Sparks, Bancroft, Rich, Brown and Stevens, among others, examined collections in England, France, Holland, Germany, Austria, and Spain. Most of the transcripts which they prepared are now either in the New York Public Library, the Library of Congress, or the Harvard College Library. After the preparation of the Carnegie guides (§ 26), the Library of Congress began a systematic program of copying photostatically the materials in England, France, Spain, Germany, and Russia. In addition, the American Council of Learned Societies in 1940 undertook to record the most important English sources; by 1949, 2,600 reels of microfilm had been assembled in the Library of Congress. See also: G. G. Griffin, *Guide to Manuscripts* (§ 26); R. R. Hill, *American Missions in European Archives* (Mexico City, 1951). For published collections, see below under the appropriate countries; also see above under the federal and state documents (§§ 45, 46).

Like the American federal and state governments, the governments of the great powers have also issued extensive series of published documents. These vary greatly in thoroughness, in regularity of appearance, and in their relevance to American history. The best guide to them is Winifred Gregory, *List of the Serial Publications of Foreign Governments 1815–1931* (N.Y., 1932). Under each country below an effort is made to list the most important series from the point of view of American history.

See also: Brown, *Manual*; Childs, *Government Document Bibliography*; and Wilcox, "New Guides." The most important diplomatic materials are included in Bemis and Griffin, *Guide to Diplomatic History* (§ 35); no attempt is made to repeat all such material here.

In general, see also: Bemis and Griffin, *Guide to Diplomatic History*, 838; *Le Bibliographe moderne; courrier international des archives et des bibliothèques* (Paris, 1897–); J. M. Meyer, ed., *Official Publications of European Governments* (Paris, 1929); *Das Öffentliche Urkundwesen der europaischen Staaten. Herausgegeben vom Ständigen Ausschusse des Internationalen Notar-Kongresses* (Leipzig, 1913).

GREAT BRITAIN AND IRELAND

The archives of Great Britain and Ireland contain the largest stores of material relevant to American history and have been most frequently used by American historians. Established in 1838, the Public Records Office, Chancery Lane, London, has since then become the central depository for all the records of the British government. Lists and indexes are available for many of these holdings; particularly useful are those for the Colonial Office (1911) and the Foreign Office (1914–29). *Calendars of State Papers* drawn from materials in the Public Records Office and elsewhere are also helpful; American historians will be particularly interested in the Colonial Series, of which vols. I, V, VII, IX deal with the North American colonies. In addition to the reprints and transcripts prepared by states, historical societies, and the Library of Congress, extensive abstracts of these records will be found in such works as J. C. Hotten, ed., *Original List of Persons of Quality . . . and Others Who Went from Great Britain to the American Plantations 1600–1700* (London, 1874); L. W. Labaree, ed., *Royal Instructions to British Colonial Governors 1670–1776* (2 vols., N.Y., 1935); Bernard Mayo, ed., "Instructions to the British Ministers to the United States 1791–1812," Am. Hist. Assoc., *Report*, 1936, III; and Essex Institute, *Abstracts of English Shipping Records Relating to Massachusetts* (5 vols., Salem, 1931–49).

There are also archives in Dublin, Belfast, and Edinburgh, and a number of local archival collections have been organized under the National Register of Archives. Such holdings are currently noted in *Archives* (London), the journal of the British Records Association, and in the *Bulletin* of the Institute of Historical Research. The following guides are helpful:

F. G. Emmison and Irvine Gray, *County Records.* London, 1948.
V. H. Galbraith, *Introduction to the Use of the Public Records.* Oxford, 1934.
V. H. Galbraith, *Studies in the Public Records.* London, 1949.
M. S. Giuseppi, ed., *Guide to the Manuscripts Preserved in the Public Records Office.* 2 vols. London, 1923–24.
Hubert Hall, ed., *British Archives and the Sources for the History of the World War.* New Haven, 1925.
Hubert Hall, ed., *Repertory of British Archives.* London, 1920.
P. E. Jones, ed., *Guide to the Records in the Corporation of London Records Office.* London, 1951.
Matthew Livingstone, ed., *Guide to the Public Records of Scotland.* Edinburgh, 1905.
Reports of the Royal Commission on Public Records of England and Wales. 3 vols. London, 1912–19.
Herbert Wood, ed., *Guide to the Records in the Public Record Office of Ireland.* Dublin, 1919.

British documentary publications are voluminous; and, as might be expected, they center about the operations of Parliament. For a general introduction to these materials, see: H. B. Lees-Smith, *Guide to Parliamentary and Official Papers* (London, 1924); and F. R. Cowell, *Brief Guide to Government Publications* (London, 1938).

Parliamentary debates were not officially recorded until the nineteenth century. For earlier years the most satisfactory compilation is William Cobbett's *Parliamentary History of England from the Earliest Period to the Year 1803* (36 vols., London, 1806–20). After 1803 reports are continuously given in *Hansard's Parliamentary Debates*. Both houses also publish journals which are indexed periodically. Especially useful to students of American history is L. F. Stock, *Proceedings and Debates of the British Parliaments Respecting North America 1452–1727* (3 vols., Wash., 1924–30).

Statutes for the period 1235–1948 may be found in *The Statutes: Third Revised Edition* (32 vols., London, 1950) with the exception of legislation for the years between 1642 and 1660 which is given in C. H. Firth and R. S. Rait, eds., *Acts and Ordinances of the Interregnum, 1642–1660* (3 vols., London, 1911). The laws of more recent years are in annual *Public General Acts* (1921–   ), as well as in such unofficial compilations as Butterworth's, Chitty's, and Halsbury's.

Since the heads of the executive departments are ministers responsible to Parliament, much of the work of those departments is reported in sessional papers presented to the House of Commons and the House of Lords. There are good files of those papers in American libraries either in microprint or in the original. These and other parliamentary materials may be traced through the following finding aids:

General Alphabetical Index to the Bills, Reports, Estimates, Accounts, Printed by Order of the House of Commons and to the Papers Presented by Command, 1801–1928/29. 8 vols. London, 1853–1931.

List of the Bills, Reports, Estimates and Accounts and Papers Printed by Order of the House of Commons and of the Papers Presented by Command with a General Alphabetical Index Thereto. London, 1920–   . — Published annually as the last volume of the sessional papers.

General Index to Sessional Papers Printed by Order of the House of Lords or Presented by Special Command. 3 vols. London, 1860–86. — Continued annually.

More specialized, but occasionally useful, is M. I. Adams, John Ewing, and James Munro, eds., *Guide to the Principal Parliamentary Papers Relating to the Dominions, 1812–1911.* Edinburgh, 1913.

Among other important publications are those of the Foreign Office, including *British and Foreign State Papers* (1812–14–   [London, 1841–   ]); G. P. Gooch and Harold Temperley, eds., *British Documents on the Origins of the War 1898–1914* (11 vols., London, 1926–38); Harold Temperley and L. M. Penson, eds., *A Century of Diplomatic Blue Books, 1814–1914* (Cambridge, Eng., 1938); and E. L. Woodward and Rohan Butler, eds., *Documents on British Foreign Policy, 1919–1939* (in process, London, 1946–   ); and the reports of Royal Commissions (which may be traced through A. H. Cole's *Finding List* [Cambridge, 1935]). The decisions of all English courts to 1866 have been assembled in *English Reports* (178 vols., Edinburgh, 1900–32); more recent cases may be found in current reports, for which see: F. C. Hicks, *Materials and Methods of Legal Research* (3 ed., Rochester, N.Y., 1942), ch. vii, App. I, II.

Between 1915 and 1921 the Stationery Office published two monthly lists of publications, one for those emanating from Parliament, the other for other official publications. Beginning with 1922, it has published a monthly *Consolidated List of Government Publications*, the December issue of which is an annual cumulation of all the public documents of the year.

Eire, since the recognition of its dominion status, has published its own documentary series, including the debates in the Dáil (1922–   ). That is also true of the Parliament of Northern Ireland (1921–   ). In general, the series of these states follow the British in form.

FRANCE

The connections between the United States and France have been long and intimate. Yet the American student will find some difficulty in using the materials in French archives outside the orbit marked out in the Leland *Guide* (§ 26).

After all, in French history, and in French archives, the United States figures only in the relatively brief modern period. In making his way to the scattered materials that might interest him in the archives in Paris and in the provinces, the historian will find a number of serviceable guides and inventories as well as some accounts of the collections in historical periodicals. The more important follow:

Annales d'histoire économique et sociale. Paris, 1929– .
Annuaire des bibliothèques et des archives. Paris, 1886– .
Archives et bibliothèques. Paris, 1935– .
H. L. Bordier, ed., *Les Archives de France.* Paris, 1855.
[Henri Courteault], *État des inventaires des archives nationales, départementales, communales, et hospitalières.* Paris, 1938.
État sommaire par series des documents conservées aux Archives nationales. Paris, 1891– .
Ernst Posner, *Archival Repositories in France.* Wash., 1943.
Revue des bibliothèques. Paris, 1891– .
UNESCO, Répertoire des bibliothèques de France (§ 16).

Perhaps more readily useful will be N. M. M. Surrey, *Calendar of Manuscripts in Paris Archives and Libraries Relating to the History of the Mississippi Valley to 1803* (2 vols., Wash., 1926–28); A. P. Nasatir, ed., *French Activities in California: an Archival Calendar-Guide* (Stanford, 1945). Occasional documents of interest are in *Collection des documents inédits sur l'histoire de France* (126 vols., Paris, 1836–).

The published French documents fall into no consistent series. Before 1789, the most important are the royal decrees, for which see: Jourdan, Isambert, Decrusy, and Taillandier, eds., *Recueil général des anciennes lois françaises* (29 vols., indexed, Paris, 1829–33). After that date fluctuations in legislative forms are reflected in frequent changes in the nature of the documents. The changes in form of government and in the constitution and powers of the legislature naturally altered the character of their publications. The *Bulletin des lois* regularly printed the laws and was indexed annually. The *Moniteur universel* (1790–) carried a variety of government decrees; various *Précis verbaux* were accounts of proceedings; and the *Annales* of the various legislative bodies were the counterparts of American *Journals.* For the period to 1839 the best edition of the debates is in a later compilation: M. J. Mavidal, *et al.*, eds., *Archives parlementaires de 1787 à 1860* (209 vols., Paris, 1879–1913). After 1870 *Le Journal officiel de la République française* is the most reliable source. It was generally issued in three parts: laws and decrees, parliamentary debates, and parliamentary documents. The journal is partially indexed and is supplemented by a number of *Annexes* of a documentary nature. In addition, there is a large body of administrative publications, including the reports of departments and bureaus, those on trade and colonies being particularly valuable for American historians.

Collections that may be useful to American historians include:

Archives diplomatiques. 193 vols. Paris, 1861–1914. — Semi-official, published monthly.
Documents diplomatiques français (1871–1914). 33 vols. Paris, 1929– .
Recueil des instructions données aux ambassadeurs et ministres de France depuis les traités de Westphalie jusqu'à la révolution française. 26 vols. Paris, 1884–1929.
L. C. Wroth and G. L. Annan, eds., *Acts of French Royal Administration Concerning Canada, Guiana, the West Indies, and Louisiana, prior to 1791.* N.Y., 1930.

SPAIN AND PORTUGAL

Spanish materials are relevant primarily for the colonial era and particularly for the sections that were at one time under the control of Spain. The archives are extensive. In the list of guides, the Chapman *Catalogue* (§ 26) is particularly useful; but see also above (§ 46) under California, Florida, Texas; below under Latin America; and the Hill and Shepherd guides above (§ 26).

Anais das bibliotecas, arquivo e museus municipais. Lisbon, 1931– .
Anais das bibliotecas e arquivos de Portugal. Coimbra, 1914– .
P. A. de Azevedo and Antonio Baião, *O Archivo da Torre do Tombo.* Lisbon, 1905.
Boletim de bibliographia portugueza e revista dos arquivos nacionaes. Coimbra, 1879– .
António Mesquita de Figueiredo, *Arquivo nacional da Torre do Tombo.* Lisbon, 1922.
Revista de archivos, bibliotecas y museos. Madrid, 1871– .
Revista de la biblioteca, archivo y museo. Madrid, 1924– .
Francisco Rodríguez Marín, *Guia histórica y descriptiva de los archivos, bibliotecas y museos arqueológicos de España.* 2 vols. Madrid, 1916.
José Torre Revello, "El Archivo General de Indias de Sevilla," Instituto de Investigaciones Historicas (Buenos Aires), *Publ.,* L (1929).

The most important published Spanish documents are the records of the Cortes (1810–). Some departmental collections are also useful. See, thus: *Boletin de la Dirección General de emigración* (Madrid, 1925–).

GERMANY

German materials are often useful for the student of American history, particularly for the nineteenth and the twentieth centuries. But they are complex and difficult to use, partly because the United States was not large in the consciousness of central Europeans until recently and partly because German governmental forms have passed through numerous transformations in the last century and a half. Those who wish to use the archives and the public documents must take account not only of those of the separate states — Prussia, Bavaria, Baden, and the like — but also of those of free cities like Frankfort and Hamburg, as well as of the central confederations. Furthermore such states as Prussia were themselves divided into provinces. Each of these entities possessed its own archives and issued its own series of publications.

A useful recent survey of archives is that issued by the United States National Archives, *Archival Repositories in Germany* (Wash., 1944). Journals like *Der Archivar* (1947–) as well as the older *Archivalische Zeitschrift* (1876–1950) will also be helpful. The extensive series of publications from archival sources, particularly Prussian, unfortunately have generally little bearing on American history. See, however: *Das Staatsarchiv* (86 vols., Berlin, 1861–1919; with a new series, 1928–).

Each of the governmental entities issued publications of laws and decrees, legislative proceedings, and reports of the ministries. An index (*Generalregister*) to the Reichstag proceedings, 1867–1895, was published in Berlin in 1896, and was continued thereafter sessionally. For the period since 1870, the *Reichsgesetzblatt* is a compendious record of government actions. For the most recent decades, the *Monatliches Verzeichnis der reichsdeutschen amtlichen Druckschriften* (Berlin, 1928–) is an essential guide. Other keys to these materials include Otto Neuberger, *Official Publications of Present-Day Germany* (Wash.,

1942); and August Wolfstieg and Karl Meitzel, *Bibliographie der Schriften über beide Häuser des Landtags in Preussen* (Berlin, 1915).

Among the general collections of value are: G. A. Gotesend, *Die Gesetze und Verordnungen . . . für den preussischen Staat und das deutsche Reich 1806–1875* (4 vols. with supplements, Köln, 1875–76); the *Vierteljahrshefte zur Statistik des deutschen Reichs* (1874–   ); and Johannes Lepsius, *et al.*, *Die Grosse Politik der europäischen Kabinette, 1871–1914* (54 vols., Berlin, 1922–27).

OTHER EUROPEAN COUNTRIES

The documentary resources of other European countries are less likely to prove rewarding to American historians. The contact with the United States has been less direct and, while all have extensive archives and published series, useful material in them is scattered and difficult to locate.

The archives are best approached through the guides listed above (§ 26) and through the periodicals published in the various countries, a good list of which will be found, *Am. Archivist*, II (1939), 77. The United States National Archives sponsored a series of helpful reports on archival establishments in Czechoslovakia, Hungary, Italy, Austria, and northwestern Europe, published in 1944 and 1945. In addition, the following works are serviceable:

Les Archives de l'État en Belgique, 1914–   .
K. A. Fink, *Das Vatikansche Archiv.* Rome, 1943.
The General State Archives and Their Contents. The Hague, 1932.
Julien van Hove, *Répertoire des organismes de documentation en Belgique.* Bruxelles, 1947.
Hilary Jenkinson and H. E. Bell, *Italian Archives during the War and at Its Close.* London, 1947.
Axel Linvald, *Dansk Arkivvæsen.* Copenhagen, 1933.
Jozef Siemiénski, *Guide des archives de Pologne.* Warsaw, 1933.
Ufficio centrale degli archivi di Stato, *Gli Archivi di Stato Italiani.* Bologna, [1944].

All these governments publish extensive series of documents emanating from their legislatures, ministries, and reports. The readiest guide is the Gregory *List* mentioned above, p. 140. Other helpful guides and indexes include:

Denmark
K. A. Hansen, *Oversigt over Beretninger, m.v. udgivet vet Statens foranstaltning i tiden 1848–1929.* Copenhagen, 1929.

Italy
Raffaello Biffoli and Camillo Montalcini, *Indice generale degli atti parlemantari 1848–97.* Rome, 1898.
Provveditorato Generale dello Stato, *Publicazioni edite dallo stato o col suo concorso (1861–1923).* Rome, 1924. — 2 supplementary vols. to 1935.
Provveditorato Generale dello Stato, *Publicazioni edite dallo stato o col suo concorso . . . 1901–1930.* 7 vols. Rome, 1926–37. — A subject index.

Norway
J. Cappelen, *et al.*, eds., *Hovedregister til Stortings-Forhandlinger (1814–1910).* 4 vols. Kristiania, 1885–1915.
Vilhelm Haffner, *Innstillinger og betenkninger fra Kongelige og parlamentariske kommisjoner, departementale komiteer m.m. 1814–1934.* 2 vols. Oslo, 1925–36.

Sakregister till Rickets Ständers Protokoll med Bihang . . . *1809–1940.* 16 vols. Stockholm, 1891–1942.

Other publications and collections vary widely in utility. The reports of the Italian and Swedish official bodies regulating immigration have an obvious importance to the students of some American problems. Investigators in the field of diplomatic history will find useful such collections as: Ludwig Bittner, *et al.*, eds., *Oesterreich-Ungarns Aussenpolitik von der bosnischen Krise, 1908, bis zum Kriegsausbruch* (9 vols., Vienna, 1930). Other students may even find profit in consulting collections of purely internal concern such as *Le Assemblee del Risorgimento* (15 vols., Rome, 1911).

LATIN AMERICA AND THE WEST INDIES

Much of the material for the years when these areas were colonial dependencies of the European powers will be found in the archives and publications of Spain, Portugal, Holland, France, and Great Britain. But each of the governmental entities in South and Central America has, in addition, developed collections and publication series of its own. The most useful general aids are the annual volumes of the *Handbook of Latin-American Studies*, edited by Lewis Hanke and others (Cambridge, 1935–   ), and the guides of Bell, Bolten, Paz, and Perez (§ 26). Both the archives and the public documents of the British West Indies are described in L. J. Ragatz, "Guide for the Study of British Caribbean History, 1763–1834," Am. Hist. Assoc., *Report*, 1930, III, 23.

The following works will be helpful in approaching the archives:

J. A. Burdon, ed., *Archives of British Honduras.* 3 vols. London, 1931–35.
C. E. Castañeda and J. A. Dabbs, eds., *Guide to the Latin American Materials in the University of Texas Library.* Cambridge, 1939.
Maria Castelo de Zavala, "El Archivo Nacional del Peru," *Revista de historia de America*, No. 20 (1945), 371.
Ricardo Donoso, "El Archivo Nacional de Chile," *ibid.*, No. 11 (1941), 47.
A. E. Gropp, ed., *Guide to Libraries and Archives in Central America and the West Indies, Panama, Bermuda, and British Guiana.* New Orleans, 1941.
R. R. Hill, ed., *National Archives of Latin America.* Cambridge, 1945.
Joaquin Llaverias, *Historia de los archivos de Cuba.* 2 ed. Havana, 1949.
Carlo Agustín Millares and J. I. Manterón, eds., *Repertorio bibliografico de los archivos mexicanos de la colecciones diplomaticas fundamentales para la historia de Mexico.* Mexico, 1948.
Richard Pattee, "Libraries and Archives for Historical Research in Ecuador," *Hispanic American Hist. Rev.*, XVII (1937), 231.
J. I. Rubio Mañe, "El Archivo General de la Nación, México," *Revista de Historia de America*, No. 9 (1940), 63.
José Torre Revello, "El Archivo General de la Nación Argentina," *ibid.*, No. 1 (1938), 41.
José Torre Revello, "El Archivo Histórico de la Provincia de Buenos Aires," *ibid.*, No. 5 (1939), 55.

Published series of value include large collections of historical documents, as well as the current records of government. Among the former are:

Archivo historico diplomatico. 32 vols. Mexico, 1923–30.
León Fernández, ed., *Colección de documentos para la historia de Costa-Rica.* 10 vols. Costa Rica, etc., 1881–1907.

J. H. Lefroy, ed., *Memorials of the Discovery and Early Settlement of the Bermudas.* 2 vols. London, 1877–79.

Heraclio Mabragaña, ed., *Los Mensajes: Historia del desenvolvimiento de la nacion argentina, redactada chronologicamente por sus gobernantes, 1810–1910.* 6 vols. Buenos Aires, 1910.

Santiago Montoto, *et al.*, eds., *Colección de documentos inéditos para la historia de Ibero-América.* 14 vols. Madrid, 1927–32.

J. F. Pacheco, Francisco de Cardenas, and Luis Torres de Mendoza, *et al.*, eds., *Colección de documentos inéditos relativos al descubrimiento, conquista y coloniza-cion de las posesiones españolas en América y Occeanía sacados . . . del real archivo de Indias.* 42 vols. Madrid, 1864–84. — Continued under the auspices of the Royal Academy of History (Madrid) in a supplementary *Colección* (25 vols., Madrid, 1885–1932). Both collections are indexed alphabetically and chronologically, Ernesto Schäfer, *Indice* (2 vols., Madrid, 1946–47).

Sesiones de los cuerpos lejislativos de la República de Chile, 1811 a 1845. 37 vols. Santiago, 1887–1908.

Among the more important current documentary series are the legislative journals for each country and for most of the colonies, the *Memoria* of each presidential adminis-tration, and the reports of colonial governors as well as a wide variety or departmental publications. Among the more helpful guides are the Gregory *List*, the Library of Congress's *Guide to the Official Publications of the Other American Republics* (Wash., 1941–   ), and the following:

J. B. Childs, ed., *Colombian Government Publications.* Wash., 1941.

J. B. Childs, ed., "Cuban Government Publications," Inter-American Bibliographical and Library Assoc., *Proc. of the Second Convention,* 1939, 122.

J. B. Childs, ed., *Memorias of the Republics of Central America and the Antilles.* Wash., 1932.

A. M. Ker, ed., *Mexican Government Publications.* Wash., 1940.

CANADA

The history of Canada has been closely related to that of the United States. The public documents of the Dominion, of its predecessors, and of its provinces are therefore of the highest value to the student of American history. The Dominion itself and each of the provinces have well-arranged archives, adequate guides to which are available. The more important are listed below. The annual reports of the archivist of Canada (1872–   ) are useful, as are those of the Province of Quebec. In addition the following works are helpful:

G. W. Brown, "Problem of Records in Canada," *Canadian Hist. Rev.,* XXV (1944), 1.

Margaret Ells, ed., *Calendar of the White Collection of Manuscripts in the Public Archives of Nova Scotia.* Halifax, 1940.

D. C. Harvey, "Archives in the Maritimes," *Dalhousie Rev.,* XXIII (1943).

H. A. McClung, "Department of Public Records and Archives of Ontario," *Am. Archivist,* X (1947), 184.

D. W. Parker, ed., *Guide to the Documents in the Manuscript Room at the Public Archives, Ottawa.* Ottawa, 1914.

P. G. Roy, ed., *Les Archives de la province et nos inventaires.* Quebec, 1926.

A good many historical documents have been published in historical collections and other works, many of which are important for students of the history of the United States. The more important include:

T. B. Akins, ed., *Selections from the Public Documents of the Province of Nova Scotia.* Halifax, 1869.

H. E. Egerton and W. P. Grant, eds., *Canadian Constitutional Development Shown by Selected Speeches and Dispatches (1763–1865).* London, 1907.

William Houston, ed., *Documents Illustrative of the Canadian Constitution*. Toronto, 1891.

William Kingsford, ed., *History of Canada (1608–1841)*. 10 vols. London, 1888–98.

P. G. Roy, ed., *Inventaire des concessions en fief et seigneurie . . . conservés aux archives de la province de Québec*. 4 vols. Beauceville, 1927–28.

Adam Shortt and A. G. Doughty, eds., *Documents Relating to the Constitutional History of Canada, 1759–1791*. Ottawa, 1907.

The Dominion and the provinces also publish extensive current series of documents. Since the provinces antedate the Dominion, their papers go back farther. In general, all these series are modeled after those of Great Britain. The Dominion publishes a *Gazette*, journals and debates of the Senate and of the House of Commons, sessional papers, the reports of special commissions and of the heads of departments. The *Canada Statistical Yearbook* (1885–   ) is helpful. Quebec, Ontario, Manitoba, British Columbia, Alberta, Saskatchewan, Newfoundland, Nova Scotia, Prince Edward's Island, and New Brunswick each has its own legislative documents and departmental papers. All these are best located through the Gregory *List*. See also:

W. C. Bowles, *et al.*, eds., *General Index to the Journals of the House of Commons of the Dominion of Canada and of the Sessional Papers of Parliament from 1867 to [1930]*. 5 vols. Ottawa, 1880–1932.

A. H. Cole, ed., *Finding-List of Royal Commission Reports in the British Dominions*. Cambridge, 1939.

M. V. Higgins, ed., *Canadian Government Publications*. Chi., 1935.

A. H. Sydère, *et al.*, eds., *General Index to the Journals and Sessional Papers of the Legislative Assembly of the Province of Ontario (1867–1927)*. 6 vols. Toronto, 1888–1927.

Alfred Todd, ed., *General Index to the Journals of the House of Assembly of . . . Upper Canada . . . 1825 . . . –1839–40*. Montreal, 1848.

Alfred Todd, ed., *General Index to the Journals of the Legislative Assembly of Canada 1841–1866*. 2 vols. Montreal, 1855–67.

INTERNATIONAL AGENCIES

Most international acts are still the acts of sovereign states, recorded in the documents of the contracting powers. But in the last half-century the appearance of several international bodies has produced a corpus of documentary sources emanating from the agencies themselves. Such agencies vary widely, ranging from permanent official bodies such as the Hague Tribunal and the Red Cross, to temporary official organizations like the International Military Tribunal and UNRRA, and to unofficial associations such as the Olympic Organization and the International Institute of Agriculture.

The most significant are those setting up an association for collective security. The League of Nations established with headquarters in Geneva after the First World War included, at one time or another, every important country except for the United States. The documents it published contain a good deal of material relevant to American history. The most valuable include its *Official Journal* (with supplements, 1920–40), and a *Monthly Summary* (1921–40), as well as regular records of the sessions of its deliberative agencies. In addition, it issued thirteen series of *Publications* and a variety of special reports, together with a subject list of its documents. All these may be traced through Hans Aufricht, *Guide to League of Nations Publications . . . 1920–1947* (N.Y., 1950); A. C. von

Breycha-Vauthier, *Sources of Information; a Handbook of the Publications of the League of Nations* (N.Y., 1939); and the older, M. J. Carroll, *Key to League of Nations Documents, 1920–* [*1936*] (5 vols., Boston, 1930–38).

The International Labor Office antedated the League of Nations, some of its activities going back to 1902. Although the I.L.O. became a constituent body within the League, it survived the dissolution of the parent organization. Through its lifetime the I.L.O. has published an impressive list of reports, studies, conferences, statistical series, and yearbooks. See: J. B. Rounds, *Research Facilities of the International Labour Office Available to American Libraries* (Chi., 1939); and *Bibliography of the International Labour Organization . . . 1919–1938* (Geneva, 1938).

The United Nations was the outgrowth of the alliance that won the Second World War. The documentary record of its formation may be found in *United Nations Documents, 1941–1945* (N.Y., [1946]). The U.N. and its constituent bodies — among them the General Assembly, the Security Council, the World Health Organization, the Economic and Social Council, and the Educational, Scientific, and Cultural Organization (UNESCO) — publish extensive series of official records, conference reports, and documents. A *Journal* (1946–   ), issued daily during Assembly sessions, contains important reports and documents. Among the more useful regular U.N. publications are its *Treaty Series* (1946–   ), a *Handbook* (1946–   ), a *Yearbook* (1946–   ), and its *Publications* (1947–   ). U.N. Secretariat, Department of Public Information, *Check List of United Nations Documents* (N.Y., 1949), is a helpful guide. The U.N. Library also publishes a *Monthly Index* to U.N. documents (1950–   ); as well as a *Reference Guide* of the Secretariat (1947–   ); and a *Catalogue of Economic and Social Projects* (1949–   ). See also: Robert Claus, "The Archives Program of the United Nations," *Am. Archivist*, XI (1948), 195; and C. C. Moor and Waldo Chamberlain, *How to Use United Nations Documents* (N.Y., 1952).

48. BOOKS OF TRAVEL AND DESCRIPTION

Travelers' accounts constitute an important source of information on the American past. They deal, in some cases, with the geographic and physiographic features of the country; in others, with its people. In either case, such accounts must, of course, be used with caution. Every student will, soon enough, become aware of the gullibility of travelers in strange lands, of their capacity for getting things wrong, of their instinct for automatic praise or automatic censure. Nevertheless, properly used, the narrations and reports of travelers — native and foreign — may be of great value to the historian. By making explicit and vivid what local residents take for granted, travelers' accounts provide a kind of color, detail, and human interest available in no other historical source. In addition, the occasional penetrating analysis by a first-rate mind may give the historian suggestive and far-reaching insights. It is often difficult to decide whether a given book is "travels" or "autobiography"; hence it would be well to search in § 54 for a given author, if not found here. Other travel information will also be found in some of the gazetteers and registers in § 24.

In the following list, descriptive words are added in a few instances, and the dates of the journey or journeys are stated when they took place some years previous to the first edition. In the case of translations, the earliest English, as well as the original, version is given; and in some cases, later, superior editions are also noted. Most of the works published in London in the nineteenth century were later reprinted — sometimes pirated — in the United States.

LISTS AND DISCUSSIONS

The following works describe some of the travelers, discuss the observations in the accounts, or list by type or section the more important works. See also (under local history by states): § 62.

Max Berger, *The British Traveller in America, 1836–1860.* N.Y., 1943.

J. G. Brooks, *As Others See Us; A Study of Progress in the United States.* N.Y., 1908.

Cambridge History of American Literature (Cambridge, 1917–21), Bk. I, ch. i; Bk. II, ch. i; Bk. III, ch. xiv.

E. M. Coulter, ed., *Travels in the Confederate States. A Bibliography.* Norman, 1947. — First volume to be published of the American Exploration and Travel Series.

E. G. Cox, *A Reference Guide to the Literature of Travel.* Seattle, 1938. — Vol. II deals with America, mostly to 1800.

J. L. Mesick, *The English Traveller in America, 1785–1835.* N.Y., 1922.

Frank Monaghan, *French Travellers in the United States, 1765–1932.* N.Y., 1933.

C. H. Sherrill, *French Memories of Eighteenth-Century America* [1775–1800]. N.Y., 1915.

Spiller, *Literary History*, III, 245.

H. T. Tuckerman, *America and Her Commentators.* N.Y., 1864.

H. R. Wagner, ed., *The Plains and the Rockies: A Bibliography of . . . Travel . . . 1800–1865.* R. by C. L. Camp. San Francisco, 1937.

Winsor, *Narrative and Critical History*, VIII, 489. — A list to 1820.

COLLECTIONS OF NARRATIVE AND TRAVELS

T. C. Blegen and P. D. Jordan, eds., *With Various Voices. Recordings of North Star Life.* St. Paul, 1949. — Selections on Minnesota.

J. L. French, ed., *The Pioneer West; Narratives.* Boston, 1923. — An illustrated anthology, 1804–86.

Oscar Handlin, ed., *This Was America.* Cambridge, 1949. — Selections from European travelers.

J. B. McMaster, ed., *The Trail Makers.* 17 vols., N.Y., 1903–05. — The series includes among its volumes the following travel accounts: A. F. Bandelier, ed., *Journey of Cabeça de Vaca and His Companions*; E. G. Bourne, ed., *Narratives of De Soto* (2 vols.); *idem*, ed., *Voyages of Champlain* (2 vols.); G. P. Winship, ed., *Journey of Coronado*; I. J. Cox, ed., *Journey of La Salle and His Companions* (2 vols.); J. B. McMaster, ed., *Lewis and Clark Expedition* (3 vols.); D. W. Harmon, *Journal of Voyages and Travels*; Alexander Mackenzie, *Voyages through North America* [1789, 1793] (2 vols.); W. F. Butler, *The Wild Northland* [1872–73].

N. D. Mereness, ed., *Travels in the American Colonies, 1690–1783.* N.Y., 1916. — Selections.

Allan Nevins, ed., *America through British Eyes.* N.Y., 1948. — Selections.

B. L. Pierce, ed., *As Others See Chicago; Impressions of Visitors, 1673–1933.* Chi., [1933].

R. G. Thwaites, ed., *Early Western Travels, 1748–1846.* 32 vols. Cleve., 1904–07. — The more important of these are listed in this *Guide* under the names of the authors.

R. G. Thwaites, ed., *Jesuit Relations and Allied Documents, 1610–1791.* 73 vols. Cleve., 1896–1901. — The French of the original editions with English translation.

S. C. Williams, ed., *Early Travels in the Tennessee Country, 1540–1800.* Johnson City, 1928. — Selections from thirty-four travelers.

Several volumes of Jameson, *Original Narratives* (§ 57) also contain travel accounts.

ALPHABETICAL LIST

The following list is a selection from the best and most representative travels in the United States, divided into four periods: from the beginning to 1789, from 1789 to 1865, from 1865 to 1900, and from 1900 to 1950.

From the Beginning to 1789

Thomas Anburey [British officer], *Travels through the Interior Parts of America* [1776–81]. 2 vols. London, 1789. — Reprinted Boston, 1923.

J. C. B., *Travels in New France* [1751–61]. S. S. Stevens, *et al.*, eds. Harrisburg, 1941.

François, Marquis de Barbé-Marbois, *Our Revolutionary Forefathers.* N.Y., 1929. — Diary and letters during residence in the United States, 1779–85, transl. from French.

William Bartram [naturalist], *Travels through North & South Carolina, Georgia, East & West Florida* [1773–78]. Phila., 1791. — Reprinted N.Y., 1940.

Charles Beattie, *Journal of a Two Months' Tour among the Frontier Inhabitants of Pennsylvania.* London, 1768.

James Birket, *Some Cursory Remarks* [Portsmouth, N.H., to Phila., 1750–51]. New Haven, 1916.

J. E. Bonnet [French émigré], *Réponse aux principales questions . . . sur les États-Unis.* 2 vols. n.p,, 1788. — Later revised editions under other titles, Lausanne, 1795, Paris, 1802 and 1816.

J. P. Brissot de Warville, *Nouveau Voyage dans les États-Unis* [1788]. 3 vols. Paris, 1791. — Transl. Dublin, 1792.

J. C. Buettner, *Narrative . . . in the American Revolution.* N.Y., 1915. — Transl. from the German.

Andrew Burnaby, *Travels through the Middle Settlements in North America* [1759–60]. London, 1775.

Jonathan Carver, *Travels through the Interior Parts of North America, 1766–68.* London, 1778.

Luigi Castiglioni [Italian naturalist], *Viaggio negli Stati Uniti dell' America, 1785–87.* 2 vols. Milan, 1790.

F. J., Marquis de Chastellux, *Voyages . . . dans l'Amérique Septentrionale* [1780–82]. 2 vols. Paris, 1786. — Transl. London, 1787; N.Y., 1827, with valuable notes by unknown translator. See: J. P. Brissot de Warville, *Examen Critique des Voyages dans l'Amérique Septentrionale, de M. le Marquis de Chastellux.* London, 1786 (transl. London, 1786).

Nicholas Cresswell, *Journal, 1774–1777* [Virginia, Ohio, New York]. N.Y., 1924.

M. G. St. Jean de Crèvecoeur, *Letters from an American Farmer* [1770–81]. London, 1782. — Many later editions.

H. H. Peckham, ed., *George Croghan's Journal of His Trip to Detroit in 1767.* Ann Arbor, 1939.

Jasper Danckaerts [Labadist], *Journal* [New Netherland, Maryland, Boston, 1679–80]. — Transl. in *Original Narratives Series.*

Durand, *Un Français en Virginie.* La Haye, 1687. — Transl. and ed. by Fairfax Harrison, *Frenchman in Virginia Being the Memoirs of a Huguenot Refugee in 1686.* Richmond, 1923.

A. W. Du Roi [Burgoyne prisoner], *Journal, 1776–78.* N.Y., 1911. — Transl. from a German ms.

William Eddis [Maryland loyalist], *Letters from America, Historical and Descriptive; Comprising Occurrences from 1769, to 1777, Inclusive.* London, 1792.

[John Farmer], "First American Journey, 1711–1714," H. J. Cadbury, ed., Am. Antiquarian Soc., *Proc.*, new ser., LIII (1943), 79.

Axel de Fersen [staff officer with Rochambeau], *Lettres à son Père* [1780–83]. Paris, 1929.

Francisco Garcés [missionary priest], *Travels through Sonora, Arizona, and California, 1775–1776.* 2 vols. N.Y., 1900.

Christopher Gist, *Journals* [Ohio and Kentucky, 1750–53]. W. M. Darlington, ed. Cleve., 1893.

Anne Grant [loyalist], *Memoirs of an American Lady; with Sketches of Manners and Scenery in America, . . . Previous to the Revolution* [chiefly upper New York]. 2 vols. London, 1808. — Later ed., Albany, 1876.

Joseph Hadfield, *An Englishman in America, 1785* [Northern states and Canada]. Toronto, 1933.

Alexander Hamilton [Maryland physician], *Itinerarium* [New York and New England, 1744]. Ed. by Carl Bridenbaugh as *Gentleman's Progress*. Chapel Hill, 1948.

Robert Honyman, *Colonial Panorama, 1775*. Philip Padelford, ed. San Marino, 1939.

Robert Hunter, Jr., *Quebec to Carolina in 1785–1786; Being the Travel Diary and Observations of . . . a Young Merchant of London*. L. B. Wright and Marion Tinling, eds. San Marino, 1943.

John Josselyn, *An Account of Two Voyages to New England* [1638, 1663]. London, 1674–75. — Reprinted, Boston, 1865; and Mass. Hist. Soc., *Coll.*, 3 ser., III (1833).

"Journal of a French Traveller in the Colonies, 1765," *Am. Hist. Rev.*, XXVI (1921), 726, XXVII (1922), 70.

Pehr Kalm [Swedish naturalist], *En Resa til Norra Amerika* [1748–51]. Stockholm, 1753–61. — Transl., London, 1770. Ed. by A. B. Benson. 2 vols. N.Y., 1937.

Sarah Knight, *Journal* [Boston to N.Y., 1704]. N.Y., 1825. — Several later editions.

John Knox, *An Historical Journal of the Campaigns in North America, 1757–60*. 2 vols. London, 1769.

G. C. Mason, "An Atlantic Crossing of the Seventeenth Century," *Am. Neptune*, XI (1951), 35.

John May, *Journal and Letters, Relative to Two Journeys to the Ohio Country* [1788–89]. Hist. and Phil. Soc. of Ohio, *Trans.*, new ser., I, Cin., 1873; supplement in *Penn. Mag. of Hist. and Biog.*, XLV (1921), 101.

Patrick M'Roberts, *A Tour through Part of the North Provinces of America, 1774–75*. Edinburgh, 1776. — Reprinted in *Penn. Mag. of Hist. and Biog.*, LIX (1935), 134.

Francisco de Miranda, *Diary, Tour of the United States* [1783–84]. Spanish text ed. by W. S. Robertson. N.Y., 1928.

Francis Moore, *Voyage to Georgia, Begun in the Year 1735*. London, 1744. — Reprinted in Georgia Hist. Soc., *Coll.*, I (1840), 79.

Moravian Journals Relating to Central New York [1745–66]. Syracuse, 1916.

William Owen, "Narrative of American Voyages and Travels [1766–71]," N.Y. Pub. Lib., *Bull.*, XXXV (1931).

Josiah Quincy, Jr., "Journals" [N.Y., Penn., and So.Car., 1773]. Mass. Hist. Soc., *Proc.*, XL (1916), 424.

Archibald Robertson [royal engineer], *Diaries and Sketches in America* [1762–80]. N.Y., 1930.

Abbé Robin [chaplain with Rochambeau], *Nouveau voyage dans l'Amérique Septentrionale* [1781]. Paris, 1782. — Transl. by Philip Freneau. Phila., 1783.

J. D. Schöpf, *Reise durch einige der mittlern und südlichen vereinigten nordamerikanischen Staaten* [1783–84]. Erlangen, 1788. — Transl. Phila., 1911.

James Smith, "Tours into Kentucky and the Northwest Territory [1783–97]," *Ohio Archeol. and Hist. Quar.*, XVI (1907), 348.

Richard Smith [N.J. lawyer], *A Tour of Four Great Rivers, the Hudson, Mohawk, Susquehanna, and Delaware, in 1769*. N.Y., 1906.

J. F. D. Smyth, *A Tour in the United States of America* [1784]. 2 vols. Dublin, 1784.

Felix-Christian Spöri [Swiss surgeon], *Americanische Reisebeschreibung nach den Caribes Insslen und Neu Engelland* [W.I. and R.I., 1661]. Zurich, 1677, 1915. — Partly transl. in *New Eng. Quar.*, X (1937), 535.

John Woolman, *Journal* (§ 54).

1789–1865

E. S. Abdy, *Journal of a Residence and Tour in the United States, 1833–34*. 3 vols. London, 1835.

Lord Acton [historian], "American Diaries" [1853], *Fortnightly Review*, CX (1921), 727, 917, CXI (1922), 63.

J. E. Alexander, *Transatlantic Sketches.* 2 vols. London, 1833.

R. B. Allardice, *Agricultural Tour in the United States and Upper Canada.* Edinburgh, 1842.

J. J. Ampère [scientist], *Promenade en Amérique* [Northeastern states, 1851–52]. 2 vols. Paris, 1855.

Francesco Arese, "Notes du Voyage" [1837–38], in Romualdo Bonfadini, *Vita di Francesco Arese* (Turin, 1894), 451. — Transl. as *A Trip to the Prairies.* N.Y., 1934.

C. D. Arfwedson, *The United States and Canada* [1832–34]. 2 vols. London, 1834.

Thomas Ashe, *Travels in America in 1806* [Ohio and Mississippi valleys]. London, 1808.

J. J. Audubon [artist and naturalist], *Journals* [Labrador, 1833; Missouri River, 1843; "episodes" from Labrador to Florida, 1808–34]. Elliott Coues, ed. 2 vols. N.Y., 1897. — Also ed. under other titles by F. C. Herrick (N.Y., 1926) and by Howard Corning (2 vols., Cambridge, 1929).

J. W. Audubon [son of above], *Western Journal, 1849–50* [N.Y., Texas, Mexico, California]. N.Y., 1852. — Also in *Mag. of Hist.*, Extra No. 41 (1915).

A. F. de Bacourt, *Souvenirs d'un diplomate: lettres intimes sur l'Amérique* [1840–42]. Paris, 1882. — Transl., N.Y., 1885.

Francis Baily, *Journal of a Tour in the Unsettled Parts of North America, 1796–97.* London, 1856.

Henry Barnard, "The South Atlantic States in 1833, as Seen by a New Englander," *Md. Hist. Mag.*, XIII (1918), 267.

J. R. Bartlett, *Personal Narrative of Explorations and Incidents in Texas, New Mexico, California, Sonora, and Chihuahua* [Boundary Commission, 1850–53]. 2 vols. N.Y., 1854.

W. E. Baxter, *America and the Americans.* London, 1855.

Félix de Beaujour, *Aperçu des États-Unis, 1800–10.* Paris, 1814. — Transl., London, 1814.

M. V. H. Dwight [Bell], *A Journey to Ohio in 1810.* Max Farrand, ed., New Haven, 1912. — Account by a Connecticut gentlewoman.

John Bernard [actor-manager], *Retrospections of America, 1797–1811.* N.Y., 1887.

Bernhard, Duke of Saxe-Weimar-Eisenach, *Reise . . . durch Nord-Amerika . . . 1825 und 1826.* Weimar, 1828. — Transl., 2 vols. Phila., 1828.

J. R. Beste, *The Wabash; or Adventures of an English Gentleman's Family in the Interior of America.* 2 vols. London, 1855.

Morris Birkbeck, *Letters from Illinois.* Phila., 1818.

Morris Birkbeck, *Notes on a Journey in America, from Virginia to Illinois.* Phila., 1817.

I. [B.] Bishop, *The Englishwoman in America.* London, 1856.

W. N. Blane, *An Excursion through the United States and Canada, 1822–23.* London, 1824.

James Boardman, *America and the Americans* [Canada also]. London, 1833.

John Bradbury [naturalist], *Travels in the Interior of America* [1809–11]. Liverpool, 1817. — In Thwaites, *Early Western Travels*, V.

Fredrika Bremer [Swedish novelist], *Hemmen i den nya Verlden* [1849–51]. 3 vols. Stockholm, 1853. — Transl. by Mary Howett. N.Y., 1853. *America of the Fifties* [selections from above]. N.Y., 1924.

W. H. Brewer, *Up and Down California in 1860–1864.* New Haven, 1930.

G. D. Brewerton, *Overland with Kit Carson, a Narrative of the Old Spanish Trail in '48.* N.Y., 1930.

Louis Bridel, *Le Pour et le Contre* [Kentucky and Western N.Y., 1803]. Paris, 1803. — Reprinted in Buffalo Hist. Soc., Publ., XVIII (1914), 257.

Traugott Bromme, *Reisen durch die Vereinigten Staaten und Ober-Canada.* 3 vols. Balt., 1834–35.

Thomas Brothers, *The United States as They Are; Being a Cure for Radicalism.* London, 1840.

Edwin Bryant, *What I Saw in California: Being the Journal of a Tour, 1846–47.* N.Y., 1848.

J. S. Buckingham [British lecturer and M.P.], *America, Historical, Statistic, and Descriptive* [1837–38]. 2 vols. N.Y., 1841.

J. S. Buckingham, *The Eastern and Western States of America* [1839–40]. 3 vols. London, 1842.

J. S. Buckingham, *The Slave States of America* [1839]. 2 vols. London, 1842.

Rebecca Burlend, *A True Picture of Emigration* [Illinois]. London, 1848.

J. D. Burn, *Three Years among the Working-Classes in the U.S. during the War.* London, 1865.

R. F. Burton, *The City of Saints and Across the Rocky Mountains to California.* London, 1861.

A. E. R. Butler, ed., "Mrs. Butler's 1853 Diary of Rogue River Valley," *Ore. Hist. Quar.,* XLI (1940), 337.

W. A. Carter, "Diary" [1857 Kansas to Wyoming], *Annals of Wyo.,* XI (1939), 75.

Théophile Cazenove [Dutch banker], "Journal" [N.J. and Penn. in 1794]. — Transl. from the French, R. W. Kelsey, ed., Haverford College, *Studies,* No. 13 (1922).

François, Vicomte de Chateaubriand, *Voyages en Amérique, en France, et en Italie* [1791–93]. 2 vols. Paris, 1828–29.

Michel Chevalier, *Lettres sur l'Amérique du Nord* [1833–35]. 2 vols. Paris, 1836. — Transl. as *Society, Manners and Politics in the United States.* Boston, 1839.

William Clark, "A Trip across the Plains in 1857," *Iowa Jour. of Hist. and Politics,* XX (1922), 163.

James Clyman, "Diaries and Reminiscences" [Gold Rush], Calif. Hist. Soc., *Quar.,* IV–VI (1925–27).

William Cobbett [English radical], *A Year's Residence in the United States of America.* 3 vols. N.Y., 1818.

E. T. Coke, *A Subaltern's Furlough* [1832]. 2 vols. London, 1833.

É. C. V. Colbert, Comte de Maulevrier, *Voyage dans l'intérieur des États-Unis et au Canada* [1798]. Balt., 1935.

Victor Collot, *A Journey in North America* [1796]. Paris, 1826. — Reprinted, Florence, 1924, in English and French.

George Combe, *Notes on the United States during a Phrenological Visit in 1838–40.* 2 vols. Phila., 1841.

Thomas Cooper, *Some Information Respecting America.* Dublin, 1794.

E. M. Cowell, *The Cowells in America.* London, 1934. — Illustrated diary by his wife, of Sam Cowell's concert tour, 1860–61.

Alexander Craig, *America and the Americans.* Paisley, 1810.

S. C. Damon, *A Journey to Lower Oregon and Upper California, 1848–49.* San Francisco, 1927.

John Davis [novelist], *Travels . . . in the United States* [1798–1802]. N.Y., 1803.

Nicholas Dawson, *California in '41. Texas in '51. Memoirs.* [Austin, 1901 ?]. — Reprinted under another title. San Francisco, 1933.

Thomas Dean, "Journal of . . . a Voyage to Indiana in 1817," Ind. Hist. Soc., *Publ.,* VI (1918), No. 2.

Alonzo Delano, *Life on the Plains and among the Diggings.* Auburn, 1854. — Reprinted with an altered title. N.Y., 1936.

Edward Dicey, *Six Months in the Federal States.* 2 vols. London, 1863.

Charles Dickens, *American Notes.* N.Y., 1842. — Many later editions.

David Douglas [botanist], *Journal during His Travels in North America, 1823–27.* London, 1914.

Gottfried Duden, *Bericht über eine Reise nach den westlichen Staaten Nordamerikas* [1824–27]. Elberfelt, 1829.

J. M. Duncan [Scots educator], *Travels through Part of the United States and Canada, 1818–19.* 2 vols. N.Y., 1823.

Ernest Duvergier de Hauranne, *Huit Mois en Amérique, 1864–65.* 2 vols. Paris, 1866.

Timothy Dwight [Yale President], *Travels in New England and New York* [1796–1815]. 4 vols. New Haven, 1821–22.

T. B. and J. G. Eastland, "To California through Texas and Mexico" [1849], Calif. Hist. Soc., *Quar.,* XVIII (1939), 99, 229.

Joseph Eder, "A Bavarian's Journey to New Orleans and Nacogdoches in 1853–1854," *La. Hist. Quar.,* XXIII (1940), 485. — Transl. and ed. by K. J. R. Arndt.

T. J. Farnham [Vermont lawyer], *Travels in the Great Western Prairies . . . and . . . Oregon Territory* [1839]. 2 vols. London, 1843. — Also in Thwaites, *Early Western Travels,* XXVIII, XXIX.

William Faux [English farmer], *Memorable Days in America* [1818–20]. London, 1823.
— Also in Thwaites, *Early Western Travels*, XI–XII.
H. B. Fearon [advance agent for immigrants], *Sketches of America. A Narrative of a Journey of Five Thousand Miles through the Eastern and Western States.* London, 1818.
G. W. Featherstonhaugh, *Excursion through the Slave States.* 2 vols. London, 1844.
Robert Ferguson, *America during and after the War* [1864–65]. London, 1866.
William Ferguson, *America by River and Rail.* London, 1856.
Isaac Fidler [English teacher], *Observations in the United States and Canada.* N.Y., 1833.
E[dmund] F[lagg], *The Far West: or, A Tour beyond the Mountains.* 2 vols. N.Y., 1838.
James Flint [Scot], *Letters from America* [1818–20]. Edinburgh, 1822. — Also in Thwaites, *Early Western Travels*, IX.
E. P. Fordham [English engineer], *Personal Narrative of Travels in Virginia, Maryland, Pennsylvania, Ohio, Indiana, Kentucky, and Illinois: 1817–1818.* Cleve., 1906.
Jacob Fowler, *Journal from Arkansas to . . .* [Arizona], *1821–22.* N.Y., 1898.
A. J. L. Fremantle, *Three Months in the Southern States: April–June, 1863.* London, 1863.
J. C. Frémont, *Report of the Exploring Expedition to the Rocky Mountains . . . Oregon, and North California* [1842–44]. Wash., 1845.
J. C. Frémont, *Memoirs of My Life.* — Ending with the third expedition in 1846.
Julius Froebel, *Aus Amerika. Erfahrungen, Reisen und Studien* [especially N.Y. and Southwest]. 2 vols. Leipzig, 1857–58. — An abridged translation, *Seven Years' Travel in the Far West.* London, 1859.
T. H. Gladstone [London *Times* correspondent], *The Englishman in Kansas.* N.Y., 1857.
Giovanni Grassi, *Notizie varie sullo stato presente della repubblica degli Stati Uniti . . . 1818.* Milan, 1819.
T. C. Grattan [British consul at Boston], *Civilized America.* 2 vols. London, 1859.
Josiah Gregg, *Commerce of the Prairies: or, The Journal of a Santa Fé Trader* [1831–39]. 2 vols. N.Y., 1844. — In Thwaites, *Early Western Travels*, XIX–XX, and 2 vols., M. M. Quaife, ed., 1941.
Theodor Griesinger, *Lebende Bilder aus Amerika.* Stuttgart, 1858.
F. J. Grund, *The Americans in Their Moral, Social, and Political Relations.* 2 vols. London, 1837.
F. J. Grund, *Aristocracy in America.* 2 vols. London, 1839.
Basil Hall, *Travels in North America* [1827–28]. 3 vols. Edinburgh, 1829. — Accompanied by *Forty Etchings from Sketches . . . in North America.* Edinburgh, 1829. A selection from Mrs. Margaret Hall's letters on the same tour have been edited by Una Pope-Hennessy as *The Aristocratic Journey.* N.Y., 1931.
Thomas Hamilton, *Men and Manners in America.* 2 vols. Phila., 1833.
Samuel Hancock, *The Narrative . . . 1845–60* [Oregon Trail]. A. D. H. Smith, ed. N.Y., 1927.
L. W. Hastings, *Emigrants' Guide to Oregon and California.* Cin., 1845.
Henry Hay, "Journal from Detroit to the Miami River" [1789–90], M. M. Quaife, ed., Wisc. Hist. Soc., *Proc.* (1914), 208.
Henri Herz [musician], *Mes Voyages en Amérique* [1846]. Paris, 1866.
Adam Hodgson, *Remarks during a Journey through North America, 1819–1821.* 2 vols. N.Y., 1823.
C. F. Hoffman, *A Winter in the Far West* [Chicago]. 2 vols. N.Y., 1835.
Issac Holmes, *Account of the United States of America, Derived from Actual Observation during a Residence of Four Years.* London, 1823.
A. B. Hulbert, ed., *Forty-Niners; the Chronicle of the California Trail.* Boston, 1931. — An anthology of many accounts woven into a connected story.
C. W. Janson, *The Stranger in America* [1793–1806]. London, 1807.
F. A. Kemble [Butler, actress], *Journal* [1823–33]. 2 vols. London, Phila., 1835.
F. A. Kemble, *Journal of a Residence on a Georgian Plantation in 1838–39.* N.Y., 1863.
E. A. Kendall, *Travels through the Northern Parts of the United States.* 3 vols. N.Y., 1809.

C. M. S. Kirkland, *A New Home — Who'll Follow? or, Glimpses of Western Life*. N. Y., 1839.

John Lambert, *Travels through Canada, and the United States* [1806–08]. 3 vols. London, 1810.

W. B. Lang, ed., *The First Overland Mail*. [East Aurora, N.Y.], 1940. — A collection of several accounts of the Butterfield Trail, 1858.

G. H. von Langsdorff, *Narrative of the Rezanov Voyage to Nueva California in 1806*. San Francisco, 1927.

Franklin Langworthy, *Scenery of the Plains, Mountains and Mines* [1850–53]. Ogdensburgh, N.Y., 1855.

François, duc de La Rochefoucauld-Liancourt, *Voyage dans les États-Unis* [1795–97]. 8 vols. Paris, 1799. — Transl. 2 vols. London, 1799.

Charles Larpenteur, *Forty Years a Fur Trader on the Upper Missouri* [1833–72]. 2 vols. N.Y., 1898.

Marquise de La Tour du Pin, *Journal d'une femme de cinquante ans* [Boston and upper N.Y., 1794–95]. 2 vols. Paris, 1913. — Transl. as *Recollections of the Revolution and the Empire*. N.Y., 1920.

B. H. Latrobe [architect], *Journal* [Penn., Va., La., Washington, 1796–1820]. N.Y., 1905.

C. J. Latrobe, *The Rambler in North America, 1832–33* [West chiefly]. 2 vols. N.Y., 1835.

C. A. Lesueur, *Artiste et savant français en Amérique de 1816 à 1839* [sketches and watercolors]. Adrien Loir, ed. Le Havre, 1920.

Henry Lewis, *Das Illustrirte Mississippithal* [1847–49]. Düsseldorf, 1857. — Colored sketches with descriptive text by G. B. Douglas. — Reprinted Leipzig, 1923.

Meriwether Lewis and William Clark, *History of the Expedition to the Sources of the Missouri, across the Rocky Mountains and down the Columbia to the Pacific* [1804–06]. 2 vols., the "Biddle" ed. Phila., 1814. — The best is *Original Journals of the Lewis and Clark Expedition, 1804–06*. R. G. Thwaites, ed. 8 vols. N.Y., 1904–05.

Francis Lieber, *The Stranger in America*. Phila., 1835.

S. H. Long [army engineer], Edwin James [botanist], *et al.*, *Account of an Expedition from Pittsburgh to the Rocky Mountains* [1819–20]. 2 vols. Phila., 1823. — Reprinted in Thwaites, *Early Western Travels*, XIV–XVII.

S. H. Long, W. H. Keating, *et al.*, *Narrative of an Expedition to the Lake of the Woods* [1823]. 2 vols. Phila., 1824.

Charles Lyell [geologist], *Travels in North America* [1841–42]. 2 vols. N.Y., 1845.

Charles Lyell, *A Second Visit to the United States* [1845–46]. 2 vols. N.Y., 1849.

C. S. Lyman [scientist], *Around the Horn to the Sandwich Islands and California* [1845–50]. New Haven, 1924.

Alexander Mackay, *The Western World; or, Travels in the United States in 1846–47*. 2 vols. Phila., 1849.

Charles Mackay, *Life and Liberty in America; or, Sketches of a Tour in the United States and Canada in 1857–58*. 2 vols. London, 1859.

S. S. Magoffin, *Down the Santa Fé Trail and into Mexico* [diary, 1846–47]. S. M. Drumm, ed. New Haven, 1926.

R. B. Marcy, *Marcy & the Gold Seekers. The Journal*. Grant Foreman, ed. Norman, 1939.

Frederick Marryat, *A Diary in America, with Remarks on Its Institutions*. 2 parts, 3 vols. each. London, 1839.

Harriet Martineau, *Society in America* [analysis, 1834–36]. 3 vols. London, 1837.

Harriet Martineau, *Retrospect of Western Travel* [travelogue, 1834–36]. 3 vols. London, 1838. — Reprinted, N.Y., 1938.

R. L. Mason [Maryland gentleman], *Narrative in the Pioneer West, 1819*. N.Y., 1915.

Ernest de Massey, "A Frenchman in the Gold Rush," Calif. Hist. Soc., *Quar.*, V (1926), 3, 139, 219, 342, VI (1927), 37.

J. W. Massie, *America: the Origin of Her Present Conflict, Illustrated by Incidents of Travel in 1863*. London, 1864.

F. B. Mayer, *With Pen and Pencil on the Frontier in 1851* [diary and sketches]. Balt., 1872.

John Melish [cartographer], *Travels in the United States* [1806–07; 1809–11]. 2 vols. Phila., 1812.

André Michaux [botanist], "Journal" [1793–96], Am. Phil. Soc., *Proc.*, XXVI (1889). — Transl. in Thwaites, *Early Western Travels*, III.

F. A. Michaux [naturalist, son of above], *Voyage à l'ouest des Monts Alléghanys* [1802]. Paris, 1804. — Transl. London, 1805. Reprinted in Thwaites, *Early Western Travels*, III.

Baron de Montlezun, *Voyage de New Yorck à la Nouvelle Orléans* [1816–17]. 2 vols. Paris, 1818.

Édouard de Montulé, *Travels in America, 1816–1817.* — Transl. by Edward Seeber. Indianapolis, 1951.

M. L. E. Moreau de Saint-Méry [Haitian émigré and bookseller], *Voyage aux États-Unis de l'Amérique* [1793–98]. New Haven, 1913. — Transl. by Kenneth and A. M. Roberts. Garden City, N.Y., 1947.

Achille Murat [Napoleonic prince], *Lettres sur les États-Unis* [1826–27]. Paris, 1830. — Transl. and greatly extended as *America and the Americans.* N.Y., 1849.

A. M. Murray [maid of honor to the Queen], *Letters from the United States, Cuba, and Canada.* 2 vols. N.Y., 1856.

C. A. Murray [master of household to the Queen], *Travels in North America, Including a Summer Residence with the Pawnees* [1834–36]. N.Y., 1839.

Peter Neilson, *Recollections of Six Years in the United States.* Glasgow, 1830.

Thomas Nuttall [ornithologist], *Journal of Travels into the Arkansas Territory* [1819]. Phila., 1821. — Reprinted in Thwaites, *Early Western Travels*, XIII.

William Oliver, *Eight Months in Illinois.* Newcastle-upon-Tyne, 1843.

F. L. Olmsted, *Journey in the Back Country* [1853–54]. N.Y., 1860.

F. L. Olmsted, *Journey in the Seaboard Slave States* [1853]. N.Y., 1856.

F. L. Olmsted, *Journey through Texas* [1853–54]. N.Y., 1857. — Olmsted's three works constitute his series *Our Slave States*, and upon them is based *The Cotton Kingdom.* 2 vols. N.Y., 1861. New ed., N.Y., 1953. A. M. Schlesinger, ed.

John Owen, *Journals and Letters* [1850–1871, Far Northwest]. 2 vols. N.Y., 1927.

A. A. Parker [of N.H.], *Trip to the West and Texas.* Concord, N.H., 1835.

Samuel Parker, *Journal of an Exploring Tour beyond the Rocky Mountains.* Ithaca, 1838.

Richard Parkinson [English agriculturist], *Tour in America* [1798–1800, mostly Va. and Md.]. London, 1805. — R. and extended, London, 1807.

Francis Parkman, *The Oregon Trail.* N.Y., 1849. — Many later editions.

John Parsons [Va. lawyer], *A Tour through Indiana in 1840.* N.Y., 1920.

J. O. Pattie [of Kentucky], *Personal Narrative* [St. Louis to California, Mexico, 1824–30]. Cin., 1831. — Reprinted in Thwaites, *Early Western Travels*, XVIII.

Théodore Pavie, *Souvenirs atlantiques; voyage aux États-Unis et au Canada.* 2 vols. Paris, 1833.

Seth Pease, "Journals to and from New Connecticutt, 1796–98," Western Reserve Hist. Soc., *Tracts*, No. 94 (1914), pt. 2.

François Péron, *Mémoires . . . sur ses voyages* [includes New England, 1797–99]. 2 vols. Paris, 1824.

F. M. Perrin du Lac, *Voyage dans les deux Louisianes* [Ohio and Mississippi Valleys, 1801–03]. Paris, 1805. — Transl. in Richard Phillips, *Collection of Modern Voyages* (London, 1807), VI.

Albert Pike, "Narrative of a Journey in the Prairie" [1831], Arkansas Hist. Assoc., *Publ.*, IV (1917), 66.

Z. M. Pike, *An Account of Expeditions to the Sources of the Mississippi* [1805–07]. 4 vols. Phila., 1810. — Elliott Coues, ed. N.Y., 1895.

John Pope, *A Tour through the Southern and Western Territories of the United States.* Richmond, 1792.

John Pope, "Report of Exploration of a Route for the Pacific Railroad . . . from the Red River to the Rio Grande" [1854], 33 Cong., 1 Sess., *H. Ex. Doc.*, No. 129, XVIII.

Tyrone Power [actor], *Impressions of America* [1833–35]. 2 vols. Phila., 1836.

Francis and Theresa Pulszky [with Louis Kossuth], *White, Red, Black: Sketches of American Society.* 2 vols. N.Y., 1853.

O. M. Raeder, *America in the Forties*. Minneapolis, 1929. — Transl. from Norwegian.

G. W. Read, *A Pioneer of 1850* [Missouri to California, 1850; N.Y. to California via Panama, 1862]. Boston, 1927.

J. C. Reid, *Reid's Tramp* [Texas to California]. Selma, Ala., 1858.

C. C. Robin [naturalist], *Voyages dans l'intérieur de la Louisiane, de la Floride Occidentale, et dans les Isles* [1802–06]. 3 vols. Paris, 1807.

Anne Royall [Washington journalist], *The Black Book; or A Continuation of Travels*. 3 vols. Wash., 1828–29.

Anne Royall, *Mrs. Royall's Pennsylvania*. 2 vols. Wash., 1829.

Anne Royall, *Mrs. Royall's Southern Tour*. 2 vols. Wash., 1830.

Anne Royall, *Letters from Alabama* [1817–1822]. Wash., 1830.

Anne Royall, *Sketches of History, Life, and Manners in the United States*. New Haven, 1826.

Osborne Russell, *Journal of a Trapper, or Nine Years in the Rocky Mountains* [1834–43]. Boise, 1914.

W. H. Russell, *American Letters to the London Times, 1861–62*. N.p., n.d.

G. A. Sala, *My Diary in America in the Midst of War*. 2 vols. London, 1865.

Patrick Shirreff [Scots farmer], *Tour through North America*. Edinburgh, 1835.

P. J. de Smet, *Letters and Sketches: with a Narrative of a Year's Residence among the Indian Tribes of the Rocky Mountains*. Phila., 1843. — Reprinted in Thwaites, *Early Western Travels*, XXVII.

P. J. de Smet, *Oregon Missions and Travels . . . in 1845–46*. N.Y., 1847. — Reprinted, Thwaites, *Early Western Travels*, XXIX.

J. S. Smith, "Journals" [1822–29]. — These are printed, together with other materials, in M. S. Sullivan, *The Travels of Jedediah Smith* (Santa Ana, Calif., 1934); H. C. Dale, *The Ashley-Smith Explorations* (r. ed., Glendale, Calif., 1941).

W. L. Smith, "Journal, 1790–91" [N.Y., New Eng., and Phila. to Charleston], Mass. Hist. Soc., *Proc.*, LI (1917), 35.

John Steele, *Across the Plains in 1850*. Chi., 1930.

James Stirling [of Glasgow], *Letters from the Slave States*. London, 1857.

James Stuart, *Three Years in North America* [1828–31]. 2 vols. Edinburgh, 1833.

Robert Stuart, *The Discovery of the Oregon Trail; Robert Stuart's Narratives* [1811–13]. P. A. Rollins, ed. N.Y., 1935.

Joseph Sturge [abolitionist], *A Visit to the United States in 1841*. London, 1842.

Robert Sutcliff, *Travels in Some Parts of North America* [1804–06]. York, Eng., 1811.

[P. A. Tabeau], *Tabeau's Narrative of Loisel's Expedition to the Upper Missouri* [1803–05]. A. H. Abel, ed. Norman, 1939.

William Tallack [Quaker], *Friendly Sketches in America*. London, 1861.

Samuel Thorne, *The Journal of a Boy's Trip on Horseback* [Charleston, So.Car. to N.Y., 1848]. N.Y., 1936.

Walter Thornton, *Criss-Cross Journeys* [U.S. on eve of Civil War]. 2 vols. London, 1873.

C. A. H. C. de Tocqueville, *De la Démocratie en l'Amérique*. 2 vols. Brussels, 1835. — Transl. as *Democracy in America*. London, 1835. Phillips Bradley, ed. 2 vols. N.Y., 1942. Additional material of value may be found in G. W. Pierson, *Tocqueville and Beaumont in America*. N.Y., 1938.

Anthony Trollope, *North America*. 2 vols. London, 1862. — Ed. with new material by Donald Smalley and B. A. Booth. N.Y., 1951.

F. M. Trollope, *Domestic Manners of the Americans*. 2 vols. London, 1832.

William Tudor, *Letters on the Eastern States*. N.Y., 1820.

Mark Twain [S. L. Clemens], *Life on the Mississippi* [1850's]. Boston, 1883.

Thomas Twining, *Travels in America 100 Years Ago* [1795–96]. N.Y., 1894.

C. F. C., comte de Volney, *Tableau du climat et du sol des États-Unis* [1783, 1795–98]. 2 vols. Paris, [1803]. — Transl. London, 1804.

J. J. Webb, *Adventures in the Santa Fé Trade, 1844–1847*. Glendale, Calif., 1931.

Isaac Weld, Jr., *Travels through North America and Canada* [1795–97]. 2 vols. London, 1799.

F. A. Wislizenus, *Ein Ausflug nach den Felsen-gebirgen im Jahre 1839*. St. Louis, 1840. — Transl. St. Louis, 1912.

Samuel Word, "Diary across the Plains, 1863," Hist. Soc. of Montana, *Contributions,* VIII (1917).

E. S. Wortley, *Travels in the United States* [Mexico and South America also]. N.Y., 1851.

Frances Wright [D'Arusmont], *Views of Society and Manners in America* [1818–20]. N.Y., 1821.

N. J. Wyeth, *Correspondence and Journals, 1831–36.* Oregon Hist. Soc., *Sources of the History of Oregon,* I (1899). Nos. 3–6.

Lorenzo de Zavala [Mexican], *Viage a los Estados-Unidos.* Paris, 1834.

1865–1900

William Archer, *America To-day: Observations and Reflections.* N.Y., 1899.

Matthew Arnold, *Civilization in the United States.* Boston, 1888.

W. H. Barneby, *Life and Labour in the Far, Far West.* London, 1884.

J. H. Beadle, *Western Wilds, and the Men Who Redeem Them* [1868–74]. Cin., 1878.

J. W. Boddam-Whetham, *Western Wanderings.* London, 1874.

Charles Boissevain, *Van 't Noorden naar 't Zuiden.* 2 vols. Haarlem, 1881–82.

Paul Bourget, *Outre-Mer: Impressions of America.* N.Y., 1895.

Samuel Bowles, *Across the Continent.* Springfield, 1866.

J. H. Bridge, *Uncle Sam at Home.* N.Y., 1888.

James Bryce, *The American Commonwealth.* 2 vols. N.Y., 1888 — Several later revisions.

George Campbell, *White and Black, the Outcome of a Visit to the United States.* N.Y., 1879.

Francesco Carego di Muricce, *In America: Stati Uniti, Avana, Portorico, Cuba, Messico.* 2 vols. Florence, 1875.

Georges Clemenceau, *American Reconstruction, 1865–1870.* Fernand Baldensperger, ed. Margaret MacVeagh, transl. N.Y., 1928. — Letters to the Paris *Temps.*

Ernest Duvergier de Hauranne, *Les États-Unis en 1867.* Paris, 1867.

Emily Faithfull [English feminist], *Three Visits to America* [1872, 1882, 1884]. N.Y., 1884.

E. A. Freeman [historian], *Some Impressions of the United States.* N.Y., 1883.

Carlo Gardini, *Gli Stati Uniti.* 2 vols. Bologna, 1887.

Giuseppe Giacosa, *Impressioni d'America.* Milan, 1908. — Account by the dramatist of a visit in 1898.

L. H. Griffin [Tory], *The Great Republic.* N.Y., 1884.

Knut Hamsun, *Fra det moderne Amerikas aandsliv.* Copenhagen, 1889.

Lady Duffus Hardy, *Through Cities and Prairie Lands.* N.Y., 1881.

E. O. Hopp, *Transatlantisches Skizzenbuch, Federzeichungen aus den amerikanischen Leben.* Berlin, 1876.

J. A., graf von Hübner [Austrian diplomat], *Promenade autour du monde, 1871.* 2 vols. Paris, 1873. — Transl. London, 1874. Most of Vol. I deals with the United States.

Claudio Jannet, *Les États-Unis contemporaines.* Paris, 1875.

Rudyard Kipling, *American Notes.* N.Y., 1891. — Many later editions.

John Leng, *America in 1876.* Dundee, 1877.

Alexander MacMillan, *A Night with the Yankees* [lecture in Cambridge, England, dealing chiefly with Massachusetts]. Ayr, Scotland, 1868.

David Macrae, *The Americans at Home.* 2 vols. Edinburgh, 1870.

W. G. Marshall, *Through America; or, Nine Months in the United States.* London, 1881.

José Marti, *En los Estados Unidos.* 2 vols. Havana, 1902–05. — A collection of articles written for newspapers in the 1880's. Also in various other editions.

A. M. Maycock, *With Mr. Chamberlain in the United States and Canada, 1887–88.* London, 1914.

Edmondo Mayor des Planches, *Attraverso gli Stati Uniti. Per l'Emigrazione Italiana.* Turin, 1913.

John Muir, *My First Summer in the Sierras* [1869]. Boston, 1911.

John Muir, *Travels in Alaska* [1879–80, 1890]. Boston, 1915.

J. F. Muirhead [Baedeker compiler], *The Land of Contrasts: A Briton's View of His American Kin.* Boston, 1898.

J. M. Murphy, *Rambles in North-western America, from the Pacific Ocean to the Rocky Mountains*. London, 1879.
J. W. Powell, *Exploration of the Colorado River* [1869–72]. Wash., 1875.
A. D. Richardson, *Beyond the Mississippi* [1857–67]. Hartford, 1867.
Richard Rose, *The Great Country*. London, 1868.
Adolfo Rossi, *Un Italiano in America* [N.Y. City and Far West]. 2 ed. Milan, 1894.
W. H. Russell, *Hesperothen; Notes from the West*. 2 vols. London, 1882.
G. A. Sala [British editor], *America Revisited*. 2 vols. N.Y., 1880.
William Saunders, *Through the Light Continent; or, the United States in 1877–8*. London, 1879.
Robert Somers, *The Southern States since the War* [1870–71]. N.Y., 1871.
G. W. Steevens, *The Land of the Dollar*. N.Y., 1897.
C. W. Stoddard, *Diary of a Visit to Molokai in 1884*. San Francisco, 1933.
P. A. Tverskoy [pseud. of P. A. Demens], *Ocherki Sievero-Amerikanskikh Soedinenykh Shtatov*. St. Petersburg, 1895.
Mark Twain [S. L. Clemens], *Roughing It* [Far West in 1860's]. Hartford, 1871.
A. P. Vivian [sporting M.P.], *Wanderings in the Western Land*. London, 1879.
H. H. Vivian, *Notes of a Tour in America* [1877]. London, 1878.
A Visit to the States [reprint of London *Times* special correspondence]. 2 vols. London, 1887–88.
C. D. Warner, *Studies in the South and West, with Comments on Canada*. N.Y., 1889.
M. T. Yelverton, viscountess Avomore, *Teresina in America*. 2 vols. London, 1875.
W. E. Youngman, *Gleanings from Western Prairies* [Kansas]. Cambridge, 1882.
Alessandro Zannini, *De l'Atlantique au Mississippi, souvenirs d'un diplomate*. Paris, 1884.
F. B. Zinke, *Last Winter in the United States* [chiefly South]. London, 1868.

1900–1951

L. A. Armer, *Southwest*. London, 1935.
A. A. Anderson, *Experiences and Impressions*. N.Y., 1933.
Simone de Beauvoir, *L'Amérique au jour le jour*. Paris, [1948].
Hilaire Belloc, *The Contrast*. London, 1923.
Arnold Bennett, *Your United States*. N.Y., 1912.
Lord Birkenhead, *My American Visit*. London, 1918.
G. A. Birmingham [pseud. of J. A. Hannay, Irish wit and clergyman], *Dublin to Chicago*. N.Y., 1914.
Sudhindra Bose [Indian scholar], *Fifteen Years in America*. Calcutta, 1920.
C. H. Bretherton, *Midas, or the United States and the Future*. N.Y., 1926.
D. W. Brogan, *The American Character*. N.Y., 1944. — R. ed. N.Y., 1950.
Elijah Brown [Alan Raleigh], *The Real America*. London, 1913.
Julio Camba, *Un Año en el otro mondo* [1916]. 3 ed. Madrid, 1927.
F. G. Carpenter, *Alaska, Our Northern Wonderland*. N.Y., 1928.
W. M. Carpenter, *So Long, Ohio*. Boston, 1935.
G. K. Chesterton, *What I Saw in America*. N.Y., 1921.
Alistair Cooke, *One Man's America*. N.Y., 1952.
Jonathan Daniels, *A Southerner Discovers New England*. N.Y., 1940.
Jonathan Daniels, *A Southerner Discovers the South*. N.Y., 1938.
Maurice Dekobra, *Sept ans chez les hommes libres*. N.Y., 1946.
Georges Duhamel, *Scènes de la vie future*. Paris, 1930. — Transl. as *America; the Menace*. Boston, 1931.
C. R. Enock, *Farthest West; Life and Travel in the United States*. London, 1910.
Paul, baron d'Estournelles de Constant, *America and Her Problems*. N.Y., 1915.
A. M. Ewing, *Seeing America First*. Ada, Ohio, 1922.
Bernard Faÿ, *The American Experiment*. N.Y., 1929.
Arthur Feiler, ed., *Amerika-Europa*. Frankfurt on Main, 1926. — Transl. as *America Seen through German Eyes*. N.Y., 1928.
W. G. Fitzgerald [Ignatius Phayre], *Can America Last?* London, 1933.
Lili Foldes, *Two on a Continent*. N.Y., 1947.
Philip Gibbs, *Land of Destiny*. N.Y., 1920.

Stephen Graham, *With Poor Immigrants to America*. N.Y., 1914.
John Gunther, *Inside U.S.A.* N.Y., 1951.
Henri Hauser [historian], *L'Amérique vivante*. Paris, 1924.
A. I. S. Hedin, *Arbetsglädje; Lärdomar från Amerika*. Stockholm, 1920.
Ilya Ilf and Eugene Petrov, *Little Golden America*. N.Y., 1937.
Henry James, *The American Scene*. N.Y., 1907.
Lennox Kerr, *Back Door Guest*. Indianapolis, 1930.
Odette Keun, *I Think Aloud in America*. N.Y., 1939.
Egon Erwin Kisch beehrt sich darzubieten: Paradies Amerika. Berlin, 1930.
Félix Klein [Catholic priest], *Au Pays de "la vie intense."* Paris, 1905. — Transl. Chi.,
    1905.
Stephen Longstreet, *The Last Man Comes Home. American Travel Journals, 1941–1942*.
    N.Y., 1942.
A. M. Low, *America at Home*. London, 1905.
A. M. Low, *The Amercian People*. 2 vols. Boston, 1909–11.
David Macrae, *America Revisited*. Glasgow, 1908.
André Maurois, *États-Unis 39 journal d'un voyage en Amérique*. Paris, 1939.
R. E. Mitchell, *America; a Practical Handbook*. London, 1935.
Ramsay Muir, *America the Golden*. London, 1927.
Hugo Münsterberg [German-American psychologist], *American Traits from the Point
    of View of a German*. Boston, 1901.
Hugo Münsterberg, *Die Amerikaner*. 2 vols. Berlin, 1904. — Transl., E. B. Holt, N.Y.,
    1904.
Ward Morehouse, *American Reveille*. N.Y., 1942.
Alva and Gunnar Myrdal, *Kontakt med Amerika*. Stockholm, [1941].
Bernard Newman, *American Journey*. London, 1943.
A. M. Peck and Enid Johnson, *Roundabout America*. 2 vols. N.Y., 1933.
W. E. and M. P. Price, *America after Sixty Years* [travel diaries of two generations of
    British parliamentarians, 1869, 1878, and 1934]. London, 1936.
P. W. Rainier, *American Hazard*. London, [1942].
E. B. Reed, ed., *The Commonwealth Fund Fellows' Impressions of America* [1925–31].
    N.Y., 1932.
George Santayana, *Character and Opinion in the United States*. N.Y., 1920.
André Siegfried, *Les États-Unis d'aujourd'hui*. Paris, 1927. — Transl. as *America Comes
    of Age*. N.Y., 1927.
J. G. Sleeswijk, *Van Menschen en Dingen in Amerika*. Amsterdam, [1933].
William Teeling, *American Stew*. London, 1933.
Ernst Toller, *Quer Durch. Reisebilder und Reden*. Berlin, 1930. — Transl. London, 1931.
N. Vasiliev, *Amerika s Chernogo Khoda*. [Moscow], 1949.
Count Vay de Vaya und Luskod [Hungarian], *The Inner Life of the United States*.
    London, 1908.
P. E. Vernon, *Coast to Coast by Motor*. London, 1930.
Enrico, marchese di Visconti-Venosta, *Impressions of America*. Chi., 1933.
Charles Wagner [author of *The Simple Life*], *My Impressions of America*. — Transl.
    from French. N.Y., 1906.
H. G. Wells, *The Future in America*. N.Y., 1906.
Edmund Wilson, *Travels in Two Democracies* [U.S.A. and U.S.S.R., 1932–35]. N.Y., 1936

49. UNOFFICIAL ANNUAL AND BIENNIAL COMPILATIONS

These compilations supply information in summary and generally with a
high degree of reliability. The usefulness of one important category of this material is discussed by C. S. Brigham, "An Account of American Almanacs and
Their Value for Historical Study," Am. Antiq. Soc., *Proc.*, new ser., XXXV
(1925), 195, and Esther Jerabek, "Almanacs as Historical Sources," *Minn. Hist.*, XV
(1934), 444. In the select list below, the titles are given first, as is usual in citing
them. All are of annual issue unless otherwise noted. The tabulation omits

statistical annuals, government yearbooks, and annual bibliographical surveys, which are treated in §§ 7, 36, 45, 46, 47.

The American Almanac and Repository of Useful Knowledge. Boston, 1830–61.

American Almanac and Treasury of Facts, Statistical, Financial, and Political. A. R. Spofford, ed. N.Y., 1878–89.

American Annual Cyclopædia. See *Appletons' Annual Cyclopædia.*

The American Annual of Photography. Boston etc., 1887– .

The American Annual Register. N.Y. etc., 1827–35.

American Art Annual. N.Y., 1898–1941.

The American Jewish Year Book. Phila., 1899– .

The American Labor Year Book. N.Y., 1916–32.

The American Year Book. S. N. D. North and later eds. N.Y., 1911–20, 1926– .

Americana Annual. A. H. McDannald and later eds. N.Y., 1923– .

Annual of Scientific Discovery: or, Year-Book of Facts in Science and Art. D. A. Wells and later eds. Boston, 1850–71.

Annual Record of Science and Industry. S. F. Baird, ed. N.Y., 1872–79.

The Annual Register. Edmund Burke and later eds. London, 1759– . — General indexes for 1758–80, 1781–92, and 1758–1819; annual indexes thereafter.

Appletons' Annual Cyclopædia. N.Y., 1862–1903. — Vols. I–XIV (1861–75), entitled *American Annual Cyclopædia,* have a separate index volume. The "New Series," embracing Vols. XV–XXXV (1876–95), has a general index in the final volume. The indexes of the "Third Series," embracing Vols. XXXVI–XLII (1896–1902), are cumulative.

An Astronomical Diary, or, an Almanack. Nathaniel Ames, ed. until 1764, followed by his son Nathaniel. Boston, 1726–75.

A Hand-Book of Politics. Edward McPherson, ed. Wash., 1868–94. — Biennial.

Information Please Almanac. John Kieran, ed. N.Y., 1947– .

The International Year Book. F. M. Colby and later eds. N.Y., 1899–1902. — Resumed as *New International Year Book.* N.Y., 1908– .

McPherson. See *A Hand-Book of Politics.*

Major Problems of United States Foreign Policy. Brookings Institution, ed. Wash., 1947– .

The Musical Year Book of the United States. Boston, 1886–93.

The National Calendar. Peter Force, ed. Wash., 1820–24, 1828–36.

Negro Year Book and Annual Encyclopedia of the Negro. M. N. Work and later eds. Tuskegee, 1912– .

New International Year Book. See *International Year Book.*

Newsweek's History of Our Times. N.Y., 1950– .

The Political Almanac. George Gallup, ed. N.Y., 1952– .

Political Handbook of the World. Title varies. W. H. Mallory, ed. N.Y., 1927– .

Poor Richard, an Almanack. Title varies. Benjamin Franklin, ed. Phila., 1732–67. — Continued thereafter under various editors and with many imitators.

Social Work Year Book. F. S. Hall and later eds. N.Y., 1929– . — Biennial.

The Statesman's Year Book. London, 1864– . — Beginning with 1906, a special section is devoted to the United States and to separate countries and dependencies.

The Theatre Book of the Year. G. J. Nathan, ed. N.Y., 1942– .

The Tribune Almanac. See *The Whig Almanac.*

United Nations Yearbook. (§ 47).

The United States in World Affairs. Walter Lippmann and later eds. N.Y., 1932– .

U.S. Camera. N.Y., 1935– .

The Whig Almanac and Politician's Register (1838), *The Politician's Register* (1839–41), and *The Whig Almanac* (1843–55). N.Y., 1843–55. — Continued as *The Tribune Almanac.* N.Y., 1856–1914.

Whitaker's Almanack. London, 1820– .

Who's Who in America, a Biographical Dictionary of Notable Living Men and Women of the United States. A. N. Marquis and later eds. Chi., 1899– . — Biennial.

The World Almanac. N.Y., 1869–77, 1887– .

The magazines and other publications issued by learned societies in history and allied fields and by state historical departments teem with material for the student. The formidable extent of this literature is indicated by the fact that C. C. Crittenden and Doris Godard, compilers of *Historical Societies in the United States and Canada* (Wash., 1944), currently catalogue 833 societies for the United States alone. In addition, scholarly journals are sometimes published independently of organizational sponsorship. The list below is highly selective. For the user's convenience an effort is made to cite general indexes to the publications where any are available. Note that historical articles appear occasionally in legal, medical, and other professional journals. For the output of universities and independent research agencies, see: § 51.

NATIONAL, REGIONAL, AND MISCELLANEOUS

Abraham Lincoln Association, *Papers.* Springfield, Ill., 1924–39. *Bulletin*, 1923–39. *Abraham Lincoln Quarterly*, 1940– . — General index to *Papers*; to *Bulletin* through 1937.

Academy of Political Science, *Proceedings.* N.Y., 1910– . *Political Science Quarterly*, 1886– . — General index to *Quarterly* through 1930, 1931–50.

Agricultural History Society, *Papers.* Wash., 1921–25. *Agricultural History*. Chi. etc., 1927– . — General index to both through 1950.

American Academy of Political and Social Science, *Annals.* Phila., 1890– . — General index through 1916; quinquennially thereafter.

American Anthropological Association, *Memoirs.* Lancaster, Penn., 1905– . *American Anthropologist*. Wash., 1888– . (Vols. I–XI were issued by the Anthropological Society of Washington.) — General index to *Anthropologist* through 1928, 1929–38.

American Antiquarian Society, *Archæologia Americana: Transactions and Collections*. Worcester, 1820–1911. *Proceedings*, 1843– . — General index to *Proceedings* through 1880.

American Association for Labor Legislation, *American Labor Legislation Review*. N.Y., 1911–42.

American Association for State and Local History, *Bulletin*. Wash., 1941– . *American Heritage*. Cooperstown, N.Y., 1947–49. Burlington, Vt., etc., 1949– .

American Association of Schools and Departments of Journalism and the American Association of Teachers of Journalism, *Journalism Quarterly*. Grand Forks, etc., 1924– . — Title varies. General index through 1948.

American Association of the History of Medicine and the Johns Hopkins Institute of the History of Medicine, *Bulletin of the History of Medicine*. Balt., 1933– . — General index through 1946.

American Bar Association, *Report*. Balt., 1878– . *Journal*, 1915– . — General index to *Journal* through 1937.

American Catholic Historical Association, *Catholic Historical Review*. Wash., 1915– . *Papers*, 1926– . *Documents*, 1933– . — General index to *Review* through 1935.

American Catholic Historical Society, *American Catholic Historical Researches*. Pitt., 1884–1912. *Records*. Phila., 1884– . — General index to *Researches*; to *Records* through 1920.

American Economic Association, *Publications*. Balt., 1886–1910. — Title varies. Continued as *American Economic Review*. Ithaca etc., 1911– . — General index to *Publications*.

American Folk-Lore Society, *Memoirs*. Boston etc., 1894– . *Journal of American Folk-Lore*, 1888– . General index to *Journal* through 1930.

American Geographical Society, *Journal*. N.Y., 1859–1900. Continued as *Bulletin*, 1901–15; then as *Geographical Review*, 1916– . *Focus*, 1950– . General index to *Bulletin*; to *Review* through 1925, 1926–35, 1936–45.

American Historical Association, *Papers.* N.Y., 1885–91. *Annual Report.* Wash., 1890– .
  American Historical Review. N.Y. etc., 1895– . — General index to *Papers* and
  Reports through 1914; decennial indexes to *Review,* 1906, 1916, 1926, 1936; "Guide
  to *Review,* 1895–1945."
American-Irish Historical Society, *Journal.* Boston etc., 1898– . *Recorder.* N.Y., 1923– .
American Jewish Historical Society, *Publications.* Balt. etc., 1893– . — General index
  through no. 20.
American Literature. Durham, 1929– .
American Neptune. Salem, Mass., 1941– .
American Philosophical Society, *Transactions.* Phila., 1771– . *Proceedings,* 1838– . —
  General index to all publications, 1940.
American Political Science Association, *Proceedings.* Lancaster, Penn., etc., 1904–14.
  American Political Science Review. Balt. etc., 1906– . — General index to *Pro-*
  ceedings through 1914; to *Review* through 1926.
American Social Science Association, *Journal of Social Science.* N.Y. etc., 1869–1909.
American Society of International Law, *Proceedings.* N.Y., 1907– . *American Journal of*
  International Law. N.Y. etc., 1907– . — General index to both through 1920.
American Society of Medical History, *Medical Life.* N.Y., 1894–1938. — Title varies.
American Sociological Society, *Papers and Proceedings.* Chi. etc., 1906–35. *American*
  Sociological Review. Menasha, 1936– .
American Speech. Balt. etc., 1925– .
American Statistical Association, *Publications.* Boston etc., 1888–1921. *Journal,* 1922– .
  — General index to both through 1939.
Annals of Medical History. N.Y., 1917–42.
Association for the Study of Negro Life and History, *Journal of Negro History.* Lancaster,
  Penn., etc., 1916– . General index through 1931.
Association of American Geographers, *Annals.* Albany, 1911– . General index through
  1935.
Association of History Teachers of the Middle States and Maryland, *Proceedings.* Balt.,
  1903– . — General index through 1931.
Business Historical Society, *Business Historical Studies.* Chi., etc., 1928. *Bulletin.* Boston,
  1926– . *Journal of Economic and Business History* (with Harvard Graduate School
  of Business Administration). Cambridge, 1928–32. — General index to *Bulletin*
  through 1941.
Canadian Historical Association, *Reports.* Ottawa, 1915– . — Title varies.
Canadian Historical Review. Toronto, 1920– . — General index through 1929, 1930–39.
Carl Schurz Memorial Foundation, *American-German Review.* Phila., 1934– .
Economic History Association, *Journal of Economic History.* N.Y., 1941– .
Friends' Historical Association, *Bulletin.* Phila., 1906– . — General index through 1921,
  1922–26, 1927–31, 1932–36.
German American Historical Society, *Americana Germanica.* N.Y., 1897–1902. Continued
  as *German American Annals.* N.Y. etc., 1903–19.
Hispanic-American Historical Review. Balt., etc., 1918–21, 1927– . — General index
  through 1945.
Historical Magazine (Dawson's). Boston, etc., 1857–75.
History Teacher's Magazine. Phila., 1909–18. Continued as *Historical Outlook,* 1918–33,
  then as *Social Studies,* 1934– . — General index through 1925.
Journal of Modern History. Chi., 1929– .
Journal of the History of Ideas. Lancaster, Penn., 1940– .
Magazine of American History. N.Y. etc., 1877–93. Revived, Mt. Vernon, N.Y., 1901–17.
  — General index through 1893.
Magazine of History. N.Y. etc., 1905–22. "Extra Numbers," 1908–35. — General indexes
  to *Magazine,* 1912, 1919; to "Extra Numbers," 1919, 1924, 1928.
Mississippi Valley Historical Association, *Proceedings.* Cedar Rapids, Ia., 1907–24. *Mis-*
  sissippi Valley Historical Review, 1914– . Clarence Walworth Alvord Memorial
  Commission, *Publications.* St. Paul, 1942– . — General index to *Review,* 1914–29,
  1929–39, 1939–49; topical guide to *Proceedings* and *Review* to 1932.
National Council for the Social Studies, *Social Education.* Crawfordsville, Ind., 1937– .

Naval History Society, *Publications*. N.Y., 1911–32.
New England Historic Genealogical Society, *New England Historical and Genealogical Register*. Boston, 1847– . — General indexes of persons (1906–07), subjects (1908), and places (1911), covering Vols. I–L; continued in D. L. Jacobus, comp., *Index to Genealogical Periodicals* (New Haven, 1932).
New England Quarterly. Balt. etc., 1928– . — General index through 1937.
Norwegian-American Historical Association, *Studies and Records*. Minneapolis etc., 1926– . *Travel and Description Series*, 1926–29.
Pacific Coast Branch, American Historical Association, *Proceedings*. Wash., 1904–30. *Pacific Historical Review*. Glendale, 1932– . — General index to *Review* through 1943.
Phi Alpha Theta, *Historian*. Albuquerque, N.M., 1938– .
Presbyterian Historical Society, *Journal*. Phila., 1901–29. Continued by Department of History, Presbyterian General Assembly, 1930– .
Protestant Episcopal Church, *Historical Magazine*. N.Y., 1932– .
Railway and Locomotive Historical Society, *Bulletin*. Boston, 1921– . — General index through 1930, 1931–42, 1943–51.
Scotch-Irish Society of America, *The Scotch-Irish in America: Proceedings of the Scotch-Irish Congress*. Cin., 1889–1901.
Society of American Archivists, *American Archivist*. Wash. etc., 1938– .
Southern Historical Association, *Journal of Southern History*. Baton Rouge etc., 1935– .
Southern Historical Society, *Papers*. Richmond, Va., 1876– . — General index through 1913.
Southern History Association, *Publications*. Wash., 1897–1907.
Southern Political Science Association, *Proceedings*. Gainesville, Fla., 1933–38. *Journal of Politics*, 1939– .
Swedish Historical Society of America, *Yearbook*. Chi. etc., 1905–26. *Swedish-American Historical Bulletin*. St. Peter, Minn., 1928–32.
United States Catholic Historical Society, *Historical Records and Studies*. N.Y., 1900– . *Monograph Series*, 1902– .
United States Infantry Association, *Infantry Journal*. Wash., 1904– .
Yivo Annual of Jewish Social Science. N.Y., 1946– .

STATE AND LOCAL
(Arranged alphabetically by states)

A — H

Alabama Historical Society, *Transactions*. Tuscaloosa, 1852, 1855, 1898–1906.
State Department of Archives and History, *Alabama Historical Quarterly*. Montgomery, 1930–31, 1940– .
State Historian of Arizona, *Arizona Historical Review*. Phoenix, 1928–36.
Arkansas Historical Association, *Publications*. Fayetteville, 1906–17. *Arkansas Historical Quarterly*, 1942– .
California Historical Society, *Quarterly*. San Francisco, 1922– .
Historical Society of Southern California, *Annual Publication*. Los Angeles, 1884–1934. Continued as *Quarterly Publication*, 1935– . Title varies. — General index through 1920.
Society of California Pioneers, *Quarterly*. San Francisco, 1924– .
State Historical Society of Colorado, *Colorado Magazine*. Denver, 1923– .
Columbia Historical Society, *Records*. Wash., 1897– . — General index through 1946.
Connecticut Historical Society, *Collections*. Hartford, 1860–1932. *Bulletin*, 1934– .
New Haven Colony Historical Society, *Papers*. New Haven, 1865–1918.
Historical Society of Delaware, *Papers*. Wilmington, 1879– . *Delaware History*, 1946– .
Florida Historical Society, *Quarterly*. Jacksonville, 1908– . — General index from beginning to 1928, 1928–36, 1936–43.
Florida State Historical Society, *Publications*. Deland etc., 1922– .
Georgia Historical Society, *Collections*. Savannah, 1840–1916. *Georgia Historical Quarterly*, 1917– . — General index to *Quarterly* from beginning to 1943.
Hawaiian Historical Society, *Annual Report*. Honolulu, 1892– . *Papers*, 1892– .

I – L

Idaho State Historical Society, *Biennial Report*. Boise, 1907–   .
Chicago Historical Society, *Collections*. Chi., 1882–1928. *Bulletin*, 1922–26, 1934–   .
   Chicago History, 1945–   .
Illinois State Historical Library, *Publications*. Springfield, 1899–1937. Continued as
   Papers in Illinois History and Transactions, 1937–   . *Collections*, 1903–   . — General index to both through 1928.
Illinois State Historical Society, *Transactions*. Springfield, 1900–36. Continued as *Papers
   in Illinois History and Transactions*, 1937–   . *Journal*, 1908–   . — General index to
   Journal through 1933.
Historical Bureau of the Indiana Library and Historical Department, *Indiana Historical
   Collections*. Indianapolis, 1916–   . *Indiana History Bulletin*, 1923–   .
Indiana Historical Society, *Publications*. Indianapolis, 1895–   .
Indiana Magazine of History (§ 51).
Historical, Memorial and Art Department of Iowa, *Annals of Iowa*. Des Moines, 1882–   .
   — General index for 1893–1909, 1909–29.
State Historical Society of Iowa, *Annals*. Iowa City, 1863–74. *Iowa Historical Record*,
   1885–1902. Continued as *Iowa Journal of History and Politics*, 1903–   . *Iowa
   Applied History Series*, 1912–   . *Iowa Biographical Series*, 1907–   . *Iowa Economic
   History Series*, 1910–   . *Iowa Social History Series*, 1915–   . *Palimpsest*, 1920–   .
   — General index to *Journal* through 1942; to *Palimpsest* through 1929.
Kansas State Historical Society, *Transactions*. Topeka, 1881–1908. Continued as *Collec-
   tions*, 1910–28. Replaced by *Kansas Historical Quarterly*, 1931–   .
Filson Club, *Publications*. Louisville, 1884–   . *History Quarterly*, 1926–   .
Kentucky State Historical Society, *Register*. Frankfort, 1903–   . — General index through
   1945.
Louisiana Historical Society, *Publications*. New Orleans, 1896–1917. Continued as
   Louisiana Historical Quarterly, 1917–   . — General index to *Publications*.

M

Maine Historical Society, *Collections*. Title varies. Portland, 1831–1906. *Proceedings*,
   1902–14. *Province and Court Records*, 1928–47. — General index to *Collections*
   through 1891.
Maryland Historical Society, *Fund Publications*. Balt., 1867–1901. *Archives of Maryland*,
   1883–   . *Maryland Historical Magazine*, 1906–   .
Colonial Society of Massachusetts, *Publications*. Boston, 1895–   . — General index
   through 1924.
Essex Institute, *Historical Collections*. Salem, 1859–   . — General index through 1930,
   1931–49.
Massachusetts Historical Society, *Collections*. Boston, 1792–   . *Proceedings*, 1879–   .
   Photostat Americana, 1919–30. *Winthrop Papers*, 1929–   . — General index to all
   publications through 1935.
Prince Society, *Publications*. Boston, 1865–1920.
Michigan Historical Commission (Pioneer Society of the State of Michigan, 1874–86;
   Pioneer and Historical Society of the State of Michigan, 1887–1912), *Historical
   Collections*. Title varies. Lansing, 1874–1929. *Michigan History Magazine*, 1917–   .
   — General index to *Historical Collections* through 1915.
Minnesota Historical Society, *Collections*. St. Paul, 1850–1920. *Minnesota History*,
   1915–   . *Narratives and Documents*, 1932–   . — General index to *Collections*
   through 1904; to *History* through 1929.
Mississippi Historical Society, *Publications*. Oxford, 1898–1914. Continued as *Centenary
   Series*, 1916–   . *Journal of Mississippi History*. Jackson, 1939–   .
Missouri Historical Society, *Collections*. St. Louis, 1880–1931. *Glimpses of the Past*,
   1933–42. *Bulletin*, 1944–   .
State Historical Society of Missouri, *Documentary Publications*. Columbia, 1920–   .
   Missouri Historical Review, 1906–   . — General index to *Review* through 1931.
Historical Society of Montana, *Contributions*. Helena, 1876–   .

N

Nebraska State Historical Society, *Transactions and Reports*. Lincoln, 1885–93. Continued as *Proceedings and Collections*, 1894–1902; then as *Publications* (title varies), 1906– . *Nebraska History* (title varies), 1918– .

Nevada Historical Society, *Report*. Carson City, 1909– . *Papers*, 1913– . *Applied History Series*, 1918– .

New Hampshire Historical Society, *Collections*. Concord etc., 1824– . *Proceedings*, 1874–1917.

New Jersey Historical Society, *Collections*. Newark, 1846– . *Proceedings*, 1847– . *New Jersey Archives*, 1880– . — General index to *Proceedings* through 1919, 1920–31.

Historical Society of New Mexico, *Publications*. Santa Fe, 1881– . *Publications in History*, 1926– . *New Mexico Historical Review*, 1926– . — General index to *Review* through 1940.

Buffalo Historical Society, *Publications*. Buffalo, 1879– .

New York Historical Society, *Collections*. N.Y., 1811–59. *John Watts de Peyster Publication Fund Series*, 1868– . *John Divine Jones Fund Series*, 1879– . *Quarterly Bulletin*, 1917– .

New York State Historical Association, *Proceedings*. N.p., 1901– . *Series*. N.Y., 1932– . *Quarterly Journal*. Albany, 1919–31. Continued as *New York History*, 1932– . — General index to *Proceedings* through 1925, 1926–35; to *Journal* through 1925, 1926–31; and to *History* through 1935.

Rochester Historical Society, *Publication Fund Series*. Rochester, 1922–49. *Scrapbook*, 1950– . — General index to *Fund Series* through 1936.

Rochester Public Library, *Rochester History*. Rochester, 1939– .

North Carolina Historical Commission (since 1943, State Department of Archives and History), *Bulletin*. Raleigh, 1907– . *North Carolina Historical Review*, 1924– .

State Historical Society of North Dakota, *Collections*. Bismarck, 1906–26. Continued as *North Dakota Historical Quarterly*, 1926– .

O — T

Historical and Philosophical Society of Ohio, *Publications*. Title varies. Cin., 1906– .

Ohio State Archæological and Historical Society, *Ohio Archæological and Historical Quarterly*. Title varies. Columbus, 1887– . *Ohio Historical Collections*, 1931– . — General index to *Quarterly* through 1934.

Oklahoma Historical Society, *Historia*. Oklahoma City, 1909–22. Continued as *Chronicles of Oklahoma*, 1921– .

Oregon Historical Society, *Quarterly*. Salem etc., 1900–26. Continued as *Oregon Historical Quarterly*, 1926– .

Historical Society of Western Pennsylvania, *Western Pennsylvania Historical Magazine*. Pitt., 1918– .

Pennsylvania-German Society, *Proceedings and Addresses*. Lancaster, etc., 1891– . — General index through 1923.

Pennsylvania Historical Association, *Pennsylvania History*. Phila., 1934– .

Pennsylvania Historical Commission, *Bulletin*. Harrisburg, 1932– . *Publications*, 1930– .

Historical Society of Pennsylvania, *Memoirs*. Phila., 1826–95. *Pennsylvania Magazine of History and Biography*, 1877– .

Rhode Island Historical Society, *Collections*. Providence, 1827–1941. *Proceedings*, 1872–92, 1900–14. *Publications*, 1893–1900. *Rhode Island History*, 1941– .

South Carolina Historical Society, *Collections*. Charleston, 1857–97. *South Carolina Historical and Genealogical Magazine*, 1900– .

State Historical Society of South Dakota, *South Dakota Historical Collections*. Aberdeen etc., 1902– . — General index through 1932.

East Tennessee Historical Society, *Publications*. Knoxville, 1929– .

Tennessee Historical Society, *Tennessee Historical Magazine*. Nashville, 1915–37. *Tennessee Historical Quarterly* (in coöperation with the Tennessee Historical Commission), 1942– . — General index to *Magazine* through 1926.

Texas State Historical Association, *Quarterly*. Austin, 1897–1912. Continued as *Southwestern Historical Quarterly*, 1912– . — General index through 1937.
West Texas Historical Association, *Year Book*. Abilene, 1925– .

U – Z

Utah State Historical Society, *Utah Historical Quarterly*. Salt Lake City, 1928– .
Vermont Historical Society, *Proceedings*. Montpelier, 1860– .
Virginia Historical Society, *Virginia Historical Register*. Richmond, 1848–53. *Virginia Historical Reporter*, 1854–60. *Collections*, 1882–92. *Virginia Magazine of History and Biography*, 1893– . — General index to the *Register* and *Magazine* through 1930 in E. G. Swem, comp., *Virginia Historical Index* (2 vols., Roanoke, 1934–36).
Virginia State Library, *Virginia Cavalcade*. Richmond, 1951– .
Washington State Historical Society, *Publications*. Olympia, 1906–14.
Washington University State Historical Society, *Washington Historical Quarterly*. Seattle, 1906–35. Continued as *Pacific Northwest Quarterly*, 1936– . — General index through 1929.
State Department of Archives and History, Charleston, *West Virginia History*, 1939– .
State Historical Society of Wisconsin, *Reports and Collections*. Madison, 1855–88. Continued as *Collections*, 1888– . *Proceedings*, 1875– . *Calendar Series*, 1915– . *Wisconsin Domesday Book*, 1922– . *History Series*, 1925– . *Wisconsin Biography Series*, 1930– . *Wisconsin Magazine of History*, 1917– . — General index to first 20 vols. of *Collections*; to *Proceedings* through 1901; to *Magazine* through 1946.
Wisconsin Academy of Sciences, Arts and Letters, *Transactions*. Madison, 1870– . — General index through 1932.
State Department of History, Wyoming, *Annals of Wyoming*. Title varies. Cheyenne, 1923– . — General index through 1942.

51. HISTORICAL SERIES OF UNIVERSITIES AND RESEARCH AGENCIES

Many valuable treatises in American history and related fields are published by universities and independent research organizations. Volumes so sponsored sometimes also contain source materials. In addition to the series listed below, it should be noted that abstracts or summaries of doctoral theses are issued by many graduate schools; frequently these works see the light of print only in this condensed form. The original theses can ordinarily be borrowed from the parent institutions through the interlibrary-loan system. For historical journals and learned-society publications, see: § 50.

American Association for International Conciliation, *International Conciliation*. N.Y., 1907–24. Continued by the Carnegie Endowment for International Peace. — General index.
American Documentation Institute, *American Documentation*. Wash., 1950– .
Baylor University, *Historical Publications*. Waco, Texas, 1940– .
Brookings Institution, Institute of Economics, *Publications*. N.Y., 1923– . Institute for Government Research, *Studies in Administration*, 1917– , and *Service Monographs of the United States Government*, 1919– .
Carnegie Endowment for International Peace, *Pamphlet Series*. Wash., 1914– . *International Conciliation*, 1924– . — General index to *International Conciliation*, Nos. 1–325 (1937).
Carnegie Institution of Washington: Department of Historical Research, *Guides* to foreign archives (§§ 26, 47). Wash., 1907–43. Department of Economics and Sociology (later Board of Research Associates in American Economic History), *Contributions to American Economic History*, 1915–33 (§ 61).
Catholic University of America, *Studies in American Church History*. Wash., 1922– . *Studies in Social Sciences*, 1922– .
Columbia University, *Studies in History, Economics, and Public Law*. N.Y., 1891– .

Columbia Legal Studies, 1925– . Studies in the History of American Agriculture, 1934– . Studies in American Culture, 1936– .

Council on Foreign Relations, The United States in World Affairs. N.Y., 1931– . Foreign Affairs, 1922– . — General index to latter through 1931.

Duke University, Publications. Durham, 1925– . Succeeding Trinity College, Publications, 1889–1924.

Fordham University, Studies, Historical Series. N.Y., 1940– .

Harvard University, Harvard Historical Studies. N.Y. and Cambridge, 1896– . Harvard Historical Monographs. Cambridge, 1932– . Harvard Economic Studies. Boston etc., 1906– . Harvard Documents in the History of Education. Cambridge, 1926– . Harvard Studies in Business History, 1931– . Harvard Political Studies. Title varies, 1914– . Harvard Studies in International Law, 1929– . Quarterly Journal of Economics, 1886– . (General index through 1935.) Harvard Business Review. Chi., 1922– .

Hebrew Union College, American Jewish Archives. Cin., 1948– .

Henry E. Huntington Library and Art Gallery, Publications. Cambridge, 1929– . Bulletin, 1931–37. Quarterly, 1937– .

Howard University, Studies in History. Wash., 1921–30. Studies in the Social Sciences, 1938– .

Indiana University, Studies. Bloomington, 1910–38. Publications: Social Science Series, 1939– . Indiana Magazine of History, 1905– . — General index to latter through 1929.

Institute of Early American History and Culture, William and Mary Quarterly, a Magazine of Early American History. Williamsburg, Va., 1944– . Scholarly studies (without serial title). Chapel Hill, 1947– . Preceded by Williamsburg Restoration Historical Studies. Williamsburg, 1940–43.

Johns Hopkins University, Studies in Historical and Political Science. Balt., 1883– . Albert Shaw Lectures on Diplomatic History, 1899– . Studies in International Thought, 1929– .

Lincoln Memorial University, Lincoln Herald, a Magazine of Education and Lincolniana. Harrogate, Tenn., 1943– .

Louisiana State University, Studies, Social Science Series. Baton Rouge, 1951– .

Museum of the American Indian, Heye Foundation, Contributions. N.Y., 1913– . Indian Notes and Monographs, 1919– .

National Bureau of Economic Research, Publications. N.Y., 1921– .

New York University, Anson G. Phelps Lectureship on Early American History. N.Y., 1932– .

Ohio State University, Contributions in History and Political Science. Columbus, 1913– . Contributions in Social Science. Title varies, 1924–28. Contributions in Economics, 1935– .

Pan American Union, American Archæology. Wash., 1927–35. History Series, 1930– . Treaty Series, 1925– .

Pennsylvania State College, Studies. State College, Penn., 1936– .

Princeton University, Public Opinion Quarterly. Princeton, 1937– .

Radcliffe College, Monographs. Boston, 1888–1911. — Titled Fay House Monographs for first four numbers.

Rutgers University, Studies in History. New Brunswick, N.J., 1938– .

Smith College, Studies in History. Northampton, 1915– .

Social Science Research Council, Social Science Abstracts. N.Y., 1929–33. — General index.

Stanford University, Publications, History and Economics. Stanford University, 1892–96. Publications, History, Economics and Political Science, 1922– .

State University of Iowa, Studies in the Social Sciences. Iowa City, 1899– .

State University of Montana, Historical Reprints, Sources of Northwest History. Missoula, 1932–39. Publications in the Social Sciences, 1942– .

University of Buffalo, Studies. Buffalo, 1919– .

University of California, Publications in History. Berkeley, 1911– . Publications in Economics, 1908– .

University of Chicago, Social Science Studies. Chi., 1924– . Social Service Series,

1924– . *Sociological Series,* 1927– . *Studies in Business Administration,* 1929– .
Journal of Political Economy, 1892– . *American Journal of Sociology,* 1895– . —
General index to last through 1935.
University of Colorado, *Historical Collections.* Boulder, 1918– . *Studies in the Social
Sciences,* 1939–46. *Series in History,* 1949– .
University of Illinois, *Studies in the Social Sciences.* Urbana, 1912– .
University of Kansas, *Political Science Series.* Lawrence, 1910–13. *Humanistic Studies,*
1912– . *Social Science Studies,* 1940– .
University of Maine, *Studies.* Orono, 1900–07, 1924– .
University of Michigan, *Publications: History and Political Science.* Title varies. Ann
Arbor, 1911– . William L. Clements Library of American History, *Bulletin,* 1924– .
University of Minnesota, *Studies in the Social Sciences.* Minneapolis, 1913–29. *Studies in
Economics and Business,* 1932– .
University of Missouri, *Studies.* Columbia, 1901–04. *Studies, Social Science Series,* 1905–
21. *Studies,* 1926– .
University of New Mexico, *Political Science Series.* Albuquerque, 1925– . *Historical
Series,* 1938– .
University of North Carolina, *Social Study Series.* Chapel Hill, 1924– . *James Sprunt
Historical Studies.* Title varies. (Published originally by North Carolina Historical
Society.) Chapel Hill, 1900– . *Social Forces.* Title varies, 1922– .
University of Notre Dame, *Review of Politics.* Notre Dame, Ind., 1938– .
University of Pennsylvania, *Series in History.* Phila., 1901–12. *American Quarterly.* Min-
neapolis etc., 1949– .
University of Southern California, *Publications: Social Science Series.* Los Angeles,
1929– .
University of Texas, *Studies in History.* Austin, 1917–25. Bureau of Research in the Social
Sciences, *Studies,* 1931–38.
University of Virginia, Institute for Research in the Social Sciences, *Institute Monographs.*
N.Y. etc., 1927– .
University of Washington, *Publications in the Social Sciences.* Seattle, 1924– .
University of Wisconsin, *Bulletin, Economics, Political Science, and History Series.* Madi-
son, 1894–99. Continued in two series: *Economics and Political Science Series,* 1904–
18, and *History Series,* 1902–18. *Studies in the Social Sciences and History,* 1918– .
William and Mary College, *William and Mary College Quarterly Historical Magazine.*
Title varies. Williamsburg, 1892–1942. For its continuation, see: Institute of Early
American History and Culture. — General index through 1930 in Swem, *Virginia
Historical Index.*
World Peace Foundation, *Pamphlet Series.* Boston, 1911–17. Continued as *A League of
Nations,* 1917–23; then as *Pamphlets,* 1923–29. Later issues unnumbered. *Interna-
tional Organization,* 1947– .
Yale University, *Yale Historical Publications.* (Subseries titled *Manuscripts; Studies;* and
Miscellany.) New Haven, 1912– . *Yale Publications in Economics, Social Science
and Government,* 1929– .

52. GENERAL MAGAZINES

Aside from specialized journals in history and cognate fields, there is considerable material important for historians in magazines addressed primarily to
other audiences. These periodicals, dating from the feeble beginnings in 1741,
are of many kinds: popular, professional, commercial, scientific, literary, religious,
propagandist, recreational. Much of the matter in these files is readily accessible
through general indexes (§ 39). Unfortunately these inventories do not cover
the advertising sections, which provide a significant key to many aspects of
American social and economic development. The appended list is confined to
magazines especially useful for historical purposes. They are arranged alphabetically in two broad chronological periods according to the dates of founding.

Fuller information in regard to these and other periodicals can be found in William Beer, "Checklist of American Periodicals, 1741–1800," Am. Antiq. Soc., *Proc.*, new ser., XXXII (1922), 330; Winifred Gregory, comp., *Union List of Serials in Libraries of the United States and Canada* (2 ed., N.Y., 1943; supplements, 1945, 1951); and F. L. Mott, *A History of American Magazines* (3 vols., N.Y. and Cambridge, 1930–38). Thanks to the University of Michigan and the Clements Library, all the extant periodicals in the United States between 1741 and 1825 inclusive have been microfilmed, thus making them available on purchase in this form to libraries throughout the country. See also: §§ 39, 40.

1787–1864

Advocate of Peace. Hartford, etc., 1837–1932. Continued as *World Affairs.* Wash., 1932– .
American Agriculturist. N.Y., etc., 1842– . — Title varies.
American Museum (Carey's). Phila., 1787–92.
American Quarterly Review. Phila., 1827–37.
American Whig Review. N.Y., 1845–52. — Title varies.
Atlantic Monthly. Boston, 1857– . — General index through 1888, 1889–1901.
Christian Examiner. Boston, etc., 1824–69. — General index.
De Bow's Review. New Orleans, 1846–64, 1866–70, 1879–80. — Title varies. General index through 1851, 1851–56.
Democratic Review. N.Y., 1837–59. — Title varies.
Dial: A Magazine for Literature, Philosophy, and Religion. Boston, 1840–44.
Eclectic Magazine of Foreign Literature, Science and Art. N.Y., etc., 1844–1907. — General index through 1881.
Frank Leslie's Illustrated Newspaper. N.Y., 1855–1922. — Title varies.
Friend of Peace. Boston, 1816–28.
Gleason's [from 1855, *Ballou's*] *Pictorial Drawing-Room Companion.* N.Y., 1851–59.
Godey's Lady's Book. Phila., 1830–98. — Title varies.
Graham's Magazine. Phila., 1826–58. — Title varies.
Harper's Monthly Magazine. N.Y., 1850– . — Title varies. General index 1852–92, 1892–1912.
Harper's Weekly. N.Y., 1857–1916. — General index through 1887. Merged with the *Independent.*
Hunt's Merchants' Magazine and Commercial Review. N.Y., 1839–70. — Title varies. General index through 1844. Merged with the *Commercial and Financial Chronicle.*
Independent. N.Y., 1848–1928. — Merged with the *Outlook.*
Knickerbocker Magazine. N.Y., 1833–65.
Literary World. N.Y., 1847–53.
Littell's Living Age. Boston, etc., 1844–1941. — Title varies. General index through 1900.
Lowell Offering. Lowell, Mass., 1840–45.
Massachusetts Magazine. Boston, 1789–96.
Methodist Review. N.Y., 1818–1931. — Title varies. Index through 1881.
New England Farmer (Fessenden's). Boston, 1822–1913.
New Englander. New Haven etc., 1843–92. — Continued as *Yale Review.* General index through 1861.
New-York Magazine. N.Y., 1790–97.
New York Mirror. N.Y., 1823–47. — Title varies.
Niles' Weekly Register. Balt., 1811–49. — Title varies. General index through 1817. See also: N. N. Luxon, *Niles' Weekly Register* (Baton Rouge, 1947).
North American Review. Boston, etc., 1815–1940. — General index through 1877, 1878–80.
Panoplist. Boston, 1805–51. — Title varies.
Peterson's Ladies' National Magazine. Phila., 1842–98. — Title varies.
Port Folio (Dennie's). Phila., 1801–27. — General index, 1816–25.
Princeton Review. N.Y., etc., 1825–88. — Title varies. General index through 1868.
Saturday Evening Post. Phila., 1821– .
Southern Literary Messenger. Richmond, 1834–64. — General index, D. K. Jackson, comp., *The Contributors and Contributions* (1936). Revived, 1939– .
Southern Quarterly Review. New Orleans, etc., 1842–57.

Western Messenger. Cin., etc., 1835–41.
Western Monthly Magazine. Vandalia, Ill., etc., 1830–37. — Title varies.

1865–1950

American Mercury. N.Y., 1924– .
American Scholar. N.Y., 1932– .
Appletons' Journal. N.Y., 1869–81.
Arena. Boston, 1889–1909.
Business Week. Greenwich, Conn., 1929– . — Supersedes *Magazine of Business.* Chi.,
    1900–29. Incorporates *The Annalist.* N.Y., 1913–40.
Catholic World. N.Y., 1865– . — General index through 1896.
Century Magazine. See: *Scribner's Monthly.*
Charities. N.Y., 1897–1909. — Title varies. Continued as *Survey,* 1909–52.
Charities Review. N.Y., 1891–1901. — General index.
Chautauquan. Meadville, N.Y., etc., 1880–1914. — Merged with *Independent.*
Christian Union. N.Y., 1870–93. — Continued as the *Outlook* (title varies), 1893–1935.
Collier's. N.Y., 1888– .
Commentary. N.Y., 1945– .
Commercial and Financial Chronicle. N.Y., 1865– .
Commonweal. N.Y., 1924– .
Current History. N.Y., 1914– . — Title varies.
Current Literature. N.Y., 1888–1912. — Continued as *Current Opinion,* 1913–25. Merged
    with *Literary Digest.*
Dial. Chi., 1881–1929.
Events. N.Y., 1937–41. — Merged with *Current History.*
Everybody's Magazine. N.Y., 1899–1929.
Fortune. N.Y., 1930– .
Forum. N.Y., 1886–1940. — Merged with *Current History.* General index through 1902.
Frontier, a Magazine of the Northwest. Missoula, Montana, 1920–33. — Continued as
    Frontier and Midland, 1933–39.
Galaxy. N.Y., 1866–78. — Merged with the *Atlantic Monthly.*
International Review. N.Y., 1874–83. — General index through 1880.
Judge. N.Y., 1881–1939.
Lend-a-Hand. Boston, 1886–97. — Merged with *Charities Review.*
Life. N.Y. etc., 1883– . — Changed from a humorous to a pictorial magazine, 1936.
Lippincott's Magazine. Phila., 1868–1916. — General index through 1881. Merged with
    Scribner's Magazine.
Literary Digest. N.Y., 1890–1938. — Merged with *Time.*
Look. N.Y., 1937– .
McClure's Magazine. N.Y., 1893–1929. — General index through April 1902.
Manufacturers' Record. Balt., 1882– .
The Masses. N.Y., 1911–17. — Superseded by *The Liberator.* N.Y., 1918–24.
Munsey's Magazine. N.Y., 1889–1929.
Nation. N.Y., 1865– . — General index through 1917; *Analytical Index to Political
    Contents* through 1882.
Nation's Business. Wash., 1912– .
New Republic. N.Y., 1914– .
New Yorker. N.Y., 1925– .
Newsweek. N.Y., 1933– .
Outing. N.Y., 1882–1923.
Outlook. See: *Christian Union.*
Overland Monthly. San Francisco, 1868–75, 1883–1935. — Title varies.
Partisan Review. N.Y., 1934– . — Title varies.
Popular Science Monthly. N.Y., 1872– . — General index through 1892.
Public Opinion. Wash., 1886–1906. — Merged with the *Literary Digest.*
Publishers' Weekly. N.Y., 1872– .
Puck. N.Y., 1877–1918.
Quarterly Register of Current History. Detroit, 1891–93. — Continued as *Cyclopedic
    Review of Current History.* Buffalo, etc., 1893–1903. Merged with *Current Literature.*

Reader's Digest. Pleasantville, N.Y., 1922– .
Reporter. N.Y., 1949– .
Review of Reviews. N.Y., 1890–1937. — Title varies.
Saturday Review of Literature. N.Y., 1924– .
Scientific American. N.Y., 1845– .
Scientific Monthly. N.Y., 1915– .
Scribner's Magazine. N.Y., 1887–1939. — General index through 1891.
Scribner's Monthly. N.Y., 1870–81. — Continued as *Century Magazine* (title varies), 1881–1930. General index through 1885. Merged with *Forum*.
Sewanee Review. Sewanee, Tenn., 1892– . — General index through 1902.
South Atlantic Quarterly. Durham, No.Car., 1902– .
Southern Review. Baton Rouge, 1935– .
Street's Pandex of the News and Cumulative Index to Current History. Chi. etc., 1903–17.
Survey. See: *Charities*.
Survey Graphic. N.Y., 1921–49. — Merged with *Survey*.
Time. N.Y., 1923– .
United Nations Weekly Bulletin. N.Y., 1946– .
U.S. News. Wash., 1933– . Title varies.
Virginia Quarterly Review. University, Va., 1925– . — General index through 1944.
Yale Review. New Haven, 1892– . — General index through 1911.

53. NEWSPAPERS

Newspapers are indispensable to the historian for both the direct and indirect information they afford. Compiled in haste and often edited with bias, they must of course be used with critical caution. Their value for the scholar is discussed by L. M. Salmon, *The Newspaper and the Historian* (N.Y., 1923); J. W. Piercy, "The Newspaper as a Source of Historical Information," *Ind. Hist. Bull.*, X (1933), 387; and D. D. Parker, *Local History*, ch. iii. See also: Ford, *Bibliography of Journalism* (§ 35). The *Journalism Quarterly* (§ 50) includes occasional historical articles, and much is also to be learned from the personal accounts by, and biographies of, editors (§§ 54, 55, 56). The following list cites some of the more important historical accounts of journalism:

GENERAL AND MISCELLANEOUS

W. G. Bleyer, *Main Currents in the History of American Journalism*. Boston, 1927.
C. S. Brigham, *Journals and Journeymen: A Contribution to the History of Early American Newspapers*. Phila., 1950.
T. D. Clark, *The Southern Country Editor*. Indianapolis, 1948. — Since the Civil War.
W. A. Dill, *Growth of Newspapers in the United States, 1704–1925*. Lawrence, Kan., 1928.
Oliver Gramling, *AP, the Story of News*. N.Y., 1940.
Sidney Kobre, *The Development of the Colonial Newspaper*. Pitt., 1944.
F. L. Mott, *American Journalism*. R. ed. N.Y., 1950.
J. C. Oswald, *Printing in the Americas*. N.Y., 1937.
J. E. Pollard, *The Presidents and the Press*. N.Y., 1947.
Victor Rosewater, *History of Cooperative News-Gathering in the United States*. N.Y., 1930.

INDIVIDUAL NEWSPAPER HISTORIES

Sam Acheson, *35,000 Days in Texas: A History of the Dallas News and Its Forbears*. N.Y., 1938.
J. C. Andrews, *Pittsburgh's Post-Gazette*. Boston, 1936. — Founded as the *Pittsburgh Gazette*.
H. W. Baehr, Jr., *The New York Tribune since the Civil War*. N.Y., 1936.

Meyer Berger, *The Story of the New York Times.* N.Y., 1951.
J. E. Chamberlin, *The Boston Transcript.* Boston, 1930.
C. M. Christian, ed., *Two Hundred Years with the Maryland Gazette, 1727–1927.* Annapolis, 1927.
Royal Cortissoz, *The New York Tribune.* N.Y., 1923.
T. E. Dabney, *One Hundred Great Years.* Baton Rouge, 1944. — The *New Orleans Times-Picayune.*
J. L. Heaton, *The Story of a Page.* N.Y., 1913. — The *New York World.*
Richard Hooker, *The Story of an Independent Newspaper.* N.Y., 1924. — The *Springfield Republican.*
G. W. Johnson, *et al., The Sunpapers of Baltimore.* N.Y., 1937.
Philip Kinsley, *The Chicago Tribune, Its First Hundred Years.* 3 vols. N.Y., 1943–46. — Covers 1847–1900.
Allan Nevins, *The Evening Post.* N.Y., 1922.
F. M. O'Brien, *The Story of the Sun.* R. ed. N.Y., 1928. — The *New York Sun.*
A. H. Shaw, *The Plain Dealer, One Hundred Years in Cleveland.* N.Y., 1942.
J. E. Smith, *One Hundred Years of Hartford's Courant.* New Haven, 1949. — To 1865.

Summaries of press opinion for the period 1811–49 appear in *Niles' Register;* for 1886–1906 in *Public Opinion;* during 1903–04 and 1908–17 in *Street's Pandex of the News;* and for 1890–1938 in the *Literary Digest* (§ 52). An important compilation for a single city is Work Projects Administration, comps., *Annals of Cleveland, a Digest and Index of the Newspaper Record of Events and Opinions* (59 vols., Cleve., 1937–38), covering the years 1818–76. The following works reprint selected editorials and news reports from colonial times to the twentieth century.

ANTHOLOGIES

J. T. Buckingham, ed., *Specimens of Newspaper Literature.* 2 vols. Boston, 1850. — Not always accurate.
O. M. Dickerson, comp., *Boston under Military Rule.* Boston, 1936. — Articles from the *New-York Journal* and *Boston Evening-Post,* 1768–69.
D. L. Dumond, ed., *Southern Editorials on Secession.* N.Y., 1931.
Laurence Greene, ed., *America Goes to Press.* Indianapolis, 1936. — News accounts from the Boston Tea Party to 1914.
Frank Moore, comp., *Diary of the American Revolution.* 2 vols. N.Y., 1858. — Selections mostly from newspapers, 1775–81.
William Nelson, comp., "Extracts from American Newspapers Relating to New Jersey," *N. J. Archives,* 1 ser., XI–XII, XIX–XX, XXIV–XXIX, XXXI. — Resumed by W. S. Stryker, *et al.,* comps., *ibid.,* 2 ser., I–V (Paterson, 1901 ff.). Covers the years 1704–82.
Allan Nevins, ed., *American Press Opinion, Washington to Coolidge.* Boston, 1928.
H. C. Perkins, ed., *Northern Editorials on Secession.* 2 vols. N.Y., 1942.
L. H. Weeks and E. M. Bacon, eds., *An Historical Digest of the Provincial Press: Massachusetts Series,* I (1689–1707). Boston, 1911. — No other vols. issued.
R. C. Wheeler, ed., *Ohio Newspapers, a Living Record.* Columbus, 1950. — Facsimile reproductions of 126 issues from 1790 to 1946.

PARTICULAR PAPERS AND CHAINS

[*Chicago Tribune*] *A Century of Tribune Editorials.* Chi., 1947. — 1857–1947.
[*Emporia Gazette*] *Forty Years on Main Street.* R. H. Fitzgibbon, comp. N.Y., 1937. — Editorials by William Allen White.
[*Hearst press*] Arthur Brisbane, *Editorials from Hearst Newspapers.* N.Y., 1906.
[*Kansas City Star*] *Roosevelt in the Kansas City Star.* Boston, 1921. — Editorials on World War I.
[*Louisville Courier-Journal*] *The Editorials of Henry Watterson.* Arthur Krock, ed. N.Y., 1923. — 1868–1919.
[*Philadelphia North American*] *The War from This Side.* 4 vols. Phila., 1915–19. — Editorials, 1914–17.

[New York *Evening Post*] *Press Time*. N.Y., 1936. — 1934–36.
[*New York Herald Tribune*] *Interpretations*. Allan Nevins, comp. 2 vols. N.Y., 1932–36.
— Selections from Walter Lippmann's syndicated column.
[*New York Tribune*] C. T. Congdon, *Tribune Essays*. N.Y., 1869. — Selections from his editorials, 1857–63.
[*New York World*] *Cobb of "The World."* J. L. Heaton, comp. N.Y., 1924. — Editorials by Frank I. Cobb, 1905–23.
[*Washington Post*] *Editorials from the Washington Post, 1917–1920*. I. E. Bennett, comp. Wash., 1921.

There is, however, no satisfactory substitute for delving into the files themselves. This is necessarily a laborious procedure, for in no respect has America been so articulate as in her daily and weekly press. Journals of the eighteenth and early nineteenth centuries are listed, with their present depositories, in C. S. Brigham, comp., *History and Bibliography of American Newspapers, 1690–1820* (2 vols., Worcester, Mass., 1947). For later files, see Winifred Gregory, comp., *American Newspapers, 1821–1936* (N.Y., 1937); N. W. Ayer, *American Newspaper Annual* (Phila., 1880–), a continuing publication; and Warren Brown, comp., *Check List of Negro Newspapers in the United States, 1827–1946* (Jefferson City, Missouri, 1946). Besides these national inventories, catalogues too numerous to cite are available for different states and cities as well as for the holdings of particular libraries. For an incomplete record of filmed newspapers, consult G. A. Schwegmann, comp., *Newspapers on Microfilm, a Union Check List* (Phila., 1948). The Library of Congress has microfilmed about 210 nineteenth-century Negro newspapers, which in this form may be borrowed or purchased from that institution.

Indexes to particular newspapers have an additional value in helping to locate like materials in other papers. Herbert Brayer has compiled a "Preliminary Guide to Indexed Newspapers in the United States, 1850–1900," *Miss. Valley Hist. Rev.*, XXXIII (1946), 237. Perhaps the most widely useful indexes are those for the *Virginia Gazette* (2 vols., L. J. Cappon and S. M. Duff, comps., Williamsburg, Va., 1950), bridging the years 1736–80; the *New York Tribune*, 1841–1907; the *New York Times*, 1851–58, 1860, 1863–1905 (all the foregoing on film), 1913– ; the *Brooklyn Daily Eagle*, 1891–1902; and the *United States Daily*, 1926–33. For the outstanding English journal, see *Palmer's Index to "The Times" Newspaper*, 1790– (London, 1868–), and the *Official Index*, 1906– (London, 1907–).

CHRONOLOGICAL LIST

Certain newspapers possess a general utility for the historian. The following select list arranges the papers by cities and dates of founding in three chronological periods. Only the short titles and principal places of publication are given.

1704–1788

[Annapolis] *Maryland Gazette*, 1745–77, 1779–1839.
[Boston] *Essex Gazette*, 1768–75; *Independent Chronicle*, 1776–1840; *Semi-Weekly Advertiser*, 1840–76.
Boston Evening-Post, 1735–75.
Boston Gazette, 1719–98.
[Boston] *Massachusetts Centinel*, 1784–90; *Columbian Centinel*, 1790–1840.
Boston News-Letter, 1704–76. — Title varies.
[Charleston] *South-Carolina Gazette*, 1732–75.

[Hartford] *Connecticut Courant*, 1764– . — Title varies.
[Lexington] *Kentucky Gazette*, 1787–1848.
Newport Mercury, 1758–75, 1780–1928; *Mercury and Weekly News*, 1928– .
New-York Gazette, 1725–44.
New-York Gazette or Weekly Post-Boy, 1747–73.
New-York Journal [Holt], 1766–76.
New-York Weekly Journal [Zenger], 1733–51.
[Philadelphia] *Pennsylvania Gazette*, 1728–1815.
[Philadelphia] *Pennsylvania Journal*, 1742–93.
Pittsburgh Gazette, 1786–1877; *Commercial Gazette*, 1877–1901; *Gazette*, 1901–06; *Gazette Times*, 1906–27; *Post-Gazette*, 1927– .
[Williamsburg] *Virginia Gazette*, 1736–80.
[Worcester] *Massachusetts Spy*, Boston, 1770–75; Worcester, 1775–1904.

1789–1865

Albany Argus, 1813–1921.
Baltimore Sun, 1837– .
[Boston] *Liberator*, 1831–65.
[Boston] *Massachusetts Mercury*, 1793–1800; *Mercury and New-England Palladium*, 1801–03; *New-England Palladium*, 1803–40.
Boston Transcript, 1830–1941.
Brooklyn Daily Eagle, 1841– .
Burlington [Iowa] *Hawk-Eye*, 1839–1933; *Hawk-Eye Gazette*, 1933– .
Charleston [S.C.] *Courier*, 1803–73; *News and Courier*, 1873– .
Charleston Mercury, 1822–68.
Chicago Times, 1854–95.
Chicago Tribune, 1847– .
Cincinnati Enquirer, 1841– .
Cleveland Plain Dealer, 1842– .
Des Moines Register, 1849– .
Detroit Free Press, 1831– .
Galveston Daily News, 1842– .
Indianapolis Journal, 1823–1904.
[Little Rock] *Arkansas Gazette*, 1819– .
Louisville Journal, 1830–68; *Courier-Journal*, 1868– .
[Milwaukee] *Herold*, 1861–1932. — Title varies.
Milwaukee Sentinel, 1837– .
[New Orleans] *Le Courrier de la Louisiane*, 1807–60.
New Orleans Picayune, 1837–1914; *Times-Picayune*, 1914– .
[New York] *Evening Post*, 1801– .
New York Herald, 1835–1924. — Merged with *Tribune*.
[New York] *Journal of Commerce*, 1827– .
[New York] *Morning Courier*, 1827–29; *Morning Courier and Enquirer*, 1829–61.
[New York] *National Anti-Slavery Standard*, 1840–64.
[New York] *Staats-Zeitung*, 1834– .
New York Sun, 1833–1950. — Merged with *World-Telegram*.
New York Times, 1851– .
New York Tribune, 1841–1924. — Merged with *Herald*.
New York World, 1860–1931; *New York World-Telegram*, 1931– .
[Philadelphia] *General Advertiser*, 1790–94; *Aurora*, 1794–1829, 1834–35.
Philadelphia Inquirer, 1829– .
[Philadelphia] *Press*, 1857–1920. — Merged with *Public Ledger*.
[Philadelphia] *Public Ledger*, 1836–1934. — Merged with *Philadelphia Inquirer*.
[Portland] *Oregonian*, 1850– .
Providence Journal, 1829– .
Richmond Dispatch, 1850–1903; *Times-Dispatch*, 1903– .
Richmond Enquirer, 1804–77.
[St. Louis] *Missouri Gazette*, 1808–22; *Missouri Republican*, 1822–88; *St. Louis Republic*, 1888–1919. — Merged with *Globe-Democrat*.

[St. Louis] *Westliche Post*, 1857–1939.
[St. Paul] *Minnesota Pioneer*, 1849–75; *Pioneer Press*, 1875– .
[Salt Lake City] *Deseret News*, 1850– .
[San Francisco] *Alta California*, 1849–91.
San Francisco Chronicle, 1865– .
Springfield Republican, 1824– .
Washington Globe, 1830–45.
[Washington] *National Era*, 1847–60.
[Washington] *National Intelligencer*, 1800–70.
[Washington] *United States Telegraph*, 1826–37.

1866–1950

Atlanta Constitution, 1868– .
[Boston] *Christian Science Monitor*, 1908– .
Chicago Inter Ocean, 1872–1914.
Denver Republican, 1876–1913.
Kansas City Star, 1880– .
Milwaukee Journal, 1882– .
New York Herald Tribune, 1924– .
New York Journal, 1882– .
[New York] *Wall Street Journal*, 1889– .
Omaha Bee, 1871–1938.
Raleigh News, 1872–80; *News and Observer*, 1880– .
[St. Louis] *Post-Dispatch*, 1878– .
Seattle Intelligencer, 1867–81; *Post-Intelligencer*, 1881– .
Washington Post, 1877– .
[Washington] *United States Daily*, 1926–33.

54. PERSONAL RECORDS

Personal records are indispensable to the historian. They offer valuable information about the development of events and they serve as stimulating reminders of the role of the individual in history. American historiography is rich in autobiographies, diaries, memoirs, collected writings and letters, and biographies. Such sources may conveniently be divided into three sections: personal records composed by participants or direct observers; collections of letters and other papers; and biographies. The present section deals with the first of these categories; the ones that follow, with the others. Necessarily, there is some overlapping. Memoirs will sometimes be found among the collected works of an author; and his letters may occasionally be woven into a biography as in the traditional "Life and Letters" pattern.

Personal records may take the form of journals or diaries kept by men contemporaneously with the events described in them; or they may be autobiographies written retrospectively after a greater or lesser interval. The utility of such documents springs from their firsthand nature. On the other hand, they may be limited in utility by inadequate perspective and special bias. Used with care, they are a source of prime importance whether they be the writings of ordinary citizens involved in commonplace events or those of great men who helped to shape the course of history. William Mathews, *American Diaries: An Annotated Bibliography of American Diaries prior to . . . 1861* (Berkeley, 1945) lists published and unpublished works in English. H. M. Forbes, *New England Diaries, 1602–1800: A Descriptive Catalogue of Diaries, Orderly Books, and Sea Journals* (Topsfield, Mass., 1923) is also useful.

Lyman Abbott, *Reminiscences*. Boston, 1915.

Louis Adamic, *Laughing in the Jungle*. N.Y., 1932.

C. F. Adams [1835–1915], *Autobiography*. W. C. Ford, ed., Boston, 1916.

Henry Adams, *The Education*. Boston, 1918, and later editions.

John Adams, "Diary and Autobiography," *Works* (§ 55), Vols. II, III.

J. Q. Adams, *Memoirs*. C. F. Adams, ed. 12 vols. Phila., 1874–77. — Allan Nevins has edited selections as *Diary*. N.Y., 1929.

Jane Addams, *Twenty Years at Hull-House*. N.Y., 1910. *The Second Twenty Years at Hull-House*. N.Y., 1930.

A. B. Alcott, *The Journals*. Odell Shepard, ed. Boston, 1938.

J. B. Angell, *Reminiscences*. N.Y., 1912.

Mary Antin, *The Promised Land*. Boston, 1912.

Francis Asbury, *Journals*. 3 vols. N.Y., 1852.

S. F. Austin, *Papers*. E. C. Barker, ed. 4 vols. Wash., Austin, 1924–28. — Vols. I, II in Am. Hist. Assoc., *Report*, 1919, 1922.

Thomas Ball, *My Threescore Years and Ten: An Autobiography*. Boston, 1891.

H. H. Bancroft, *Literary Industries*. San Francisco, 1890. — Also in *History of the Pacific States*, Vol. XXXIV; and *Works*, Vol. XXXIX.

P. T. Barnum, *Life . . . Written by Himself*. N.Y., 1855.

C. W. Barron, *They Told Barron*. Arthur Pound and S. T. Moore, eds. N.Y., 1930. *More . . .* Arthur Pound and S. T. Moore, eds., N.Y., 1931.

Clara Barton, *Story of My Childhood*. N.Y., 1907.

John Bascom, *Things Learned by Living*. N.Y., 1913.

Edward Bates, "Diary," H. K. Beale, ed. Am. Hist. Assoc., *Report*, 1930, IV.

William Bentley, *Diary*. 4 vols. Salem, 1905–14.

T. H. Benton, *Thirty Years' View*. 2 vols. N.Y., 1854–56.

John Bigelow, *Retrospections of an Active Life*. 5 vols. N.Y., 1909–13.

G. A. Birmingham, *From Dublin to Chicago*. N.Y., 1914.

J. G. Blaine, *Twenty Years of Congress: From Lincoln to Garfield*. 2 vols. Norwich, Conn., 1884–86.

Edward Bok, *The Americanization of . . .* N.Y., 1920.

O. N. Bradley, *A Soldier's Story*. N.Y., [1951].

O. H. Browning, *Diary . . . 1850–1881*. T. C. Pease and J. G. Randall, eds. 2 vols. Springfield, Ill., 1925–31.

W. G. Brownlow, *Rise, Progress, and Decline of Secession; with Narrative of Personal Adventure Among the Rebels*. Phila., 1862.

O. A. Brownson, *The Convert*. N.Y., 1857.

W. J. Bryan, *Memoirs*. Phila., 1925.

James Buchanan, *Mr. Buchanan's Administration on the Eve of the Rebellion*. N.Y., 1866.

Luther Burbank and Wilbur Hall, *Harvest of the Years*. Boston, 1927.

B. F. Butler, *Autobiography and Personal Reminiscences*. Boston, 1892.

William Byrd, *The Secret Diary of William Byrd of Westover, 1709–1712*. L. B. Wright and Marion Tinling, eds. Richmond, 1941. *Another Secret Diary of William Byrd of Westover, 1739–1741, with Letters and Literary Exercises, 1696–1726*. M. H. Woodfin and Marion Tinling, eds. Richmond, 1942. *Writings*. J. S. Bassett, ed. N.Y., 1901.

J. F. Byrnes, *Speaking Frankly*. N.Y., [1947].

Charles Caldwell, *Autobiography*. H. W. Warner, ed. Phila., 1855.

Andrew Carnegie, *Autobiography*. J. C. Van Dyke, ed. Boston, 1920.

Peter Cartwright, *Autobiography*. N.Y., 1929.

J. J. Chapman, *Memories and Milestones*. N.Y., 1915.

S. P. Chase, "Diary and Correspondence," Am. Hist. Assoc., *Report*, 1902, II.

M. B. Chesnut, *A Diary from Dixie*. I. D. Martin and M. L. Avary, eds. N. Y., 1905, 1929.

Champ Clark, *My Quarter Century of American Politics*. 2 vols. N.Y., 1920.

J. F. Clarke, Autobiography, *Diary and Correspondence*. E. E. Hale, ed. Boston, 1891.

Levi Coffin, *Reminiscences*. Cin., 1876.

M. D. Conway, *Autobiography, Memories and Experiences*. 2 vols. Boston, 1904.

Calvin Coolidge, *Autobiography*. N.Y., 1929.
J. M. Cox., *Journey Through My Years*. N.Y., 1946.
C. N. Crittenton, *The Brother of Girls*. Chi., 1910.
David Crockett, *A Narrative . . . Written by Himself*. Phila., 1834.
S. M. Cullom, *Fifty Years of Public Service; Personal Recollections*. Chi., 1911.
Walter Damrosch, *My Musical Life*. N.Y., 1923.
C. A. Dana, *Recollections of the Civil War*. N.Y., 1898.
Pascal D'Angelo, *Son of Italy*. N.Y., 1924.
Josephus Daniels, *Tar Heel Editor*. Chapel Hill, 1939. *Editor in Politics*. Chapel Hill,
    1941.
J. J. Davis, *The Iron Puddler: My Life in the Rolling Mills and What Came of It*.
    Indianapolis, 1922.
F. W. Dawson, *Reminiscences of Confederate Service*. Charleston, 1882.
Henry Dearborn, *Revolutionary War Journals . . . 1775-1783*. L. A. Brown and H. H.
    Peckham, eds. Chi., 1939.
C. M. Depew, *My Memories of Eighty Years*. N.Y., 1922.
George Dewey, *Autobiography*. N.Y., 1913.
Jonathan Dickinson's Journal. E. W. and C. M. Andrews, eds. New Haven, 1945.
Frederick Douglass, *Narrative of the Life of . . . an American Slave*. Boston, 1845.
Neal Dow, *Reminiscences . . . Recollections of Eighty Years*. Portland, Me., 1898.
Daniel Drake, *Pioneer Life in Kentucky, a Series of Reminiscential Letters*. C. M. Drake,
    ed. Cin., 1870.
Theodore Dreiser, *Dawn*. N.Y., 1931. *A Book About Myself*. N.Y., [1922]. *A Traveler
    at Forty*. N.Y., 1913. *A Hoosier Holiday*. N.Y., 1916.
John Drew, *My Years on the Stage*. N.Y., 1922.
Isadora Duncan, *My Life*. N.Y., 1927.
J. A. Early, *Autobiographical Sketch*. Phila., 1912.
M. L. Eaton, *Autobiography of Peggy Eaton*. N.Y., 1932.
M. S. Eccles, *Beckoning Frontiers*. N.Y., 1951.
M. F. Egan, *Recollections of a Happy Life*. N.Y., 1924.
D. D. Eisenhower, *Crusade in Europe*. N.Y., 1948.
R. W. Emerson, *Journals*. E. W. Emerson and W. E. Forbes, eds. 10 vols. Boston,
    1909-14.
J. A. Farley, *Behind the Ballots*. N.Y., [1938]. *Jim Farley's Story*. N.Y., [1948].
C. G. Finney, *Memoirs . . . Written by Himself*. N.Y., 1876.
P. V. Fithian, *Journal & Letters . . . 1773-1774*. H. D. Farish, ed. Williamsburg, 1945.
    — J. R. Williams, ed. (Princeton, 1900) covers a longer period and contains some-
    what different selections.
Timothy Flint, *Recollections of the Last Ten Years*. Boston, 1826.
E. J. Flynn, *You're the Boss*. N.Y., 1947.
J. B. Foraker, *Notes of a Busy Life*. 2 vols. Cin., 1916.
Mrs. J. B. Foraker, *I Would Live It Again*. N.Y., 1932.
J. L. Ford, *Forty-Odd Years in the Literary Shop*. N.Y., 1921.
James Forrestal, *The Forrestal Diaries*. Walter Millis and E. S. Duffield, eds. N.Y., 1951.
J. W. Foster, *Diplomatic Memoirs*. 2 vols. Boston, 1909.
Benjamin Franklin, *Memoirs. Parallel Text Edition*. Max Farrand, ed. Berkeley, 1949. —
    Many other editions of this autobiography are available.
J. C. Frémont, *Memoirs of My Life*. Chi., 1887.
O. B. Frothingham, *Recollections and Impressions, 1822-90*. N.Y., 1891.
Margaret Fuller [Ossoli], *Memoirs*. R. W. Emerson, *et al.*, eds. 2 vols. Boston, 1852.
Frederick Funston, *Memories of Two Wars; Cuba and Philippine Experiences*. N.Y., 1911.
Hamlin Garland, *Trail-Makers of the Middle Border*. N.Y., 1926. *A Son of the Middle
    Border*. N.Y., 1917. *A Daughter of the Middle Border*. N.Y., 1921. *Back-Trailers
    from the Middle Border*. N.Y., 1928. *Roadside Meetings*. N.Y., 1930. *Companions
    on the Trail*. N.Y., 1931. *My Friendly Contemporaries*. N.Y., 1932. *Afternoon
    Neighbors*. N.Y., 1934.
James Gibbons, *A Retrospect of Fifty Years*. Balt., 1916.
Washington Gladden, *Recollections*. Boston, 1909.

Samuel Gompers, *Seventy Years of Life and Labor.* 2 vols. N.Y., 1925.

S. G. Goodrich, *Recollections of a Lifetime.* N.Y., 1856.

J. B. Gough, *Autobiography and Personal Recollections.* Springfield, Mass., 1869.

U. S. Grant, *Personal Memoirs.* 2 vols. N.Y., 1885–86.

Alexander Graydon, *Memoirs of a Life, Chiefly Passed in Pennsylvania, within the Last Sixty Years.* Harrisburg, 1811. — Later edition, Phila., 1846.

Horace Greeley, *Recollections of a Busy Life.* N.Y., 1868.

J. C. Grew, *Ten Years in Japan.* N.Y., 1944.

J. B. Grinnell, *Men and Events of Forty Years.* Boston, 1891.

E. E. Hale, *A New England Boyhood and Other Bits of Autobiography.* Boston, 1900. *Memories of a Hundred Years.* 2 vols. N.Y., 1902–04.

G. S. Hall, *Life and Confessions of a Psychologist.* N.Y., 1923.

J. A. Hamilton, *Reminiscences . . . during Three Quarters of a Century.* N.Y., 1869.

Townsend Harris, *Complete Journal.* M. E. Cosenza, ed. N.Y., 1930.

C. C. Harrison, *Recollections Grave and Gay.* N.Y., 1911.

F. R. Hassler, *Memoirs.* Emil Zschokke, ed. Aarau, Switzerland, 1877. Transl. Nice, 1882.

R. B. Hayes, *Diary and Letters.* C. R. Williams, ed. 5 vols. Columbus, 1922–26.

William Heath, *Memoirs.* Boston, 1798. William Abbatt, ed. N.Y., 1901.

T. W. Higginson, *Cheerful Yesterdays.* Boston, 1898.

G. F. Hoar, *Autobiography of Seventy Years.* 2 vols. N.Y., 1903.

W. W. Holden [Governor of No.Car.], *Memoirs.* W. K. Boyd, ed. Durham, N.C., 1911.

Phillip Hone, *Diary . . . 1828–1851.* Allan Nevins, ed. N.Y., 1927.

Herbert Hoover, *Memoirs.* 2 vols., N.Y., 1951.

E. M. House, *Intimate Papers.* Charles Seymour, ed. 4 vols. Boston, 1926–28.

O. O. Howard, *Autobiography.* 2 vols. N.Y., 1907.

J. W. Howe, *Reminiscences.* Boston, 1899.

W. D. Howells, *Life in Letters.* Mildred Howells, ed. 2 vols. N.Y., 1928. *Years of My Youth.* N.Y., 1916. *Literary Friends and Acquaintances.* N.Y., 1900.

Henry Holt, *Garrulities of an Octogenarian Editor.* Boston, 1923.

W. C. Hudson, *Random Recollections of an Old Political Reporter.* N.Y., 1911.

Cordell Hull, *Memoirs.* 2 vols. N.Y., 1948.

H. L. Ickes, *The Autobiography of a Curmudgeon.* N. Y., [1943].

Washington Irving, *Journal . . . 1823–1824.* S. T. Williams, ed. Cambridge, 1931.

Henry James, *A Small Boy and Others.* N.Y., 1913. *Notes of a Son and Brother.* N.Y., 1914. *The Middle Years.* N.Y., 1917.

John Jay, *Diary, during Peace Negotiations of 1782.* Frank Monaghan, ed. New Haven, 1934.

Joseph Jefferson, *Autobiography.* N.Y., 1890.

R. U. Johnson, *Remembered Yesterdays.* Boston, 1923.

T. L. Johnson, *My Story.* N.Y., 1911.

J. E. Johnston, *Narrative of Military Operations.* N.Y., 1874.

Jesse Jones, *Fifty Billion Dollars: My Thirteen Years with the R.F.C., 1932–1945.* N.Y., 1951.

J. B. Jones, *A Rebel War Clerk's Diary at the Confederate States Capitol.* 2 vols. Phila., 1866. R. ed., Howard Swiggett, ed. 2 vols. N.Y., 1935.

Mother [M. H.] Jones, *Autobiography.* M. F. Parton, ed. Chi., 1925.

D. S. Jordan, *The Days of a Man; Being Memories of a Naturalist, Teacher, and Minor Prophet of Democracy.* 2 vols. Yonkers, N.Y., 1922.

Younghill Kang, *East Goes West.* N.Y., 1937.

Amos Kendall, *Autobiography.* William Stickney, ed. N.Y., 1872.

G. E. King, *Memories of a Southern Woman of Letters.* N.Y., 1932.

G. P. Körner, *Memoirs . . . 1809–1896.* T. J. McCormack, ed. Cedar Rapids, Ia., 1909.

Marquis de Lafayette, *Mémoires.* 6 vols. Paris, 1837–38.

R. M. LaFollette, *Autobiography.* Madison, 1913. R. ed., 1919.

F. H. LaGuardia, *The Making of an Insurgent.* Phila., [1948].

Robert Lansing, *The Peace Negotiations: A Personal Narrative.* Boston, 1921. *War Memoirs.* Indianapolis, 1935.

Lucy Larcom, *A New England Girlhood.* Boston, 1889.

B. H. Latrobe, *Journal*. N.Y., 1905.
Amos Lawrence, *Extracts from the Diary and Correspondence*. W. R. Lawrence, ed. Boston, 1855.
W. D. Leahy, *I Was There*. N.Y., [1950].
M. B. Leavitt, *Fifty Years in Theatrical Management*. N.Y., 1912.
Joseph LeConte, *Autobiography*. W. D. Armes, ed. N.Y., 1903. *Journal of Ramblings through the High Sierra of California*. San Francisco, 1930.
R. E. Lee, *Recollections and Letters*. N.Y., 1904.
C. G. Leland, *Memoirs*. N.Y., 1893.
Ludwig Lewisohn, *Upstream*. N.Y., 1922. *Mid-Channel*. N.Y., 1929.
H. C. Lodge, *Early Memories*. N.Y., 1913.
J. D. Long, *America of Yesterday, as Reflected in the Journal of John Davis Long*. L. S. Mayo, ed. Boston, 1923.
Benjamin Lundy, *The Life, Travels and Opinions*. Thomas Earle, ed. Phila., 1847.
W. G. McAdoo, *Crowded Years*. Boston, 1931.
G. B. McClellan, *McClellan's Own Story*. N.Y., 1887.
S. S. McClure, *My Autobiography*. N.Y., 1914.
James McCosh, *The Life of . . . .* W. M. Sloane, ed. N.Y., 1896.
Hugh McCulloch, *Men and Measures of Half a Century*. N.Y., 1888.
William Maclay, *Journal . . . 1789–1791*. E. S. Maclay, ed. N.Y., 1890. — New ed. N.Y., 1927.
D. B. MacMillan, *How Peary Reached the Pole, the Personal Story of His Assistant*. Boston, 1934.
James Madison, "Autobiography," Douglass Adair, ed., *William and Mary Quar.*, 3 ser., II (1945), 191.
A. T. Mahan, *From Sail to Steam; Recollections of a Naval Life*. N.Y., 1907.
William Mason, *Memories of a Musical Life*. N.Y., 1901.
Cotton Mather, "Diary," W. C. Ford, ed., Mass. Hist. Soc., *Coll.*, 7 ser., VII–VIII (1911–12).
J. B. Matthews, *These Many Years, Recollections of a New Yorker*. N.Y., 1917.
Hans Mattson, *Reminiscences*. St. Paul, 1891.
H. S. Maxim, *My Life*. London, 1915.
S. J. May, *Recollections of Our Anti-Slavery Conflict*. Boston, 1869.
Philip Mazzei, *Memoirs . . . 1730–1861*. Transl. by H. R. Marraro. N.Y., 1942.
Seth Metcalf, *Diary and Journal (1755–1807)*. Boston, 1939.
N. A. Miles, *Serving the Republic; Memoirs of . . . Civil and Military Life*. N.Y., 1911.
E. P. Mitchell, *Memoirs of an Editor, Fifty Years of American Journalism*. N.Y., 1924.
Maria Mitchell, *Life, Letters, and Journals*. P. M. Kendall, comp. Boston, 1896.
Raymond Moley, *After Seven Years*. N.Y., 1939.
Henry Morgenthau, *All in a Life-Time*. N.Y., 1922.
Gouverneur Morris, *Diary and Letters*. A. C. Morris, ed. 2 vols. N.Y., 1888. *A Diary of the French Revolution*. B. C. Davenport, ed. 2 vols. Boston, 1939. — The earlier edition is the more comprehensive (1789–1816); the later (1789–1793) is more accurate.
S. F. B. Morse, *Letters and Journals*. E. L. Morse, ed. 2 vols. Boston, 1914.
J. J. Most [anarchist], *Memorien, Erlebtes, Erforschtes und Erdachtes*. 2 vols. N.Y., 1903.
R. R. Moton, *Finding a Way Out*. N.Y., 1920.
H. M. Muhlenberg, *Journals*. T. G. Tappert and J. W. Doberstein, eds. 2 vols. Phila., 1942–45.
John Muir, *The Story of My Boyhood and Youth*. Boston, 1913.
Simon Newcomb, *Reminiscences of an Astronomer*. Boston, 1903.
George Nichols, *Salem Shipmate and Merchant*. Martha Nichols, ed. Salem, [1913].
T. L. Nichols, *Fifty Years of American Life*. 2 vols. London, 1864. — New ed., N.Y., 1937.
G. W. Norris, *Fighting Liberal*. N.Y., 1945.
J. H. Noyes, *Religious Experience*. G. W. Noyes, ed. N.Y., 1923. *The Putney Community*. G. W. Noyes, ed. Oneida, N.Y., 1931.
Bill [E. W.] *Nye, His Own Life Story*. F. W. Nye, comp. N.Y., [1926].

William Cardinal O'Connell, *Recollections of Seventy Years*. Boston, 1934.

G. H. Palmer, *Autobiography of a Philosopher*. Boston, 1930.

Francis Parkman, *Journals*. Mason Wade, ed. 2 vols. N.Y., 1947.

J. P. Peabody, *Diary and Letters*. C. H. Baker, ed. Boston, 1925.

Joseph Pennell, *Adventures of an Illustrator*. Boston, 1925.

S. W. Pennypacker, *Autobiography of a Pennsylvanian*. Phila., 1918.

Gifford Pinchot, *Breaking New Ground*. N.Y., 1947.

Allan Pinkerton, *Criminal Reminiscences and Detective Sketches*. N.Y., 1879. *Thirty Years a Detective*. N.Y., 1884.

T. C. Platt, *Autobiography*. L. J. Lang, ed. N.Y., 1910.

J. K. Polk, *Diary*. M. M. Quaife, ed. 4 vols. Chi., 1910. — Extracts edited by Allan Nevins. N.Y., 1929.

T. V. Powderly, *Thirty Years of Labor*. Columbus, 1889. *The Path I Trod*. H. J. Carman, Henry David, and P. N. Guthrie, eds. N.Y., 1940.

Raphael Pumpelly, *My Reminiscences*. 2 vols. N.Y., 1918. *Travels and Adventures of Raphael Pumpelly, Mining Engineer, Geologist, Archeologist, and Explorer*. O. S. Rice, ed., N.Y., 1920.

M. I. Pupin, *From Immigrant to Inventor*. N.Y., 1933.

Herbert Quick, *One Man's Life*. Indianapolis, 1925.

Josiah Quincy, *Figures of the Past, from the Leaves of Old Journals*. Boston, 1883. — New ed., Boston, 1926.

C. S. Rafinesque, *A Life of Travels and Researches in North America and South Europe*. Phila., 1836.

M. E. Ravage, *An American in the Making*. N.Y., 1917.

A. M. Rihbany, *Far Journey*. Boston, 1914.

J. A. Riis, *The Making of an American*. N.Y., 1901.

W. S. Robinson, *"Warrington" Pen-Portraits*. Boston, 1877.

K. K. Rockne, *Autobiography*. Indianapolis, 1931.

Robert Rogers, *Journals*. London, 1765. F. B. Hough, ed. Albany, 1883.

Theodore Roosevelt, *Autobiography*, N.Y., 1913.

S. I. Rosenman, *Working with Roosevelt*, N.Y., [1952].

S. B. Royce, *A Frontier Lady*. R. H. Gabriel, ed. New Haven, 1932.

Benjamin Rush, *Autobiography . . . Together with His Commonplace Book for 1789–1813*. G. W. Corner, ed. Princeton, 1948.

Richard Rush, *Narrative of a Residence at the Court of London* [1817–18]. London, 1833. — Am. ed., *Memoranda of a Residence*. Phila., 1833. *A Residence at the Court of London, Second Series* [1819–25]. 2 vols. London, 1845. — Am. ed., *Memoranda of a Residence*. Phila., 1845.

Augustus Saint-Gaudens, *Reminiscences*. Homer Saint-Gaudens, ed. 2 vols. N.Y., 1913.

F. B. Sanborn, *Recollections of Seventy Years*. 2 vols. Boston, 1909.

W. S. Schley, *Forty-five Years under the Flag*. N.Y., 1904.

Carl Schurz, *Reminiscences*. 3 vols. N.Y., 1907–08.

Winfield Scott, *Memoirs*. 2 vols. N.Y., 1864.

E. W. Scripps, *Damned Old Crank*. C. R. McCabe, ed. N.Y., [1951].

Raphael Semmes, *Memoirs of Service Afloat, during the War between the States*. Balt., 1869.

Ambrose Serle, *American Journal . . . 1776–1778*. San Marino, Calif., 1940.

Samuel Sewall, "Diary," Mass. Hist. Soc., *Coll.*, 5 ser., V–VII (Boston, 1878–82). — Mark Van Doren, ed. N.Y., 1927 (selections).

F. W. Seward, *Reminiscences, 1830–1915*. N.Y., 1916.

W. H. Seward, *Autobiography . . . from 1801 to 1834*. F. W. Seward, ed. 3 vols. N.Y., 1877–91.

N. S. Shaler, *Autobiography . . . with a Supplementary Memoir by His Wife*. Boston, 1909.

A. H. Shaw, *The Story of a Pioneer*. N.Y., [1915].

P. H. Sheridan, *Personal Memoirs*. 2 vols. N.Y., 1888.

John Sherman, *Recollections of Forty Years in the House, Senate and Cabinet*. 2 vols. Chi., 1895.

W. T. Sherman, *Memoirs.* 2 vols. N.Y., 1875. — R. ed., N.Y., 1886.

M. B. Smith, *The First Forty Years of Washington Society.* Gaillard Hunt, ed. London, 1906.

H. M. Stanley, *Autobiography.* Dorothy Stanley, ed. Boston, 1909.

Elizabeth Cady Stanton, as Revealed in Her Letters, Diary and Reminiscences. Theodore Stanton and H. S. Blatch, eds. 2 vols. N.Y., [1922].

E. A. Steiner, *From Alien to Citizen.* N.Y., 1914.

A. H. Stephens, *Recollections* [and] *Diary Kept when a Prisoner, 1865.* M. L. Avary, ed. N.Y., 1910.

Gertrude Stern, *My Mother and I.* N.Y., 1917.

Ezra Stiles, *Literary Diary.* F. B. Dexter, ed. 3 vols. N.Y., 1901. *Extracts from Itineraries . . . with Selections from His Correspondence.* F. B. Dexter, ed. New Haven, 1916.

H. L. Stimson, *On Active Service in Peace and War.* N.Y., [1948].

R. H. Stoddard, *Recollections, Personal and Literary.* N.Y., 1903.

O. S. Straus, *Under Four Administrations, from Cleveland to Taft.* Boston, 1922.

G. T. Strong, *Diary.* Allan Nevins and M. H. Thomas, eds. 4 vols. N.Y., 1952.

L. H. Sullivan, *Autobiography of an Idea.* N.Y., 1924.

William Sullivan, *Familiar Letters on Public Characters and Public Events* [1783–1815]. Boston, 1834.

J. A. Sutter, *Sutter's Own Story.* N.Y., 1936.

Theodore Thomas, *A Musical Autobiography.* G. P. Upton, ed. 2 vols. Chi., 1905.

George Ticknor, *Life, Letters and Journals.* G. S. Hillard, ed. 2 vols. Boston, 1876.

L. F. Tooker, *The Joys and Tribulations of an Editor.* N.Y., 1924.

G. F. Train, *My Life in Many States and Foreign Lands.* N.Y., 1902.

E. L. Trudeau, *An Autobiography.* Garden City, N.Y., 1916.

H. S. Truman, *Mr. President.* William Hillman, ed. N.Y., [1952].

John Trumbull [1756–1843], *Autobiography, Reminiscences, and Letters.* N.Y., 1841.

Mark Twain [S. L. Clemens], *Autobiography.* A. B. Paine, ed. 2 vols. N.Y., 1924. *Mark Twain in Eruption.* Bernard DeVoto, ed. N.Y., [1940].

O. W. Underwood, *Drifting Sands of Party Politics.* N.Y., 1928. — 2 ed. with biographical sketch by C. G. Bowers. N.Y., 1931.

Martin Van Buren, "Autobiography," J. C. Fitzpatrick, ed., Am. Hist. Assoc., *Report,* 1918, II.

Matthew Vassar, *Autobiography and Letters.* E. H. Haight, ed. N. Y., 1916.

Henry Villard, *Memoirs of . . . [a] Journalist and Financier.* 2 vols. Boston, 1904.

Henry Wallace [1836–1916], *Uncle Henry's Own Story of His Life.* 3 vols. Des Moines, 1917–19.

Lew Wallace, *An Autobiography.* 2 vols. N.Y., 1906.

Lester Wallack, *Memories of Fifty Years.* N.Y., 1889.

William Warren, *Life and Memoirs.* Boston, 1889.

B. T. Washington, *Up from Slavery, an Autobiography.* N.Y., 1901. *My Larger Education.* Garden City, N.Y., 1911.

George Washington, *Diaries, 1748–1799.* J. C. Fitzpatrick, ed. 4 vols. Boston, 1925.

Elkanah Watson, *Men and Times of the Revolution; or, Memoirs.* N.Y., 1856.

Henry Watterson, *"Marse Henry": An Autobiography.* 2 vols. N.Y., 1919.

Thurlow Weed, "Autobiography," H. A. Weed, *Life of Thurlow Weed* (Boston, 1884), I.

Gideon Welles, *Diary.* 3 vols. Boston, 1911.

A. D. White, *Autobiography.* 2 vols. N.Y., 1905.

Walter White, *A Man Called White.* N.Y., 1948.

W. A. White, *Autobiography.* N.Y., 1946.

Brand Whitlock, *Forty Years of It.* N.Y., 1925.

James Wilkinson, *Memoirs of My Own Times.* 3 vols. Phila., 1816.

H. L. Wilson, *Diplomatic Episodes in Mexico, Belgium and Chile.* Garden City, N.Y., 1927.

William Winter, *Other Days; Being Chronicles and Memories of the Stage.* N.Y., 1908. *Old Friends; Being Literary Recollections of Other Days.* N.Y., 1909. *The Wallet of Time.* 2 vols. N.Y., 1913.

J. S. Wise, *The End of an Era.* Boston, 1899.

Sarah Wister, *Journal, a True Narrative; Being a Quaker Maiden's Account of Her Experiences with Officers of the Continental Army, 1777–1778.* A. C. Myers, ed. Phila., 1902.

John Woolman, *Journal.* Phila., 1774. A. M. Gummere, ed. N.Y., 1922. Janet Whitney, ed. Chi., 1950.

F. L. Wright, *Autobiography.* N.Y., 1932.

55. COLLECTIONS OF WRITINGS

The works included in this section embrace a variety of materials. Among them are personal and official letters, speeches and sermons, papers written for specific occasions, and formal books, essays, and poems. That such works follow no uniform pattern is a reflection of the diversity of the men who are the subjects of American history as well as of the editors who prepared these papers for publication. A good deal of similar material is often also included in the biographies listed in § 56. See also: § 57.

Abigail Adams, *Letters.* 4 ed. C. F. Adams, ed. Boston, 1848. *New Letters.* Stewart Mitchell, ed. Boston, 1947. — See also: John Adams.

C. F. and Henry Adams, *A Cycle of Adams Letters, 1861–65.* W. C. Ford, ed. 2 vols. Boston, 1920.

Henry Adams, *Letters.* W. C. Ford, ed. Boston, 1930. — See also: C. F. Adams.

John Adams, *Works* (C. F. Adams, ed., 10 vols., 1850–56).

John and Abigail Adams, *Familiar Letters.* C. F. Adams, ed. N.Y., [1875].

John and J. Q. Adams, *The Selected Writings.* Adrienne Koch and William Peden, eds. N.Y., 1946.

J. Q. Adams, *Writings* [1779–1823]. W. C. Ford, ed. 7 vols. N.Y., 1913–17. — See also: John Adams.

Samuel Adams, *Writings.* H. A. Cushing, ed. 4 vols. N.Y., 1904–08.

Alexander Agassiz, *Letters and Recollections.* George Agassiz, ed. Boston, 1913.

Fisher Ames, *Works.* Seth Ames, ed. 2 vols. Boston, 1854.

Robert Anderson, *An Artillery Officer in the Mexican War* . . . *Letters.* E. A. Lawton, ed. N.Y., 1911.

Nicholas Biddle, *Correspondence.* R. C. McGrane, ed. Boston, 1919.

C. F. Browne. See: Artemus Ward.

O. A. Brownson, *Works.* H. F. Brownson, ed. 20 vols. Detroit, 1882–1907.

L. D. Brandeis, *Social and Economic Views.* Alfred Lief, ed. N.Y., [1930].

James Buchanan, *Works.* J. B. Moore, ed. 12 vols. Phila., 1908–11.

B. F. Butler, *Correspondence* . . . *during the Period of the Civil War.* 5 vols. Norwood, Mass., 1917.

J. C. Calhoun, *Works.* R. K. Crallé, ed. 6 vols. N.Y., 1853–55. "Correspondence," J. F. Jameson, ed., Am. Hist. Assoc., *Report*, 1899, II, 71.

Robert Carter, *Letters* . . . *1720–1727.* L. B. Wright, ed. San Marino, 1940.

W. E. Channing, *Works.* One vol. ed. Boston, 1875.

L. M. Child, *Letters.* H. W. Sewall, ed. Boston, 1883.

Rufus Choate, *Works* . . . *with a Memoir of His Life.* S. G. Brown, ed. 2 vols. Boston, 1862.

W. C. C. Claiborne, *Official Letter Books* . . . *1801–1816.* Dunbar Rowland, ed. 6 vols. Jackson, Miss., 1917.

G. R. Clark, "Papers, 1771–81," J. A. James, ed., *Ill. Hist. Coll.*, VIII (1912), XIX (1926).

C. M. Clay, *Life* . . . *Written and Compiled by Himself.* Cin., 1886.

Henry Clay, *Private Correspondence.* Calvin Colton, ed. N.Y., 1855. *Works.* Calvin Colton, ed. 6 vols. N.Y., [1857].

George Clinton, *Public Papers.* Hugh Hastings and J. A. Holden, eds. 10 vols. N.Y., 1899–1914.

Cadwallader Colden, "Letters and Papers . . . 1711–1775," N.Y. Hist. Soc., *Coll.*, L–LVI, LXVII–LXVIII (1918–37).

J. F. Cooper, *Correspondence*. J. F. Cooper, ed. 2 vols. New Haven, 1922. *Works*. 33 vols. N.Y., 1895–1900.

J. S. Copley and Henry Pelham, "Letters and Papers," Mass. Hist. Soc., *Colls.*, LXXI (1914).

Stephen Crane, *Works*. Wilson Follet, ed. 12 vols. N.Y., 1925–26.

Samuel Curwen, *Journal and Letters*. G. A. Ward, ed. Boston, 1842.

Jefferson Davis, *Jefferson Davis, Constitutionalist, His Letters, Papers, and Speeches*. Dunbar Rowland, ed. 10 vols. Jackson, Miss., 1923.

R. H. Davis, *Adventures and Letters*. C. B. Davis, ed. N.Y., 1917. *Writings*. 12 vols. N.Y., 1916.

E. V. Debs, *Writings and Speeches*. A. M. Schlesinger, Jr., ed. N.Y., 1948.

Joseph Dennie, "Letters . . . 1768–1812," L. G. Pedder, ed., Univ. of Maine, *Studies*, XXXVII (1936).

C. M. Depew, *Orations, Addresses, and Speeches*. J. D. Champlin, ed. 8 vols. N.Y., 1910.

Emily Dickinson, *Bolts of Melody*. N.Y., 1945. *Letters*. M. L. Todd, ed. N.Y., 1931. *Poems*. M. D. Bianchi and A. L. Hampson, eds. Boston, 1937.

Robert Dinwiddie, *Official Records . . . 1751–1758*. R. A. Brock, ed. 2 vols. Richmond, 1883–84.

Millard Fillmore, "Papers," F. H. Severance, ed., Buffalo Hist. Soc., *Publ.*, X–XI (1907).

John Fiske, *Letters*. E. F. Fiske, ed. N.Y., 1940. *Personal Letters*, Cedar Rapids, 1939. *Unpublished Orations*. Boston, 1909. *Writings*. 24 vols. Cambridge, 1902.

Charles Follen, *Works*. E. L. Follen, ed. 5 vols. Boston, 1841.

G. V. Fox, *Confidential Correspondence . . . 1861–65*. R. M. Thompson and Richard Wainwright, eds. 2 vols. N.Y., 1918–19.

Jonathan Edwards, *Works*. 8 vols. Leeds, 1806–11. — Often reprinted.

R. W. Emerson, *Complete Works*. Centenary Ed. 12 vols. Boston, 1903–04. *Uncollected Writings*. C. C. Bigelow, ed. N.Y., 1912. *Letters*. R. L. Rusk, ed. 6 vols. N. Y., 1939.

W. M. Evarts, *Arguments and Speeches*. Sherman Evarts, ed. 3 vols. N.Y., 1919.

Benjamin Franklin, *Letters to the Press, 1758–1775*. V. W. Crane, ed. Chapel Hill, 1950. *The Letters of Benjamin Franklin and Jane Mecom*. Carl Van Doren, ed. Princeton, 1950. *Writings*. A. H. Smyth, ed. 10 vols. N.Y., 1905–07. *Benjamin Franklin and Catherine Ray Greene: Their Correspondence*. W. G. Roelker, ed. Phila., 1949.

Philip Freneau, *Poems*. F. L. Pattee, ed. 3 vols. Princeton, 1902–07.

Margaret Fuller, *Writings*. Mason Wade, ed. N.Y., 1941.

H. H. Furness, *Letters*. H. H. F. Jayne, ed. 2 vols. Boston, 1922.

Thomas Gage, *Correspondence*. C. E. Carter, ed. 2 vols. New Haven, 1931–33.

Albert Gallatin, *Writings*. Henry Adams, ed. 3 vols. Phila., 1879.

Henry George, *Complete Works*. 10 vols. Garden City, N.Y., 1906–11.

J. W. Gibbs, *Collected Works*. W. R. Longley and R. G. Van Name, eds. N.Y., 1928.

U. S. Grant, *Letters . . . to His Father and His Youngest Sister, 1857–1878*. J. G. Cramer, ed. N.Y., 1912.

Asa Gray, *Letters*. J. L. Gray, ed. 2 vols. Boston, 1893.

Horatio Greenough, *Letters . . . to His Brother Henry Greenough*. F. B. Greenough, ed. Boston, 1887.

Josiah Gregg, *Diary and Letters*. M. G. Fulton, ed. 2 vols. Norman, Okla., 1941–44.

Angelina and Sarah Grimké. See: T. D. Weld.

Alexander Hamilton, *Works*. J. C. Hamilton, ed. 7 vols. N.Y., 1850–51. *Works*. H. C. Lodge, ed. 12 vols. N.Y., 1904. *Industrial and Commercial Correspondence*. A. H. Cole, ed. Chi., 1928. — Neither edition of the *Works* is complete; and each has material not in the other.

J. C. Harris, *Joel Chandler Harris: Editor and Essayist*. Chapel Hill, 1931.

Bret Harte, *Letters*. G. B. Harte, ed. Boston, 1926. *Works*. 25 vols. N.Y., 1914.

Nathaniel Hawthorne, *The American Notebooks*. Randall Stewart, ed. New Haven, 1932. *Complete Works*. G. P. Lathrop, ed. 12 vols. Boston, 1883. *The English Notebooks*. Randall Stewart, ed. N.Y., 1941.

John Hay, *Letters . . . and Extracts from Diary*. Henry Adams, ed. 3 vols. Wash., 1908.

Joseph Henry, "Scientific Writings," Smithsonian Inst., *Misc. Coll.*, XXX (1886).

T. W. Higginson, *Letters and Journals*. M. T. Higginson, ed. Boston, 1921.

O. W. Holmes, *Writings*. 13 vols. Boston, 1891.
O. W. Holmes, Jr., *Holmes-Pollock Letters . . . 1874–1932*. M. D. Howe, ed. 2 vols.
  Cambridge, 1941. *Dissenting Opinions*. Alfred Lief, ed. N.Y., [1929].
Herbert Hoover, *State Papers*. W. S. Myers, ed. 2 vols. Garden City, N.Y., 1934.
S. G. Howe, *Letters and Journals*. L. E. Richards, ed. 2 vols. Boston, 1906–09.
Isaac Hull, *Papers*. G. W. Allen, ed. Boston, 1929.
J. G. Huneker, *Intimate Letters*. N.Y., 1924. *Letters*. 2 vols. N.Y., 1922. — Both edited
  by Josephine Huneker.
Thomas Hutchinson, *Diary and Letters*. P. O. Hutchinson, ed. 2 vols. London, 1883–86.
J. J. Ingalls, *Collection of . . . Writings*. W. E. Connelley, ed. Kansas City, Mo., 1902.
R. G. Ingersoll, *Works*. 12 vols. N.Y., 1900. *Letters*. E. I. Wakefield, ed. N.Y., 1951.
Washington Irving, *Works*. 12 vols. N.Y., 1881.
Ralph Izard, *Correspondence*. A. I. Deas, ed. N.Y., 1844.
Andrew Jackson, *Correspondence*. J. S. Bassett and J. F. Jameson, eds. 7 vols. Wash.,
  1926–35.
Henry James [1843–1916], *Letters*. Percy Lubbock, ed. 2 vols. N.Y., 1920.
William James [1842–1910], *Letters*. Henry James, ed. 2 vols. Boston, 1920.
John Jay, *Correspondence and Public Papers*. H. P. Johnston, ed. 4 vols. N.Y., 1890–93.
Thomas Jefferson and P. S. Du Pont de Nemours, *Correspondence*. Gilbert Chinard, ed.
  Balt., 1931. — A less complete collection, but with the French letters translated
  into English, Dumas Malone, ed. Boston, 1930.
Thomas Jefferson, *Papers*. J. P. Boyd, *et al.*, eds. 5 vols. Princeton, 1950–52. *Writings*.
  P. L. Ford, ed. 10 vols. N.Y., 1892–99. *Writings*, A. A. Lipscomb and A. E. Bergh,
  eds. 20 vols. Wash., 1903. — The Liscomb and Bergh is fuller but less accurate
  than the Ford. See also: Lafayette.
Andrew Johnson, *Speeches*. Frank Moore, ed. Boston, 1865.
Samuel Johnson, *Samuel Johnson, President of King's College: His Career and Writings*.
  Herbert and Carol Schneider, eds. 4 vols. N.Y., 1929.
William Johnson, *Papers*. J. Sullivan, A. C. Flick and M. W. Hamilton, eds. 11 vols.
  Albany, 1921–53.
Joyce Kilmer, *Poems, Essays and Letters*. R. C. Holliday, ed. 2 vols. N.Y., 1918.
Lafayette and Thomas Jefferson, *Letters*. Gilbert Chinard, ed. Balt., 1929.
Lafayette, *Letters . . . to Washington, 1777–1779*. Louis Gottschalk, ed. N.Y., 1944.
M. B. Lamar, *Papers*. C. A. Gulick, *et al.*, eds. 6 vols. Austin, 1921–27.
F. K. Lane, *Letters*. A. W. Lane and L. H. Hall, eds. Boston, 1922.
Sidney Lanier, *Centennial Edition* [of Works and Letters]. C. R. Anderson, ed. 10 vols.
  Balt., 1945.
Charles Lee, "Papers," N. Y. Hist. Soc., *Coll.*, IV–VII (1871–74).
R. H. Lee, *Letters*. J. C. Ballagh, ed. 2 vols. N.Y., 1911–14.
William Lee, *Letters*. W. C. Ford, ed. 3 vols. Brooklyn, 1891.
Francis Lieber, *Miscellaneous Writings*. 2 vols. Phila., 1881.
Abraham Lincoln, *Collected Works*. R. P. Basler, ed. 8 vols. New Brunswick, 1953.
  Complete Works. J. G. Nicolay, John Hay, and F. D. Tandy, eds. 12 vols. N.Y.,
  1905. *Uncollected Letters*. G. A. Tracy, ed. Boston, 1917. *New Letters*. P. M. Angle,
  ed. Boston, 1930.
H. C. Lodge and Theodore Roosevelt, *Selections from the Correspondence*. 2 vols. N.Y.,
  1925.
James Logan. See: William Penn.
H. W. Longfellow, *Works*. Samuel Longfellow, ed. 14 vols. Boston, 1886–91.
J. R. Lowell, *Complete Writings*. 16 vols. Cambridge, 1904. *New Letters*. M. A. DeW.
  Howe, ed. N.Y., 1932.
James Madison, *Writings*. Gaillard Hunt, ed. 9 vols. N.Y., 1900–10.
Jane Mecom. See: Benjamin Franklin.
Herman Melville, *Collected Poems*. H. P. Vincent, ed. Chi., 1945. *Works*. R. M. Weaver,
  ed. 16 vols. London, 1922–24.
James Monroe, *Writings*. S. M. Hamilton, ed. 7 vols. N.Y., 1898–1903.
W. V. Moody, *Poems and Plays*. J. M. Manly, ed. 2 vols. Boston, 1912. *Some Letters*.
  D. G. Mason, ed. Boston, 1913.

J. L. Motley, *Correspondence.* G. W. Curtis, ed. 2 vols. N.Y., 1889. *Writings.* G. W. Curtis, ed. 17 vols. N.Y., 1900.

John Muir, *Writings.* W. F Badè, ed. 10 vols. Boston, 1916–24.

F. G. Newlands, *Public Papers.* A. B. Darling, ed. 2 vols. Boston, 1932.

[Benjamin] Frank[lin] Norris, *Complete Works.* 10 vols. Garden City, N.Y., 1928.

C. E. Norton, *Letters.* Sarah Norton and M. A. DeW. Howe, eds. 2 vols. Boston, 1913.

James Otis, "Some Political Writings," C. F. Mullett, ed., Univ. of Mo., *Studies,* IV (1929), Nos. 3, 4.

Thomas Paine, *Complete Writings.* P. S. Foner, ed. 2 vols. N.Y., 1945. *Writings.* M. D. Conway, ed. 4 vols. N.Y., 1894–96.

Theodore Parker, *Works.* Centenary Ed. 15 vols. Boston, 1907–13.

Francis Parkman, *Works.* Centenary Ed. 12 vols. Boston, 1922.

J. P. Peabody, *Collected Poems.* K. L. Bates, ed. Boston, 1927. *Collected Plays.* G. P. Baker, ed. Boston, 1927.

Henry Pelham. See: J. S. Copley.

William Penn, *A Collection of the Works.* Joseph Besse, ed. 2 vols. London, 1726.

William Penn and James Logan, "Correspondence," Deborah Logan and Edward Armstrong, eds., Hist. Soc. of Penn., *Publ.,* IX–X (1870–72).

Wendell Phillips, *Speeches, Lectures, and Letters.* Boston, 1863.

G. E. Pickett, *Soldier of the South . . . Letters to His Wife.* A. C. Inman, ed. Boston, 1928.

E. A. Poe, *Complete Works.* J. A. Harrison, ed. 17 vols. N.Y., 1902.

W. S. Porter, *The Complete Works of O. Henry.* Garden City, N.Y., 1937.

W. H. Prescott, *Correspondence . . . 1833–1847.* Roger Wolcott, ed. Boston, 1925. *Prescott: Unpublished Letters.* C. L. Penney, ed. N.Y., 1927. *Works.* W. H. Munro, ed. 22 vols. Phila., 1904.

J. W. Riley, *Complete Works.* E. H. Eitel, ed. 6 vols. Indianapolis, 1913. *Letters.* W. L. Phelps, ed. Indianapolis, 1930.

Caesar Rodney, *Letters . . . 1756–1784.* G. H. Ryden, ed. Phila., 1933.

F. D. Roosevelt, *F.D.R. His Personal Letters.* Elliott Roosevelt, ed. 4 vols. N.Y., 1947–50. *The Public Papers and Addresses.* S. I. Rosenman, ed. 13 vols. N. Y., 1938–50.

Theodore Roosevelt, *Letters.* E. E. Morison, *et al.,* eds. 8 vols. Cambridge, 1951–54. *Works.* 24 vols. N.Y., 1923–26.

Thomas Ruffin, *Papers.* J. G. deR. Hamilton, ed. 4 vols. Raleigh, 1918–20.

Benjamin Rush, *Letters.* L. H. Butterfield, ed. 2 vols. Princeton, 1951.

Carl Schurz, *Speeches, Correspondence and Political Papers.* Frederic Bancroft, ed. 6 vols. N.Y., 1913.

W. H. Seward, *Works.* G. E. Baker, ed. 5 vols. N.Y., 1853–54.

W. T. Sherman, *Home Letters.* M. A. DeW. Howe, ed. N.Y., 1909.

William Shirley, *Correspondence . . . 1731–1760.* C. H. Lincoln, ed. 2 vols. N.Y., 1912.

John Smith, *Works.* Edward Arber and A. G. Bradley, eds. 2 vols. Edinburgh, 1910.

Alexander Spotswood, *The Official Letters . . . 1710–1722.* R. A. Brock, ed. 2 vols. Richmond, Va., 1882–85.

A. H. Stephens. See: Howell Cobb.

John Sullivan, *Letters and Papers.* O. G. Hammond, ed. 2 vols. Concord, N.H., 1930–31.

Charles Sumner, *Works.* 15 vols. Boston, 1870–83.

J. C. Symmes, *Correspondence.* B. W. Bond, Jr., ed. N.Y., 1926.

Zachary Taylor, *Letters . . . from the Battle-fields of the Mexican War.* Intro. by W. H. Samson. Rochester, N.Y., 1908.

H. D. Thoreau, *Writings.* Walden Ed. 20 vols. Boston, 1906.

John Tipton, *Papers.* N. A. Robertson, *et al.,* eds. 3 vols. Indianapolis, 1942.

Robert Toombs. See: Howell Cobb.

Mark Twain, *Letters.* A. B. Paine, ed. 2 vols. N.Y., 1917. *Writings.* A. B. Paine, ed. 37 vols. N.Y., 1922–25.

A. H. Vandenberg, *Private Papers.* A. H. Vandenberg, Jr. and J. H. Morris, eds. Boston, 1952.

Artemus Ward [Charles Farrar Browne], *His Works, Complete.* N.Y., 1875.

James and Mercy [Otis] Warren, "Warren-Adams Letters," W. C. Ford, ed., 2 vols., Mass. Hist. Soc., *Coll.*, LXXII–LXXIII (1917–25).
George Washington, *Writings*. J. C. Fitzpatrick, ed. 39 vols. Wash., 1931–44.
Daniel Webster, *Letters*. C. H. Van Tyne, ed. N.Y., 1902. *Writings and Speeches*. J. W. McIntyre, ed., 18 vols. Boston, 1903.
T. D. Weld, A. G. Weld, and Sarah Grimké, *Letters . . . 1822–1844*. G. H. Barnes and D. L. Dumond, eds. 2 vols. N.Y., 1934.
Walt Whitman, *Complete Writings*. H. L. Traubel, *et al.*, eds. 10 vols. N.Y., 1902.
J. G. Whittier, *Writings*. H. E. Scudder, ed. 7 vols. Boston, 1894.
Roger Williams, *Writings*. 6 vols. Providence, 1866–74.
Woodrow Wilson, *Public Papers*. R. S. Baker and W. E. Dodd, eds. 6 vols. Garden City, N.Y., 1925–27. *Selected Literary and Political Papers*. 3 vols. N.Y., 1925–27.
John Winthrop, *Papers*. A. B. Forbes, ed. 5 vols. Boston, 1929–47. — In process.
Chauncey Wright, *Letters*. J. B. Thayer, ed. Cambridge, 1878.

56. BIOGRAPHIES

American historical literature is particularly rich in biographies. The most important biographical cyclopedia is Allen Johnson and Dumas Malone, eds., *Dictionary of American Biography* (22 vols., N.Y., 1928–44, including a general index and a supplementary volume), which supersedes all earlier compilations of this character. Some of its sketches are superior to longer biographies published separately; its bibliographies offer more complete information than the limits of the *Guide* permit. In briefer compass, Webster's *Biographical Dictionary* (Springfield, 1943) is a handy reference tool.

There are many single volumes of biographical essays by one or more authors. Their variety is indicated by the following: S. C. Beach, *Daughters of the Puritans* (Boston, 1905); Royal Cortissoz, *American Artists* (N.Y., 1923); J. T. Flexner, *Doctors on Horseback, Pioneers of American Medicine* (N.Y., 1937); B. J. Hendrick, *The Lees of Virginia* (Boston, 1935); D. S. Jordan, ed., *Leading American Men of Science* (N.Y., 1910); H. W. Odum, ed., *American Masters of Social Science* (N.Y., 1927); C. E. Merriam, *Four American Party Leaders* (N.Y., 1926); C. M. Rourke, *Trumpets of Jubilee* (N.Y., 1927); and S. P. Sherman, *Americans* (N.Y., 1922). Of particular value are the "psychographs" or biographical sketches by Gamaliel Bradford, including the following: *Confederate Portraits* (Boston, 1912); *Damaged Souls* (Boston, 1923); *Portraits of American Women* (Boston, 1917); *Saints and Sinners* (Boston, 1932); and *Union Portraits* (Boston, 1914). These are based upon an intensive study of the subjects, and seek to reveal the essential character of each person in relation to the life of his times.

Fuller treatments may be found either in independent volumes or as parts of larger coöperative works. Among the more notable biographical series are *American Men of Energy* (N.Y., 1900–1907); *American Religious Leaders* (7 vols., Boston, 1889–92); Elliott Coues, ed., *American Explorers Series* (N.Y., 1898–1903), which includes documentary accounts; W. D. Lewis, ed., *Great American Lawyers* (8 vols., Phila., 1907–09); M. A. DeW. Howe, ed., *The Beacon Biographies* (31 vols., Boston, 1899–1910); Laurence Hutton, ed., *American Actor Series* (Boston, 1881–82); *Makers of America* (17 vols., N.Y., 1890–93); Carlos Martyn, ed., *American Reformers* (N.Y., 1890–96); J. T. Morse, Jr., ed., *American Statesmen* (32 vols., including a general index vol., Boston, 1882–1900; 2nd series, 1905–16); Allan Nevins, ed., *American Political*

Leaders (N.Y., 1930–   ); E. P. Oberholtzer, ed., *American Crisis Biographies* (15 vols., Phila., 1904–15); W. H. Smith, *Speakers of the House* (Balt., 1928); Mark Van Doren, *et al.*, eds., *American Men of Letters Series* (N.Y., 1948–   ); an earlier series under the same title (C. D. Warner, ed., Boston, 1881–1906); and J. G. Wilson, ed., *Great Commanders Series* (18 vols., N.Y., 1892–1902). Individual volumes of these series are cited in the list below. Somewhat different in character, Bemis, *American Secretaries of State* (§ 59), depicts the work of the men concerned while in charge of the Department of State.

The critical student will wish to familiarize himself with two recent discussions of the evolution of American biographical writing: D. K. Merrill, *The Development of American Biography* (Portland, Me., 1932), and E. H. O'Neill, *A History of American Biography, 1800–1935* (Phila., 1935). N. O. Ireland, *Historical Biographies for Junior and Senior High Schools, Universities and Colleges* (Phila., 1933), offers a list of biographies covering European as well as American history.

A variety of other sources will supply the student with biographical information about persons many of whom are not prominent enough to have whole volumes devoted to them. *Who's Who in America* provides factual data in regard to living or recently deceased persons, furnished by the subjects. *Who Was Who in America* (2 vols. Chi., 1942–50), compiled from the foregoing, covers the years, 1897–1950. *Current Biography* (Maxine Block, *et al.*, eds., N.Y., 1940–   ) is a monthly with annual cumulations (index, 1940–50 in 1950) that prints longer accounts of "newsworthy" individuals. Other compilations, from time to time, deal with particular localities, professions, or ethnic groups; and many local histories (§ 62) have extensive biographical sections. Various registers supply information on government officials, officers of the armed forces, the alumni of many colleges, and the members of learned societies. Sometimes, however, the only such information available is in newspaper obituaries or in newspaper morgues.

The more helpful guides and collections include:

"Biographical Directory of the American Congress, 1774–1949," 81 Cong., 2 Sess., H. *Doc.*, No. 607.
Biography Index. — A continuing series (§ 39).
Marion Dargan, *Guide to American Biography*. Albuquerque, 1949.
Index to the Obituary Notices in the Boston Transcript [1875–1930]. 5 vols. Boston, n.d.
T. H. S. Hamersly, *Complete Army and Navy Register*. N.Y., 1888.
R. B. Mosher, *Executive Register of the United States, 1789–1802*. Balt., [1903].
O'Neill, *Biography by Americans* (§ 35).

The following list is highly selective. Privately printed or very scarce works, brief sketches in composite works, memoirs in the publications of learned and professional societies, obituaries, and campaign biographies are omitted. Such of them as have historical value are noted later in the *Guide* in connection with the relevant subject matter. Some important names will be found wanting, because no adequate life of them exists; some less important ones are included because their biographies or writings contain material useful to the student of American civilization. The list takes into account many varieties of achievement. If scientists, businessmen, and women seem few, compared with figures in other walks of life, it is because few adequate biographies of them have been published. In cases where there is more than one biography of a person, the best, or those that are written from different points of view are mentioned.

E. V. Lucas, *Edwin Austin Abbey, Royal Academician. The Record of His Life and Work.* 2 vols. N.Y., 1921.

Janet Whitney, *Abigail Adams.* Boston, 1947.

C. F. Adams, *Charles Francis Adams* [1807–86]. Boston, 1900.

C. F. Adams, *Life of John Adams.* 2 vols. Phila., 1874. Gilbert Chinard, *Honest John Adams.* Boston, 1933.

S. F. Bemis, *John Quincy Adams and the Foundations of American Foreign Policy.* N.Y., 1949.

J. C. Miller, *Sam Adams.* Boston, 1936. W. V. Wells, *The Life and Public Services of Samuel Adams.* 3 vols. Boston, 1865.

J. W. Linn, *Jane Addams.* N.Y., 1935.

L. A. Patton, *Elizabeth Cary Agassiz.* Boston, 1919.

E. C. Agassiz, *Louis Agassiz, His Life and Correspondence.* 2 vols. Boston, 1885. Jules Marcou, *Life, Letters and Works of Louis Agassiz.* 2 vols. N.Y., 1896.

F. B. Sanborn and W. T. Harris, *A. Bronson Alcott, His Life and Philosophy.* 2 vols. Boston, 1893. Odell Shepard, *Pedlar's Progress.* Boston, 1937.

Katharine Anthony, *Louisa May Alcott.* N.Y., 1938. E. D. Cheney, *Louisa May Alcott: Her Life, Letters, and Journals.* Boston, 1889.

N. W. Stephenson, *Nelson W. Aldrich, a Leader in American Politics.* N.Y., 1930.

Ferris Greenslet, *Life of Thomas Bailey Aldrich.* Boston, 1908.

John Pell, *Ethan Allen.* Boston, 1929.

J. B. Flagg, *Life and Letters of Washington Allston.* N.Y., 1892.

Harry Barnard, *"Eagle Forgotten." The Life of John Peter Altgeld.* Indianapolis, [1938].

J. C. Long, *Lord Jeffery Amherst.* N.Y., 1933.

H. G. Pearson, *Life of John A. Andrew.* 2 vols. Boston, 1904.

I. H. Harper, *Life and Work of Susan B. Anthony.* 3 vols. Indianapolis, 1898–1908.

E. A. Talbot, *Samuel Chapman Armstrong* [educator]. N.Y., 1904.

I. N. Arnold, *Life of Benedict Arnold.* Chicago, 1880. C. C. Sellers, *Benedict Arnold.* N.Y., 1930.

G. F. Howe, *Chester A. Arthur.* N.Y., 1934.

E. S. Tipple, *Francis Asbury, the Prophet of the Long Road.* N.Y., 1916. Herbert Asbury, *A Methodist Saint.* N.Y., 1927.

James Parton, *Life of John Jacob Astor.* N.Y., 1865. K. W. Porter, *John Jacob Astor, Business Man.* 2 vols. Cambridge, 1931.

F. H. Herrick, *Audubon the Naturalist.* 2 vols. N.Y., 1917. M. R. Audubon, *Audubon and His Journals.* Elliott Coues, ed. 2 vols. N.Y., 1897, 1900. C. M. Rourke, *Audubon.* N.Y., 1936.

E. C. Barker, *Life of Stephen F. Austin, Founder of Texas.* Nashville, 1926.

T. J. Wertenbaker, *Torchbearer of the Revolution* [Nathaniel Bacon]. Princeton, 1940.

W. H. Dall, *Spencer Fullerton Baird.* Phila., 1915.

M. A. DeW. Howe, *Life and Letters of George Bancroft.* 2 vols. N.Y., 1908. R. B. Nye, *George Bancroft.* N.Y., 1944.

C. B. Todd, *Life and Letters of Joel Barlow.* N.Y., 1886. T. A. Zunder, *Early Days of Joel Barlow.* New Haven, 1934.

John Fulton, *Memoirs of Frederick A. P. Barnard.* N.Y., 1896.

M. R. Werner, *Barnum.* N.Y., 1923.

W. E. Barton, *Life of Clara Barton.* 2 vols. Boston, 1922.

William Darlington, *Memorials of John Bartram and Humphrey Marshall.* Phila., 1849. Ernest Earnest, *John and William Bartram.* Phila., 1940.

R. S. and J. B. Baker, *An American Pioneer in Science* [William James Beal]. Amherst, Mass., 1925.

J. S. Myer, *Life and Letters of Dr. William Beaumont.* St. Louis, 1912.

Hamilton Basso, *Beauregard, the Great Creole.* N.Y., 1933.

Paxton Hibben, *Henry Ward Beecher, an American Portrait.* N.Y., 1927. Lyman Abbott, *Henry Ward Beecher.* Boston, 1903.

W. C. Klein, *Johann Conrad Beissel . . . 1690–1786.* Phila., 1942.

Catherine Mackenzie, *Alexander Graham Bell.* Boston, 1928.

J. H. Parks, *John Bell of Tennessee.* Baton Rouge, 1930.

A. E. Morgan, *Edward Bellamy*. N.Y., 1944.

Thomas Beer and E. S. Bellows, *George W. Bellows; His Lithographs*. N.Y., 1927. E. S. Bellows, *The Paintings of George Bellows*. N.Y., 1929.

Roberts Vaux, *Memoirs of the Life of Anthony Benezet* [philanthropist]. Phila., 1817.

Pierce Butler, *Judah P. Benjamin*. Phila., 1907. R. G. Osterweis, *Judah P. Benjamin, Statesman of the Lost Cause*. N.Y., 1933. R. D. Meade, *Judah P. Benjamin*. N.Y., 1943.

D. C. Seitz, *The James Gordon Bennetts, Father and Son*. Indianapolis, 1928.

W. M. Meigs, *Life of Thomas Hart Benton*. Phila., 1904.

C. G. Bowers, *Beveridge and the Progressive Era*. Boston, 1932.

Grace King, *Jean Baptiste le Moyne, Sieur de Bienville*. N.Y., 1892.

Carey McWilliams, *Ambrose Bierce*. N.Y., 1929.

Margaret Clapp, *Forgotten First Citizen: John Bigelow*. Boston, 1947.

F. H. Garrison, *John Shaw Billings*. N.Y., 1916.

C. C. Binney, *Life of Horace Binney, with Selections from His Letters*. Phila., 1903.

William Birney, *James G. Birney and His Times*. N.Y., 1890.

Ferdinand Schevill, *Karl Bitter; a Biography*. Chi., 1917.

D. S. Muzzey, *James G. Blaine*. N.Y., 1934.

D. E. Motley, *Life of Commissary James Blair, Founder of William and Mary College*. Balt., 1901.

W. V. Byars, *An American Commoner* [R. P. Bland]. Columbia, Mo., 1900.

E. S. Bradley, *George Henry Boker, Poet and Patriot*. Phila., 1927.

H. A. Bruce, *Daniel Boone and the Wilderness Road*. N.Y., 1910.

William Winter, *Life and Art of Edwin Booth*. N.Y., 1893.

V. Y. Bowditch, *Life and Correspondence of Henry Ingersoll Bowditch*. 2 vols. Boston, 1902.

G. S. Merriam, *Life and Times of Samuel Bowles*. 2 vols. N.Y., 1885.

C. M. Newlin, *The Life and Writings of Hugh Henry Brackenridge*. Princeton, 1932.

D. C. Seitz, *Braxton Bragg, General of the Confederacy*. Columbia, So. Car., 1924.

A. T. Mason, *Brandeis*. N.Y., 1946.

L. E. Richards, *Laura Bridgman*. N.Y., 1928.

A. V. G. Allen, *Life and Letters of Phillips Brooks*. 2 vols. N.Y., 1900.

O. G. Villard, *John Brown*. N.Y., 1943.

C. F. Browne. See: Artemus Ward.

E. M. Coulter, *William G. Brownlow*. Chapel Hill, 1937.

H. F. Brownson, *Orestes A. Brownson*. 3 vols. Detroit, 1898–1900. A. M. Schlesinger, Jr., *Orestes A. Brownson*. Boston, 1939.

M. R. Werner, [William Jennings] *Bryan*. N.Y., 1929.

Parke Godwin, *A Biography of William Cullen Bryant, with Extracts from His Private Correspondence*. 2 vols. N.Y., 1883.

G. T. Curtis, *Life of James Buchanan*. 2 vols. N.Y., 1883.

C. A. Place, *Charles Bulfinch, Architect and Citizen*. Boston, 1925.

H. S. Williams, *Luther Burbank, His Life and Work*. N.Y., 1915.

E. B. de Fonblanque, *Political and Military Episodes Derived from the Life and Correspondence of John Burgoyne*. London, 1876.

Charles Moore, *Daniel H. Burnham, Architect, Planner of Cities*. 2 vols. Boston, 1921.

M. L. Davis, *Memoirs of Aaron Burr with Miscellaneous Selections from His Correspondence*. 2 vols. N.Y., 1836–37. Idem, *Private Journal of Aaron Burr During His Residence of Four Years in Europe, with Selections from His Correspondence*. 2 vols. N.Y., 1838. James Parton, *The Life and Times of Aaron Burr*. N.Y., 1858. S. H. Wandell and Meade Minnigerode, *Aaron Burr*. 2 vols. N.Y., 1925. W. F. McCaleb, *The Aaron Burr Conspiracy*. N.Y., 1936. Nathan Schachner, *Aaron Burr*. N.Y., 1937.

M. E. Curti, *The Learned Blacksmith* [Elihu Burritt]. N.Y., 1937.

Clara Barrus, *Life and Letters of John Burroughs*. 2 vols. Boston, 1925. Idem, *Our Friend, John Burroughs*. Boston, 1914.

M. B. Cheney, *Life and Letters of Horace Bushnell*. N.Y., 1880. T. T. Munger, *Horace Bushnell*. N.Y., 1899.

A. W. H. Eaton, *The Famous Mather Byles*. Boston, 1914.
R. C. Beatty, *William Byrd of Westover*. Boston, 1932.
L. L. C. Biklé, *George W. Cable, His Life and Letters*. N.Y., 1928.
H. C. Lodge, *Life and Letters of George Cabot*. Boston, 1877.
W. M. Meigs, *The Life of John Caldwell Calhoun*. 2 vols. N.Y., 1917. C. M. Wiltse, *John C. Calhoun*. 3 vols. Indianapolis, 1944–51.
W. H. Browne, *George Calvert and Cecilius Calvert, Barons of Baltimore*. N.Y., 1890.
Robert Richardson, *Memoirs of Alexander Campbell*. 2 vols. Phila., 1868–70.
H. G. Connor, *John Archibald Campbell*. Boston, 1920.
Virginius Dabney, *Dry Messiah: The Life of Bishop [James] Cannon [Jr.]*. N.Y., 1949.
L. W. Busbey, *Uncle Joe Cannon*. N.Y., 1927.
William Elder, *Memoir of Henry C. Carey*. Phila., 1880.
K. W. Rowe, *Mathew Carey, a Study in American Economic Development*. Balt., 1933.
B. J. Hendrick, *The Life of Andrew Carnegie*. 2 vols. N.Y., 1932. J. K. Winkler, *Incredible Carnegie*. N.Y., 1931.
K. M. Rowland, *Life of Charles Carroll of Carrollton, 1737–1832, with His Correspondence and Public Papers*. 2 vols. N.Y., 1898. E. H. Smith, *Charles Carroll*. Cambridge, 1942.
P. K. Guilday, *Life and Times of John Carroll*. 2 vols. N.Y., 1922.
E. L. Sabin, *Kit Carson Days*. R. ed. 2 vols. N.Y., 1935.
A. C. McLaughlin, *Lewis Cass*. Boston, 1899.
Achille Ségard, *Un Peintre des enfants et des mères, Mary Cassatt*. Paris, 1913.
Morris Bishop, *Champlain, the Life of Fortitude*. N.Y., 1948.
W. C. Harris, *Public Life of Zachariah Chandler, 1851–1875*. Lansing, Mich., 1917.
J. W. Chadwick, *William Ellery Channing*. Boston, 1903.
M. A. DeW. Howe, *John Jay Chapman and His Letters*. Boston, 1937.
A. B. Hart, *Salmon P. Chase*. Boston, 1899. J. W. Schuckers, *Life and Public Services of Salmon P. Chase*. N.Y., 1874.
E. S. Martin, *Life of Joseph Hodges Choate*. 2 vols. N.Y., 1920.
C. M. Fuess, *Rufus Choate, the Wizard of the Law*. N.Y., 1928.
G. L. Nute, *Caesars of the Wilderness: Médard Chouart . . . and Pierre Esprit Radisson, 1618–1710*. N.Y., 1943.
J. A. James, *Life of George Rogers Clark*. Chi., [1928].
Carl Schurz, *Life of Henry Clay*. 2 vols. Boston, 1887. Bernard Mayo, *Henry Clay [to 1812]*. Boston, 1937. G. G. Van Deusen, *The Life of Henry Clay*. Boston, 1937.
Samuel L. Clemens. See: Mark Twain.
Allan Nevins, *Grover Cleveland; a Study in Courage*. N.Y., 1932.
W. W. Campbell, *Life and Writings of De Witt Clinton*. N.Y., 1933.
Z. T. Johnson, *Political Policies of Howell Cobb*. Nashville, 1929.
L. L. Noble, *Life and Works of Thomas Cole*. N.Y., 1856.
S. E. Morison, *Admiral of the Ocean Sea*. 2 vols. Boston, 1942. Justin Winsor, *Christopher Columbus*. Boston, 1891. Cesare de Lollis, *Cristoforo Colombo*. R. ed. Milan, 1931. J. B. Charcot, *Christophe Colomb vu par un Marin*. Paris, 1928. Washington Irving, *The Life and Voyages of Christopher Columbus*. R. ed. 3 vols. N.Y., 1848–49. J. B. Thacher, *Christopher Columbus*. 3 vols. N.Y., 1903–04.
Heywood Broun and Margaret Leech, *Anthony Comstock, Roundsman of the Lord*. N.Y., 1927.
C. K. Shipton, *Roger Conant*. Cambridge, 1944.
A. R. Conkling, *Life and Letters of Roscoe Conkling*. N.Y., 1889. D. B. Chidsey, *The Gentleman from New York: A Life of Roscoe Conkling*. New Haven, 1935.
M. J. Moses, *Life of Heinrich Conried*. N.Y., 1916.
E. P. Oberholtzer, *Jay Cooke, Financier of the Civil War*. 2 vols. Phila., 1907. H. M. Larson, *Jay Cooke, Private Banker*. Cambridge, 1936.
W. A. White, *A Puritan in Babylon: Calvin Coolidge*. N.Y., 1938.
T. R. Lounsbury, *James Fenimore Cooper*. Boston, 1882. R. E. Spiller, *Fenimore Cooper*. N.Y., 1931.
R. W. Raymond, *Peter Cooper*. Boston, 1901.
Dumas Malone, *Public Life of Thomas Cooper, 1783–1839*. New Haven, 1926.

H. F. Osborn, *Cope, Master Naturalist*. Princeton, 1931.

M. B. Amory, *Domestic and Artistic Life of John Singleton Copley*. Boston, 1882.

H. E. Bolton, *Coronado*. N.Y., 1949.

Philip Horton, *Hart Crane*. N.Y., 1937.

Thomas Beer, *Stephen Crane, a Study in American Letters*. N.Y., 1923. John Berryman, *Stephen Crane*. [N.Y., 1950].

M. H. Elliott, *My Cousin, F. Marion Crawford*. N.Y., 1934.

Thomas Hicks, *Thomas Crawford; Career, Character, and Works*. N.Y., 1858.

J. E. D. Shipp, *Giant Days; or, the Life and Times of William H. Crawford*. Americus, Ga., 1909.

A. M. B. Coleman, *Life of John J. Crittenden*. 2 vols. Phila., 1871.

A. T. Volwiler, *George Croghan and the Westward Movement, 1741–82*. Cleve., 1926.

H. T. Peters, *Currier and Ives, Printmakers to the American People*. 2 vols. N.Y., 1925–31.

E. A. Alderman and A. C. Gordon, *J. L. M. Curry*. N.Y., 1911.

B. R. Curtis, *A Memoir of Benjamin Robbins Curtis . . . with Some of His Professional and Miscellaneous Writings*. 2 vols. Boston, 1879.

Edward Cary, *George William Curtis*. Boston, 1894.

C. M. Fuess, *Life of Caleb Cushing*. 2 vols. N.Y., 1923.

Emma Stebbins, *Charlotte Cushman: Her Letters and Memories of Her Life*. Boston, 1878.

F. S. Dellenbaugh, *George Armstrong Custer*. N.Y., 1917.

W. P. and J. P. Cutler, *Life, Journals, and Correspondence of Rev. Manasseh Cutler*. 2 vols. Cin., 1888.

S. D. Smedes, *Memorials of a Southern Planter* [T. S. G. Dabney]. Balt., 1887.

G. M. Dallas, *Life and Writings of Alexander James Dallas*. Phila., 1871. Raymond Walters, Jr., *Alexander James Dallas*. Phila., 1943.

J. F. Daly, *Life of Augustin Daly*. N.Y., 1917.

D. C. Gilman, *The Life of James Dwight Dana, Scientific Explorer, Mineralogist, Geologist, Zoologist*. N.Y., 1899.

C. F. Adams, *Richard Henry Dana* [1815–1882]. 2 vols. Boston, 1890–91.

B. C. Steiner, *Life of Henry Winter Davis*. Balt., 1916.

W. E. Dodd, *Jefferson Davis*. Phila., 1907. V. H. Davis, *Jefferson Davis*. 2 vols. N.Y., 1890. R. M. McElroy, *Jefferson Davis, the Unreal and the Real*. 2 vols., N.Y., 1937.

G. L. Clark, *Silas Deane*. N.Y., 1913.

David Karsner, *Debs: His Authorized Life and Letters*. N.Y., 1919. Ray Ginger, *The Bending Cross: Debs*. New Brunswick, 1949.

Daniel De Leon, The Man and His Work; a Symposium. N.Y., 1920.

H. M. Ellis, *Joseph Dennie and His Circle*. Austin, 1915.

J. D. Phillips, *Life and Times of Richard Derby, Merchant of Salem, 1712 to 1783*. Cambridge, 1929.

William Harper, *Memoir of the Life, Character, and Public Services, of the Late Hon. Henry William De Saussure*. Charleston, 1841.

M. D. Bianchi, *Life and Letters of Emily Dickinson*. Boston, 1924. G. F. Whicher, *This Was a Poet*. N.Y., 1938.

C. J. Stillé, *Life and Times of John Dickinson*. Phila., 1891.

L. K. Koontz, *Robert Dinwiddie*. Glendale, Calif., 1941.

H. E. Marshall, *Dorothea Dix: Forgotten Samaritan*. Chapel Hill, 1937.

Morgan Dix, *Memoirs of John Adams Dix*. 2 vols. N.Y., 1883.

Allen Johnson, *Stephen A. Douglas*. N.Y., 1908. G. F. Milton, *The Eve of Conflict: Stephen A. Douglas and the Needless War*. Boston, 1934.

B. T. Washington, *Frederick Douglass*. Phila., 1907.

C. C. Sellers, *Lorenzo Dow*. N.Y., 1928.

Otto Juettner, *Daniel Drake and His Followers*. Cin., [1909].

Donald Fleming, *John William Draper and the Religion of Science*. Phila., 1950.

R. H. Elias, *Theodore Dreiser, Apostle of Nature*. N.Y., 1949.

Everett Kimball, *The Public Life of Joseph Dudley*. N.Y., 1911.

J. W. Jenkins, *James B. Duke, Master Builder*. N.Y., 1927.

B. G. Brawley, *Paul Lawrence Dunbar*. Chapel Hill, 1936.

O. S. Coad, *William Dunlap, a Study of His Life and Works*. N.Y., 1917.

B. G. du Pont, *Life of Eleuthère Irenée du Pont*. 12 vols. Newark, Dela., 1923–26.

H. A. du Pont, *Rear-Admiral Samuel Francis du Pont*. N.Y., 1926.

Norman Heermann, *Frank Duveneck*. Boston, 1918.

G. W. Cooke, *John Sullivan Dwight, Brook-Farmer, Editor and Critic of Music*. Boston, 1898.

C. E. Cunningham, *Timothy Dwight, 1752–1817*. N.Y., 1942.

Louis How, *James B. Eads*. Boston, 1900.

Queena Pollack, *Peggy Eaton* [O'Neale]. N.Y., 1931.

E. S. Bates and J. V. Dittemore, *Mary Baker Eddy, the Truth and the Tradition*. N.Y., 1932. E. F. Dakin, *Mrs. Eddy*. R. ed. N.Y., 1930. L. P. Powell, *Mary Baker Eddy*. N.Y., 1930.

F. L Dyer and T. C Martin, *Edison, His Life and Inventions* N.Y., 1910. R. ed., 1929.

A. V. G. Allen, *Jonathan Edwards*. Boston, 1891. Perry Miller, *Jonathan Edwards*. N.Y., 1949.

N. W. Edwards, *History of Illinois from 1778 to 1833; and Life and Times of Ninian Edwards*. Springfield, Ill., 1870.

G. C. Eggleston, *The First of the Hoosiers: Reminiscences of Edward Eggleston*. Phila., 1903. W. P. Randel, *Edward Eggleston*. N.Y., 1946.

C. W. Eliot, *Charles Eliot, Landscape Architect*. Boston, 1902.

Henry James, *Charles W. Eliot*. 2 vols. Boston, 1930. W. A. Neilson, *Charles W. Eliot, the Man and His Beliefs*. 2 vols. N.Y., 1926.

C. V. C. Mathews, *Andrew Ellicott, His Life and Letters*. N.Y., 1908.

W. G. Brown, *The Life of Oliver Ellsworth*. N.Y., 1905.

J. E. Cabot, *Memoir of Ralph Waldo Emerson*. 2 vols. Boston, 1887. G. E. Woodberry, *Ralph Waldo Emerson*. N.Y., 1907. R. L. Rusk, *The Life of Ralph Waldo Emerson*. N.Y., 1949.

T. A. Emmet, *Memoir of Thomas Addis and Robert Emmet*. 2 vols. N.Y., 1915.

L. S. Mayo, *John Endecott, a Biography*. Cambridge, 1936.

P. K. Guilday, *Life and Times of John England*. 2 vols. N.Y., 1927.

W. C. Church, *Life of John Ericsson*. 2 vols. N.Y., 1890.

A. H. Heusser, *The Forgotten General, Robert Erskine, Geographer*. Paterson, 1928.

L. H. Gipson, *Lewis Evans*. Phila., 1939.

Brainerd Dyer, *The Public Career of William M. Evarts*. Berkeley, 1933. C. L. Barrows, *William M. Evarts*. Chapel Hill, 1941.

P. R. Frothingham, *Edward Everett, Orator and Statesman*. Boston, 1925.

A. T. Mahan, *Admiral Farragut*. N.Y., 1892. C. L. Lewis, *David Glasgow Farragut*. 2 vols. Annapolis, 1941–43.

V. F. O'Daniel, *The Right Rev. Edward Dominic Fenwick*. Wash., 1920.

R. F. Perrin, *Life and Works of Thomas Green Fessenden*. Orono, Me., 1925.

Francis Fessenden, *Life and Public Services of William Pitt Fessenden*. 2 vols. Boston, 1907.

I. F. Judson, *Cyrus W. Field, His Life and Work*. N.Y., 1896.

E. A. Field, *Record of the Life of David Dudley Field, His Ancestors and Descendants*. Denver, 1931.

Slason Thompson, *Life of Eugene Field*. N.Y., 1927.

C. B. Swisher, *Stephen J. Field, Craftsman of the Law*. Wash., 1930.

A. A. Fields, *James T. Fields, Biographical Notes and Personal Sketches*. Boston, 1881.

W. E. Griffis, *Millard Fillmore*. Ithaca, N.Y., 1915.

Allan Nevins, *Hamilton Fish; the Inner History of the Grant Administration*. N.Y., 1936.

T. S. Perry, *John Fiske*. Boston, 1906. H. S. Commager, "John Fiske," Mass. Hist. Soc., *Proc.*, LXVI (1942), 332. J. S. Clark, *The Life and Letters of John Fiske*. 2 vols. Boston, 1917.

H. S. White, *Willard Fiske, Life and Correspondence*. N.Y., 1925.

M. J. Moses and Virginia Gerson, *Clyde Fitch and His Letters*. Boston, 1924.

Arthur Mizener, *The Far Side of Paradise: A Biography of F. Scott Fitzgerald*. Boston, 1951.

Harvey Wish, *George Fitzhugh*. Baton Rouge, 1943.

C. H. Ambler, *Life and Diary of John Floyd*. Richmond, 1918.

Everett Walters, *Joseph Benson Foraker*. Columbus, Ohio, 1948.

S. F. Hughes, *Letters and Recollections of John Murray Forbes*. 2 vols. Boston, 1899. H. G. Pearson, *An American Railroad Builder*. Boston, 1911.

K. T. Sward, *The Legend of Henry Ford*. N.Y., 1948.

W. R. Alger, *Life of Edwin Forrest*. 2 vols. Phila., 1877. M. J. Moses, *The Fabulous Forrest*. Boston, 1929.

J. H. Mathes, *General Forrest*. N.Y., 1902. A. N. Lytle, *Bedford Forrest and His Critter Company*. N.Y., 1931.

J. T. Howard, *Stephen Foster, America's Troubadour*. N.Y., 1934. Raymond Walters, *Stephen Foster*. Princeton, 1937.

Carl Becker, *Benjamin Franklin*. Ithaca, 1946. James Parton, *Life and Times of Benjamin Franklin*. 2 vols. N.Y., 1864. Carl Van Doren, *Benjamin Franklin*. N.Y., 1938. Carl Van Doren, *et al., Meet Dr. Franklin*. Phila., 1943.

W. H. Stephenson, *Isaac Franklin, Slave Trader*. University, La., 1938.

Allan Nevins, *Frémont, the West's Greatest Adventurer*. 2 vols. N.Y., 1928.

Lewis Leary, *That Rascal Freneau*. New Brunswick, 1941.

George Harvey, *Henry Clay Frick*. N.Y., 1928.

Mason Wade, *Margaret Fuller*. N.Y., 1940. M. B. Stern, *Life of Margaret Fuller*. N.Y., 1942.

W. L. King, *Melville Weston Fuller*. N.Y., 1950.

H. W. Dickinson, *Robert Fulton, Engineer and Artist; His Life and Works*. London, 1913.

J. R. Alden, *General Gage in America*. Baton Rouge, 1948.

Henry Adams, *Life of Albert Gallatin*. Phila., 1879.

T. C. Smith, *Life and Letters of James Abram Garfield*. 2 vols. New Haven, 1925. R. G. Caldwell, *James A. Garfield, Party Chieftain*. N.Y., 1931.

F. J. and W. P. Garrison, *William Lloyd Garrison, 1805–1879*. 4 vols. N.Y., 1885–89. Lindsay Swift, *William Lloyd Garrison*. Phila., 1911. Ralph Korngold, *Two Friends of Man . . . William Lloyd Garrison and Wendell Phillips*. Boston, 1950.

I. M. Tarbell, *Life of Elbert H. Gary*. N.Y., 1925.

S. W. Patterson, *Horatio Gates*. N.Y., 1941.

Henry George, Jr., *Life of Henry George*. N.Y., 1900. A. A. De Mille, *Henry George*. Chapel Hill, 1950.

J. T. Austin, *Life of Elbridge Gerry*. 2 vols. Boston, 1827–29.

J. T. Ellis, *The Life of Cardinal Gibbons*. 2 vols. Milwaukee, 1953.

L. P. Wheeler, *Josiah Willard Gibbs*. New Haven, 1951.

G. W. Julian, *Life of Joshua R. Giddings*. Chi., 1892.

D. R. Anderson, *William Branch Giles*. Menasha, Wisc., 1914.

Fabian Franklin, *The Life of Daniel Coit Gilman*. N.Y., 1910.

Rollo Ogden, *Life and Letters of Edwin Lawrence Godkin*. 2 vols. N.Y., 1907.

J. B. and Farnham Bishop, *Goethals; Genius of the Panama Canal*. N.Y., 1930.

R. H. Harvey, *Samuel Gompers, Champion of the Toiling Masses*. Stanford Univ., Calif., 1935.

C. H. Whitaker, *Bertram Grosvenor Goodhue, Architect and Master of Many Arts*. N.Y., 1925.

R. F. Wolf, *India Rubber Man: The Story of Charles Goodyear*. Caldwell, Idaho, 1939.

M. D. Gorgas and B. J. Hendrick, *William Crawford Gorgas; His Life and Work*. N.Y., 1924. J. M. Gibson, *Physician to the World*. Durham, No. Car., 1950.

H. W. Morrow, *Tiger! Tiger! The Life Story of John B. Gough*. N.Y., 1930.

Gentry Dugat, *Life of Henry W. Grady*. Edinburg, Texas, 1927.

Adam Badeau, *Military History of U. S. Grant*. 3 vols. N.Y., 1868–81. W. B. Hesseltine, *U. S. Grant, Politician*. N.Y., 1935. Lloyd Lewis, *Captain Sam Grant*. Boston, 1950.

D. C. Seitz, *Horace Greeley, Founder of the New York Tribune*. N.Y., 1926. W. A Linn, *Horace Greeley*. N.Y., 1903. W. H. Hale, *Horace Greeley*. N.Y., [1950].

G. W. Greene, *The Life of Nathanael Greene*. 3 vols. N.Y., 1867–71.

Allene Gregory, *John Milton Gregory*. Chi., 1923.

C. H. Birney, *The Grimké Sisters*. Boston, 1885.

J. T. DuBois and G. S. Mathews, *Galusha A. Grow*. Boston, 1917.

E. E. Hale, Jr., *The Life and Letters of Edward Everett Hale*. 2 vols. Boston, 1917.

H. P. Johnston, *Nathan Hale*. R. ed., New Haven, 1914.

R. E. Finley, *The Lady of Godey's, Sarah Josepha Hale*. Phila., 1931.

J. M. Clarke, *James Hall . . . Geologist and Paleontologist*. Albany, 1921.

H. C. Lodge, *Alexander Hamilton*. Boston, 1882. Nathan Schachner, *Alexander Hamilton*. N.Y., 1946.

B. A. Konkle, *The Life of Andrew Hamilton, 1676–1741*. Phila., 1941.

C. E. Hamlin, *Life and Times of Hannibal Hamlin*. Cambridge, 1899.

W. T. Baxter, *The House of Hancock. Business in Boston, 1724–1775*. Cambridge, 1945. H. S. Allan, *John Hancock*. N.Y., 1948.

F. A. Walker, *General* [Winfield Scott] *Hancock*. N.Y., 1894.

H. D. Croly, *Marcus Alonzo Hanna*. N.Y., 1912. Thomas Beer, *Hanna*. N.Y., 1929.

J. L. Howard, *Seth Harding, Mariner: A Naval Picture of the Revolution*. New Haven, 1930.

Johnson Brigham, *James Harlan*. Iowa City, 1913.

T. W. Goodspeed, *William Rainey Harper*. Chi., 1928.

George Kennan, *E. H. Harriman*. 2 vols. Boston, 1922.

J. C. Harris, *The Life and Letters of Joel Chandler Harris*. Boston, 1918. A. F. Harlow, *Joel Chandler Harris*. N.Y., 1941.

J. S. Roberts, *William T. Harris*. Wash., 1924.

Carl Bridenbaugh, *Peter Harrison, First American Architect*. Chapel Hill, 1949.

Freeman Cleaves, *Old Tippecanoe; William Henry Harrison*. N.Y., 1939.

G. R. Stewart, Jr., *Bret Harte*. Boston, 1931.

Florian Cajori, *The Chequered Career of Ferdinand Rudolph Hassler*. Boston, 1929.

E. F. Brown, *Joseph Hawley, Colonial Radical*. N.Y., 1931.

G. E. Woodberry, *Nathaniel Hawthorne*. Boston, 1902. Newton Arvin, *Hawthorne*. Boston, 1929.

W. R. Thayer, *Life and Letters of John Hay*. 2 vols. Boston, 1915. Tyler Dennett, *John Hay*. N.Y., 1933.

C. R. Williams, *Life of Rutherford Birchard Hayes*. 2 vols. Boston, 1914. H. J. Eckenrode, *Rutherford B. Hayes, Statesman of Reunion*. N.Y., 1930.

T. D. Jervey, *Robert Y. Hayne and His Times*. N.Y., 1909.

Elizabeth Bisland, *Life and Letters of Lafcadio Hearn*. 2 vols. Boston, 1906. E. L. Tinker, *Lafcadio Hearn's American Days*. N.Y., 1924. Vera McWilliams, *Lafcadio Hearn*. Boston, 1946.

Oliver Carlson and E. S. Bates, *Hearst, Lord of San Simeon*. N.Y., 1936.

William Elliott, *Life of Father Hecker*. N.Y., 1891.

Carl Wittke, *Against the Current; the Life of Karl Heinzen*. Chi., 1945.

William Yarrow and Louis Bouche, *Robert Henri, His Life and Works*. N.Y., 1921.

O. Henry. See: W. S. Porter.

W. W. Henry, *Patrick Henry: Life, Correspondence and Speeches*. 3 vols. N.Y., 1891. Jacob Axelrad, *Patrick Henry*. N.Y., 1947.

T. B. Mott, *Myron T. Herrick, Friend of France*. N.Y., 1929.

Allan Nevins, *Abram S. Hewitt: With Some Account of Peter Cooper*. N.Y., 1935.

M. I. Pupin, *In Memoriam of Peter Cooper Hewitt*. N.Y., 1921.

F. J. Wilstach, *Wild Bill Hickok*. Garden City, N.Y., 1926.

Bliss Perry, *Life and Letters of Henry Lee Higginson*. Boston, 1921.

J. G. Pyle, *The Life of James J. Hill*. 2 vols. N.Y., 1917.

W. G. Land, *Thomas Hill*. Cambridge, 1933.

F. H. Gillett, *George Frisbie Hoar*. Boston, 1934.

J. T. Morse, Jr., *Life and Letters of Oliver Wendell Holmes* [1809–1894]. 2 vols. Boston, 1896. M. A. DeW. Howe, *Holmes of the Breakfast Table*. N.Y., 1939.

Silas Bent, *Justice Oliver Wendell Holmes* [1841–1935]. Garden City, N.Y., 1932. Felix Frankfurter, ed., *Mr. Justice Holmes*. N.Y., 1931.

W. H. Downes, *The Life and Works of Winslow Homer*. Boston, 1911.

H. H. Thom, *Johns Hopkins; a Silhouette*. Balt., 1929.

J. H. Denison, *Mark Hopkins; a Biography*. N.Y., 1935.

G. E. Hastings, *Life and Works of Francis Hopkinson*. Chi., 1926. O. G. Sonneck, *Francis Hopkinson and James Lyon*. Wash., 1905.

B. A. Konkle, *Joseph Hopkinson, 1770–1842*. Phila., 1931.

Marquis James, *The Raven, a Biography of Sam Houston*. Indianapolis, [1929].

L. E. Richards and M. H. Elliott, *Julia Ward Howe*. 2 vols. Boston, 1916.

L. E. Richards, *Samuel Gridley Howe*. N.Y., 1935.

D. G. Cooke, *William Dean Howells*. N.Y., 1922.

M. J. Pusey, *Charles Evans Hughes*. 2 vols. N.Y., 1951.

H. A. Brann, *Most Rev. John Hughes*. N.Y.; 1892.

H. F. Clarke, *John Hull*. Portland, 1940.

H. M. Knowlton, *Art-Life of William Morris Hunt*. Boston, 1899.

H. H. Simms, *Life of Robert M. T. Hunter; a Study in Sectionalism and Secession*. Richmond, 1935.

I. F. Marcosson, *A Little Known Master of Millions* [Henry E. Huntington]. Boston, 1914.

F. L. Greeno, *Obed Hussey*. Rochester, N.Y., 1912.

W. K. Rugg, *Unafraid: A Life of Anna Hutchinson*. Boston, 1930.

J. K. Hosmer, *The Life of Thomas Hutchinson*. Boston, 1896.

C. T. Burnett, *Hyde of Bowdoin; a Biography of William DeWitt Hyde*. Boston, 1931.

C. B. Reed, *The First Great Canadian* [Pierre le Moyne, Sieur d'Iberville]. Chi., 1910.

W. E. Connelley, [John James] *Ingalls of Kansas*. Topeka, 1909.

W. M. Meigs, *Life of Charles J. Ingersoll*. Phila., 1897.

L. H. Gipson, *Jared Ingersoll; a Study of American Loyalism*. New Haven, 1920.

George Inness, Jr., *Life, Art, and Letters of George Inness*. N.Y., 1917.

G. J. McRee, *Life and Correspondence of James Iredell*. 2 vols. N.Y., 1857–58.

S. T. Williams, *Life of Washington Irving*. 2 vols. N.Y., 1935.

J. S. Bassett, *Life of Andrew Jackson*. 2 vols. N.Y., 1925. James Parton, *Life of Andrew Jackson*. 3 vols. N.Y., 1860. Marquis James, *Andrew Jackson*. 2 vols. Indianapolis, [1933–37].

J. J. Putnam, *Memoir of Dr. James Jackson*. Boston, 1905.

G. F. R. Henderson, *Stonewall Jackson and the American Civil War*. 2 vols. London, 1898.

Ruth Putnam, *Life and Letters of Mary Putnam Jacobi*. N.Y., 1925.

Austin Warren, *The Elder Henry James* [1811–1882]. N.Y., 1934.

Pelham Edgar, *Henry James*. London, 1927.

R. B. Perry, *The Thought and Character of William James*. 2 vols., Boston, 1935.

Robertus Love, *The Rise and Fall of Jesse James*. N.Y., 1926.

Frank Monaghan, *John Jay*. N.Y., 1935.

Bayard Tuckerman, *William Jay and the Constitutional Movement for the Abolition of Slavery*. N.Y., 1893.

William Winter, *Life and Art of Joseph Jefferson*. N.Y., 1894.

H. S. Randall, *Life of Thomas Jefferson*. 3 vols. N.Y., 1858. Marie Kimball, *Jefferson*. 3 vols., in process, N.Y., 1943–50. Dumas Malone, *Jefferson and His Time*. 2 vols., in process, Boston, 1948–52. Adrienne Koch, *Jefferson and Madison*. N.Y., 1950.

F. O. Matthiessen, *Sarah Orne Jewett*. Boston, 1929.

M. J. Scott, *Isaac Jogues, Missioner and Martyr*. N.Y., 1927. J. J. Birch, *Saint of the Wilderness: Isaac Jogues*. N.Y., 1936.

L. P. Stryker, *Andrew Johnson; a Study in Courage*. N.Y., 1929.

P. S. Flippin, *Herschel V. Johnson*. Richmond, 1931.

B. C. Steiner, *Life of Reverdy Johnson*. Balt., 1914.

L. W. Meyer, *Life and Times of Col. Richard M. Johnson of Kentucky*. N.Y., 1932.

E. E. Beardsley, *Life and Correspondence of Samuel Johnson, D.D.* 2 ed. N.Y., 1874.

E. S. Delaplaine, *Life of Thomas Johnson* [Governor of Maryland]. N.Y., 1927.

W. L. Stone, *Life and Times of Sir William Johnson, Bart.* 2 vols. Albany, 1865.

E. E. Beardsley, *Life and Times of William Samuel Johnson*. 2 ed. N.Y., 1886. G. C. Groce, Jr., *William Samuel Johnson: A Maker of the Constitution*. N.Y., 1937.

W. P. Johnston, *Life of General Albert Sidney Johnston*. N.Y., 1878.

Jean Delanglez, *Life and Voyages of Louis Jolliet*. Chi., 1948.

Anna De Koven, *Life and Letters of John Paul Jones*. 2 vols. N.Y., 1913.

Francis Wayland, *Memoir of the Life and Labors of the Rev. Adoniram Judson.* 2 vols. Boston, 1853.

G. J. Clarke, *George W. Julian.* Indianapolis, 1923.

Friedrich Kapp, *The Life of John Kalb.* N.Y., 1884.

J. W. de Peyster, *Personal and Military History of Philip Kearny, Major-General.* N.Y., 1869.

Bernard Bailyn, "The *Apologia* of Robert Keayne," *William and Mary Quar.*, VII (1950), 568.

E. W. Kirby, *George Keith, 1638–1716.* N.Y., 1942.

J. T. Horton, *James Kent.* N.Y., 1939.

Hall Harrison, *Life of the Right Rev. John Barrett Kerfoot.* 2 vols. N.Y., 1886.

C. R. King, *Life and Correspondence of Rufus King.* 6 vols. N.Y., 1894–1900.

H. E. Bolton, *Rim of Christendom; a Biography of Eusebio Francisco Kino.* N.Y., 1936.

D. E. Clark, *Samuel Jordan Kirkwood.* Iowa City, 1917.

Noah Brooks, *Henry Knox, A Soldier of the Revolution.* N.Y., 1900. F. S. Drake, *Life and Correspondence of Henry Knox.* Boston, 1873.

Edmund Jezierski, *Tadeusz Kościuszko.* Warsaw, 1918. M. M. Gardner, *Kościuszko.* London, 1920. Miecislaus Haiman, *Kosciuszko in the American Revolution.* N.Y., 1943. *Idem, Kosciuszko, Leader and Exile.* N.Y., 1946.

John Hemmenway, *The Apostle of Peace. Memoir of William Ladd.* Boston, 1872.

Royal Cortissoz, *John La Farge.* Boston, 1911.

Brand Whitlock, *La Fayette.* 2 vols. N.Y., 1929. Louis Gottschalk, *Lafayette Comes to America.* Chi., 1935. *Idem, Lafayette Joins the American Army.* Chi., 1937. *Idem, Lafayette and the Close of the American Revolution.* Chi., 1942. *Idem, Lafayette between the American and the French Revolution.* Chi., 1950.

M. V. Charnley, *Jean Lafitte, Gentleman Smuggler.* N.Y., 1934.

Edward Mayes, *Lucius Q. C. Lamar: His Life, Times, and Speeches.* Nashville, 1896. W. A. Cate, *Lucius Q. C. Lamar; Secession and Reunion.* Chapel Hill, 1935.

H. P. Gambrell, *Mirabeau Buonaparte Lamar: Troubadour and Crusader.* Dallas, 1934.

A. H. Starke, *Sidney Lanier.* Chapel Hill, 1933.

D. D. Addison, *Lucy Larcom: Life, Letters, and Diary.* Boston, 1894.

Francis Parkman, *La Salle and the Discovery of the Great West.* Boston, 1879. Maurice Constantin-Weyer, *The French Adventurer, the Life and Exploits of La Salle.* N.Y., 1931.

J. E. Semmes, *John H. B. Latrobe and His Times.* Balt., 1917.

D. D. Wallace, *Life of Henry Laurens.* N.Y., 1915.

William Lawrence, *Life of Amos A. Lawrence with Extracts from His Diary and Correspondence.* Boston, 1888.

E. S. Bradley, *Henry Charles Lea.* Phila., 1931.

C. H. Lee, *A Vindication of Arthur Lee.* Richmond, Va., 1894.

J. R. Alden, *General Charles Lee.* Baton Rouge, 1951.

T. H. Boyd, *Light-Horse Harry Lee.* N.Y., 1931.

F. B. Maurice, *Robert E. Lee, the Soldier.* Boston, 1925. D. S. Freeman, *R. E. Lee, a Biography.* 4 vols. N.Y., 1934–35.

Linda Rhea, *Hugh Swinton Legaré, a Charleston Intellectual.* Chapel Hill, 1934.

E. R. Pennell, *Charles Godfrey Leland; a Biography.* Boston, 1906.

T. S. Perry, *Life and Letters of Francis Lieber.* Boston, 1882. Frank Freidel, *Francis Lieber.* Baton Rouge, 1947.

M. E. Hirst, *Life of Friedrich List, and Selections from His Writings.* London, 1909.

W. H. Herndon and J. W. Weik, *Herndon's Lincoln.* 3 vols. Chi., 1889. J. G. Nicolay, and John Hay, *Abraham Lincoln: A History.* 10 vols. N.Y., 1890. A. J. Beveridge, *Abraham Lincoln, 1809–1858.* 2 vols. Boston, 1928. Lord Charnwood, *Abraham Lincoln.* London, 1916. Carl Sandburg, *Abraham Lincoln.* 6 vols. N.Y., 1926–39. J. G. Randall, *Lincoln the President.* 2 vols. N.Y., 1945. *Idem, Lincoln the Liberal Statesman.* N.Y., 1947. B. P. Thomas, *Abraham Lincoln.* N.Y., 1952.

W. B. Hatcher, *Edward Livingston.* University, La., 1940.

C. D. Lloyd, *Henry Demarest Lloyd, 1847–1903.* 2 vols. N.Y., 1912.

Henry Adams, *Life of George Cabot Lodge.* Boston, 1911.

T. W. Richards, *The Scientific Work of Morris Loeb.* Cambridge, 1913.

G. F. Dawson, *Life and Services of General John A. Logan.* Chi., 1887.

C. K. London, *The Book of Jack London.* 2 vols. N.Y., 1921. Joan London, *Jack London and His Times.* N.Y., 1939. Irving Stone, *Sailor on Horseback.* Boston, 1938.

Harry Rogoff, *An East Side Epic: The Life . . . of Meyer London.* N.Y., 1930.

Samuel Longfellow, *Life of Henry Wadsworth Longfellow with Extracts from His Journals and Correspondence.* 3 vols. Boston, 1891. J. T. Hatfield, *New Light on Longfellow.* Boston, 1933. Lawrance Thompson, *Young Longfellow, 1807–1843.* N.Y., 1938.

J. D. Wade, *Augustus Baldwin Longstreet.* N.Y., 1924.

S. M. Pargellis, *Lord Loudoun in North America.* New Haven, 1933.

B. R. C. Low, *Seth Low.* N.Y., 1925.

S. F. Damon, *Amy Lowell.* Boston, 1935.

H. E. Scudder, *James Russell Lowell.* 2 vols. Boston, 1901. Ferris Greenslet, *James Russell Lowell.* Boston, 1905.

W. R. Stewart, *The Philanthropic Work of Josephine Shaw Lowell.* N.Y., 1911.

A. L. Lowell, *Biography of Percival Lowell.* N.Y., 1935. Louise Leonard, *Percival Lowell.* Boston, 1921.

H. H. Ravenel, *Life and Times of William Lowndes of South Carolina.* Boston, 1901.

B. B. Gilchrist, *Life of Mary Lyon.* Boston, 1910.

W. S. Myers, *A Study in Personality: General George Brinton McClellan.* N.Y., 1934.

J. M. Farley, *The Life of John, Cardinal McCloskey.* N.Y., 1918.

W. T. Hutchinson, *Cyrus Hall McCormick.* 2 vols. N.Y., 1930–35.

Lawrence Gilman, *Edward MacDowell.* N.Y., 1909. J. F. Porte, *Edward MacDowell.* London, 1922.

Melancthon Tope, *A Biography of William Holmes McGuffey.* Bowerston, Ohio, 1929. H. C. Minnich, *William Holmes McGuffey and His Readers.* N.Y., 1936.

B. C. Steiner, *Life and Correspondence of James McHenry.* Cleve., 1907.

Frank Cousins and P. M. Riley, *Samuel McIntire, the Wood-Carver of Salem.* Boston, 1916.

R. C. McKay, *Some Famous Sailing Ships and Their Builder, Donald McKay.* N.Y., 1928.

Percy MacKaye, *Epoch, the Life of Steele MacKaye.* 2 vols. N.Y., 1927.

Charles Moore, *The Life and Times of Charles Follen McKim.* Boston, 1929.

C. S. Olcott, *Life of William McKinley.* 2 vols. Boston, 1916.

R. C. Johnson, *John McLoughlin, Patriarch of the Northwest.* Portland, Ore., 1935. R. G. Montgomery, *The White-Headed Eagle, John McLoughlin.* N.Y., 1935.

W. E. Dodd, *Life of Nathaniel Macon.* Raleigh, No. Car., 1903.

F. J. Zwierlein, *Life and Letters of Bishop McQuaid.* 3 vols. Rochester, N.Y., 1925–27.

Gaillard Hunt, *Life of James Madison.* N.Y., 1920. Irving Brant, *James Madison.* 3 vols. Indianapolis, 1941–50. See also: Thomas Jefferson.

C. C. Taylor, *The Life of Admiral Mahan.* London, 1920.

Mary Mann, *Life and Works of Horace Mann.* R. ed. 5 vols. Boston, 1891. — The *Life* also appeared separately, Boston, 1865.

William Winter, *Life and Art of Richard Mansfield.* 2 vols. N.Y., 1910.

R. G. Thwaites, *Father Marquette.* N.Y., 1902.

A. J. Beveridge, *Life of John Marshall.* 4 vols. Boston, 1916–19. Edward S. Corwin, *John Marshall and the Constitution.* N.Y., 1919. J. B. Thayer, *John Marshall.* Boston, 1901.

Cyrus Adler, *Louis Marshall.* N.Y., 1931.

K. M. Rowland, *Life of George Mason, 1725–1792.* 2 vols. N.Y., 1892.

Virginia Mason, *Public Life and Diplomatic Correspondence of James M. Mason.* Roanoke, Va., 1903.

L. T. Hemans, *Life and Times of Stevens Thomson Mason, the Boy Governor of Michigan.* Lansing, Mich., 1920.

Barrett Wendell, *Cotton Mather.* N.Y., 1891. R. P. and Louise Boas, *Cotton Mather.* N.Y., 1928.

K. B. Murdock, *Increase Mather.* Cambridge, 1925.

C. L. Lewis, *Matthew Fontaine Maury.* Annapolis, 1927.

Alden Bradford, *Memoir of the Life and Writings of Rev. Jonathan Mayhew*. Boston, 1838.

G. G. Meade, *The Life and Letters of George Gordon Meade*. 2 vols. N.Y., 1913.

Jean Simon, *Herman Melville*. Paris, 1939. W. E. Sedgwick, *Herman Melville*. Cambridge, 1944. Jay Leyda, *The Melville Log; a Documentary Life*. 2 vols. N.Y., 1951. Newton Arvin, *Herman Melville*. [N.Y.], 1950.

H. D. Capers, *Life and Times of C. G. Memminger*. Richmond, Va., 1893.

M. A. DeW. Howe, *George von Lengerke Meyer*. N.Y., 1919.

C. C. Wilson, *Robert Mills, Architect*. Columbia, So. Car., 1919. H. M. Gallagher, *Robert Mills, Architect of the Washington Monument*. N.Y., 1935.

Elsie Glück, *John Mitchell, Miner*. N.Y., 1929.

A. R. Burr, *Weir Mitchell, His Life and Letters*. N.Y., 1929.

C. R. Hall, *A Scientist in the Early Republic, Samuel Latham, Mitchill*. N.Y., 1934.

W. P. Cresson, *James Monroe*. Chapel Hill, 1946.

W. R. Moody, *Dwight L. Moody*. N.Y., 1930. Gamaliel Bradford, *D. L. Moody, a Worker in Souls*. Garden City, N.Y., 1927.

D. D. Henry, *William Vaughn Moody*. Boston, 1934.

Lewis Corey, *The House of Morgan*. N.Y., 1930. H. L. Satterlee, *The Life of J. Pierpont Morgan*. N.Y., 1937. F. L. Allen, *The Great Pierpont Morgan*. N.Y., 1949.

J. H. McIlvaine, *The Life and Works of Lewis H. Morgan*. Rochester, 1882. B. J. Stern, *Lewis Henry Morgan, Social Evolutionist*. Chi., 1931.

W. B. Parker, *The Life and Public Services of Justin Smith Morrill, 1810–1898*. Boston, 1924.

Daniel Walther, *Gouverneur Morris, Witness of Two Revolutions*. N.Y., 1934.

E. P. Oberholtzer, *Robert Morris, Patriot and Financier*. N.Y., 1903.

Harold Nicolson, *Dwight Morrow*. N.Y., 1935.

Carleton Mabie, *The American Leonardo, a Life of Samuel F. B. Morse*. N.Y., 1943.

R. M. McElroy, *Levi Parsons Morton, Banker, Diplomat and Statesman*. N.Y., 1930.

W. D. Foulke, *Life of Oliver P. Morton*. 2 vols. Indianapolis, 1899.

Rudolph Rocker, *Johann Most*. Berlin, 1924.

O. W. Holmes, *John Lothrop Motley*. Boston, 1879.

A. D. Hallowell, *James and Lucretia Mott, Life and Letters*. Boston, 1884. L. C. M. Hare, *The Greatest American Woman, Lucretia Mott*. N.Y., 1937.

W. J. Mann, *Life and Times of Henry Melchior Mühlenberg*. Phila., 1887. P. A. W. Wallace, *The Muhlenbergs of Pennsylvania*. Phila., 1950.

E. W. Hocker, *The Fighting Parson of the American Revolution; a Biography of General Peter Muhlenberg*. Phila., 1936.

W. W. Newton, *Dr. [William Augustus] Muhlenberg*. Boston, 1890.

L. M. Wolfe, *Son of the Wilderness . . . John Muir*. N.Y., 1945.

A. B. Paine, *Th. Nast, His Period and His Pictures*. N.Y., 1904.

M. W. Odland, *The Life of Knute Nelson*. Minneapolis, 1926.

Isaac Goldberg, *Major Noah: American Jewish Pioneer*. Phila., 1936.

Gustav Eckstein, *Noguchi*. N.Y., 1931.

Franklin Walker, *Frank Norris*. Garden City, N.Y., 1932. Ernest Marchand, *Frank Norris*. Stanford, 1942.

G. B. Grinnell, *Two Great Scouts and Their Pawnee Battalion; . . . Frank J. North and Luther H. North*. Cleve., 1928.

O. W. Firkins, *Cyrus Northrop*. Minneapolis, 1925.

R. A. Parker, *A Yankee Saint; John Humphrey Noyes and the Oneida Community*. N.Y., 1935.

L. F. Church, *Oglethorpe: A Study of Philanthropy in England and Georgia*. London, 1932. A. A. Ettinger, *James Edward Oglethorpe, Imperialist Idealist*. Oxford, 1936.

Broadus Mitchell, *Frederick Law Olmsted*. Balt., 1924.

Henry James, *Richard Olney*. Boston, 1923.

J. J. Roche, *Life of John Boyle O'Reilly*. N.Y., 1891.

R. W. Chamberlain, *There is No Truce; a Life of Thomas Mott Osborne*. N.Y., 1935.

D. R. Fox, *Herbert Levi Osgood; an American Scholar*. N.Y., 1924.

Harvey Cushing, *Life of Sir William Osler*. 2 vols. Oxford, 1925.

S. E. Morison, *Life and Letters of Harrison Gray Otis*. 2 vols. Boston, 1913.
William Tudor, *Life of James Otis*. Boston, 1823.
R. W. Leopold, *Robert Dale Owen*. Cambridge, 1940.
Rosewell Page, *Thomas Nelson Page*. N.Y., 1923.
B. J. Hendrick, *Life and Letters of Walter Hines Page*. 3 vols. Garden City, N.Y., 1922–25.
    Idem, The Training of an American. Boston, 1928.
M. D. Conway, *The Life of Thomas Paine*. 2 vols. N.Y., 1892. Hesketh Pearson, *Tom*
    Paine, Friend of Mankind. N.Y., 1937.
G. H. Palmer, *The Life of Alice Freeman Palmer*. Boston, 1908.
F. H. Foster, *Life of Edward Amasa Park*. N.Y., 1935.
C. S. Parker, *An American Idyll: The Life of Carleton H. Parker*. Boston, 1919.
G. W. Chadwick, *Horatio Parker*. New Haven, 1921.
John Weiss, *Life and Correspondence of Theodore Parker*. 2 vols. N.Y., 1864. H. S. Com-
    mager, *Theodore Parker*. Boston, 1936.
Mason Wade, *Francis Parkman*. N.Y., 1942.
L. C. Wroth, *William Parks, Printer and Journalist*. Richmond, 1926.
Theophilus Parsons, Jr., *Memoir of Theophilus Parsons*. Boston, 1859.
M. D. Learned, *The Life of Francis Daniel Pastorius*. Phila., 1908.
Samuel Crowther, *John H. Patterson, Pioneer in Industrial Welfare*. Garden City, N.Y.,
    1923.
W. I. Paulding, *Literary Life of James K. Paulding*. N.Y., 1867. A. L. Herold, *James Kirke*
    Paulding. N.Y., 1926.
R. P. Chiles, *John Howard Payne*. Wash., 1930.
C. C. Sellers, *Charles Willson Peale*. 2 vols. Phila., 1947.
J. L. M. Curry, *Sketch of George Peabody and a History of the Peabody Education Fund*.
    Cambridge, 1898.
W. H. Hobbs, [Robert Edwin] *Peary*. N.Y., 1936.
R. C. Archibald, *Benjamin Peirce, 1809–1880*. Oberlin, 1925.
Theodore Thayer, *Israel Pemberton, King of the Quakers*. Phila., 1943.
D. J. Mays, *Edmund Pendleton, 1721–1803*. 2 vols. Cambridge, 1952.
S. M. Janney, *The Life of William Penn*. 2 ed. Phila., 1852. W. I. Hull, *William Penn, a*
    Topical Biography. N.Y., 1937. W. W. Comfort, *William Penn*. Phila., 1944. E. C. O.
    Beatty, *William Penn as Social Philosopher*. N.Y., 1939.
E. M. Barrows, *The Great Commodore; the Exploits of Matthew Galbraith Perry*. In-
    dianapolis, 1935.
J. P. Carson, *Life, Letters and Speeches of James Louis Petigru, the Union Man of South*
    Carolina. Wash., 1920.
C. E. Russell, *The Story of Wendell Phillips*. Chi., 1914. Carlos Martyn, *Wendell Phillips,*
    the Agitator. N.Y., 1890. See also: William Lloyd Garrison.
A. L. Pickens, *Skyagunsta, the Border Wizard Owl, Major-General Andrew Pickens*.
    Greenville, So. Car., 1934.
Octavius Pickering and C. W. Upham, *The Life of Timothy Pickering*. 4 vols. Boston,
    1867–73. H. P. Prentiss, *Timothy Pickering as the Leader of New England Federal-
    ism, 1800–1815*. Salem, 1934.
R. F. Nichols, *Franklin Pierce*. Phila., 1931.
F. W. Allsopp, *Albert Pike*. Little Rock, Ark., 1928.
H. H. Ravenel, *Eliza Pinckney*. N.Y., 1896.
C. C. Pinckney, *Life of General Thomas Pinckney*. Boston, 1895.
R. C. Washburn, *The Life and Times of Lydia E. Pinkham*. N.Y., 1931.
T. O. Mabbott and F. L. Pleadwell, *The Life and Works of Edward Coote Pinkney*. N.Y.,
    1926.
L. A. Coolidge, *An Old-Fashioned Senator: Orville H. Platt*. N.Y., 1910.
William Plumer, Jr., *Life of William Plumer*. Boston, 1856.
G. E. Woodberry, *The Life of Edgar Allan Poe*. R. ed. 2 vols. Boston, 1909. A. H. Quinn,
    Edgar Allan Poe. N.Y., 1941.
H. E. Putnam, *Joel Roberts Poinsett*. Wash., 1935.
E. I. McCormac, *James K. Polk*. Berkeley, 1922.
W. M. Polk, *Leonidas Polk, Bishop and General*. R. ed., 2 vols. N.Y., 1915.

H. H. Peckham, *Pontiac and the Indian Uprising*. Princeton, 1947.
D. D. Porter, *Memoir of Commodore David Porter*. Albany, 1875.
J. R. Soley, *Admiral* [David Nixon] *Porter*. N.Y., 1903.
C. A. Smith, *O. Henry* [William Sydney Porter]. Garden City, N.Y., 1916.
C. A. W. Pownall, *Thomas Pownall, M. P., F. R. S., Governor of Massachusetts Bay*. London, 1908.
George Ticknor, *Life of William Hickling Prescott*. Boston, 1864.
Anne Holt, *Life of Joseph Priestley*. London, 1931. E. F. Smith, *Priestley in America, 1794–1804*. Phila., [1920].
D. C. Seitz, *Joseph Pulitzer, His Life and Letters*. N.Y., 1924.
Bailey Willis, *Biographical Memoir of Raphael Pumpelly, 1837–1923*. Wash., 1934.
G. H. Putnam, *A Memoir of George Palmer Putnam*. N.Y., 1903.
C. D. Abbott, *Howard Pyle*. N.Y., 1925.
Josiah Quincy, *Memoir of the Life of Josiah Quincy, Jun*. [1744–75]. Boston, 1825.
Edmund Quincy, *Life of Josiah Quincy* [1772–1864]. Boston, 1867.
J. F. H. Claiborne, *Life and Correspondence of John A. Quitman*. 2 vols. N.Y., 1860.
Stanley Vestal, *King of the Fur Traders . . . Pierre Esprit Radisson*. Boston, 1940. See also: Médard Chouart.
T. J. Fitzpatrick, *Rafinesque: A Sketch of His Life with Bibliography*. Des Moines, 1911.
M. D. Conway, *Omitted Chapters of History, Disclosed in the Life and Papers of Edmund Randolph*. N.Y., 1888.
R. N. Toppan and A. T. S. Goodrick, *Edward Randolph; Including His Letters and Official Papers . . . 1676–1703*. 7 vols. Boston, 1898–1909.
W. C. Bruce, *John Randolph of Roanoke*. 2 vols. N.Y., 1922.
E. F. Brown, *Raymond of the Times*. N.Y., 1951.
C. R. Woodward, *Ploughs and Politics: Charles Read of New Jersey*. New Brunswick, 1941.
W. T. Read, *Life and Correspondence of George Read*. Phila., 1870.
W. L. Stone, *Life and Times of Red-Jacket, or Sa-go-ye-wat-ha*. N.Y., 1841.
C. F. Horner, *Life of James Redpath and the Development of the Modern Lyceum*. N.Y., 1926.
Granville Hicks, *John Reed; the Making of a Revolutionary*. N.Y., 1936.
W. B. Reed, *Life and Correspondence of Joseph Reed*. 2 vols. Phila., 1847.
S. W. McCall, *The Life of Thomas Brackett Reed*. Boston, 1914. W. A. Robinson, *Thomas B. Reed*. N.Y., 1930.
H. A. Kelly, *Walter Reed and Yellow Fever*. R. ed. Balt., 1923.
Royal Cortissoz, *The Life of Whitelaw Reid*. 2 vols. N.Y., 1921.
R. W. G. Vail, *Frederic Remington, Chronicler of the Vanished West*. N.Y., 1929.
W. A. Noyes and J. F. Norris, *Biographical Memoir of Ira Remsen*. Wash., 1931.
E. H. Goss, *The Life of Colonel Paul Revere*. 2 vols. Boston, 1891. Esther Forbes, *Paul Revere and the World He Lived In*. Boston, 1942.
L. A. White, *Robert Barnwell Rhett, Father of Secession*. N.Y., [1931].
M. A. DeW. Howe, *James Ford Rhodes, American Historian*. N.Y., 1929.
N. E. Dionne, *Gabriel Richard, Sulpicien, Curé et Second Fondateur de la Ville de Détroit*. Quebec, 1911.
H. R. Hitchcock, *The Architecture of H. H. Richardson and His Times*. N.Y., 1936.
Marcus Dickey, *The Youth of James Whitcomb Riley*. Indianapolis, 1919. *Idem, The Maturity of James Whitcomb Riley*. Indianapolis, 1922.
O. B. Frothingham, *George Ripley*. Boston, 1882.
C. H. Ambler, *Thomas Ritchie; a Study in Virginia Politics*. Richmond, 1913.
Edward Ford, *David Rittenhouse*. Phila., 1946.
Hamilton Schuyler, *The Roeblings, a Century of Engineers, Bridge-Builders and Industrialists*. Princeton, 1931.
E. K. Lindley, *Franklin D. Roosevelt*. Indianapolis, [1931]. Frank Freidel, *Franklin D. Roosevelt*. Boston, 1952. — In process, 1 vol. published.
H. F. Pringle, *Theodore Roosevelt*. N.Y., 1931.
P. C. Jessup, *Elihu Root*. 2 vols. N.Y., 1938.
Harriet Monroe, *John Wellborn Root*. Boston, 1896.

R. W. G. Vail, *Susanna Haswell Rowson, the Author of Charlotte Temple.* Worcester, Mass., 1933.

A. O. Craven, *Edmund Ruffin, Southerner.* N.Y., 1932.

N. G. Goodman, *Benjamin Rush, Physician and Citizen, 1746–1813.* Phila., 1934.

R. H. Barry, *Mr. Rutledge of South Carolina.* N.Y., 1942.

C. E. Russell, *Haym Salomon and the Revolution.* N.Y., 1930.

Evan Charteris, *John Sargent.* N.Y., 1927. W. H. Downes, *John S. Sargent, His Life and Works.* Boston, 1925.

Cyrus Adler, *Jacob H. Schiff: His Life and Letters.* 2 vols. N.Y., 1928.

C. M. Fuess, *Carl Schurz, Reformer.* N.Y., 1932.

Bayard Tuckerman, *Life of General Philip Schuyler.* N.Y., 1903.

A. D. H. Smith, *Old Fuss and Feathers, the Life . . . of Winfield Scott.* N.Y., 1937.

N. D. Cochran, *E. W. Scripps.* N.Y., 1933. Gilson Gardner, *Lusty Scripps; the Life of E. W. Scripps.* N.Y., 1932.

E. E. Beardsley, *Life and Correspondence of the Right Rev. Samuel Seabury.* Boston, 1881.

Colyer Meriwether, *Raphael Semmes.* Phila., 1913.

G. E. Foster, *Sequoyah, the American Cadmus and Modern Moses. A Complete Biography of the Greatest of Redmen.* Phila., 1885.

Francisco Palou, *Life and Apostolic Labors of the Venerable Father Junipero Serra.* G. W. James, ed. C. S. Williams, transl. Pasadena, 1913. Agnes Repplier, *Junípero Serra, Pioneer Colonist of California.* Garden City, N.Y., 1933.

C. S. Driver, *John Sevier, Pioneer of the Old Southwest.* Chapel Hill, 1932. F. M. Turner, *Life of General John Sevier.* N.Y., 1910.

N. H. Chamberlain, *Samuel Sewall and the World He Lived in.* Boston, 1897.

Frederic Bancroft, *Life of W. H. Seward.* 2 vols. N.Y., 1900.

Stewart Mitchell, *Horatio Seymour.* Cambridge, 1938.

F. H. Chase, *Lemuel Shaw, Chief Justice of the Supreme Judicial Court of Massachusetts.* Boston, 1918.

Joseph Hergesheimer, [Philip H.] *Sheridan.* Boston, 1931.

T. E. Burton, *John Sherman.* Boston, 1906.

Jacob Zeitlin and Homer Woodbridge, *Life and Letters of Stuart P. Sherman.* 2 vols. N.Y., 1929.

B. H. Liddell Hart, [William Tecumseh] *Sherman — Soldier, Realist, American.* N.Y., 1929.

G. A. Wood, *William Shirley, Governor of Massachusetts.* N.Y., 1920.

G. S. Haight, *Mrs. [Lydia Howard] Sigourney, the Sweet Singer of Hartford.* New Haven, 1930.

W. B. Parker, *Edward Rowland Sill, His Life and Work.* Boston, 1915.

G. P. Fisher, *Life of Benjamin Silliman.* 2 vols. N.Y., 1866. J. F. Fulton and E. H. Thomson, *Benjamin Silliman, 1779–1864.* N.Y., [1947].

W. P. Trent, *William Gilmore Simms.* Boston, 1892.

E. E. Morison, *Admiral Sims and the Modern American Navy.* Boston, 1942.

Stanley Vestal, *Sitting Bull.* Boston, 1932.

G. S. White, *Memoir of Samuel Slater, the Father of American Manufactures.* Phila., 1836.

J. H. Morison, *Life of the Hon. Jeremiah Smith, LL.D.* Boston, 1845.

J. G. Fletcher, *John Smith — also Pocahontas.* N.Y., 1928.

J. H. Evans, *Joseph Smith, an American Prophet.* N.Y., 1933. F. M. Brodie, *No Man Knows My History: The Life of Joseph Smith.* N.Y., 1945.

E. L. Pond, *Junius Smith, a Biography of the Father of the Atlantic Liner.* N.Y., 1927.

M. A. Wyman, *Two American Pioneers, Seba Smith [Major Jack Downing] and Elizabeth Oakes Smith.* N.Y., 1927.

H. W. Smith, *Life and Correspondence of the Rev. William Smith, D.D.* 2 vols. Phila., 1880.

H. B. Adams, *Life and Writings of Jared Sparks.* 2 vols. Boston, 1893.

G. C. Gorham, *Life and Public Services of Edwin M. Stanton.* 2 vols. Boston, 1899.

Laura Stedman and G. M. Gould, *Life and Letters of Edmund Clarence Stedman.* 2 vols. N.Y., 1910.

Louis Pendleton, *Alexander H. Stephens*. Phila., 1908. Rudolph Von Abele, *Alexander H. Stephens*. N.Y., 1946.

A. D. Turnbull, *John Stevens, an American Record*. N.Y., 1928.

T. F. Woodley, *Thaddeus Stevens*. Harrisburg, 1934. R. N. Current, *Old Thad Stevens*. Madison, 1942. J. A. Woodburn, *Thaddeus Stevens*. N.Y., 1913.

W. W. Story, *Life and Letters of Joseph Story*. 2 vols. Boston, 1851.

Henry James, *William Wetmore Story and His Friends*. 2 vols. Boston, 1903.

Forrest Wilson, *Crusader in Crinoline: The Life of Harriet Beecher Stowe*. Phila., 1941. Catherine Gilbertson, *Harriet Beecher Stowe*. N.Y., 1937.

J. H. Morgan, *Gilbert Stuart*. 4 vols. N.Y., 1926. W. T. Whitley, *Gilbert Stuart*. Cambridge, 1932.

J. W. Thomason, Jr., *Jeb* [J. E. B.] *Stuart*. N.Y., 1930.

T. C. Amory, *Life of James Sullivan*. 2 vols. Boston, 1859.

A. S. Blackwell, *Lucy Stone, Pioneer of Woman's Rights*. Boston, 1930.

M. A. DeW. Howe, *Portrait of an Independent, Moorfield Storey*. Boston, 1932.

R. F. Dibble, *John L. Sullivan*. Boston, 1925.

Hugh Morrison, *Louis Sullivan, Prophet of Modern Architecture*. N.Y., 1935.

Edward Biddle and Mantle Fielding, *The Life and Works of Thomas Sully*. Phila., 1921.

E. L. Pierce, *Memoir and Letters of Charles Sumner*. 4 vols. Boston, 1877–93. G. H. Haynes, *Charles Sumner*. Phila., 1909. Carl Schurz, *Charles Sumner*. A. R. Hogue, ed. Urbana, 1951.

J. P. Zollinger, [John Augustus] *Sutter the Man and His Empire*. N.Y., 1939.

L. F. Swift and Arthur Van Vlissingen, Jr., *Yankee of the Yards: The Biography of Gustavus F. Swift*. N.Y., 1927.

H. F. Pringle, *The Life and Times of William Howard Taft*. 2 vols. N.Y., [1939].

C. S. Hall, *Benjamin Tallmadge*. N.Y., 1943.

C. B. Swisher, *Roger B. Taney*. N.Y., 1935. C. W. Smith, *Roger B. Taney, Jacksonian Jurist*. Chapel Hill, 1936.

Lewis Tappan, *The Life of Arthur Tappan*. N.Y., 1870.

R. C. Beatty, *Bayard Taylor, Laureate of the Gilded Age*. Norman, Okla., 1936.

F. B. Copley, *Frederick W. Taylor, Father of Scientific Management*. 2 vols. N.Y., 1923.

E. T. Mudge, *The Social Philosophy of John Taylor of Caroline*. N.Y., 1939.

Holman Hamilton, *Zachary Taylor*. 2 vols. Indianapolis, [1941–51]. Brainerd Dyer, *Zachary Taylor*. Baton Rouge, 1946.

A. F. C. Wallace, *King of the Delawares: Teedyuscung 1700–1763*. Phila., 1949.

C. E. Russell, *The American Orchestra and Theodore Thomas*. Garden City, N.Y., 1927.

Freeman Cleaves, *Rock of Chickamauga: The Life of General George H. Thomas*. Norman, Okla., 1948.

J. A. Thompson, *Count Rumford of Massachusetts* [Sir Benjamin Thompson]. N.Y., 1935.

H. S. Canby, *Thoreau*. Boston, 1939. F. B. Sanborn, *Life of Henry D. Thoreau*. Boston, 1917.

John Bigelow, *The Life of Samuel J. Tilden*. 2 vols. N.Y., 1895. A. C. Flick and G. S. Lobrano, *Samuel Jones Tilden*. N.Y., 1939.

G. T. Winston, *Builder of the New South . . . Daniel Augustus Tompkins*. Garden City, N.Y., 1920.

U. B. Phillips, *Life of Robert Toombs*. N.Y., 1913. W. W. Brewton, *Son of Thunder; an Epic of the South*. Richmond, 1936.

Alexander Cowie, *John Trumbull: Connecticut Wit*. Chapel Hill, 1936.

J. F. Weir, *John Trumbull* [artist]. N.Y., 1901.

Jonathan Trumbull, *Jonathan Trumbull, Governor of Connecticut*. Boston, 1919.

Horace White, *Life of Lyman Trumbull*. Boston, 1913.

J. M. Blum, *Joe Tumulty and the Wilson Era*. Boston, 1951.

A. B. Paine, *Mark Twain*. 3 vols. N.Y., 1912. Condensed 1920. Bernard DeVoto, *Mark Twain's America*. Boston, 1932. *Idem, Mark Twain at Work*. Cambridge, 1942. E. C. Wagenknecht, *Mark Twain*. New Haven, 1935. Dixon Wecter, *Sam Clemens of Hannibal*. Boston, 1952.

L. G. Tyler, *Letters and Times of the Tylers* [John Tyler, 1747–1813, and President Tyler]. 3 vols. Richmond, 1884–96.

H. M. Jones, *The Life of Moses Coit Tyler*. Ann Arbor, 1933.

A. B. Paine, *Theodore N. Vail*. N.Y., 1929.

Holmes Alexander, *The American Talleyrand . . . Martin Van Buren*. N.Y., 1935. E. M. Shepard, *Martin Van Buren*. R. ed. Boston, 1899.

Joseph Dorfman, *Thorstein Veblen and His America*. N.Y., 1934. J. A. Hobson, *Veblen*. London, 1936.

W. I. Bartlett, *Jones Very*. Durham, 1942.

Stefan Zweig, *Amerigo* [Vespucci], *a Comedy of Errors in History*. N.Y., 1942.

J. P. Munroe, *Life of Francis Amasa Walker*. N.Y., 1923.

W. E. Dodd, *Robert J. Walker, Imperialist*. Chi., 1914.

Laurence Greene, *The Filibuster: The Career of William Walker*. Indianapolis, 1937.

H. A. Gibbons, *John Wanamaker*. 2 vols. N.Y., 1926.

D. C. Seitz, *Artemus Ward*. N.Y., 1919.

T. R. Lounsbury, *Biographical Sketch of Charles Dudley Warner*. Hartford, 1905.

Alice Brown, *Mercy Warren*. N.Y., 1896.

H. P. Arnold, *Memoir of John Collins Warren*. Boston, 1882.

Richard Frothingham, *Life and Times of Joseph Warren*. Boston, 1865.

William Bailie, *Josiah Warren, the First American Anarchist*. Boston, 1906.

Gaillard Hunt, *Israel, Elihu, and Cadwallader Washburn*. N.Y., 1925.

B. J. Mathews, *Booker T. Washington*. Cambridge, 1948.

J. C. Fitzpatrick, *George Washington Himself*. Indianapolis, 1933. Bernhard Knollenberg, *Washington and the Revolution*. N.Y., 1940. D. S. Freeman, *George Washington*. 5 vols. N.Y., 1948–52. N. W. Stephenson and W. H. Dunn, *George Washington*. 2 vols. N.Y., 1940. T. G. Frothingham, *Washington, Commander in Chief*. Boston, 1930. C. H. Ambler, *George Washington and the West*. Chapel Hill, 1936. H. C. Lodge, *George Washington*. 2 vols. Boston, 1889.

C. V. Woodward, *Tom Watson, Agrarian Rebel*. N.Y., 1938.

H. E. Wildes, *Anthony Wayne*. N.Y., 1941.

F. E. Haynes, *James Baird Weaver*. Iowa City, 1919.

C. M. Fuess, *Daniel Webster*. 2 vols. Boston, 1930. H. C. Lodge, *Daniel Webster*. Boston, 1882.

H. R. Warfel, *Noah Webster: Schoolmaster to America*. N.Y., 1936. E. C. Shoemaker, *Noah Webster, Pioneer of Learning*. N.Y., 1936.

T. W. Barnes, *Life of Thurlow Weed*. 2 vols. Boston, 1884. G. G. Van Deusen, *Thurlow Weed*. Boston, 1947.

P. A. W. Wallace, *Conrad Weiser, 1696–1760*. Phila., 1945.

Simon Flexner and J. T. Flexner, *William Henry Welch and the Heroic Age of American Medicine*. N.Y., 1941.

M. A. DeW. Howe, *Barrett Wendell*. Boston, 1924.

H. G. Prout, *Life of George Westinghouse*. N.Y., 1921. F. E. Leupp, *George Westinghouse*. Boston, 1918.

E. R. and Joseph Pennell, *Life of James McNeill Whistler*. R. ed. Phila., 1919.

Allan Nevins, *Henry White: Thirty Years of American Diplomacy*. N.Y., 1930.

C. C. Baldwin, *Stanford White*. N.Y., 1931.

Luke Tyerman, *The Life of the Rev. George Whitefield*. 2 vols. London, 1930. A. D. Belden, *George Whitefield*. London, 1930.

H. S. Canby, *Walt Whitman*. Boston, 1943. Bliss Perry, *Walt Whitman: His Life and Work*. Boston, 1906. H. L. Traubel, *With Walt Whitman in Camden*. 3 vols. Boston and N.Y., 1906–14.

E. T. Brewster, *Life and Letters of Josiah Dwight Whitney*. Boston, 1909.

Albert Mordell, *Quaker Militant, John Greenleaf Whittier*. Boston, 1933. A. T. Pickard, *Life and Letters of John Greenleaf Whittier*. R. ed. 2 vols. Boston, 1907.

Joseph Barnes, [Wendell] *Willkie*. N.Y., 1952.

T. R. Hay and M. R. Werner, *The Admirable Trumpeter . . . General James Wilkinson*. N.Y., 1941.

J. E. Ernst, *The Political Thought of Roger Williams*. Seattle, 1929. S. H. Brockunier, *The Irrepressible Democrat: Roger Williams*. N.Y., 1940.

H. A. Beers, *Nathaniel Parker Willis*. Boston, 1885.

C. B. Going, *David Wilmot, Free-Soiler*. N.Y., 1924.

J. S. Wilson, *Alexander Wilson: Poet-Naturalist*. N.Y., 1906.

R. S. Baker, *Woodrow Wilson, Life and Letters*. 6 vols. Garden City, N.Y., 1927–37. A. S. Link, *Wilson*. Princeton, 1947. H. C. F. Bell, *Woodrow Wilson and the People*. Garden City, N.Y., 1945.

J. P. Kennedy, *Memoirs of the Life of William Wirt, Attorney-General of the United States*. 2 vols. Phila., 1849.

V. L. Collins, *President* [John] *Witherspoon*. 2 vols. Princeton, 1925.

Hermann Hagedorn, *Leonard Wood*. 2 vols. N.Y., 1931.

E. H. Woods, *Robert A. Woods, Champion of Democracy*. N.Y., 1929.

Janet Whitney, *John Woolman*. Boston, 1942.

W. R. Waterman, *Frances Wright*. N.Y., 1924.

J. A. Garraty, *Silas Wright*. N.Y., 1949.

F. C. Kelly, *The Wright Brothers: Fathers of Flight*. N.Y., 1943.

J. W. DuBose, *Life and Times of William Lowndes Yancey*. Birmingham, 1892.

M. R. Werner, *Brigham Young*. N.Y., 1925. F. L. Cannon and G. L. Knapp, *Brigham Young and His Mormon Empire*. N.Y., 1913. S. Y. Gates and L. D. Widtsoe, *The Life Story of Brigham Young*. London, 1930.

J. T. McManis, *Ella Flagg Young and a Half-Century of the Chicago Public Schools*. Chi., 1916.

Livingston Rutherfurd, *John Peter Zenger*. N.Y., 1904.

A. G. Spangenberg, *Life of Nicolas Lewis, Count Zinzendorf*. Samuel Jackson, transl. London, 1838.

57. MISCELLANEOUS COLLECTIONS OF ORIGINAL SOURCES

The most important compilations of sources have generally been issued by public bodies or by historical societies (§§ 41–47, 50). But there are a large number of useful unofficial documentary collections. Individual editors and compilers have felt free to follow their own inclinations in considerable degree, so that these volumes follow no regular pattern. Often they illustrate a particular theme or supply information on a particular series of events. Others of these collections are devised as teaching instruments. A list of the most useful, arranged alphabetically, follows:

Edith Abbott, ed., *Historical Aspects of the Immigration Problem*. Chi., 1926.

Edith Abbott, ed., *Immigration; Select Documents and Case Records*. Chi., [1924].

Henry Adams, ed., *Documents Relating to New England Federalism, 1800–1815*. Boston, 1877.

R. B. Anderson, ed., *The Norse Discovery of America*. London, 1907.

R. J. Bartlett, ed., *The Record of American Diplomacy*. N.Y., 1950.

Henry Beston, ed., *American Memory; Being a Mirror of the Stirring and Picturesque Past of Americans and the American Nation*. N.Y., [1937].

R. A. Billington, B. J. Loewenberg, and S. H. Brockunier, eds., *The Making of American Democracy; Readings and Documents*. 2 vols. N.Y., 1950.

J. L. Blau, ed., *Social Theories of Jacksonian Democracy; Representative Writings of the Period 1825–1850*. N.Y., 1947.

E. C. Boykin, ed., *Living Letters from American History*. N.Y., [1942].

E. C. Burnett, ed., *Letters of Members of the Continental Congress*. 8 vols. Wash., 1921–38.

P. L. Bush, ed., *Democracy in Action; the Basic Documents of Our Government*. Dallas, [1940].

G. S. Callender, ed., *Selections from the Economic History of the United States, 1765–1868*. Boston, [1909].

H. R. Casgrain, ed., *Collection de documents inédits sur le Canada et l'Amérique, publiés par le Canada-français*. 3 vols. Quebec, 1888–90.

Champlain Society, *Publications*. 31 vols. Toronto, 1907–52.

H. S. Commager, ed., *Documents of American History.* 5 ed. N.Y., [1949].

J. R. Commons, *et al.*, eds., *Documentary History of American Industrial Society.* 10 vols. Cleve., 1910–11.

A. O. Craven, Walter Johnson, and F. R. Dunn, eds., *A Documentary History of the American People.* Boston, [1951].

F. G. Davenport, ed., *European Treaties Bearing on the History of the United States and Its Dependencies.* 4 vols. Wash., 1917–37.

L. B. Evans, ed., *Cases on American Constitutional Law.* R. ed., C. G. Fenwick, ed. Chi., 1948.

W. L. Fleming, ed., *Documentary History of Reconstruction . . . 1865 to the Present Time.* 2 vols. Cleve., 1906–07.

Felix Flügel and H. U. Faulkner, eds., *Readings in the Economic and Social History of the United States.* N.Y., 1929.

Peter Force, ed., *Tracts and Other Papers Relating Principally to the Colonies in North America.* 4 vols. Wash., 1836–46; reprinted, 1947.

P. L. Ford and W. C. Ford, eds., *Winnowings in American History.* 15 vols. Brooklyn, 1890–91.

Gorges Society, *Publications.* 5 vols. Portland, 1884–93. — Relate to northern New England.

L. M. Hacker and H. S. Zahler, eds., *The Shaping of the American Tradition.* N.Y., 1947.

Hakluyt Society, *Works Issued by the . . . Society.* 196 vols. London, 1847–1951. — Perhaps half the volumes deal with America.

A. B. Hart, ed., *American History Told by Contemporaries.* 5 vols. N.Y., 1897–1929.

F. L. Hawks and W. S. Perry, eds., *Documentary History of the Protestant Episcopal Church in the United States of America.* 2 vols. N.Y., 1863–64.

Ebenezer Hazard, ed., *Historical Collections; Consisting of State Papers and Other Authentic Documents.* 2 vols. Phila., 1792–94.

Historical Manuscripts in the Public Library of the City of Boston. 5 vols. Boston, 1900–04. — A miscellaneous collection.

J. M. Jacobson, ed., *The Development of American Political Thought, a Documentary History.* N.Y., [1932].

J. F. Jameson, ed., *Original Narratives of Early American History.* 19 vols. N.Y., 1906–17. Reprinted N.Y., 1952. — This is the most useful series for colonial times; it includes travel accounts, explorations, chronicles, contemporary history, and literature. The individual volumes are: J. E. Olson and E. G. Bourne, eds., *The Northmen, Columbus and Cabot;* F. W. Hodge and T. H. Lewis, eds., *Spanish Explorers in the Southern United States;* H. S. Burrage, ed., *Early English and French Voyages;* W. L. Grant, ed., *Voyages of Champlain;* L. G. Tyler, ed., *Narratives of Early Virginia;* W. T. Davis, ed., *Bradford's History of Plymouth Plantation;* J. K. Hosmer, ed., *Winthrop's Journal,* 2 vols.; J. F. Jameson, ed., *Narratives of New Netherland; idem, Johnson's Wonder-Working Providence;* and *idem, Journal of Jasper Danckaerts;* A. S. Salley, ed., *Narratives of Early Carolina;* C. C. Hall, ed., *Narratives of Early Maryland;* L. P. Kellogg, ed., *Early Narratives of the Northwest;* H. E. Bolton, ed., *Spanish Exploration in the Southwest;* G. L. Burr, ed., *Narratives of the Witchcraft Cases;* C. H. Lincoln, ed., *Narratives of the Indian Wars;* C. M. Andrews, ed., *Narratives of the Insurrections* [of 1675–1689]; A. C. Myers, ed., *Narratives of Early Pennsylvania, West New Jersey and Delaware.*

Alexander Johnston and J. A. Woodburn, eds., *American Orations: Studies in American Political History.* 4 vols. R. ed. N.Y., 1896–97.

S. S. Jones, *et al.*, eds., *Documents on American Foreign Relations, 1938–50.* 12 vols. Boston and Princeton, 1939–51.

J. D. Lawson, ed., *American State Trials.* 17 vols. St. Louis, 1914–36.

William MacDonald, ed., *Documentary Source Book of American History, 1606–1926.* R. ed. N.Y., 1934.

William MacDonald, ed., *Select Charters and Other Documents Illustrative of American History, 1606–1775.* N.Y., 1899.

William MacDonald, ed., *Select Documents Illustrative of the History of the United States, 1776–1861.* R. ed. N.Y., 1905.

William MacDonald, ed., *Select Statutes and Other Documents Illustrative of the History of the United States, 1861–1898.* N.Y., 1903.

T. H. McKee, ed., *National Conventions and Platforms of All Political Parties, 1789 to 1904.* Balt., 1904.

T. G. Manning, D. M. Potter, and W. E. Davies, eds., *Select Problems in Historical Interpretation, 1775–Present.* 2 vols. N.Y., 1949–50.

A. T. Mason, ed., *Free Government in the Making; Readings in American Political Thought.* N.Y., 1949.

M. A. Musmanno, ed., *Proposed Amendments to the Constitution.* Wash., 1929.

Allan Nevins and H. S. Commager, *Heritage of America.* Boston, 1939.

Hezekiah Niles, ed., *Principles and Acts of the Revolution in America.* Balt., 1822. Reprinted, N.Y., 1876.

Old South Leaflets. 8 vols. Boston, 1883–

S. M. Pargellis, ed., *Military Affairs in North America, 1748–1765; Selected Documents from the Cumberland Papers in Windsor Castle.* N.Y., [1936].

The People Shall Judge. Readings in the Formation of American Policy. 2 vols. Chi., 1949.

W. S. Perry, ed., *Historical Collections Relating to the American Colonial Church.* 5 vols. Hartford, 1870–78.

J. D. Richardson, ed., *Compilation of the Messages and Papers of the Confederacy, Including the Diplomatic Correspondence.* 2 vols. Nashville, 1905.

L. B. Schmidt and E. D. Ross, eds., *Readings in the Economic History of American Agriculture.* N.Y., 1925.

Buckingham Smith, *Colección de varios documentos* (§ 46).

State Papers and Publick Documents of the United States from the Accession of George Washington . . . Exhibiting a Complete View of Our Foreign Relations since That Time. 10 vols. Boston, 1817. R. ed. 1819.

C. C. Tansill, ed., *Documents Illustrative of the Formation of the Union* (§ 45).

F. W. Taussig, ed., *State Papers and Speeches on the Tariff.* Cambridge, 1893.

J. W. Thornton, ed., *The Pulpit of the American Revolution.* Boston, 1860.

Willard Thorp, Merle Curti, and Carlos Baker, eds., *American Issues.* 2 vols. Chi., 1941.

H. R. Warfel, R. H. Gabriel, and S. T. Williams, eds., *The American Mind.* N.Y., 1937.

B. F. Wright, ed., *A Source Book of American Political Theory.* N.Y., 1929.

58. CYCLOPEDIAS OF AMERICAN HISTORY

General compilations treating topics succinctly in alphabetical order are handy for quick reference. Occasionally they contain a better account of a subject than can be found elsewhere. Certain of these works are of particular interest to the student of American history. The appended list, which indicates only the more important, follows the usual practice of citing the titles first:

Biographical Directory of the American Congress (§ 56).

Cyclopædia of Political Science, Political Economy, and of the Political History of the United States. J. J. Lalor, ed. 3 vols. Chicago, 1881–84.

Cyclopedia of American Agriculture. L. H. Bailey, ed. 4 vols. N.Y., 1907–09.

Cyclopedia of American Government. A. C. McLaughlin and A. B. Hart, eds. 3 vols. N.Y., 1914.

Dictionary of American History. J. T. Adams, ed. 5 vols. and index vol. N.Y., 1940.

Dictionary of American Politics. E. C. Smith and A. J. Zurcher, eds. R. ed. N.Y., 1946.

Encyclopaedia of the Social Sciences. E. R. A. Seligman, ed. 15 vols. N.Y., 1930–34.

Encyclopedia of American History. R. B. Morris, ed. N.Y., 1953.

The New Dictionary of American History. Michael Martin and Leonard Gelber, eds. N.Y., 1952.

The New Encyclopedia of Social Reform. W. D. P. Bliss, ed. R. ed. N.Y., 1908.

59. LARGER COMPREHENSIVE HISTORIES

This list is confined to standard multivolumed works on American history of both single and plural authorship.

[1800–1817]   Henry Adams, *History of the United States*. 9 vols. N.Y., 1889–91. — Reprinted, 4 vols., N.Y., 1930, with intro. by H. S. Commager.

[1492–1763]   C. M. Andrews, *The Colonial Period of American History*. 4 vols. New Haven, 1934–38.

[1492–1806]   E. M. Avery, *A History of the United States and Its People*. 7 vols. and index vol. Cleve. and Tarrytown, N.Y., 1904–15.

[1492–1782]   George Bancroft, *History of the United States*. 10 vols. Boston, 1834–74. — An edition in 6 vols., bearing the subtitle *Author's Last Revision,* carries the work to 1789. N.Y., 1883–85.

[1501–1890]   H. H. Bancroft, *History of the Pacific States of North America*. 34 vols. San Francisco, 1882–90. Also *Native Races of the Pacific States of North America*. 5 vols. N.Y., 1874–76. — In method of preparation, a coöperative history. The whole was reissued as *Works*. 39 vols. San Francisco, 1883–90.

[1789–1925]   S. F. Bemis, ed., *The American Secretaries of State and Their Diplomacy*. 10 vols. N.Y., 1927–29.

[1000–1865]   Edward Channing, *A History of the United States*. 6 vols. N.Y., 1905–25. Separate index vol. (N.Y., 1932).

[1607–1941]   Henry David, *et al.*, eds., *The Economic History of the United States*. 5 vols. N.Y., 1945–51. — To be completed in 4 more vols.

[1492–1914]   W. E. Dodd, ed., *The Riverside History of the United States*. 4 vols. Boston, 1915.

[1492–1760]   J. A. Doyle, *The English in America*. 5 vols. London, 1882–1907. — Reprinted with different pagination as *English Colonies in America*. N.Y., 1882–1907.

[1606–1912]   Herbert Fisher, *et al.*, eds., *Home University Library of Modern Knowledge* (5 vols., N.Y., 1912–14) form a connected history of the United States, as follows: C. M. Andrews, *The Colonial Period* (XLVII); T. C. Smith, *The Wars between England and America* (LXXXII); William MacDonald, *From Jefferson to Lincoln* (LXVII); F. L. Paxson, *The Civil War* (XXV); P. L. Haworth, *Reconstruction and Union* (XXXIX).

[1000–1865]   John Fiske, *The Discovery of America*. 2 vols. Boston, 1892. — The following continue the account, with important gaps: *Old Virginia and Her Neighbours* (2 vols., Boston, 1897); *The Beginnings of New England* (Boston, 1889); *The Dutch and Quaker Colonies in America* (2 vols., Boston, 1899); *New France and New England* (Cambridge, 1902); *The American Revolution* (2 vols., Boston, 1891–92); *The Critical Period of American History* (Boston, 1888); *The Mississippi Valley in the Civil War* (Boston, 1900).

[1748–1775]   L. H. Gipson, *The British Empire before the American Revolution*. 7 vols. Caldwell, Idaho and N.Y., 1936–49. — To be continued in 4 additional vols., with general index in XI.

[1300–1907]   A. B. Hart, ed., *The American Nation: A History*. 26 vols. and index vol. N.Y., 1904–08. — A supplementary vol., F. A. Ogg, *National Progress* (N.Y., 1918) continues the work to 1917.

[1492–1821]   Richard Hildreth, *The History of the United States*. 6 vols. N.Y., 1849–56. — R. ed., 1880–82.

[1750–1861]   H. E. von Holst, *The Constitutional and Political History of the United States*. Transl. from the German by J. J. Lalor, A. B. Mason, and Paul Shorey. 7 vols. and index vol. Chi., 1876–92.

[1492–1920]   Allen Johnson, ed., *The Chronicles of America Series*. 50 vols. New Haven,

1918–21. — 6 supplementary vols. (New Haven, 1950–51), Allan Nevins, ed., continue the account to 1945.

[1000–1905]   G. C. Lee and F. N. Thorpe, eds., *The History of North America*. 20 vols. Phila., 1903–07. — General index in XX.

[1783–1861]   J. B. McMaster, *A History of the People of the United States from the Revolution to the Civil War*. 8 vols. N.Y., 1883–1913. — *A History of the People of the United States during Lincoln's Administration* (N.Y., 1927) continues the narrative through 1865.

[1865–1901]   E. P. Oberholtzer, *A History of the United States since the Civil War*. 5 vols. N.Y., 1917–37.

[1606–1763]   H. L. Osgood, *The American Colonies in the Seventeenth Century*. 3 vols. N.Y., 1904–07. *The American Colonies in the Eighteenth Century*. 4 vols. N.Y., 1924–25.

[1512–1763]   Francis Parkman, *France and England in North America*. 9 vols. Boston, 1865–92. Supplemented by *The Conspiracy of Pontiac*. 2 vols. Boston, 1851. — Reprinted in *Works* (§ 55).

[1913–1923]   F. L. Paxson, *American Democracy and the World War*. 3 vols. Boston and Berkeley, Calif., 1936–48.

[1850–1877]   J. F. Rhodes, *History of the United States from the Compromise of 1850*. 7 vols. N.Y., 1893–1906. — Two supplementary works continue the account to 1909: *History of the United States from Hayes to McKinley* (N.Y., 1919); and *The McKinley and Roosevelt Administrations* (N.Y., 1922). These were later added to the original set as VIII and IX.

[1492–1941]   A. M. Schlesinger and D. R. Fox, eds., *A History of American Life*. 13 vols. N.Y., 1927–48.

[1783–1865]   James Schouler, *History of the United States under the Constitution*. 6 vols. N.Y., 1880–99. — A r. ed. continues the work to 1877 (7 vols. N.Y., 1894–1913) with a general index in VII.

[1607–1909]   *The South in the Building of the Nation*. 12 vols. and index vol. Richmond, 1913. — A coöperative work.

[1607–1946]   W. H. Stephenson and E. M. Coulter, eds., *A History of the South*. 6 vols. Baton Rouge and Austin, Texas, 1948–53. — To be completed in 4 more vols.

[1900–1925]   Mark Sullivan, *Our Times*. 6 vols. N.Y., 1926–35.

[1600–1841]   George Tucker, *The History of the United States*. 4 vols. Phila., 1856–57.

[1783–   ]   Sumner Welles and D. C. McKay, eds., *The American Foreign Policy Library*. 13 vols. Cambridge, 1945–53. — Each vol. affords a historical approach to America's relations with one or more other countries. To be completed in 12 additional vols.

[1492–1900]   Woodrow Wilson, *A History of the American People*. 5 vols. N.Y., 1902.

[1000–1850]   Justin Winsor, ed., *Narrative and Critical History of America*. 8 vols. Boston, 1884–89.

60. SHORTER SURVEYS AND TEXTBOOKS

The following list consists of textbooks, volumes of essays, and similar short works that treat American history generally over a long period. See also: § 18.

J. T. Adams, *The Epic of America*. Boston, 1931.
C. A. Beard and M. R. Beard, *The Rise of American Civilization*. 4 vols. N.Y., 1927–42.
R. A. Billington, B. J. Loewenberg, and S. H. Brockunier, *The United States: American Democracy in World Perspective, 1492–1947*. N.Y., 1947.
O. P. Chitwood, *History of Colonial America*. N.Y., 1948.
M. E. Curti, *et al.*, *An American History*. 2 vols. N.Y., 1950.

F. R. Dulles, *Twentieth Century America*. N.Y., 1945.
H. U. Faulkner, *American Political and Social History*. R. ed. N.Y., 1949.
L. M. Hacker and B. B. Kendrick, *The United States since 1865*. R. ed. N.Y., 1939.
J. D. Hicks, *The American Nation from 1865 to the Present*. Boston, [1941].
J. D. Hicks, *The Federal Union; a History of the United States to 1865*. Boston, 1952.
J. D. Hicks, *Short History of American Democracy*. Boston, 1946.
H. C. Hockett, *Political and Social Growth of the American People, 1492–1865*. R. ed. N.Y., 1943.
H. C. Hockett and A. M. Schlesinger, *Land of the Free, a Short History of the American People*. N.Y., 1944.
S. E. Morison and H. S. Commager, *The Growth of the American Republic*. 2 vols. R. ed. N.Y., 1950.
C. P. Nettels, *The Roots of American Civilization*. N.Y., 1938.
H. B. Parkes, *The American Experience*. N.Y., 1947.
Max Savelle, *Seeds of Liberty*. N.Y., 1948.
Max Savelle, *The Foundations of American Civilization*. N.Y., 1942.
A. M. Schlesinger, *New Viewpoints*. N.Y., 1922.
A. M. Schlesinger, *Paths to the Present*. N.Y., 1949.
A. M. Schlesinger, *The Rise of Modern America, 1865–1951*. R. ed. N.Y., 1951.
G. M. Stephenson, *American History*. 2 vols. N.Y., 1939–40.
F. J. Turner, *The Frontier in American History*. N.Y., [1950].
F. J. Turner, *The Significance of Sections in American History*. Intro. by Max Farrand. N.Y., 1950.
Harvey Wish, *Contemporary America, the National Scene since 1900*. N.Y., [1945].

61. WORKS ON SPECIAL SUBJECTS

Apart from the works which attempt to present a summary account of the whole of American history, and apart from those which focus on a narrow time span, an extensive body of historical literature is devoted to special topics which run through long chronological periods. The list below contains a selection of the most useful of such books, arranged alphabetically within their subject categories. The term special is not used here in any precise sense. It may refer to the history of sections or to topics of greater or lesser generality. It can thus include histories of the whole economy, of manufacturing, and of the woolen industry. The primary basis of selection is the treatment of a single subject across a rather extensive time period.

Agriculture   P. W. Bidwell and J. I. Falconer, *History of Agriculture in the Northern United States, 1620–1860*. Wash., 1925.
R. A. Clemen, *The American Livestock Industry*. N.Y., 1923.
E. E. Dale, *The Range Cattle Industry*. Norman, Okla., 1930.
N. S. B. Gras, *History of Agriculture in Europe and America*. N.Y., 1925.
L. C. Gray, *History of Agriculture in the Southern United States to 1860*. 2 vols. Wash., 1933.
Meyer Jacobstein, *The Tobacco Industry in the United States*. N.Y., 1907.
Louis Pelzer, *The Cattlemen's Frontier*. Glendale, Calif., 1936.
J. C. Robert, *The Story of Tobacco in America*. N.Y., 1949.
E. S. Osgood, *The Day of the Cattleman*. Minneapolis, 1929.

Art and   Virgil Barker, *American Painting, History and Interpretation*. N.Y., 1950.
Architecture Cahill, *American Folk Art* (§ 18).
T. F. Hamlin, *The American Spirit in Architecture*. New Haven, 1926.
Samuel Isham, *The History of American Painting*. New ed., with supplemental chapters by Royal Cortissoz. N.Y., 1927.
O. W. Larkin, *Art and Life in America*. N.Y., 1949.
Lewis Mumford, *Sticks and Stones*. N.Y., 1924.

Lorado Taft, *The History of American Sculpture.* New ed. N.Y., 1930.
T. E. Tallmadge, *The Story of Architecture in America.* R. ed. N.Y., 1936.

Automobiles H. L. Barber, *The Story of the Automobile.* Chi., 1917.
R. C. Epstein, *The Automobile Industry.* Chi., 1928.
E. D. Kennedy, *The Automobile Industry.* N.Y., 1941.

Aviation N. L. Smith, *Airways: The History of Commercial Aviation in the United States.* N.Y., 1942.

Banking and Finance C. A. Conant and Marcus Nadler, *A History of Modern Banks of Issue.* 6 ed. N.Y., 1927.
D. R. Dewey, *Financial History of the United States.* 12 ed. N.Y., 1934.
Gustavus Myers, *History of the Great American Fortunes.* 3 vols. N.Y., 1910.
W. J. Schultz and M. B. Caine, *Financial Development of the United States.* N.Y., 1937.

Book Publishing Hellmut Lehmann-Haupt, *The Book in America.* R. ed. N.Y., 1951.

Civil Liberties R. K. Carr, *Federal Protection of Civil Rights.* N.Y., 1947.
M. R. Konvitz, *The Constitution and Civil Rights.* N.Y., 1947.
Gustavus Myers, *History of Bigotry in the United States.* N.Y., 1943.

Commerce Clive Day, *A History of Commerce of the United States.* N.Y., 1925.
J. H. Frederick, *The Development of American Commerce.* N.Y., 1932.
L. C. Hunter, *Steamboats on the Western Rivers.* Cambridge, 1949.
E. R. Johnson, *et al., History of Domestic and Foreign Commerce of the United States.* 2 vols. Wash., 1915.
J. C. Mills, *Our Inland Seas, Their Shipping and Commerce for Three Centuries.* Chi., 1910.

Congress F. L. Burdette, *Filibustering in the Senate.* Princeton, 1940.
W. S. Holt, *Treaties Defeated by the Senate.* Balt., 1933.

Conservation C. R. Van Hise, *The Conservation of Natural Resources in the United States.* N.Y., 1924.

Constitutional History Dean Alfange, *The Supreme Court and the National Will.* Garden City, N.Y., 1937.
H. C. Hockett, *The Constitutional History of the United States.* 2 vols. N.Y., 1939.
A. H. Kelly and W. A. Harbison, *The American Constitution.* N.Y., 1948.
C. B. Swisher, *American Constitutional Development.* Boston, [1943].

Diplomatic History T. A. Bailey, *A Diplomatic History of the American People.* 4 ed. N.Y., 1950.
S. F. Bemis, *American Secretaries of State* (§ 59).
S. F. Bemis, *A Diplomatic History of the United States.* R. ed. N.Y., 1950.
S. F. Bemis, *The Latin American Policy of the United States.* N.Y., 1943.
Tyler Dennett, *Americans in Eastern Asia.* N.Y., 1941.
F. R. Dulles, *China and America; the Story of Their Relations since 1784.* Princeton, 1946.
F. R. Dulles, *The Road to Teheran; the Story of Russia and America. 1781–1943.* Princeton, 1946.
A. W. Griswold, *The Far Eastern Policy of the United States.* N.Y., 1938.
Dexter Perkins, *Hands Off; a History of the Monroe Doctrine.* Boston, 1941.
P. J. Treat, *Diplomatic Relations between the United States and Japan, 1853–1905.* 3 vols. Stanford, 1932–38.
A. K. Weinberg, *Manifest Destiny.* Balt., 1935.
B. H. Williams, *Economic Foreign Policy of the United States.* N.Y., 1929.

Drama M. G. Mayorga, *A Short History of the American Drama.* N.Y., 1932.
A. H. Quinn, *A History of the American Drama.* R. ed. N.Y., 1943.

Economic
History

David, *et al., Economic History* (§ 59).
Joseph Dorfman, *The Economic Mind in American Civilization*. 3 vols. N.Y., 1946–49.
H. U. Faulkner, *American Economic History*. 6 ed. N.Y., 1949.
E. C. Kirkland, *A History of American Economic Life*. R. ed. N.Y., 1951.
F. A. Shannon, *America's Economic Growth*. R. ed. N.Y., 1951.
H. F. Williamson, ed., *The Growth of the American Economy*. N.Y., 1951.

Education

W. C. Ryan, *Studies in Early Graduate Education*. N.Y., 1939.
E. P. Cubberley, *Public Education in the United States*. R. ed. Boston, 1934.
E. D. Ross, *Democracy's College*. Ames, Iowa, 1942.
D. G. Tewksbury, *The Founding of American Colleges and Universities before the Civil War*. N.Y., 1932.
Thomas Woody, *A History of Women's Education in the United States*. 2 vols. N.Y., 1929.

Etiquette

A. M. Schlesinger, *Learning How to Behave*. N.Y., 1946.

Family

A. W. Calhoun, *A Social History of the American Family*. 3 vols. Cleve., 1917–19.

Fashions

A. M. Earle, *Two Centuries of Costume in America*. 2 vols. N.Y., 1903.

Fisheries

E. P. Hohman, *The American Whaleman*. N.Y., 1928.
H. A. Innis, *The Cod Fisheries*. New Haven, 1940.
Raymond McFarland, *A History of the New England Fisheries*. N.Y., 1911.
W. S. Tower, *A History of the American Whale Fishery*. Phila., 1907.

Food

R. O. Cummings, *The American and His Food*. Chi., 1940.

Frontier

R. A. Billington, *Westward Expansion, a History of the American Frontier*. N.Y., 1949.
R. C. Buley, *The Old Northwest: Pioneer Period, 1815–1840*. 2 vols. Indianapolis, 1950.
T. D. Clark, *The Rampaging Frontier*. Indianapolis, 1939.
Katherine Coman, *Economic Beginnings of the Far West*. 2 vols. N.Y., 1925.
W. J. Ghent, *The Early Far West*. N.Y., 1931.
L. R. Hafen and C. C. Rister, *Western America*. N.Y., 1941.
F. L. Paxson, *History of the American Frontier*. Boston, 1924.
Turner, *Frontier in American History* (§ 60).
W. P. Webb, *The Great Plains*. Boston, 1931.

Fur Trade

H. M. Chittenden, *The American Fur Trade of the Far West*. 3 vols. N.Y., 1902.

Humor

Murrell, *American Graphic Humor* (§ 18).
Nevins and Weitenkampf, *Political Cartoons, 1800–1900* (§ 18).
C. M. Rourke, *American Humor*. N.Y., 1931.

Immigration

Louis Adamic, ed., *The Peoples of America Series*. Phila., 1947– . — Includes works on immigrants from Holland by Arnold Mulder; from Hungary by Emil Lengyel; from Norway by L. N. Bergmann; from Sweden by A. B. Benson and Naboth Hedin; from England by G. W. Johnson; from Mexico by Carey McWilliams; from Japan by Bradford Smith; on Indians by D'Arcy McNickle; and on Negroes by J. S. Redding.
T. C. Blegen, *Norwegian Migration to America*. 2 vols. Northfield, Minn., 1931–40.
A. B. Faust, *German Element in the United States*. 2 vols. Boston, 1909.
Oscar Handlin, *The Uprooted*. Boston, 1951.
M. L. Hansen, *The Atlantic Migration, 1607–1860*. A. M. Schlesinger, ed. Cambridge, 1940.
M. L. Hansen, *The Immigrant in American History*. A. M. Schlesinger, ed. Cambridge, 1941.

M. L. Hansen, *The Mingling of the Canadian and American Peoples.* New Haven, 1940.

C. C. Qualey, *Norwegian Settlement in the United States.* Northfield, Minn., 1938.

Carl Wittke, *We Who Built America; the Saga of the Immigrant.* N.Y., 1939.

Indians
Angie Debo, *The Rise and Fall of the Choctaw Republic.* Norman, Okla., 1934.

Angie Debo, *The Road to Disappearance.* Norman, Okla., 1941.

D'Arcy McNickle, *They Came Here First.* Phila., 1949.

Paul Radin, *Story of the American Indian.* N.Y., 1927.

Clark Wissler, *Indians of the United States.* N.Y., 1940.

Intellectual History
M. E. Curti, *The Growth of American Thought.* N.Y., 1943.

R. H. Gabriel, *The Course of American Democratic Thought.* N.Y., 1940.

V. L. Parrington, *Main Currents in American Thought.* 3 vols. N.Y., 1927–30.

Dixon Wecter, *The Hero in America.* N.Y., 1941.

M. G. White, *Social Thought in America.* N.Y., 1949.

C. M. Wiltse, *The Jeffersonian Tradition in American Democracy.* Chapel Hill, 1935.

Harvey Wish, *Society and Thought in America.* 2 vols. N.Y., 1950–52.

Inventions
Roger Burlingame, *March of the Iron Men.* N.Y., 1938.

W. B. Kaempffert, ed., *Popular History of American Invention.* 2 vols. N.Y., 1924.

Cyrus McCormick, *The Century of the Reaper.* Boston, 1931.

Labor
J. R. Commons, *et al.*, *History of Labour in the United States.* 4 vols. N.Y., 1918–35.

F. R. Dulles, *Labor in America.* N.Y., 1949.

Felix Frankfurter and Nathan Greene, *The Labor Injunction.* N.Y., 1930.

Selig Perlman, *A History of Trade Unionism in the United States.* N.Y., 1922.

Samuel Yellen, *American Labor Struggles.* N.Y., 1936.

Land
Jenks Cameron, *The Development of Governmental Forest Control in the United States.* Balt., 1928.

B. H. Hibbard, *A History of Public Land Policies.* N.Y., 1924.

John Ise, *The United States Forest Policy.* New Haven, 1920.

E. L. Peffer, *The Closing of the Public Domain.* Stanford, 1951.

R. M. Robbins, *Our Landed Heritage, the Public Domain 1776–1936.* Princeton, [1942].

A. M. Sakolski, *The Great American Land Bubble.* N.Y., 1932.

Language
H. L. Mencken, *The American Language.* R. ed. N.Y., 1936. — Supplement I–II. N.Y., 1945–48.

Law
Homer Cummings and Carl McFarland, *Federal Justice.* N.Y., 1937.

J. W. Hurst, *The Growth of American Law.* Boston, 1950.

Charles Warren, *A History of the American Bar.* Boston, 1911.

Literature
Van Wyck Brooks, *Makers and Finders; a History of the Writer in America, 1800–1915.* 5 vols. N.Y., 1936–52. — Published separately under various titles.

J. D. Hart, *The Popular Book.* N.Y., 1950.

F. O. Matthiessen, *American Renaissance.* N.Y., 1941.

R. E. Spiller, *et al.*, *Literary History of the United States.* 3 vols. N.Y., 1948.

W. P. Trent, *et al.*, *Cambridge History of American Literature.* 4 vols. N.Y., 1917–21.

Lumber Industry
J. E. Defebaugh, *History of the Lumber Industry of America.* 2 vols. Chi., 1906–07.

A. M. Larson, *History of the White Pine Industry.* Minneapolis, 1949.

Magazines	Mott, *American Magazines* (§ 52).
Manufacturing	J. L. Bishop, *History of American Manufactures from 1608 to 1860.* 3 vols. Phila., 1861–68.
	V. S. Clark, *History of Manufactures in the United States, 1607–1860.* R. ed. 3 vols. Wash., 1929.
	A. H. Cole, *The American Wool Manufacture.* 2 vols. Cambridge, 1926.
	A. H. Cole and W. F. Williamson, *The American Carpet Manufacture.* Cambridge, 1941.
	M. T. Copeland, *The Cotton Manufacturing Industry in the United States.* Cambridge, 1912.
	C. B. Kuhlmann, *Development of the Flour Milling Industry in the United States.* Boston, 1929.
	R. M. Tryon, *Household Manufactures in the United States, 1640–1860.* Chi., 1917.
	L. H. Weeks, *A History of Paper Manufacturing in the United States 1690–1916.* N.Y., 1916.
Maritime History	R. G. Albion, *Square Riggers on Schedule.* N.Y., 1938.
	H. I. Chappelle, *The History of American Sailing Ships.* N.Y., 1935.
	A. H. Clark, *The Clipper Ship Era.* N.Y., 1911.
	C. C. Cutler, *Greyhound of the Sea; the Story of the American Clipper Ship.* N.Y., 1930.
	J. G. B. Hutchins, *The American Maritime Industries and Public Policy, 1789–1914; an Economic History.* Cambridge, 1941.
	J. R. Spears, *The Story of the American Merchant Marine.* R. ed. N.Y., 1915.
Medicine	Albert Deutsch, *The Mentally Ill in America; a History of Their Care and Treatment from Colonial Times.* Garden City, N.Y., 1937.
	F. R. Packard, *History of Medicine in the United States.* 2 vols. N.Y., 1931.
	H. E. Sigerist, *American Medicine.* Hildegard Nagel, transl. N.Y., 1934.
Mining	T. A. Rickard, *The History of American Mining.* N.Y., 1932.
Mormons	W. A. Linn, *The Story of the Mormons.* N.Y., 1902.
Motion Pictures	Lewis Jacobs, *The Rise of the American Film, a Critical History.* N.Y., 1939.
Music	T. P. Coffin, *British Traditional Ballad in North America.* Phila., 1950.
	J. T. Howard, *Our American Music.* R. ed. N.Y., 1946.
	G. M. Laws, *Native American Balladry.* Phila., 1950.
National Defense	C. S. Alden, *The United States Navy, a History.* R. ed. Chi., 1945.
	H. I. Chappelle, *The History of the American Sailing Navy.* N.Y., 1949.
	W. A. Ganoe, *The History of the United States Army.* N.Y., 1942.
	D. W. Knox, *A History of the United States Navy.* R. ed. N.Y., 1948.
	C. H. Metcalf, *A History of the United States Marine Corps.* N.Y., 1939.
	D. W. Mitchell, *History of the Modern Navy, from 1883 through Pearl Harbor.* N.Y., 1946.
	O. L. Spaulding, *The United States Army in War and Peace.* N.Y., 1937.
	H. H. and Margaret Sprout, *The Rise of American Naval Power, 1776–1918.* Princeton, 1939.
Negro	J. H. Franklin, *From Slavery to Freedom: A History of American Negroes.* N.Y., 1947.
	E. F. Frazier, *The Negro in the United States.* N.Y., 1949.
	Gunnar Myrdal, *An American Dilemma.* 2 vols. N.Y., 1944.
	U. B. Phillips, *American Negro Slavery.* N.Y., 1929.
New England	J. T. Adams, *The Founding of New England.* Boston, 1921.
	J. T. Adams, *New England in the Republic. 1776–1850.* Boston, 1926.
	J. T. Adams, *Revolutionary New England, 1691–1776.* Boston, 1923.
	E. C. Kirkland, *Men, Cities and Transportation; a Study in New England History, 1820–1900.* 2 vols. Cambridge, 1948.

Mathews, *The Expansion of New England* (§ 23).
W. B. Weeden, *Economic and Social History of New England, 1620–1789.*
2 vols. Boston, 1890.

Newspapers　§ 53.

Oil Industry　John Ise, *United States Oil Policy.* New Haven, 1926.
C. C. Rister, *Oil! Titan of the Southwest.* Norman, Okla., 1949.

Patriotism　M. E. Curti, *Roots of Loyalty.* N.Y., 1946.
Nathaniel Weyl, *The Battle Against Disloyalty.* N.Y., 1951.
Nathaniel Weyl, *Treason; the Story of Disloyalty and Betrayal in American History.* Wash., 1950.

Peace Movement　M. E. Curti, *Peace or War: The American Struggle. 1636–1936.* N.Y., 1936.

Philosophy　I. W. Riley, *American Thought from Puritanism to Pragmatism and Beyond.* N.Y., 1923.
W. H. Werkmeister, *A History of Philosophical Ideas in America.* N.Y., 1949.

Politics　W. E. Binkley, *American Political Parties; Their Natural History.* N.Y., 1943.
Richard Hofstadter, *The American Political Tradition and the Men Who Made It.* N.Y., 1948.
Harold Zink, *City Bosses in the United States.* Durham, 1930.

Political Theory　E. R. Lewis, *A History of American Political Thought from the Civil War to the World War.* N.Y., 1937.
C. E. Merriam, *A History of American Political Theories.* N.Y., 1920.

Presidency　W. E. Binkley, *President and Congress.* Garden City, N.Y., 1947.
G. F. Milton, *The Use of Presidential Power, 1789–1943.* Boston, 1944.
Pollard, *Presidents and the Press* (§ 53).
B. M. Rich, *The Presidents and Civil Disorder.* Wash., 1941.
Edward Stanwood, *History of the Presidency.* 2 vols. R. ed. Boston, 1921.
K. H. Young and Lamar Middleton, *Heirs Apparent.* N.Y., 1948.

Prisons　Blake McKelvey, *American Prisons.* Chi., 1936.

Prohibition　J. A. Krout, *The Origins of Prohibition.* N.Y., 1925.

Radio　Paul Schubert, *The Electric World; the Rise of Radio.* N.Y., 1928.

Railroads　G. H. Burgess and M. C. Kennedy, *Centennial History of the Pennsylvania Railroad Company.* Phila., 1949.
L. H. Haney, *Congressional History of Railways* [to 1887]. 2 vols. Madison, 1908–1910.
S. H. Holbrook, *The Story of American Railroads.* N.Y., 1947.
R. C. Overton, *Burlington West.* Cambridge, 1941.
R. E. Riegel, *The Story of the Western Railroads.* N.Y., 1926.
N. C. Wilson and F. J. Taylor, *Southern Pacific.* N.Y., 1952.

Recreation　Herbert Asbury, *Sucker's Progress. An Informal History of Gambling.* N.Y., 1938.
F. R. Dulles, *America Learns to Play; a History of Popular Recreation, 1607–1940.* N.Y., 1940.
J. A. Krout, *Annals of American Sport.* New Haven, 1929.
Robert Smith, *Baseball. A Historical Narrative of the Game.* N.Y., 1947.
A. G. Spalding, *America's National Game.* N.Y., 1911.
A. M. Weyand, *American Football. Its History and Development.* N.Y., 1926.
H. W. Wind, *The Story of American Golf.* N.Y., 1948.

Reform　Daniel Aaron, *Men of Good Hope, a Story of American Progressives.* N.Y., 1951.
A. E. Bestor, Jr., *Backwoods Utopias.* Phila., 1950.

	R. B. Nye, *Midwestern Progressive Politics*. East Lansing, Mich., 1951. A. M. Schlesinger, *The American as Reformer*. Cambridge, 1950.
Religion	E. B. Greene, *Religion and the State*. N.Y., 1941. Philip Schaff, H. C. Potter, S. M. Jackson, eds., *The American Church History Series*. 13 vols. N.Y., 1893–98. A. P. Stokes, *Church and State in the United States*. 3 vols. N.Y., 1950. W. W. Sweet, *The Story of Religion in America*. R. ed. N.Y., 1939.
Science	Bernard Jaffe, *Men of Science in America*. N.Y., 1944. D. J. Struik, *Yankee Science in the Making*. Boston, 1948.
Socialism	D. D. Egbert and Stow Persons, *Socialism and American Life*. 2 vols. Princeton, 1952. Morris Hillquit, *History of Socialism in the United States*. R. ed. N.Y., 1910. J. H. Noyes, *History of American Socialisms*. Phila., 1870.
Society	Dixon Wecter, *The Saga of American Society*. N.Y., 1937.
South	W. J. Cash, *The Mind of the South*. N.Y., 1941. Clement Eaton, *A History of the Old South*. N.Y., 1949. Stephenson and Coulter, *History of the South* (§ 59).
Suffrage	K. H. Porter, *A History of Suffrage in the United States*. Chi., 1918.
Supreme Court	Louis Boudin, *Government by Judiciary*. 2 vols. N.Y., 1932. R. K. Carr, *The Supreme Court and Judicial Review*. N.Y., 1942. Charles Warren, *The Supreme Court in United States History*. R. ed. 2 vols. Boston, 1937.
Tariff	Edward Stanwood, *American Tariff Controversies*. 2 vols. Boston, 1903. F. W. Taussig, *The Tariff History of the United States*. 7 ed. N.Y., 1923.
Taxation	Sidney Ratner, *American Taxation*, N.Y., 1942.
Theater	O. S. Coad and Edwin Mims, Jr., *The American Stage*. New Haven, 1929. Arthur Hornblow, *A History of the Theatre in America*. 2 vols. Phila., 1919. Carl Wittke, *Tambo and Bones; a History of the American Minstrel Stage*. Durham, 1930.
Transportation	B. H. Meyer, *et al.*, *History of Transportation in the United States before 1860*. Wash., 1917.
Travel	Seymour Dunbar, *History of Travel in America*. 4 vols. Indianapolis, 1915. A. M. Earle, *Stage-Coach and Tavern Days*. N.Y., 1900. A. B. Hulbert, *Historic Highways of America*. 16 vols. Cleve., 1902–05.
Veterans	Dixon Wecter, *When Johnny Comes Marching Home*. Boston, 1944.
Women	E. A. Hecker, *A Short History of Women's Rights*. N.Y., 1910. Elizabeth Stanton, S. B. Anthony, and M. J. Gage, eds., *History of Woman Suffrage*. 6 vols. N.Y. and Rochester, 1881–[1922].

62. STATE AND LOCAL HISTORY

The earliest American histories dealt with local themes. Not till the nineteenth century did the developing sense of national consciousness induce students to emphasize the national aspects of their past and to treat important subjects on a more general basis. The emergence of the school of scientific history toward the end of the century reinforced that trend, drawing attention to the questions most readily treated on the national level. Nevertheless, local history continues to be written and still serves a valid function. The strength of the state and local historical societies testifies to its vitality (§ 4).

Local history often has unique and valuable characteristics. A single community can serve as a case study which throws light on very general problems; and its story can be told with the concreteness and vividness that makes for interesting reading. To the residents of a locality, its history often has a clearer relevance and more incisive meaning than the doings of remote statesmen on the national scene. Local histories, not so involved with politics as the national ones, are likely to devote a good deal of space to social and economic themes.

Much of the writing in this field has been in the hands of dedicated amateurs, a circumstance that has advantages as well as disadvantages. Such books too often show an amateurism in research and a clumsiness in composition, as well as parochialism and isolation from the central problems of American historiography. The poorest of them also are distracted by irrelevancies and spend an undue amount of time on the role of local figures in wars and in other national events better described elsewhere. To compensate, local historians bring to their work a spirit of devotion that leads them to invest large amounts of time and money in the quest. Hence their histories, if weak in interpretation, are often rewarding in factual detail. In some cases, they are elaborately printed with extensive quotations from the sources, thus making available large bodies of local records.

In a somewhat special category are a large number of state, county, and urban histories, commonly known as "mug books." The production of these volumes began in the last quarter of the nineteenth century and continued into the 1930's. Turned out by publishing firms that specialized in this work, they are generally multivolumed, large, well-printed, and expensive. Their reason for being is the long section, in each, devoted to the biographies of the locally prominent, who doubtless subscribed for the sake of seeing themselves photographed and extolled in print. Nevertheless these books occasionally have historical sections of considerable value, and even the biographical volumes may provide information not elsewhere available.

The general guides to local history include T. L. Bradford and S. V. Henkels, *Bibliographer's Manual of American History, Containing an Account of All State, Territory, Town and County Histories* (5 vols., Phila., 1907–10); A. P. C. Griffin, *Index of Articles upon American Local History in Historical Collections* (Boston, 1889); A. P. C. Griffin, *Index of the Literature of American Local History, in Collections Published in 1890–1895* (Boston, 1896); C. S. Peterson, *Bibliography of County Histories of the 3111 Counties in the 48 States* (Balt., 1946); C. L. Stocker, "Genealogical Material and Local Histories in the St. Louis Public Library," *St. Louis Public Library Monthly Bull.,* XXV (1927), 193; A. H. Clark Company, *The United States; a Catalogue of Books Relating to the History of Its Various States, Counties and Cities and Territories* (Cleve., 1928); F. B. Perkins, *Check List for American Local History* (Boston, 1876); J. L. Rader, ed., *South of Forty from the Mississippi to the Rio Grande: A Bibliography* (Norman, Okla., 1947).

In addition, the journals of the state historical societies (§ 50) contain many articles of value, traceable through their indexes. The Writers' Project of the WPA undertook a large number of studies in this field, few of which were however published. Some such material was also included in the various state guide books put out by the WPA. For the remainder, see: M. E. Colby, *Final Report on Disposition of Unpublished Materials of the WPA Writers' Program* (§ 26).

The list which follows is selected and illustrative. Within each state and territory, guides and bibliographies are mentioned first, then general state histories, and finally, local histories. Additional titles are listed on page 545.

Alabama

T. M. Owen, "Bibliography of Alabama," Am. Hist. Assoc., *Report*, 1897, 777.

         ✸   ✸   ✸

Memorial Record of Alabama. 2 vols. Madison, 1893.
A. B. Moore, *History of Alabama.* University, [1935].
M. B. Owen, *Our State, Alabama.* Montgomery, 1927.
T. M. Owen, *History of Alabama and Dictionary of Alabama Biography.* 4 vols. Chi., 1921.

         ✸   ✸   ✸

P. J. Hamilton, *Colonial Mobile.* Boston, 1910.
Jefferson County and Birmingham, Alabama. Birmingham, 1887.
Nina Leftwich, *Two Hundred Years of Muscle Shoals.* Tuscumbia, 1935.
J. B. Little, *The History of Butler County, Alabama.* Cin., 1885.
F. H. W. Moss, *Building Birmingham and Jefferson County.* Birmingham, [1947].

Alaska

W. H. Dall and Marcus Baker, "Partial List of Charts, Maps, and Publications Relating to Alaska and the Adjacent Region," U.S. Coast and Geodetic Survey, *Pacific Coast Pilot* (1892), 165.
James Wickersham, *A Bibliography of Alaskan Literature.* Cordova, 1927.

         ✸   ✸   ✸

C. L. Andrews, *The Story of Alaska.* Caldwell, 1938.
H. H. Bancroft, *Alaska.* (*History of the Pacific States*, Vol. XXVIII.) San Francisco, 1886.
J. P. Nichols, *Alaska.* Cleve., 1924.
S. R. Tompkins, *Alaska.* Norman, 1945.

Arizona

Hector Alliot, *Bibliography of Arizona.* Los Angeles, 1914.

         ✸   ✸   ✸

H. H. Bancroft, *Arizona and New Mexico.* (*History of the Pacific States*, Vol. XII.) San Francisco, 1888.
T. E. Farish, *History of Arizona.* 8 vols. Phoenix, 1915.
Cleve Hallenbeck, *Land of the Conquistadores.* Caldwell, 1950.
R. E. Sloan and W. R. Adams, *History of Arizona.* 4 vols. Phoenix, 1930.
R. K. Wyllys, *Arizona: The History of a Frontier State.* Phoenix, 1950.

Arkansas

D. T. Herndon, *Arkansas History Catalog.* Ft. Smith, 1923.

         ✸   ✸   ✸

John Hallum, *Biographical and Pictorial History of Arkansas.* Vol. I. Albany, 1887.
W. S. McNutt, O. E. McKnight, and G. A. Hubbell, *A History of Arkansas.* [Little Rock, 1933].
D. Y. Thomas, *Arkansas and Its People, 1541–1930.* N.Y., 1930.

California

Ethel Blumann and M. W. Thomas, *California Local History, a Centennial Bibliography.* Stanford, 1950.
R. E. Cowan, *A Bibliography of the History of California.* 3 vols. San Francisco, 1933. — New ed. Columbus, Ohio, 1952.

         ✸   ✸   ✸

Gertrude Atherton, *California, an Intimate History.* N.Y., 1914.
H. H. Bancroft, *California.* 7 vols. (*History of the Pacific States*, Vols. XIII–XIX.) San Francisco, 1884-1890.

J. W. Caughey, *California.* N.Y. 1953.
C. E. Chapman, *A History of California, the Spanish Period.* N.Y., 1921.
R. G. Cleland, *A History of California, the American Period.* N.Y., 1922.
Z. S. Eldredge, *History of California.* 5 vols. N.Y., [1915].
R. D. Hunt and N. V. Sanchez, *A Short History of California.* N.Y., [1929].
Josiah Royce, *California from the Conquest in 1846 to the Second Vigilance Committee in San Francisco.* Boston, 1886. — R. G. Cleland, ed., 1948.

o   o   o

Walter Bean, *Boss Ruef's San Francisco.* Berkeley, 1952.
P. E. Benedict, *History of Beverly Hills.* Beverly Hills, 1934.
Isaac Cox, *The Annals of Trinity County.* San Francisco, 1858. — New ed. Eugene, 1940.
C. C. Dobie, *San Francisco, a Pageant.* N.Y., 1934.
W. W. Ferrier, *Berkeley, California.* Berkeley, 1933.
Morrow Mayo, *Los Angeles.* N.Y., 1933.
F. C. Merritt, *History of Alameda County, California.* 2 vols. Chi., 1928.
Max Miller, *Harbor of the Sun. The Story of the Port of San Diego.* N.Y., 1940.
E. O. Palmer, *History of Hollywood.* 2 vols. Hollywood, 1937.
J. E. Pleasants, *History of Orange County, California.* 3 vols. Los Angeles, 1931.
Santa Barbara. N.Y., 1941. — WPA Writers' Project.
Frank Soulé, J. H. Gihon, and James Nisbet, *The Annals of San Francisco.* N.Y., 1855. — Index, comp. by C. F. Griffin, San Francisco, 1935.
Boyle Workman, *The City that Grew.* Los Angeles, 1935.
J. P. Young, *San Francisco, a History of the Pacific Coast Metropolis.* 2 vols. San Francisco, [1913].

Colorado

F. L. Paxson, *A Preliminary Bibliography of Colorado History.* Boulder, 1906.

o   o   o

H. H. Bancroft, *Nevada, Colorado, and Wyoming.* (*History of the Pacific States,* Vol. XX.) San Francisco, 1890.
P. S. Fritz, *Colorado, the Centennial State.* N.Y., 1941.
L. R. Hafen, *Colorado, the Story of a Western Commonwealth.* Denver, 1933.
W. F. Stone, *History of Colorado.* 3 vols. Chi., 1918.

o   o   o

David Boyd, *A History: Greeley, and the Union Colony of Colorado.* Greeley, 1890.
J. C. Smiley, *History of Denver.* Denver, 1903.
M. S. Wolle, *Stampede to Timberline.* Boulder, [1949].

Connecticut

C. A. Flagg, "Reference List of Connecticut Local History," *New York State Library, Bull.,* No. 53 (1900).
J. H. Trumbull, *List of Books Printed in Connecticut, 1709–1800.* [Hartford], 1904.

o   o   o

C. W. Burpee, *The Story of Connecticut.* 4 vols. N.Y., 1939.
G. L. Clark, *A History of Connecticut.* N.Y., 1914.
Forrest Morgan, *Connecticut as a Colony and as a State, or One of the Original Thirteen.* 4 vols. Hartford, 1904.
J. M. Morse, *A Neglected Period of Connecticut's History, 1818–1850.* New Haven, [1933].
N. G. Osborn, *History of Connecticut in Monographic Form.* 5 vols. N.Y., 1925.
Odell Shepard, *Connecticut Past and Present.* N.Y., 1939.
Benjamin Trumbull, *A Complete History of Connecticut.* 2 vols. New London, 1898. — Originally published 1818.

o   o   o

F. O. Allen, *The History of Enfield, Connecticut.* 3 vols. Lancaster, 1900.
Joseph Anderson, *The Town and City of Waterbury, Connecticut, from the Aboriginal Period to the Year Eighteen Hundred and Ninety-Five.* 3 vols. New Haven, 1896.
E. E. Atwater, *History of the Colony of New Haven to Its Absorption into Connecticut.* New Haven, 1881.
J. M. Bailey, *History of Danbury, Connecticut, 1684–1896.* N.Y., 1896.
C. W. Bowen, *The History of Woodstock, Connecticut.* 4 vols. Norwood, 1926–1932.
Isabella Brayton, *The Story of Hartford, a History.* Hartford, 1929.
F. M. Caulkins, *History of New London, from the First Survey of the Coast in 1612.* New London, 1852.
F. M. Caulkins, *History of Norwich, from Its Possession by the Indians to 1873.* [Hartford], 1874.
C. M. Green, *History of Naugatuck, Connecticut.* New Haven, [1948].
Samuel Orcutt, *The History of the Old Town of Derby, Connecticut, 1642–1880.* Springfield, Mass., 1880.
Samuel Orcutt, *A History of the Old Town of Stratford and the City of Bridgeport, Connecticut.* 2 vols. [New Haven], 1886.
Epaphroditus Peck, *A History of Bristol, Connecticut.* Hartford, 1932.
E. H. Schenck, *The History of Fairfield, Connecticut, 1639–1818.* 2 vols. N.Y., 1889.
B. C. Steiner, *History of the Plantation of Menunkatuck and of the Original Town of Guilford, Connecticut, Comprising the Present Towns of Guilford and Madison.* Balt., 1897.
H. R. Stiles, *History and Genealogies of Ancient Windsor, 1635–1891.* 2 vols. Hartford, 1891–1892.

Delaware

G. H. Ryden, *Bibliography of Delaware History.* [Newark, 1927.]

* * *

H. C. Conrad, *History of the State of Delaware.* 3 vols. Wilmington, 1908.
Amandus Johnson, *Swedish Settlements on the Delaware, 1638–1664.* 2 vols. Phila., 1911.
W. A. Powell, *A History of Delaware.* Boston, [1928].
H. C. Reed, ed., *Delaware: A History of the First State.* 3 vols. N.Y., 1947.
J. T. Scharf, *History of Delaware, 1609–1888.* 2 vols. Phila., 1888.

* * *

F. A. Cooch, *Little Known History of Newark, Delaware, and Its Environs.* Newark, 1936.
A. T. Lincoln, *Wilmington, Delaware, 1609–1937.* Rutland, [1937].
History of Wilmington. Wilmington, 1894.

District of Columbia

W. B. Bryan, *A History of the National Capital.* 2 vols. N.Y., 1914–16.
William Tindall, *Standard History of the City of Washington.* Knoxville, 1914.
W. B. Webb and John Wooldridge, *Centennial History of the City of Washington, D.C.* Dayton, 1892.

Florida

C. M. Brevard and J. A. Robertson, *A History of Florida, from the Treaty of 1763 to Our Own Times.* 2 vols. Deland, 1924.
W. T. Cash and Dorothy Dodd, *Florida Becomes a State.* Tallahassee, 1945.
Paul Gaffarel, *Histoire de la Floride Française.* Paris, 1875.
K. A. Hand, *Florida, Land of Change.* Chapel Hill, 1948.
S. W. Martin, *Florida during the Territorial Days.* Athens, 1944.

* * *

Isidor Cohen, *Historical Sketches and Sidelights of Miami, Florida.* Miami, 1925.
T. F. Davis, *History of Jacksonville, Florida and Vicinity, 1513 to 1924.* [Jacksonville], 1925.

W. W. Dewhurst, *History of Saint Augustine, Florida.* N.Y., 1881.
K. H. Grismer, *The Story of Sarasota.* Tampa, 1946.

Georgia

T. H. Jack, "Historiography in Georgia," Georgia Hist. Assoc., *Proc.,* 1917, 21.
E. M. Thornton, *Finding List of Books and Pamphlets Relating to Georgia and Georgians.* Atlanta, 1928.
Oscar Wegelin, *Books Relating to the History of Georgia.* Savannah, 1911.

     ❖   ❖   ❖

J. C. Bonner and L. E. Roberts, *Georgia History and Government.* Athens, 1940.
E. M. Coulter, *Georgia, a Short History.* Chapel Hill, 1947.
Amanda Johnson, *Georgia, as Colony and State.* Atlanta, 1938.
C. C. Jones, *History of Georgia.* 2 vols. Boston, 1883.
A. B. Saye, *New Viewpoints in Georgia History.* Athens, 1943.
G. G. Smith, *The Story of Georgia and the Georgia People, 1732 to 1860.* Macon, 1900.

     ❖   ❖   ❖

G. M. Battey, *A History of Rome and Floyd County, 1540–1922.* Atlanta, 1922.
W. G. Cooper, *Official History of Fulton County.* [Atlanta, 1934.]
L. J. Cunyus, *The History of Bartow County.* [N.p., 1933.]
B. S. Hart, *The Official History of Laurens County, Georgia, 1807–1941.* Dublin, 1941.
Folks Huxford, *The History of Brooks County, Georgia.* Quitman, 1948.
T. H. Martin, *Atlanta and Its Builders.* 2 vols. Atlanta, 1902.
W. P. Reed, *History of Atlanta.* Syracuse, 1889.
S. B. G. Temple, *The First Hundred Years, a Short History of Cobb County in Georgia.* Atlanta, 1935.
Adelaide Wilson, *Historic and Picturesque Savannah.* Boston, 1889.

Hawaii

List of Books on the Hawaiian Islands. Honolulu, 1928.
U.S. Library of Congress. Division of Bibliography. *The Hawaiian Islands; a Bibliographical List.* Wash., 1931.

     ❖   ❖   ❖

S. K. Stevens, *American Expansion in Hawaii, 1842–1898.* Harrisburg, 1945.
R. S. Kuykendall and A. G. Day, *Hawaii.* N.Y., 1948.
H. W. Bradley, *American Frontier in Hawaii.* Stanford, 1942.
M. C. Alexander, *Story of Hawaii.* N.Y., 1912.

Idaho

J. E. Rees, *Idaho Chronology, Nomenclature, Bibliography.* Chi., 1918.

     ❖   ❖   ❖

J. H. Hawley, *History of Idaho, the Gem of the Mountains.* 4 vols. Chi., 1920.
C. J. Brosnan, *History of the State of Idaho.* N.Y., [1918].
M. D. Beal, *A History of Southeastern Idaho.* Caldwell, 1942.
Thomas Donaldson, *Idaho of Yesterday.* Caldwell, 1941.
M. A. Elsensohn, *Pioneer Days in Idaho County.* Caldwell, 1947.
Vardis Fisher, ed., *Idaho Encyclopedia.* Caldwell, 1938.
W. J. McConnell, *Early History of Idaho.* Caldwell, 1913.

     ❖   ❖   ❖

J. B. Brown, *Fort Hall, on the Oregon Trail.* Caldwell, 1932.
A. L. Bird, *Boise, the Peace Valley.* Caldwell, 1934.

Illinois

P. M. Angle, *Suggested Readings in Illinois History; with a Selected List of Historical Fiction.* Springfield, 1935.

     ❖   ❖   ❖

C. W. Alford, ed., *The Centennial History of Illinois.* 5 vols. Springfield, 1918–20.
P. M. Angle and R. L. Beyer, *A Handbook of Illinois History.* Springfield, 1943.
E. G. Mason, *Chapters from Illinois History.* Chi., 1901.

❊   ❊   ❊

A. T. Andreas, *History of Chicago.* 3 vols. Chi., 1885.
Newton Bateman and Paul Selby, *Historical Encyclopedia of Illinois, with Histories of St. Clair, Lake, Dupage, Sangamon, Lundy, Cass, Rock Island, Christian, Mc-Donough, Lee, McLean, Carroll and Fulton Counties.* 23 vols. Chi., 1902–18.
Herma Clark, *The Elegant Eighties when Chicago Was Young.* Chi., [1941].
J. L. Hasbrouck, *History of McLean County, Illinois.* 2 vols. Topeka, 1924.
Lloyd Lewis and H. J. Smith, *Chicago, the History of Its Reputation.* N.Y., [1929].
B. L. Pierce, *A History of Chicago.* 2 vols. N.Y., 1937–40. — In progress.
J. M. Rice, *Peoria City and County, Illinois.* 2 vols. Chi., 1912.
J. W. Spencer and J. M. D. Burrows, *The Early Days of Rock Island and Davenport.* Chi., 1942.

Indiana

Logan Esarey, "Indiana Local History: A Guide," Ind. University Extension Division, *Bull.*, I, No. 7 (1916).
L. E. Henley, "Bibliography of Indiana Local History," *Ind. Quar. Mag. Hist.*, VI (1910), 43.
L. E. Henley, "Bibliography of Town and City Histories," *Ind. Quar. Mag. Hist.*, VI (1910), 91.

❊   ❊   ❊

W. M. Cockrum, *Pioneer History of Indiana.* Oakland City, 1907.
J. B. Dillon, *A History of Indiana from Its Earliest Exploration by Europeans to the Close of the Territorial Government in 1816.* Indianapolis, 1859.
J. P. Dunn, *Indiana and Indianans.* 5 vols. Chi., 1919.
Logan Esarey, *A History of Indiana.* 2 vols. Indianapolis, 1915–18.
J. H. Levering, *Historic Indiana.* N.Y., 1910.
W. H. Smith, *History of the State of Indiana.* 2 vols. Indianapolis, 1897.

❊   ❊   ❊

John Ade, *Newton County.* Indianapolis, [1911].
W. A. Brice, *History of Fort Wayne.* Fort Wayne, 1868.
George Hazzard, *History of Henry County, Indiana, 1822–1906.* 2 vols. New Castle, 1906.
History of Wayne County, Indiana. 2 vols. Chi., 1884.

Iowa

J. E. Briggs, *Iowa, Old and New.* Lincoln, [1939].
Cyrenus Cole, *A History of the People of Iowa.* Cedar Rapids, 1921.
Cyrenus Cole, *Iowa through the Years.* Iowa City, 1940.
B. F. Gue, *History of Iowa from the Earliest Times.* 4 vols., N.Y., [1903].
G. F. Parker, *Iowa Pioneer Foundations.* 2 vols. Iowa City, 1940.
Henry Sabin and E. L. Sabin, *The Making of Iowa.* Chi., [1900].
William Salter, *Iowa, the First Free State in the Louisiana Purchase.* Chi., 1905.
B. F. Shambaugh, *The Constitutions of Iowa.* Iowa City, 1934.

Kansas

W. E. Connelley, *History of Kansas.* 5 vols. Chi., 1928.
History of the State of Kansas. Chi., 1883.
D. W. Wilder, *Annals of Kansas.* Topeka, 1875. — Another ed. 1886.

❊   ❊   ❊

F. W. Giles, *Thirty Years in Topeka: A Historical Sketch.* Topeka, 1886.
G. W. Harrington, *Annals of Brown County, Kansas.* Hiawatha, 1903.
C. C. Lowther, *Dodge City, Kansas.* Phila., [1940].

Kentucky

J. W. Coleman, Jr., *A Bibliography of Kentucky History.* Lexington, 1949.

* * *

W. E. Connelley and E. M. Coulter, *History of Kentucky.* 5 vols. Chi., 1922.
T. D. Clark, *A History of Kentucky.* N.Y., 1937.
Lewis Collins, *History of Kentucky.* R. and enlarged by his son, R. H. Collins. 2 vols. Covington, 1878.
F. G. Davenport, *Ante-bellum Kentucky.* Oxford, Miss., 1943.
R. M. McElroy, *Kentucky in the Nation's History.* N.Y., 1909.
Z. F. Smith, *History of Kentucky.* Louisville, 1886.
F. A. Wallis and Hambleton Tapp, *A Sesqui-Centennial History of Kentucky.* Hopkinsville, 1945.

* * *

A. P. Johnson, *A Century of Wayne County, Kentucky, 1800-1900.* Louisville, [1939].
I. M. McMeekin, *Louisville, the Gateway City.* N.Y., [1946].
G. W. Ranck, *History of Lexington, Kentucky.* Cin., 1872.
O. A. Rothert, *A History of Muhlenberg County.* Louisville, 1913.
G. L. Willis, Sr., *History of Shelby County, Kentucky.* Louisville, 1929.

Louisiana

François Barbé-Marbois, *Histoire de la Louisiane et de la Cession.* Paris, 1829. — Transl. as *The History of Louisiana, Particularly of the Cession of That Colony to the United States.* Phila., 1830.
Alcée Fortier, *History of Louisiana.* 4 vols. N.Y., 1904.
Charles Gayarré, *History of Louisiana.* R. ed. 4 vols. New Orleans, 1903.
Eugène Guénin, *La Louisiane.* Paris, 1904.
Pierre Heinrich, *La Louisiane sous la Compagnie des Indes, 1717-1731.* Paris, [1908].
F. X. Martin, *History of Louisiana.* 2 vols. New Orleans, 1827-29. — Reprinted (with continuation to 1861 by J. F. Condon), New Orleans, 1882.
J. A. Robertson, *Louisiana under the Rule of Spain, France and the United States, 1785-1807.* 2 vols. Cleve., 1911. — Contemporary accounts by Paul Alliot and others.
Vicente Rodriguez, *Primeros años de dominación española en la Luisiana.* Madrid, 1942.
Marc de Villiers du Terrage, *Les Dernières années de la Louisiane française.* Paris, [1904].

* * *

Grace King, *New Orleans, the Place and the People.* N.Y., 1895.
S. A. Marchand, *The Flight of a Century 1800-1900 in Ascension Parish, Louisiana.* Donaldsonville, 1936.
M. G. O'Pry, *Chronicles of Shreveport.* Shreveport, [1928].
Henry Rightor, *Standard History of New Orleans, Louisiana.* Chi., 1900.
Lyle Saxon, *Fabulous New Orleans.* N.Y., 1939.
Harold Sinclair, *The Port of New Orleans.* Garden City, N.Y., 1942.

Maine

D. B. Hall, "Reference List on Maine Local History," New York State Library, *Bull.,* No. 63 (1910).
A. J. Huston, *A Check List of Maine Local Histories.* Portland, 1915.
Joseph Williamson, *A Bibliography of the State of Maine, from the Earliest Period to 1891.* 2 vols. Portland, 1896.

* * *

J. S. C. Abbott and E. H. Elwell, *History of Maine.* Augusta, 1892.
L. C. Hatch, *Maine: A History.* 3 vols. N.Y., 1919.
W. H. Rowe, *The Maritime History of Maine.* N.Y., [1948].
James Sullivan, *History of the District of Maine.* Boston, 1795.
H. M. Sylvester, *Maine Pioneer Settlements.* Boston, 1909.
W. D. Williamson, *History of the State of Maine.* 2 vols. Hallowell, 1832.

* * *

C. E. Allen, *History of Dresden, Maine*. [Augusta], 1931.
F. S. Chase, *Wiscasset in Pownalborough*. Wiscasset, 1941.
R. P. T. Coffin, *Kennebec: Cradle of Americans*. N.Y., [1937].
F. B. Greene, *History of Boothbay, Southport and Boothbay Harbor, Maine*. Portland, 1906.
R. W. Hale, *The Story of Bar Harbor*. N.Y., [1949].
Helen Hamlin, *Pine, Potatoes and People*. N.Y., [1948].
W. C. Hatch, *A History of the Town of Industry, Franklin County, Maine*. Farmington, 1893.
H. W. Owen, *History of Bath*. Bath, 1936.
W. H. Rowe, *Ancient North Yarmouth and Yarmouth, Maine*. Yarmouth, 1937.
Joseph Williamson and Alfred Johnson, *History of the City of Belfast*. 2 vols. Boston, 1913.
William Willis, *The History of Portland, from 1632 to 1864*. Portland, 1865.

Maryland

B. C. Steiner, "Descriptions of Maryland," Johns Hopkins University, *Studies*, XXII, Nos. 11–12 (1904).

o   o   o

M. P. Andrews, *The Founding of Maryland*. N.Y., 1933.
M. P. Andrews, *History of Maryland: Province and State*. Garden City, N.Y., 1929.
Elizabeth Baer, *Seventeenth Century Maryland*. Balt., 1949.
Dieter Cunz, *The Maryland Germans*. Princeton, 1948.
James McSherry, *History of Maryland, 1634–1848*. Balt., 1849.
N. D. Mereness, *Maryland as a Proprietary Province*. N.Y., 1901.
H. D. Richardson, *Side-lights on Maryland History*. 2 vols. Balt., 1903.
J. T. Scharf, *History of Maryland from the Earliest Period to the Present Day*. 3 vols. Balt., 1879.
B. C. Steiner, *Maryland during the English Civil Wars*. 2 vols. Balt., 1906–07.
B. C. Steiner, *Maryland under the Commonwealth 1649–1658*. Balt., 1911.

o   o   o

Charles Hirschfeld, *Baltimore, 1870–1900: Studies in Social History*. Balt., 1941.
George Johnston, *History of Cecil County, Maryland*. Elkton, 1881.
Elias Jones, *Revised History of Dorchester County, Maryland*. Balt., 1925.
Hamilton Owens, *Baltimore on the Chesapeake*. Garden City, N.Y., 1941.
J. T. Scharf, *Chronicles of Baltimore*. Balt., 1874.
A. L. Sioussat, *Old Baltimore*. N.Y., 1931.
Oswald Tilghman, *History of Talbot County, Maryland, 1661–1861*. 2 vols. Balt., 1915.

Massachusetts

Boston Public Library. Tercentenary Celebration, 1630–1930, *The Massachusetts Bay Colony and Boston; a Selected List of Works*. Boston, 1930.
Jeremiah Colburn, *Bibliography of the Local History of Massachusetts*. Boston, 1871.
C. A. Flagg, *Guide to Massachusetts Local History*. Salem, [1907].

o   o   o

Brooks Adams, *The Emancipation of Massachusetts*. Boston, 1887.
C. F. Adams, *Massachusetts, Its Historians and Its History*. Boston, 1893.
C. F. Adams, *Three Episodes of Massachusetts History*. 2 vols. Boston, 1892.
William Bradford, *Of Plymouth Plantation, 1620–47*. Many eds., esp. W. C. Ford's, 2 vols., Boston, 1912, and S. E. Morison's, N.Y., 1952.
A. B. Hart, *Commonwealth History of Massachusetts*. 5 vols. N.Y., 1927–30.
Thomas Hutchinson, *The History of the Colony and Province of Massachusetts Bay*. New ed. 3 vols., Cambridge, 1936.
D. L. Marsh and W. H. Clark, *The Story of Massachusetts*. 4 vols. N.Y., [1938].
G. R. Minot, *Continuation of the History of the Province of Massachusetts Bay, from the Year 1748 to 1765*. 2 vols. Boston, 1798–1803.

S. E. Morison, *Maritime History of Massachusetts. 1783–1860*. Boston, 1921.
J. F. Sly, *Town Government in Massachusetts, 1620–1930*. Cambridge, 1930.
John Winthrop, *The History of New England 1630–1649*. James Savage, ed. 2 vols. Boston, 1853. — Identical with his *Journal*, J. K. Hosmer, ed., 2 vols., N.Y., 1908.

* * *

C. F. Adams, *History of Braintree, the North Precinct of Braintree, and the Town of Quincy*. Cambridge, 1891.
C. E. Banks, *The History of Martha's Vineyard*. 3 vols. Boston, 1911–25.
C. K. Bolton, *Brookline*. Brookline, 1897.
Boston Looks Seaward. Boston, 1941. — WPA Writers' Project.
Mellen Chamberlain, *A Documentary History of Chelsea*. 2 vols. Boston, 1908.
G. W. Chase, *History of Haverhill*. Haverhill, 1861.
G. K. Clarke, *History of Needham, Massachusetts, 1711–1911*. [Cambridge, 1912.]
M. C. Crawford, *Romantic Days in Old Boston*. Boston, 1910.
J. J. Currier, *History of Newbury, Massachusetts*. Boston, 1902.
J. J. Currier, *History of Newburyport, Massachusetts*. 2 vols. Newburyport, 1909.
J. G. Curtis, *History of the Town of Brookline, Massachusetts*. Boston, 1933.
John Daggett, *Sketch of the History of Attleborough*. Dedham, 1834.
W. T. Davis, *Ancient Landmarks of Plymouth*. Boston, 1883.
S. G. Drake, *History of Middlesex County*. 2 vols. Boston, 1880.
J. B. Felt, *History of Ipswich, Essex, and Hamilton*. Cambridge, 1834.
Frederick Freeman, *History of Cape Cod*. 2 vols. Boston, 1860–62.
C. M. Green, *Holyoke*. New Haven, 1939.
S. A. Green, *Groton Historical Series*. 4 vols. Groton, 1887–99.
E. M. Herlihy, *et al.*, *Fifty Years of Boston*. Boston, [1932].
Oscar Handlin, *Boston's Immigrants*. Cambridge, 1941.
History of the Town of Hingham. 3 vols. Hingham, 1893.
J. G. Holland, *History of Western Massachusetts*. 2 vols. Springfield, 1855.
Charles Hudson, *History of the Town of Lexington*. 2 vols. Boston, 1913.
A. S. Hudson, *History of Concord*. Concord, 1904.
J. F. Hunnewell, *A Century of Town Life: A History of Charlestown, Massachusetts, 1775–1887*. 2 vols. Boston, 1888.
Sylvester Judd, *History of Hadley*. Northampton, 1863. — New ed. by George Sheldon, Springfield, 1905.
L. C. Kellogg, *History of Greenfield, 1900–1929*. 3 vols. Greenfield, 1931.
J. H. Lockwood, *Westfield*. 2 vols. Springfield, 1922.
J. H. Lockwood, *et al.*, *Western Massachusetts; a History 1636–1925*. 4 vols. N.Y., 1926.
R. H. Lord, *et al.*, *History of the Archdiocese of Boston*. 3 vols. N.Y., 1944.
Joseph Merrill, *History of Amesbury and Merrimac*. Haverhill, 1880.
L. R. Paige, *History of Cambridge, 1630–1877*. Boston, 1877.
H. C. Parsons, *A Puritan Outpost*. N.Y., 1937. — Northfield.
G. F. Partridge, *History of the Town of Bellingham, Massachusetts, 1719–1919*. Bellingham, 1919.
Sidney Perley, *The History of Salem*, 2 vols. Salem, 1924–26.
J. D. Phillips, *Salem and the Indies*. Boston, 1947.
J. D. Phillips, *Salem in the Seventeenth Century*. Boston, 1933.
J. D. Phillips, *Salem in the Eighteenth Century*. Boston, 1937.
H. K. Rowe, *Tercentenary History of Newton, 1630–1930*. Newton, 1930.
Townsend Scudder, *Concord*. Boston, 1947.
George Sheldon, *History of Deerfield*. 2 vols. Deerfield, 1895–1896.
J. E. A. Smith, *History of Pittsfield, 1734–1876*. Boston and Springfield, 1869–76.
Frank Smith, *A History of Dedham, Massachusetts*. Dedham, 1936.
E. C. Smith and P. M. Smith, *A History of the Town of Middlefield, Massachusetts*. [Menasha, Wisc.], 1924.
C. J. Taylor, *History of Great Barrington*. Gt. Barrington, 1928.
F. M. Thompson, *History of Greenfield*. 3 vols. Greenfield, 1904.
T. F. Waters, *Ipswich in the Massachusetts Bay Colony*. 2 vols. Ipswich, 1905–17.

Thomas Weston, *History of the Town of Middleboro, Massachusetts*. Boston, 1906.
Justin Winsor, *Memorial History of Boston, 1630–1880*. 4 vols. Boston, 1880–81.

Michigan

F. B. Streeter, *Michigan Bibliography; a Partial Catalogue of Books, Maps, Manuscripts and Miscellaneous Materials Relating to the Resources, Development and History of Michigan from Earliest Times to July 1, 1917, together with Citation of Libraries in which the Materials May Be Consulted, and a Complete Analytic Index by Author and Subject*. 2 vols. Lansing, 1921.

o   o   o

J. V. Campbell, *Outlines of the Political History of Michigan*. Detroit, 1876.
G. N. Fuller, *Economic and Social Beginnings of Michigan*. Lansing, 1916.
Calvin Goodrich, *The First Michigan Frontier*. Ann Arbor, 1940.
M. M. Quaife and Sidney Glazer, *Michigan from Primitive Wilderness to Industrial Commonwealth*. N.Y., 1948.
W. R. Riddell, *Michigan under British Rule*. Lansing, 1926.
N. V. Russell, *The British Régime in Michigan and the Old Northwest 1760–1796*. Northfield, [1939].
F. B. Streeter, *Political Parties in Michigan, 1837–1860*. Lansing, 1918.
H. M. Utley and B. M. Cutcheon, *Michigan as a Province, Territory and State, the Twenty-sixth Member of the Federal Union*. 4 vols. N.Y., 1906.

o   o   o

History of Upper Peninsula of Michigan. Chi., 1883.
Arthur Pound, *Detroit, Dynamic City*. N.Y., 1940.

Minnesota

T. C. Blegen and Lewis Beeson, *Minnesota, Its History and Its People; a Study Outline with Topics and References*. Minneapolis, 1937.

o   o   o

W. W. Folwell, *A History of Minnesota*. 4 vols. St. Paul, 1921–30.
L. F. Hubbard, *et al.*, *Minnesota in Three Centuries, 1655–1908*. 4 vols. N.Y., 1908.
Meridel Le Sueur, *North Star Country*. N.Y., [1945].

o   o   o

Isaac Atwater, *History of the City of Minneapolis*. 2 vols. N.Y., 1893.
H. A. Castle, *History of St. Paul and Vicinity*. 3 vols. Chi., 1912.
A. B. Easton, *History of the Saint Croix Valley*. 2 vols. Chi., 1909.
C. R. Walker, *American City, a Rank-and-File History*. N.Y., [1937]. — Minneapolis.

Mississippi

T. M. Owen, "Bibliography of Mississippi," Am. Hist. Assoc., *Report*, 1899, I, 633.
J. F. H. Claiborne, *Mississippi as a Province, Territory, and State*. Jackson, 1880.
Robert Lowry and W. H. McCardle, *History of Mississippi*. Jackson, 1891.
Dunbar Rowland, *History of Mississippi, the Heart of the South*. 2 vols. Chi., 1925.

o   o   o

H. T. Kane, *Natchez on the Mississippi*. N.Y., 1947.
W. L. Lipscomb, *A History of Columbus, Mississippi, during the Nineteenth Century*. Birmingham, 1909.

Missouri

H. L. Conard, *Encyclopedia of the History of Missouri*. 6 vols. N.Y., 1901.
F. A. Culmer, *A New History of Missouri*. Mexico, [1938].
Louis Houck, *History of Missouri, from the Earliest Explorations . . . until the Admission of the State into the Union*. 3 vols. Chi., 1908.
Houck, *Spanish Régime in Missouri*.

W. B. Stevens, *Centennial History of Missouri, One Hundred Years in the Union, 1820–1921*. 6 vols. St. Louis, 1921.

• • •

J. E. Ford, *A History of Jefferson City and of Cole County*. Jefferson City, [1938].
J. T. Scharf, *History of Saint Louis, City and County, from the Earliest Periods to the Present Day*. 2 vols. Phila., 1883.
W. B. Stevens, *St. Louis, the Fourth City, 1764–1909*. 3 vols. St. Louis, 1909.
C. W. Whitney, *Kansas City, Missouri, Its History and Its People 1808–1908*. 3 vols. Chi., 1908.

Montana

H. H. Bancroft, *Washington, Idaho, and Montana*. (*History of the Pacific States*, Vol. XXVI.) San Francisco, 1890.
C. P. Connolly, *The Devil Learns to Vote, the Story of Montana*. N.Y., [1938].
C. B. Glasscock, *The War of the Copper Kings*. Indianapolis, [1935].
J. K. Howard, *Montana, High, Wide and Handsome*. New Haven, 1943.
Tom Stout, *Montana, Its Story and Biography*. 3 vols. Chi., 1921.

• • •

Copper Camp, Stories of the World's Greatest Mining Town, Butte, Montana. N.Y., [1943]. — WPA Writers' Project.

Nebraska

History of the State of Nebraska. Chi., 1882.
J. S. Morton, *et al.*, *Illustrated History of Nebraska*. 3 vols., Lincoln, 1905–06.

• • •

A. B. Hayes and S. D. Cox, *History of the City of Lincoln*. Lincoln, 1889.
Alfred Sorenson, *The Story of Omaha*. Omaha, 1923.
D. P. Stough, *History of Hamilton and Clay Counties, Nebraska*. 2 vols. Chi., 1921.

Nevada

S. P. Davis, *The History of Nevada*. 2 vols. Reno, 1913.
R. G. Lillard, *Desert Challenge, an Interpretation of Nevada*. N.Y., 1942.
E. M. Mack, *Nevada, a History of the State from the Earliest Times through the Civil War*. Glendale, 1936.

• • •

Max Miller, *Reno*. N.Y., 1941.

New Hampshire

O. G. Hammond, *Checklist of New Hampshire Local History*. Concord, 1925.

• • •

Jeremy Belknap, *History of New Hampshire*. 3 vols. Boston, 1791–92. — 2 ed., Boston, 1813.
W. H. Fry, *New Hampshire as a Royal Province*. N.Y., 1908.
J. N. McClintock, *History of New Hampshire*. Boston, 1888.
Hobart Pillsbury, *New Hampshire*. 4 vols. N.Y., 1927.
E. S. Stackpole, *History of New Hampshire*. 4 vols. N.Y., [1916].
R. F. Upton, *Revolutionary New Hampshire*. Hanover, [1936].

• • •

C. H. Bell, *History of the Town of Exeter*. Exeter, 1888.
Benjamin Chase, *History of Old Chester*. Auburn, 1869.
J. R. Eastman, *History of the Town of Andover, N.H.* Concord, 1910.
L. W. Leonard and J. L. Seward, *The History of Dublin, New Hampshire*. Dublin, 1920.
[City History Commission], *History of Concord, New Hampshire*. Concord, 1903.
J. O. Lyford, *History of the Town of Canterbury*. 2 vols. Concord, 1912.

Ralph May, *Early Portsmouth History*. Boston, 1926.
R. W. Musgrove, *History of the Town of Bristol*. Bristol, 1904.
M. N. Rawson, *New Hampshire Borns a Town*. N.Y., 1942. — Alstead.
M. T. Runnels, *History of Sanbornton*. 2 vols. Boston, 1882.
H. H. Saunderson, *History of Charlestown*. Claremont, 1876.
Ezra Stearns, *History of Rindge, 1736–1874*. Boston, 1875.
W. A. Wallace, *The History of Canaan, New Hampshire*. Concord, 1910.

New Jersey

T. F. Chambers, *The Early Germans of New Jersey*. Dover, 1895.
W. R. Fee, *The Transition from Aristocracy to Democracy in New Jersey, 1789–1829*. Somerville, 1933.
E. J. Fisher, *New Jersey as a Royal Province 1738 to 1776*. N.Y., 1911.
T. F. Gordon, *History of New Jersey, from Its Discovery by Europeans to the Adoption of the Federal Constitution*. Trenton, 1834.
D. L. Kemmerer, *Path to Freedom, the Struggle for Self-Government in Colonial New Jersey, 1703–1776*. Princeton, 1940.
F. B. Lee, *New Jersey as a Colony and as a State*. 4 vols. N.Y., 1902.
Leonard Lundin, *Cockpit of the Revolution, the War for Independence in New Jersey*. Princeton, 1940.
R. P. McCormick, *Experiment in Independence, New Jersey in the Critical Period 1781–1789*. New Brunswick, 1950.
I. S. Mulford, *Civil and Political History of New Jersey*. Camden, 1848.
Samuel Smith, *History of the Colony of Nova-Caesaria, or New Jersey*. Burlington, 1765.
E. P. Tanner, *The Province of New Jersey 1664–1738*. N.Y., 1908.
H. F. Wilson, *et al., Outline History of New Jersey*. New Brunswick, 1950.

¤ ¤ ¤

Joseph Atkinson, *History of Newark*. Newark, 1878.
George De Cou, *Burlington: A Provincial Capital*. Phila., [1945].
Entertaining a Nation. Long Branch, 1940. — WPA Writers' Project.
J. F. Hageman, *History of Princeton*. 2 vols. Phila., 1879.
E. F. Hatfield, *History of Elizabeth*. N.Y., 1868.
A. M. Heston, *Absegami: Annals of Eyren Haven and Atlantic City, 1609–1904*. 2 vols. [Camden], 1904.
A. M. Heston, *South Jersey, a History 1664–1924*. 4 vols. N.Y., 1924.
A History of the City of Newark, New Jersey. 3 vols. N.Y., 1913.
A. D. Mellick, Jr., *The Story of an Old Farm*. Somerville, 1889.
O. E. Monnette, *First Settlers of Ye Plantations of Piscataway and Woodbridge Olde East New Jersey, 1664–1714*. 4 vols. Los Angeles, 1930–35.
J. S. Sickler, *The History of Salem County, New Jersey*. Salem, [1937].
E. R. Walker, *et al., A History of Trenton, 1679–1929*. 2 vols. Princeton, 1929.
F. A. Westervelt, *History of Bergen County, New Jersey, 1630–1923*. 3 vols. N.Y., 1923.

New Mexico

Bancroft, *Arizona and New Mexico*.
A. F. Bandelier and F. R. Bandelier, *Historical Documents Relating to New Mexico, Nueva Vizcaya, and Approaches thereto, to 1773*. 3 vols. Wash., 1923.
Erna Fergusson, *New Mexico, a Pageant of Three Peoples*. N.Y., 1951.
R. E. Twitchell, *The Leading Facts of New Mexican History*. 5 vols. Cedar Rapids, 1911.

New York

C. A. Flagg and J. T. Jennings, "Bibliography of New York Colonial History," N.Y. State Library, *Bull.*, No. 56, "Bibliography, 24" (1901).

¤ ¤ ¤

D. S. Alexander, *A Political History of the State of New York, 1774–1882*. 3 vols. N.Y., 1906–09.
W. J. van Balen, *Holland aan de Hudson*. Amsterdam, 1943.

J. R. Brodhead, *History of the State of New York.* 2 vols. Vol. I, 1609–1664, N.Y., 1853; Vol. II, 1664–1691, N.Y., 1871.

A. C. Flick, ed., *History of the State of New York.* 10 vols. N.Y., 1933–37.

D. R. Fox, *Yankees and Yorkers.* N.Y., 1940.

F. W. Halsey, *The Old New York Frontier, 1614–1800.* N.Y., 1901.

J. D. Hammond, *History of Political Parties in the State of New York.* 2 vols. Cooperstown, 1846.

E. L. Raesly, *Portrait of New Netherland.* N.Y., 1945.

G. W. Schuyler, *Colonial New York: Phillip Schuyler and His Family.* 2 vols. N.Y., 1885.

o   o   o

R. G. Albion, *The Rise of New York Port, 1815–1860.* N.Y., 1939.

C. W. Baird, *History of Rye, New York.* N.Y., 1871.

R. W. Bingham, *The Cradle of the Queen City, a History of Buffalo to the Incorporation of the City.* Buffalo, 1931.

M. L. Booth, *History of the City of New York.* N.Y., 1880.

Hugh Bradley, *Such Was Saratoga.* N.Y., 1940.

A. A. Chapin, *Greenwich Village.* N.Y., 1917.

J. A. Dix, *History of the Parish of Trinity Church in the City of New York.* 5 vols. N.Y., 1898–1950.

Robert Ernst, *Immigrant Life in New York City, 1825–1863.* N.Y., 1949.

E. R. Foreman, *Centennial History of Rochester, New York.* 4 vols. Rochester, 1931–34.

Frank Hasbrouck, *The History of Dutchess County, New York.* Poughkeepsie, 1909.

J. T. Horton, *History of Northwestern New York.* 3 vols., N.Y., [1947].

G. R. Howell, *Early History of Southampton, L.I.* 2 ed. Albany, 1887.

M. J. Lamb, *History of the City of New York.* 2 vols. N.Y., 1877–80.

Blake McKelvey, *Rochester: The Water-Power City 1812–54: The Flower City 1855–90.* 2 vols. Cambridge, 1945–49. — In progress.

Frank Monaghan and Marvin Lowenthal, *This Was New York, the Nation's Capital in 1789.* Garden City, N.Y., 1943.

J. H. Monroe, *Schenectady, Ancient and Modern 1661–1914.* Geneva, 1914.

Jacqueline Overton, *Long Island's Story.* Garden City, N.Y. [1929].

James Riker, *Revised History of Harlem.* N.Y., 1904.

E. M. Ruttenber, *History of the County of Orange . . . with a History of the Town and City of Newburgh.* Newburgh, 1875.

J. T. Scharf, *History of Westchester County, New York.* 2 vols. Phila., 1886.

Marius Schoonmaker, *History of Kingston, New York, from Its Early Settlement to the Year 1820.* N.Y., 1888.

W. R. Shepherd, *The Story of New Amsterdam.* N.Y., [1926].

Esther Singleton, *Social New York under the Georges 1714–1776.* N.Y., 1902.

H. R. Stiles, *The Civil, Political, Professional and Ecclesiastical History and Commercial and Industrial Record of the City of Brooklyn, New York, 1683–1884.* N.Y., [1884].

H. R. Stiles, *History of the City of Brooklyn.* 3 vols. Brooklyn, 1867–70.

I. N. P. Stokes, *Iconography of Manhattan Island.* 6 vols. N.Y., 1895–1928.

H. C. Syrett, *The City of Brooklyn, 1865–1898.* N.Y., 1944.

B. F. Thompson, *History of Long Island.* 3 vols. N.Y., 1918.

Orsamus Turner, *History of the Pioneer Settlement of Phelps and Gorham's Purchase.* Rochester, 1870.

Orsamus Turner, *Pioneer History of the Holland Purchase.* Buffalo, 1849.

M. G. Van Rensselaer, *History of the City of New York in the Seventeenth Century.* 2 vols. N.Y., 1909.

Epher Whitaker, *History of Southold, L.I.: Its First Century.* Southold, 1881. R. ed., C. E. Craven, ed., Princeton, 1931.

J. G. Wilson, ed., *Memorial History of the City of New York.* 4 vols. N.Y., 1892–93.

North Carolina

W. K. Boyd and J. G. deR. Hamilton, *A Syllabus of North Carolina History, 1584–1876.* Durham, 1913.

o   o   o

S. A. Ashe, *History of North Carolina.* 2 vols. Greensboro, 1908.
W. K. Boyd, *History of North Carolina 1783–1860.* 2 vols. Chi., 1919.
H. T. Lefler, *North Carolina History Told by Contemporaries.* Chapel Hill, 1934.
G. G. Johnson, *Ante-Bellum North Carolina; a Social History.* Chapel Hill, 1937.
C. L. Raper, *North Carolina; a Study in English Colonial Government.* N.Y., 1904.
David Schenck, *North Carolina · 1780–'81.* Raleigh, 1889.
Hugh Williamson, *History of North Carolina.* 2 vols. Phila., 1812.

❋ ❋ ❋

W. C. Allen, *The Annals of Haywood County, North Carolina.* N.p., 1935.
J. P. Arthur, *Western North Carolina; a History (from 1730 to 1913).* Raleigh, 1914.
W. K. Boyd, *The Story of Durham, City of the South.* Durham, 1925.
C. L. Hunter, *Sketches of Western North Carolina.* Raleigh, 1877.
J. C. Leonard, *Centennial History of Davidson County, North Carolina.* 2 vols. Raleigh, 1927.
J. B. O'Neall and J. A. Chapman, *The Annals of Newberry.* Newberry, 1892.
Jethro Rumple, *A History of Rowan County, North Carolina.* Salisbury, 1881. — Reprinted, Salisbury, [1929].
W. L. Sherrill, *Annals of Lincoln County, North Carolina.* Charlotte, 1937.
F. A. Sondley, *A History of Buncombe County, North Carolina.* Asheville, 1930.
James Sprunt, *Chronicles of the Cape Fear River, 1660–1916.* Raleigh, 1916.
D. A. Thompkins, *History of Mecklenburg County and the City of Charlotte, 1740–1903.* Charlotte, 1903.

North Dakota

M. K. Armstrong, *The Early Empire Builders of the Great West.* St. Paul, 1901.
Compendium of History and Biography of North Dakota. Chi., 1900.
C. A. Lounsberry, *Early History of North Dakota.* Wash., 1919.

Ohio

W. D. Overman, "Index to Materials for the Study of Ohio History," *Ohio Arch. and Hist. Quar.*, XLIV (1935), 138.
P. G. Thomson, *A Bibliography of the State of Ohio; being a Catalogue of the Books and Pamphlets Relating to the History of the State, with Collations and Bibliographical and Critical Notes.* Cin., 1880.
P. G. Thomson, *Catalogue of Books Relating to the State of Ohio, the West and Northwest.* Cin., 1890.

❋ ❋ ❋

Henry Howe, *Historical Collections of Ohio.* Cin., 1847. — Also the Centennial Ed., 3 vols. Columbus, 1889–91.
E. O. Randall and D. J. Ryan, *History of Ohio, the Rise and Progress of an American State.* 5 vols. N.Y., 1912.
E. H. Roseboom and F. P. Weisenburger, *A History of Ohio,* Columbus, 1953.
Carl Wittke, ed., *The History of the State of Ohio.* 6 vols. Columbus, 1941–44.

❋ ❋ ❋

Henry Bushnell, *History of Granville, Licking County, Ohio.* Columbus, 1889.
C. L. de Chambrun, *Cincinnati, Story of the Queen City.* N.Y., 1939.
H. W. Crew, ed., *History of Dayton.* Dayton, 1889.
H. A. and K. B. Ford, *History of Cincinnati.* Cleve., 1881.
C. T. Greve, *Centennial History of Cincinnati.* 2 vols. Chi., 1904.
E. T. Heald and Edward Thornton, *The Stark County Story.* Canton, 1949.
A. H. Heiser, *Hamilton in the Making.* Oxford, 1941.
J. C. Hover, *et al.*, *Memoirs of the Miami Valley.* 3 vols. Chi., 1919.
J. H. Kennedy, *History of the City of Cleveland.* Cleve., 1896.
S. P. Orth, *A History of Cleveland, Ohio.* 3 vols. Chi., 1910.
F. H. Reighard, *A Standard History of Fulton County, Ohio.* 2 vols. Chi., 1920.
W. G. Rose, *Cleveland, the Making of a City.* Cleve., [1950].

T. J. Summers, *History of Marietta*. Marietta, 1903.
W. A. Taylor, *Centennial History of Columbus and Franklin County, Ohio*. 2 vols. Chi., 1909.
[The Samuel Bissell Memorial Library Association], *Twinsburg, Ohio, 1817–1917*. Twinsburg, 1917.
H. T. Upton, *History of the Western Reserve*. 3 vols. Chi., 1910.
N. O. Winter, *A History of Northwest Ohio*. 3 vols. Chi., 1917.

Oklahoma

E. E. Dale and M. L. Wardell, *Outline and References for Oklahoma History*. [Norman, 1924.]

◦   ◦   ◦

J. S. Buchanan and E. E. Dale, *A History of Oklahoma*, [Chi., 1924.]
E. E. Dale and M. L. Wardell, *History of Oklahoma*. N.Y., 1948.
Grant Foreman, *A History of Oklahoma*. Norman, 1942.
L. B. Hill, *History of the State of Oklahoma*. 2 vols. Chi., 1908.
J. B. Thoburn and M. H. Wright, *Oklahoma, a History of the State and Its People*. 4 vols. N.Y., 1929.

◦   ◦   ◦

Angie Debo, *Tulsa: From Creek Town to Oil Capital*. Norman, 1943.

Oregon

C. W. Smith, *Pacific Northwest Americana, a Check-List of Books and Pamphlets Relating to the History of the Pacific Northwest*. Olympia, 1909. — Rev. by Isabel Mayhew, Portland, 1950.

◦   ◦   ◦

H. H. Bancroft, *Oregon*. 2 vols. (*History of the Pacific States*, Vols. XXIV, XXV.) San Francisco, 1886–88.
H. H. Bancroft, *The Northwest Coast*. 2 vols. (*History of the Pacific States*, Vols. XXII, XXIII.) San Francisco, 1884.
C. H. Carey, *A General History of Oregon prior to 1861*. 2 vols. Portland, 1935–36.
J. W. Caughey, *History of the Pacific Coast*. Los Angeles, 1933.
G. W. Fuller, *A History of the Pacific Northwest*. 2 ed. N.Y., 1938.
Joseph Gaston, *The Centennial History of Oregon, 1811–1912*. Chi., 1912.
Washington Irving, *Astoria*. 2 vols. Phila., 1839.
H. S. Lyman, *History of Oregon*. 4 vols. N.Y., 1903.
Joseph Schafer, *A History of the Pacific Northwest*. N.Y., 1918.
H. W. Scott, *History of the Oregon Country*. 6 vols. Cambridge,.1924.

◦   ◦   ◦

Orvil Dodge, *Pioneer History of Coos and Curry Counties, Oregon*. Salem, 1898.
L. W. Moore, N. W. McCormack, G. W. McCready, *The Story of Eugene*. N.Y., 1949.

Pennsylvania

L. M. Bausman, *A Bibliography of Lancaster County, Pennsylvania, 1745–1912*. Phila., [1917].
A. C. Bining, "A Selected Bibliography of Secondary Works on Pennsylvania History," *Penn. Library Notes*, XIII (1933), 355.
C. W. Garrison, "The C.W.A. Survey of Historical Source Material in Pennsylvania," *Penn. Hist.*, I (1934), 217.
L. W. H. Johnston, "The Government-Supported Historical Survey of Pennsylvania in the Western Counties," *Western Penn. Hist. Mag.*, XVIII (1935), 209.
Pennsylvania State Library, *Check-List of Pennsylvania County, Town, and Township Histories, 1794–1892*. Harrisburg, 1892.

◦   ◦   ◦

A. S. Bolles, *Pennsylvania, Province and State, 1609–1790*. 2 vols. Phila., 1899.
W. F. Dunaway, *A History of Pennsylvania*. N.Y., 1948.

Samuel Hazard, *Annals of Pennsylvania, from the Discovery of the Delaware, 1609–1682.* Phila., 1850.
H. M. Jenkins, *Pennsylvania; Colonial and Federal; a History, 1608–1903.* 3 vols. Phila., 1903.
C. P. Keith, *Chronicles of Pennsylvania from the English Revolution to the Peace of Aix-la-Chapelle, 1688–1748.* 2 vols. Phila., 1917.
P. S. Klein, *Pennsylvania Politics, 1817–1832; a Game without Rules.* Phila., 1940.
Robert Proud, *History of Pennsylvania, from . . . 1681, till after the Year 1742.* 2 vols. Phila., 1797–98.
Isaac Sharpless, *History of Quaker Government in Pennsylvania.* 2 vols. Phila., 1898–99.
W. R. Shepherd, *History of Proprietary Government in Pennsylvania.* N.Y., 1896.

＊   ＊   ＊

R. W. Albright, *Two Centuries of Reading, Pennsylvania, 1748–1948.* Reading, 1948.
L. D. Baldwin, *Pittsburgh, the Story of a City.* Pitt., 1937.
J. H. Bausman, *History of Beaver County, Pennsylvania and Its Centennial Celebration.* 2 vols. N.Y., 1904.
S. J. Buck and E. H. Buck, *The Planting of Civilization in Western Pennsylvania.* Pitt., 1939.
Struthers Burt, *Philadelphia, Holy Experiment.* Garden City, N.Y., 1945.
H. L. Collins, *Philadelphia, a Story of Progress.* 4 vols. N.Y., 1941.
W. W. H. Davis, *The History of Bucks County, Pennsylvania.* Doylestown, 1876.
G. T. Fleming, *History of Pittsburgh and Environs.* 4 vols. N.Y., 1922.
James Hadden, *A History of Uniontown.* Uniontown, 1913.
C. F. Heverly, *History of the Towandas, 1770–1886.* Towanda, 1886.
N. H. Keyser, *et al., History of Old Germantown.* Germantown, 1907.
H. M. J. Klein, *Lancaster County, Pennsylvania, a History.* 4 vols. N.Y., 1924.
W. J. McKnight, *A Pioneer Outline History of Northwestern Pennsylvania.* Phila., 1905.
J. I. Mombert, *Authentic History of Lancaster County.* Lancaster, 1869.
J. B. Nolan, *The Foundation of the Town of Reading in Pennsylvania.* Reading, 1929.
E. P. Oberholtzer, *Philadelphia, a History of the City and Its People.* 4 vols. Phila., [1912].
Agnes Repplier, *Philadelphia, the Place and the People.* N.Y., 1898.
William Riddle, *The Story of Lancaster: Old and New.* Lancaster, 1917.
J. T. Scharf and Thompson Westcott, *History of Philadelphia, 1609–1884.* 3 vols. Phila., 1884.
J. F. Watson, *Annals of Philadelphia and Pennsylvania, in the Olden Time.* 2 vols. Phila., 1857.
H. B. Wright, *Historical Sketches of Plymouth.* Phila., 1873.
J. R. Young, *Memorial History of City of Philadelphia.* 2 vols. N.Y., 1895–98.

Rhode Island

J. R. Bartlett, *Bibliography of Rhode Island.* Providence, 1864.
C. S. Brigham, "List of Books upon Rhode Island History," *Rhode Island Educational Circulars,* Hist. Ser. I (1908).
C. S. Brigham, *Bibliography of Rhode Island History.* [Boston], 1902.

＊   ＊   ＊

S. G. Arnold, *History of Rhode Island.* 2 vols. N.Y., 1859.
T. W. Bicknell, *The History of the State of Rhode Island and Providence Plantations.* 4 vols. N.Y., 1920.
H. M. Chapin, *Documentary History of Rhode Island.* 2 vols. Providence, 1916–19.
Edward Field, *State of Rhode Island and Providence Plantations at the End of the Century: A History.* 3 vols. Boston, 1902.
I. B. Richman, *Rhode Island, Its Making and Its Meaning.* 2 vols. N.Y., 1902.
W. B. Weeden, *Early Rhode Island: A Social History of the People.* N.Y., [1910].

＊   ＊   ＊

M. A. DeW. Howe, *Bristol.* Cambridge, 1930.
G. S. Kimball, *Providence in Colonial Times.* Boston, [1912].

W. H. Munro, *Tales of an Old Sea Port*. Princeton, 1917.
E. R. Potter, *Early History of Narragansett*. Providence, 1835.
C. O. F. Thompson, *Sketches of Old Bristol*. Providence, 1942.

South Carolina

J. H. Easterby, *Guide to the Study and Reading of South Carolina History*. Columbia, 1950.

❋ ❋ ❋

A. H. Hirsch, *The Huguenots of Colonial South Carolina*. Durham, 1928.
Edward McCrady, *The History of South Carolina 1670–1783*. 4 vols. N.Y., 1897–1902.
R. L. Meriwether, *The Expansion of South Carolina, 1729–65*. Kingsport, 1940.
David Ramsay, *History of South Carolina, from its First Settlement in 1670, to the Year 1808*. 2 vols. Charleston, 1809.
W. R. Smith, *South Carolina as a Royal Province, 1719–1776*. N.Y., 1903.
Yates Snowden, *History of South Carolina*. 5 vols. Chi., 1920.
D. D. Wallace, *The History of South Carolina*. 4 vols. N.Y., 1934.

❋ ❋ ❋

W. W. Boddie, *History of Williamsburg*. Columbia, 1923.
E. L. Green, *A History of Richland County, 1732–1805*. Columbia, 1932.
T. J. Kirkland and R. M. Kennedy, *Historic Camden*. 2 vols. Columbia, 1905–25.
H. H. Ravenel, *Charleston, the Place and the People*. N.Y., 1906.
R. G. Rhett, *Charleston, an Epic of Carolina*. Richmond, 1940.
A. S. Salley, *The History of Orangeburg County, South Carolina*. Orangeburg, 1898.
W. W. Sellers, *A History of Marion County, South Carolina*. Columbia, 1902.

South Dakota

O. W. Coursey, *Literature of South Dakota*. 4 ed. Mitchell, [1925].
Doane Robinson, *History of South Dakota*. 2 vols. [N.p.], 1904.
H. S. Schell, *South Dakota, Its Beginnings and Growth*. N.Y., [1942].
G. M. Smith, *South Dakota, Its History and Its People*. 5 vols. Chi., 1915.

Tennessee

T. P. Abernethy, *From Frontier to Plantation in Tennessee*. Chapel Hill, 1932.
W. H. Combs and W. E. Cole, *Tennessee, a Political Study*. Knoxville, 1940.
J. W. Caldwell, *Studies in the Constitutional History of Tennessee*. Cin., 1907.
W. T. Hale and D. L. Merritt, *A History of Tennessee and Tennesseans*. 8 vols. Chi., 1913.
P. M. Hamer, ed., *Tennessee; a History, 1673–1932*. 4 vols. N.Y., 1933.
J. T. Moore and A. P. Foster, *Tennessee, the Volunteer State, 1769–1923*. 4 vols. Chi., 1923.

❋ ❋ ❋

R. E. Barclay, *Ducktown Back in Raht's Time*. Chapel Hill, [1946].
G. M. Capers, *The Biography of a River Town; Memphis, Its Heroic Age*. Chapel Hill, 1939.
Shields McIlwaine, *Memphis, Down in Dixie*. N.Y., [1948].
Henry McRaven, *Nashville, Athens of the South*. Chapel Hill, 1949.
E. I. Williams, *Historic Madison, the Story of Jackson and Madison County, Tennessee*. Jackson, 1946.
John Wooldridge, ed., *History of Nashville, Tennessee*. Nashville, 1890.

Texas

C. W. Raines, *A Bibliography of Texas; being a Descriptive List of Books, Pamphlets, and Documents Relating to Texas in Print and Manuscript since 1536*. Austin, 1896.
E. W. Winkler, *Check List of Texas Imprints 1846–1860*. Austin, 1949.

❋ ❋ ❋

H. H. Bancroft, *North Mexican States and Texas*. 2 vols. (*History of the Pacific States*, Vols. X, XI.) San Francisco, 1883–89.

J. H. Brown, *History of Texas.* 2 vols. St. Louis, [1892–93].
F. W. Johnson, *A History of Texas and Texans.* 5 vols. Chi., 1914.
L. W. Newton and H. P. Gambrell, *Texas Yesterday and Today.* Dallas, [1949].
R. N. Richardson, *Texas, the Lone Star State.* N.Y., 1943.
J. H. Smith, *The Annexation of Texas.* N.Y., 1911.
D. G. Wooten, ed., *A Comprehensive History of Texas.* Dallas, 1898.
L. J. Wortham, *A History of Texas from Wilderness to Commonwealth.* 5 vols. Fort Worth, 1924.
J. W. Rogers, *The Lusty Texans of Dallas.* N.Y., 1951.
I. T. Taylor and N. A. Taylor, *The Cavalcade of Jackson County.* San Antonio, [1938].
Owen White, *Out of the Desert, the Historical Romance of El Paso.* El Paso, 1923.

Utah

J. C. Alter, *Utah, the Storied Domain.* 3 vols. Chi., 1932.
H. H. Bancroft, *Utah.* (*History of the Pacific States,* Vol. XXI.) San Francisco, 1889.
M. R. Hunter, *Utah in Her Western Setting.* Salt Lake City, 1943.
M. R. Hunter, *Utah, the Story of Her People, 1540–1947.* Salt Lake City, 1946.
O. F. Whitney, *History of Utah.* 4 vols. Salt Lake City, 1892–1904.
L. E. Young, *The Founding of Utah.* N.Y., 1923.

Vermont

M. D. Gilman, *Bibliography of Vermont.* Burlington, 1897.
M. B. Jones, *List of Additions to Gilman's Bibliography of Vermont.* Boston, 1926.

◦   ◦   ◦

Ira Allen, *Natural and Political History of the State of Vermont.* London, 1798.
W. H. Crockett, *Vermont, the Green Mountain State.* 4 vols. N.Y., 1921.
B. H. Hall, *History of Eastern Vermont, from its Earliest Settlement to the Close of the Eighteenth Century.* N.Y., 1858.
Hiland Hall, *History of Vermont, from Its Discovery to Its Admission into the Union in 1791.* Albany, 1868.
J. P. Lee, *Uncommon Vermont.* Rutland, [1926].
D. M. Ludlum, *Social Ferment in Vermont, 1791–1850.* N.Y., 1939.
E. W. Newton, *The Vermont Story.* Montpelier, 1949.
C. M. Thompson, *Independent Vermont.* Boston, 1942.
[Vermont Historical Society], *Essays in the Early History of Vermont.* Montpelier, 1943.
[Vermont Historical Society], *Essays in the Social and Economic History of Vermont.* Montpelier, 1943.
Chilton Williamson, *Vermont in Quandary: 1763–1825.* Montpelier, 1949.

◦   ◦   ◦

E. L. Bogart, *Peacham.* Montpelier, 1948.
M. R. Cabot, *Annals of Brattleboro, 1681–1895.* 2 vols. Brattleboro, 1921.
A. E. Cudworth, *The History with Genealogical Sketches of Londonderry.* Montpelier, [1935].
W. M. Newton, *History of Barnard, Vermont.* 2 vols. [Burlington, 1928.]
H. H. Vail, *Pomfret.* 2 vols. Boston, [1930].
[Vermont Historical Society], *The Upper Connecticut.* Montpelier, 1943.

Virginia

L. J. Cappon, *Bibliography of Virginia History since 1865.* Charlottesville, 1930.
E. G. Swem, "A Bibliography of Virginia," Va. State Library, *Bull.,* VIII, Nos. 2–4, X, Nos. 1–4, XII, Nos. 1–2, XVII, No. 2 (1915–32).

◦   ◦   ◦

M. P. Andrews, *The Soul of a Nation.* N.Y., 1943.
M. P. Andrews, *Virginia the Old Dominion.* Garden City, N.Y., 1937.
L. C. Bell, *The Old Free State.* 2 vols. Richmond, [1927].

Robert Beverley, *History of Virginia, in Four Parts (1584–1720)*. 2 ed. London, 1722. —
New ed., L. B. Wright, ed., Chapel Hill, 1947.
Alexander Brown, *The First Republic in America*. Boston, 1898.
P. A. Bruce, *Economic History of Virginia in the Seventeenth Century*. 2 vols. N.Y., 1896.
P. A. Bruce, *Institutional History of Virginia in the Seventeenth Century*. 2 vols. N.Y.,
1910.
C. W. Sams, *The Conquest of Virginia*. 4 vols. Norfolk, 1916–39.
William Stith, *History of the First Discovery and Settlement of Virginia*. Williamsburg,
1747.
T. J. Wertenbaker, *Patrician and Plebian in Virginia*. Charlottesville, 1910.
T. J. Wertenbaker, *The Planters of Colonial Virginia*. Princeton, 1922.
T. J. Wertenbaker, *Virginia under the Stuarts, 1607–1688*. Princeton, 1914.

o   o   o

S. M. Ames, *Studies of the Virginia Eastern Shore in the Seventeenth Century*. Richmond,
1940.
Alfred Bagly, *King and Queen County, Virginia*. N.Y., 1908.
J. B. Boddie, *Seventeenth Century Isle of Wight County, Virginia*. Chi., [1938].
W. A. Christian, *Richmond, Her Past and Present*. Richmond, 1912.
M. C. Clement, *The History of Pittsylvania County, Virginia*. Lynchburg, 1929.
Dinwiddie County. [Richmond, 1942.] — W.P.A. Writers' Project.
H. C. Forman, *Jamestown and St. Mary's Buried Cities of Romance*. Balt., 1938.
K. G. Greene, *Winchester, Virginia and Its Beginnings, 1743–1814*. Strasburg, 1926.
J. H. Gwathmey, *Twelve Virginia Counties*. Richmond, 1937.
J. N. Harman, *Annals of Tazewell County, Virginia 1800–1922*. 2 vols. Richmond, 1922.
[Fairfax Harrison], *Landmarks of Old Prince William*. 2 vols. Richmond, 1924.
D. E. Johnston, *History of Middle New River Settlements*. Huntington, 1906.
Samuel Kercheval, *History of the Valley of Virginia*. Winchester, 1833. 4 ed. Strasburg,
1925.
G. M. Moore, *Seaport in Virginia*. Richmond, [1949].
Prince William, the Story of Its People and Its Places. [Richmond, 1941.] — W.P.A.
Writers' Project.
H. J. Eckenrode, ed., *Richmond, Capital of Virginia*. [Richmond], 1938.
J. A. Waddell, *Annals of Augusta County, Virginia*. Richmond, 1886.
T. J. Wertenbaker, *Norfolk Historic Southern Port*. Durham, 1931.
Marshall Wingfield, *A History of Caroline County, Virginia*. Richmond, 1924.
J. C. Wise, *Ye Kingdome of Accawmacke or the Eastern Shore of Virginia in the Seven-
teenth Century*. Richmond, 1911.

Washington (see also: Oregon)

H. E. Barko and Catherine Bullard, *History of the State of Washington*. Boston, [1947].
Herbert Hunt and F. C. Kaylor, *Washington West of the Cascades*. Chi., 1917.
C. A. Snowden, *History of Washington*. 4 vols. N.Y., 1909.

o   o   o

C. H. Hanford, *Seattle and Environs 1852–1924*. Chi., 1924.

West Virginia

"Bibliography of West Virginia," State Dept. of Archives and Hist., *Report*, 1938.

o   o   o

C. H. Ambler, *West Virginia, the Mountain State*. N.Y., 1940.
T. C. Miller, *West Virginia and Its People*. 3 vols. N.Y., 1913.
[Sylvester Myers], *Myers' History of West Virginia*. 2 vols. [Wheeling, 1915.]
M. P. Shawkey, *West Virginia in History, Life, Literature and Industry*. 5 vols. Chi., 1928.

o   o   o

M. K. Bushong, *A History of Jefferson County, West Virginia*. Charles Town, 1941.
J. T. Peters and J. B. Carden, *History of Fayette County, West Virginia*. Charleston, 1926.
E. C. Smith, *A History of Lewis County, West Virginia*. Weston, 1920.

Wisconsin

Leroy Schlinkert, comp., *Subject Bibliography of Wisconsin History*. Madison, 1947.

❖ ❖ ❖

H. C. Campbell, ed., *Wisconsin in Three Centuries, 1634–1905*. 4 vols. N.Y., [1906].
History of Northern Wisconsin. Chi., 1881.
L. P. Kellogg, *The British Régime in Wisconsin and the Northwest*. Madison, 1935.
L. P. Kellogg, *The French Régime in Wisconsin and the Northwest*. Madison, 1925.
Frederick Merk, *Economic History of Wisconsin during the Civil War Decade*. Madison, 1916.
W. F. Raney, *Wisconsin, a Story of Progress*. N.Y., 1940.
R. G. Thwaites, *Wisconsin; the Americanization of a French Settlement*. Boston, 1908.
E. B. Usher, *Wisconsin, Its Story and Biography, 1848–1913*. 8 vols. Chi., 1914.

❖ ❖ ❖

D. S. Durrie, *History of Madison*. Madison, 1874.
E. H. Neville, S. G. Martin, and D. B. Martin, *Historic Green Bay, 1634–1840*. Green Bay, 1893.
Theodore Roemer, *St. Joseph in Appleton*. Appleton, 1943.
A. H. Sanford and H. J. Hirshheimer, *A History of La Crosse, Wisconsin, 1841–1900*. La Crosse, 1951.
Joseph Schafer, *Four Wisconsin Counties, Prairie and Forest*. Madison, 1927.
Bayrd Still, *Milwaukee, the History of a City*. Madison, 1948.

Wyoming

H. H. Bancroft, *Nevada, Colorado, and Wyoming*. (*History of the Pacific States*, Vol. XX.) San Francisco, 1890.
C. G. Coutant, *History of Wyoming*. Vol. I. Laramie, 1899.
Velma Linford, *Wyoming, Frontier State*. Denver, 1947.

❖ ❖ ❖

A. J. Mokler, *History of Natrona County Wyoming, 1888–1922*. Chi., 1923.
Nolie Mumey, *The Teton Mountains, Their History and Tradition*. Denver, 1947.

63. SCHOLARLY USES OF HISTORICAL FICTION

A historical novel, as generally understood, is a work of fiction which deals with bygone days in a manner intended to convey historical verisimilitude. The author usually poses a story of imaginary characters against a background of actual men and events. A variant of the type is fictionalized biography, which treats only real historical figures. Gertrude Atherton's portrayal of Alexander Hamilton as *The Conqueror* (1902) and Catherine Drinker Bowen's delineation of Justice Oliver Wendell Holmes as the *Yankee from Olympus* (1944) are notable examples. This genre involves special difficulties for the author, who is constantly tempted to invent conversations, thoughts, and acts unsupported by documentary evidence. The reader, for his part, never knows where history ends and fancy begins.

Even historical novels of the conventional sort vary greatly in factual accuracy. Nevertheless, such writings have often awakened in young people their first interest in the past and have enabled their elders to imbibe their history painlessly. The best historical fiction rests on conscientious research. W. D. Edmonds, for example, describes the way he gathered data for *Drums along the Mohawk* in "How You Begin a Novel," *Atlantic Monthly*, CLVIII (1936), 189, and Elizabeth Page appends a bibliography of some 240 items to her *Tree of Liberty*. How well one of S. Weir Mitchell's romances meets scholarly standards is shown by Max Farrand in "Hugh Wynne, a Historical Novel," *Wash. Hist. Quar.*, I (1906–07), 101. For a more recent example, see Grace L. Nute's critique of Kenneth Roberts' *Northwest Passage*, in *Minn. Hist.*, XIX (1938), 76. Even when a much larger factor of error enters in, these works may still impart a substantially true impression of the times and of the reasons men acted as they did. With the exception of a few earlier writers, like Hawthorne who excelled in this department of letters as in others, the historical novel has reached its highest development in the aging twentieth century. Though there are exceptions, the modern tendency is to reject a romantic or drum-and-trumpet treatment for a homelier and more believable re-creation of the past. The writers seek to spotlight the common experience rather than the exploits of the great or the notorious.

For the scholar, however, this type of historical fiction has less value than two others which are not ordinarily so labeled. One consists of novels that helped make history. On first meeting Harriet Beecher Stowe, President Lincoln is reported to have said, "So you are the little woman who wrote the book that made this great war!" Volumes like *Uncle Tom's Cabin* are primary sources for studying the factors that influenced political or social action. Keyed to an emotional pitch, and reaching an enormous number of readers, they have often proved more potent agencies of propaganda than the utterances of statesmen.

The other kind comprises novels and stories which depict human situations in the author's time for their own sake. With the passage of years these portrayals become grist for the historian as firsthand accounts of other days. Broadly speaking, such works repay the historical student to the extent they are realistic, that is, to the extent they picture persons, emotions, and conditions with fidelity to fact. But there are nearly as many shades and degrees of realism as there are authors. In the hands of a William Dean Howells such writings deal with the commonplace rather than the unusual: Howells sought to delineate the "work-worn, care-worn, brave, kindly face" of the everyday world. Since the 1890's a growing number of novelists have stressed the grim and sordid in human relations. Many volumes of this latter sort shade off into the category described in the preceding paragraph.

While both of these types of literature must be used with critical caution, they form a body of historical data too often neglected by the professional scholar.

64. SELECT LIST OF HISTORICAL NOVELS AND SHORT STORIES

There are numerous guides to historical fiction. For the scholar perhaps the most rewarding are E. E. Leisy, *The American Historical Novel* (Norman, 1950), which is confined to tales that treat of earlier times than those in which the authors lived, and O. W. Coan and R. C. Lillard, eds., *America in Fiction* (3 ed., Stanford, 1949), which provides an annotated list of all three types of these writings as defined in § 63. More specialized are F. P. Donovan, *The Railroad in Literature* (Boston, 1940), and R. W. Smith, comp., "Catalogue of the Chief Novels and Short Stories Dealing with the Civil War and Its Effects, 1861–99," *Bull. Bibliog.*, XVI (1939), 193, XVII (1940), 10, 33, 53.

The select list below includes both novels and volumes of short stories. These are grouped in broad periods according to the chronological setting of the plots, and are arranged within each period alphabetically by author. When no time or incident is indicated after the title, the action is contemporaneous with the writer's life. The first date of publication in book form is cited. Titles marked with asterisks (°) indicate volumes of a socially purposeful or opinion-forming character. A dagger (†) designates a volume valuable particularly for social documentation of the author's own time. It should be borne in mind that the distinction between these two is often difficult to draw.

1607–1783

Edward Bellamy (1850–98), *The Duke of Stockbridge* (1900), Shays's rebellion.

James Boyd (1888–1944), *Drums* (1925), the Revolution.

Roger Burlingame (1889–   ), *Three Bags Full* (1936), the Revolution.

LeGrand Cannon, Jr. (1899–   ), *Look to the Mountain* (1942) and *Come Home at Even* (1951), 18th-century New England.

R. W. Chambers (1865–1933), *Cardigan* (1901), *The Maid-at-Arms* (1902), and *The Reckoning* (1905), the Revolution.

Winston Churchill (1871–1947), *Richard Carvel* (1899), the Revolution.

John Esten Cooke (1830–86), *The Virginia Comedians* (1854), pre-Revolutionary Virginia.

James Fenimore Cooper (1789–1851), *The Spy* (1821), the Revolution; *The Pioneers* (1823), *The Last of the Mohicans* (1826), *The Pathfinder* (1840), and *The Deerslayer* (1841), 18th-century New York frontier.

W. S. Davis (1877–1930), *Gilman of Redford* (1927), the Revolution around Boston.

W. D. Edmonds (1903–   ), *Drums along the Mohawk* (1936), the New York frontier in the Revolution.

Inglis Fletcher (1888–   ), *Raleigh's Eden* (1940) and *Toil of the Brave* (1946), North Carolina in the Revolution.

Esther Forbes (1891–   ), *A Mirror for Witches* (1928) and *Paradise* (1937), 17th-century Massachusetts; *Johnny Tremain* (1943), Boston on the eve of the Revolutionary War.

P. L. Ford (1865–1902), *Janice Meredith* (1899), the Revolution.

Harold Frederic (1856–98), *In the Valley* (1890), the Mohawk Valley during the Revolution.

Caroline Gordon (1895–   ), *Green Centuries* (1941), the pre-Revolutionary frontier of Tennessee and Kentucky.

Nathaniel Hawthorne (1804–64), *Twice-Told Tales* (2 vols. 1837–42) and *The Scarlet Letter* (1850), colonial Massachusetts.

Washington Irving (1783–1859), *A History of New York by Diedrich Knickerbocker* (1809), New Netherland.

Mary Johnston (1870–1936), *To Have and to Hold* (1900), early 17th-century Virginia; *Audrey* (1902), early 18th-century Virginia.

J. P. Kennedy (1795–1870), *Horse-Shoe Robinson* (1835), the Revolution in the Carolinas.

Bruce Lancaster (1896–   ), *Guns of Burgoyne* (1939) and *Trumpet to Arms* (1944), the Revolution.

S. Weir Mitchell (1829–1914), *Hugh Wynne, Free Quaker* (1897), the Revolution.

Honoré W. Morrow (1880–1940), *Let the King Beware!* (1936), the Revolution.

Elizabeth Page (1889–   ), *The Tree of Liberty* (1939), Virginia, 1754–1806.

Kenneth Roberts (1885–   ), *Arundel* (1930), *Rabble in Arms* (1933), and *Oliver Wiswell* (1940), the Revolution; *Northwest Passage* (1937), the French and Indian War and later.

William Gilmore Simms (1806–70), *The Yemassee* (1835), a South Carolina Indian conspiracy, 1715; *The Partisan* (1835), *The Scout* (1841), and *The Forayers* (1855), South Carolina during the Revolution.

Maurice Thompson (1844–1901), *Alice of Old Vincennes* (1900), the George Rogers Clark expedition of 1779.

Samuel Hopkins Adams (1871–   ), *The Gorgeous Hussy* (1934), the Jacksonian period.

Hervey Allen (1889–1949), *Action at Aquila* (1938), the Civil War.

T. S. Arthur (1809–85), °*Six Nights with the Washingtonians* (1842), and °*Ten Nights in a Bar-room* (1854), the evils of intemperance.

J. G. Baldwin (1815–64), †*The Flush Times of Alabama and Mississippi* (1853), contemporary backwoods life.

Ambrose Bierce (1842–1914), *In the Midst of Life* (1898), the Civil War.

James Boyd (1888–1944), *Marching On* (1927), the Civil War; *The Long Hunt* (1930), post-Revolutionary North Carolina and Tennessee.

H. H. Brackenridge (1748–1816), *Modern Chivalry* (1792–1815), post-Revolutionary times in western Pennsylvania.

Louis Bromfield (1896–   ), *The Farm* (1933), Ohio from 1815 to 1915; *Wild Is the River* (1941), New Orleans during the Civil War.

Charles Brockden Brown (1771–1810), *Arthur Mervyn* (1799–1800), the Philadelphia yellow-fever epidemic in the 1790's; *Edgar Huntley* (1799), the frontier.

George W. Cable (1844–1925), *The Grandissimes* (1880), New Orleans in the early 19th century; *Dr. Sevier* (1885), New Orleans during the Civil War.

Carl Carmer (1893–   ), *Genesee Fever* (1941), the Genesee Valley of New York in the 1790's.

Winston Churchill (1871–1947), *The Crisis* (1901), Missouri during the Civil War; *The Crossing* (1904), the Old Northwest in the Revolutionary and Federalist eras; *Coniston* (1906), New Hampshire politics in the Jackson era.

James Fenimore Cooper (1789–1851), *The Prairie* (1827), the trans-Mississippi frontier.

Stephen Crane (1871–1900), *The Red Badge of Courage* (1895), the Civil War.

August Derleth (1909–   ), *Bright Journey* (1940), fur trading in the Old Northwest, 1812–43.

Clifford Dowdey (1904–   ), *Bugles Blow No More* (1937), Richmond during the Civil War; *Tidewater* (1943), the West Tennessee frontier after 1837.

W. D. Edmonds (1903–   ), *Rome Haul* (1929) and *Erie Water* (1933), the Erie Canal in the early days.

Edward Eggleston (1837–1902), *The Hoosier Schoolmaster* (1871) and *The Circuit Rider* (1874), backwoods life in Indiana and Ohio in first half of the 19th century.

Leonard Ehrlich (1905–   ), *God's Angry Man* (1932), John Brown.

William Faulkner (1897–   ), *"Absalom, Absalom!"* (1936), Mississippi plantation life in the 1830's.

Esther Forbes (1891–   ), *The Running of the Tide* (1948), Salem about 1800.

John Fox, Jr. (1863–1919), *The Little Shepherd of Kingdom Come* (1903), Kentucky during the Civil War.

G. W. Gabriel (1890–   ), *I, James Lewis* (1932), an expedition around Cape Horn to Oregon in 1811.

Ellen Glasgow (1874–   ), *The Battle-Ground* (1902), Virginia during the Civil War.

Herbert Gorman (1893–   ), *The Wine of San Lorenzo* (1945), the Mexican War.

A. B. Guthrie (1901–   ), *The Big Sky* (1947), the trans-Mississippi West in the 1830's; *The Way West* (1949), the Oregon Trail in the 1840's.

Edward Everett Hale (1822–1909), °*The Man without a Country* (1863), the Burr conspiracy.

Nathaniel Hawthorne (1804–64), *The House of the Seven Gables* (1851), Salem in the early 19th century; †*The Blithedale Romance* (1852), Brook Farm.

Joseph Hergesheimer (1880–   ), *Java Head* (1919), Salem in the 1840's.

Emerson Hough (1857–1923), *The Covered Wagon* (1922), an overland journey from Missouri to Oregon in 1848.

Mary Johnston (1870–1936), *Lewis Rand* (1908), Burr's conspiracy; *The Long Roll* (1911) and *Cease Firing* (1912), the Civil War.

MacKinlay Kantor (1904–   ), *Long Remember* (1934) and *Arouse and Beware!* (1936), the Civil War.

J. P. Kennedy (1795–1870), *Swallow Barn* (1832), Virginia plantation life about 1800.

Bruce Lancaster (1896–   ), *For Us the Living* (1940), Lincoln's early life and environment; *No Bugles Tonight* (1948), Georgia during the Civil War.

A. B. Longstreet (1790–1870), †*Georgia Scenes* (1835), contemporary backwoods life.

Herman Melville (1819–91), †*White-Jacket* (1850), life on a warship; †*Moby Dick* (1851), whaling.

Caroline Miller (1903–   ), *Lamb in His Bosom* (1933), backwoods Georgia, 1810–65.

S. Weir Mitchell (1829–1914), *In War Time* (1885) and *Roland Blake* (1886), the Civil War; *The Red City* (1907), Philadelphia in the 1790's.

J. K. Paulding (1778–1860), *Westward Ho!* (1832), frontier Kentucky.

Conrad Richter (1890–   ), *The Trees* (1940), *The Fields* (1946), and *The Town* (1950), western Pennsylvania and Ohio about 1800–1840.

Elizabeth M. Roberts (1886–1941), *The Great Meadow* (1930), frontier Kentucky.

Kenneth Roberts (1885–   ), *The Lively Lady* (1931) and *Captain Caution* (1934), the War of 1812 on the sea.

Evelyn Scott (1893–   ), *The Wave* (1929), the Civil War.

Upton Sinclair (1878–   ), *Manassas* (1904), the Civil War and before.

Harriet Beecher Stowe (1811–1896), °*Uncle Tom's Cabin* (1852) and °*Dred* (1856), slave life in the South; *Oldtown Folks* (1869), Massachusetts about 1790.

T. S. Stribling (1881–   ), *The Forge* (1931), Alabama during the Civil War.

Robert Penn Warren (1905–   ), *World Enough and Time* (1950), Kentucky in the 1820's.

Mary S. Watts (1868–   ), *Nathan Burke* (1910), the Mexican War.

Stewart Edward White (1873–1946), *Gold* (1913) and *Gray Dawn* (1915), California, 1849–56; *The Long Rifle* (1932) and *Folded Hills* (1934), California slightly earlier.

Stark Young (1881–   ), *So Red the Rose* (1934), Mississippi during the Civil War.

1865–1900

Edward Bellamy (1850–98), °*Looking Backward* (1888) and °*Equality* (1897), Utopian novels.

James Boyd (1888–1944), *Bitter Creek* (1939), Wyoming cowboy life in the 1880's and 1890's.

George W. Cable (1844–1925), *John March, Southerner* (1894), the New South.

Abraham Cahan (1860–1951), *The Rise of David Levinsky* (1917), success story of a Russian Jewish immigrant, in America from 1885.

Willa Cather (1875–1947), *O Pioneers!* (1913) and *My Antonia* (1918), immigrant life on the prairies toward the end of the 19th century.

W. Van T. Clark (1909–   ), *The Ox-Bow Incident* (1940), Nevada in 1885.

S. L. Clemens (1835–1910) and C. D. Warner (1829–1900), †*The Gilded Age* (1873), politics and business after the Civil War.

Theodore Dreiser (1871–1945), *The Financier* (1912) and *The Titan* (1914), big business and high finance in the 1870's and later.

Edna Ferber (1887–   ), *Showboat* (1926), the Mississippi River in the 1880's and 1890's.

P. L. Ford (1865–1902), †*The Honorable Peter Stirling* (1894), New York politics in the 1870's and after.

Mary E. Wilkins Freeman (1852–1930), †*A Humble Romance* (1887) and †*A New England Nun* (1891), New England rural life.

H. B. Fuller (1857–1929), †*The Cliff-Dwellers* (1893), middle-class life in Chicago.

Hamlin Garland (1860–1940), †*Main-Travelled Roads* (1891), †*A Little Norsk* (1892), and †*Rose of Dutcher's Coolly* (1895), farm life in Middle West; *The Captain of the Gray-Horse Troop* (1902), Montana in the 1890's.

Ellen Glasgow (1874–   ), *The Voice of the People* (1900) and *The Deliverance* (1904), Virginia after the Civil War.

Frank Harris (1855–1931), *The Bomb* (1908), the Haymarket riot.

Bret Harte (1836–1902), *The Luck of Roaring Camp* (1870), California mining camp after the Civil War.

Emerson Hough (1857–1923), *North of 36* (1923), the Chisholm Trail soon after the Civil War.

E. W. Howe (1854–1937), †*The Story of a Country Town* (1883), contemporary village
life in Kansas.
William Dean Howells (1837–1920), †*A Modern Instance* (1882), †*The Rise of Silas
Lapham* (1885), †*A Hazard of New Fortunes* (1890), and †*The World of Chance*
(1893), contemporary middle-class life in the East; °*A Traveller from Altruria*
(1894), Utopian novel.
Helen Hunt Jackson (1830–1885), °*Ramona* (1884), mistreatment of Indians in Cali-
fornia.
Henry James (1843–1916), †*The American* (1877), †*Daisy Miller* (1879), †*The Portrait
of a Lady* (1881), and †*The Ambassadors* (1903), contemporary Americans in
European settings; †*The Bostonians* (1886), feminism and reform stirrings in
Boston.
Sarah Orne Jewett (1849–1909), †*Deephaven* (1877), †*A White Heron* (1886), and
†*The Country of the Pointed Firs* (1896), contemporary New England.
Charles King (1844–1933), *An Army Wife* (1895), *A Daughter of the Sioux* (1902), and
An Apache Princess (1903), contemporary army life on the plains.
Ross Lockridge (1914–48), *Raintree County* (1947), Indiana, 1844–92.
J. P. Marquand (1893–   ), †*The Late George Apley* (1937), Boston's Beacon Hill
aristocracy, 1866–1933.
Margaret Mitchell (1903–50), *Gone with the Wind* (1936), Civil War and Reconstruc-
tion in Georgia.
Frank Norris (1870–1902), †*The Octopus* (1901), contemporary wheat farmers and
railroads in California; †*The Pit* (1903), Chicago wheat speculation.
Thomas Nelson Page (1853–1922), *Red Rock* (1898), Virginia during Reconstruction.
W. H. Page (1855–1918), *The Southerner* (1909), the New South.
Herbert Quick (1861–1925), *Vandemark's Folly* (1922), *The Hawkeye* (1923), and
The Invisible Woman (1924), Iowa in the second half of the 19th century.
O. E. Rolvaag (1876–1931), *Giants in the Earth* (1927), Norwegian pioneer life in
Dakota, 1873–91.
C. M. Sheldon (1857–1941), °*In His Steps* (1896), Middle Western religious life.
T. S. Stribling (1881–   ), *The Store* (1932), Southern tenancy after the Civil War.
Booth Tarkington (1869–1946), *The Gentleman from Indiana* (1899), Indiana politics
in the 1890's.
A. W. Tourgée (1838–1905), °*A Fool's Errand* (1879), Reconstruction period in South.
Mark Twain. See Clemens.
Edith Wharton (1862–1937), *The House of Mirth* (1905), New York society in the
late 19th century; *The Age of Innocence* (1920), patrician New York in the 1870's.
Owen Wister (1860–1938), *The Virginian* (1902), cowboy life in Wyoming in the
1870's and 1880's.

1900–1950

Samuel Hopkins Adams (1871–   ), †*Revelry* (1926), the Harding era.
Sherwood Anderson (1876–1941), †*Winesburg, Ohio* (1919) and †*The Triumph of the
Egg* (1921), small-town life in the Middle West.
Thomas Bell (1903–   ), †*Out of This Furnace* (1941), Slovak immigrants in Pennsyl-
vania steel mills.
Erskine Caldwell (1903–   ), †*Tobacco Road* (1932) and †*God's Little Acre* (1933),
Georgia poor whites.
W. E. M. Campbell (1894–   ), †*Company K* (1933), World War I.
Robert Cantwell (1908–   ), †*The Land of Plenty* (1934), lumber-mill workers during
the Great Depression.
Winston Churchill (1871–1947), †*Mr. Crewe's Career* (1908), New Hampshire politics;
†*The Dwelling Place of Light* (1917), Massachusetts factory city.
James Gould Cozzens (1903–   ), *Guard of Honor* (1948), World War II.
Floyd Dell (1887–   ), *Moon Calf* (1920), a small factory town in Missouri.
John Dos Passos (1896–   ), †*The 42nd Parallel* (1930), †*1919* (1932), and †*The Big
Money* (1936), aspects of American life from 1900.
J. H. Downing (1888–   ), *A Prayer for Tomorrow* (1938), South Dakota, 1890–1930.

James T. Farrell (1904–   ), †*Young Lonigan* (1932), †*The Young Manhood of Studs Lonigan* (1934), †*Judgment Day* (1935), and †*A World I Never Made* (1936), slum life in Chicago.

William Faulkner (1897–   ), †*As I Lay Dying* (1930) and †*Light in August* (1932), Southern poor whites.

Vardis Fisher (1895–   ), †*Toilers in the Hills* (1928), Idaho dry farmers in the early 20th century.

F. Scott Fitzgerald (1896–1940), †*This Side of Paradise* (1920) and †*The Great Gatsby* (1925), the Jazz Age.

Zona Gale (1874–1938), †*Miss Lulu Bett* (1920), village life in Wisconsin.

Ellen Glasgow (1874–   ), †*Barren Ground* (1925), Virginia poor whites.

Paul Green (1894–   ), †*This Body the Earth* (1935), Southern sharecroppers.

Albert Halper (1904–   ), †*The Foundry* (1934), foundry workers.

Ernest Hemingway (1896–   ), †*A Farewell to Arms* (1929), World War I.

James Jones (1921–   ), †*From Here to Eternity* (1951), World War II.

Ring W. Lardner (1885–1933), *Round Up* (1929), American manners.

Alfred Henry Lewis (1857–1914), †*The Boss* (1903), machine politics.

Sinclair Lewis (1885–1950), †*Main Street* (1920), and †*Babbitt* (1922), middle-class life in the Midwest; †*Elmer Gantry* (1927), clerical life; †*Arrowsmith* (1925), the medical profession.

Norman Mailer (1923–   ), †*The Naked and the Dead* (1948), World War II.

William March. See Campbell, W. E. M.

J. A. Michener (1907–   ), †*Tales of the South Pacific* (1947), World War II.

David Graham Phillips (1867–1911), *The Cost* (1904) and *The Deluge* (1905), high finance; *Light-Fingered Gentry* (1907), the New York insurance scandals; *The Plum Tree* (1905) and *The Conflict* (1911), political corruption.

Ernest Poole (1880–   ), †*The Harbor* (1915), industrial conditions in New York.

Upton Sinclair (1878–   ), *The Jungle* (1906), Chicago packing-house conditions; *The Money-Changers* (1908), the financial panic of 1908; *Boston* (1928), the Sacco-Vanzetti trial.

Lillian Smith (1897–   ), †*Strange Fruit* (1944), race relations in a Georgia town.

John Steinbeck (1902–   ), *The Grapes of Wrath* (1939), migratory farm workers in California during the Great Depression.

T. S. Stribling (1881–   ), †*The Store* (1932) and †*Unfinished Cathedral* (1934), social conditions in an Alabama town.

Ruth Suckow (1892–   ), †*The Folks* (1934), a small Iowa town.

Dorothy Thomas (1899–   ), †*The Home Place* (1936), a Nebraska farm during the Great Depression.

Lionel Trilling (1905–   ), †*The Middle of the Journey* (1947), Communism and the intellectuals.

Robert Penn Warren (1905–   ), *Night Riders* (1939), Kentucky in the early 1900's; †*All the King's Men* (1946), the Huey Long regime in Louisiana.

Richard Wright (1908–   ), †*Native Son* (1940), race relations.

65. HISTORICAL POEMS, SONGS, AND PLAYS

Poems, songs, and plays illuminate many aspects of American development. As in the case of historical fiction (§ 63), verse falls into three categories in this respect. Practically all the standard poets treat historical themes; some sought to fire the popular conscience against existing injustices; and much of their writing concerns the spirit and conditions of their times. Philip Freneau, a patriot bard during the Revolution, later became a keen satirist of Federalist policies; John Greenleaf Whittier, besides dealing with retrospective subjects, won fame as the "poet laureate of the antislavery crusade"; and Walt Whitman lives on to our own day as the trumpeter of an exuberant democracy. In the twentieth century such writers as Vachel Lindsay, Edwin Markham, and Carl Sandburg have similarly voiced social criticism. Certain European poets have also exerted an influence on American thinking, notably Rudyard Kipling whose "The White Man's Burden" (1899) argued persuasively for colonial imperialism.

A sampling of the collected works of a given author is the best introduction to this extensive literature. For reasons of space, only poems of considerable length are noted here:

Joel Barlow (1754–1812), *The Vision of Columbus* (1787), later expanded into *The Columbiad* (1807), the discovery, settlement, independence, and future of America.
Stephen Vincent Benét (1898–1943), *John Brown's Body* (1928), the Civil War.
Henry Wadsworth Longfellow (1807–82), *Evangeline* (1847), Acadia; *The Song of Hiawatha* (1855), Indian lore; *The Courtship of Miles Standish* (1858), early Plymouth.
James Russell Lowell (1819–91), *The Biglow Papers* (1848), the Mexican War; *The Biglow Papers* (2 ser., 1862), the Civil War.
Archibald MacLeish (1892–   ), *Conquistador* (1932), the conquest of Mexico.
Edgar Lee Masters (1869–   ), *Spoon River Anthology* (1915), contemporary life in a Middle Western small town.
John G. Neihardt (1881–   ), *The Song of Hugh Glass* (1915) and *The Song of Three Friends* (1919), the trans-Missouri fur trade.
John Trumbull (1750–1831), *M'Fingal* (1775–82), the Revolution.

Ballads are of comparable interest to the historian for a variety of reasons. Patriotic refrains have helped bolster the nation's morale in time of war and rumors of war; religious songs reveal spiritual sentiments; political songs evidence partisan attitudes; popular ditties mirror changing manners and interests; while folk ballads attest the experiences and feelings of ethnic, regional, and occupational groups. The following list cites examples of anthologies of all these types of music. For more extensive catalogues, see Spiller *et al.*, *Literary History*, III, 192–201 (for folk songs), and M. E. Sears, comp., *Song Index: An Index to More than 12,000 Songs in 177 Song Collections* (N. Y., 1926), with a supplement (1934) listing 7000 additional items.

F. D. Allan, comp., *Allan's Lone Star Ballads. A Collection of Southern Patriotic Songs Made during Confederate Times.* Galveston, 1874.
W. F. Allen *et al.*, eds., *Slave Songs of the United States.* N.Y., 1867; new ed., 1929.
W. E. Barton, ed., *Old Plantation Hymns.* Boston, 1899.
T. C. Blegen and M. B. Ruud, eds., *Norwegian Emigrant Songs and Ballads.* Minn., 1936.
E. M. Butterfield, "American Political Songs," *N. Y. Hist.*, XXX (1949), 409. — In the period 1800–1948.
Carl Carmer, ed., *Songs of the Rivers of America.* N.Y., 1942.
J. C. Colcord, comp., *Roll and Go, Songs of American Sailormen.* Boston, 1924.
J. H. Cox, ed., *Folk Songs of the South.* Cambridge, 1924. — Mostly mountain whites.
S. F. Damon, ed., *Series of Old American Songs.* Providence, 1936. — Facsimile reproductions of sheet music, 1759–1858.
A. K. Davis, Jr., ed., *Traditional Ballads of Virginia.* Cambridge, 1929.
William Doerflinger, ed., *Shantymen and Shantyboys.* N.Y., 1951. — Sailors and lumbermen.
E. A. Dolph, ed., *Sound Off: Soldier Songs from Yankee Doodle to Parley-Voo.* N. Y., 1929.
G. C. Eggleston, ed., *American War-Ballads and Lyrics.* 2 vols. N. Y., 1889.
R. P. Gray, *Songs and Ballads of the Maine Lumberjacks.* Cambridge, 1924.
W. C. Handy and Abbe Niles, eds., *Blues: An Anthology of Jazz Music from the Early Negro Folk Blues to Modern Music.* N. Y., 1926.
G. S. Jackson, ed., *Early Songs of Uncle Sam.* Boston, 1933. — From popular collections, 1825–50.

George Korson, comp., *Minstrels of the Mine Patch*. Phila., 1938. — Anthracite miners.

E. H. Linscott, comp., *Folk Songs of Old New England*. N. Y., 1939.

J. A. Lomax, comp., *Cowboy Songs, and Other Frontier Ballads*. R. ed., N. Y., 1916. *Songs of the Cattle Trail and Cow Camp*, 1919. With Alan Lomax, *American Ballads and Folk Songs*. N. Y., 1934.

Julius Mattfeld, ed., *The Folk Music of the Western Hemisphere*. N. Y., 1925. — Negroes, cowboys, lumberjacks, sailors, mountaineers, miners, etc.

Frank Moore, ed., *The Civil War in Song and Story*. N. Y., 1889. *Songs and Ballads of the American Revolution*. N. Y., 1856. *Songs and Ballads of the Southern People*. N. Y., 1886.

R. W. Neeser, ed., *American Naval Songs and Ballads*. New Haven, 1938. — From the Revolution to 1882.

W. A. Owens, ed., *Texas Folk Songs*. Dallas, 1950.

Dailey Paskman and Sigmund Spaeth, *Gentlemen, Be Seated; a Parade of the Old-Time Minstrels*. N. Y., 1928.

Vance Randolph, ed., *Ozark Folksongs*. 4 vols. Columbia, Mo., 1946–50.

C. C. Sellers, ed., "A Garland of Brickbats," *Poet Lore*, XXXVII (1926), 396. — Songs of the fire companies in the early 19th century.

Sigmund Spaeth, *Read 'Em and Weep*. Garden City, 1926. *Weep Some More, My Lady*. N. Y., 1927. — Popular songs.

N. I. White, ed., *American Negro Folk-Songs*. Cambridge, 1928.

S. A. Witherbee, ed., *Spanish-American War Songs*. Detroit, 1898.

From pre-Revolutionary times onward, the stage also affords a running commentary on the American scene. Thus, playwrights like William Dunlap (1766–1839) and Clyde Fitch (1865–1909) deal with historical incidents; others like James A. Herne (1839–1901) and Paul Green (1894–　) treat regional themes with varying degrees of realism; Bronson Howard (1842–1908) and George E. Kelly (1887–　) exemplify the preoccupation with manners; while the work of Maxwell Anderson (1888–　) and Clifford Odets (1906–　) illustrates the socially purposeful drama. Some plays, like "Uncle Tom's Cabin," "Ten Nights in a Bar-room," and Charles Klein's "The Lion and the Mouse," probably did more to shape popular attitudes toward the problems with which they were concerned than did the books which suggested them. A scholarly account, stressing aesthetic considerations, is Quinn, *History of the American Drama*.

Unfortunately, many of the scripts of the earlier productions have not survived. The following collections are convenient:

John Gassner, ed., *Best Plays of the Modern Theatre*. 2 vols. N. Y., 1939–47.

A. G. Halline, ed., *American Plays*. N. Y., 1935. — 1787–1927.

Burns Mantle *et al.*, eds., *The Best Plays Series*. 33 vols. and general index vol. Boston and N. Y., 1920–50. — Condensed texts, 1899–1950, generally in annual vols.

M. J. Moses, ed., *Representative Plays by American Dramatists*. 3 vols. N. Y., 1918–25. — 1765–1917.

A. H. Quinn, ed., *Representative American Plays from 1767*. R. ed. N. Y., 1938.

E. B. Watson and Benfield Pressey, eds., *Contemporary Drama*. 2 vols. N. Y., 1931–38.

66. SOUND RECORDINGS AND THE HISTORIAN

Thanks to the phonograph, sound recordings are adding a new dimension to the historian's knowledge of the past as well as providing him with a new means of making history live in the classroom. For many years after Edison's invention in 1878 the makers of disks specialized on pure entertainment, but in the twentieth century they have given increasing attention to public addresses and notable occasions. As a result the student can often hear for himself what he formerly could only have read in print, or have learned about at second hand from others. Moreover, many record albums reproduce instrumental and vocal music from early times to the present, and scholars have used the phonograph to transcribe folk speech and folk songs.

All the commercial companies issue catalogues of their offerings. There is also available a monthly *American Record Guide* (Pelham, N. Y., founded in 1935 as *American Music Lover*), which discusses current releases. Among the more recent albums appealing to the historian are "Then Came War: 1939" (Elmer Davis, ed., World Book Co., Yonkers, 1940), which invokes the voices of the major actors in that crisis; and "'I Can Hear It Now'" (3 vols., E. R. Murrow and F. W. Friendly, eds., Columbia Masterworks, N. Y., 1948–50), which covers the principal events from 1919 to 1949. An important series illustrating the kind of music the early settlers heard and sang includes "Early American Psalmody," "Ballads of Colonial America," and "Instrumental Music of Colonial America" (C. S. Smith, ed., New Records, N. Y., 1951). The American Archive of Folk Song in the Library of Congress leads in its field. Its holdings are catalogued in *Check-List of Recorded Songs in the English Language* (3 vols., Wash., 1942) and *Folk Music of the United States and Latin America* (Wash., 1948).

The radio has provided still a different type of sound recordings, many of which have been preserved for permanent use. The Federal Communications Commission, for example, has files of tape recordings and scripts of broadcasts. *The Catalog of Radio Recordings* (Office of Educ., Wash., 1950) lists selected transcriptions by federal agencies and commercial stations and networks on such subjects as foreign relations, World War II, conservation projects, folk music, and the activities of immigrant and racial groups. Further information regarding this variety of material is obtainable from the national offices of the networks.

PART III

Colonial History and the Revolution
1492–1788

Chapter Six

FROM PREHISTORIC TIMES TO 1600

67. PHYSIOGRAPHY AND GEOGRAPHY OF NORTH AMERICA

Summary — Physical conformation of North America: characteristics of different regions, their soils, mineral deposits, climate, rainfall. — Effects of this environment on mankind, and of "sequent occupance" on the land. — The oceans and American development. — Historical geography of the United States. — Map collections and atlases (§§ 19–23).

General — Physiography: Atwood, *Physiographic Provinces;* N. M. Fenneman, "Physiographic Divisions of the United States" (3 ed., with map), Assoc. Am. Geog., *Annals*, XVIII (1928), 261, and *Physiography of the Western United States* (1931), and *Physiography of the Eastern United States* (1938). ❡ Oceanography: H. B. Bigelow, *Oceanography, Its Scope, Problems, and Economic Importance* (1931); James Johnstone, *Study of the Oceans* (1926), chs. iii–vi; Rachel Carson, *Sea Around Us* (1951); H. U. Sverdrup, *et al., Oceans, Their Physics, Chemistry, and General Biology* (1942). ❡ Geography and History: G. J. Miller and A. E. Perkins, *Geography of North America* (1946); E. G. Ashton, *North America* (1939); J. R. Smith and Phillips, *North America;* D. R. Jones and P. W. Bryan, *North America, Its Historical, Economic and Regional Geography* (9 ed., 1950); C. L. White and E. J. Foscue, *Regional Geography of North America* (1943); A. J. Wright, *United States and Canada: An Economic Geography* (1948); J. R. Whitaker and Edward Ackerman, *American Resources* (1951); R. H. Brown, *Historical Geography of the United States* (1948); Erwin Raisz, "Outline of History of American Cartography," *Isis*, XXVI (1937), 373; C. P. Lucas, *et al., Historical Geography of the British Colonies* (7 vols., 1888–1920), II, V; Dexter Perkins, "Geographical Influences in American History," *Geog. Jour.* (London), CIX (1947), 26. ❡ Sequent Occupance: D. S. Whittlesey, Assoc. Am. Geog., *Annals*, XIX (1929), 162; J. O. M. Broek, *Santa Clara Valley, a Study in Landscape Changes* (1932); H. S. Kemp, " 'Queen City of the Lakes' [Buffalo] a Geographic Pageant," *Jour. Geog.*, XXX (1931), 93; G. T. Trewartha, "The Prairie du Chien Terrace," Assoc. Am. Geog., *Annals*, XII (1932), 119; J. R. Whitaker, *Negaunee, Michigan* (1931); H. F. Wilson, *The Hill Country of Northern New England* (1936); L. E. Klimm, *Relations between Population Changes and Physical Environment in Massachusetts, 1790–1925* (1933). ❡ Boundaries: Paullin, *Atlas*, 52–87, plates 89–101; Douglas, "Boundaries, Areas, Geographical Centers."

Special — Morse, *American Geography;* Thomas Hutchins, *A Topographical Description of Virginia, Pennsylvania, Maryland, and North Carolina* (1778; F. C. Hicks, ed., 1904); H. L. Shapiro, "The French Population of Canada; a Study of the Effects of Environment," *Natural Hist.*, XXXII (1932), 341; C. O. Sauer, "A Geographic Sketch of Early Man in America," *Geog. Rev.*, XXXIV (1944), 529.

Bibliography — L. C. Karpinski, *Early Maps of Carolina* (catalogue of Kendall collection, 1930), and *Bibliography of Printed Maps of Michigan,* and *Cartographical Collections in America* (1935); P. L. Phillips, *List of Maps of America;* E. G. Swem, *Maps Relating to Virginia* (1914); LeGear, *United States Atlases;* Edmund Thompson, *Maps of Connecticut before 1800* (1940), and *Maps of Connecticut for 1801–1860* (1942).

68. NORTH AMERICAN ARCHAEOLOGY

Summary — Were there people in America before the Indians? — The Mound Builders and Red Paint People. — Dating of archaeological remains by radiocarbon and other methods. — Stratification of human remains in the Southwest. — Ancient civilizations of Mexico; the Maya, Toltec, and Aztec. — The Maya calendar and hieroglyphics. — Extent and dating of the Maya Empire.

General — P. S. Martin, *et al., Indians before Columbus* (1947); Frederica deLaguna, "Prehistory of Northern North America," Soc. for Am. Arch., *Memoir,* No. 3, pt. 2 (1947); *Essays on Archaeological Methods,* J. B. Griffin, ed., University of Mich. Museum of Anthropology, *Papers,* No. 8 (1951); W. W. Taylor, *Study of Archaeology* (1943).

Special — Kenneth MacGowan, *Early Man in New World* (1950); E. H. Sellards, *Early Man in America* (1940); H. M. Wormington, *Ancient Man in North America* (1939); E. W. Haury, *Stratigraphy and Archaeology of Ventana Cave* (1950); Frederick Johnson, "Radiocarbon Dating," *Am. Archeol.,* XXVII (1951), No. 1, pt. 2. ❡ Eastern United States and the Plains: B. B. King, *Under Your Feet, Story of Mound Builders* (1939); H. C. Shetrone, *Mound Builders* (1930); J. A. Ford and G. R. Willey, "Interpretation of Prehistory of Eastern United States," *Am. Anthropologist,* XLIII (1941), 325; Philip Phillips, *et al., Archaeological Survey in Lower Mississippi Alluvial Valley,* Peabody Museum, *Papers,* XXV (1951); W. S. Webb and D. L. de Jarnette, *Archaeological Survey of Pickwick Basin . . . of Alabama, Mississippi, and Tennessee* (1942); W. S. Webb and C. E. Snow, *Adena People* (1945); J. O. Brew, *Archaeology of Alkali Ridge, Utah, with Prehistory of Mesa Verde and Observations on Archaeological Systematics,* Peabody Museum, *Papers,* XXI (1946); W. R. Wedel, *Introduction to Pawnee Archaeology* (1936); B. W. Knoblock, *Banner Stones of North American Indian* (1939); A. V. Kidder, *Introduction to Study of Southwestern Archaeology* (1924), and *Artifacts of Pecos* (1932); R. G. Montgomery, Watson Smith, and J. O. Brew, *Franciscan Awatovi,* Peabody Museum, *Papers,* XXXVI (1949); R. F. Heizer and S. F. Cook, *Archaeology of Central California* (1949). ❡ Mexico and the Mayas: H. J. Spinden, *Ancient Civilizations of Mexico and Central America* (1917); G. C. Vaillant, *Aztecs of Mexico* (1941); J. E. S. Thompson, *Mexico before Cortez* (1933); *The Maya and Their Neighbors* (Alfred Tozzer *Festschrift,* 1940); A. V. Kidder, *Artifacts of Uaxactun, Guatemala* (1947); J. L. Stephens, *Incidents of Travel in Yucatan* (1843), and *Incidents of Travel in Central America, Chiapas and Yucatan* (1841; r. ed., 1949); S. G. Morley, *Introduction to Study of Maya Hieroglyphs* (1915). ❡ Periodicals and Publications of Learned Societies: *Am. Antiquity; Am. Anthropologist;* Am. Museum of Natural Hist., *Anthropological Papers;* Chi. Natural Hist. Soc., *Publ.;* Peabody Museum of Am. Archaeol. and Ethnology, *Memoirs,* and *Papers;* Museum of the Am. Indian, N.Y., Heye Foundation, *Publ.,* and *Indian Notes and Monographs;* Quivera Soc., *Publ.;* Smithsonian Inst., *Misc. Coll.; Southwestern Jour. of Anthropology;* Tulane University, Middle Am. Res. Inst., *Publ.;* University of Calif., *Publ. in Am. Arch. and Ethnology;* University of Mich. Museum of Anthropology, *Anthropological Papers;* University of Penn. Museum, *Publ.;* U.S. Bur. of Ethnology, *Reports;* Yale University, *Publ. in Anthropology.*

Bibliography — J. O. Brew, *Selected Bibliography of American Archaeology East of Rocky Mountains,* Excavators' Club, *Papers,* II (1943); Irving Rouse and J. M. Goggin, *Anthropological Bibliography of Eastern Seaboard* (1947); Hanke, *Handbook of Latin American Studies.*

69. NORTH AMERICAN INDIANS

Summary — Origin of the North American Indians, dates and circumstances of migration; how they spread. — Indian characteristics, culture, and religion. — Indian artifacts, agriculture, contributions to world economy. — Social condition of Indians on Atlantic seaboard, 1500–1600. — Effects of the coming of the Europeans. — Treatment of the Indian problem by the Spanish, French, English, and Portuguese colonists (§§ 74, 79).

General — Clark Wissler, *American Indian* (1917); Fred Eggan, ed., *Social Anthropology of North American Tribes* (1937); Frederick Johnson, ed., *Man in Northeastern North America* (1946); Hodge, *Handbook of American Indians*; Luis Pericot y García, *América Indígena*, Antonio Ballestros y Beretta, ed., *Historia de América* (1936), I.

Special — Lewis Hanke, *Spanish Struggle for Justice in Conquest of America* (1949), and *Bartolomé de Las Casas, Bookman, Scholar and Propagandist* (1952); J. H. Kennedy, *Jesuit and Savage in New France* (1950); C. C. Willoughby, *Antiquities of New England Indians* (1935); F. G. Speck, *Penobscot Man* (1940); F. H. Eckstorm, "Attack on Norridgewock," *New Eng. Quar.*, VII (1934), 541 and "Pigwacket and Parson Symmes, *ibid.*, IX (1936), 378, and *Old John Neptune* (1945); H. M. Chapin, *Sachems of Narragansetts* (1931); J. W. Lyddeker, *Faithful Mohawks* (1938); L. H. Morgan, *League of Iroquois* (1851; 2 ed., 1901); G. T. Hunt, *Wars of Iroquois* (1940); F. G. Speck, *Naskapi* (1935); Diamond Jenness, *Indians of Canada* (1934); James Mooney, *Siouan Tribes of East* (1894); D. L. Rights, *American Indian in North Carolina* (1947); J. R. Swanton, *Early History of Creek Indians* (1922), and *Indian Tribes of Lower Mississippi* (1911); Emmet Starr, *History of Cherokee* (1921); W. H. Gilbert, *Eastern Cherokees*, Bur. Am. Ethnology, *Bull.*, No. 133 (1943); W. V. Kinietz, *Indians of Western Great Lakes, 1615–70* (1940); L. P. Kellogg, *Fox Indians During French Regime*, Wisc. Hist. Soc., *Proc.* (1907), 142; R. H. Lowie, *Crow Indians* (1935); A. C. Fletcher, *Omaha Tribe* (1911); Paul Radin, *Winnebago Tribe* (1923); A. B. Thomas, *Plains Indians and New Mexico, 1751–1778* (1940); G. A. Reichard, *Social Life of Navajo Indians* (1928); Clyde Kluckhohn and Dorothea Leighton, *Navajo* (1946); J. T. Hack, *Changing Physical Environment of Hopi Indians* (1942); Leslie Spier, *Yuman Tribes of Gila River* (1933); E. F. Castetter, *Yuman Indian Agriculture* (1951); Bancroft, *Native Races of Pacific States*.

Periodicals and Publications of Learned Societies — See: § 68; Diego de Landa, *Relación de las Cosas de Yucatan* (A. M. Tozzer, ed.), Peabody Museum, *Papers*, XVIII (1941).

Sources — Lewis Hanke, *Cuerpo de documentos del siglo XVI sobre los derechos de España en las Indias y las Filipinas* (1943); R. G. Thwaites, ed., *Jesuit Relations* (73 vols., 1866–1901).

Bibliography — G. P. Murdock, *Ethnographic Bibliography of North America* (1941); A. L. Kroeber, *Cultural and Natural Areas of Native North America* (1939); J. C. Pilling, *Bibliography of Algonquian Languages* (1891), *Iroquoian Languages* (1888), *Siouan Languages* (1887); Juan Comas. *Bibliografía selectiva de las culturas indigenas de America* (1953).

70. PRE-COLUMBIAN DISCOVERIES

Summary — Geographical knowledge of the ancients; theories of Eratosthenes, Strabo, and others. — Middle Ages. — Fabulous Islands and Mythical Voyages by Basques, Brothers Zeno, and others. — A.D. 1000, the Norse discovery. — Later voyages to Vinland. — Authenticity of the Sagas. — Questionable relics: Newport round tower; Kensington rune stone; and Beardmore weapons.

General — J. Fiske, *Discovery of America*, I, 148; Winsor, *Narrative and Critical History*, I, ch. ii; Fridtjof Nansen, *In Northern Mists* (2 vols., 1911); Egmont Zechlin, "Das

Problem der vorkolumbischen Entdeckung Amerikas u. die Kolumbusforschung," *Historische Zeitschrift*, CLII (1935), 1.

Special — Norsemen: A. M. Reeves, *Finding of Wineland and the Good* (1890); Halldór Hermannsson, "Problem of Wineland," *Islandica*, XXV, 1936; Einar Haugen, *Voyages to Vinland* (1942); Joseph Fischer, *Discoveries of Norsemen in America* (1903); A. A. Bjørnbo and C. S. Petersen, *Anecdota Cartographica Septentrionalia* (1908); A. A. Bjørnbo, "Cartographia Groenlandica," *Meddelelser om Grønland*, XLVIII (1912); H. P. Steensby, *Norsemen's Route from Greenland to Wineland* (1918); A. W. Brögger, *Vinlandsferdene* (1937); J. T. Honti, "Vinland," *Acta Ethnologia*, III (1938), 17, and *Modern Language Notes*, LIV (1939), 159, and *Modern Language Quar.*, I (1940), 339; Vilhjalmur Stefansson, ed., *Three Voyages of Martin Frobisher* (1938), and *Unsolved Mysteries of Arctic* (1939), and *Ultima Thule* (1940); M. M. Mjelde, "Norse Discoveries of America: The Eyktarstadr Problem," *Saga-Book of Viking Society*, X, pt. 1 (1928), 57; P. A. Means, *Newport Tower* (1942); W. S. Godfrey, Jr., "Newport Tower," *Arch.*, II (1949), 146, and *ibid.*, III (1950), 183. ❡ Greenland: *Meddelelser om Grønland*, LXVII (1924), summary in *Geog. Rev.*, XV (1925), 605, and *Am. Scand. Rev.*, XI (1923), 547. ❡ Kensington Rune Stone, pro: H. R. Holand, *Westward from Vinland* (1940), and *America: 1355–1364* (1946); S. N. Hagen, "Kensington Runic Inscription," *Speculum*, XXV (1950), 321; William Thalbitzer, "Two Runic Stones from Greenland and Minnesota," *Smithsonian Misc. Coll.*, CXVI (1951), No. 3. ❡ Kensington Rune Stone, con: L. M. Larson, "Kensington Rune Stone," *Minn. Hist.*, XVII (1936), 20; J. M. Armstrong, "Numerals on Kensington Stone," *ibid.*, XVIII (1937), 185; M. M. Quaife, "Kensington Myth," *Mich. Hist.*, XXXI (1947), 129; Eric Moltke, "The Kensington Stone," *Antiquity*, XXV, No. 98 (1951), 87; Erik Wahlgren, "The Runes of Kensington," in *Studies in Honor of A. M. Sturtevant* (1952), 57. ❡ Beardmore Relics: O. C. Elliott and C. T. Currelly, "Case of Beardmore Relics," *Canadian Hist. Rev.*, XXII (1941), 254. ❡ Irish: Joseph Dunn, "Brendan Problem," *Cath. Hist. Rev.*, VI (1921), 395; J. F. Kenney, "Legend of St. Brendan," Royal Soc. Canada, *Proc.*, 3 ser., XIV (1920), § 2, 51; Paul Gaffarel, *Les Irlandais en Amerique avant Colomb* (1890); Hugh Hencken, "Irish Monastery at New Salem, N. H.," *New Eng. Quar.*, XII (1939), 492. ❡ Miscellaneous: Sofus Larsen, *Discovery of America Twenty Years before Columbus* (1925); R. H. Major, ed., *Voyages of Nicolò & Antonio Zeno* (Hakluyt Soc., 1873); F. W. Lucas, *Annals of the Brothers Zeno, a Criticism and Indictment* (1898); W. H. Hobbs, "Zeno and Cartography of Greenland," *Imago Mundi*, VI (1949), 15; L. D. Scisco, "Pre-Columbian Discovery by Basques," Royal Soc. Canada, *Proc.*, 3 ser., XVIII (1924), § 2, 51; W. H. Babcock, *Legendary Islands of the Atlantic* (1922); Richard Hennig, "Atlantische Fabelinseln u. Entdeckung Amerikas," *Historische Zeitschrift*, CLIII (1936), 461. — For Portuguese claims, see: § 71.

Sources — Reeves, *Wineland*, has text of Vinland sagas and Eng. transl., reprinted in J. E. Olson and E. G. Bourne, *Northmen, Columbus, and Cabot* ("Original Narratives" series, 1906); another transl. in Haugen, *Voyages*, and another text in Halldór Hermannsson, "Vinland Sagas," *Islandica* (1944).

Bibliography — Winsor, *Narrative and Critical History*, I, 76; Halldór Hermannsson, "Northmen in America," *Islandica*, II (1909), 1.

71. EUROPEAN BACKGROUND AND APPROACH TO AMERICAN DISCOVERY

Summary — Revival of European interest in exploration. — The Renaissance, economic revolution, and discovery. — Marco Polo and the partial reopening of Asia. — Voyages of Vivaldi and Malocello. — Rediscovery of Canaries and Cape Verde Islands. — Discovery of Azores. — Prince Henry the Navigator. — Evolution in shipbuilding; the caravel. — Growth of scientific navigation. — Portuguese voyages in Africa. — Martin Behaim. — Question of pre-Columbian discoveries by Portuguese.

General — E. P. Cheyney, *European Background of American History* (1904), chs. i–vi; E. G. Bourne, *Spain in America* (1905), ch. i; Edgar Prestage, *Portuguese Pioneers*

(1933), chs. i–x; S. E. Morison, *Portuguese Voyages to America in Fifteenth Century* (1940); W. C. Abbott, *Expansion of Europe* (1938), chs. i, ii; R. B. Merriman, *Rise of Spanish Empire* (1918–34), I, ch. iii, II, ch. xvi; J. N. L. Baker, *History of Geographical Discovery and Exploration* (1931), chs. i–iv; Beazley, *Dawn of Modern Geography*.

Special — Geography and Navigation: W. H. Tillinghast, "Geographical Knowledge of Ancients," in Winsor, *Narrative and Critical History*, I, ch. i; G. H. T. Kimble, *Geography in Middle Ages* (1938); J. K. Wright, *Geographical Lore of Time of Crusades* (1925); Segundo de Ispizúa, *Historia de la geografía y de la cosmografía en las edades antigua y media* (2 vols., 1922–26); Leonardo Olschki, *Marco Polo's Precursors* (1943); E. G. Ravenstein, *Martin Behaim, His Life and Globe* (1908). ❧ African Voyages: C. G. M. B. de La Roncière, *La découverte de l'Afrique au moyen âge* (3 vols., 1924–27); J. W. Blake, *European Beginnings in West Africa* (1937); A. H. Lybyer, "Influence of Turks upon Routes of Oriental Trade," Am. Hist. Assoc., *Report*, 1914, I, 125. ❧ Navigation and Shipbuilding: L. C. Wroth, *Way of a Ship* (1937); Joaquim Bensaude, *Histoire de la science nautique portugaise, résumé* (1917); Abel Fontoura da Costa, *Science nautique des Portugais à l'époque des découvertes* (1935; a résumé of his *Marinharia dos Descobrimentos* (1933); Stevenson, *Atlas of Portolan Charts*, No. 82; Heinrich Winter, "Late Portolan Charts," *Imago Mundi*, VII (1950), 37; A. E. Nordenskiöld, *Periplus: An Essay on Early History of Charts and Sailing-Directions* (1897); Gervasio de Artiñano y de Galdácano, *Arquitectura naval Española* (1920); Quirino da Fonseca, *Caravela Portuguesa* (1934); F. C. Lane, *Venetian Ships and Shipbuilders of Renaissance* (1934); Auguste Jal, *Archéologie navale* (2 vols., 1840). ❧ Portuguese Voyages: J. P. Oliveira Martins, *Golden Age of Prince Henry the Navigator* (1914), and *Historia da colonização portuguesa do Brasil*, I (Oporto, 1921); Armando Cortesão, *Cartografia e Cartógrafos Portugueses dos Seculos XV e XVI* (2 vols., 1935). ❧ The Economic revolution of 1400–1600: Henri Pirenne, *Economic and Social History of Medieval Europe* (1936); Henri Sée, *Modern Capitalism* (1928); Tawney, *Religion and Rise of Capitalism*; F. L. Nussbaum, *History of Economic Institutions of Modern Europe* (1933), pts. 1–3; Henri Hauser, *Les débuts du capitalisme* (1927); G. F. von Schmoller, *Mercantile System* (1931); Richard Ehrenberg, *Capital and Finance in Age of Renaissance* (H. M. Lucas transl., 1928); Miriam Beard, *History of Business Man* (1938). ❧ Spanish Civilization: E. D. Salmon, *Imperial Spain* (1931); Merriman, *Rise of Spanish Empire*, II, chs. xii–xv; Rafael Altamira y Crevea, *Historia de España* (1900–30), II, 369–549.

Sources — *Book of Ser Marco Polo* (best eds. are the Cordier-Yule, 2 vols., 1903, and the Penzer, 1937); d'Ailly, *Imago Mundi; Alguns documentos do Archivo Nacional da Torre do Tombo* (1892); Gomes Eannes de Azurara, *Conquests and Discoveries of Henry the Navigator* (abridgment of his *Chronicle*, 1936); Davenport, *European Treaties*, I, 9; Duarte Pacheco Pereira, *Esmeraldo de situ Orbis*, Hakluyt Soc., *Publ.*, LXXIX (1937); *Voyages of Cadamosto* (G. R. Crone, ed.), *ibid.*, LXXX (1937); *Voyage of Pedro Álvares Cabral* (W. B. Greenlee, ed.), *ibid.*, LXXXI (1938).

72. CHRISTOPHER COLUMBUS AND HIS DISCOVERIES

Summary — Birth and early career of Columbus. — What was he trying to do? — Question of Toscanelli's assistance. — Nature of Columbus's contract. — Pinzon's help or hindrance. — The Ships. — 1492–93, First Voyage. — 1493–05, Second Voyage, discovery of Lesser Antilles, exploration of Cuban coast. — Early maps showing discoveries. — Who was Vespucci and what voyages did he really make? — Bulls and treaties of demarcation. — Columbus as a colonizer. — 1498, Third Voyage; discovery of the mainland. — 1502–04, Fourth Voyage, Jamaica.

General — Bourne, *Spain in America*, chs. ii–iv; H. I. Priestley, *Coming of White Man, 1492–1848* (1929), ch. i; Fiske, *Discovery of America*, I, 335; D. L. Molinari, *La Empresa columbina* (1938), and *El Nacimento del nuevo mundo 1492–1534* (1941).

Special — Biographies of Columbus: Irving, *Life and Voyages of Columbus*; Morison,

Admiral of the Ocean Sea; J. B. Thacher, *Christopher Columbus* (3 vols., 1903–04); de Lollis, *Cristoforo Colombo*; Charcot, *Christophe Colomb*; J. Winsor, *Columbus*; Paolo Revelli, *Il Genovese* (1951); Armando Alvárez Pedroso, *Cristóbal Colón* (1944); Ferdinand Columbus, *Historie della vita e dei fatti di Cristoforo Colombo* (1569; partly translated in John Pinkerton, *Collection of Voyages* [1808–14], XII; best modern ed., Renaldo Caddeo [2 vols., 1930]. Hernan Pérez de Oliva's early biography, never printed, is summarized by Leonard Olschki in *Hispanic Am. Hist. Rev.*, XXIII (1943), 165. ⊄ Columbus' motives: Henry Vignaud, *Histoire critique de la grande entreprise de Christophe Colomb* (2 vols., 1911; summarized in his *Columbian Tradition*, [1920]); R. D. Carbia, *La Nueva Historia del Descubrimiento de América* (1936); Henry Harrisse, *Christophe Colomb* (2 vols., 1884–85); Nunn, *Geographical Conceptions of Columbus*; Otto Schoenrich, ed., *Legacy of Columbus* (2 vols., 1949–50); C. H. Haring, "Genesis of Royal Government in Spanish Indies," *Hispanic Am. Hist. Rev.*, VII (1927), 141; Alberto Magnaghi, "La Sigla e la Firma di C. Colombo," *Rivista Geog. Ital.*, XXXVIII (1931), 53; Ramon Menéndez Pidal, "La Lengua de Colón," *Bulletin Hispanique*, XLII (1940), 1; S. E. Morison, "Columbus's Colonial Policy," Pan-Am. Union, *Bull.*, LXXVI (1942), 543, and "Route of Columbus along Coast of Haiti and Site of Navidad," Am. Philos. Soc., *Trans.* (n.s.), XXXI, iv (1940), 239; Ángel de Altolaguirre y Duvale, "Evidence that Columbus was an Italian," *Inter-America*, IX (1925), 149; H. R. Wagner, "Marco Polo's Narrative Becomes Propaganda," *Imago Mundi*, VI (1949), 3. ⊄ Ships, Crew, and Navigations: Morison, *Admiral*, I, chs. ix–xiii; J. F. Guillén y Tato, *La Carabela Santa María* (1927); R. C. Anderson, "The Santa Maria," *Mariner's Mirror*, XVI (1930), 187; Heinrich Winter, *Die Kolumbusschiffe* (1944); A. B. Gould, "Nueva lista documentada de los tripulantes de Colón en 1492," Real Acad. de la Hist., *Boletin*, LXXXV–CXV (1924–44); J. W. McElroy, "Ocean Navigation of Columbus on First Voyage," *Am. Neptune*, I (1940), 209; S. E. Morison, "Colón y la Polar," *Anuario de Historia Argentina* (1941), 1; Heinrich Winter, "Who Invented the Compass?," *Mariner's Mirror*, XXIII (1937), 95; *Imago Mundi* (1935–   ). ⊄ Toscanelli question: Molinari, *Empresa*; de Lollis, *Colombo*; N. Sumien, *Correspondence de Toscanelli avec Christophe Colomb* (1927); Henry Vignaud, *Toscanelli and Columbus* (1902); Ángel de Altolaguirre y Duvale, *Cristóbal Colón y Pablo del Pozzo Toscanelli* (1903); C. E. Nowell, "Toscanelli Letters," *Hispanic Am. Hist. Rev.*, XVII (1937), 346. ⊄ Landfalls: J. B. Murdock, "Cruise of Columbus in Bahamas," U. S. Naval Inst., *Proc.*, X (1884), 449; R. T. Gould, "Landfall of Columbus," *Geog. Jour.*, LXIX (1927), 403; Rudolf Cronau, *Discovery of America, Landfall and Last Resting Place of Columbus* (1921); W. H. Hobbs, "Track of Columbus Caravels," *Mich. Alumni Quar. Rev.*, LVI (1950), 118; P. Verhoog, *Guanahani Again* (1947); J. L. Montalvo-Guenard, *El descubrimiento de Boriquén* (1933). ⊄ Vespucci and the name America: Bourne, *Spain in America*, ch. vii; Alberto Magnaghi, *Amerigo Vespucci: studio critico* (Rome, 1926); Roberto Almagià, *Gli Italiani, primi esploratori dell' America* (1937); Roberto Levillier, *América la bien llamada* (2 vols., 1949); G. T. Northrup, ed., *Vespucci Reprints* (7 vols., 1916); Martin Waldseemüller, *Cosmografiae Introductio* (1506, facsimile reproduction, 1907); *Oldest Map with Name America*, Joseph Fischer and Franz von Wieser, eds., 1903); H. N. Stevens, *First Delineation of New World* (London, 1928). ⊄ Papal Bulls and Treaty of Tordesillas: Henry Harrisse, *Diplomatic History of America* (1897); Herman vander Linden, "Alexander VI and the Bulls of Demarcation," *Am. Hist. Rev.*, XXII (1916), 1; F. G. Davenport, *European Treaties*, I, 56; P. Gottschalk, *Earliest Diplomatic Documents on America* (1927). ⊄ Maps: Paullin, *Atlas*, plates 8–10; E. D. Fite and Archibald Freeman, *Book of Old Maps* (1926), nos. 3–5; Konrad Kretschmer, *Die Entdeckung Amerika's Atlas* (1892); Real Academia de Historia, *Mapas Españoles de América* (1951); Armando Cortesão, *Historia da colonização portuguesa* (§ 71) I; G. E. Nunn, *Mappemonde of Juan de la Cosa*.

Sources — The Italian government's great *Raccolta di Documenti e Studi* (14 vols., 1892–96), contains the best texts; Giovanni Monleone (comp. for the City of Genoa), *Christopher Columbus Documents and Proofs of His Genoese Origin* (1932); L. C. Jane, *Four Voyages of Columbus* and *Voyages of Columbus* (London, 1930); Olson and Bourne, *Northmen, Columbus and Cabot*; Maria del Rosario, Duquesa de Berwick y Liria y Alba, *Autógrafos de Colón* (1892), and *Nuevos Autógrafos* (1902); C. Columbus His Own *Book of Privileges*, B. F. Stevens, ed. (1893); Pacheco, *Colección*, 2 ser., VII, VIII;

Memorias de la Real Academia de Historia, X (1883), 163. — For contemporary historians, see: § 74.

Bibliography — Winsor, *Narrative and Critical History,* II, 46; H. P. Biggar, "Recent Books on Columbus," *Canadian Hist. Rev.,* XII (1931), 59; Wilberforce Eames, "Columbus Letter," N.Y. Public Library, *Bull.,* XXVIII (1924), 594; C. E. Nowell, "Columbus Question, a Survey of Recent Literature," *Am. Hist. Rev.,* XLIV (1939), 802; D. H. Mugridge, *Christopher Columbus: Selected List of Books and Articles by American Authors, 1892-1950* (1950).

73. CABOTS AND CORTE-REALS

Summary — 1497, John Cabot's first voyage. — 1498, second voyage; question of landfall and extent of coasting; veracity of Sebastian Cabot. — Early sixteenth century voyages by Bristol-Azorean syndicate. — Problem of the voyage of João Fernandez "the Labrador." — 1499-1502, the three voyages of Gaspar and Miguel Corte-Real; exploitation of Newfoundland fisheries by Portuguese.

General — Bourne, *Spain in America,* ch. v; Nansen, *In Northern Mists,* chs. xiv, xv; A. P. Newton, ed., *Great Age of Discovery* (1932), ch. vi; Morison, *Portuguese Voyages,* ch. i.

Special — J. A. Williamson, *Voyages of Cabots and English Discovery of North America* (1929); H. P. Biggar, *Voyages of Cabots and Corte-Reals* (1903); Henry Harrisse, *Discovery of North America,* and *Découverte et évolution cartographique de Terre Neuve* (1900), and *John Cabot and Sebastian His Son* (1896), and *Les Corte-Real* (1883); S. E. Dawson, "Voyages of the Cabots; Latest Phases," Royal Soc. of Canada, *Proc.,* 2 ser., III, § 2 (1897), 139; W. F. Ganong, "Crucial Maps in Early Cartography of Canada," *ibid.,* 3 ser., XXIII, § 2 (1929), 135; G. E. Nunn, *The La Cosa Map and the Cabot Voyages* (1946); D. Gernez, "Les Cartes avec échelle de latitudes auxiliaires pour la Région de Terre-Neuve," Académie de Marine de Belgique, *Communications,* VI (1952), 93–117; Eileen Power and M. M. Postan, eds., *Studies in English Trade in XV Century* (1933), ch. v; Henrique Braz and José Agostinho, "Fernandez-Barcellos and Diogo de Tieve Voyages," Instituto Historico de Ilha Terceira, *Boletim,* I (1943), 7, II (1944), 1, 276, III (1945), 259, IX (1951), 211. ❡ Maps: Stevenson, *Maps Illustrating Early Discovery* includes a detailed photograph of the Cantino Map (1502); a facsimile of the Contarini (1506) was issued by the British Museum (1924); the Sebastian Cabot Map of 1544 is best reproduced in Dawson's "Voyages of the Cabots."

Sources — Williamson, *Voyages;* Olson and Bourne, *Northmen, Columbus and Cabot,* 421; H. P. Biggar, ed., *Precursors of Cartier, 1497-1535, Documents Relating to Early History of Canada* (1911).

Bibliography — Charles Dean in Winsor, *Narrative and Critical History,* III, ch. i; G. P. Winship, *Cabot Bibliography* (1900).

74. THE SPANISH COLONIAL EMPIRE

Summary — The great conquests. — Mexico, Peru, Chile, New Granada. — Discovery of the Pacific; Magellan's voyage, conquest of the Philippines. — Political organization of the empire. — The Catholic Church and the Indians (§ 69). — Trade and navigation. — The founding of universities; culture, learning, and literature.

General — C. H. Haring, *Spanish Empire in America* (1952); Bourne, *Spain in America,* chs. x-xxi; B. W. Diffie, *Latin American Civilization, Colonial Period* (1945); Molinari, *Nacimiento del nuevo mundo;* Priestley, *Coming of White Man,* chs. ii, iv-vii; F. A. Kirkpatrick, *Spanish Conquistadores* (1934); Washington Irving, *Companions of Columbus* (1831); W. H. Prescott, *Conquest of Mexico* (1843), and *Conquest of Peru* (1847); George Frederici, *Charakter der Entdeckung u. Eroberung Amerikas durch die*

Europaër (3 vols., 1925–36); Silvio Zavala, *New Viewpoints on Spanish Colonization of America* (1943); Hanke, *Spanish Struggle for Justice*; Bernard DeVoto, *Course of Empire* (1952).

Special — Contemporary historians: Peter Martyr d'Anghiera, *De orbe novo decades* (1516; English transl. by Richard Eden [1555], reprinted in Edward Arber, ed., *First Three English Books on America* [1885]); Andrés Bernáldez, *Historia de Fernando y Isabel* (2 vols., 1869); Antonio de Herrera, *Historia General de los hechos de los Castellanos* (1601–15); López de Gómara, *Historia general de las Indias* (2 vols., 1932); Fernández de Oviedo, *Historia general y natural de las Indias* (4 vols., 1851–55); Bartolomé de las Casas, *Historia de las Indias* (3 vols., 1927) and *Apologética historia de las Indias* (Serrano y Sanz, ed. 1909); Hanke, *Las Casas*. ❡ The Pacific: J. T. Medina, *Descubrimiento del Océano Pacífico* (3 vols., 1914–20); Ángel de Altolaguirre y Duvale, *Vasco Nuñez de Balboa* (1914); Pablo Pastells and Constantino Bayle, *Descubrimiento estrecho de Magallanes* (2 vols., 1920); F. H. H. Guillemard, *Magellan* (1890); J. A. de M. J., Visconde de Lagôa, *Fernão de Magalhãs* (2 vols., 1938); G. E. Nunn, "Magellan's Route in Pacific," *Geog. Rev.*, XXIV (1934), 615; W. L. Schurz, *Manila Galleon* (1939); *Encyclopedia of Philippines*, VIII, *History* (1936). ❡ Provinces and Viceroyalties: Carlos Pereyra, *La Obra de España en América* (1920); I. A. Wright, *Early History of Cuba, 1492–1586* (1916); H. I. Priestley, *Mexican Nation, a History* (1923); H. H. Bancroft, *History of Mexico* (6 vols., 1883–88), and *History of Central America* (3 vols., 1882–87); Bernard Moses, *Spanish Dependencies in South America* (2 vols., 1914); J. A. Villacorte, *Historia de la capitanía general de Guatemala* (1942); R. B. Cunninghame Graham, *Pedro de Valdivia, Conqueror of Chile* (1926), and *Life of Quesada* (1922), and *Conquest of New Granada* (1922); Germán Arciniegas, *Germans in the Conquest of America* (1943); P. A. Means, *Fall of Inca Empire and Spanish Rule in Peru 1530–1780* (1932); F. A. Encina, *Historia de Chile* (1940–45), I–IV. ❡ The Church: Robert Ricard, *La Conquête spirituelle du Méxique 1523 à 1572* (1933); G. R. G. Conway, *An Englishman and Mexican Inquisition 1556–1560* (1927); H. C. Lea, *Inquisition in the Spanish Dependencies* (1922); J. L. Mecham, *Church and State in Latin America* (1934); chs. i–iii. ❡ Institutions and Economy: C. H. Haring, *Trade and Navigation between Spain and Indies* (1915), and "Genesis of Royal Government in Spanish Indies"; J. H. Parry, *Spanish Theory of Empire in Sixteenth Century* (1940); E. J. Hamilton, *American Treasure and the Price Revolution in Spain* (1934); Lewis Hanke, *First Social Experiments* (1935); J. P. Rubio, *El Piloto Mayor de la casa contratación* (1923); L. B. Simpson, *Encomienda in New Spain* (1950), and *Repartimiento System* (1938), and *Emancipation of Indian Slaves* (1940). ❡ Intellectual History: J. T. Lanning, *Academic Culture in Spanish Colonies* (1940); Alfred Coester, *Literary History of Spanish America* (1928); Pedro Henríquez Ureña, *Literary Currents in Hispanic America* (1945); I. A. Leonard, *Books of the Brave* (1949) and *Don Carlos de Sigüenza y Góngora* (1939); José Torre Revello, *El Libro, la imprenta y el periodismo en América* (1940); Felipe Barreda Laos, *Vida intelectual del virreinato del Peru* (1937). ❡ Fine Arts: Diego Angulo Iñíguez, *Historia del arte hispano-americano* (1945–50), I–II; Pál Kelemen, *Baroque and Rococo in Latin America* (1951); Manuel Toussaint, *Arte colonial en México* (1948); H. E. Wethey, *Colonial Architecture and Sculpture in Peru* (1949); Felipe Cossío del Pomar, *Pintura colonial* (1928); Lawrence Anderson, *Art of Silversmith in Mexico 1519–1936* (2 vols., 1941). ❡ Education: Constantino Bayle, *España y la educación popular en América* (1934); Priestley, *Mexican Nation*, chs. v–x; C. B. de la Plaza y Jaén, *Crónica de la Universidad de México* (2 vols., 1931).

Sources — Pedro de Cieza de Leon, *His Chronicle of Peru* (C. R. Markham, transl., 2 vols., 1864–83); Pascual de Andagoya, *Narrative of Pedrarias Davila* (C. R. Markham, transl., 1865); Garcilaso de la Vega, *First Part of Royal Commentaries of Yncas* (C. R. Markham, transl., 2 vols., 1869–71); C. R. Markham, ed., *Reports on Discovery of Peru* (1872); P. F. de Queiros, *Voyages* (C. R. Markham, transl., 2 vols., 1904), and *Historia del descubrimiento de las regiones australes* (3 vols., 1876–82); Bernal Diaz del Castillo, *Discovery and Conquest of Mexico* (A. P. Maudslay, transl., 1928); Pedro Pizarro, *Relation of Discovery and Conquest of Peru* (P. A. Means, ed., 2 vols., 1921); Antonio Pigafetta, *Magellan's Voyage Around the World* (J. A. Robertson, transl., 2 vols., 1906);

Gaspar de Carvajal, *Discovery of Amazon* (H. C. Heaton, ed., 1934); Pacheco, *Colección*; Montoto, *Colección;* E. H. Blair and J. A. Robertson, eds., *Philippine Islands 1493–1898* (55 vols., 1903–09).

Bibliography — C. K. Jones, *Bibliography of Latin American Bibliographies* (1942); Winsor, *Narrative and Critical History*, II, chs. ii–ix; A. C. Wilgus, *Histories and Historians of Hispanic America* (1936); Hanke, *Handbook of Latin America Studies*; P. A. Means, *Biblioteca Andina* (1928), pt. 1, and "Chroniclers," Conn. Acad. Arts and Sci., *Trans.*, XXIX (1928), 271; S. R. Clemence, ed., *Calendar of Documents, Harkness Coll.*, *Library of Congress* (2 vols., 1932–36); Pedro Torres y Lanzas, *Catálogo de los documentos relativas a las Filipinas* (9 vols., 1925–36); G. F. Cruz, *Bibliografía de D. José Toribio Medina* (1931); Robert Streit, ed., *Bibliotheca Missionum* (17 vols., 1916–39), II; Emilio Valton, *Impresos mexicanos del siglo XVI* (1935); J. T. Medina, *La Imprenta en México* (8 vols., 1907–12), and *La Imprenta en Lima* (4 vols., 1904–07).

75. SPANISH EXPLORATIONS AND SETTLEMENTS IN THE UNITED STATES TO 1660

Summary — The Adelantado and the Frontier Mission as institutions. — 1513–60, Expeditions of Ponce de Leon, Cabeza de Vaca, Coronado, De Soto, and other explorations of the Interior. — Earliest explorations of Lower and Upper California. — Spanish voyages along the west coast of Mexico and the United States. — 1524–65, Gómez' and other Spanish voyages along the Atlantic coast. — Province of Guale, slave hunting, mission station on Chesapeake Bay. — 1565, St. Augustine and other presidios in Florida; missions in Florida and the Carolina coast. — 1595, Oñate's conquest of New Mexico; exploration of the Pimería Alta. — Spanish archeology. — Later developments (§§ 100, 140, 164).

General — H. E. Bolton, *Spanish Borderlands* (1921), chs. i–vi; Priestley, *Coming of White Man*, ch. iii; Channing, *History*, I, 59; Bancroft, *North Mexican States and Texas*, I, chs. i–vii, xiv, and *Arizona and New Mexico*, chs. i–viii; Brebner, *Explorers of North America*, chs. i–vi.

Special — Harrisse, *Discovery of North America*, pt. 1, bks. 6, 7; J. T. Medina, *El Portugués Esteban Gómez al servicio de España* (1908); E. L. Stevenson, "Early Spanish Cartography of New World," Am. Antiq. Soc., *Proc.*, n.s., XIX (1909), 369; H. E. Bolton, "Mission as Frontier Institution," *Am. Hist. Rev.*, XXIII (1917), 42; Winsor, *Narrative and Critical History*, II, ch. iv; Woodbury Lowery, *Spanish Settlements within Present Limits of United States 1513–61* (1901), and *Spanish Settlements in Florida 1562–74* (1905); A. G. de Barcia, *Ensayo cronológico de la Florida* (1723; Anthony Kerrigan, transl., 1951); V. E. Chatelain, *Defenses of Spanish Florida 1565–1763* (1941); Maynard Geiger, *Franciscan Conquest of Florida, 1573–1618* (1937); J. T. Lanning, *Spanish Missions of Georgia* (1935; but see E. M. Coulter, *Georgia's Disputed Ruins*, 1937). Constantino Bayle, *Pedro Menéndez de Avilés* (1928); L. D. Scisco, "Track of Ponce de Leon in 1513," Am. Geog. Soc., *Bull.*, XLV (1913), 721; Cleve Hallenbeck, *Alvar Nuñez Cabeza de Vaca* (1940); R. B. Cunninghame Graham, *Hernando de Soto* (1903); Bolton, *Coronado;* G. P. Hammond, *Don Juan de Oñate and Founding of New Mexico* (1927); Twitchell, *New Mexico History*, I (1911), chs. i–vii; Wagner, *Spanish Voyages to Northwest Coast*, and *Cartography of Northwest Coast*, I, chs. i–xiv; Chapman, *History of California*; H. E. Bolton, "Spanish Occupation of Texas, 1519–1690," *Southwest Hist. Quar.*, XVI (1912), 1; C. E. Castañeda, *Catholic Heritage in Texas*, I, *The Finding, 1519–1693* (1936).

Sources — Bolton, *Spanish Exploration in Southwest;* Hodge and Lewis, eds., *Spanish Explorers in Southern United States;* Bourne, *Narratives of Hernando de Soto;* G. P. Hammond and Agapito Rey, eds., *Narratives of Coronado Expedition, 1540–42* (1940); C. W. Hackett, ed., *Historical Documents Relating to New Mexico* (2 vols., 1923–37); Eugenio Ruidíaz y Caravia, ed., *La Florida* (2 vols., 1893); G. S. de Merás, *Pedro*

Menéndez de Avilés Memorial (J. T. Connor, transl.), Fla. State Hist. Soc., *Publ.*, III (1923); Connor, *Colonial Records of Spanish Florida;* H. I Priestley, ed., *Luna Papers* (2 vols.), Fla. State Hist. Soc., *Publ.*, VIII (1928); A. P. Whitaker, ed., *Documents Relating to Commercial Policy of Spain in Floridas*, Fla. State Hist. Soc., *Publ.*, X (1931).

Bibliography — H. R. Wagner, *Spanish Southwest, 1542–1794. An Annotated Bibliography* (2 vols., r. ed., 1937); Alliot, *Bibliography of Arizona;* Cowan, *Bibliography of California;* J. A. Robertson, "Spanish MSS. of the Florida State Historical Society," Am. Antiq. Soc., *Proc.*, n.s., XXXIX (1929), 16. — See also: § 74.

76. FRENCH EXPLORATION OF THE AMERICAS TO 1608

Summary — Were French fishermen on the American coast before Columbus? — 1524, Verrazano's voyage. — Norumbega, Saguenay, and other mythical kingdoms. — 1533–41, Cartier's and Roberval's voyages. — 1560, French corsairs sack Trujillo. — 1562–65, Ribaut, Laudonnière, and the French attempts on Florida. — 1565, Menendez (§ 75) founds St. Augustine. — 1555–58, Villegagnon's colony in Brazil. — 1589, renewed activity in the north. — 1598, De la Roche's colony on Sable Island. — 1599, Pontgravé at the Saguenay. — 1603, Champlain's first voyage. — 1604, Sieur de Monts founds St. Croix and Port Royal. — Later developments (§§ 79, 97).

General — Francis Parkman, *Pioneers of France in New World* (r. ed., 1885); G. M. Wrong, *Rise and Fall of New France* (1928), I, ch. iv; Winsor, *Narrative and Critical History*, IV, chs. i, ii; N. M. Crouse, *French Pioneers in West Indies, 1624–64* (1940); C. G. M. B. de La Roncière, *Histoire de la marine française* (1906–10) III, 129, 307, IV, 10, 46, 307, 338.

Special — J. P. Baxter, *Jacques Cartier* (1906); C. G. M. B. de La Roncière, *Jacques Cartier* (1931); H. P. Biggar, *Early Trading Companies of New France* (1901); J. E. King, "Glorious Kingdom of Saguenay," *Canadian Hist. Rev.*, XXXI (1950), 390; Sigmund Diamond, "Norumbega," *Am. Neptune*, XI (1951), 95. ❡ Maps: Stevenson, *Maps Illustrating Early Discovery*, No. 12; W. F. Ganong, "Crucial Maps in Early Cartography of Canada," Royal Soc. Canada, *Proc.*, 3 ser., XXV (1931), § ii, 169, XXVII (1933), § ii, 149, XXVIII (1934), § ii, 149, XXIX (1935), § ii, 101.

Sources — Biggar, *Precursors of Cartier* (1911); "Verrazano's Letter on His Voyages," (three versions: Hakluyt's *Voyages*, VIII; N.Y. Hist. Soc., *Coll.*, 2 ser., I [1841], 37; and Amer. Scenic and Hist. Preservation Soc., *Report*, XV [1910], App. A); H. P. Biggar, ed., *Voyages of Jacques Cartier*, Public Archives of Canada, *Publ.*, No. 11 (1924), and *Collection of Documents, Cartier and Roberval*, Public Archives of Canada, *Publ.*, No. 14 (1930); W. I. Morse, *Acadiensia Nova*, II (1935), ch. iii (for La Roche); Jean de Léry, *Histoire d'un voyage en Brésil* (1578; Paul Gaffarel, ed., 1880, 1927); André Thevet, *Les singularitez de la France antarctique* (1558; Paul Gaffarel, ed., 1878); Jean Ribaut, *Whole and True Discouerye of Terra Florida* (1563; in Hakluyt, *Divers Voyages*, 1582, and in facsimile in Fla. State Hist. Soc., *Publ.*, VII [1927]); M. M. Basanier, *L'histoire notable de la Floride* (in Hakluyt, *Voyages*, VIII, IX). — See also: § 75.

Bibliography — Winsor, *Narrative and Critical History*, II, ch. iv, IV, chs. i, ii, viii, 391; Channing, *History*, I, 112; Staton and Tremaine, *Bibliography of Canadiana;* G. M. Wrong, *et al.*, *Review of Historical Publications Relating to Canada* (22 vols., 1896–1918); Streit, *Bibliotheca Missionum* II, III.

77. CAUSES AND BACKGROUND OF ENGLISH EXPANSION

Summary — Heritage of Wars of the Roses. — Sixteenth century changes in English society: woolens trade; foreign investment; deposit banking; bills of exchange; regulated and joint-stock companies; "dress rehearsal for the industrial revolution." — 1497–1603,

The Tudor Dynasty: Henry VII and VIII; Edward VI, Mary I, and Elizabeth I; their attitudes toward overseas enterprise. — 1521, the breach with Rome; phases of the Protestant Reformation, its effect on business. — 1564–1603, Richard Eden, John Dee, the two Hakluyts, Humphrey Gilbert, and the literary encouragement to overseas expansion.

General — E. P. Cheyney, *European Background*, chs. vii, viii, and *History of England* (2 vols., 1913–26); A. L. Rowse, *England of Elizabeth* (1950); J. A. Williamson, "England and Opening of Atlantic," J. H. Rose, *et al.*, eds., *Cambridge History of British Empire* (7 vols., 1929–30), I, ch. ii; Andrews, *Colonial Period*, I, chs. i–iii; G. L. Beer, *Origins of British Colonial System* (1908), chs. i–iii; G. N. Clark, *Seventeenth Century*, chs. i–iv.

Special — Geography: Edward Lynam, ed., *Richard Hakluyt and His Successors* (1946); G. P. Parks, *Richard Hakluyt and English Voyages* (1928); E. G. R. Taylor, *Late Tudor and Early Stuart Geography* (1934); F. T. McCann, *English Discovery of America to 1585* (1952). ❡ Economic Development: Ephraim Lipson, *Economic History of England* (1931), II, ch. ii; W. R. Scott, *Constitution and Finance of Joint Stock Companies* (1910–12; 1951), I, II; A. P. Usher, *Introduction to Industrial History of England* (1920); E. F. Heckscher, *Mercantilism* (2 vols., 1935); J. U. Nef, *Industry and Government in France and England, 1540–1640* (1940); R. H. Tawney, *Agrarian Problem in Sixteenth Century* (1912); W. E. Lingelbach, *Merchant Adventurers of England* (1902); George Unwin, *Studies in Economic History* (1927), 133; F. R. Salter, *Sir Thomas Gresham* (1925); Inna Lubimenko, *Relations commerciales et politiques de l'Angleterre avec la Russie avant Pierre le Grand* (1933). ❡ Religion and Capitalism: Weber, *Protestant Ethic*; H. M. Robertson, *Aspects of Rise of Economic Individualism* (1933); Tawney, *Religion and Rise of Capitalism*.

Sources — Voyages: Richard Hakluyt, *Principal Navigations, Voyages of English Nation* (8 vols., 1927), I, V, VI (contains Gilbert, "Discourse," Carleil, "Briefe and Summarie Discourse," and Peckham, "Discourse"); Alexander Brown, *Genesis of United States* (2 vols., 1890); E. G. R. Taylor, ed., *Writings and Correspondence of Two Richard Hakluyts* (1935). ❡ English Economy and Social Life: William Harrison, *Description of England* (1577, reprinted 1889); C. T. Carr, ed., *Select Charters of Trading Companies* (1913); R. H. Tawney and Eileen Power, *Tudor Economic Documents* (3 vols., 1924); W. H. Dunham and Stanley Pargellis, *Complaint and Reform in England, 1436–1714* (1938).

Bibliography — R. H. Tawney, "Bibliography of Rise of Capitalism," *Econ. Hist. Rev.*, IV (1933), 336; Conyers Read, *Bibliography of British History, Tudor Period* (1933); Godfrey Davies, *Bibliography of British History, Stuart Period* (1928).

78. ENGLISH VOYAGES AND SETTLEMENTS, 1527–1606

Summary — 1527, Thorne's "Declaration" and Rut's Voyage; 1553, Muscovy Company chartered. — 1554, African voyages begun. — 1562–68, Three voyages of John Hawkins. — 1570–73, Drake in the West Indies. — 1577–80, Drake's circumnavigation. — 1576, Company of Catay (Frobisher). — 1578–87, Voyages of Gilbert and John Davis. — 1584, Raleigh's Virginia charter. — 1585–90, The Grenville and John White colony at Roanoke and its fate. — 1595, Raleigh's voyage to Guiana. — 1602–15, New England voyages of Gosnold, Pring, and Weymouth. — 1606, The Virginia Company.

General — Andrews, *Colonial Period*, I, chs. ii–iv; Channing, *History*, I, ch. v; Cheyney, *History of England*, I, pt. iii; Sir William Foster, *England's Quest of Eastern Trade* (1933), chs. iii–v, x, xi; J. A. Williamson, *Age of Drake* (1938); *Cambridge History of British Empire*, I, 47; Winsor, *Narrative and Critical History*, III, chs. iii, iv, vi; David Hannay, *Great Chartered Companies* (1926); W. F. Craven, *Southern Colonies in Seventeenth Century* (1949), chs. i, ii.

Special — Elizabethan Seamen: J. A. Williamson, *Sir John Hawkins* (1927); A. L. Rowse, *Sir Richard Grenville* (1937); Frank Aydelotte, "Elizabethan Seamen in Mexico and Ports of Spanish Main," *Am. Hist. Rev.*, XLVIII (1942), 1; W. G. Gosling, *Sir Humphrey Gilbert* (1911); J. S. Corbett, *Drake and Tudor Navy* (2 vols., 1917); H. R. Wagner, *Sir Francis Drake's Voyage Around World* (1926); E. G. R. Taylor, "More Light on Drake," *Mariner's Mirror*, XVI (1930), 134; R. P. Bishop, "Drake's Course in North Pacific," *British Columbia Hist. Quar.*, III (1939), 351; R. F. Heizer, *Drake and California Indians* (1947); George Davidson, *Identification of Drake's Anchorage* (1890); H. E. Bolton, *Drake's Plate of Brass* (1937); H. R. Wagner, "Creation of Rights of Sovereignty," *Pacific Hist. Rev.*, VII (1938), 297; J. A. Williamson, *et al.*, "Drake's Plate of Brass," *Geog. Jour.*, XCI (1938), 543, XCIV (1939), 54, XCV (1940), 159; R. B. Haselden, "Drake's Plate," *Am. Hist. Rev.*, XLII (1937), 863, XLIV (1939), 879. ⁅ Raleigh colonies: Ashe, *History of North Carolina*, I, chs. ii–iv; D. B. Quinn, *Raleigh and British Empire* (1949); R. D. W. Connor, *Raleigh's Settlements on Roanoke* (1907); W. F. Gookin, "Bart. Gosnold," *William and Mary Quar.*, 3 ser., VI (1949), 398. ⁅ Ships and Seafaring Conditions: John Masefield, introduction, Hakluyt, *Principle Navigations, Voyages*; E. K. Chatterton, *English Seamen and Colonization of America* (1930; Am. ed., *Seed of Liberty*); A. H. Markham, introduction, John Davis, *Voyages and Works* (1880); Michael Oppenheim, *Administration of Royal Navy* (1896), I. ⁅ Voyages and Narratives: H. P. Biggar, "English Expedition in 1527," *Mélanges d'histoire offerts à Charles Bémont* (1913), 459. ⁅ Maps: E. G. R. Taylor, *Tudor Geography 1485–1583* (1930); Fite and Freeman, *Book of Old Maps*, Nos. 25–28; R. P. Bishop, "Gilbert Map of c. 1582–83," *Geog. Jour.*, LXXII (1928), 235.

Sources — Voyages: Hakluyt, *Principle Navigations, Voyages*; Francis Fletcher, *World Encompassed by Sir Francis Drake* (1628; Sir R. C. Temple, ed., 1926); Thomas Maynarde, *Sir Francis Drake His Voyage, 1595* (W. D. Cooley, ed., 1849); Zelia Nuttall, ed., *New Light on Drake* (1914); I. A. Wright, ed., *Spanish Documents concerning English Voyages to Spanish Main, 1569–1580* (1932), and *Further English Voyages to Spanish America, 1583–94* (1951); Taylor, *Writings of Two Hakluyts*; D. B. Quinn, ed., *Voyages and Colonising Enterprises of Sir Humphrey Gilbert* (1940); H. S. Burrage, ed., *Early English and French Voyages* (1906); Samuel Purchas, *Hakluytus Posthumus or Purchas His Pilgrimes* (1625; 20 vols., 1905–07); Sir Richard Hawkins, *Observations in His Voyage into South Sea, 1593* (J. A. Williamson, ed., 1933); Thomas Hariot, *Briefe and True Report of New Found Land of Virginia* (1588; De Bry ed., 1590, with engravings of John White's drawings; often reprinted); Stefansson, *Three Voyages of Martin Frobisher*. ⁅ Documents: Brown, *Genesis of United States*, I; "Despatches of Castelnau de la Mauvissière," *Am. Hist. Rev.*, XXXI (1926), 285; *Calendar of State Papers Colonial*, I (*America and the West Indies 1574–1660*), IX (*Addenda 1574–1674*), and the *Spanish* series.

Bibliography — Winsor, *Narrative and Critical History*, III, chs. ii, iii, iv, vi; *Cambridge History of British Empire*, I, 847; R. G. Adams, *Brief Account of Raleigh's Roanoke Colony* (1935); J. A. Williamson, "Books on Drake," *History*, n.s., XII (1928), 310; W. J. Harte, "Some Recent Views on Drake's Voyage Round World," *ibid.*, n.s., XX (1936), 348; F. W. Bateson, ed., *Cambridge Bibliography of English Literature* (1941), I, 763.

Chapter Seven

THE PLANTING OF THE DUTCH, FRENCH, AND ENGLISH IN NORTH AMERICA TO 1660

79. NEW FRANCE

Summary — French explorations (§ 76). — 1603, De Monts and his patent. — 1604, Settlements on the Bay of Fundy. — Champlain on the New England coast. — 1608, Champlain founds Quebec; 1609, discovers Lake Champlain; 1615, Lake Huron. — 1629, Sir Thomas Kirke captures Quebec. — 1632, Treaty of St. Germain; New France, Acadia, and Canada confirmed to France. — The Hundred Associates. — 1632–1633, La Tour and D'Aulnay, claimants to Acadia. — Society and culture in Quebec. — Canadian feudal system. — Fur trade. — Church and the Indians (§ 69). — Later developments (§ 97).

General — Channing, *History*, I, 100; Francis Parkman, *Pioneers of New France*, pt. 2, and *Jesuits in North America* (1867), and *Old Régime in Canada* (1874); G. M. Wrong, *Rise and Fall of New France*, I, chs. vi–xiv; Gabriel Hanotaux and Alfred Martineau, *Histoire des colonies françaises* (1929), I, 41, 191; Émile Salone, *La Colonisation de la Nouvelle-France* (1905); J. F. Saintoyant, *La Colonisation française sous l'ancien régime* (1929), I, § 11, chs. ii–iii; F. X. Garneau, *Histoire du Canada* (1858; new ed., 1946; rev. by A. L. Burt, *Am. Hist. Rev.*, LII [1946], 155); *Cambridge History British Empire*, VI, chs. i–iii.

Special — Biggar, *Early Trading Companies of New France*; C. G. M. B. de La Roncière, *Histoire de la marine française*, IV, 319, 629, V, 226, and "La compagnie française au pôle arctique au temps de Henry IV," *Bibliothèque de l'École des Chartes*, LXXVIII (1917), 154; Lucas, *Historical Geography*, V (1), chs. ii–iii; Bishop, *Champlain*; J. B. Brebner, *New England's Outpost, Acadia before Conquest* (1927), ch. i; Émile Lauvrière, *La Tragédie d'un peuple; histoire du peuple acadien* (1922), I, chs. i–iv, vi, and *Deux traîtres d'Acadie et leur victime* (1932); Azarie Couillard Després, *Charles de la Tour, gouverneur en Acadie 1593–1666* (1932); Fr. Candide de Nant, *Pages glorieuses de l'épopée canadienne. Une mission capucine en Acadie* (1927); Nute, *Caesars of Wilderness*, chs. i–v; Donatien Frémont, *Pierre Radisson, voi des coureurs de bois* (1933); W. B. Munro, *Seignorial System in Canada* (1907), chs. i, ii; D. A. Heneker, *Seignorial Régime in Canada* (1927); J. Delalande, *Le conseil souverain de la Nouvelle-France* (1927); Camille de Rochemonteix, *Les Jésuites et la Nouvelle-France aux XVII° siècle* (3 vols., 1895–96); Kennedy, *Jesuit and Savage in New France*; Auguste Gosselin, *L'Instruction au Canada sous le régime français* (1911); Birch, *Isaac Jogues*; L. M. Spell, "Music in New France in Seventeenth Century," *Canadian Hist. Rev.*, VIII (1927), 119; Antoine Roy, *Lettres, sciences, arts au Canada sous le régime français* (1930); François Dollier de Casson, *History of Montreal 1640–72* (Ralph Flenley, transl., 1928); E. Z. Massicotte, "Les colons de Montréal de 1642 à 1667," *Bull. des Recherches Historiques*, XXXIII

(1927); Seraphin Marion, *Un pionnier canadien: Pierre Boucher* (1927); W. B. Munro, "The coureurs de bois," Mass. Hist. Soc., *Proc.*, LVII (1924), 192.

Sources — Samuel de Champlain, *Works* (H. P. Biggar, ed., 6 vols. and portfolio of plates and maps, 1922–36); W. L. Grant, ed., *Voyages of Samuel de Champlain* (1907); Marc Lescarbot, *Histoire de la Nouvelle France* (1609; H. P. Biggar, ed., 3 vols., 1907–14), and *Nova Francia* (1609; H. P. Biggar, ed., 1928), and *Les Muses de la Nouvelle France* (1609; transl. by H. T. Richardson as, *Theatre of Neptune*, 1927); W. B. Munro, ed., *Documents Relating to Seignorial Tenure in Canada 1598–1854* (1908); Thwaites, *Jesuit Relations*; Edna Kenton, ed., *Indians of North America* (2 vols., 1925, a selection from Thwaites); Mère Marie de L'Incarnation, *Écrits spirituels et historiques publiés par dom Claude* [Martin], (Albert Jamet, ed., 3 vols., 1929); Pierre Boucher, *Histoire véritable et naturelle des moeurs et productions du pays de la Nouvelle France* (1664; often reprinted); "Isaac Jogues Papers," N. Y. Hist. Soc., *Coll.*, 2 ser., III (1857), 161; *Rapport de l'Archiviste de Québec* (1929–   ); *Nova Francia*, I–VII (1925–32); Pierre Margry, *Découvertes et établissements des français, 1614–1754. Mémoires et documents originaux* (6 vols., 1876–86).

Bibliography — Winsor, *Narrative and Critical History*, IV, 130, 149; Staton and Tremaine, *Bibliography of Canadiana*; Wrong, *Review of Historical Publications*; W. C. Ford, "French Royal Edicts on America," Mass. Hist. Soc., *Proc.*, LX (1927), 250.

80. NEW NETHERLAND AND NEW SWEDEN

Summary — The Dutch Republic and sea power; exploits in the Far East and West Indies. — 1609, Henry Hudson and his explorations. — 1614, The United Netherland Company. — 1621, The Dutch West India Company; its objects and government. — 1629, The Charter of Privileges to Patroons. — The Dutch and the Indians. — Internal affairs. — 1647–64, Governor Stuyvesant; relations with the Swedes and English. — Dutch architecture, schools, and the Dutch Reformed Church. — Willem Usselinx and founding of New Sweden. — Finnish contribution to the colony. — The log cabin. — 1655, conquest of New Sweden by New Netherland. — Dutch activities in the West Indies and South America, capture of Brazil, Curaçao, and Dutch Guiana. — Exploits of Piet Hein. — Later developments (§§ 93, 95).

General — Andrews, *Colonial Period*, III, 70; Osgood, *American Colonies in Seventeenth Century*, II, ch. v; Channing, *History*, I, chs. xvi, xvii; Charles de Lannoy, *Histoire de l'expansion coloniale des peuples européens* (1907–21), II, chs. i–vi, III; Pierre Bonnasieux, *Les Grandes compagnies de commerce* (1892), 69; T. J. Wertenbaker, *Founding of American Civilization. The Middle Colonies* (1938), ch. ii.

Special — Raesly, *New Netherland*; Fox, *Yankees and Yorkers*, chs. ii–iv; G. A. Ballard, *Rulers of Indian Ocean* (1927), chs. vii–x; Peter Geyl, *Netherlands Divided, 1609–48* (S. A. Bindoff, transl., 1936); S. van Brakel, *De Hollandsche handelscompagnieën de XVII eeuw* (1908); Llewellyn Powys, *Henry Hudson* (1928); L. J. Burpee, "Fate of Henry Hudson," *Canadian Hist. Rev.*, XXI (1940), 401; Brodhead, *History of New York*, I; E. B. O'Callaghan, *History of New Netherlands* (2 vols., 1846–48); Flick, *New York*, I, chs. vi–x; V. H. Paltsits, "Founding of New Amsterdam in 1626," Am. Antiq. Soc., *Proc.*, n. s., XXXIV (1924), 39; A. E. McKinley, "English and Dutch Towns of New Netherlands," *Am. Hist. Rev.*, VI (1900), 1; S. G. Nissenson, *Patroon's Domain* (1937); Van Rensselaer, *History of City of New York*, I; W. H. Kilpatrick, *Dutch Schools of New Netherland* (1912); E. J. De Forest, *A Walloon Family in America* (1914), I, chs. i–iv; J. F. Jameson, "Willem Usselinx," Am. Hist. Assoc., *Papers*, II, pt. 3; Amandus Johnson, *Swedish Settlements on Delaware 1638–44* (2 vols., 1911); Christopher Ward, *Dutch and Swedes on Delaware, 1609–64* (1930); E. A. Louhi, *Delaware Finns* (1925); A. H. Buffinton, "New England and Western Fur Trade," Col. Soc. Mass., *Publ.*, XVIII (1917), 165; H. R. Shurtleff, *Log Cabin Myth* (1939), ch. vii; Hugh Morrison, *Early American Architecture* (1952), ch. iv.

Sources — J. F. Jameson, ed., *Narrative of New Netherland, 1609–1664* (1909); A. C. Myers, ed., *Narratives of Early Pennsylvania, West New Jersey, and Delaware* (1912); A. J. F. Van Laer, ed., *Van Rensselaer Bowier Mss.* (1908), and *Court Minutes of Fort Orange and Beverwyck 1652–1660* (2 vols., 1920–23), and *Minutes of Court of Rensselaerwyck 1648–1652* (1922), and *Documents relating to New Netherland in Huntington Library* (1924); Maria Van Rensselaer, *Correspondence, 1669–1689* (A. J. F. Van Laer, ed., 1935); Jeremias Van Rensselaer, *Correspondence, 1651–1674* (A. J. F. Van Laer, ed., 1935); Amandus Johnson, *Instruction for Johan Printz*; Stokes, *Iconography of Manhattan*, I, ch. i, II, chs. i–iv, IV, ch. i; Harold Köhlin, "First Maps of Delaware," *Imago Mundi*, V (1948) 78.

Bibliography — Winsor, *Narrative and Critical History*, IV, chs. viii, ix; *Encyclopaedie van Nederlansch West-Indië* (1914), 224; Amandus Johnson, *Swedish Settlements*, II, 767; H. N. Stevens, "Bibliography of De Bry's Publications of Early Dutch Voyages," *Wilberforce Eames, a Tribute* (1924), 269.

81. VIRGINIA COMPANY AND VIRGINIA, 1606–1624

Summary — James I and colonization. — 1606, organization of the Virginia Companies of London and Plymouth (§ 84). — Conflict of Smyth, Sandys, and Warwick factions in the Company; were English politics involved? — 1607, Founding of Jamestown. — 1608–10, Years of suffering. — Question of Captain John Smith's reliability. — 1609, Gates's fleet, shipwreck at Bermuda. — 1611, Dale's Laws. — 1612, Third charter. — 1616, Tobacco export and tenant farming. — 1618, Charter of Liberties and other innovations. — 1619, first Assembly, head-right system, "hundreds," attempt to establish industries and a college. — 1619, first Negroes arrive; slaves or servants? — 1622, Indian massacre. — 1624, Dissolution of Virginia Company; Virginia a royal province. — Later developments (§§ 89, 91).

General — Andrews, *Colonial Period*, I, 98; Channing, *History*, I, chs. vi, vii; Osgood, *American Colonies in Seventeenth Century*, I, pt. 1, chs. ii–iv, III, ch. ii; Craven, *Southern Colonies*, chs. iv, v; Fiske, *Old Virginia*, chs. ii–vii; Wertenbaker, *Planters of Colonial Virginia*, chs. i, ii; M. C. Tyler, *History of American Literature* (1878; 1 vol. ed., 1949), I, chs. ii, iii.

Special — Government and society: Beer, *Origins of British Colonial System*; Bruce, *Economic History of Virginia in Seventeenth Century*, I, chs. i–iv, viii–ix, and *Institutional History of Virginia in Seventeenth Century*, I, 343, II, 229; Alexander Brown, *English Politics in Virginia* (1901), and *First Republic*, and *Genesis*, II, 811; W. F. Craven, *Dissolution of the Virginia Company* (1932); Sams, *Conquest of Virginia*, IV. ◀ John Smith: L. L. Kropf, "Communication," *Am. Hist. Rev.*, III (1897), 737; J. M. Morse, "John Smith and His Critics," *Jour. Southern Hist.*, I (1935), 123; William Randel, "Captain John Smith's Attitudes toward Indians," *Va. Mag. Hist.*, XLVII (1939), 218; Keith Glenn, "Captain John Smith and the Indians," *ibid.*, LII (1944), 228–48; Scott, *Constitution and Finance of Joint-Stock Companies*, II, 246; George Arents, "Seed from which Virginia Grew," *William and Mary Quar.*, 2 ser., XIX (1939), 123. ◀ Negroes; slaves or servants: J. C. Ballagh, *History of Slavery in Virginia* (1902), 28; J. H. Russell, Free Negro in Virginia (1913), 16; S. M. Ames, *Virginian Eastern Shore in Seventeenth Century* (1940), 101; Oscar and M. F. Handlin, "Origins of Southern Labor System," *William and Mary Quar.*, 3 ser., VII (1950), 199. ◀ Maps: Robert Tyndall, "Draughte of Virginia, 1608," Mass. Hist. Soc., *Proc.*, LVIII (1925), 244; Fite and Freeman, *Book of Old Maps*, No. 32; Paullin, *Atlas*; P. L. Phillips, *Virginia Cartography, a Bibliographical Description* (1896); Swem, "Maps Relating to Virginia."

Sources — Kingsbury, *Records of the Virginia Company*; Brown, *Genesis of United States*; Captain John Smith, *Travels and Works* (Edward Arber, ed., 2 vols., 1884; A. G. Bradley, ed., 1910); L. G. Tyler, ed., *Narratives of Early Virginia, 1606–1626* (1907); William Strachey, *Historie of Travaile into Virginia Britannia* (1849); John Rolfe, *True*

Relation of State of Virginia in 1616 (reprinted, *Americana Nautica Ser.*, 1951); Force, *Tracts*; Stock, *Proceedings*, I; Wallace Notestein, ed., *Commons Debates 1621* (7 vols., 1935); C. H. Firth, ed., *An American Garland* (1915); I. A. Wright, ed., "Documents on Spanish Policy," *Am. Hist. Rev.*, XXV (1920), 448, and Mass. Hist. Soc., *Proc.*, LIV (1922), 61; W. C. Ford, "Captain Wollaston, Humphrey Rasdell and Thomas Weston," *ibid.*, LI (1918), 219; "Note of the Shipping, Men and Provisions sent to Virginia by Treasurer and Company, 1619," Mass. Hist. Soc., *Photostat Americana*, 2 ser., 1936.

Bibliography — Winsor, *Narrative and Critical History*, III, 153; Kingsbury, *Records of Virginia Company*, I, 119.

82. BERMUDA, BARBADOS, AND THE CARIBBEE ISLANDS

Summary — Situation in Lesser Antilles in 1600. — 1604–20, the English approach via Guiana; Charles Leigh, Robert Harcourt, Roger North, Amazon Company. — 1605, *Olive Branch*. — 1609, Gates and Somers shipwrecked on Bermuda. — 1615, Somers Islands (Bermuda) Company. — 1624, Thomas Warner and Pierre d'Esnambuc in St. Kitts. — 1627, The Courteens' settlement in Barbados, Carlisle charter. — 1629, Spanish attack on St. Kitts. — 1630, Warwick and Pym's Old Providence colony; settlement of Leeward Islands, buccaneers in Tortuga. — 1634, Van Welbeck seizes Curaçao group. — 1635, French occupy Guadeloupe and Martinique; Compagnie des Isles. — 1638, French and Dutch partition St. Martin's. — 1641–60, Effect of the English Civil War. — 1649, Royalist revolt in Bermuda; William Sayle starts colony in Bahamas. — 1651, French take St. Croix. — West Indian Economy; tobacco, salt, sugar; indentured labor, and African slave trade. — Raleigh in Guiana (§ 78); Cromwell's Western Design and the conquest of Jamaica (§ 89); West Indies after 1660 (§ 98).

General — *Cambridge History of British Empire*, I; A. P. Newton, *European Nations in West Indies* (1933), chs. viii–xiv; Andrews, *Colonial Period*, I, chs. xi–xii, II, ch. vii, III, ch. i; La Roncière, *Histoire de la marine française*, IV, 649; F. R. Hart, *Admirals of the Caribbean* (1922), chs. i–ii; Beer, *Origins of British Colonial System*.

Special — Henry Wilkinson, *Adventurers of Bermuda* (1933); Lefroy, *Memorials of the Bermudas*; Fulmer Mood, "Henry Robinson and the Bahama Articles of 1647," Col. Soc. Mass., *Publ.*, XXXII (1934), 155; V. T. Harlow, *History of Barbados 1625–85* (1926); R. H. Schomburck, *History of Barbados* (1847); J. A. Williamson, *Caribbee Islands under Proprietary Patents* (1936); Aucher Werner, *Sir Thomas Warner* (1933); Crouse, *French Pioneers in West Indies 1624–64*; A. P. Newton, *Colonizing Activities of English Puritans* (1914); Bryan Edwards, *History of British West Indies* (3 ed., 1801), I, II.

Sources — *Calendar of State Papers, Colonial, America and West Indies*, I (1574–1660), IX (Addenda, 1574–1674); *Acts of Privy Council, Colonial Series*, I (1613–80); Elizabeth Donnan, ed., *Documents Illustrative of History of Slave Trade to America* (2 vols., 1930–35), I; Stock, *Proceedings*, I; V. T. Harlow, ed., *Colonizing Expeditions to West Indies and Guiana* (1925); Lewis Hughes, "Goodnes of God towards the Sommer Ilands," (W. F. Craven, ed.), *William and Mary Quar.*, 2 ser., XVII (1937), 56.

Bibliography — Frank Cundall, *Bibliography of West Indies (Excluding Jamaica)* (1909); "List of Works relating to West Indies," N. Y. Public Library, *Bull.*, XVI (1912), nos. 1, 3–8.

83. ENGLISH PURITANISM AND BACKGROUND OF PURITAN MIGRATION

Summary — Puritanism as the left wing of the English Reformation. — Non-Conformists, Brownists, Separatists. — Attitude of Elizabeth I, James I, and Charles I to the Puritans. — The Puritan creed. — Influence of Continental theologians and of Petrus

Ramus. — Puritanism in the English and Scottish universities. — Puritan appeal to the merchants of London and to the rural population of East Anglia and the West Country. — Connection of Puritanism with the Opposition to royal absolutism. — 1604, Millenary Petition and the Hampton Court Conference. — Movement of Puritan congregations to Holland. — 1628, William Laud becomes Bishop of London. — 1629, Foreign and domestic situation turns Puritan thoughts to migration.

General — Channing, *History*, I, ch. x, 421; Andrews, *Colonial Period*, I; G. N. Clark, *Seventeenth Century* (1929), chs. xii, xiii, xviii; T. J. Wertenbaker, *Puritan Oligarchy* (1947), ch. i; Parrington, *Main Currents*, I; Fiske, *Beginnings of New England*, 50; J. G. Palfrey, *History of New England* (5 vols., 1858–90), I, chs. iii, vii.

Special — H. J. C. Grierson, *Cross-Currents in English Literature of Seventeenth Century* (1929), chs. i, v, vi; Murdock, *Literature and Theology in Colonial New England*, ch. i; Perry Miller, *Orthodoxy in Massachusetts* (1933), chs. i–iv, and *New England Mind* (1939), chs. i, ii, v; R. G. Usher, *Presbyterian Movement in Reign of Elizabeth* (1905), and *Reconstruction of English Church* (2 vols., 1910), and *Rise and Fall of High Commission* (1913); H. M. Dexter, *Congregationalism as Seen in Its Literature* (1880); H. W. Clark, *History of English Nonconformity* (1911), I, bk. 2, chs. i–iii; Champlin Burrage, *Early English Dissenters* (2 vols., 1912); A. F. S. Pearson, *Church and State, Political Aspects of Sixteenth Century Puritanism* (1928), and *Thomas Cartwright and Elizabethan Puritanism* (1925); J. W. Allen, *History of Political Thought* (1928), pt. 2, chs. viii–ix; J. R. Tanner, *English Constitutional Conflicts of Seventeenth Century* (1928); David Masson, *Life of John Milton* (7 vols., 1859–94), I, chs. iv–vi; F. J. Powicke, *Henry Barrowe and Exiled Church of Amsterdam* (1900); Newton, *Colonizing Activities of English Puritans*, ch. ii; N. M. Crouse, "Causes of Great Migration," *New Eng. Quar.*, V (1932), 3; R. P. Stearns, "New England Way in Holland," *ibid.*, VI (1933), 747; S. E. Morison, *Founding of Harvard College* (1935), chs. iii–x; C. E. Banks and S. E. Morison, "Persecution as a Factor in Emigration," Mass. Hist. Soc., *Proc.*, LXIII (1930), 136; Hart, *Commonwealth History of Massachusetts*, I, ch. iii; H. D. Foster, "Calvin's Programme for a Puritan State," and "Political Theories of Calvinists," *Collected Papers* (1929); George Unwin, *Industrial Organization in Sixteenth and Seventeenth Centuries* (1904); Scott, *Constitution and Finance of English Joint-Stock Companies*, I, chs. viii–xi, II, division ii, ch. iii; also § 77.

Sources — Perry Miller and T. H. Johnson, eds., *Puritans* (1938); Winthrop, *Papers*, I, II; Benjamin Hanbury, ed., *Historical Memorials Relating to Independents or Congregationalists* (3 vols., 1839–44); Williston Walker, *Creeds and Platforms of Congregationalism* (1893); M. M. Knappen, ed., *Two Elizabethan Puritan Diaries* (of Richard Rogers and Samuel Ward, 1933); Sir Simonds D'Ewes, *Autobiography and Correspondence* (2 vols., 1845; 1 vol. ed., 1923); Philip Henry, *Diaries and Letters* (M. H. Lee, ed., 1882); William Ames, *Cases of Conscience* (1630), and *Marrow of Sacred Divinity* (1627), both transl. from Latin, 1638, 1639, 1643; Bulstrode Whitelock, *Memorials of English Affairs* (3 vols., 1853).

Bibliography — Read, *Bibliography of Tudor Period*; Davies, *Bibliography of Stuart Period*; H. M. Dexter, *Congregationalism*, App.; Miller, *Orthodoxy*, 317.

84. NEW ENGLAND SETTLEMENTS TO 1630

Summary — c. 1550–1630, English fisheries on the coast. — 1602–19, coastal explorations by Gosnold, Pring, Champlain, Weymouth, John Smith, Hudson, Block, and others. — 1607, the Popham Colony at Sagadahoc. — 1613, Argall's suppression of French settlements. — 1620–29, the Pilgrim Fathers, voyage of Mayflower, vicissitudes of the Plymouth Colony. — 1620, Sir Ferdinando Gorges, the Council for New England, and its grants. — 1622–29, trading factories and fishing stations in Maine, New Hampshire, and Massachusetts. — 1623, Dorchester adventurers. — 1628, the Massachusetts Bay Company. — 1629, Gov. Endecott Colony at Salem.

General — Channing, *History*, I, chs. x, xi, 356; Andrews, *Colonial Period*, I, chs. iv, xii–xvii; Osgood, *American Colonies in Seventeenth Century*, I, 98, 290; Parkman, *Pioneers of France*, chs. vi–viii; H. F. Howe, *Prologue to New England* (1943); Tyler, *History of American Literature*, I, ch. v, §§ 1, 2, 3.

Special — Early settlement: Winsor, *Narrative and Critical History*, III, ch. vi; Diamond, "Norumbega"; R. A. Preston, "Fishing and Plantation, New England in Parliament of 1621," *Am. Hist. Rev.*, XLV (1939), 29; J. T. Adams, *Founding of New England*, chs. iii, v; S. E. Morison, *Builders of Bay Colony* (1930), chs. i, ii; Fiske, *Beginnings of New England*, 72; Burrage, *Beginnings of Colonial Maine*; May, *Early Portsmouth History*; S. F. Haven, "Grants under Council for New England," *Lectures on Early History of Massachusetts* (1869). ❧ Plymouth Colony: G. F. Willison, *Saints and Strangers* (1945); Bradford Smith, *Bradford of Plymouth* (1951); R. G. Usher, *Pilgrims and Their History* (1918); H. M. and Morton Dexter, *England and Holland of Pilgrims* (1905); W. S. Nickerson, *Land Ho! — 1620* (1931); S. E. Morison, "The Pilgrim Fathers' Significance in History," *By Land and By Sea* (1953), ch. x; D. E. Leach, "Military System of Plymouth," *New Eng. Quar.*, XXIV (1951), 342; Daniel Plooij, *Pilgrim Fathers from a Dutch Point of View* (1932); C. E. Banks, *English Ancestry and Homes of Pilgrims* (1929). ❧ Massachusetts Bay Company and Settlement: Frances Rose-Troup, *Massachusetts Bay Company and Its Predecessors* (1930); A. G. Lapham, *Old Planters of Beverly* (1930); Mayo, *John Endecott*, chs. ii–iv; C. F. Adams, *Three Episodes of Massachusetts History*, I; C. E. Banks, *Winthrop Fleet* (1930); H. R. Shurtleff, *Log Cabin Myth*, 83.

Sources — C. H. Levermore, ed., *Forerunners and Competitors of Pilgrims and Puritans* (2 vols., 1912); G. P. Winship, ed., *Sailors' Narratives of Voyages Along New England Coast 1524–1624* (1905); § 78; Bradford, *Plymouth Plantation*; "Bradford's Letter-Book," Mass. Hist. Soc., *Coll.*, III (1794), and separately (1906); Alexander Young, *Chronicles of Pilgrim Fathers* (1844); Edward Arber, ed., *Story of Pilgrim Fathers* (1897); MacDonald, *Select Charters*, 23, 50; R. E. Moody, ed., "Versions of Mayflower Compact," *Old South Leaflet* No. 225 (1951); Jameson, *Narratives of New Netherland*, 102 (Isaack de Rasieres's letter on Plymouth); Champlin Burrage, ed., *John Pory's Lost Description of Plymouth Colony* (1918); *Founding of Massachusetts* (1930); *Winthrop Papers*; "Records of Council for New England," Am. Antiq. Soc., *Proc.*, 1867; C. E. Banks, ed., "Popham Expedition Documents," *ibid.*, n.s., XXXIX (1929), 307; Maine Hist. Soc., *Documentary History of Maine* (1869–1916), I–IV; Notestein, *Commons Debates 1621*; Thomas Morton, *New English Canaan* (Amsterdam, 1637; C. F. Adams, ed., 1883).

Bibliography — Winsor, *Narrative and Critical History*, III, 184, 283, 340, 381; annual bibliography of New England history, *New Eng. Quar.*, II– (1929–); *Dictionary American Biography*, II, 563 (Bradford's writings).

85. MASSACHUSETTS BAY COLONY, 1630–1660

Summary — 1629, Cambridge Agreement, John Winthrop elected governor, Thomas Dudley deputy, of Massachusetts Bay Company. — 1630, voyage of Winthrop fleet to Salem, transfer of charter, eight towns started. — 1631, great Puritan migration sets in; sources and motives, dispersal of settlement about the Bay, origin of township system, church-member franchise. — 1632, Watertown protest. — 1634, representatives elected to General Court, local self-government. — Was the Bay Colony a theocracy, oligarchy, or aristocracy? — 1635, public schools, proceedings against charter, Roger Williams banished, migration to the Connecticut River (Haynes and Hooker). — 1636, Henry Vane, governor, Harvard College founded. — 1637, Antinomian movement, defeat of Governor Vane, banishment of Anne Hutchinson. — 1641, emigration stops; economic crisis, start of local fishing industry, West Indies trade and shipbuilding; attempts at economic autarchy. — 1643, Confederation. — 1644, bicameral system, trouble with Gorton and the Narragansetts, LaTour supported against d'Aulnay, Governor Endecott. — 1645, Hingham militia dispute, Winthrop's speech on Liberty. — 1646, Presbyterian remonstrance, Eliot begins missionary work. — 1656, persecution of Quakers and Baptists. — earlier developments (§ 84); Pequot War (§ 88); New England Confederation (§ 89); economic and social aspects, including land system (§ 90).

General — Andrews, *Colonial Period*, I, chs. xvii–xxii; Channing, *History*, I, chs. xii, xiii, 432, 518; Osgood, *American Colonies in Seventeenth Century*, I, pt. 2, chs. i–v, xi, xii, xiii; Palfrey, *History of New England*, I, chs. viii–xv, II, chs. iii, iv, vi, viii, x; Tyler, *History of American Literature*, I, chs. v–x.

Special — G. E. Ellis, *Puritan Age and Rule* (1888); Stokes, *Church and State in United States*, I, ch. iii; J. T. Adams, *Founding of New England*, chs. vi–vii, xi; C. F. Adams, *Three Episodes*, I, II; Gertrude Huehns, *Antinomianism in English History* (1951), chs. i–iv, x; Miller, *Orthodoxy*, chs. vi–viii, and *New England Mind*; S. E. Morison, *Builders of Bay Colony*, chs. iii, iv, vii, viii, and "William Pynchon," *Mass. Hist. Soc., Proc.*, LXIV (1931), 81; R. C. Winthrop, *Life and Letters of John Winthrop* (2 vols., 1869); E. A. J. Johnson on the Economic, and Stanley Gray on the Political Thought of Winthrop, *New Eng. Quar.*, III (1930), 235, 681; E. A. J. Johnson, "Mercantilism in Massachusetts Bay," *ibid.*, I (1928), 371; E. E. Brennan, "Massachusetts Council of Magistrates," *ibid.*, IV (1931), 54; Bailyn, "Apologia of Keayne"; Hart, *Commonwealth of Massachusetts*, I, chs. iii, iv, xviii; W. L. Sachse, "Migration of New Englanders to England, 1640–1660," *Am. Hist. Rev.*, LIII (1948), 251; Rugg, *Anne Hutchinson*; R. P. Hallowell, *Quaker Invasion of Massachusetts* (1883); R. M. Jones, *Quakers in American Colonies* (1911), bk. 1; M. B. Jones, *Thomas Maule and Free Speech* (1936); A. H. Buffinton, "Isolationist Policy of Colonial Massachusetts," *New Eng. Quar.*, I (1928), 158; G. L. Kittredge, "Dr. Robert Child the Remonstrant," *Col. Soc. Mass., Publ.*, XXI (1919), 1; Sly, *Town Government in Massachusetts*, chs. i–iii; R. B. Morris, "Massachusetts and Common Law," *Am. Hist. Rev.*, XXXI (1926), 443, and *Studies in History of American Law* (1930); A. B. Seidman, "Church and State in the Early Years of Bay Colony," *New Eng. Quar.*, XVIII (1945), 211; M. D. Howe and L. F. Eaton, Jr., "Supreme Judicial Power in Massachusetts Bay," *ibid.*, XX (1947), 291; G. L. Haskins, "Beginnings of the Recording System," *Boston University Law Rev.*, XXI (1941), 281; G. F. Dow, *Every Day Life in Massachusetts Bay Colony* (1935), chs. i–ii; C. A. Duniway, *Development of Freedom of Press in Massachusetts* (1906), chs. i–iv.

Sources — John Winthrop, *Papers*, and his "Journal" published as *History of New England*; Thomas Lechford, *Plain Dealing* (1642; reprinted 1867), and "Note Book," Am. Antiq. Soc., *Trans.*, VII (1885); William Wood, *New England's Prospect* (1634; reprinted 1865); Hutchinson, *Collection of Papers*, and *History of Massachusetts-Bay*, I, App.; Edward Johnson, *Wonder Working Providence* (J. F. Jameson, ed., 1910); Shurtleff, *Records of Governor and Company*; Alexander Young, ed., *Chronicles of Massachusetts Bay* (1846); Thomas Shepard, "Autobiography," *Col. Soc. Mass., Publ.*, XXVII (1932), 345; Max Farrand, ed., *Laws and Liberties of Massachusetts* (reprinted from 1648 ed., 1929); Whitmore, *Colonial Laws of Massachusetts*; § 46.

86. NORTHERN ENGLISH COLONIES, FROM NEWFOUNDLAND TO NEW HAMPSHIRE, TO 1700

Summary — 1583, Gilbert takes possession of St. Johns; continuous attempts at settlement and use of Newfoundland coasts by fishermen. — 1610, John Guy and Newfoundland Company, the Vaughan tract. — 1623–28, Calvert's Avalon colony, succeeded by the Kirkes. — 1621–29, Sir William Alexander's grant of Nova Scotia, settlement at Port Royal. — 1629, Piscataqua region granted to John Mason; southern Maine to Gorges. — 1635, Council for New England divides up the area and disbands. — 1641, Gorges' charter of Agamenticus (York, Me.). — Fishing and trading stations at Castine, Monhegan, Pemaquid, Damariscove, Richmond Isles, Saco. — 1639–58, settlement on the Piscataqua; 1649–52, Province of Maine; statute of religious liberty; "plebiscites" attach these settlements to Massachusetts Bay. — 1664, Province of Sagadahoc (east of Kennebec) in Duke of York's Grant. — 1665, Maine proper confirmed to Gorges. — 1669,

Hudson's Bay Company chartered. — 1675–77, Philip's War wipes out northern settlements. — 1677, Massachusetts buys Gorges' title. — 1680, Royal Province of New Hampshire. — 1688, Dominion of New England. — 1689–97, King William's War, northern settlements again wiped out. — 1691, Maine and Sagadahoc annexed to Massachusetts Bay. — 1692, Fort Pemaquid. — Events before 1630 (§ 84); later events (§§ 90, 99).

General — Andrews, *Colonial Period*, I, chs. xv, xvi, xix; Osgood, *American Colonies in Seventeenth Century*, I, 119, 371; *Cambridge History of British Empire*, I; G. L. Beer, *Old Colonial System* (2 vols., 1912), II, ch. x; Palfrey, *History of New England*, I, 516, 587, II, 383.

Special — R. G. Albion, *Forests and Sea Power* (1926), ch. vi; D. W. Prowse, *History of Newfoundland* (1895), chs. v–viii; B. C. Steiner, "Baltimore and His Colonial Projects," Am. Hist. Assoc., *Report*, 1905, I, 109; R. G. Lounsbury, "Yankee Trade at Newfoundland," *New Eng. Quar.*, III (1930), 607, and *British Fishery at Newfoundland 1634–1763* (1934); J. D. Rogers, "Newfoundland," C. P. Lucas, *Historical Geography of British Colonies* (1911), V, pt. 4; G. C. Moore Smith, "Robert Hayman and Newfoundland," *Eng. Hist. Rev.*, XXXIII (1918), 21; H. J. Berkley, "Lord Baltimore's Contest with Sir David Kirke," *Md. Hist. Mag.*, XII (1917), 107; L. D. Scisco, "Kirke's Memorial on Newfoundland," *Canadian Hist. Rev.*, VII (1926), 46; G. P. Insh, *Scottish Colonial Schemes 1620–86* (1922), chs. i–iii; H. S. Burrage, *Beginnings of Colonial Maine* (1914), and *Gorges and Grant of Province of Maine* (1923); J. P. Baxter, *George Cleeve of Casco Bay 1630–67* (1885); Henry Gardiner, *New England's Vindication* (1660; Gorges Soc. ed., 1884); J. F. Baldwin, "Feudalism in Maine," *New Eng. Quar.*, V (1932), 352; W. D. Spencer, *Pioneers on Maine Rivers* (1930); F. B. Sanborn, *New Hampshire* (1904), chs. i–iv; O. G. Hammond, "Mason Title," Am. Antiq. Soc., *Proc.*, n.s., XXVI (1916), 245; C. E. Banks, *History of York, Maine* (1931), I; J. P. Baxter, *Sir Ferdinando Gorges and His Province of Maine* (3 vols., 1890); C. W. Tuttle, *Captain John Mason, Founder of New Hampshire* (1887); E. F. Slafter, *Sir William Alexander and American Colonization* (1873); C. H. Bell, *John Wheelwright* (1876); P. E. Moyer, "Settlement of New Hampshire," *Granite Monthly*, LIV (1922), 153; E. L. Page, "A.D. 1623," *ibid.*, 205; John Scales, "First Permanent Settlement," *ibid.*, 269; C. T. Libby, "Who Planted New Hampshire," *ibid.*, 364; Levermore, *Forerunners of Pilgrims*; § 78.

Sources — *Calendar of State Papers, Colonial*, I, V, VII–XVIII; *Acts of the Privy Council*, I, II; Baxter, *Gorges*; Tuttle, *Mason*; Slafter, *Alexander*; C. W. Tuttle, *Captain Francis Champernowne, the Dutch Conquest of Acadia* (1889); Morse, *Acadiensia Nova*, I, 55; Christopher Levett, "Voyage of 1622–23," Maine Hist. Soc., *Coll.*, II (1847), 74; Banks, "Popham Expedition Documents"; Maine Hist. Soc., *Documentary History of Maine*; C. T. Libby, ed., *Province and Court Records of Maine* (2 vols., 1928–31); Bouton, *Documents and Records and State Papers of New Hampshire*.

Bibliography — Winsor, *Narrative and Critical History*, III, 363; Williamson, *Bibliography of Maine*; Prowse, *Newfoundland*, 166.

87. MARYLAND IN THE SEVENTEENTH CENTURY

Summary — Settlements prior to 1630. — The Calvert family. — 1632, the Maryland charter; institutional background; vague boundaries. — 1634, voyage of *Ark and Dove*, settlement at St. Mary's; early proportion of Catholics and Protestants. — Religious and economic motives of the second Lord Baltimore. — 1639–44, troubles with Virginia, the Jesuits, the Indians, and William Claiborne. — Powers of Governor Leonard Calvert. — 1638, mixed assembly. — Council, local institutions, manors. — Plantation economy and the labor system. — 1642–44, Puritan migration and rebellion. — 1648, Governor William Stone. — 1649, Toleration Act; controversy as to motives and responsibilities. — 1654, Parliamentary commissioners depose Stone; Battle of the Severn. — 1658, Proprietor's powers restored; Governor Charles Calvert. — 1674, Indian War. — 1682, Assembly reasserts itself. — 1684, Boundary dispute with Pennsylvania. — 1688–89, Coode Rebellion. — 1692–1715, Royal Province of Maryland, Governor Lionel Copley; Church of England established. — Society and economy (§ 91).

General — Andrews, *Colonial Period*, II, chs. viii, ix; Channing, *History*, I, ch. ix, 499, 519, II, 209, 226, 423; Craven, *Southern Colonies*, ch. vi; Osgood, *American Colonies in Seventeenth Century*, II, chs. ii–iv, xii–xvi, III, ch. xvi.

Special — G. T. Lapsley, *County Palatine of Durham* (1900); Andrews, *Founding of Maryland*; B. C. Steiner, *Beginnings of Maryland* (1903), and *Maryland during English Civil Wars* (1906), and *Maryland under the Commonwealth*; Mereness, *Maryland as Proprietary Province*; C. J. Rohr, *Governor of Maryland* (1932); Browne, *George and Cecilius Calvert*; John Johnson, *Old Maryland Manors* (1883); D. R. Randall, *Puritan Colony in Maryland* (1886); M. S. Morriss, *Colonial Trade of Maryland 1689–1715* (1914); Pierre Brodin, *Les Quakers en Amérique au XVIIᵉ siècle* (1935), 183; K. L. Carroll, "Maryland Quakers and Slavery," *Md. Hist. Mag.*, XLV (1950), 215; Raphael Sommes, *Captains and Mariners of Early Maryland* (1937); J. H. Latané, *Early Relations between Virginia and Maryland* (1895); F. E. Sparks, *Causes of Revolution of 1689 in Maryland* (1896); B. B. James, *Labadist Colony in Maryland* (1899); Dieter Cunz, *Maryland Germans* (1948), chs. i–iv; Thomas Hughes, *History of Society of Jesus in North America* (1907), I; G. B. Stratemeier, *Thomas Cornwaleys, Commissioner of Maryland* (1922). ❧ Maps: Fite and Freeman, *Book of Old Maps*, No. 40.

Sources — C. C. Hall, ed., *Narratives of Early Maryland 1633–84* (1910); Force, *Tracts*, II, III; Gerald Johnson, ed., *Maryland Act of Religious Toleration* (1949); Dankaerts, *Journal*; George Alsop, *Character of Province of Maryland* (1666; N. D. Mereness, ed., 1902); Hughes, *History Documents*, pt. 1; Henry Foley, *Records of English Province of Society of Jesus* (1878), III, 320; B. C. Steiner, ed., "Religious Freedom in Provincial Maryland," *Am. Hist. Rev.*, XXVIII (1923), 258; L. C. Wroth, "Maryland Muse, by Ebenezer Cooke," Am. Antiq. Soc., *Proc.*, n.s., XLIV (1934), 267; *Archives of Maryland* (§ 47); C. T. Bond, ed., *Proceedings of Maryland Court of Appeals 1695–1729* (1933); *Calvert Papers*, Md. Hist. Soc., *Fund Publ.*, Nos. 28, 34–35 (1889–99); Beverly McAnear, ed., "Mariland's Grevances Wiy They Have Taken Op Arms" (1689), *Jour. Southern Hist.*, VIII (1942), 392.

Bibliography — Winsor, *Narrative and Critical History*, III, ch. xiii; L. C. Wroth, "Maryland Colonization Tracts," *Essays Offered to Herbert Putnam* (1929), 539; Baer, *Seventeenth Century Maryland*; E. B. Mathews, *Maps and Map-Makers of Maryland* (1898).

88. SOUTHERN NEW ENGLAND COLONIES TO 1663

Summary — Rhode Island: Roger Williams; ideas as to religious liberty, democracy, and justice to the Indians; 1636, banished from Massachusetts, founds Providence Plantation; 1638, Anne Hutchinson (§ 85), founds Portsmouth; 1639, William Coddington founds Newport, and Samuel Gorton, Warwick; 1643, Providence Plantations patent; unique constitutional development; 1663, royal charter of Rhode Island and Providence Plantations; relations with Narragansetts; opening of West India trade (§ 90). — Dutch and Pilgrims on Connecticut River: 1635, Saybrook founded; 1635–36, John Haynes and Thomas Hooker found Hartford, Windsor, and Wethersfield; motives; 1638, the "Fundamental Orders"; development of representative government; 1637, Pequot War; expansion to interior and Long Island; 1662, royal charter of Connecticut; continuity of government, "Land of Steady Habits." — New Haven: 1637, John Davenport, Theophilus Eaton and a London congregation emigrate to Boston; 1638, they found New Haven; 1639, "Fundamental Articles"; 1643, form of government; "Blue Laws"; expansion along Long Island Sound; rivalry with New Netherland, and fur-trading ventures; 1662, New Haven included in Connecticut.

General — Channing, *History*, I, 362, ch. xiv; Andrews, *Colonial Period*, II, chs. i–v; Osgood, *American Colonies in Seventeenth Century*, I, chs. iv, vii–viii, xi–xiii; Tyler, *History of American Literature*, I; Parrington, *Colonial Mind*, 51; J. T. Adams, *Founding of New England*, 163; Fiske, *Beginnings of New England*, 122; Palfrey, *History of New England*, I, 444, 511, 528, 600, II, 112, 207, 344, 371.

Special — Richman, *Rhode Island*; John Callender, *Historical Discourse on Rhode Island* (1739; reprinted, R. I. Hist. Soc., *Coll.*, IV [1838]); Trumbull, *History of Connecticut*, I; I. M. Calder, *New Haven Colony* (1934); C. H. Levermore, *Republic of New Haven* (1886); B. C. Steiner, *History of Guilford* (1897); W. deL. Love, *Colonial History of Hartford* (1914); W. F. Prince, "Peter's Blue Laws," Am. Hist. Assoc., *Report*, 1898, 97; C. M. Andrews, *et al.*, Tercentenary Commission of Connecticut, *Fundamental Orders* (1933), and *Beginnings of Connecticut* (1933), and *Connecticut and the British Government* (1933), and *Connecticut Intestacy Law* (1933), and *Charter of Connecticut* (1933); Dorothy Deming, *Settlement of Connecticut Towns* (1933); R. V. Coleman, *Fundamental Orders* (1934), and *Old Patent* (1936), and *Roger Ludlow* (1934); Howard Bradstreet, *War with the Pequots* (1933); L. W. Labaree, *Milford* (1933); G. L. Walker, *Thomas Hooker* (1891); H. E. Turner, *William Coddington* (1878); Rugg, *Anne Hutchinson*, chs. xix–xxii; Ernst, *Political Thought of Roger Williams;* Brockunier, *Roger Williams;* L. G. Janes, *Samuel Gorton* (1896); H. B. Parkes, "Cotton and Williams Debate Toleration," *New Eng. Quar.*, IV (1931), 735; Perry Miller, "Hooker and Democracy of Early Connecticut," *ibid.*, 663, and *Orthodoxy;* G. A. Stead, "Williams and Massachusetts," *New Eng. Quar.*, VII (1934), 235; S. E. Baldwin, "Secession of Springfield," Col. Soc. Mass., *Publ.*, XII (1908), 55; Morison, "William Pynchon"; C. P. Nettels, "Beginnings of Money in Connecticut," Wisc. Acad. Sci., *Trans.*, XXIII (1927), 1; E. L. Ullman, "Eastern Boundary of Rhode Island," State College of Washington, *Research Studies*, IV (1936), 67; I. M. Calder, "Earl of Stirling and Colonization of Long Island," in *Essays Presented to C. M. Andrews* (1931).

Sources — Roger Williams, "Writings," I–VI; *Colonial Records of Rhode Island 1636–1792* (10 vols., 1856–65); Trumbull and Hoadly, *Public Records of Connecticut 1636–1776*; Hoadly, *New Haven Records, 1638–1664*; Chapin, *Documentary History of Rhode Island;* John Mason, "Brief History of Pequot War," (1736), Mass. Hist. Soc., *Coll.*, 2 ser., VIII (1819), 120; John Underhill, "News from America, containing a True Relation of Their War-like Proceedings," (1638), *ibid.*, 3 ser., VI (1837), 1; S. G. Drake, *Old Indian Chronicle* (1867); A. C. Bates, ed., "Wyllys Papers," Conn. Hist. Soc., *Coll.*, XXI (1924).

89. THE ENGLISH CIVIL WAR AND THE COLONIES, 1641–1660

Summary — Attempts of Warwick Commission on Plantations to bring Barbados and Virginia into line. — Governor Bennett imposed on Virginia; the Puritan regime there. — 1655, Cromwell's Western Design and the conquest of Jamaica. — Relations of Long Parliament and Cromwell with New England colonies. — 1643, New England Confederation; relations between its members, threats of war, support of education and of Eliot's missionary work. — 1644, Roger Williams and the Providence Plantations Patent. — 1646, the Child Remonstrance. — 1651, First Navigation Act. — 1654, First Dutch War. — West Indies (§ 82); Maryland (§ 87).

General — Channing, *History*, I, chs. xv, xviii–xix; Andrews, *Colonial Period*, II, 253, 310, III, ch. 1, IV, ch. ii; Beer, *Origins British Colonial System*, chs. xi–xii; Craven, *Southern Colonies*, chs. vii, viii; Osgood, *American Colonies in Seventeenth Century*, I, ch. x, III, ch. v; Palfrey, *History of New England*, II, chs. ii–xii.

Special — Southern colonies: L. A. Harper, *English Navigation Laws* (1939), chs. i–iv; Harlow, *History of Barbados*, chs. ii–iii; G. P. Gooch, *English Democratic Ideas* (H. J. Laski, ed., 1927); G. N. Clark, "Navigation Act of 1651," *History*, n.s., VII (1923), 282; George Edmundson, *Anglo-Dutch Rivalry* (1911), ch. vi; C. M. Andrews, *British Committees of Trade, 1622–75* (1908), chs. i–iii; Frank Strong, "The Causes of Cromwell's West Indian Expedition," *Am. Hist. Rev.*, IV (1898), 228, and "Forgotten Danger to the New England Colonies," Am. Hist. Assn. *Report*, 1898, 77; I. A. Wright, "Spanish Resistance to English in Jamaica," Royal Hist. Soc., *Trans.*, 4 ser., XIII (1930), 117; Wertenbaker, *Virginia under Stuarts;* Bruce, *Economic History of Virginia*, chs. vi, ix, xv. — New England: Morison, *Builders of Bay Colony*, chs. vii, viii, x; Kittredge, "Robert Child"; Hart, *Commonwealth History*, I, chs. ix, xviii; Buffinton, "Fur Trade," Col. Soc. Mass., *Publ.*, XVIII (1916), 160; S. R. Weaver, "Negotiations for Reciprocity," *Jour. Pol. Econ.*, XIX (1911), 411; S. E. Morison, *Founding of Harvard*, ch. xxi, and *Harvard College in Seventeenth Century* (2 vols., 1936), I, chs. ii, xiv–xvii.

Sources — Stock, *Proceedings*, I, 100; *Calendar of State Papers, Colonial, America and West Indies*, I, IX; General Robert Venables, *Narrative of Expedition to West Indies* (C. H. Firth, ed., 1900); I. A. Wright, ed., *Spanish Narratives of the English Attack on Santo Domingo 1655* (Camden Miscellany, XIV, 1926); Shurtleff, *Records of New Plymouth*, IX, X; G. P. Winship, ed., *New England Company of 1649 and John Eliot* (1920); J. W. Ford, ed., *Some Correspondence between New England Company in London and Commissioners of the United Colonies* (1897); John Eliot, "Diary," Boston Record Commissioners, *Sixth Report* (1889), and *New Eng. Hist. Gen. Register*, XXXIII (1879–80), 62, 236, 295, 413.

90. NEW ENGLAND IN THE SEVENTEENTH CENTURY: SOCIAL, ECONOMIC, INSTITUTIONAL

Summary — Development of trade, agriculture, and domestic manufacture. — John Winthrop, Jr., iron works, other industrial experiments. — Attempts at economic autarchy. — Sumptuary and other legislation to preserve social lines. — Social control in the towns, "warning out," regulation of wages; indented servants, poor relief, slavery; — Methods of making new settlements and partitioning land; proprietors and settlers. — Development of law and legal concepts; the Body of Liberties (1641) and Laws and Liberties (1648). — Influence of Puritanism on the New England mind; contributions to theology and ecclesiastical polity by the clergy (John Cotton, Thomas Shepard, Thomas Hooker, Roger Williams, Peter Bulkeley, Solomon Stoddard). — The Cambridge and Boston printing press, booksellers, and libraries; the literature of Puritanism. —Anne Bradstreet, the Almanac Poets, Benjamin Tompson, Edward Taylor; the historians, Bradford, Hubbard, Nathaniel Morton, the Mathers. — Contemporary interest in natural science; Increase Mather, William Brattle, and Charles Morton. — Development of primary and grammar schools; the Harvard curriculum and social life; medicine and physicians. — Architecture, painting, and domestic arts; John Hull and the silversmiths. — 1652, the Pine Tree Shilling.

General — T. J. Wertenbaker, *First Americans* (1927), chs. iii–vii, and *Puritan Oligarchy*, chs. iii–ix; Channing, *History*, I, chs. xv, xix; Tyler, *History American Literature*, I, chs. v–x, II, chs. xi–xv; A. H. Quinn, ed., *Literature of American People* (1951), chs. iii–v (by K. B. Murdock); R. B. Perry, *Puritanism and Democracy* (1944).

Special — Perry Miller, *New England Mind*, and *Orthodoxy*, chs. v–viii, and "Marrow of Puritan Divinity," Col. Soc. Mass., *Publ.*, XXXII (1935), 247, and "Half-Way Covenant," *New Eng. Quar.*, VI (1933), 676; Murdock, *Literature and Theology in Colonial New England;* R. P. Stearns, "Assessing the New England Mind," *Church History*, X (1941), 3; E. S. Morgan, *Puritan Family* (1944); C. K. Shipton, "Puritanism and Modern Democracy," *New England Hist. Geneal. Reg.*, CI (1947), 181; E. A. J. Johnson, *American Economic Thought in Seventeenth Century* (1932); Weeden, *Economic and Social History of New England*, I, chs. iii–viii; Hutchinson, *History of Massachusetts Bay*, I, chs. iv, v; Hart, *Commonwealth History of Massachusetts*, I, ch. xv, II, 192; Matthews, *Expansion of New England*, chs. ii–iii; S. E. Morison, *Puritan Pronaos* (1936), chs. ii–x, and *Builders of Bay Colony*, chs. v, ix, xi; A. M. Earle, *Child Life* (1899), and *Colonial Dames* (1896); E. A. Dexter, *Colonial Women* (1924); T. G. Wright, *Literary Culture in Early New England* (1920), pts. 1, 2; G. N. Winship, *Cambridge Press, 1638–92* (1945); N. H. Dawes, "Titles as Symbols of Prestige," *William and Mary Quar.*, 3 ser.,

VI (1949), 69; Morrison Sharp, "Leadership and Democracy in Early New England Defense," *Am. Hist. Rev.*, L (1945), 244; R. R. Walcott, "Husbandry in Colonial New England," *New Eng. Quar.*, IX (1936), 218; Carl Bridenbaugh, *Cities in Wilderness* (1938), pt. 1, 218; A. H. Buffinton, "Sir Thomas Temple in Boston," Col. Soc. Mass., *Publ.*, XXVII (1929), 308, and "Fur Trade"; F. X. Moloney, *Fur Trade in New England 1620–76* (1931); Deane Phillips, *Horse Raising in Colonial New England* (1922); Murdock, *Increase Mather;* E. B. Carpenter, "Huguenot Influence in Rhode Island," and "John Saffin His Book," *South County Studies* (1924); H. B. Parkes, "Morals and Law Enforcement in Colonial New England," *New Eng. Quar.*, V (1932), 431; M. W. Jernegan, *Laboring and Dependent Classes in Colonial America* (1931), pt. 2; R. W. Kelso, *History of Public Poor Relief in Massachusetts* (1922), chs. i–iii; C. K. Shipton, "Secondary Education in Puritan Colonies," *New Eng. Quar.*, VII (1934), 646; R. W. Hale, *Tercentenary History of Roxbury Latin School* (1946); Morison, *Harvard in Seventeenth Century;* A. O. Norton, "Harvard Text-Books," Col. Soc. Mass., *Publ.*, XXVIII (1933), 361; P. A. Scholes, *Puritans and Music* (1934); Morrison, *Early American Architecture,* chs. i–iii; A. N. B. Garvan, *Architecture and Town Planning in Colonial Connecticut* (1951); J. F. Kelly, *Early Domestic Architecture of Connecticut* (1927); Wallace Nutting, *Furniture of Pilgrim Century* (1921); H. F. Clarke, *John Hull* (1940), and *John Coney, Silversmith* (1932), and *Jeremiah Dummer, Craftsman and Merchant* (1935); H. M. Forbes, *Gravestones of Early New England* (1927); J. T. Flexner, *First Flowers of Our Wilderness* (1947), chs. i, ii; Louisa Dresser, *XVIIth Century Painting in New England* (1935); Dow, *Every Day Life in Massachusetts Bay Colony;* G. F. Donovan, *Pre-Revolutionary Irish in Massachusetts. 1620–1775* (1932); L. J. Greene, *Negro in Colonial New England* (1942); Morris, *Studies in American Law,* chs. ii, iv; T. L. Wolford, "Laws and Liberties of 1648," *Boston University Law Rev.*, XXVIII (1948), 426; Julius Goebel, "King's Law and Local Custom in Seventeenth Century New England," *Columbia Law Rev.*, XXXI (1931), 416; Zechariah Chafee, Jr., introd. to *Records of Suffolk County Court 1671–80*, Col. Soc. Mass., *Publ.*, XXIX (1933); Osgood, *American Colonies in Seventeenth Century,* I, ch. xi; R. H. Akagi, *Town Proprietors of New England* (1924), pt. i; J. H. Benton, *Warning Out in New England* (1911); W. de L. Love, *Fast and Thanksgiving Days in New England* (1895); V. F. Barnes, "Richard Wharton," Col. Soc. Mass., *Publ.*, XXVI (1925), 238; O. W. Holmes, *Lectures in the Early History of Massachusetts* (1869), 257; H. R. Viets, "Features of Medicine in Massachusetts," *Isis*, XXIII (1935), 391, and *Brief History of Medicine in Massachusetts* (1930), chs. i–ii.

Sources — Miller and Johnson, *Puritans;* G. F. Dow, ed., *Records and Files of Quarterly Courts of Essex County, 1636–1683* (8 vols., 1911–21); *Records of Suffolk County Court 1671–80,* Col. Soc. Mass., *Publ.*, XXIX, XXX (1933); *Records of Court of Assistants;* Samuel Sewall, "Diary," Mass. Hist. Soc., *Coll.*, 5 ser., V–VII, and "Letter Book," *ibid.*, 6 ser., I–II (1878–88); Cotton Mather, *Magnalia Christi* (1702; reprinted, 2 vols., 1853), and "Diary"; K. B. Murdock, ed., *Selections from Cotton Mather* (1926); Donnan, *Documents Illustrative of Slave Trade,* I, III; H. M. Chapin, ed., *Letter Book of Peleg Sanford of Newport, 1666–68* (1928); R. P. Stearns, "Correspondence of John Woodbridge, Jr., and Richard Baxter, 1669–72," *New Eng. Quar.*, X (1937), 557; "Harvard College Records," Col. Soc. Mass., *Publ.*, XV, XVI, XXXI (1925–35); Anne Bradstreet, *Works* (J. H. Ellis, ed., 1887); H. J. Hall, ed., *Benjamin Tompson, His Poems* (1924); Edward Taylor, *Poetical Works* (T. H. Johnson, ed., 1940); K. B. Murdock, ed., *Handkerchiefs from Paul* (1927); Charles Morton, *Compendium Physicae* (1685), Col. Soc. Mass., *Publ.*, XXXIII (1940). — See also: § 46.

91. CHESAPEAKE COLONIES IN THE SEVENTEENTH CENTURY: SOCIAL, ECONOMIC, INSTITUTIONAL

Summary — 1624–52, institutional development of Virginia as royal province: Council, Assembly, County Courts, Parishes, Sheriff, Governors Harvey and Berkeley. — 1634–92, proprietary institutions in Maryland; economic development; the head-right system and dispersed location; "particular plantations"; manors. — Was this area largely yeoman farms or large plantations before 1675, were the gentry imported or native? — Tobacco; attempts of English government to diversify crops; relations between planter and merchant; effect of Acts of Trade. — Anglicanism and dissent; social implications of Maryland Toleration Act. — Laws regulating labor. — Education; literary culture; libraries; 1693, College of William and Mary (also, §§ 81, 87).

General — Andrews, *Colonial Period*, I, chs. ix, x; Channing, *History*, I, 225, 517, II, 80; Craven, *Southern Colonies*, chs. vii, viii; Osgood, *American Colonies in Seventeenth Century*, II, chs. iii–iv, III, chs. iv, ix; T. J. Wertenbaker, *First Americans*, ch. ii, and *Old South* (1942), chs. ii, iii; U. B. Phillips, *Life and Labor in Old South* (1929), ch. ii; Beer, *Origins of British Colonial System*, 241, and *Old Colonial System*, II, ch. viii; Quinn, *Literature of American People*, chs. i–v; Tyler, *History of American Literature*, I, chs. ii–iv.

Special — L. B. Wright, *First Gentlemen of Virginia* (1940); P. A. Bruce, *Economic History of Virginia*, and *Institutional History of Virginia*, and *Social Life of Virginia* (1927); M. N. Stanard, *Colonial Virginia* (1917); Wertenbaker, *Patrician and Plebeian*, and *Virginia under Stuarts*, and *Planters of Colonial Virginia;* P. S. Flippin, *Royal Government in Virginia* (1919), and *Financial Administration in Virginia* (1915); Bond, *Proceedings of Maryland Court of Appeals*, intro. and 1; C. H. Karraker, *Seventeenth-Century Sheriff* (1930); A. P. Scott, *Criminal Law in Colonial Virginia* (1930); O. P. Chitwood, *Justice in Colonial Virginia* (1905); R. B. Morris, *Studies in History of American Law*, ch. ii; E. E. MacQueen, "Commissary in Colonial Maryland," *Md. Hist. Mag.*, XXV (1930), 190; B. W. Bond, *Quit-Rent System* (1919), chs. vii–viii; A. W. Lauber, *Indian Slavery in Colonial Times* (1913), § ii; Jernegan, *Laboring and Dependent Classes*, chs. ix–xii; J. C. Ballagh, *White Servitude in Virginia* (1895); A. E. Smith, *Colonists in Bondage* (1947); P. C. Mason, "Jayle Birds in Colonial Virginia," *Va. Mag. Hist.*, LIII (1945), 37; Bishop William Meade, *Old Churches of Virginia* (2 vols., 1857); (also § 87); G. M. Brydon, *Virginia's Mother Church* (2 vols., 1947), I; H. R. McIlwaine, *Struggle of Protestant Dissenters for Toleration* (1894); Shurtleff, *Log Cabin Myth;* C. R. Edwards, *Frontier Policy of Colony of Virginia* (1915); A. O. Craven, *Soil Exhaustion as Factor in Virginia* (1925), chs. i–ii; E. A. J. Johnson, *American Economic Thought;* L. C. Gray, "Market Surplus Problems of Colonial Tobacco," *Ag. Hist.*, II (1928), 1; V. J. Wyckoff, "Seventeenth Century Maryland Prices," *ibid.*, XII (1938), 299; W. B. Blanton, *Medicine in Virginia* (1930); L. B. Wright, "The 'Gentlemen's Library' in Early Virginia," *Huntington Library Quar.*, I (1937), 1; Hendrick, *Lees of Virginia*, pt. i; A. K. Davis, Jr., *Traditional Ballads of Virginia;* F. Harrison, *Landmarks of Old Prince William*, I, chs. i–xiii, and *Virginia Land Grants* (1925); J. S. Bassett, "Virginia Planter and London Merchant," *Am. Hist. Assoc., Report*, 1901, I, 551; Morrison, *Early American Architecture*, ch. v; S. F. Kimball, *Domestic Architecture of American Colonies* (1927), 1; J. C. Spruill, *Women's Life and Work in Southern Colonies* (1938); (also § 90); S. P. Moorehead, "The Castle," *Va. Mag. Hist.*, XLII (1934), 298, and "Christ's Cross," *ibid.*, XLIII (1935), 1.

Sources — McIlwaine has edited and the Commonwealth published, *Journals of the House of Burgesses*, and *Executive Journals of Council*, and *Minutes of Council and General Court;* Sir William Berkeley, *Discourse and View of Virginia* (1663; reprinted 1914); § 87; Beverley, *History of Virginia;* Durand, *Frenchman in Virginia;* Force, *Tracts*, I–III; *Bristol and America, a Record of the First Settlers 1654–85* (1929; M. M. Lorenz, ed., lists thousands of servants).

Bibliography — Swem, *Virginia Historical Index.*

Chapter Eight

FROM THE STUART RESTORATION TO THE
TREATY OF UTRECHT 1660–1713

92. THE RESTORATION AND ENGLISH COLONIAL POLICY

Summary — § 89; 1660, Colonial policy of Charles II; closer economic control, emigration no longer favored. — 1660, 1662, 1663, 1672, 1696, 1699, Acts of Trade and Navigation. — Enforcement before establishment of Admiralty courts. — 1707, Scotland admitted to system. — Organs of English government dealing with colonies: King, Privy Council, Parliament, Secretary of State of Southern Department, Lords of Trade, Board of Trade and Plantations, Admiralty, Treasury. — The Royal Disallowance and Judicial Appeals. — Writs of Assistance. — Colonial considerations in English foreign policy. — 1688, The "Glorious Revolution"; effect on the colonial system. — William III and his advisers. — Money supply and currency. — English attitude toward colonial manufacturing. — English politics. — Later developments (§ 101).

General — Beer, *Old Colonial System*, I, chs. i–iv; Channing, *History*, II, chs. i, viii–ix; Andrews, *Colonial Period*, III, ch. ii, IV, chs. i–x; Craven, *Southern Colonies*, chs. viii, x; Osgood, *American Colonies in Seventeenth Century*, III, chs. vi–vii, and *American Colonies in Eighteenth Century*, I, ch. i, iv–vi; David Ogg, *England in Reign of Charles II* (1934), I, chs. iv, vi, II, ch. xviii; *Cambridge History British Empire*, I, chs. viii–x, xiv; Lipson, *Economic History of England*, II, 352, III, 116.

Special — Colonial Policy: Harper, *English Navigation Laws*, chs. v–xvii; O. M. Dickerson, *American Colonial Government 1696–1765* (1912), chs. i, ii; Andrews, *British Committees of Trade and Plantations*, chs. iv, v; R. P. Bieber, *Lords of Trade. 1675–96* (1919); G. A. Jacobsen, *William Blathwayt* (1932); G. H. Guttridge, *Colonial Policy of William III* (1922); M. A. Thomson, *Secretaries of State, 1681–1782* (1932); E. B. Russell, *Review of American Colonial Legislation by King in Council* (1915); W. T. Root, *Relations of Pennsylvania with British Government 1696–1765* (1912); C. M. Andrews, "The Royal Disallowance," Am. Antiq. Soc., *Proc.*, n.s., XXIV (1914), 342; G. A. Washburn, *Imperial Control of Administration of Justice 1684–1776* (1923); E. R. Turner, *Privy Council 1603–1784* (1928), I; A. M. Schlesinger, "Colonial Appeals to Privy Council," *Pol. Sci. Quar.*, XXVIII (1913), 279, 433; H. J. Crump, *Colonial Admiralty Jurisdiction* (1931); Emily Hickman, "Colonial Writs of Assistance," *New Eng. Quar.*, V (1932), 83; St. G. L. Sioussat, "Extension of English Statutes to Plantations," *Select Essays in Anglo-American Legal History* (1907), I, 416; Theodora Keith, "Scottish Trade with Plantations before 1707," *Scottish Hist. Rev.*, VI (1908), 32; C. P. Nettels, "Menace of Colonial Manufacturing, 1690–1720," *New Eng. Quar.*, IV (1931), 230, and "Economic Relations of Boston, Philadelphia, and New York, 1680–1715," *Jour. Econ. and Bus. Hist.*, III (1931), 185, and *Money Supply of American Colonies before 1720* (1934). ❡ English Politics: Keith Feiling, *History of Tory Party 1640–1714* (1924);

L. F. Brown, *First Earl of Shaftesbury* (1933); James Ferguson, *Robert Ferguson the Plotter* (1887); Theodora Keith, "Economic Causes for Scottish Union," *Eng. Hist. Rev.*, XXIV (1909), 44.

Sources — Labaree, ed., *Royal Instructions*; Stock, *Proceedings*, I–III; *Calendar of State Papers, Colonial, America and West Indies* (includes Journal of Commissioners of Trade and Plantations until 1704, when a separate series begins); *Acts of Privy Council, Colonial*, I–II, VI; *Calendar of Treasury Books* (1660–1685; 7 vols., 1904–16); "Clarendon Papers," N.Y. Hist. Soc., *Coll.*, 1869; MacDonald, *Select Charters*, Nos. 22, 23, 25, 28, 34, 43; A. M. Davis, ed., *Colonial Currency Reprints 1682–1751* (4 vols., 1910).

93. NEW YORK

Summary — § 80; 1660, English merchants move to seize New Netherland. — 1664, Duke of York's grant; seizure of New Netherland by Colonel Richard Nicolls. — Dutch inhabitants retain rights and property. — 1665, The Duke's Laws promulgated to appease English in Long Island. — 1673, Captain Evertsen captures New York City; 1674, restored to English; Governor Edmund Andros. — 1680, William Dyer sued for taxation without representation. — The Iroquois alliance, French attacks of 1665–66. — 1683, Governor Thomas Dongan calls first assembly; Charter of Liberties disallowed by James II. — 1684, Albany Conference, relations with Canada. — 1685, New York a Royal Province. — 1688–91, Dominion of New England and Leisler regime (§ 96). — 1691, Governor Sloughter summons Assembly. — 1697–1708, Governors Fletcher, Bellomont, Cornbury, and Hunter. — 1690–1700, the pirates, Teach, Quelch, and Kidd.

General — Andrews, *Colonial Period*, III, 35, 96; Channing, *History*, II, 263, 294, chs. ii, v; Osgood, *American Colonies in Seventeenth Century*, II, chs. vi–vii, 309, 356, 367, 386, III, 143, ch. xii; Flick, *New York*, II, chs. i–iv.

Special — Brodhead, *History of New York*, I, 734, II, chs. i–viii; E. B. O'Callaghan, *Origin of Legislative Assemblies in New York* (1861); A. E. McKinley, "Transition from Dutch to English Rule," *Am. Hist. Rev.*, VI (1900), 693; Peter Wraxall, *Abridgment of Indian Affairs* (C. H. McIlwain, ed., 1915), pp. xxxv, 1; Van Rensselaer, *City of New York*, II; C. R. Hildeburn, *Printers and Printing in New York* (1895); Wilberforce Eames, *First Year of Printing in New York* (1928); J. H. Kennedy, *Thomas Dongan* (1930); W. C. Abbott, "Colonel John Scott of Long Island," *Conflicts with Oblivion* (1924), 281; Stokes, *Iconography of Manhattan*, I, ch. ii, IV, ch. ii; also §§ 62, 92.

Sources — O'Callaghan and Fernow, *New York Colonial Documents*, II; O'Callaghan, ed., *Documentary History of New York*; Paltsits, *Minutes of Executive Council*; Trumbull and Hoadly, *Public Records of Connecticut (1636–1776)*, II–III; *Minutes of Common Council of City of New York*, I; town records (§ 46); Morris, ed., *Select Cases of Mayor's Court*; Jeremias Van Rensselaer, *Correspondence*; A. J. F. Van Laer, ed., *Minutes of Court of Albany 1668–1685* (3 vols., 1926–32); Daniel Denton, *Description of New York* (1670; reprinted 1937); J. F. Jameson, ed., *Privateering and Piracy in Colonial Period* (1923), 190; § 46.

94. THE CAROLINAS

Summary — 1629, Carolina grant; New England trade, and settlement at Cape Fear River. — 1663, 1665, Carolina charters; Lord Ashley (Shaftesbury) and Sir John Colleton. — 1663, Hilton's voyage. — 1664, Province of Albemarle, nucleus of North Carolina early settlers. — 1669, John Locke and the Fundamental Constitutions. — The Baronies. — 1670, Port Royal, 1680, Charleston, founded. — Spanish and Indian relations, the peltry trade, trade with West Indies. — Virginian, Barbadian, English, Scots, Swiss, and Huguenot immigrants. — Discontent with proprietary rule. — Beginnings of rice culture in the southern province; tobacco and naval stores in the north. — Society and culture in early Charleston. — Conflicts with Spain (§ 96).

General — Andrews, *Colonial Period*, III, chs. v, vi; Channing, *History*, II, 13, ch. xii; Osgood, *American Colonies in Seventeenth Century*, chs. ix, x; *Cambridge History British Empire*, I, 607; Beer, *Old Colonial System*, ch. ix.

Special — R. D. W. Connor, *North Carolina: Colonial and Revolutionary Periods, 1584–1783* (1919); Ashe, *History of North Carolina*, I, chs. vii–xv; W. J. Rivers, *History of South Carolina to 1719* (1856); Edward McCrady, *History of South Carolina under Proprietary Government* (1897); Wallace, *South Carolina*, I; Brown, *First Earl of Shaftesbury*, ch. x; H. F. Russell Smith, *Harrington and His Oceana* (1914), ch. vii; G. D. Bernheim, *German Settlements in North and South Carolina* (1872); Hirsch, *Huguenots of South Carolina*; Frederick Dalcho, *Historical Account of Protestant Episcopal Church in South Carolina* (1820); H. A. M. Smith, "Town of Dorchester," *So. Car. Hist. Mag.*, VI (1905), 62, and "Baronies of South Carolina," *ibid.*, XI (1910)–XV (1914), XVIII (1917); Leah Townsend, *South Carolina Baptists, 1670–1805* (1935); J. P. Thomas, "Barbadians in Early South Carolina," *So. Car. Hist. Mag.*, XXXI (1930), 75; A. S. Salley, "Spanish Settlement at Port Royal," *ibid.*, XXVI (1925), 31, and *Introduction of Rice Culture into South Carolina* (1919); Insh, *Scottish Colonial Schemes*, ch. vi; W. P. Cumming, "Earliest Permanent Settlement in Carolina," *Am. Hist. Rev.*, XLV (1939), 82; R. E. Moody, "Massachusetts Trade with Carolina, 1686–1709," *No. Car. Hist. Rev.*, XX (1943), 43; V. W. Crane, *Southern Frontier 1670–1732* (1928); St. J. R. Childs, "Cavaliers and Burghers of Carolina Low Country," E. F. Goldman, *Historiography and Urbanization* (1941); St. J. R. Childs, *Malaria and Colonization in Carolina Low Country* (1940); Sanford Winston, "Indian Slavery in Carolina Region," *Jour. of Negro Hist.*, XIX (1934), 431; Edward McCrady, "Slavery in South Carolina," *Am. Hist. Assoc., Report*, 1895, 629; F. J. Klingberg, *Negro in Colonial South Carolina* (1941); Ravenel, *Charleston;* E. L. Pennington, "The Library in Charles Town," *Am. Antiq. Soc., Proc.*, n.s., XLIV (1935), 159; Phillips, *Life and Labor in Old South*, ch. iii; F. P. Bowes, *Culture of Early Charleston* (1942); also § § 62, 96.

Sources — A. S. Salley, ed., *Narratives of Early Carolina, 1650–1708* (1911; includes *Discovery of New Brittaine* (1650), William Hilton, *Relation* (1664), *Brief Description* (1666), Robert Sandford, *Relation* (1666), Thomas Ashe and Samuel Wilson, *Carolina* (1682), William Pratt, *Journal* (1695–1701), Daniel Defoe, *Party-Tyranny in Carolina* (1705), John Archdale, *New Description* (1707); William Byrd, *Histories of Dividing Line* (W. K. Boyd, ed., 1929), and *Writings*, and *Secret Diary*; John Lawson, *History of Carolina* (1718), and *New Voyage to Carolina* (1709; reprinted, 1860); W. A. Courtenay, *Genesis of South Carolina, 1562–1670* (1907); Christopher von Graffenried, *Account of Founding of New Bern* (V. H. Todd, ed., 1920); Langdon Cheves, ed., "Shaftesbury Papers," *So. Car. Hist. Soc., Coll.*, V (1897); Salley, ed., *Records in British Public Record Office Relating to South Carolina, 1663–1710;* Saunders, *Colonial Records of North Carolina, 1662–1712*, I; Salley, *Journal of Grand Council*, and *Journals of Commons House of Assembly*, and *Commissions and Instructions*, and *Journal of Commissioners of Indian Trade*, and *Warrants for Lands in South Carolina 1672–1711;* F. J. Klingberg, ed., *Carolina Chronicle: the Papers of Commissary Gideon Johnston 1707–16* (1946); § 46.

Bibliography — Winsor, *Narrative and Critical History*, V, ch. v; W. C. Ford, "Early Maps of Carolina," *Geog. Rev.*, XVI (1926), 264; Karpinsky, *Early Maps of Carolina;* J. H. Easterby, *South Carolina Bibliographies* (1950), No. 2.

95. NEW JERSEY, PENNSYLVANIA, AND DELAWARE

Summary — Quakers: George Fox and the Society of Friends. — New Jersey: 1664, Duke of York's grant to Berkeley and Carteret, settlement of Newark, Monmouth, and Middletown; 1665, Concessions and Agreements; 1668, First assembly; 1673, Fenwick and Byllynge buy Berkeley's half (West New Jersey). — 1676, William Penn and three other Quakers acquire Carteret's half (East New Jersey), issue Concessions and Agreements; 1682, Quaker propriety for both Jersies; 1702, Royal Province; Governor Cornbury; confusion over land titles, controversies with New York. — Delaware: (§ 80); 1655,

New Netherland annexes New Sweden; 1664, Delaware area included in Duke's grant. — Pennsylvania: Early life and conversion of William Penn; 1681, Pennsylvania Charter, and ducal grant of Delaware; Penn's ideals for his "holy experiment"; his advertisements for colonists; 1682, Penn arrives, founds Philadelphia, calls first assembly; his land system; English, Irish, and Dutch Quaker migrations; 1683, Pastorius and the Mennonites found Germantown; 1682, 1683, 1696, Penn's Frames of Government; 1701, his Charter of Privileges; wranglings among Penn's governors, the Lloyds, and the Assembly; early trade and prosperity of the province; 1692, Pennsylvania a Royal Province; Governor Fletcher; — 1694, propriety restored; 1697, Governor Markham and the pirates; 1704, Lower Counties (Delaware) acquire separate Assembly; 1718, death of Penn; liberal Quaker penal code replaced.

General — Andrews, *Colonial Period*, III, chs. iv, vii; Channing, *History*, II, 44, ch. iv, 313; Osgood, *American Colonies in Seventeenth Century*, II, chs. viii, xi, 341, and *American Colonies in Eighteenth Century*, I, ch. xii, 537, II, 87, 121, ch. xxiv; R. M. Jones, *Quakers in American Colonies*; Wertenbaker, *Founding of American Civilization*, chs. iv–vii; Tyler, *History of American Literature*, II, 225.

Special — Tanner, *Province of New Jersey 1664–1738*, chs. i–viii; J. E. Pomfret, "Proprietors of West New Jersey, 1674–1702," *Penn. Mag. Hist.*, LXXV (1951), 117, and "West New Jersey, a Quaker Society," *William and Mary Quar.*, 3 ser., VIII (1951), 493; R. G. Johnson, "John Fenwicke," *N. J. Hist. Soc., Proc.*, IV (1849), 53; William Nelson, *Discovery and Early History of New Jersey* (1912); H. L. Carlson, "Genesis of Charter of Pennsylvania," *Penn. Mag. Hist.*, XLIII (1919), 289; N. B. Wainwright, "Mystery of Pennsylvania's Royal Charter," *ibid.*, LXXIII (1949), 415; F. H. Kane, "Early Pennsylvania Promotion Literature," *ibid.*, LXIII (1939), 144; Keith, *Chronicles of Pennsylvania*, I; Janney, *William Penn*; S. G. Fisher, *True William Penn* (1900); W. I. Hull, *William Penn*, and *Penn and Dutch Quaker Migration* (1935); M. R. Brailsford, *Making of William Penn* (1930); C. H. Smith, *Mennonite Immigration to Pennsylvania* (1929); H. S. Bender, "Founding of Mennonite Church at Germantown," *Mennonite Quar. Rev.*, VII (1933), 227; A. C. Myers, *Immigration of Irish Quakers into Pennsylvania, 1682–1750* (1902); C. H. Browning, *Welsh Settlement of Pennsylvania* (1912); Knittle, *Early Eighteenth Century Palatine Emigration*; F. B. Tolles, *Meeting House and Counting House, Quaker Merchants of Colonial Philadelphia* (1948), chs. i, ii; W. F. Dunaway, "English Settlers in Colonial Pennsylvania," *Penn. Mag. Hist.*, LII (1928), 317, LIII (1929), 322; J. de L. Leonard, "Organization and Procedure of Pennsylvania Assembly, 1682–1776," *ibid.*, LXXI (1948), 215, 376; Learned, *Pastorius*; R. S. Rodney, "Early Relations of Delaware and Pennsylvania," *Penn. Mag. Hist.*, LIV (1930), 209; B. A. Konkle, "A Grant Yet Not a Grant," *ibid.*, LIV (1930), 241; Scharf, *Delaware*, I, chs. iv–xii; Russell Smith, *Harrington and His Oceana*, ch. vii; § 62. ❡ Maps: Oliver Hough, "Captain Thomas Holme," *Penn. Mag. Hist.*, XIX (1895), 413, XX (1896), 128, 248; W. C. Ford, "First Separate Map of Pennsylvania," *Mass. Hist. Soc., Proc.*, LVII (1923), 172; Gipson, *Lewis Evans*.

Sources — Myers, *Narratives of Early Pennsylvania, West Jersey and Delaware* (includes *Present State of Colony of West-Jersey* [1681]; and William Penn, *Some Account of Pennsilvania* [1681]; and *Letter to Free Society of Traders* (1683); and *Further Account of Pennsylvania* [1685]; and Thomas Paschall, *Letter* [1683]; and Richard Frame, *Short Description* [1692]; and Gabriel Thomas, *Historical and Geographical Account of Pennsilvania and West-New-Jersey* [1698]; and F. D. Pastorius, *Sichere Nachricht* "Positive Information" [1684]; and *Umständige Geographische Beschreibung* "Circumstantial Geographical Description" [1700]); MacDonald, *Select Charters*, Nos. 30, 31, 35–41, 44, 46; William Penn and James Logan, "Correspondence"; Thomas Budd, *Good Order Established in Pennsylvania and New Jersey* (1685; reprinted 1865, 1902); Jonathan Dickinson, *God's Protecting Providence* (1699; E. W. and C. McL. Andrews, eds., 1945); Leaming and Spicer, *Grants, Concessions, and Original Constitutions*; "Scots East Jersey Proprietors' Letters, 1683–84," *N. J. Hist. Soc., Proc.*, n.s., VII (1922), 4, 119; J. E. Pomfret, ed., "Edward Byllynge's Proposed Gift of Land," *Penn. Mag. Hist.*, LXI (1937), 88.

Bibliography — Winsor, *Narrative and Critical History*, III, 449, 495, V, 242; M. K. Spence, "William Penn: A Bibliography," Penn. Hist. Commission, *Bull.*, No. 1 (1932); Bining, "Selected Bibliography on Pennsylvania History"; H. P. Beers, "Pennsylvania Bibliographies," *Penn. Hist.*, II (1935), 104, 178, 239, III (1936), 46; Emil Meynen, *Bibliography on German Settlements.*

96. WARS, INSURRECTIONS, AND OTHER DISTURBANCES, 1675–1692

Summary — 1675–76, King Philip's War: causes; strategy and tactics; destruction; effect on New England and on the Indians. — 1675, Bacon's Rebellion: causes; events, suppression; results for Virginia; 1677, Culpeper Rebellion in North Carolina. — New England: 1676, Edward Randolph's reports on New England trade; 1684, Massachusetts Bay Charter vacated; 1685, Dominion of New England, Joseph Dudley, president; 1686, Edmund Andros, Governor General; Dominion annexes Rhode Island, Connecticut, and New York; policy as to trade, taxes, religion, and learning. — 1688, "Glorious Revolution" in England; 1689, revolutions in Boston and New York; charter governments resumed in Rhode Island and Connecticut; 1689–92, rise and fall of Jacob Leisler. — Witchcraft: 1691–92, outbreak at Salem Village (Danvers, Massachusetts); popular belief in witchcraft; question of spectral evidence, of influence of the Mathers and other ministers, of Governor William Phips; the frenzy ended; attitude of the judges and the provincial government.

General — Channing, *History*, II, chs. iii, v–vii, 456, 527; Osgood, *American Colonies in Seventeenth Century*, I, ch. xiv, III, chs. viii–ix, xiii–xvi, 223; Beer, *Old Colonial System*, ch. xii; G. S. Graham, *Empire of North Atlantic, the Maritime Struggle for North America* (1950), chs. i–iv; Palfrey, *New England*, III, chs. iv–v, xii–xiv, IV, 96; J. T. Adams, *Founding of New England*, chs. xv–xvi.

Special — Wertenbaker, *Planters of Colonial Virginia*, chs. v–vii, and *Torchbearer*; V. F. Barnes, *Dominion of New England* (1923), and "Rise of William Phips," *New Eng. Quar.*, I (1928), 271, 523; Toppan, *Edward Randolph*; Duniway, *Freedom of Press in Massachusetts*, 58; F. W. Gookin, *Daniel Gookin* (1912); Ashe, *History of North Carolina*, I, chs. x–xi; A. L. Ferguson, "Susquehannock Fort on Piscataway Creek," *Md. Hist. Mag.*, XXXVI (1941), 1; Van Rennselaer, *City of New York*, II; Brodhead, *History of New York*, II; Faust, *German Element*, I, 13. ❡ Witchcraft: E. W. Taylor, "Some Medical Aspects of Witchcraft," *Problems of Personality* (C. M. Campbell, *et al.*, eds., 1925), 167, and "Witchcraft Episode," Hart, *Commonwealth History of Massachusetts*, II, 29; C. W. Upham, *Salem Witchcraft* (2 vols., 1867); M. L. Starkey, *Devil in Massachusetts* (1949); G. L. Kittredge, *Witchcraft in Old and New England* (1928); ch. xviii; G. L. Burr, "New England's Place in Witchcraft," Am. Antiq. Soc., *Proc.*, n.s., XXI (1911), 185; Morison, *Puritan Pronaos*, 248; Murdock, *Increase Mather*; Winsor, *History of Boston*, II, ch. iv; C. K. Shipton, "Plea for Puritanism," *Am. Hist. Rev.*, XL (1935), 459; F. N. Parke, *Witchcraft in Maryland* (1937).

Sources — C. H. Lincoln, ed., *Narratives of the Indian Wars, 1675–1699* (1913; contains John Easton, *Relacion* [1675], Nathaniel Saltonstall, *Present State of New England* [1675], and *New and Further Narrative* [1676], Mary Rowlandson, *Captivity* [1682], and Cotton Mather, *Decennium Luctuosum* [1699]); Cadwallader Colden, *History of the Five Indian Nations* (1747; 2 vols., 1922), chs. iv–xiii; C. M. Andrews, ed., *Narratives of the Insurrections, 1675–1690* (1915; contains Thomas Mathew, *Beginning of Bacon's Rebellion* [1705], *History of Bacon's and Ingram's Rebellion* [1676], the *True Narrative by Royal Commissioners* [1677], and *Declaration of Protestant Subjects in Maryland* [1689]); "Aspinwall Papers," Mass. Hist. Soc., *Coll.*, 4 ser., IX (1871), 162; "Bacon's Rebellion: Eggleston MSS.," *William and Mary Quar.*, IX (1900), 1; Ebenezer Cooke, "Maryland Muse" (1731), on the Rebellion, Am. Antiq. Soc., *Proc.*, n.s., XLIV (1934), 309. ❡ New England: R. N. Toppan, ed., "Dudley Records," Mass. Hist. Soc., *Proc.*, 2 ser., XIII (1899), 222; R. N. Toppan, ed., "Andros Records," Am. Antiq. Soc., *Proc.*, n.s., XIII (1899–1900), 237, 463; J. H. Tuttle, ed., "Land Warrants under Andros," Col.

Soc. Mass., *Publ.*, XXI (1919), 292; Hutchinson, *Collection of Papers*, II, 210; Perry, *Historical Collections*, III, 1; *Andros Tracts* (3 vols., 1868–74); John Usher, "Report on Northern Colonies, 1698," *William and Mary Quar.*, 3 ser., VII (1950), 95. ❧ New York: "Documents on Leisler Administration," N.Y. Hist. Soc., *Coll.*, I (1868), 237; "Papers Relating to Administration of Leisler," O'Callaghan, *Documentary History of New York*, II, 3; Brodhead, *Documents Relating to Colonial History of New York*, III. ❧ Witchcraft: G. L. Burr, ed., *Narratives of Witchcraft Cases, 1648–1706* (1914; includes Robert Calef, *More Wonders of Invisible World* [1700], Richard Chamberlain, *Lithobolia* [1698], Deodat Lawson, *Brief and True Narrative of Witchcraft at Salem Village* [1692]; W. E. Woodward, ed., *Records of Salem Witchcraft* (2 vols., 1864); David Levin, ed., *What Happened in Salem?* (1952); Zoltan Haraszti, "Cotton Mather and Witchcraft Trials," *More Books*, XV (1940), 179; Mather, "Diary," VII, 143, 150, 160; Dankaerts, *Journal*.

Bibliography — T. J. Holmes, *Cotton Mather, a Bibliography* (3 vols., 1940), and *Increase Mather, a Bibliography* (1931), I, 115; Burr, "New England's Place in Witchcraft"; Starkey, *Devil in Massachusetts*.

97. FRENCH ACTIVITIES IN NORTH AMERICA; FOUNDING OF LOUISIANA, 1665–1713

Summary — § 79; 1664, Canada a royal province; policy of Colbert and Louis XIV; the Carignan-Salières regiment; influence of the Church; the fur trade; hostilities with Iroquois. — 1668, Acadia restored to France; foundation of Sault Ste. Marie. — 1669, Hudson's Bay Company. — 1672–85, 1689–98, Frontenac, governor; relations with other officials, the Iroquois, the English colonies. — Robert Cavelier de la Salle, 1669–72; plans and early journeys. — 1673, Joliet and Marquette reach the Mississippi. — 1678–83, the "Grand Enterprise," passage of the Lakes; Hennepin, descent of the Mississippi, Apr. 9, 1682, takes possession of the Great Valley for Louis XIV, returns to France. — 1699, d'Iberville founds first Louisiana settlement at Biloxi. — 1700, settlements in the Illinois country. — 1702, Bienville transfers Louisiana colony to Mobile. — 1683–1701, LeSueur in the Sioux country. — 1694–1704, Cadillac at Michilimacinac, founding of Detroit, Outagamie War. — 1703–13, Queen Anne's War. — 1714, Juchereau explores the Red River. — Wars of 1692–1713 (§ 99); Pensacola and the Texas frontier (§ 100); Louisiana after 1713 (§ 106).

General — Francis Parkman, *Frontenac and New France under Louis XIV*, and *Old Regime in Canada*, and *La Salle and Discovery of the Great West*, and *Half-Century of Conflict* (1892), I, chs. i–viii, xiv, xv; Gipson, *British Empire before American Revolution*, V, chs. i–iii; Channing, *History*, II, ch. v, 527, 552; Ernest Lavisse, *et al.*, *Histoire de France* (11 vols., 1900–11), VII, pt. 1, 233; La Roncière, *Histoire de la marine française*, VI, 243, 473, V, 302, 647; F. X. Garneau, *Histoire du Canada* (§ 79); Wrong, *Rise and Fall of New France*, I, chs. xviii–xx, II, chs. xxi–xxiii; Salone, *Nouvelle-France; Cambridge History British Empire*, VI, ch. iv.

Special — Louisiana: Francis Parkman II, "French Policy in Lower Mississippi Valley, 1697–1712," Col. Soc. Mass., *Publ.*, XXVIII (1932), 225; Ella Lonn, "French Council of Commerce and American Trade," *Miss. Valley Hist. Rev.*, VI (1920), 192; W. E. Dunn, *Spanish and French Rivalry in Gulf Region* (1917); W. T. Morgan, "English Fear of 'Encirclement'," *Canadian Hist. Rev.*, X (1929), 4, and "Crisis in History of Hudson's Bay Company," *No. Dakota Hist. Quar.*, V (1931), 197; G. N. Clark, *Dutch Alliance and War against French Trade 1688–97* (1923); Gayarré, *History of Louisiana*, I; Fortier, *History of Louisiana*, I, chs. ii–iv; Hamilton, *Colonial Mobile*, pt. 2; C. G. M. B. de La Roncière, *Une Épopée Canadienne* (1930); Grace King, *Le Moyne de Bienville* (1892). ❧ Canada and the West: John Finley, *French in Heart of America* (1915), chs. i–vi; L. P. Kellogg, "France and Mississippi Valley," *Miss. Valley Hist. Rev.* (1931), 3, and *French Régime in Wisconsin and Northwest*, chs. vii–xiii; H. R. Casgrain, *Les Sulpiciens en Acadie* (1897); M. B. Sulte, "Le Régiment de Carignan," Royal Soc. Canada, *Proc.*,

2 ser., VIII (1902), § 1, 25; A. C. Laut, *Cadillac* (1931); Wraxall, *Abridgment*, intro., ch. ii; H. P. Biggar, "Frontenac's Projected Attempt on New York in 1689," N.Y. State Hist. Assoc., *Quar. Jour.*, V (1924), 139; G. B. Selden, "Expedition of Denonville against Senecas, 1687," Rochester Hist. Soc., *Publ. Fund Ser.*, IV (1925), 1; Goodrich, *First Michigan Frontier*; W. R. Riddell, "When Detroit Was French," *Mich. Hist. Mag.*, XXIII (1939), 37.

Sources — Narratives and Documents: Margry, *Découvertes et établissements des français;* L. P. Kellogg, ed., *Early Narratives of Northwest, 1634–1699* (1917); J. G. Shea, *Discovery and Exploration of Mississippi Valley* (1852); Thwaites, *Jesuit Relations* (§ 79); W. I. Morse, ed., *Acadiensia Nova* (2 vols., 1935); Sieur de Dièreville, *Voyage du Port Royal* (1686; J. C. Webster, ed., 1933); I. J. Cox, ed., *Journeys of La Salle* (2 vols., 1905); Rowland and Sanders, *Mississippi Provincial Archives: French Dominion*, I; J. J. Thompson, "Illinois: Cradle of Christianity, a Documentary History," *Ill. Cath. Hist. Rev.*, IX–XI (1926–29); Wroth and Annan, *Acts of French Royal Administration Concerning Canada, Guiana, West Indies and Louisiana to 1791.* ❬ Contemporary Histories: Pierre de Charlevoix, *Histoire et description générale de la Nouvelle France* (1744; J. G. Shea, transl., 1880); Louis Hennepin, *Description de la Louisiana* (1683; J. G. Shea, ed., 1880).

Bibliography — Winsor, *Narrative and Critical History*, IV, chs. v–vii, V, ch. i; Raymond Thomassy, *Géologie pratique de la Louisiane* (1860), 205; Morse, *Acadiensia Nova*. II.

98. THE WEST INDIES, 1660–1775

Summary — West Indies before 1660 (§ 82). — 1664, Colbert's Compagnie des Portelles. — 1665–67, Anglo-Dutch war. — 1670, Royal grant of Bahamas. — French obtain foothold on Hispaniola. — 1697, Treaty of Ryswick, St. Domingue ceded to France. — Buccaneers turn filibusters; Morgan's raids on Panama. — 1685, Bermuda a royal province. — 1698–99, Scots colony at Darien. — 1713, Treaty of Utrecht, England gains Asiento and whole of St. Kitts. — 1718, Gov. Woodes Rogers in the Bahamas. — Clandestine trade of Jamaica with logwood coast and Spanish colonies. — Wars (§§ 106–08, 118); islands frequently change hands. — Plantation organization and society; replacement of tobacco by sugar; constitutional struggles in Jamaica and Barbados; planters' influence in Parliament; Molasses Act of 1735; African slave trade.

General — *Cambridge History British Empire*, I, 239, chs. xi, xv, xviii, xx, xxii; Newton, *European Nations*, chs. xv–xxiii; Hart, *Admirals of Caribbean*, chs. iii–vi; Beer, *Old Colonial System*, chs. v–vii; Gipson, *British Empire before American Revolution*, II, chs. vii–x; Lucas, *Historical Geography of the British Colonies* (1905), II; La Roncière, *Histoire de la marine française*, VI; (§ 93).

Special — C. H. Haring, *Buccaneers in West Indies in Seventeenth Century* (1910); V. T. Harlow, *History Barbados*, chs. iv–vii, and *Christopher Codrington* (1928); C. S. S. Higham, *Development of Leeward Islands under Restoration* (1921); Richard Pares, *War and Trade in West Indies, 1739–1763* (1936), and *West-India Fortune* (1950); F. W. Pitman, *Development of British West Indies 1700–1763* (1917), and "Slavery on British West Indies Plantations," *Jour. Negro Hist.*, XI (1926), 584; L. J. Ragatz, *Old Plantation System in British Caribbean* (1925), and *Fall of Planter Class in Caribbean, 1763–1833* (1928), chs. i–iv; L. M. Penson, *Colonial Agents of British West Indies* (1924), and "London West Indies Interest in the Eighteenth Century," *Eng. Hist. Rev.*, XXXVI (1921), 373; G. P. Insh, *Company of Scotland Trading to Africa and Indies* (1932); F. R. Hart, *Disaster of Darien, 1699–1701* (1929); N. M. Crouse, *French Struggle for West Indies 1665–1713* (1943); S. L. Mims, *Colbert's West India Policy* (1912); G. F. Zook, *Company of Royal Adventurers Trading into Africa* (1919); I. A. Wright, "Coymans Asiento, 1685–1689," *Bijdragen voor Vaderlandsche Geschiednis*, VI, § 1 (1924), 23; Frank Cundall, *Historic Jamaica* (1915), and *Governors of Jamaica in Seven-*

teenth Century (1936), and *Governors of Jamaica in First Half of Eighteenth Century* (1937); A. M. Whitson, *Constitutional Development of Jamaica 1660–1729* (1929), and "Outlook of Continental Colonies on British West Indies," *Pol. Sci. Quar.*, XLV (1930), 56; K. G. Davies, "Origins of Commission System," *Royal Hist. Soc., Trans.*, 5 ser., II (1952), 89; Henry Wilkinson, *Adventurers of Bermuda* (1923), chs. xvi–xviii, and *Bermuda in Old Empire 1684–1784* (1950).

Sources — Documents: *Calendar of State Papers, Colonial, America and West Indies*, V, VII, IX–XL; *Acts of Privy Council, Colonial*, II–VI; *Journals of Commissioners of Trade and Plantations* (11 vols., 1920–35); Stock, *Proceedings*, III–IV; E. Donnan, *Documents Illustrative of Slave Trade*, I, II. ❧ Memoirs and Voyages: Christopher Jeaffreson, *Young Squire of the Seventeenth Century* (J. C. Jeaffreson, ed., 2 vols., 1878); J. B. Labat, *Voyage aux isles d'Amérique* (6 vols., 1722, 1742; abridged ed., 2 vols., 1931); [Janet Schaw], *Journal of a Lady of Quality, 1774–1776* (E. W. and C. M. Andrews, eds., 1921); A. O. Esquemeling, *History of Bucaniers of America* (1684; many reprints); William Dampier, *New Voyage Round World* (1697; N. M. Penzer, ed., 1931). ❧ Contemporary Histories: Edwards, *British West Indies*, I–III; Edward Long, *History of Jamaica* (3 vols., 1774); Dalby Thomas, *Rise and Growth of West India Colonies* (1690; reprinted, *Harleian Miscellany*, II, 340); Thomas Southey, *Chronological History of West Indies* (3 vols., 1827); M. L. É. Moreau de Saint-Méry, *Description de la partie française de l'isle Saint-Domingue* (2 vols., 1797).

Bibliography — Ragatz, *Planter Class*, 461, and *Guide for Study of British Caribbean History*; *Cambridge History British Empire*, I, 872; Frank Cundall, *Bibliographia Jamaicensis* (1902; Supplement, to same, 1908), and *Bibliography of West Indies*; American Geographical Society, *Catalogue of Maps of Hispanic America* (1930), I, 259.

99. VIRGINIA, NEW ENGLAND, AND WARS ON NORTHERN FRONTIER, 1689–1713

Summary — 1692–97, conclusion of King William's War; Treaty of Ryswick; 1692–1722, Governors Andros, Nicholson, and Spotswood in Virginia; 1692–1719, Governors Fletcher, Bellomont, Cornbury, and Hunter in New York; 1692–1715, Governors Phips, Bellomont, and Dudley in Massachusetts Bay. — Piracy. — Payment for frontier forts; plans for colonial union; Albany merchants and the Iroquois Confederacy. — Queen Anne's War (1702–13); 1704, assaults on Deerfield and Haverhill; 1704–10, attacks on Port Royal and Placentia; conquest of Acadia; 1711, Hill-Walker expedition against Quebec; 1713, Treaty of Utrecht, important territorial changes. — See also: §§ 96, 97.

General — Parkman, *Half-Century of Conflict*, I, chs. i–ix; Osgood, *American Colonies in Eighteenth Century*, I, chs. iii, vii–x, xiii, xiv, xvi, II, chs. xix–xxiv; G. S. Graham, *Empire of North Atlantic*, ch. v; J. T. Adams, *Revolutionary New England*, chs. iv–v, and *Provincial Society* (1928), chs. i–vi; Channing, *History*, II, 263.

Special — Turner, *Frontier in American History*, ch. ii; A. H. Buffinton, "Dudley and Treaty of Neutrality," Col. Soc. Mass., *Publ.*, XXVI (1925), 211; Kimball, *Joseph Dudley*, ch. vi; J. C. Webster, *Samuel Vetch* (1929); Wraxall, *Abridgment* (§ 97), intro., ch. ii; Nettels, "Economic Relations of Boston, Philadelphia, and New York"; S. M. Reed, *Church and State in Massachusetts 1691–1740* (1914); Perry Miller, "Solomon Stoddard," *Harvard Theological Rev.*, XXXIV (1941), 277; Duniway, *Freedom of Press in Massachusetts*, ch. v; C. K. Shipton, "Immigration to New England, 1680–1740," *Jour. Pol. Econ.*, XLIV (1936), 225, and "New England Frontier," *New Eng. Quar.*, X (1937), 25, and "New England Clergy in Glacial Age," Col. Soc. Mass., *Publ.*, XXXII (1933), 24; J. L. Sibley, *Harvard Graduates* (continued by C. K. Shipton, 8 vols., 1873–1951); Morison, *Harvard in Seventeenth Century*, II, chs. xxiii, xxiv; Leonidas Dodson, *Alexander Spotswood* (1932); Fairfax Harrison, "Western Explorations in Virginia," *Va. Mag. Hist.*, XXX (1922), 323; W. T. Morgan, "Attempts at Imperial Coöperation during Reign of Queen Anne," *Royal Hist. Soc., Trans.*, 4 ser., X (1927), 171, and "Economic Aspects of

Ryswick Negotiations," *ibid.*, XIV (1931), 225, and "Origins of South Sea Company," *Pol. Sci. Quar.*, XLIV (1929), 16, and "South Sea Company and Canadian Expedition," *Hispanic Am. Hist. Rev.*, VIII (1928), 143, and "Queen Anne's Canadian Expedition of 1711," Queen's University, *Bull.*, No. 56 (1928), and "Five Nations and Queen Anne," *Miss. Valley Hist. Rev.*, XIII (1927), 169.

Sources — Virginia: Henry Hartwell, *et al.*, *Present State of Virginia and the College* (1697; H. D. Farish, ed., 1940); Beverley, *History of Virginia*; R. A. Brock, ed., "Official Letters of Governor Spotswood," Va. Hist. Soc., *Coll.*, n.s., I–II (1882–85); William Byrd, *Writings*, and *Secret Diary 1709–12*, and "Letters 1683–91," *Va. Mag. Hist.*, XXIV–XXVIII (1916–20); William Fitzhugh, "Letters, 1679–99," *ibid.*, I–VI (1893–99); "Papers Relating to Governor Nicholson and Founding of William and Mary," *ibid.*, VII–IX (1899–1902); Durand, *Frenchman in Virginia*; McIlwaine, *Journals of House of Burgesses*, III, IV, and *Executive Journals of Council*, II, III. ❆ New York and New England: Sewall, "Diary"; Mather, "Diary"; *Acts and Resolves of Province of Massachusetts Bay*, I, II; Colden, *Five Indian Nations*; Wraxall, *Abridgment*; Miller and Johnson, *Puritans*; *Calendar of State Papers, Colonial, America and West Indies*; J. F. Jameson, *Privateering and Piracy in Colonial Period*, 147.

100. SPANISH BORDERLANDS, 1660–1713

Summary — 1662, Governor Peñalose and Quivira. — 1680, Pueblo Revolt and Massacre. — 1684, La Salle's colony in Texas. — 1687–1707, Father Kino and the Pimería Alta. — 1690, Alonso de León founds first Spanish mission in Texas. — 1692, reconquest of New Mexico begun by Vargas. — 1701, Albuquerque founded, New Mexico subdued. — 1690–1713, Carolina-Florida frontier in King William's and Queen Anne's Wars; struggle for Pensacola, for control of Creek, Cherokee, Choctaw and Chickasaw tribes. — See also: §§ 97, 165, 166.

General — Parkman, *La Salle*, chs. xxiv–xxix; Bolton, *Spanish Borderlands*, chs. vii, viii; H. E. Bolton and T. M. Marshall, *Colonization of North America* (1936), chs. xiii, xvi; Andrews, *Colonial Period*, III, 203; Bancroft, *North Mexican States and Texas*, I, chs. viii, x–xiv, and *Arizona and New Mexico*, chs. viii–xi, xv.

Special — Crane, *Southern Frontier*, chs. i–vi; H. E. Bolton, *Spain's Title to Georgia* (1925), and "Spanish Resistance to Carolina Traders," *Ga. Hist. Quar.*, IX (1925), 115, and *Rim of Christendom*, and "Location of La Salle's Colony on the Gulf," *Southwest Hist. Quar.*, XXVII (1924), 171; J. G. Johnson, "Spanish Colonies in Georgia and South Carolina," *Ga. Hist. Quar.*, XV (1931), 301, and "Spanish Southeast in Seventeenth Century," *ibid.*, XVI (1932), 17; Dunn, *Spanish and French Rivalry*; J. M. Espinosa, *Crusaders of Rio Grande: D. Diego de Vargas* (1942); L. C. Ford, *Triangular Struggle for Spanish Pensacola 1689–1739* (1939); Lanning, *Spanish Missions of Georgia*, chs. vii–ix; I. A. Leonard, ed., *Spanish Approach to Pensacola, 1689–1693* (1939); M. F. Boyd, "Mission Sites in Florida," Fla. Hist. Soc., *Quar.*, XVII (1939), 255; Chatelain, *Defenses of Spanish Florida*, chs. xīii, xiv; J. A. Morfi, *History of Texas 1673–1779* (C. E. Castañeda, tr., 1935), chs. i–iv; C. E. Castañeda, *Catholic Heritage in Texas*: II, *The Winning, 1693–1731* (1936); Wagner, *Cartography of Northwest Coast*, I, chs. xv–xx; Hart, *Disaster of Darien*.

Sources — Bolton, *Spanish Exploration in Southwest*; E. F. Kino, *Historical Memoir of Pimería Alta* (H. E. Bolton, ed., 2 vols., 1919); G. J. de Solís, "Diary of Visit of Inspection of Texas Missions, 1767–68," M. A. Hatcher, ed., *Southwest Hist. Quar.*, XXXV (1931), 28; Carlos de Sigüenza y Góngora, *Mercurio Volante; Expedition of Diego de Vargas into New Mexico, 1692* (I. A. Leonard, tr., 1932); J. M. Espinosa, ed., *First Expedition of Vargas into New Mexico, 1692* (1940); Otto Maas, ed., "Documentos sobre las misiones del Nuevo Méjico," *Archivo ibero-americano*, XIX (1923), 41, XX (1923), 195, XXI (1924), 96, 369, XXXII (1929), 76, 226, 365, XXXIII (1930), 81, 251, 374; A. B. Thomas, ed., *After Coronado, Spanish Exploration Northeast of New Mexico 1696–1727, Documents* (1935); Serrano y Sang, *Documentos Históricos*.

Bibliography — J. L. Mecham, "Northern Expansion of New Spain, 1522–1822," *Hispanic Am. Hist. Rev.*, VII (1927), 233; Lyle Saunders, *Guide to Materials Bearing on Cultural Relations of New Mexico* (1944); F. R. Hart, ed., "List of Spanish Documents on Scots Settlement at Darien," Mass. Hist. Soc., *Proc.*, LXIII (1930), 154. — See also: § 75.

Chapter Nine

FROM THE TREATY OF UTRECHT TO THE REVOLUTION

101. BRITISH COLONIAL POLICY AND ADMINISTRATION, 1713–1760

Summary — Colonial policy of George I and II. — New Acts of Trade and Navigation and their enforcement. — Efforts to regulate colonial iron and hat industries. — Bounties on naval stores, indigo, pig iron, and other colonial products. — Organs of English government dealing with the colonies: King and Privy Council, Parliament, Secretary of State, Board of Trade and Plantations (its development under Halifax), Admiralty, Treasury, Board of War. — The Royal Governor in the colonies; his rights, prerogatives, and limitations; legal force of his instructions. — Greenwich hospital money and impressment. — The Colonial Agents in England. — Money supply and currency. — Administration of Church of England in the Colonies. — Administration of Indian affairs. — The King's Woods.

General — Andrews, *Colonial Period*, IV, chs. ix–xi; L. W. Labaree, *Royal Government in America* (1930); Channing, *History*, II, chs. viii, ix, xvii; Osgood, *American Colonies in Eighteenth Century*, II, 293, III, chs. x, xi, xvii, IV; Gipson, *British Empire before American Revolution*, III, ch. xi.

Special — § 92; G. L. Beer, *British Colonial Policy 1754–65* (1907); O. M. Dickerson, *Navigation Acts and the American Revolution* (1951), chs. i–v; Harper, *English Navigation Laws* (1939), chs. xviii–xxiv; A. H. Basye, *Lords Commissioners of Trade and Plantations 1748–1782* (1925); J. D. Doty, *British Admiralty Board in Colonial Administration 1689–1763* (1932); Ella Lonn, *Colonial Agents of Southern Colonies* (1945); M. P. Wolff, *Colonial Agency of Pennsylvania 1712–1757* (1933); J. J. Burns, *Colonial Agents of New England* (1935); Marguerite Appleton, "Richard Partridge: Colonial Agent," *New Eng. Quar.*, V (1932), 293; Beverley McAnear, "Income of Royal Governors of Virginia," *Jour. Southern Hist.*, XVI (1950), 196; G. C. Smith, "Pistole Fee," *Va. Mag. Hist.*, XLVIII (1940), 209; Bond, *Quit-Rent System*; M. P. Clarke, "Parliamentary Privilege," and D. M. Clark, "Impressment of Seamen," *Essays Presented to Charles M. Andrews* (1931); A. B. Forbes, "Greenwich Hospital Money," *New Eng. Quar.*, III (1930), 519; Justin Williams, "English Mercantilism and Carolina Naval Stores," *Jour. Southern Hist.*, I (1935), 169; Albion, *Forests and Sea Power*, chs. vi–vii; L. S. Mayo, *John Wentworth* (1921), ch. v; Elizabeth Donnan, "Eighteenth Century English Merchants: Micajah Perry," *Jour. of Econ. and Bus. Hist.*, IV (1931), 70; A. C. Bining, *British Regulation of Colonial Iron Industry* (1933); H. L. Shaw, *British Regulation of the Southern Indians* (1931), chs. i–ii; A. L. Cross, *Anglican Episcopate and American Colonies* (1902), chs. iii–v; Norman Sykes, *Edmund Gibson, Bishop of London* (1926), ch. x.

Sources — See: § 92; MacDonald, *Select Charters* No. 50.

102. POLITICAL AND CONSTITUTIONAL DEVELOPMENT, 1713–1760

Summary — Controversies between colonial assemblies and royal governors over finance, commerce, the judiciary, military affairs, and matters of prestige. — Liberty of the press; James Franklin and the *Courant*, the Zenger case. — Quit rents and other permanent revenue. — Relations of church and state, growth of toleration. — Politics and local institutions in individual colonies. — Position of the proprietors and politics in Pennsylvania, Delaware and Maryland. — The autonomous colonies of Connecticut and Rhode Island. — British part in this development (§ 101).

General — Channing, *History*, II, chs. x–xiii, 473; Labaree, *Royal Government in America*; Osgood, *American Colonies in Eighteenth Century*, II, pt. 2, III, IV; E. B. Greene, *Provincial America* (1905), chs. xii, xiii; Morris, *History of American Law*.

Special — J. F. Burns, *Controversies between Royal Governors and Assemblies in Northern Colonies* (1923); Reed, *Church and State in Massachusetts*; Duniway, *Freedom of the Press in Massachusetts*, chs. vi, vii; Rutherfurd, *Zenger*; Konkle, *Andrew Hamilton*; Fry, *New Hampshire as Royal Province*; C. K. Shipton, "Shaping of Revolutionary New England, 1680–1740," *Pol. Sci. Quar.*, L (1935), 584; C. M. Andrews, "Connecticut Intestacy Law," *Select Essays in Anglo-American Legal History* (1907–09), I, 431; Flick, *History of New York*, III, chs. i, iv, v; E. J. Fisher, *New Jersey as Royal Province*, chs. i–ix; W. R. Shepherd, *Proprietary Government in Pennsylvania* (1896), pt. 1, ch. vii, pt. 2; Arthur Pound, *Penns of Pennsylvania and England* (1932), bk. 3; Isaac Sharpless, *Political Leaders of Provincial Pennsylvania* (1919); C. P. Keith, *Provincial Councillors of Pennsylvania* (1883); Root, *Relations of Pennsylvania with British Government*; R. S. Rodney, *Colonial Finances in Delaware* (1928); St. G. L. Siousset, *Economics and Politics in Maryland, 1720–1750* (1903); P. S. Flippin, *Royal Government in Virginia*, and "William Gooch, Governor of Virginia," *William and Mary Quar.*, 2 ser., V (1925), 225, VI (1926), 1; Ashe, *History of North Carolina*, I, chs. xvi–xx; Raper, *North Carolina*; L. F. London, "Representation Controversy in Colonial North Carolina," *No. Car. Hist. Rev.*, XI (1934), 255; C. C. Crittenden, "Surrender of Charter of Carolina," *ibid.*, I (1924), 383; J. P. Boyd, "Sheriff in Colonial North Carolina," *ibid.*, V (1928), 151; Florence Cook, "Procedure in North Carolina Assembly, 1731–1770," *ibid.*, VIII (1931), 258; McCrady, *South Carolina*, II, chs. i–xviii; W. R. Smith, *South Carolina as Royal Province*, § ii, chs. i–vi; Cross, *Anglican Episcopate and the American Colonies*; Dickerson, *American Colonial Government*; Basye, *Lords Commissioners of Trade and Plantations*; Thomson, *Secretaries of State 1681–1782*. ❡ Albany Congress: L. H. Gipson, *British Empire before American Revolution*, V, chs. iv, v, and "Thomas Hutchinson and Framing of Albany Plan of Union," *Penn. Mag. Hist.*, LXXIV (1950), 5; V. W. Crane, "Letter on Albany Congress Plan," *ibid.*, LXXV (1951), 350.

Sources — Franklin, *Writings; Calendar of State Papers, Colonial, America, and West Indies*; James Logan, "State of the British Plantations" (1732), J. E. Johnson, ed., *Penn. Mag. Hist.*, LX (1936), 97; Colden, *Papers;* "Papers of Lewis Morris, Governor of New Jersey 1738–1746," N. J. Hist. Soc., *Coll.*, IV (1852); Shirley, *Correspondence;* Labaree, *Royal Instructions; Trial of John Peter Zenger* (1752; 1765 ed., reprinted Calif. State Library, 1940; 1770 ed., reprinted, P. W. Chandler, *American Criminal Trials* [1841], I); W. K. Boyd, ed., *Some Eighteenth Century Tracts concerning North Carolina* (1927); see § 101.

Bibliography — Labaree, *Royal Government*, 449.

103. SOCIAL AND ECONOMIC DEVELOPMENT, NORTHERN COLONIES
1713–1760

Summary — Economic growth: first capitalist enterprises; ironmasters of the Middle Colonies; currency and paper money, 1741, Land Bank suppressed; — land speculation and new methods of settlement; "Old West" in New England and Middle Colonies; — immigration of Germans, Scotch-Irish, Swiss, Jews; growth of seaports. — Cultural development: groups in Philadelphia, New York, Boston, and Newport; growth of Harvard and Yale; rise of scientific studies (Franklin, John Winthrop, Rittenhouse, the Mathers, Thomas Prince; foundation of Princeton, 1746; Philadelphia Academy, 1751; King's, 1754; Franklin and the Junto; schools and schoolmasters; libraries; printing; law and medicine; beginnings of American drama; literature of the period; artists, architects, joiners, glass-makers, potters; American music. — Humanitarian movements; crime and servitude, slavery, Quakers. — Religion: Great Awakening, Jonathan Edwards and George Whitefield; Presbyterians, Baptists, Moravians, Lutherans; Anglican missionary efforts, the S. P. G. and S. P. C. K.; efforts to convert the Indians. — The press and Zenger (§ 102).

General — Channing, History, II, chs. xiii–xviii; Gipson, British Empire before American Revolution, III, IV, chs. v–vi; Turner, Frontier in American History, chs. i, ii; Osgood, American Colonies in Eighteenth Century, II, ch. vi, III, ch. xvi, 540, ch. xvii, 406, IV, 24; Tyler, History of American Literature, chs. xi–xvi; Parrington, Colonial Mind, 118, 148; Quinn, Literature of American People, chs. vi, vii; I. W. Riley, American Philosophy, Early Schools (1907); Weeden, Economic and Social History of New England, I, ch. xi, II, chs. xii–xvii; T. J. Wertenbaker, Golden Age of Colonial Culture (1942); Bridenbaugh, Cities in Wilderness, chs. ix–xii; Colonial Craftsmen (1950); L. B. Wright, Atlantic Frontier (1947), chs. iii–v; J. T. Adams, Provincial Society (1927); Savelle, Seeds of Liberty; Curti, Growth of American Thought, chs. ii–v; Van Doren, Franklin.

Special — Law, Literature, Fine Arts: Morris, History of American Law; Julius Goebel, Law Enforcement in Colonial New York (1944); Warren, American Bar, chs. i–ix; Rutherfurd, Zenger; L. C. Wroth, An American Bookshelf, 1755 (1934), and Colonial Printer (1938); Brigham, Journals and Journeymen; L. N. Richardson, History of Early American Magazines (1931); Hart, Popular Book, chs. ii–iii; H. M. Jones, "American Prose Style, 1700–1770," Ideas in America (1944); C. K. Shipton, "Literary Leaven in New England," New Eng. Quar., IX (1936), 203; Morrison, Early American Architecture, chs. ix, x, xiv–xvi; Kimball, Domestic Architecture, 53; Bridenbaugh, Peter Harrison; Larkin, Art and Life in America, pts. 1, 2; A. C. Prime, Arts and Crafts in Philadelphia, Maryland and North Carolina 1721–85 (2 vols., 1929); Sellers, Charles Willson Peale, I; H. W. Foote, Robert Feke (1936); Quinn, History of American Drama, ch. i; G. L. Heiges, Henry William Stiegel (1937). ❡ Music: David Ewen, Music Comes to America (1947); O. G. Sonneck, Early Concert-Life in America, 1731–1800 (1907); Penn. Soc. of Colonial Dames, Church Music and Musical Life in Pennsylvania (3 vols., 1926–47); H. C. Macdougall, Early New England Psalmody (1940); H. T. David, "Ephrata and Bethlehem: A Comparison," Int. College of Musicology of 1939, Papers (1944), 97; W. T. Upton, "Secular Music in United States One Hundred and Fifty Years Ago," ibid., 105–11. ❡ Religion and Great Awakening: C. H. Maxson, Great Awakening in Middle Colonies (1920); Allen, Jonathan Edwards; Perry Miller, Jonathan Edwards, and "Jonathan Edwards and Great Awakening," Daniel Aaron, ed., America in Crisis (1952); F. I. Carpenter, "Radicalism of Edwards," New Eng. Quar., IV (1931), 629; E. E. White, "Decline of Great Awakening in New England," ibid., XXIV (1951), 35; Joseph Haroutunian, Piety vs. Moralism (1932); L. W. Labaree, "Conservative Attitude toward Great Awakening," William and Mary Quar., 3 ser., I (1944), 331; L. J. Trinterud, Reexamination of Colonial Presbyterianism (1949); E. B. Greene, "Anglican Outlook on American Colonies," Am. Hist. Rev., XX (1914), 64; C. F. Pascoe, Two Hundred Years of S. P. G. (1901); Edward Midwinter, "Society for Propagation of Gospel," Protestant Episcopal Church Hist. Mag., IV (1935), 67; Cross, Anglican Episcopate and American Colonies; F. J. Klingberg, "Sir William Johnson and S. P. G.," Protestant Episcopal Church Hist. Mag., VIII (1939), 4, and Anglican Humanitarianism in Colonial New York (1940). ❡ Land, business, shipping: R. H. Akagi, Town Proprietors of New England Colonies (1924); Albion, Forests and Sea Power, chs. ii, iv, vi; Baxter, House of Hancock; A. W. Griswold, "Three Puritans on Prosperity," New Eng. Quar., VII (1934), 475; B. M. Bigelow, "Aaron Lopez, Colonial Merchant of Newport," ibid., IV (1931), 757; W. D. Miller, "Narragansett Planters," Am. Antiq. Soc., Proc., n.s., XLIII (1933), 49; Carpenter, South County Studies; V. D. Harrington, New York Merchant on Eve of Revolution; Flick, History of New York, II, chs. vii–x; G. F. Warren.

F. A. Pearson, and H. M. Stoker, *Wholesale Prices 1720 to 1932* (1932), pt. 2, 201; R. L. Higgins, *Expansion in New York* (1931), chs. iv–vii; Shepherd, *Proprietary Government in Pennsylvania*, pt. 1; M. A. Hanna, *Trade of Delaware District before Revolution* (1917); Volwiler, *Croghan;* Wallace, *Weiser;* Wraxall, *Abridgment*, intro., lxiv, 96; Tolles, *Meeting House and Counting House;* A. C. Bining, *British Regulation of Colonial Iron Industry*, and *Pennsylvania Iron Manufacture in Eighteenth Century* (1938); C. S. Boyer, *Early Forges and Furnaces in New Jersey* (1931); Anne Bezanson, *et al., Prices in Colonial Pennsylvania* (1935); Edward Edelman, "Thomas Hancock," *Jour. Econ. and Bus. Hist.*, I (1928–29), 77; J. B. Hedges, *Browns of Providence Plantations* (1952); Dorfman, *Economic Mind*, I, chs. viii–x. ❧ Currency Questions: Nettels, *Roots of American Civilization*, 530, 596; § 92; R. A. Lester, "Currency Issues to Overcome Depressions," *Jour. Pol. Econ.*, XLVI (1938), 324, XLVII (1939), 182; K. L. Behrens, *Paper Money in Maryland, 1727–89* (1923). ❧ Education and Science: E. E. Slosson, *American Spirit in Education* (1921), chs. i, iii–v; S. E. Morison, *Three Centuries of Harvard* (1936), chs. iv–vi; Edwin Oviatt, *Beginnings of Yale (1701–1726)* (1916); T. J. Wertenbaker, *Princeton 1746–1896* (1946); ch. i; Schneider, *Samuel Johnson;* E. P. Cheyney, *History of University of Pennsylvania* (1940), chs. i–iii; A. F. Gegenheimer, *William Smith, Educator and Churchman* (1943); L. B. Richardson, *History of Dartmouth College* (1932), chs. i–iii; Packard, *History of Medicine*, I, chs. i–iii; Viets, *Medicine in Massachusetts*, ch. iii; Theodore Hornberger, "Science of Thomas Prince," *New Eng. Quar.*, IX (1936), 26, and *Science and New World* (1937), and *Scientific Thought in American Colleges 1638–1800* (1945); F. G. Kilgour, "Rise of Scientific Activity in Colonial New England," *Yale Jour. Biol. and Med.*, XXII (1949), 123; E. M. Tilton, "Lightning-Rods and Earthquake of 1755," *New Eng. Quar.*, XIII (1940), 86; W. W. Kemp, *Support of Schools in Colonial New York* (1913); J. J. Walsh, *Education of Founding Fathers, Scholasticism in Colonial Colleges* (1935); Archibald Alexander, *Biographical Sketches of Founder and Alumni of Log College* (1845); F. L. Broderick, "Curriculum of College of New Jersey, 1746–94," *William and Mary Quar.*, 3 ser., VI (1949), 42; Beverley McAnear, "Selection of an Alma Mater by Pre-Revolutionary Students," *Penn. Mag. Hist.*, LXXIII (1949), 429; R. F. Seybolt, "Schoolmasters of Colonial Philadelphia," *ibid.*, LII (1928), 361, and *Public Schools* (1935), and *Public Schoolmasters of Colonial Boston* (1939); Thomas Woody, ed., *Quaker Education in New Jersey* (1923); I. B. Cohen, *Some Early Tools of American Science* (1950), chs. i–iii, and *Benjamin Franklin's Experiments* (1941), and "Franklin and Transit of Mercury," Am. Philos. Soc., *Proc.*, XCIV (1950), No. 3, and "Anguetil-Duperron, Franklin, and Ezra Stiles," *Isis*, XXXIII (1941), 17; Struik, *Yankee Science*, ch. 1. ❧ Immigration and Non-English Peoples: A. E. Smith, *Colonists in Bondage;* Hansen, *Atlantic Migration*, ch. ii; Wittke, *We Who Built America*, pt. 1; S. G. Fisher, *Making of Pennsylvania* (1896; reprinted 1932); W. A. Knittle, *Early Eighteenth Century Palatine Emigration* (1936); J. S. Klett, *Presbyterians in Colonial Pennsylvania* (1937); H. J. Ford, *Scotch-Irish in America* (1915); Faust, *German Element*, I, chs. iii–vi; Fredric Klees, *Pennsylvania Dutch* (1950); Hull, *William Penn and Dutch Quaker Migration;* F. R. Diffenderffer, *German Immigration into Pennsylvania through Philadelphia, 1700–1775*, pt. 2, *Redemptioners* (1900); R. B. Strassburger and W. J. Hinke, "Pennsylvania German Pioneers," Penn.-German Soc., *Proc.*, XLII–XLIV (1934); L. M. Friedman, *Early American Jews* (1934); A. V. Goodman, *American Overture: Jewish Rights in Colonial Times* (1947); F. J. F. Schantz, *Domestic Life of Pennsylvania German Pioneers* (1900); E. M. Fogel, *Beliefs and Superstitions of Pennsylvania Germans* (1915); J. F. Sachse, *German Sectarians of Pennsylvania* (2 vols., 1899–1900); J. J. Sessler, *Communal Pietism among Early American Moravians* (1933); C. H. Smith, "Mennonite Immigration"; W. F. Dunaway, "Pennsylvania as an Early Distributing Center of Population," *Penn. Mag. Hist.*, LV (1931), 134; E. R. Turner, *Negro in Pennsylvania* (1910), chs. i–v; C. A. Herrick, *White Servitude in Pennsylvania* (1926). ❧ Crime and Humanitarianism: R. H. Fox, *Dr. John Fothergill and His Friends* (1919); L. H. Gipson, *Crime and Punishment in Provincial Pennsylvania* (1935); Edith Philips, *Good Quaker in French Legend* (1932); G. S. Brooks, *Friend Anthony Benezet* (1937).

Sources — Kalm, *En Resa;* Bridenbaugh, *Gentleman's Progress;* John Cuthbertson, "Diary," W. L. Fisk, Jr., ed., *Penn. Mag. Hist.*, LXXIII (1949), 441; Gottlieb Mittelberger, *Journey to Pennsylvania in 1750* (C. T. Eben, tr., 1898); "Correspondence of James Logan and Thomas Story, 1724–41," Friends Hist. Assoc., *Bull.*, XV (1926), No. 2; Murdock, *Selections from Cotton Mather;* Mather, "Diary"; Sewall, "Diary"; C. H. Faust and T. H. Johnson, eds., *Jonathan Edwards* (1935); *Letter-Book of James Browne of Providence, Merchant, 1735–38* (1929); "Letter-Book of John Watts, Merchant and Councillor of New York," N. Y. Hist. Soc., *Coll.*, LXI (1928); "Belcher Papers," Mass. Hist. Soc., *Coll.*, 6 ser., VI–VII (1893–94); "Commerce of Rhode Island, 1726–1774," *ibid.*, 7 ser., IX (1915); "Wolcott Papers," Conn. Hist. Soc., *Coll.*, XVI (1916); "Fitch Papers," *ibid.*, XVII–XVIII (1918–20); "Pitkin Papers," *ibid.*, XIX (1921); "Wyllys Papers," *ibid.*, XXI (1924); "Law Papers," *ibid.*, XI, XIII, XV (1907, 1911, 1914); Ernest Hawkins, ed., *Historical Notices of Missions of Church of England* (1845); H. S. Tapley, ed., *Early Coastwise and Foreign Shipping of Salem* (1934); G. F. Dow, *Arts and Crafts in New England, 1704–75, Gleanings from Boston Newspapers* (1927); J. P. Boyd, ed., *Susquehannah Company Papers* (1930), I, II; Mereness, ed., *Travels in American Colonies;* I. M. Calder, ed., *Colonial Captivities, Marches and Journeys* (1935); E. L. Coleman, *New England Captives to Canada* (2 vols., 1925); John Bartram, *Observations on Soil, Rivers* (London, 1751); Gist, *Journals;* Thwaites, *Early Western Travels,* I; Woolman, *Journal.*

Bibliography — Evans, *American Bibliography,* I, II; Brigham, *History and Bibliography of American Newspapers;* Matthews, *American Diaries Prior to 1861;* Vail, *Old Frontier;* Spiller, *Literary History of the United States,* III; S. M. Pargellis and D. J. Medley, *Bibliography of British History: Eighteenth Century, 1714–1789* (1951), 452; O. G. Sonneck, *Bibliography of American Secular Music* (W. T. Upton, ed., 1945).

104. SOCIAL AND ECONOMIC DEVELOPMENT, SOUTHERN COLONIES 1713–1765

Summary — Economic Growth: land speculation; development of the slave-tilled tobacco plantation system in Virginia, of rice and indigo culture in South Carolina and Georgia; grain culture in Maryland; trade with Great Britain and the West Indies; rise of Norfolk. — Settlement: "Old West" south of Mason and Dixon Line; settlement of the Piedmont and beginnings in the Valley; Germans, Swiss, Scotch-Irish, and Huguenots. — Culture: spread of log dwellings on the frontier; Georgian architecture in the towns and great plantations; nuclei of culture and the arts in Annapolis, Williamsburg, and Charleston; horse racing and other sports; science, botany (Bartram, Clayton); College of William and Mary; private schools, law and medicine. — The Great Awakening in the South; Anglican and Presbyterian missionary activity. — See also: §§ 90, 94, 99, 101, 103, 105, 106.

General — Channing, *History,* II, chs. xiii–xvii; Turner, *Frontier in American History,* ch. iii; Wertenbaker, *Golden Age of Colonial Culture,* 85, and *Old South,* 92; J. T. Adams, *Provincial Society,* chs. vii–xi; Gipson, *British Empire before American Revolution,* II, chs. i–vi; Tyler, *History of American Literature,* ch. xvii; Osgood, *American Colonies in Eighteenth Century,* III, chs. x–xi, 468, IV, chs. vii–ix, xi; Carl Bridenbaugh, *Myths and Realities* (1952).

Special — Spruill, *Women's Life and Work in Southern Colonies;* Herbert Aptheker, *American Negro Slave Revolts* (1943), ch. viii; M. W. Jernegan, "Slavery and Conversion in Colonies," *Am. Hist. Rev.*, XXI (1916), 504; C. P. Gould, *Land System in Maryland, 1720–65* (1913), and *Money and Transportation in Maryland* (1915), and "Economic Causes of Rise of Baltimore," *Essays Presented to C. M. Andrews* (1931), 225; E. I. McCormac, *White Servitude in Maryland* (1904); Matilda Edgar, *A Colonial Governor* [Horatio Sharpe] *in Maryland* (1912); H. W. Hill, *Maryland's Colonial Charm Portrayed in Silver* (1938); J. T. Wheeler, "Reading Interests in Colonial Maryland," *Md. Hist. Mag.*, XXXVI (1941), 281, XXXVII (1942), 26, 291, XXXVIII (1943), 37, 167, 273; Behrens, *Paper Money in Maryland, 1727–89;* Sioussat, *Economics and Politics in Maryland;* P. H. Giddens, "Trade and Industry in Colonial Maryland, 1753–69," *Jour. Econ. and Bus. Hist.*, IV (1932), 512; C. A. Barker, "Property Rights in Provincial System of

Maryland," *Jour. Southern Hist.*, II (1936), 211; Freeman, *Washington*, I, ch. iv; Wright, *First Gentlemen of Virginia*, 249; Earnest, *John and William Bartram*; Louis Morton, *Robert Carter of Nomini Hall* (1941); Kathleen Bruce, *Virginia Iron Manufacture in Slave Era* (1930); W. M. Gewehr, *Great Awakening in Virginia, 1740–90* (1930); C. R. Lingley, *Transition in Virginia* (1910), ch. 1; Fairfax Harrison, *Virginia Land Grants*, and *Equine F.F.V.'s, English Horses Imported into Virginia* (1928); G. M. Brydon, "Huguenots of Manakin Town," *Va. Mag. Hist.*, XLII (1934), 325, and "Bristol Iron Works," *ibid.*, XLII (1934), 97, and *Virginia's Mother Church*, II; Anne Maury, *Memoirs of a Huguenot Family* [Fontaine] (1872); S. M. Ames, "Virginia Business Man N. L. Savage," *Jour. Econ. and Bus. Hist.*, III (1931), 407; St. G. L. Sioussat, "Virginia and English Commercial System," Am. Hist. Assoc., *Report*, 1905, I, 71; W. W. Scott, "Knights of Horseshoe," *William and Mary Quar.*, 2 ser., III (1923), 145; R. H. Land, "First Williamsburg Theatre," *ibid.*, 3 ser., V (1948), 359; C. H. Ambler, *Sectionalism in Virginia* (1910), ch. i; T. P. Abernethy, *Three Virginia Frontiers* (1940), ch. ii; L. K. Koontz, *Virginia Frontier, 1754–63* (1925); Kercheval, *History of Valley of Virginia*, chs. iii–v, xii, xvi–xxix; W. B. Blanton, *Medicine in Virginia in Eighteenth Century* (1931); D. D. Oliver, "Society for Propagation of Gospel in North Carolina," James Sprunt Hist. Publ., IX (1910); E. L. Pennington, "Thomas Bray's Associates' Work among Negroes," Am. Antiq. Soc., *Proc.*, n.s., XLVIII (1938), 311; J. S. Bassett, *Slavery and Servitude in Colony of North Carolina* (1896); S. C. Hughson, "Carolina Pirates and Colonial Commerce, 1670–1740," *Johns Hopkins Studies*, XII (1894), v–vii; McCrady, *South Carolina*, II, chs. viii, ix, xiii–xvii, xx–xxvi; Eola Willis, *Charleston Stage in Eighteenth Century* (1924), chs. i–ii; Ravenel, *Eliza Pinckney*, chs. i–xii; G. R. Taylor, "Wholesale Commodity Prices at Charleston, 1732–1791," *Jour. Econ. and Bus. Hist.*, IV (1932), 356; Slosson, *American Spirit in Education*, ch. iii; E. W. Knight, *Public Education in South* (1922), chs. i–iii; J. P. Corry, "Education in Colonial Georgia," *Ga. Hist. Quar.*, XVI (1932), 136; Morrison, *Early American Architecture*, chs. xi–xiii; also §§ 90, 101, 103.

Sources — Mereness, ed., *Travels in American Colonies;* Charles Carroll, "Accounts and Letter Books, 1735–55," *Md. Hist. Mag.*, XX–XXVII (1925–32); Hugh Jones, *Present State of Virginia* (1724; reprinted 1865); G. M. Brydon, ed., "Virginia Clergy: Governor Gooch's Letters to Bishop of London, 1727–49," *Va. Mag. Hist.*, XXXII (1924), 209, 321, XXXIII (1925), 51; "Letters of William Byrd II and Sir Hans Sloane," *William and Mary Quar.*, 2 ser., I (1921), 186; Robert Carter, *Letters, 1720–27;* Byrd, *Another Secret Diary;* R. A. Brock, ed., "Documents Relating to Huguenots," Va. Hist. Soc., *Coll.*, n.s., V (1886); A. L. Fries, ed., *Records of Moravians in North Carolina* (7 vols., 1922–47); B. R. Carroll, ed., *Historical Collections of South Carolina* (2 vols., 1836); Hawkins, *Historical Notices of Missions in Colonies;* "Letters of Henry Laurens 1747–49," *So. Car. Hist. Mag.*, XXVIII–XXXI (1927–30); "Letters of Peter Manugault, 1750–54," *ibid.*, XXXI–XXXIII (1930–32); F. N. Mason, ed., *John Norton & Sons, Merchants of London and Virginia* (1937); James Adair, *History of American Indians* (1755; reprinted, 1930); J. F. Gronovius, *Flora Virginia, exhibens Plantas quas Johannes Clayton in Virginia observavit atque collegit* (1739, 1762); E. W. Knight, ed., *Documentary History of Education in South before 1860* (4 vols., 1949–53), I, 368.

Bibliography — Cappon and Duff, *Virginia Gazette Index.*

105. GEORGIA AND FLORIDA, 1730–1775

Summary — Early English plans for the area. — The Bray-Coram-Percival group of philanthropists. — Oglethorpe and prison reform; philanthropic and imperial motives. — 1732, Charter of the Georgia Trustees. — Question of human materials; poor debtors or rugged yeomen? — Settlement of Savannah, Ebenezer, Frederica. — Land system, antislavery, and prohibition. — Visits of Wesleys and Whitefield. — 1752, Royal province. — Rice, silk, indigo culture. — Spanish outposts (§ 100); Louisiana and War of Jenkins' Ear (§ 106); 1758–63, French and Indian War (§ 108). — 1763, Cession of Florida to Great Britain. — 1763–75, The Provinces of East and West Florida.

General — Coulter, *Georgia, a Short History*, chs. i–x; J. E. Callaway, *Early Settlement of Georgia* (1948), chs. i–vi; Osgood, *American Colonies in Eighteenth Century*, III, ch. ix, IV, ch. xiii; Gipson, *British Empire before American Revolution*, II, ch. vi, IV, ch. ii; Justin Winsor, *Narrative and Critical History*, V, ch. vi; C. L. Mowat, *East Florida as British Province, 1763–84* (1943); Cecil Johnson, *British West Florida 1763–83* (1943); C. N. Howard, *British Development of West Florida, 1763–69* (1947).

Special — A. B. Saye, *New Viewpoints*, and *Constitutional History of Georgia, 1732–1845* (1948), chs. i–iii; E. M. Coulter and A. B. Saye, *List of Early Settlers of Georgia* (1949); J. R. McCain, *Georgia as Proprietary Colony* (1917); P. S. Flippin, "Royal Government in Georgia, 1752–1776," *Ga. Hist. Quar.*, VIII–XIII (1924–29); C. C. Jones, *History of Georgia;* R. C. Strickland, *Religion and State in Georgia* (1939); Church, *Oglethorpe;* Ettinger, *James Edward Oglethorpe;* A. E. Clark-Kennedy, *Stephen Hales* (1929); J. D. Wade, *John Wesley* (1930); E. L. Pennington, "John Wesley's Georgia Ministry," *Church History*, VIII (1939), 231; R. B. Flanders, *Plantation Slavery in Georgia* (1933), chs. i–iii; P. A. Strobel, *Salzburgers and Their Descendants* (1855); A. L. Fries, *Moravians in Georgia* (1905); F. J. Klingberg, "Humanitarian Spirit in Eighteenth-Century England," *Penn. Mag. Hist.*, LXVI (1942), 260; V. W. Crane, "Projects for Colonization in South," (§ 94), and "Philanthropists and Genesis of Georgia," *Am. Hist. Rev.*, XXVI (1921), 63, and *Promotion Literature of Georgia* (1925); J. R. Alden, *John Stuart and Southern Colonial Frontier, 1754–75* (1944); J. P. Corry, *Indian Affairs in Georgia, 1732–1756* (1936); H. B. Fant, "Indian Trade Policy of Trustees," *Ga. Hist. Quar.*, XV (1931), 207, and "Labor Policy of Trustees," *ibid.*, XVI (1932), 1, and "Thomas Coram," *ibid.*, XXXII (1948), 77; A. P. Tankersley, "Midway District, Puritanism in Colonial Georgia," *ibid.*, XXXII (1948), 149; E. M. Coulter, "When Wesley Preached in Georgia," *ibid.*, IX (1925), 317, and *Georgia's Disputed Ruins;* M. B. Hamer, "Silk Industry in Georgia," *No. Car. Hist. Rev.*, XII (1935), 125; C. N. Howard, "Military Government in West Florida," *La. Hist. Quar.*, XXII (1939), 18, and "Military Occupation of West Florida," *Fla. Hist. Quar.*, XVII (1939), 181, and "Governor Johnstone," *ibid.*, XVII (1939), 281, and "Colonial Pensacola," *ibid.*, XIX (1940–41), 109, 246, 368; M. F. Boyd, "Remote Frontier," *ibid.*, XIX (1941), 179, 402, XX (1941), 82, 203, XX (1942), 293, 382, XXI (1942), 44, 135; W. H. Siebert, "Slavery and White Servitude in East Florida, 1726–76," *ibid.*, X (1931), 3.

Sources — Ga. Hist. Soc., *Coll.*, I–III (1840–1873), VII (1909), VIII (1913); Candler, *Colonial Records of Georgia*, I–XXVI; John Percival, Earl of Egmont, *Manuscripts* (Royal Hist. MSS. Commission, 3 vols., 1920–23); John Wesley, *Journal* (Nehemiah Curnock and John Telford, eds., 8 vols., 1909–16), I; John Bartram, *Diary of Journey through Carolinas, Georgia and Florida 1765–66* (Francis Harper, ed.), Am. Phil. Soc., *Trans.*, XXXIII, pt. 1 (1942); William Bartram, *Travels in Georgia and Florida 1773–74* (Francis Harper, ed.), *ibid.*, XXXIII, pt. 2 (1943).

Bibliography — Winsor, *Narrative and Critical History*, V, 392; Azalea Clizbee, ed., *Catalogue of Wymberley Jones de Renne Georgia Library* (Wormsloe, Ga., 1931); *Ga. Hist. Quar.*, XIII (1929), 410, XIV (1930), 122, XVIII (1934), 27; J. A. Robertson, "Archival Distribution of Florida Manuscripts," *Fla. Hist. Quar.*, X (1931), 35, and "Spanish Manuscripts of Florida State Historical Society"; C. L. Mowat, "Material Relating to British East Florida in Clements Library," *Fla. Hist. Quar.*, XVIII (1939), 46; L. C. Wroth, "Source Materials of Florida History in John Carter Brown Library," *ibid.*, XX (1941) 3; A. C. Manucy, "Florida History in Spanish Records of North Carolina State Archives," *ibid.*, XXV (1947), 319, XXVI (1947), 77; "Union Catalog of Floridiana" (maintained at Rollins College, Winter Park, Fla.).

106. LOUISIANA AND SPANISH BORDERLANDS, 1713–1760

Summary — Earlier history (§§ 100, 105); 1713–48, development of Louisiana; 1717, Compagnie des Indes; 1718, New Orleans founded; trade with the Mississippi Valley, France, and the West Indies; John Law and the Mississippi Bubble. — 1713–48, French in the Illinois country. — Spanish missions in Texas. — 1715, Yamasee War. — 1736, French war with the Chickasaw. — 1739, War of Jenkins' Ear, naval warfare in the Caribbean, Vernon's attack on Cartagena, Oglethorpe's victory of the Bloody March, St. Simon's Island. — 1713–48, New Mexico in mid-eighteenth century; the Pimería Alta.

General — Bolton, *Spanish Borderlands*, chs. viii, ix; Osgood, *American Colonies in Eighteenth Century*, III, 395, 491; *Cambridge History British Empire*, I, 336, ch. xii; Lavisse, *Histoire de France*, VIII, pt. 2, 21; Bancroft, *North Mexican States and Texas*, I, chs. xxii, xxiii, and *Arizona and New Mexico*, chs. xi, xii, xv.

Special — Marc de Villiers, "Histoire de la fondation de la Nouvelle-Orléans (1717)," Warrington Dawson, transl., *La. Hist. Quar.*, III (1920), 157; Émile Lauvrière, *Histoire de la Louisiane française 1673–1939* (1940); Heinrich, *Louisiane sous la compagnie des Indes*; C. W. Alvord, *Illinois Country 1673–1818* (1920), chs. vi–ix; N. W. Caldwell, *French in Mississippi Valley 1740–50* (1941); Crane, *Southern Frontier*, chs. vii–xi; J. G. Johnson, "Colonial Southeast, 1732–63," University of Colorado, *Studies*, XIX (1932), 163; N. M. M. Surrey, *Commerce of Louisiana during French Régime* (1916); Grace King, "Review," *La. Hist. Quar.*, V (1922), 19; N. M. M. Surrey, "Development of Industries in Louisiana during French Regime," *Miss. Valley Hist. Rev.*, IX (1923), 227; C. P. Gould, "Trade between Windward Isles and French Continental Colonies," *ibid.*, XXV (1939), 473; H. P. Dart, "Legal Institutions of Louisiana," *La. Hist. Quar.*, II (1919), 72; Wilfrid Bovey, "Notes on Arkansas Post and St. Philippe," Royal Soc. Canada, *Proc.*, 3 ser., XXXIII (1939), §§ 2, 29; Georges Oudard, *Amazing Life of John Law* (1928); H. E. Bolton, *Texas in Middle Eighteenth Century* (1915); Morfi, *History of Texas*, chs. v–viii; C. W. Hackett, "Spanish Policy regarding French Encroachments from Louisiana, 1721–62," *New Spain and Anglo-American West*, I, 107–45. ❡ War of Jenkins' Ear: J. O. McLachlan, *Trade and Peace with Old Spain, 1667–1750* (1940); J. T. Lanning, *Diplomatic History of Georgia, Epoch of Jenkins' Ear* (1936), chs. vii–x; Meriwether, *Expansion of South Carolina*; M. L. Shaggs, *North Carolina Boundary Disputes Involving Her Southern Line* (1941); H. W. Richmond, *Navy in War of 1739–48* (3 vols., 1920), I, chs. i–iii, vi, xii, III, ch. v; F. R. Hart, "Struggle for Control of America," *Jour. of Am. Hist.*, II [1] (1908), 315; Richard Pares, *War and Trade in West Indies*, chs. i–x, and "American Versus Continental Warfare, 1739–63," *Eng. Hist. Rev.*, LI (1936), 429; Albert Harkness, "Americanism and Jenkins' Ear," *Miss. Valley Hist. Rev.*, XXXVII (1950), 61; M. D. Cate, "Fort Frederica and Battle of Bloody Marsh," *Ga. Hist. Quar.*, XXVII (1943), 111; N. W. Caldwell, "Southern Frontier in King George's War," *Jour. Southern Hist.*, VII (1941), 37; § 100.

Sources — Margry, *Découvertes et éstablissements français*, V, VI; H. H. Cruzat and H. P. Dart, eds., "Records of the Superior Council of Louisiana," *La. Hist. Quar.*, II–XXVI (1919–43); Houck, *Spanish Régime in Missouri*; Rowland and Sanders, *Mississippi Provincial Archives: French Dominion*; H. H. Cruzat, ed., "Concession at Natchez," *La. Hist. Quar.*, VIII (1925), 389, and "Documents Concerning Chaouachaous Plantation," *ibid.*, 594; L. B. Bloom, ed., "Campaign against Moqui Pueblos," *New Mexico Hist. Rev.*, VI (1931), 158; Caroline and Eleanor Dunn, eds., "Indiana's First War" (Bienville's account), Ind. Hist. Soc., *Publ.*, VIII, No. 2 (1924).

Bibliography — Wagner, *Spanish Southwest*.

107. KING GEORGE'S WAR AND NOVA SCOTIA, 1745–1755

Summary — 1745–48, King George's War (Austrian Succession). — Naval war in the Caribbean. — 1745, capture of Louisbourg. — 1746–47, border conflicts. — Great Lakes Frontier. — The Six Nations. — 1748, Peace of Aix-la-Chapelle. — Settlement of Nova Scotia. — 1755, expulsion of the Acadians. — War on the southern frontier (§§ 105, 106).

General — Gipson, *British Empire before American Revolution*, IV, chs. v–viii, V, chs. iii, vi, VI, chs. viii–x; Parkman, *Half-Century of Conflict*, II, chs. xvii–xxiv; Osgood,

American Colonies in Eighteenth Century, III, ch. iii, IV, chs. vi, x; Wrong, *New France,* II, chs. xxiv–xxvi; Graham, *Empire of North Atlantic,* chs. vi, vii; Mahan, *Influence of Sea Power,* chs. vi, vii; J. B. Perkins, *France under Louis XV* (1897), I, chs. v–viii; Lavisse, *Histoire de France,* VIII, pt. 1, 143; *Cambridge History of British Empire,* VI, 91.

Special — J. S. McLennan, *Louisbourg from Its Foundation to Its Fall* (1918), chs. i–xi; Richmond, *Navy in War of 1739–48,* II, chs. ix, x, III, chs. i–v, viii, App. B.; Georges Lacour-Gayet, *La marine militaire sous le règne de Louis XV* (1910), chs. viii, xii; H. M. Chapin, *Privateering in King George's War* (1928); N. W. Caldwell, *French in Mississippi Valley;* Wood, *Shirley;* A. H. Buffinton, "Canadian Expedition of 1746," *Am. Hist. Rev.,* XLV (1940), 552; Walton, *Weiser,* chs. i–xi; Volwiler, *Croghan,* chs. i–ii; K. P. Bailey, *Ohio Company of Virginia and Westward Movement* (1939); Archibald Henderson, "Dr. Thomas Walker and Loyal Company," *Am. Antiq. Soc., Proc.,* n.s., LXI (1931), 77; T. P. Abernethy, *Western Lands and American Revolution* (1937), ch. i; J. C. Webster, *Forts of Chignecto* (1930). ❧ Settlement of Nova Scotia: Brebner, *New England's Outpost, Acadia before Conquest of Canada;* W. O. Sawtelle, "Acadia: Pre-Loyalist Migration and Philadelphia Plantation," *Penn. Mag. Hist.,* LI (1927), 244; W. O. Raymond, "Nova Scotia under English Rule, 1710–1760," *Royal Soc. Canada, Trans.,* 3 ser., IV (1910), 55, and "Alexander McNutt and Pre-Loyalist Settlements of Nova Scotia," *ibid.,* V (1911), 23, VI (1912), 201; A. W. H. Eaton, "Settling of Colchester County," *ibid.,* VI (1912), 221; Casgrain, *Sulpiciens en Acadie.* ❧ Expulsion of the Acadians: A. G. Doughty, *Acadian Exiles* (1916); Édouard Richard, *Acadie* (Henri d'Arles, ed., 1916–21), III.

Sources — Shirley, *Correspondence;* L. E. De Forest, ed., *Louisbourg Journals, 1745* (1932); Sir William Johnson, *Papers,* I; "Letters relating to Expedition against Cape Breton," *Mass. Hist. Soc., Coll.,* 1 ser., I (1792); "Pepperell Papers," *ibid.,* 6 ser., X (1899); Conrad Weiser, "Journal," Thwaites, ed., *Early Western Travels,* I, 21; Wraxall, *Abridgment,* 164; Nova Scotia Hist. Soc., *Coll.,* I–IV (1879–85; Samuel Vetch, John Winslow, and other deportation papers); A. M. Macmechan, ed., *Minutes of H. M. Council at Annapolis Royal, 1720–39* (1908); Akins, *Public Documents of Nova Scotia;* Adam Shortt and V. K. Johnston, eds., *Documents Relating to Nova Scotia 1675–1758* (1933).

108. POLITICS AND WAR, 1749–1763

Summary — 1748, Ohio Company. — 1749, expedition of Céleron de Bienville; French forts on the Alleghany and Ohio. — 1753–54, Washington's expeditions to the Ohio; Fort Necessity. — 1754, Albany Congress and Plan of Union. — 1755, French and Indian War (Seven Years' War in Europe); Braddock's defeat; panic on the Virginia Frontier; Battle of Lake George (Sir William Johnson). — 1756–57, Montcalm captures Oswego and Fort William Henry; Newcastle Ministry; responses of the colonies to appeals from England for assistance. — Colonial politics and the royal governors, Shirley, Dinwiddie, Fauquier, Clinton. — 1758, William Pitt in power; new strategic plan; capture of Louisbourg by Amherst, Wolfe, and Boscawen, of Fort Frontenac by Bradstreet, of Fort du Quesne by Forbes. — 1759, year of victories; capture of Fort Niagara by Johnson, of Ticonderoga by Amherst; of Quebec by Wolfe and Saunders (Sept. 13, Battle of Plains of Abraham); of Guadeloupe. — 1760, surrender of Montreal and all Canada; death of George II. — 1761, Family Compact, France and Spain. — 1762, war declared on Spain (§ 105); capture of Martinique and other French islands, of Havana, and Manila. — 1763, Peace of Paris; expulsion of France from North America.

General — Channing, *History,* II, ch. xix; Wrong, *Rise and Fall of New France,* II, ch. xxvii; *Cambridge History of British Empire,* VI, 91–120; Beer, *British Colonial Policy, 1754–56;* Francis Parkman, *Montcalm and Wolfe* (2 vols., 1884); Gipson, *British Empire before American Revolution,* V, chs. i–vii, xi, VI, VII; Bancroft, *History of United States,* IV; Mahan, *Influence of Sea Power,* ch. viii; Graham, *Empire of North Atlantic,* chs. viii, ix; J. S. Corbett, *England in Seven Years War* (2 vols., 1907).

Special — Politics during the war: Osgood, *American Colonies in Eighteenth Century*, III, 566, IV, chs. xi–xiv; Palfrey, *New England*, V, chs. ix–xi, xiii; Flick, *History of New York*, II, chs. v–vi; Dunaway, *History of Pennsylvania*, ch. vi; Root, *Relations of Pennsylvania with British Government*, ch. x; Bolles, *Pennsylvania*, I, ch. v. ❡ War in Europe: Lavisse, *Histoire de France*, VIII, pt. 2; Perkins, *France under Louis XV*, chs. xii–xv. ❡ War in America: Freeman, *Washington*, I, chs. vi–xii, 540; S. M. Pargellis, *Loudoun in North America* and "Braddock's Defeat," *Am. Hist. Rev.*, XLI (1936), 253; F. T. Nichols, "Organization of Braddock's Army," *William and Mary Quar.*, 3 ser., IV (1947), 127; McLennan, *Louisbourg*, chs. xi–xv; Max Savelle, *Diplomatic History of Canadian Boundary 1749–63* (1940); A. G. Doughty, *Siege of Quebec* (6 vols., 1901); G. M. Wrong, *Fall of Canada 1759–60* (1914); C. W. Alvord, *Mississippi Valley in British Politics* (1916), I, ch. ii; E. I. McCormac, *Colonial Opposition to Imperial Authority during French and Indian War* (1911); Koontz, *Virginia Frontier*; R. C. Downes, *Council Fires on Upper Ohio* (1940), chs. i–vii; W. R. Jacobs, *Diplomacy and Indian Gifts* (1950); Walton, *Conrad Weiser*, chs. xii–xvi; Wallace, *King of Delaware*; Alden, *John Stuart and Southern Frontier*, pt. 1; Abernethy, *Western Lands and American Revolution*, chs. i, ii; B. H. Liddell Hart, "General Wolfe, Grandsire of United States," *Blackwood's*, CCXXI (1927), 336; Thomas Chapais, *Le Marquis de Montcalm* (1911); Basil Williams, *Life of William Pitt* (2 vols., 1913), II; Hubert Hall, "Chatham's Colonial Policy," *Am. Hist. Rev.*, V (1900), 659; Long, *Lord Jeffrey Amherst*; R. H. Mahon, *Life of General James Murray* (1921); J. B. Brebner, *Neutral Yankees of Nova Scotia* (1937), chs. i, ii; Pares, *War and Trade in West Indies*, chs. vii–xii; F. R. Hart, *Siege of Havana, 1762* (1931); Marshall Smelser, "Insular Campaign of 1759: Guadeloupe," *Am. Neptune*, VII (1947), 21; W. L. Grant, "Canada vs. Guadeloupe," *Am. Hist. Rev.*, XVII (1912), 735; M. C. Tyler, *Literary History of the American Revolution* (2 vols., 1897), I, ch. vii; Fort Ticonderoga Museum, *Bull.* (S. H. P. Pell, ed., 1927–). ❡ Albany Congress and Plan: Richard Frothingham, *Rise of Republic* (1872), ch. iv; J. R. Alden, "Albany Congress and Indian Superintendencies," *Miss. Valley Hist. Rev.*, XXVII (1940), 193; § 102.

Sources — Pargellis, *Military Affairs in North America*; G. S. Kimball, ed., *Correspondence of William Pitt with Colonial Governors* (2 vols., 1906); Shirley, *Correspondence*, II; Sir William Johnson, *Papers*, I–IV; Colden, *Papers*, V–VI, IX; "Fitch Papers"; Dinwiddie, *Official Records*; Horatio Sharpe, "Correspondence, 1753–1761," *Md. Archives*, VI, IX (1888, 1890); Knox, *Historical Journal of Campaigns in North America*; Jeffrey Amherst, *Journal* (J. C. Webster, ed., 1931); James Murray, *Journal of Siege of Quebec* (1871); William Wood, ed., *Logs of Conquest of Canada* (1909); L. J., Marquis de Montcalm, *Journal* (H. R. Casgrain, ed., 1895), and "Correspondence," Public Archives of Canada, *Report*, 1929, 31; Washington, *Diaries*, I, and *Writings*, I, II; S. M. Hamilton, ed., *Letters to Washington* (1898), I; Franklin, *Writings*, II, III; Abijah Willard, "Journal," J. C. Webster, ed., New Brunswick Hist. Soc., *Coll.*, No. 13 (1930); C. B. Galbreath, "Expedition of Céleron," *Ohio Arch. Hist. Quar.*, XXIX (1920), 330; "La Mission de M. de Bougainville," Archiviste de Québec, *Rapport* (1924); Sigmund Samuel, *Seven Years' War in Canada, Records and Illustrations* (1934); T. C. Pease and Ernestine Jenison, eds., *Illinois on Eve of Seven Years' War 1747–55* (1940); MacDonald, *Select Charters*, Nos. 51, 52, 54.

Bibliography — Winsor, *Narrative and Critical History*, V, 450, 560; *Northcliffe Collection* (Calendar of Generals Townshend and Monckton MSS., 1926); J. C. Long, comp., *Plimpton Collection French and Indian War Items Amherst College* (1934).

Chapter Ten

THE REVOLUTIONARY ERA, 1760–1789

109. THE AMERICAN REVOLUTION, INTRODUCTORY AND GENERAL

Summary — Underlying influences, causes and background. — Constitutional issues. — Comparison of American Revolution with other modern revolutions. — General histories of the era. — Influence on Europe. — Intellectual and cultural influences (§ 120).

General — Introduction and Essays: — C. M. Andrews, *Colonial Background of the American Revolution* (1924); Beer, *British Colonial Policy, 1754–1765*; Carl Becker, *Eve of the Revolution* (1911); Lord Acton, "American Revolution," *Lectures on Modern History* (1921), ch. xix, and *History of Freedom and Other Essays* (1922), chs. i, ii, xvi; Schlesinger, *New Viewpoints*, ch. vii; H. E. Egerton, *Causes and Character of the American Revolution* (1923); R. A. Humphreys, "Rule of Law and American Revolution," *Law Quar. Rev.*, LIII (1937), 80; C. H. McIlwain, *American Revolution: A Constitutional Interpretation* (1923); R. L. Schuyler, *Parliament and British Empire* (1929); R. B. Morris, "Legalism *versus* Revolutionary Doctrine," *New Eng. Quar.*, IV (1931), 195; C. F. Mullett, *Fundamental Law and American Revolution* (1933). ❡ General Accounts: Channing, *History*, III; Bancroft, *History of United States*, III; E. B. Greene, *Revolutionary Generation, 1763–90* (1943); Fiske, *American Revolution*; J. C. Miller, *Origins of American Revolution* (1943), and *Triumph of Freedom* (1948); C. H. Van Tyne, *Causes of War of Independence* (1922), and *American Revolution* (1905); A. C. McLaughlin, *Confederation and Constitution* (1905); G. O. Trevelyan, *Early History of Charles James Fox* (1901), and *American Revolution* (4 vols., 1909–12), and *George III and Charles Fox* (2 vols., 1912–14); Henry Belcher, *First American Civil War, 1775–78* (2 vols., 1911); Arthur Johnston, *Myths and Facts of American Revolution* (1908).

Special — Social and Cultural: Gipson, *British Empire before American Revolution*, I; Tyler, *Literary History of American Revolution*; Quinn, *Literature of American People*, chs. viii–xi; Parrington, *Colonial Mind*, 164. ❡ Political: Philip Davidson, *Propaganda and American Revolution 1763–83* (1941); R. G. Adams, *Political Ideas of American Revolution* (1922); Z. S. Fink, *Classical Republicans* (1945); A. C. McLaughlin, *Foundations of American Constitutionalism* (1932); B. F. Wright, *American Interpretations of Natural Law* (1931), chs. i–vi; C. M. Walsh, *Political Science of John Adams* (1915); Caroline Robbins, "Sidney's Discourses on Government," *William and Mary Quar.*, 3 ser., IV (1947), 267, and "Library of Liberty," *Harvard Library Bull.*, V (1951), 5, 181; Clinton Rossiter, "Political Theory of Benjamin Franklin," *Penn. Mag. Hist.*, LXXVI (1952), 259. ❡ Effect on British Empire: G. M. Wrong, *Canada and the American Revolution 1760–1776* (1935); Brebner, *Neutral Yankees of Nova Scotia*; Reginald Coupland, *American Revolution and British Empire* (1930). ❡ Classes and Groups: A. M. Schlesinger, *Colonial Merchants and American Revolution* (1918); Harrington, *New York Merchants*; A. M. Baldwin, *New England Clergy and American Revolution* (1928), and

"Sowers of Sedition, Presbyterian Clergy," *William and Mary Quar.*, 3 ser., V (1948), 53; Cross, *Anglican Episcopate and American Colonies*; Clinton Rossiter, "Jonathan Mayhew," *William and Mary Quar.*, VII (1950), 531; R. J. Hooker, "Mayhew Controversy," *Church Hist.*, V (1936), 239; Dickerson, *Navigation Acts and American Revolution*; J. F. Jameson, *American Revolution as Social Movement* (1940); Elizabeth Cometti, "Women in Revolution," *New Eng. Quar.*, XX (1947), 329; Faust, *German Element*, I, chs. x, xi; C. A. Hanna, *Scotch-Irish* (1902), I, ch. i; M. J. O'Brien, *Hidden Phase of American History* (1919); and Miecislaus Haiman, *Poland and American Revolutionary War* (1932); L. M. Hacker, "First American Revolution," *Columbia University Quar.*, XXVII (1935), 239, and "American Revolution: Economic Aspects," *Marxist Quar.*, I (1937), 46. ❧ Regional: Palfrey, *New England*, V; J. T. Adams, *Revolutionary New England*, chs. xiii–xviii, and *New England in Republic*, chs. i–vii; Upton, *Revolutionary New Hampshire*; Oscar Zeichner, *Connecticut's Years of Controversy* (1950); Carl Becker, *Political Parties in New York 1760–66* (1909); W. C. Abbott, *New York in American Revolution* (1929); Lundin, *Cockpit of Revolution*; C. H. Lincoln, *Revolutionary Movement in Pennsylvania 1760–76* (1901); C. A. Barker, *Background of Revolution in Maryland* (1940); P. A. Crowl, *Maryland during and after Revolution* (1943); H. J. Eckenrode, *Revolution in Virginia* (1916); C. C. Crittenden, *Commerce of North Carolina, 1763–89* (1936); McCrady, *South Carolina*, II–IV; §§ 111, 120.

Sources — Niles, *Principles and Acts of Revolution*; Force, *American Archives*, 4 ser., I; Moore, *Diary of American Revolution*; S. E. Morison, ed., *Sources and Documents Illustrating the American Revolution, 1764–1788* (1929); Callender, *Selections from Economic History of United States*; MacDonald, *Select Charters*; J. C. Wahlke, ed., *Causes of Revolution* (1949); Earl Latham, ed., *Declaration of Independence and Constitution* (1949); Burnett, *Letters of Members of Continental Congress*; Ford, *Journals of Continental Congress*; George III, *Letters to Lord Bute, 1756–66* (Romney Sedgwick, ed., 1939), and *Correspondence 1760–1783* (Sir J. W. Fortescue, ed., 6 vols., 1927–28; see: L. B. Namier, *Additions and Corrections* [1937]); John Almon, *Remembrancer* (17 vols., 1775–84), and *Collection of Papers Relating to Dispute between Great Britain and America* (*Prior Documents*, 1777); writings of Washington, Franklin, John Adams, Samuel Adams, Jefferson, Hamilton, and Jay (§§ 54, 55); "Jeremy Belknap Papers," *Mass. Hist. Soc., Coll.*, 5 ser., II, III (1877), 6 ser., IV (1891); "William Heath Papers," (including Winthrop-Adams and Warren-Adams correspondence), *ibid.*, 5 ser., IV (1878), 7 ser., IV, V (1904–05); "Trumbull Papers," *ibid.*, 5 ser., IX, X (1885–88), 7 ser., II, III (1902); "Bowdoin-Temple Papers," *ibid.*, 6 ser., IX (1897), 7 ser., VI (1907); "Jefferson Papers," *ibid.*, 7 ser., I (1900); "Commerce of Rhode Island 1726–1800," *ibid.*, 7 ser., IX, X (1914–15); "Pelham-Copley Letters," *ibid.*, LXXI (1914); Warren, "Warren-Adams Letters"; Colden, *Papers*, VII; "Huntington Papers, 1771–1783," Conn. Hist. Soc., *Coll.*, XX (1923); "Pitkin Papers"; Deane, "Papers" (§ 114); William Johnson, *Papers*, IV–VIII; John Rowe, *Letters and Diary 1759–1779* (A. R. Cunningham, ed., 1903); John Boyle, "Journal of Occurrences in Boston, 1759–78," *New Eng. Hist. Geneal. Register*, LXXXIV (1930), 142, 248, 357, LXXXV (1931), 5, 117.

Bibliography — Winsor, *Narrative and Critical History*, VI–VII; Miller, *Triumph of Freedom*, 689; Greene, *Revolutionary Generation*, ch. xvii; Morison and Commager, *Growth of American Republic*, I, 755.

110. RENEWED ACTIVITY IN SPANISH BORDERLANDS

Summary — Louisiana: 1759, Carlos III and his colonial policy. — 1762, Louisiana. — 1763, Floridas ceded to Great Britain (§ 108). — 1764, founding of St. Louis. — 1766–69, Governor Ulloa; rebellion in New Orleans; suppression by Governor O'Reilly. — 1776, Governor Gálvez. — Society and economy in Louisiana: Indian relations; immigration of Germans and Acadian French; 1773, removal of settlers on Texas border to San Antonio; 1781, Spanish expedition across Illinois, capture of St. Joseph. — New Mexico: 1769, Rivera and Portolá expeditions to Upper California; Fr. Junípero Serra founds San Diego mission; 1770, Portolá discovers San Francisco Bay; presidio and mission at Monterey; 1775–76, Anza Expedition and founding of San Francisco (§§ 164, 165). — Spanish Indian policy; founding of missions. — 1783–89, relations between Spain and American frontiersmen; balance of power among the Indians, wars with Creeks and Cherokees, danger of Western secession. — Spanish diplomacy and the Revolution (§ 117). — The West in general (§ 111).

General — H. E. Bolton, *Spanish Borderlands*, chs. ix, x, and *Outpost of Empire* (1931), and *Athanase de Mezières and Louisiana-Texas Frontier, 1768–1780* (2 vols., 1914), and *Texas in Middle Eighteenth Century*, pt. 5, and *Fray Juan Crespi* (1927); Bancroft, *California*, I, chs. iv–xxii; C. E. Chapman, *Founding of Spanish California* (1916); A. P. Whitaker, *Spanish American Frontier: 1783–1795* (1927), chs. i–viii; J. F. Yela Utrilla, *España ante la independencia de los Estados Unidos* (2 vols., 1925); Manuel Danvila y Collado, *Reinado de Carlos III* (1893–96), IV, chs. ii, v–vii, V, chs. i–v.

Special — H. I. Priestley, *José de Gálvez* (1916); L. E. Fisher, *Intendant System in Spanish America* (1929); Gayarré, *History of Louisiana*, I; Fortier, *History of Louisiana*, I, chs. viii–xi, II; J. W. Caughey, *Bernardo de Gálvez in Louisiana, 1776–1783* (1934); J. E. Winston, "Revolution of 1768 in Louisiana," *La. Hist. Quar.*, XV (1932), 181; E. W. Lyon, *Louisiana in French Diplomacy 1759–1804* (1934); J. H. Deiler, *German Coast of Louisiana* (1909); Wagner, *Cartography of Northwest Coast*, I, chs. xx–xxxix; Siebert, "Slavery and White Servitude in East Florida"; *New Spain and Anglo-American West: Contributions to H. E. Bolton* (1932), I; A. P. Nasatir, "Anglo-Spanish Frontier in Illinois, 1779–1783," Ill. Hist. Soc., *Jour.*, XXI (1928), 291; V. L. Brown, "Anglo-Spanish Relations in America," *Hispanic-Am. Hist. Rev.*, V (1922), 329, 479; J. A. James, "Spanish Influence in West during Revolution," *Miss. Valley Hist. Rev.*, IV (1918), 193; F. J. Teggart, "Capture of St. Joseph, Michigan, by Spaniards in 1781," *Missouri Hist. Rev.*, V (1911), 214; C. W. Alvord, "Conquest of St. Joseph, Michigan, by Spaniards in 1781," *Michigan Hist. Mag.*, XIV (1930), 398; Lawrence Kinnaird, "Spanish Expedition against Fort St. Joseph," *Miss. Valley Hist. Rev.*, XIX (1933), 173.

Sources — H. E. Bolton, ed., *Anza's California Expeditions* (5 vols., 1930); A. B. Thomas, ed., *Forgotten Frontiers* (1932); Francisco Palóu, *Noticias de la Nueva California* (H. E. Bolton, ed., 4 vols., 1926); G. W. James, ed., *Vida de Junípero Serra* (1913); T. H. Hittell, *History of California* (1885–97), I, bk. 3, chs. i–xii; Morfi, *History of Texas*, chs. ix–x; Robertson, *Louisiana*, I, 235; Serrano y Sanz, *Documentos Historicos de la Florida y la Luisiana*; Whitaker, *Documents Relating to Commercial Policy of Spain in Floridas*.

Bibliography — *Hispanic-Am. Hist. Rev.*, V (1922), 329, 479.

111. WEST IN THE AMERICAN REVOLUTION

Summary — 1763: Western postwar problems: Pontiac Rebellion; land speculation; fur traders and frontiersmen; treaties of Fort Stanwix and Hard Labor; Indian relations; Ohio, Loyal, Susquehanna, Walpole (Vandalia), Indiana, Wabash, Illinois, Transylvania, land companies; Lyman Military Adventurers. — British Policy: Proclamation of 1763; Shelburne's Plan of 1764; Board of Trade Report of 1768; Royal Instructions of February 3, 1774 (§ 113); Dunmore's war. — Internal Problems: under-representation of western counties, Paxton Boys, Regulators in the Carolinas. — Confederation period: pressure groups in the Continental Congress; western state-making (Franklin) during the war; George Rogers Clark Expedition; proposals to divide trans-Appalachia between Spain and Great Britain; territorial policy, Ordinances of 1784, 1785, 1787. — Western questions in the Federal Convention. — Vermont (§ 119); the Southwest (§ 110).

General — Turner, *Frontier in American History*, ch. iii, and *Significance of Sections*, ch. iv; Paxson, *American Frontier*, chs. i–vi; Parkman, *Conspiracy of Pontiac*; Billington, *Westward Expansion*, chs. vii–ix; C. W. Alvord, *Mississippi Valley in British Politics*, I, chs. ii, vi–xii, and *Centennial History of Illinois: I, The Illinois Country 1673–1818*

(1920), chs. xi–xv; Beer, *British Colonial Policy, 1754–1765,* chs. ix, xii; Theodore Roosevelt, *Winning of the West* (6 vols., 1889–96), I, II.

Special — Abernethy, *Western Lands and American Revolution,* and *From Frontier to Plantation,* chs. i–vii; Alden, *John Stuart and Southern Colonial Frontier;* Freeman, *George Washington,* III, chs. v–vii, 215, 245, 256, chs. xiii, xiv; Peckham, *Pontiac;* C. E. Carter, *Great Britain and Illinois Country, 1763–1774* (1910), and "British Policy toward Indians in South, 1763–68," *Eng. Hist. Rev.,* XXXIII (1918), 37; G. E. Lewis, *Indiana Company 1763–1798* (1941); Bailey, *Ohio Company of Virginia and Westward Movement;* B. A. Hinsdale, *Old Northwest* (1891), chs. viii–x; W. S. Lester, *Transylvania Company* (1935); Alden, *General Gage,* chs. vi, viii; C. H. Metzger, *Quebec Act* (1936), and "Shelburne's Western Policy," *Mid-America,* VIII (1937), 169; Wrong, *Canada and American Revolution,* chs. iv, xii; F. H. Hart, *Valley of Virginia in American Revolution* (1942); J. S. Bassett, "Regulators in North Carolina," *Am. Hist. Assoc., Report,* 1894, 141; Archibald Henderson, "Origin of Regulation in North Carolina," *Am. Hist. Rev.,* XXI (1916), 320; McCrady, *South Carolina,* II, chs. xvi–xvii, xxxii, III, chs. ii, v, ix, xxvii; Kellogg, *British Régime in Wisconsin,* chs. vii–xii; J. D. Barnhart, *Henry Hamilton and George Rogers Clark* (1951); Philip Davidson, "Southern Backcountry on Eve of Revolution," *Essays in Honor of William E. Dodd* (1935), 1; A. B. Hulbert, *Boone's Wilderness Road* (1903); C. A. Hanna, *Wilderness Trail* (2 vols., 1911); Driver, *John Sevier;* S. C. Williams, *History of Lost State of Franklin* (1933), and *Dawn of Tennessee Valley and Tennessee History* (1937); J. A. James, *George Rogers Clark,* and *Oliver Pollock* (1937); R. G. Thwaites, *Daniel Boone* (1902); Edna Kenton, *Simon Kenton* (1930); Max Farrand, "Indian Boundary Line," *Am. Hist. Rev.,* X (1905), 782; Matthews, *Expansion of New England,* 96; Higgins, *Expansion in New York,* chs. viii, ix, xii; L. S. Shimmell, *Border Warfare in Pennsylvania during Revolution* (1901); J. P. Boyd, *Susquehannah Company* (1935); W. R. Smith, "Sectionalism in Pennsylvania," *Pol. Sci. Quar.,* XXIV (1909), 208; Brooke Hindle, "March of Paxton Boys," *William and Mary Quar.,* 3 ser., III (1946), 461; R. G. Thwaites and L. P. Kellogg, *Revolution on Upper Ohio* (1908); J. A. James, "Indian Diplomacy and Opening of Revolution in West," Wisc. Hist. Soc., *Proc.* (1909), 125, and "Problems of Northwest in 1779," *Essays in American History Dedicated to F. J. Turner* (1910), 57; R. C. Downes, *Council Fires on Upper Ohio,* chs. viii–xii, and "Dunmore's War," *Miss. Valley Hist. Rev.,* XXI (1934), 311; W. H. Mohr, *Federal Indian Relations 1774–1788* (1933); Max Savelle, *George Morgan* (1932).

Sources — Morison, *Sources and Documents,* 1, 9, 54, 83, 97, 203, 226, 270; Shortt and Doughty, *Documents,* 93, 374; R. G. Thwaites and L. P. Kellogg, eds., *Dunmore's War* (1905); "Documents of the Regulation," *North Carolina Colonial Records,* VIII (1890); Boyd, *Eighteenth Century Tracts concerning North Carolina,* Nos. vi, viii, ix, x; Herman Husband, "Continuation of Impartial Relation," Archibald Henderson, ed., *No. Car. Hist. Rev.,* XVIII (1941), 48; Gage, *Correspondence;* William Johnson, *Papers,* IV–VIII; John Stuart, "Observations," *Am. Hist. Rev.,* XX (1915), 815; Boyd, *Susquehannah Company Papers;* Gist, *Journals;* Thomas Walker, "Journal (1750)," J. S. Johnston, ed., *First Explorations of Kentucky* (1898); Richard Smith, *Tour;* C. W. Alvord, ed., *Cahokia Records,* Ill. Hist. Coll., II (1907), and *Kaskaskia Records, ibid.,* V (1909); G. R. Clark, "Papers, 1771–1781"; Franklin, *Works,* III, 278, IV, 22, 243, 416, V, 433, VI, 3.

Bibliography — F. J. Turner and Frederick Merk, *References on History of West* (1922), §§ 9, 10; Winsor, *Narrative and Critical History,* VI, chs. viii–ix.

112. BRITISH POLICY AND COLONIAL RESISTANCE, 1761–1766

Summary — 1761, order to enforce Molasses Act; Writs of Assistance. — 1763, Parsons' Cause and Royal Proclamation; decision to leave garrisons in colonies. — 1764, Sugar Act, Otis' *Rights of the* Colonies. — 1765, Stamp Act, question of necessity, of constitutionality. — Acts of resistance. — Virginia Resolves, Stamp Act Congress. — 1766, repeal of Stamp Act; Declaratory Act.

General — Andrews, *Colonial Background,* chs. iii, iv; Channing, *History,* III, chs. i–iii; Beer, *British Colonial Policy 1754–1765* chs. x–xiv; Van Tyne, *Causes,* v–ix; Tyler, *Literary History of American Revolution,* I, 1, 223.

Special — The Controversy: Carl Bridenbaugh, *Seat of Empire* (1950); A. P. Scott, "Constitutional Aspects of Parsons' Cause," *Pol. Sci. Quar.,* XXXI (1916), 558; G. C. Smith, "Parsons' Cause," *Tyler's Quar.,* XXI (1940), 140, 291; A. M. Schlesinger, "Colonial Newspapers and Stamp Act," *New Eng. Quar.,* VIII (1935), 63; F. J. Ericson, "British Opposition to Stamp Act," Mich. Ac. Sci., *Papers,* XXIX (1943), 489; W. T. Laprade, "Stamp Act in British Politics," *Am. Hist. Rev.,* XXXV (1930), 735; E. S. and H. M. Morgan, *Stamp Act Crisis* (1953); L. H. Gipson, *Jared Ingersoll,* chs. v–vii, and "Connecticut Taxation and Parliamentary Aid," *Am. Hist. Rev.,* XXXVI (1931), 721; Zeichner, *Connecticut's Years of Controversy,* ch. iii; V. W. Crane, *Benjamin Franklin, Englishman and American* (1936), and "Franklin and Stamp Act," *Col. Soc. Mass., Publ.,* XXXII (1937), 56; Carl Becker, *Political Parties in New York,* chs. i–ii, and *Declaration of Independence* (1922), 1; Schlesinger, *Colonial Merchants,* chs. i, ii; C. F. Mullett, *Fundamental Law and the American Revolution,* and *Colonial Claims to Home Rule 1764–1775* (1927); Wright, *American Interpretations of Natural Law,* ch. iv; Humphreys, "Rule of Law and American Revolution"; R. G. Adams, *Political Ideas,* chs. ii–iv; Root, *Relations of Pennsylvania with British Government,* chs. xi–xii; Eckenrode, *Revolution in Virginia,* ch. i; J. T. Adams, *Revolutionary New England,* 268; Miller, *Sam Adams,* chs. ii, iii; Van Doren, *Franklin,* chs. xii–xvi; Alden, *General Gage,* chs. v–vii; R. D. W. Connor, *Cornelius Harnett* (1909); Henry, *Patrick Henry,* I, chs. ii–iv; W. E. Foster, *Stephen Hopkins* (1884); Wallace, *Henry Laurens,* chs. viii, ix. ❡ British Politics, 1760–83: G. H. Guttridge, *English Whiggism and American Revolution* (1942); L. B. Namier, *England in Age of American Revolution* (1930), and *Structure of Politics at Accession of George III* (2 vols., 1929); D. G. Barnes, *George III and William Pitt* (1939), chs. i, ii; Herbert Butterfield, *George III, Lord North and People, 1779–80* (1949).

Sources — Morison, *Sources and Documents,* 4; MacDonald, *Select Charters,* Nos. 56–60; John Adams, *Works,* II, 108; Samuel Adams, *Writings,* I; Franklin, *Writings,* III, IV; Otis, *Some Political Writings,* 261; Colden, *Papers,* VI; "State of the Trade, 1763," Col. Soc. Mass., *Publ.,* XIX (1918), 379; Edward Channing and A. C. Coolidge, eds., *Barrington-Bernard Correspondence* (1912), 30; C. H. Hull and H. W. V. Temperley, eds., "Debates on Repeal of Stamp Act," *Am. Hist. Rev.,* XVII (1912), 563; George III, *Correspondence;* "Bowdoin — Temple Papers"; Jasper Mauduit, "Papers," *ibid.,* LXXIV (1918); Dennys De Berdt, "Letters," Col. Soc. Mass., *Publ.,* XIII (1911), 293; Charles Garth, "Correspondence," J. W. Barnewell, ed., *So. Car. Hist. Mag.,* XXVI (1925), 67, XXVIII (1927), 79, 226, XXIX (1928), 41, 115, 212, 295, XXX (1929), 27, 105, 168, 215, XXXI (1930), 46, 124, 226; "Stamp Act Papers," *Md. Hist. Mag.,* VI (1911), 282; Carl Van Doren, ed., *Letters of Franklin and Richard Jackson* (1947); V. W. Crane, ed., *Franklin's Letters to Press, 1758–1775* (1950), 20; E. S. Morgan, ed., "New York Declarations of 1764," *Old South Leaflet,* No. 224 (1948), and "Stamp Act Congress Declarations and Petitions," *ibid.,* No. 223 (1948).

113. FROM PASSIVE TO ACTIVE RESISTANCE, 1767–1774

Summary — 1767, Chatham-Grafton Ministry, Townshend Acts, and Commissioners of the Customs; non-importation agreements. — 1768, Massachusetts' Circular Letter, John Hancock and sloop *Liberty.* — 1769, Virginia Resolves. — 1770, North Ministry, repeal of Townshend duties. — Boston Massacre. — 1772, Burning of *Gaspee.* — 1773, new tea acts, Virginia Resolves, Boston Tea Party, reception of tea elsewhere. — 1774, Coercive Acts, Quebec Act, First Continental Congress, the Association, proposals of federal union by John Adams, Galloway, Jefferson, and Wilson. — The settlement of Nova Scotia and its loyalty. — English politics (§ 112).

General — Channing, *History,* III, chs. iv, v; Miller, *Origins,* chs. x–xvi; Van Tyne, *Causes,* chs. x–xvi; W. A. Brown, *Empire or Independence, a Study in Failure of Rec-*

onciliation 1774–83 (1941), chs. i–vi; Dickerson, *Navigation Acts and American Revolution*, 195; Tyler, *Literary History of American Revolution*, I, chs. x–xii, xviii; Parrington, *Main Currents*, I, 164; Trevelyan, *American Revolution*, I, chs. i–vii; E. C. Burnett, *Continental Congress* (1941), chs. i–iii; Bancroft, *United States*, IV (1896), chs. i–xix.

Special — R. G. Adams, *Political Ideas*, chs. iv–viii; Alvord, *Mississippi Valley in British Politics*, II; A. M. Schlesinger, *Colonial Merchants*, chs. iii–xi, and "Politics, Propaganda, and Philadelphia Press," *Penn. Mag. Hist.*, LX (1936), 309, and "Propaganda and Boston Press," Col. Soc. Mass., *Publ.*, XXXII (1937), 396; Frothingham, *Rise of Republic*, chs. vi–ix; J. P. Boyd, *Anglo-American Union: Joseph Galloway's Plans* (1941); C. M. Andrews, "Boston Merchants and Non-Importation," Col. Soc. Mass., *Publ.*, XIX (1917), 159; E. D. Collins, "Committees of Correspondence," Am. Hist. Assoc., *Report*, 1901, I, 243; D. M. Clark, "American Board of Customs, 1767–85," *Am. Hist. Rev.*, XLV (1940), 777; R. A. Humphreys, "Lord Shelburne and British Colonial Policy, 1766–68," *Eng. Hist. Rev.*, L (1935), 257; H. C. Bell, "West Indian Trade before Revolution," *Am. Hist. Rev.*, XXII (1917), 272; J. T. Adams, *Revolutionary New England*, chs. xv–xvi; Baldwin, *New England Clergy and Revolution*, ch. viii; E. L. Page, "King's Powder," *New Eng. Quar.*, XVIII (1945), 83; Zeichner, *Connecticut's Years of Controversy*, chs. iv–ix; Becker, *Declaration of Independence*, ch. iii; Abbott, *New York in Revolution*, chs. iv–vi; T. J. Wertenbaker, *Father Knickerbocker Rebels* (1948), chs. i–iv; Flick, *History of New York*, III, ch. vii; Eckenrode, *Revolution in Virginia*, chs. ii–v; W. E. Dodd, "Virginia Takes Road to Revolution," in Carl Becker, *et al.*, *Spirit of '76 and Other Essays* (1927), 101; McCrady, *South Carolina*, II, chs. xxix–xl; Ashe, *History of North Carolina*, I, chs. xxi–xxii; P. W. Postgate, *That Devil Wilkes* (1929); S. F. Duff, "Case against the King," *William and Mary Quar.*, 3 ser., VI (1949), 383; Forbes, *Paul Revere and World He Lived In*, chs. iv–vi. ❡ Biographies: Zoltán Haraszti, *John Adams and Prophets of Progress* (1952), chs. i–iii; Miller, *Sam Adams*, chs. v–xiii; Stillé, *John Dickinson*, chs. iv–v; Van Doren, *Franklin*, chs. xvii, xviii; Alden, *General Gage*, chs. ix, x; Mays, *Edmund Pendleton*, I, chs. x–xvii; Henry, *Patrick Henry*, I, chs. v–x; Dumas Malone, *Jefferson*, I, chs. ix–xiv; Wallace, *Henry Laurens*, chs. x–xiii; Rowland, *George Mason*, I, chs. iv–v; Brant, *James Madison*, I, chs. v–vii; Freeman, *Washington*, III, 194, 248, chs. xv, xvi; Mayo, *John Wentworth*, chs. iv–xi. ❡ Nova Scotia, 1763–83: Brebner, *Neutral Yankees of Nova Scotia*; V. F. Barnes, "Governor Francis Legge of Nova Scotia," *New Eng. Quar.*, IV (1931), 420; E. P. Weaver, "Nova Scotia and New England during Revolution," *Am. Hist. Rev.*, X (1904), 52; Margaret Ells, "Clearing Decks for Loyalists," Canadian Hist. Assoc., *Reports* (1933), 43, and "Settling Loyalists in Nova Scotia," *ibid.* (1934), 105; W. B. Kerr, *Maritime Provinces and American Revolution* (1941); J. S. Martell, "Second Expulsion of Acadians," *Dalhousie Rev.*, XIII (1934), 359; Sawtelle, "Acadia, the pre-Loyalist Migration," 244; *Cambridge History British Empire*, VI, ch. vii.

Sources — Morison, *Sources and Documents*, 34; John Adams, *Works*, II, 328, IV, 11; Warren, "Warren-Adams Letters"; Franklin, *Writings*, IV, V, and *Letters to the Press*, 108; Hutchinson, *Diary and Letters*, I, 78–338; John Dickinson, "Letters from a Farmer in Pennsylvania, (1768)" *Writings* (P. L. Ford, ed., 1895), 277; James Wilson, "Considerations on Authority of Parliament (1774)," *Works* (J. D. Andrews, ed., 1896), II, 522; Jefferson, *Writings*, I, 421, and *Papers*, I; William Knox, "Controversy Reviewed (1769)," *Old South Leaflet*, No. 210; *Glorious Ninety-Two: Selections from Journals of House, Massachusetts-Bay 1767–1768* (1949); Dickerson, *Boston under Military Rule*; Bradford, *Speeches of Governors*, 196; Hutchinson, *History of Massachusetts Bay*, III, 215; Samuel Adams, *Writings*, I, 114, II, III; "Bowdoin Temple Papers"; Force, *American Archives*, 4 ser., I; George III, *Correspondence*, I, 432, II, 161; Josiah Quincy, Jr., "London Journal and Correspondence, 1774–75," Mass. Hist. Soc., *Proc.*, L (1917), 433; Gage, *Correspondence*, I, 119, II, 403; Burnett, *Letters of Members of Continental Congress*, I; Cobbett, *Parliamentary History*, XVIII, 198, 319; Edmund Burke, *Speeches and Letters on American Affairs* (1908); Colden, "Papers," VII; Rush, *Letters*, I.

114. FROM JANUARY 1775, THROUGH THE DECLARATION OF INDEPENDENCE

Summary — Situation at the beginning of 1775. — "Cold war" in Massachusetts and Virginia. — Gage's forces in Boston; armed clashes narrowly averted. — Apr. 19, Lexington and Concord. — May 1775, Second Continental Congress; appointment of Washington commander-in-chief; Declaration of Causes, authorization of Canada Expedition, Olive Branch Petition, counter-measures in England. — Theory of war against "ministerial army." — 1776, movement toward independence; Paine's *Common Sense,* Virginia Resolves. — Declaration of Independence: sources of doctrine; preparation of draft; July 2, R. H. Lee's independence resolve adopted; July 4, Declaration adopted; when and by whom signed; the grievances. — Mecklenburg and other spurious Declarations of Independence. — Military-Naval Campaigns: — First American Navy. — Siege of Boston. — May 10, 1775, capture of Fort Ticonderoga. — June 17, Bunker Hill. — Oct. 17, burning of Falmouth (Portland, Me.). — Mar. 17, 1776, evacuation of Boston. — Opposing forces converge on New York. — September 1775, Canada Expedition (Montgomery and Arnold); Nov. 13, Montreal surrenders; Dec. 31, Quebec assaulted, Montgomery killed. — Dec. 9, 1775, Battle of Great Bridge, Va. — Jan. 1, 1776, burning of Norfolk, Va. — Mar. 26, Battle of Moore's Creek, No. Car. — June 28, Clinton and British fleet repulsed before Charleston, So. Car. — Later events (§ 116).

General — Channing, *History,* III, chs. vi–viii; Freeman, *Washington,* III, chs. xv–xxii, IV, chs. i–v; W. M. Wallace, *Appeal to Arms, a Military History of Revolution* (1951), chs. i–ii; Christopher Ward, *War of Revolution* (J. R. Alden, ed., 2 vols., 1952), I, chs. iii–xvi; C. P. Nettels, *Washington and American Independence* (1951), chs. iii–xii; Frothingham, *Washington,* 37; Becker, *Declaration of Independence;* Burnett, *Continental Congress,* chs. iii–ix; Tyler, *Literary History of American Revolution,* I, chs. xix–xxiii, II, chs. xxiv–xxvi; Bancroft, *United States,* IV, Epoch 3.

Special — Military events: Allen French, *First Year of American Revolution* (1934); Alden, *General Gage,* chs. xiv–xvii; F. W. Coburn, *Battle of April 19, 1775* (1922); Harold Murdock, *The 19th of April 1775* (1923); Elizabeth Merritt, "Lexington Alarm, Messages Sent to Southward," *Md. Hist. Mag.,* XLI (1946), 89; Richard Frothingham. *Siege of Boston* (1849); D. W. Knox, *Naval Genius of Washington* (1932), chs. i–iv; L. H. Butterfield, "Psychological Warfare in 1776," Am. Phil. Soc., *Proc.,* XCIV (1950), No. 3; O. W. Stephenson, "Supply of Gunpowder in 1776," *Am. Hist. Rev.,* XXX (1925), 271; E. A. Leonard, "Paper as Critical Commodity," *Penn. Mag. Hist.,* LXXIV (1950), 488; Wrong, *Canada and American Revolution,* ch. xiii; Pell, *Ethan Allen;* J. H. Smith, *Arnold's March to Quebec* (1903), and *Struggle for Fourteenth Colony* (2 vols., 1907); Kerr, *Maritime Provinces and American Revolution;* Barnes, "Francis Legge"; H. P. Johnston, "Campaign of 1776 around New York," Long Island Hist. Soc., *Memoirs* (1878). ❧ Declaration of Independence: Edward Dumbauld, *Declaration of Independence and What It Means Today* (1950); Malone, *Jefferson,* chs. xiii–xvi; Gaillard Hunt, "Cardinal Bellarmine and Virginia Bill of Rights," *Catholic Hist. Rev.,* III (1917), 276; D. S. Schaff, "Bellarmine-Jefferson Legend," Am. Soc. of Church Hist., *Papers,* 2 ser., VIII (1928), 239; Ashe, *History of North Carolina,* I, ch. xxvi; A. S. Salley, Jr., "Mecklenburg Declaration," *Am. Hist. Rev.,* XIII (1908), 16; W. H. Hoyt, *Mecklenburg Declaration* (1907). ❧ Local Movements: Abbott, *New York in Revolution,* chs. vi–ix; Becker, *Political Parties in New York,* chs. viii–ix; Schlesinger, *Colonial Merchants,* chs. xii–xv; Lincoln, *Revolutionary Movement in Pennsylvania,* chs. xi–xiv; Reed, *Life of Joseph Reed,* I, chs. iii–x; B. L. Whitaker, *Provincial Council and Committee of Safety in North Carolina* (1908).

Sources — Morison, *Sources and Documents,* 137; MacDonald, *Select Charters,* 367; J. P. Boyd, *Anglo-American Union,* and "Authorship of Declaration of Causes," *Penn. Mag. Hist.,* LXXIV (1950), 51, and *Declaration of Independence, Evolution of Text* (1945); Jefferson, *Papers,* I, 298, 413; Paine, *Complete Writings,* I; Franklin, *Writings,* VI; Silas Deane, "Papers," Charles Isham, ed., N. Y. Hist. Soc., *Coll.,* xix–xxiii (1887–90), and Conn. Hist. Soc., *Coll.,* xxiii (1930); John Adams, *Works,* II, III, and *Familiar*

Letters; Washington, *Writings,* III–V; Wharton, *Revolutionary Diplomatic Correspondence,* II, 139; Force, *American Archives,* 4 ser., I–VI, 5 ser., I–III; Burnett, *Letters of Members of Continental Congress,* I; Gage, *Correspondence* I, 390, II, 179, 665; Governor Samuel Ward (of Rhode Island), *Correspondence* (Bernhard Knollenberg, ed., 1952); T. E. Hansard, *Parliamentary History* (36 vols., 1806–20), XVIII, 149, 319; M. W. Willard, ed., *Letters on American Revolution 1774–76* [in English newspapers] (1925); P. V. Fithian, *Journal 1775–76* (R. G. Albion, ed., 1934).

115. THE LOYALISTS

Summary — Different classes of Loyalists; their numbers. — Lack of organization; persecution and suppression, before and after Independence. — Early migrations from Norfolk and Boston. — 1776–83, New York City and adjacent territory under British and Loyalist rule. — 1775–83, formation of Loyalist military units, Rawdon's "Volunteers of Ireland," Tarleton's "Legion." — Raids from New York on Long Island Sound. — Loyalist element in the Southern campaigns. — Loyalist privateers. — Confiscatory legislation by States during and after the war. — Dispersal of Loyalists, voluntary and otherwise; settlements in Canada, the Floridas, Bahamas; Nova Scotia and New Brunswick (§ 113). — Tories in Bristol and London. — Claims and pensions. — Loyalist literature and poetry. — 1783–1800, return of many Loyalists to the United States. — Careers of prominent Loyalists abroad.

General — Channing, *History,* III, 361; C. H. Van Tyne, *Loyalists in American Revolution* (1929), and *Causes,* 448, and *War of Independence* (1929), ch. ii; Trevelyan, *American Revolution,* I, 186, 373, III, 231; Tyler, *Literary History of American Revolution,* I, chs. xiii–xviii, II, xxvii–xxix, 394; Parrington, *Main Currents,* I, 194, 248; Wrong, *Canada and American Revolution,* chs. xviii–xxiii; Carl Wittke, *History of Canada* (1941), ch. vi.

Special — Lewis Einstein, *Divided Loyalties* (1933); Lorenzo Sabine, *Biographical Sketches of Loyalists* (2 vols., 1864); L. W. Labaree, "Nature of American Loyalism," Am. Antiq. Soc., *Proc.,* LIV (1944), 15; Davidson, *Propaganda and American Revolution,* chs. xiv–xvii. ❡ Regionally: J. H. Stark, *Loyalists of Massachusetts* (1910); W. H. Siebert, "Loyalist Troops of New England," *New Eng. Quar.,* IV (1931), 108; F. T. Bowles, "Loyalty of Barnstable," Col. Soc. Mass., *Publ.,* XXV (1924), 265; Jonathan Smith, "Toryism in Worcester County," Mass. Hist. Soc., *Proc.,* XLVIII (1915), 15; O. G. Hammond, *Tories of New Hampshire* (1917); Epaphroditus Peck, *Loyalists of Connecticut* (1934); A. C. Flick, *Loyalism in New York* (1901); O. T. Barck, *New York City during War for Independence* (1931); Abbott, *New York in American Revolution,* chs. viii–xi; Wertenbaker, *Father Knickerbocker Rebels,* chs. v, ix–xi; Howard Swiggett, *War out of Niagara, Butler and the Tory Rangers* (1933); G. W. Kyte, "Plans for Loyalist Stronghold in Middle Colonies," *Penn. Hist.,* XVI (1949), 177; E. A. Cruikshank, "King's Royal Regiment," Ontario Hist. Soc., *Papers,* XXVII (1931), 193; E. A. Jones, "Loyalists of New Jersey," N. J. Hist. Soc., *Proc.,* XI, XII (1926–27); H. B. Hancock, *Delaware Loyalists* (1940); I. S. Harrell, *Loyalism in Virginia* (1926); R. O. DeMond, *Loyalists in North Carolina* (1940). ❡ Biographies: J. B. Johnson, *Robert Alexander, Maryland Loyalist* (1942); R. P. Baker, "Poetry of Jacob Bailey, Loyalist," *New Eng. Quar.,* II (1929), 58; R. R. Beirne, "Governor Robert Eden," *Md. Hist. Mag.,* XLV (1950), 153, 294; Catherine Fennelly, "Governor William Franklin of New Jersey," *William and Mary Quar.,* VI (1949), 361; E. H. Baldwin, "Joseph Galloway," *Penn. Mag. Hist.,* XXVI (1902), 161, 289, 417; Hosmer, *Thomas Hutchinson;* Sibley, *Harvard Graduates,* VII, 464, VIII, 149, 737; Gipson, *Jared Ingersoll;* J. E. Alden, "John Mein; Scourge of Patriots," Col. Soc. Mass., *Publ.,* XXXIV (1942), 571; James Murray, *Letters* (N. M. Tiffany, ed., 1901); S. F. Batchelder, "Adventures of John Nutting," *Bits of Cambridge History* (1930), ch. iv; G. E. Ellis, *Benjamin Thompson, Count Rumford* (1871); J. A. Thompson, *Count Rumford;* M. deL. Haywood, *Governor Tryon* (1903); H. C. Van Schaack, *Life of Peter Van Schaack* (1842). ❡ Confiscation, Dispersal, and Reintegration: Merrill Jensen, *New Nation* (1950), 265; W. S. Wallace, *United Empire*

Loyalists (1914); A. G. Bradley, *Colonial Americans in Exile* (1932); W. H. Siebert, *Loyalists in East Florida* (2 vols., 1929), and "Dispersion of American Tories," *Miss. Valley Hist. Rev.*, I (1914), 185, and "Loyalists in West Florida," *ibid.*, II (1916), 465, and "Kentucky's Struggle," *ibid.*, VII (1920), 113, and "Legacy of American Revolution to British West Indies," Ohio State University, *Bull.*, XVII (1913), No. 27, and "Exodus of Loyalists from Penobscot," *ibid.*, XVIII (1914), No. 26, and "Loyalist Refugees of New Hampshire," *ibid.*, XXI (1916), No. 2, and "Loyalists of Pennsylvania," *ibid.*, XXIV (1920), No. 23, and "Loyalists in Prince Edwards Island," (with F. E. Gilliam), Royal Soc. of Canada, *Trans.*, IV (1910), § 2, 109, and "American Loyalists in Eastern Quebec," *ibid.*, VII (1913), § 2, 1, and "Loyalist Settlements on Gaspé," *ibid.*, VIII (1914), § 2, 399, and "Loyalists in Niagara Peninsula," *ibid.*, IX (1915), § 2, 79, and "Refugee Loyalists in Connecticut," *ibid.*, X (1916), § 2, 75, and *Flight of American Loyalists to British Isles* (1911); A. M. Davis, *Confiscation of John Chandler's Estate* (1903); S. E. Morison, "Property of Harrison Gray," Col. Soc. Mass., *Publ.*, XIV (1913), 320; F. W. C. Hersey, "Misfortunes of Dorcas Griffiths," *ibid.*, XXXIV (1943), 13; H. B. Yoshpe, *Disposition of Loyalist Estates in Southern District of New York* (1939); Oscar Zeichner, "Rehabilitation of Loyalists in Connecticut," *New Eng. Quar.*, XI (1938), 308, and "Loyalists Problem in New York after the Revolution," *N. Y. Hist.*, XXI (1940), 284.

Sources — "Proceedings of Commissioners on Loyalist Claims," Ontario Bureau of Archives, *Second Report* (2 vols., 1905); D. P. Coke, *Notes on Royal Commission on Losses and Services of American Loyalists* (H. E. Egerton, ed., 1915); Hawks and Perry, *Documentary History*; E. A. Jones, *Loyalists of Massachusetts, Memorials, Petitions and Claims* (1930); *Minutes of Committee for Detecting Conspiracies* (N.Y. Hist. Soc., *Coll.*, 2 vols., 1924–25); "Sufferings and Losses of Jolley Allen," Mass. Hist. Soc., *Proc.*, XVI (1878), 69–99; Jonathan Boucher, *View of Causes and Consequences of American Revolution* (1797), and *Reminiscences of an American Loyalist* (1925); David Fanning, *Narrative of Exploits as Loyalist of North Carolina* (1865); Alexander Chesney, *Journal* (E. A. Jones, ed., Ohio State Univ., *Bull.*, XXVI [1921], No. 4); Ward Chipman, "Diary," J. B. Berry, ed., Essex Inst., *Hist. Coll.*, LXXXVII (1951), 211; Curwen, *Journal and Letters;* Eddis, *Letters from America;* Joseph Galloway, *Candid Examination of Mutual Claims of Great Britain and Colonies* (1775), and *Claim of American Loyalists* (1788), and *Historical and Political Reflections on Rise and Progress of American Rebellion* (1780); Ann Hulton, *Letters of a Loyalist Lady* (1927); Thomas Hutchinson, *Strictures upon the Declaration* (1776), and *Diary and Letters;* E. L. Johnston, *Recollections of a Georgia Loyalist* (1901); James Moody, *Narrative of Exertions and Sufferings* (1783); Samuel Seabury, *Letters of a Westchester Farmer* (C. H. Vance, ed., Westchester Co. Hist. Soc., *Publ.*, VIII [1930]); Winthrop Sargent, ed., *Loyalist Poetry of Revolution* (1857), and *Loyal Verses of Joseph Stansbury and Dr. Jonathan Odell* (1860); W. O. Raymond, ed., *Winslow Papers* (1901); J. J. Talman, ed., *Loyalist Narratives from Upper Canada* (1946).

Bibliography — Winsor, *Narrative and Critical History*, VII, 185.

116. THE WAR OF INDEPENDENCE, 1776–1781

Summary — Administration: § 114; British and American strategy; organization of the armies, the regiment, battalion, legion, light infantry corps; Congress' attitude on enlistments and bounties; Washington's authority; methods of raising troops and procuring supplies; British recruiting and logistics difficulties; German mercenaries; French logistic aid prior to the Treaty; flags and weapons; Von Steuben and Army reorganization; other European volunteers: Lafayette, Duportail, Pulaski, Kosciuszko; Conway Cabal and other military intrigues against Washington; American generals, Gates, Green, Knox, Lincoln, Stirling, Sullivan; treason of Arnold and Charles Lee. — Campaigns and battles: Aug. 27, 1776, Long Island and retreat to Manhattan; Nov.–Jan., 1777, Jersey campaign, Trenton and Princeton; July–Oct., Howe transfers army to the Chesapeake; Brandywine and Germantown; Sept. 27, Howe occupies Philadelphia; 1777–78, Washington winters at Valley Forge; July–Oct., 1777, Northern Campaign, Oriskany, Bennington, Freeman's Farm,

Bemis Heights; Oct. 17, Burgoyne surrenders to Gates at Saratoga; June 1778, Philadelphia evacuated; July–Sept., Monmouth, Wyoming, Cherry Valley; Dec. 29, British take Savannah; 1778–79, G. R. Clark conquers Illinois country; 1779, Stony Point, American defeats at Savannah and the Penobscot, Sullivan defeats the Mohawks; 1780–81, Southern campaigns; May 12, 1780, British take Charleston; Aug. 16, Camden; Oct. 7, King's Mountain; Jan. 17, 1781, Cowpens; March 15, Guilford; Sept. 8, Eutaw. — Yorktown Campaign and naval operations (§ 118).

General — Channing, *History*, III, 210; Freeman, *Washington*, IV, chs. vi–xxiv; Miller, *Triumph of Freedom*, chs. viii–xiv, xx, xxiii–xxv; Frothingham, *Washington Commander in Chief*, 121; Wallace, *Appeal to Arms*; Trevelyan, *American Revolution*, II, III, IV, chs. xviii, xxiii, xxviii–xxxv, and *George III and Charles Fox*, I, chs. viii–ix, II, chs. x, xv–xvi, xxi; F. V. Greene, *Revolutionary War* (1911), chs. ii–vi; J. W. Fortescue, *History of the British Army* (1899–1930), III, chs. ix–xvii; H. B. Carrington, *Battles of American Revolution* (1876).

Special — L. C. Hatch, *Administration of American Revolutionary Army* (1904); W. L. Dorn, *Competition for Empire* (1940), ch. iii; C. K. Bolton, *Private Soldier under Washington* (1902); Allen Bowman, *Morale of American Revolutionary Army* (1943); Flick, *History of New York*, IV, ch. iv; J. W. Wright, "Notes on the Continental Army," *William and Mary Quar.*, XI (1931), 81, 185, and "Corps of Light Infantry," *Am. Hist. Rev.*, XXXI (1926), 454; J. G. W. Dillin, *Kentucky Rifle* (1924), ch. xiv; Felix Reichmann, "Pennsylvania Rifle," *Penn. Mag. Hist.*, LXIX (1945), 3; E. E. Curtis, *Organization of British Army in American Revolution* (1936); C. T. Atkinson, "British Forces in North America 1774–81," *Jour. Soc. Army Hist. Research*, XVI (London, 1937), 3, XIX (1940), 163; G. H. Guttridge, "Lord George Germain in Office," *Am. Hist. Rev.*, XXXIII (1928), 23; F. E. Schermerhorn, *American and French Flags of Revolution* (1948); E. J. Lowell, *Hessians in Revolution* (1884); Max von Eelking, *German Allied Troops in War of Independence* (J. G. Rosengarten, tr., 1893); Carl Van Doren, *Secret History of American Revolution* (1941), and *Mutiny in January* (1943); Knollenberg, *Washington and the Revolution*; Greene, *Nathanael Greene*; J. M. Palmer, *General von Steuben* (1937); T. S. Anderson, *Command of Howe Brothers* (1936); L. V. L. Naisawald, "Howe's Activities in South Carolina and Georgia," *Ga. Hist. Quar.*, XXXV (1951), 23; Malone, *Jefferson*, I, chs. xxiii–xxiv; Gottschalk, *Lafayette Joins American Army*; Boyd, *Light-Horse Harry Lee*; Alden, *General Charles Lee*; Hoffman Nickerson, *Turning Point of Revolution* (1928); Jane Clark, "Responsibility for Failure of Burgoyne Campaign," *Am. Hist. Rev.*, XXXV (1930), 542; A. H. Bill, *Campaign of Princeton* (1948), and *Valley Forge* (1952); W. S. Stryker, *Battle of Monmouth* (1927), and *Trenton and Princeton* (1898); McCrady, *South Carolina*, III, chs. xiv–xxxvii; B. J. Lossing, *Pictorial Field-Book of Revolution* (2 vols., 1851).

Sources — Washington, *Writings*, V–XX; Burnett, *Letters of Members of Continental Congress*, II–V; "Calendar of American Manuscripts in the Royal Institute," Historical Manuscripts Commission, *Reports* (4 vols., 1904–09); Henri Doniol, *Histoire de la participation de la France à l'établissement des États-Unis d'Amérique* (5 vols., 1886–92); Lafayette, *Mémoires*; John Sullivan, *Journals of Expedition against Six Nations* (1887), and "Letters and Papers"; Dearborn, *War Journals*; Henry Lee, *Memoirs of War in Southern Department* (R. E. Lee, ed., 1869); Jefferson, *Papers*, III–V; James Thacher, *Military Journal* (1827); Frederick MacKenzie, *Diary* (2 vols., 1930); William Moultrie, *Memoirs* (2 vols., 1802); Baroness F. C. L. von Riedesel, *Letters and Memoirs* (1827); R. W. Pettengill, ed., *Letters from America of Brunswick, Hessian and Waldeck Officers* (1924); Joel Shepard, "Autobiography," *New Eng. Quar.*, I (1928), 335, 476; Banastre Tarleton, *Campaigns* (1787), chs. i–iii; "Huntington Papers"; Carl Baurmeister, *Letters during the Philadelphia Campaign* (B. A. Uhlendorf and Edna Vosper, eds., 1937); James Murray, *Letters from America 1773–80* (Eric Robson, ed., 1951); Rush, *Letters*, I, 91.

Bibliography — Winsor, *Narrative and Critical History*, VI; R. G. Adams, *British Headquarters Maps and Sketches, a Descriptive List* (1928).

117. INTERNATIONAL ASPECTS OF THE REVOLUTIONARY ERA

Summary — 1775, debates on foreign relations in the Second Continental Congress, first mission to France. — 1776–77, Beaumarchais and secret French aid. — 1778, reasons for French change of policy; treaties of Alliance and Commerce; the Carlisle peace mission. — 1779–81, Franco-Spanish Alliance, Spain's relation to the war; western intrigues, Haldimand's negotiations with Vermont. — 1780, Netherlands and Armed Neutrality League. — 1781, Imperial Mediation. — 1781–82, Peace negotiations in Paris; question of credentials; impact of Adams and Jay; question of Vergennes' fairness; preliminary articles. — 1783, Treaty of Peace. — 1783–88, Foreign policy of R. R. Livingston. — British, French, and Dutch commercial policy toward the United States. — Impact of Canada on British policy. — Fisheries and the Western Posts. — Jefferson in France. — American negotiations with Netherlands, Austria, Sweden, Prussia, and Barbary States. — Influence of the Revolution on Ireland, England, and the British Empire. — Later developments (§ 128).

General — S. F. Bemis, *Diplomacy of American Revolution* (1935), and *Diplomatic History*, chs. ii–v; A. B. Darling, *Our Rising Empire 1763–1803* (1940), chs. i–v; Bailey, *Diplomatic History*, chs. ii–iv; Jensen, *New Nation*, ch. vii; E. S. Corwin, *French Policy and American Alliance* (1916); Bancroft, *United States*, IV, ch. xxiii, V, chs. x, xvi–xvii, xx–xxii, and (in "epoch v"), chs. i, v–vii; Lavisse, *Histoire de France*, IX, pt. 1, 91.

Special — Spain and the West: (§ 110); P. C. Phillips, *West in Diplomacy of American Revolution* (1913); Yela Utrilla, *España*, I; Whitaker, *Spanish-American Frontier*, chs. i–viii; Valentin Urtasun, *Historia Diplomática de América* (2 vols., 1920–24); S. F. Bemis, *Pinckney's Treaty* (1926), chs. i–v. ❧ Northern Powers and Armed Neutrality: Friedrich Edler, *Dutch Republic and American Revolution* (1911); P. J. van Winter, *Het Aandell van den amsterdamschen Handel aan den Opbouw van het amerikaansche Gemeenebest* (2 vols., 1927–33); Paul Fauchille, *La Diplomatie française et la ligue des neutres de 1780* (1893); A. B. Benson, *Sweden and American Revolution* (1926). ❧ British and Canadian Relations: Brown, *Empire or Independence*, chs. viii–x; Van Doren, *Secret History of Revolution*, chs. iii, iv; N. R. Einhorn, "Reception of the British Peace Offer of 1778," *Penn. Hist.*, XVI (1949), 191; A. L. Burt, *United States, Great Britain and British North America* (1940), chs. i–vi; Williamson, *Vermont in Quandary*, chs. vii–x; W. B. Kerr, *Bermuda and American Revolution* (1936); G. S. Graham, *British Policy and Canada 1774–91* (1930); Coupland, *American Revolution and British Empire*; D. M. Clark, *British Opinion and American Revolution* (1930); E. G. P. Fitzmaurice, *Life of Shelburne* (1875–76), III, chs. iv–vi; G. H. Guttridge, *David Hartley* (1926). ❧ French Relations: E. E. Hale, *Franklin in France* (2 vols., 1887); Van Doren, *Franklin*, chs. xx–xxiv; Wladimir d'Ormesson, *La Première mission officielle de la France aux États-Unis, C.-A. Gérard* (1924); J. J. Meng, *Comte de Vergennes, European Phases of His American Diplomacy* (1932); Kathryn Sullivan, *Maryland and France 1774–89* (1936), ch. iv; R. H. Lee, *Life of Arthur Lee* (2 vols., 1829); Malone, *Jefferson*, II, chs. i–viii; Wallace, *Laurens*, chs. xx–xxi, xxiv–xxv. ❧ Peace Negotiations: John Adams, *Works*, I; Winsor, *Narrative and Critical History*, VII, ch. ii; Monaghan, *Jay*. ❧ Miscellaneous Relations: Michael Kraus, "America and Irish Revolutionary Movement," R. B. Morris, ed., *Era of American Revolution* (1939), 332; E. C. Burnett, "Negotiations with Austria," *Am. Hist. Rev.*, XVI (1911), 567; Edmond Buron, "Statistics on Franco-American Trade," *Jour. Econ. and Bus. Hist.*, IV (1932), 571; Gaston Martin, "Commercial Relations between Nantes and the Colonies," *ibid.*, IV, 812; F. L. Nussbaum, "French Colonial Arrêt of 1784," *So. Atlantic Quar.*, XXVII (1928), 62; Henri Sée, "Commerce between France and United States," *Am. Hist. Rev.*, XXXI (1926), 732; J. S. Reeves, "Prussian-American Treaties," *Am. Jour. Int. Law*, XI (1917), 475; R. W. Irwin, *Diplomatic Relations of United States with Barbary Powers 1776–1816* (1931); H. R. Marraro, *Philip Mazzei, Virginia's Agent in France* (1935). ❧ Cultural Relations: Bernard Faÿ, *Revolutionary Spirit in France and America* (1927); Roland Thomas, *Richard Price* (1924); Richard Price, *Observations on Importance of American Revolution* (1784); Otto Vossler, *Die amerikanischen Revolutionsideale in ihrem Verhältnis zu den Europäischen* (1929).

Sources — Wharton, *Revolutionary Diplomatic Correspondence*; Henri Doniol, *Histoire de la participation de la France*, and "Le Ministère des affaires étrangères sous le Comte de Vergennes," *Revue d'Histoire Diplomatique*, VII (1893), 528; W. G. Leland and E. C. Burnett, eds., "Letters from Lafayette to Luzerne," *Am. Hist. Rev.*, XX (1915), 341, 576; "Calendar of Correspondence Politique, États-Unis," Public Archives of Canada, *Report*, 1912, 162, 1913, 152; C. A. Gérard, *Despatches and Instructions* (J. J. Meng, ed., 1939); Yela Utrilla, *España*, II; B. F. Stevens, ed., *Facsimiles of Manuscripts in European Archives Relating to America 1773–1783* (25 vols., 1889–95); George III, *Correspondence*, IV–VI; James Harris (Lord Malmesbury), *Diaries and Correspondence* (1845); I; "Landsdowne Manuscripts Calendar," Historical Manuscripts Commission, *Fifth Report*, 215; "Strachey Manuscripts Calendar," *ibid.*, *Sixth Report*, 399; Deane, "Papers"; J. B. Scott, ed., *Armed Neutralities of 1780 and 1800* (1918); John Adams, *Works*, II–III, VII–VIII; Franklin, *Writings*; Warren, *Warren-Adams Letters*; John and Abigail Adams, *Familiar Letters*; Jay, *Correspondence*, I–III; Jay, *Diary*; William Greene, "Diary, 1778," Mass. Hist. Soc., *Proc.*, LIV (1920), 84; "Carlisle Peace Mission Documents, Calendar," Historical Manuscripts Commission, *Fifteenth Report*, Appendix, pt. 6; Mereness, *Travels in American Colonies*, 569.

Bibliography — Bemis and Griffin, *Guide to Diplomatic History*, chs. i–iii; Winsor, *Narrative and Critical History*, VII, chs. i–ii.

118. NAVAL WARFARE AND THE YORKTOWN CAMPAIGN, 1775–1782

Summary — 1775, Oct. 13, birth of United States Navy; state navies. — 1776, March 3, Esek Hopkins takes Nassau; Oct. 11, Valcour Island on Lake Champlain. — 1777, loss of the *Delaware*; British blockade forces commerce destroying on American naval forces. — Privateering, its military and economic aspects. — Value of French, Spanish, and West Indies bases. — 1777–81, exploits of John Barry, Joshua Barney, Nicholas Biddle, Lambert Wickes, and J. P. Jones in British and American waters. — 1779, Sept. 23, Battle of Flamboro' Head. — French and British navies compared; French naval policy and the war; overriding interest in the West Indies. — 1778–79, Comte d'Estaing's fleet in American waters; fiasco off Newport, victories in West Indies, defeat at Savannah. — 1781, Rodney and Hood in West Indies, capture of St. Eustatius. — 1781, Yorktown Campaign; Cornwallis entrenches, Washington and Rochambeau move south, Aug. 29, De Grasse arrives at Chesapeake, Sept. 5, beats Graves off the Capes; Oct. 19, surrender of Cornwallis. — 1782, Apr. 12, Battle of the Saints; siege of Gibraltar lifted; British clean-up of American privateers.

General — Channing, *History*, III, 175, 308; Knox, *Naval Genius of Washington*; Frothingham, *Washington Commander in Chief*, 330; Lacour-Gayet, *Marine militaire sous Louis XVI*; Herbert Richmond, *Statesmen and Sea Power* (1946), 140; Mahan, *Influence of Sea Power*, chs. ix–xiii; Chappelle, *History of American Sailing Navy*, chs. i, ii; Graham, *Empire of North Atlantic*, ch. x.

Special — Major fleets and operations: G. W. Allen, *Naval History of American Revolution* (2 vols., 1913), and "Captain Hector McNeill," Mass. Hist. Soc., *Proc.*, LV (1922), 46; A. T. Mahan, *Major Operations of Navies in War of American Independence* (1913); W. M. James, *British Navy in Adversity, a Study of War of Independence* (1926); J. B. Perkins, *France in American Revolution* (1911), chs. viii, xiv, xix–xxi; W. L. Clowes, *Royal Navy* (1897–1903), III, chs. xxx–xxxi, IV, ch. xxxii; Vicomte A.M.R.A. de Noailles, *Marins et soldats français en Amérique* (1903); J. S. Corbett, "Signals and Instructions, 1776–1794," Navy Records Soc., *Publ.*, XXXV (1908); R. G. Usher, "Royal Navy Impressment during American Revolution," *Miss. Valley Hist. Rev.*, XXXVII (1951), 673; W. B. Willcox, "Rhode Island in British Strategy, 1780–81," *Jour. Modern Hist.*, XVII (1945), 304; Gershom Bradford, "Nelson in Boston Bay," *Am. Neptune*, XI (1951), 239; Albion, *Forests and Sea Power*, ch. vii; G. A. R. Callender, "With Grand Fleet in 1780," *Mariner's Mirror*, IX (1923), 258, 290; DeKoven, *John Paul Jones* (1913); W. B. Clark, *Lambert Wickes* (1932); R. D. Paine, *Joshua Barney* (1924); Joseph Gurn, *Commodore*

John Barry (1933); W. B. Clark, *Captain Dauntless: Story of Nicholas Biddle* (1949); M. V. Brewington, "Battle of Delaware Bay, 1782," U. S. Naval Inst., *Proc.*, LXV (1939), 231; Malcolm Lloyd, Jr., "Taking of Bahamas in 1776," *Penn. Mag. Hist.*, XLIX (1925), 349. ❧ Privateering: E. S. Maclay, *History of American Privateers* (1899), pt. 1; S. G. Morse, "State or Continental Privateers?" *Am. Hist. Rev.*, LII (1947), 68, and "Yankee Privateersman of 1776," *New Eng. Quar.*, XVII (1944), 71; O. T. Howe, "Beverly Privateers," Col. Soc. Mass., *Publ.*, XXIV (1922), 318; Howard, *Seth Harding*; J. F. Jameson, "St. Eustatius in Revolution," *Am. Hist. Rev.*, VIII (1903), 638; Hubertis Cummings, "Robert Morris and Polacre *Victorious*," *Penn. Mag. Hist.*, LXX (1946), 239; R. H. Stewart, *Virginia's Navy* (1933); L. F. Middlebrook, *History of Maritime Connecticut during Revolution* (2 vols., 1925); W. E. Davies, "Privateering around Long Island during Revolution," *N. Y. Hist.*, XX (1939), 283; J. D. Phillips, "Salem Revolutionary Privateers Condemned at Jamaica," Essex Inst., *Hist. Coll.*, LXXVI (1940), 46. ❧ Yorktown Campaign: H. F. Landers, *Virginia Campaign and Blockade and Siege of Yorktown* (1931); H. P. Johnston, *Yorktown Campaign* (1881); DeB. R. Keim, *Rochambeau* (1907); H. A. Larrabee, "Claude-Anne, Marquis de Saint-Simon," *Jour. des Américanistes*, XXIV (1932), 245; R. G. Adams, "View of Cornwallis' Surrender," *Am. Hist. Rev.*, XXXVII (1932), 25; C. L. Lewis, *Admiral de Grasse and American Independence* (1945); W. B. Willcox, "British Road to Yorktown," *Am. Hist. Rev.*, LII (1947), 1.

Sources — Major Operations and Yorktown Campaign: F. E. Chadwick, ed., *Graves Papers and Other Documents relating to Naval Operations of Yorktown Campaign* (1916); *Operations of French Fleet under Count de Grasse* (Bradford Club ser. No. 3, 1864); Samuel Hood, *Letters* (David Hannay, ed., 1895); C. M. Barham, *Letters and Papers* (J. K. Laughton, ed., 3 vols., 1907–11), I, 120; G. B. Rodney, *Letter-Books and Order-Book* (2 vols., 1932); K. J. Tornquist, *Naval Campaigns of Count de Grasse* (1787; Amandus Johnson, tr., 1942); J. B. Scott, *De Grasse à Yorktown* (1931); Count William Deux-Points, *Campaigns in America* (S. A. Greene, ed., 1868); de Fersen, *Lettres à son père*; J. B. D. de V., Comte de Rochambeau, *Mémoires* (2 vols., 1809), I, 237; J. E. Weelen, *Rochambeau* (1934); C. A., Marquis de Saint-Simon, "Journal," *Revue d'histoire diplomatique*, XLII (1928), 384, and "La Prise de Saint-Christophe," *Revue historique des Antilles*, I (1929), 17; William Feltman, *Journal* (1853); S. A. Harrison, *Memoir of Tench Tilghman, Containing His Journal* (1876); St. George Tucker, "Journal," *William and Mary Quar.*, V (1948), 375. ❧ Miscellaneous: C. O. Paullin, ed., *Out-Letters of Continental Marine Committee and Board of Admiralty* (2 vols., 1914); R. W. Neeser, ed., *Letters and Papers relating to Cruises of Gustavus Conyngham 1777–79* (1915); R. W. Neeser, ed., *Despatches of Molyneux Shuldham, Vice-Admiral of the Blue* (1913); Nathaniel Fanning, "Narrative" (1806), *Mag. of Hist.*, *Extra Numbers*, VI (1913), No. 21; J. S. Barnes, ed., *Logs of Serapis-Alliance-Ariel under Jones' Command* (1911); George Williams, "Revolutionary Letters to Timothy Pickering," Essex Inst., *Hist. Coll.*, XLII (1906), 313, XLIII (1907), 7, 199, XLIV (1908), 313, XLV (1909), 119, 286; Esek Hopkins, *Letter Book and Correspondence 1775–77* (1932); Nicholas Biddle, "Letters," W. B. Clark, ed., *Penn. Mag. Hist.*, LXXIV (1950), 348.

Bibliography — Winsor, *Narrative and Critical History*, VI, 589; Allen, *Naval History*, II, Appendix I; G. E. Manwaring, *Bibliography of British Naval History* (1929); Neeser, *Statistical and Chronological History*; Keim, *Rochambeau*, 607; C. H. Lincoln, *Naval Records of American Revolution* (1906); "H. H.," "Naval History, Admiral Mahan and His Successors," *Military Historian and Economist*, III (1918), 7; Pargellis and Medley, *Bibliography of British History*, ch. viii.

119. POLITICAL AND CONSTITUTIONAL HISTORY OF THE STATES, 1775–1788

Summary — 1776–83, State constitutions and governments. — Basic ideas; natural law, separation of powers, influence of Locke, Montesquieu and other publicists. — 1776, George Mason, the Virginia Bill of Rights, later bills of rights and their sources. — The Virginia pattern of legislative supremacy. — 1776, Franklin, Thomas Young, and the Pennsylvania unicameral constitution; the Pennsylvania anti-constitutionalists. — 1779,

J. M. Scott, John Jay, and the New York Constitution. — 1778–81, John Adams, the "Essex Result," and struggle for a constitution in Massachusetts; popular discussion and ratification. — Legal reforms in states. — Articles of Confederation and state finances (§ 121); social and economic movements (§ 120); western state making (§ 111).

General — Channing, *History*, III, ch. xiv; Allan Nevins, *American States during and after the Revolution* (1924), chs. ii–ix, xii–xiii; M. B. Macmillan, *War Governors in American Revolution* (1943).

Special — J. F. Jameson, *Introduction to Study of Constitutional and Political History of States* (1886), and *Essays in Constitutional History* (1889); W. C. Morey, "First State Constitutions," Am. Acad. Pol. and Soc. Sci., *Annals,* IV (1893), 201; T. F. Moran, *Rise and Development of Bicameral System in America* (1895). ❡ Political Theory: Georg Jellinek, *Declaration of Rights of Man* (Max Farrand, tr., 1901); B. F. Wright, *American Interpretations of Natural Law,* ch. vi, and "Origins of Separation of Powers in America," *Economica,* XIII (1933), 169; Gilbert Chinard, *Thomas Jefferson, Apostle of Americanism* (1929); Haraszti, *John Adams,* chs. ii, vii, viii; C. J. Friedrich, "Separation of Powers," and John Dickinson, "Checks and Balances," in *Encyclopaedia of Social Sciences*; Fernand Cattelain, *L'Influence de Montesquieu dans les constitutions américaines* (1927); J. P. Selsam and J. G. Rayback, "French Comment on the Pennsylvania Constitution of 1776," *Penn. Mag. Hist.,* LXXVI (1952), 311; P. M. Spurlin, *Montesquieu in America 1760–1801* (1940); R. E. Delmage, "American Idea of Progress, 1750–1860," Am. Philos. Soc., *Proc.,* XCI (1947), 309; Russell Smith, *Harrington and His Oceana,* ch. viii; F. L. Windolph, *Leviathan and Natural Law* (1951). ❡ Sectional and Personal Studies: Baldwin, *New England Clergy and the Revolution,* chs. x–xi; J. T. Adams, *New England in Republic,* ch. iv; Upton, *Revolutionary New Hampshire,* chs. iii–v, x–xiv; Williamson, *Vermont in Quandary,* chs. i–vi; Pell, *Ethan Allen;* C. M. Thompson, *Independent Vermont;* J. B. Wilbur, *Ira Allen* (1928), I, chs. ii–viii; Oscar and M. F. Handlin, *Commonwealth: Massachusetts 1774–1861* (1947), chs. i, ii; S. E. Morison, "Struggle over Adoption of Constitution of Massachusetts, 1780," Mass. Hist. Soc., *Proc.,* L (1917), 353; J. C. Meyer, *Church and State in Massachusetts* (1930), ch. iv; Brown, *Joseph Hawley,* chs. vi–ix; A. E. Morse, *Federalist Party in Massachusetts* (1909), ch. ii; R. J. Purcell, *Connecticut in Transition* (1918), ch. v; Field, *State of Rhode Island,* I, ch. xv; Fox, *Yankees and Yorkers,* chs. vi, vii; T. C. Cochran, *New York in Confederation* (1932); C. Z. Lincoln, *Constitutional History of New York* (5 vols., 1906), I, ch. ii; E. W. Spaulding, *New York in Critical Period 1783–1789* (1932); Flick, *History of New York,* IV, ch. v; McCormick, *Experiment in Independence: New Jersey;* Lincoln, *Revolutionary Movement in Pennsylvania,* chs. x–xvi; J. P. Selsam, *Pennsylvania Constitution of 1776* (1936); R. L. Brunhouse, *Counter-Revolution in Pennsylvania 1776–1790* (1942); Reed, *Life of Joseph Reed,* II; F. M. Green, *Constitutional Development in South Atlantic States 1776–1860* (1930), chs. i–iii; J. A. Silver, *Provisional Government of Maryland, 1774–1777* (1895); B. W. Bond, *State Government in Maryland, 1777–1781* (1905); H. J. Eckenrode, *Revolution in Virginia,* chs. v–ix, and *Separation of Church and State in Virginia* (1910); H. B. Grigsby, *Virginia Convention of 1776* (1855); Rowland, *George Mason,* I, chs. vii–x; Malone, *Jefferson,* I, chs. xvii–xxviii; Brant, *Madison,* I, chs. xii, xiii; *William and Mary Quar.,* VIII (Jan., 1951); Frank Nash, "North Carolina Constitution of 1776," *James Sprunt Hist. Publ.,* XI (1912), No. 2; Ashe, *History of North Carolina,* I, ch. xxxii; S. B. Weeks, *Church and State in North Carolina* (1893); McRee, *James Iredell,* I, chs. ix–xi; McCrady, *South Carolina,* III, chs. vi, x, xi, xiii, IV, chs. xxiv–xxv.

Sources — John Locke, *Second Treatise of Civil Government* (J. W. Gough, ed., 1946); C. L. de S., baron de Montesquieu, *Spirit of Laws* (1758); John Adams, *Works,* IV; Jefferson, *Papers,* II; King, *Rufus King,* I; Parsons, *Memoir of Theophilus Parsons,* 359; Poore, *Federal and State Constitutions*; Thorpe, *Federal and State Constitutions*; also, § 47.

Bibliography — Nevins, *American States,* 679.

120. ECONOMIC, SOCIAL, AND INTELLECTUAL MOVEMENTS

Summary — Impact of Independence on the American mind and character. — Influence on Europe. — Hostility to hereditary principle; the Society of the Cincinnati. — War economy (iron, clothing manufacture); development of new industries. — 1783–85, the depression; how extensive, and when did it end? — New lines of trade, to Russia, India, China. — Effect of the Revolution on religious sects. — Adjustment of Catholic, Anglican, and Presbyterian churches to independence. — Effects on slavery; slaves and free Negroes in the army; antislavery opinions of leaders; efforts to curb slave trade; abolition by judicial opinion in Massachusetts (Quaco and Mom Bet cases), gradual emancipation elswhere; Phyllis Wheatley. — Literature: Noah Webster's nationalism, Hartford Wits; Freneau, Hopkinson, and other poets, Royal Tyler and the drama; contemporary writers of memoirs; historians. — Colonial colleges during the war and their presidents (Stiles, Willard, Witherspoon); founding of new colleges, medical and law schools; natural sciences of the period; founding of learned societies; painting: Copley and West in England, John Trumbull and C. W. Peale. — Music (§ 103); political theory (§ 119).

General — Greene, *Revolutionary Generation*; Channing, *History*, III, ch. xviii; Curti, *Growth of American Thought*, chs. vi–vii; Jameson, *American Revolution as Social Movement*; Wish, *Society and Thought in America*, I, ch. vii; Michael Kraus, *Atlantic Civilization: Eighteenth Century Origins* (1949), and *Inter-colonial Aspects of American Culture on Eve of Revolution* (1928); James Schouler, *Americans of 1776* (1906); McMaster, *History*, I, chs. i–iv; Tyler, *Literary History of American Revolution*, I, chs. i, vii–ix, xix–xx, II, xxviii–xxxii, xxxiv, xxxvi, xxxvii, xxxix; Parrington, *Main Currents*, I, 248; Quinn, *Literature of American People*, chs. viii, x; Spiller, *Literary History*, I, chs. ix–xv.

Special — Nevins, *American States*, ch. x; Werner Stark, *America: Ideal and Reality: United States of 1776 in Contemporary European Philosophy* (1947); S. I. Pomerantz, "Patriot Newspaper and the American Revolution," Morris, *Era of American Revolution*; Winslow Warren, *Society of Cincinnati* (1929); E. E. Hume, "Early Opposition to Cincinnati," *Americana*, XXX (1936), 597; W. E. Davies, "Society of Cincinnati in New England," *William and Mary Quar.*, V (1948), 1. ❡ Economics: R. A. East, *Business Enterprise in American Revolutionary Era* (1938); Weeden, *Economic and Social History of New England*, II, chs. xx–xxiii; Kenneth Scott, "Price Control in New England during Revolution," *New Eng. Quar.*, XIX (1946), 453; Oscar and M. F. Handlin, "Revolutionary Economic Policy in Massachusetts," *William and Mary Quar.*, IV (1947), 3, and "Radicals and Conservatives in Massachusetts," *New Eng. Quar.*, XVII (1944), 343; Bruce, *Virginia Iron Manufacture*, ch. 1. ❡ Religion: W. W. Sweet, *Story of Religion*, chs. xii–xiii, and *Religion in Development of American Culture* (1952), chs. i–iii; W. P. Trent, "Constitution-Making in American Churches," Jameson, *Essays in Constitutional History*, ch. iv; Stokes, *Church and State*, I, chs. iv, v; E. F. Humphrey, *Nationalism and Religion in America, 1774–89* (1924); Brant, *Madison*, I, ch. xv; R. B. Semple, *Rise and Progress of Baptists in Virginia* (1810); Gewehr, *Great Awakening in Virginia*, chs. v–xi; Baldwin, "Sowers of Sedition"; S. M. Janney, *Religious Society of Friends* (1867), III, chs. xv–xvi, xviii; E. H. Gillett, *History of Presbyterian Church* (1864), chs. x–xiii; G. A. Koch, *Republican Religion* (1933), ch. i; Faÿ, *Revolutionary Spirit*, chs. ii–iii; Guilday, *John Carroll*, I, chs. v–xxiii; M. A. Ray, *American Opinion of Roman Catholicism* (1936), chs. vii–ix; A. J. Riley, *Catholicism in New England to 1788* (1936). ❡ Slavery and the Slave Trade: M. S. Locke, *Anti-Slavery Sentiment in America 1619–1808* (1901); J. R. Brackett, "Status of Slave, 1775–89," Jameson, *Essays in Constitutional History*, ch. v; W. E. B. DuBois, *Suppression of African Slave Trade* (1896), ch. v; Elizabeth Donnan, "New England Slave Trade after Revolution," *New Eng. Quar.*, III (1930), 251; G. H. Moore, *Notes on Slavery in Massachusetts* (1866). ❡ Arts, Letters, Education, Science: Warfel, *Noah Webster*; Zunder, *Joel Barlow*; Goodman, *Benjamin Rush*, chs. iii–vii; O. G. Sonneck, *Report on Yankee Doodle* (1909), and *Francis Hopkinson and James Lyon*; Hastings, *Francis Hopkinson* (1926); Phyllis Wheatley, *Poems and Letters* (C. F. Heartman, ed., 1915); Quinn, *History of American Drama*, chs. ii–iv; Willis, *Charleston Stage*, chs. iii–vii; Wertenbaker, *Princeton*, chs. ii–iii; Collins, *President Witherspoon*, I, chs. iv–vi,

II, i–iv; Richardson, *Dartmouth College*, chs. iii–iv; J. H. Easterby, *History of College of Charleston* (1935), chs. i, ii; G. C. Groce, *William Samuel Johnson*; J. E. Ford, *David Rittenhouse* (1946); Morison, *Three Centuries of Harvard*, 133; Edward Warren, *Life of John Warren*, M. D. (1874), chs. v–ix; Cowie, *John Trumbull*; B. N. Parker and A. B. Wheeler, *John Singleton Copley* (1938); Weir, *John Trumbull*; Theodore Sizer, *Works of Colonel John Trumbull* (1950); Sellers, *Charles Willson Peale*, I; Struik, *Yankee Science*, chs. ii–iv; Cohen, *Some Early Tools of American Science*.

Sources — Contemporary Histories of the Revolution: David Ramsay, *American Revolution* (2 vols., 1789), and *Revolution of South Carolina* (2 vols., 1785), and *History of South Carolina*; Hugh McCall, *History of Georgia* (1784; 2 vols., 1811–16; 1 vol., 1909); Hutchinson, *History of Massachusetts Bay*, III; Belknap, *History of New Hampshire*; L. S. Mayo, "Jeremy Belknap," *New Eng. Quar.*, II [1929], 183); G. R. Minot, *Continuation of History of Massachusetts Bay*, and *History of the Insurrections in Massachusetts* (1788); Edmund Randolph, "Essay on Revolutionary History of Virginia," *Va. Mag. Hist.*, LXIII (1935), 115, 209, 315, XLIV (1936), 35, 105, 223, 312, XLV (1937), 46; William Gordon, *History of Independence of United States* (4 vols., 1788; see: "William Gordon — Historian," *Mass. Hist. Soc., Proc.*, LXIII [1930], 303; O. G. Libby, "*Critical Examination of Gordon's History*," Am. Hist. Assoc., *Report*, 1899, I, 367); Warren, *History of American Revolution*; Isaac Backus, *History of New England, with Particular Reference to Baptists* (3 vols., 1777–96); Charles Stedman, *History of Origin, Progress, and Termination of American War* (2 vols., 1794); Filippo Mazzei, *Récherches historiques et politiques sur les États-Unis avec quatre lettres d'un Bourgeois* [Condorcet] *de New-Haven* (4 vols., 1788). ❡ Contemporary Memoirs of the Revolution: Graydon, *Memoirs*; Lee, *Memoirs of War*; Moultrie, *Memoirs*; W. H. Drayton, *Memoirs* (composed 1773–76, published by his son John, 2 vols., 1821); Grant, *Memoirs of an American Lady*; Margaret Coghlan, *Memoirs Interspersed with Anecdotes of Late American War* (2 vols., 1794). ❡ Other Sources: Stiles, *Literary Diary*, and *Itineraries*; Rush, *Letters*, I; St. Jean de Crèvecoeur, *Sketches of Eighteenth Century America* (1925), and *Letters from an American Farmer* (1782); Woolman, *Journal*; Cutler, *Manasseh Cutler*, I, chs. i–x; Bentley, *Diary*, I; Moore, *Songs and Ballads of American Revolution*; Freneau, *Poems*; Miranda, *Diary*; "Charles Bellini, First Professor of Modern Languages," *William and Mary Quar.*, V (1925), 1; J. D. Schoepf, *Travels in Confederation* (2 vols., 1911); Cresswell, *Journal 1774–1777*; Smyth, *Tour*; writings of Franklin, Jefferson, and John Adams (§ 55); Thornton, *Pulpit of American Revolution*; Charles Deane, ed., "Letters and Documents on Slavery in Massachusetts," *Mass. Hist. Soc., Coll.*, 5 ser., III (1877), 375.

Bibliography — Spiller, *Literary History*, III, 86.

121. CONFEDERATION, 1777–1788

Summary — 1777–81, Articles of Confederation, sources, amendments in Congress, struggle to ratify; influence of land question; cessions and ratification. — Nature of government; congressional committees and boards; forerunner of Supreme Court; ministers of finance and foreign affairs. — Western policy (also § 111); resolves of 1780, ordinances of 1784, 1785, 1787; influence of Ohio Company. — Interstate disputes and restrictive tariffs. — Dishonoring of congressional requisitions. — Proposed Amendments, the 5 per cent (1781) and import (1783) fail. — State and federal finances; war debts and currency, 1782–87; debtor-creditor conflict, stay and tender laws, "banks" of paper money, especially in Rhode Island. — 1782–87, Shays's Rebellion, its effect on the nationalist movement. — 1786–88, revival of trade in New England. — 1786, Annapolis Convention. — Foreign affairs (§ 117); social and economic movements (§ 120).

General — Channing, *History*, III, chs. xiii–xviii; MacLaughlin, *Foundations of American Constitutionalism*, and *Confederation and Constitution*, chs. iii–xi; Merrill Jensen, *Articles of Confederation* (1948), and *New Nation*; Fiske, *Critical Period of American History*; Bancroft, *United States*, VI.

Special — H. B. Dawson, "Motley Letter," *Hist. Mag.*, 2 ser., IX (1871), 157; Callender, *Selections from Economic History of United States*; C. A. Beard, *Economic Interpretation of Constitution* (1913), chs. ii–v; J. F. Jameson, "Predecessor of Supreme Court," *Essays in Constitutional History*, and "Old Federal Court of Appeal," Am. Hist. Assoc., *Papers*, III (1889), 383; E. C. Burnett, "Committee of States," Am. Hist. Assoc., *Report*, 1913, I, 141; St. G. L. Sioussat, "Luzerne and Ratification of Articles by Maryland," *Penn. Mag. Hist.*, LX (1936), 391; Elizabeth Cometti, "Civil Servants of Revolutionary Period," *ibid.*, LXXV (1951), 159; L. B. Dunbar, *Study of "Monarchical" Tendencies in United States 1776–1801* (1923). ❆ Territorial Policy: Philbrick, *Laws of Illinois Territory*, intro.; J. A. Barrett, *Evolution of Ordinance of 1787* (1891); P. J. Treat, *National Land System* (1910), ch. iii; H. B. Adams, *Maryland's Influence upon Land Cessions* (1885); Henry Tatter, "State and Federal Land Policy during Confederation Period," *Ag. Hist.*, IX (1935), 176. ❆ Trade Revival: Morison, *Maritime History*, chs. iii–vii; Phillips, *Salem and Indies*, chs. ii–iv; F. W. Howay, "Voyages of 'Columbia' to Northwest Coast 1787–90 and 1790–93," Mass. Hist. Soc., *Coll.*, LXXIX (1941). ❆ Finances, Federal and State: Dewey, *Financial History*, ch. ii; C. J. Bullock, *Finances of United States 1775–1789* (1895), and "Finances and Financial Policy of Massachusetts 1780–1905," Am. Econ. Assoc., *Publ.*, VIII (1907), 269; W. G. Sumner, *Financier* [Robert Morris] *and Finances of American Revolution* (2 vols., 1891); Oberholtzer, *Robert Morris*; King, *Rufus King*, I, chs. v–vi; F. G. Bates, *Rhode Island and Formation of Union* (1899), chs. iii–iv; E. R. Potter and S. S. Rider, *Paper Money of Rhode Island* (1880), chs. xii, xiii; Nettels, *Roots of American Civilization*, 673; E. J. Ferguson, "State Assumption of Federal Debt during Confederation," *Miss. Valley Hist. Rev.*, XXXVIII (1951), 403; R. V. Harlow, "Economic Conditions in Massachusetts," Col. Soc. Mass., *Publ.*, XX (1918), 163, and "Aspects of Revolutionary Finance," *Am. Hist. Rev.*, XXXV (1929), 46; W. B. Norton, "Paper Currency in Massachusetts during Revolution," *New Eng. Quar.*, VII (1934), 43; McCormick, *New Jersey in Critical Period*; W. F. Dodd, "Effect of Adoption of Constitution on Finances of Virginia," *Va. Mag. Hist. and Biog.*, X (1903), 360. ❆ Shays's Rebellion: J. T. Adams, *New England in Republic*, chs. v–vi; Holland, *History of Western Massachusetts*, I, chs. xvi–xviii; Jonathan Smith, *Some Features of Shays's Rebellion* (1903; reprinted, *William and Mary Quar.*, V [1948], 77); Morse, *Federalist Party in Massachusetts*, ch. iii; J. P. Warren, "Confederation and Shays Rebellion," *Am. Hist. Rev.*, XI (1905), 42; R. E. Moody, "Samuel Ely: Forerunner of Shays," *New Eng. Quar.*, V (1932), 105–34; W. A. Dyer, "Embattled Farmers," *ibid.*, IV (1931), 460; Handlin, *Commonwealth*, ch. ii; J. E. A. Smith, *Pittsfield*, I, chs. xxi, xxii:

Sources — J. B. Scott, *United States: Study in International Organization* (1920); Ford, *Journals of Continental Congress*; Burnett, *Letters of Members of Continental Congress*; Department of State, *Diplomatic Correspondence of United States, 1783–1789* (7 vols., 1833–34); Wharton, *Revolutionary Diplomatic Correspondence*; Madison, *Writings*, II, 361; Phineas Bond, "Letters," J. F. Jameson, ed., Am. Hist. Assoc., *Report*, 1896, I, 513, 1897, 454; Stephen Higginson, "Letters," J. F. Jameson, ed., *ibid.*, 1896, I, 704; Callender, *Selections from Economic History of United States*, 168; Morison, *Sources and Documents*, 178, 203; J. P. Warren, ed., "Documents relating to Shays Rebellion," *Am. Hist. Rev.*, II (1897), 693; E. F. Brown, ed., "Shays's Rebellion," *ibid.*, XXXVI (1931), 776; Minot, *History of Insurrections*.

122. FEDERAL CONVENTION AND RATIFICATION OF THE CONSTITUTION, 1787–1789

Summary — 1787, Feb. 21, call of Convention by Congress; choice of delegates; preconvention meeting, Randolph or Virginia plan; May 25–Sept. 17, Convention sits. — Procedure and methods. — Great or Connecticut Compromise; other compromises. — Economic motives and considerations; sectional divisions; judicial review. — Reasons for Mason, Gerry, and New York delegation voting against Constitution. — Dec., 1787–July, 1788, ratification in the states. — *Federalist* and other controversial writing. — Movement for a new convention thwarted. — Bills of Rights drafted. — 1789–90, North Carolina and Rhode Island ratify.

General — McLaughlin, *Confederation and Constitution*, chs. xii–xviii; Bancroft, *United States*, VI, pts. 3–5; McMaster, *History*, I, 436; Channing, *History*, III, ch. xvi; Carl Van Doren, *Great Rehearsal* (1948); Max Farrand, *Framing of Constitution* (1913); Charles Warren, *Making of Constitution* (1928); R. L. Schuyler, *Constitution of United States* (1923); Beard, *Economic Interpretation of Constitution*; Schlesinger, *New Viewpoints*, ch. viii; Fiske, *Critical Period of American History*, chs. vi, vii; Jensen, *New Nation*, ch. xx; Brant, *Madison*, III, chs. i–xvii; Edwin Mims, Jr., *Majority of People* (1941); Walton Hamilton and Douglass Adair, *Power to Govern* (1937); W. W. Crosskey, *Politics and Constitution* (2 vols., 1953).

Special — Libby, *Geographical Distribution of Vote*; Nevins, *American States*, ch. xiii; Beveridge, *John Marshall*, I, chs. ix–xii; J. B. Walker, *New Hampshire Convention 1788* (1888); S. B. Harding, *Contest over Ratification in Massachusetts* (1896); Handlin, "Radicals and Conservatives"; Bates, *Rhode Island and Formation of Union*; H. M. Bishop, "Why Rhode Island Opposed Federal Constitution," *R. I. Hist.*, VIII (1949), 33, 115; G. H. Hollister, *History of Connecticut* (1855), II, ch. xix; C. E. Miner, *Ratification of Federal Constitution in New York* (1921); J. B. McMaster and F. D. Stone, *Pennsylvania and Federal Constitution* (1888); B. C. Steiner, "Maryland's Adoption of Federal Constitution," *Am. Hist. Rev.*, V (1900), 22, 297; P. A. Crowl, "Anti-Federalism in Maryland," *William and Mary Quar.*, IV (1947), 446; Ambler, *Sectionalism in Virginia*, 53; Mays, *Edmund Pendleton*, II, chs. xiii–xvi; Hart, *Valley of Virginia*, chs. ix, x; L. I. Trenholme, *Ratification of Federal Constitution in North Carolina* (1932); J. H. Robinson, *Original and Derived Features of United States Constitution* (1890). ⊄ Judicial Review: C. A. Beard, *Supreme Court and Constitution* (1922); C. G. Haines, *American Doctrine of Judicial Supremacy* (1932); Boudin, *Government by Judiciary*, I; E. S. Corwin, *Doctrine of Judicial Review and Other Essays* (1914); J. B. Thayer, "Origin and Scope of American Doctrine of Constitutional Law," *Legal Essays* (1908). ⊄ Critiques of Beard: E. C. Barker, "Economic Interpretation of Constitution," *Texas Law Rev.*, XXII (1944), 373; Douglass Adair, "Tenth Federalist Revisited," *William and Mary Quar.*, VIII (1951), 48; Richard Hofstadter, "Beard and Constitution, History of an Idea," *Am. Quar.*, II (1950), 195; Latham, *Declaration of Independence and Constitution*.

Sources — Farrand, *Records of Federal Convention*; Dept. of State, Bur. of Rolls and Library, *Documentary History of Constitution*; Tansill, *Documents Illustrative of Formation of Union*; Elliot, *Debates*; P. L. Ford, ed., *Pamphlets on the Constitution of United States* (1888), and *Essays on Constitution* (1892); C. A. Beard, *Enduring Federalist* (1948); Madison, *Writings*, II–IV; Hamilton, *Works*, I, 413; King, *Rufus King*, I, 259, 311; George Bancroft, *History of the Formation of Constitution* (2 vols., 1882), II; H. E. Bourne, "Correspondence of Comte de Moustier with Comte de Montmorin," *Am. Hist. Rev.*, VIII (1903), 709, IX (1904), 86; Bond, "Letters"; Theodore Foster, *Minutes of Convention at South Kingston, Rhode Island 1790* (R. C. Cotner, ed., 1929).

Bibliography — P. L. Ford, *Pamphlets on Constitution*, 383; Winsor, *Narrative and Critical History*, VII, 255.

PART IV

National Growth, 1789–1865

Chapter Eleven

ESTABLISHMENT OF THE REPUBLIC

123. THE SOCIAL BACKGROUND, 1789-1820

Summary — Origins (§§ 103–4, 120). — Economic Growth: revival of trade, with Europe, China, West Indies; establishment of banking system (§ 125); insurance; speculation; origins of transportation system, turnpikes, steamships, canals; corporations (§ 125); extension of agriculture; beginnings of industry; immigration; labor (§ 128). — Cultural nationalism: education; the daily press; magazines; literature, Hartford Wits; theater; painting; architecture, federal, Greek revival. — Republican ideas: progress; perfectibility; conceptions of government; reaction to French revolution; conservatism. — Science: medicine; societies; Benjamin Silliman; chemistry; professional trends. — Religion: deism; unitarianism; Universalism; revivalism; the mission movement. — Humanitarian stirrings: temperance movement; slavery (§ 128). — Sectional aspects (§§ 140, 141). — Later developments (§§ 148–153).

General — J. A. Krout and D. R. Fox, *Completion of Independence* (1944), chs. i–xiv; Channing, *History*, IV, chs. i, iii, iv; McMaster, *History*, I, II; Henry Adams, *United States*, I, IX; Wish, *Society and Thought*, I, chs. viii–x; Curti, *Growth of American Thought*, chs. vi–xi; J. T. Adams, *New England in Republic*, chs. viii–x.

Special — Economic growth: East, *Business Enterprise*, ch. xiii; W. B. Smith and A. H. Cole, *Fluctuations in American Business* (1935); Anne Bezanson, *Wholesale Prices in Philadelphia* (1936); A. H. Cole, *Wholesale Commodity Prices* (1938); Meyer, *History of Transportation*, chs. i–v; Earle, *Stage-Coach and Tavern Days*; U. B. Phillips, *History of Transportation in Eastern Cotton Belt* (1908); J. A. Durrenberger, *Turnpikes* (1931); F. J. Wood, *Turnpikes of New England* (1919); Dunbar, *History of Travel*, I–III; Christopher Roberts, *Middlesex Canal* (1938); L. D. Baldwin, *Keelboat Age on Western Waters* (1941); C. H. Ambler, *History of Transportation in Ohio Valley* (1932); J. S. Davis, *Essays in Earlier History of American Corporations* (2 vols., 1917); Handlin, *Commonwealth*, chs. ii–vi, and "Origins of American Business Corporation," *Jour. Econ. Hist.*, V (1945), 1; E. R. Johnson, *History of Domestic and Foreign Commerce*, I, ch. xix, II, chs. xxii, xxiii; Frederick, *Development of American Commerce*, chs. v, vii; Spears, *Story of American Merchant Marine*, chs. vi–viii; W. L. Marvin, *American Merchant Marine* (1902), chs. iv–vi; Morison, *Maritime History*, chs. iv–xii; K. S. Latourette, "Early Relations between United States and China," Conn. Ac. Arts and Sci., *Trans.*, XXII (1917), 1; Dennett, *Americans in Eastern Asia*, chs. i–iii; Bradley, *American Frontier in Hawaii*, ch. i; Adele Ogden, *California Sea Otter Trade* (1941), chs. i–iv; F. R. Dulles, *Old China Trade* (1930), chs. i–ii; N. S. Buck, *Development of Anglo-American Trade* (1925); M. E. Martin, *Merchants and Trade of Connecticut Valley* (1939); Porter, *John Jacob Astor*, I; King, *Rufus King*, IV; V. S. Clark, *History of Manufactures*, chs. xi–xx; Tryon, *Household Manufactures*, chs. iv–vii; C. F. Ware, *Early New England Cotton Manufacture* (1931), ch. i; Bishop, *American Manufactures*, II, ch. i; White, *Samuel*

Slater, chs. i–iv; Cole, *American Wool Manufacture*, I; Bidwell and Falconer, *History of Agriculture in Northern United States*, chs. xi–xii; H. F. Wilson, *Hill Country*, ch. i; U. P. Hedrick, *History of Agriculture in State of New York* (1933), chs. v–xi; Gray, *History of Southern Agriculture*, I, chs. xix–xxiv, II, chs. xxv–xxxv; S. I. Pomerantz, *New York 1783–1803* (1938); § 141. ❡ Cultural Nationalism: education (§ 141); Warfel, *Noah Webster*; Shoemaker, *Noah Webster*; Spiller, *Literary History*, I, chs. ix–xxii; Trent, *Cambridge History of American Literature*; Parrington, *Main Currents*, II; Leary, *Freneau*; Ellis, *Joseph Dennie*; Godwin, *Bryant*; William Dunlap, *Life of Charles B. Brown* (2 vols., 1815); H. M. Jones, *America and French Culture* (1927), chs. x–xiii; Leon Howard, *Connecticut Wits* (1942); H. R. Brown, *Sentimental Novel in America* (1940), chs. i–vi; biographies and writings of Washington Irving, J. F. Cooper (§§ 54–6); Lehmann-Haupt, *Book in America*, 84; C. R. Nichols, *Isaiah Thomas* (1912); M. W. Hamilton, *Country Printer* (1936); Quinn, *History of American Drama*, I, chs. iii–viii; William Dunlap, *History of American Theatre* (1832); Hornblow, *History of Theatre*, I, chs. viii–xii; Mott, *American Journalism*, chs. vi–viii; R. W. Jones, *Journalism in the United States* (1947), chs. xvii–xxiv; Nevins, *Evening Post*, chs. i–iv; Andrews, *Pittsburgh's Post-Gazette*, ch. i; Mott, *History of American Magazines*, I, pts. 1, 2; Larkin, *Art and Life in America*, pt. 2; William Dunlap, *History of the Arts of Design* (1834; F. W. Bayley and C. E. Goodspeed, eds., 3 vols., 1918), I, II; Oskar Hagen, *Birth of American Tradition in Art* (1940); Barker, *American Painting*, chs. xxx–xl; Isham, *American Painting*, chs. v–x; G. C. Mason, *Life and Works of Gilbert Stuart* (1879); Mabee, *American Leonardo*, chs. i–xii; Wehle, *American Miniatures*; A. T. Gardner, *Yankee Stonecutters* (1945); I. T. Frary, *Thomas Jefferson, Architect* (1931); Place, *Charles Bulfinch*; Aymar Embury, *Asher Benjamin* (1917); T. F. Hamlin, *Greek Revival Architecture* (1944); Howard, *Our American Music*, chs. v–vi. ❡ Ideas: D. J. Boorstin, *Lost World of Thomas Jefferson* (1948); G. A. Koch, *Republican Religion*; Adrienne Koch, *Philosophy of Thomas Jefferson* (1943); Dorfman, *Economic Mind*, I, chs. xiii–xviii; Mudge, *John Taylor*; Parsons, *Theophilus Parsons*; C. D. Hazen, *Contemporary American Opinion of French Revolution* (1897); E. P. Link, *Democratic Republican Societies* (1942); W. T. Utter, "Saint Tammany in Ohio," *Miss. Valley Hist. Rev.*, XV (1928), 321; Ludlum, *Social Ferment in Vermont.* ❡ Science: W. M. and Mabel Smallwood, *Natural History and American Mind* (1941); Struik, *Yankee Science*; Fisher, *Benjamin Silliman*; Holt, *Priestley*, chs. xi, xii; E. F. Smith, *Priestley in America*, and *James Woodhouse* (1918); Herrick, *Audubon*; G. L. Vose, *Sketch of Loammi Baldwin* (1885); Goodman, *Benjamin Rush*; Hall, *S. L. Mitchell*; Alexander Young, *Discourse on Nathaniel Bowditch* (1838); J. W. Harshberger, *Botanists of Philadelphia* (1899); R. H. Shryock, *Development of Modern Medicine* (1947), chs. ii–ix; H. B. Shafer, *American Medical Profession* (1936). ❡ Religion: Albert Post, *Popular Free Thought in America* (1943); H. M. Morais, *Deism in Eighteenth Century America* (1934); N. H. Sonne, *Liberal Kentucky* (1939); John and J. S. Murray, *Life of Rev. John Murray* (1870); Richard Eddy, *Universalism in America* (1884–86), I; F. H. Foster, *Genetic History of New England Theology* (1907); Vernon Stauffer, *New England and the Bavarian Illuminati* (1918); J. K. Morse, *Jedidiah Morse* (1939); Stephen West, *Sketches of Samuel Hopkins* (1805); Cunningham, *Timothy Dwight*; Malone, *Thomas Cooper*; Thomas Belsham, *Memoirs of Theophilus Lindsay* (1872), ch. ix; W. W. Sweet, *Religion on American Frontier* (1931–39), I, and *Revivalism in America* (1944), 119; F. M. Davenport, *Primitive Traits in Religious Revivals* (1905); C. C. Cleveland, *Great Revival in West* (1916); Gewehr, *Great Awakening in Virginia*; Haroutuinian, *Piety vs. Moralism*; Sellers, *Lorenzo Dow*; C. R. Keller, *Second Great Awakening in Connecticut* (1942); D. R. Fox, "Protestant Counter-Reformation," *N. Y. Hist.*, XVI (1935), 19; E. B. Greene, "Puritan Counter-Reformation," *Am. Antiq. Soc., Proc.*, XLII (1932), 17; Guilday, *John Carroll*, II; § 141. ❡ Humanitarianism: Krout, *Origins of Prohibition*, ch. i; (§ 152).

Sources — Writings of John Adams, Jefferson, Hamilton, Paine (§ 55); Ames, *Works*, I; Bentley, *Diary*; Rush, *Letters*, and *Autobiography*; Finney, *Memoirs*; Trumbull, *Autobiography*; *Niles' Weekly Register* (1811–20); *Port Folio* (1801–15); *North Am. Rev.* (1815–20); *Am. Medical Recorder* (1818–20); *Medical Repository* (1797–1820); *New Eng. Jour. of Medicine and Surgery* (1812–20); Newspapers (§ 53); W. W. Sweet, *Congregationalists* (1939); Knight, *Documentary History of Education*, II, III, chs. i–iii;

M. J. Moses and J. M. Brown, *American Theatre* (1934), 21; Samuel Breck, *Recollections* (1877); La Rochefoucauld-Liancourt, *Voyage*; Handlin, *This Was America*, pt. 1; William Priest, *Travels* (1802); Faux, *Memorable Days*; Dwight, *Travels*.

Bibliography — Bidwell and Falconer, *History of Agriculture*, 454, 462; Mott, *American Journalism*, 163; Krout and Fox, *Completion of Independence*, 430.

124. ORGANIZATION OF THE THREE DEPARTMENTS OF GOVERNMENT, 1789–1793

Summary — Precedents: English (§ 77); colonial government (§ 102); state governments (§ 119); Continental Congress (§ 121); writers on political theory (§ 123). — Preliminaries: 1788–89, first national elections; place of meeting. — Legislative department: 1789, Apr. 1, 6, the two houses organized; question of instructions; salaries; relations with the president; relations with the cabinet; speaker; committees; leaders. — Executive department: 1789, Apr. 30, inauguration of Washington; question of title; ceremonies; salary; appointments; question of removal of officers; 1792, first veto; 1796, question of submitting papers. — Executive heads: practice of the Confederation; creation of heads of departments; the cabinet; patronage; opinions and discussions. — Judiciary: previous federal courts (§ 121); 1789, Sept. 24, judiciary act; supreme court; inferior courts; attorney-general; appointments of judges; questions of appeal jurisdiction; extra-judicial opinions; 1793, Chisholm v. Georgia.

General — (§ 123); L. D. White, *Federalists* (1948); L. M. Short, *Development of National Administrative Organization* (1923); James Hart, *American Presidency in Action 1789* (1948); C. P. Patterson, *Presidential Government in United States* (1947); F. F. Stephens, *Transitional Period, 1788–1789* (1909); C. K. Burdick, *Law of Constitution* (1926), chs. iv–vi; A. N. Holcombe, *Our More Perfect Union* (1950); Swisher, *American Constitutional Development*, chs. iii–vi; Hockett, *Constitutional History of United States*, I, chs. xii–xiv; E. S. Corwin, *Constitution and What It Means Today* (1948); H. W. Horwill, *Usages of American Constitution* (1925); J. S. Bassett, *Federalist System* (1906), ch. i; Dunbar, *"Monarchical" Tendencies*, ch. vi; L. K. Caldwell, *Administrative Theories of Hamilton and Jefferson* (1944); J. Q. Adams, *Jubilee of Constitution* (1839); general histories of Channing, McMaster (§ 59); biographies of Washington, Jefferson, Hamilton (§ 54); McLaughlin and Hart, *Cyclopedia of American Government*, by subjects; J. T. Adams, *Album of American History*, II, chs. i, ii; D. M. Matteson, "Organization of Government," U. S. Constitution Sesquicentennial Commission, *Formation of the Union under the Constitution* (1941), 141.

Special — Legislative Department: R. V. Harlow, *History of Legislative Methods before 1825* (1917); D. S. Alexander, *History and Procedure of House of Representatives* (1916); L. G. McConachie, *Congressional Committees* (1898); M. P. Follett, *Speaker* (1896); G. H. Haynes, *Senate* (1938); C. H. Kerr, *Origin and Development of United States Senate* (1895); Samuel Oppenheim, *Early Congressional Debates and Reporters* (1889); J. R. Hayden, *Senate and Treaties 1789–1817* (1920), chs. i–iv. ⁋ Executive Department: E. S. Corwin, *President, Office and Powers* (1948), and *President's Removal Power* (1927), and *President's Control of Foreign Relations* (1917); W. E. Binkley, *Powers of President* (1937), chs. i–ii; Milton, *Use of Presidential Power*; C. C. Thach, *Creation of Presidency, 1775–1789* (1922); R. W. Griswold, *Republican Court* (1855); C. A. Berdahl, *War Powers of Executive* (1921); H. B. Learned, *President's Cabinet* (1912); M. L. Hinsdale, *President's Cabinet* (1911); Jameson, *Essays in Constitutional History*, No. 3; L. F. Schmeckebier, *Customs Service* (1924); Cummings and McFarland, *Federal Justice*; G. D. Harmon, *Sixty Years of Indian Affairs* (1941); W. E. Rich, *History of the Post Office to 1829* (1924); F. W. Powell, comp., *Control of Federal Expenditures* (1939); Gaillard Hunt, *Department of State* (1914), and "Office Seeking," *Am. Hist. Rev.*, I (1896), 270, II (1897), 241; L. C. Hatch, *History of Vice-Presidency* (1934), chs. i–ix; J. B. McMaster, *With the Fathers* (1896), 150; Monaghan and Lowenthal, *This Was New York*. ⁋ Judiciary: Hurst, *Growth of American Law*, ch. vi; S. E. Baldwin, *American Judiciary* (1905), ch. ix; Charles Warren, *Supreme Court*, I, chs. i–iii, and *Congress*,

Constitution, and Supreme Court (1930), and "Judiciary Act of 1789," *Harvard Law Rev.*, XXXVII (1923), 49; Henry Flanders, *Lives and Times of Chief Justices* (1875), I, chs. xiv–xvi; Monaghan, *John Jay*, ch. xv; Brown, *Oliver Ellsworth*, chs. v, vi; McRee, *James Iredell*, II, chs. xxiii–xxxii; § 143.

Sources — Debates: *Annals of Congress*, I–III; T. H. Benton, *Abridgment of Debates of Congress, 1789–1856* (16 vols., 1857–61), I; Elliot, *Debates*, IV, 343; Thomas Lloyd, *Congressional Register of Debates of First House (1789–1790)* (1792); Maclay, *Journal*; John Adams, *Works*, III, 407. ❡ Official Documents: *Statutes at Large*, I; *Annals of Congress*, II, III; *Am. State Papers, Misc.*, I; Richardson, *Messages and Papers*, I, 42, 64, 81, 103; Allen Johnson, ed., *Readings in Constitutional History* (1912), chs. xvi–xxiii. ❡ Contemporary Writings: Washington, *Writings*, XXX–XXXVI and *Diaries*, IV; Jefferson, *Writings*, VIII, IX; Hamilton, *Works* (Lodge, ed.), II; Madison, *Writings*, V, 248; Fisher Ames, *Works*, I, and *Speeches in Congress* (1871); King, *Rufus King*, I, chs. xix, xx; Jared Sparks, *Life of Gouverneur Morris* (1832), III, 363; Jay, *Correspondence*, III, 363; Steiner, *James McHenry*, chs. viii–x.

Bibliography — Winsor, *Narrative and Critical History*, VII, 299, 323; Bassett, *Federalist System*, ch. xx; Burchfield, *Student's Guide to Materials in Political Science*.

125. FINANCIAL AND COMMERCIAL QUESTIONS, 1789–1797

Summary — Financial situation in 1789 (§§ 119, 121). — Revenue: 1789, July 4, first tariff act; tonnage duties and other revenues; 1790–1800, increases in tariff. — Debt: 1790, Jan. 14, Hamilton's report on public credit; question of funding; foreign debt; domestic debt. — Assumption of state debts: question of site of national capital; Jefferson's compromise; protests. — Expenditures. — Bank of the United States: banking (§ 121); 1790, Dec. 14, Hamilton's report; 1791, Feb., question of constitutionality (§ 143); Feb. 25, act approved; successful operation of the bank; State banks. — Financial progress (§§ 149, 155). — Commerce: (§ 121); registry of shipping; bounties; coasting trade; lighthouses; entry and clearance; consuls. — Business: coinage; copyright; patents; report on manufactures; post office. — Criticism of the Treasury: funding; 1793, Giles resolutions; 1795, Jan. 31, Hamilton retires. — Whisky Rebellion: 1791, Mar. 3, first excise; 1792, May 8, revision; violence; May 2, act for summoning militia; 1794, July, armed outbreak; Aug. 7, president's proclamation; Oct., military expedition; 1795, Feb. 28, second act for summoning militia; treason trials; pardons; Washington on "self-constituted societies"; later taxation troubles (§ 156).

General — Channing, *History*, IV, chs. iii, iv, 138; C. G. Bowers, *Jefferson and Hamilton* (1936), chs. iii–ix; Bassett, *Federalist System*, chs. ii–vii; Dewey, *Financial History*, chs. iv, v; A. S. Bolles, *Financial History* (1879–86), Bk. 1, chs. i–xi; Lodge, *Alexander Hamilton*, chs. v, vi; Schachner, *Alexander Hamilton*, chs. xix–xxii; W. G. Sumner, *Alexander Hamilton* (1890), chs. x–xiii; J. C. Hamilton, *Alexander Hamilton* (1834–40); H. C. Lodge, *George Washington* (1898), 110; W. C. Rives, *History of the Life and Times of James Madison* (1868–73), III, 447; Brant, *James Madison*, III, chs. xix–xxviii; King, *Rufus King*, I, chs. xix–xxii; Henry Adams, *Albert Gallatin*, Bk. 2, 86; Malone, *Jefferson*, II, chs. xxiii–xxviii; George Tucker, *Thomas Jefferson* (1837), I, chs. xiii–xvi; George Gibbs, *Memoirs of the Administrations of Washington and Adams* (1846), I, chs. ii, iii, vi, vii, x, xiii. See also: the general histories, McMaster, Schouler (§ 59).

Special — Tariff: Stanwood, *Tariff Controversies*, I, chs. iii, iv; Sumner, *Financier and Finances*, II, chs. xxxi, xxxii; William Hill, *First Stages of Tariff Policy* (1893), ch. iv; Harold Hutcheson, *Tench Coxe* (1938). ❡ Government Finance: Ratner, *American Taxation*, chs. i, ii; B. U. Ratchford, *American State Debts* (1941), ch. iii. ❡ Banking: J. T. Holdsworth, *First Bank of United States* (1910); J. O. Wettereau, "New Light on First Bank," *Penn. Mag. of Hist.*, LXI (1937), 263, and "Branches of First Bank," *Jour. Econ. Hist.*, II (1942), 66; E. R. Taus, *Central Banking Function of United States Treasury* (1943), ch. i; W. G. Sumner, *History of Banking in All Nations* (1896), I, ch. iii; B. A. Konkle, *Thomas Willing* (1937), chs. xv–xviii; Fritz Redlich, *Molding of American*

Banking (1947–51), I, chs. ii, iii; H. E. Miller, *Banking Theories before 1860* (1927), chs. i–vii; D. R. Dewey, *State Banking before the Civil War* (1910); J. S. Davis, *Essays in the Earlier History of American Corporations*, II, ch. ii; Handlin, *Commonwealth*, chs. iv, v; N. S. B. Gras, *Massachusetts First National Bank* (1937), chs. i–v; Louis Hartz, *Economic Policy and Democratic Thought* (1948), Pt. 2, ch. ii. ❡ Currency: A. B. Hepburn, *History of Currency* (1915), ch. v; J. L. Laughlin, *History of Bimetalism* (1900), ch. ii; Director of Mint, *Report*, 1895, 116. ❡ Other Commercial Regulations: V. G. Setser, *Commercial Reciprocity Policy of United States, 1774–1829* (1937), ch. iv; G. A. Weber, *Patent Office* (1924), ch. i; L. W. Maxwell, *Discriminating Duties and American Merchant Marine* (1926), chs. i–v. ❡ National Capital: Bryan, *National Capital*, I, chs. i–vi. ❡ Whisky Rebellion: L. D. Baldwin, *Whiskey Rebels* (1939); R. J. Ferguson, *Early Western Pennsylvania Politics* (1938), ch. v; Buck, *Planting of Civilization in Western Pennsylvania*, ch. xix. ❡ Maps: Paullin, *Atlas*, plates 112 A, 112 B.

Sources — Debates: *Annals of Congress*, I–VI; Benton, *Abridgment*, I; Lloyd, *Congressional Register*. ❡ Official Documents: *Statutes at Large*, I; *Annals of Congress*, II–VI, Apps.; *American State Papers, Finance*, I, *Post Office*, I, *Claims*, I, *Commerce*, I, *Misc.*, I; 28 Cong., 1 sess., *H. Ex. Doc.*, II, No. 15. ❡ Collections of Documents: Hazard, *Pennsylvania Archives*, 2 ser., IV; William Findley, *History of Insurrection in Western Pennsylvania* (1796); Francis Wharton, *State Trials* (1849), 102; Dallas, A. J. Dallas, 29, 149; Hart, *American History Told by Contemporaries*, III, §§ 76, 78, 80, 82; MacDonald, *Select Documents*, Nos. 6, 8–11; C. F. Dunbar, *Laws Relating to Currency* (1897), 7; National Monetary Commission, *Laws Concerning Money* (1910), 3, 269, 474; Richardson, *Messages and Papers*, I, 124, 158, 179. ❡ Contemporary Writings: Hamilton, *Works* (Hamilton, ed.), III–V, VI, 632, and (Lodge, ed.), II, III, V, 471, VI, 3, and *Industrial and Commercial Correspondence*; Felix Flügel, *Documents Relating to American Economic History* (1929); Gallatin, *Writings*, I, III; Washington, *Writings*, XXX–XXXVI; Maclay, *Journal*, chs. ii, v–xi, xiv; Madison, *Writings*, V, 339, VI; Jefferson, *Writings*, III, VII, IX.

Bibliography — P. L. Ford, *Bibliotheca Hamiltoniana* (1896); Winsor, *Narrative and Critical History*, VII, 308, 328; A. P. C. Griffin, *List of Works Relating to First and Second Banks* (1908); H. B. Meyer and W. A. Slade, comps., *Select List of References on Monetary Question* (1913), 116; Dewey, *Financial History*, §§ 33, 42; Larned, *Literature of American History*, 319; Setser, *Commercial Reciprocity Policy*, 261; Hepburn, *History of Currency*, 479; Baldwin, *Whiskey Rebels*, 305; U. S. Tariff Commission, *Tariff*.

126. DOCTRINE OF IMPLIED POWERS

Summary — Constitution (§ 122): general clauses; "necessary and proper" clause. — Bank question: 1791, Feb., question of constitutionality; opinions of the cabinet. — Doctrines of powers of Congress: "implied powers"; "resulting powers"; "sovereignty of Congress." — Applications: 1789, protection (§ 125); 1791, bank (§ 125); later applications (§§ 134, 143).

General — Burdick, *Law of Constitution*, ch. vi, § 59; T. M. Cooley, *General Principles of Constitutional Law* (1880), ch. iv, § 15; W. W. Willoughby, *Constitutional Law* (1929), §§ 45–75; A. V. Dicey, *Introduction to the Study of Law of Constitution* (1889; 1939), ch. iii; Warren, *Supreme Court*, I, ch. xii; Beveridge, *John Marshall*, IV, ch. vi.

Special — Joseph Story, *Commentaries on Constitution* (2 ed., 1851), 430, 497, 638, 910, 1236, 1329; James Kent, *Commentaries on American Law* (1826–30; 1884), I, lect. 12; J. R. Tucker, *Constitution* (1899), §§ 179–183, 222–234, 248, 249, 294; J. N. Pomeroy, *Introduction to Constitutional Law* (1888), §§ 259–269; McLaughlin and Hart, *Cyclopedia of American Government*, by subject.

Sources — Notable Cases: M'Culloch *v.* Maryland (1819), 4 *Wheaton* 316; Martin *v.* Hunter's Lessee (1816), 1 *Wheaton* 304; "Legal Tender Cases" (1871), 12 *Wallace*

457; — *In re* Neagle (1890), 135 *United States* 1; Juilliard *v.* Greenman (1884), 110 *United States* 421; Fong Yue Ting *v.* United States (1893), 149 *United States* 698; Kansas *v.* Colorado (1907), 206 *United States* 46; (§ 45). ❡ Collections of Cases: Evans, *Cases*, ch. i, §§ 4, 5; J. B. Thayer, *Cases on Constitutional Law* (1894–95), 123, 271, 335, 343, 1346 n., 1799, 2237, 2255. ❡ Contemporary Discussions: Hamilton, *Works* (Hamilton, ed.), IV, 103, (Lodge, ed.), III, 179; Jefferson, *Writings*, VII, 555; Madison, *Writings*, IX, 411; M. S. Clarke and D. A. Hall, *Legislative and Documentary History of Bank of United States* (1832), 85.

Bibliography — Burdick, *Law of Constitution*, § 59; Evans, *Cases*, 87 n.

127. POLITICAL PARTIES, 1789–1793

Summary — Origin of parties: colonial (§ 102); Revolutionary patriots and Tories (§§ 109, 115); 1783–88, factions in Congress (§ 121); 1787–89, Federalists and Anti-Federalists (§ 124); state parties. — 1788–89, first national elections; 1789–92, genesis of parties in Congress; in the cabinet. — 1793, Republican and Federalist parties forming; effect of the French Revolution (§ 123); "Democrats"; "British party"; "monarchical faction"; "corrupt treasury squadron."

General — Binkley, *American Political Parties*, chs. i–iii; E. E. Robinson, *American Political Parties* (1924), chs. iii, iv; Alexander Johnston and J. A. Woodburn, *American Political History* (1912), I, ch. xi; W. O. Lynch, *Fifty Years of Party Warfare* (1931), ch. i; Malone, *Jefferson*, II, chs. xxiii–xxviii; Lodge, *George Washington*, II, ch. v, and *Alexander Hamilton*, 72, 134; Sumner, *Alexander Hamilton*, chs. ix, xii; Schachner, *Alexander Hamilton*, chs. xvii–xx; Randall, *Thomas Jefferson*, I, ch. xv, II, chs. i–iii; Brant, *James Madison*, III, chs. xxii–xxviii; Anderson, *William Branch Giles*, ch. ii; Austin, *Elbridge Gerry*, II, ch. iv; Brown, *Oliver Ellsworth*, 223; Stanwood, *Presidency*, I, chs. i–iii; McLaughlin and Hart, *Cyclopedia of American Government*, by subjects; general histories of Channing, McMaster, Schouler (§ 59).

Special — C. A. Beard, *Economic Origins of Jeffersonian Democracy* (1915), chs. iii–ix; Bowers, *Jefferson and Hamilton*, chs. iii–ix; G. D. Luetscher, *Early Political Machinery* (1903); Harlow, *Legislative Methods before 1825*, chs. viii, ix; O. G. Libby, "Political Factions in Washington's Administrations," University of North Dakota, *Quar. Jour.*, III (1913), 293; Gibbs, *Administrations of Washington and John Adams*, I, chs. ii–iv; S. E. Forman, *Political Activities of Freneau* (1902), ch. iii; Link, *Democratic-Republican Societies*; W. A. Robinson, *Jeffersonian Democracy in New England* (1916), ch. i; Morse, *Federalist Party in Massachusetts*, ch. v; Alexander, *Political History of New York*, I, chs. v, vi; M. I. Ostrogorski, *Democracy and Organization of Political Parties* (1908), II, 3; Martin Van Buren, *Inquiry into Origin of Political Parties* (1867), chs. ii, iv; Merriam, *American Political Theories*, 122; Hazen, *American Opinion of French Revolution*.

Sources — Debates: *Annals of Congress*, I–III; Benton, *Abridgment*, I. ❡ Contemporary Writings: Hamilton, *Works* (Hamilton, ed.), IV, V, VII, (Lodge, ed.), VI, VIII; Jefferson, *Writings* (Liscomb and Bliss, eds.), III, 359, IX, 87, (Ford, ed.), I, 154, V, 328, VI; John Adams, *Works*, VI, VIII; Warren, "Warren-Adams Letters," LXXIII; Abigail Adams, *New Letters;* Washington, *Writings* (Fitzpatrick ed.), XXX–XXXIII; Madison, *Writings*, VI, 46; Henry, *Patrick Henry*, III, 387; King, *Rufus King*, I, chs. xxiii, xxiv; Hamilton, *Alexander Hamilton*, IV, chs. lx, lxxi–lxxvi; "South Carolina Federalist Correspondence," *Am. Hist. Rev.*, XIV (1909), 776; Hart, *American History Told by Contemporaries*, III, ch. xiii.

Bibliography — Burchfield, *Student's Guide to Political Science*, 87; Claflin, *Political Parties;* Lynch, *Fifty Years of Party Warfare*, 479; Library of Congress, *Political Parties in United States* (1936); Bassett, *Federalist System*, 310; Winsor, *Narrative and Critical History*, VII, 294.

128. TERRITORIAL AND SLAVERY QUESTIONS, 1789-1802

Summary — New states and territories (§§ 62, 111); questions under the Confederation (§ 119). — Western cessions: 1790, North Carolina cession; 1795, Yazoo grants (§§ 129, 135); 1800, Western Reserve cession (jurisdiction); 1802, Georgia cession. — Slavery question: under the Confederation (§§ 119, 120); issue revived; state restrictions on the slave trade; 1793, fugitive slave act; 1794, regulation of trade. — 1793, the cotton gin. — Seat of government: 1790, site fixed by compromise (§ 125); selected by Washington; 1800, first occupied. — Progress of territorial questions (§§ 134, 135, 148). — Progress of slavery questions (§ 159).

General — Bassett, *Federalist System,* chs. xii, xiii; Paxson, *American Frontier,* chs. vi–x; Billington, *Westward Expansion,* ch. x; general histories by Channing, Schouler, McMaster (§ 59); Krout and Fox, *Completion of Independence,* ch. vi.

Special — Western Cessions: Hinsdale, *Old Northwest,* chs. xii, xiii, xvi–xix; B. W. Bond, *Foundations of Ohio* (1941), chs. xii–xiv, and *Civilization of Old Northwest* (1934); Abernethy, *Frontier to Plantation in Tennessee,* chs. viii–xii; Driver, *John Sevier,* chs. vi–ix; Paullin, *Atlas,* Plates 45–47, pp. 34–36. ❡ Slavery: Phillips, *American Negro Slavery,* chs. vii–ix; Dubois, *Slave-Trade,* ch. vii; Locke, *Anti-Slavery Sentiment,* chs. iv–viii; M. G. McDougall, *Fugitive Slaves* (1891), 16; T. E. Drake, *Quakers and Slavery* (1950), chs. vi, vii; Holland Thompson, *Age of Invention* (1921), ch. ii; Burlingame, *March of Iron Men,* ch. xi; Allan Nevins and Jeannette Mirsky, *Eli Whitney* (1952). ❡ Maps: Paullin, *Atlas,* plates 67, 68, 123; Bassett, *Federalist System,* 184. ❡ Seat of Government: Bryan, *National Capital,* I, chs. i–xiv.

Sources — Debates: *Annals of Congress,* I–XI; Benton, *Abridgment,* I, II. ❡ Official Documents: *Statutes at Large,* I; *Annals of Congress,* I–XI, Apps.; Richardson, *Messages and Papers,* I, 94, 100, 102; *American State Papers, Public Lands,* I, *Misc.,* I; Carter, *Territorial Papers,* II, III; T. C. Pease, ed., *Laws of Northwest Territory 1788–1800* (1925). ❡ Contemporary Writings: Arthur St. Clair, *Papers* (W. H. Smith, ed., 2 vols., 1882), II; S. C. Williams, ed., "Executive Journal of Sevier," East Tenn. Hist. Soc., *Publ.,* I (1929), 95, II (1930), 135, III (1931), 154, IV (1932), 138; John Sevier, "Journal," J. H. DeWitt, ed., *Tenn. Hist. Mag.,* V (1919–20), 156, 232, VI (1920), 18; Jackson, *Correspondence,* I, 1; Eli Whitney, "Correspondence," *Am. Hist. Rev.,* III (1897), 90; S. K. Padover, ed., *Thomas Jefferson and National Capital* (1946).

Bibliography — Bassett, *Federalist System,* 307; H. C. Hockett, *Western Influences on Political Parties* (1917), 145; R. C. Downes, *Frontier Ohio* (1935), 253–268; Driver, *John Sevier,* 219; McDougall, *Fugitive Slaves,* App. E; Locke, *Anti-Slavery Sentiment,* 199.

129. FOREIGN AND INDIAN RELATIONS, 1789-1798

Summary — France: 1778, treaties (§ 117); 1788, consular convention; 1789, revolution; 1793, neutrality declared; Genêt episode; capture of American vessels; 1794, Monroe episode; 1796, Monroe's recall; Pinckney episode. — Spain: 1786, Mississippi question (§ 117); 1789, Yazoo grants (§§ 128, 135); Indian intrigues; 1795, Oct. 27, Pinckney's treaty. — England: 1789, outstanding questions under the treaty of 1783 (§ 117); 1790, Nootka Sound; 1792, discovery of the Columbia River (§ 123); 1793, outbreak of European war; 1794, aggressions on neutral trade; impressments; war threatened; Nov. 19, Jay's treaty; 1795, Jay's treaty opposed; "Dispatch No. 10"; 1796, treaty accepted by the House; posts surrendered; 1797, Blount conspiracy; 1798, negotiations on claims and boundaries. — Barbary powers: treaties of tribute. — Indians: Western settlements (§§ 107, 111); British and Spanish influence; 1789, Jan. 9, Fort Harmar treaty; 1790, Aug. 7, Creek treaty; Miami expedition; 1791, St. Clair's defeat; 1793–94, Wayne's campaign; 1795, Aug. 3, Greenville treaty; 1792–93, defeat of the Cherokees; 1795, Georgia's protest. — Later controversies (§§ 130, 134, 136–140, 154).

General — Bemis, *American Secretaries of State*, II, 3, and *Diplomatic History*, ch. vi; Bailey, *Diplomatic History*, chs. v, vi; J. B. Moore, *American Diplomacy* (1905), 34–57, and *Arbitrations*, I, chs. ix, x, II, ch. xix, V, 4399, and *Adjudications*, I–IV; Bowers, *Jefferson and Hamilton*, chs. x–xii, xv; Brant, *James Madison*, III, chs. xix, xxiii; Lodge, *George Washington*, II, 83, ch. iv, and *Alexander Hamilton*, 151, 185; Gibbs, *Administrations of Washington and John Adams*, I, chs. iv, v, vii–xii; Justin Winsor, *Westward Movement* (1897), chs. xvii, xix–xxv; Roosevelt, *Winning of West*, III, chs. vii, viii, IV, chs. i, ii, iv, V, chs. ii–v, VI, ch. ii; McMaster, Schouler (§ 59).

Special — France: Channing, *History*, IV, chs. v, vii; C. M. Thomas, *American Neutrality in 1793* (1931); Turner, *Significance of Sections*, chs. iii, v; Beveridge, *John Marshall*, II, 214; S. F. Bemis, "Washington's Farewell Address," *Am. Hist. Rev.*, XXXIX (1934), 263; E. W. Lyon, "Directory and United States," *Am. Hist. Rev.*, XLIII (1938), 514; Hazen, *American Opinion of the French Revolution;* Pickering and Upham, *Timothy Pickering*, III, chs. v–vii; Chinard, *John Adams*, bk. 3, chs. ii, iii. ❡ Spain: A. P. Whitaker, *Spanish-American Frontier*, and *Mississippi Question* (1934), chs. i–v, and "Treaty of San Lorenzo," *Miss. Valley Hist. Rev.*, XV (1929), 435, and "Godoy's Knowledge," *Am. Hist. Rev.*, XXXV (1930), 804; Bemis, *Pinckney's Treaty;* T. M. Green, *Spanish Conspiracy* (1891), chs. xix–xxii; J. R. Jacobs, *Tarnished Warrior* (1938), chs. v–vii. ❡ Great Britain: S. F. Bemis, *Jay's Treaty* (1923); Burt, *United States, Great Britain, and British North America*, chs. vii–ix; Monaghan, *John Jay*, chs. xvii–xix; A. T. Mahan, *Sea Power in Its Relations to War of 1812* (1905), I, 42–99; W. R. Manning, "Nootka Sound Controversy," Am. Hist. Assoc., *Report*, 1904, 279; W. S. Robertson, *Miranda* (1929), I, ch. v; Wilbur, *Ira Allen*, chs. xix–xxiii; Williamson, *Vermont in Quandary*, chs. xiv, xv; Wildes, *Anthony Wayne* chs. xvi–xix; Conway, *Edmund Randolph*, chs. xxi–xxxv; W. R. Riddell, *John Graves Simcoe* (1926), chs. v–xx. ❡ Barbary Powers: C. O. Paullin, *Diplomatic Negotiations of American Naval Officers* (1912), chs. ii–v; Irwin, *Diplomatic Relations of United States with Barbary Powers*, chs. iii–vi; F. L. Humphreys, *Life and Times of David Humphreys* (1917), II, chs. ix–xi. ❡ Indians: Downes, *Council Fires on Upper Ohio*, ch. xiii; W. E. Stevens, *Northwest Fur Trade* (1928), chs. iv–vii; J. R. Jacobs, *Beginnings of United States Army*, chs. iii–vii; J. W. Caughey, *McGillivray of Creeks* (1938); Harmon, *Sixty Years of Indian Affairs*, chs. iii–vi. ❡ Maps: Paullin, *Atlas*, plates 91–93, and pp. 55–58; Bassett, *Federalist System*, 58, 70; Avery, *History of United States*, VII, 96.

Sources — Debates: *Annals of Congress*, I–VI; Benton, *Abridgment*, I. ❡ Official Documents: *Statutes at Large*, I; *Annals of Congress*, I–VI, Apps.; *American State Papers, Foreign*, I, *Misc.*, I, *Indian*, I, *Military*, I; Richardson, *Messages and Papers*, I; Miller, *Treaties*, II; C. J. Kappler, *Indian Affairs*, II, 13. ❡ Diplomatic Correspondence: F. J. Turner, ed., "Correspondence of French Ministers," Am. Hist. Assoc., *Report*, 1903, II, 43, and "Mangourit Correspondence," *ibid.*, 1897, 569, and "Correspondence of Clark and Genêt," *ibid.*, 1896, I, 930; Whitaker, *Documents Relating to Commercial Policy of Spain in Floridas*, 102; Lawrence Kinnaird, ed., "Spain in the Mississippi Valley," Am. Hist. Assoc., *Report*, 1945, II–IV; Manning, *Diplomatic Correspondence: Canadian Relations*, I; Mayo, "Instructions to British Ministers," III, 1; J. G. Simcoe, *Correspondence with Allied Documents* (E. A. Cruikshank, ed., 5 vols., 1923–31); Peter Russell, *Correspondence with Allied Documents Relating to Government of Upper Canada during Term of Lieut.-Governor Simcoe* (E. A. Cruikshank and A. F. Hunter, eds., 3 vols., 1932–36); Historical Manuscripts Commission, *Report on Manuscripts of J. B. Fortescue at Dropmore* (1899), III; F. J. Turner, ed., "Blount Conspiracy," *Am. Hist. Rev.*, X (1905), 574. ❡ Indian Affairs: St. Clair, *Papers*, II; John Askin, *Papers* (M. M. Quaife, ed., 2 vols., 1929–31), I; Benjamin Hawkins, *Letters* (1916); Howay, "Voyages of Columbia." ❡ Contemporary Writings: Washington, *Writings*, XXXII–XXXVI; V. H. Paltsits, ed., *Washington's Farewell Address* (1935); Steiner, *James McHenry*, ch. xi; Ames, *Works*, I, II, and *Speeches in Congress;* Morris, *Diary and Letters*, I, chs. xxiii–xxvi, II, chs. xxvii–xxx; Jay, *Correspondence*, IV; Hamilton, *Works* (Hamilton, ed.), IV, 355, V, VII (Lodge, ed.), IV; Jefferson, *Writings* (Liscomb and Bergh, eds.), III, IV, IX (Ford, ed.), I, 179, V, 198, VI, VII, 1; James Monroe, *Writings*, I, 250, II, III, 1, 383, VII, 277, and *View of Conduct of Executive* (1797); Trumbull, *Autobiography*, chs.

xii–xiv; William Cobbett, *Porcupine's Works* (12 vols., 1801), II; King, *Rufus King,* I, chs. xxiv–xxxi, II, chs. ii–xi; Madison, *Writings* (Hunt ed.), VI, 125; Sparks, *Gouverneur Morris,* II, III; Edmund Randolph, *Vindication* (1795); Bond, "Letters"; Higginson, "Letters," I, 765; J. Q. Adams, *Writings,* I, II.

Bibliography — Bemis and Griffin, *Guide to Diplomatic History,* ch. iv; Bassett, *Federalist System,* 305, 306; Harmon, *Sixty Years of Indian Affairs,* 383.

130. JOHN ADAMS AND THE BREACH WITH FRANCE, 1797–1800

Summary — Change of Administrations: 1796, Washington's farewell address; election of John Adams; trouble with the cabinet. — X. Y. Z. episode: 1796, French grievances (§ 129); Pinckney not received (§ 129); 1797, demand for a bribe; 1798, June 21, Adams on the crisis. — War with France: 1798, July 9, authorization to capture French vessels; 1798–99, naval battles; privateers. — 1798, the Miranda project; Santo Domingo. — Internal troubles: question of Hamilton's command; 1798, July 14, direct tax. — Peace: 1799, French overtures; 1800, Sept. 30, convention negotiated; "French spoliation claims." — Effect on Adams (§ 132). — Subsequent relations (§§ 134, 137, 154).

General — Bemis, *American Secretaries of State,* II, 208, and *Diplomatic History,* ch. vii; Bailey, *Diplomatic History,* ch. vi; Channing, *History,* IV, ch. vii; Bassett, *Federalist System,* chs. ix, xiv–xvi; Gibbs, *Administrations of Washington and John Adams,* I, chs. xiii–xv, II, chs. i–vi; Beveridge, *John Marshall,* II, chs. iv, vi–ix; Bowers, *Jefferson and Hamilton,* chs. xvi–xviii; Chinard, *John Adams,* 259; Brown, *Oliver Ellsworth,* 264; Hamilton, *Alexander Hamilton,* VI, chs. cxxxii–cxxxv, VII, chs. cxxxvi–cxlvii; Austin, *Elbridge Gerry,* II, chs. v–viii; Morison, *Harrison Gray Otis,* I, ch. x.

Special — Moore, *Arbitrations,* V, 4421, and *Digest of International Law,* V, 593; J. A. James, "French Opinion Preventing War," *Am. Hist. Rev.,* XXX (1924), 44; G. A. King, "French Spoliation Claims," 64 Cong., 1 sess., *Sen. Doc.,* No. 451; Hayden, *Senate and Treaties,* 114; Charles Warren, "History of Laws Prohibiting Correspondence with a Foreign Government," 64 Cong., 2 sess., *Sen. Doc.,* No. 696. ❡ Naval War: G. W. Allen, *Our Naval War with France* (1909); Knox, *United States Navy,* ch. v; Porter, *Commodore David Porter,* chs. ii, iii; E. S. Maclay, *History of United States Navy* (1902), I, 155.

Sources — Debates: *Annals of Congress,* VII–X; Benton, *Abridgment,* II. ❡ Official Documents: *American State Papers, Foreign,* II, *Military,* I, *Naval,* I, *Commerce,* I; *Annals of Congress,* IX, X, Apps.; Richardson, *Messages and Papers,* I, 213, 228, 264, 266, 288, 306; Naval Records and Library Office, *Naval Documents related to the Quasi-War.* ❡ Collections of Documents: J. B. Scott, ed., *Controversy over Neutral Rights between United States and France 1797–1800* (1917); Turner, "Correspondence of French Ministers," II, 968; Miller, *Treaties,* II, 457; H. V. Ames and J. B. McMaster, *XYZ Letters* (1899). ❡ Contemporary Writings: John Adams, *Works,* VIII, 520, IX, 3; J. Q. Adams, *Writings,* II; Washington, *Writings,* XXXIII–XXXVI; John Marshall, *Life of George Washington* (1804–07; n. ed., 1832), V, ch. ix; Hamilton, *Works* (Hamilton, ed.), VI; Steiner, *James McHenry,* chs. xii–xiv; Madison, *Writings* (Hunt, ed.), VI; Monroe, *Writings,* III, 98, 249; Pickering and Upham, *Timothy Pickering,* III, chs. ix–xi; W. V. Murray, "Letters to J. Q. Adams," W. C. Ford, ed., *Am. Hist. Assoc., Report,* 1912, 343; Elbridge Gerry, *Some Letters* (W. C. Ford, ed., 1896), 9; Lewis Goldsmith, *Exposition of Conduct of France toward America* (1810); King, *Rufus King,* II, chs. xii–xxxiv, III, chs. i–xxviii, Apps. ii, iii; Stephen Higginson, "Letters," I, 797; Jefferson, *Writings* (Liscomb and Bergh, eds.), IV (Ford, ed.), I, 272, VII, 89; S. E. Morison, ed., "DuPont, Talleyrand, and French Spoliations," Mass. Hist. Soc., *Proc.,* XLIX, (1915), 63.

Bibliography — Bemis and Griffin, *Guide to Diplomatic History,* 73; Allen, *Naval War with France,* 283; Bassett, *Federalist System,* 306.

131. ALIEN AND SEDITION ACTS, AND VIRGINIA AND KENTUCKY RESOLUTIONS, 1798–1800

Summary — The states previous to 1798 (§§ 119, 123). — The Statutes: 1798, June 18, naturalization act; June 25, alien act; June 27, bank fraud act; July 6, alien enemies act; July 14, sedition act. — Principles involved: status of aliens; status of bank; freedom of speech and press; common-law jurisdiction; federal criminal law; truth a defense; personal liberty; president's powers; powers of states. — State resolutions: 1798, Nov. 19, first Kentucky resolutions; 1798, Dec. 21, Virginia resolutions; 1799, Nov. 22, second Kentucky resolutions; 1799, replies of other states; 1800, Madison's report. — Principles involved: powers of Congress; implied powers; supremacy of the Constitution; arbiter in disputes; "interposition"; "nullification"; ultimate use of force. — Cases under the acts: no aliens expelled; 1798–1800, Cooper, Callender, Lyon, and other sedition cases. — 1800–01, expiration of the acts. — Subsequent controversies (§§ 135, 139, 143, 156).

General — J. C. Miller, *Crisis in Freedom* (1951); Channing, *History*, IV, ch. viii; Bassett, *Federalist System*, chs. xvii, xviii; Bowers, *Jefferson and Hamilton*, chs. xvi, xvii; Nathan Schachner, *Thomas Jefferson* (1951), II, chs. xli–xliv; Randall, *Thomas Jefferson*, II, chs. viii–x; Brant, *James Madison*, III, ch. xxxiv; Koch, *Jefferson and Madison*, chs. vi, vii; Hamilton, *Alexander Hamilton*, VII, chs. cxlii, cxlvii, cxlviii; Henry Adams, *Albert Gallatin*, 189, and *John Randolph* (1882), ch. ii; Anderson, *William Branch Giles*, ch. v; Davis, *Confederate Government*, I, ch. xiv.

Special — A. C. McLaughlin, "Social Compact and Constitutional Construction," *Am. Hist. Rev.*, V (1900), 467; F. M. Anderson, "Contemporary Opinion of Resolutions," *ibid.*, V, 45, 225; E. D. Warfield, *Kentucky Resolutions of 1798* (1887); E. P. Powell, *Nullification and Secession* (1897), ch. ii; C. W. Loring, *Nullification, Secession* (1893), ch. iv; Ambler, *Sectionalism in Virginia*, 66; C. F. Carroll, "Freedom of Press in Federalist Period," *Mich. Law Rev.*, XVIII (1920), 615; Burdick, *Law of Constitution*, §§ 126, 130; F. M. Anderson, "Enforcement of Alien and Sedition Laws," *Am. Hist. Assoc., Report*, 1912, 115; Story, *Commentaries*, §§ 1880–92; Leon Whipple, *Story of Civil Liberty in United States* (1927), 18; Malone, *Thomas Cooper*, chs. iii, iv; J. F. McLaughlin, *Matthew Lyon* (1900), chs. v, vi. ❧ Maps: Paullin, *Atlas*, plate 112C.

Sources — Debates: *Annals of Congress*, VIII, IX; Benton, *Abridgment*, II. ❧ Official Documents: *Annals of Congress*, IX, App. ❧ Collections of Documents: A. B. Hart and Edward Channing, eds., *American History Leaflets* (1892–1911), No. 15; H. V. Ames, *State Documents on Federal Relations* (1907), 15; Elliot, *Debates*, IV, 528. ❧ Contemporary Writings: Jefferson, *Writings* (Lipscomb and Bergh, eds.), IX, (Ford, ed), VII, 244; Madison, *Writings*, VI; Hamilton, *Works* (Hamilton, ed.), VI; Wharton, *State Trials*, 322, 659; Johnston and Woodburn, *American Orations*, I, 131.

Bibliography — Schroeder, *Free Speech Bibliography*, pt. 3; Library of Congress, Division of Bibliography, *List of References on Alien and Sedition Laws, 1798* (1925); Zechariah Chafee, *Free Speech in United States* (1948), 569.

132. FALL OF THE FEDERALISTS, 1799–1801

Summary — Earlier party relations (§§ 121, 122, 127). French war; taxes; 1799, Robbins' case; 1799, Fries's insurrection; 1800, judiciary act; 1801, judicial appointments. — Internal quarrels; 1799, cabinet breaks up; 1800, Hamilton's attack on Adams; Oliver Wolcott. — Election of 1800: Adams and Jefferson candidates; Hamilton's intrigues; no electoral choice. — Election of 1801: Burr and Jefferson; Feb. 17, Jefferson elected. — Subsequent history of the Federalists (§§ 133, 135, 139, 144).

General — Bassett, *Federalist System*, ch. xix; Channing, *History*, IV, ch. viii; Bowers, *Jefferson and Hamilton*, chs. xix–xxi; Schachner, *Thomas Jefferson*, II, chs. xlv–xlvi, and *Alexander Hamilton*, chs. xx–xxvi; Hamilton, *Alexander Hamilton*, VII, chs. cxlix–clvii;

C. F. Adams, *John Adams*, ch. x. See also: McMaster, Schouler, and other general histories (§ 59).

Special — Beard, *Jeffersonian Democracy*, chs. xi–xiv; Hockett, *Western Influences*, 36, 51; Alexander, *History of New York*, I, ch. ix; Robinson, *Jeffersonian Democracy*, ch. ii; Purcell, *Connecticut in Transition*, chs. vi, vii; Stauffer, *New England and Bavarian Illuminati;* Koch, *Republican Religion;* H. M. Tinkcom, *Republicans and Federalists in Pennsylvania* (1950); Ferguson, *Early Western Pennsylvania Politics*, chs. vi, vii; U. B. Phillips, "South Carolina Federalists," *Am. Hist. Rev.*, XIV (1909), 529, 731; Max Farrand, "Judiciary Act," *ibid.*, V (1900), 682; Gibbs, *Administrations of Washington and John Adams*, II, chs. vi, vii; Luetscher, *Early Political Machinery*, chs. iii, iv; Monaghan, *John Jay*, 415; Spaulding, *George Clinton*, chs. xvii, xix; Bernard Faÿ, *Two Franklins* (1933), 264. ❡ Maps: Paullin, *Atlas*, plate 102D; Bassett, *Federalist System*, 168, 176, 290.

Sources — Debates: *Annals of Congress*, IX, X; Benton, *Abridgment*, II. ❡ Official Documents: *Annals of Congress*, X, App.; Richardson, *Messages and Papers*, I, 286, 303. ❡ Contemporary Writings: John Adams, *Works*, VIII, IX; Jefferson, *Writings* (Liscomb and Bergh, eds.), IV, 203 (Ford, ed.), VII, 376; Hamilton, *Works* (Hamilton, ed.), V, VII; Madison, *Writings* (Hunt, ed.), VI, 406; Monroe, *Writings*, III, 219, 244; Steiner, *James McHenry*, chs. xv, xvi; Lodge, *George Cabot*, chs. vii, viii; Davis, *Aaron Burr*, II, chs. iv, v; DeWitt Clinton, *Vindication of Thomas Jefferson* (1800); Jay, *Correspondence*, IV, 265; Wharton, *State Trials*, 392; Sparks, *Gouverneur Morris*, III, 115; Ames, *Works*, I, 224; J. Q. Adams, *Writings*, II; William Linn, *Serious Considerations on Election of a President* (1800); J. A. Bayard, *Documents relating to Presidential Election of 1801* (1831).

Bibliography — J. W. Cronin and W. H. Wise, comps., *Bibliography of John Adams and John Quincy Adams* (1935), 4, and *Bibliography of Thomas Jefferson* (1935).

Chapter Twelve

REPUBLICAN SUPREMACY, 1801–1815

133. THE JEFFERSONIAN SYSTEM, 1801–1805

Summary — Jefferson's personality: early career (§§ 120, 123, 124, 127, 131); republican simplicity; varied intellectual interests. — Political principles. — Civil service: cabinet; "midnight appointments"; principle of equalization. — Gallatin's financial policy: views on public debt; retrenchment and its effects on public finance, army and navy. — Federal judiciary: 1802, March 8, judiciary act of 1801 repealed; 1803, Marbury *v.* Madison; 1804, Judge Pickering impeached; 1805, impeachment of Judge Chase fails; judicial appointments (§ 143). — National capital.

General — Henry Adams, *United States,* I, chs. i–xii, II, chs. vii, x; Edward Channing, *History,* IV, chs. ix, x, and *Jeffersonian System* (1906), chs. i, ii, ix; McMaster, *History,* II, 583–620, III, 146–183; Allen Johnson, *Jefferson and His Colleagues* (1921), chs. i, ii; Binkley, *Powers of President,* ch. iii; Schachner, *Thomas Jefferson,* II, chs. xlvii–l, lv; Chinard, *Thomas Jefferson,* bks. 3, 4, 5, ch. i; Hofstadter, *American Political Tradition,* ch. ii; L. D. White, *Jeffersonians* (1951); Schachner, *Alexander Hamilton,* ch. xxvi; Hamilton, *Alexander Hamilton,* VII, chs. clviii–clxi; Henry Adams, *Albert Gallatin,* bk. 3, and *John Randolph,* ch. iii; Hunt, *James Madison,* ch. xxviii; Dodd, *Nathaniel Macon,* ch. xii; Dorfman, *Economic Mind,* I, ch. xiv.

Special — Politics: Beard, *Jeffersonian Democracy,* ch. xiv; Parrington, *Main Currents,* II, 3; Wiltse, *Jeffersonian Tradition;* Harlow, *Legislative Methods,* ch. x; Merriam, *American Political Theories,* ch. iv; D. R. Fox, *Decline of Aristocracy in Politics of New York* (1919), chs. i–v; Robinson, *Jeffersonian Democracy,* chs. iii, iv; W. R. Fell, *Transition from Aristocracy to Democracy* (1933), chs. iii–iv; D. H. Gilpatrick, *Jeffersonian Democracy in North Carolina* (1931); Purcell, *Connecticut in Transition;* H. C. Hockett, "Federalism and West," *Essays in American History Dedicated to Frederick Jackson Turner* (1910), 113; Stanwood, *Presidency,* I, ch. vi; H. C. Adams, *Taxation, 1789–1816* (1884); Dewey, *Financial History,* §§ 54–57; Josiah Quincy, *Memoir of John Quincy Adams* (1858), ch. ii; Plumer, *William Plumer,* chs. vii, viii. ❦ Civil Service: Hunt, "Office-Seeking"; J. M. Merriam, "Jefferson's Use of Executive Patronage," Am. Hist. Assoc., *Papers,* II (1887), No. 1, 47; C. R. Fish, *Civil Service and Patronage* (1904), ch. ii. ❦ Federal Judiciary: Beveridge, *John Marshall,* III, chs. i–iv; W. S. Carpenter, *Judicial Tenure in United States* (1918), 57, 101; Anderson, *William Branch Giles,* ch. vi; Corwin, *Judicial Review,* ch. i; A. C. McLaughlin, *Courts, Constitution and Parties* (1912), ch. i; Haines, *American Doctrine of Judicial Supremacy;* Warren, *Supreme Court,* I, chs. iv–vi, and *Congress, Constitution and Supreme Court,* chs. ii–iv; Beard, *Supreme Court;* Brinton Coxe, *Judicial Power and Unconstitutional Legislation* (1893); Boudin, *Government by Judiciary;* Thayer, *Legal Essays,* 1. ❦ National Capital: Bryan, *National Capital,* I, chs. xiii–xix.

Sources — Debates: *Annals of Congress,* XI–XV; Benton, *Abridgment,* II, III. ❦ Official Documents: *Annals of Congress,* XI–XIV, Apps.; *American State Papers, Finance,*

I, II; Richardson, *Messages and Papers*, I, 321, 342, 369, 378; Dunbar, *Currency, Finance, and Banking*, 49; National Monetary Commission, *Laws Concerning Money*, 57, 283. ❡ Contemporary Writings: J. Q. Adams, *Memoirs*, I, and *Writings*, III; Jefferson, *Writings* (Liscomb and Bergh, eds.), IV, VIII, (Ford, ed.), I, 291, VIII; Jefferson and DuPont de Nemours, *Correspondence*; Thomas Jefferson, *Some Correspondence* (W. C. Ford, ed., 1902), 76; Monroe, *Writings*, III, IV; Gallatin, *Writings*, I; Hamilton, *Works* (Hamilton, ed.), VI, VII; K. P. Battle, ed., *Letters of Nathaniel Macon, John Steele and William Barry Grove* (1902); Nathaniel Macon, "Correspondence" (W. E. Dodd, ed.), *John P. Branch Hist. Papers*, III (1909), No. 1, 27; E. B. Williston, *Eloquence of United States* (1827), II, 76, IV, 261. ❡ Personal and Reminiscence: S. N. Randolph, *Domestic Life of Thomas Jefferson* (1939); Theodore Dwight, *Character of Thomas Jefferson* (1839); Sparks, *Gouverneur Morris*, III, 163; Morris, *Diary and Letters*, II, chs. xli–xlv; M. B. Smith, *Forty Years of Washington Society*, 5, 65, 383; L. B. Cutts, ed., *Memoirs and Letters of Dolly Madison* (1886), chs. iv–vi. ❡ Travels: Bradbury, *Travels;* Davis, *Travels*; Dwight, *Travels*; Parkinson, *Tour in America*. For other travels, see: § 48. — National Capital: Padover, *Thomas Jefferson and National Capital*.

Bibliography — H. B. Tompkins, *Bibliotheca Jeffersoniana* (1887); Cronin and Wise, *Bibliography of Thomas Jefferson*; Channing, *Jeffersonian System*, ch. xxi; Winsor, *Narrative and Critical History*, VII, 300, 337, 338; Haines, *American Doctrine of Judicial Supremacy*, 663; Felix Frankfurter and J. M. Landis, *Business of the Supreme Court* (1927), 24.

134. FOREIGN AFFAIRS DURING JEFFERSON'S FIRST TERM

Summary — Tripolitan war: character of Barbary states; the war; results. — Gunboat system. — Purchase of Louisiana: previous territorial history (§§ 106, 110, 128, 129); 1800, Oct., retrocession to France; 1802, Oct., "deposit" withdrawn; threat of Jefferson; 1803, Monroe mission; Napoleon's offer of the whole. — The treaty: boundaries; payment. — Party contest over the purchase: Federalist opposition; "incorporation" in the Union; implied powers (§ 126); Jefferson's projected amendment. — West Florida boundary question: controversy with Spain; 1808, revolution; 1810, Western part annexed; 1812, remainder annexed; 1814, Mobile occupied. — Texas boundary: Northern; Western; later adjustments (§ 167). — Organization: 1804, territory of Orleans; 1805, representative territorial government. — Exploration of Louisiana and the Far West (§ 164); 1803–1806, Lewis and Clark's expedition; 1811, Astoria founded; later Oregon adjustment (§ 166); Pike's expeditions.

General — Henry Adams, *United States*, I, chs. xiii–xvii, II, chs. i–vi, xi–xviii, III, chs. ii, v, vi, V, ch. xv; Bailey, *Diplomatic History*, ch. vii; Bemis, *American Secretaries of State*, III, 3, and *Diplomatic History*, ch. viii; Channing, *History*, IV, chs. xi, xii, and *Jeffersonian System*, chs. iii–vii; McMaster, *History*, II, 588, 601, 620; Allen Johnson, *Jefferson and His Colleagues*, chs. iii–v; Hunt, *James Madison*, ch. xxix; Henry Adams, *John Randolph*, ch. iv, and *Albert Gallatin*, bk. 3; Schachner, *Thomas Jefferson*, II, chs. li–liv; Billington, *Westward Expansion*, ch. xi.

Special — Louisiana Purchase: Whitaker, *Mississippi Question;* Louis Pelzer, "Economic Factors in Acquisition of Louisiana," *Miss. Valley Hist. Assoc., Proc.*, VI (1912), 109; E. W. Lyon, *Louisiana*, and *Man Who Sold Louisiana* (1942); Gayarré, *History of Louisiana*, III, IV; T. L. Stoddard, *French Revolution in San Domingo* (1914); C. C. Tansill, *United States and Santo Domingo* (1938), chs. i–iii; R. W. Logan, *Diplomatic Relations of United States with Haiti* (1941), chs. ii–iv; Ralph Korngold, *Citizen Toussaint* (1944); E. S. Brown, *Constitutional History of Louisiana Purchase* (1920); Burdick, *Law of Constitution*, §§ 100–105; Story, *Commentaries*, §§ 1282–1288, 1314–1321; T. M. Marshall, *History of Western Boundary of Louisiana Purchase* (1914); I. J. Cox, "Louisiana-Texas Frontier," *Texas State Hist. Assoc., Quar.*, X (1907), 1, and *Southwestern Hist. Quar.*, XVII (1914), 1, 140. ❡ West Florida Question: I. J. Cox, *West Florida Controversy* (1918); H. E. Chambers, *West Florida* (1898); H. B. Fuller, *Purchase of Florida* (1906), chs. iii–v. ❡ Explorations: R. B. Guinness, "Purpose of Lewis and Clark Expedition," *Miss. Valley Hist. Rev.*, XX (1933), 90; Brebner, *Explorers of North America*, ch. xxiv; Coman, *Economic Beginnings of Far West*, I, 231; F. J. Teggart, "Notes Supplementary," Am. Hist. Assoc., *Report*, 1908, I, 183; I. J. Cox, *Early Explorations of Louisiana* (1906); W. E. Hollon, *Lost Pathfinder* (1949). ❑ Barbary Wars: L. B. Wright and J. H. Macleod, *First Americans in North Africa* (1945); Irwin, *Diplomatic Relations of United States with Barbary Powers*, chs. vii–xiii; Émile Dupuy, *Américains et Barbaresques* (1910), chs. viii–xvii; C. O. Paullin, *Diplomatic Negotiations*, chs. ii–iv, and *John Rodgers* (1909); G. W. Allen, *Our Navy and Barbary Corsairs* (1905); Knox, *United States Navy*, chs. vi, vii; Maclay, *United States Navy*, I, 214–302; C. L. Lewis, *Romantic Decatur* (1937), chs. iv–viii. ❑ Maps: Paullin, *Atlas*, plates 28–32, 39AB, 49; *Harper's Atlas*, 15, 25–27, 30; E. M. Avery, *History of United States*, VII, 348.

Sources — Debates: *Annals of Congress*, XII, XIII; Benton, *Abridgment*, II, III. ❑ Official Documents: *American State Papers, Foreign*, II, *Public Lands*, I; *Annals of Congress*, XII, App.; Richardson, *Messages and Papers*, I, 346, 357, 367, 384, 389, 430, 480, 484, 488; Miller, *Treaties*, II, 498, 585, 617; Moore, *Digest of International Law*, I, § 101, V, 613; Thomas Donaldson, *Public Domain* (1884), 89. ❑ Contemporary Writings: Jefferson, *Writings* (Liscomb and Bergh, eds.), IV, VIII, (Ford, ed.), VIII, 61, 143, 172, 188, 349, 379; Madison, *Writings* (Hunt, ed.), VI, 448–464, VII, 1–156; Monroe, *Writings*, IV; Gallatin, *Writings*, I; William Plumer, *Memorandum of Proceedings in Senate, 1803–07* (E. S. Brown, ed., 1923); Barbé-Marbois, *Louisiane*; Claiborne, *Official Letter Books*, I–VI; Robertson, *Louisiana*; "Despatches from United States Consulate in New Orleans," *Am. Hist. Rev.*, XXXII (1927), 801, XXXIII (1928), 331, XXXVIII (1933), 291; J. A. Pichardo, *Treatise on the Limits of Louisiana and Texas* (4 vols., C. W. Hackett, ed., 1931–46). ❑ Exploration: Lewis and Clark, expedition accounts (Biddle, ed., Thwaites, ed., § 48); M. M. Quaife, ed., *Journals of Lewis and Ordway* (1916); Pike, *Account of Expeditions* (Coues, ed., § 48); M. M. Quaife, ed., *Southwestern Expedition of Zebulon M. Pike* (1925); Z. M. Pike, *Arkansaw Journal* (S. H. Hart and A. B. Hulbert, eds., 1932); Z. M. Pike, "Papers" (H. E. Bolton, ed.), *Am. Hist. Rev.*, XIII (1908), 798; William Dunbar, *Documents Relating to Purchase and Exploration of Louisiana* (1904).

Bibliography — Bemis and Griffin, *Guide to Diplomatic History*, chs. v, vi; Lyon, *Louisiana*, 253; Brown, *Constitutional History of Louisiana Purchase*, 197; Irwin, *Diplomatic Relations of United States with Barbary Powers*, 205; Winsor, *Narrative and Critical History*, VII, 546–562.

135. JEFFERSON'S DOMINATION OF THE REPUBLICAN PARTY, 1804–1808

Summary — Presidential election of 1804; Burr read out of Republican party; triumph of Jefferson. — Northern secession project; New England discontent; New York gubernatorial contest; Burr's defeat; Burr-Hamilton duel. — Burr's Western expedition; intrigues in Washington; 1806, Dec., descent of the Ohio; Wilkinson at New Orleans; Pike's expedition (§ 134); Jefferson's proclamation; Burr treason trial; definition of legal proof of treason; Jefferson's part in the trial. — John Randolph and the Quids; issue of strict construction; the Yazoo lands question.

General — Henry Adams, *United States*, II, chs. viii, ix, xvii, III, chs. i, vii–xv, xix, IV, chs. vi, xvi–xx; Channing, *History*, IV, chs. xii, xiii; McMaster, *History of United States*, III, ch. xv; Schouler, *History*, II, 67, 98, 122; Schachner, *Thomas Jefferson*, II, chs. lvi, lix, lxi; Randall, *Thomas Jefferson*, III, chs. iv, v; Tucker, *Thomas Jefferson*, II, chs. ix–xi; Hamilton, *Alexander Hamilton*, VII, chs. clxvii, clxviii; Henry Adams, *John Randolph*, chs. v–viii; Bruce, *John Randolph*, I, chs. vi, vii; Dodd, *Nathaniel Macon*, ch. xiii.

Special — Beveridge, *John Marshall*, III, chs. vi–x; Corwin, *John Marshall*, ch. iv; I. J. Cox, "General Wilkinson and His Later Intrigues," *Am. Hist. Rev.*, XIX (1914), 794; McCaleb, *Aaron Burr Conspiracy*; Schachner, *Aaron Burr*, chs. xvi–xxvi; Bassett, *Andrew Jackson*, I, ch. iv; Parton, *Andrew Jackson*, I, chs. xxviii–xxx, and *Aaron Burr*, chs. xviii–xxvi; W. H. Safford, *Harman Blennerhassett* (1850); Morison, *Harrison Gray Otis*, I, ch. xv; C. R. Brown, *Northern Confederacy* (1915), ch. iii; Theodore Roosevelt, *Gouverneur Morris* (1898), ch. xiii; Ambler, *Thomas Ritchie*, ch. ii. ❡ Maps: Paullin, *Atlas*, plate 102E.

Sources — Official Documents: *American State Papers, Misc.*, I; Richardson, *Messages and Papers*, I, 404, 412, 429, 435; *Annals of Congress*, XVI, XVII, Apps. ❡ Contemporary Writings: Davis, *Aaron Burr*, II, chs. v–xxi; Aaron Burr, "Some Papers" (W. C. Ford, ed.), *Am. Antiq. Soc., Proc.*, XXIX (1919), 43; Jefferson, *Writings* (Liscomb and Bergh, eds.), IV, V, (Ford ed.), I, 318, VIII, IX; Madison, *Writings* (Congress ed., 1865), II, 393; Hamilton, *Works*, VI, VII, 851; Claiborne, *Official Letter Books*, III–V; W. H. Safford, ed., *Blennerhassett Papers* (1861); Wilkinson, *Memoirs*, II, chs. viii, ix; T. Carpenter, *Trial of Aaron Burr* (4 vols., 1807); William Wirt, *Two Principle Arguments on Trial of Aaron Burr* (1808); John Marshall, *Writings* (1839), 3; Williston, *Eloquence of the United States*, IV, 384; Henry Adams, *New England Federalism*; Lodge, *George Cabot*, 317; King, *Rufus King*, IV, ch. xxv; William Coleman, *Death of Alexander Hamilton* (1804).

Bibliography — Cronin and Wise, *Bibliography of Jefferson*; S. H. Wandell, *Aaron Burr in Literature* (1936); H. B. Tompkins, *Burr Bibliography* (1892); Schachner, *Aaron Burr*, 547.

136. NEUTRAL TRADE, 1793–1807

Summary — Previous difficulties (§§ 129, 130). — Four limitations on neutral trade: "blockade," "contraband," "free ships, free goods," "rule of 1756." — Early difficulties (§ 127); 1800–02, King's negotiations; 1800, 1803, treaties with France (§ 130); impressments. — Complaints against the United States: harboring deserters; false papers; continuous voyages; coasting. — Aggressions renewed; 1803, war between England and France; decisions of English admiralty courts; 1807, Jay treaty expires. — British orders in council and French decrees: Napoleon's "continental system"; 1805, Trafalgar; 1806, May 16, British blockade order; Nov. 21, Berlin Decree; 1807, Jan., Mar., both sides prohibit coasting trade; Nov. 11, general blockade order; Dec. 17, Milan Decree. — Jefferson's policy: 1803–07, "gunboat system" (§ 137); 1806, Apr. 18, conditional non-importation act; 1806, Dec. 31, Monroe-Pinkney treaty with England; 1807, treaty withheld; 1807, June, Leopard-Chesapeake affair; negotiations for West Florida (§ 134). — Damage done to the United States: number of impressments; English captures; French captures. — Subsequent difficulties (§ 137).

General — Henry Adams, *United States*, III, chs. ii, iv, xvi–xviii, IV, chs. i–vi; Bemis, *American Secretaries of State*, III, 80; Channing, *History*, IV, ch. xiii, and *Jeffersonian System*, chs. xiii–xv; Schachner, *Thomas Jefferson*, II, chs. lvii, lviii, lx, lxii, lxiii; A. T. Mahan, *Sea Power in War of 1812*, I, 99, and *Influence of Sea Power upon French Revolution* (1892), II, chs. xvii, xviii; R. D. Paine, *Old Merchant Marine* (1920), ch. vi; Sprout, *Rise of American Naval Power*, chs. iii–v; Spears, *Story of American Merchant Marine*, ch. viii.

Special — F. E. Melvin, *Napoleon's Navigation System* (1919), chs. i–v; E. F. Heckscher, *Continental System* (1922), pt. 2, chs. i–iii; A. C. Clauder, *American Commerce as Affected by the Wars of the French Revolution* (1932), chs. ii, iii; W. F. Galpin, *Grain Supply of England* (1925), ch. viii; W. E. Lingelbach, "England and Neutral Trade," *Military Historian and Economist*, II (1917), 153; H. W. Briggs, *Doctrine of Continuous Voyage* (1926), chs. i, ii; Moore, *Digest of International Law*, §§ 317, 318, 828, 1179, 1180, 1195, 1270, 1336; J. F. Zimmerman, *Impressment of American Seamen* (1925); I-mien Tsiang, *Question of Expatriation in America Prior to 1907* (1942); Morison, *Maritime History*, ch. xii; R. G. Albion and J. B. Pope, *Sea Lanes in Wartime* (1942), chs. iii, v; Hutchins, *American Maritime Industries*, chs. vi–viii.

Sources — Debates: *Annals of Congress*, XIV–XVI; Benton, *Abridgment*, II, III. ❡ Official Documents: *American State Papers, Foreign*, II, III, especially 147–51, 262–94,

Commerce, I; *Annals of Congress,* XV, XVI, Apps.; Richardson, *Messages and Papers,* I, 361, 383, 388, 395, 402, 422. ❡ Contemporary Writings: Jefferson, *Writings* (Liscomb and Bergh, eds.), IV, (Ford ed.), I, 307, VIII, 319, IX; Gallatin, *Writings,* I; Madison, *Writings* (Congress ed.), II, 189, (Hunt ed.), VI, 423, VII; Monroe, *Writings,* IV, V; King, *Rufus King,* III, chs. xxix–xxxv, IV; Sparks, *Gouverneur Morris,* III, 229; J. Q. Adams, *Memoirs,* I, and *Writings,* III; Tench Coxe, *Examination of the Conduct of Great Britain* (1802); Theodore Dwight, *History of the Hartford Convention* (1833), 44; Mathew Carey, *Olive Branch* (1815); James Stephen, *War in Disguise* (1805); Alexander Baring [baron Ashburton], *Inquiry into the Causes and Consequences of the Orders in Council* (1808); Basil Hall, *Voyages and Travels* (1895), ch. xi; Thomas Barclay, *Selection from the Correspondence* (G. L. Rives, ed., 1894), chs. iv, v.

Bibliography — Bemis and Griffin, *Guide to Diplomatic History,* ch. v; H. H. B. Meyer, *List of References on Embargoes* (1917); L. M. Sears, *Jefferson and Embargo* (1927), 321; Melvin, *Napoleon's Navigation System,* 378; Clauder, *American Commerce as Affected by French Revolution,* 245; Galpin, *Grain Supply of England,* 259; Winsor, *Narrative and Critical History,* VII, 457, 519, 520; Channing, *History,* IV, 374.

137. EMBARGO AND NON-INTERCOURSE, 1807–1811

Summary — Previous difficulties (§§ 129, 130, 136). — Embargo act: 1807, Dec. 22, act passed; 1808, supplementary acts; question of constitutionality. — Enforcement: evasions by New England shipowners; overland trade; collisions with troops; treason trials; 1809, Jan., Giles's enforcement acts. — effects: economic depression; 1809, Henry's mission; question of New England loyalty; Embargo repealed. — Non-intercourse: 1809, Mar. 1, act passed; Mar. 4, Madison becomes president; Apr. 19, Erskine agreement; June 10, intercourse with England renewed; 1810, Mar. 23, French decree of Rambouillet, Aug. 5, of Trianon, and 1811, Apr. 28, of St. Cloud; May 1, "Macon Bill No. 2"; unsuccessful missions of Jackson and Rose; 1811, Mar. 2, non-intercourse renewed. — Pinkney mission to England: question whether the French decrees were withdrawn; 1811, Feb., Pinkney demands passports; July, Foster's mission to Washington.

General — Henry Adams, *United States,* IV, chs. vii–xx, V, and *Albert Gallatin,* 355; Channing, *History,* IV, chs. xiv, xv; Allen Johnson, *Jefferson and His Colleagues,* chs. viii, ix; K. C. Babcock, *Rise of American Nationality* (1906), chs. i–iii; Mahan, *Sea Power in War of 1812,* I, 182; Bemis, *Diplomatic History,* chs. ix, x; Bailey, *Diplomatic History,* chs. viii, ix; Moore, *Arbitrations,* V, 4451–6; Randall, *Thomas Jefferson,* III, chs. vi–ix; Tucker, *Thomas Jefferson,* II, chs. x–xiii; C. G. Bowers, *Jefferson in Power* (1936), chs. xx–xxiii; Hunt, *James Madison,* ch. xxx; Dodd, *Nathaniel Macon,* chs. xiv, xv; Anderson, *William Branch Giles,* chs. vii–x; Schurz, *Henry Clay,* I, ch. iv; Mayo, *Henry Clay,* chs. ix, x; Quincy, *Josiah Quincy,* chs. vi–ix; Bruce, *John Randolph,* I, chs. vi, vii; Pickering and Upham, *Timothy Pickering,* IV, chs. iv, v. See also: general histories (§ 59) for this period.

Special — Sears, *Jefferson and Embargo*; W. F. Galpin, *Grain Supply of England,* ch. viii, and "American Grain Trade," *Jour. Econ. and Bus. Hist.,* II (1929), 71; Clauder, *American Commerce as Affected by French Revolution,* chs. iv–viii; G. S. Graham, *Sea Power and British North America* (1941), pt. 4; Albion and Pope, *Sea Lanes in Wartime,* ch. iv; W. W. Jennings, *American Embargo* (1921); G. W. Daniels, "American Cotton Trade under the Embargo," *Am. Hist. Rev.,* XXI (1916), 276; Cole, *Wholesale Commodity Prices,* and *Statistical Supplement*; Warren, Pearson, and Stoker, "Wholesale Prices"; A. G. Peterson, *Historical Study of Prices Received by Producers of Farm Products in Virginia* (1929); Thomas Tooke, *History of Prices* (6 vols., 1838–57), 1, 255; Marvin, *American Merchant Marine,* ch. vii; Story, *Commentaries* (2 ed.), §§ 1289–91; D. W. Brown, *Commercial Power of Congress* (1910), ch. xii; E. A. Cruikshank, *Political Adventures of John Henry* (1936); Paullin, *John Rodgers,* ch. ix; Stanwood, *Presidency,* I, ch. vii. See also: works cited § 136. ❡ Maps: Paullin, *Atlas,* plate 112D.

Sources — Debates: *Annals of Congress,* XVII–XXII; Benton, *Abridgment,* III, IV. ❡ Official Documents: *Statutes at Large,* II; *American State Papers, Foreign,* III, *Com-*

merce, I; *Annals of Congress*, XVIII–XXII, Apps.; Richardson, *Messages and Papers*, I.
❧ Contemporary Writings: Jefferson, *Writings* (Liscomb and Bergh, eds.), V, VIII,
(Ford ed.), IX, 167; J. Q. Adams, *Memoirs*, I, 491, and *Writings*, III, 164; Barclay,
Correspondence, ch. vi; Gallatin, *Writings*, I, II, 198; King, *Rufus King*, V, chs. iii–xiii,
App. 1; Madison, *Writings* (Congress ed.), II, 410, (Hunt ed.), VIII; Monroe, *Writings*,
V, 22, 353; John Howe, "Secret Reports," *Am. Hist. Rev.*, XVII (1911–12), 70, 332;
Story, *Joseph Story*, I, ch. vi; John Taylor, "Letters," *John P. Branch Hist. Papers*, II, 290.

Bibliography — See: § 136.

138. WAR OF 1812, 1812–1815

Summary — Rise of the war party: problem of neutral rights and impressments (§ 136);
Indian troubles in the West; expansionism; Congressional election of 1810; "Young Republicans"; affair of the *President* and *Little Belt*; Madison and the "War Hawks"; declaration of war; British "Orders" withdrawn; reëlection of Madison, 1812. — American un-
preparedness for war; weakness of administration; financial weakness. — 1812, Campaign
against Canada; Detroit; Niagara; Lake Champlain; loss of Astoria. — 1813, Second campaign against Canada; Lake Erie; Thames River; Niagara frontier. — 1814, Brown at
Niagara; Plattsburg; Washington burned; invasion of Maine. — 1815, Battle of New
Orleans. — War at sea: successful naval duels; American coast blockaded; prowess of
privateers. — Peace: 1812, Russian mediation; 1814, meeting at Ghent; questions of
conquered territory, navigation of Mississippi and St. Lawrence; Indians; impressment;
Dec. 24, treaty signed. — Later diplomacy (§§ 146, 147, 154, 162, 166, 173).

General — Henry Adams, *United States*, VI, chs. ii–xx, VII, VIII, IX, chs. i–iii, and
Albert Gallatin, 443; F. F. Beirne, *War of 1812* (1949); Channing, *History*, IV, chs.
xvi–xx; Allen Johnson, *Jefferson and His Colleagues*, chs. x–xii; R. D. Paine, *Fight for a
Free Sea* (1920); Babcock, *Rise of American Nationality*, chs. iv–viii, x, xi; Hunt, *James
Madison*, chs. xxxi–xxxiv; Schurz, *Henry Clay*, I, chs. v, vi; Mayo, *Henry Clay*, chs. ix–
xiii; Wiltse, *Calhoun*, I, chs. iv–vii; Bemis, *John Quincy Adams*, chs. viii–x; J. H. Parks,
Felix Grundy (1940), chs. iii, iv; Dodd, *Nathaniel Macon*, ch. xvi; Follett, *Speaker*,
§§ 41–46. See also: general histories (§ 59) for this period.

Special — The West and The War: J. W. Pratt, *Expansionists of 1812* (1949), and
"Western Aims," *Miss. Valley Hist. Rev.*, XII (1925), 36, and "Fur Trade Strategy," *Am.
Hist. Rev.*, XL (1935), 246; L. M. Hacker, "Western Land Hunger," *Miss. Valley Hist.
Rev.*, X (1924), 365; Billington, *Westward Expansion*, ch. xiii; Burt, *United States, Great
Britain and British North America*, chs. xi–xv; Weinberg, *Manifest Destiny*; W. H. Good-
man, "Origins of the War of 1812," *Miss. Valley Hist. Rev.*, XXVIII (1942), 171; D. B.
Goebel, *William Henry Harrison* (1926), chs. iii–vi; Cleaves, *Old Tippecanoe*, chs. v–xvii;
E. T. Raymond, *Tecumseh* (1915), chs. vi–x; M. M. Quaife, *Chicago and the Old North-
west* (1913), chs. viii–xi; Cox, *West Florida Controversy*, chs. ix–xvii; Porter, *John Jacob
Astor*, I, chs. viii–xi; Kellogg, *British Régime in Wisconsin*, chs. xvii–xx; L. A. Tohill,
Robert Dickson (1927), chs. iv–x. ❧ Military History: Fortescue, *History of the British
Army*, VIII, ch. xvi, IX, ch. x, X, chs. xix, xx; C. P. Lucas, *Canadian War of 1812* (1906);
Matilda Edgar, *General Brock* (1926); Emory Upton, *Military Policy of the United
States* (1904), chs. ix–xii; L. L. Babcock, *War of 1812 on the Niagara Frontier* (1927);
B. J. Lossing, *Pictorial Field Book of the War of 1812* (1868); William James, *Full and
Correct Account of the Military Occurrences* (2 vols., 1818); Bassett, *Andrew Jackson*, I,
chs. vi–xiii; Eron Rowland, *Andrew Jackson's Campaign against the British* (1926).
❧ Naval History: A. T. Mahan, *Sea Power in War of 1812*; Theodore Roosevelt, *Naval
War of 1812* (1882); Sprout, *Rise of American Naval Power*, chs. v, vi; Allan Westcott,
ed., *American Sea Power Since 1775* (1947), chs. iv–vi; Maclay, *United States Navy*, I,
305, and *American Privateers*, pt. 2; Knox, *United States Navy*, chs. viii–xii; George
Coggeshall, *American Privateers* (1861); Paullin, *John Rodgers*, chs. x, xi; Lewis, *Romantic Decatur*, chs. ix–xiii; Chapelle, *American Sailing Ships*, chs. ii, iii; William James,
Full and Correct Account of the Naval Occurrences (1817); Gomer Williams, *History of
the Liverpool Privateers* (1897), pt. 1, ch. vi. ❧ Finances: Dewey, *Financial History*,

§§ 59–64; P. R. Nielson, *Financial History, 1811–1816* (1926); H. C. Adams, *Public Debts* (1887), pt. 2, ch. i, and *Taxation in the United States*; Henry Adams, *Albert Gallatin*, 426; J. B. McMaster, *Life and Times of Stephen Girard* (2 vols., 1918), II, chs. ix, x; Porter, *John Jacob Astor*, I, ch. xi. ❡ Peace: Bemis, *American Secretaries of State*, III, 266, and *John Quincy Adams*, ch. x, and *Diplomatic History*, ch. x; Bailey, *Diplomatic History*, ch. x; Mahan, *Sea Power in War of 1812*, II, ch. xviii; F. A. Updyke, *Diplomacy of the War of 1812* (1915), chs. iii–xi; Moore, *Arbitrations*, I, ch. xi; J. C. Hildt, *Early Diplomatic Negotiations of the United States with Russia* (1906), chs. iii, iv. ❡ Maps: Paullin, *Atlas*, plates 47A, 102G, 113A; Babcock, *Rise of American Nationality*, 6, 88, 136, 276; Henry Adams, *United States*, VI–VIII; Shepherd, *Atlas*, 200.

Sources — Debates: *Annals of Congress*, XXIII–XXVIII; Benton, *Abridgment*, IV, V. ❡ Official Documents: *Statutes at Large*, II, III; *American State Papers, Foreign*, III, *Finance*, II, *Misc.*, II, 938, *Commerce*, I, *Military*, I, *Naval*, I; Richardson, *Messages and Papers*, I; Miller, *Treaties*, II, 557. ❡ Collections of Documents: William Wood, *Select British Documents of the Canadian War of 1812* (4 vols., 1920–28); C. K. Webster, *British Diplomacy 1813–1815* (1921); Manning, *Diplomatic Correspondence Canadian Relations*, I, 617; E. A. Cruikshank, ed., *Documentary History of the Campaign on the Niagara Frontier* (9 vols., 1896–1908), and *Documents Relating to the Invasion of Canada and the Surrender of Detroit* (1912); C. O. Paullin, *Battle of Lake Erie* (1918); Moore, *Digest of International Law*, §§ 319–20, 829, 1167, 1217, 1219, and *Adjudications, Modern*, VI; J. B. Scott, ed., *Prize Cases* (3 vols., 1923), I, II; Dunbar, *Currency, Finance, and Banking*, 62; National Monetary Commission, *Laws Concerning Money*, 72, 491; T. H. Palmer, ed., *Historical Register* (4 vols., 1814–16); *Niles' Weekly Register*, I–VIII. ❡ Contemporary Writings: J. Q. Adams, *Memoirs*, II, III, and *Writings*, IV, V; Gallatin, *Writings*, I; J. A. Bayard, "Papers," Am. Hist. Assoc., *Report*, 1913; II, 202; Jonathan Russell, "Letters," Mass. Hist. Soc., *Proc.*, XLIV (1911), 305; Jefferson, *Writings* (Liscomb and Bergh, eds.), VI, (Ford ed.), IX, 337; Madison, *Writings* (Congress ed.), II, 523, III, 373, (Hunt ed.), VIII, 173; Monroe, *Writings*, V, 205, 364, VII, 93; Clay, *Works*, I, ch. ix, IV, ch. i; Daniel Mallory, ed., *Henry Clay* (2 vols., 1843), I; Calhoun, *Works*, II, V; W. H. Harrison, "Messages and Letters," *Ind. Hist. Coll.*, VII, IX (1922); Jackson, *Correspondence*, I, II; D. D. Tompkins, *Public Papers* (3 vols., 1898–1902); Dallas, *A. J. Dallas*, 234; Arthur Wellesley, duke of Wellington, *Supplementary Despatches* (1858–72), IX; James Gallatin, *Diary* (1916); pts. 1, 2; Williston, *Eloquence of the United States*, III; Carey, *Olive Branch*; M. B. Smith, *Forty Years of Washington Society*, 89.

Bibliography — Bemis and Griffin, *Guide to Diplomatic History*, 147; Pratt, *Expansionists of 1812*, 275; Winsor, *Narrative and Critical History*, VII, 420, 457, 485, 486, 521; J. W. Cronin and W. H. Wise, *Bibliography of Madison and Monroe* (1935); Nielson, *Financial History*, 104; C. T. Harbeck, *Contribution to Bibliography of History of United States Navy* (1906), 15–39; G. W. Allen, comp., *List of Articles Relating to United States Navy* (2 vols., 1915); Lewis, *Romantic Decatur*, 258; Library of Congress, *List of References on Illegal Trade between United States and Great Britain during War of 1812* (1915).

139. OPPOSITION TO THE WAR, 1811–1815

Summary — Party opposition (§§ 127, 132, 133): John Randolph (§135); Federalists; peace Republicans; DeWitt Clinton. — New England sectionalism; militia question; attitude toward government loans. — Trade: New England and the British blockade; overland trade from North to South; dealings with the enemy. — Hartford Convention: 1814, Oct., called by Massachusetts; states represented; temper of the convention; proposed amendments to the Constitution; projected second convention; collapse on news of the peace (§ 138).

General — Henry Adams, *United States*, VI, chs. vii, xviii–xx, VIII, chs. i, viii–xi; Morison, *Harrison Gray Otis*, II, chs. xx–xxviii; Babcock, *Rise of American Nationality*, ch. ix; Hunt, *James Madison*, ch. xxxiii. See also: general histories (§ 59) for this period.

Special — F. M. Anderson, "Opposition to War of 1812," Miss. Valley Hist. Assoc., *Proc.*, VI (1912–13), 176; Robinson, *Jeffersonian Democracy*, ch. v; Alexander, *History of New York*, I, ch. xviii; Lodge, *George Cabot*, chs. x–xiii; Quincy, *Josiah Quincy*, chs. ix–xiv; Pickering and Upham, *Timothy Pickering*, IV, ch. vi, vii; Bruce, *John Randolph*, I, 368; G. T. Curtis, *Life of Daniel Webster* (1870), I, chs. iv–vi; Dorothie Bobbé, *DeWitt Clinton* (1933), 180; T. C. Smith, "War Guilt in 1812," Mass. Hist. Soc., *Proc.*, LXIV (1932), 319; J. T. Adams, *New England in Republic*, ch. xii. ◖ Maps: Paullin, *Atlas*, plates 102, 113A.

Sources — Official Documents: *Annals of Congress*, XXIV, XXV, XXVIII, Apps.; Richardson, *Messages and Papers*, I, 516, II, 226. ◖ Collections of Documents: Ames, *State Documents*, No. 2; *Niles' Weekly Register*, II–VIII; Dwight, *Hartford Convention*; Henry Adams, *New England Federalism*; Carey, *Olive Branch*. ◖ Contemporary Writings: Sparks, *Gouverneur Morris*, III, 273; King, *Rufus King*, V, chs. xiv–xxv, Apps. ii–iv; Steiner, *James McHenry*, ch. xix; S. E. Morison, "Massachusetts Embassy to Washington," Mass. Hist. Soc., *Proc.*, XLVIII (1915), 343; H. G. Otis, "Two Letters on the Hartford Convention," *ibid.*, LX (1926), 24; Sullivan, *Familiar Letters*, letters lx–lxx; Goodrich, *Recollections*, I, letters xxvii–xxx, II, letter xxxi.

Bibliography — Morison, *Harrison Gray Otis*, II, 313; Winsor, *Narrative and Critical History*, VII, 320–322, 343, 522.

140. SETTLEMENT OF THE WEST, 1789–1820

Summary — Frontier in 1790 (§ 128). — The geographic base. — Influence of Indian wars and foreign relations (§ 129); 1795, Greenville treaty; Indian cessions under Jefferson; extinction of Indian title after War of 1812. — Public land and speculation (§§ 123, 128): 1796, Cleaveland and Western Reserve; Virginia Military Tract; Yazoo lands; credit system of 1800; Panic of 1819; relief bills; 1820, cash system adopted (§ 142). — Regional settlements and frontier; pioneer agriculture; rise of a trans-Allegheny agricultural surplus; home market argument; Ohio and Mississippi river trade; demand for internal improvements (§§ 142, 149); River and lake transportation (§ 123). — Banking (§ 123). — Pioneer society: ideals; religion. — Immigration (§ 150). — Government: admission of new states: 1791, Mar. 4, Vermont; 1792, June 1, Kentucky; 1796, June 1, Tennessee; 1803, Ohio; 1812, Apr. 30, Louisiana (§ 134); 1816, Dec. 11, Indiana; 1816, Dec. 10, Mississippi; 1818, Dec. 3, Illinois; 1819, Dec. 14, Alabama (22d). — Territories formed: 1789, Aug. 7, Northwest confirmed; 1790, May 26, South of the Ohio; 1798, Apr. 7, Mississippi; 1800, May 7, Indiana; 1804, May 26, Orleans (§ 134); 1805, Jan. 11, Michigan; Mar. 3, Louisiana; 1809, Feb. 3, Illinois; 1812, June 4, Missouri; 1817, Mar. 3, Alabama; 1819, Mar. 2, Arkansas. — Later frontier history and settlements (§§ 145, 148). — Later states and territories (§ 152).

General — Paxson, *American Frontier*, chs. viii–xxvi; Channing, *History*, V, chs. i, ii; Billington, *Westward Expansion*, chs. xii–xvii; R. E. Riegel, *America Moves West* (1930), chs. v–xiv; D. E. Clark, *West in American History* (1937), chs. xii–xxvi; Roosevelt, *Winning of West*, IV, chs. iii, v, VI, chs. i, iii; Winsor, *Westward Movement*, chs. xviii, xxii; Hockett, *Western Influences*; Callender, *Selections from Economic History of United States*, 313, 597, 617, 666; L. C. Gray, *Agriculture in Southern United States*, I, ch. xix, II, chs. xxix–xxxviii; Everett Dick, *Dixie Frontier* (1948); Bidwell and Falconer, *Agriculture in Northern United States*, chs. xi–xix; K. W. Colegrove, "Attitude of Congress toward the Pioneers," *Iowa Jour. of Hist. and Pol.*, VIII (1910), 3; § 123.

Special — Geographic Base (§§ 20–22, 67): Smith and Phillips, *North America*, chs. xii–xxii; Bowman, *Forest Physiography*, chs. xxiv, xxv, xxxii, xxxiii; Brigham, *Geographic Influences*, chs. iv–vi; Jedidiah Morse, *Universal Geography* (2 vols., 1802), I; Peck, *New Guide to West*; Timothy Flint, *Condensed Geography of Western States* (2 vols., 1828); H. H. Bennett, *Soils of Southern States* (1921); Vance, *Human Geography of South*; H. W. Odum, *Southern Regions* (1936); G. D. Hubbard, "Geographic Influence," Am. Geog. Soc., *Bull.*, XXXVI (1904), 145; H. H. Barrows, "Geography of Middle Illinois

Valley," Ill. State Geol. Surv., *Bull.*, No. 15 (1916); Frank Leverett, "Surface Geology of Michigan," Mich. Geol. Biol. Surv., *Publ.*, XXV (1917). ❡ Indian Problems (§ 129): A. H. Abel, "Indian Consolidation," Am. Hist. Assoc., *Report*, 1906, I, chs. i–iv; H. P. Beers, *Western Military Frontier* (1935), chs. i–v; E. B. Wesley, *Guarding the Frontier* (1935); F. J. Turner, *Early Writings* (1938), 87; I. A. Johnson, *Michigan Fur Trade* (1919), chs. iv–x; R. B. Way, "Factory System for Trading," *Miss. Valley Hist. Rev.*, VI (1920), 220. ❡ Public Land Laws and Speculation: Robbins, *Our Landed Heritage*, ch. ii; Hibbard, *Public Land Policies*, chs. i–iv; Treat, *National Land System*, chs. iv–xiv; Donaldson, *Public Domain*; J. S. Davis, *Earlier History of American Corporations*, I, chs. v–viii; Shaw Livermore, *Early American Land Companies* (1939), ch. v; Turner, *Phelps and Gorham's Purchase*; P. D. Evans, *Holland Land Company* (1924), and "Pulteney Purchase," N. Y. State Hist. Assoc., *Quar. Jour.*, III (1922), 83; H. I. Cowan, *Charles Williamson* (1941); C. H. Haskins, "Yazoo Land Companies," Am. Hist. Assoc., *Papers*, V (1891), 393; Sakolski, *Great American Land Bubble*, chs. iii–ix; Turner and Merk, *References on History of West*, chs. xiii–xix. ❡ Settlement: Buck, *Planting of Civilization in Western Pennsylvania*, chs. x–xxi; Hedrick, *Agriculture in New York*; Bond, *Civilization of Old Northwest*; Buley, *Old Northwest*; Esarey, *Indiana*, I, chs. v–x, xv; Alvord, *Illinois Country*, chs. xviii–xxi; S. J. Buck, *Illinois in 1818* (1917); T. C. Pease, *Frontier State* (1918), chs. i–v; A. C. Boggess, *Settlement of Illinois* (1908); Edwards, *Illinois*; Fuller, *Economic and Social Beginnings of Michigan*, chs. i–iv; T. M. Cooley, *Michigan* (1905), chs. viii, x; Kellogg, *British Regime in Wisconsin*, chs. xiv–xx; Joseph Schafer, *History of Agriculture in Wisconsin* (1922), chs. i, ii; Harvey Wish, "French of Old Missouri," *Mid-America*, XXIII (1941), 167; Jonas Viles, "Missouri before 1804," *Mo. Hist. Rev.*, V (1911), 189; E. M. Violette, *History of Missouri* (1918), chs. iii–v; Houck, *Missouri*; Savelle, *George Morgan*, chs. ix, x; T. D. Clark, *Kentucky*, chs. vii–x; Connelley and Coulter, *Kentucky*, I, chs. xxxvi–xlv, II, chs. xlvi–lxi; T. P. Abernethy, *Frontier to Plantation*, chs. vii–xiv, and *Formative Period in Alabama* (1922); Rowland, *History of Mississippi*, I, chs. ix–xii. See also: § 62. ❡ Immigration: See: § 123. ❡ Transportation and Trade: A. B. Hulbert, *Paths of Inland Commerce* (1920), and *Historic Highways*, VIII–XII; Meyer, *History of Transportation*, chs. i–v; Dunbar, *History of Travel*, I, chs. x–xviii, II, chs. xix–xxv; Durrenberger, *Turnpikes*, chs. iii–vi; W. A. Pusey, *Wilderness Road* (1921); J. W. Coleman, *Stage Coach Days in Blue Grass* (1935), chs. i–x; A. F. Harlow, *Old Towpaths* (1926); Baldwin, *Keelboat Age*; Hunter, *Steamboats on Western Rivers*, pts. 1, 2; Ambler, *Transportation in Ohio Valley*, 17; J. T. Flexner, *Steamboats Come True* (1944); Dickinson, *Robert Fulton*; Turnbull, *John Stevens*; T. A. Boyd, *Poor John Fitch* (1935); Rich, *United States Post Office*, ch. v; Malcolm Keir, *March of Commerce* (1927), chs. iii, iv. ❡ For the issue of internal improvements, see: § 125. ❡ See also: § 149. ❡ Banking and Currency: See §§ 123, 125. ❡ Pioneer Society: Turner, *Frontier in American History*, chs. i, xi; Henry Adams, *United States*, I, 52, 156, 184; Roscoe Pound, *Spirit of Common Law* (1921), ch. v; J. E. Wright and D. S. Corbett, *Pioneer Life* (1940); J. M. Miller, *Genesis of Western Culture* (1938); Meredith Nicholson, *Hoosiers* (1915); J. C. Campbell, *Southern Highlanders* (1921), chs. ii–iv; Phillips, *Life and Labor in Old South*, chs. v, xiv, xvi, xvii; A. B. Hart, *Southern South* (1910), ch. iii; W. W. Sweet, *Story of Religion*, chs. xiv–xvii, and *Methodism in American History* (1933), chs. viii–xi; Asbury, *Methodist Saint*, chs. x–xv; W. B. Posey, *Development of Methodism in Old Southwest* (1933); Cleveland, *Great Revival in West*; T. T. McAvoy, *Catholic Church in Indiana* (1940); Sonne, *Liberal Kentucky*; C. B. Goodykoontz, *Home Missions on American Frontier* (1939), chs. iv, v; O. W. Elsbree, *Rise of Missionary Spirit in America* (1928); P. G. Mode, *Frontier Spirit in American Christianity* (1923). ❡ Government: Douglas, "Boundaries"; Bond, *Civilization Old Northwest*. ❡ Maps: Paullin, *Atlas*, plate 76; *Twelfth Census, Statistical Atlas*, plates 2–5; Mathews, *Expansion of New England*, 174, 178, 182, 206; Bur. of Ethnology, *Annual Report*, XVIII (1896–97), pt. 2; Avery, *History of United States*, VII, 264; *Harper's Atlas*, 23, 24, 28, 32–34, 36; Shepherd, *Atlas*, 202, 203.

Sources — Official Documents: *American State Papers, Public Lands*, I–III, *Indian Affairs*, I, II, *Misc.*, I, 724; Kappler, *Indian Affairs*, II; Richardson, *Messages and Papers*, I, II; *Congressional Globe*, 25 Cong., 3 sess., App. 52, 53. ❡ For references to Congressional debates, see: Colgrove, "Attitude of Congress toward Pioneers"; Carter, *Territorial Papers*, II–XVIII. ❡ Collections of Documents: Pease, *Laws of Northwest Territory*; Philbrick, *Laws of Illinois Territory*, and *Laws of Indiana Territory*; W. W. Woollen, *et al.*, eds., "Executive Journal of Indiana Territory," Ind. Hist. Soc., *Publ.*, III, No. 3 (1900); "Documents Relating to Detroit, 1805–1813," *Mich. Hist. Coll.*, XL (1929); Rowland, *Mississippi Territorial Archives*, I; Claiborne, *Official Letter Books*; A. B. Hulbert, ed., *Records of Ohio Company* (2 vols., 1917); Rowena Buell, *Memoirs of Rufus Putnam* (1903); Symmes, *Correspondence*; Askin, *Papers*; I. J. Cox and R. C. McGrane, eds., "Documents Relating to Zachariah Cox," Ohio Hist. and Phil. Soc., *Publ.*, VIII (1913), Nos. 2, 3; Hawkins, *Letters*; Sweet, *Religion on American Frontier*, I–IV. ❧ Travels: (§ 48); S. S. Forman, *Narrative of a Journey in 1789–90* (1888); James Smith, "Tours into Kentucky"; Brissot de Warville, *Nouveau voyage*, I, letters xviii, xxvi, xliv; Baily, *Journal*; Melish, *Travels*, II; Audubon, *Journals*; Weld, *Travels*; Thwaites, *Early Western Travels*, III–V, VIII–XII. ❧ Reminiscences: Crèvecoeur, *Letters from an American Farmer*, letters ii, xii; *American Husbandry* (2 vols., 1775; H. J. Carman, ed., 1939); David Zeisberger, "Diaries" (A. B. Hulbert and W. N. Schwarze, eds.), *Ohio Archeol. and Hist. Quar.*, XXI (1912), 1, and *Diary* (E. F. Bliss, ed., 2 vols., 1885); Weed, "Autobiography," ch. ii; W. C. Howells, *Recollections* (1895); J. M. Peck, *Forty Years of Pioneer Life* (1864); Birkbeck, *Letters from Illinois*; Ninian Edwards, *Papers* (E. B. Washburne, ed., 1884); John Owen, *Journal and Letters*; Gideon Lincecum, "Autobiography," Miss. Hist. Soc., *Publ.*, VIII (1904), 443; M. J. Welsh, "Recollections of Pioneer Life in Mississippi," *ibid.*, IV (1901), 343; E. S. Tipple, *Heart of Asbury's Journal* (1916); Cartwright, *Autobiography*; Commons, *Documentary History*, II, 165; Hart, *American History Told by Contemporaries*, III, ch. xxi; E. D. Mansfield, *Personal Memories* (1879), chs. i–iii; Flint, *Recollections*.

Bibliography — Turner and Merk, *References on History of West*, chs. xiii, xv–xxiii; F. J. Turner, *Rise of New West* (1906), 336, 341; E. E. Edwards, *Bibliography of History of Agriculture*, and *References on Frontier*, and *References on Mountaineers of Southern Appalachians* (1935); Gray, *Agriculture in Southern United States*, II, 945; Abernethy, *Frontier to Plantation*, 365; S. J. Buck, *Travel and Description* (1914), 35; Hulbert, *Paths of Inland Commerce*, 197; Abel, "Indian Consolidation," 413; Beers, *Western Military Frontier*, 178.

141. THE ATLANTIC SEABOARD, 1789–1820

Summary — Agriculture: Northern staples; attempts at diversification; merino sheep craze; Southern staples, tobacco, rice, indigo; sea island cotton; 1792, invention of the cotton gin, effects on Southern economy (§ 123). — Foreign markets: effect of wars of French Revolution; Embargo and War of 1812; depression of 1819 (§§ 136–8). — Land tenure: tenancy; decline of aristocracy in North; effect of opening of the West; emigration. — Communication: problems of marketing; the turnpike era (§ 123). — Foreign and domestic commerce (§ 123); privateering (§ 136); packet service. — Industry, lumbering, and fishing. — Education; religion, growth of deism, revivalism; separation of church and state (§ 123). — Literature and the fine arts: national beginnings (§ 123).

General — Krout and Fox, *Completion of Independence*; Henry Adams, *United States*, I, IX; McMaster, *History*, II; R. H. Brown, *Mirror for Americans* (1943).

Special — Agriculture: P. W. Bidwell, "Rural Economy in New England," *Conn. Ac. Arts and Sci.*, XX (1916), 245; Bidwell and Falconer, *Agriculture in Northern United States*; Gray, *Agriculture in Southern United States*, I, chs. xix–xxiv, II, chs. xxv–xxxv; H. F. Wilson, *Hill Country*, ch. i; L. D. Stilwell, *Migration from Vermont* (1948); M. R. Pabst, "Agricultural Trends in Connecticut Valley," *Smith College Studies in History*, XXVI (1941); Purcell, *Connecticut in Transition*; Hedrick, *Agriculture in New York*; Fox, *Decline of Aristocracy in New York*, chs. i–ix; D. M. Ellis, *Landlords and Farmers in Hudson-Mohawk Region* (1946); N. A. McNall, *First Half Century of Wadsworth Tenancy* (1945), and *Genesee Country* (1952); C. R. Woodward, *Development of Agriculture in New Jersey* (1927); S. W. Fletcher, *Pennsylvania Agriculture and Country Life* (1950); Craven, *Soil Exhaustion*, ch. iii. ❧ Communication: § 123. ❧ Commerce: § 123. ❧ Education: Cubberley, *Public Education in United States*, chs. v–xi; M. E. Curti, *Social*

Ideas of American Educators (1935), chs. ii–v; C. F. Thwing, *History of Higher Education in America* (1906), chs. vii–xv; Morison, *Three Centuries of Harvard*, chs. viii–x; Wertenbaker, *Princeton;* V. L. Collins, *Princeton* (1914), chs. iv, v; E. M. Coulter, *College Life in Old South* (1928); Warfel, *Noah Webster;* Slosson, *American Spirit in Education*, chs. vi–viii. ❡ Religion: § 123; Goodykoontz, *Home Missions*, chs. iv, v; Elsbree, *Rise of Missionary Spirit;* R. H. Gabriel, *Elias Boudinot* (1941). ❡ Church and state: Greene, *Religion and State*, ch. iv; Stokes, *Church and State*, I, chs. vii–xiii, II, chs. xiv, xv; Meyer, *Church and State in Massachusetts*, chs. v–ix; M. L. Greene, *Development of Religious Liberty in Connecticut* (1905); Eckenrode, *Separation of Church and State in Virginia;* Strickland, *Religion and State in Georgia.*

Sources — Works cited §§ 123, 140, 151; J. Q. Adams, *Memoirs*, and *Writings*, III; Ruffin, *Papers; American State Papers, Finance*, II, 425; Adam Seybert, *Statistical Annals* (1818); Timothy Pitkin, *Statistical View* (1835).

Bibliography — Krout and Fox, *Completion of Independence*, ch. xvi; Spiller, *Literary History*, III.

Chapter Thirteen

THE NEW NATIONALISM, 1815–1829

142. ECONOMIC NATIONALISM, 1816–1820

Summary — Banking: state banks; 1817, specie payment restored; 1819, commercial crisis; Second Bank of the United States, 1814, bills of Dallas and Calhoun, 1815, Madison's veto, 1816, Apr. 10, charter; later history (§ 155). — Tariff: early acts (§ 125); 1812, July 1, tariff rates doubled; growth of manufactures; 1815, deluge of British goods; 1816, protective tariff act; 1818, iron act; 1820, tariff bill fails; later history (§§ 147, 156). — Internal improvements: 1811–18, Cumberland Road opened to the Ohio; 1807, Coast Survey; 1807–12, rise of steam navigation; 1808, Gallatin's report; 1817, Mar. 3, Madison's veto of the Bonus bill; 1822, May 4, Monroe's veto; Clay's American system (§§ 123, 140, 148). — Commerce: Anglo-American maritime rivalry; growth of internal commerce; river and lake trade. — Diplomacy of commerce: 1815, Algerine conflict; 1816, peace; 1815, commercial convention with England; 1818, fisheries convention; question of West Indies trade; retaliatory legislation. — 1817, Rush-Bagot agreement.

General — Turner, *New West*, ch. xiii; Channing, *History*, V, chs. i, x; Babcock, *Rise of American Nationality*, chs. xii–xiv; Callender, *Selections from Economic History of United States*, 387, 432, 487; Hockett, *Constitutional History*, I, ch. xvii, and *Western Influences*, chs. iv, v; A. C. McLaughlin, *Constitutional History* (1935), ch. xxvii; Dorfman, *Economic Mind*, I, ch. xviii; Schurz, *Henry Clay*, I, 126; Wiltse, *Calhoun*, I, chs. viii–xvii; Meigs, *Calhoun*, I chs. ix, x; Fuess, *Daniel Webster*, I, ch. vii; Dodd, *Nathaniel Macon*, 291; Ambler, *Thomas Ritchie*, chs. iii, iv. — See also general histories (§ 59).

Special — Banking: Dewey, *Financial History*, ch. vii, and *State Banking before Civil War*, 5; R. C. H. Catterall, *Second Bank of United States* (1903), chs. i–iv; C. C. Huntington, "Banking and Currency in Ohio," *Ohio Archeol. and Hist. Quar.*, XXIV (1915), chs. i–iv; W. G. Sumner, *History of American Currency* (1874), 61; also § 123. ❡ Tariff: Taussig, *Tariff History*, 17; Stanwood, *Tariff Controversies*, I, chs. v, vi; M. R. Eiselen, *Rise of Pennsylvania Protectionism* (1932), chs. ii, iii; Jervey, *Robert Y. Hayne*, ch. ix; V. S. Clark, *History of Manufactures*, chs. xi, xii; Bishop, *American Manufactures*, II, 177; Ware, *Early New England Cotton Manufacture*, ch. v. ❡ Internal Improvements: A. B. Hulbert, *Cumberland Road* (1904); P. D. Jordan, *National Road* (1948). ❡ Foreign Relations: R. W. Irwin, *Diplomatic Relations of United State with Barbary Powers*, ch. xii; Allen, *Navy and Barbary Corsairs*, chs. xvi, xvii; Maclay, *United States Navy*, II, ch. i; Lewis, *Romantic Decatur*, ch. xiv; Bemis, *John Quincy Adams*, chs. xi, xii; Setser, *Commercial Reciprocity Policy*, ch. vi; F. L. Benns, *American Struggle for British West India Carrying Trade* (1923), chs. ii–iv; McFarland, *New England Fisheries*; E. A. Ackerman, *New England's Fishing Industry* (1941); Innis, *Cod Fisheries*, chs. viii–x; Moore, *Digest of International Law*, §§ 164, 830–832; M. A. Hess, *American Tobacco and Central European Policy* (1948), chs. iii–v; J. M. Callahan, *Neutrality of American Lakes* (1898); J. H. Powell, *Richard Rush* (1942), chs. iv–vi.

Sources — Debates: *Annals of Congress*, XXIX–XXXVI. ❡ Official Documents: *Statutes at Large*, III; *American State Papers, Finance*, III, *Commerce*, II, *Naval*, I, *Public Lands*, II, III, *Misc.*, I, 724; Richardson, *Messages and Papers*, I, II; Miller, *Treaties*, I. ❡ Collections of Documents: Ames, *State Documents*, Nos. 42–47; Dunbar, *Currency, Finance, and Banking*, 79; National Monetary Commission, *Laws Concerning Money*, 97, 288; Clarke and Hall, *Bank of United States*, chs. iii–vi; 42 Cong., 2 Sess., *H. Ex. Doc.*, No. 109; Manning, *Diplomatic Correspondence, Canadian Relations*, I. ❡ Contemporary Writings: Clay, *Works*, I, ch. xix, II, ch. vi, IV, ch. ii; Calhoun, *Works*, II; Gallatin, *Writings*, I, 690, II; Madison, *Writings* (Congress ed.), III, (Hunt ed.), VIII, 335; King, *Rufus King*, V, ch. xxvii, App. vi. ❡ Economic Writings: *Niles' Weekly Register*, I–X; Seybert, *Statistical Annals*; John Bristed, *Resources of United States* (1818); [S. A.] *Mitchell's Compendium of Internal Improvements* (1835); Blane, *Excursion Through United States*; Cobbett, *Year's Residence*.

Bibliography — Winsor, *Narrative and Critical History*, VII, 278; Dewey, *Financial History*, § 65; Griffin, *List of Works relating to First and Second Banks*; U.S. Tariff Commission, *Tariff*, 41; V. S. Clark, *History of Manufactures*, 625; Meyer, *History of Transportation*, 609; G. H. Fuller and F. S. Hellman, *Waterways in United States* (1938); E. R. Johnson, *Domestic and Foreign Commerce*, II, 352; Setser, *Commercial Reciprocity Policy*, 261–280; Ragatz, "Guide for Study of British Caribbean History"; H. H. B. Meyer and W. A. Slade, comps., *Select List of References on the Monetary Question* (1913), 116.

143. THE GREAT CONSTITUTIONAL DECISIONS, 1792–1824

Summary — Supreme Court under Washington and Adams (§ 124); under Jefferson (§ 133). — Declaring acts of Congress void: 1803, Marbury *v.* Madison (§ 133). — Limiting the states: 1793, Chisholm *v.* Georgia; 1794, Eleventh Amendment; 1809, United States *v.* Judge Peters (inferior authority of states); 1810, Fletcher *v.* Peck (Yazoo land case); 1816, Martin *v.* Hunter's Lessee (state act unconstitutional); 1819, Sturges *v.* Crowninshield and Dartmouth College case (impairment of contracts); 1821, Cohens *v.* Virginia (appeals from state courts sustained); 1827, Brown *v.* Maryland (foreign commerce); 1832, Worcester *v.* Georgia (jurisdiction over Indians; § 154). — Implied powers of Congress asserted (§ 126): 1796, Hylton *v.* United States (carriage tax); 1819, M'Culloch *v.* Maryland (bank); 1820, Houston *v.* Moore (militia); 1821, Anderson *v.* Dunn (judicial authority of Congress); 1824, Gibbons *v.* Ogden (commerce); 1824, Osborn *v.* Bank of the United States (bank); 1827, Martin *v.* Mott (militia). — Later cases (§§ 153, 154, 177).

General — McLaughlin, *Constitutional History*, chs. xxiii, xxx; Hockett, *Constitutional History*, I, chs. xiv, xv, xvii, xviii; Warren, *Supreme Court*, I, chs. v–xvi; Corwin, *John Marshall*, chs. iii–vii; Thayer, *John Marshall*; Beveridge, *John Marshall*, III, chs. iii, x, IV, chs. i–ix; C. B. Swisher, *American Constitutional Development*, chs. viii–xi; C. G. Haines, *Role of Supreme Court, 1789–1835* (1944), chs. iv–xiv; Van Buren, *Inquiry into Political Parties*, ch. vi; Boudin, *Government by Judiciary*, I, chs. i–xii.

Special — Felix Frankfurter, *Commerce Clause under Marshall, Taney, and Waite* (1937), ch. i; G. G. Reynolds, *Distribution of Power to Regulate Interstate Carriers* (1928), ch. ii; B. F. Wright, *Contract Clause* (1938), chs. i, ii; J. M. Shirley, *Dartmouth College Causes* (1879); W. B. Hunting, *Obligation of Contracts Clause* (1919); E. L. Bogart, "Taxation of Second Bank," *Am. Hist. Rev.*, XVII (1912), 312; U. B. Phillips, "Georgia and State Rights," Am. Hist. Assoc., *Report*, 1901, II, 24; W. E. Dodd, "Marshall and Virgina," *Am. Hist. Rev.*, XII (1907), 776; Story, *Commentaries*, §§ 1033–44, 1259–81, 1374–97, 1685–8; Burdick, *Law of Constitution*, chs. v, vii, viii, xxii; Roscoe Pound, *Formative Era of American Law* (1938), chs. i–iii; C. G. Haines, *Conflict over Judicial Powers* (1909), chs. ii–iv; C. A. M. Ewing, *Judges of Supreme Court* (1938). ❡ Biographies: Story, *Joseph Story*, I, chs. vii–xv; Lewis, *Great American Lawyers*, III, 121; Fuess, *Daniel Webster*, I, chs. ix, x; Kennedy, *William Wirt*, II, chs. v, ix; Horton, *James Kent*; also § 133.

Sources — Contemporary Writings: Webster, *Writings*, X, XI; Dallas, *A. J. Dallas*, 59; Spencer Roane, "Papers," *John P. Branch Historical Papers*, I (1904), 325, II, 78; Madison, *Writings* (Hunt ed.), VIII, 447, IX, 58; Jefferson, *Writings* (Ford ed.), X, 140, 188, 189; John Taylor, *Construction Construed* (1820); Kendall, *Autobiography*, ch. vii; Ames, *State Documents*, 7, 45, 93. ❡ Cases: United States *v.* Judge Peters (1809): 5 *Cranch*, 115; Marshall, *Writings*, 119. — Fletcher *v.* Peck (1810): 6 *Cranch*, 87; 2 *Curtis*, 328; Thayer, *Cases*, 114; Marshall, *Writings*, 126. — Martin *v.* Hunter's Lessee (1816): 1 *Wheaton*, 304; 3 *Curtis*, 562; Thayer, *Cases*, 123; Marshall, *Writings*, 525. — Sturges *v.* Crowninshield (1819): 4 *Wheaton*, 122; 4 *Curtis*, 362; Marshall, *Writings*, 147. — Dartmouth College *v.* Woodward (1819): 4 *Wheaton*, 518; 4 *Curtis*, 463; Marshall, *Writings*, 188. — M'Culloch *v.* Maryland (1819): 4 *Wheaton*, 316; 4 *Curtis*, 415; Thayer, *Cases*, 271, 1340; Marshall, *Writings*, 160. — Cohens *v.* Virginia (1821): 6 *Wheaton*, 264; 5 *Curtis*, 82; Thayer, *Cases*, 285; Marshall, *Writings*, 221. — Anderson *v.* Dunn (1821): 6 *Wheaton*, 204; 5 *Curtis*, 61; Marshall, *Writings*, 603. — Gibbons *v.* Ogden (1824): 9 *Wheaton*, 1; 6 *Curtis*, 1; Thayer, *Cases*, 1799; Marshall, *Writings*, 287–314. — Osborn *v.* Bank (1824): 9 *Wheaton*, 738; 6 *Curtis*, 251; Marshall, *Writings*, 315. — Martin *v.* Mott (1827): 12 *Wheaton*, 19; 7 *Curtis*, 10; Thayer, *Cases*, 2290; Marshall, *Writings*, 611.

Bibliography — Hockett, *Constitutional History*, I, 381; Burchfield, *Student's Guide to Political Science*, 17; M. R. Senior, comp., *Supreme Court* (1937); H. H. B. Meyer, comp., *List of Works Relating to Supreme Court* (1909).

144. ERA OF GOOD FEELINGS, 1817–1825

Summary — Monroe's presidency: election of 1816; cabinet; civil service; opposition of Clay; disappearance of Federalists; 1820, unopposed reëlection; four years' tenure act. — East Florida: 1810, 1812, annexation of West Florida (§ 134); 1814, Jackson in Pensacola; 1816, Seminole war; 1818, Jackson in St. Marks and Pensacola; Arbuthnot affair; Rhea letter; Jackson exonerated. — Negotiations with Spain: 1802, unratified convention; East Florida; Texas; 1819, treaty signed; line to the Pacific; Floridas ceded; 1821, ratification; Jackson, governor of Florida. — Oregon question: 1817, Astoria restored; 1818, convention of joint occupation; negotiations (§ 147).

General — Turner, *New West*; Babcock, *Rise of American Nationality*, chs. xv–xvii; George Dangerfield, *Era of Good Feelings* (1952); McMaster, *History*, IV, chs. xxxii–xxxviii; Channing, *History*, V, ch. x; Schouler, *History*, III, 1, 189; C. S. Sydnor, "One-Party Period of American History," *Am. Hist. Rev.*, LI (1946), 439; Schurz, *Henry Clay*, I, 146; Van Deusen, *Henry Clay*, chs. vii–x; Wiltse, *Calhoun*, I, chs. viii–xxxi; Meigs, *Calhoun*, I, chs. x, xi; Bruce, *John Randolph*, I, ch. x; Cresson, *James Monroe*, chs. xxix–xxxiv; Bassett, *Andrew Jackson*, I, chs. xiv–xvi; James, *Andrew Jackson*, I, chs. xviii–xx; Tucker, *Thomas Jefferson*, II, chs. xvi–xxi; Hockett, *Western Influences on Political Parties*, chs. iv, v.

Special — Executive: Fish, *Civil Service and Patronage*, 52; Stanwood, *Presidency*, I, chs. ix, x; Shipp, *William H. Crawford*. ❡ Foreign Relations: Bemis, *John Quincy Adams*, chs. xii–xvi, xxix, and *American Secretaries of State*, IV, 3, 86, and *Diplomatic History*, ch. xi; Bailey, *Diplomatic History*, ch. xi; C. C. Griffin, *United States and Disruption of the Spanish Empire* (1937), chs. i, vi–viii; P. C. Brooks, *Diplomacy and Borderlands* (1939); Harry Bernstein, *Origins of Inter-American Interest* (1945), chs. iii–vii; Marshall, *Western Boundary of Louisiana Purchase*, ch. iii; Frederick Merk, "Genesis of Oregon Question," *Miss. Valley Hist. Rev.*, XXXVI (1950), 583, and "Negotiations of 1818," *Am. Hist. Rev.*, LV (1950), 530. ❡ Maps: Paullin, *Atlas*, plates 93B, 95A, 103; Miller, *Treaties*, III, 41.

Sources — Debates: *Annals of Congress*, XXXI–XLII; *Register of Debates*, I; Benton, *Abridgment*, VI. ❡ Official Documents: *Statutes at Large*, III, IV; *American State Papers, Foreign*, IV, V, *Military*, I, *Misc.*, II; *Annals of Congress*, XXXII, XXXIV, XXXVI, XXXVII, Apps.; Miller, *Treaties*, III, 3; Richardson, *Messages and Papers*, I, 505, II.

❧ Contemporary Writings: Monroe, *Writings*, V, 341, VI, VII, 1, 173, 209; J. Q. Adams, *Memoirs*, IV–VI, and *Writings*, VI, VII, and *James Monroe* (1831); Clay, *Works*, I, ch. xii, IV, ch. ii; Jefferson, *Writings* (Liscomb and Bergh, eds.), VII; Calhoun, *Works*, V, VI, 349, and "Correspondence," 136, 251, 314, 343; Luis de Onís, *Memoir* (1821); Moore, *Digest of International Law*, §§ 102, 215, 216, 884; Pichardo, *Treatise;* "Panton, Leslie & Co. and John Forbes & Co., Papers," Fla. Hist. Soc., *Quar.*, IX–XVIII (1930–40).

Bibliography — Claflin, *Political Parties;* Library of Congress, *Political Parties in United States;* Brooks, *Diplomacy and Borderlands,* 220; Winsor, *Narrative and Critical History,* VII, 344, 438.

145. THE MISSOURI COMPROMISE

Summary — Slavery before 1800 (§ 128). — Slavery after 1800: 1803, slavery in Louisiana; 1807, slave trade prohibited; 1818, movement for new fugitive act; 1819, fugitive act; 1820, piracy act. — Antislavery: southern and middle state societies; American Convention; propaganda; churches; slave insurrections; cotton. — Colonization: 1816, American Society; 1819, government aid; 1820, Liberia; failure. — Missouri question: growth of population and application for statehood; Tallmadge amendment; sectional clash; Maine-Missouri bill; Thomas amendment; Compromise of 1820; Clay and the second compromise. — Questions raised: slavery issue; sectional predominance; constitutionality of restriction; danger to the Union; 1836, extension of Missouri boundary; operation to 1854 (§§ 159–60, 170–8).

General — Turner, *New West*, chs. ix, x; A. B. Hart, *Slavery and Abolition* (1906), ch. xi; C. S. Sydnor, *Development of Southern Sectionalism* (1948), ch. v; McLaughlin, *Constitutional History*, ch. xxix; von Holst, *History*, I, 324; Schurz, *Henry Clay*, I, ch. viii; Meigs, *Thomas Hart Benton*, ch. ix; Dodd, *Nathaniel Macon*, 310; Wiltse, *Calhoun*, I, ch. xv; Cresson, *James Monroe*, ch. xxxii; H. A. Garland, *Life of John Randolph* (2 vols., 1856), II, chs. xi–xiii; also general histories (§ 59) for this period.

Special — F. C. Shoemaker, *Missouri's Struggle for Statehood* (1916); F. H. Hodder, "Missouri Compromise," Am. Hist. Assoc., *Report*, 1909, 151; N. D. Harris, *History of Negro Servitude in Illinois* (1904), chs. i–v; E. L. Fox, *American Colonization Society* (1919); C. H. Huberich, *Political and Legislative History of Liberia* (2 vols., 1947), I, 19; state histories of Missouri and Maine (§ 62). ❧ Maps: Paullin, *Atlas*, plate 113D.

Sources — Debates: *Annals of Congress*, XXXVI, XXXVII; Benton, *Abridgment*, VI. ❧ Official Documents: *Statutes at Large*, III; *Annals of Congress*, XXXVI, XXXVII, Apps.; Richardson, *Messages and Papers*, II, 63, 95. ❧ Collections of Documents: Allen Johnson, *Readings in Constitutional History*, ch. xxxiii; Ames, *State Documents*, 193; Johnston and Woodburn, *American Orations*, II, 33, 63; Williston, *Eloquence of United States*, III. — Contemporary Writings: J. Q. Adams, *Memoirs*, V, VI, XII, and *Writings*, VI, VII; Clay, *Works*, I, chs. x, xiii; Jefferson, *Writings* (Liscomb and Bergh, eds.), VII, (Ford ed.), IX, 151; Madison, *Writings* (Congress ed.), III, 121, (Hunt ed.), VIII, 425, 439, IX, 1; King, *Rufus King*, VI, ch. xv, App. iv; E. S. Brown, *Missouri Compromises and Presidential Politics* (1926); *Niles' Weekly Register;* T. M. Marshall, *Life and Papers of Frederick Bates* (1926), II.

Bibliography — H. A. Trexler, *Slavery in Missouri* (1914), 241; Turner, *New West*, 344–5; Winsor, *Narrative and Critical History*, VII, 325; A. D. Adams, *Neglected Period of Anti-Slavery* (1908), App. D; Sydnor, *Southern Sectionalism*, 346; "List of Works Relating to American Colonization Society," New York City Public Library, *Bull.*, VI (1902), 265.

146. THE MONROE DOCTRINE

Summary — Spanish colonies: previous status (§§ 75, 100, 110, 129, 134); 1806, Miranda; 1806, British attack on La Plata; 1809, first revolts; 1814, Bourbons restored; 1817, San Martín crosses the Andes; 1818, second series of revolts; Clay's interest; commercial interest; 1822, American recognition. — "European system": tradition of noninterference in Europe by the United States; 1815, Holy Alliance; 1818, Congress of Aix la Chapelle; 1822, Congress of Verona. — "Intervention": 1820, Bourbons in Naples; 1821, revolt of Greece; 1823, French in Spain; Spain asks for aid against the colonies; Oct. 16, Russian dispatch on political system; 1823, Spain asks for a congress; Aug., Sept., Canning's proposition for a joint declaration; Oct. 9, pacific declaration of Polignac. — "Colonization": 1790, Nootka Sound convention (§ 129); 1821, Russia's ukase on the Northwest coast and sea; 1823, July 17, J. Q. Adams's protest. — Preparation of message: Adams and Monroe; cabinet discussion; effect of previous recognition. — Doctrine: 1823, Dec. 2, Monroe's message; new states; recognition; status; ambition of France; colonization; intervention; political system; effects on Europe; 1824, Apr. 17, American boundary treaty with Russia; 1825, Feb. 28, English boundary treaty with Russia. — Later applications: 1826, Panama Congress (§ 147); 1845, Oregon (§ 166); 1850, the Isthmus (§ 173); 1854, Cuba (§ 173); 1865, Mexico (§§ 187, 194); 1881, Peru (§ 220); 1895, Venezuela (§ 220); 1903, the Canal (§ 238); collection of debts (§ 238).

General — Dexter Perkins, *Monroe Doctrine 1823–1826* (1927), and *Hands Off*, chs. i, ii; A. P. Whitaker, *United States and Independence of Latin America* (1941); Bemis, *American Secretaries of State*, IV, 36, and *John Quincy Adams*, chs. xvii–xix, and *Latin American Policy of United States*, chs. iii–vi, and *Diplomatic History*, ch. xii, Bailey, *Diplomatic History*, ch. xii; Griffin, *United States and Disruption of Spanish Empire*; E. H. Tatum, *United States and Europe* (1936); Julius Goebel, *Recognition Policy of United States* (1915), ch. v; also general histories (§ 59) for this period.

Special — C. K. Webster, *Foreign Policy of Castlereagh 1815–1822* (1925), chs. viii, ix; H. W. V. Temperley, *Foreign Policy of Canning* (1925), chs. v–vii, ix; J. F. Rippy, *Rivalry of United States and Great Britain over Latin America* (1929), and *Joel R. Poinsett*, chs. iv–ix; John Rydjord, *Foreign Interest in Independence of New Spain* (1935); W. S. Robertson, *France and Latin American Independence* (1939); W. R. Manning, *Early Diplomatic Relations Between United States and Mexico* (1916), chs. i–viii; H. C. Evans, *Chile and Its Relations with United States* (1927), chs. i–iii; L. F. Hill, *Diplomatic Relations between United States and Brazil* (1932), chs. i, ii; Hildt, *Early Diplomatic Negotiations with Russia*; B. P. Thomas, *Russo-American Relations, 1815–1867* (1930), ch. iii; Frederick Merk, *Albert Gallatin and Oregon Problem* (1950), ch. iii; M. A. Cline, *American Attitude Toward Greek War of Independence* (1930). ❧ Privateering and Piracy: G. W. Allen, *Our Navy and West Indian Pirates* (1929); F. B. C. Bradlee, "Suppression of Piracy," *Essex Inst. Hist. Coll.*, LVIII (1922), 297, LIX (1923), 33, 105, 217, 305. ❧ Maps: *Harper's Atlas*, 35; Turner, *New West*, 208.

Sources — Official Documents: *American State Papers, Foreign*, IV, V; *Annals of Congress*, XXXII, XXXIX, Apps.; Richardson, *Messages and Papers*, II, 13, 14, 43, 44, 58, 59, 77, 88, 89, 105, 116, 192, 193, 209, 217, 260; Miller, *Treaties*, III. ❧ Collections of Documents: Manning, *Diplomatic Correspondence Concerning Latin American Nations*; Moore, *Digest of International Law*, §§ 28–36, 61; *Niles' Weekly Register*, XIV–XXV; J. W. Gantenbein, *Evolution of Latin-American Policy* (1950), 7, 301; C. K. Webster, *Britain and the Independence of Latin America* (2 vols., 1938); Alaska Boundary Tribunal, "Proceedings," 58 Cong., 2 Sess., Sen. Doc., No. 162, II, 31; T. S. Currier, *Los Corsarios del Río de la Plata* (1929); C. F. Goodrich, "Our Navy and West Indian Pirates," U. S. Naval Inst., *Proc.*, XLII (1916), 1171, XLIII (1917), 83. ❧ Contemporary Writings: J. Q. Adams, *Memoirs*, IV–VI, and *Writings*, VI, VII; Monroe, *Writings*, VI, 31, 92, 151, 207, 304; King, *Rufus King*, IV, ch. xxxii, App., 577–86; W. C. Ford, "J. Q. Adams and Monroe Doctrine," *Am. Hist. Rev.*, VII (1902), 676, VIII (1902), 28, and "Some Original Documents on Monroe Doctrine," Mass. Hist. Soc., *Proc.*, 2 ser., XV (1902), 373, and "Correspondence of Russian Ministers," *Am. Hist. Rev.*, XVIII (1913), 309, 537; Rush, *Residence at Court of London*; Webster, *Writings*, V, 60.

Bibliography — Bemis and Griffin, *Guide to Diplomatic History*, 172; Griffin, *United States and Disruption of Spanish Empire*, 289; Perkins, *Monroe Doctrine 1823–1826*, 263; Rydjord, *Foreign Interest in New Spain*, 309; H. H. B. Meyer, Comp., *List of References on Monroe Doctrine* (1919); Phillips Bradley, *Bibliography of Monroe Doctrine* (1929).

147. ADMINISTRATION OF JOHN QUINCY ADAMS

Summary — Previous public service (§§ 129, 133, 144, 147). — Election of 1824: rival candidates; methods of nomination; no electoral choice; House election of 1825; Feb. 9, Adams chosen over Jackson. — Adams's presidency: cabinet; charges of a "corrupt bargain"; criticisms of the first message; criticisms of appointments. — Emergence of new parties: Adams-Clay coalition; rival coalition of Jackson and Calhoun; position of Crawford group; effects of factionalism. — Panama Congress: 1825, invitation; special envoys nominated; 1826, opposition in House; the Congress fails. — Internal improvements: earlier history (§ 142); Adams's policy; 1824, survey act; 1825, extension of Cumberland Road (§ 142); harbors. — Indian question: previous status (§§ 129, 140, 144); 1821–25, policy and cessions; 1825, fraudulent treaty of Indian Springs; conflict of authority between the United States and Georgia; 1826, new Indian treaty; 1827, Georgia defies the United States; later developments (§§ 154, 158). — Tariff: previous status (§ 144); 1824, revised act; 1827, Mallary's woolens bill; Harrisburg convention; 1828 tariff bill; Southern objection; "tariff of abominations"; May 20, act passes. — Foreign policy: commercial treaties; West Indian trade question; 1824, draft slave-trade convention; spoliation claims. — Oregon question: renewal of convention of joint occupation.

General — Turner, *New West*, chs. xiv–xix; Channing, *History*, V, ch. xi; McMaster, *History*, V, chs. xlii, xliv, xlvi, li, lii; Schouler, *History*, III, 293; Lynch, *Fifty Years of Party Warfare*, chs. vi, vii; Schurz, *Henry Clay*, I, chs. ix–xi; Bassett, *Andrew Jackson*, I, chs. xvii, xviii; James, *Andrew Jackson*, II, chs. i–vii; J. T. Morse, *John Quincy Adams* (1882), 163; Bemis, *John Quincy Adams*, chs. xx–xxvi; Wiltse, *Calhoun*, I, chs. xxv–xxx; Meigs, *Calhoun*, I, chs. xi–xiii; Lodge, *Daniel Webster*, chs. v, vi; Curtis, *Daniel Webster*, I, chs. x–xiv; Theodore Roosevelt, *Thomas H. Benton* (1887), ch. iii; Bruce, *John Randolph*, I, ch. x.

Special — Political Problems: Stanwood, *Presidency*, I, ch. xi; F. W. Dallinger, *Nominations for Elective Office* (1897), ch. i; A. R. Newsome, *Presidential Election of 1824 in North Carolina* (1939); Binkley, *Powers of President*, ch. iii; Fish, *Civil Service and Patronage*, 70. ❡ Economic Problems: Dewey, *Financial History*, §§ 78, 79; Taussig, *Tariff History*, 68; Stanwood, *Tariff Controversies*, I, chs. vii, viii; C. W. Wright, *Wool-Growing and Tariff* (1910), ch. iii. ❡ Foreign Relations: Perkins, *Monroe Doctrine 1823–1826*, 204; Bemis, *American Secretaries of State*, IV, 115; Rippy, *Rivalry over Latin America*, 227; Setser, *Commercial Reciprocity Policy*, ch. vi; Benns, *West India Carrying Trade*, chs. iv, v; Ragatz, *Fall of Planter Class*, ch. x; Merk, *Albert Gallatin and Oregon Problem*. ❡ Indians: Abel, "Indian Consolidation," 296; Phillips, "Georgia and State Rights," 39. ❡ Maps: Turner, *New West*, 232, 242, 260; Paullin, *Atlas*, plate 103B.

Sources — Debates: *Register of Debates*, I–V; Benton, *Abridgment*, VIII, IX. ❡ Official Documents: *Statutes at Large*, IV; *American State Papers, Foreign*, VI, *Finance*, V, *Indian*, II; *Register of Debates*, I–V, Apps.; Richardson, *Messages and Papers*, II, 216, 234, 255, 256, 280, 292; Miller, *Treaties*, III. ❡ Collections of Documents: Ames, *State Documents*, 113; Taussig, *State Papers on Tariff*; Williston, *Eloquence of United States*, IV; Manning, *Diplomatic Correspondence Concerning Latin-American Nations*; Fabian Velarde and F. J. Escobar, *Congreso de Panamá* (1922); Frederick Merk, *Fur Trade and Empire: George Simpson's Journal* (1932); *Niles' Weekly Register*, XXV–XXXV. ❡ Contemporary Writings: J. Q. Adams, *Memoirs*, VI, VII; Benton, *Thirty Years' View*, I, chs. xvii–xxxvii; Clay, *Works*, I, chs. xiv–xviii, IV, chs. iii–v; Calhoun, "Correspondence," 202; A. R. Newsome, ed., "Correspondence Relating to Campaigns of 1824," *No. Car. Hist. Rev.*, VII (1930), 477; W. P. Mangum, *Papers* (H. T. Shanks, ed., 1950), I; Buchanan, *Works*, I, 80; Henry Adams, *Albert Gallatin*, 586; Gallatin, *Writings*, II; Webster, *Letters*, 89, and *Writings*, V, VI, and *Private Correspondence* (Fletcher Webster, ed., 2 vols., 1857), I, 345; Levi Woodbury, *Writings* (3 vols., 1852), I. ❡ Reminiscences: B. P. Poore, *Perley's Reminiscences* (2 vols., 1886), I, chs. i–v; Quincy, *Fig-*

ures of Past, 188; M. B. Smith, *Forty Years of Washington Society,* 162, 238; Hall, *Travels.*

Bibliography — Turner, *New West,* ch. xx; Claflin, *Political Parties;* Library of Congress, *Political Parties;* U.S. Tariff Commission, *Tariff,* 41; Ames, *State Documents,* 113; Bemis and Griffin, *Guide to Diplomatic History,* 182, 230; Benns, *West India Carrying Trade,* 189; Ragatz, *Guide for Study of British Caribbean History,* pt. 9.

Chapter Fourteen

SOCIAL AND ECONOMIC EXPANSION, 1820–1860

148. GROWTH OF AMERICAN SOCIETY, 1820–1860

Summary — Geographic base (§ 67). — Indian problem: removal policy; plains reservations. — Public land legislation and speculation: preëmption; graduation; military bounties; speculation; panics of 1837 and 1857 (§ 149); homestead-law agitation. — Regional settlement. — Northern states: migration of crops; effect on the East; migration of wool growing; pioneer farming; farm machinery; McCormick reaper. — Southern states: Westward migration of slaves; black belts of the West; effect of Western competition; agricultural depression in the tidewater; plantation economy; special crops; cotton; sugar; tobacco; stock raising; cattle droving; meat packing in the Ohio Valley. — Immigration: origins; ethnic elements; distribution; amalgamation; nativism. — Internal improvements: federal policy (§§ 142, 147, 153, 154); river improvements; state policy and results. — River and lake carriers; river rafts; steamboat life. — Canals: Erie; other Middle State systems; Western; Southern; decay. — Roads: National; state and local; corporate toll roads and bridges; macadamizing process; stage travel. — Railroads: state activity in building; rivalry for Western trade; Calhoun's plans; 1836, Nashville convention; Eastern capital in Western enterprises; 1845, Memphis convention; 1847, Chicago convention; 1850–60, extension of trunk lines; opening the prairies; 1850, railroad land grants; agitation for a Pacific railway; improvements in equipment; express; rates; control. — Communications: post office; legislation on routes; railroad mail; pony express; telegraph; first Atlantic cable.

General — Turner, *United States*, chs. i–vii, and *Frontier in American History*, chs. i, iv–xiii, and *Significance of Sections*, chs. ii, vi, vii; Paxson, *American Frontier*, chs. xxi–l; Billington, *Westward Expansion*, chs. xiv–xix; Riegel, *America Moves West*, chs. xii–xxxii; C. R. Fish, *Rise of Common Man* (1937), chs. i, iv, vi; A. C. Cole, *Irrepressible Conflict* (1934), chs. i, ii, v, vi; Channing, *History*, V, chs. i, ii, v, xv; McMaster, *History*, IV, ch. xxxiii, V, ch. xliv, VI, chs. lvi, lxiii, VII, chs. lxxi, lxxiii, lxxv, lxxvi, lxxxiv; William MacDonald, *Jacksonian Democracy* (1906), chs. i, viii, xv, xvi; Hart, *Slavery and Abolition*, chs. iii, vii; T. C. Smith, *Parties and Slavery* (1906), chs. v; J. R. Smith and Phillips, *North America*, chs. xi–xxii; G. R. Taylor, *Transportation Revolution* (1951).

Special — Indian Problem: Grant Foreman, *Last Trek of Indians* (1946), and *Indian Removal* (1932), and *Advancing the Frontier* (1933), and *Five Civilized Tribes* (1934); F. E. Stevens, *Black Hawk War* (1903); A. W. Hoopes, *Indian Affairs* (1932). ❡ Public Lands: Robbins, *Our Landed Heritage*, chs. iii–xii; R. G. Wellington, *Political and National Influence of Public Lands, 1826–1842* (1914); G. M. Stephenson, *Political History of Public Lands, 1840–1862* (1917); H. S. Zahler, *Eastern Workingmen and Land Policy, 1829–1862* (1941); P. W. Gates, "Public Domain in Illinois," *Jour. Econ. and Bus. Hist.*, III (1931), 216, and "Land Policy and Tenancy," *Jour. of Econ. Hist.*, I (1941), 60; A. C. Cole, "Variations in Sale of Public Lands," *Rev. Econ. Stat.*, IX (1927), 41. ❡ Northern States: Bidwell and Falconer, *Agriculture in Northern United*

States, chs. xi–xxxix; Joseph Schafer, *Social History of American Agriculture* (1936); H. L. Carter, "Rural Indiana in Transition," *Ag. Hist.,* XX (1946), 107; W. V. Pooley, *Settlement of Illinois* (1908), ch. xiv; P. W. Gates, *Illinois Central Railroad and Its Colonization Work* (1934), chs. i–xiii; J. G. Thompson, *Rise and Decline of Wheat Growing in Wisconsin* (1909), 13; B. H. Hibbard, *History of Agriculture in Dane County* (1904); L. G. Connor, "Sheep Industry," Am. Hist. Assoc., *Report,* 1918, I, 102; Wright, *Wool-Growing and the Tariff,* chs. iii–v; W. C. Edgar, *Story of a Grain of Wheat* (1903); Paul Weatherwax, *Story of the Maize Plant* (1923); Hutchinson, *Cyrus Hall McCormick;* T. S. Berry, *Western Prices before 1861* (1943); J. E. Boyle, *Chicago Wheat Prices* (1922); Clemen, *American Livestock Industry,* chs. i–vi; B. L. Pierce, *Chicago,* II, 90; Kuhlmann, *Flour-Milling Industry,* 38; Hedrick, *Agriculture in New York,* chs. xi–xx; McKelvey, *Rochester,* I, ch. vii; H. F. Wilson, *Hill Country,* chs. ii–iv. See: state histories (§ 62). ❧ Southern States: Gray, *Agriculture in Southern United States,* I, chs. xix–xxiv, II, chs. xxvii–xxxix; W. E. Dodd, *Cotton Kingdom* (1921), chs. i–iii; Phillips, *Life and Labor in Old South,* chs. vi–xviii; R. S. Cotterill, *Old South* (1939); Eaton, *History of Old South;* M. B. Hammond, *Cotton Industry* (1897), 67, 243; A. H. Stone, "Cotton Factorage System," *Am. Hist. Rev.,* XX (1915), 557; F. P. Gaines, *Southern Plantation* (1924); J. C. Robert, *Tobacco Kingdom* (1938); B. H. Clark, *Tennessee Yeomen, 1840–1860* (1942); Herbert Weaver, *Mississippi Farmers, 1850–1860* (1945); P. H. Buck, "Poor Whites of Ante-Bellum South," *Am. Hist. Rev.,* XXXI (1925), 41; Horace Kephart, *Our Southern Highlanders* (1913); Dick, *Dixie Frontier;* DuBois, *Slave Trade,* chs. ix, x; Frederic Bancroft, *Slave Trading in Old South* (1931); Stephenson, *Isaac Franklin;* § 159. ❧ Migration: Hansen, *Atlantic Migration,* chs. iv–xiii, and *Immigrant in American History,* chs. vii, ix; G. M. Stephenson, *History of American Immigration* (1926), chs. i–xi; Wittke, *We Who Built America,* pt. 2; Faust, *German Element,* I, chs. xii–xviii; J. A. Hawgood, *Tragedy of German-America* (1940); W. F. Adams, *Ireland and Irish Emigration* (1932); M. G. Kelly, *Catholic Immigrant Colonization Projects* (1939); Blegen, *Norwegian Migration;* Qualey, *Norwegian Settlement,* chs. i–v; F. E. Janson, *Background of Swedish Immigration* (1931), chs. i–vi; J. S. Lindberg, *Background of Swedish Emigration* (1930), chs. i–vii; B. H. Wabeke, *Dutch Emigration, 1624–1860* (1944), chs. iv, v; Fuess, *Carl Schurz,* chs. ii–vi; Stilwell, *Migration from Vermont,* chs. v–viii; Mathews, *Expansion of New England,* chs. vii–x; Buley, *Old Northwest,* I, ch. i, II, ch. x; S. H. Holbrook, *Yankee Exodus* (1950); Joseph Schafer, "Yankee and Teuton in Wisconsin," *Wisc. Mag. Hist.,* VI (1922), 125. ❧ Transportation: Dunbar, *History of Travel,* II, chs. xxx–xxxii, III, IV; Hulbert, *Paths of Inland Commerce,* chs. viii–xi; W. J. Lane, *Indian Trail to Iron Horse* (1939), chs. vii–xiii, and *Commodore Vanderbilt* (1942); J. V. Frederick, *Ben Holladay, Stagecoach King* (1940); Durrenberger, *Turnpikes,* chs. iii–x. ❧ Canals: Harlow, *Old Towpaths;* N. E. Whitford, *History of Canal System of New York* (2 vols., 1906); D. M. Ellis, "New York Central and Erie Canal," *N. Y. Hist.,* XXIX (1948), 268; A. L. Bishop, *State Works of Pennsylvania* (1907); Roberts, *Middlesex Canal;* W. S. Sanderlin, *Great National Project; Chesapeake and Ohio Canal* (1946); W. F. Dunaway, *History of James River and Kanawha Company* (1922); E. L. Bogart, *Internal Improvements and State Debt in Ohio* (1924); Logan Esarey, "Internal Improvements in Indiana," Ind. Hist. Soc., *Publ.,* V (1915), No. 2; J. W. Putnam, *Illinois and Michigan Canal* (1918); R. C. McGrane, *Foreign Bondholders and American State Debts* (1935), chs. i–xii; L. H. Jenks, *Migration of British Capital* (1927), chs. iii, iv; Ratchford, *American State Debts,* chs. iv, v; § 153. ❧ River and Lake Transport: Hunter, *Steamboats on Western Rivers;* Ambler, *Transportation in Ohio Valley,* 17; W. J. Petersen, *Steamboating on Upper Mississippi* (1937); Baldwin, *Keelboat Age;* Mills, *Our Inland Seas,* chs. vi–xiv. ❧ Railroads: Meyer, *Transportation before 1860,* chs. vi–xvii; Kirkland, *Men, Cities and Transportation,* I, chs. iv–x; F. W. Stevens, *Beginnings of New York Central Railroad* (1926); Edward Hungerford, *Story of Baltimore and Ohio Railroad* (1928), I, and *Men and Iron: The New York Central* (1938), chs. i–xii; Paxson, "Railroads of Old Northwest"; Overton, *Burlington West,* chs. i–viii; A. L. Kohlmeier, *Old Northwest* (1938); H. G. Brownson, *History of Illinois Central Railroad* (1915); C. J. Corliss, *Main Line of Mid-America* (1950), chs. i–xii; Phillips, *Transportation in Eastern Cotton Belt;* J. G. Van Deusen, *Economic Bases of Disunion in South Carolina* (1928), ch. vi, and *Ante-Bellum Southern Commercial Conventions* (1926); S. M. Derrick, *Centennial History of South Carolina Railroad*

(1930), chs. i–xiii; H. D. Dozier, *History of Atlantic Coast Line Railroad* (1920), chs. i–vi; Haney, *Congressional History of Railways*, I, bks. 1, 2, II, chs. i–v; J. B. Sanborn, *Congressional Grants in Aid of Railways* (1899), chs. i–iv. ❧ Technical Development: Kaempffert, *American Invention*, I, ch. i; W. H. Brown, *History of First Locomotives in America* (1874); J. E. Watkins, "American Rail and Track," Smithsonian Institution, *Report*, 1889, 651; David Stevenson, *Civil Engineering of North America* (1838); H. G. Tyrrell, *History of Bridge Engineering* (1911). ❧ Communications: "History of Railway Mail Service," 48 Cong., 2 sess., *Sen. Ex. Doc.*, No. 40; G. G. Tunell, *Railway Mail Service* (1902); A. L. Stimson, *History of Express Business* (1881), chs. i–vi; L. R. Hafen, *Overland Mail* (1926); G. D. Bradley, *Story of Pony Express* (1913); Mabie, *American Leonardo;* R. L. Thompson, *Wiring a Continent* (1947); Judson, *Cyrus W. Field;* H. M. Field, *History of Atlantic Telegraph* (1867), chs. i–xii.

Sources — General: *Hunt's Merchants' Magazine*, I–XLIII (1839–60); *De Bow's Review*, I–XXIX (1846–60); *Niles' Weekly Register*, XVII–LXXVI (1820–49); *Hazard's United States Commercial and Statistical Register* (1839–42); also state documents (§§ 42, 46), gazetteers (§ 24), and travels (§ 48). ❧ Indian and Land: Wilson Lumpkin, *Removal of Cherokee* (1907); Tipton, *Papers;* Donaldson, *Public Domain;* G. L. Nute, *Documents Relating to Northwest Missions 1815–27* (1942). ❧ Agriculture: Commissioner of Patents, *Annual Report* (on agriculture, 1837–61; general index by Dept. of Agriculture); *Eighth Census* (1860), *Agriculture*, especially Introduction; *Am. Agriculturist* (1842–60); *Prairie Farmer* (1840–60), *The Cultivator* (1834–60); James Caird, *Prairie Farming* (1859); James Hall, *Notes on Western States* (1838); H. A. Kellar, ed., *Solon Robinson* (1936); H. J. Carman, *Jesse Buel* (1947); Greeno, *Obed Hussey;* Commons, *Documentary History*, I, II; J. H. Easterby, *South Carolina Rice Plantation;* U. B. Phillips and J. D. Glunt, eds., *Florida Plantation Records* (1927); J. S. Bassett, *Southern Plantation Overseer* (1925). See also: §§ 150, 159. ❧ Population and Immigration: W. S. Rossiter, *Century of Population Growth* (1909), and *Twelfth Census, Statistical Atlas;* Immigration Commission, "Reports," 61 Cong., 3 Sess., *Sen. Doc.*, Nos. 747, 748, 756; Commissioner-General of Immigration, *Report*, 1907, charts; Bureau of Foreign and Domestic Commerce, "One Hundred Years of American Immigration," *Commerce Reports*, XXII (1919), No. 254; Abbott, *Immigration, Select Documents*, and *Immigration Problem;* Birkbeck, *Journey in America*, and *Letters from Illinois;* Thwaites, *Early Western Travels*, IX–XXX; Handlin, *This Was America*, pt. 2; Blegen and Jordan, *With Various Voices*, chs. iii–viii. See also: § 150. ❧ Transportation and Communication: I. D. Andrews, "Report on Trade and Commerce (1853)," 32 Cong., 1 Sess., *H. Ex. Doc.*, No. 136; *American Railroad Journal;* H. V. Poor, *History of Railroads and Canals* (1860); Mitchell, *Compendium of Internal Improvements;* Tanner, *American Traveller;* Alexander Trotter, *Observations on Financial Position of Such of States as Have Contracted Public Debts* (1839); Morse, *Letters and Journals;* state documents (§§ 42, 43, 46), and railroad company reports (§ 7).

Bibliography — Turner and Merk, *References on the History of West*, chs. xv, xvi, xviii–xxi; Edwards, *Bibliography of History of Agriculture;* L. B. Schmidt, *Topical Studies* (1923), chs. xiii–xxi; Bidwell and Falconer, *Agriculture in Northern United States*, 474; Gray, *Agriculture in Southern United States*, II, 945; Stephenson, *History of American Immigration*, 283; Qualey, *Norwegian Settlement*, 255; Meyer, *History of Transportation*, 609; Durrenberger, *Turnpikes*, 166; Fuller and Hellman, *Waterways in United States;* T. R. Thomson, *Publications on American Railroads Before 1841* (1942); Kirkland, *History of American Economic Life*, 690, 693, 702; A. L. Demaree, *American Agricultural Press* (1941).

149. DEVELOPMENT OF INDUSTRY AND COMMERCE, 1820–1860

Summary — Manufacturing: earlier (§§ 120, 123); effect of tariff (§§ 125, 142, 156); factory system; fall-line water power; cotton and woolen textiles; improvements in machinery, dyes, location; metals and machinery, iron and steel, anthracite, coke, and bituminous smelting. — Lumbering: supply, diminution in Northeast, Great Lakes pineries, Southern naval stores, interior hardwood, Pacific coast forests; demand. — Mining: coal; iron ore, beginning of Lake Superior development; copper; lead; gold (§ 165); quarries; beginning of petroleum industry; methods of mining. — Fisheries: Canadian coast; Grand Banks; whaling. — Foreign commerce: character; ship-building, clippers; trade with Orient; Atlantic ocean steamers, liners, Collins; Pacific steamers; subsidy; facilities; coast survey. — Coast-wise trade: American monopoly; coal trade; California; Isthmian transit. — Commercial organization: corporations (§ 153); insurance, credit, bankruptcy, panics (§§ 162, 178); capitalists, Astor, Girard; retail trade, A. T. Stewart (§ 150). — Labor: conditions, apprentices, child labor, woman labor, legislation; beginning of organization, Loco-foco movement; strikes. See also: §§ 152, 160.

General — Turner, *New West*, chs. ii, iii, vii, xvii, and *United States*, chs. iii, iv; Channing, *History*, V, chs. iii, iv, vi; Krout and Fox, *Completion of Independence*, ch. ix; Fish, *Rise of Common Man*, ch. iv; Cole, *Irrepressible Conflict*, chs. i, vii; McMaster, *History*, IV, ch. xxxvii, V, ch. xliii, VII, ch. lxxiv; Cole, *Wholesale Commodity Prices 1700–1861*; Bezanson, *Wholesale Prices in Philadelphia*; W. B. Smith and Cole, *Fluctuations in American Business 1790–1860*; Samuel Rezneck, "Depression of 1819–1822," *Am. Hist. Rev.*, XXXIX (1933), 28, and "Social History of an American Depression, 1837–1843," *ibid.*, XL (1935), 662, and "Rise of Industrial Consciousness," *Jour. Econ. Bus. Hist.*, IV (1932), 784; E. C. Kirkland, *History American Economic Life*, chs. vi–xi.

Special — Manufacturing: V. S. Clark, *History of Manufactures*, chs. xi–xx; Tryon, *Household Manufactures*, chs. vii, viii; Bishop, *American Manufactures*, II, III; C. M. Depew, *One Hundred Years of American Commerce* (1895); Isaac Lippincott, *History of Manufactures in Ohio Valley* (1914), chs. iii, iv; Kaempffert, *American Inventions*, pt. 4, chs. i–v, pt. 5, chs. iii, iv. ❧ Textiles: Ware, *Early New England Cotton Manufacture*, chs. iv–x; Vera Shlakman, *Economic History of a Factory Town: Chicopee* (1935), chs. ii–vi; Green, *Holyoke*, chs. i–iii; Cole, *American Wool Manufacture*, I, chs. v–xx; Cole and Williamson, *American Carpet Manufacture*, chs. i–vi; B. E. Hazard, *Organization of Boot and Shoe Industry* (1921). ❧ Metals and Machinery: J. M. Swank, *History of Manufacture of Iron in All Ages* (1892), chs. xvii–xxxvi, xli–xliv, xlviii; L. C. Hunter, "Influence of Market upon Technique in the Iron Industry," *Jour. Econ. and Bus. Hist.*, I (1929), 241, and "Financial Problems," *ibid.*, II (1930), 520; Nevins, *Abram S. Hewitt*, chs. iv–xi; Bruce, *Virginia Iron Manufacture*, chs. ii–ix; Broadus Mitchell, *William Gregg* (1928); L. J. Cappon, "Southern Iron Industry," *Jour. Econ. and Bus. Hist.*, II (1930), 353; G. S. Gibb, *Saco-Lowell Shops* (1950), chs. i–vi; T. R. Navin, *Whitin Machine Works* (1950), chs. i, ii; Jack Rohan, *Yankee Arms Maker* (1935); W. G. Lathrop, *Brass Industry* (1926), chs. i–vi. ❧ Mining: Rickard, *American Mining*; H. N. Eavenson, *First Century and a Quarter of American Coal Industry* (1942); Eliot Jones, *Anthracite Coal Combination* (1914), chs. i, ii; C. L. Jones, *Economic History of Anthracite-Tidewater Canals* (1908); W. R. Ingalls, *Lead and Zinc* (1908); P. H. Giddens, *Birth of Oil Industry* (1938), chs. i–v; L. M. Fanning, *Rise of American Oil* (1936). ❧ Lumbering: Defebaugh, *Lumber Industry*, I, chs. xxvi, xxx, xxxi, II; R. G. Wood, *History of Lumbering in Maine* (1935); A. G. Hempstead, *Penobscot Boom* (1931); W. F. Fox, "Lumber Industry in New York," Dept. of Ag., Bur. of Forestry, *Bull.*, No. 34 (1902); Larson, *White Pine Industry*, chs. i–vi; Merk, *Economic History of Wisconsin*, chs. ii, iii. ❧ Fisheries: Lorenzo Sabine, "Report on Principal Fisheries," 32 Cong., 2 sess., *Sen. Ex. Doc.*, No. 22, 325; G. B. Goode, *et al.*, *Fisheries and Fishery Industries* (1884–87), § 5; Alexander Starbuck, *History of American Whale Fishery* (1878), 95, 230; Tower, *American Whale Fishery*, chs. iv–viii; Hohman, *American Whaleman*, chs. v–xii; A. H. Verrill, *Real Story of the Whaler* (1916). ❧ Commerce: E. R. Johnson, *Domestic and Foreign Commerce*, I, chs. xii–xxi, II, chs. xxiv, xxix, xxx, xxxvii–xli; Hutchins, *American Maritime Industries*, chs. vi–xi; Marvin, *American Merchant Marine*, chs. viii–xiii; Spears, *American Merchant Marine*, chs. ix, xi–xv; Morison, *Maritime History*, chs. xiv–xxiii; Albion, *New York Port*, and *Square-Riggers*; Rowe, *Maritime History of Maine*; W. S. Robertson, *Hispanic-American Relations with United States* (1923), ch. vi; F. R. Rutter, *South American Trade of Baltimore* (1897), chs. i, ii; J. W. Livingood, *Philadelphia-Baltimore Trade Rivalry* (1947); Porter, *John*

Jacob Astor, II; R. O. Cummings, *American Ice Harvests* (1949), chs. i–iv. ❡ Organization: R. W. Hidy, *House of Baring* (1949); N. S. Buck, *Development of Anglo-American Trade* (1925); J. C. Brown, *Hundred Years of Merchant Banking* (1909); G. R. Putnam, *Lighthouses* (1933), chs. ii–viii; Lewis, *Matthew Fontaine Maury*. ❡ Ships: A. H. Clark, *Clipper Ship Era;* Cutler, *Greyhounds of Sea*, chs. ix–xxxiii; Chapelle, *American Sailing Ships*, chs. iv–vii; A. K. Laing, *Clipper Ship Men* (1944); D. B. Tyler, *Steam Conquers Atlantic* (1939); Royal Meeker, *History of Shipping Subsidies* (1905), 150; M. M. McKee, *Ship Subsidy Question* (1922), chs. ii, iii. ❡ Internal Trade Organization: F. M. Jones, *Middlemen in Domestic Trade of United States 1800–1860* (1937); M. G. Myers, *New York Money Market* (1931), I, chs. i–x; Larson, *Jay Cooke*, chs. ii–vi; E. N. Vose, *Seventy-five Years of R. G. Dun & Co.* (1916), chs. i–iii; W. H. Hillyer, *James Talcott* (1937), chs. ii–vi; Tappan, *Arthur Tappan*, chs. iv, v, xvii; J. E. Boyle, *Cotton and New Orleans Cotton Exchange* (1934), chs. i–vii; L. C. Hunter, *Studies in Economic History of Ohio Valley* (1934); R. T. Thompson, *Colonel James Neilson* (1940); Gras, *Massachusetts First National Bank*, chs. vi–viii. ❡ Labor: Commons, *History of Labour*, I; Perlman, *Trade Unionism*, ch. i; M. R. Beard, *Short History of American Labor Movement* (1920), chs. i–vi; F. T. Carlton, *Organized Labor in American History* (1920), chs. ii–viii; N. J. Ware, *Industrial Worker, 1840–1860* (1924); Dulles, *Labor in America*, chs. ii–vi; Dorfman, *Economic Mind*, II, ch. xxiv; Edith Abbott, *Women in Industry* (1910), chs. iv–xii, Apps. A–E; Hannah Josephson, *Golden Threads* (1949); E. L. Otey, "Beginnings of Child Labor Legislation," 61 Cong., 2 sess., *Sen. Doc.*, No. 645, VI; H. L. Sumner, "Women in Industry," *ibid.*, IX; J. B. Andrews and W. D. P. Bliss, "Women in Trade Unions," *ibid.*, X, chs. i–iii; H. W. Farnam, *Chapters in History of Social Legislation in United States to 1860* (1938), chs. xi, xvii–xx; S. M. Kingsbury, ed., *Labor Laws and Their Enforcement* (1911), 3; J. K. Towles, *Factory Legislation of Rhode Island* (1908); A. M. Edwards, *Labor Legislation of Connecticut* (1907); Carter Goodrich and Sol Davidson, "Wage Earner in Westward Movement," *Pol. Sci. Quar.*, L (1935), 161, LI (1936), 61; Joseph Schafer, "Safety Valve for Labor," *Miss. Valley Hist. Rev.*, XXIV (1937), 299; Handlin, *Boston's Immigrants*, ch. iii; Ernst, *Immigrant Life in New York City;* also § 153.

Sources — Manufacturing, Mining, and Commerce: § 148; *Eighth Census, Manufactures;* "Report on Manufactures," 22 Cong., 1 sess., *H. Ex. Doc.*, No. 308; Nathan Appleton, *Introduction of Power Loom* (1858); Samuel Batchelder, *Introduction and Early Progress of Cotton Manufacture* (1863); James Montgomery, *A Practical Detail* (1840); Greville and Dorothy Bathe, *Oliver Evans* (1935); Commissioner of Patents, *Annual Reports* (1837–60); T. M. Marshall, *Early Records of Gilpin County* (1920). ❡ Foreign Commerce: Treasury Department, *Commerce and Navigation* (annual reports, 1821–60); Coast Survey, *Annual Reports* (1834–60); 49 Cong., 2 sess., *Sen. Misc. Doc.*, No. 91; R. H. Dana, *Two Years before Mast* (1840); J. M. Forbes, *Letters and Recollections* (1899), I, chs. iii–vi; R. B. Forbes, *Personal Reminiscences* (1878); K. W. Porter, *Jacksons and Lees* (1937); W. C. Hunter, "Fan Kwae at Canton (1938). ❡ Internal Trade: I. D. Andrews, "Report on Trade," 32 Cong., 1 sess., *Sen. Ex. Doc.*, No. 112; Mark Twain, *Life on Mississippi*. — Labor: Commons, *Documenatry History*, III–VIII; "Report on Wholesale Prices, Wages, and Transportation (Aldrich Report)," 52 Cong., 2 sess., *Sen. Report*, No. 1394; E. M. Stewart, "History of Wages from Colonial Times to 1928," U. S. Bur. Labor Stat., *Bull.*, No. 604 (1934); Ethelbert Stewart, *Documentary History of Early Organizations of Printers* (1907).

Bibliography — V. S. Clark, *History of Manufactures*, 624; Tryon, *Household Manufactures*, 377; Ware, *Early New England Cotton Manufacture*, 325; Bruce, *Virginia Iron Manufacture*, 431; Eliot Jones, *Anthracite Coal Combination*, 238; Kuhlmann, *Flour-Milling*, 325; McFarland, *New England Fisheries*, ch. xx; Albion, *New York Port*, 425; Hutchins, *American Maritime Industries*, 585; Dennett, *Americans in Eastern Asia*, ch. xxxv; Myers, *New York Money Market*, I, 437; Commons, *History of Labour*, II, 541; Farnam, *Social Legislation*, 271; Kirkland, *History of American Economic Life*, 694; Krout and Fox, *Completion of Independence*, ch. xvi; Kuhlman, *Guide to Material on Crime*, 431; L. G. Reynolds and C. C. Killingsworth, *Trade Unions Publications* (3 vols., 1945).

150. DEVELOPMENT OF LABOR AND OCCUPATIONS

Summary — People: population at each census; westward and interstate movement, lines of transportation; immigration (§ 148); distribution of population, rural, old states, frontier (§ 140), villages, towns, county seats, railroad towns; cities, development, new centers, governments (§ 153), conveniences and safety (§ 153); health and disease (also, § 151). — Occupations: cityward drift; freedom of choice; professions, clergy (§ 148), professors and teachers (§ 151), lawyers, doctors, artists, musicians, scientific men, engineers, literary men (§ 151); status of professional men, social consideration; foreign and domestic training (§ 151), condition of labor (§ 149). — Commercial methods: commercial organization (§ 149), wholesale trade; middlemen; retail trade, A. T. Stewart; payment in kind, barter, one price; country stores and politics; irregular currency; purchases in Eastern cities. — Later development (§§ 200, 202, 205, 206, 228).

General — Channing, *History*, V, chs. i–iii, VI, ch. i; McMaster, *History*, V, 121, VI; Hart, *Slavery and Abolition*, ch. i; Schouler, *History*, III, ch. xiii, § 2; Fish, *Rise of Common Man*, chs. vi, vii; Cole, *Irrepressible Conflict*, 21, 79, ch. viii; Taylor, *Transportation Revolution*, chs. xii, xiii, 388; E. D. Branch, *Sentimental Years* (1934); Meade Minnigerode, *Fabulous Forties* (1924); Kirkland, *History of American Economic Life*, 254. See also: state and local histories (§ 62), especially Green (Naugatuck), Pierce (Chi.), Green (Holyoke), Handlin (Boston), Kane (Natchez), Flick (N.Y.), Ernst (N.Y.), McKelvey (Rochester), Capers (Memphis), and Still (Milwaukee).

Special — People: W. S. Thompson and P. K. Whelpton, *Population Trends* (1933), ch. i; A. F. Weber, *Growth of Cities* (1899), 20; Rossiter, *Century of Population Growth*; E. W. Martin, *Standard of Living in 1860* (1942); A. H. Hansen, "Trend of Real Wages," *Am. Econ. Rev.*, XV (1925), 32; Bogart, *Peacham*, ch. x; G. G. Johnson, *Ante-Bellum North Carolina*, chs. ii–xv; M. C. Boyd, *Alabama in Fifties* (1931); George Tucker, *Progress of United States* (1855); Farnam, *Social Legislation*, chs. ix–xii; R. H. Shryock, "Origins and Significance of Public Health Movement," *Annals Medical Hist.*, I (1929), 645; J. S. Chambers, *Conquest of Cholera* (1938); § 148. ❡ Occupations: Freeman Hunt, *Lives of American Merchants* (1856–58); W. O. Stoddard, *Men of Business* (1894); J. A. Scoville, *Old Merchants of New York City* (1863–70); J. D. McCabe, *Great Fortunes* (1871); Warren, *American Bar*, chs. x–xx; Lewis, *Great American Lawyers*, II–VI; S. D. Gross, *Lives of Eminent American Physicians and Surgeons* (1861); Shafer, *American Medical Profession*; W. F. Norwood, *Medical Education before Civil War* (1944); Flexner, *Doctors on Horseback*; educators and clergy (§ 151); Henry Barnard, *Educational Biography* (1861); W. B. Sprague, *Annals of American Pulpit* (1857–69), IV–VIII. ❡ Commercial Methods: Myers, *Great American Fortunes*, I, II; Brown, *Merchant Banking*, chs. ii–viii, xi, xii, xiv, xvi; Hidy, *House of Baring*; McMaster, *Stephen Girard*; Vincent Nolte, *Fifty Years* (1854); Porter, *Jacksons and Lees*, II, 1395; L. E. Atherton, "Itinerant Merchandising," Bus. Hist. Soc., *Bull.*, XIX (1945), 53, and *Pioneer Merchant* (1939), and *Southern Country Store, 1800–1860* (1949); F. M. Jones, *Middlemen in Domestic Trade*; §§ 148, 149.

Sources — General: *Niles' Weekly Register*; *North Am. Rev.*; *Hunt's Merchants' Mag.*; *De Bow's Rev.*; *Hazard's Register*; newspapers, magazines, and registers (§§ 24, 52, 53). ❡ Travel accounts by Abdy, Bernhard, Bremer, Chevalier, Dicey, Grund, Kemble, Lyell, Martineau, Pulszky, De Tocqueville, Trollope, and others (§ 48). ❡ People: federal and state censuses (§ 7); B. W. McCready, *On Influence of Trades in Disease* (1837); W. S. Forest, *Great Pestilence in Virginia* (1856); Abbott, *Immigration Problem*; Friedrich Kapp, *Immigration and Commissioners of Emigration* (1870); Jesse Chickering, *Immigration into United States* (1848); E. E. Hale, *Letters on Irish Emigration* (1852); W. J. Bromwell, *History of Immigration* (1856); references on migration, § 148; Manning, Potter, Davies, *Select Problems*, I, ch. iv. ❡ Occupations: R. W. Pomeroy, *Young Merchant* (1841); Lawrence, *Diary and Correspondence*. ❡ Commercial Methods: Theophilus Parsons, *Law of Business* (1857); B. F. Foster, *Merchant's Manual* (1838); S. H. Terry, *Retailer's Manual* (1869); R. G. Hazard, "Railroad Corporations and Public," *Hunt's Merchants' Mag.*, XXI (1849), 622; A. B. Johnson, "Private Corporations," *ibid.*,

XXIII (1850), 626; B. V. Abbott, *General Digest of Law of Corporations* (1869); J. K. Angell and Samuel Ames, *Law of Private Corporations* (1831); § 149, 153.

Bibliography — Fish, *Rise of Common Man*, 352; Cole, *Irrepressible Conflict*, 423; Turner, *New West*, 334; MacDonald, *Jacksonian Democracy*, 322; A. P. C. Griffin, ed., *List of Books on Immigration* (1907); Channing, *History*, VI, 37.

151. INTELLECTUAL AND CULTURAL DEVELOPMENTS, 1820–1860

Summary — Education: public, common schools, Horace Mann, high schools, normal schools, higher education; professional and technical schools; beginnings of coeducation; intellectual organization; learned societies, national scientific institutions; lyceums; libraries. — Literature: New England school; New York school; Southern writers; Western writers; periodicals; newspapers, metropolitan, country, telegraph. — Fine arts: painting, sculpture, architecture, music, theater. — Science: natural history, geology, chemistry, botany; medicine, anesthesia (§ 150). — Religion: sects; transformation of Calvinism; Unitarian movement; doctrinal disputes; Mormons; Millerites; Catholics; Jews; national organization; split on slavery (§ 159). — Philosophy: Transcendentalism, Emerson. — Political, economic, and social thought (§ 153). — Social life: foreign observers; American critics; fashions; morals; societies, benevolent, secret orders; amusements, watering places, beginning of sports; life insurance. — Later development (§§ 214, 216–19).

General — Channing, *History*, V, chs. vii–ix; Fish, *Rise of Common Man*, chs. vii, ix–xi; Cole, *Irrepressible Conflict*, chs. viii–x; McMaster, *History*, IV, ch. xxxviii, V, chs. xliv, xlvii–xlix, VII, ch. lxxiii; H. M. Jones, *America and French Culture*; Curti, *Growth of American Thought*, chs. xii–xiv, xvi; Parrington, *Main Currents*, II.

Special — Education: Cubberley, *Public Education in the United States*, chs. v–xii; Slosson, *American Spirit in Education*, chs. ix–xiv; Paul Monroe, *Founding of American Public School System* (1940), I, chs. viii–xv; S. L. Jackson, *America's Struggle for Free Schools* (1941); Curti, *Social Ideas of American Educators*, chs. ii–v; Aaron, *America in Crisis*, ch. v; F. T. Carlton, *Economic Influences upon Educational Progress* (1908); A. D. Mayo, "Common Schools," Commissioner of Education, *Reports*, 1895–1901; B. A. Hinsdale, "Foreign Influence upon Education," *ibid.*, 1897–98, I, 591; Woody, *Women's Education in United States*, I, chs. vii–xi, II, chs. i–ix; J. P. Wickersham, *History of Education in Pennsylvania* (1886), chs. xiii–xxiv; E. A. Miller, *History of Educational Legislation in Ohio, 1803–1850* (1918); R. G. Boone, *History of Education in Indiana* (1892), chs. ii–xvi; Knight, *Public Education in South*, chs. iv–viii. ❡ Phases of Education: R. D. Mosier, *Making the American Mind: McGuffey Readers* (1947); E. E. Brown, *Making of Our Middle Schools* (1907), chs. x–xv; E. D. Grizzell, *Origin of High School in New England before 1865* (1923), chs. ii–xvi; G. F. Miller, *Academy System of New York* (1922); V. L. Mangun, *American Normal School* (1928), chs. i–x; J. P. Gordy, *Rise and Growth of Normal School Idea* (1891), chs. i–vii; Thwing, *Higher Education in America*, chs. x–xv; J. M. Taylor, *Before Vassar Opened* (1914); C. G. Woodson, *Education of Negro prior to 1861* (1919), chs. v–xiii; C. A. Bennett, *Manual and Industrial Education up to 1870* (1926), chs. iv–xi; S. M. Smith, *Relation of State to Religious Education in Massachusetts* (1926), chs. v–x; J. A. Burns, *Growth of Catholic School System* (1912), chs. vii–ix; G. W. Knight, "Land Grants for Education in Northwest Territory," Am. Hist. Assoc., *Papers*, I (1885), 79. ❡ Institutions and Leaders: B. A. Hinsdale, *Horace Mann* (1898); R. B. Culver, *Horace Mann and Religion in Massachusetts Public Schools* (1929); W. S. Monroe, *Educational Labors of Henry Barnard* (1893); J. J. McCadden, *Education in Pennsylvania* (1937); Alma Lutz, *Emma Willard* (1929); Cornelius Van Santvoord, *Eliphalet Nott* (1876); Morison, *Three Centuries of Harvard*, chs. x–xii; P. A. Bruce, *History of University of Virginia* (1920–22), I–III; R. S. Fletcher, *History of Oberlin College* (1943); A. O. Hansen, *Early Educational Leadership in the Ohio Valley* (1923); C. H. Rammelkamp, *Illinois College* (1928), chs. i–viii; C. E. Payne, *Josiah Bushnell Grinnell* (1938), chs. iv–xvi; Coulter, *College Life in the Old South*. ❡ Intellectual Organization: G. B. Goode, ed., *Smithsonian Institution* (1897), and "Origin of National Scientific and Educational Institutions," Am. Hist. Assoc., *Report*, 1889, 53, and *Papers*,

IV (1890), 95; R. S. Bates, *Scientific Societies in United States* (1946); Edward Edwards, *Free Town Libraries* (1869), bk. 3, chs. i–v; U. S. Bur. of Education, *Public Libraries* (1876), pt. 1; Johnston, *Library of Congress*, I; Lydenberg, *New York Public Library*; C. B. Hayes, *American Lyceum* (1932); Harriette Smith, *Lowell Institute* (1898). ❡ Literature: Trent, *Cambridge History of American Literature*; Spiller, *Literary History*, I, II, chs. xvi–xlvii; V. W. Brooks, *Makers and Finders: Flowering of New England* (1936), and *World of Washington Irving* (1944); O. W. Long, *Literary Pioneers* (1935); Matthiessen, *American Renaissance*; M. J. Moses, *Literature of South* (1910), chs. vii–xii; Carl Holliday, *History of Southern Literature* (1906), ch. iv; Wade, *Augustus Baldwin Longstreet*; R. L. Rusk, *Literature of Middle Western Frontier* (1925); D. A. Dondore, *Prairie* (1926), chs. iv–vi; M. H. Elliott, *Uncle Sam Ward* (1938); Bassett, *Middle Group of American Historians*; Walter Blair, *Native American Humor* (1937), 3–124, 199–549; Rourke, *American Humor*; J. R. Tandy, *Crackerbox Philosophers* (1925), chs. i–vi; G. R. Stewart, *John Phoenix* (1937); F. J. Meine, ed., *Tall Tales of Southwest* (1930), intro.; G. P. Krapp, *English Language in America* (2 vols., 1925); Mencken, *American Language*; Warfel, *Noah Webster* (§ 56); Hans Kurath, *et al.*, *Handbook of Linguistic Geography of New England* (1939). ❡ Individual Authors: Hervey Allen, *Israfel* (2 vols., 1926); Newton Arvin, *Hawthorne* and *Whitman* (1938); Williams, *Washington Irving*; Katharine Anthony, *Margaret Fuller* (1920); Wade, *Fuller*; R. B. Nye, *George Bancroft* (1944), chs. i–iii, vi; biographies of J. F. Cooper, W. C. Bryant, R. W. Emerson, H. W. Longfellow, J. G. Whittier, O. W. Holmes, J. R. Lowell, H. D. Thoreau, Emily Dickinson, Herman Melville, W. G. Simms, George Bancroft, W. H. Prescott, Jared Sparks, J. L. Motley, Francis Parkman. ❡ Periodicals: Mott, *American Magazines*, I, II, and *American Journalism*, chs. ix–xix; A. H. Smyth, *Philadelphia Magazines* (1892), 86; B. B. Minor, *Southern Literary Messenger* (1905); Luxon, *Niles' Weekly Register*; R. W. Jones, *Journalism*, chs. xxv–xxix; Bleyer, *American Journalism*, chs. v–x; A. M. Lee, *Daily Newspaper in America* (1937); Rosewater, *Cooperative News-Gathering in United States*, chs. i–xii; Nevins, *Evening Post*, chs. v–xi; O'Brien, *Sun*, chs. i–vii. ❡ Publishing Organization: E. L. Bradsher, *Mathew Carey* (1912); Lehmann-Haupt, *Book in America*, 58; J. H. Harper, *House of Harper* (1912), chs. i–xv; Hart, *Popular Book*, chs. v–viii; S. P. Ladas, *International Protection Literary Artistic Property* (1938), I, 3, 4, 21; R. R. Shaw, *Literary Property* (1950). ❡ Fine Arts: Suzanne LaFollette, *Art in America* (1929), § 2; Isham, *American Painting*; Alan Burroughs, *Limners and Likenesses* (1936), chs. v, vi; C. H. Caffin, *Story of American Painting* (1907), chs. iii–vii; Frank Weitenkampf, *American Graphic Art* (1924); Taft, *American Sculpture*, pts. 1, 2; Robert Taft, *Photography 1839–1889* (1938); Larkin, *Art and Life in America*, bk. 4; F. J. Mather, *et al.*, *American Spirit in Art* (1927); Tallmadge, *Architecture in America*, chs. iv, v; Hamlin, *American Spirit in Architecture*; Dunlap, *Arts of Design*, III; Howard, *Our American Music*, chs. iv–viii; L. C. Elson, *History of American Music* (1925); H. C. Lahee, *Annals of Music* (1922), chs. iii–v; F. J. Metcalf, *American Writers and Compilers of Sacred Music* (1925). ❡ Drama: Quinn, *American Drama*, I, chs. vi–xii; M. C. Crawford, *Romance of American Theatre* (1940), chs. iv–xiii, xv; Hornblow, *History of Theatre*, chs. xii–xxiv; G. C. D. Odell, *Annals of New York Stage* (15 vols., 1927–49), III–VII; T. A. Brown, *History of New York Stage* (3 vols., 1903), I; Wittke, *Tambo and Bones*, chs. i–iv; L. S. Driver, *Fanny Kemble* (1933); Coad and Mims, *American Stage*. ❡ Thought and Religion: H. C. Goddard, *Studies in New England Transcendentalism* (1908); O. B. Frothingham, *Transcendentalism in New England* (1876); I. W. Riley, *American Thought* (1923), chs. iv–vi; H. W. Schneider, *History of American Philosophy* (1946), chs. iii–v; H. A. Pochmann, *New England Transcendentalism and St. Louis Hegelianism* (1948); Shepard, *Pedlar's Progress*. ❡ Religion: Schaff, *American Church History Series*; Sweet, *Story of Religion*, chs. xiv–xix; H. K. Rowe, *History of Religion* (1924), chs. v–viii; Commager, *Theodore Parker*; G. W. Cooke, *Unitarianism in America* (1902), chs. v–vii; S. E. Mead, *Nathaniel William Taylor* (1942); W. W. Manross, *Episcopal Church in the United States, 1800–1840* (1938); F. D. Nichol, *Midnight Cry* (1944); C. E. Sears, *Days of Delusion* (1924); B. H. Roberts, *Comprehensive History of Church of Jesus Christ of Latter-Day Saints* (6 vols., 1930), I–III; W. E. LaRue, *Foundations of Mormonism* (1919); Brodie, *No Man Knows My History*; Werner, *Brigham Young*; I. W. Riley, *Founder of Mormonism* (1902); M. M. Quaife, *Kingdom of St. James: A Narrative of the Mormons* (1930); J. G. Shea, *History of Catholic Church in the United States*

(1886–92), III, IV; T. T. McAvoy, "Founding of Catholic Minority," *Rev. of Politics*, X (1948), 13; J. N. Norwood, *Schism in Methodist Church, 1844* (1923); Lewis Tappan, *History of American Missionary Association* (1855); W. R. Cross, *Burned-Over District* (1950); Goodykoontz, *Home Missions*, chs. vi–ix; Post, *Popular Freethought*. ❧ Science: Struik, *Yankee Science*; Jaffe, *Men of Science*, chs. iv–xii; E. S. Dana, *et al.*, *Century of Science in America* (1918); E. F. Smith, *Chemistry in America* (1914), chs. viii–x; R. T. Young, *Biology in America* (1922); A. S. Packard, "Century's Progress in American Zoology," *Am. Naturalist*, X (1876), 591; G. P. Merrill, *First Hundred Years of American Geology* (1924), chs. ii–v; S. W. Geiser, *Naturalists of Frontier* (1948); Shryock, *Modern Medicine*, chs. vi–xii; Packard, *History of Medicine*, I, chs. iii–ix, II; N. S. Davis, *Contributions to History of Medical Education* (1877); J. A. Taylor, *History of Dentistry* (1922); A. W. Lufkin, *History of Dentistry* (1938), chs. xiv–xvi; W. J. Rhees, *An Account of Smithsonian Institution, Its Founder* (1857); T. C. Johnson, *Scientific Interests in the Old South* (1936); J. F. Fulton and E. H. Thomson, *Benjamin Silliman* (1947); Fisher, *Benjamin Silliman*; A. B. Gould, *Louis Agassiz* (1901); John Burroughs, *John James Audubon* (1902); Lewis, *Matthew Fontaine Maury*; Morse, *Oliver Wendell Holmes*; Frances Taylor, *Crawford W. Long* (1928). ❧ Social Life: Calhoun, *American Family*, II; Minnigerode, *Fabulous Forties*; Phillips, *Life and Labor in Old South*; Dodd, *Cotton Kingdom*; Edward Ingle, *Southern Sidelights* (1896); T. N. Page, *Social Life in Old Virginia before War* (1897); E. M. Ripley, *Social Life in Old New Orleans* (1912); A. C. Cole, "Our Sporting Grandfathers," *Atlantic Monthly*, CL (1932), 88; Krout, *Annals of American Sport*; C. K. Knight, *Life Insurance in United States to 1870* (1920), chs. iii, iv; §§ 150, 159.

Sources — Education: *American Journal of Education* (1855–70); *Massachusetts Teacher* (1848–79); *New York Teacher* (1852–67); *Ohio Journal of Education* (1852–60); reports of state commissioners (§ 46); also, 16 Cong., 2 sess., *Sen. Doc.*, No. 85; 22 Cong., 1 sess., *Sen. Doc.*, No. 142; 21 Cong., 1 sess., *H. Reports*, No. 312; 35 Cong., 1 sess., *H. Reports*, No. 261; 25 Cong., 2 sess., *H. Ex. Doc.*, No. 136; 33 Cong., 1 sess., *H. Ex. Doc.*, No. 52; 30 Cong., 2 sess., *H. Misc. Doc.*, No. 18; S. S. Randall, *Common School System of State of New York* (1851); Knight, *Documentary History of Education*, III, chs. iv–vii, IV; Mann, *Horace Mann*; F. G. Freedman, ed., *Walt Whitman Looks at Schools* (1950); A. O. Norton, ed., *First State Normal School in America; Journals of Cyrus Peirce and Mary Swift* (1926); M. F. Lansing, ed., *Mary Lyon* (1937); Edward Eggleston, *Hoosier Schoolmaster* (1871). ❧ Intellectual Organization: W. J. Rhees, ed., *Smithsonian Institution: Documents, 1835–1889* (1901); C. C. Jewett, *Notices of Public Libraries* (1851). ❧ Literature: §§ 54, 55. ❧ Religion: W. E. Channing, *Works*; Lyman Beecher, *Autobiography* (2 vols., 1864–65); Perry Miller, *Transcendentalists* (1950); Finney, *Memoirs*; Cartwright, *Autobiography*; Mode, *Source Book for American Church History*, chs. xx–xxii; Sweet, *Religion on American Frontier*; American Home Missionary Society, *Reports* (1827–   ); American Board of Commissioners for Foreign Missions, *Annual Reports* (1810–   ); *Home Missionary* (1828–   ). ❧ Social Customs: *Godey's Lady's Book*; Trollope, *Domestic Manners*; W. H. Venable, *Buckeye Boyhood* (1911); Manfield, *Personal Memories*; W. D. Howells, *Boy's Town* (1890); Quincy, *Figures of Past*; Larcom, *New England Girlhood*; G. F. Hoar, *A Boy Sixty Years Ago* (1898), and *Autobiography*, I, chs. iv, vi, vii; A. B. Longstreet, *Georgia Scenes* (1835); J. G. Baldwin, *Flush Times of Alabama* (1853); Mark Twain, *Tom Sawyer* (1876), and *Huckleberry Finn* (1884). ❧ Others: Morse, *Letters and Journals*, I, chs. ix–xx, II, ch. xxii; Emerson, *Letters*, I–V; *New Eng. Jour. of Medicine and Surgery* (1820–   ); *Medical Repository* (1820–   ); *Am. Medical Recorder* (1818–   ); Moses and Brown, *American Theatre*, 50.

Bibliography — Fish, *Rise of Common Man*, ch. xvi; Cole, *Irrepressible Conflict*, ch. xvi; Mott, *American Magazines*, I, II, and *American Journalism*, 209, 324; O. O. Winther, *Trans-Mississippi West: Guide to Periodical Literature* (1942); Cubberley, *Public Education in United States*; Woody, *Women's Education in United States*, II, 481; Spiller, *Literary History*, III; Trent, *Cambridge History of American Literature*, I, 468, II, 411, IV, 635; Rusk, *Literature of Middle Western Frontier*, II, 39; Blair, *Native American Humor*, 163; Isham, *American Painting*, 593; Mode, *Source Book for American Church*

History, chs. xiii–xxviii; H. G. Townsend, *Philosophical Ideas in United States* (1934), 267; P. R. Anderson and M. H. Fisch, *Philosophy in America* (1939), 545; Meisel, *Bibliography of American Natural History*; Packard, *History of Medicine,* II, 1243.

152. THE REFORM IMPULSE, 1820–1860

Summary — Intellectual, social, economic background (§§ 148, 149, 150, 151): English and other European influences; religious impulse (§ 151); Quakers; relationship among reforms; individual reformers, S. G. Howe, W. L. Garrison, Gerrit Smith, Tappan brothers, Theodore Parker. — Temperance: early drinking habits; religious opposition; temperance societies; American Temperance Society; 1833, United States Temperance Union; cold water army; Washingtonian Movement; J. B. Gough; Father Matthew; Neal Dow; 1851, Maine Law; immigrant attitudes. — Women's Rights: legal position; Frances Wright, Grimké sisters; Ernestine Rose; Lucretia Mott, Elizabeth C. Stanton, Margaret Fuller; Lucy Stone; 1840, World Anti-Slavery Convention; property rights; 1848, Seneca Falls Convention; Bloomerism. — Labor Reform: § 149; ten-hour-day movement; 1840, in federal employment; legal status; Commonwealth v. Hunt; G. H. Evans; Loco-Foco Movement; imprisonment for debt (§ 153). — Prison Reform: English influence; prison reform associations; Pennsylvania (solitary) system; New York (silent) system; Auburn Prison. — Peace: Quaker activity; 1828, American Peace Society; Elihu Burritt; arbitration; 1843, World Peace Congress. — Care of dependents: insane, Dorothea L. Dix, 1839 Boston Lunatic Hospital; diseased; other hospitals (§ 151); paupers; blind, deaf. — Abolition of dueling, lotteries. — Education: § 151. — Abolition of Slavery: § 160. — Communitarian experiments: Utopian democracy; relation to democracy, to immigration, to intellectual unrest; types, Brook Farm, Hopedale, Fourierism and Phalanxes, New Harmony, Zoar, Amana, Mormons (§ 151), Icaria, Oneida; effects. — Political democracy: §§ 151, 153, 155.

General — Channing, *History,* chs. iv, vi, vii; McMaster, *History,* VI, 96; Fish, *Rise of Common Man,* ch. xii; Cole, *Irrepressible Conflict,* ch. vii; Curti, *Growth of American Thought,* chs. xii, xv; Taylor, *Transportation Revolution,* chs. xii, xiii; F. L. Pattee, *Feminine Fifties* (1940); Schlesinger, *American as Reformer,* ch. ii; Gilbert Seldes, *Stammering Century* (1928); Parrington, *Main Currents,* II; A. F. Tyler, *Freedom's Ferment* (1944), chs. xi–xiii, xv, xvi; Gabriel, *American Democratic Thought,* ch. xiii; personal accounts of individual reformers, §§ 54, 55, 56.

Special — Temperance: Daniel Dorchester, *Liquor Problem* (1884); Krout, *Origins of Prohibition*; E. H. Cherington, *Evolution of Prohibition* (1920); J. F. Maguire, *Father Matthew* (1898). ⦅ Women's Rights: Stanton, Anthony, and Gage, *Woman Suffrage*; Hecker, *Women's Rights,* ch. viii; Harper, *Susan B. Anthony*; A. G. Violette, *Economic Feminism* (1925); Blackwell, *Lucy Stone*; Alma Lutz, *Created Equal* (1940); M. I. Ostrogorski, *Rights of Women* (1893); A. J. G. Perkins and Theresa Wolfson, *Frances Wright* (1939). ⦅ Labor Reform: A. M. Schlesinger, Jr., *Brownson,* and *Age of Jackson* (1945), chs. xi, xxiv; Commons, *History of Labour,* I, pt. 2; Ware, *Industrial Worker*; William Trimble, "Social Philosophy of Loco-Foco Democracy," *Am. Jour. Sociol.,* XXVI (1921), 705; Walter Nelles, "Commonwealth v. Hunt," *Columbia Law Rev.,* XXXII (1932), 1128; Farnam, *Social Legislation,* chs. xvii–xx. ⦅ Prison Reform: McKelvey, *American Prisons,* chs. i, ii; F. H. Wines, *Punishment and Reformation* (1895); Clapp, John Bigelow, ch. iv; O. F. Lewis, *American Prisons and Prison Customs* (1922), chs. ix–xxv; H. E. Barnes, *Evolution of Penology in Pennsylvania* (1927); Philip Klein, *Prison Methods in New York State* (1920). ⦅ Peace Movement: M. E. Curti, *Peace or War,* ch. i, and *American Peace Crusade* (1929); Edson Whitney, *American Peace Society* (1928); Curti, *Learned Blacksmith*; W. E. Galpin, *Pioneering for Peace* (1933); C. G. Phelps, *Anglo-American Peace Movement* (1930). ⦅ Care of Dependents: F. B. Sanborn, Howe (1891); L. S. Selling, *Men against Madness* (1940); Kelso, *Poor Relief in Massachusetts* (chs. iv–vi); Albert Deutsch, *Mentally Ill in America* (1937), chs. vii–xiii; Marshall, *Dorothea Dix,* chs. iii–ix; D. M. Schneider, *History of Public Welfare in New York State* (1938); L. H. Feder, *Unemployment Relief* (1936), ch. ii; H. M. Hurd, *et al., Institutional Care of Insane* (4 vols., 1916–17); D. T. McColgan, *Joseph Tuckerman* (1940).

❡ Communitarian Experiments: Egbert and Persons, *Socialism and American Life*, I, chs. iv–v; A. E. Bestor, "Education and Reform at New Harmony," Ind. Hist. Soc., *Publ.*, XV (1948), 283, and *Backwoods Utopias*; Noyes, *American Socialisms*; Charles Nordhoff, *Communistic Societies of United States* (1875); W. A. Hinds, *American Communities and Co-operative Colonies* (1908); Hillquit, *History of Socialism*, 29; Leopold, *Robert Dale Owen*, chs. i–vii; Lindsay Swift, *Brook Farm* (1900); B. M. H. Shambaugh, *Amana* (1923); Albert Shaw, *Icaria* (1884); J. A. Geddes, *United Order among Mormons* (1924); A. E. McBee, *Utopia to Florence* (1947); G. B. Lockwood, *New Harmony Movement* (1905).

Sources — General: Travel accounts, particularly Abdy, Bremer, Dickens, Lyell, Martineau, Tocqueville, Trollope (§ 48); memoirs, correspondence and works of A. B. Alcott, T. D. Weld, W. E. Channing, Lyman Beecher, S. G. Howe, J. Q. Adams (§§ 54, 55); magazines, including *North Am. Rev.*, *Democratic Rev.* (§ 52); newspapers, especially *National Intelligencer* (Wash.) and *N.Y. Tribune* (§ 53). ❡ Temperance: American Temperance Society, *Reports*; American Temperance Union, *Jour.* (1837–65); Dow, *Reminiscences*; H. S. Clubb, *Maine Liquor Law* (1856); Gough, *Autobiography*. ❡ Prison Reform: Prison Discipline Society, *Annual Report* (1826–36). ❡ Women's Rights: M. F. Ossoli, *Woman in Nineteenth Century* (1855); *Elizabeth Cady Stanton as Revealed in Her Letters*. ❡ Peace: *The Harbinger of Peace* (later *The Calumet*, 1828–35. — Communitarian experiments: G. W. Noyes, ed., *John Humphrey Noyes* (1931); Blau, *Jacksonian Democracy*.

Bibliography — Tyler, *Freedom's Ferment*, 551; Fish, *Rise of Common Man*, 358; Cole, *Irrepressible Conflict*, 434; Curti, *Growth of American Thought*, 778; Egbert and Persons, *Socialism and American Life*, II; Bestor, *Backwoods Utopias*, 245.

153. POLITICAL AND CONSTITUTIONAL DEVELOPMENT, 1820–1860

Summary — (See: §§121, 122, 123, 126, 143–45, 156, 180). — Political conceptions: individualism; democracy; equality; perfectibility of mankind; balance of sections; "manifest destiny" (see also: § 152). — Popular government: suffrage and officeholding, exclusions reduced, white manhood suffrage, votes of aliens; expatriation, naturalization; party development; nomination methods, caucuses, mass meetings, tours of candidates; elections, *viva voce*, written ballot. — Federal government: increase in powers; internal improvements (§ 158); enlargement of presidency; activity of Congress; court review of state and federal activities; Taney (§ 157); strict and loose construction (§§ 125, 143); states rights (§§ 123, 131, 139, 156, 180); proposed constitutional amendments; civil service (§§ 123, 133, 154). — New territories: 1836, Wisconsin; 1838, Iowa; 1848, Oregon; 1849, Minnesota; 1850, Utah; 1850, New Mexico; 1853, Washington; 1854, Nebraska and Kansas. — New states: 1820, Maine; 1821, Missouri; 1836, Arkansas; 1837, Michigan; 1845, Florida and Texas; 1846, Iowa; 1848, Wisconsin; 1850, California; 1858, Minnesota; 1859, Oregon. — State governments: controversies over boundaries; constitutions, democratization; legislatures, influence of speakers, corruption; character and powers of governors; state civil service; courts, elected judiciaries, appeals to federal courts; interstate comity, rendition, fugitive slaves (§§ 161, 172), privileges and immunities of citizens of other states; territorial governments. — State economic activities: finances; loans; repudiation; public works; regulation. — Local government: cities, charters, administration by councils, mayors, police, water, fire protection, public sanitation, gas, subsidies for transportation; town government; county government; mixed systems. — Growth of law; Joseph Story; James Kent; law schools; movement for codification. — Later development (§§ 189, 190, 192, 203).

General — Turner, *New West*, chs. i–v, and *United States*, chs. i–viii, and *Significance of Sections*, ch. ii; Fish, *Rise of Common Man*, chs. i, iii, xiii; MacDonald, *Jacksonian Democracy*, chs. xiv, xv; McMaster, *History*, V, ch. i, VII, 162; Swisher, *American Constitutional Development*, chs. ix–xiv; J. B. McMaster, *Acquisition of Political, Social, and Industrial Rights* (1903); Taylor, *Transportation Revolution*, ch. xvi; Warren, *Supreme Court*, III; Haines, *Role of Supreme Court*, chs. xv–xvii; Boudin, *Government by Judiciary*, I, chs. xiii–xix; Schlesinger, Jr., *Age of Jackson*, chs. xii–xvi; McLaughlin, *Courts, Con-*

stitution and Parties, 111; Ostrogorski, *Democracy and Political Parties*, chs. i–iii; Stanwood, *Presidency*, I, ch. xiv; Sydnor, *Southern Sectionalism*, chs. xii, xiv.

Special — Political conceptions: W. S. Carpenter, *Development of American Political Thought* (1930); R. G. Gettell, *History of American Political Thought* (1928), chs. viii–x; Merriam, *American Political Theories*, chs. v–vii; Weinberg, *Manifest Destiny*, chs. i–vii; Wright, "Political Institutions and Frontier"; Oscar Handlin, Louis Hartz, and Milton Heath, "Laissez-Faire Thought," *Tasks of Economic History*, III (1943); Dorfman, *Economic Mind*, II, ch. xxii; Wiltse, *Calhoun*, III, chs. xxviii–xxix; J. T. Carpenter, *South as a Conscious Minority* (1930), chs. i–iv; E. S. Corwin, "Due Process before Civil War," *Harvard Law Rev.*, XXIV (1911), 366, 460. ❡ Popular Government: Porter, *Suffrage in United States*, chs. iii–v; Dallinger, *Nominations for Elective Office*; Bradsher, *Mathew Carey*; Freidel, *Francis Lieber*; Malone, *Thomas Cooper*; F. G. Franklin, *Legislative History of Naturalization* (1906), chs. vii–xiv; E. M. Carroll, *Origins of Whig Party* (1925); also: §§ 154, 160, 163, 171, 176. ❡ Federal Government: Binkley, *Powers of President*, chs. iv, v; Corwin, *President's Control of Foreign Relations*; Short, *National Administrative Organization*, chs. iv, x; D. C. Fowler, *Cabinet Politician* (1943), chs. i–v; H. M. Wriston, *Executive Agents in American Foreign Relations* (1929); Bolles, *Financial History*, II; Fish, *Civil Service and Patronage*, chs. iii–viii; Baldwin, *American Judiciary*; Frankfurter and Landis, *Business of Supreme Court*, ch. i, and *Commerce Clause*, ch. ii; E. S. Corwin, *Twilight of Supreme Court* (1934), ch. ii; Swisher, *Roger B. Taney*; F. P. Weisenburger, *John McLean* (1937); H. V. Ames, "Proposed Amendments," Am. Hist. Assoc., *Report*, 1896, II; Carter Goodrich, "National Planning," *Pol. Sci. Quar.*, LXIII (1948), 16, and "Revulsion against Internal Improvements," *Jour. of Economic Hist.*, X (1950), 145. ❡ New Territories and States: Bayrd Still, "Statehood Process, 1800 to 1850," *Miss. Valley Hist. Rev.*, XXIII (1936), 189; § 62, by states. ❡ State Government: J. Q. Dealey, *Growth of American State Constitutions* (1915), chs. iv, v; James Schouler, *Constitutional Studies* (1897), pt. 3; J. A. Jameson, *Constitutional Convention* (1867); Charles Borgeaud, *Adoption and Amendment of Constitutions* (1895), 146; W. F. Dodd, *Revision and Amendment of State Constitutions* (1910), ch. ii; Beveridge, *John Marshall*, IV, ch. ix; C. S. Lobingier, *People's Law* (1909), chs. xiii–xviii; E. C. Griffith, *Gerrymander* (1907); G. H. Evans, *Business Incorporations* (1948); F. E. Jewett, *Financial History of Maine* (1937); Handlin, *Commonwealth: Massachusetts 1774–1861*; Bullock, "Finances of Massachusetts"; A. B. Darling, *Political Changes in Massachusetts* (1925); Morse, *Neglected Period of Connecticut's History*; A. M. Mowry, *Dorr War* (1901); Flick, *History of New York*, VI, chs. i–iv; H. L. McBain, *De Witt Clinton and Spoils System* (1907); Fox, *Decline of Aristocracy in New York*, chs. vii–xiv; J. W. Cadman, *Corporation in New Jersey* (1949); Klein, *Pennsylvania Politics*, chs. ii–iv; H. R. Mueller, *Whig Party in Pennsylvania* (1922); Hartz, *Economic Policy and Democratic Thought*; Cole, *Whig Party in South*; Paul Murray, *Whig Party in Georgia, 1825–53* (1948); Green, *Constitutional Development in South Atlantic States*, chs. iv–vii; Ambler, *Sectionalism in Virginia*, chs. iv–x; H. H. Simms, *Rise of Whigs in Virginia* (1929); Carter Goodrich, "Virginia System of Mixed Enterprise," *Pol. Sci. Quar.*, LXIV (1949), 355; C. C. Norton, *Democratic Party in Ante-Bellum North Carolina* (1930); Abernethy, *Frontier to Plantation in Tennessee*, chs. xvii–xxii; E. L. Bogart, *Internal Improvements and State Debt in Ohio*, and *Financial History of Ohio* (1912); R. C. McGrane, *Panic of 1837* (1924), and *Foreign Bondholders and State Debts*, chs. i–xiii; Ratchford, *American State Debts*; R. T. Ely, *Taxation in American States and Cities* (1888); state histories (§ 61). ❡ Local Government: local histories (§ 61) especially city histories listed in § 150; T. H. Reed, *Municipal Government* (1934), ch. v; J. A. Fairlie, *Local Government in Counties, Towns and Villages* (1906), ch. iii; G. E. Howard, *Local Constitutional History* (1889), chs. iv, x; C. P. Huse, *Financial History of Boston* (1916), chs. i–iii; Quincy, *Josiah Quincy*, ch. xvi; Gustavus Myers, *Tammany Hall* (1917), chs. vii–xxi; Pierce, *Chicago*, I, chs. x, xi. ❡ Law: Schlesinger, Jr., *Age of Jackson*, ch. xxv; Horton, *James Kent*; M. R. Cohen, "Legal Philosophy in America," *Law: A Century of Progress* (1937), II, 266; Wright, *American Interpretations of Natural Law*, chs. vii–xi; Corwin, *John Marshall*; Hurst, *American Law*; Chase, *Lemuel Shaw*; Warren, *American Bar*; E. K. Bauer, *Commentaries on the Constitution 1790–1860* (1952); §§ 150, 151. ❡ Maps: Paullin, *Atlas*, plates 103–05.

Sources — John Taylor, *Construction Construed*, and *New Views of the Constitution* (1823); Thomas Sargeant, *Constitutional Law* (1822); William Rawle, *Constitution* (1825); Kent, *Commentaries*; Joseph Story, *Commentaries*, and *Conflict of Laws* (3 ed., 1846); A. P. Upshur, *Brief Inquiry into Our Federal Government* (1840); James Bayard, *Exposition* (1833), and *Lectures on Constitutional Jurisprudence* (2 ed., 1856); Henry Baldwin, *General View* (1837); Timothy Walker, *Introduction to American Law* (1837); H. St. G. Tucker, *Lectures on Constitutional Law* (1843); E. F. Smith, *Commentaries* (1848); Theodore Sedgwick, *Treatise* (1857); Tocqueville, *Democracy in America*; G. T. Poussin, *Principe démocratique qui régit l'union américaine* (1841); Achille Murat, *Principes du gouvernement républicain* (1833); Francis Lieber, *On Civil Liberty* (1859); A. G. de Gurowski, *America and Europe* (1857), chs. iii, iv, vi; M. D. Howe, *Readings in American Legal History* (1949), chs. iv, v; Manning, Potter, Davies, *Select Problems*, I, ch. ix. ❡ Travels (§ 48), especially Chevalier, Grund, Martineau, and Raumer. ❡ Periodicals (§§ 52, 53), especially *Niles' Weekly Register*. Charles Kettleborough, ed., *State Constitutions and Organic Laws of Territories* (1918); other public records (§§ 45, 46).

Bibliography — Larned, *Literature of American History*, 302; Claflin, *Political Parties in United States*; Library of Congress, *Political Parties in United States*.

Chapter Fifteen

JACKSONIAN DEMOCRACY, 1829–1840

154. ANDREW JACKSON

Summary — Life: 1767, birth; 1790–1804, offices; 1797–98, U.S. senator; 1804–14, Indian fighter; 1815, Battle of New Orleans (§ 138); 1818, Seminole War (§ 144); 1824–25, defeated for presidency (§ 147); 1828, elected. — Character: self-confidence; belligerency; insubordination; uprightness; "retrenchment"; opposition to monopolies and corporations; public spirit. — Supporters: Lewis; Van Buren; Benton; Kendall; Blair; cabinet, "kitchen cabinet"; Eaton episode; popularity. — Opponents: Clay, Adams, Calhoun, Webster, coalition. — Civil service: inaugural, "task of reform," condition of the service (§§ 133, 147, 153); dismissals, appointments, number of changes. — Foreign policy: French spoliation claims; countervailing policy; Maine and Oregon boundaries (§ 166); Texas (§ 167); Isthmian canal (§ 173). — Judiciary: previous status (§ 143); 1831, Peck impeachment; 1832, Worcester *v.* Georgia; new appointments, 1834, Taney, chief justice; 1837, Briscoe *v.* Kentucky. — Parties: Jackson men; "Democratic"; "Whig"; "Anti-Masonic" (§ 153).

General — Hofstadter, *American Political Tradition*, ch. iii; Channing, *History*, V, ch. xii; McMaster, *History*, V, 513, VI, ch. lvii; Turner, *United States*, ch. ix; MacDonald, *Jacksonian Democracy*, chs. ii–iv, xii, xiv, xviii; C. G. Bowers, *Party Battles of Jackson Period* (1922), chs. i–vii; Binkley, *American Political Parties*, ch. vi, and *Powers of President*, chs. iv–v; Parton, *Andrew Jackson*; Bassett, *Andrew Jackson*, I, chs. i–iii, v, II, chs. xix–xxii, xxiv, xxv, xxx, xxxii; James, *Andrew Jackson*, I, II, chs. i–x, xviii; Schlesinger, Jr., *Age of Jackson*, chs. i–vi; Stanwood, *Presidency*, I, ch. xii.

Special — Shepard, *Van Buren*, chs. vi, vii; Meigs, *Benton*, 73, 141, 254, and *Calhoun*, I, ch. xiv; Schurz, *Clay*, I, chs. xii, xiii; Swisher, *Roger B. Taney*, chs. vii, viii; Nye, *Bancroft*, ch. iv; Curtis, *Buchanan*, I, chs. v, vi, ix, xii; W. E. Smith, *Francis Preston Blair Family in Politics* (1933), I, chs. vi–x; Wiltse, *Calhoun*, II, chs. i–iii; Dorfman, *Economic Mind*, II, ch. xxiii; Carroll, *Origins of Whig Party*; Abernethy, *Frontier to Plantation*, chs. x–xviii; Bailey, *Diplomatic History*, ch. xiii; Bemis, *American Secretaries of State*, IV; R. A. McLemore, *Franco-American Diplomatic Relations: 1816–1836* (1941); E. B. White, *American Opinion of France* (1927); Hatcher, *Livingston*; Herman Hailperin, "Pro-Jackson Sentiment in Pennsylvania," *Penn. Mag. of Hist. and Biog.*, L (1926), 193; Klein, *Pennsylvania Politics*, chs. vii–xii; Charles McCarthy, "Anti-Masonic Party," Am. Hist. Assoc., *Report*, 1902, I, 365; Myers, *History of Bigotry*, chs. xii; L. M. Salmon, "Appointing Power," Am. Hist. Assoc., *Papers* (1886), I, ch. v; Fish, *Civil Service and Patronage*, chs. iv, v, viii; E. M. Eriksson, "Official Newspaper Organs," *Tenn. Hist. Mag.*, VIII (1925), 231, IX (1926), 37, and "Federal Civil Service under Jackson," *Miss. Valley Hist. Rev.*, XIII (1927), 517; Beveridge, *John Marshall*, IV, ch. x; Haines, *Role of Supreme Court*, ch. xvi; Moore, *Arbitrations*, V, 4456.

Sources — Congressional debates (§ 45); Richardson, *Messages and Papers*, II, III; Moore, *Adjudications*, V; Jackson, *Correspondence*; J. Q. Adams, *Memoirs*, VIII, IX;

J. A. Hamilton, *Reminiscences*, chs. iv–viii; Benton, *Thirty Years' View*, chs. xxxviii–lxviii; Blau, *Jacksonian Democracy*; Miller, *Treaties*, III; Webster, *Writings and Speeches*, VII, 152; Webster, *Letters*, 141; Calhoun, *Works*, II, III, V; Calhoun, "Correspondence," 271, 290, 793; Clay, *Works*, I, II, IV, chs. vii–xi; Van Buren, "Autobiography," chs. xx–xxi, xxvi, xxvii, xxix; Kendall, *Autobiography*, chs. x–xiv; Quincy, *Figures of Past*, 352; Hart, *American History Told by Contemporaries*, III; §§ 158, 160.

Bibliography — Winsor, *Narrative and Critical History*, VIII, 287, 348; Larned, *Literature of American History*, 181; Hofstadter, *American Political Tradition*, 353; W. H. Wise and J. W. Cronin, *Bibliography of Andrew Jackson and Martin Van Buren* (1935).

155. JACKSON'S WAR ON THE BANK, 1829–1832

Summary — Status of the bank: previous history (§ 142); President Biddle; amount of government deposits; relations to Treasury; branches. — Jackson's attitude: 1829, Portsmouth Branch affair; Hill's influence; Ingham's correspondence; the attack on the bank. — Recharter controversy: 1829–1830, report; 1832, Jan., petition of the bank; July 2, recharter bill passes; 1832, July 10, Jackson's veto message; race-horse drafts; management. — Election of 1832: 1831, Dec., Clay nominated; 1832, May, first national convention (Jackson); Nov., Jackson re-elected; doctrine of a popular mandate.

General — Channing, *History*, V, ch. xiv; Schouler, *History*, IV, ch. xiii, § 3; MacDonald, *Jacksonian Democracy*, chs. vii, xi; von Holst, *History*, II, 31; Turner, *United States*, 402; Kirkland, *History of American Economic Life*, 271; Taylor, *Transportation Revolution*, ch. xiv; Kelly and Harbison, *American Constitution*, ch. xiii; Swisher, *American Constitutional Development*, ch. ix; Fish, *Rise of Common Man*, 50; Stanwood, *Presidency*, I, ch. xiii; Bowers, *Party Battles*, chs. viii–ix; James, *Andrew Jackson*, II, chs. xi, xiii, xv–xvii.

Special — Schlesinger, Jr., *Age of Jackson*, chs. vii–x; Bray Hammond, "Jackson, Biddle, and the Bank," *Jour. Econ. Hist.*, VII (1947), 1; Dewey, *Financial History*, §§ 86, 87; J. T. Holdsworth and D. R. Dewey, *First and Second Banks* (1910), 248, 296; Catterall, *Second Bank*, chs. iv–xi, xvi–xix; McGrane, *Panic of 1837*; Miller, *Banking Theories*; W. B. Smith, *Economic Aspects of Second Bank* (1953); Redlich, *Molding of American Banking*; M. G. Madeleine, *Monetary and Banking Theories of Jacksonian Democracy* (1943); Bassett, *Andrew Jackson*, II, chs. xxvii, xxviii; W. G. Sumner, *Andrew Jackson* (1882), chs. xi–xiii; Schurz, *Clay*, I, ch. xiii; Parton, *Andrew Jackson*, III, chs. xxix–xxxi; Swisher, *Roger B. Taney*, chs. ix, x; Meigs, *Benton*, 183, 271; W. E. Smith, *Blair Family*, I, chs. ix, xii; G. R. Taylor, *Jackson Versus Biddle* (1949).

Sources — Debates (§ 45); *Niles' Weekly Register*, XXXV–XLIV; 22 Cong., 1 sess., *H. Report*, No. 460; 23 Cong., 1 sess., *H. Ex. Doc.*, No. 523; Richardson, *Messages and Papers*, II; J. Q. Adams, *Memoirs*, VIII; Benton, *Thirty Years' View*, I, chs. xl, xli, lxvi–lxviii; Clay, *Works*, IV, chs. vii, viii, VI, 94–105; Webster, *Writings and Speeches*, V, 35, VI, 124; Van Buren, "Autobiography," chs. xxv, xxviii, xxxiv; J. A. Hamilton, *Reminiscenses*, chs. vi–viii; Jackson, *Correspondence*, IV, V; Biddle, *Correspondence* (§ 55); W. M. Gouge, *Paper Money and Banking* (1833); William Leggett, *Political Writings* (1840).

Bibliography — A. P. C. Griffin, *List of Works Relating to First and Second Banks*; Catterall, *Second Bank*, 513; MacDonald, *Jacksonian Democracy*, 324; Winsor, *Narrative and Critical History*, VII, 348; Meyer and Slade, *References on Monetary Question*, 116.

156. THE TARIFF AND NULLIFICATION, 1828–1833

Summary — Early threats of nullification: previous status; tariff of 1824 (§§·121, 131, 147); 1825–28, South Carolina protests. — Nullification movement: 1828, tariff act (§ 147); 1828, Calhoun's *Exposition*; Madison's opposition; 1828–29, Georgia and South Carolina declare act unconstitutional; Foote resolution and western lands; 1830, Jan., Webster-Hayne debate; Apr. 13, Jackson's Union toast; May, breach with Calhoun;

1831, July, address of South Carolina legislature; 1832, June, Gallatin's memorial; debates; July 14, tariff act passed; 1832, Oct., South Carolina convention summoned; Nov. 24, Ordinance of Nullification; "Exposition" and "Address"; Dec., Calhoun resigns vicepresidency. — Coercion: 1832, Dec. 11, Jackson's proclamation; Dec. 20, South Carolina statutes; military preparation; 1833, Jan. 6, nullification message; Jan., Feb., force bill; Webster-Calhoun debate. — Compromise of 1833: Feb. 12, Clay's proposition; March 2, force act passed and compromise tariff passed; March 16, Nullification Ordinance repealed. — Later development: fate of the tariff (§§ 163, 169); secession (§ 180).

General — Channing, *History*, V, ch. xiii; McMaster, *History*, VI, chs. liv, lviii; von Holst, *History*, I, ch. xii; MacDonald, *Jacksonian Democracy*, chs. v, vi, ix; Bowers, *Party Battles*, ch. x; Sydnor, *Southern Sectionalism*, chs. viii, ix; *South in Building of Nation*, II, 66, IV, 454; Schouler, *History*, IV, ch. xiii, § iii; Haines, *Role of Supreme Court*, ch. xv; Aaron, *America in Crisis*, ch. iv; Dorfman, *Economic Mind*, II, chs. xxvi–xxx.

Special — Wiltse, *Calhoun*, I, chs. xxix–xxxi, II, chs. iv–xv; Meigs, *Calhoun*, I, chs. xii, xiii, xv, II, ch. i; Lodge, *Daniel Webster*, chs. vi, vii; James, *Andrew Jackson*, II, chs. xii, xiv; Bassett, *Andrew Jackson*, II, ch. xxvi; Schurz, *Clay*, II, ch. xiv; Van Deusen, *Henry Clay*; McLaughlin, *Cass*, 139; Meigs, *Benton*, 246; L. A. White, *Rhett*, chs. ii–iv, and "Fate of Calhoun's Convention," *Am. Hist. Rev.*, XXXIV (1929), 757; Malone, *Thomas Cooper*; D. F. Houston, *Critical Study of Nullification* (1896); Ambler, *Sectionalism in Virginia*, 202; Frederic Bancroft, *Calhoun and the South Carolina Nullification Movement* (1928); C. S. Boucher, *Nullification Controversy in South Carolina* (1916); Van Deusen, *Disunion in South Carolina*, ch. i; R. R. Russel, *Economic Aspects Southern Sectionalism* (1924); Dewey, *Financial History*, ch. viii; Eiselen, *Pennsylvania Protectionism*, chs. iv–vi; Stanwood, *Tariff Controversies*, I, chs. vii–x; Taussig, *Tariff History*, pt. 1, ch. iii; W. T. Miller, "Nullification in Georgia and South Carolina," *Georgia Hist. Quar.*, XIV (1930), 286; R. G. Wellington, "Tariff and Public Lands," Am. Hist. Assoc., *Report*, 1911, I, 177. ❡ Maps: Paullin, *Atlas*, plate 114.

Sources — Debates (§ 45); Richardson, *Messages and Papers*, II; *Niles' Weekly Register*, XXXV–XLIV; F. W. Taussig, *State Papers on Tariff*, 108; Jackson, *Correspondence*, IV, V; Clay, *Works*, II, chs. vi–xii, IV, chs. viii, ix, V, 640, VI, 5; J. Q. Adams, *Memoirs*, VIII; Calhoun, *Works*, II, VI; Calhoun, "Correspondence," II, 219, 269; Webster, *Writings and Speeches*, V, 248, VI, 3, 181; Webster, *Letters*; Benton, *Thirty Years' View*, I, chs. xlvi, lxix, lxxviii; Madison, *Writings*, IX; Van Buren, "Autobiography," ch. xxx.

Bibliography — Dewey, *Financial Hist.*, § 77; MacDonald, *Jacksonian Democracy*, 325; Library of Congress, *Tariff in Its Relation to South* (1929); U.S. Tariff Commission, *Tariff*.

157 REMOVAL OF THE DEPOSITS, 1833–1837

Summary — Status: 1816, Bank Act clause (§ 142); 1832, veto of bank recharter (§ 155); House resolution affirming safety. — Removal: 1833, controversy over French draft; July, plan for state bank deposits; Sept. 18, "paper read to the cabinet"; Sept. 23, Secretary Duane removed; Sept. 26, Secretary Taney gives the order; question of contract, secretary's discretion, presidential responsibility. — Controversy with Senate: 1833, Dec. 3, Jackson's defense; Dec. 10, 26, Clay's resolution of censure; 1834, March 28, modified resolution passed; Apr. 15, Jackson's protest; May 12, Senate's counter protest; 1837, Jan. 16, expunging resolutions. — Fate of bank: 1836, charter expires; Pennsylvania charter; 1837, 1839, failure (§ 162). — Currency: state banks; government deposits in pet banks; 1834, June 28, 16 to 1 ration act; hard money; Loco-Foco faction (§ 162); 1836, July 11, "Specie Circular."

General — Channing, *History*, V, 446; von Holst, *History*, II, 52; Schouler, *History*, IV, ch. xiv, § i; McMaster, *History*, VI, ch. lix; MacDonald, *Jacksonian Democracy*, ch. xiii; Bowers, *Party Battles*, chs. xi–xii; also references in § 155.

Special — Schlesinger, Jr., *Age of Jackson*, 97; James, *Andrew Jackson*, II, chs. xiv, xxi; Bassett, *Andrew Jackson*, II, ch. xxix; Sumner, *Andrew Jackson*, chs. xiii, xiv; Parton, *Andrew Jackson*, III, chs. xxxvi–xxxix; Schurz, *Clay*, II, chs. xv, xviii; Meigs, *Benton*, 225, 258; Swisher, *Roger B. Taney*, chs. xi, xii; W. E. Smith, *Blair Family*, chs. ix, xii; Meigs, *Calhoun*, II, chs. ii, v; Wiltse, *Calhoun*, II, chs. xvi, xvii; Catterall, *Second Bank*, chs. xii–xv; Dewey, *Financial History*, §§ 88–90; also § 155.

Sources — Debates (§ 45); Richardson, *Messages and Papers*, II, 600, III, 5, 30, 36, 39, 69, 108, 163, 246, 282, 301; *Niles' Weekly Register*, XLVI–L; J. Q. Adams, *Memoirs*, IX; Benton, *Thirty Years' View*, I, chs. xcii–cxi; Calhoun, *Works*, II, III; Calhoun, "Correspondence," II, 329, 368; Clay, *Works*, IV, chs. ix, x, VI, 145, 264; Webster, *Writings and Speeches*, V, VI, 239, VII, 3, 200, 235, VIII, 3, 30, 36; Leggett, *Political Writings*; Buchanan, *Works*, III, 114; Kendall, *Autobiography*, ch. xiv; Van Buren, "Autobiography," chs. xl–xliv.

Bibliography — § 155.

158. TERRITORIAL QUESTIONS AND SURPLUS REVENUE, 1829-1841

Summary — Indians: Creek conflict (§ 147); 1826–29, Cherokee conflict; 1830, Tassel's case; 1831, Cherokee Nation *v.* Georgia; 1832, Worcester *v.* Georgia (§ 154); 1832, Black Hawk War; 1834, Indian Territory created; 1835, removal; Seminole War begins; later conditions (§ 165). — Internal improvements: previous status (§ 147); 1830, Maysville Road veto; 1831–32, increased expenditure. — Public lands: previous status (§ 142); 1820–31, normal sales; 1830, Foote resolution (§ 156); 1832–36, speculative sales; connection with wildcat banks; 1836, specie circular (§ 157); 1834–41, land grants; 1837, panic (§ 162); 1841, preëmption act. — Surplus: of 1806 (§ 133); of 1819 (§ 142); of 1836–37; connection with the tariff (§ 156); distribution, Clay's policy, Calhoun's attitude; 1833, pocket veto of Clay's act; 1836, "deposit act"; 1837, Calhoun's bill; payment of three installments; effects of financial crisis (§ 162); fate of remaining "deposit."

General — Channing, *History*, V, 453; McMaster, *History*, VI, chs. lv, lxii, lxiii; Schouler, *History*, IV, ch. xiv, § ii; von Holst, *History*, II, 177; Billington, *Westward Expansion*, 312; MacDonald, *Jacksonian Democracy*, chs. viii, x, xv, xvi.

Special — Bassett, *Andrew Jackson*, II, chs. xxiii, xxxi; James, *Andrew Jackson*, II, 244, 280; Schlesinger, Jr., *Age of Jackson*, 350; Beveridge, *John Marshall*, IV, ch. x; Meigs, *Benton*, 164; E. G. Bourne, *Surplus Revenue of 1837* (1885); Dewey, *Financial History*, §§ 91–94; Wellington, *Political Influence of Public Lands*; Hibbard, *Public Land Policies*, chs. vi, x; Zahler, *Eastern Workingmen and National Land Policy*; Stevens, *Black Hawk War*; Cyrenus Cole, *I Am a Man: The Indian Black Hawk* (1938); Phillips, "Georgia and States Rights," 73; Miller, "Nullification in Georgia and South Carolina," 286; Abel, "Indian Consolidation," ch. viii; Lumpkin, *Removal of Cherokee Indians*; Foreman, *Indian Removal*, and *Last Trek of Indians*, ch. iv, and *Advancing Frontier*; M. L. Starkey, *Cherokee Nation* (1946); Dunbar, *History of Travel*, II, chs. xxvi–xxix. — Maps: Paullin, *Atlas*, plate 114.

Sources — Debates (§ 45); 23 Cong., 1 sess., *Sen. Doc.*, No. 512; *American State Papers, Indian Affairs*, II, and *Public Lands*, VI–VIII, and *Military Affairs*, IV–VII; Richardson, *Messages and Papers*, II, III; *Niles' Weekly Register*; Moore, *Digest of International Law*, §§ 15–17; Benton, *Thirty Years' View*, I, chs. xliv, li, lxx, lxxi, xc, cxxii–cxxviii, cxxxvi–cxliii, cxlvi, cliv–clxi; Calhoun, *Works*, II, III, V, and "Correspondence," II, 349; Clay, *Works*, IV, VI; Webster, *Writings and Speeches*, IV, VII, 252, VIII, 50, 129, 261; J. Q. Adams, *Memoirs*, VIII–X; Van Buren, "Autobiography," chs. xxii–xxiv; Black Hawk, *Autobiography* (1833).

Bibliography — Abel, "Indian Consolidation," 413; Foreman, *Indian Removal*, 389; Dewey, *Financial History.*, § 85; T. H. McKee, *Reports of Committees on Public Lands 1815 to 1887* (1887); MacDonald, *Jacksonian Democracy*, 323; Winsor, *Narrative and Critical History*, VII, 322; Larned, *Literature of American History*, 319; § 155.

Chapter Sixteen

MANIFEST DESTINY AND SLAVERY, 1830–1848

159. NEGRO SLAVERY, 1830–1860

Summary — Southern whites: large and small slaveholders, independent farmers, poor whites, immigrants; social and political leadership. — Negro: origins; conditions, physical, intellectual, religious; character; associations; Mulattoes; race mixture; free Negroes; political and social discriminations. — Slavery system: clothing; houses; food; cost of maintenance; families, recreations; old age; sickness and death; education; slave codes; laws regulating manumission; variety of employment; hiring out; overseers; drivers; tasks, punishments; privileges; degree of efficiency; in industry. — Slave trade: private sales; auction; hardships, reënslavement for jail fees; market value; dealers (§ 161). — Insurrections: colonial (§ 91); 1800, Gabriel's; 1822, Denmark Vesey's; 1831, Nat Turner's; 1859, John Brown (§ 177); fear of insurrections; fugitives (§§ 161, 172).

General — Channing, *History*, V, ch. v, VI, 10; McMaster, *History*, VIII, 228; Rhodes, *History*, I, ch. iv; Cole, *Irrepressible Conflict*, chs. ii, iii; Sydnor, *Southern Sectionalism*, ch. xi; Kirkland, *History of American Economic Life*, 160; Curti, *Growth of American Thought*, ch. xvii; Allan Nevins, *Ordeal of Union* (1947), I, chs. xiii–xv; *South in Building of Nation*, IV, 198, 226, V, 73, 108, 152, 398; Hart, *Slavery and Abolition*, ch. iv–ix; Dodd, *Cotton Kingdom*; Farnam, *Social Legislation*, chs. xiii–xvi; Franklin, *Slavery to Freedom*, chs. xiii–xiv.

Special — Economics of Slavery: Gray, *Agriculture in Southern United States*; Phillips, *Life and Labor in Old South*, and *American Negro Slavery*, chs. ix–xxiii; Bruce, *Virginia Iron Manufacture*, ch. vi; Hammond, *Cotton Industry*, bk. 1, chs. i–iii; Robert, *Tobacco Kingdom*, pt. 1; V. A. Moody, *Slavery on Louisiana Sugar Plantations* (1924); J. D. Hill, "Economic Aspects of Slavery," *So. Atlantic Quar.*, XXVI (1927), 161; W. H. Yarbrough, *Economic Aspects of Slavery* (1932); F. L. and H. C. Owsley, "Economic Basis of Society," *Jour. Southern Hist.*, VI (1940), 24, and "Economic Structure of Rural Tennessee," *ibid.*, VIII (1942), 162; J. C. Bonner, "Profile of a Late Ante-Bellum Community," *Am. Hist. Rev.*, XLIX (1944), 663. ❡ Biographical Studies: Craven, *Ruffin*, chs. iii, iv; Wiltse, *Calhoun*, II, chs. xx, xxv. ❡ State Studies: J. R. Brackett, *Negro in Maryland* (1889), chs. iii–v; C. S. Sydnor, *Slavery in Mississippi* (1933); Ballagh, *Slavery in Virginia*; G. G. Johnson, *Ante-Bellum North Carolina*, chs. xvi–xviii, xx; R. H. Taylor, *Slaveholding in North Carolina* (1926); B. R. Holt, *Supreme Court of North Carolina and Slavery* (1927); Flanders, *Plantation Slavery in Georgia*; J. W. Coleman, *Slave Times in Kentucky* (1940); J. B. Sellers, *Slavery in Alabama* (1950); R. W. Shugg, *Origins of Class Struggle in Louisiana* (1939), chs. i–v; Trexler, *Slavery in Missouri*, chs. i–iv. ❡ Poor Whites: Buck, "Poor Whites," 41; A. O. Craven, "Poor Whites and Negroes," *Jour. of Negro Hist.*, XV (1930), 14; B. H. Clark, *Tennessee Yeomen*; F. L. Owsley, *Plain Folk of Old South* (1949); Coulter, *Brownlow*, chs. i–vi. ❡ Free Negroes: J. M. Wright, *Free Negro in Maryland* (1921); Russell, *Free Negro in Virginia*; J. M. England, "Free Negro in Ante-Bellum Tennessee," *Jour. Southern Hist.*, IX (1943),

37; R. B. Flanders, "Free Negro in Georgia," *No. Car. Hist. Rev.*, IX (1932), 250; J. H. Franklin, *Free Negro in North Carolina* (1943); L. P. Jackson, *Free Negro in Virginia* (1942). ❪ Other Topics: B. W. Doyle, *Etiquette of Race Relations* (1931); C. H. Wesley, *Negro Labor* (1927), chs. i–iii; W. E. B. DuBois and A. G. Dill, *Negro American Artisan* (1912), ch. iii; C. G. Woodson, *Education of Negro;* L. H. Hirsch, "Negro and New York," *Jour. Negro Hist.*, XVI (1931), 382; D. R. Fox, "Negro Vote in Old New York," *Pol. Sci. Quar.*, XXXII (1917), 252; Turner, *Negro in Pennsylvania*, chs. vii–xiii; W. E. B. DuBois, *Philadelphia Negro* (1899), chs. iii, iv; Bancroft, *Slave-Trading in Old South;* W. S. Drewry, *Slave Insurrections in Virginia* (1900); Clement Eaton, "Mob Violence in Old South," *Miss. Valley Hist. Rev.*, XXIX (1942), 351; Aptheker, *American Negro Slave Revolts.* ❪ Maps: Shepherd, *Atlas*, 206, 207; Paullin, *Atlas*, plates 66–9.

Sources — Documents: H. T. Catterall, ed., *Judicial Cases Concerning American Slavery* (4 vols., 1926–36); J. C. Sitterson, ed., "Magnolia Plantation," *Miss. Valley Hist. Rev.*, XXV (1938), 197; J. H. Easterby, ed., *South Carolina Rice Plantation* (1945); Phillips and Glunt, *Florida Plantation Records;* Commons, *Documentary History*, I, II; F. L. Riley, "Diary of a Mississippi Planter," *Miss. Hist. Soc., Publ.*, X (1909), 305; C. G. Woodson, ed., "Negro Owners of Slaves," *Jour. of Negro Hist.*, IX (1924), 41; Omar ibn Said, "Autobiography," J. F. Jameson, ed., *Am. Hist. Rev.*, XXX (1925), 787; Bassett, *Southern Plantation Overseer.* ❪ Travelers' Accounts: particularly, Lyell, Olmsted, Stuart (§ 48); Gurowski, *America and Europe*, ch. v. ❪ Periodicals: (§§ 52, 53); also *Southern Cultivator* (1843–   ); *American Cotton Planter* (1853–56); *DeBow's Review.* ❪ Southern Views: H. R. Helper, *Impending Crisis* (1857); Benton, *Thirty Years' View*, II, ch. xxxii; Smedes, *Memorials of a Southern Planter;* Calhoun, *Works*, II–VI; William Harper, *et al., Pro-Slavery Argument* (1852); T. R. R. Cobb, *Law of Negro Slavery* (1858). ❪ Northern Views: Frederick Douglass, *Life and Times* (1881), pt. i; F. A. Kemble, *Journal of Residence on Georgia Plantation;* Nehemiah Adams, *South Side View of Slavery* (1854); F. C. Adams, *Uncle Tom at Home* (1853); K. E. R. Pickard, *Kidnapped and Ransomed* (1856); Solomon Northrup, *Twelve Years a Slave* (1853); E. H. Botume, *First Days among the Contrabands* (1893); William Goodell, *American Slave Code* (1853). ❪ Other Sources: Manning, Potter, Davies, *Select Problems*, I, ch. vi.

Bibliography — Kirkland, *History of American Economic Life*, 692; Work, *Bibliography of the Negro;* Cole, *Irrepressible Conflict*, 417; Channing, *History*, VI, 38; Turner and Merk, *References on History of West*, § 18; Sydnor, *Southern Sectionalism*, 355.

160. THE ABOLITION MOVEMENT, 1830–1850

Summary — Pro-slavery argument: scriptural; ancient precedent; Negro inferiority; good of the Negro; good of the whites; basis of democracy; economic advantages. — Anti-slavery argument: unchristian; uneconomic; degrading; demoralizing to masters; inhuman; contrary to rights of man; encourages political oligarchies; sectional. — Rise of abolitionists; early history (§§ 120, 127, 145); 1816, American Colonization Society (§ 145). — Foreign influences; 1830, 1837, British abolition; 1848, French abolition. — Eastern movement: Benjamin Lundy; 1831, W. L. Garrison, *Liberator;* 1837, Wendell Phillips; Gerrit Smith; J. G. Whittier; 1845, Theodore Parker; J. R. Lowell. — Western movement: 1826, Western Reserve College; 1832, Lane Seminary; 1833, Oberlin College; S. P. Chase; early fugitive cases; Southern abolitionists; 1834, J. G. Birney; Grimké sisters; C. M. Clay. — Organization: 1832, state and local societies; English agitators; George Thompson; 1833, American Anti-Slavery Society; 1840, separation of national society; 1840, American and Foreign Anti-Slavery Society; 1840, "Liberty Party." — Opposition: 1831–34, Negro schools destroyed in north; 1834–38, northern riots; 1837, Lovejoy; 1838, Pennsylvania Hall; Southern legislation; demands on the North for restrictions; slave codes; disappearance of anti-slavery sentiment; pro-slavery propaganda. — Congressional struggles: antislavery men in Congress, Miner, Slade, J. Q. Adams, Giddings; 1801–25, movements for emancipation in District of Columbia; fugitives, other aspects of District slavery (§§ 159, 161); "incendiary publications" in mails; 1835, Aug., Postmaster-General Kendall's letter; 1836, Calhoun's bill; "freedom of the press." — Abolition petitions: earlier objections (§ 180); 1820–30, on District of Columbia; J. Q. Adams' attitude; 1836, Calhoun's proposition; Buchanan's compromise; Gag resolutions in the House; 1836, Pinckney's; 1837, Hawes's; 1837, Patton's; 1838, Atherton's; 1840, Johnson's; 1844, repeal; attempted censures; 1837, J. Q. Adams; 1842, Adams; 1842, Giddings.

General — Rhodes, *History*, I, 38; Channing, *History*, V, 140; Schouler, *History*, IV, ch. xiv, § ii; Fish, *Rise of Common Man*, 276; Cole, *Irrepressible Conflict*, ch. ix; McMaster, *History*, VI, chs. lxi, lxvii; von Holst, *History*, II, 80, 219; Hart, *Slavery and Abolition* (1900), chs. x, xii–xviii; T. C. Smith, *Liberty and Free Soil Parties* (1897), chs. ii–v; Jesse Macy, *Anti-Slavery Crusade* (1919), chs. i–vi; Merriam, *American Political Theories*, ch. vi; Hofstadter, *American Political Tradition*, ch. vi; Nevins, *Ordeal of Union*, I, 137; Sydnor, *Southern Sectionalism*, ch. x; Dorfman, *Economic Mind*, II, ch. xxxii.

Special — G. H. Barnes, *Anti-Slavery Impulse* (1933); Tyler, *Freedom's Ferment*, chs. xvii, xviii; D. L. Dumond, *Antislavery Origins Civil War* (1939); R. K. Nuermberger, *Free Produce Movement* (1942); Fletcher, *Oberlin*, I, chs. xviii–xxvii; Hart, *Commonwealth History of Massachusetts*, IV, ch. ix; M. H. Rice, *American Catholic Opinion in Slavery Controversy* (1944); F. E. Gibson, *Attitudes of New York Irish* (1951), ch. iv; W. H. Lofton, "Abolition and Labor," *Jour. Negro Hist.*, XXXIII (1948), 249; U. B. Phillips, *Course of South to Secession* (1939), chs. v, vi; Ambler, *Sectionalism in Virginia*, 185; Clement Eaton, *Freedom of Thought in Old South* (1940); A. E. Martin, *Anti-Slavery Movement in Kentucky* (1918); W. S. Jenkins, *Pro-Slavery Thought* (1935); J. C. Robert, *Road from Monticello* (1941); K. M. Stampp, "Fate of Southern Anti-Slavery Sentiment," *Jour. Negro Hist.*, XXVIII (1943), 10; R. G. Osterweis, *Romanticism and Nationalism in Old South* (1949); T. C. Johnson, *Scientific Interests in Old South;* G. G. Johnson, *Ante-Bellum North Carolina*, ch. xix; Gaines, *Southern Plantation*, chs. i–iii; Flanders, *Plantation Slavery in Georgia*, ch. xii; R. B. Nye, *Fettered Freedom* (1945), chs. i–v; Cash, *Mind of South;* B. B. Kendrick and A. M. Arnett, *South Looks at Its Past* (1935); Dodd, *Cotton Kingdom*, ch. iii; Fox, *American Colonization Society* (1919); J. P. Bretz, "Economic Background of Liberty Party," *Am. Hist. Rev.*, XXXIV (1929), 250; W. S. Savage, *Controversy over Distribution of Abolition Literature* (1938); B. B. Munford, *Virginia's Attitude toward Slavery* (1909), chs. viii, ix, xv–xvii, xxxi; Harris, *Negro Servitude in Illinois*, chs. vi–x; J. E. Cutler, *Lynch Law* (1905), ch. iv; Mary Tremaine, *Slavery in District of Columbia* (1892), chs. iii, iv. ❧ Biographies: Birney, *Birney*, chs. xii–xvii; Julian, *Giddings*, chs. i–iii; Tappan, *Arthur Tappan*, chs. viii–xx; Weiss, *Parker*, II, ch. xviii; Commager, *Parker;* Mordell, *Whittier;* Schurz, *Clay*, II, chs. xvii, xxi; Van Deusen, *Henry Clay*, ch. xix; Story, *Story*, I, ch. xi; Morse, *J. Q. Adams*, ch. iii; Pierce, *Sumner*, III, ch. xxx; Meigs, *Calhoun*, II, ch. iv; Craven, *Ruffin*, chs. v, vi; Martyn, *Phillips;* Garrison, *Garrison;* Wish, *Fitzhugh.*

Sources — Periodicals: *Liberator; Anti-Slavery Standard; Emancipator; Niles' Weekly Register; National Era; N.Y. Tribune; Richmond Whig; Charleston Mercury* (§ 53); reports of anti-slavery societies. ❧ Public Documents: Debates (§ 45); Richardson, *Messages and Papers*, III, 175. ❧ Contemporary Tracts and Speeches: J. R. Giddings, *Speeches* (1853); Webster, *Writings and Speeches*, VIII, 109; Wendell Phillips, *Speeches* (1891); G. B. Cheever, *Guilt of Slavery* (1860); Albert Barnes, *Inquiry into Slavery* (1846); L. M. Child, *The Oasis* (1834); William Jay, *Miscellaneous Writings* (1853); Edward Beecher, *Narrative of Riots at Alton* (1838); George Fitzhugh, *Cannibals All* (1857); Samuel Seabury, *American Slavery* (1861). ❧ Personal Accounts: B. P. Poore, *Perley's Reminiscences*, I, ch. xv; George Thompson, *Prison Life* (1847); Levi Coffin, *Reminiscences;* J. F. Clarke, *Anti-Slavery Days* (1883); May, *Recollections;* Parker Pillsbury, *Acts of Anti-Slavery Apostles* (1883); Clay, *Life*, I, chs. i–iv; G. H. Barnes and D. L. Dumond, eds., *Weld-Grimké Letters* (1934); D. L. Dumond, ed., *Birney Letters* (1938); J. Q. Adams, *Memoirs*, IX, X; Chase, "Dairy," 107, 459; Calhoun, "Correspondence," and *Works*, II–VI; Clay, *Works*, IV, VI; Benton, *Thirty Years' View*, I, chs. cxxix–cxxxi, II, chs. xxxiii, xxxvi, xxxvii. ❧ Others: Manning, Potter, Davies, *Select Problems*, I, chs. vii, viii; Jacobson, *American Political Thought*, ch. v.

Bibliography — Hart, *Slavery and Abolition*, ch. xxii; Tyler, *Freedom's Ferment*, 582; Samuel May, Jr., *Catalogue of Anti-Slavery Publications* (1864); Larned, *Literature of American History*, 181.

161. INTERNATIONAL AND INTERSTATE STATUS OF SLAVERY
1830–1850

Summary — Role of federal goverment: District of Columbia (§ 160); territories (§§ 170, 171, 174, 177); extradition of fugitives; domestic trade; rights of colored citizens; foreign relations. — Fugitives (§§ 159, 172): usual methods; advertisements; return in slave states; "underground railroad," "personal liberty" bills. — Important cases: 1837, Matilda; 1840, Van Zandt; 1842, Prigg; 1842, Latimer; 1847, Kennedy. — Interstate extradition: 1835, Williams; 1837, Maine-Georgia; 1839, New York-Virginia; 1859, Kentucky v. Dennison. — Free Negroes: 1822, 1835, South Carolina Negro seaman acts; 1844, Hoar's mission; question of temporary sojourn; transit of slaves through free states (§ 172). — Foreign relations: Haiti; Liberia (§ 145); Negroes carried away by troops (§ 138); fugitives to Mexico and Canada; slave-trade regulations; 1841, Quintuple treaty; 1842, Ashburton treaty on joint cruising (§ 166). — Slave vessel cases: 1830, Comet; 1834, Encomium and Enterprise; 1839, L'Amistad; 1840, British indemnity; 1841, Creole.

General — McMaster, *History*, VII, 248; von Holst, *History*, II, 312; Hart, *Slavery and Abolition*, ch. xix; Macy, *Anti-Slavery Crusade*, ch. viii.

Special — Bancroft, *Seward*, I, 101; Pierce, *Sumner*, II, ch. xxiv; G. F. Dowe, *Slave Ships and Slaving* (1927); W. L. Mathieson, *Great Britain and Slave Trade* (1929); Hill, *United States and Brazil*, ch. v; H. G. Soulsby, *Right of Search and Slave Trade in Anglo-American Relations, 1814–1862* (1933); Moore, *Arbitrations*, I, 408; Julian, *Giddings*, chs. iv–vi; M. G. McDougall, *Fugitive Slaves*, ch. ii; W. H. Collins, *Domestic Slave Trade* (1904); W. H. Siebert, *Underground Railroad* (1898); DuBois, *Slave Trade*, chs. ix–xi; Warren, *Supreme Court*, III, 73, ch. xxv. — Maps: Hart, *Slavery and Abolition*, 126, 230; Siebert, *Underground Railroad*, 113; Shepherd, *Atlas*, 206.

Sources — Debates: (§ 45). ❡ Documents: J. B. Moore, *Digest of International Law*, §§ 208, 310; 27 Cong., 3 sess., *Sen. Docs.*, I; 27 Cong., 2 sess., *H. Ex. Docs.*, II, No. 116, V, No. 242; 28 Cong., I sess., *H. Ex. Docs.*, IV, No. 83; 35 Cong., 1 sess., *Sen. Reports*, I, No. 36; Miller, *Treaties*, III, iv; Richardson, *Messages and Papers*, II, 204, 243, 250, IV, 232; *Niles' Weekly Register*; Hall, *Opinions of the Attorneys-General*, I, 659, II, 426. ❡ Contemporary Writings: J. C. Hurd, *Law of Freedom and Bondage* (1858–62), I, chs. ii, vii–xiii; A. H. Stephens, *Constitutional View of Late War between the States*, (1868–70), II, colloquy xiv; Jay, *Miscellaneous Writings*, 207; J. Q. Adams, *Memoirs*, VIII–X; Benton, *Thirty Years' View*, II, chs. xlix, xcviii; H. C. Carey, *Slave Trade* (1853); Calhoun, *Works*, III–V; Webster, *Writings and Speeches*, VII, 230, XI, XII, 3, 65, XIV, 373, 403, XV, 171; Levi Woodbury, *Writings*, II, 400; William Still, *Underground Railroad* (1872; r. ed., 1879).

Bibliography — DuBois, *Slave Trade*, App. C; §§ 159, 160.

162. VAN BUREN'S ADMINISTRATION, 1837–1841

Summary — Election of 1836: no Whig nomination; Jackson's influence; Van Buren elected. — Parties (§ 153): Whig opposition; Loco-Focos; conservatives; 1839, New Jersey contested elections. — Foreign policy: 1836, question of Texas (§ 167); 1837, Caroline affair; 1838–39, Aroostook War (§ 166); 1841, McLeod incident. — Finances: 1837, panic; "deposit act" suspended (§ 158); 1839, second crisis; 1840, Independent Treasury established; 1841, repealed; 1846, reëstablished (§ 169). — Slavery questions (§§ 160, 161). — State finances: internal improvements (§§ 149, 150, 153); repudiations. — Sectional contest for the west: railroad plans (§ 149); land politics (§ 149). — Labor and politics (§§ 149, 150, 152, 153).

General — Channing, *History*, V, 453; Turner, *United States*, ch. x; Schlesinger, Jr., *Age of Jackson*, chs. xvii–xxi; McMaster, *History*, VI, chs. lxiv–lxvi, lxviii; von Holst, *History*, II, 146, 194; Schouler, *History*, IV, ch. xv; MacDonald, *Jacksonian Democracy*, ch. xvii; Hart, *Slavery and Abolition*, ch. xx; Bowers, *Party Battles*, ch. xv; Stanwood, *Presidency*, I, chs. xiv, xv.

Special — Biographies: Alexander, *Van Buren;* Shepard, *Van Buren*, chs. viii–x; Schurz, *Clay*, II, chs. xix, xx; Meigs, *Benton*, 264; Bancroft, *Seward*, I, 111; Curtis, *Buchanan*, I, chs. xiii–xv; Meigs, *Calhoun*, II, ch. vi; Wiltse, *Calhoun*, II, chs. xviii–xix, xxvi, xxvii; Van Deusen, *Henry Clay*, ch. xviii; W. E. Smith, *Blair Family*, I, ch. xiii. ❡ Finances: Dewey, *Financial History*, §§ 96–101, 104, and *State Banking before Civil War;* Taus, *Central Banking Functions*, ch. ii; David Kinley, *Independent Treasury* (1910), chs. ii–vi; Van Deusen, *Disunion in South Carolina*, ch. iv; Taylor, *Transportation Revolution*, 338; McGrane, *Panic of 1837;* Rezneck, "American Depression, 1837–1843"; W. A. Scott, *Repudiation of State Debts* (1893), ch. ii. ❡ Politics: Myers, *Tammany Hall*, chs. xii–xiv; Hammond, *Political Parties in New York*, II, chs. xl, xli; Alexander, *History of New York*, II, ch. ii; Fish, *Civil Service and Patronage*, ch. vi. ❡ Diplomacy: J. M. Callahan, *American Foreign Policy in Canadian Relations* (1937); J. B. Brebner, *North Atlantic Triangle* (1945), ch. viii; O. E. Tiffany, "United States and Canadian Rebellion of 1837," Buffalo Hist. Soc., *Publ.*, VIII (1905), 1; A. B. Corey *Crisis of 1830–1842 in Canadian-American Relations* (1941); H. L. Keenleyside and G. S. Brown, *Canada and United States* (1952); W. P. Shortridge, "Canadian American Frontier," *Canadian Hist. Rev.*, VII (1926), 16; Alastair Watt, "Alexander McLeod," *ibid.*, XII (1931), 165. ❡ Maps: Paullin, *Atlas*, plate 114.

Sources — Debates (§ 45); Benton, *Abridgment*, XIII, XIV; Miller, *Treaties*, IV; Richardson, *Messages and Papers*, III, 313; *Niles' Weekly Register*, LI–LVIII; Dunbar, *Currency, Finance, and Banking*, 118; A. T. Huntington and R. J. Mawhinney, comps., *Laws Concerning Money, Banking and Loans* (1910), 117, 323, 633. ❡ Contemporary Writings: J. Q. Adams, *Memoirs*, IX, X; Van Buren, "Autobiography"; Benton, *Thirty Years' View*, II, chs. i–lix; Calhoun, *Works*, III, and "Correspondence," 371; Leggett, *Political Writings;* Richard Hildreth, *Banks, Banking, and Paper Currencies* (1840), chs. xxii–xxv; Clay, *Works*, IV, chs. x, xi, VI, 279; Webster, *Writings and Speeches*, VI, VIII; Woodbury, *Writings*, I; Buchanan, *Works*, III, IV; Poore, *Perley's Reminiscences*, I, chs. xiv–xvi; F. Byrdsall, *History of the Loco-Foco Party* (1842); Greeley, *Recollections*, ch. xvi; Nathan Appleton, *Remarks on Currency* (1841).

Bibliography — Dewey, *Financial History*, § 95; Bemis and Griffin, *Guide to Diplomatic History*, 277; Wise and Cronin, *Bibliography of Jackson and Van Buren*, 57.

163. THE WHIGS AND TYLER, 1840–1844

Summary — Election of 1840: Van Buren; Harrison; "Tippecanoe and Tyler too"; Harrison elected. — 1841, President Harrison; cabinet; policy; Apr. 4, death. — 1841, Tyler's breach with the Whigs: Clay's schemes; subtreasury repeal (§ 162); "Fiscal Bank" veto; "Fiscal Corporation" veto; resignation of the cabinet; Webster remains. — Tyler's policy: cabinet changes; 1843, Webster retires; "corporal's guard." — Tariff of 1842: 1833–41, effect of the Compromise of 1833 (§ 156); lack of revenue; 1841, temporary tariff; 1842, tariff vetoes; tariff act passed; effect (§ 169). — Slavery questions (§§ 160, 161). — Foreign affairs (§ 166). — State questions: 1842, Dorr rebellion in Rhode Island; 1839–46, anti-rent agitation in New York.

General — McMaster, *History*, VI, chs. lxix, lxx, VII, chs. lxxi, lxxii; von Holst, *History*, II, chs. v, vi; Schouler, *History*, IV, chs. xvi, xvii; Stanwood, *Presidency*, I, ch. xvi; Binkley, *American Political Parties*, ch. vii; Turner, *United States*, ch. xi; Schlesinger, Jr., *Age of Jackson*, chs. xxii, xxiii, xxx–xxxii.

Special — Curtis, *Buchanan*, I, ch. xvi; H. A. Wise, *Seven Decades* (1876), chs. viii–xii; Tyler, *Tylers*, I, ch. xx, II, chs. i–vi, III, 84–114; Schurz, *Clay*, II, chs. xxii, xxiii;

Van Deusen, *Henry Clay*, chs. xx, xxi; W. E. Smith, *Blair Family*, I, chs. xiv, xv; Meigs, *Calhoun*, II, ch. vii; Wiltse, *Calhoun*, III, chs. i–iii, vi; Cleaves, *Old Tippecanoe*, chs. xxii–xxiv; Goebel, *Harrison*, chs. x, xi; Curtis, *Daniel Webster*, II, chs. xxvi, xxvii; G. R. Poage, *Clay and Whig Party* (1936), chs. ii–viii; Stanwood, *Tariff Controversies*, II, ch. xi; Dewey, *Financial History*, §§ 102, 103; Eiselen, *Pennsylvania Protectionism*, ch. vii; Kinley, *Independent Treasury*, chs. ii–vi; Ostrogorski, *Democracy and Political Parties*, II, 71; Fish, *Civil Service and Patronage*, ch. viii; Van Deusen, *Southern Sectionalism*, chs. ii, iii; Weyl, *Treason*, ch. x; Garraty, *Wright*; Mowry, *Dorr War*; Dan King, *Life and Times of Thomas Wilson Dorr* (1859); E. P. Cheyney, *Anti-Rent Agitation in New York* (1887); Flick, *History of New York*, VI, ch. ix; Henry Christman, *Tin Horns and Calico* (1945); Ellis, *Landlords and Farmers in Hudson-Mohawk Region*. See also: § 153.

Sources — Debates and Documents (§ 45); Benton, *Abridgment*, XIV, XV; Richardson, *Messages and Papers*, IV; *Niles' Weekly Register*, LVIII–LXIII; Moore, *Digest of International Law*, § 217. ⚓ Contemporary Writings: E. R. Potter, *Considerations on Questions in Rhode Island* (1842); Webster, *Writings and Speeches*, III, VIII, XI, 217, XV; Clay, *Works*, II, chs. xiv–xvi, IV, ch. xi, VI, 406; Calhoun, *Works*, III, IV, and "Correspondence," 448, 816, 844; Benton, *Thirty Years' View*, II, chs. lviii–cxxxiv; J. Q. Adams, *Memoirs*, X, XI; Woodbury, *Writings*, I, 212; Poore, *Perley's Reminiscences*, I, chs. xvii–xxiii; Nathan Sargent (Oliver Oldschool, pseud.), *Public Men and Events 1817 to 1853* (1875), II, chs. v, vi.

Bibliography — Winsor, *Narrative and Critical History*, VII, 353–355; J. W. Cronin and W. H. Wise, *Bibliography of Harrison, Tyler, Polk* (1935); Turner and Merk, *References on History of West*, §§ 22–24; U.S. Tariff Commission, *Tariff*.

164. EXPLORATION OF THE FAR WEST TO 1850

Summary — Geographic provinces: prairies and the Great Plains; Rocky Mountains; Columbia Plateau; Colorado Plateau; Interior Basin (the Desert); Pacific Coast. — Western Indians. — Exploration by sea (§§ 75, 78, 134): 1542–43, Cabrillo and Ferrelo; 1579, Drake; 1602–03, Vizcaíno and Aguilar; 1741, Bering; 1769, Pérez; 1778, Cook; 1792, Gray, the *Columbia*; 1792, Vancouver. — Exploration by land: French and the Sea of the West (§ 76); 1714, Saint Denis; 1724, Bourgmont; 1740, Mallet brothers; 1731–1743, Vérendrye family. — Spanish in California: 1769, Portolá and Father Junípero Serra; 1776, foundation of the presidio and mission of San Francisco. — American explorations: 1803–06, Lewis and Clark (§ 134); 1806–07, Pike (§ 134); 1811–12, the Astorians (§ 134); 1820, Long; Hudson's Bay Company in the Oregon country; Rocky Mountain fur traders; 1823–24, Ashley's men; 1826–29, Jedediah Smith; 1842–46, Frémont.

General — Billington, *Westward Expansion*, chs. xx–xxiii; Cardinal Goodwin, *Trans-Mississippi West* (1922), chs. i–iv, vii; Justin Winsor, *Mississippi Basin* (1895), 30, 193; Parkman, *Half Century of Conflict*, I, ch. xv, II, ch. xvi; Livingston Farrand, *Basis of American History* (1904), chs. iv, viii, ix, xii; Turner, *New West*, ch. viii; Schafer, *Pacific Northwest*, chs. i–viii; Caughey, *Pacific Coast*, chs. i–xiv; Webb, *Great Plains*, ch. ii–v; Everett Dick, *Vanguards of Frontier* (1941), chs. i–viii; Priestley, *Coming of White Man*.

Special — Geography: Powell, *Physiographic Regions*, 85; Brigham, *Geographic Influences*, chs. viii–x; Isaiah Bowman, *Forest Physiography* (1911), chs. ix–xxiii; W. D. Johnson, "High Plains and Their Utilization," U.S. Geolog. Survey, *Report*, XXI (1899–1900), pt. 4, XXII (1900–01), pt. 4; W. E. Smythe, *Conquest of Arid America* (1907); A. G. McAdie, *Climatology of California* (1903). ⚓ Explorers and traders: Bernard De Voto, *Year of Decision* (1943), chs. i, ii, and *Across Wide Missouri* (1947); Bolton, *Spanish Exploration*, and *Anza's California Expedition*; G. D. Lyman, *John Marsh, Pioneer* (1930), chs. vii–xxvii; O. O. Winther, *Great Northwest* (1947), ch. vi; G. R. Hebard, *Pathbreakers* (1933); R. G. Cleland, *This Reckless Breed; Trappers of the Southwest* (1950); Hodge, *Handbook of American Indians*; A. C. Laut, *Story of Trapper* (1902), chs. i–viii, and *Conquest of Great Northwest* (1908), I, ch. xx, II; C. A. Vandiveer, *Fur Trade* (1929); George Bryce, *Remarkable History of Hudson's Bay Company* (1900), chs. xxxix, xl; Douglas MacKay, *Honourable Company* (1936); Bancroft, *California*, I, chs. iii, vi, and *Pacific Northwest*, and *Nevada, Colorado, and Wyoming*, ch. ii, and *Utah*, ch. ii; H. M. Chittenden, *American Fur Trade*, and *History of Early Steamboat Navigation on Missouri* (2 vols., 1903); Washington Irving, *Captain Bonneville*, and *Astoria*; I. B. Richman, *California* (1911), chs. i–vi; Nevins, *Frémont*, chs. vi–xv; Porter, *John Jacob Astor*, II, chs. xiv–xvi. ❧ Maps: Paullin, *Atlas*, plates 38, 39; Shepherd, *Atlas*, 210; A. B. Hulbert, *Transcontinental Trails* (6 vols., 1925–28); Richman, *California*. — Most of the accounts of exploration contain valuable maps.

Sources — Champlain Society, *Publ.*, Hudson's Bay series (1938–   ); Margry, *Découvertes et établissements des français*; R. P. Bieber and L. R. Hafen, eds., *Southwest Historical Series* (12 vols., 1931–43); Palou, *Noticias*; Pedro Font, *Complete Diary* (H. E. Bolton, ed., 1931); Gaspar de Portolá, "Account," "Diary," and "Narrative," Ac. of Pacific Coast Hist., *Publ.*, I (1910), II (1911); Pedro Fages, *Historical Description of California* (H. I. Priestley, ed., 1937); Thwaites, *Early Western Travels*, XIV–XXX; A. B. Hulbert, *Overland to Pacific* (1933–41), I–IV; Long and James, *Account of an Expedition*; H. M. Brackenridge, *Journal of Voyage up Missouri* (1815); Dale, *Ashley-Smith Explorations*; Nute, "Calendar of the American Fur Company's Papers"; Merk, *Fur Trade and Empire*; Blegen and Jordan, *With Various Voices*, chs. i–ii; Elliott Coues, ed., *New Light on Greater Northwest* (Alexander Henry and David Thompson Journals, 3 vols., 1897); Edward Harris, *Up Missouri with Audubon* (J. F. McDermott, ed., 1951); Tabeau, *Narrative*; Larpenteur, *Forty Years a Fur Trader*; Porter, *John Jacob Astor*, II, 1143; George Catlin, *Illustrations of Manners, Customs and Condition of the North American Indians* (7 ed., 1848); R. I. Dodge, *Our Wild Indians: Thirty-three Years Personal Experience* (1882); *Annals of Congress*, XXXVIII, 416, XLI, 450; 19 Cong., 1 sess., *H. Ex. Doc.*, No. 117; 24 Cong., 1 sess., *H. Ex. Doc.*, No. 181; 28 Cong., 2 sess., *S. Ex. Doc.*, No. 174; 29 Cong., 1 sess., *S. Ex. Doc.*, No. 438; Stuart, *Discovery of Oregon Trail*; Charles Wilkes, *Narrative of United States Exploring Expedition* (5 vols., 1845); Parkman, *Oregon Trail*; Frémont, *Report*; P. T. Tyson, *Geology and Industrial Resources of California* (1851); W. H. Emory, *Notes on Military Reconnoissance to San Diego* (1848; Ross Calvin, ed., 1951); *California Guide Book* (1849); J. H. Simpson, *Explorations across Great Basin in 1859* (1876); J. N. Macomb, *Report of Exploring Expedition from Santa Fé in 1859* (1876); P. St. G. Cooke, *Scenes and Adventures in Army* (1859); R. B. Marcy, *Thirty Years of Army Life* (1866); [James Hildreth], *Dragoon Campaign to Rocky Mountains* (1836); Parker, *Journal*; John McLoughlin, *Letters* (1948); Eugène Duflot de Mofras, *Travels on Pacific Coast* (1844; M. E. Wilbur, ed., 2 vols., 1937).

Bibliography — Turner, *New West*, 337; Billington, *Westward Expansion*, 802; Turner and Merk, *References on the History of West*, §§ 26–31; Blumann and Thomas, *California Local History*; Cowan, *Bibliography of California*; Bancroft, *Pacific Northwest*, I, pp. xvii–xxxiii; Richman, *California*, 361; A. R. Hasse, *Reports of Explorations Printed in Documents of Government* (1899). See also: § 165.

165. TRADE AND SETTLEMENT IN THE FAR WEST TO 1860

Summary — Rocky Mountain fur trade (§ 164); Santa Fe trail. — Texas: Spanish settlements; French claims (§§ 76, 134); 1819, 1828, boundary treaties; American invasions, 1800, Nolan, 1806, Burr's project (§ 134), 1812, Gutierrez and Magee, 1819, Long; the empresarios; 1821, Stephen Austin; colonization laws of 1824, 1825, 1830; 1826–27, Fredonian War; Mexican revolutions; 1829, slavery abolished in Mexico, relation to Texas; 1836, Texan war, Goliad, siege of Alamo, declaration of independence, battle of San Jacinto; effect in United States (§ 167). — Oregon: 1834–36, Wyeth and missionaries, Lee, Whitman; 1842, Whitman's ride; "saving Oregon"; question of occupation (§ 166), 1838–43, Linn's territorial bills; 1842–43, overland migrations. — Utah: 1823, Joseph Smith and the Mormons in Palmyra, 1830, in Kirtland, Ohio, 1831–46, in Missouri, Illinois, Wisconsin, and Michigan (§ 151); 1839, Nauvoo; 1843, "revelation" on polygamy; 1844, killing of Smith, succession of Brigham Young (§ 151); 1846–47, migration to Great Salt

Lake; 1846–48, Mormons in the Mexican War; 1848, cession of Utah (§ 168); 1849, State of Deseret; the church and irrigation; Mormon War (§ 178). — California (§§ 168, 170, 171): Russian settlements; Spanish and Mexican regimes, missions, land grants, ranches, Yankee trade, remoteness of central government; 1841, Bidwell, and the first immigrant train; diplomatic relations, 1842, temporary seizure of Monterey, 1846, Frémont and Bear Flag Republic; 1846–48, conquest and cession (§ 168); 1848, discovery of gold; 1849, rush to California; effects; mining camps. — Significance of American colonization of Pacific Coast.

General — Channing, History, V, 487, ch. xvi, VI, ch. ii; Billington, Westward Expansion, chs. xxiv–xxvii; Turner, United States, 1830–1850, ch. viii; McMaster, History, V, 3, VI, 250, VII, 216, 422, 585; Schouler, History, IV, 250, 445, 510, 528, V, 130; Coman, Economic Beginnings of Far West, II, pts. 3, 4; Dick, Vanguards of Frontier, chs. ix, x; Fuller, Pacific Northwest, chs. viii–xvii; Caughey, Pacific Coast, chs. xv–xx; Goodwin, Trans-Mississippi West, chs. v, vi, viii, ix, xii, xiii.

Special — Western Trade and Indian Problems: Abel, "Indian Consolidation," chs. v–viii; Grant Foreman, Last Trek of Indians, and Advancing Frontier, and Indians and Pioneers (1936), and Five Civilized Tribes; Charles Kelly, Salt Desert Trail (1930); Hafen, Overland Mail; R. L. Duffus, Santa Fe Trail (1930); Mack, Nevada, 59. ❧ Texas: N. W. Stephenson, Texas and Mexican War (1921), chs. i–v; W. C. Binkley, Texas Revolution (1952); C. E. Castañeda, ed., Mexican Side of Texas Revolution (1928); W. R. Hogan, Texas Republic (1946); J. W. Schmitz, Texan Statecraft (1941); H. P. Gambrell, Anson Jones (1948); J. D. Hill, Texas Navy (1937); E. C. Barker, Mexico and Texas, 1821–35 (1928), and Austin, and "Texan Declaration of Causes," Texas Hist. Assoc., Quar., XV (1912), 173, and "African Slave Trade in Texas," ibid., VI (1902), 145, and "Finances of the Texas Revolution," Pol. Sci. Quar., XIX (1904), 612, and "President Jackson and Texas Revolution," Am. Hist. Rev., XII (1907), 788; E. Z. Rather, Recognition of Republic of Texas (1911), and "DeWitt's Colony," Texas Hist. Assoc., Quar., VIII (1904), 95, and "Influence of Slavery in Colonization of Texas," Miss. Valley Hist. Rev., XI (1924), 3; Wooten, Texas, I, pt. 1, chs. vii–xxix, pt. 2, chs. i–xiii; Bancroft, North Mexican States and Texas, I, chs. xii, II, chs. ii–x, and Mexico, V, ch. vii; E. D. Adams, British Interests in Texas (1910); H. G. Warren, Sword Was Their Passport: Filibustering in Mexican Revolution (1943); Cox, "Louisiana-Texas Frontier," 1; B. F. Lathrop, Migration into East Texas (1949); L. G. Bugbee, "Difficulties of a Texas Empresario," Southern Hist. Assoc., Publ., III (1899), 95; R. L. Biesele, German Settlements in Texas (1930); Faust, German Element, I, 490; James, Houston; also § 167. ❧ Oregon: Bancroft, Oregon, I, II; Lyman, Oregon, I, II; W. J. Ghent, Road to Oregon (1929); DeVoto, Year of Decision, ch. vi; Winther, Great Northwest, chs. vii, viii; C. M. Drury, Henry Harmon Spaulding (1936), and Elkanah and Mary Walker (1940); R. C. Johnson, McLaughlin; Montgomery, McLaughlin; E. G. Bourne, Essays in Historical Criticism (1901), 3; W. A. Mowry, Marcus Whitman (1901); Theressa Gay, Life and Letters of Mrs. Jason Lee (1936); J. H. Gilbert, Trade and Currency in Early Oregon (1907), chs. i–iii. ❧ Utah: § 151; Bancroft, Utah, chs. viii–xvii; DeVoto, Year of Decision, ch. iii; Linn, Mormons; W. J. McNiff, Heaven on Earth (1940); M. H. Cannon, "Migration of English Mormons," Am. Hist. Rev., LII (1947), 436; Lowry Nelson, Mormon Village (1952); L. H. Creer, Utah and Nation (1929); G. O. Larson, Prelude to Kingdom: Mormon Desert Conquest (1947); C. H. Brough, Irrigation in Utah (1898), chs. i–xi, xiv–xvi; Roberts, Church of Latter Day Saints; Werner, Young. ❧ California: Bancroft, California, I–VI; Royce, California; Ogden, California Sea Otter Trade; R. G. Cleland, From Wilderness to Empire (1944), and California; Cardinal Goodwin, Establishment of State Government (1914); M. F. Williams, History of San Francisco Committee of Vigilance (1921); Priestley, Coming of White Man, ch. vii; Zephyrin Engelhardt, Missions and Missionaries of California (4 vols., 1908–15; also new series, 1932–); J. S. Hildrup, Missions of California (1907); R. G. Cleland, Cattle on a Thousand Hills (1941); R. A. Rydell, Cape Horn to Pacific (1952); Hector Chevigny, Lost Empire: Life of Rezánov (1937); W. B. Okun, Russian-American Company (1951); R. L. Underhill, From Cowhides to Golden Fleece (1946); J. W. Caughey, Gold Is Cornerstone (1948); J. H. Jackson, Anybody's Gold

(1941); R. W. Paul, *California Gold* (1947); Bernard Moses, *Establishment of Municipal Government in San Francisco* (1889); J. A. B. Scherer, *Lion of Vigilantes* (W. T. Coleman, 1939); Nevins, *Frémont*, chs. xvi–xxii; Lyman, *Marsh*, chs. xxviii–xxxviii; Zollinger, *Sutter.* ❡ Maps: *Twelfth Census Statistical Atlas*, plates 5–8; Channing, *History*, V, 500, 519; McMaster, *History*, V, 12; Foreman, *Advancing Frontier*, 174, 190, 330. See also: maps, §§ 164, 166, 167.

Sources — Western Trade: Gregg, *Commerce of Prairies*, and *Diary*; Thwaites, *Early Western Travels*, XIX, XX; Magoffin, *Santa Fé Trail.* ❡ Texas: Austin, *Papers*; Lamar, *Papers*; H. S. Foote, *Texas and Texans* (2 vols., 1841); Frédéric Leclerc, *Texas and Its Revolution* (1840; J. L. Shepherd, ed., 1950); W. B. Dewees, *Letters from an Early Settler of Texas* (1854); Anson Jones, *Memoranda Relating to Republic of Texas* (1859); William Kennedy, *Texas* (2 vols., 1841), bks. 1, 2; E. D. Adams, *British Correspondence Concerning Texas*; Calhoun, "Correspondence"; Jackson, *Correspondence*; Polk, *Diary*; J. Q. Adams, *Memoirs*; Hackett, *Documents Relating to New Mexico*; Sam Houston, *Writings* (A. W. Williams and E. C. Barker, eds., 8 vols., 1938–43); Binkley, *Correspondence of Texan Revolution*; G. P. Garrison, ed., *Texan Diplomatic Correspondence* (3 vols., 1908–11). See also: Texas Documents, § 46. ❡ Oregon: Thwaites, *Early Western Travels*, VII; Hulbert, *Overland to Pacific*, V–VIII; N. J. Wyeth, "Papers," 25 Cong., 3 sess., *H. Reports*, No. 101, App. 1; Daniel Lee and J. H. Frost, *Ten Years in Oregon* (1844); Jesse Applegate, *Day With the Cow Column* (Joseph Schafer, ed., 1934); Medorem Crawford, *Journal* (1897); P. H. Burnett, *Recollections* (1880), chs., iii–v. ❡ Utah: 31 Cong., 1 sess., *H. Misc. Docs.*, Nos. 18, 43, and *H. Reports*, No. 219; Brigham Young, *et al.*, *Journal of Discourses* (26 vols., 1854–86); M. M. Quaife, *Kingdom of Saint James* (1930); *Millenial Star*; *Deseret News*; Mode, *Source Book for American Church History*, ch. xxiii. ❡ California: Dana, *Two Years before Mast*; Font, *Complete Diary*; D. M. Brown, ed., *China Trade Days in California: Thompson Papers* (1947); Walter Colton, *Three Years in California* (1850); S. B. Dakin, *Scotch Paisano* (1939); W. D. Wyman, ed., *California Emigrant Letters* (1952); Hastings, *Emigrant's Guide*; T. O. Larkin, *Papers* (G. D. Hammond, ed., 3 vols., 1951–52); T. A. Barry and B. A. Patten, *Men and Memories of San Francisco* (1850); G. W. Read and Ruth Gaines, eds., *Gold Rush: Papers J. Goldsborough Bruff* (2 vols., 1944); D. M. Potter, ed., *Trail to California* (1945); C. E. Pancoast, *Diary of a Quaker Forty-Niner* (A. P. Hannum, ed., 1930); C. de L. Canfield, ed., *Diary of a Forty-Niner* (1906); O. T. Howe, *Argonauts of '49* (1923); J. T. Brooks, *Four Months Among Gold-Finders* (1849); Enos Christman, *One Man's Gold* (1930); Hancock, *Narrative*; Grant Foreman, ed., *Marcy & the Gold Seekers* (2 vols., 1939); William Downie, *Hunting for Gold* (1893); Burnett, *Recollections*, chs. vi–ix; Irving McKee, ed., *Alonzo Delano's California Correspondence* (1952); Édouard Auger, *Voyage en Californie* (1854); Porter Garnett and M. F. Williams, eds., *Papers of San Francisco Committee of Vigilance* (3 vols., 1910–19).

Bibliography — Larned, *Literature of American History*, 206; Priestley, *Coming of White Man*, 365; Cole, *Irrepressible Conflict*, 419; Turner and Merk, *References on History of West*, §§ xxxii, xxxiii, xxxiv, xxxv; Billington, *Westward Expansion*, 803; Wagner, *Spanish Southwest*; Bancroft, *North Mexican States and Texas*, and *California*; Raines, *Bibliography of Texas*; C. W. Smith, *Check-List Relating to Pacific Northwest*; Mode, *Source Book for American Church History*; also: § 164.

166. NORTHEASTERN AND NORTHWESTERN BOUNDARIES, 1783–1846

Summary — Northern boundary: 1783, in the treaty (§ 117), "Northwest angle," "St. Croix," "Source of St. Croix," "highlands," "Source of Connecticut," "Forty-fifth Parallel"; 1794, in the Jay treaty (§ 128); 1798, St. Croix established; 1803, draft boundary treaty; 1814, boundary in the treaty (§ 138); 1818, boundary west of the Lake of the Woods; 1822, lower lake boundary completed; 1827–31, arbitration by the King of the Netherlands; 1831, decision ignored; 1838–39, hostile attitude on the border; the McLeod Case; the *Caroline.* — Ashburton treaty: 1842, British mission; Webster negotiations, treaty

proclaimed; boundaries; slave trade; extradition; right of visit; "battle of the maps." —
Oregon controversy: claims to Oregon (§ 134); exploration and settlement (§§ 164, 165);
1818, joint occupation; 1819–21, Spanish claims extinguished; 1824, Russian claims extinguished; 1827, joint occupation continued; 1842, question in Ashburton negotiation;
1843, Linn's bill (§ 165); 1844, "fifty-four-forty or fight" (§ 167); 1845, arbitration
declined; 1846, June 15, treaty signed; connection with Mexican war (§ 168).

General — McMaster, *History*, V, 18, 463, VI, 429, 513, VII, 271, 407; Channing,
History, V, 534; Bemis, *Diplomatic History*, chs. xv, xvi; Bailey, *Diplomatic History*, chs.
xiv, xv; von Holst, *History*, III, chs. ii, vi; Callahan, *American Foreign Policy in Canadian
Relations*, chs. vii–x; Bemis, *American Secretaries of State*, V, 3, 245; Keenleyside and
Brown, *Canada and United States*, ch. v; J. S. Reeves, *American Diplomacy under Tyler
and Polk* (1907), chs. i–ii, viii–x.

Special — Northeastern: Corey, *Crisis of 1830–1842*; J. R. Baldwin, "Ashburton-
Webster Settlement," Canadian Hist. Assoc., *Report*, 1938, 121; Brebner, *North Atlantic
Triangle*, chs. vii, viii; Lodge, *Daniel Webster*, ch. viii; Curtis, *Daniel Webster*, II, chs.
xxviii, xxix, xxxii; Wiltse, *Calhoun*, III, ch. v; H. S. Burrage, *Maine in Northeastern Bound-
ary Controversy* (1919); R. N. Current, "Webster's Propaganda and Ashburton Treaty,"
Miss. Valley Hist. Rev., XXXIV (1947), 187; Thomas LeDuc, "Maine Frontier," *Am. Hist.
Rev.*, LIII (1947), 30; Moore, *Arbitrations*, I, chs. i–vi. ❧ Northwestern: Meigs, *Benton*,
ch. xvi; Bancroft, *Pacific Northwest*, II, chs. xv–xvii, and *Oregon*, I, ch. xiv; Winther, *Great
Northwest*, ch. ix; McCormac, *Polk*, ch. xxi; C. M. Drury, *Marcus Whitman* (1937);
Frederick Merk, *Gallatin and Oregon*, and "British Corn Crisis of 1845–46 and Oregon
Treaty," *Ag. Hist.*, VIII (1934), 95, and "British Government Propaganda," *Am. Hist.
Rev.*, XL (1934), 38, and "British Party Politics and the Oregon Treaty," *ibid.*, XXXVII
(1932), 667, and "Genesis of Oregon Question," and "Oregon Pioneers and Boundary,"
Am. Hist. Rev., XXIX (1924), 683, and "Snake Country Expedition," *Miss. Valley Hist.
Rev.*, XXI (1934), 49, 63; Dexter Perkins, *Monroe Doctrine, 1826–1867* (1933), ch. ii;
F. W. Howay, *et al.*, *British Columbia and United States* (1942), chs. i–vi; J. W. Pratt,
"James K. Polk and John Bull," *Canadian Hist. Rev.*, XXIV (1943), 341. ❧ Maps:
Channing, *History*, V, 537, 539; Paullin, *Atlas*, plate 91; Albert Gallatin, *Memoir on
North-Eastern Boundary* (1843); W. F. Ganong, *Boundaries of New Brunswick* (1901);
25 Cong., 2 sess., *Sen. Doc.*, VI, No. 502; Shepherd, *Atlas*, 206; Winsor, *Narrative and
Critical History*, VII, 172.

Sources — Debates, American and English (§§ 45, 47); Benton, *Abridgment*, XV;
Richardson, *Messages and Papers*, II–IV; Malloy, Redmond, and Treworth, *Treaties, Con-
ventions*, I, 593; Miller, *Treaties*, IV, V; Moore, *Digest of International Law*, II, 930, V,
§§ 834, 835; 17 Cong., 1 sess., *H. Ex. Doc.*, No. 112; 19 Cong., 1 sess., *H. Ex. Doc.*,
No. 65; 20 Cong., 1 sess., *Sen. Doc.*, No. 171, *H. Ex. Doc.*, No. 199; 25 Cong., 2 sess.,
Sen. Doc., Nos. 319, 502, 3 sess., *H. Report*, No. 101; 26 Cong., 1 sess., *Sen. Doc.*,
Nos. 107, 174, 382, *H. Ex. Doc.*, Nos. 189, 223, 245, 2 sess., *Sen. Doc.*, No. 173; 27 Cong.,
2 sess., *Sen. Doc.*, Nos. 84, 97, 3 sess., *Sen. Doc.*, No. 1, *H. Ex. Doc.*, No. 31, *H. Report*,
No. 157; 29 Cong., 1 sess., *Sen. Doc.*, Nos. 274, 489, *H. Ex. Doc.*, No. 105; 44 Cong., 1 sess.,
Sen. Doc., No. 41; *American State Papers, Foreign*, I, III, VI; *Treaties and Agreements
Affecting Canada 1814–1925* (1927). ❧ Contemporary Accounts: Polk, *Diary*; Buchanan,
Works, VI; Webster, *Writings and Speeches*, III, 109, IX, 60, 78, XII, 21, XIII, 310,
XIV, 392, 593; Benton, *Thirty Years' View*, II, chs. ci–civ, cxliii; Hone, *Diary*; Calhoun,
Works, IV, V, and "Correspondence," 653, 1065; J. Q. Adams, *Memoirs*, XII; Rufus
Choate, *Works*, II, 125; W. P. Preble, *Decisions of King of Netherlands* (1831); Robert
Greenhow, *History of Oregon* (1844); Travers Twiss, *Oregon Territory* (1846); Wynd-
ham Robertson, *Oregon Right and Title* (1846).

Bibliography — Winsor, *Narrative and Critical History*, VII, 172, 525, 555, 562; Larned,
Literature of American History, 206; Bemis and Griffin, *Guide to Diplomatic History*,
ch. xi; R. W. Van Alstyne, "International Rivalries in the Pacific Northwest," *Oregon
Hist. Quar.*, XLVI (1945), 185.

167. ANNEXATION OF TEXAS, 1836–1846

Summary — Territorial history: French claim; Spanish claim; Mexican boundary; northern boundary; effect of Louisiana cession (§ 134); 1819, treaty with Spain (§ 144); 1825–29, attempts to purchase; 1828, confirmatory treaty with Mexico. — Settlement and independence (§ 165); Texas asks admission into the Union; 1837, Texas recognized. — Agitation for annexation: 1838, resolutions; 1842, temporary occupation of Monterey; 1843, Adams's address of warning. — Annexation treaty: 1843, proposed to Texas; 1844, promise of military aid; Feb. 28, explosion on *Princeton*; Mar. 29, Calhoun secretary of state; Pakenham correspondence on England's position; April 12, treaty signed; June 8, treaty rejected; June 10, Benton's bill. — Election of 1844: Tyler's hopes; Liberty party; Oregon question (§ 166); annexation question; Clay committed; Van Buren set aside. — Annexation: 1844, Dec., Tyler plan; 1845, Mar. 1, joint resolution passes; Mar. 3, Tyler offers annexation; British attitude; discussion in Texas; Dec. 3, annexation act. — Effect on Mexico (§ 168).

General — Channing, *History*, V, 520, 541; Rhodes, *History*, I, 75; McMaster, *History*, V, 540, VI, 260, 458, VII, 304; T. C. Smith, *Liberty and Free Soil Parties*, ch. vi; McCormac, *Polk*, chs. xii–xvi; Stephenson, *Texas and Mexican War*, chs. iv–ix; Bailey, *Diplomatic History*, ch. xvi; Bemis, *American Secretaries of State*, V, and *Diplomatic History*, ch. xiii; Turner, *United States*, ch. xii; J. C. N. Paul, *Rift in the Democracy* (1951); Schouler, *History*, II, ch. xvii, § ii; Stanwood, *Presidency*, I, xvii; G. P. Garrison, *Westward Extension* (1906), chs. i, ii, vi–x; von Holst, *History*, II, 513.

Special — E. C. Barker, *Austin*, and "Annexation of Texas," *Southwestern Hist. Quar.*, L (1946), 49; Manning, *Diplomatic Relations between United States and Mexico*; G. L. Rives, *United States and Mexico* (1913), I, chs. i–xxiii; J. M. Callahan, *American Foreign Policy in Mexican Relations* (1932); M. K. Chase, *Négociations de la république du Texas en Europe* (1932); J. H. Smith, *Annexation of Texas*; Bancroft, *North Mexican States, Texas*, chs. i, xii–xiv; Henderson Yoakum, *History of Texas* (1856), chs. xxx–xxxvi; W. C. Binkley, *Expansionist Movement in Texas* (1925); E. D. Adams, *British Interests in Texas*; Barker, "Jackson and Texas"; J. E. Winston, "Annexation of Texas and Mississippi Democrats," *Southwestern Hist. Quar.*, XXV (1921), 1; James, *Andrew Jackson*, II, chs. xix; Tyler, *Tylers*, II, 250, III, 115; Curtis, *Daniel Webster*, I, ch. xxiv, II, chs. xxx–xxxii; Wiltse, *Calhoun*, III, vii–xiii, xv–xvii; Meigs, *Calhoun*, II, chs. viii, ix; L. A. White, *Rhett*, ch. vi; L. M. Sears, "Nicholas P. Trist," *Miss. Valley Hist. Rev.*, XI (1924), 85; Goebel, *Recognition Policy*, ch. vi; O. P. Chitwood, *John Tyler* (1939), ch. xxii; Shepard, *Van Buren*, ch. xi; Bassett, *Andrew Jackson*, II, 734; Meigs, *Benton*, ch. xviii; McLaughlin, *Cass*, ch. vii; Julian, *Giddings*, chs. vi, vii; Schurz, *Clay*, II, chs. xxiv, xxv; Poage, *Clay and Whig Party*, ch. x; Van Deusen, *Clay*, ch. xxii; Quincy, *John Quincy Adams*, chs. xiii, xiv; Curtis, *Buchanan*, I, chs. xvii, xix. ◄ Maps: MacDonald, *Jacksonian Democracy*, 214; Garrison, *Westward Extension*, 104, 282; § 165.

Sources — Debates: § 45; Benton, *Abridgment*, XIV, XV; contemporary newspapers (§ 53). ◄ Documents: congressional documents (§ 45), especially, 24 and 28 Cong.; "Documents on Texas Boundary," 61 Cong., 3 sess., *Sen. Report*, No. 940, and *H. Report*, No. 1883; Richardson, *Messages and Papers*, III; Manning, *Diplomatic Correspondence: Inter-American Affairs*, XII; Garrison, *Diplomatic Correspondence of Texas*; E. D. Adams, *British Correspondence Concerning Texas*; Texas documents (§ 46); Ames, *State Documents*, 224; Moore, *Digest of International Law*, §§ 10, 62, 103; *Niles' Weekly Register*, especially, LXV–LXIX. ◄ Contemporary Writings: Polk, *Diary*; J. Q. Adams, *Memoirs*, XI, XII; Benton, *Thirty Years' View*, I, chs. cxliv, cxlv, II, chs. xxiv, cxxxv–cxlii, cxlviii; Webster, *Writings and Speeches*, III, 217, IV–VI, IX, 55, XII, 96, 153; Calhoun, *Works*, IV, V, and "Correspondence," 497, 829; U. B. Phillips, ed., "Correspondence of Toombs, Stephens, and Cobb," *Am. Hist. Assoc., Report*, 1911, II; Clay, *Works*, IV, chs. xi, xii; Austin, *Papers*; Houston, *Writings*; Woodbury, *Writings*, I, 355; Buchanan, *Works*, VI, VIII; William Jay, *Review of Mexican War* (1849); J. R. Lowell, *Anti-Slavery Papers* (1902), I, 3; Poore, *Perley's Reminiscences*, I, ch. xxiv; Kennedy, *Texas*, bk. 3; "Van Buren-Bancroft Correspondence," *Mass. Hist. Soc., Proc.*, XLII (1909), 381; also § 165.

Bibliography — Winsor, *Narrative and Critical History*, VII, 550; Garrison, *Westward Extension*, ch. xxi; Raines, *Bibliography of Texas*; J. H. Smith, *Annexation of Texas*, 471; Hogan, *Texas Republic*; Cronin and Wise, *Bibliography of Harrison, Tyler, Polk*, 45; Turner and Merk, *References on History of West*, § xxiv; Billington, *Westward Expansion*, 810; § 165.

168. THE MEXICAN WAR, 1846–1848

Summary — Causes: 1826–44, claims; 1836–44, encouragement to Texas; 1845, annexation of Texas (§ 167); 1846, Texan boundaries; 1846, designs on California (§ 165); extension of slave territory. — Outbreak: 1845, July, Taylor's advance to Corpus Christi; Sept. to Dec., Slidell mission; 1846, Jan., Taylor ordered forward; Mar., Slidell not recognized; Polk determines on war; Oregon question settled (§ 166); Apr. 24, attack on Taylor; May 11, Polk's war message; May 13, war declared. — Campaigns: 1846–47, Taylor's northern campaign; New Mexico taken; California taken; Scott's central campaign; City of Mexico taken. — Treaty of peace: 1846, "two million bill"; 1847, Trist in Mexico; 1848, Feb. 2, treaty of Guadeloupe Hidalgo (Texas, New Mexico, California, indemnity to Mexico). — Boundary troubles: 1853, Gadsden purchase.

General — Channing, *History*, V, chs. xvii, xviii; McMaster, *History*, VII, 423, 506; Nevins, *Ordeal of Union*, I, ch. i; Schouler, *History*, IV, 518, V, ch. xviii, §§ ii, iii; Garrison, *Westward Extension*, chs. xiii–xv; Billington, *Westward Expansion*, ch. xxviii; Stephenson, *Texas and Mexican War*, chs. x–xiv; J. F. Rippy, *United States and Mexico* (1931), chs. vii, viii; Callahan, *American Foreign Policy in Mexican Relations*, chs. iv–vii; Bailey, *Diplomatic History*, ch. xvii; Reeves, *Diplomacy under Tyler and Polk*, chs. xi–xiii; Bemis, *American Secretaries of State*, V, 265, and *Diplomatic History*, chs. xiii, xiv, and *Latin-American Policy of United States*, ch. vi; A. M. Carreño, *La Diplomacia extraordinaria entre México y Estados Unidos* (1951), I, chs. xvi–xix, II, chs. i–viii; von Holst, *History*, III, chs. iii–xii; Upton, *Military Policy*, ch. xv; Knox, *United States Navy*, ch. xvi; De Voto, *Year of Decision*, chs. iv, v, vii–ix; Schlesinger, Jr., *Age of Jackson*, ch. xxxiii.

Special — Vito Alessio Robles, *Coahuila y Texas desde la independencia hasta Guadalupe Hidalgo* (2 vols., 1945–46); A. H. Bill, *Rehearsal for Conflict* (1947); J. H. Smith, *War with Mexico* (2 vols., 1919); Rives, *United States and Mexico*, I, chs. xxiv–xxvii, II; Bancroft, *Mexico*, V; Hittell, *California*, II, 435; Meigs, *Calhoun*, II, ch. x; Wiltse, *Calhoun*, III, ch. xix; Curtis, *Buchanan*, I, chs. xx–xxii; Hamilton, *Taylor*, I, chs. xi–xviii; McCormac, *Polk*, chs. xvii–xx; George Tays, "Frémont," *Pacific Hist. Rev.*, IX (1940), 157; Freeman, *Lee*, I; Rowland, *Davis*, II, III; L. M. Sears, "Nicholas P. Trist," and *John Slidell* (1925), ch. iii; Dyer, *Taylor*, chs. vii–xi; A. D. H. Smith, *Old Fuss and Feathers*, bk. 4; Beveridge, *Lincoln*, I, chs. vii, viii; Nye, *Bancroft*, ch. v; R. C. Winthrop, Jr., *Memoir of Robert C. Winthrop* (1897), 44; Schurz, *Clay*, II, ch. xxv; Nichols, *Pierce*, chs. xx–xxii; Pierce, *Sumner*, III, ch. xxxii; R. R. Stenberg, "Failure of Polk's Mexican War Intrigue," *Pacific Hist. Rev.*, IV (1935), 39, and "Polk and Frémont," *ibid.*, VII (1938), 211; W. P. Webb, *Texas Rangers* (1935); J. D. P. Fuller, *Movement for Acquisition of All Mexico* (1936); C. S. Ellsworth, "American Churches and Mexican War," *Am. Hist. Rev.*, XLV (1940), 301; E. D. Adams, "English Interest in California," *ibid.*, XIV (1909), 744; P. N. Garber, *Gadsden Treaty* (1923). ❡ Maps: Bill, *Rehearsal for Conflict*, 78, 144, 226, 268; J. H. Smith, *War with Mexico*; Shepherd, *Atlas*, 201; Alessio Robles, *Coahuila y Texas*; Paullin, *Atlas*, plates 94, 95.

Sources — Debates (§ 45); Benton, *Abridgment*, XV, XVI; newspapers and magazines (§§ 52, 53); Richardson, *Messages and Papers*, III, IV; Malloy, Redmond, and Treworth, *Treaties*, I, 1082; Miller, *Treaties*, V, 236, VI, 293; Moore, *Digest of International Law*, §§ 21, 857, 858; Manning, *Diplomatic Correspondence: Inter-American Affairs*, VI, pts. 5, 6, VII–IX; Gantenbein, *Latin-American Policy*, 545; Nasatir, *French Activities in California*. ❡ Congressional Documents: 29 Cong., 1 sess., *Sen. Ex. Doc.*, Nos. 337, 368, 388, 392, 395, 439, *H. Ex. Doc.*, No. 196, 2 sess., *Sen. Ex. Doc.*, No. 107, *H. Ex. Doc.*, No. 19; 30 Cong., 1 sess., *Sen. Ex. Doc.*, Nos. 52, 60, *H. Ex. Doc.*, Nos. 8, 69. ❡ Contemporary

Accounts: Polk, *Diary*, I–III; Buchanan, *Works*, VI–VIII; J. M. Roa Bárcena, *Recuerdos de la invasión norteamericana* (3 vols., 1947); Calhoun, *Works*, IV, and "Correspondence," 671, 960, 1067, 1083; Webster, *Writings and Speeches*, IX, 253, X, 3, XIII, 345; Benton, *Thirty Years' View*, II, chs. cxlix, clxi; Phillips, "Correspondence of Toombs, Stephens, and Cobb"; J. Q. Adams, *Memoirs*, XII; A. L. de Santa Anna, "Letters Relating to War" (J. H. Smith, ed.), Am. Hist. Assoc., *Report*, 1917, 355; G. B. McClellan, *Mexican War Diary* (W. S. Myers, ed., 1917); Taylor, *Letters*; Anderson, *Letters*; Scott, *Memoirs*; John Sedgwick, *Correspondence* (1902–03), I; Grant, *Memoirs*, I, chs. iii–xiii; J. T. Hughes, "Doniphan's Expedition," 63 Cong., 2 sess., *Sen. Doc.*, No. 608; E. K. Smith, *To Mexico with Scott* (1917); Meade, *Life and Letters*, I, pt. 2; Sherman, *Memoirs*, I, ch. i; Coleman, *Crittenden*, I, chs. xix–xxii; Poore, *Perley's Reminiscences*, I, ch. xxv; F. A. Golder, *et al.*, eds., *March of Mormon Battalion* (1928); Calderón de la Barca, *Life in Mexico* (1843).

Bibliography — Larned, *Literature of American History*, 204; Channing, *History*, V, 584, 615; J. H. Smith, *War with Mexico*; Billington, *Westward Expansion*, 815; H. E. Haferkorn, *War with Mexico* (1914).

169. FINANCIAL AND COMMERCIAL QUESTIONS, 1845–1849

Summary — Conditions in 1845 (§§ 158, 163): revenue; currency; banks; tariff; shipping; waterways (§ 149); public lands; commercial prosperity. — Treasury: 1846, Aug. 6, Independent Treasury (§ 162) revived. — Tariff: 1845, Dec. 3, Walker's report; specific and ad valorem duties; question of revenue; 1846, July 31, act passed; Aug. 6, warehouse act. — Internal improvements; earlier status (§ 158); 1837–45, poverty of the Treasury; land grants for canals; 1841–45, Tyler's vetoes; 1846–47, Polk's vetoes; 1847, Dec. 21, House resolutions affirming the right; state internal improvements (§ 149). — State finances (§ 153): taxation; debts, repudiations (§ 162); accounts; state-owned banks, state-chartered banks.

General — Dewey, *Financial History*, §§ 107–112; Schouler, *History*, IV, 418, 515, V, 81, 120; von Holst, *History*, II, 529, III, 277. See also: §§ 155–8.

Special — Coleman, *Crittenden*, I, ch. xix; Meigs, *Calhoun*, II, ch. vii; Wiltse, *Calhoun*, III, ch. xviii; Sumner, *American Currency*, I, 161; J. J. Knox, *United States Notes* (1884), chs. vi, vii; Bishop, *American Manufactures*, II, 381; Stanwood, *Tariff Controversies*, II, ch. xii; Taussig, *Tariff History*, 112; McCormac, *Polk*, ch. xxiii; Going, *Wilmot*, ch. vi; Kinley, *Independent Treasury*; Taus, *Central Banking Functions*, chs. ii, iii; Eiselen, *Pennsylvania Protectionism*, chs. viii–x. ◀ Maps: Paullin, *Atlas*, plate 114.

Sources — Debates (§ 45); Benton, *Abridgment*, XV, XVI; Congressional Documents, especially, 29 Cong., 1 sess., *Sen. Doc.*, II, Nos. 2, 6, III, No. 5, VIII, No. 437, IX, No. 444, *H. Ex. Doc.*, No. 5, 2 sess., *Sen. Doc.*, I, No. 2, III, No. 105, *H. Ex. Doc.*, III, No. 25; Richardson, *Messages and Papers*, IV; *Niles' Weekly Register*, LXIX, 233; Taussig, *State Papers on Tariff*, 214; *De Bow's Review*, I–VI; *Hunt's Merchants' Mag.*, XII–XX. ◀ Contemporary Writings: Polk, *Diary*; Calhoun, *Works*, IV, and "Correspondence," 673, 700, 1049, 1081, 1085; J. Q. Adams, *Memoirs*, XII; Webster, *Writings and Speeches*, IX, 161, 244; Webster, *Letters*, 332; Kendall, *Autobiography*, chs. xv, xvi; Curtis, *Memoir*, II, 93.

Bibliography — Dewey, *Financial History*, § 106; Larned, *Literature of American History*, 319; U. S. Tariff Commission, *Tariff*.

Chapter Seventeen

THE YEARS OF DECISION, 1848–1861

170. THE TERRITORIES, 1846–1849

Summary — Wilmot proviso: 1846, Aug. 8, fails in Senate: 1847, Feb. 13, added to the "three million bill"; advocated by Northern legislatures; 1847, Dec., R. C. Winthrop chosen Speaker; 1848, Feb. 28, proviso tabled by the House. — Abolition activity: 1839, Giddings in the House (§ 160); 1847, J. P. Hale in the Senate; 1848, resolution against slave trade in the District of Columbia; 1849, Abraham Lincoln's emancipation bill; fugitive slave cases (§ 172). — Election of 1848: "Barnburner" split in New York; May, Cass nominated; June, Taylor nominated; Aug., Van Buren nominated by Free Soilers; Nov., Taylor chosen. — Theories of control of the territories: (1) complete power of Congress; (2) "popular sovereignty"; (3) application of the Constitution; (4) decision by the Supreme Court; (5) compromise line. — Specific questions: Oregon, New Mexico, California, Texas claims; 1848, Aug. 14, Oregon organized as a free territory; deadlock between Taylor and Southern Whigs.

General — Nevins, *Ordeal of Union*, I, chs. ii, iii; McMaster, *History*, VII, chs. lxxxi, lxxxiii, lxxxv; Turner, *United States*, ch. xiii; Garrison, *Westward Extension*, chs. xvi, xvii, xix; Stanwood, *Presidency*, I, ch. xviii; Cole, *Irrepressible Conflict*, ch. iv; Coman, *Economic Beginnings of Far West*, pt. 5; von Holst, *History*, III, chs. xi–xiv; Schouler, *History*, V, ch. xviii, § iii.

Special — Schurz, *Clay*, II, ch. xxv; Going, *Wilmot*, chs. vii–xx; Curtis, *Daniel Webster*, II, chs. xxxiii–xxxv; Poage, *Clay and Whig Party*, chs. xii, xiii; Hamilton, *Taylor*, II, chs. v–xv, xvii–xxvii; Dyer, *Taylor*, chs. xii–xiv; McCormac, *Polk*, ch. xxii; McLaughlin, *Cass*, ch. viii; Meigs, *Benton*, 369; Hart, *Chase*, 94; Bancroft, *Seward*, I, 156; Dodd, *Davis*, 104; C. F. Adams, *Charles Francis Adams*, chs. iv–vi; Nichols, *Pierce*, chs. xxiii–xxiv; W. E. Smith, *Blair Family*, ch. xviii; J. A. Woodburn, *Thaddeus Stevens* (1913), ch. v; Julian, *Giddings*, 206; Wiltse, *Calhoun*, III, chs. xx–xxii, xxiv, xxv; Phillips, *Toombs*, chs. iii–iv; Milton, *Eve of Conflict*, ch. iii; Van Deusen, *Weed*, chs. x–xii; Nicolay and Hay, *Lincoln*, I, chs. xiv–xvi; R. M. Johnston and W. H. Browne, *A. H. Stephens* (1878), chs. xxi, xxii; R. C. Winthrop, Jr., *R. C. Winthrop*, 65; Haynes, *Sumner*, 103; Winther, *Great Northwest*, ch. x; T. C. Smith, *Liberty and Free Soil Parties*, chs. v–x; R. R. Stenberg, "Motivation of Wilmot Proviso," *Miss. Valley Hist. Rev.*, XVIII (1932), 535; W. O. Lynch, "Anti-Slavery Tendencies of Democratic Party," *ibid.*, XI (1924), 319; C. W. Ramsdell, "Natural Limits of Slavery Expansion," *ibid.*, XVI (1929), 151; A. C. Cole, *Era of Civil War* (*Centennial History of Illinois*, III, 1919), ch. iii; H. D. A. Donovan, *Barnburners* (1925); C. E. Magoon, *Reports on Law of Civil Government in Territory Subject to Military Occupation* (1902), 121; D. Y. Thomas, *History of Military Government* (1904), bk. 2; C. E. Persinger, "Bargain of 1844 and Wilmot Proviso," Am. Hist. Assoc., *Report*, 1911, I, 189. ❡ Maps: G. P. Garrison, *Westward Extension*, 282; Shepherd, *Atlas*, 202, 203.

Sources — Debates and Documents (§ 45); Benton, *Abridgment*, XVI; Congressional Documents, especially 29 Cong., 1 sess., *Sen. Doc.*, III, No. 25; 30 Cong., 1 sess., *H. Ex. Doc.*, VIII, No. 70, 2 sess., *H. Ex. Doc.*, I, No. 1; Richardson, *Messages and Papers*, IV; Ames, *State Documents*, 241. ℂ Contemporary Newspapers: especially *National Era* (Wash.), *N. Y. Tribune*, *N. Y. Times*, *N. Y. Evening Post*, *Boston Whig*, *Liberator*. ℂ Contemporary Writings: Polk, *Diary*, II–IV; Calhoun, *Works*, IV, 303, and "Correspondence," 709, 1036; Webster, *Writings and Speeches*, IV, 145, X, 34; Webster, *Letters*, 351; Chase, "Diary," 116, 467; Phillips, "Correspondence of Toombs, Stephens, and Cobb"; Fillmore, *Papers; Jefferson Davis, Constitutionalist* (Rowland, ed.), I; Benton, *Thirty Years' View*, II, chs. clxvi–clxxxiii; Pierce, *Sumner*, III, ch. xxxiii; Stephens, *War between the States*, II, colloquy xiv; Coleman, *Crittenden*, I, chs. xxi. xxiv–xxviii; Jay, *Miscellaneous Writings*, 491; J. R. Lowell, *Anti-Slavery Papers*, I, 52, II, 3, and *Biglow Papers* (1848).

Bibliography — Larned, *Literature of American History*, 181; W. H. Wise and J. W. Cronin, *Bibliography of Taylor, Fillmore, Pierce, Buchanan* (1935); Turner and Merk, *References on History of West*, § xxix.

171. COMPROMISE OF 1850

Summary — Administration: 1849, Mar. 5, President Taylor; 1850, July 10, President Fillmore; influence of Seward, Clay, Webster, Calhoun. — New anti-slavery forces in Congress: 1849, Chase, Seward; 1851, Sumner, Wade. — California organizes itself: 1848, discovery of gold (§ 165); 1849, Sept., constitutional convention (anti-slavery); Dec., provisional state government. — Compromise proposed: 1849–50, speakership contest; 1850, Jan. 29, Clay's plan; Mar. 4, Calhoun's speech; Mar. 7, Webster's speech; Mar. 11, Seward's speech; Mar. 13, Jefferson Davis' demand; Mar. 26, Chase's speech; Feb. 4, House yields; May 8, "Omnibus Bill"; Taylor holds out. — Compromise accepted: 1850, July 9, death of Taylor; (1) Aug. 9, Texas bill; (2) Aug. 15, New Mexico bill; (3) Sept. 7, California bill; (4) Sept. 9, Utah bill; (5) Sept. 12, fugitive-slave bill; (6) Sept. 14, District of Columbia slave-trade bill. — Results: "Cotton Whigs" and "Conscience Whigs"; "higher law"; danger to the Union; Calhoun's attitude; Southern legislatures; 1850, Nashville convention; Union sentiment prevails.

General — Channing, *History*, VI, ch. iii; Rhodes, *History*, I, ch. ii; von Holst, *History*, III, chs. xv, xvi; Schouler, *History*, V, chs. xix, xx, § 1; Nevins, *Ordeal of Union*, I, chs. viii–xii; Garrison, *Westward Extension*, ch. xx.

Special — Schlesinger, Jr., *Age of Jackson*, ch. xxxiv; Curtis, *Daniel Webster*, II, chs. xxxvi, xxxvii; Going, *Wilmot*, chs. xxi–xxiii; Lodge, *Daniel Webster*, ch. ix; Bancroft, *Seward*, I, chs. xiii–xv; Hermann von Holst, *J. C. Calhoun* (1882), ch. ix; Meigs, *Calhoun*, II, ch. xi; Wiltse, *Calhoun*, III, chs. xxv–xxx; H. V. Ames, "Calhoun and Secession 1850," Am. Antiq. Soc., *Proc.*, n.s. XXVIII (1918), 19; McLaughlin, *Cass*, ch. ix; Meigs, *Benton*, ch. xx; W. E. Dodd, *Davis*, 113, and *Statesmen of Old South* (1911), 157; Hart, *Chase*, 112; Johnston and Browne, *Stephens*, chs. xxiii, xxiv; R. C. Winthrop, Jr., *Robert C. Winthrop*, 96; Schurz, *Clay*, II, ch. xvi; Van Deusen, *Clay*, chs. xxiii–xxiv; Poage, *Clay and Whig Party*, chs. xiv–xvi; G. D. Harmon, "Douglas and Compromise of 1850," Ill. State Hist. Soc., *Jour.*, XXI (1929), 453; Milton, *Eve of Conflict*, chs. iii–v; W. E. Smith, *Blair Family*, I, ch. xix; Beveridge, *Lincoln*, II, chs. i, ii; Dyer, *Taylor*, chs. xv–xvi; J. B. Ranck, *Albert Gallatin Brown* (1937), chs. i–iii; Phillips, *Toombs*, chs. iv, v; Flippin, *Johnson*, ch. ii; Von Abele, *Stephens*, ch. iii; Ambler, *Sectionalism in Virginia*, 244; Bancroft, *California*, VI, chs. xii, xiii; Hittell, *California*, II, chs. viii, xi, xiv; T. C. Smith, *Liberty and Free-Soil Parties*, chs. xi–xv; Cole, *Whig Party in South*, ch. v; McDougall, *Fugitive Slaves*, §§ 29–32; Herbert Wender, *Southern Commercial Conventions* (1930); Van Deusen, *Ante-Bellum Southern Commercial Conventions*; Carpenter, *South as Conscious Minority*, ch. iv; R. H. Shryock, *Georgia and Union in 1850* (1926); N. W. Stephenson, "Southern Nationalism in South Carolina, in 1851," *Am. Hist. Rev.*, XXXVI (1931), 314; R. S. Cotterill, "Memphis Railroad Convention," *Tenn. Hist. Mag.*, IV

(1918), 83, and "Early Agitation for a Pacific Railroad," *Miss. Valley Hist. Rev.*, V (1919), 396; St. G. L. Sioussat, "Tennessee, Compromise of 1850, and Nashville Convention," *Miss. Valley Hist. Rev.*, II (1915), 313. ❡ Maps: Hart, *Slavery and Abolition*, 126; Garrison, *Westward Extension*, 328; T. C. Smith, *Parties and Slavery*, 6; Paullin, *Atlas*, plate 114.

Sources — Debates and Documents: *Congressional Globe*, 31 Cong., 1 sess.; Benton, *Abridgment*, XVI; 31 Cong., 1 sess., *Sen. Ex. Doc.*, IX, No. 18, XIII, Nos. 55, 56, 60, XIV, Nos. 67, 74, 76, *Sen. Misc. Docs.*, *Sen. Reports*, I, No. 123, *H. Ex. Doc.*, III, No. 5, V, No. 17, VII, No. 39; Richardson, *Messages and Papers*, V; MacDonald, *Select Documents*, Nos. 78–83; Ames, *State Documents*, 253. ❡ Contemporary Writings: Benton, *Thirty Years' View*, II, chs. clxxxiv–cxcvii; C. S. Boucher and R. P. Brooks, eds., *Correspondence to Calhoun* (1930); Calhoun, *Works*, IV, 542, and "Correspondence," 764, 1197; Chase, "Diary," 188; Fillmore, *Papers*, II, 321; Stephens, *War between States*, II, colloquies xv, xvi; Clay, *Works*, IV, chs. xiii, xiv, VI, 601; Buchanan, *Works*, VIII, 369; Webster, *Writings and Speeches*, X, 56, 105, 113, 144, 281, and *Private Correspondence*, II, 353, and *Letters*, 374; Jefferson Davis, *Confederate Government* (1881), I, chs. ii, iii, and *Jefferson Davis, Constitutionalist*, I; H. A. Wise, *Seven Decades* (1876), ch. xiii; E. D. Keyes, *Fifty Years' Observation* (1884), ch. xiii; Pierce, *Sumner*, III, chs. xxxiv, xxxv; Phillips, "Correspondence of Toombs, Stephens, and Cobb"; Hart, *American History Told by Contemporaries*, III, §§ 19–22; Lowell, *Anti-Slavery Papers*, II, 58; Poore, *Perley's Reminiscences*, chs. xxvii–xxx; Grant, *Personal Memoirs*, I, chs. xiv, xv; G. W. Julian, *Political Recollections* (1884), ch. iv, v.

Bibliography — Garrison, *Westward Extension*, 345; Wise and Cronin, *Bibliography of Taylor, Fillmore, Pierce, Buchanan*, 25.

172. FUGITIVE SLAVES AND ANTI-SLAVERY PROPAGANDA, 1850–1860

Summary — Status of runaway slaves: causes (§ 159); in slave states (§ 161); in free states (§ 161); in territories (§ 170); in foreign countries (§ 161). — National action: act of 1793 (§ 128); negotiations of 1826 (§ 161); act of 1850 (§ 171); question of constitutionality. — Personal liberty acts: early state statutes; 1842, Prigg decision (§ 161); statutes; application; Southern complaints. — "Underground Railroad": southern termini; colored, white agents; crossing to Canada; number aided; prosecutions; defiance of law; purchase of fugitives. — Famous cases: before 1850 (§ 161); 1850, Hamlet; 1851, Shadrach rescue; Sims, Christiana (Castner Hanway trial), Jerry McHenry rescue; 1854, Burns; 1855, Passmore Williamson; 1856, Garner; 1858, Oberlin-Wellington rescue; 1858, John Brown in Kansas (§ 175). — 1855–59, Wisconsin decision (Abelman *v.* Booth); 1861, "Contrabands" (§ 188). — Anti-slavery literature: *Liberator; National Era; Uncle Tom's Cabin;* poets; J. R. Lowell's satires. — Societies: American Colonization Society (§ 145); Garrison's society (§ 160); others; conventions. — Political action: pledging candidates; third parties; balance of power in Congress; 1849–1852, Free Democrats. — Action of churches.

General — Channing, *History*, VI, ch. iv; Cole, *Irrepressible Conflict*, ch. x, 262; Horace Greeley, *American Conflict* (1864–67), I, ch. xvi; Stephens, *War between States*, II, 44; Schouler, *History*, V, ch. xx; von Holst, *History*, IV, V, 61; Rhodes, *History*, I, 207, 222, 363, 498, II, 73, 360; T. C. Smith, *Parties and Slavery*, 22, 196, 206, 280; Kelly and Harbison, *American Constitution*, chs. xiv, xv; Swisher, *American Constitutional Development*, ch. x.

Special — McDougall, *Fugitive Slaves*, chs. iii–vi; Siebert, *Underground Railroad*; Franklin, *Slavery to Freedom*, ch. xv; Nye, *Fettered Freedom*, chs. vi–viii; Still, *Underground Railroad*; P. S. Foner, *Business and Slavery* (1941); W. J. Carnathan, "Proposal to Reopen African Slave Trade," *So. Atlantic Quar.*, xxv (1926), 410; Swisher, *Roger B. Taney*, ch. xxv; Allen Johnson, "Constitutionality of Fugitive Slave Acts," *Yale Law Jour.*, XXXI (1921), 161; Fred Landon, "Negro Migration to Canada," *Jour. Negro Hist.*, V

(1920), 22; Herbert Aptheker, *Essays in History of American Negro* (1945), chs. i, iii; C. H. Wesley, *Richard Allen* (1935); R. V. Harlow, *Gerrit Smith* (1939); Weiss, *Parker*, II, chs. xix, xx; Commager, *Parker*, chs. x, xi; Woodburn, *Stevens*, ch. vi; W. U. Hensel, *Christiana Riots* (1911); Warren, *Supreme Court*, III, chs. xxv, xxvii; C. F. Adams, *Dana*, I, chs. x, xiv, xv; Milton, *Eve of Conflict*, chs. xi–xii; Beveridge, *Lincoln*, II, chs. iii, IV; Hart, *Chase*, 163; Schuckers, *Chase*, ch. ix, xv, xxi; M. T. Higginson, *T. W. Higginson* (1914), ch. viii; Washington, *Douglass*; T. C. Smith, *Liberty and Free Soil Parties*, ch. xvi; Cole, *Whig Party in South*, ch. vi; *South in Building of Nation*, IV, 398. — See: biographies of anti-slavery men in §§ 54–6, 160. ❡ Maps: Hart, *Slavery and Abolition*, 230; Siebert, *Underground Railroad*, 113.

Sources — Debates and Documents: *Congressional Globe*; Ames, *State Documents*, 286, 303; Richardson, *Messages and Papers*, V; contemporary newspapers, especially, the *Liberator*. ❡ Contemporary Writings: Douglass, *Narrative*; S. G. Howe, *Refugees from Slavery in Canada* (1864); Garrison, *Garrison*, III, ch. xv; Woodbury, *Writings*, I, 533, III, 345; Benjamin Drew, *Refugee* (1856); *Jefferson Davis, Constitutionalist*, I, II; Coleman, *Crittenden*, I, ch. xxv; Fillmore, "Papers," I, 333, 362, II, 312; *Calendar of Gerrit Smith Papers in Syracuse University Library* (1942), II; May, *Recollections*; Coffin, *Reminiscences*; C. E. Stevens, *Anthony Burns* (1856); Pillsbury, *Anti-Slavery Apostles*; W. G. Eliot, *Archer Alexander* (1885); Charles Stearns, *Henry Box Brown* (1849); W. G. Hawkins, *Lunsford Lane* (1863); Northrup, *Twelve Years a Slave*; C. G. Woodson, *Mind of Negro as Reflected in Letters* (1926); W. H. Marsh, *God's Law Supreme: A Sermon* [on] *Fugitive Slave Law* (1850); E. W. Andrews, *Oration* (1851); J. H. Van Evrie, *Negroes and Negro "Slavery"* (1853); Am. and Foreign Anti-Slavery Soc., *Annual Reports*; Hart, *American History Told by Contemporaries*, IV, ch. v; Johnston and Woodburn, *American Orations*, II, 219, 268. ❡ Cases (see also § 161): Cobb, *Law of Slavery*, chs. vii–xi; Prigg *v.* Pennsylvania (1842), 16 Peters, 539; Ableman *v.* Booth (1859), 21 Howard, 506; Kentucky *v.* Dennison (1861), 24 Howard, 66; J. J. Robins, *Report of Trial of Castner Hanway* (1852); *History of Trial of Castner Hanway* (1852); Joel Parker, *Personal Liberty Laws* (1861); Hurd, *Law of Freedom and Bondage*; R. C. Hurd, *Treatise on Personal Liberty and Habeas Corpus* (1858), 598; Mode, *Source Book for American Church History*, ch. xxvii. — See: §§ 134, 135, 160.

Bibliography — McDougall, *Fugitive Slaves*, App. E; Siebert, *Underground Railroad*, App. D; T. C. Smith, *Parties and Slavery*, 323; Channing, *History*, VI, 116; Mode, *Source Book for American Church History*, 576.

173. AMERICAN DIPLOMACY, 1844–1860

Summary — Cuba and slavery: 1807, Jefferson suggests annexation; 1814–22, revolt of Spanish colonies (§ 146); 1826, Panama Congress (§ 147); 1849–51, filibustering; López' expeditions; 1850, Taylor's proclamation; right of search and the slave trade; 1854, *Black Warrior* episode, Ostend Manifesto; effect of Kansas-Nebraska bill (§ 174); 1859, purchase debate. — Latin America: earlier relations (§ 146, 147); 1846, Isthmian Treaty with New Granada; 1848, Yucatan episode; 1849, Hise's and Squier's draft treaties; 1850, Clayton-Bulwer treaty; 1851–60, controversy with England; 1851, intervention in Haiti; 1851, Panama Railroad; 1857, Walker in Nicaragua; 1857–60, Buchanan's Mexican policy; 1858, Paraguay incident; later relations (§§ 194, 220, 222, 224, 225). — Canada: early fishery questions (§§ 117, 142); renewal of controversy; 1854, June 5, reciprocity treaty; later controversies (§§ 194, 224). — Orient: 1844, Chinese treaty; 1854, proposed annexation of Hawaii; 1854, Perry in Japan, treaty; 1858, Chinese treaty; 1858, Japanese treaty; attitude during Arrow War; Townsend Harris; 1860, Japanese embassy, later relations (§§ 187, 194, 221). — European relations: 1849, Mann in Hungary; 1850, Huelsemann episode; 1851, Kossuth's visit; 1853, Koszta incident; 1853, court-dress circular; 1854–56, Crimean War neutrality; 1856, Declaration of Paris; 1857, Apr. 17, Sound dues treaty; later relations (§§ 187, 194, 223, 224).

General — Nevins, *Ordeal of Union*, I, ch. xiii; II, ch. x; Garrison, *Westward Extension*, ch. xviii; T. C. Smith, *Parties and Slavery*, ch. vi; McMaster, *History*, VII, ch.

lxxxiv; Schouler, *History*, V; Rhodes, *History*, I, 199, 294, 393, II, 1, 120, 186, 289, 351; von Holst, *History*, IV, ch. ii, V, chs. i, x, VI, 151, 330; Bemis, *Diplomatic History*, chs. xvii–xx; Bailey, *Diplomatic History*, chs. xviii–xx; Paullin, *Diplomatic Negotiations of Naval Officers*, chs. vii–ix; J. W. Foster, *American Diplomacy in the Orient* (1903), chs. ii–vii; Bemis, *American Secretaries of State*, VI; Moore, *Arbitrations*, I, chs. xii, xiii, II, chs. xxviii, xxx, xxxii, xxxiii, xxxvi, V, chs. H–J.

Special — Cuba: G. B. Henderson, "Southern Designs on Cuba," *Jour. Southern Hist.*, V (1939), 371; R. G. Caldwell, *López Expeditions* (1915); A. A. Ettinger, *Mission to Spain of Pierre Soulé* (1932); Basil Rauch, *American Interests in Cuba* (1948); R. W. Van Alstyne, "British Right of Search and African Slave Trade," *Jour. of Modern Hist.*, II (1930), 39. ❡ Latin America: J. H. Kemble, *Panama Route* (1943); Perkins, *Monroe Doctrine, 1826–1867*, chs. i–iv; Gerstle Mack, *Land Divided* (1944); W. O. Scroggs, *Filibusters and Financiers* (1916); R. W. Van Alstyne, "British Diplomacy and Clayton-Bulwer Treaty," *Jour. of Modern Hist.*, XI (1939), 149, and "Anglo-American Relations, 1853–1857," *Am. Hist. Rev.*, XLII (1937), 491; M. W. Williams, *Anglo-American Isthmian Diplomacy* (1916), chs. i–viii; W. R. Sherman, *Diplomatic Relations of United States and Chile* (1926), chs. ii–iii; E. T. Parks, *Colombia and United States* (1935), chs. iv–xii. ❡ Canada: Brebner, *North Atlantic Triangle*, ch. ix; D. C. Master, *Reciprocity Treaty of 1854* (1937); L. B. Shippee, *Canadian-American Relations, 1849–1874* (1939), chs. i–v; Callahan, *American Foreign Policy in Canadian Relations*, ch. xi; C. D. Allin and G. M. Jones, *Annexation, Preferential Trade and Reciprocity* (1912). ❡ Orient: Dennett, *Americans in Eastern Asia*, chs. i–xxii; Treat, *Diplomatic Relations between United States and Japan*, I, chs. i–xi; Inazo Itobe, *Intercourse between United States and Japan* (1891); Arthur Walworth, *Black Ships off Japan* (1946); H. B. Morse, *International Relations of Chinese Empire* (3 vols., 1910–1918; abridged by H. F. McNair as *Far Eastern International Relations*, 1931); Dulles, *Old China Trade*; Eldon Griffin, *Clippers and Consuls* (1938); Latourette, "Early Relations between United States and China"; H. W. Bradley, "Hawaiian Islands and Pacific Fur Trade," *Pacific Northwest Quar.*, XXX (1939), 275; S. W. Livermore, "Early Relations with East Indies," *Pacific Hist. Rev.*, XV (1946), 31. ❡ Europe: M. E. Curti, "Young America," *Am. Hist. Rev.*, XXXII (1926), 34, and *Austria and United States* (1926); Gibson, *Attitudes of New York Irish*, ch. ii; J. G. Gazley, *American Opinion of German Unification* (1926); Handlin, *Boston's Immigrants*, ch. v. ❡ Biographies: Butler, *Benjamin*, 179; Curtis, *Buchanan*, I, ch. xxii, II, chs. iv–vii; Fuess, *Cushing*; P. C. Kuo, "Caleb Cushing," *Jour. of Modern Hist.*, V (1933), 34; Carl Crow, *He Opened Door of Japan* (1939; Harris); C. S. Alden, *Lawrence Kearny* (1936), chs. v–vii; Nichols, *Pierce*, chs. xliii–xlv; Claiborne, *Quitman*; Bancroft, *Seward*, I, chs. xvii, xxii; Hamilton, *Taylor*, II, chs. xvi, xxviii; Greene, *Filibuster* (Walker); Curtis, *Daniel Webster*, II, 533. ❡ Maps: T. C. Smith, *Parties and Slavery*, 246; L. M. Keasbey, *Nicaragua Canal* (1896).

Sources — Documents: Richardson, *Messages and Papers*, III, 272, IV, 211, 358, 398, 511, 555, 581, V; Sen. *Ex. Doc.* of each congressional session contain diplomatic correspondence; 33 Cong., 2 sess., H. *Ex. Doc.*, No. 93; Manning, *Diplomatic Correspondence Inter-American Affairs*, I–VII, XI; Moore, *Digest of International Law*, §§ 41, 50, 51, 65, 72, 75, 108, 118–120, 131, 134, 164, 165, 218, 224, 336–340, 343–8, 351–6, 368, 490–1, 550, 639, 640, 643, 686, 797–8, 837, 845–7, 860, 882, 905–6, 941–2, 1023–4, 1168, 1221, 1300; Miller, *Treaties*, IV–VIII; P. H. Clyde, ed., *United States Policy Toward China, 1838–1939* (1940), Nos. 1–11; Gantenbein, *Latin-American Policy*, 425, 497, 879. ❡ Contemporary Writings: J. Q. Adams, *Memoirs*, XI; Buchanan, *Works*, VIII; *Jefferson Davis, Constitutionalist*, III; Calhoun, *Works*, and "Correspondence"; G. M. Dallas, *Letters from London* (1869); Fillmore, "Papers"; Harris, *Complete Journal*; F. L. Hawks, *Narrative of Expedition to China Seas and Japan* (1850); A. B. Cole, ed., *Scientist with Perry* (1947; James Morrow); Polk, *Diary*; J. S. Sewall, "With Perry in Japan," *Century Mag.*, LXX (1905), 358; A. H. Abel and F. J. Klingberg, eds., *Sidelight on Anglo-American Relations* (1927; Lewis Tappan correspondence); Webster, *Writings and Speeches*, X, 45, XII, 137, 162, 187, 265, XIII, 452, XIV, 416. — See also: *De Bow's Rev.*; and other newspapers and magazines (§§ 52, 53).

Bibliography — Bemis and Griffin, *Guide to Diplomatic History*, chs. viii, ix, xi, xii; A. P. C. Griffin, *List of Books Relating to Cuba* (1898), and *List of Books Relating to Hawaii* (1898), and *Select List of Books, with References to Periodicals on Reciprocity with Canada* (1907); H. A. Morrison, *List Relating to Interoceanic Routes* (1900).

174. KANSAS-NEBRASKA ACT, 1854

Summary — Western territory: 1820, left without organization (§ 145); 1845, "Indian Country"; 1836, corner added to Missouri; 1845–53, bills for organizing; railroad interests (§ 149). — "Popular Sovereignty": 1847–48, suggested by Leake, Dickinson, and Cass (§ 170); 1850, not stated in Compromise (§ 171); 1854, Douglas' version. — Nebraska bill: election of 1852 (§ 176); 1853, Dec., House report; 1853–54, Douglas' bills; 1854, Pierce's attitude; Jan. 16, Dixon amendment; Jan. 19, "Appeal of the Independent Democrats"; Mar. 2, Chase's amendment; Mar. 3, bill passes Senate; May 20, passes House; compromise of 1820 repealed, or "superseded," or "inoperative." — Issues: power of Congress over territorial slavery; question of indirect repeal in 1850; demands of the South; extent of "squatter sovereignty"; principle of non-intervention. — Effects: annexation of Cuba killed (§ 173); Republican party formed (§ 176); Kansas struggle (§ 175); Douglas' career (§ 178); contest accelerated (§ 179).

General — Channing, *History*, VI, ch. vi; T. C. Smith, *Parties and Slavery*, ch. viii; Rhodes, *History*, I, ch. v; von Holst, *History*, IV, chs. vi–viii; Schouler, *History*, V, 279; J. W. Draper, *Civil War* (1867–70), I, ch. xxiv; L. W. Spring, *Kansas* (1885), chs. i, ii; Nevins, *Ordeal of the Union*, II, ch. ii.

Special — P. O. Ray, *Repeal of Missouri Compromise* (1909); F. H. Hodder, "Genesis of Kansas-Nebraska Act," Wisc. Hist. Soc., *Proc.*, 1912, 69, and "Railroad Background of Kansas-Nebraska Act," *Miss. Valley Hist. Rev.*, XII (1925); Riegel, *Western Railroads*, chs. ii–iv; R. R. Russel, "Pacific Railway Issue," *Miss. Valley Hist. Rev.*, XII (1925), 187; Joseph Ellison, "Designs for a Pacific Republic," *Ore. Hist. Quar.*, XXXI (1930), 319; Friedrich Kapp, *Geschichte der Sklaverei* (1861), ch. xii; Allen Johnson, "Genesis of Popular Sovereignty," *Iowa Jour. of Hist. and Politics*, III (1905), 3; Cole, *Era of Civil War*, ch. v, and *Whig Party in South*, ch. ix; Meigs, *Benton*, 409; McLaughlin, *Cass*, 287; Hart, *Chase*, 131; Milton, *Eve of Conflict* (Douglas), chs. vii–x; Allen Johnson, *Douglas*, chs. viii, xi; Nichols, *Pierce*, chs. xxv–xlii; Bancroft, *Seward*, I, ch. xviii; W. E. Smith, *Blair Family*, I, ch. xxiii; Flippin, *Johnson*, chs. iii–iv; Van Deusen, *Weed*, ch. xiii. — See also: histories of Kansas, Nebraska, and Colorado (§ 62), and other biographies of Douglas, Chase, Seward, Hale, Sumner (§ 56). ◖ Maps: Paullin, *Atlas*, plate 115; T. C. Smith, *Parties and Slavery*, 106.

Sources — Debates (§ 45); 33 Cong., 1 sess., *Sen. Report*, No. 15, *H. Report*, No. 80; MacDonald, *Select Documents*, Nos. 85–88; H. V. Ames, *State Documents*, 280–286. ◖ Contemporary Writings: Horace Greeley, *Slavery Extension* (1856), 71; Reverdy Johnson, *Remarks on Popular Sovereignty* (1859); J. S. Pike, *First Blows of Civil War* (1879), 188; Stephens, *War between the States*, I, 625, II, 241; Jefferson Davis, *Constitutionalist*, II; Pierce, *Sumner*, III, ch. xxxviii; Chase, "Diary," 254; Garrison, *Garrison*, III, ch. xiv; J. M. Cutts, *Treatise on Party Questions* (1866), 123; Parker, *Works*, V, VI.

Bibliography — Channing, *History*, VI, 179; Ray, *Repeal of Missouri Compromise*, App. F.

175. THE KANSAS STRUGGLE, 1854–1861

Summary — Status of Kansas: northern immigration; 1854–55, Massachusetts and New England Emigrant Aid societies; Lawrence founded; John Brown; Southern emigration; "Border Ruffians"; pro-slavery towns; 1856, Buford's Company. — Territorial government: 1854, Governor Reeder; 1855, Mar., fraudulent election for legislature; July, Shawnee legislature, slave code; 1855, July, Governor Shannon; 1856, Governor Geary; 1857, Nov., Governor Walker; 1858, Governor Denver. — Free state movement:

1855, Topeka Convention; July 4, legislature dispersed by troops. — Violence: 1855, "Wakarusa War"; 1856, sack of Lawrence; John Brown's fights; Pottowatomie massacre; "treaty of Lawrence"; 1859, Brown's aid to fugitives (§ 172). — Lecompton Constitution: 1855–57, Republican majority in the House (§ 176); 1857, Buchanan president; instructions to Walker; Lecompton Convention; popular vote for constitution with slavery; 1858, Douglas objects; "English Bill"; Kansas rejects; Lincoln-Douglas debate (§ 178). — Admission as a free state: 1859, Wyandotte Convention; 1861, Jan. 21, state admitted.

General — Channing, *History*, VI, 160; Rhodes, *History*, II; von Holst, *History*, V, chs. iii, v, vi, viii, VI, chs. ii, iv, v; Schouler, *History*, V, ch. xxi, § ii, ch. xxii, § i; R. F. Nichols, *Disruption of American Democracy* (1948), chs. iv–vii, ix; Allan Nevins, *Ordeal of the Union*, II, ch. ix, xi, xii, and *Emergence of Lincoln* (1950), chs. v–vi, ix–xi; T. C. Smith, *Parties and Slavery*, chs. ix, xi, xv, xvi; Macy, *Anti-Slavery Crusade*, chs. x–xii.

Special — J. C. Malin, "Proslavery Background of the Kansas Struggle," *Miss. Valley Hist. Rev.*, X (1923), 285; R. V. Harlow, "Rise and Fall of Kansas Aid Movement," *Am. Hist. Rev.*, XLI (1935), 1; S. A. Johnson, "Genesis of New England Emigrant Aid Company," *New Eng. Quar.*, III (1930), 95, and "Emigrant Aid Company," *Kan. Hist. Quar.*, I (1932), 429; J. C. Malin, *John Brown and Legend of Fifty-Six* (1942); R. E. Moody, "First Year of Emigrant Aid Company," *New England Quar.*, IV (1931), 148; G. R. Gaeddert, *Birth of Kansas* (1940); F. H. Hodder, "English Bill," Am. Hist. Assoc., *Report*, 1906, I, 201; W. H. Isely, "Sharps Rifle Episode," *Am. Hist. Rev.*, XII (1907), 546; W. L. Fleming, "Buford Expedition to Kansas," *ibid.*, VI (1900), 38; Villard, *Brown*, chs. i–ix; Curtis, *Buchanan*, II, 197; Milton, *Eve of Conflict* (Douglas), chs. xiii, xvii, xviii; Higginson, *Higginson*, ch. x; Nichols, *Pierce*, chs. lvi–lxxi; F. W. Blackmar, *Charles Robinson* (1902), chs. iii–vii, xii; Bancroft, *Seward*, I, 398; Phillips, *Toombs*, chs. vi, vii; J. N. Holloway, *History of Kansas* (1868); Connelley, *Kansas*, I, chs. xvii–xxxvi, II, chs. xxxvii–xl; Trexler, *Slavery in Missouri*, ch. vi; Eli Thayer, *Kansas Crusade* (1889); Wilder, *Kansas*; J. H. Gihon, *Geary and Kansas* (1857); Kan. State Hist. Soc., *Coll.* (see § 50); state histories of Kansas (§ 62). ❡ Maps: T. C. Smith, *Parties and Slavery*, 126.

Sources — Debates and documents (§ 45, 46); "Howard Committee Report," 34 Cong., 1 sess., *H. Ex. Doc.*, II, No. 200; Richardson, *Messages and Papers*, V; Kan. State Hist. Soc., *Coll.*; MacDonald, *Select Documents*, Nos. 90, 92; Ames, *State Documents*, 289, 299. ❡ Contemporary Writings: Buchanan, *Works*, X, 105, and *Mr. Buchanan's Administration*, 28–56; Dr. Albert Morrall, "Statement and Autobiography," Kan. State Hist. Soc., *Coll.*, XIV (1918), 123; P. W. Bidwell, ed., "New England Emigrant Aid Company" (F. L. Olmsted letters), *Am. Hist. Rev.*, XXIII (1917), 114; Blackmar, *Robinson*, App. B; Franklin Pierce, "Some Papers," *Am. Hist. Rev.*, X (1904–05), 124, 350; Sumner, *Works*, IV; W. A. Phillips, *Conquest of Kansas* (1856); Stephens, *War between States*, II, colloquy xvii; F. B. Sanborn, *Life and Letters of John Brown* (1885), chs. vii–xi; S. T. D. L. Robinson, *Kansas* (1899); Gladstone, *Englishman in Kansas*; John Sherman, *Recollections*, I, ch. v; Sanborn, *Recollections*, I, 48–133; Hart, *American History Told by Contemporaries*, IV, §§ 36–40; contemporary newspapers (§ 53), especially *N. Y. Tribune*.

Bibliography — T. C. Smith, *Parties and Slavery*, ch. xxi; Kan. State Hist. Soc., *Coll.*, VI, 385; Ames, *State Documents*, 289; Malin, *Brown*, 765.

176. RISE OF THE REPUBLICAN PARTY, 1852–1858

Summary — End of the Whigs: 1850–52, "Finality Resolutions"; 1852, Scott's candidacy; Free Democrats (§ 172); 1852, Pierce elected; Free Soil vote reduced. — Know-Nothings: immigration (§ 148); early nativism; 1835–44, "American Republican" movement; 1852, Order of the Star Spangled Banner; antiforeign principles; anti-Catholic principles; 1854–55, American Party success; 1855, split on slavery; 1856–60, disintegration. — Republican party: membership; 1854, May 23, anti-Nebraska conference; organization; July, first use of the name; state successes; 1855, anti-Nebraska majority in the House; 1856, Banks, speaker; investigation of Kansas (§ 175). — Election of 1856: Know-Nothings divided; nomination of Fillmore; May 22, assault on Charles Sumner; June, Buchanan nominated by Democrats; Frémont nominated by Republicans; Aug., congressional deadlock over Kansas; Nov., Buchanan elected. — Later policy of Republicans: 1857, on Dred Scott decision (§ 177); on Lecompton Constitution (§ 175); gains in election of 1858; 1859, Speaker Pennington (§ 178); success in 1860 (§ 178).

General — Channing, *History*, VI, ch. v; Rhodes, *History*, I, 206, 243, II, chs. vii, viii; Cole, *Irrepressible Conflict*, 272; von Holst, *History*, IV, chs. iii, iv, V, ch. i, ii, iv, vii, ix; Schouler, *History*, V, ch. xxi, § ii, ch. xxii, § i; Stanwood, *Presidency*, I, chs. xix, xx; Nevins, *Ordeal of the Union*, II, chs. i, ii, xiii, xiv, and *Emergence of Lincoln*, I, ch. iii; Binkley, *American Political Parties*, chs. viii, ix; G. M. Stephenson, *American Immigration*, chs. x, xi; Wittke, *We Who Built America*, ch. xix; Myers, *History of Bigotry*, chs. xiii–xx; T. C. Smith, *Parties and Slavery*, chs. ii–iv, viii, x, xii, and *Liberty and Free Soil Parties*, chs. xiv–xx.

Special — Party Structure: R. F. Nichols, *Disruption of American Democracy*, chs. i–iii, viii–x, and *Democratic Machine 1850–1854* (1923). ❧ Regional Works: Cole, *Whig Party in South*, chs. vii–x; Alexander, *History of New York*, II, chs. xiii–xvii; Cole, *Era of Civil War*, ch. vi; Kinsley, *Chicago Tribune*, I, pt. i, chs. xi–xvi; E. H. Roseboom, *Civil War Era*, in Wittke, ed., *Ohio* (1944), IV, chs. x–xii; H. C. Hubbart, *Older Middle West* (1936), chs. i, v, vi. ❧ Biographies: Clapp, *John Bigelow*, ch. ix; Birney, *Birney*, chs. xxviii, xxix; W. E. Smith, *Blair Family*, chs. xxi, xxiv; Curtis, *Buchanan*, II, chs. vi, viii–xi; Fuess, *Cushing*, II, chs. xii–xiii; Dodd, *Davis*, ch. viii; Milton, *Eve of Conflict* (Douglas), chs. xii, xiv–xvi; Nevins, *Frémont*, chs. xxvi–xxviii; F. H. Harrington, "Frémont and North Americans," *Am. Hist. Rev.*, XLIV (1939), 842; J. A. Isely, *Horace Greeley and Republican Party* (1947); Nicolay and Hay, *Lincoln*, I, chs. xviii–xxi; Beveridge, *Lincoln*, II, chs. v–vi; Weiss, *Parker*, II, chs. xxi, xxii; Nichols, *Pierce*, chs. xxv–xxxii; Bancroft, *Seward*, I, 291, 363, 410; L. M. Sears, "Slidell and Buchanan," *Am. Hist. Rev.*, XXVII (1922), 709; Current, *Stevens*, chs. i–vii; Phillips, *Toombs*, chs. vi, vii; Van Deusen, *Weed*, ch. xv; Going, *Wilmot*, chs. xxvii–xxix; R. C. Winthrop, Jr., *Robert C. Winthrop*, 142. ❧ Nativism: R. A. Billington, *Protestant Crusade* (1938); G. M. Stephenson, "Nativism in Forties and Fifties," *Miss. Valley Hist. Rev.*, IX (1922), 185; A. W. Thompson, "Political Nativism in Florida," *Jour. Southern Hist.*, XV (1949), 39; Carl Brand, "Know Nothing Party in Indiana," *Ind. Mag. Hist.*, XVIII (1922), 47, 177, 266; L. F. Schmeckebier, *Know-Nothing Party in Maryland* (1899); Handlin, *Boston's Immigrants*, ch. vii; W. G. Bean, "Puritan and Celt," *New Eng. Quar.*, VII (1934), 70; Gibson, *Attitudes of New York Irish*, ch. iii; L. D. Scisco, *Political Nativism in New York* (1901); Charles Stickney, *Know-Nothingism in Rhode Island* (1894); A. G. McGann, *Nativism in Kentucky* (1944); W. D. Overdyke, *Know-Nothing Party in South* (1950); Sister Paul of the Cross McGrath, *Political Nativism in Texas* (1930), ch. v. ❧ Maps: T. C. Smith, *Parties and Slavery*, 132, 158; Cole, *Whig Party in South*, 368.

Sources — Debates and documents (§ 45); Ames, *State Documents*, 293; Richardson, *Messages and Papers*, 202, 222, 397. ❧ Contemporary Writings: Bates, "Diary"; Browning, *Diary*, II; Buchanan, *Works*, VIII, 426, IX, 457, 485, X, XI, 494; Chase, "Diary," 220, 264; Coleman, *Crittenden*, II, chs. vi–x; Fillmore, "Papers," II; Garrison, *Garrison*, III, chs. xvi–xviii; Lincoln, *Collected Works*, II; Pike, *First Blows*, 260; Poore, *Perley's Reminiscences*, I, chs. xxxvi–xliv; Quincy, *Josiah Quincy*, ch. xx; W. S. Rand, "Southern Rights and Union Congress," *Hunt's Merchants' Mag.*, XXXV (1856), 309; Seward, *Works*, IV, 223; Stephens, *War between States*, II, colloquy xvii; Charles Sumner, *Works*, III, IV; Pierce, *Sumner*, III, chs. xxxix, xl; Webster, *Letters*, 475; Wise, *Seven Decades*, ch. xiii.

Bibliography — Library of Congress, *Political Parties United States;* Wise and Cronin, *Bibliography of Taylor, Fillmore, Pierce, Buchanan*, 37, 51; Stephenson, *History of Immigration*, 290; Billington, *Protestant Crusade*, 445.

177. DRED SCOTT DECISION AND JOHN BROWN'S RAID, 1857–1859

Summary — Status of Supreme Court: early decisions (§ 143); changes under Jackson (§ 154); 1842–56, decisions on slavery (§§ 161, 172); desire to settle the controversy; 1857, Buchanan's announcement. — Dred Scott Case: 1834–38, Scott taken to Illinois and the Indian country; 1838, returned to Missouri; 1847–53, Scott's three suits against his owner; backing of the Blair family; 1856, suit before the Supreme Court; 1857, Mar. 10, decision. — Principles: application of state law; Negro citizenship denied; residence in free territory not decisive; power of Congress denied; Missouri Compromise disallowed; restrictions by territorial legislatures denied. — Effects: popular sovereignty denied (§ 174); Douglas ignored (§ 178); 1858, Lincoln's disavowal (§ 178); 1862, decision ignored by Congress (§ 188). — John Brown's raid: John Brown in Kansas (§ 175); character; early plans for a slave insurrection; support in New England; 1857–58, plans for raid; 1859, Oct., capture of Harpers Ferry; Oct.–Dec., trial and execution; Republican disavowals; effect on South.

General — Nevins, *Emergence of Lincoln*, I, chs. iii–iv, II, chs. i, iii, iv, App. 1; Channing, *History*, VI, 219, ch. vii; Macy, *Anti-Slavery Crusade*, chs. xiii, xiv; T. C. Smith, *Parties and Slavery*, ch. xiv; Rhodes, *History*, II, 242, 384; von Holst, *History*, VI, ch. i.

Special — Dred Scott Case: C. W. Smith, *Taney*; Warren, *Supreme Court*, III, chs. xxvi, xxvii; Kelly and Harbison, *American Constitution*, chs. xiv, xv; Boudin, *Government by Judiciary*, II, ch. xx; E. S. Corwin, "Dred Scott Decision," *Am. Hist. Rev.*, XVII (1911), 52; H. T. Catterall, "Some Antecedents of Dred Scott Case," *ibid.*, XXX (1924), 56; F. H. Hodder, "Dred Scott Case," *Miss. Valley Hist. Rev.*, XVI (1929), 3; E. I. McCormac, "Justice Campbell and Dred Scott Decision," *ibid.*, XIX (1933), 565; R. R. Stenberg, "Political Aspects Dred Scott Case," *ibid.*, XIX (1933), 571; Swisher, *Roger B. Taney*, chs. xxiii, xxiv; V. C. Hopkins, *Dred Scott's Case* (1951); Beveridge, *Lincoln*, II, ch. vii; Parker, *Personal Liberty Laws*, 53; Hurd, *Law of Freedom and Bondage*, §§ 489–539; Nicolay and Hay, *Lincoln*, II, chs. iv, v; Philip Auchanpaugh, "James Buchanan, the Court, and the Dred Scott Case," *Tenn. Hist. Mag.*, IX (1928), 231; H. H. Hagan, "Dred Scott Decision," *Georgetown Law Jour.*, XV (1927), 95; W. E. Smith, *Blair Family*, I, ch. xxii; Milton, *Eve of Conflict* (Douglas), chs. xvii–xix; Haines, *Conflict over Judicial Powers*, 145; Henry Wilson, *Slave Power*, II, ch. xxxix; Van Buren, *Political Parties*, ch. viii. ❡ John Brown: Villard, *Brown*, chs. xi–xv; Aaron, *America in Crisis*, ch. vi; R. V. Harlow, "Gerrit Smith and Brown Raid," *Am. Hist. Rev.*, XXXVIII (1932), 32; Harvey Wish, "Slave Insurrection Panic of 1856," *Jour. Southern Hist.*, V (1939), 206; Fred Landon, "Canadian Negroes and John Brown Raid," *Jour. of Negro Hist.*, VI (1921), 174; James Redpath, *Public Life of John Brown* (1860), 229; W. E. B. DuBois, *John Brown* (1909); Hermann von Holst, *John Brown* (1889); Higginson, *Higginson*, ch. xi; F. T. Hill, *Decisive Battles of Law* (1907), ch. iii; M. J. Wright, "Trial," Am. Hist. Assoc., *Papers* (1890), IV, 439; Washington, *Douglass*, 182; B. H. Wise, *Life of Henry A. Wise* (1899), ch. xiv; Capers, *Memminger*, 238. ❡ Maps: F. E. Chadwick, *Causes of Civil War* (1906), 80.

Sources — Text of the Dred Scott Decision: 19 Howard, 399, and 2 Miller, 1; extracts in *American History Leaflets*, No. 23; MacDonald, *Select Documents*, No. 91; Thayer, *Cases*, 480. ❡ Debates and Documents: *Congressional Globe*; 36 Cong., 1 sess., Sen. *Ex. Doc.*, II, No. 2; Richardson, *Messages and Papers*, V, 431, 553; Lawson, *American State Trials*, VI, 700 (record); Ames, *State Documents*, 295, 306. ❡ Contemporary Writings: Lincoln, *Collected Works*, II; Sanborn, *Brown*, chs. xii–xvii, and *Recollections*, I, chs. v–ix; Jefferson Davis, *Constitutionalist*, III; Browning, *Diary*, 270; James Redpath, *Echoes of Harpers Ferry* (1860); Pike, *First Blows*, 420; Douglass, *Life and Times*, pt. 2, chs. viii–x; Garrison, *Garrison*, III, ch. xix; Poore, *Perley's Reminiscences*, II, ch. iii; *Mr. Buchanan's Administration*; Johnston and Woodburn, *American Orations*, III, 129, 154; Hart, *American History Told by Contemporaries*, IV, §§ 41–3, 47, 48; T. H. Benton, *Historical and Legal Examination* (1857); S. A. Foot, *Examination of Case of Dred Scott* (1859); Horace Gray and John Lowell, *Legal Review of Case of Dred Scott* (1877).

Bibliography — Ames, *State Documents*, 295, 306, 307; Villard, *Brown*, 689; Chadwick, *Causes of Civil War*, 350; Nevins, *Emergence of Lincoln*, II, 491.

178. PRESIDENTIAL ELECTION OF 1860

Summary — Parties in 1857 and 1858 (§ 176); Buchanan's presidency; 1857, new tariff; commercial panic; homestead question; Pacific railroads (§§ 174, 197); revival of the slave trade; Kansas (§ 175); 1858, Mormon War; 1859–60, Southern commercial conventions. — Lincoln-Douglas debates: Douglas against the Lecompton Constitution (§ 175); Lincoln Republican candidate for senatorship; 1858, June 16, "House divided" speech; joint debates; Aug. 27, Douglas' "Freeport doctrine"; Douglas successful; 1858, Seward's "Irrepressible conflict" speech. — Congress: 1859–60, Douglas out of favor; speakership contest; Helper's *Impending Crisis*; "Covode investigation." — Nominations of 1860: Feb. 2, Jefferson Davis' resolutions in the Senate on state rights and slavery; Apr. 23–May 3, Charleston Convention; May 10, Constitutional Unionists nominate Bell (1); May 16, Republican convention; hopes of Seward, Cameron, and Chase; May 17, Lincoln (2) nominated; May 24, Davis' resolutions voted on; June 22, Baltimore convention nominates Douglas (3); June 28, Seceders' convention nominates Breckinridge (4). — Issues: spoils of office; tariff; Kansas (§ 175); territorial slavery (§ 170, 174, 177); abolition; disunion (§ 180). — Result: Nov. 6, Lincoln elected; Nov. 20, South Carolina secedes (§ 181).

General — Nevins, *Emergence of Lincoln*, I, chs. vii, xii–xiv, II, chs. iv, vi–x, 478; Channing, *History*, VI, 197, ch. viii, xix; Rhodes, *History*, II, chs. x, xi; von Holst, *History*, VI, chs. iii, vi, vii, VII, chs. ii–vi; T. C. Smith, *Parties and Slavery*, chs. xvii, xviii; Chadwick, *Causes of Civil War*, chs. vi–vii; Stanwood, *Presidency*, I, ch. xxi; Nichols, *Disruption of American Democracy*, chs. x–xix.

Special — Biographies: Sandburg, *Lincoln*, II, chs. civ–cxviii, cxxix, cxliii–cxlvi; Beveridge, *Lincoln*, II, chs. viii–x; Herndon, *Lincoln*; Bancroft, *Seward*, I, 432, chs. xxiii, xxiv; Going, *Wilmot*, ch. xxxi; Clapp, *John Bigelow*, ch. x; C. V. Easum, *Americanization of Schurz* (1929), ch. ix; Fuess, *Schurz*, ch. vii; W. E. Smith, *Blair Family*, ch. xxvi; Van Deusen, *Weed*, ch. xvi; Dodd, *Davis*, 163; Milton, *Eve of Conflict* (Douglas), chs. xix–xxix; Allen Johnson, *Douglas*, chs. xvi–xviii; Hart, *Chase*, ch. vii; Linn, *Greeley*, 170; Phillips, *Toombs*, ch. viii; Flippin, *Johnson*, ch. v; Current, *Stevens*; Helen Nicolay, *Lincoln's Secretary* (Nicolay; 1949), ch. iv; Curtis, *Buchanan*, II, chs. xii, xiii; D. V. Smith, "Chase and Election 1860," *Ohio Archeol. and Hist. Quar.*, XXXIX (1930), 515, 769. ❡ Economic Issues: Kinley, *Independent Treasury*, ch. vii; C. F. Dunbar, *Economic Essays* (1904), 266; G. W. Van Vleck, *Panic of 1857* (1943); Dewey, *Financial History*, §§ 113–115; Hans Rosenberg, *Die Weltwirtschaftskrisis von 1857–1859* (1934); Taylor, *Transportation Revolution*, 345; Eiselen, *Pennsylvania Protectionism*, chs. xi–xii; T. M. Pitkin, "Western Republicans and Tariff in 1860," *Miss. Valley Hist. Rev.*, XXVII (1940), 401. ❡ Mormon War: Juanita Brooks, *Mountain Meadows Massacre* (1950); Linn, *Mormons*, 458; Bancroft, *Utah*, chs. xviii, xix. ❡ Election of 1860: Ollinger Crenshaw, *Slave States in Presidential Election of 1860* (1945); R. H. Luthin, *First Lincoln Campaign* (1944); D. Y. Thomas, "Southern Non-Slaveholders in Election of 1860," *Pol. Sci. Quar.*, XXVI (1911), 222; E. D. Fite, *Presidential Campaign of 1860* (1911). ❡ Local studies: Cole, *Era of Civil War*, chs. vii, viii; Hubbart, *Older Middle West*, chs. vii, viii; Kinsley, *Chicago Tribune*, I, pt. 1, chs. xvii–xx; Ambler, *Sectionalism in Virginia*, 308. ❡ Maps: Paullin, *Atlas*, plates 103, 115.

Sources — Debates (§ 45); Richardson, *Messages and Papers*, V, 433; 32 Cong., 1 sess., *H. Ex. Doc.*, Nos. 25, 33; 35 Cong., 1 sess., *H. Ex. Doc.*, No. 138, *Sen. Ex. Doc.*, Nos. 11, 67, 2 sess., *Sen. Ex. Doc.*, II, No. 1; 36 Cong., 1 sess., *H. Ex. Doc.*, No. 78; *Sen. Ex. Doc.*, No. 32; Works of Lincoln, Seward, Buchanan, Davis (§ 55); C. F. Adams, *Autobiography*, ch. ii; Browning, *Diary*, 389; Bates, "Diary"; Chase, "Diary," 275, 477; John Sherman, *Recollections*, I, ch. viii; Coleman, *Crittenden*, II, chs. x, xii; Stephens, *War between States*, II; Poore, *Perley's Reminiscences*, II, ch. iv; Schurz, *Reminiscences*, II; *Hunt's*

Merchants' Mag., XXXVII, XXXVIII, XL; G. F. Train, *Young America in Wall Street* (1857); Amasa Walker, *Nature and Uses of Money* (1857); *Report of Committee of Boston Board of Trade* (1858); H. C. Carey, *Financial Crises* (1864); D. H. Evans, *History of Commercial Crisis, 1857–58* (1859).

Bibliography — Works cited in § 176; U. S. Tariff Commission, *Tariff*.

Chapter Eighteen

THE CIVIL WAR

179. THE SECTIONS COMPARED, 1861

Summary — (§§ 141, 148–51, 159, 165). — Geography: areas of free states, border states, and seceding states; status of territories; of Pacific states. — Military conditions: distances; coast line; Appalachian range; inside lines; hills; forested areas; the South on the defensive. — Economic differences: (§§ 148, 149); agriculture; manufactures; mines; commerce; wealth; means of communications. — Social differences: (§§ 148, 150); population; Northern border states, Confederate; Negroes and whites; cities; education. — Military differences: number of troops, Northern and Southern; Confederates from loyal states; Northern troops from seceding states; regular army; military administration; military aptitude; officers; the Northern and Southern volunteer; military supplies, military preparation; use of Negroes (§§ 185, 188). — Expectation of foreign aid: "King Cotton"; sympathy of England and France; tariff question; effects of the blockade (§§ 184, 187). — Slavery as a cause of difference (§§ 159–161, 170, 171, 174, 177, 178). — General causes: the Northern view; the Southern view; "revisionism"; opposition to "revisionism."

General — H. K. Beale, "Causes of Civil War," Soc. Sci. Res. Coun., *Bull.*, No. 54 (1946), 53; Nevins, *Emergence of Lincoln*, I, chs. i, ii, viii, xii, and *Ordeal of Union*, II, ch. xv; von Holst, *History*, VII, chs. vii, viii; J. G. Randall, *Civil War and Reconstruction* (1937), chs. i–v; Nicolay and Hay, *Lincoln*, III, chs. i, ii; J. C. Ropes and W. R. Livermore, *Story of Civil War* (1894–1913), I, chs. vii, viii; Chadwick, *Causes of Civil War*, ch. ii; J. K. Hosmer, *Appeal to Arms* (1907), ch. i; Semple, *American History and Its Geographic Conditions*, ch. xiv; W. G. Brown, *Lower South in American History* (1902), ch. i; *South in Building of Nation*, IV, 59, 338, 382, 500, 544, V, 656; John Formby, *American Civil War* (1910), ch. v.

Special — The Sections: Carpenter, *South as Conscious Minority*, ch. i; A. O. Craven, "Agricultural Reformers," *Am. Hist. Rev.*, XXXIII (1928), 302; W. C. Bagley, *Soil Exhaustion and the Civil War* (1942); P. G. Davidson, "Industrialism in South," *So. Atlantic Quar.*, XXVII (1928), 405; Davenport, *Kentucky* (§ 62); Kohlmeier, *Old Northwest*; Frederick Phisterer, *Statistical Record of Armies of United States* (1883), pt. 1; T. L. Livermore, *Numbers and Losses in Civil War* (1901); biographies and personal narratives, §§ 180–187. ❅ Cultural and Social Divisions: Cole, *Irrepressible Conflict*; Sweet, *Methodism*, ch. xiii; Norwood, *Schism in Methodist Church*. ❅ Foreign Accounts: L. P. A. d'O., Comte de Paris, *History of Civil War* (4 vols., 1875–88), I, 6, 16, 76, 172, 257; James Spence, *American Union* (1862), ch. vii; H. C. Fletcher, *History of American War* (1865), I, ch. iii; Gurowski, *America and Europe*; J. E. Cairnes, *Slave Power* (1862); Agenor de Gasparin, *Uprising of a Great People* (1861). ❅ Northern Interpretations: T. S. Goodwin, *Natural History of Secession* (1864); Blaine, *Twenty Years*, I, ch. xiv; S. S. Cox, *Three Decades of Federal Legislation* (1885), chs. iv, v. ❅ Southern Interpretations: Jefferson Davis, *Confederate Government*, I, 301, 471, II, 705; R. L. Dabney, *Defence of Virginia* (1867). ❅ Revisionist Interpretations: Phillips, *Course of*

South to Secession; A. O. Craven, "Coming of War," *Jour. Southern Hist.*, II (1936), 303, and *Repressible Conflict* (1939); C. W. Ramsdell, "Changing Interpretation of Civil War," *Jour. Southern Hist.*, III (1937), 3; J. G. Randall, "Civil War Restudied," *ibid.*, VI (1940), 439; F. L. Owsley, "Fundamental Cause of Civil War," *ibid.*, VII (1941), 3. ❡ Other Interpretations: Beard, *Rise of American Civilization*, II, chs. xvii, xviii; E. C. Rozwenc, *Slavery as Cause of Civil War* (1949); R. H. Shryock, "Nationalistic Tradition of Civil War," *So. Atlantic Quar.*, XXII (1933), 294; A. M. Schlesinger, Jr., "Causes of Civil War," *Partisan Rev.*, XVI (1949), 969; Dumond, *Anti-Slavery Origins of Civil War*; Cole, *Irrepressible Conflict*; T. P. Govan, "Slavery and Civil War," *Sewanee Rev.*, XLVIII (1940), 533; Osterweis, *Romanticism and Nationalism in Old South.* ❡ Maps: Chadwick, *Causes of Civil War*, 8, 20, 60; Hosmer, *Appeal to Arms*, 4.

Sources — Debates: *Congressional Globe*, especially 36 Cong., 2 sess., 12, 72, 134, 624, 721, 943, 1467. ❡ Documents: census publications (§ 7); 36 Cong., 2 sess., *Sen. Ex. Doc.*, II, III, VIII, *H. Ex. Doc.*, II, IX, No. 53, X, No. 77; 37 Cong., 1 sess., *Sen. Ex. Doc.*, Nos. 1, 2, 19, 85, *H. Ex. Doc.*, Nos. 1, 14, *Sen. Report*, No. 1; *Appletons'* (*Am.*) *Annual Cyclopedia, 1861*, 26, 490; *ibid.*, *1863*, 268, 361. ❡ Contemporary Writings: travel accounts (§ 48); Sherman, *Memoirs*, II, ch. xxv; Olmsted, *Cotton Kingdom*; Helper, *Impending Crisis*; Richard Hildreth, *Despotism in America* (1854); J. D. B. De Bow, *Industrial Resources of Southern and Western States* (3 vols., 1852–53); G. M. Weston, *Progress of Slavery* (1857); "Barbarossa" [John Scott], *Lost Principle* (1860); Augustin Cochin, *Results of Slavery* (1863), bk. 1; Manning, Potter, Davies, *Select Problems*, I, ch. xi; L. B. Schmidt and E. D. Ross, *Readings in History of American Agriculture* (1925), ch. xv.

Bibliography — Chadwick, *Causes of Civil War*, 351; *South in Building of Nation*, V, 667.

180. SECESSION IN THEORY

Summary — Status of state before 1789 (§§ 114, 119, 121, 122). — Effect of ratifications of the Constitution (§ 122): revocable or irrevocable; "supreme law," "more perfect union"; reserved rights. — Threats of secession: 1795, *Connecticut Courant;* 1798, Virginia and Kentucky (§ 131); 1803, 1811, 1814, New England (§ 139); 1832, sentiment in South Carolina (§ 156); 1833, differentiation from nullification; 1844, Bluffton movement; 1850, threats in the Compromise debate (§ 171); 1856, meeting of the governors at Raleigh; 1860, threats in the presidential election (§ 178). — Enunciations of secession doctrine: 1798–99, Virginia and Kentucky doctrine (§ 131); 1803, Tucker's *Blackstone*; 1811, Josiah Quincy's speech; 1825, Rawle's *View of the Constitution*; 1832, South Carolina resolutions (§ 156); 1845, Garrison's doctrine (§ 160); 1850, Calhoun's speech (§ 171); 1860, Feb. 2, Jefferson Davis' resolutions (§ 178). — Questions in 1860: constitutionality; expediency; effectiveness; legal effect of ordinances of secession (§ 181).

General — Merriam, *American Political Theories*, ch. vii; Chadwick, *Causes of Civil War*, chs. i, iii.

Special — Historical Discussions: D. L. Dumond, *Secession Movement* (1931), ch. i; Carpenter, *South as Conscious Minority*, chs. v, vi; C. S. Boucher, *South Carolina and the South* (1919); H. T. Shanks, *Secession Movement in Virginia* (1934); Spence, *American Union*, ch. vi; White, *Rhett*, chs. v, vii–ix; Wiltse, *Calhoun*, III, chs. xxviii, xxix; also biographies §§ 181, 182. ❡ Adverse Legal Accounts: Cooley, *Constitutional Law*, ch. ii; Story, *Commentaries*; Willoughby, *Constitutional Law*, I, ch. iv. ❡ Defense of Doctrine: Jefferson Davis, *Confederate Government*, I, pt. 1; B. F. Grady, *Case of South* (1899); Stephens, *War between States*; *South in Building of Nation*, IV, 466; also § 181.

Sources — Debates (§ 45); Richardson, *Messages and Papers*, V; *Mr. Buchanan's Administration*; Texas v. White, 7 Wallace, 700; White v. Hart, 13 Wallace, 646; Sprott *v.* U. S., 20 Wallace, 419; Keith *v.* Clark, 92 U.S., 461; *Jefferson Davis, Constitutionalist,* IV; James Williams, *Rise and Fall of "Model Republic"* (1863); also works cited § 153.

Bibliography — Library of Congress, *List of Books on Secession* (1914).

181. THE ACT OF SECESSION, 1860–1861

Summary — Previous threats (§ 180). — Causes: § 179; desire for independence; political supremacy; economic handicaps; slavery. — Grievances of South: general discontent; difference in interpretation of the Constitution; economic differences; apprehension from Lincoln's election; Northern opposition to slavery. — South Carolina: 1860, Oct. 5, Governor Gist's letter; Nov. 5, legislature called; Nov. 6, election day; Nov. 7, resignation of federal officials; Nov. 12, act calling convention; Dec. 17–20, Secession Convention; Dec. 20, Secession Ordinance; Dec. 24, accompanying appeals; effect on the Union. — Other cotton states: movement; Nov. 14, Stephen's Union speech; 1861, Jan. 5, resolutions of secession congressmen; Jan. 9, Mississippi; Jan. 10, Florida; Jan. 10, Alabama; Jan. 11, Georgia; Jan. 26, Louisiana; Jan. 28, Texas. — Feb. 4–18, Southern Confederacy formed (§ 184).

General — Channing, *History,* VI, ch. x; Rhodes, *History,* III, 115, 192, 272; von Holst, *History,* VII, chs. vii, viii; Schouler, *History,* V, 469; T. C. Smith, *Parties and Slavery,* chs. xix, xx; Randall, *Civil War and Reconstruction,* chs. vi–vii; Nevins, *Emergence of Lincoln,* I, chs. xv, xvi, II, ch. xi; Nichols, *Disruption of American Democracy,* ch. xx; W. G. Shotwell, *Civil War* (1923), I, chs. vii–viii; N. W. Stephenson, *Abraham Lincoln and Union* (1918), chs. i–v; A. O. Craven, *Coming of Civil War* (1942), chs. xvi, xvii; E. M. Coulter, *Confederate States of America* (1950), ch. i.

Special — State and local histories (§ 62); A. C. Cole and J. G. de R. Hamilton, "Lincoln's Election an Immediate Menace to Slavery in the States?," *Am. Hist. Rev.,* XXXVI (1931), 740, XXXVII (1932), 700; Sandburg, *Lincoln,* III, ch. i; Craven, *Ruffin,* ch. viii; Milton, *Eve of Conflict,* ch. xxx; White, *Rhett,* chs. vii–ix; Ranck, *Brown,* chs. iv–vi; Elizabeth Merritt, *James Henry Hammond* (1923), ch. v, vi; Capers, *Memminger;* Fuess, *Cushing,* II, ch. xiv; von Abele, *Stephens,* ch. iv; L. M. Sears, *John Slidell* (1925), ch. vii; Flippin, *Johnson;* Meade, *Benjamin,* ch. viii; P. G. Auchampaugh, *Robert Tyler* (1934), ch. vi; Phillips, *Toombs,* ch. ix; Current, *Stevens,* ch. ix; other biographies, §§ 182, 183, 184; Dumond, *Secession Movement,* chs. ii–vii, x; P. L. Rainwater, *Mississippi, Storm-Center of Secession, 1856–1861* (1938); C. P. Denman, *Secession Movement in Alabama* (1933); L. A. Kibler, "Unionist Sentiment in South Carolina in 1860," *Jour. of Southern Hist.,* IV (1938), 346; W. M. Caskey, *Secession and Restoration in Louisiana* (1938), chs. i–ii; Carpenter, *South as Conscious Minority,* ch. vi; E. C. Smith, *Borderland in Civil War* (1927), ch. iv; Russel, *Southern Sectionalism,* ch. ix; M. J. White, *Secession Movement 1847–1852* (1910); § 184.

Sources — Debates (§ 45); 36 Cong., 2 sess., *Sen. Ex. Docs.,* I, No. 1, IV, No. 5, *H. Ex. Docs.,* VI, No. 26, IX, Nos. 61, 72, *H. Reports,* I, No. 50, II, Nos. 79, 87, 88, 91; 37 Cong., 3 sess., *H. Ex. Docs.,* III, No. 1; 38 Cong., 1 sess., *Sen. Ex. Docs.,* I, No. 3; Winkler, *Journal of Secession Convention Texas,* and other state convention reports (§ 46); *War of Rebellion,* 1 ser., I, 4 ser., I; *Mr. Buchanan's Administration,* chs. iv–vi, ix–xi; Lincoln, *Collected Works,* III–IV; Jefferson Davis, *Confederate Government,* I; Stephens, *War between States,* I, II; H. V. Johnson, "From the Autobiography," *Am. Hist. Rev.,* XXX (1925), 311; *Jefferson Davis, Constitutionalist,* V; Cox, *Three Decades,* ch. vi; Dumond, *Southern Editorials on Secession.*

Bibliography — § 180.

182. ABRAHAM LINCOLN AND THE OUTBREAK OF WAR, 1860–1861

Summary — Potential policies: (1) "let the erring sisters go in peace"; (2) resistance; (3) compromise. — Buchanan's attitude: 1860, Oct. 29, "General Scott's Views"; Nov. 20, opinion of Attorney-General Black; Dec. 3, Buchanan's message; Dec. 9, "Memorandum" of South Carolina members; Dec. 11, instructions to Major Anderson; Dec. 15, resignation of Secretary Cass. — First period of compromise: precedents (§§ 145, 156, 171); Dec. 6-Jan. 14, House Committee of 33; Dec. 14, Southern address; Dec. 20-28, Senate Committee of 33; Davis ultimatum; Seward ultimatum; Lincoln's influence defeats compromise. — First Sumter episode: Dec. 27-29, cabinet crisis, Floyd resigns; Dec. 29, Buchanan yields to Black; Dec. 31, decision to hold Sumter; Jan. 9, *Star of the West* fired upon; Jan. 14-Feb. 6, correspondence with South Carolina commission. — Second period of compromise: Jan. 14, Crittenden compromise defeated; Feb. 7, Vallandigham's plan; Feb. 4-27, peace conference; March 2, Corwin amendment. — Advent of Lincoln: 1809, birth; 1847-49, in Congress (§ 170); 1854-56, on Kansas; 1858, Douglas Debate (§ 178); 1860, Cooper Union Speech, elected president (§ 178); Dec. 22, letter to Stephens; journey to Washington. — Crisis: Mar. 4, inaugural; Mar. 5, cabinet; Mar. 12, confederate commission; Campbell's intervention; cabinet advice; decision to reinforce Sumter; Apr. 1, Seward proposes foreign war; Apr. 6, notice to South Carolina; Apr. 12, attack on Fort Sumter; Apr. 13, surrender. — War: Apr. 15, call for volunteers; blockade proclamations. — Border secessions: Apr. 17, Virginia; May 6, Arkansas; May 7, Tennessee; May 20, North Carolina; status of loyal slave states, of East Tennessee, West Virginia, and Virginia eastern shore.

General — Channing, *History*, VI, ch. xi; Cole, *Irrepressible Conflict*, ch. xiii; D. M. Potter, *Lincoln and His Party in Secession Crisis* (1942); K. M. Stampp, *And the War Came* (1950); Nevins, *Emergence of Lincoln*, II, chs. xii-xv; Rhodes, *History*, III; Schouler, *History*, V, ch. xxii, § ii; von Holst, *History*, VII, ch. xi; G. F. Milton, *Conflict* (1941), chs. i-iii; Randall, *Civil War and Reconstruction*, chs. viii-ix; Shotwell, *Civil War*, I, chs. ix-xi; J. F. Rhodes, *History of Civil War* (1917), ch. i; Stephenson, *Lincoln and Union*, chs. vi-ix; Coulter, *Confederate States*, ch. ii.

Special — E. C. Smith, *Borderland in Civil War*, chs. i-iii, v-xi; Hubbart, *Older Middle West*, chs. ix, x; W. W. Ryle, *Missouri, Union or Secession* (1931); Russel, *Southern Sectionalism*, ch. xi; Munford, *Virginia's Attitude*; Shanks, *Secession in Virginia*; Dumond, *Secession Movement*, chs. viii, ix, xi, xii; J. C. Sitterson, *Secession Movement in North Carolina* (1939); Hofstadter, *American Political Tradition*, ch. v; C. W. Ramsdell, "Lincoln and Fort Sumter," *Jour. of Southern Hist.*, III (1937), 259; Mary Scrugham, *Peaceable Americans of 1860-1861* (1921); G. G. Glover, *Immediate Pre-Civil War Compromise Efforts* (1934); Frederic Bancroft, "Final Efforts at Compromise, 1860-61," *Pol. Sci. Quar.*, VI (1891), 401; C. E. Knox, "Possibilities of Compromise in Senate Committee of Thirteen," *Jour. of Negro Hist.*, XVII (1932), 437; Sandburg, *Lincoln*, III, chs. iii-viii; Randall, *Lincoln*, I; Going, *Wilmot*, ch. xxxiii; P. G. Auchampaugh, *James Buchanan and His Cabinet* (1926), chs. iv-vi; L. A. White, "Sumner and Crisis of 1861," A. O. Craven, ed., *Essays in Honor of William E. Dodd* (1935); Milton, *Eve of Conflict*, chs. xxxi, xxxii; Bancroft, *Seward*, II, chs. xxv, xxviii, xxix; A. D. H. Smith, *Old Fuss and Feathers* (Scott), bk. 5; Nicolay, *Lincoln's Secretary*, chs. v-vi; W. E. Smith, *Blair Family*, II, ch. xxviii; Current, *Stevens*, chs. viii, ix; Woodburn, *Stevens*, chs. vii, viii; Pearson, *Andrew*, I, chs. iv, v; § 184; also other biographies of Lincoln, Seward, Chase, Crittenden, Toombs, Jefferson Davis (§ 56). ❡ Map: Nevins, *Emergence of Lincoln*, II, 348.

Sources — Congressional papers and debates (§ 45); *Opinions of the Attorneys-General*, IX, 522; *War of Rebellion, Official Records*, 1 ser., I, 4 ser., I; *Naval Records*, I, IV; Richardson, *Messages and Papers*, V, VI; Perkins, *Northern Editorials on Secession*; J. E. Walmsley, ed., "Change of Secession Sentiment in Virginia," *Am. Hist. Rev.*, XXXI (1925), 82; *Mr. Buchanan's Administration*, chs. vii, viii; Kendall, *Autobiography*, ch. xix; Seward, *Works*, IV; F. W. Seward, *Reminiscences* (1916), 134; Lincoln, *Collected Works*; Chase, "Diary," 290, 483; John Sherman, *Recollections*, I, chs. x, xi; *Jefferson Davis, Constitutionalist*, V; Stephens, *War between States*, II; Jefferson Davis, *Confederate Government*, I; Bates, "Diary"; Welles, *Diary*, I, ch. 1; Browning, "Diary"; C. F. Adams, *Autobiography*, ch. iii; Henry Adams, *Education*, ch. vii; Ruffin, *Papers*, III, 120; Johnson Hagood, *Memoirs of War* (1910); Manning, Potter, Davies, *Select Problems*, I, ch. x.

Bibliography — Nevins, *Emergence of Lincoln*, II, 491; Jay Monaghan, comp., *Lincoln Bibliography* (2 vols., 1943–45); D. C. Mearns, *Lincoln Papers* (2 vols., 1948).

183. THE NORTH, 1861–1865

Summary — Administration: President (§ 182); cabinet; Secretary Stanton; civil service; war governors; generals. — Parties: Republicans; Union Party; War Democrats; Peace Democrats; election of 1862; Republican opposition to Lincoln; cabinet changes. — New states: 1863, West Virginia; 1864, Nevada. — Raising troops: regulars; volunteers; guerrillas; spies; terms; reënlistment; officers' commissions; recruiting; bounties; drafts; 1863, draft riots. — Supplies: arms; commissariat; medical and hospital; clothing, "shoddy"; contracts. — Volunteer aid: Christian Commission; Sanitary Commission; fairs. — Arbitrary government: "Copperheads"; other opposition; efforts at peace; 1861, Apr. 27, Lincoln suspends habeas corpus; May 25, Merryman case; Aug. 6, indemnity act; 1863, Mar. 3, act authorizing suspensions; arbitrary confinements; 1863, May, Vallandigham tried by a military tribunal; Vallandigham sent south; the opposition press; provost marshalships in northern states; 1864, Milligan case. — Social, religious, and cultural conditions. — Economic development: commercial prosperity; homestead act; tariff, banks (§ 186); immigration legislation; land-grant colleges. — Lincoln: popularity; influence on Congress; 1863, Nov. 19, Gettysburg speech; 1864, June, renominated; Nov. 8, reëlected; 1865, Mar. 4, second inauguration and address; April 14, assassinated.

General — Channing, *History*, VI, ch. xi; Cole, *Irrepressible Conflict*, ch. xiv; Schouler, *History*, V, ch. i, §§ viii, xiv, ch. ii, §§ i, ii, v, viii, xi; Rhodes, *History*, III, 438, 553, IV, 163, 221, 408, 456, 507, V, ch. xxvii, and *Civil War*, chs. iv, v, viii, xi; Randall, *Civil War and Reconstruction*, chs. xiv–xvii, xxv–xxvii; Milton, *Conflict*, chs. viii, xx, xxi; C. R. Fish, *American Civil War* (1937), chs. iv–vi, xvi; Stephenson, *Lincoln and Union*, ch. xi; Curti, *Growth of American Thought*, ch. xviii; Greeley, *American Conflict*, I, chs. xxxii, xxxiv, II, chs. xxi, xxx; Swisher, *American Constitutional Development*, chs. xiii, xiv; Kelly and Harbison, *American Constitution*, ch. xvi; Boudin, *Government by Judiciary*, II, ch. xxi.

Special — Administration and Politics: Sandburg, *Lincoln*, IV, chs. xlvii, xlix, V, chs. l, lii–lx, VI, chs. lxii–lxiv, lxxii–lxxvi; Herndon, *Lincoln*; Randall, *Lincoln*, II, III; Thomas, *Lincoln*; Charnwood, *Lincoln*; W. E. Smith, *Blair Family*, I, ch. xxvii, II, xxxi–xxxvi; Harris, *Chandler*, chs. vii–ix; Hart, *Chase*, ch. xii; D. V. Smith, *Chase and Civil War Politics* (1931), ch. xv; Fuess, *Cushing*, II, ch. xv; Nevins, *Frémont*, chs. xxx, xxxi, xxxiii; R. R. Fahrney, *Horace Greeley and Tribune in Civil War* (1936); Tyler Dennett, *John Hay* (1933), chs. iv, v; D. H. Donald, *Lincoln's Herndon* (1948); Stryker, *Johnson*, chs. vii–xxiii; Foulke, *Morton*, I, chs. xii–xxxi; Nicolay, *Lincoln's Secretary*, chs. vii–xx; A. D. H. Smith, *Old Fuss and Feathers* (Scott), bk. 5; Bancroft, *Seward*, II, chs. xxxiv, xxxvii; Gorham, *Stanton*, I, ch. xxxvi, II, chs. lxxi, lxxv–lxxvii, lxxx–lxxxii, lxxxiv, lxxxvii; Current, *Stevens*, chs. x–xiv; Woodburn, *Stevens*, ch. x; Swisher, *Roger B. Taney*, ch. xxvi; Stanwood, *Presidency*, I, ch. xxii; Binkley, *American Political Parties*, chs. x, xi, and *Powers of President*, ch. vi; Jefferson Davis, *Confederate Government*, II; Pollard, *Presidents and Press*, 312; Fowler, *Cabinet Politician*, ch. vi; Upton, *Military Policy*, chs. xvii–xxix; T. H. Williams, *Lincoln and Radicals* (1941); B. J. Hendrick, *Lincoln's War Cabinet* (1946); W. B. Hesseltine, *Lincoln and War Governors* (1948); H. J. Carman and R. H. Luthin, *Lincoln and Patronage* (1943); Fish, *Civil Service and Patronage*, 169. ❡ Raising Troops: Louis Smith, *American Democracy and Military Power* (1951), ch. xi; F. A. Shannon, *Organization and Administration of Union Army* (2 vols., 1928); A. H. Meneely, *War Department: 1861* (1928); E. N. Wright, *Conscientious Objectors in Civil War* (1931); S. A. Pleasants, *Fernando Wood* (1948), ch. ix; Gibson, *Attitudes of New York Irish*, chs. v, vi; Ella Lonn, *Desertion during the Civil War* (1928), chs. ix–xvi; C. R. Fish, "Conscription," *Am. Hist. Rev.*, XXI (1915), 100; W. F. Raney, "Recruiting in Canada," *Miss. Valley Hist. Rev.*, X (1923), 21. ❡ Opposition to the War and Arbitrary Government: J. G. Randall, *Constitutional Problems under Lincoln* (1926); Warren, *Supreme Court*, III, ch. xxxiii; Weyl, *Battle Against Disloyalty*, chs. iv, v, and *Treason*, chs. xiv–xv;

G. F. Milton, *Abraham Lincoln and Fifth Column* (1942); Wood Gray, *Hidden Civil War* (1942); Pleasants, *Wood*, chs. vii–viii; Mayo Fesler, "Secret Political Societies," *Ind. Mag. Hist.*, XIV (1918), 183; Shotwell, *Civil War*, I, chs. xxv, xxx; E. C. Smith, *Borderland in Civil War*, ch. x; Hubbart, *Older Middle West*, chs. xi–xiii; Otto Eisenschiml, *Why Was Lincoln Murdered?* (1937); Nott, *American Journalism*, chs. xx–xxiv; E. C. Kirkland, *Peacemakers of 1864* (1927). ❧ Economic Development: E. D. Fite, *Social and Industrial Conditions in North* (1910); Going, *Wilmot*, ch. xxxvii; St. G. L. Sioussat, "Andrew Johnson and Homestead," *Miss. Valley Hist. Rev.*, V (1918), 253; W. W. Belcher, *Economic Rivalry St. Louis and Chicago* (1947), chs. i–ix; Riegel, *Western Railroads*, ch. v; V. S. Clark, "Manufacturing Development during the Civil War," *Military Historian and Economist*, III (1918), 92; Frederick Merk, "Eastern Antecedents of Grangers," *Ag. Hist.*, XXIII (1949), 1; Thomas Weber, *Northern Railroads in Civil War* (1952); F. P. Summers, *Baltimore and Ohio in Civil War* (1939). ❧ Social Conditions: M. B. Greenbie, *Lincoln's Daughters of Mercy* (1944); C. R. Fish, "Social Relief in Northwest," *Am. Hist. Rev.*, XXII (1917), 309; N. J. Ware, *Labor Movement in United States 1860–1895* (1929), chs. i, ii; J. P. Grossman, *William Sylvis* (1945), chs. i–vii; Slosson, *American Spirit in Education*, ch. xv; William Wood and R. H. Gabriel, *In Defense of Liberty* (1928); L. G. Vander Velde, *Presbyterian Churches* (1932); Sweet, *Methodism*, ch. xiv; B. W. Korn, *American Jewry and Civil War* (1951). ❧ Local Histories: J. R. Lane, *Political History of Connecticut during Civil War* (1941); Pearson, *Andrew*, I, chs. vi–viii, II; Hart, *Commonwealth History Massachusetts*, V, chs. xvii, xviii; E. E. Ware, *Political Opinion in Massachusetts during Civil War and Reconstruction* (1916); Folwell, *History of Minnesota*, II; Alexander, *History of New York*, III, chs. i–ix; Nevins, *Evening Post*, chs. xii, xiii; C. M. Knapp, *New Jersey Politics during Civil War* (1924), chs. iii–vi; E. M. Coulter, "Effects of Secession upon Mississippi Valley," *Miss. Valley Hist. Rev.*, III (1916), 275; Roseboom, *Civil War Era* (Wittke, *Ohio*, V), chs. xiii–xiv; Ambler, *West Virginia*, chs. xvii–xxii; A. A. Taylor, "Making West Virginia Free," *Jour. Negro Hist.*, VI (1921), 131; Cole, *Era of Civil War*, chs. xi–xvi; Kinsley, *Chicago Tribune*, I, pt. II, chs. i–viii; Frederick Merk, *Economic History of Wisconsin*; W. B. Rice, *Los Angeles Star* (1947), chs. xxii–xxvi; Margaret Leech, *Reveille in Washington* (1941).

Sources — Richardson, *Messages and Papers*, VI; Congressional debates and documents (§ 45); *Official Opinions of Attorneys-General*, X, XI; R. G. Thwaites, A. C. Tilton, and Frederick Merk, eds., *Civil War Messages of Wisconsin Governors* (1912); other state documents (§ 46); Frank Moore, ed., *Rebellion Record* (11 vols., 1861–65). ❧ Contemporary Writings: Sherman, *Recollections*, I, ch. xv; Lincoln, *Collected Works*; Welles, *Diary*, I, II; Buchanan, *Works*, XI; Blaine, *Twenty Years*, I, chs. xvii, xx, xxi, xxiii; William Salter, *James W. Grimes* (1876), 139; Coleman, *Crittenden*, II, ch. xviii; C. L. Vallandigham, *Record on Abolition, Union and Civil War* (1863); Seward, *Works*, V; Sumner, *Works*, V–IX; John Hay, *Lincoln and Civil War* (Tyler Dennett, ed., 1939); Cox, *Three Decades*, chs. xi–xii; Bates, "Diary"; Browning, *Diary*; Seward, *Reminiscences*, 155; H. W. Davis, *Speeches and Addresses* (1867); Franklin Pierce, "Papers," 110, 350; Julian, *Recollections*, chs. ix–xi; A. G. Riddle, *Recollections* (1895); Noah Brooks, *Washington in Lincoln's Time* (1895); F. B. Carpenter, *Inner Life of Abraham Lincoln. Six Months at the White House* (1867); Forbes, *Letters and Recollections*, I, chs. ix–xiii, II, xvi–xviii; K. P. Wormeley, *Other Side of War* (1888); C. J. Stillé, *History of United States Sanitary Commission* (1866); Lemuel Moss, *Annals of the Christian Commission* (1868).

Bibliography — Milton, *Conflict*, 399; Mott, *American Journalism*, 407.

184. THE SOUTHERN CONFEDERACY, 1861–1865

Summary — Formation: 1798–1860, antecedents (§§ 180–1); 1836, *The Partisan Leader*; 1861, Jan. 7, call by Alabama; Feb. 4, Montgomery Congress; Feb. 8, provisional constitution; Feb. 18, Davis inaugurated president; Mar. 11, permanent constitution submitted; 1862, Feb. 18, permanent constitution in force. — The Constitution: modeled on the federal Constitution; delegated powers; cabinet ministers in Congress; no protective tariffs or national internal improvements; veto of appropriation items; two-thirds vote for export tax and new states; slave trade prohibited; slavery, right of transit, and territorial slavery acknowledged; 1861, Mar. 21, Vice-President Stephens' "corner-stone" speech. — Administration: cabinet ministers; civil officials; Davis' predominance; rivalry of Stephens; secret sessions; no Supreme Court. — Finances: loans; foreign loans; paper money; requisition; taxes. — Conscription: successive acts; difficulty with Georgia; desertion; Unionist opposition. — Foreign relations (§ 187). — Relations with federal government: pirates and traitors; prisoners of war; border intercourse; attempts at peace negotiations. — Economic and social conditions: manufactures; transportation; exhaustion of the country; effect of the blockade. — Legal status: a government *de facto*; acts legally void; effect of Fourteenth Amendment (§§ 189, 190).

General — Coulter, *Confederate States*, chs. iii–viii, x–xv, xvii–xxii; Rhodes, *History*, III, 291, 320, 543, V, chs. xxviii, xxix; Schouler, *History*, VI, ch. i, § iii, ch. iii, § i; Cole, *Irrepressible Conflict*, chs. xii, xv; Randall, *Civil War and Reconstruction*, chs. xiii, xxix; Rhodes, *Civil War*, ch. xii; Milton, *Conflict*, chs. xvii, xxiv; Chadwick, *Causes of Civil War*, ch. xv; Brown, *Lower South*, pt. 3; N. W. Stephenson, *Day of Confederacy* (1919); S. S. Cox, *Three Decades*, ch. xv; D. S. Freeman, *South to Posterity* (1939); *South in Building of Nation*, IV, V.

Special — Confederate Government: W. M. Robinson, *Justice in Grey* (1941); Carpenter, *South as Conscious Minority* (1930), ch. vii; Upton, *Military Policy*, chs. xxx, xxxi; F. L. Owsley, *States Rights in Confederacy* (1925); C. H. Wesley, *Collapse of Confederacy* (1937); R. W. Patrick, *Jefferson Davis and His Cabinet* (1944); J. L. M. Curry, *Government of Confederate States* (1901); E. A. Pollard, *Lost Cause* (1866), chs. v, vii, x. ❧ Local histories: W. L. Fleming, *Civil War and Reconstruction in Alabama* (1905), pts. 1, 2; T. C. Bryan, *Confederate Georgia* (1953); Caskey, *Secession and Restoration in Louisiana*, chs. iii–vii; Shugg, *Class Struggle in Louisiana*, ch. vi; J. K. Bettersworth, *Confederate Mississippi* (1943); J. W. Patton, *Unionism and Reconstruction in Tennessee* (1934); Claude Elliott, "Union Sentiment in Texas," *Southwestern Hist. Quar.*, L (1947), 449; § 62. ❧ Biographies: B. J. Hendrick, *Statesmen of Lost Cause* (1939); Bradford, *Confederate Portraits*; Dodd, *Davis*, chs. xiii–xxi; V. H. Davis, *Davis*, II; Meade, *Benjamin*, chs. ix–xvii; H. M. Rice, *Life of Jonathan M. Bennett* (1943); Ranck, *Brown*, ch. vii; Coulter, *Brownlow*, chs. vii–xiii; Merritt, *Hammond*, ch. vii; Flippin, *Johnson*, ch. vii; Capers, *Memminger*, 300; von Abele, *Stephens*, ch. v; Phillips, *Toombs*, ch. x; Du Bose, *Yancey*, chs. xxv–xxvii. ❧ Economic and Social Conditions: J. C. Schwab, *Confederate States* (1901); Russel, *Southern Sectionalism*, ch. x; Ratner, *American Taxation*, ch. vi; J. L. Sellers, "Economic Incidence of War in South," *Miss. Valley Hist. Rev.*, XIV (1927), 179; R. E. Riegel, "Federal Operation of Southern Railroads," *ibid.*, IX (1922), 126; R. C. Black, *Railroads of the Confederacy* (1952); R. S. Cotterill, "Southern Railroads," *ibid.*, X (1924), 396; C. W. Ramsdell, "Confederate Government and Railroads," *Am. Hist. Rev.*, XXII (1917), 794, and "Control of Manufacturing," *Miss. Valley Hist. Rev.*, VIII (1921), 231; Ella Lonn, *Salt in the Confederacy* (1933); A. S. Roberts, "Federal Government and Confederate Cotton," *Am. Hist. Rev.*, XXXII (1927), 262; F. B. Simkins and J. W. Patton, *Women of Confederacy* (1940); Ella Lonn, *Foreigners in Confederacy* (1940); A. H. Abel, *American Indian as Slaveholder and Secessionist* (2 vols., 1915–19); B. I. Wiley, *Plain People of Confederacy* (1943); also § 188. ❧ Conscription and Disloyalty: A. B. Moore, *Conscription and Conflict in the Confederacy* (1924); Wright, *Conscientious Objectors*; Bessie Martin, *Desertion of Alabama Troops* (1932); G. L. Tatum, *Disloyalty in Confederacy* (1934); Lonn, *Desertion*, chs. i–viii; A. S. Roberts, "Peace Movement in North Carolina," *Miss. Valley Hist. Rev.*, XI (1924), 190; L. H. Gipson, "Collapse of Confederacy," *Miss. Valley Hist. Rev.*, IV (1918), 437. ❧ Military Affairs (§ 185). ❧ Diplomacy (§ 187).

Sources — Documents: *American Annual Cyclopedia*, 1861–65; Stephens, *War between States*, II, 714; Edward McPherson, *Political History of United States during the Rebellion* (1865); Richardson, *Messages and Papers*, VI, 237, 260, and *Messages and Papers of Confederacy*, I; *Journal of Congress of Confederate States*; D. S. Freeman, ed., *Calendar of Confederate Papers* (1908); *War of Rebellion, Official Records*, 1 ser., 2 ser., 4 ser.; 39 Cong., 1 sess., *H. Ex. Doc.*, XII, No. 3; Moore, *Rebellion Record*; Southern

Hist. Soc., *Papers;* J. M. Matthews, ed., *Statutes at Large of the Confederate Congress* (1862–64); C. W. Ramsdell, ed., *Laws and Joint Resolutions of Last Session* (1941); §§ 45, 46; Moore, *Digest of International Law,* §§ 22, 38, 66; Mode, *Source Book for American Church History,* ch. xxviii. ⫧ Contemporary Writings: Jefferson Davis, *Confederate Government,* I, II; *Jefferson Davis, Constitutionalist,* V, VI; Stephens, *War between States;* Ruffin, *Papers,* III, 158; J. H. Reagan, *Memoirs* (1906), chs. ix–xvi; G. C. Eggleston, *Rebel's Recollections* (1875); J. B. Jones, *Rebel Diary;* Wise, *End of Era;* Chestnut, *Diary from Dixie;* S. A. Pryor, *Reminiscences of Peace and War* (1905), chs. ix–xxvi; E. F. Andrews, *War Time Journal of a Georgia Girl* (1908); C. R. Holmes, ed., *The Burckmyer Letters, 1863–65* (1926); T. C. De Leon, *Four Years in Rebel Capitals* (1890); J. L. Peyton, *American Crisis* (2 vols., 1867), I, chs. i–v; Dabney, *Defence of Virginia;* Heros von Borcke, *Memoirs of Confederate War for Independence* (2 vols., 1866; 2 ed., 1938); Charles Girard, *États Confédérés d'Amérique* (1864); Cox, *Three Decades,* ch. xv. ⫧ Newspapers (§ 53): especially *Richmond Examiner; Richmond Enquirer; Charleston Mercury; Charleston Courier.*

Bibliography — Schwab, *Confederate States,* App. 2; *South in Building of Nation,* IV, 498, 499, V, 151, 426, 457, 482, 497, 677; H. A. Morrison, "Bibliography of Official Literature of Rebellion," Bibliog. Soc. of Am., *Proc. and Papers,* III (1908), 92; Coulter, *Confederate States,* 569; Mode, *Source Book for American Church History,* 604; Cole, *Irrepressible Conflict,* 446; C. N. Baxter and J. M. Dearborn, *Confederate Literature* (1917).

185. MILITARY EVENTS OF THE CIVIL WAR, 1861–1865

Summary — Preparations: regular army, navy; resignations of officers; military stores; fortifications; theater of war (§ 179); effect of Fort Sumter episode (§ 182). — Eastern campaigns: 1861, July 21, Bull Run; 1862, May–July, Peninsula campaign; Aug. 24, second Bull Run; Sept. 16, 17, Antietam; Dec. 13, Fredericksburg; 1863, May 3–5, Chancellorsville; July 1–3, Gettysburg; 1864, May 5–9, Wilderness; May–June, Grant's Virginia campaign; June, investment of Petersburg and Richmond; Aug.–Nov., Sheridan's Valley campaigns. — Western campaigns: 1861, Missouri held; Nov. 7, Belmont; 1862, Feb. 6–16, Forts Henry and Donelson; Apr. 6, 7, Pittsburg Landing; Oct. 8, Perryville; Dec. 31, Stone River; 1863, July 4, Vicksburg surrenders; Sept. 19, 20, Chickamauga; Nov. 23–25, Chattanooga; 1864, May–July, Sherman's Georgia campaign; Sept. 2, Atlanta; Nov.–Dec., march to the sea; Dec. 15, 16, Nashville. — Naval warfare: 1861–65, blockade; 1862, Mar. 9, 10, *Merrimac* and *Monitor;* Apr. 23, New Orleans; 1863, July, Mississippi opened; 1864, June 19, *Kearsarge* and *Alabama;* Aug. 4–22, Mobile. — Finale: 1865, Jan.–Apr., Sherman's northward march; Apr. 2, 3, Richmond abandoned; Apr. 9, Lee surrenders at Appomattox; Apr. 26, Johnson surrenders; dissolution of Southern organization; 1865–66, disbandment of Northern armies (§ 184).

General — Channing, *History,* I, chs. xi, xiii, xv, xvi; Rhodes, *History,* III–V, and *Civil War,* chs. iii, v, vi, viii–x, xii, xiv; Cole, *Irrepressible Conflict,* ch. xv; Schouler, *History,* VI; Milton, *Conflict,* chs. iii–v, ix, x, xiv–xx, xxi–xxiv; Randall, *Civil War and Reconstruction,* chs. x–xii, xx–xxiv; Coulter, *Confederate States,* chs. xvi, xix; Shotwell, *Civil War,* I, chs. xii–xxiv, xxvi–xxix, xxxi, II, xxxii–xxxvi, xxxviii–xli, xliii–lv; John Formby, *American Civil War;* Ropes and Livermore, *Civil War;* Comte de Paris, *Civil War;* Fletcher, *American War,* I–III; C. A. Evans, ed., *Confederate Military History* (12 vols., 1899); R. V. Johnson and C. C. Buel, eds., *Battles and Leaders of Civil War* (4 vols., 1887); B. J. Lossing, *History of Civil War* (1912).

Special — War on Land: K. P. Williams, *Lincoln Finds a General* (3 vols., 1949–52); C. E. Macartney, *Lincoln and His Generals* (1925); T. H. Williams, *Lincoln and His Generals* (1952); Bruce Catton, *Mr. Lincoln's Army* (1951), and *Glory Road* (1952); Sir Frederick Maurice, *Statesmen and Soldiers of Civil War* (1926); D. S. Freeman, *Lee's Lieutenants* (3 vols., 1942–44), and *Lee;* F. S. Haydon, *Aeronautics in Union and Confederate Armies* (1941); E. S. Miers and R. A. Brown, *Gettysburg* (1948); S. F.

Horn, *Army of Tennessee* (1941); T. R. Hay, *Hood's Tennessee Campaign* (1929); John Bigelow, *Chancellorsville* (1910); R. M. Johnston, *Bull Run* (1912); C. C. Anderson, *Fighting by Southern Federals* (1912); J. F. C. Fuller, *Generalship of Grant* (1929); and *Grant and Lee* (1933); Badeau, *Grant;* A. L. Conger, *Rise of U. S. Grant* (1931); Lloyd Lewis, *Sherman* (1932); Liddell Hart, *Sherman;* Hergesheimer, *Sheridan;* Myers, *McClellan;* Seitz, *Bragg;* F. H. Harrington, *Fighting Politician N. P. Banks* (1948); A. D. H. Smith, *Old Fuss and Feathers* (Scott), bk. 5; Cleaves, *Rock of Chickamauga* (G. E. Thomas); Nevins, *Frémont*, chs. xxix, xxxii; Basso, *Beauregard;* Lytle, *Forrest;* E. W. Sheppard, *Bedford Forrest* (1930); J. A. Wyeth, *Nathan Bedford Forrest* (1899); U. R. Brooks, *Butler and His Cavalry* (1909); Harrison Trow, *Charles W. Quantrell* (1923); Henderson, *Stonewall Jackson;* Thomason, *Stuart;* A. M. Stickles, *Simon Bolivar Buckner* (1940), chs. vi–xvi; H. J. Eckenrode and Bryan Conrad, *James Longstreet* (1936); Kinsley, *Chicago Tribune*, I, pt. 2, chs. xv–xxxii; Fletcher, *Oberlin*, II, chs. xlix–li. ❡ War on Sea: Sprout, *Rise of American Naval Power*, ch. x; Westcott, *American Sea Power*, chs. viii–xiii; Knox, *United States Navy*, chs. xvii–xviii; J. D. Hill, *Sea Dogs of Sixties* (1935); F. B. C. Bradlee, *Blockade Running during Civil War* (1925); J. T. Scharf, *History of Confederate Navy* (1894); J. P. Baxter, *Introduction of Ironclad Warship* (1933); R. S. McCordock, *Yankee Cheese Box* (1938); S. F. Horn, *Gallant Rebel: Cruise of Shenandoah* (1947); W. M. Robinson, *Confederate Privateers* (1928); Meriwether, *Semmes;* Lewis, *Farragut*, II; W. M. Robinson, "*Alabama-Kearsarge* Battle," Essex Inst., *Hist. Coll.*, LX (1924), 97, 209. ❡ Other Biographies: (§§ 183, 184); Sandburg, *Lincoln*, IV, chs. xxxvii–xlvi, V, li, VI, lxv–lxvii; Nicolay and Hay, *Lincoln*, IV–IX; C. R. Ballard, *Military Genius of Lincoln* (1926); W. E. Smith, *Blair Family*, II, chs. xxix–xxx; Gorham, *Stanton*, pts. 4–8; Meredith, *Lincoln's Camera Man Brady.* ❡ Other Subjects: B. I. Wiley, *Life of Johnny Reb* (1943), and *Life of Billy Yank* (1952); G. W. Adams, *Doctors in Blue* (1952), and "Confederate Medicine," *Jour. Southern Hist.*, VI (1939), 151; Barton, *Barton;* C. J. Stillé, *History of the United States Sanitary Commission* (1866); W. B. Hesseltine, *Civil War Prisons* (1930); Southern Hist. Soc., *Papers.* ❡ Pictures: Miller, *Photographic History of Civil War;* David Donald, ed., *Divided We Fought* (1952); A. H. Guernsey and H. M. Alden, *Harper's Pictorial History of Great Rebellion* (1866). ❡ Statistics: B. A. Gould, *Investigations in Military Statistics* (1869); J. H. Baxter, *Statistics, Medical and Anthropological, of Provost-Marshal-General's Bureau* (2 vols., 1875); W. F. Fox, *Regimental Loss* (1889); Livermore, *Numbers and Losses.* ❡ Maps: Ropes and Livermore, *Civil War;* Comte de Paris, *Civil War, Atlas; War of the Rebellion, Official Records, Atlas;* Milton, *Conflict*, 393; Rhodes, *History*, III–V; Paullin, *Atlas*, plates 163–4; Shepherd, *Atlas*, 208; see also: C. E. LeGear, "Hotchkiss Map Collection," Library of Congress, *Quar. Jour. of Acquisitions*, VI (1948), 16.

Sources — Debates: Congressional Globe, 37, 38 Congs. ❡ Congressional Investigations: "Report on Conduct of the War," (8 vols., 1863–66), 37 Cong., 3 sess., *Sen. Report*, No. 108, 38 Cong., 2 sess., *Sen. Report*, No. 142. ❡ Reports of the Secretaries of War and Navy: 37 Cong., 2 sess., *Sen. Ex. Doc.*, II–V, 37 Cong., 3 sess., *H. Ex. Doc.*, IV–VIII, 38 Cong., 1 sess., *H. Ex. Doc.*, IV, V, VII, IX, XIII, XV; 38 Cong., 2 sess., *H. Ex. Doc.*, VI, VII, XII–XIV, *Sen. Ex. Doc.*, 38 Cong., special sess., *Sen. Ex. Doc.*, 39 Cong., 1 sess., *H. Ex. Doc.*, III, V, XII–XVI. ❡ Documents: Richardson, *Messages and Papers*, VI; 37 Cong., 2 sess., *H. Ex. Doc.*, I, V, VII, IX, X, 3 sess., *H. Ex. Doc.*, IV; 38 Cong., 1 sess., *Sen. Report, H. Report*, I, Nos. 65, 67, 2 sess., *Sen. Report, H. Report, H. Misc. Doc.*, I, No. 39; M. R. Robinton, *Introduction to Papers of New York Prize Court* (1945); McPherson, *Rebellion*, 417; Moore, *Rebellion Record;* G. B. McClellan, *Army of the Potomac Report* (1864); *War of the Rebellion, Official Records; Official Records of Union and Confederate Navies;* J. K. Barnes, *et al.*, *Medical and Surgical History of War of Rebellion* (6 vols., 1870–88). ❡ Works of Statesmen: Lincoln, *Collected Works;* Welles, *Diary*, I, II; Blaine, *Twenty Years*, I, chs. xv–xvii, xxiii–xxxv; Cox, *Three Decades*, chs. viii–x; Jefferson Davis, *Confederate Government*, I, 352, II; Jefferson Davis, *Constitutionalist*, V, VI; G. V. Fox, *Confidential Correspondence* (R. M. Thompson and Richard Wainwright, eds., 2 vols., 1918–19); Bates, "Diary"; §§ 183, 184. ❡ Works of Commanders: Grant, *Memoirs;* Sherman, *Memoirs*, I, II, and *Home Letters*, chs. vii–x; Sheridan, *Memoirs;* McClellan, *McClellan's Own Story;* Meade, *Life and Letters*, I, pts. 4–6, II; J. D. Cox, *Military Reminiscences* (1900); J. M. Schofield, *Forty-*

six Years in Army (1897), chs. iii–xviii; Howard, *Autobiography*, chs. viii–xlv; Butler, *Correspondence;* Schurz, *Reminiscences*, II, chs. vii, viii, III, chs. i, ii, iv; Lee, *Recollections;* Horace Porter, *Campaigning with Grant* (1897); Heros von Borcke, *Dispatches to Jefferson Davis* (D. S. Freeman, ed., 1915), and *Memoirs;* J. E. Johnston, *Military Operations;* G. H. Gordon, *War Diary* (1882); J. B. Hood, *Advance and Retreat* (1880); James Longstreet, *Manassas to Appomattox* (1896); E. P. Alexander, *Military Memoirs* (1907); Richard Taylor, *Destruction and Reconstruction* (1879), chs. ii–xiv; Semmes, *Memoirs;* Sedgwick, *Correspondence*, II; Pickett, *Soldier of South;* J. S. Mosby, *War Reminiscences* (1887). ❡ Narratives of Participants: C. F. Adams, *Autobiography*, ch. iv; Dana, *Recollections;* O. W. Holmes, Jr., *Touched with Fire: Civil War Letters* (1946); J. C. Gray and J. C. Ropes, *War Letters* (1927); P. R. de Trobriand, *Four Years with Army of Potomac* (1889); Bryan Grimes, *Extracts of Letters* (Pulaski Cowper, ed., 1883); Carlton McCarthy, *Detailed Minutiae of a Soldier's Life* (1882); J. C., C. H., and H. R. Dalton, *Letters* (1923); D. D. Porter, *Incidents and Anecdotes of Civil War* (1885); G. H. Perkins, *Letters* (1886); H. M. Calvert, *Reminiscences of a Boy in Blue* (1920); W. A. Cate, ed., *Two Soldiers* (1938); John Gibbon, *Personal Recollections of Civil War* (1928); Theodore Lyman, *Meade's Headquarters, 1863–1865* (G. R. Agassiz, ed., 1922); E. P. McKinney, *Life in Tent and Field* (1922); S. E. Nicholas, *"Your Soldier Boy Samuel"* (C. S. Underhill, ed., 1929); J. K. Hosmer, *Color-Guard* (1864); G. A. Townsend, *Campaigns of a Non-Combatant* (1866); J. H. Browne, *Four Years in Secessia* (1865); J. H. Chamberlayne, *Letters and Papers* (1932); R. A. Shotwell, *Papers* (J. G. deR. Hamilton, ed., 3 vols., 1929–36), I, II; M. B. Toney, *Privations of a Private* (1907); W. A. Fletcher, *Rebel Private* (1908); A. B. Ford, *Life in Confederate Army* (1910); Frank Mixon, *Reminiscences* (1910); E. A. Moore, *Story of a Cannoneer* (1907); W. B. Hazen, *Narrative of Military Service* (1885); J. E. Cooke, *Wearing the Gray* (1867); Robert Stiles, *Four Years under Marse Robert* (1903); Eggleston, *Rebel's Recollections;* Frank Wilkeson, *Recollections of a Private Soldier* (1886); W. H. Morgan, *Personal Reminiscences* (1911); C. H. Lynch, *Civil War Diary* (1915); John Wilkinson, *Narrative of a Blockade Runner* (1877); J. W. Morgan, *Recollections of a Rebel Reefer* (1917); T. E. Taylor, *Running the Blockade* (1896); F. E. Vandiver, ed., *Confederate Blockade Running through Bermuda* (1947); M. A. DeW. Howe, *Marching with Sherman* (1927); Otto Eisenschiml and Ralph Newman, eds., *American Iliad* (1947); H. S. Commager, *Blue and Gray* (2 vols., 1951). ❡ Chaplains, Doctors, and Nurses: Cornelia Hancock, *South after Gettysburg* (H. S. Jacquette, ed., 1937); Jonathan Letterman, *Medical Recollections* (1886); J. H. Brinton, *Personal Memoirs* (1914); F. E. Daniel, *Recollections of Rebel Surgeon* (1901); J. A. Wyeth, *With Sabre and Scalpel* (1914); W. H. Reed, *Hospital Life* (1866); C. A. Humphreys, *Field Camp, Hospital and Prison* (1918); Mary Phinney, *Adventures of an Army Nurse* (1903). ❡ Foreign Observers: W. H. Russell, *My Diary, North and South* (1863); S. P. Day, *Down South* (2 vols., 1862); Dicey, *Six Months in Federal States;* Fremantle, *Three Months in Southern States.* ❡ Illustrative Material: *Harper's Weekly; Frank Leslie's.* See also: §§ 63, 64, 65. ❡ Periodicals: see §§ 30, 40, 52. ❡ Newspapers: see § 53, especially *New York Tribune, New York Times, New York World, New York Evening Post, Springfield Republican, Boston Advertiser, Chicago Tribune, Cincinnati Commercial.* — See also: § 188.

Bibliography — U. S. War Department, *Bibliography of State Participation in Civil War* (1913); Milton, *Conflict*, 399; Cole, *Irrepressible Conflict*, 444; Channing, *History* VI, 331, 395; Poore, *Catalogue of Government Publications*, 790; J. R. Bartlett, *Literature of the Rebellion* (1866); Larned, *Literature of American History*, 213; Wiley, *Johnny Reb.*

186. FINANCING THE CIVIL WAR, 1861–1865

Summary — Earlier financial conditions (§§ 169, 178). — Financial status in 1861: outgo; taxes; debt; estimates. — Financial administration: 1861, Mar. 5, Secretary Chase; 1864, July 4, Secretary Fessenden; finance committees. — Taxes: import duties raised; gold duties; internal revenue acts; stamp duties; direct tax; income tax; miscellaneous taxes; proceeds. — Legal tender: Chase's policy; legal tender acts; amount issued; 1862–

79, gold speculation (§§ 191, 201); 1870–71, 1884, Supreme Court decisions (§§ 191, 201). — Loans: "seven-thirties," "six-forties," "five-twenties"; amount of principal; proceeds; gold interest; actual interest; transfer of greenbacks. — National banks: old state banks (§ 169); 1863, Feb. 25, 1864, June 3, National Bank Acts; number of banks; services to the government; circulation; exclusion of state bank notes. — Expenditures: military; civil; Pacific railroads (§ 197); methods, accounts; state accounts. — Postwar finances (§ 191). — Land policy: earlier history (§§ 158, 170, 171, 174); relation to railroad policy; 1854, Graduation Act; 1862, May 20, Homestead Act; July 2, Morrill Land Grant Act for agricultural education; later policy (§ 196).

General — Rhodes, *History*, III–V; Randall, *Civil War and Reconstruction*, ch. xviii; Milton, *Conflict*, ch. xi; Stephenson, *Lincoln and Union*, ch. x; Shotwell, *Civil War*, II, ch. xxxvii; Fish, *American Civil War*, ch. xv; Schouler, *History*, VI, 152, 282; Sumner, *American Currency*, 189; Stanwood, *Tariff Controversies*, II, ch. xiii; Taussig, *Tariff History*, pt. 2, ch. i; Dewey, *Financial History*, § 114, chs. xii, xiii; Ratner, *American Taxation*, chs. iv, v; Hibbard, *Public Land Policies*, chs. xvii–xviii.

Special — Nicolay and Hay, *Lincoln*, VI, chs. xi, xii, IX, ch. iv; Sandburg, *Lincoln*, IV, ch. xlviii; Hart, *Chase*, 215, 274; Parker, *Morrill*, chs. v, vi; Woodburn, *Stevens*, ch. xi; Oberholtzer, *Cooke*, I, chs. iv–xii; Larson, *Jay Cooke*; Fessenden, *Fessenden*, I, chs. iv–vi; Comte de Paris, *Civil War*, II, 654, III, 403; J. L. Sellers, "Interpretation of Civil War Finance," *Am. Hist. Rev.*, XXX (1925), 282; A. M. Davis, *Origin of the National Banking System* (1910–11); Fite, *Social and Industrial Conditions*, ch. i; T. J. Middleton, "Andrew Johnson and Homestead Law," *Sewanee Rev.*, XV (1907), 316; E. J. James, *Origins of Land Grant Act of 1862* (1910); W. C. Mitchell, *History of Greenbacks* (1903); D. C. Barrett, *Greenbacks and Resumption* (1931); § 183.

Sources — Debates: *Congressional Globe*, 37 Cong., 39 Cong. ❡ Finance Reports: 37 Cong., 2 sess., *Sen. Ex. Doc.*, No. 2, 3 sess., *Sen. Ex. Doc.*, No. 1; 38 Cong., 1 sess., *H. Ex. Doc.*, VI, No. 3, VII, Nos. 4, 8, IX, No. 36, XV, No. 84; 38 Cong., 2 sess., *H. Ex. Doc.*, VII, VIII, XIII, No. 73; 39 Cong., 1 sess., *H. Ex. Doc.*, VI, XII, No. 74. ❡ Other Documents: 37 Cong., 2 sess., *H. Ex. Doc.*, I, III, Nos. 36, 44, IX, No. 122, 3 sess., *H. Ex. Doc.*, V, No. 25; 38 Cong., 1 sess., *Sen. Ex. Doc.*, I, Nos. 35, 50, 52; *H. Ex. Doc.*, No. 66, *H. Misc. Doc.*, III, No. 28, *H. Report*, II, No. 140, 2 sess., *H. Ex. Doc.*, VIII, No. 16; 39 Cong., 1 sess., *Sen. Misc. Doc.*, Nos. 100, 112, 117; *H. Ex. Doc.*, VII, No. 26, XII, No. 95; 48 Cong., 2 sess., *H. Ex. Doc.*, XVII, No. 4; 51 Cong., 2 sess., *Sen. Report*, No. 2130; Richardson, *Messages and Papers*, VI; *American Annual Cyclopedia*, 1861–65; McPherson, *Rebellion*, 358. ❡ Statutes: *Statutes at Large*, XII, XIII; Dunbar, *Currency, Finance, and Banking*, 155; Huntington and Mawhinney, *Laws Concerning Money*, 161, 327, 518, 634; MacDonald, *Select Statutes*, Nos. 3, 4, 10, 14, 16, 19, 25, 29, 30, 33, 37, 39. ❡ Contemporary Writings: John Sherman, *Recollections*, I, chs. xii, xiii, and *Selected Speeches* (1879); McCulloch, *Men and Measures*, chs. xv–xvii; R. B. Warden, *Chase* (1874), chs. xxvi–xlii; Schuckers, *Chase*, chs. xxx, xxxvii–xxxix; Chase, "Diary," 312; Cox, *Three Decades*, ch. vii; Blaine, *Twenty Years*, I, chs. xviii, xix, xxii; L. E. Chittenden, *Personal Reminiscences* (1893), chs. xxxiii, xxxiv; Sumner, *Works*, VI, 319, VII, 84, 148, 166, VIII, 419, 471, IX, 26, 229, 336; § 183.

Bibliography — Dewey, *Financial History*, §§ 116, 126; Larned, *Literature of American History*, 319; Mitchell, *Greenbacks*; indexes to public documents (§ 41); Meyer and Slade, *References on Monetary Question*, 123.

187. THE CIVIL WAR AND INTERNATIONAL RELATIONS, 1861–1865

Summary — Earlier foreign affairs (§ 173). — Administration of foreign affairs: Lincoln; Secretary Seward; Senator Sumner; controversies with Navy Department; foreign representatives. — Blockade: 1861, Apr. 19, 27, Lincoln's proclamations; blockade runners (§ 184); captures (§ 185); effect on foreign cotton industry. — Recognition of belligerency: precedents; 1861, May 13, English neutrality proclamation; others; independence of Confederacy not recognized; 1863, Dec. 3, the Pope's letter to Davis. — Trent affair: 1861, Nov. 8, seizure of Slidell and Mason by Wilkes; Dec. 23, English ultimatum; Dec. 25, cabinet agrees to surrender Mason and Slidell. — Alabama question: 1861, May 13, Minister C. F. Adams in London; Confederate sympathies of the governing class and English colonies; Union sympathies of the working class; 1862, Feb. 8, to Mar. 22, Adams' protest against the *Oreto* (*Florida*); June 23 to July 29, Adams' protest against the "290" (*Alabama*); 1863, the *Japan* (*Georgia*); 1864, the *Sea King* (*Shenandoah*); depredations of the cruisers (§§ 184, 185); effect on American merchant marine; Alabama claims; question of indirect damages (§ 194). — Captures of English vessels: blockade-runners (§ 185); "continuous voyages"; Stephen Hart (*Bermuda*), Springbok, and *Peterhoff* cases. — Mexico: 1861, English, French, and Spanish convention; 1862, French invasion; 1863, Sept. 20, Seward's protest; 1864, Apr. 4, House resolution on monarchical governments; Maximilian's empire; 1865–67, Napoleon III compelled to withdraw (§ 194).

General — Channing, *History*, VI, ch. xii; Hosmer, *Appeal to Arms*, ch. xx; Schouler, *History*, VI, ch. i, §§ vi, xiii, ch. ii, § vi; Rhodes, *History*, III, 417, 519, IV, 76, ch. xxii, V, 205, and *Civil War*, chs. ii, vii; Randall, *Civil War and Reconstruction*, chs. xix, xxviii; Milton, *Conflict*, ch. vi; Fish, *American Civil War*, ch. vii; Stephenson, *Lincoln and Union*, ch. xii; Coulter, *Confederate States*, ch. ix; F. L. Owsley, *King Cotton Diplomacy* (1931); J. M. Callahan, *Diplomatic History of Southern Confederacy* (1901); Bemis, *American Secretaries of State*, VII, and *Diplomatic History*, chs. xxi–xxii; Bailey, *Diplomatic History*, ch. xxi–xxiii; Goebel, *Recognition Policy*, ch. vii.

Special — Biographies: Nicolay and Hay, *Lincoln*, IV, ch. xv, V, ch. ii, VI, chs. ii, iv, VII, ch. xiv, VIII, ch. x; Jay Monaghan, *Diplomat in Carpet Slippers* (1945); Randall, *Lincoln*, II, ch. xvi; Sandburg, *Lincoln*, IV, ch. xxxvi; Bancroft, *Seward*, II, chs. xxx–xxxiii, xxxv, xxxvi, xxxviii; C. F. Adams, *Charles Francis Adams* (1900), 144; Pierce, *Sumner*, IV, chs. xliv–xlviii; Fuess, *Schurz*, ch. viii; Clapp, *John Bigelow*; T. W. L. Newton, *Lord Lyons* (1913), I, chs. ii–iv; Mason, *Mason*, chs. viii–xx; Sears, *Slidell*, ch. viii; Beckles Willson, *Slidell in Paris* (1932); E. C. Corti, *Maximilian* (2 vols., 1928). ❦ Neutrality: E. D. Adams, *Great Britain and American Civil War* (2 vols., 1925); J. P. Baxter, "British Government and Neutral Rights," *Am. Hist. Rev.*, XXXIV (1928), 9, 77; *Cambridge History British Foreign Policy* (1923), II, III; F. L. Owsley, "America and Freedom of Seas," Craven, *Essays in Honor of Dodd*, 196; M. L. Bonham, *British Consuls in Confederacy* (1911); *History of* [London] *Times* (1935–47), II, ch. xviii; Brougham Villiers and W. H. Chesson, *Anglo-American Relations, 1861–65* (1919); T. L. Harris, *Trent Affair* (1896); Albion and Pope, *Sea Lanes in Wartime*, ch. vi; Briggs, *Doctrine of Continuous Voyage*; L. B. Schmidt, "Influence of Wheat and Cotton on Anglo-American Relations," *Iowa Jour. of Hist. and Pol.*, XVI (1918), 400; Eli Ginzberg, "Economics of British Neutrality," *Ag. Hist.*, X (1936), 147; M. P. Clausen, "Peace Factors in Anglo-American Relations," *Miss. Valley Hist. Rev.*, XXVI (1940), 511. ❦ Foreign Opinion: §§ 182–5; H. D. Jordan and E. J. Pratt, *European Opinion on the American Civil War* (1931). ❦ Mexican Affair: Perkins, *Monroe Doctrine, 1826–67* (1933), chs. v–viii; Callahan, *American Foreign Policy in Mexican Relations*, chs. viii, ix; H. M. Hyde, *Mexican Empire* (1946); Carreño, *Diplomacia*, chs. x–xiii; F. E. Lally, *French Opposition to Mexican Policy* (1931); S. A. MacCorkle, *American Policy of Recognition towards Mexico* (1933); Rippy, *United States and Mexico*, chs. xiii, xiv; H. W. Casper, *American Attitudes toward Napoleon III* (1947); White, *American Opinion of France*, ch. v; Ollinger Crenshaw, "Knights of the Golden Circle," *Am. Hist. Rev.*, XLVII (1941), 23. ❦ Others: Moore, *Arbitrations*, I, ch. xiv; Treat, *Diplomatic Relations between United States and Japan*, chs. vi–xi; Shippee, *Canadian-American Relations*, chs. vi–viii; Brebner, *North Atlantic Triangle*, ch. ix; Callahan, *American Foreign Policy in Canadian Relations*, chs. xii, xiii; J. W. Headley, *Confederate Operations in Canada* (1906), chs. viii–xxix; John Bigelow, *France and Confederate Navy* (1888); Gazley, *American Opinion of German Unification*, chs. vii–viii; H. L. Ferris, "Relations of United States with South America during Civil War," *Hispanic-Am. Hist. Rev.*, XX (1941), 51; Hill, *United States and Brazil*, chs. vi, vii.

Sources — Diplomatic Correspondence: *Foreign Relations*, 1861–64; *Official Records of Union and Confederate Navies*, 2 ser., III; 37 Cong., 2 sess., *Sen. Ex. Doc.*, I, 3 sess., *Sen. Ex. Doc.*, I; 38 Cong., 1 sess., *H. Ex. Doc.*, I, II, 2 sess., *H. Ex. Doc.* I–IV; 39 Cong., 1 sess., *H. Ex. Doc.*, I; *British and Foreign State Papers*, LV. ⟐ Other Official Documents: Richardson, *Messages and Papers*, VI, and *Messages and Papers of Confederacy*, II; Miller, *Treaties*, VIII; 37 Cong., 2 sess., *H. Ex. Doc.*, III, No. 46, VIII, Nos. 100, 104, *H. Report*, III, No. 122, *Sen. Ex. Doc.*, IV, Nos. 8, 14, 18, V, No. 57, 3 sess., *H. Ex. Doc.*, V, No. 23, VI, No. 54, *Sen. Ex. Doc.*, Nos. 27, 49, 50; 38 Cong., 1 sess., *H. Ex. Doc.*, VII, No. 10, XV, No. 92, *Sen. Ex. Doc.*, I, Nos. 30, 47, 54, 2 sess., *Sen. Ex. Doc.*, I, Nos. 2, 33; 39 Cong., 1 sess., *H. Ex. Doc.*, VII, No. 36, *H. Report*, I, No. 100, *Sen. Ex. Doc.*, I, No. 5; *Case of the United States before* [Geneva] *Tribunal of Arbitration* (1872). ⟐ Other Collections: Carlton Savage, *Policy of United States toward Maritime Commerce in War* (1934), I, ch. xi; MacDonald, *Select Statutes*, No. 34; McPherson, *Rebellion*, 150, 338; Moore, *Rebellion Record*, Sup. I; Moore, *Digest of International Law*, § 860, chs. xxvi–xxviii; Bartlett, *American Diplomacy*, chs. xvi, xvii; *American Annual Cyclopedia*, 1861–64; Pitt Cobbett, *Leading Cases on International Law* (5 ed., 1931), I, §§ 32–34, II; M. O. Hudson, *Cases on International Law* (2 ed., 1936), chs. ii, xv. ⟐ Contemporary Writings: Lincoln, *Collected Works;* Seward, *Works*, V; Conway, *Autobiography*, I, ch. xxvi; John Bright, *Speeches on American Question* (1865); Jefferson Davis, *Confederate Government*, II, 245, 367; Gideon Welles, *Lincoln and Seward*, (1874), and *Diary*, I, II; C. G. Loring and E. W. Field, *Correspondence on Present Relations between Great Britain and the United States* (1862); Bigelow, *Retrospections*, I–III; S. A. Goddard, *Letters on American Rebellion* (1870); Cox, *Three Decades*, chs. xiii, xiv; C. F. and Henry Adams, *Cycle of Letters;* Sumner, *Works*, VI–IX; Schurz, *Reminiscences*, II, 273; Forbes, *Letters and Recollections*, II, chs. xiv, xv; Benjamin Moran, "Extracts from Diary," *Mass. Hist. Soc., Proc.*, XLVIII (1915), 431; *Jefferson Davis, Constitutionalist*, V, VI; Lord John Russell, *Later Correspondence* (1925), II, 317; "Letters of Richard Cobden to Charles Sumner, 1862–1865," *Am. Hist. Rev.*, II (1897), 306; Henry Adams, *Education*, chs. viii–xi; Karl Marx and Frederick Engels, *Civil War in United States* (1937); L. M. Case, ed., *French Opinion on United States and Mexico* (1936); F. A. Golder, ed., "American Civil War through Eyes of a Russian Diplomat," *Am. Hist. Rev.*, XXVI (1921), 454; C. F. Adams, "Trent Affair," *Mass. Hist. Soc., Proc.*, XLV (1911), 35, and "Negotiation of 1861," *ibid.*, XLVI, 23, and "Crisis in Downing Street," *ibid.*, XLVII (1914), 372; Brooks Adams, "Seizure of the Laird Rams," *ibid.*, XLV (1911), 243; J. D. Bulloch, *Secret Service of Confederate States in Europe* (2 vols., 1883). ⟐ Periodicals: *Times* (London); *Economist* (London); *Blackwood's Mag.* (London); *Harper's Weekly* (N. Y.); *N. Y. Tribune; Index* (London).

Bibliography — Bemis and Griffin, *Guide to Diplomatic History*, ch. xiii.

188. THE NEGRO AND SLAVERY DURING THE WAR

Summary — Status in 1861: in border slave states; territories; District of Columbia; government posts; fugitive slaves; 1861, Feb. 11, House resolution; Mar. 2, Corwin amendment (§ 182); July 22, House on purpose of the war. — Fugitives and slaves of combatants: 1861, May, Butler's "contraband of war"; Aug. 6, confiscation act; 1862, Mar. 13, return by officers forbidden; July 2, second confiscation act; 1864, June 28, act of 1850 repealed. — District of Columbia: 1862, Apr. 26, District compensated emancipation act; June 19, territorial prohibition act. — Negro troops: 1861, Dec., Cameron's message; 1862, Hunter's regiment; July 17, enlistments authorized; services. — Slave trade: 1862, June 7, treaty with England; 1864, July 7, domestic trade forbidden. — Emancipation Proclamation: 1861–62, Lincoln's attitude; influence of border states; 1861, Aug. 30, Frémont's order; 1862, May 9, Hunter's order; 1862, Sept. 22, preliminary proclamation; 1863, Jan. 1, final proclamation; legal, political, diplomatic effects. — Proposed colonization: Lincoln's plans; Chiriqui; Haiti; failure. — State emancipation: Lincoln's schemes of compensation; 1862, Apr. 10, joint resolution; 1862–63, border states refuse; 1862, Mar. 21, West Virginia abolishes; 1863, June 24, Missouri emancipates;

1864, Oct. 13, Maryland abolishes; 1865, Dec., abolition in Kentucky and Delaware by Thirteenth Amendment. — Thirteenth Amendment: 1864, Apr. 8, passes Senate; 1864, June 15, fails in House; 1865, Jan. 31, passes the House; Dec. 18, declared in force.

General — Rhodes, *History*, III–V; Hosmer, *Appeal to Arms*, ch. xiv; Schouler, *History*, VI, 214, 276, 400, 528; Franklin, *Slavery to Freedom*, ch. xvi; Herbert Aptheker, *To Be Free* (1948), 75, and *History of American Negro*, 161; Wesley, *Negro Labor*, ch. iv; G. S. Merriam, *Negro and Nation* (1906), chs. xxvi, xxvii; Shotwell, *Civil War*, II, ch. xlii; Randall, *Civil War and Reconstruction*, chs. xx, xxi; Milton, *Conflict*, ch. xiii; Fish, *American Civil War*, ch. xi.

Special — Biographies: Sandburg, *Lincoln*, IV, ch. xxxiv, VI, ch. lxi; Nicolay and Hay, *Lincoln*, IV, chs. xxii, xxiv, V, ch. xii, VI, chs. vi, viii, xvii, xix, xx, VIII, chs. xvi, xx, X, ch. iv; Pearson, *Andrew*, II, ch. x; Hart, *Chase*, ch. x; Garrison, *Garrison*, IV, chs. i–vi; Higginson, *Higginson*, ch. xii; Nicolay, *Lincoln's Secretary*, ch. xiv; Gorham, *Stanton*, II, 73, 86; Woodburn, *Stevens*, ch. ix; Pierce, *Sumner*, IV, chs. xlviii–l. ❡ Local Studies: Trexler, *Slavery in Missouri*, ch. vii. ❡ Others: B. I. Wiley, *Southern Negroes 1861–1865* (1938); C. H. Wesley, "Employment of Negroes as Soldiers in Confederate Army," *Jour. of Negro Hist.*, IV (1919), 239; T. R. Hay, "South and Arming Slaves," *Miss. Valley Hist. Rev.*, VI (1920), 34; T. L. Spraggins, "Mobilization of Negro Labor," *No. Car. Hist. Rev.*, XXIV (1947), 160; G. W. Williams, *History of Negro Troops in the War* (1888); McDougall, *Fugitive Slaves*, §§ 85–105; Tremain, *Slavery in District of Columbia*, 92; C. F. Adams, "John Quincy Adams and Emancipation through Martial Law," *Mass. Hist. Soc., Proc.*, 2 ser., XV (1877), 436. ❡ Maps: Hosmer, *Appeal to Arms*, 214.

Sources — Debates: *Congressional Globe*. ❡ Newspapers: *N. Y. Tribune, N. Y. Times, N. Y. Herald, Boston Advertiser, Chicago Tribune* (§ 53). ❡ Documents: Miller, *Treaties*, VIII, 228, 237; 37 Cong., 2 sess., *Sen. Ex. Doc.*, V, No. 42, VI, No. 68, *Sen. Report*, No. 12, *H. Ex. Doc.*, V, No. 69, X, Nos. 133, 143, *H. Report*, III, No. 58, IV, Nos. 120, 148; 38 Cong., 1 sess., *Sen. Report*, Nos. 8, 17, 24, 25; *H. Ex. Doc.*, IX, No. 42, *H. Report*, I, No. 2, 38 Cong., 2 sess., *Sen. Report*, I, No. 137, *H. Ex. Doc.*, VIII, No. 38, *H. Report*, No. 9, *H. Misc. Doc.*; 39 Cong., 1 sess., *Sen. Ex. Doc.*, II, No. 55. ❡ Collections: *American Annual Cyclopedia*, 1861, 641; *idem*, 1862, 720, 736, 752, 786; *idem*, 1863, 268, 304, 425, 831; *idem*, 1864, 219, 387; *idem*, 1865, 205, 370; Richardson, *Messages and Papers*, VI; MacDonald, *Select Statutes*, Nos. 6, 11, 15, 17, 20, 24, 28, 38, 45, 48; Moore, *Digest of International Law*, II, 941; McPherson, *Rebellion*, 195; Moore, *Rebellion Record*, V–XI. ❡ Contemporary Writings: Lincoln, *Collected Works*, IV–VIII; Sumner, *Works*, VI–IX; Sherman, *Recollections*, I, ch. xiv; Chase, "Diary"; Riddle, *Recollections*, 129; G. S. Boutwell, *Speeches and Papers* (1867); Douglass, *Life and Times*, chs. xi, xii; Goddard, *Letters on American Rebellion*; Brooks, *Washington in Lincoln's Time*, ch. vi; A. K. McClure, *Lincoln and Men of War Times* (1892), 88; Carpenter, *Inner Life of Abraham Lincoln*; Botume, *First Days among Contrabands*; T. W. Higginson, *Army Life in a Black Regiment* (1869); Hart, *American History Told by Contemporaries*, IV, ch. xxi; Blaine, *Twenty Years*, I, chs. xx, xxi; Jefferson Davis, *Confederate Government*, II, 158, 460; Cox, *Three Decades*, ch. xvi; A. J. Wilcox, *Powers of Federal Government over Slavery* (1862); S. G. Fisher, *Trial of Constitution* (1862), ch. iv.

Bibliography — McDougall, *Fugitive Slaves*; Bartlett, *Literature of Rebellion*.

PART V

The Rise of Modern America

1865–1900

Chapter Nineteen

LIQUIDATION OF THE CIVIL WAR, 1865–1880

189. PRESIDENTIAL AND CONGRESSIONAL RECONSTRUCTION, 1863–1868

Summary — Impact of peace: demobilization; economic unsettlement; crime; political conditions in North; economic and social disorganization of the South. — Northern theories of status of seceded states: unimpaired rights (Democrats); state suicide (Sumner); conquered provinces (Stevens); forfeited rights (Congress). — Lincoln's efforts at reconstruction, 1862–65; Thirteenth Amendment. — Johnson's breach with Congress over Southern policy. — Submission of Fourteenth Amendment; restoration of Tennessee, 1866. — Congressional elections of 1866. — Military reconstruction by Congress, 1867–68; attitude of Supreme Court; restoration of seven more states, 1868. — Impeachment of Johnson, 1868. — Presidential election of 1868. — Religious and educational aspects of Reconstruction.

General — H. K. Beale, "Rewriting Reconstruction History," 807; C. G. Bowers, *Tragic Era* (1929), chs. i–ix, xi; P. H. Buck, *Road to Reunion* (1937), chs. i–iv; J. W. Burgess, *Reconstruction and Constitution* (1902), chs. i–ix; W. E. B. Du Bois, *Black Reconstruction* (1935), chs. vi–ix, xv; W. A. Dunning, *Reconstruction* (1907), chs. i–vii; W. L. Fleming, *Sequel of Appomattox* (1919), chs. i–vii; Franklin, *Slavery to Freedom*, ch. xvii; R. S. Henry, *Reconstruction* (1938), chs. i–xxxv; W. B. Hesseltine, *History of South* (1936), chs. xxii–xxiii; Matthew Josephson, *Politicos* (1938), 3; McMaster, *History of United States during Lincoln's Administration*, 511, 631; Allan Nevins, *Emergence of Modern America* (1927), 1; Oberholtzer, *History*, I, chs. i–iii, vii, II, chs. x–xi; Randall, *Civil War and Reconstruction*, chs. xxx–xxxv; Rhodes, *History*, IV, 484, V, 47, 132, 516, VI, 1, 168; Schouler, *History*, VII, ch. i; F. B. Simkins, "Southern Reconstruction," and *South Old and New* (1947), chs. xi–xii.

Special — Impact of Peace: Wecter, *When Johnny Comes Marching Home*, pt. 2; D. S. and H. E. Jordan, *War's Aftermath* (1914); R. F. Nichols, "United States vs. Jefferson Davis," *Am. Hist. Rev.*, XXXI (1926), 266; R. H. Dana, "Reasons for Not Prosecuting Jefferson Davis," Mass. Hist. Soc., *Proc.*, LXIV (1932), 201; A. V. House, "Northern Congressional Democrats as Defenders of South," *Jour. Southern Hist.*, VI (1940), 46; Edith Abbott, "Civil War and Crime Wave of 1865–70," *Social Service Rev.*, I (1927), 212; Ware, *Public Opinion in Massachusetts*, ch. vi; H. A. Stebbins, *Political History of New York, 1865–1869* (1913); Knapp, *New Jersey Politics*, chs. vii–viii; W. S. Myers, *Self-Reconstruction of Maryland* (1909); C. H. Moore, "Ohio in National Politics," *Ohio Arch. and Hist. Quar.*, XXXVII (1928), 220; H. M. Dilla, *Politics of Michigan* (1912), chs. ii–vii; Cole, *Era of Civil War*, chs. xvi–xix; E. M. Coulter, *Civil War and Readjustment in Kentucky* (1933), chs. xv–xix; Sellers, "Economic Incidence of War in South"; G. L. Anderson, "South and Post-Civil War Finance," *Jour. Southern Hist.*, IX (1943), 181; L. F. Hill, "Confederate Exodus to Latin America," *Southwestern Hist. Quar.*, XXXIX (1935), 100. ❧ Constitutional Aspects: McLaughlin, *Constitutional*

History, chs. xlv–xlvii; W. A. Dunning, *Essays on Civil War and Reconstruction* (1904), 63; Warren, *Supreme Court,* II, chs. xxx, xxxii; Lewis, *American Political Thought,* chs. i–iv; Swisher, *American Constitutional Development,* ch. xv; Hockett, *Constitutional History,* II, chs. xvii–xviii; Boudin, *Government by Judiciary,* II, chap. xii; H. E. Flack, *Adoption of Fourteenth Amendment* (1908); J. B. James, "Immediate Purpose of Fourteenth Amendment," *Ind. Mag. Hist.,* XXXIX (1943), 345. ❡ Reconstruction under Lincoln: C. H. McCarthy, *Lincoln's Plan of Reconstruction* (1901); E. G. Scott, *Reconstruction during Civil War* (1895), chs. xiii–xx. ❡ Under Johnson: G. F. Milton, *Age of Hate* (1930); C. E. Chadsey, *Struggle between Johnson and Congress* (1897); H. K. Beale, *Critical Year* (1930); L. H. Gipson, "Statesmanship of Johnson," *Miss. Valley Hist. Rev.,* II (1915), 363; B. B. Kendrick, *Journal of Joint Committee on Reconstruction* (1914), pt. 2; R. E. McClendon, "Status of Ex-Confederate States as Seen in Readmission of Senators," *Am. Hist. Rev.,* XLI (1936), 703; J. T. Dorris, "Pardoning Leaders of Confederacy," *Miss. Valley Hist. Rev.,* XV (1928), 3, and "Pardon Seekers and Brokers," *Jour. Southern Hist.,* I (1935), 276; W. N. Brigance, "Jeremiah Black and Johnson," *Miss. Valley Hist. Rev.,* XIX (1932), 205; J. M. Mecklin, "Black Codes," *So. Atlantic Quar.,* XVI (1917), 248; P. S. Peirce, *Freedmen's Bureau* (1904); D. M. Dewitt, *Impeachment and Trial of Johnson* (1903); E. G. Ross, *Impeachment of Johnson* (1896). ❡ Election of 1868: Stanwood, *Presidency,* I, ch. xxii; C. H. Coleman, *Election of 1868* (1933); C. M. Destler, *American Radicalism* (1946), chs. ii–iii; M. L. Shipley, "Background of Pendleton Plan," *Miss. Valley Hist. Rev.,* XXIV (1938), 329. ❡ Religious and Educational Aspects: Sweet, *Story of Religion,* ch. xx; Vander Velde, *Presbyterian Churches,* pt. 2, ch. vii, pts. 3, 6; O. S. Heckman, "Presbyterian Church in U. S. A. in Reconstruction," *No. Car. Hist. Rev.,* XX (1943), 219; H. D. Farish, *Circuit Rider Dismounts* (1938), ch. iv; R. S. Rust, *Freedmen's Aid Society of Methodist Episcopal Church* (1880); W. A. Russ, Jr., "Influence of Methodist Church upon Reconstruction," Susquehanna Univ., *Studies,* I (1937), 51, and "Anti-Catholic Agitation during Reconstruction," Am. Cath. Hist. Soc., *Recs.,* XLV (1934), 312; Mark Mohler, "Episcopal Church and Conciliation," *Pol. Sci. Quar.,* XLI (1926), 567; C. G. Woodson, *Negro Church* (1921), chs. ix–xi; E. W. Knight, *Influence of Reconstruction on Education in South* (1913); H. L. Swint, *Northern Teacher in South* (1941). ❡ Reconstruction in Separate States: Fleming, *Civil War and Reconstruction in Alabama,* chs. v–xxiv; F. G. Bromberg, *Reconstruction Period in Alabama* (1911–14); H. M. Bond, "Alabama Reconstruction," *Jour. Negro Hist.,* XXIII (1938), 290; T. S. Staples, *Reconstruction in Arkansas* (1923); D. Y. Thomas, *Arkansas in War and Reconstruction* (1926), chs. xxvi–xxix; W. W. Davis, *Civil War and Reconstruction in Florida* (1913), chs. xiii–xxvii; C. M. Thompson, *Reconstruction in Georgia* (1915); Caskey, *Secession and Restoration in Louisiana,* chs. iv–x; Ella Lonn, *Reconstruction in Louisiana after 1868* (1918); F. P. Burns, "White Supremacy in South," *La. Hist. Quar.,* XVIII (1935), 581; J. W. Garner, *Reconstruction in Mississippi* (1901); J. S. McNeily, "War and Reconstruction in Mississippi," Miss. Hist. Soc., *Publ.* (*Centenary Ser.*), II (1918), 165; V. L. Wharton, "Negro in Mississippi," *James Sprunt Studies in History and Political Science* (1947), chs. i–xiv; J. G. deR. Hamilton, *Reconstruction in North Carolina* (1914); F. B. Simkins and R. H. Woody, *South Carolina during Reconstruction* (1932); A. A. Taylor, *Negro in South Carolina during Reconstruction* (1924); E. L. Wells, *Hampton and Reconstruction* (1907); H. M. Jarrell, *Hampton and the Negro* (1949); L. J. Webster, *Freedmen's Bureau in South Carolina* (1916); Patton, *Unionism and Reconstruction in Tennessee,* chs. iv–x; T. B. Alexander, *Political Reconstruction in Tennessee* (1950); C. R. Hall, *Andrew Johnson, Military Governor of Tennessee* (1916); A. A. Taylor, *Negro in Tennessee* (1941); C. W. Ramsdell, *Reconstruction in Texas* (1910); H. J. Eckenrode, *Virginia during Reconstruction* (1904); A. A. Taylor, *Negro in Reconstruction of Virginia* (1926). ❡ Northern Biographies: R. C. McGrane, *William Allen* (1925), 169; Muzzey, *Blaine,* 48, 57; Edward Stanwood, *Blaine* (1905), chs. iv–v; W. E. Smith, *Blair Family,* II, chs. xxxix–xliii; Harris, *Chandler,* chs. ix–xi; Hart, *Chase,* chs. xiii–xiv; Conkling, *Conkling,* chs. xiv–xvii; Chidsey, *Conkling,* chs. x–xxxiv; Barrows, *Evarts,* chs. x–xii; Dyer, *Evarts,* chs. vi–vii; Fessenden, *Fessenden,* II, chs. vii–x; Hesseltine, *Grant,* chs. iii–vi, xi; Adam Badeau, *Grant in Peace* (1887), chs. ii–xvii; R. W. Winston, *Andrew Johnson* (1928), 325; Stryker, *Johnson,* chs. xxiv–lxxxiv; Clarke, *Julian,* chs. xi–xii; Nicolay and Hay, *Lincoln,* VI, ch. xvi, VIII, chs. xvi–xx, IX, chs. v, xix; Parker, *Morrill,* ch. ix;

Foulke, *Morton*, I, chs. xxxii–xxxv, II, chs. i–ii, v–vi; Fuess, *Schurz*, chs. xii–xiii; Joseph Schafer, *Schurz* (1930), chs. xv–xvii; Mitchell, *Seymour*, chs. xvi–xix; Bancroft, *Seward*, II, chs. xxxvi, xli; Burton, *Sherman*, ch. vii; Gorham, *Stanton*, II, chs. xc–cxviii; Current, *Stevens*, chs. xvi–xvii; A. B. Miller, *Stevens* (1939), chs. xvi–xxvi; Pierce, *Sumner*, IV, chs. l–liii; Haynes, *Sumner*, 283–328; Horace White, *Trumbull*, chs. xiv–xxi. ❦ Southern Biographies: Ranck, *Brown*, ch. viii; Herbert Fielder, *J. E. Brown* (1883), chs. xiii–xiv; Coulter, *Brownlow*, chs. xii–xvi; McElroy, *Davis*, II, chs. xxvii–xxix; V. H. Davis, *Davis*, II, chs. lvi–lvii; Mathes, *Forrest*, ch. xx; H. J. Pearce, Jr., *B. H. Hill* (1928); chs. vii–xi; Flippin, *Johnson*, chs. viii–ix; Mayes, *Lamar*, ch. xii; Cate, *Lamar*, chs. viii–xii; Freeman, *Lee*, IV, chs. xiv–xxvii; F. L. Riley, ed., *Lee after Appomattox* (1922); C. H. Ambler, *Pierpont* (1937), chs. xx–xxvi; Johnston and Browne, *Stephens*, chs. xxxix–xli; Pendleton, *Stephens*, ch. xvii; Phillips, *Toombs*, ch. xi.

Sources — Official Documents: *Congressional Globe* and *Congressional Doc.*, 39, 40 Congs.; 39 Cong., 1 Sess., *Sen. Ex. Doc.*, I, No. 2, II, No. 43 (reports of Grant, Schurz, and B. C. Truman), and *H. Report*, II, No. 30; 40 Cong., 1 Sess., *H. Report*, No. 7; and 2 Sess., *H. Misc. Doc.*, II, Nos. 89, 91–2, 101, 107, 134, and *Sen. Misc. Doc.*, Nos. 42–3 (trial of Johnson); Richardson, *Messages and Papers*, VI; *Statutes at Large*, XIII, 507, 737, 744, 758, 760, XIV, esp. 27, 173, 364, 428, 430, 432, 486, 571, 811, XV, 2, 14, 41, 72, 73, 85, 193, 257, 344, 711. ❦ Cases: *Ex parte* Milligan (1867), 4 *Wallace*, 2; Cummings *v.* Missouri (1867), *ibid.*, 277; *Ex parte* Garland (1867), *ibid.*, 333; Mississippi *v.* Johnson (1867), *ibid.*, 475; Georgia *v.* Stanton (1867), 6 *Wallace*, 50; White *v.* Cannon (1868), *ibid.*, 443. ❦ State Action: Department of State, *Documentary History of Constitution* (1894–1905), II, 520, V, 495; Thorpe, *Federal and State Constitutions*. ❦ Unofficial Collections: Fleming, *Documentary History*; Edward McPherson, *Reconstruction* (1871), and *Handbook of Politics*; Kendrick, *Journal of Joint Committee*, pt. 1; *American Annual Cyclopædia*; Commager, *Documents*, II, 1; Nevins and Commager, *Heritage of America*, ch. xxvi; K. H. Porter, *Party Platforms* (1924), 64. ❦ Education, Churches, and Negro Relief: Fleming, *Documentary History*, II, chs. ix–x; reports of Freedmen's Aid Societies. ❦ Correspondence and Memoirs: G. S. Boutwell, *Reminiscences* (1902), II, chs. xxx–xxxii; Butler, *Autobiography*, ch. xx; Chase, "Diary," 382; Blaine, *Twenty Years*, II, chs. i, iii–xii, xiv; Clemenceau, *American Reconstruction*; Cox, *Three Decades* (1885), chs. xvi–xxxiv; Cullom, *Fifty Years*, chs. viii–ix; *Jefferson Davis, Constitutionalist*, VII; Douglass, *Life and Times*, pt. 2, chs. xii–xiv; J. A. Garfield, *Works* (1882–83), I; Howard, *Autobiography*, II, pt. 3; Julian, *Recollections*, chs. xii–xiv; Koerner, *Memoirs*, II, chs. xliv–xlvi; Lincoln, *Collected Works*, VIII; McCulloch, *Men and Measures*, chs. xxv–xxvi; Poore, *Perley's Reminiscences*, II, chs. xvi–xxi; Schofield, *Forty-six Years in Army*, chs. xix, xxi–xxii; Schurz, *Reminiscences*, III, chs. vi–x, and *Speeches, Correspondence*, I, 252; Sheridan, *Memoirs*, II, chs. x–xi; Sherman, *Recollections*, I, chs. xvi, xix; John and W. T. Sherman, *Letters* (1894), 245; A. H. Stephens, *War between States*, II, colloquies xxiii–xxiv, and *Reviewers Reviewed* (1872), 226, and *Recollections*, pts. 2–3; W. M. Stewart, *Reminiscences* (1908), chs. xx, xxii, xxiv; Sumner, *Works* (1870–83), VI–XV; Taylor, *Destruction and Reconstruction*, ch. xv; S. J. Tilden, *Writings and Speeches* (1885), I, 395, and *Letters* (1908); Welles, *Diary*, II–III. ❦ Contemporary Descriptions: Sidney Andrews, *South since War* (1866); M. L. Avary, *Dixie after War* (1906); Virginia Clay-Clopton, *Belle of Fifties* (1905), chs. xviii–xxix; V. V. Clayton, *White and Black* (1899); J. H. Kennaway, *On Sherman's Track* (1867); Henry Latham, *Black and White* (1867); Macrae, *Americans at Home*; E. W. Pearson, *Letters from Port Royal* (1906); J. S. Pike, *Prostrate State* (1935); E. A. Pollard, *Lost Cause*, ch. xliv, and *Lost Cause Regained* (1868); Whitelaw Reid, *After the War* (1866); Somers, *Southern States since War*; J. T. Trowbridge, *South* (1866).

Bibliography — E. M. Coulter, *South during Reconstruction* (1947), 392; Nevins, *Emergence of Modern America*, ch. xv; Randall, *Civil War and Reconstruction*, 881; Beale, *Critical Year*, 407; Du Bois, *Black Reconstruction*, 731.

190. CARPETBAG RULE AND ITS OVERTHROW, 1868–1877

Summary — Union Leagues; Carpetbaggers; Scalawags. — Fifteenth amendment and restoration of last four states, 1869–70. — Ku Klux Klan and other undercover movements; federal repressive measures, 1870–72. — Amnesty Act, 1872. — Actions of carpetbag regimes. — Gradual recovery of Southern white supremacy, 1869–77. — Civil Rights Act, 1875. — Attitude of Supreme Court. — Religious and educational aspects (§ 189). — Rise of New South (§ 195).

General — C. G. Bowers, *Tragic Era*, chs. x, xv, xvii, xxi, xxiv; Burgess, *Reconstruction*, chs. x–xiii; Du Bois, *Black Reconstruction*, chs. x–xiv; Dunning, *Reconstruction*, chs. xi, xiii, xv–xvii, xix; Fleming, *Sequel of Appomattox*, chs. viii–xiii; Franklin, *Slavery to Freedom*, ch. xviii; Henry, *Reconstruction*, chs. xxxvi–li; W. B. Hesseltine, *History of South*, ch. xxiv, and "Economic Factors in Abandonment of Reconstruction," *Miss. Valley Hist. Rev.*, XXII (1935), 191; Paul Lewinson, *Race, Class, & Party* (1932), ch. iii; Merriam, *Negro and Nation*, chs. xviii–xxxvi; Oberholtzer, *History*, II, ch. ix, 258, ch. xiii, III, ch. xx; Randall, *Civil War and Reconstruction*, chs. xxxvi–xxxvii; Rhodes, *History*, VI, 200, 244, 284, 390, VII, 74; Schouler, *History*, VII, 43, 243, 352; Simkins, *South Old and New*, chs. xiii–xiv; *South in Building of Nation*, IV, 601, 632; G. W. Williams, *Negro Race* (1883), II, chs. xxi, xxiii.

Special (§ 189). — Carpetbag and Negro Rule: W. A. Russ, Jr., "Registration and Disfranchisement under Radical Reconstruction," *Miss. Valley Hist. Rev.*, XXI (1934), 163, and "Negro and White Disfranchisement," *Jour. Negro Hist.*, XIX (1934), 171; S. A. Walker, "Carpetbaggers," *ibid.*, XIV (1929), 44; C. M. Thompson, "Carpetbaggers in United States Senate," *Studies in Southern History and Politics* (1920), 161; W. L. Fleming, *Freedmen's Savings Bank* (1927); J. M. Harrell, *Brooks and Baxter War* (1893); John Wallace, *Carpetbag Rule in Florida* (1888); W. W. Ball, *State That Forgot* (1932), chs. xxii–xxiii; H. A. Herbert, *et al.*, *Why the Solid South?* (1890), chs. ii–vi, viii, xii–xiv; J. M. Mathews, *Legislative and Judicial History of Fifteenth Amendment* (1909). ❦ Ku Klux Klan and Election Frauds: J. C. Lester and D. L. Wilson, *Ku Klux Klan* (1905); S. F. Horn, *Invisible Empire* (1939); Eyre Damer, *When the Ku Klux Rode* (1912); Brown, *Lower South*, ch. iv; W. A. Sinclair, *Aftermath of Slavery* (1905), chs. ii–vi; H. O. Lestage, Jr., "White League in Louisiana," *La. Hist. Quar.*, XVIII (1935), 617; W. W. Davis, "Enforcement Acts," *Studies in Southern History and Politics*, 205; L. E. Murphy, "Civil Rights Law of 1875," *Jour. Negro Hist.*, XII (1927), 110; Warren, *Supreme Court*, chs. xxxiii–xxxiv. ❦ Establishment of White Rule (§ 193): H. T. Thompson, *Ousting Carpetbagger from South Carolina* (1926); A. B. Williams, *Hampton and His Red Shirts* (1935); G. W. McGinty, *Louisiana Redeemed* (1941); F. Z. L. Bone, "Louisiana in Disputed Election," *La. Hist. Quar.*, XIV (1931), 408, 549, XV (1932), 93, 234; C. V. Woodward, *Reunion and Reaction* (1951).

Sources (§ 189). — Official: *Congressional Globe*, 40 Cong., 3 Sess.-42 Cong., 3 Sess.; *Congressional Record*, 43–44 Congs.; *Congressional Doc.*, esp. 42 Cong., 1 Sess., *Sen. Report*, No. 1, 2 Sess., *ibid.*, II, No. 41; 45 Cong., 2 Sess., *H. Misc. Doc.*, V, No. 52; F. T. Wilson, "Federal Aid in Domestic Disturbances," 57 Cong., 2 Sess., *Sen. Doc.*, XV, No. 209, chs. v–viii; *Statutes at Large*, XVI, 3, 6, 7, 40, 59, 62, 140, 363, 433, XVII, 13, 142, 348, XVIII, 325, XXI, 113; Richardson, *Messages and Papers*, VII. ❦ Cases: *Ex parte* McCardle (1869), 7 *Wallace*, 506; Texas *v.* White (1869), *ibid.*, 700; White *v.* Hart (1872), 13 *Wallace*, 646; Gunn *v.* Barry (1873), 15 *Wallace*, 610; Slaughter House cases (1873, 1884), 16 *Wallace*, 36, and 111 *U.S.*, 746; United States *v.* Reese (1876), 92 *U.S.*, 214; United States *v.* Cruikshank (1876), *ibid.*, 542; Williams *v.* Bruffy (1878), 96 *U.S.*, 176; Strauder *v.* West Virginia (1880), 100 *U.S.*, 303; *Ex parte* Siebold (1880), *ibid.*, 371; United States *v.* Harris (1883), 106 *U.S.*, 629; Civil Rights cases (1883), 109 *U.S.*, 3. ❦ Descriptions and Reminiscences: W. A. Allen, *Governor Chamberlain's Administration* (1888); Shotwell, *Papers*, II, III; Campbell, *White and Black*; W. L. Clowes, *Black America* (1891); R. H. Gillet, *Democracy in United States* (1868), 297; Edward King, *Great South* (1875); F. B. Leigh, *Ten Years on Georgia Plantation* (1883); J. A. Leland, *Voice from South Carolina* (1879); R. G. M'Clellan, *Republicanism in America* (1868); Charles Nordhoff, *Cotton States* (1876); J. A. Payne, "Reconstruction on Lower Mississippi," *Miss. Valley Hist. Rev.*, XXI (1934–35), 387; L. F. Post, "A 'Carpetbagger' in South Carolina," *Jour. Negro Hist.*, X (1925), 10; J. C. Reed, *Old and New South*

(1876); L. P. Scarborough, "So It Was When Life Began," *La. Hist. Rev.*, XIII (1930), 428.

Bibliography (§ 241). — M. N. Work, *Bibliography of Negro* (1928), 370; Peirce, *Freedmen's Bureau*, 175.

191. FINANCIAL RECONSTRUCTION, 1865–1872

Summary — Public debt and forms of taxation, 1865; House resolution to retire green-backs; Funding and Contraction Act, 1866. — Inflated prices; debtor discontent; theories of resumption of specie payment. — Repeal of contraction, 1868; "Ohio Idea" in presidential campaign of 1868 (§ 189); Public Credit Act, 1869. — Refunding legislation, 1870–71. — Supreme Court decisions regarding greenbacks, 1870–84. — Gold purchases; Black Friday, 1869. — Wells commission report, 1866; reduction of internal revenue taxes, 1866–70; lowering of income tax, 1870. — Tariff controversy: sectional and party attitudes; legislation, 1867–72; in campaign of 1872 (§ 192). — Later financial problems (§ 201).

General — Dewey, *Financial History*, chs. xiv, xvi; Dunning, *Reconstruction*, 131, 220; A. D. Noyes, *Forty Years of American Finance* (1909), 1; Oberholtzer, *History*, I, 26, 189, 265, II, 159, 272; W. M. Persons, *et al.*, "Business and Financial Conditions Following the Civil War," *Rev. Econ. Statistics*, II (1920), suppl. 2; Ratner, *American Taxation*, ch. vii; Rhodes, *History*, VI, 158, 215, 241, 273, 424; Schultz and Caine, *Financial Development*, ch. xv.

Special — Greenbacks: Hepburn, *History of Currency*, chs. xii, xiv; Barrett, *Greenbacks and Resumption*, 79; W. C. Mitchell, *Greenbacks*, pt. 2, and *Gold, Prices, and Wages under Greenback Standard* (1908); Knox, *United States Notes*, ch. xi; Horace White, *Money and Banking* (1935), chs. ix, x; Laughlin, *Bimetallism*, ch. vi; J. K. Upton, *Money in Politics* (1884), chs. xiv–xv; C. J. Bullock, *Monetary History* (1900), pt. 1, ch. vii; M. S. Wildman, *Money Inflation* (1905), ch. v; F. D. Graham, "International Trade under Depreciated Paper," *Quar. Jour. Econ.*, XXXVI (1922), 220. ❡ Constitutionality of Greenbacks: Warren, *Supreme Court*, II, ch. xxxi; H. H. Neill, "Legal Tender Question," *Pol. Sci. Quar.*, I (1866), 250; B. T. De Witt, "Are Our Legal-Tender Laws Ex Post Facto?" *ibid.*, XV (1900), 96; Sidney Ratner, "Was Supreme Court Packed by Grant?" *ibid.*, L (1935), 343; D. H. Chamberlain and T. H. Talbot, "Legal Tender Decision of 1884," *Am. Law Rev.*, XVIII (1884), 410, 618. ❡ Funding: R. A. Bayley, *National Loans* (1882), 85, 165; W. F. De Knight, *Currency and Loans* (1897), 98, 120. ❡ Banking and Independent Treasury: J. J. Knox, *History of Banking in United States* (1903), 101, 137, 270, 295. ❡ Internal Revenue and Tariff: H. E. Smith, *United States Internal Tax History from 1861 to 1871* (1914); F. C. Howe, *Taxation and Taxes under Internal Revenue System* (1896), chs. iii–vii; Taussig, *Tariff History*, 171; Stanwood, *Tariff Controversies* (1903), II, ch. xiv; I. M. Tarbell, *Tariff in Our Times* (1911), chs. ii–iii; Wright, *Wool-Growing and Tariff*, ch. vii; J. D. Goss, *Tariff Administration* (1891), ch. iv. ❡ Leading Figures: H. R. Ferleger, *Wells and Revenue System* (1942); F. B. Joyner, *Wells* (1939), chs. iii–viii; H. S. Schell, "Hugh McCulloch and Treasury Department, 1865–69," *Miss. Valley Hist. Rev.*, XVII (1930), 404; Burton, *Sherman*, chs. viii–x; Fessenden, *Fessenden*, II, 103, 289; Foulke, *Morton*, II, 13, 65; Hart, *Chase*, chs. xi, xv; T. C. Smith, *Garfield*, I, 387.

Sources — General: *Congressional Globe* and *Congressional Docs.*, 40–42 Congs.; Richardson, *Messages and Papers*, VI–VII; *Report on Finances* (annual, 1865–72); A. P. Andrew, *Statistics for United States, 1867–1909* (1910), pts. 2–4; Dunbar, *Currency, Finance, and Banking*, 199; *American Annual Cyclopædia*. ❡ Cases: Lane County *v.* Oregon (1869), 7 *Wallace*, 71; Pacific Insurance Co. *v.* Soule (1869), *ibid.*, 433; Veazie Bank *v.* Fenno (1870), 8 *Wallace*, 533; Hepburn *v.* Griswold (1870), *ibid.*, 603; Legal Tender cases (1871), 12 *Wallace*, 457; Scholey *v.* Rew (1875), 23 *Wallace*, 331; Springer *v.* United States (1881), 102 *U.S.*, 586; Juilliard *v.* Greenman (1884), 110 *U.S.*, 421.

❡ Tariff: R. G. Proctor, "Tariff Acts, 1789–1897," 55 Cong., 2 Sess., *H. Doc.*, LXXII, No. 562; J. S. Morrill, "Tariff on Imports," 48 Cong., 1 Sess., *Sen. Report*, I, No. 12; Edward Young, *Customs-Tariff Legislation* (1872), pp. cxxxviii–cxcviii; D. A. Wells, *Reports of Revenue Commission* (1867–70). ❡ Reminiscences: McCulloch, *Men and Measures*, 170, 193, 234; Boutwell, *Reminiscences*, II, chs. xxxiii, xxxv–xxxvi; Sherman, *Recollections*, I, chs. xvii, xx–xxi.

Bibliography — Dewey, *Financial History*, pp. xxiv–xxv, 331, 359, 383.

192. REPUBLICAN DISCORD AND POLITICAL SHAME, 1869–1875

Summary — President Grant's difficulties: Southern policy (§ 190); civil-service reform; the tariff. — Liberal Republican movement from 1870; presidential election of 1872. — Panic of 1873 (§ 201). — Political scandals, 1872–76: Credit Mobilier inquiry; "salary grab"; "moiety system"; Whisky Ring; Belknap affair; Mulligan letters. — Democratic tidal wave, 1874. — Tariff of 1875. — Later political developments (§ 193).

General — Binkley, *American Political Parties*, 278; Dunning, *Reconstruction*, chs. xii, xv, xviii; Josephson, *Politicos*, 78; D. T. Lynch, *Wild Seventies* (1941), chs. xx–xxvii; Oberholtzer, *History*, II, 268, 292, 598, III, 1, 129; Rhodes, *History*, VI, ch. xxxix, VII, 1, 64, 175; Schouler, *History*, VII, 202, 262, 287.

Special — Civil Service: Fish, *Civil Service and Patronage*, 209; L. M. Salmon, "Appointing Power," 87; H. C. Lodge, *Historical and Political Essays* (1892), 114. ❡ Tariff: Stanwood, *Tariff Controversies*, II, ch. xiv; Taussig, *Tariff History*, 171; Tarbell, *Tariff*, 71. ❡ Liberal Republicans and 1872 Election: Stanwood, *Presidency*, I, ch. xxiv; T. S. Barclay, *Liberal Republican Movement in Missouri* (1926); E. D. Ross, *Liberal Republican Movement* (1919); F. E. Haynes, *Third Party Movements* (1916), chs. ii–iv. ❡ Scandals: D. G. Loth, *Public Plunder* (1938), ch. x; J. B. Crawford, *Credit Mobilier* (1880), chs. vii–xi; Rowland Hazard, *Credit Mobilier* (1881), 24; Nelson Trottman, *Union Pacific* (1923), ch. iv; L. E. Guese, "St. Louis and the Great Whiskey Ring," *Mo. Hist. Rev.*, XXXVI (1942), 160; R. C. Prickett, "Malfeasance of Belknap," *No. Dak. Hist.*, XVII (1950), 5. ❡ Biographies: Muzzey, *Blaine*, 66; Stanwood, *Blaine*, chs. v–vi; Merriam, *Bowles*, II, chs. xxxvi–xxxvii, xxxix, xlii; O. J. Hollister, *Schuyler Colfax* (1886), chs. xi–xiv; Cary, *Curtis*, chs. xv–xviii; J. H. Wilson, *C. A. Dana* (1907), chs. xxv–xxvi; Nevins, *Fish*, chs. xxvii, xxxii–xxxiv; T. C. Smith, *Garfield*, I, ch. xv; Caldwell, *Garfield*, ch. xii; Hesseltine, *Grant*, chs. xiii, xvi–xvii, xix, xxii–xxiv; Hale, *Greeley*, chs. xvi–xvii; H. L. Stoddard, *Greeley* (1946), chs. xxviii–xxx; Hamlin, *Hamlin*, chs. xxxix–xl; Moorfield Storey and E. W. Emerson, *E. R. Hoar* (1911), ch. v; Gillett, *Hoar*, ch. vi; Foulke, *Morton*, II, chs. x, xii, xiv; Fuess, *Schurz*, chs. xiv–xvi; Frederic Bancroft and W. A. Dunning in Schurz, *Reminiscences*, III, 315; Moorfield Storey, *Sumner* (1900), ch. xxiv; Horace White, *Trumbull*, chs. xxiii, xxv–xxvi.

Sources — Official: *Congressional Globe* and *Congressoinal Record* and *Congressional Doc.*, 41–44 Congs. ❡ Corruption: 42 Cong., 3 Sess., *H. Report*, II, Nos. 77, 78, and *Sen. Report*, III, No. 519; 44 Cong., 1 Sess., *H. Report*, I, No. 186, II, No. 345, V, No. 784, VI, Nos. 789, 791, 793, VII, No. 794; *H. Misc. Doc.*, V, No. 167, IX, No. 186, X, No. 193; *Congressional Record*, IV, 2724, 3602. ❡ Unofficial Compilations: McPherson, *Handbook of Politics*; Porter, *Party Platforms*, 71; *American Annual Cyclopædia*. ❡ Personal: Blaine, *Twenty Years*, II, chs. xxii, xxiv; Boutwell, *Reminiscences*, II, chs. xxxvii–xxxviii; Roeliff Brinkerhoff, *Recollections* (1900), chs. xvi–xvii; G. W. Curtis, *Orations and Addresses* (1894), II, Nos. 1–4; Garfield, *Works*, I, 499, II, 30; Hoar, *Autobiography*, I, chs. xxi–xxv; Julian, *Recollections*, ch. xv; A. K. McClure, *Our Presidents* (1900), 221; John McDonald, *Great Whiskey Ring* (1880); Watterson, "*Marse Henry*," I, ch. xi; A. D. White, *Autobiography*, I, ch. x.

Bibliography — Fish, *Civil Service and Patronage*, 252–66.

193. THE DISPUTED ELECTION AND AFTER, 1876–1879

Summary — Presidential campaign of 1876: issues; candidates; disputed returns; Electoral Commission, 1877; seating of Hayes. — Withdrawal of troops and restoration of white rule in Louisiana, South Carolina, and Florida, 1877 (§ 190). — Republican factionalism: reasons; Halfbreeds and Stalwarts; Hayes and civil-service reform. — Democratic strategy: Potter committee; efforts to repeal election laws; capture of both houses of Congress, 1878. — Later political developments (§ 203).

General — Dunning, *Reconstruction*, chs. xix–xxi; Josephson, *Politicos*, 213; Oberholtzer, *History*, III, 247, IV, 37, 45; Rhodes, *History*, VII, 206, VIII, 1, 88; Schouler, *History*, VII, 290, 301; E. E. Sparks, *National Development* (1907), 84, 154.

Special — Election of 1876–77: P. L. Haworth, *Hayes-Tilden Disputed Election* (1906); Stanwood, *Presidency*, ch. xxv; A. K. McClure, *Our Presidents*, 244; McLaughlin, *Constitutional History*, ch. xlviii; C. V. Woodward, *Reunion and Reaction*, and *Origins of New South* (1951), chs. i–iii; J. H. Dougherty, *Electoral System* (1906), ch. v; J. S. Black, "Electoral Conspiracy," *No. Am. Rev.*, CXXV (1877), 1; E. W. Stoughton, " 'Electoral Conspiracy' Bubble Exploded," *ibid.*, 193; John Bigelow, *Supreme Court and Electoral Commission* (1903); G. F. Edmunds, "Presidential Elections," *Am. Law Rev.*, XII (1877), 1; Manton Marble, *Secret Chapter* (1878); A. M. Gibson, *A Political Crime* (1885). ❡ Republican Factionalism: J. W. Burgess, *Administration of Hayes* (1916); V. L. Shores, *Hayes-Conkling Controversy* (1919); Lee Newcomer, "Arthur's Removal from Custom House," *N. Y. Hist.*, XVIII (1937), 401; L. N. Richardson and C. W. Garrison, "Curtis, Hayes, and Civil Service Reform," *Miss. Valley Hist. Rev.*, XXXII (1945), 235. ❡ Biographies: Howe, *Arthur*, chs. vi–vii; C. C. Tansill, *Congressional Career of Bayard* (1946), chs. v–viii; Clapp, *John Bigelow*, 273; Muzzey, *Blaine*, ch. vi; Gail Hamilton (M. A. Dodge), *Blaine* (1895), ch. xiv; Merriam, *Bowles*, II, 259, 278, 350; L. B. Richardson, *Chandler* (1940), 173; Conkling, *Conkling*, chs. xxvi–xxvii; Chidsey, *Conkling*, chs. xx–xxv; J. H. Wilson, *Dana*, ch. xxvi; Barrows, *Evarts*, chs. xx–xxii; Dyer, *Evarts*, ch. xi; Nevins, *Fish*, ch. xxxv, and *Abram S. Hewitt*, chs. xvii–xxi; T. C. Smith, *Garfield*, I, ch. xvii; Williams, *Hayes*, I, chs. xxiii–xxvi, xxix; Eckenrode, *Hayes*, chs. vi–ix; Gillett, *Hoar*, ch. vii; Cate, *Lamar*, chs. xiv–xvi; Charles Fairman, *Mr. Justice Miller and Supreme Court* (1939), ch. xii; Foulke, *Morton*, II, chs. xix–xxiv; Paine, *Nast*, chs. xxxviii–xxxix, xliv; Fuess, *Schurz*, 215; Bigelow, *Tilden*, I, 293, II, chs. i–iii, vi; Flick, *Tilden*, chs. xxiii–xxxiii.

Sources — Official (general): *Congressional Record*, and *Congressional Doc.*, 44 Cong., 2 Sess.-45 Cong.; Richardson, *Messages and Papers*, VII, 439. ❡ Hayes-Tilden Contest: 44 Cong., 2 Sess., *Sen. Ex. Doc.*, I, No. 2, *Sen. Report*, I, Nos. 536, 548, 561, 598, 627, 678, 704, IV, No. 701, *Sen. Misc. Doc.*, I, Nos. 1, 5, 8, 16, 18, 23, 25, 40, II, No. 14, III, Nos. 44, 45, *H. Ex. Doc.*, IX, No. 30, *H. Report*, I, Nos. 100, 108, 143, 156, II, No. 175, *H. Misc. Doc.*, I, Nos. 6, 26, 31, 34, 35, 38, II, No. 13; 45 Cong., 3 Sess., *H. Report*, I, No. 140, *H. Misc. Doc.*, IV–V; *Proceedings of Congress and Electoral Commission* (also in *Congressional Record*, V, pt. 4); *Statutes at Large*, XIX, 227. ❡ Unofficial Compilations: McPherson, *Handbook of Politics*; *Appletons' Annual Cyclopædia*; Porter, *Party Platforms*, 86. ❡ Personal: Blaine, *Twenty Years*, II, chs. xxv–xxvi, xxviii; J. P. Bradley, *Miscellaneous Writings* (1902), 8, 165; Cox, *Three Decades*, chs. xxxvi–xxxvii; Garfield, *Works*, II, 393, 543, 655; Hayes, *Diary and Letters*, III, chs. xxxii–xxxviii; Hoar, *Autobiography*, I, ch. xxvii, II, chs. ii–vi; Hudson, *Recollections*, 53; McCulloch, *Men and Measures*, ch. xxvii; Schurz, *Speeches, Correspondence*, III, 222; Sherman, *Recollections*, I, ch. xxviii; Tilden, *Writings*, II, 354, and *Letters*; Watterson, "*Marse Henry*," I, 277.

Bibliography — N. Y. Public Library, *Political Parties* (1915), 22, 32, 56.

194. POSTWAR FOREIGN RELATIONS, 1865–1875

Summary — Earlier diplomatic relations (§ 173). — French in Mexico (§ 187): United States policy and French withdrawal, 1866–67. — Relations with Great Britain: Fenian movement, 1866; Senate's rejection of Johnson treaty, 1869; Treaty of Washington, 1871; Geneva and other arbitrations, 1872–77. — Expatriation controversy. — Expansionist sentiment: purchase of Alaska, 1867; Danish West Indies question, 1867; Santo Domingo question, 1869–70; Cuban insurrection and *Virginius* incident, 1873; reciprocity treaty with Hawaii, 1875. — Isthmian negotiations (§ 222). — Chinese exclusion question (§ 211). — Relations with other countries. — Later foreign affairs (§§ 220–5).

General — Bailey, *Diplomatic History*, chs. xxiv–xxv; Bemis, *American Secretaries of State*, VII, 102, and *Diplomatic History*, 349, 388, 432; Dunning, *Reconstruction*, ch. x; J. W. Foster, *Century of American Diplomacy* (1900), ch. xi; J. B. Henderson, Jr., *Diplomatic Questions* (1901), 389, 513; J. H. Latané and D. M. Wainhouse, *American Foreign Policy* (1934), chs. xvii–xviii; Nevins, *Fish*, chs. vi–xxiv, xxvi, xxviii, xxxvi; Oberholtzer, *History*, I, ch. viii, II, ch. xiv, III, 123; Rhodes, *History*, VI, 205, ch. xxxviii, VII, 29; Schouler, *History*, VII, 161, 194.

Special — Mexico: P. F. Martin, *Maximilian in Mexico* (1914), ch. xxxiii; Rippy, *United States and Mexico*, 265; Callahan, *American Foreign Policy in Mexican Relations*, 305; Perkins, *Monroe Doctrine, 1826–1867*, ch. ix; Hilarión Frías y Soto, *México y los Estados Unidos durante la Intervención Francesa* (1901); Lalley, *French Opposition to Mexican Policy*; H. L. Hoskins, "French View of Monroe Doctrine and Mexican Expedition," *Hispanic Am. Hist. Rev.*, IV (1921), 677; Bancroft, *Seward*, II, ch. xl; E. B. White, *American Opinion of France*, 150. ❡ Great Britain and Canada: Shippee, *Canadian-American Relations*, chs. ix–xx; Keenleyside and Brown, *Canada and United States*, 137, 267, 301; Callahan, *American Foreign Policy in Canadian Relations*, chs. xiii–xvi; J. A. MacDonald, *Troublous Times in Canada* (1910); G. A. Smith, *Treaty of Washington* (1941); R. C. Clark, "Diplomatic Mission of Sir John Rose," *Pacific Northwest Quar.*, XXVII (1936), 227; J. P. Baxter, "British High Commissioners at Washington, 1871," *Mass. Hist. Soc., Proc.*, LXV (1940), 334; Moore, *Arbitrations*, I, 495, 712, V, 4639; Ferdinand Grimm, *Northwest Water Boundary* (Hunter Miller, ed., 1942); C. F. Adams, Jr., *Charles Francis Adams*, chs. xvii–xix; Barrows, *Evarts*, chs. xiv–xv; Dyer, *Evarts*, ch. viii; Pierce, *Sumner*, IV, 160, 383, 488; Haynes, *Sumner*, ch. xvii; D. H. Chamberlain, *Charles Sumner and Treaty of Washington* (1902); Andrew Lang, *Sir Stafford Northcote* (1890), II, ch. xii; Edmond Fitzmaurice, *Earl Granville* (1905), II, ch. iii; John Morley, *Gladstone* (1903), II, bk. 6, ch. ix; Egidio Reale, *L'Arbitrage International. Le Règlement Judiciaire du Conflit de l'Alabama* (1929). ❡ Expatriation: Tsiang, *Expatriation*, 84; R. L. Morrow, "Anglo-American Treaty of 1870," *Am. Hist. Rev.*, XXXIX (1934), 663; Jeannette Keim, *German-American Political Relations* (1919), ch. iii; Friedrich Kapp, "Der Deutsch-Amerikanische Vertrag," *Preussische Jahrbuch*, XXXV (1875), 509, 660. ❡ Expansionist Sentiment: T. C. Smith, "Expansion after Civil War," *Pol. Sci. Quar.*, XVI (1901), 412; J. P. Smith, *Republican Expansionists of Early Reconstruction Era* (1933); R. E. Sandborn, "United States and British Northwest," *No. Dak. Hist. Quar.*, VI (1931), 5; Brainerd Dyer, "R. J. Walker on Acquiring Greenland and Iceland," *Miss. Valley Hist. Rev.*, XXVII (1940), 263; A. C. Wilgus, "Official Manifest Destiny Sentiment Concerning Hispanic America," *La. Hist. Quar.*, XV (1932), 486; Stevens, *American Expansion in Hawaii*, chs. v–vi; D. M. Dozer, "Anti-Expansionism during Johnson Administration," *Pacific Hist. Rev.*, XII (1943), 253. ❡ Alaska: B. P. Thomas, *Russo-American Relations*, ch. ix; V. J. Farrar, *Purchase of Alaska* (1937); F. A. Golder, "Purchase of Alaska," *Am. Hist. Rev.*, XXV (1920), 411; R. H. Luthin, "Sale of Alaska," *Slavic and East European Rev.*, XVI (1937), 168; T. A. Bailey, "Why United States Purchased Alaska," *Pacific Hist. Rev.*, III (1934), 39; V. H. Reid, *Purchase of Alaska: Contemporary Opinion* (1939); J. M. Callahan, *Alaska Purchase and Americo-Canadian Relations* (1908); Bancroft, *Seward*, II, ch. xlii. ❡ West Indies: Dexter Perkins, *Monroe Doctrine, 1867–1907* (1937), 8; C. C. Tansill, *Purchase of Danish West Indies* (1932), chs. i–iii, and *United States and Santo Domingo*, chs. vii–x; Sumner Welles, *Naboth's Vineyard* (1928), I, ch. v; Logan, *Relations of United States with Haiti*, 315; F. E. Chadwick, *United States and Spain* (1909), I, chs. xiv–xix; J. M. Callahan, *Cuba and International Relations* (1899), 350; Rudolph de Cordova, "'Virginius' Incident," *Nineteenth Century*, LX (1906), 976; Haynes, *Sumner*, ch. xvi; Pierce, *Sumner*, IV, 328, 425. ❡ Other Countries: E. M. Cable, *United States Korean Relations, 1866–71* (1939);

A. J. May, "Crete and United States, 1866–69," *Jour. Mod. Hist.*, XVI (1944), 286; H. R. Marraro, "Closing of Diplomatic Mission to Vatican," *Cath. Hist. Rev.*, XXXIII (1948), 423.

Sources — General: *Congressional Globe*, and *Congressional Record*, 39–44 Congs.; Moore, *Digest of International Law*, §§ 40, 67, 104, 390–400, 475, 907, 957–9; *Foreign Relations, 1865–1875* (*General Index*, 1861–99); Malloy, Redmond, and Treworth, *Treaties, Conventions*; Welles, *Diary*, II–III; Richardson, *Messages and Papers*, VI–VII; Bartlett, *American Diplomacy*, 305. ❪ Mexico: 40 Cong., 1 Sess., *Sen. Ex. Doc.*, No. 20, 2 Sess., *H. Ex. Doc.*, VII, No. 25; Matiás Romero, *Correspondencia durante la Intervención* (1870–92); Bigelow, *Retrospections*, III, chs. xv–xviii. ❪ Great Britain and Canada: Dept. of State, *Correspondence Concerning Claims against Great Britain* (1869–71), and *Correspondence Respecting Geneva Arbitration* (1872), and *Papers Relating to Treaty of Washington* (1872–74); *Washington Treaty Debate* (in Canadian House of Commons, May 1872); Caleb Cushing, *Treaty of Washington* (1873); J. C. B. Davis, *Fish and Alabama Claims* (1893); T. W. Balch, *Alabama Arbitration* (1900); F. W. Hackett, *Reminiscences of Geneva Tribunal* (1911). ❪ Alaska: 40 Cong., 2 Sess., *H. Ex. Doc.*, No. 177; Hunter Miller, "Russian Opinion on Cession of Alaska," *Am. Hist. Rev.*, XLVIII (1943), 521. ❪ Santo Domingo: 41 Cong., 3 Sess., *Sen. Ex. Docs.*, Nos. 17, 34, *H. Ex. Docs.*, Nos. 42, 43; A. D. White, *Autobiography*, I, chs. ix, xi, xxviii; Howe, *Letters and Journals*, II, ch. xviii.

Bibliography — Bemis and Griffin, *Guide to Diplomatic History*, 349, 397, 510; Bailey, *Diplomatic History*, 404, 425.

Chapter Twenty

ECONOMIC REVOLUTION, 1865–1880

195. EMERGENCE OF THE NEW SOUTH, 1865–1880

Summary — Postwar economic disorganization in South (§ 189). — Recovery of white supremacy (§ 190). — Problem of state debts. — Readjustment of agriculture: breakup of large plantations; tenant farming; debt peonage; improved farming methods; new commercial crops. — Railway extension. — Industrial development: cotton textiles; iron and steel; tobacco products. — Human factors: former aristocracy; poor whites; mountaineers; child labor; immigrants; race relations (§ 212). — Rise of agrarian discontent (§ 209). —Reconciliation of North and South.

General — P. A. Bruce, *Rise of New South* (1905), chs. i–xxi, xxx; Cash, *Mind of South*, bk. 2; E. Q. Hawk, *Economic History of South* (1934), ch. xvi; W. B. Hesseltine, *History of South*, ch. xxv, and *Confederate Leaders in New South* (1950); Oberholtzer, *History*, IV, 506, 555, 564; Shannon, *America's Economic Growth*, ch. xviii; Simkins, *South Old and New*, ch. xvi; *South in Building of Nation*, VI; Holland Thompson, *New South* (1919), chs. iv–vi; Woodward, *Origins of New South*, chs. iv–viii.

Special — State Debts: Ratchford, *American State Debts*, 162; Scott, *Repudiation of State Debts*, 55, 67, 167; McGrane, *Foreign Bondholders and State Debts*, ch. xiv; B. C. Randolph, "Foreign Bondholders and Repudiated Debts of Southern States," *Am. Jour. Int. Law*, XXV (1931), 63; C. C. Pearson, *Readjuster Movement in Virginia* (1935). ⟨ Agriculture: F. A. Shannon, *Farmer's Last Frontier* (1945), chs. iv–v; B. I. Wiley, "Southern Agriculture since Civil War," *Ag. Hist.*, XIII (1939), 65, and "Farming in Lower Mississippi Valley," *Jour. Southern Hist.*, III (1937), 441; Oscar Zeichner, "Transition from Slave to Free Labor," *Ag. Hist.*, XIII (1939), 22; C. W. Tebeau, "Aspects of Planter-Freedman Relations," *Jour. Negro Hist.*, XXI (1936), 130; E. C. Brooks, *Story of Cotton* (1911), chs. xi–xvii; H. C. Nixon, "New South and Old Crop," Craven, *Essays in Honor of Dodd*, 320; H. W. Grady, "Cotton and Its Kingdom," *Harper's Mag.*, LXIII (1881), 719; J. L. Waller, "Overland Movement of Cotton," *Southwestern Hist. Quar.*, XXXV (1931), 137; Jacobstein, *Tobacco Industry*, 68; R. P. Brooks, *Agrarian Revolution in Georgia* (1914), chs. i–iii; E. M. Banks, *Economics of Land Tenure in Georgia* (1905), chs. ii–vi; G. W. McGinty, "Changes in Louisiana Agriculture," *La. Hist. Quar.*, XVIII (1935), 407. ⟨ Railroads: C. R. Fish, *Restoration of Southern Railroads* (1919); E. G. Campbell, "Indebted Railroad," *Jour. Southern Hist.*, VI (1940), 167; A. B. Moore, "Railroad Building in Alabama during Reconstruction," *ibid.*, I (1935), 421; P. S. McGuire, "Railroads of Georgia," *Ga. Hist. Quar.*, XVI (1932), 179. ⟨ Manufactures: Copeland, *Cotton Manufacturing*, 32; Broadus Mitchell, *Rise of Cotton Mills in South* (1921); Holland Thompson, *From Cotton Field to Cotton Mill* (1906), chs. iv, vi, xii; T. M. Young, *American Cotton Industry* (1902), chs. vii–x; H. C. Nixon, "Rise of Cotton-seed Oil Industry," *Jour. Pol. Econ.*, XXXVIII (1930), 73; D. A. Tompkins, *Cotton and Cotton Oil* (1901); Ethel Armes, *Story of Coal and Iron in Alabama* (1910), chs. xiv–xxv; Jacobstein, *Tobacco Industry*, ch. iii; Robert, *Story of Tobacco*, 121; Boyd, *Durham*, chs. iv–v.　❡ Social Groups: S. A. Hamilton, "New Race Question in South," *Arena*, XXVII (1902), 352; C. W. Stiles, *Report upon Prevalence and Distribution of Hookworm Disease* (1903); W. G. Frost, "Our Contemporary Ancestors in Southern Mountains," *Atlantic Monthly*, LXXXIII (1899), 311; S. T. Wilson, *Southern Mountaineers* (1906); Kephart, *Our Southern Highlanders*; R. T. Berthoff, "Southern Attitudes toward Immigration," *Jour. Southern Hist.*, XVII (1951), 328; B. J. Loewenberg, "Efforts of South to Encourage Immigration," *South Atlantic Quar.*, XXXIII (1934), 363.　❡ Reconciliation of North and South: Buck, *Road to Reunion*, chs. v–xiii; Ella Lonn, "Reconciliation between North and South," *Jour. Southern Hist.*, XIII (1947), 3.　❡ Biographies: Jenkins, *Duke*, chs. ii–vi; R. B. Nixon, *Henry W. Grady* (1943), chs. v–xi; N. M. Blake, *William Mahone of Virginia* (1935), chs. iv–x; Hendrick, *Page*, I, chs. i–iii, and *Training of an American*, chs. i–viii; Winston, *Tompkins*, chs. ii–xv; Baker, *Woodrow Wilson*, I, chs. ii–viii.

Sources — Official Documents: Census reports, esp. *Tenth Census*, V; *Statistical Abstract* (annual, since 1878).　❡ Unofficial Compilation: *Appletons' Annual Cyclopædia*. ❡ Contemporary Accounts and Commentaries: "A Georgia Plantation," *Scribner's Monthly*, XXI (1881), 830; W. M. Barrows, *New South* (1884); M. B. Hillyard, *New South* (1887); J. W. Johnston, *Emancipation of Southern Whites* (1887); W. D. Kelley, *Old South and New* (1888); A. K. McClure, *South* (1886).

Bibliography — Edwards, *Bibliography of History of Agriculture*, esp. 75; Cappon, *Bibliography of Virginia History*.

196. DEVELOPMENT OF THE MINING FRONTIER, 1859–1880

Summary — New mineral discoveries: Pike's Peak (Colorado), the Comstock Lode (Virginia City, Nevada), and Arizona, 1859; Lewiston (Idaho), 1860–61; western Montana, 1862–64; Wyoming, 1867; Black Hills (Dakota), 1875. — Mining-camp traits. — Mechanization of mining. — Formation of territories: Colorado, 1861 (admitted, 1876); Nevada, 1861 (admitted 1864; see: § 183); Dakota, 1861; Arizona and Idaho, 1863; Montana, 1864; Wyoming, 1876. — Mining in the South (§ 195). — Lake Superior ore beds (§ 207). — Rise of silver question (§ 209).

General — Billington, *Westward Expansion*, ch. xxx; E. D. Branch, *Westward* (1930), 485, 503; D. E. Clark, *West in American History*, ch. xxxiii; Hafen and Rister, *Western America*, chs. xxiv–xxv; Emerson Hough, *Passing of Frontier* (1921), ch. v; Oberholtzer, *History*, I, 280, 334, III, 366; F. L. Paxson, *American Frontier*, 441, 554, and *Last American Frontier* (1910), chs. ix–x; Rickard, *American Mining*, chs. v–vi, viii–ix, xi–xv.

Special — Mineral Finds: H. E. Briggs, *Frontiers of Northwest* (1940), ch. i; W. J. Trimble, *Mining Advance into Inland Empire* (1914), and "Gold Discoveries in Northwest," *Miss. Valley Hist. Rev.*, V (1918), 70; Winther, *Great Northwest*, ch. xiv; A. D. Anderson, *Silver Country, or Great Southwest* (1877), ch. ii; E. S. Mead, *Story of Gold* (1908), chs. vi–vii; G. C. Quiett, *Pay Dirt* (1936), chs. v–vii, ix–xiii, xvi–xviii; L. E. Young, *Mine Taxation in United States* (1917), 25–121.　❡ By Territories and States: Bancroft, *Pacific States*; Paul, *California Gold*, chs. xiv–xvi; M. G. Burlingame, *Montana Frontier* (1942), ch. iv; G. H. Smith, *History of Comstock Lode* (1943); G. D. Lyman, *Ralston's Ring: California Plunders Comstock Lode* (1934); Oscar Lewis, *Silver Kings* (1947); N. C. Wilson, *Silver Stampede* (1937); C. H. Shinn, *Story of Mine* (1896); De Voto, *Mark Twain's America*, ch. vi; G. F. Willison, *Here They Dug Gold* (1932); A. D. Tallent, *Black Hills* (1899); H. E. Briggs, "Black Hills Gold Rush," *No. Dak. Hist. Quar.*, V (1930), 71; G. W. Stokes and H. R. Driggs, *Deadwood Gold* (1926); § 62.　❡ Mining Camps: J. D. Hill, "Early Mining Camp," *Pacific Hist. Rev.*, I (1932), 295; Dick, *Vanguards of Frontier*, ch. xi; H. A. Trexler, *Flour and Wheat in Montana Gold Camps* (1918); S. J. Coon, "Gold Camps and Development of Western Montana," *Jour. Pol. Econ.*, XXXVIII (1930), 580; T. J. Dimsdale, *Vigilantes of Montana* (1882); N. P. Langford, *Vigilante Days and Ways* (1890).　❡ Territorial Government: E. S. Pomeroy, *Territories, 1861–90* (1947).

Sources — Official Documents and Contemporary Reports: *Congressional Globe, Congressional Record,* and *Congressional Docs.,* 36–46 Congs.; *Census Reports,* 1860–80, also *Twelfth Census, Statistical Atlas* (1900), plates 10–11; Clarence King, "Mining Laws and Regulations," *Tenth Census* (1880), XIV; U. S. Mint, *Reports* (1859–80), and *Report on Production of Precious Metals* (1880); Eliot Lord, "Comstock Mining and Miners," Geol. Surv., *Monographs,* IV (1883); R. W. Raymond, *Mining Industry of Rocky Mountains* (1874), and *Statistics of Mines and Mining* (1875); J. R. Browne, *Mineral Resources West of Rocky Mountains* (1868), and *Resources of Pacific Slope;* W. A. Jones, *Report upon Reconnaissance of Northwestern Wyoming* (1875). ❡ Guidebooks, Descriptions, and Reminiscences: John Mullan, *Miners' and Travelers' Guide* (1865); F. Fry, *Traveler's Guide* (1865); E. H. Hall, *Great West* (1864); L. P. Brockett, *Our Western Empire* (1881), pt. 1, chs. x–xi, pt. 2, ch. iv; R. E. Strahorn, *Handbook of Wyoming* (1877), and *Resources and Attractions of Idaho Territory* (1881); H. N. Maguire, *Resources of Montana* (1868), and *New Map and Guide to Dakota and Black Hills* (1877); J. R. Hinton, *Hand-book to Arizona* (1878); F. C. Young, *Across the Plains in '65* (1905); Mark Twain, *Roughing It;* Samuel Bowles, *Across Continent,* chs. iii–vii, xiv–xvi, xxvii–xxx, and *Our New West* (1869); A. D. Richardson, *Beyond the Mississippi,* and *Our New States and Territories* (1866); A. K. McClure, *Three Thousand Miles through Rocky Mountains* (1869); W. F. Rae, *Westward by Rail* (1871); W. A. Bell, *New Tracks in North America* (1869); A. S. Duniway, *From the West to the West* (1905); Clarence King, *Mountaineering in Sierra Nevada* (1871), ch. xiv; William Wright (Dan De Quille), *Big Bonanza* (1877; new ed., 1947); G. T. Ingham, *Digging Gold among the Rockies* (1880); L. R. Hafen, ed., *Pike's Peak Guide Books of 1859* (1941), and *Overland Routes to Gold Fields, 1859* (1942), and *Colorado Gold Rush* (1941); W. A. Goulder, *Reminiscences* (1909); W. T. Stoll and H. W. Whicker, *Silver Strike* (1932); M. M. Mathews, *Ten Years in Nevada* (1880); Stewart, *Reminiscences,* chs. xiv–xvii; A. J. Larsen, ed., "Black Hills Gold Rush," *No. Dak. Hist. Quar.,* VI (1932), 302.

Bibliography — Bancroft, *Pacific States;* Quiett, *Pay Dirt,* 483; Billington, *Westward Expansion,* 821; Crane, *Index of Mining Engineering Literature.*

197. WESTERN RAILROADS, 1861–1872

Summary — Earlier history of railroads (§ 148). — Overland stage and pony express. — Pacific railroads: sectional dispute in 1850's over location (§ 174); Congressional charters to Central Pacific, Union Pacific, Southern Pacific, and other companies, 1862–71. — Construction of Central Pacific and Union Pacific, 1864–69: their rivalry; Huntington, Stanford, Crocker, and Hopkins; Credit Mobilier (§ 192). — Extension of Middle Western railroads to the prairies. — Development of trunk lines. — Later history (§§ 200, 207).

General — Billington, *Westward Expansion,* ch. xxxi; Branch, *Westward,* chs. xxv, xxix; D. E. Clark, *West in American History,* chs. xxxii, xxxiv; Hafen and Rister, *Western America,* chs. xxvi, xxix; John Moody, *Railroad Builders* (1919), ch. vi; Nevins, *Emergence of Modern America,* 50; Oberholtzer, *History,* I, 296, II, 474, 519; Paxson, *Last American Frontier,* chs. xi–xiii, xix, and *American Frontier,* 427, 459, 494; Riegel, *Western Railroads,* 65; J. W. Starr, Jr., *One Hundred Years of American Railroading* (1928), chs. xiii–xv; Slason Thompson, *Short History of American Railways* (1925), 166.

Special — Nonrail Communication: Hafen, *Overland Mail;* O. O. Winther, *Via Western Express & Stagecoach* (1945); Arthur Chapman, *Pony Express* (1932); W. L. Visscher, *Pony Express* (1908); A. F. Harlow, *Old Waybills* (1934), chs. xiii–xiv; Frederick, *Ben Holladay;* G. R. Hebard and E. A. Brininstool, *Bozeman Trail* (1922), I, 59; R. N. Richardson and C. C. Rister, *Greater Southwest* (1935), ch. x; F. A. Root and W. B. Connelley, *Overland Stage to California* (1901); H. E. Briggs, "Early Freight and Stage Lines in Dakota," *No. Dak. Hist. Quar.,* III (1928–29), 229; E. A. Wiltsee, *Pioneer Miner and the Pack Mule Express* (1931); Edward Hungerford, *Wells Fargo* (1947), chs. i–viii; Stimson, *Express Business,* chs. xix–xx; R. L. Thompson, *Wiring a Continent,* chs. xiv–xv.

❡ Pacific Railroads: G. C. Quiett, *They Built the West* (1934), chs. i–vii; Haney, *Congressional History of Railways*, II, 49; J. D. Galloway, *First Transcontinental Railroad* (1950); E. L. Sabin, *Building the Pacific Railway* (1919); H. K. White, *Union Pacific* (1895), chs. i–v; Trottman, *Union Pacific*, chs. i–iii; Crawford, *Credit Mobilier*, chs. i–vi; H. J. Carman and C. H. Mueller, "Contract and Finance Corporation and Central Pacific," *Miss. Valley Hist. Rev.*, XIV (1927), 326; Oscar Lewis, *Big Four* (1938); G. T. Clark, *Leland Stanford* (1931), chs. vi–ix; J. R. Perkins, *Trails, Rails and War* (1929), chs. ix–xiv, xvi; L. L. Waters, *Steel Rails to Santa Fé* (1950), 23. ❡ Middle Western Lines: Gates, *Illinois Central*, chs. v–xiv; Corliss, *Main Line of Mid-America*, chs. xiii–xxx; Overton, *Burlington West*, chs. vii–xiii; J. W. Cary, *Chicago, Milwaukee and St. Paul* (1893); H. G. Pearson, *American Railroad Builder* (1911), ch. v; C. F. Adams, *Railroads* (1878), 80; P. J. Green, "Railroad Building," Univ. of No. Dak., *Quar. Jour.*, XIX (1928), 59; Merk, *Economic History of Wisconsin*, chs. x–xi.

Sources — (See also: §§ 199–200) — Official: 42 Cong., 2 Sess., *H. Ex. Doc.*, XII, No. 213, *H. Misc. Doc.*, IV, No. 228, 3 Sess., *H. Report*, II, Nos. 77, 78; Pacific Railway Commission, "Report," 50 Cong., 1 Sess., *Sen. Ex. Doc.*, No. 51; *Pacific Railroad, Congressional Proceedings in the 37th, 38th, and 41st Congresses* (1875). ❡ Unofficial: H. V. Poor, *Manual of Railroads* (1868–   ), esp. intro. in 1881; *American Annual Cyclopædia*. ❡ Personal Accounts: C. T. Blake, "Working for Wells Fargo," Calif. Hist. Soc., *Quar.*, XVI (1937), 30, 172; Bowles, *Across Continent*, ch. xxiv; G. M. Dodge, *How We Built Union Pacific Railway* (1910); W. F. Hooke, *Bullwhacker* (1925); Alexander Majors, *Seventy Years on Frontier* (1893), chs. xix–xxii, xxvi; H. S. Rumfield, "Letters of Overland Mail Agent in Utah," Am. Antiq. Soc., *Proc.*, XXXVIII (1928), 227; C. A. Strahorn, *Fifteen Thousand Miles by Stage* (1911).

Bibliography — Billington, *Westward Expansion*, 823; Riegel, *Western Railroads*, 321; F. A. Cleveland and F. W. Powell, *Railroad Promotion* (1909), 295.

198. INDIAN RELATIONS, 1860–1886

Summary — Earlier situation (§ 165). — Indian wars in the Pacific Northwest, the Southwest, and the Great Plains, 1860–65. — Guarding the roads to the mines, 1866; Red Cloud; Spotted Tail; Fort Philip Kearny; Fetterman massacre. — Guarding the railroads. — Peace commissions, 1867–68; creation of Board of Indian Commissioners, 1869. — Decimation of the buffalo herds. — Hostilities in 1876–77; Custer massacre; Chief Joseph's retreat. — Apache difficulties in Arizona and New Mexico, 1882–86. — Later Indian relations (§ 212).

General — Billington, *Westward Expansion*, ch. xxxii; D. E. Clark, *West in American History*, 572; Hafen and Rister, *Western America*, chs. xxvii–xxviii; Hough, *Passing of Frontier*, ch. vii; W. C. Macleod, *American Indian Frontier* (1928), ch. xxxiii; D. M. McNicol, *Amerindians* (1937), chs. xii–xvi; G. W. Manypenny, *Our Indian Wards* (1880), chs. vii–xix; Nevins, *Emergence of Modern America*, 101; Oberholtzer, *History*, I, ch. vi, III, 380, IV, 631; Paxson, *Last American Frontier*, chs. ii, viii, xiv–xix, xxi, and *American Frontier*, 485, 502; Sparks, *National Development*, ch. xvi.

Special — Plains Life of Aborigines: Clark Wissler, *North American Indians of Plains* (1920) and *American Indian* (1917), 218; Radin, *American Indian*, ch. xiii; Webb, *Great Plains*, ch. iii; W. H. Miner, *American Indians* (1917), chs. iv–v; R. I. Dodge, *Plains of Great West* (1877), pt. 3; Dane and M. R. Coolidge, *Navajo Indians* (1930); G. B. Grinnell, *Cheyenne Indians* (1923); Hodge, *Handbook of American Indians*. ❡ Border Warfare (inclusive): P. I. Wellman, *Death on Horseback* (1947), sect. 1, chs. i–ix, sect. 2, chs. iv–ix; F. W. Seymour, *Story of Red Man* (1929), chs. xv–xvii; F. D. Downey, *Indian-Fighting Army* (1941); G. A. Forsyth, *Story of Soldier* (1900), chs. vi–xvi. ❡ Border Warfare (particular): C. C. Rister, *Border Command: General Phil Sheridan* (1944); C. E. DeLand, "Sioux Wars," *So. Dak. Hist. Coll.*, XV (1930), 9, XVII (1934), 177; W. F. Johnson, *Red Record of Sioux* (1891); Vestal, *Sitting Bull*, chs.

i-xxx; E. A. Brininstool, *et al.*, "Chief Crazy Horse," *Neb. Hist. Mag.*, XII (1929), 4; G. R. Hebard, *Washakie* (1930), 93; Fred Dustin, *Custer Tragedy* (1939); C. F. Roe, *Custer's Last Battle* (1927); W. A. Graham, *Story of Little Big Horn* (1926); F. F. Van de Water, *Glory-Hunter* (1934), pts. 2, 3; J. E. Cox, "Soldiering in Dakota in Seventies," *No. Dak. Hist. Quar.*, VI (1931), 63; P. E. Byrne, "Custer Myth," *ibid.*, 187; W. M. Wemett, "Custer's Expedition," *ibid.*, 292; Hebard and Brininstool, *Bozeman Trail*, I, 179, II; J. P. Dunn, *Massacres of Mountains* (1886); G. F. Brimlow, *Bannock Indian War of 1878* (1938); R. R. Arnold, *Indian Wars of Idaho* (1932); C. A. Fee, *Chief Joseph* (1936); N. C. Titus, "Last Stand of Nez Percés," *Wash. Hist. Quar.*, VI (1915), 145; G. O. Shields, *Battle of Big Hole* (1889); R. J. Walsh, *Making of Buffalo Bill* (1928), chs. ix–xi, xv; G. E. Hyde, *Red Cloud's Folk* (1937), chs. vii–xvi; G. B. Grinnell, *Fighting Cheyennes* (1915), chs. xi–xxxi; C. C. Rister, *Southwestern Frontier* (1928), 19; Richardson and Rister, *Greater Southwest*, chs. xiii–xiv; Webb, *Texas Rangers*, chs. vii–xviii; R. N. Richardson, *Comanche Barrier to South Plains Settlement* (1933), 267–397; F. C. Lockwood, *Apache Indians* (1938), chs. ix–xiv; W. C. Barnes, "Apaches' Last Stand in Arizona," *Ariz. Hist. Rev.*, III (1930–31), No. 4, 36; H. W. Daly, "Geronimo Campaign," *ibid.*, No. 2, 26. ❧ Destruction of Buffalo: M. S. Garretson, *American Bison* (1938), chs. viii–xiii; E. D. Branch, *Hunting of Buffalo* (1929); M. G. Burlingame, "Buffalo in Trade and Commerce," *No. Dak. Hist. Quar.*, III (1929), 262; Briggs, *Frontiers of Northwest*, ch. ii; H. A. Trexler, "Buffalo Range of Northwest," *Miss. Valley Hist. Rev.*, VII (1920), 348; C. C. Rister, "Destruction of Buffalo in Southwest," *Southwestern Hist. Quar.*, XXXIII (1929), 34. ❧ United States Indian Policy: L. B. Priest, *Uncle Sam's Stepchildren* (1942), chs. viii–xii; Foreman, *Last Trek of Indians*, pt. 2; E. W. Hayter, "Ponca Removal," *No. Dak. Hist. Quar.*, VI (1932), 262; Stanley Clark, "Ponca Publicity," *Miss. Valley Hist. Rev.*, XXIX (1943), 495; Roy Gittinger, *Formation of Oklahoma* (1939), chs. vi–vii; E. E. Dale, *Indians of Southwest* (1949), chs. vi–ix; R. H. Ogle, *Federal Control of Western Apaches* (1940); F. D. Reeve, "Government and Navaho," *N. Mex. Hist. Rev.*, XVIII (1943), 17; F. W. Seymour, *Indian Agents* (1941), chs. i–xvii; Woodworth Clum, *Apache Agent* (1936), chs. iii–xxxvii; H. H. Jackson, *Century of Dishonor* (1881).

Sources — Official: Bur. of Ethnology, *Eighteenth Annual Report* (1899), pt. 2; Kappler, *Indian Affairs*; annual *Reports* of Commissioner of Indian Affairs, of Board of Indian Commissioners, of Secretary of War, and of Bureau of Engineering; *Record of Engagements with Hostile Indians within the Military Division of the Missouri from 1868 to 1882* (1883). ❧ Personal: J. C. Birge, *Awakening of Desert* (1912), chs. xiv–xxx; J. G. Bourke, *On Border with Crook* (1891); J. R. Browne, *Adventures in Apache Country* (1869); C. E. Campbell, "Down among Red Men," *Kan. State Hist. Soc., Coll.*, XVII (1928), 623; F. C. Carrington, *My Army Life* (1910); J. P. Clum, "Geronimo," *N. Mex. Hist. Rev.*, III (1928), 1, 121, 217; W. F. Cody, *Adventures of Buffalo Bill* (1904), and *Story of Wild West* (1902); J. H. Cook, *Fifty Years on Old Frontier* (1891); J. R. Cook, *Border and Buffalo* (1907); George Crook, *Autobiography* (1946), chs. v–vii; E. B. Custer, *Tenting on Plains* (1895), and *Boots and Saddles* (1885), and *Following the Guidon* (1890); G. A. Custer, *My Life on Plains* (1874); Britton Davis, *Truth about Geronimo* (1929); Dodge, *Our Wild Indians;* W. F. Drannan, *Thirty-One Years on Plains* (1908), chs. x–xliv; J. F. Finerty, *War Path and Bivouac* (1890); Geronimo, *Story of His Life* (1906); O. O. Howard, *My Life and Experiences among Hostile Indians* (1907); C. A. Windolph, *I Fought with Custer* (1947); R. W. Johnson, *Soldier's Reminiscences* (1886); Charles King, *Campaigning with Crook* (1880); Luther Standing Bear, *My People the Sioux* (1928), chs. i–viii; James McLaughlin, *My Friend the Indian* (1910); Anton Mazzanovich, *Trailing Geronimo* (1926); N. A. Miles, *Personal Recollections* (1896), chs. x–xxi; M. A. Otero, *My Life on Frontier* (1935–39); D. C. Poole, *Among the Sioux* (1881); Sheridan, *Memoirs*, II, chs. xii–xiv; John and W. T. Sherman, *Letters*, 287, 296, 317; Z. T. Sutley, *Last Frontier* (1930); Stanley Vestal, ed., *New Sources of Indian History* (1934); H. W. Wheeler, *Buffalo Days* (1925).

Bibliography — Billington, *Westward Expansion*, 825; Hodge, *Handbook of American Indians*, II, 1179; Dunn, *Massacres of Mountains*, 757; Rister, *Southwestern Frontier*, 311.

199. LANDS AND AGRICULTURE, 1862–1880

Summary — Earlier history of public lands (§§ 158, 169). — Federal legislation: Homestead Act, 1862; Timber Culture Act, 1873; Desert Land Act, 1877; Free Timber and Timber and Stone Acts, 1878. — Evasions; Land Commission, 1879. — Encouragement of settlers. — Railroad land sales. — Government promotion of farming; Department of Agriculture, 1862; Morrill Land Grant Act for agricultural colleges, 1862; state agricultural departments, beginning with Georgia, 1874. — Mechanization of farming. — Western development, 1862–80: prairie farming; extension of wheat culture; advance of North Central states. — Rural life. — Lawlessness (§ 214). — Granger movement (§ 200). — Southern agriculture (§ 195). — Decline of New England agriculture. — Later developments (§§ 207–9).

General — L. H. Bailey, *Cyclopedia of American Agriculture* (1907–09); Billington, *Westward Expansion*, ch. xxxv; E. L. Bogart, *Economic History of American Agriculture* (1923), ch. vii; E. E. Edwards, "American Agriculture — the First 300 Years," *Yearbook of Ag.*, 1940, 171; Schmidt and Ross, *Readings in American Agriculture*, pt. 3; Shannon, *Farmer's Last Frontier*, chs. ii–iii, vi–viii, xi–xii.

Special — Land Legislation and Administration: Hibbard, *Public Land Policies*, 324, 358, 457; Robbins, *Our Landed Heritage*, chs. xiii–xviii; H. H. Dunham, *Government Handout* (1941), chs. i–viii; Sanborn, *Grants in Aid of Railways*, App. A; Haney, *Congressional History of Railways*, II, chs. ii–iii; Stephenson, *Political History*, chs. xiii–xv; Dubois and Mathews, *Grow*, 183, 254; P. W. Gates, "Homestead Law in an Incongruous Land System," *Am. Hist. Rev.*, XLI (1936), 652; J. T. Ganoe, "Origin of National Reclamation Policy," *Miss. Valley Hist. Rev.*, XVIII (1931), 34, and "Desert Land Act in Operation," *Ag. Hist.*, XI (1937), 142; W. F. Raney, "Timber Culture Acts," Miss. Valley Hist. Assoc., *Proc.*, X (1921), 219; Ise, *Forest Policy*, 31; Cameron, *Governmental Forest Control*, ch. vii; R. H. Hess, "Beginnings of Irrigation," *Jour. Pol. Econ.*, XX (1912), 807. ❧ Encouragement of Settlers: T. C. Blegen, "Competition of Northwestern States for Immigrants," *Wisc. Mag. Hist.*, III (1919), 3, and "Minnesota's Campaign for Immigrants," Swedish Hist. Soc., *Year Book*, XI (1926), 3; H. S. Schell, "Immigration Activities of Dakota," *No. Dak. Hist. Quar.*, VII (1932), 5; M. L. Hansen, "Encouragement of Immigration to Iowa," *Iowa Jour. Hist. and Pol.*, XIX (1921), 159; A. J. Brown, "Promotion of Emigration to Washington," *Pacific Northwest Quar.*, XXXVI (1945), 3; Riegel, *Western Railroads*, ch. xviii; Overton, *Burlington West*, ch. xiii; Gates, *Illinois Central*, chs. xii, xiv; G. D. Bradley, *Santa Fé* (1920), ch. v; J. B. Hedges, *Villard and Railways of Northwest* (1930), ch. vi; Waters, *Steel Rails to Santa Fe*, 218; H. F. Peterson, "Projects of Northern Pacific," *Minn. Hist.*, X (1929), 127, and "Early Minnesota Railroads and Quest for Settlers," *ibid.*, XIII (1932), 25; E. M. Parker, "Southern Pacific Railroad and Settlement in Southern California," *Pacific Hist. Rev.*, VI (1937), 103. ❧ Government Promotion of Agriculture: Edward Wiest, *Agricultural Organization* (1923), chs. ii, x; T. S. Harding, *Two Blades of Grass* (1947), chs. iii, iv; E. D. Ross, "Department of Agriculture during Commissionership," *Ag. Hist.*, XX (1946), 129; A. C. True, *History of Agricultural Education* (1937), 41, 67; James, *Land Grant Act*; W. B. Parker, *J. S. Morrill* (1924), ch. xi; B. F. Andrews, *Land Grant Act of 1862 and Land Grant Colleges* (1918); Ross, *Democracy's College*, chs. v–vii. ❧ Mechanization of Farming: R. L. Ardrey, *American Agricultural Implements* (1894); H. W. Quaintance, *Influence of Farm Machinery* (1904); Leo Rogin, *Introduction of Farm Machinery in Relation to Productivity of Labor* (1931); W. G. Moody, *Land and Labor* (1883), ch. i; Kaempffert, *American Invention*, II, ch. vii; George Iles, *Leading American Inventors* (1912), 276; Hutchinson, *Cyrus H. McCormick*, II, chs. iii, x–xi, xiii–xv; F. B. Swingle, "Invention of Twine Binder," *Wisc. Mag. Hist.*, X (1926), 35; Webb, *Great Plains*, 280; E. W. Hayter, "Barbed Wire Fencing," *Ag. Hist.*, XIII (1939), 189. ❧ Western Agriculture: Brockett, *Our Western Empire*, pt. 1, chs. xii–xiv, pt. 2, chs. vi–vii; Finlay Dun, *American Farming and Food* (1881); R. P. Porter, *West from Census of 1880* (1882); Moody, *Land and Labor*, chs. ii–iv; W. D. Emerson, *Indian Corn and Its Culture* (1878), chs. v, xii–xvi; Briggs, *Frontiers of Northwest*, 485; Schafer, *Agriculture in Wisconsin*, 93; H. M. Larson, *Wheat Market and Farmer in Minnesota* (1926), chs. i–vi; Wilder,

Kansas, 310; J. C. Malin, *Winter Wheat in Kansas* (1944), chs. ii–x; Osgood Hardy, "Agricultural Changes in California," Pacific Coast Br., Am. Hist. Assoc., *Proc.,* 1929, 216. ❡ Rural Life (also § 200): Briggs, *Frontiers of Northwest,* 564; Everett Dick, *Sod-House Frontier* (1937), chs. viii–ix, xv–xxi, xxxiii–xxxv; N. W. Ross, *Westward the Women* (1945), chs. vi–xi; E. V. Smalley, "Isolation of Life on Prairie Farms," *Atlantic Monthly,* LXXII (1893), 375; John Ise, *Sod and Stubble* (1936); N. H. Egleston, *Village and Village Life* (1878), chs. iv–v; T. D. Clark, *Pills, Petticoats and Plows: the Southern Country Store* (1944); W. M. Raine, *Guns of Frontier* (1940), chs. vii–xiii. ❡ New England: H. F. Wilson, *Hill Country,* chs. v–ix; W. H. Brewer, *Brighter Side of New England Agriculture* (1890); F. H. Chase, "Is Agriculture Declining in New England?" *New Eng. Mag.,* II (1890), 448; J. D. Long, *et al.,* "Future of New England Country," *ibid.,* III (1891), 661.

Sources — Public Domain: Donaldson, *Public Domain;* 47 Cong., 2 Sess., *H. Misc. Docs.,* XVI–XVIII ([Land] *Laws of United States, Local or Temporary,* and *Existing Laws*); 46 Cong., 2 Sess., *H. Ex. Doc.,* No. 46, 3 Sess., *ibid.,* No. 47; General Land Office, *Reports.* ❡ Agriculture: *Reports* of U. S. Commissioner of Agriculture and of State agricultural boards; culture in Census Bureau, *Reports* (on agriculture); "Agricultural Progress of Fifty Years," *Twelfth Census* (1900), pp. xvi–xxv; Dept. of Ag., Division of Stat., "Wages of Farm Labor, 1866–1892," Misc. Ser., *Reports,* No. 4 (1892); Dept. of Ag., *Yearbook,* 1899; "Agricultural Implements," 46 Cong., 3 Sess., *H. Ex. Doc.,* No. 42, pt. 5. ❡ Maps: Paullin, *Atlas,* plates 57–8, 63–4, 143–7; Dept. of Ag., *Atlas of American Agriculture* (1918–35). ❡ Personal: M. L. T. Baily, "Prairie Homesteading," *Palimpsest,* XXIII (1942), 229; Hamlin Garland, *Boy Life on Prairie* (1899), and *Son of the Middle Border,* chs. i–xx; E. W. Howe, *Story of a Country Town* (1883); L. A. Ide, "In a Prairie Schooner," *Wash. Hist. Quar.,* XVIII (1927), 122, 191; Quick, *One Man's Life,* chs. ix–x; E. R. Orpen, *Old Emigrant Days in Kansas* (1928); Howard Ruede, *Sod-House Days* (1937); W. D. Wyman, "Reminiscences," *Neb. Hist.,* XXVIII (1947), 187.

Bibliography — Edwards, *Bibliography of History of Agriculture;* Shannon, *Farmer's Last Frontier,* ch. xvi; L. B. Schmidt, *Topical Studies and References on History of American Agriculture* (1940), pt. 3; R. B. Handy and M. A. Cannon, *Publications of U. S. Department of Agriculture* (1902); Hasse, *Index of Economic Material;* Bercaw, *Bibliography on Land Settlement,* 16–200; Milton Conover, *General Land Office* (1923), 178; A. C. True, *Agricultural Education,* 397; H. F. Wilson, *Hill Country,* 403.

200. TRANSPORTATION AND THE GRANGERS, 1867–1880

Summary — Rapid expansion of railroads (§ 197) and of agriculture (§ 199) in Middle West. — Causes of agrarian discontent. — Patrons of Husbandry (Grangers), founded in 1867; coöperative undertakings. — Farmers in politics: local parties; state regulation of railways and grain elevators, beginning with Illinois, 1870. — Railway rate legislation in the East. — Agitation for federal regulation: Windom report and McCrary bill, 1874; Hopkins bill, 1876; Reagan report and bill, 1878. — Supreme Court decisions in the Granger cases, 1877. — Railway receiverships, 1876–80; reaction in favor of companies. — Relation of Granger movement to later railway regulation (§ 206).

General — S. J. Buck, *Agrarian Crusade* (1920), chs. i–iv, and *Granger Movement* (1913); Haynes, *Third Party Movements,* chs. vi–vii; Nevins, *Emergence of Modern America,* 154, 371; Oberholtzer, *History,* III, 96; L. B. Schmidt, "Granger Movement," *Prairie Farmer,* XCIII (1921), Nos. 4–8; Wiest, *Agricultural Organization,* chs. xvi–xvii.

Special — Agrarian Unrest and Political Revolt: T. B. Veblen, "Price of Wheat since 1867," *Jour. Pol. Econ.,* I (1892), 68; Frederick Merk, "Eastern Antecedents of Grangers," *Ag. Hist.,* XXIII (1949), 1; W. A. Anderson, "Granger Movement in Middle West," *Iowa Jour. Hist. and Pol.,* XXII (1924), 3; A. E. Paine, *Granger Movement in Illinois* (1904); Larson, *Wheat Market,* ch. iv; H. S. Schell, "Grange and Credit Problem in Dakota," *Ag. Hist.,* X (1936), 59; O. F. Ander, "Immigrant Church and Patrons of Husbandry," *ibid.*, VIII (1934), 155; R. L. Hunt, *Farmer Movements in Southwest* (1935), 7; R. A. Smith, "Grange Movement in Texas," *Southwestern Hist. Quar.*, XLII (1939), 297; J. S. Ferguson, "Grange and Farmer Education in Mississippi," *Jour. Southern Hist.*, VIII (1942), 497; J. H. Easterby, "Granger Movement in South Carolina," *So. Car. Hist. Assoc., Proc.*, I (1931), 21. ❡ Coöperatives: E. W. Bemis, "Cooperative Distribution," *U. S. Dept. Labor, Bull.*, I (1895–96), 610; E. W. Bemis, *et al.*, *Cooperation in United States* (1888), 33, 263, 316, 333, 369, 382, 502; A. H. Hirsch, "Grange Efforts in Middle West to Control Price of Farm Machinery," *Miss. Valley Hist. Rev.*, XV (1929), 473. ❡ Movement for Rate Regulation: E. R. Johnson and T. W. Van Metre, *Principles of Railroad Transportation* (1921), ch. xxv; C. F. Adams, Jr., *Railroads*, 116; A. T. Hadley, *Railroad Transportation* (1889), ch. vii; A. B. Stickney, *Railway Problem* (1891), chs. viii–x; William Larrabee, *Railroad Question* (1893), chs. x–xi; Edward Stanwood, "Farmers and Railroads," *Old and New*, VIII (1873), 335; C. R. Detrick, "Effects of Granger Acts," *Jour. Pol. Econ.*, XI (1903), 237; J. H. Gordon, *Illinois Railway Legislation and Commission Control* (1904), chs. i–viii; Merk, *Economic History of Wisconsin*, chs. ix, xii–xiii; R. S. Saby, *Railroad Legislation in Minnesota* (1912), chs. vii–xvi; A. G. Warner, "Railroad Problems," *Pol. Sci. Quar.*, VI (1891), 66; C. R. Aldrich, "Repeal of Granger Law in Iowa," *Iowa Jour. Hist. and Pol.*, III (1905), 256; E. J. James, "Agitation for Federal Regulation," *Am. Econ. Assoc., Publ.*, II (1887–88), 236; Haney, *Congressional History of Railways*, II, ch. xix. ❡ Rate Regulation and the Courts: Warren, *Supreme Court*, II, 574; J. F. Hudson, *Railways and the Republic* (1889), ch. iv; J. K. Edsall, "Granger Cases and Police Power," *Am. Bar Assoc., Report*, X (1887), 288; W. H. Dunbar, "State Regulation of Prices and Rates," *Quar. Jour. Econ.*, IX (1895), 305; H. S. Smalley, "Railway Rate Control in Its Legal Aspects," *Am. Econ. Assoc., Publ.*, VII (1906), 327.

Sources (also § 199) — Public Documents: *Congressional Globe*, 41 Cong., 2 Sess., 239, 868; 42 Cong., 3 Sess., App. 56; *Congressional Record*, II, 1945, 2147, 2427, 2493, App., 6, 56, 163; "[Windom] Report on Transportation Routes to the Seaboard," 43 Cong., 1 Sess., *Sen. Report*, III, No. 307; reports of state railway commissions and labor bureaus. ❡ Rate Cases: Munn *v.* Illinois (1877), 94 *U. S.*, 113; Chicago, Burlington and Quincy Railroad *v.* Iowa (1877), *ibid.*, 155; Peik *v.* Chicago and Northwestern Railroad (1877), *ibid.*, 164; Chicago, Milwaukee and St. Paul Railroad *v.* Ackley (1877), *ibid.*, 179; Winona and St. Peter Railroad *v.* Blake (1877), *ibid.*, 180; Stone *v.* Wisconsin (1877), *ibid.*, 181; Ruggles *v.* Illinois (1883), 108 U. S., 526. ❡ Other Contemporary Documents: Commons, *Documentary History*, X, ch. vi; Patrons of Husbandry, *Proceedings* (state and national); railway reports, esp. of the Chicago, Burlington, and Quincy, the Chicago, Milwaukee, and St. Paul, and the Chicago Northwestern; *American (Appletons') Annual Cyclopædia*; McPherson, *Handbook of Politics*; C. F. Adams, Jr., "Granger Movement," *No. Am. Rev.*, CXX (1875), 394; O. H. Kelley, *Origin and Progress of Patrons of Husbandry* (1875); E. W. Martin (J. D. McCabe, Jr.), *History of Grange Movement* (1874); Jonathan Periam, *Groundswell* (1874); S. R. Smith, *Grains for Grangers* (1873); G. F. Root and Mrs. S. M. Smith, *Trumpet of Reform* (1874); E. S. Carr, *Patrons of Husbandry on Pacific Coast* (1875); J. J. Woodman, "Reminiscences," *Am. Grange Bull.*, XXX–XXXII (1900–02).

Bibliography (also § 199) — Buck, *Granger Movement*, 315; Bur. of Railway Econ., *Railway Economics* (1912), 22, 141.

201. FINANCIAL PROBLEMS, 1873–1880

Summary — Earlier financial history (§ 191). — Panic of 1873 and ensuing depression. — President Grant's veto of inflation bill, 1874. — Tariff of 1875. — Resumption Act, 1875. — Greenback party, formed in 1875. — Silver agitation: demonetization of silver ("Crime of 1873"); increased production (§ 196); demonetization abroad, 1871–75; sectional attitudes in Congress; Bland-Allison Act, 1878. — Specie payment achieved, 1879. — Later developments (§§ 209–10).

General — Dewey, *Financial History*, 370, 403; Hepburn, *History of Currency*, chs.

xii, xv; Nevins, *Emergence of Modern America,* 290, 370; Noyes, *Forty Years,* 17; Oberholtzer, *History,* III, 79, 112, IV, 1, 22; Rhodes, *History,* VII, 37, VIII, 93, 104; Schultz and Caine, *Financial Development,* chs. xvi–xvii; Sparks, *National Development,* 137; Horace White, *Money and Banking,* 257.

Special — H. G. Roach, "Sectionalism in Congress, 1870 to 1890," *Am. Pol. Sci. Rev.,* XIX (1925), 500. ❢ Panic and Depression: E. R. McCartney, *Crisis of 1873* (1935); Rendig Fels, "American Business Cycles, 1865–79," *Am. Econ. Rev.,* XLI (1951), 325; O. V. Wells, "Depression of 1873–79," *Ag. Hist.,* XI (1937), 237; O. M. W. Sprague, *Crises* (1910), ch. i; O. C. Lightner, *Business Depressions* (1922), chs. xvii–xviii; D. A. Wells, *Recent Economic Changes* (1889), ch. i; Conant, *Modern Banks of Issue,* 453, 509; Horace White, "Financial Crisis," *Fortnightly Rev.,* XXV (1876), 810; Feder, *Unemployment Relief,* ch. iii; Samuel Rezneck, "Distress, Relief, and Discontent during Depression of 1873–78," *Jour. Pol. Econ.,* LVIII (1950), 494. ❢ Greenback Question and Resumption: Mitchell, *Gold, Prices, and Wages;* Barrett, *Greenbacks and Resumption,* 173; Knox, *U. S. Notes,* 139; Haynes, *Third Party Movements,* chs. ix–xiii; Buck, *Agrarian Crusade,* ch. vi; O. G. Libby, "Greenback Movement," Wisc. Ac., *Trans.,* XII (1898–99), 530; C. M. Destler, "Influence of Edward Kellogg," *Jour. Pol. Econ.,* XL (1932), 338; G. L. Anderson, "Western Attitude toward National Banks," *Miss. Valley Hist. Rev.,* XXIII (1936), 205; R. C. McGrane, "Ohio and Greenback Movement," *ibid.,* XI (1925), 526; E. B. Usher, *Greenback Movement* (1911); C. O. Ruggles, "Greenback Movement in Iowa and Wisconsin," Miss. Valley Hist. Assoc., *Proc.,* VI (1912), 142; J. A. Leach, "Inflation Movement in Missouri," *Mo. Hist. Rev.,* XIV (1930), 379; R. C. Martin, "Greenback Party in Texas," *Southwestern Hist. Quar.,* XXX (1927), 161. ❢ Silver Question: Laughlin, *Bimetallism,* chs. vii, x–xi, xiii–xiv; D. K. Watson, *American Coinage* (1899), chs. viii–xi, xvii; F. W. Taussig, *Silver Situation* (1893), pt. 1, chs. i–iii, vii; H. B. Russell, *International Monetary Conferences* (1898), chs. ii–v; C. F. Adams, Jr., "Currency Debate of 1873–74," *No. Am. Rev.,* CXIX (1874), 111; J. P. Nichols, "Sherman and Silver Drive of 1877–78," *Ohio State Arch. and Hist. Quar.,* XLVI (1937), 148. ❢ Biographies: McGrane, *Allen,* ch. ix; Byars, *American Commoner,* ch. xii; Larson, *Jay Cooke,* chs. xix–xx; Oberholtzer, *Cooke,* II, ch. xviii; E. N. Dingley, *Nelson Dingley* (1902), chs. x–xi; Nevins, *Abram S. Hewitt,* 281; Williams, *Hayes,* I, ch. xxii, II, ch. xxx; Foulke, *Morton,* II, ch. xv; Burton, *Sherman,* chs. x–xii; Haynes, *Weaver,* chs. vi–x.

Sources — Official: *Congressional Record,* and *Congressional Docs.,* 43–46 Congs.; Richardson, *Messages and Papers,* VII; *Report on the Finances* (annual, from 1873); *Statistical Abstract* (annual, from 1878); "History of Coinage Act of 1873," 41 Cong., 2 Sess., *Sen. Misc. Doc.,* No. 132; National Monetary Commission of 1876, *Laws Concerning Money,* 230, 417, 530, 572, 680. ❢ Unofficial and Personal: Dunbar, *Currency, Finance, and Banking,* 210, 241, 295; Am. Bankers Assoc., *Annual Reports* (from 1875); Monetary Commission of Indianapolis Convention, *Report* (1898), 138, 205, 214, 250, 423; Blaine, *Twenty Years,* II, 556, 602; Garfield, *Works,* II, 329; Sherman, *Recollections,* I, 459, 488, II, 603; *American (Appletons') Annual Cyclopædia;* McPherson, *Handbook of Politics.*

Bibliography — Dewey, *Financial History,* 359, 402; T. E. Burton, *Financial Crises* (1902), 369; Schultz and Caine, *Financial Development,* 732.

202. EXPANSION OF COMMERCE AND BUSINESS, 1865–1880

Summary — Trade and industry during the Civil War (§§ 183, 184). — External commerce: decline of merchant marine; directions of foreign trade; changes in imports and exports; effect of tariffs (§§ 191, 201). — Internal commerce: extension of railways (§§ 195, 197); coastwise shipping; canal and river transportation; refrigerator system; Great Lakes shipping. — Manufactures: reasons for growth; development in the East; extension in the South (§ 195) and the West; leading industries; tendencies toward concentration. — Finance: growth of Wall Street; speculation (also § 191); relation of banking to business; Panic of 1873 (§ 201); new fortunes. — Later developments (§§ 206, 210).

General — Depew, *One Hundred Years of Commerce*, I–II; Day, *History of Commerce*, chs. li–liii; L. M. Hacker, *Triumph of American Capitalism* (1940), ch. xxvi; Émile Levasseur, *American Workman* (1900), ch. i; Nevins, *Emergence of Modern America*, 31, 190, 395; Oberholtzer, *History*, II, 538; Persons, "Business and Financial Conditions following Civil War"; Schlesinger, *New Viewpoints*, ch. xi; Shannon, *America's Economic Growth*, chs. xxiii–xxv; Sparks, *National Development*, 16, 53, 305.

Special — Merchant Marine: Hutchins, *American Maritime Industries*, chs. xii–xv; Marvin, *American Merchant Marine*, chs. xiv–xvi; Spears, *American Merchant Marine*, ch. xvi; F. C. Matthews, *American Merchant Ships* (1930–31); F. C. Bowen, *Century of Atlantic Travel* (1930), chs. iv–v; D. A. Wells, *Our Merchant Marine* (1887), chs. ii–iii, ix–x; Henry Fry, *North Atlantic Steam Navigation* (1896), chs. xxiii, xxxi; J. D. J. Kelley, *Question of Ships* (1884), chs. i–vi, App. i–ii. ❧ Foreign Commerce: E. R. Johnson, *Domestic and Foreign Commerce*, II, ch. xxvi; J. L. Laughlin and H. P. Willis, *Reciprocity* (1903), chs. i–ii; Chalfont Robinson, *History of Two Reciprocity Treaties* (1904), pt. 2. ❧ Internal Commerce: Julius Grodinsky, *Iowa Pool* (1950); L. D. H. Weld, *Private Freight Cars* (1908), chs. i–ii; L. F. Nickerson, "Refrigeration," *National Provisioner*, III (1891), No. 8; Joseph Husband, *Story of Pullman Car* (1917), chs. iii–v, vii; E. R. Johnson, *Domestic and Foreign Commerce*, I, chs. xvi–xvii, xx; G. G. Tunell, "Transportation on Great Lakes," *Jour. Pol. Econ.*, IV (1896), 332, and "Diversion of Flour and Grain Traffic to Railroads," *ibid.*, V (1897), 340; Hunter, *Steamboats on Western Rivers*, 561; Ambler, *Transportation in Ohio Valley*, 265, 310; M. L. Hartsough, *From Canoe to Steel Barge on Upper Mississippi* (1934), 170, 185. ❧ Manufacturing: V. S. Clark, *History of Manufactures*, II, chs. vi–xlv; Malcolm Keir, *Manufacturing Industries* (1920), 56, 122, 195, 230; T. C. Cochran and William Miller, *Age of Enterprise* (1942), 119; B. J. Hendrick, *Age of Big Business* (1919), chs. i–iii; Kaempffert, *American Invention*, II; E. W. Byrn, *Progress of Invention* (1900), chs. xix, xxix–xxxi. ❧ Cordage: S. E. Morison, *Ropemakers of Plymouth* (1950), 61. ❧ Explosives: A. P. Van Gelder and Hugo Schlatter, *Explosives Industry* (1927), 121, 315, 375; J. K. Winkler, *Du Pont Dynasty* (1935), ch. ii; W. S. Dutton, *Du Pont* (1942), 107. ❧ Food: Clemen, *American Livestock Industry*, 146, 190, 269, 451; O. E. Anderson, *Refrigeration in America* (1953), chs. iii–v; Harper Leech and J. C. Carroll, *Armour and His Times* (1938), chs. viii–ix; T. R. Pirtle, *Dairy Industry* (1926), 73; Edward Wiest, *Butter Industry* (1916), 11, 38, 77, 139, 214; Schafer, *Agriculture in Wisconsin*, ch. ix; Kuhlmann, *Flour-Milling Industry*, ch. iv, 288; H. J. Thornton, *Quaker Oats Company* (1933), chs. ii, iv, vii; J. H. Collins, *Canned Foods* (1924), chs. ii–xiii; P. L. Vogt, *Sugar Refining Industry* (1908), 8. ❧ Iron and Steel: H. N. Casson, *Romance of Steel* (1907), 1, 72; J. R. Smith, *Iron and Steel* (1908), chs. vi–vii; J. G. Butler, Jr., *Fifty Years of Iron and Steel* (1923), 1; Roger Burlingame, *Engines of Democracy* (1940), ch. iv; Hendrick, *Carnegie*, I, chs. ix–xii; Nevins, *Abram S. Hewitt*, chs. xiii–xiv, 420. ❧ Liquor: J. P. Arnold and Frank Penman, *Brewing Industry* (1933), 73. ❧ Lumber: Defebaugh, *Lumber Industry*, I, 491, 532, II; G. W. Hotchkiss, *Lumber and Forest Industry of Northwest* (1898). ❧ Paper: Weeks, *Paper Manufacturing*, chs. xiii–xiv. ❧ Petroleum: I. M. Tarbell, *Standard Oil Company* (1904), I, chs. ii–viii, II, ch. ix; G. H. Montague, *Standard Oil Company* (1903), 1–88; P. H. Giddens, *Birth of Oil Industry*, chs. iv–v, and *Early Days of Oil* (1948); A. A. Lawrence, *Petroleum Comes of Age* (1938), chs. vi–xvii; H. D. Lloyd, *Wealth against Commonwealth* (1894), chs. v–ix; Allan Nevins, *Rockefeller* (1940), I, chs. ix–xxvii. ❧ Shoes: F. J. Allen, *Shoe Industry* (1922), ch. ii; F. A. Gannon, *Shoemaking* (1912), chs. vii–xii. ❧ Textiles: Hammond, *Cotton Industry*, chs. iv–vi, xi, App. i; Copeland, *Cotton Manufacturing*; H. F. Williamson, *Edward Atkinson* (1934), 33, 57; Cole, *American Wool Manufacture*, I, ch. xx, II; R. J. Woodruff, "American Hosiery Industry," *Jour. Econ. and Bus. Hist.*, IV (1931), 18. ❧ Tobacco: W. N. Baer, *Cigar Industry* (1933), pt. 3. ❧ Wall Street and Speculation: John Moody, *Masters of Capital* (1919), 1, 52; C. F. and Henry Adams, *Chapters of Erie* (1871), 1, 135; Meade Minnigerode, *Certain Rich Men* (1927), 51; Matthew Josephson, *Robber Barons* (1935), chs. ii–iii, v–viii; T. C. Cochran, "Legend of Robber Barons," *Penn. Mag. Hist. and Biog.*, LXXIV

(1950), 307; Corey, *House of Morgan*, chs. ix–xiii; Carl Hovey, *J. P. Morgan* (1911), chs. iii–v; J. K. Winkler, *Morgan the Magnificent* (1930), chs. v–vi; Oberholtzer, *Cooke*, II, chs. xiv–xvii; Larson, *Jay Cooke*, chs. xiv–xviii; Bouck White, *Book of Daniel Drew* (1910), chs. xxi–xl; Lane, *Vanderbilt*, chs. ix–xiii; R. H. Fuller, *Jubilee Jim* (1928), 118; Myers, *Great American Fortunes*, pt. 3; A. P. Youngman, *Economic Causes of Great Fortunes* (1909), ch. iii.

Sources — Official: *Commerce and Navigation; Statistical Abstract* (from 1878); *Commercial Relations* (annual); *Consular Reports* (monthly from 1880); census publications (§ 7); 52 Cong., 2 Sess., Sen. Report, III, No. 1394; Bur. Stat., Treasury Dept., *Monthly Summary of Commerce and Finance* (from 1866). ❡ Unofficial: *American (Appletons')* *Annual Cyclopædia*; reports of boards of trade and chambers of commerce; P. H. Giddens, *Pennsylvania Petroleum, a Documentary History* (1947); *Financial Review* (annual). ❡ Contemporary Accounts: Andrew Carnegie, *Autobiography*, chs. ix–xiv, and *Triumphant Democracy* (1886), chs. x–xiii; Henry Clews, *Fifty Years in Wall Street* (1908), chs. ii–v, xii–xvii, xx–xxvii, xxxiv–xxxvi; A. M. Eaton, "Oil Regions of Pennsylvania, 1865," *Western Penn. Hist. Mag.*, XVIII (1935), 189; Forbes, *Letters and Recollections*, II, ch. xx; Villard, *Memoirs*, II, chs. xxxviii–xlii; Wells, *Recent Economic Changes*, chs. ii–vi.

Bibliography — E. R. Johnson, *Domestic and Foreign Commerce*, II, 352; V. S. Clark, *History of Manufactures*, II, 841; Shannon, *America's Economic Growth*, 883, 893; F. C. Hicks, *High Finance in Sixties* (1929), 405.

Chapter Twenty-one

NATIONAL POLITICS AND ECONOMIC TRENDS
1880–1900

203. THE REPUBLICAN TURN TO REFORM, 1880–1884

Summary — Political background (§§ 192–3) — Presidential election of 1880. — Garfield's administration, 1881: patronage problems; contest with Conkling; Star Route frauds; assassination; accession of Arthur, Sept. 19. — "Surplus financiering," 1881–82: debt retirement; lavish spending; pension legislation. — Tariff agitation: causes; Tariff Commission, 1882; Act of 1883. — Pendleton Act for civil-service reform, 1883. — Recession of 1884. — Passage of Morrison tariff bill by Democratic House, 1884. — Later developments (§ 204).

General — H. J. Ford, *Cleveland Era* (1919), 13; Josephson, *Politicos*, 276; Oberholtzer, *History*, IV, 58; Rhodes, *History*, VIII, 109, 161, 197; Robinson, *Political Parties*, 195; Sparks, *National Development*, chs. xi–xii, xvii; H. C. Thomas, *Return of Democratic Party* (1919), chs. iii–vii.

Special — Garfield's Election and Presidency: Stanwood, *Presidency*, I, ch. xxvi; J. I. Davenport, *Forged "Morey Letter"* (1884); C. W. Stein, *Third-Term Tradition* (1943), ch. vi; H. L. Dawes, "Garfield and Conkling," *Century*, n.s., XXV (1894), 341; T. B. Connery, "Garfield-Conkling Tragedy," *Cosmopolitan*, XXIII (1897), 145; J. M. Klotsche, "Star Route Cases," *Miss. Valley Hist. Rev.*, XXII (1935), 407; Stewart Mitchell, "Man Who Murdered Garfield," *Mass. Hist. Soc.*, *Proc.*, LXVII (1944), 452. ❡ Fiscal Policies under Arthur: Dewey, *Financial History*, 415; Noyes, *Forty Years*, ch. iv; W. H. Glasson, *Federal Military Pensions* (1918), chs. i–ii; J. W. Oliver, *Civil War Military Pensions* (1917), 80, 90; Taussig, *Tariff History*, ch. iv; Tarbell, *Tariff*, ch. v; Stanwood, *Tariff Controversies*, II, 197; C. L. Miller, *Old Northwest and Tariff* (1929), 118. ❡ Civil Service: J. G. Van Deusen, "Did Republicans 'Colonize' Indiana in 1879?" *Ind. Mag. Hist.*, XXX (1934), 335; F. M. Stewart, *National Civil Service Reform League* (1929), 23; A. B. Sageser, *Two Decades of Pendleton Act* (1935), ch. ii; Henry Lambert, *Progress of Civil Service Reform* (1885), 10. ❡ Recession of 1884: Sprague, *Crises*, 108; Lightner, *Business Depressions*, ch. xix. ❡ Biographies: Howe, *Arthur*, chs. ix–xxii; Muzzey, *Blaine*, chs. viii–ix; J. A. Barnes, *Carlisle* (1931), chs. iv–v; Conkling, *Conkling*, chs. xxxi–xxxv; Chidsey, *Conkling*, chs. xxvii–xxxii; Cary, *Curtis*, chs. xx, xxii; Dingley, *Nelson Dingley*, chs. xii–xiv; T. C. Smith, *Garfield*, II, chs. xxv–xxx; Caldwell, *Garfield*, chs. xiv–xvi; Hesseltine, *Grant*, ch. xxvi; Badeau, *Grant in Peace*, chs. xxxvii–xl; Greenslet, *Lowell*, 191.

Sources — Official: *Congressional Record*, and *Docs.*, 46 Cong., 3 Sess.-48 Cong.; Richardson, *Messages and Papers*, VIII; Civil Service Commission, *First Report* (1884); Tariff Commission of 1882, "Report," 47 Cong., 2 Sess., *H. Misc. Doc.*, No. 6. ❡ Personal: Blaine, *Twenty Years*, II, ch. xxix; G. S. Boutwell, *Reminiscences*, II, ch. xl; S. M. Cullom, *Fifty Years*, ch. xv; Curtis, *Orations and Addresses*, III, ch. x; Depew, *Memories*, chs. viii–ix; Garfield, *Works*, II, 723; Hoar, *Autobiography*, I, chs. xxviii–xxix; A. K. McClure,

Recollections (1902), 106; Platt, *Autobiography*, chs. vi–viii; Sherman, *Recollections*, II, chs. xl–xlvii; John and W. T. Sherman, *Letters*, 350; A. D. White, *Autobiography*, I, chs. xi–xii. ❦ Unofficial Compilations: Porter, *Party Platforms*, 99; *Appletons' Annual Cyclopædia*; McPherson, *Handbook of Politics*; National Civil Service Reform League, *Proc.* and *Civil Service Record* (both from 1881).

Bibliography — Sparks, *National Development*, 352; Howe, *Arthur*, 292; Caldwell, *Garfield*, 365; Dewey, *Financial History*, 414; Fish, *Civil Service and Patronage*, 252.

204. THE DEMOCRATS IN POWER, 1884–1889

Summary — Campaign of 1884: candidates; Mugwumps; issues; outcome. — Civil service and election laws: Cleveland's patronage policy; Presidential Succession Act, 1886; Electoral Count Act and repeal of Tenure of Office Act, 1887. — Silver question (§ 209). — Government policy toward labor (§ 205). — Land policy. — Dawes Severalty Act (§ 212) and Interstate Commerce Act (§ 206), 1887. — Measures to reduce the surplus revenue. — Cleveland's pension vetoes. — Tariff: Democratic differences; Cleveland's message of 1887; Mills bill, 1888. — Campaign of 1888: nominees; issues; Harrison's close victory. — Progress of ballot reform. — Later political developments (§ 209).

General — D. R. Dewey, *National Problems* (1907), chs. ii, iv–v, viii; Ford, *Cleveland Era*, chs. iii–vi; Josephson, *Politicos*, 346; Oberholtzer, *History*, IV, 159, 309, 426, 504, V, ch. xxxiii; H. T. Peck, *Twenty Years of Republic* (1906), chs. i–ii, iv; Rhodes, *History*, VIII, 205, 292; Robinson, *Political Parties*, 204; Sparks, *National Development*, ch. xix; Thomas, *Return of Democratic Party*, chs. viii–xi.

Special — Presidential Elections: Stanwood, *Presidency*, I, chs. xxvii–xxix; C. M. Fuess, "Schurz, Lodge and Campaign of 1884," *New Eng. Quar.*, V (1932), 453; P. P. Chase, "Protestant Clergy in Massachusetts, 1884," *Mass. Hist. Soc., Proc.*, LXIV (1930–32), 467; F. W. Mack, "Rum, Romanism and Rebellion," *Harper's Wkly.*, XLVIII (1904), 1140; Tansill, *Bayard*, ch. xii; J. C. Malin, "Roosevelt and Elections of 1884 and 1888," *Miss. Valley Hist. Rev.*, XIV (1927), 25; R. C. Buley, "Campaign of 1888 in Indiana," *Ind. Mag. Hist.*, X (1914), No. 2, 30; F. A. Ogg, "Dollars behind the Ballots," *World To-Day*, XV (1908), 946. ❦ Civil Service: Sageser, *Pendleton Act*, ch. iii. ❦ Land Policy: Robbins, *Our Landed Heritage*, 278, 291; J. B. Rae, "Commissioner Sparks and Railroad Land Grants," *Miss. Valley Hist. Rev.*, XXV (1938), 211; D. M. Ellis, "Forfeiture of Railroad Land Grants," *ibid.*, XXXIII (1946), 27; Dunham, *Government Handout*, chs. ix–xiv. ❦ Pensions: Glasson, *Military Pensions*, 190; D. L. McMurry, "Pension Question," *Miss. Valley Hist. Rev.*, IX (1922), 19. ❦ Tariff: Taussig, *Tariff History*, 251; Tarbell, *Tariff*, chs. vi–vii; Stanwood, *Tariff Controversies*, II, 220; Miller, *Northwest and Tariff*, 156; C. F. Randolph, "Surplus Revenue," *Pol. Sci. Quar.*, III (1888), 226; E. L. Godkin, *Problems of Modern Democracy* (1896), 98. ❦ Biographies: Muzzey, *Blaine*, 271, ch. xiv; Stanwood, *Blaine*, ch. ix; Barnes, *Carlisle*, chs. vi–vii; Nevins, *Cleveland*, chs. x–xv, xvii–xxiv; R. M. McElroy, *Grover Cleveland* (1923), I, chs. iv–viii, xi; D. T. Lynch, *Cleveland* (1932), chs. xlvi–lxiv; Cary, *Curtis*, 279; Matilda Gresham, *Life of W. Q. Gresham* (1919), II, 500, 561; Cate, *Lamar*, ch. xviii; Mayes, *Lamar*, ch. xxix; Paine, *Nast*, chs. liii, lv–lvii, lix; Pringle, *Roosevelt*, 79, 117; Fuess, *Schurz*, chs. xxi–xxii; W. D. Foulke, *Lucius B. Swift* (1930), 15, 131; Gibbons, *Wanamaker*, I, ch. xxiv. ❦ Ballot Reform: E. C. Evans, *Australian Ballot System* (1917), chs. ii–v; J. B. Bishop, "Secret Ballot," *Forum*, XII (1892), 589; R. H. Dana, "Sir William Harcourt and Australian Ballot Law," *Mass. Hist. Soc., Proc.*, LVIII (1925), 401.

Sources — Official: *Congressional Record*, and *Congressional Docs.*, 48–50 Congs.; Richardson, *Messages and Papers*, VIII; U. S. Civil Service Commission, *Annual Reports*. ❦ Personal: Perry Belmont, *American Democrat* (1940), ch. ix; Grover Cleveland, *Presidential Problems* (1904), ch. i, and *Writings and Speeches* (1892), chs. i–iv, xi–xii, xv–xx, and *Letters* (1933), chs. iii–vii; Cullom, *Fifty Years*, ch. xvi; Foraker, *Notes*, I, ch. xiv, xxi–xxiii; W. D. Foulke, *Fighting the Spoilsmen* (1919), ch. iii; R. W. Gilder, *Cleveland*

(1910), 3; Benjamin Harrison and J. G. Blaine, *Correspondence* (1940), ch. i; Hoar, *Autobiography*, I, chs. xxix–xxx, II, chs. xi, xiv; Hudson, *Recollections*, 150; G. F. Parker, *Recollections* (1919), chs. iv–vii; Platt, *Autobiography*, chs. ix–xii; Lodge and Roosevelt, *Correspondence*, I, 1; C. E. Russell, *Shifting Scenes* (1914), ch. vii; Sherman, *Recollections*, II, chs. xlvii, l–li; John and W. T. Sherman, *Letters*, 357; A. E. Stevenson, *Men I Have Known* (1909), ch. xviii; A. T. Volwiler, ed., "Tariff Strategy and Propaganda, 1887–88," *Am. Hist. Rev.*, XXXVI (1930), 76; A. D. White, *Autobiography*, I, 201. ❧ Unofficial Compilations: Porter, *Political Platforms*, 113; *Appletons' Annual Cyclopædia*; McPherson, *Handbook of Politics*; National Civil Service Reform League, *Proc.*, and *Civil Service Record* (both from 1881).

Bibliography — Dewey, *National Problems*, 329, and *Financial History*, 414; N. Y. Public Library, *Political Parties*, 23, 32, 56; G. A. Weber, *Bureau of Pensions* (1923), 100.

205. THE LABOR MOVEMENT, 1865–1892

Summary — Postwar trends in labor organization: increase of wage earners (§ 202); local and national craft unions; Railroad Brotherhoods, formed 1863–83; National Labor Union, 1866–73. — National labor parties from 1872. — Knights of Labor: founded, 1869; membership; aims; increasing radicalism; decline in late 1880's. — Rise of American Federation of Labor from 1881: composition; program; rivalry with the Knights; activities. — Employers' associations. — Conflicts: Molly Maguires, 1862–76; railway strikes, 1877; "Great Upheaval," 1885–86; Homestead and Cœur d'Alene strikes, 1892. — Ameliorative efforts: profit sharing; model factory towns; trade agreements. — Government and labor: federal eight-hour law, 1868; state legislation; attitude of courts; federal Bureau of Labor, 1884 (called Department, 1888–1905); federal arbitration act, 1888. — Anticapitalist ideologies: spread of socialism from 1867, with Socialist Labor party in 1877; anarchism and the Haymarket riot, 1886; Utopian fiction, especially Edward Bellamy's *Looking Backward* (1888). — Single tax: Henry George's *Progress and Poverty* (1879) and its influence. — Later developments (§ 210).

General — Commons, *History of Labour*, II; Dewey, *National Problems*, ch. iii, 247; Dulles, *Labor in America*, 95; Nathan Fine, *Labor and Farmer Parties* (1928), chs. iv–v; Herbert Harris, *American Labor* (1938), 65; F. E. Haynes, *Social Politics* (1924), chs. iii, v–vi; Levasseur, *American Workman*, chs. iii–ix; Nevins, *Emergence of Modern America*, 69, 380; Oberholtzer, *History*, IV, 10, 411, V, 210, 742; S. P. Orth, *Armies of Labor* (1919), 63, 133, 229; Perlman, *Trade Unionism*, 44, 152; Rhodes, *History*, VIII, 13, 269, 386; Sparks, *National Development*, ch. v; I. M. Tarbell, *Nationalizing of Business* (1936), chs. vii, ix–x, 273; C. D. Wright, *Industrial Evolution* (1895), 245, 269, 297, chs. xxvii–xxix.

Special — Working Conditions: D. W. Douglas, "Ira Steward on Consumption and Unemployment," *Jour. Pol. Econ.*, XL (1932), 532; D. A. Wells, *Relation of Tariff to Wages* (1888); Moody, *Land and Labor*, chs. vii–viii, xii–xiv, xvii; Jacob Schoenhof, *Industrial Situation* (1885), chs. xiii–xvi; George Gunton, *Wealth and Progress* (1887), 35, 205, 347; Mitchell, *Gold, Prices and Wages*; F. A. Shannon, "Homestead Act and Labor Surplus," *Am. Hist. Rev.*, XLI (1936), 637; M. C. Cahill, *Shorter Hours* (1932), 31, 68, 95, 137. ❧ Organizations: William Kirk, *National Labor Federations* (1906), pt. 1; W. M. Burke, *Central Labor Unions* (1899), 33, 70; Leo Wolman, *Growth of Trade Unions* (1924); D. D. Lescohier, *Knights of St. Crispin* (1910); E. M. Chamberlin, *Sovereigns of Industry* (1875); Charlotte Todes, *William H. Sylvis and National Labor Union* (1942); Ware, *Labor Movement*; H. J. Browne, *Catholic Church and Knights of Labor* (1949); L. L. Lorwin, *American Federation of Labor* (1933), 7; A. P. James, "First Convention of American Federation of Labor," *Western Penn. Hist. Mag.*, VI (1923), 201; L. S. Reed, *Labor Philosophy of Gompers* (1930); Andrew Roy, *History of Coal Miners* (1907), chs. v–xxv; Chris Evans, *History of United Mine Workers* (1918–20), I, II, chs. i–xii; F. T. Stockton, *International Molders Union* (1921); J. S. Robinson, *Amalgamated Association of Iron, Steel and Tin Workers* (1920); A. E.

Galster, *Labor Movement in Shoe Industry* (1924), chs. iii–v; F. S. Deibler, *Amalgamated Wood Workers' International Union* (1912); E. C. Robbins, *Railway Conductors* (1914). ❧ Labor Coöperatives: Bemis, *Cooperation in United States*, 37, 56, 162, 243, 302, 394, 500; R. H. Newton, *Social Studies* (1886), 85; T. S. Adams and H. L. Sumner, *Labor Problems* (1905), ch. x. ❧ Employers' Associations: C. E. Bonnett, *Employers' Associations* (1922), 21, chs. ii, viii–ix. ❧ Conflicts: Yellen, *American Labor Struggles*, chs. i, iii–iv; Louis Adamic, *Dynamite* (1931), chs. i–ix; Florence Peterson, *Strikes in United States* (1938), chs. ii–iii; R. W. Rowan, *Pinkertons* (1931), chs. xvii–xviii, xxi; J. W. Coleman, *Molly Maguire Riots* (1936); F. P. Dewees, *Molly Maguires* (1877); P. A. Slaner, "Railroad Strikes of 1877," *Marxist Quar.*, I (1937), 214; J. A. Dacus, *Annals of the Great Strikes* (1877); E. W. Martin (J. D. McCabe), *History of the Great Riots* (1877); R. A. Allen, *Great Southwest Strike* (1942); A. G. Burgoyne, *Homestead* (1893); J. H. Bridge, *Carnegie Steel Company* (1903), chs. xiv–xvi; Stoll and Whicker, *Silver Strike*, chs. xx–xxvii. ❧ Ameliorative Efforts: N. P. Gilman, *Profit Sharing* (1889), ch. vii, and *Socialism and American Spirit* (1893), ch. ix; Paul Monroe, "Profit Sharing," *Am. Jour. Sociol.*, I (1896), 685; R. T. Ely, "Pullman," *Harper's Mag.*, LXX (1885), 452; Cahill, *Shorter Hours*, 224; C. D. Wright, *Industrial Conciliation and Arbitration* (1881); A. E. Suffern, *Conciliation and Arbitration in Coal Industry* (1915), 1, 203, and *Coal Miners' Struggle* (1926), chs. ii–iii. ❧ Government and Labor: F. J. Stimson, *Labor in Its Relations to Law* (1895), 17, and *Handbook to Labor Law* (1896); T. S. Adams and H. L. Sumner, *Labor Problems*, ch. xii; G. G. Groat, *Attitude of Courts in Labor Cases* (1911), chs. iv–xxii. ❧ Anticapitalist Movements: Dorfman, *Economic Mind*, III, chs. ii, vi; Hillquit, *History of Socialism*, 156; H. H. Quint, *Forging of American Socialism* (1953), chs. i–vi; Hinds, *American Communities*, 422, 444; E. M. Schuster, *Native American Anarchism* (1932), 136; Henry David, *Haymarket Affair* (1936); Yellen, *American Labor Struggles*, ch. ii; E. L. Bogart and C. M. Thompson, *Industrial State* (1920), ch. viii; D. D. Lum, *Chicago Anarchists* (1886); Harvey Wish, "Altgeld Pardons Anarchists," *Ill. State Hist. Soc., Jour.*, XXXI (1938), 424; J. P. Altgeld, *Reasons for Pardoning* (1893); Everett Carter, "Haymarket Affair in Literature," *Am. Quar.*, II (1950), 270. ❧ Utopian Fiction: A. B. Forbes, "Literary Quest for Utopia," *Social Forces*, VI (1927), 179; V. L. Parrington, Jr., *American Dreams* (1947), chs. viii–xxi; W. F. Taylor, *Economic Novel* (1942), 189, 237; A. E. Morgan, *Philosophy of Bellamy* (1945); J. H. Franklin, "Bellamy and Nationalist Movement," *N. Eng. Quar.*, XI (1938), 739; Elizabeth Sadler, "One Book's Influence," *ibid.*, XVII (1944), 530; Gilman, *Socialism and American Spirit*, ch. vi. ❧ Single Tax: G. R. Geiger, *Philosophy of Henry George* (1931); A. N. Young, *Single Tax Movement* (1916), chs. i–vii; Washington Gladden, *Tools and the Man* (1893), ch. iii. ❧ Biographies: Barnard, *Altgeld*, chs. viii–xxvi; W. R. Browne, *Altgeld* (1924), chs. viii–xi; Morgan, *Bellamy*, chs. vii–xiv; Hendrick, *Carnegie*, I, chs. xix–xx; Harvey, *Frick*, chs. viii–xiii; A. G. de Mille, *Henry George* (1950), chs. viii–xxix; L. F. Post, *Prophet of San Francisco* (1930); Harvey, *Gompers*, 27; Gresham, *Gresham*, I, chs. xiii–xiv, 409; Lloyd, *Lloyd*, I, chs. iv–vii; Grossman, *Sylvis*, chs. vi–xii.

Sources — Official: *Congressional Docs.*, esp. 48 Cong., 1 Sess., *Sen. Report*, No. 820; 49 Cong., 2 Sess., *H. Report*, III, No. 4174; 50 Cong., 1 Sess., *H. Misc. Doc.*, XV, No. 572, 2 Sess., *H. Report*, IV, No. 4147; 52 Cong., 2 Sess., *Sen. Report*, No. 1280; 57 Cong., 2 Sess., *Sen. Doc.*, No. 209; reports of federal Commissioner (Secretary) of Labor from 1886, and of state bureaus of labor statistics from 1870; Penn. General Assembly, Comm. to Investigate Railroad Riots, *Report* (1878). ❧ Unofficial Compilations: Commons, *Documentary History*, IX, chs. ii–iv; *American (Appletons') Annual Cyclopædia*; proceedings of national labor bodies. ❧ Personal: J. R. Buchanan, *Story of Labor Agitator* (1903); Carnegie, *Autobiography* (1920), ch. xvii; C. S. Darrow, *My Life* (1932), chs. xii–xiii; George, *Works*, I–VIII; Emma Goldman, *Living My Life* (1936), I, chs. ix–xvii; Gompers, *Seventy Years*, I, chs. iv–xvi; R. B. Hayes, "Notes of Four Cabinet Meetings," *Am. Hist. Rev.*, XXXVII (1932), 286; Powderly, *Path I Trod*, chs. iii–xiii, xviii–xxix, and *Thirty Years*; Russell, *Shifting Scenes*, ch. vi; Caroline Ticknor, *Glimpses of Authors* (1922), ch. viii; Sigmund Zeisler, "Reminiscences of Anarchist Case," *Ill. Law Rev.*, XXI (1927), 224. ❧ Polemic Writings: Edward Bellamy, *Looking Backward* (1888), and *Talks on Nationalism* (1938); Henry George, *Progress and Poverty* (1879);

Laurence Gronlund, *Coöperative Commonwealth* (1884); A. R. Parsons, *Anarchism* (1887); Ira Steward, *Eight-Hour Movement* (1865); W. G. Sumner, *What Social Classes Owe to Each Other* (1883); B. R. Tucker, *Instead of a Book* (1893). ❡ Contemporary Accounts: R. T. Ely, *Recent American Socialism* (1885), and *Labor Movement* (1886); G. E. McNeill, ed., *Labor Movement* (1887), chs. v–xv, xvii–xxii; Wells, *Recent Economic Changes*, chs. ix–x.

Bibliography — Commons, *History of Labour*, II, 541, 571; Dept. of Labor, *Index of All Reports Issued by Bureaus of Labor Statistics* (1902); G. E. Barnett, *Trial Bibliography of Trade Union Publications* (1907); Helen Marot, *Handbook of Labor Literature* (1899); Reynolds and Killingsworth, *Trade Union Publications*.

206. BUSINESS CONSOLIDATION, 1880–1892

Summary — Earlier history (§ 202). — Consolidating movement: reasons; advantages; evils. — Railway combinations: rate wars; secret rebates and other discriminations; rate agreements; pools; Wabash decision, 1886; Interstate Commerce Act, 1887; difficulties of enforcement. — Industrial combinations: destructive competition; Standard Oil and other trusts, 1879–87; efforts at state regulation; Sherman Antitrust Act, 1890; New York and Ohio decisions against trusts, 1890–92. — Concentration of banking. — Growth of commercial advertising. — Concentration of wealth. — Later developments (§ 210).

General — Cochran and Miller, *Age of Enterprise*, chs. vii–viii; Dewey, *National Problems*, chs. vi, xii; Oberholtzer, *History*, IV, 384, 445, V, 112; Rhodes, *History*, VIII, 288, 358; Tarbell, *Nationalizing of Business*, chs. iii–vi, xii.

Special — Trend toward Consolidation: W. F. Willoughby, "Concentration of Industry," *Yale Rev.*, VII (1898), 72, and "Integration of Industry," *Quar. Jour. Econ.*, XVI (1901), 94; Levasseur, *American Workman*, ch. ii; J. H. Bridge, *The Trust: Its Book* (1902), chs. vi–vii; J. L. Laughlin, *Industrial America* (1906), chs. iv–v. ❡ Railway Combinations: F. H. Spearman, *Strategy of Great Railroads* (1904); Moody, *Railroad Builders*, chs. viii–x; C. S. Langstroth and Wilson Stilz, *Railway Co-operation* (1899), 31, 131; Riegel, *Western Railroads*, ch. xi, 217, 289; E. R. Johnson and T. W. Van Metre, *Principles of Railroad Transportation*, chs. xviii, xxvi; B. H. Meyer, *Railway Legislation* (1898), 189; W. Z. Ripley, *Railroads: Rates and Regulation* (1915), ch. xiii; Haney, *Congressional History of Railways*, II, chs. xxii–xxiv; I. L. Sharfman, *Interstate Commerce Commission* (1931–37), I, 11; H. S. Drinker, *Interstate Commerce Act* (1909), I, 53, II, 565; J. R. Dos Passos, *Inter-State Commerce Act* (1887). ❡ Industrial Combinations: Hendrick, *Age of Big Business*, 52, 106; A. S. Dewing, *Corporate Promotions and Reorganizations* (1914), 49, 72, 112, 165, 412; Sullivan, *Our Times*, II, 299; Ernst von Halle, *Trusts* (1895), chs. ii–viii; S. C. T. Dodd, *Trusts* (1889); J. W. Jenks and W. E. Clark, *Trust Problem* (1917), chs. xiii–xiv; Lloyd, *Wealth against Commonwealth*; George Gunton, *Trusts and Public* (1899), chs. i–iii; W. Z. Ripley, ed., *Trusts, Pools and Corporations* (1916), chs. i–ii, iv; Tarbell, *Standard Oil Company*, II, chs. x–xvii; Montague, *Standard Oil Company*, 77; Vogt, *Sugar Refining Industry*, chs. iv–vii; Herbert Myrick, *American Sugar Industry* (1899), 31; J. W. Jenks, "Michigan Salt Association," *Pol. Sci. Quar.*, III (1888), 78, and "Whiskey Trust," *ibid.*, IV (1889), 296; Jacobstein, *Tobacco Industry*, 86; Eliot Jones, *Anthracite Coal Combination*, 40; H. N. Casson, *Romance of Steel*, ch. iv, and *History of Telephone* (1910), chs. iii, v; Horace Coon, *American Tel & Tel* (1939), chs. v, x; Bridge, *Carnegie Steel*, chs. vii–xii; Morison, *Ropemakers of Plymouth*, 61; W. M. Springer, "Telegraph Monopoly," *No. Am. Rev.*, CXXXII (1881), 369; O. W. Knauth, *Policy of United States toward Industrial Monopoly* (1914), ch. i; E. P. Prentice, *Federal Power over Carriers and Corporations* (1907), 156; Jenks and Clark, *Trust Problem*, 241; C. G. Washburn, "Sherman Antitrust Act," *Boston Univ. Law Rev.*, VIII (1928), 95; A. H. Walker, *Sherman Law* (1910), chs. i–iv; Edward Berman, *Labor and Sherman Act* (1930), chs. i–iii; G. F. Edmunds, "Interstate Trust and Commerce Act," *No. Am. Rev.*, CXCIV (1911), 801. ❡ Courts and Big Business: Warren, *Supreme Court*, II, chs. xxxv–xxxvi; Swisher, *American Constitutional De-*

velopment, 401; Lewis, *American Political Thought*, 85; A. C. McLaughlin, "Court, Corporation and Conkling," *Am. Hist. Rev.*, XLVI (1940), 45; Frankfurter, *Commerce Clause* (1937), ch. iii; W. M. Daniels, "Constitutional Growth under Fourteenth Amendment," *So. Atl. Quar.*, XXIX (1930), 16; A. J. Eddy, *Law of Combinations* (1901), I, pts. 3–5, II, pts. 6–8. ❡ Concentration of Banking and Wealth: Moody, *Masters of Capital*, 19, 49, 58, 88; C. B. Spahr, *Present Distribution of Wealth* (1896), chs. iii, v–vii; C. D. Wright, "Are the Rich Growing Richer?" *Atl. Monthly*, LXXX (1897), 300. ❡ Commercial Advertising: Frank Presbrey, *History and Development of Advertising* (1929), chs. xxxv–xlvii; R. M. Hower, *History of Advertising Agency* (1939), ch. iv; S. A. Sherman, "Advertising," Am. Stat. Assoc., *Publ.*, VII (1900), 119. ❡ Biographies: Mackenzie, *Bell*, chs. xiv–xv; Hendrick, *Carnegie*, I, ch. xv; Jenkins, *Duke*, 65; Swisher, *Field*, ch. ix; Harvey, *Frick*, chs. vi–vii; Kennan, *Harriman*, I, chs. iii–v; Allen, *Morgan*, chs. iv–vi; Hovey, *Morgan*, chs. vi–vii; Corey, *House of Morgan*, chs. xiv–xvii; Crowther, *Patterson*, chs. vi–viii; W. H. Allen, *Rockefeller* (1930), chs. xx–xxiii, xli; J. T. Flynn, *God's Gold* (1932), 248; Nevins, *Rockefeller*, II, chs. xxviii–xxxiii; Burton, *Sherman*, 336, 353; A. R. Burr, *Portrait of Banker* (1927) (James Stillman), chs. iv–vi; A. B. Paine, *In One Man's Life* (1921) (T. N. Vail), chs. xx–xxiv, xxviii, xxx; Gibbons, *Wanamaker*, I, ch. xxii, II, chs. i–iii; J. H. Appel, *Wanamaker* (1930), chs. vii–viii, xxvi; Leupp, *Westinghouse*, chs. vii–xii.

Sources — Official: *Congressional Record*, 46–52 Congs.; *Congressional Docs.*, esp. 49 Cong., 1 Sess., *Sen. Report*, No. 46; 50 Cong., 1 Sess., *H. Report*, No. 3112; 51 Cong., 1 Sess., *Sen. Report*, No. 829; 52 Cong., 2 Sess., *H. Report*, Nos. 2278, 2601; 57 Cong., 2 Sess., *Sen. Doc.*, XIV, No. 147; *Statutes at Large*, XXIV, 379, XXVI, 209; U. S. Industrial Commission, *Report* (1900–02), I–II, IV, IX, XIII, XIX, 259, 595; Interstate Commerce Commission, *Annual Reports* (from 1887), and *Reports and Decisions* (from 1887); N. Y. *Sen. Docs.*, V (1888), No. 50, X (1889), No. 64. ❡ Judicial: San Mateo County *v.* Southern Pacific (1885), 116 *U.S.*, 138; Santa Clara County *v.* Southern Pacific (1886), 118 *ibid.*, 394; Wabash and Pacific *v.* Illinois (1886), *ibid.*, 557; Pembina Mining Co. *v.* Pennsylvania (1888), 125 *ibid.*, 181; Minnesota and St. Louis *v.* Beckwith (1889), 129 *ibid.*, 26; Chicago, Milwaukee, and St. Paul *v.* Minnesota (1890), 134 *ibid.*, 418; People *v.* North Sugar Refining Co. (1890), 121 *N.Y.*, 582; Distilling and Cattle Feeding Co. *v.* People (1890), 156 *Ill.*, 448; State *v.* Standard Oil Co. of Ohio (1892), 49 *Ohio State*, 137. ❡ Personal: Cullom, *Fifty Years*, 254, ch. xxi; A. D. Noyes, *Market Place* (1938), 23; R. F. Pettigrew, *Triumphant Plutocracy* (1921), chs. vi–vii; J. D. Rockefeller, *Random Reminiscences* (1933), ch. iv; G. P. Rowell, *Forty Years an Advertising Agent* (1906); John Sherman, *Recollections*, II, 1071. ❡ Unofficial Compilations: National Convention of Railroad Commissioners, *Annual Proc.* (from 1889); *Appletons' Annual Cyclopædia*

Bibliography — Ripley, *Trusts, Pools, and Corporations*, ch. xviii; H. R. Seager and C. A. Gulick, Jr., *Trust and Corporation Problems* (1929), 685; Bur. of Railway Economics, *Railway Economics*, 141; Joshua Bernhardt, *Interstate Commerce Commission* (1923), 155.

207. THE NEW NORTHWEST AND THE GREAT LAKES REGION, 1880–1892

Summary — Earlier history (§§ 196–200, 202). — Completion of railroads to the Pacific: Northern Pacific, 1883; Oregon Short Line, 1884; Canadian Pacific, 1885; Great Northern, 1893. — Progress of settlement: diminution of public domain; maladministration of land laws (also § 204); occupation of semiarid west of Kansas and Nebraska. — Increased silver production, decline in price (§ 209). — Cattle and sheep raising in the central and northern plains, 1866–92. — Frontier lawlessness (§ 214). — Advance of farmers' frontier: conflicts with cattlemen; fencing; new wheat and corn areas; droughts; falling prices (§ 209). — Arid West (§ 208). — Lumbering, fisheries, and fruit culture in the Pacific Northwest. — New states: North and South Dakota, Montana, and Washington, 1889; Idaho and Wyoming, 1890. — Great Lakes area: development of Lake Superior iron fields, 1873–92; widening of Sault Ste. Marie Canal; increased rail and water traffic. — Later developments (§§ 209–10).

General — Billington, *Westward Expansion*, chs. xxxiii–xxxv; Branch, *Westward*, ch. xxxi, 588; Briggs, *Frontiers of Northwest*, chs. iii–iv, 410; Hafen and Rister, *Western America*, chs. xxx–xxxi; Hough, *Passing of Frontier*, chs. ii–iv, viii–ix; Oberholtzer, *History*, IV, 592, 598, 606, 653; Riegel, *America Moves West*, ch. xxxvii, 512, 520; A. M. Schlesinger, *Rise of City* (1933), 23, 51; Shannon, *Farmer's Last Frontier*, chs. ix–x.

Special — New Northwest: Brigham, *Geographic Influences*, chs. ix–x; Sidney Warren, *Farthest Frontier* (1949), chs. vii–viii; Bancroft, *Oregon*, II, chs. xxiii–xxiv, and *Washington, Idaho, and Montana*, 287, 535, 719, and *Nevada, Colorado, and Wyoming*, 224, 446, 504, 750, 783; other state histories (§ 62). ❡ Railway Extension (also § 206): Moody, *Railroad Builders*, 138, 165; Starr, *One Hundred Years of Railroading*, ch. xvii; Spearman, *Strategy of Great Railroads*, 49, 177; Riegel, *Western Railroads*, ch. xiii; Winther, *Great Northwest*, ch. xvi; E. A. Bryan, *Orient Meets Occident* (1936), chs. v–x; Hedges, *Villard and Railways of Northwest*, chs. iii–v, vii–ix; Haney, *Congressional History of Railways*, II, ch. x; E. V. Smalley, *Northern Pacific Railroad* (1883), chs. xxv–xxxi; Pyle, *Hill*, I, chs. viii–xxi. ❡ Cattle and Sheep Raising (also § 208): Clemen, *American Livestock Industry*, ch. viii; E. E. Dale, *Range Cattle Industry*, chs. iv–v, viii, and *Cow Country* (1942), chs. i–vii, x–xi; Osgood, *Day of Cattleman*; P. I. Wellman, *Trampling Herd* (1939); Pelzer, *Cattlemen's Frontier*, 71; Webb, *Great Plains*, 225; F. W. Powell, *Bureau of Animal Industry* (1927), 1, 121; Burlingame, *Montana Frontier*, ch. xii; J. O. Oliphant, "Livestock Industry in Pacific Northwest," *Ore. Hist. Quar.*, XLI (1948), 3; J. G. McCoy, *Cattle Trade* (1874), chs. i–xvii, xix; Brockett, *Western Empire*, pt. 1, chs. xv–xvi, pt. 2, chs. viii–ix; Walter von Richthofen, *Cattle Raising on Plains* (1885); J. S. Brisbin, *Beef Bonanza* (1885); James Macdonald, *Food from Far West* (1878), chs. xiii, xv, xxiii; P. A. Rollins, *Cowboy* (1936); Emerson Hough, *Story of Cowboy* (1897); R. M. Wright, *Dodge City* (1913); W. H. Miller, *Kansas City* (1881), ch. xiv; E. D. Branch, *Cowboy and His Interpreters* (1926); Hermann Hagedorn, *Roosevelt in Bad Lands* (1921); C. W. Towne and E. N. Wentworth, *Shepherd's Empire* (1945), chs. vii–viii; E. N. Wentworth, *America's Sheep Trails* (1948), chs. xi–xxv; E. A. Carman, et al., *Sheep Industry* (1892); Wright, *Wool-Growing and Tariff*, ch. vii. ❡ Lands and Agriculture (also §§ 204, 209): Hibbard, *Public Land Policies*, chs. xix–xxi, xxiii; H. H. Dunham, "Crucial Years of General Land Office," *Ag. Hist.*, XI (1937), 117; Raney, "Timber Culture Acts," 219; Schmidt and Ross, *Readings in American Agriculture*, chs. xvi–xx; C. W. Thompson, "Movement of Wheat Growing," *Quar. Jour. Econ.*, XVIII (1904), 570; J. G. Thompson, *Wheat Growing in Wisconsin*, ch. iv; G. N. Lamphere, "Wheat Raising in Red River Valley," Minn. Hist. Soc., *Coll.*, X (1900), 1; E. V. Robinson, *Early Economic Conditions and Agriculture in Minnesota* (1915), ch. iv. ❡ Statehood: R. E. Albright, "Western Statehood Movement," *Pacific Hist. Rev.*, III (1934), 296; F. L. Paxson, "Admission of Omnibus States," Wisc. Hist. Soc., *Proc.*, 1911, 77; J. D. Hicks, *Constitutions of Northwest States* (1923). ❡ Great Lakes Area: Casson, *Romance of Steel*, 49; H. R. Mussey, *Combination in Mining Industry* (1905), ch. iv; R. D. Williams, *Peter White* (1907), chs. xviii–xx; Rickard, *American Mining*, ch. x; N. H. and H. V. Winchell, *Iron Ores of Minnesota* (1891); F. P. Wirth, *Minnesota Iron Lands* (1937); Hotchkiss, *Lumber and Forest Industry*; Mills, *Our Inland Seas*, chs. xvii, xxii; D. H. Kelton, *Sault Ste. Marie Canal* (1888).

Sources — Official: *Congressional Record*, and *Docs.*, 47–52 Congs.; *Statistical Abstract*; Richardson, *Messages and Papers*, VIII–IX; Dept. of Ag., *Yearbook*, 1899; census reports. ❡ Cattle and Sheep: Clarence Gordon, "Cattle, Sheep, and Swine," *Tenth Census* (1880), III, 952; J. B. Grinnell, "Cattle Interests West of the Mississippi," Bur. Animal Industry, *Report* (1884), I, 233; J. H. Fullinwider, "Cattle Interests of the West," *ibid.*, 271; H. M. Taylor, "Range Industry," *ibid.* (1885), 293, and *ibid.* (1886), 105; Joseph Nimmo, "Range and Ranch Cattle Business," 48 Cong., 2 Sess., *H. Ex. Doc.*, No. 267; 50 Cong., 1 Sess., *H. Ex. Doc.*, No. 232. ❡ Lands and Agriculture: 48 Cong., 1 Sess., *Sen. Ex. Doc.*, VI, No. 127, *H. Ex. Doc.*, XXVI, No. 119, *H. Report*, V, No. 1325, 2 Sess., *Sen. Report*, I, No. 979; 49 Cong., 2 Sess., *H. Ex. Doc.*, XXIV, No. 166; Commissioner General Land Office, *Annual Reports*; Public Lands Commission, *Report*, 58 Cong., 3 Sess., *Sen. Doc.*, IV, No. 189; F. H. Newell, "Agriculture by Irrigation," *Eleventh Census*, III; "Agricultural Progress of Fifty Years," *Twelfth Census*, V, pp. xvi–xxxv

❡ Great Lakes Area: C. H. Keep and S. G. Brock, "Commerce and Shipping of Great Lakes," 52 Cong., 1 Sess., *H. Ex. Doc.*, XXVII–XXVIII; G. G. Túnell, "Statistics of Lake Commerce," 55 Cong., 2 Sess., *H. Doc.*, LI, No. 277; Bur. Statistics, *Reports on Internal Commerce (Commerce and Navigation, 1876–1891*, pt. 2); Detroit Deep Waterways Convention, *Proc.* (1891).   ❡ Personal: Reginald Aldridge, *Life on a Ranch* (1884); John Baumann, "On a Western Ranche," *Fortnightly Rev.*, XLVII (1887), 516; Mrs. R. O. Brandt, "Prairie Pioneering," *Norwegian-Am. Stud. and Rec.*, VII (1933), 1; E. B. Bronson, *Reminiscences of Ranchman* (1908); John Clay, *My Life on Range* (1924); J. L. Hill, *End of Cattle Trail* (n.d.), 49; Frederic Remington, *Pony Tracks* (1895); Theodore Roosevelt, *Autobiography*, ch. iv, and *Ranch Life* (1888); William Shepherd, *Prairie Experiences in Handling Cattle and Sheep* (1884); Villard, *Memoirs*, II, chs. xxxix–xli; Frank Wilkeson, "Cattle Raising," *Harper's Mag.*, LXXII (1886), 788.   ❡ Contemporary Accounts: Julian Ralph, *Our Great West* (1893); Paul de Rousiers, *American Life* (1892), chs. v–x; Winser, *Great Northwest*; F. J. Rowbotham, *Trip to Prairie-Land* (1885); F. T. Gilbert, *Resources, Business, and Business Men of Montana* (1888); [Northern Pacific Railroad], *Great Northwest* (1886); J. L. Onderdonk, *Idaho* (1885); [Ore. Immigration Board], *Pacific Northwest*; [Pacific Northwest Immigration Board], *Pacific Northwest*; W. M. Thayer, *Marvels of New West* (1888); [Union Pacific Railroad], *Wealth and Resources of Oregon and Washington* (1889); F. F. Victor, *Atlantis Arisen* (1891); Stanley Wood, *Over the Range to the Golden Gate* (1895).   ❡ Maps: Paullin, *Atlas*, plates 58, 64–5, 141, 143–7.

Bibliography — Edwards, *Bibliography of History of Agriculture*, 82; Shannon, *Farmer's Last Frontier*, 398; C. W. Smith, *Pacific Northwest Americana*; Pelzer, *Cattlemen's Frontier*, 315; Powell, *Bureau of Animal Industry*, 157; Herman Kahn, "Records in National Archives Relating to Range Cattle Industry," *Ag. Hist.*, XX (1946), 187.

208. THE GREAT SOUTHWEST, 1880–1892

Summary — Earlier history (§§ 196–9, 202). — Extension of railroads: Southern Pacific, 1881; Santa Fe System, Denver and Rio Grande, Texas Pacific, and Missouri Pacific, 1883. — Advance of settlement. — Mining in the Southwest. — Rise of cattle industry from 1866; extension to the Northwest (§ 207). — Sheep raising (§ 207). — Frontier lawlessness (§ 214). — Arid America: beginnings of irrigation; Forest Reserves Act and repeal of Preëmption and Timber Culture Acts, 1891; Carey Act, 1894. — Utah: economic progress; the Mormon question; growth of non-Mormon element; Edmunds Antipolygamy Act, 1882; Edmunds-Tucker Act, 1887; official abandonment of polygamy, 1890; statehood, 1896. — Indian Territory: cattle leases; opening of Oklahoma, 1889; formation of Oklahoma Territory, 1889. — Growth of Texas. — Development of California. — Later developments (§§ 209–10).

General — Hough, *Passing of Frontier*, chs. ii–iv, viii; Oberholtzer, *History*, IV, 594, 602, 662; Paxson, *American Frontier*, 515, chs. lvi, lix, 546; Richardson and Rister, *Greater Southwest*, chs. xv–xx; Schlesinger, *Rise of City*, 32, 423; Sparks, *National Development*, 21, ch. xv.

Special — Great Southwest: Bancroft, *Arizona and New Mexico*, 530, 569, 582, 752; A. T. Steinel and D. W. Working, *Agriculture in Colorado* (1926), 107, 197; other state histories (§ 62).   ❡ Railway Extension (also § 207): Riegel, *Western Railroads*, chs. xi–xii; Moody, *Railroad Builders*, ch. viii; Haney, *Congressional History of Railways*, II, ch. ix; Stuart Daggett, *Chapters on Southern Pacific* (1922), chs. vii–viii, xi–xii; Waters, *Steel Rails to Santa Fe*, 51; Bradley, *Santa Fe*, chs. iv, vi–xi; W. C. Holden, *Alkali Trails* (1930), 63, 186; S. B. McAllister, "Building the Texas and Pacific West of Fort Worth," *West Texas Hist. Assoc.*, *Yearbook*, IV (1928), 50; L. B. Lesley, "Transcontinental Railroad into California," *Pacific Hist. Rev.*, V (1936), 52.   ❡ Cattle Industry (also § 207): Dale, *Range Cattle Industry*, chs. iii, vi–vii, and *Cow Country*, chs. viii–ix; Pelzer, *Cattlemen's Frontier*, 37; Clemen, *American Livestock Industry*, 174; C. C. Rister, *Southwestern Frontier*, 267, and *Southern Plainsmen* (1938), ch. x; J. F. Dobie, *Longhorns* (1941); Wellman, *Trampling Herd*; C. M. Love, "Cattle Industry in Southwest," *Southwestern*

Hist. Quar., XIX (1916), 370, XX (1916), 1; S. P. Ridings, *Chisholm Trail* (1936); T. U. Taylor, *Chisholm Trail and Other Routes* (1936); Everett Dick, "Long Drive," Kan. State Hist. Soc., *Coll.*, XVII (1926), 27; T. J. Cauley, "Early Business Methods in Texas Cattle Industry," *Jour. Econ. and Bus. Hist.*, IV (1932), 461; Bert Haskett, "Early Cattle Industry in Arizona," *Ariz. Hist. Rev.*, VI (1935), No. 4, p. 3; R. J. Morrisey, "Early Range Cattle Industry in Arizona," *Ag. Hist.*, XXIV (1950), 151; O. B. Peake, *Colorado Range Cattle Industry* (1937); McCoy, *Cattle Trade*, ch. xviii; Macdonald, *Food from Far West*, chs. vi–xii; T. U. Taylor, *Jesse Chisholm* (1939); J. E. Haley, *Charles Goodnight* (1939), chs. vii–xxv; E. C. McMechen, "John Hittson," *Colo. Mag.*, XI (1934), 164. ❡ Arid America: Webb, *Great Plains*, chs. viii–ix; Smythe, *Arid America*, 77, 106, 150; R. C. Morris, "Notion of Great American Desert," *Miss. Valley Hist. Rev.*, XIII (1926), 190; J. T. Ganoe, "Origin of Reclamation Policy," 34, and "Beginnings of Irrigation," *ibid.*, XXV (1938), 59, and "Desert Land Act," 142; Ise, *Forest Policy*, 74; J. P. Kinney, *Forest Law* (1917); Raney, "Timber Culture Acts," 219; J. W. Powell, "Institutions for Arid Lands," *Century Mag.*, XVIII (1890), 111. ❡ Utah and Mormons: Bancroft, *Utah*, 677, 720, 759; Linn, *Mormons*, bk. 6, ch. xxiv; Nels Anderson, *Desert Saints* (1942), ch. xii; Smythe, *Arid America*, 51, 161; Brough, *Irrigation in Utah*, pt. 1, chs. v–viii; George Thomas, *Development of Institutions under Irrigation* (1920), 53, 138, 231; Hamilton Gardner, "Cooperation among Mormons," *Quar. Jour. Econ.*, XXXI (1917), 461, and "Communism among Mormons," *ibid.*, XXXVII (1922), 134; G. O. Larson, "Perpetual Emigration Fund," *Miss. Valley Hist. Rev.*, XVIII (1931), 184. ❡ Oklahoma: Grant Foreman, *Oklahoma* (1942), chs. xvii–xix; Gittinger, *Formation of Oklahoma*, chs. vii–xi; C. C. Rister, *Land Hunger* (1942); D. W. Peery, "Crocker and Boomer Movement," *Chronicles Okla.*, XIII (1935), 273, and "Payne," *ibid.*, XIII, 438, and "First Two Years," *ibid.*, VII (1929), 278, 419; E. E. Brown, "No Man's Land," *ibid.*, IV (1926), 89; H. S. Wicks, "Opening of Oklahoma," *ibid.*, IV (1926), 129; J. B. Milam, "Opening of Cherokee Outlet," *ibid.*, IX (1931), 268, 454, X (1932), 115; E. B. Smith, "Provisional Governments in Oklahoma," *Southwestern Soc. Sci. Quar.*, XIII (1933), 353. ❡ California: Bancroft, *California*, VII, chs. xv–xvi, xxi; Hittell, *California*, IV, bk. 12, chs. xi–xiv; Caughey, *California*, chs. xxvi–xxviii; Cleland, *Wilderness to Empire*, ch. xx; D. S. Jordan, "California," *Atl. Monthly*, LXXXII (1898), 793; E. W. Maslin, ed., *Resources of California* (1893); C. D. Warner, *Our Italy* (1891).

Sources — Official: *Congressional Record* and *Docs.*, 47–52 Congs.; Richardson, *Messages and Papers*, VII–IX; *Statutes at Large*, esp. XXII, 30, XXIV, 635, XXVIII, pt. 1, 422; census reports; J. W. Powell, *Report on Lands of Arid Region* (1879); F. H. Newell, *Report on Agriculture by Irrigation* (1894), and "Irrigation on Great Plains," Dept. of Ag., *Yearbook*, 1896, 167; H. L. Bentley, "Cattle Rangers of Southwest," Dept. of Ag., *Farmers' Bull.*, No. 72 (1898). ❡ Personal: J. M. Hunter, ed., *Trail Drivers of Texas* (1925); Andy Adams, *Log of Cowboy* (1903); E. G. Barnard, *Rider of Cherokee Strip* (1936); William French, *Recollections of Western Ranchman* (1928); J. C. Henderson, "Reminiscences of Range Rider," *Chronicles Okla.*, III (1925), 253; S. K. Humphrey, "Rushing the Cherokee Strip," *Atl. Monthly*, CXLVII (1931), 566; M. J. Jaques, *Texan Ranch Life* (1894); J. W. Moffitt, "Diary of an Eighty-Niner," *Chronicles Okla.*, XV (1937), 66; Rufus Phillips, "Cowboy Life in Arkansas Valley," *Colo. Mag.*, VII (1930), 165; Frank Tanberg, "Cowboy Life in Colorado," *ibid.*, XII (1935), 23. ❡ Travelers' Accounts of Mormons: Faithful, *Three Visits*, chs. xi–xii; Willard Glazier, *Ocean to Ocean* (1895), ch. xxvii; Marshall, *Through America*, chs. vii–xi; Sala, *America Revisited*, II, ch. xxi; Steevens, *Land of Dollar*, ch. xxiv.

Bibliography — Riegel, *Western Railroads*, 330; Edwards, *Bibliography of History of Agriculture*, 44, 97, 106; Dale, *Range Cattle Industry*, 199; Inst. for Government Research, *U. S. Reclamation Service* (1913), 132; Gittinger, *Formation of Oklahoma*, 231.

209. THE FARMERS' REVOLT AND NATIONAL POLITICS, 1889–1900

Summary — Agrarian unrest in 1880's: economic, social, and psychological causes; Farmers' Alliances; elections of 1890. — New drive for free silver (§ 201): reasons; Sherman Silver Purchase Act, 1890, and its effects. — Harrison and the civil service. — "Czar"

Reed and the House of Representatives. — Sherman Antitrust Act (§ 206). — Continuance of surplus problem (§ 204): Dependent Pension Act and McKinley Tariff, 1890; refund of direct war tax, 1891. — Campaign of 1892: advent of People's (Populist) party; candidates and issues; Cleveland's election. — Panic of 1893 and ensuing depression (§ 210). — Drain on gold reserve; deficit; repeal of Silver Purchase Act, 1893; bond sales and Morgan syndicate, 1894–96. — Labor troubles (§§ 205, 210). — Taxation problems (§ 204): Wilson-Gorman Tariff, 1894; invalidation of income tax, 1895. — Republican gains in 1894. — Election of 1896: silver issue in party conventions; candidates and campaign; McKinley's victory. — Dingley Tariff, 1897. — Decline of silver agitation: reasons; Gold Standard Act, 1900.

General — Dewey, *National Problems*, chs. v, ix, xi, xiv–xvii, xx; Ford, *Cleveland Era*, ch. ix; Josephson, *Politicos*, 434; Oberholtzer, *History*, IV, 365, V, 75, 126, 169, 300, 364, 448; Peck, *Twenty Years*, 166, 193, 252, 389, 437; Rhodes, *History*, VIII, 328, 365, 380, 456, IX, 1, 119; Stanwood, *Presidency*, I, chs. xxx–xxxi; Sullivan, *Our Times*, I, chs. vi–ix; Tarbell, *Nationalizing of Business*, 195, 244.

Special — T. A. Bailey, "Party Irregularity in Senate, 1869–1901," *Southwestern Soc. Sci. Quar.*, XI (1931), 355, and "West and Radical Legislation, 1890–1930," *Am. Jour. Sociol.*, XXXVIII (1933), 603; L. F. Cox, "Agricultural Wage Earner, 1865–1900," *Ag. Hist.*, XXII (1948), 95. ❡ Civil Service and Pensions (§ 204): Sageser, *Pendleton Act*, chs. iv–v; Glasson, *Military Pensions*, 225; D. L. McMurry, "Pension Question," 19, and "Pension Bureau during Harrison," *Miss. Valley Hist. Rev.*, XIII (1926), 343. ❡ Congressional Organization: Follett, *Speaker*, 112, 190; H. B. Fuller, *Speakers of House* (1909), ch. viii. ❡ Tariff and Income Tax: Ratner, *American Taxation*, 144; Tarbell, *Tariff*, chs. viii–x; Taussig, *Tariff History*, chs. v–vii; Stanwood, *Tariff Controversies*, II, chs. xvi–xviii; William Hill, "Votes on McKinley and Wilson Bills," *Jour. Pol. Econ.*, II (1894), 290; E. R. A. Seligman, *Income Tax* (1914), pt. 2, chs. iv–v; Swisher, *American Constitutional Development*, 440; R. G. and G. C. Blakey, *Federal Income Tax* (1940), ch. i; George Tunell, "Second Income Tax," *Jour. Pol. Econ.*, III (1895), 311; J. K. Beach, "Income Tax Decision," *Yale Rev.*, V (1896), 58. ❡ Silver Question: Dewey, *Financial History*, ch. xix; Hepburn, *Currency*, chs. xvi, xx; Noyes, *Forty Years*, chs. vi–vii, ix–x; J. P. Hütter, *Question de la monnai d'argent* (1938), chs. iv–vii; Wildman, *Money Inflation*, ch. vi; Bullock, *Monetary History* (1900), pt. 1, ch. viii; Laughlin, *Bimetallism*, chs. xvi–xvii; F. W. Taussig, *Silver Situation* (1896), 18, and "Treasury in 1894–96," *Quar. Jour. Econ.*, XIII (1899), 204; Russell, *International Monetary Conferences*, chs. vii–ix; W. C. Ford, "Foreign Exchanges and Movement of Gold, 1894–95," *Yale Rev.*, IV (1895), 128; Fred Wellborn, "Silver Republican Senators, 1889–91," *Miss. Valley Hist. Rev.*, XIV (1928), 462; J. A. Barnes, "Gold-Standard Democrats and Party Conflict," *ibid.*, XVII (1930), 422; J. P. Nichols, "Silver Diplomacy," *Pol. Sci. Quar.*, XLVIII (1933), 565, and "Silver Repeal in Senate," *Am. Hist. Rev.*, XLI (1935), 26. ❡ Rural Life (§ 199): Schlesinger, *Rise of City*, 57; J. C. Malin, *Dust Storms* (1946), 49; J. E. Briggs, "Grasshopper Plagues in Iowa," *Iowa Jour. Hist.*, XIII (1915), 349; H. S. Schell, "Drought in Eastern Dakota," *Ag. Hist.*, V (1931), 162; W. C. Holden, "West Texas Drouths," *Southwestern Hist. Quar.*, XXXII (1928), 103; E. W. Hayter, "Patent System and Agrarian Discontent," *Miss. Valley Hist. Rev.*, XXXIV (1947), 59; F. A. Shannon, "Midwestern Farmer in 1900," *ibid.*, XXXVII (1950), 491; J. W. Bookwalter, "Farmer's Isolation," *Forum*, XII (1891), 50; Smalley, "Isolation on Prairie Farms," 378; N. H. Egleston, *Home and Its Surroundings* (1883), chs. i–vi, xxv; Josiah Strong, *New Era* (1893), ch. viii; C. F. Emerick, "Agricultural Discontent," *Pol. Sci. Quar.*, XI (1896), 433, 601, XII (1897), 93; J. R. Elliott, *American Farms* (1890). ❡ Farmers' Alliances and Populism: J. D. Hicks, *Populist Revolt* (1931); F. L. McVey, *Populist Movement* (1896); Buck, *Agrarian Crusade*, chs. vii–xiii; Haynes, *Third Party Movements*, pt. 4; Shannon, *Farmer's Last Frontier*, ch. xiii; Samuel Proctor, "National Farmers' Alliance Convention of 1890," *Fla. Hist. Quar.*, XXVIII (1950), 161; J. M. Klotsche, "'United Front' Populists," *Wisc. Mag. Hist.*, XX (1937), 375; H. C. Nixon, "Cleavage within Alliance Movement," *Miss. Valley Hist. Rev.*, XV (1928), 22; N. A. Dunning, *Farmers' Alliance History* (1891); W. S. Morgan, *Wheel and Alliance, and Impending Revolution* (1889). ❡ By Regions and States: Hallie Farmer, "Economic

Background of Frontier Populism," *Miss. Valley Hist. Rev.*, X (1924), 406, and "Railroads and Frontier Populism," *ibid.*, XIII (1926), 387, and "Economic Background of Southern Populism," *So. Atl. Quar.*, XXIX (1930), 77; E. D. Stewart, "Populist Party in Indiana," *Ind. Mag. Hist.*, XIV (1918), 332, XV (1919), 53; Destler, *American Radicalism*, chs. viii–ix, xi (Ill.); W. S. Tryon, "Agriculture and Politics in South Dakota," *So. Dak. Hist. Coll.*, XIII (1926), 284; H. C. Nixon, "Populist Movement in Iowa," *Iowa Jour. Hist.*, XXIV (1926), 3; Homer Clevenger, "Farmers' Alliance in Missouri," *Mo. Hist. Rev.*, XXXIX (1944), 24; W. P. Harrington, "Populist Party in Kansas," *Kan. State Hist. Soc.. Coll.*, XVI (1923–25), 403; Connelley, *Kansas*, II, 1137; J. D. Barnhart, "Rainfall and Populist Party in Nebraska," *Am. Pol. Sci. Rev.*, XIX (1925), 527; L. W. Fuller, "Colorado's Revolt against Capitalism," *Miss. Valley Hist. Rev.*, XXI (1934), 343; C. O. Johnson, "Silver Politics in Idaho," *Pacific Northwest Quar.*, XXXIII (1942), 283; Marion Harrington, *Populist Movement in Oregon* (1940); C. H. Wooddy, "Populism in Washington," *Wash. Hist. Quar.*, XXI (1930), 103; H. F. Taggart, "California and Silver Question," *Pacific Hist. Rev.*, VI (1937), 249; Woodward, *Origins of New South*, chs. ix–x; W. D. Sheldon, *Populism in Old Dominion* (1935); S. A. Delap, "Populist Party in North Carolina," *Trinity Coll. Hist. Soc., Papers*, XIV (1922), 40; F. B. Simkins, *Tillman Movement in South Carolina* (1926), chs. iii–vii; A. M. Arnett, *Populist Movement in Georgia* (1922); J. O. Knauss, "Farmers' Alliance in Florida," *So. Atl. Quar.*, XXV (1926), 300; D. M. Robison, *Bob Taylor and Agrarian Revolt in Tennessee* (1935); J. B. Clark, *Populism in Alabama* (1927); Shugg, *Class Struggle in Louisiana*, chs. vii–ix; L. E. Daniel, "Louisiana People's Party," *La. Hist. Quar.*, XXVI (1943), 1055; R. C. Martin, *People's Party in Texas* (1933). ❧ Campaign of 1892: G. H. Knoles, *Presidential Campaign and Election of 1892* (1942); D. M. Dozer, "Harrison and Campaign of 1892," *Am. Hist. Rev.*, LIV (1948), 49. ❧ Campaign of 1896: Elmer Ellis, "Silver Republicans in 1896," *Miss. Valley Hist. Rev.*, XVIII (1932), 519; Harvey Wish, "Altgeld and Election of 1896," *ibid.*, XXIV (1938), 503; J. A. Barnes, "Myths of Bryan Campaign," *ibid.*, XXXIV (1947), 367; Steevens, *Land of Dollar*, chs. x, xiii, xv, xix, xxvi, xxx–xxxii; "Cost of National Campaigns," *World's Work*, I (1900), 77. ❧ Biographies: Stephenson, *Aldrich*, chs. v–x; Barnard, *Altgeld*, chs. xxxiii–xxxv; S. H. Acheson, *Joe Bailey* (1932), chs. iv–viii; Muzzey, *Blaine*, chs. xvi–xvii; Paxton Hibben, *Peerless Leader* (1929), chs. xii–xvii; Werner, *Bryan*, 24; W. C. Williams, *Bryan* (1923), chs. vi–ix; Byars, *American Commoner*, chs. xviii–xxvii; Barnes, *Carlisle*, chs. x–xviii; McElroy, *Cleveland*, II, chs. i, iv, vii–viii; Nevins, *Cleveland*, chs. xxviii–xxix, xxxi–xxxii, xxxv–xxxvii; E. N. Dingley, *Nelson Dingley*, chs. xvii–xxii; J. D. Hicks, "Ignatius Donnelly," *Miss. Valley Hist. Rev.*, VIII (1921), 80; Gresham, *Gresham*, II, chs. xl–xlv; M. A. Tyner, "Gresham," *Ind. Mag. Hist.*, XXIX (1933), 297; Croly, *Hanna*, chs. xiii–xix; Beer, *Hanna*, 110; Herbert Gambrell, "J. S. Hogg," *Southwestern Rev.*, XIII (1928), 338; H. H. Kohlsaat, *From McKinley to Harding* (1923), chs. ii–xiii; Lloyd, *Lloyd*, I, ch. xii; Olcott, *McKinley*, I, chs. ix–x, xiv–xix; Hovey, *Morgan*, chs. viii–ix; Corey, *House of Morgan*, ch. xviii; J. C. Olson, *J. S. Morton* (1942), chs. xviii–xxvi; Stuart Noblin, *L. L. Polk* (1949), chs. viii–xviii; McCall, *Reed*, chs. xiii–xix; Robinson, *Reed*, chs. xiii–xviii; Pringle, *Roosevelt*, chs. x, xii; Burton, *Sherman*, 336; Elmer Ellis, *H. M. Teller* (1941), chs. vii–xix; F. B. Simkins, *Pitchfork Ben Tillman* (1944), chs. vi–xxii; Gibbons, *Wanamaker*, I, chs. xxv–xxviii; Woodward, *Watson*, chs. v–xvii; Haynes, *Weaver*, chs. xiv–xvi; Walter Johnson, *W. A. White's America* (1947), chs. iii–v; M. D. Hirsch, *W. C. Whitney* (1948), chs. ix–xv.

Sources — Official: *Congressional Record* and *Docs.*, 51–56 Congs.; Richardson, *Messages and Papers*, IX; *Statutes at Large*, esp. XXVI, 182, 289, 567, 822, XXVIII, 4, 509, XXX, 151; 51 Cong., 2 Sess., *H. Report*, III, No. 3732; 52 Cong., 1 Sess., *ibid.*, VIII–IX; "Report on Real Estate Mortgages, 1890," 52 Cong., 1 Sess., *H. Misc. Doc.*, L, No. 340, pt. 23; "Condition of Cotton Growers," 53 Cong., 3 Sess., *Sen. Report*, No. 986; *Finance Report* (annual); *Statistical Abstract* (annual); National Monetary Commission, *Laws Concerning Money*, 245, 439, 589, 698; U. S. Industrial Commission, *Report*, X–XI; Dept. of Ag., *Yearbook*. ❧ Judicial: Field *v.* Clark (1892), 143 *U.S.*, 649; United States *v.* Ballin (1892), 144 *ibid.*, 1; Pollock *v.* Farmers' Loan and Trust Co. (1895), 158 *ibid.*, 601; United States *v.* Realty Company (1896), 163 *ibid.*, 427. ❧ Unofficial: Civil Service Reform League, *Proc.*, and *Civil Service Record* (to 1892), and *Good Government* (from

1892); N. Y. Reform Club, *Sound Currency* (1894–1905); *Appletons' Annual Cyclopædia*; Porter, *Political Platforms*, 159. ❡ Personal: Ball, *State That Forgot*, chs. xiv–xviii; Belmont, *American Democrat*, ch. xv; W. J. Bryan, *First Battle* (1896), and *Memoirs*, 99; Cleveland, *Letters*, chs. x–xiv, and *Presidential Problems*, ch. iii; C. G. Dawes, *Journal* (1950), ch. iii; Foraker, *Notes*, I, chs. xxvii–xxix; Foulke, *Fighting the Spoilsmen*, chs. iv–v, ix; Garland, *Son of Middle Border*, chs. ix–xxi, xxxi–xxxii; Harrison and Blaine. *Correspondence*, chs. ii–v; Hoar, *Autobiography*, II, ch. xxii; Parker, *Recollections*, chs. viii–xi; Pettigrew, *Triumphant Plutocracy*, ch. iv; Platt, *Autobiography*, I, chs. xiii–xiv; Quick, *One Man's Life*, chs. ix–xxvii; Lodge and Roosevelt, *Correspondence*, I, 74; Russell, *Shifting Scenes*, chs. xii–xiii; Sherman, *Recollections*, II, chs. lvii, lix–lxv; Stewart, *Reminiscences*, chs. xxxi–xxxvi; A. D. White, *Autobiography*, I, 224; W. A. White, *Autobiography*, chs. xxxvi–xlv. ❡ Polemic Writings: W. A. Peffer, *Farmer's Side* (1891); W. H. Harvey, *Coin's Financial School* (1894), and *Coin's Financial School Up-to-Date* (1895); J. L. Laughlin, *Facts about Money* (1895); Willard Fisher, " 'Coin' and His Critics," *Quar. Jour. Econ.*, X (1896), 187. — *Arena; Atlantic Monthly; Forum; No. Am. Rev.; Pol. Sci. Quar.*; and other periodicals.

Bibliography — Hicks, *Populist Revolt*, 447; Dewey, *National Problems*, 329; Schlesinger, *Rise of City*, 439; N. Y. Public Library, *Political Parties*, 32, 53; Weber, *Bureau of Pensions*, 100; Seligman, *Income Tax*, 687.

210. ECONOMIC DEPRESSION AND RECOVERY, 1893–1900

Summary — Panic of 1893: causes (§§ 206–9); economic prostration; maintenance of the gold standard (§ 209); problem of the unemployed; Coxey's army and allied movements; tramps (§ 214). — Organized labor (§ 205): Pullman strike of 1894, Cleveland's intervention, judicial extension of Sherman Anti-trust Act to labor combinations, 1895; other strikes; progress of labor; Interstate Commerce Arbitration Act, 1898; Socialist schisms. — Industrial growth (§ 206): Supreme Court interpretation of Antitrust Act in Knight case (1895), Trans-Missouri Freight case (1897), Addyston Pipe case (1899), and others; business recovery from depression; consolidation in industry and in rail transport, 1898–1900. — Gold discoveries in the Klondike and Alaska, 1897–98.

General — Dewey, *National Problems*, 201, 253, 288; Josephson, *Robber Barons*, chs. xvi–xvii; Oberholtzer, *History*, V, 254, 285, 623, 678; Rhodes, *History*, VIII, 395, 424; Tarbell, *Nationalizing of Business*, 220, 262.

Special — Panic of 1893: W. J. Lauck, *Causes of Panic of 1893* (1907); F. P. Weberg, *Background of Panic of 1893* (1929); Lightner, *Business Depressions*, chs. xx–xxi; Noyes, *Forty Years*, chs. viii, xi; Feder, *Unemployment Relief*, chs. iv–vii; F. D. Watson, *Charity Organization Movement* (1922), 248; C. C. Closson, Jr., "Unemployed in Cities," *Quar. Jour. Econ.*, VIII (1894), 168, 257, 453, 499; "Relief of Unemployed during Winter of 1893–94," *Jour. Soc. Sci.*, XXXII (1894), 1; D. L. McMurry, *Coxey's Army* (1929); Henry Vincent, *Story of Commonweal* (1894); T. B. Veblen, "Army of Commonweal," *Jour. Pol. Econ.*, II (1894), 456. ❡ Labor Movement and Pullman Strike: Commons, *History of Labour*, II, 500; Dulles, *Labor in America*, 171; Wright, *Industrial Evolution*, ch. xxvi; Lorwin, *American Federation of Labor*, 35; P. H. Douglas, *Real Wages* (1930), chs. xiii–xv; Almont Lindsey, *Pullman Strike* (1942); Yellen, *American Labor Struggles*, ch. iv; Harvey Wish, "Pullman Strike," Ill. State Hist. Soc., *Jour.*, XXXII (1939), 288; Edward Berman, *Labor Disputes and President* (1924), chs. i–ii, and *Labor and Sherman Act*, 58, 284; W. J. Ashley, *Railroad Strike of 1894* (1895); W. H. Carwardine, *Pullman Strike* (1894); W. F. Burns, *Pullman Boycott* (1894); W. H. Dunbar, *Government by Injunction* (1898); B. M. Rastall, *Cripple Creek District* (1908), pt. 1, chs. i–iv; J. P. Gazzam, "Leadville Strike of 1896," Mo. Hist. Soc., *Bull.*, VII (1950), 89; Hillquit, *History of Socialism*, 284; Quint, *Forging American Socialism*, chs. vii–x; ❡ Industrial Combinations: Ripley, *Trusts, Pools, and Corporations*, chs. iii–iv; Dewing, *Corporate Promotions*, 16, 59, 76, 140, 174, 205, 249, 269, 305, 418; Willoughby, "Integration of Industry," 94; Knauth, *Policy of United States towards Industrial Monopoly*, 66, 93;

Walker, *Sherman Law*, chs. v–vi; C. F. Randolph, "Federal Trust Legislation," *Pol. Sci. Quar.*, XII (1897), 622; J. B. Clark, "Trusts," *ibid.*, XV (1900), 181; Eliot Jones, *Anthracite Coal Combination*, 54; Mussey, *Combination in Mining*, ch. v; Tarbell, *Standard Oil Company*, 124; Bridge, *Carnegie Steel Company*, chs. xix–xx; Myrick, *American Sugar Industry*, 143. ❡ Railroad Consolidations: E. G. Campbell, *Reorganization of Railroad System, 1893–1900* (1938); Langstroth and Stilz, *Railway Co-operation*, 149; Daggett, *Railroad Reorganization*; Bryan, *Orient Meets Occident*, 197; Moody, *Railroad Builders*, 110, 162, 187, and *Masters of Capital*, 27, 89; Edward Hungerford, *Baltimore and Ohio Railroad* (1928), II, ch. xi; H. W. Schotter, *Pennsylvania Railroad* (1927), 236; T. C. Cochran, "Social Attitudes of Railroad Administrators," Bus. Hist. Soc., *Bull.*, XVII (1943), 15. ❡ Alaska Gold Rush: H. W. Clark, *Alaska* (1930), 100; Quiett, *Pay Dirt*, chs. xiv–xv; A. W. Greely, *Handbook of Alaska* (1909). ❡ Biographies: Browne, *Altgeld*, chs. xii–xvi; Hendrick, *Carnegie*, II, chs. i–iv; McElroy, *Cleveland*, II, ch. v; Nevins, *Cleveland*, ch. xxxiii; Karsner, *Debs*, ch. vii; McAlister Coleman, *Debs* (1930), chs. viii–xi; Jenkins, *Duke*, 94; Harvey, *Frick*, 178; Tarbell, *Gary*, 72; Kennan, *Harriman*, I, 91, 185; Pyle, *Hill*, I, ch. xx, II, ch. xxii; London, *London*, I, chs. xi–xii, xv–xviii; Corey, *House of Morgan*, ch. xix; Allen, *Morgan*, chs. vii–viii; James, *Olney*, chs. iv–vi; Crowther, *Patterson*, chs. ix, xi; Nevins, *Rockefeller*, II, chs. xxxvii–xl; Burr, *Portrait of Banker* (Stillman), chs. vii–x; Prout, *Westinghouse*, chs. vii–viii, xv.

Sources — Official: *Congressional Record* and *Docs.*, 53–57 Congs.; U.S. Strike Commission, "Report on Chicago Strike," 53 Cong., 3 Sess., *Sen. Ex. Doc.*, No. 7; F. T. Wilson, "Federal Aid in Domestic Disturbances," 228, 347; Sprague, *Crises*, ch. iv; U.S. Industrial Commission, *Report*, I–II, IV–V, VII–VIII, XII–XIV, XVII, XIX; *Annual Reports* of federal Secretary of Labor and of state labor commissioners. ❡ Judicial: U.S. *v.* E. C. Knight Co. (1895), 156 *U.S.*, 1; *In re.* Debs (1895), 158 *ibid.*, 564; U.S. *v.* Trans-Missouri Freight Assoc. (1897), 166 *ibid.*, 290; *In re.* Lennon (1897), *ibid.*, 548; U.S. *v.* Joint Traffic Assoc. (1898), 171 *U.S.*, 505; Stock Yards cases (1898), *ibid.*, 578, 604; Addyston Pipe and Steel Co. *v.* U.S. (1899), 175 *ibid.*, 211. ❡ Personal: Tappen Adney, *Klondike Stampede* (1899); Cleveland, *Letters*, 357, and *Presidential Problems*, ch. ii; M. L. Davis, *Sourdough Gold* (1933); Dawes, *Journal*, chs. iv, vi; Debs, *Writings and Speeches*, 1, 43, 140, 167; Hamlin Garland, *Trail of the Goldseekers* (1899); Joseph Grinnell, *Gold Hunting in Alaska* (1901); Gompers, *Seventy Years*, I, ch. xx; W. B. Haskell, *Two Years in Klondike* (1898); Angelo Heilprin, *Alaska and Klondike* (1899); Jack London, "Diary," *Palimpsest*, VII (1926), 129; C. A. Margeson, *Gold Hunters in Alaska* (1899); Noyes, *Market Place*, 101. ❡ Unofficial Compilation: *Appletons' Annual Cyclopædia*.

Bibliography — Commons, *History of Labour*, II, 541, 576; Dept. of Labor, *Index of Reports by Bureaus of Labor Statistics*; McMurry, *Coxey's Army*, 311; Ripley, *Trusts, Pools, and Corporations*, ch. xviii; Bur. of Railway Economics, *Railway Economics*, 141.

Chapter Twenty-two

SOCIAL AND INTELLECTUAL GROWTH, 1865–1900

211. IMMIGRATION AND FEDERAL RESTRICTION, 1865–1900

Summary — Earlier immigration (§ 148). — Changes in immigration from Europe after Civil War: foreign and American causes; promotional work of state and railroad agencies (§ 199); mounting numbers; additions from Central and Southern European sources; differences between old and new types. — Geographic distribution in the United States. — Social, economic, and political aspects (§§ 205, 213–4, 224). — Religious effects (§ 216). — Nativist opposition (§ 216). — Federal regulation of European immigration: reasons; increasing limitations from 1875 onward; Cleveland's veto of literacy test, 1897. — Chinese immigration: Burlingame treaty, 1868; anti-Chinese agitation in California; treaty of 1880; exclusion legislation, 1882–93; treaty of 1894; laws of 1898 and 1890 (Chinese immigration to Hawaii). — Later developments (§ 226).

General — J. R. Commons, *Races and Immigrants* (1907), chs. iv–ix; H. P. Fairchild, *Immigration* (1925), chs. v–xvi; R. L. Garis, *Immigration Restriction* (1927), 86, 203, 288; Oberholtzer, *History*, I, 246, II, 506, IV, 213, 397, 499, V, 710, 727; Peter Roberts, *New Immigration* (1912), chs. i–xx; Stephenson, *American Immigration*, 140, 196, chs. xix–xx; F. J. Warne, *Immigrant Invasion* (1916), chs. i–iv, vi–xi; Wittke, *We Who Built America*.

Special — E. N. Saveth, *American Historians and European Immigrants* (1948). ❡ Qualitative Effects: E. A. Walcott, "Effect of Immigration on Population," Commonwealth Club of Calif., *Trans.*, XVII (1922), 366; J. J. Spengler, "New England Puritans: an Obituary," *Jour. Heredity*, XXIII (1932), 71. ❡ Distribution: K. H. Claghorn, "Agricultural Distribution of Immigrants," U. S. Industrial Commission, *Reports*, XV, 492, and "Foreign Immigrant in New York City," *ibid.*, XV, 449; F. A. Bushee, *Ethnic Factors in Population of Boston* (1903). ❡ Dutch: G. F. Huizinga, *What Dutch Have Done in West* (1909), 31; Arnold Mulder, *Americans from Holland* (1947). ❡ French Canadians: A. R. M. Lower, "New France in New England," *N. Eng. Quar.*, II (1929), 278; D. M. A. Magnan, *Histoire de la Race Française aux États-Unis* (1912), pt. 3, chs. ii–ix; E. Hamon, *Canadiens-Français de la Nouvelle Angleterre* (1891); C. E. Amaron, *Your Heritage: or New England Threatened* (1891). ❡ Germans: A. B. Faust, *German Element* (1927), I, chs. xvi–xvii, II; Rachel Davis-DuBois and Emma Schweppe, *Germans in American Life* (1936), chs. ii–x. ❡ German Russians: Richard von Sallet, *Russland-deutsche Siedlungen in den Vereinigten Staaten* (1931); C. H. Smith, *Coming of Russian Mennonites* (1927); Georg Leibbrandt, "Emigration of German Mennonites from Russia," *Mennonite Quar. Rev.*, VI (1932), 205, VII (1933), 5. ❡ Greeks: Thomas Burgess, *Greeks in America* (1913). ❡ Irish: "Power of Irish in Cities," *Littell's Living Age*, CLXXI (1886), 382; J. P. Bocock, "Irish Conquest of Cities," *Forum*, XVII (1894), 186; H. C. Merwin, "Irish in American Life," *Atl. Monthly*, LXXVII (1896), 289. ❡ Italians: R. F. Foerster, *Italian Immigration* (1919), chs. i–vii, xvii–xx; Eliot Lord, *et al.*, *Italian in America* (1905); Eugene Schuyler, "Italian Immigration," *Pol. Sci.*

434

Quar., IV (1889), 480. ❧ Jews: Peter Wiernik, *Jews in America* (1931), chs. xxvii–xxxv, xli–xliv; Samuel Joseph, *Jewish Immigration* (1914); Oscar and M. F. Handlin, "Century of Jewish Immigration," *Am. Jewish Yearbook*, L (1948), 1; C. S. Bernheimer, ed., *Russian Jew in United States* (1905). ❧ Scandinavians: K. C. Babcock, *Scandinavian Element* (1914), chs. vii–xii; O. N. Nelson, ed., *Scandinavians* (1899); Blegen, *Norwegian Migration*, II; Qualey, *Norwegian Settlement*; A. B. Benson and Naboth Hedin, *Americans from Sweden* (1950), chs. vii–xxxv; Lindberg, *Background of Swedish Emigration*, chs. ii–xiii; Janson, *Background of Swedish Immigration*, chs. vii–xii; G. M. Stephenson, *Religious Aspects of Swedish Immigration* (1932), chs. xxi–xxiii; O. F. Ander, "Americanization of Swedish Immigrant," Ill. State Hist. Soc., *Jour.*, XXVI (1933–34), 136. ❧ Slavs: E. G. Balch, *Our Slavic Fellow Citizens* (1910), pt. 2; F. J. Warne, *Slav Invasion and Mine Workers* (1904), chs. i–viii; Thomas Čapek, *Čechs [Bohemians] in America* (1920), 31; K. D. Miller, *Czecho-Slovaks in America* (1922), ch. i. ❧ Chinese: M. R. Coolidge, *Chinese Immigration* (1909); F. W. Williams, *Anson Burlingame and First Chinese Mission* (1912), 73; Tien-Lu Li, *Congressional Policy of Chinese Immigration* (1916), chs. i–x; E. C. Sandmeyer, *Anti-Chinese Movement in California* (1939); Lucile Eaves, *California Labor Legislation* (1910), chs. iii–vi; I. B. Cross, *Labor Movement in California* (1935), chs. vi–vii; J. A. Whitney, *Chinese and Chinese Question* (1880); G. F. Seward, *Chinese Immigration* (1881); Bryce, *American Commonwealth*, III, ch. xc; McNeill, *Labor Movement*, ch. xvi.

Sources — Official: *Congressional Record*, 44–56 Congs.; *Congressional Docs.*, esp. 44 Cong., 2 Sess., *Sen. Report*, III, No. 689; 46 Cong., 2 Sess., *H. Report*, II, No. 572; 49 Cong., 1 Sess., *H. Ex. Doc.*, XXX, No. 102, 2 Sess., *H. Ex. Doc.*, XXIV No. 157; 50 Cong., 1 Sess., *H. Misc. Doc.*, XV, No 572, 2 Sess., *H. Report*, I, No. 3792; 51 Cong., 2 Sess., *H. Report*, II, No. 3472; 52 Cong., 1 Sess., *H. Ex. Doc.*, XXXVII, No. 235, *H. Report*, XII, No. 2090, 2 Sess., *Sen. Report*, II, No. 1333; 54 Cong., 1 Sess., *Sen. Report*, II, 290; *Statutes at Large*, XVIII, pt. 3, 477, XXII, 58, 214, XXIII, 332, XXVI, 1084; *Consular Reports* (monthly, from 1880); Bur. Statistics, *Annual Reports*; Supt. (Commissioner General) of Immigration, *Annual Reports* (from 1892); U.S. Industrial Commission, *Report*, XV; "Emigration and Immigration," 49 Cong., 2 Sess., *H. Ex. Doc.*, XXIV, No. 157. ❧ Unofficial and Personal: Abbott, *Immigration Problem*, 155, 361, 526, 638, 838, and *Immigration: Select Documents*, 42, 164; Clyde, *United States Policy toward China*, chs. xi–xv, xxii; Antin, *Promised Land*; Blegen, "Minnesota's Campaign for Immigrants," 29; G. M. Stephenson, ed., "Typical 'America Letters,'" Swedish Hist. Soc., *Year-Book*, VII (1921), 52; A. G. Carlson, *En Emigrants Resa* (1894); R. L. Stevenson, *Amateur Emigrant* (1895), and *Across the Plains* (1892); Immigration Restriction League, *Reports* (from 1894); *American (Appletons') Annual Cyclopædia*. ❧ Maps: Paullin, *Atlas*, plates 70–5.

Bibliography — F. J. Brown and J. S. Roucek, eds., *One America* (1945), 660; D. F. Bowers, ed., *Foreign Influences in American Life* (1944), 175; Stephenson, *American Immigration*, 283; W. C. Smith, *Americans in the Making* (1939), 433; R. E. Cowan and Boutwell Dunlap, *Bibliography of Chinese Question* (1909).

212. ASSIMILATION OF NEGRO AND INDIAN, 1877–1900

Summary — The Negro during Reconstruction (§§ 189–90). — Freedmen's struggle with poverty and ignorance: hands-off policy of federal government from 1877; croplien system; progress toward farm ownership; other occupations; color line in education; leadership of Booker T. Washington and Tuskegee from 1881; aid from Peabody Fund (1867), Slater Fund (1882), and Daniel Hand Fund (1888); decline of illiteracy. — Negro religious life. — Race relations: Negro exodus of 1879; spread of "Jim Crow" laws from 1875; early methods of disfranchisement; defeat of Force bill in Congress, 1890; flexible literacy tests and "grandfather clauses" of the 1890's; lynchings. — Indian problem: removal of tribes to reservations (§§ 198, 207–8); reservation life; abuses of administration; direct federal aid to education from 1873; agitation for Indian reform; Dawes Severalty Act (1887) and its effects; dissolution of Five Civilized Tribes; Messiah craze, 1889–91; last uprising (Minnesota), 1898. — Later developments (§ 226).

General — Dewey, *National Problems*, 6, 162; Oberholtzer, *History*, IV, 525, 573, 585, 642, V, 116, 121, 712; Schlesinger, *Rise of City*, 368.

Special — M. E. Carpenter, *Treatment of Negro in American History School Textbooks* (1941). ❡ Over-all Accounts of Negro: Franklin, *Slavery to Freedom*, chs. xviii, xxi; Frazier, *Negro in United States*, chs. viii, xii–xix; B. G. Brawley, *Social History of Negro* (1921), 278; *South in Building of Nation*, IV, 617, 638, VI, 41, X, 166; Woodward, *Origins of New South*, ch. viii; Holland Thompson, *New South*, chs. ii, vii; B. T. Washington, *Story of Negro* (1909), II, chs. ii–xv, and (with others) *Negro Problem* (1903), and *Negro in South* (1907); J. A. Tillinghast, *Negro in Africa and America* (1902), pt. 3; Buck, *Road to Reunion*, ch. xii; Calhoun, *American Family*, III, chs. ii–iii; "Negro Progress in Fifty Years," Am. Ac. Pol. and Soc. Sci., *Annals*, XLIX (1913). ❡ Negro Economic Life: Wesley, *Negro Labor*, 211; Carl Kelsey, *Negro Farmer* (1903); Zeichner, "Transition from Slave to Free Labor," 22; W. E. B. Du Bois, *Negro in Business* (1899), and *Philadelphia Negro;* P. A. Bruce, *Plantation Negro as Freeman* (1889). ❡ Negro Education and Religion: J. L. M. Curry, *Education of Negroes since 1860* (1894); Kelly Miller, "Education of Negro," U. S. Commissioner Educ., *Report*, 1900–01, I, 731; "Education of Colored Race," *ibid.*, 1894–95, II, 1331, and 1895–96, II, 2081; A. D. Mayo, "Northern Churches in Education of Negro," *ibid.*, 1902, I, 285; W. E. B. Du Bois, *Negro Common School* (1901); J. L. M. Curry, *Peabody*, and (with others) "Slater Fund," U. S. Commissioner Educ., *Report*, 1894–95, II, 1367; D. O. W. Holmes, *Evolution of Negro College* (1934), chs. iv–xiii; F. G. Peabody, *Education for Life* (1918), chs. iv–x; Walter Dyson, *Howard University* (1941), chs. iii–vii; M. B. Thrasher, *Tuskegee* (1900); Vernon Loggins, *Negro Author* (1931), chs. vii–viii; Woodson, *Negro Church*, chs. x–xiii; Farish, *Circuit Rider Dismounts*, chs. v–vi. ❡ Race Relations: C. G. Woodson, *Negro Migration* (1918), ch. vii; J. G. Van Deusen, "Exodus of 1879," *Jour. Negro Hist.*, XXI (1936), 111; Frederick Douglass, "Negro Exodus," *Jour. Soc. Sci.*, XI (1880), 1; R. T. Greener, "Emigration of Colored Citizens," *ibid.*, XI, 22; W. M. Brewer, "Poor Whites and Negroes since Civil War," *Jour. Negro Hist.*, XV (1930), 26; Franklin Johnson, *State Legislation Concerning Free Negro* (1918); S. J. Folmsbee, "Origin of First 'Jim Crow' Law," *Jour. Southern Hist.*, XV (1949), 235; Cutler, *Lynch-Law*, chs. vi–ix. ❡ Negro Disfranchisement: Lewinson, *Race, Class, & Party*, chs. iv–v; Dunning, *Essays*, 353; Porter, *Suffrage in United States*, 191; V. O. Key, *Southern Politics* (1949), ch. xxv; F. G. Caffey, "Suffrage Limitations at South," *Pol. Sci. Quar.*, XX (1905), 53; C. G. Woodson, "Fifty Years of Negro Citizenship," *Jour. Negro Hist.*, VI (1921), 1; W. F. Nowlin, *Negro in National Politics* (1931), chs. i, iii–vi; S. D. Smith, *Negro in Congress* (1940). ❡ Indians: Seymour, *Story of Red Man*, chs. xviii–xix; W. K. Moorehead, *American Indian* (1914), chs. xx, xxvi–xxvii; L. F. Schmeckebier, *Office of Indian Affairs* (1927), 66, 121; F. A. McKenzie, *Indian in Relation to White Population* (1908), 11; R. A. Gallaher, "Indian Agent," *Iowa Jour. Hist.*, XIV (1916), 184; J. P. Kinney, *Continent Lost* (1937), 163; Priest, *Uncle Sam's Stepchildren*, chs. xiii–xix; Angie Debo, *And Still the Waters Run* (1940), chs. i–iv; L. N. Brown, "Dawes Commission," *Chronicles Okla.*, IX (1931), 71; N. M. Butler, ed., *Education in United States* (1900), II, 941; Vestal, *Sitting Bull*, chs. xxxv–xxxix; L. H. Roddis, "Last Indian Uprising," *Minn. Hist. Bull.*, III (1919–20), 273. ❡ Biographical: Talbot, *Armstrong*, chs. vi–x; McElroy, *Cleveland*, I, ch. ix; Alderman and Gordon, *Curry*, chs. xv, xvii; M. A. DeW. Howe, *Bishop Hare* (1911), chs. iii–vii; E. G. Eastman, *Pratt* (1935), chs. v–xix; W. L. Fleming, "'Pap' Singleton," *Am. Jour. Sociol.*, XV (1909), 61; Mathews, *B. T. Washington*, chs. iii–xi; E. J. Scott and L. B. Stowe, *B. T. Washington* (1916), chs. i–iii.

Sources — Negroes (Official): W. E. B. Du Bois, "Negro Farmer," *Supplementary Analysis and Derivative Tables* (*Twelfth Census, Special Report*), 185, and 511; *Negro Population, 1790–1915;* 46 Cong., 2 Sess., Sen. Report, No. 693; U. S. Commissioner Educ., *Annual Reports.* ❡ Negroes (Unofficial): A. G. Haygood, *Our Brother in Black* (1881); T. T. Fortune, *Black and White* (1884); A. W. Tourgée, *Appeal to Caesar* (1884); G. W. Cable, *Silent South* (1885), and *Negro Question* (1888); H. M. Field, *Bright Skies and Dark Shadows* (1890); S. J. Barrows, "What the Negro Is Doing for Himself," *Atl. Monthly*, LXVII (1891), 805; James Bryce, "Thoughts on Negro Problem," *No. Am. Rev.*, CLIII (1891), 641; T. N. Page, *Old South* (1892), 277; W. H. Crogman, *Talks for the Times* (1896); F. L. Hoffman, *Race Traits and Tendencies* (1896); B. T. Washington, *Story of My Life* (1900), and *Up from Slavery*. ❡ Indians (Official): *Congressional Record*, esp. 49–55 Congs.; K. S. Murchison, "Digest of Decisions Relating to Indian Affairs," 56 Cong., 2 Sess., *H. Ex. Doc.*, No. 538; Richardson, *Messages and Papers*, VII–IX; *Statutes at Large*, esp. XXIV, 388 (1887), XXVI, 794 (1891), XXIX, 506 (1897), XXX, 495 (1898); Commissioner Indian Affairs, *Annual Reports* (from 1865); Board Indian Commissioners, *Annual Reports* (from 1870). ❡ Indians (Unofficial): Indian Rights Assoc., *Annual Reports* (from 1882); Lake Mohonk Conference of Friends of Indian, *Proc.* (from 1883); *Appletons' Annual Cyclopædia;* D. W. Risher, ed., *Indian and White Man* (1880); Jackson, *Century of Dishonor*, chs. i, x; R. I. Dodge, *A Living Issue* (1882); H. S. Pancoast, ed., *Opinions of the Press on Legislation for Indians* (1885); William Barrows, *Indian's Side* (1887); J. B. Harrison, *Studies on Indian Reservations* (1887); A. C. Fletcher, *Indian Education* (1888); Robert Weil, *Legal Status of Indian* (1888); E. E. White, *Service on Indian Reservations* (1893); H. L. Dawes, "Have We Failed with Indian?" *Atl. Monthly*, LXXXIV (1899), 280; H. B. Whipple, *Lights and Shadows* (1900), chs. xi–xxxviii.

Bibliography — Work, *Bibliography of Negro*, 384; C. G. Woodson, *African Background Outlined* (1936), 307, 345, 379, 416, 450; E. F. Frazier, *Negro in United States*, 715; Schmeckebier, *Office of Indian Affairs*, 537.

213. ADVENT OF GREAT CITIES, 1865–1900

Summary — Urban trend: causes (§§ 205–6, 209, 211); decline of rural New England (§ 199). — Urban improvements: elevated system (1868), cable car (1873), trolley car (1888), and subway (1897); Brooklyn Bridge, 1870–83; water gas (1873), Brush's arc light (1878), and Edison's incandescent light (1880); telephone (1876) and central switchboard (1878) and other devices; brick and asphalt paving; more efficient sewage and garbage disposal; extension of waterworks; better fire protection. — Apartment house, department store, and skyscraper (§ 218); typewriter (1868) and other new office equipment. — Society life: the "Four Hundred"; social climbing; international marriages; fashionable resorts. — Municipal politics: sources of corruption; Tweed Ring (1868–71) and other scandals; reform efforts. — Urban social problems (§ 214). — City expositions: Philadelphia Centennial, 1876; Chicago World's Fair, 1893. — Growth of suburban districts. — Later developments (§§ 226, 231).

General — Nevins, *Emergence of Modern America*, 74, 92, 182, 306; Oberholtzer, *History*, I, 230, 241, 269, II, 549, 581, V, 687; Rhodes, *History*, VI, 392, VII, 48, VIII, 414; Schlesinger, *Rise of City*, 78, 150, 283, 389; Sparks, *National Development*, 4, 29, 37; Tarbell, *Nationalizing of Business*, 43, 265.

Special — Urban Trend: A. F. Weber, *Growth of Cities*, 20, and "Suburban Annexations," *No. Am. Rev.*, CLXVI (1898), 612; N. S. Shaler, ed., *United States* (1894), II, ch. v; S. L. Loomis, *Modern Cities* (1887), chs. i–ii; Josiah Strong, *Our Country* (1891), ch. xi, and *New Era*, chs. viii–ix; F. J. Kingsbury, "Tendency to Live in Cities," *Jour. Soc. Sci.*, XXXIII (1895), 1. ❡ Particular Cities: Willard Glazier, *Peculiarities of American Cities* (1883); Karl Baedeker, ed., *United States* (1893; rev., 1899); Stokes, *Iconography of Manhattan Island*, III, 748, V, 1914; H. C. Brown, *Last Fifty Years in New York* (1926), and *New York in Elegant Eighties* (1926), and *In Golden Nineties* (1928); McKelvey, *Rochester*, II, chs. iv–xiii; Young, *Philadelphia*, I, 537; Hirschfield, *Baltimore*; G. B. Catlin, *Detroit* (1923), chs. ci–cvi; Lewis and H. J. Smith, *Chicago*, pt. 1, chs. x–xiv, pt. 2, chs. i–vii; Belcher, *Rivalry between St. Louis and Chicago*, chs. ix–xi; Still, *Milwaukee*, chs. xi–xv; Alice Lanterman, "Kansas City as Grain and Milling Center," *Mo. Hist. Rev.*, XLII (1947), 20; Capers, *Memphis*, chs. vii–ix; O. O. Winther, "Rise of Metropolitan Los Angeles," *Huntington Library Quar.*, X (1947), 391. ❡ Urban Improvements: J. A. Fairlie, *Municipal Administration* (1901), 86, pt. 2; Charles Zueblin, *American Municipal Progress* (1902); E. W. Bemis, ed., *Municipal Monopolies* (1899); Burlingame, *Engines of Democracy*, chs. vi–vii, xi; Kaempffert, *American Invention*, I,

106, 320, 539; Byrn, *Progress of Invention*, chs. vi–viii, xiv; Depew, *One Hundred Years of Commerce*, I, chs. xx, xxii, xlii, II, ch. liv; George Iles, *Flame, Electricity and Camera* (1900), chs. x, xvii; T. C. Martin and S. L. Coles, *Electricity* (1919–22), I, chs. iii–vi; A. F. Harlow, *Old Wires and New Waves* (1936), chs. xvii–xx; J. B. Walker, *Fifty Years of Rapid Transit* (1918), chs. v–xiii; W. F. Reeves, "Elevated Lines in New York," N. Y. Hist. Soc., *Quar. Bull.*, XVIII (1935), 59, XIX (1935), 3; H. G. Tyrrell, *Bridge Engineering* (1911), chs. x–xiv; Henry Schroeder, *Electric Light* (1923), 25; E. Greenwood, "Behind the Veil," National Electric Light Assoc., *Bull.*, XVI (1929), 632; Casson, *Telephone*, chs. i–ii, iv; Hendrick, *Age of Big Business*, ch. iv; G. W. Tillson, *Street Pavements* (1900), chs. ix–x; N. P. Lewis, "Modern City Roadways," *Pop. Sci. Mo.*, LVI (1900), 524; H. P. Eddy, *et al.*, "Development of Sanitary Engineering," Am. Soc. Civil Engineers, *Trans.*, XCII (1928), 1207; G. E. Waring, Jr., *Sanitary Drainage* (1876), chs. iii–x, and *Modern Methods of Sewage Disposal* (1894), and *Street-Cleaning* (1897); G. W. Rafter and M. N. Baker, *Sewage Disposal* (1894); M. N. Baker, *Municipal Engineering* (1901); W. F. Morse, *Municipal Waste* (1908), 99. ❡ Department Stores and other Innovations: R. M. Hower, *Macy's of New York* (1943), chs. iii–xi; J. W. Tebbel, *Marshall Fields* (1947), ii–iv; H. W. Roby, *Invention of Typewriter* (1925); Iles, *Leading American Inventors*, 315; Herkimer County Hist. Soc., *Story of Typewriter* (1923), chs. iii–viii. ❡ Society Life: Dixon Wecter, *Saga of American Society* (1937), chs. iv–xii; M. K. Van Rensselaer and Frederic Van de Water, *Social Ladder* (1924), chs. iv–viii; Harvey O'Connor, *Astors* (1941), ch. iv; A. S. Crockett, *Peacocks on Parade* (1931), chs. i–xi; Schlesinger, *Learning How to Behave*, ch. iv; Godkin, *Problems*, 311; J. D. Champlin, Jr., "Manufacture of Ancestors," *Forum*, X (1891), 565. ❡ Municipal Politics: C. W. Patton, *Battle for Municipal Reform* (1940); Hendrick, *Age of Big Business*, ch. v; D. B. Eaton, *Government of Municipalities* (1899), chs. i–xi; S. P. Orth, *Boss and Machine* (1919), chs. v–vi; Bryce, *American Commonwealth*, I, chs. l–lii, II, chs. lxiii–lxiv, lxviii, lxxxviii–lxxxix; Lincoln Steffens, *Struggle for Self-Government* (1906), 40, 161, and *Shame of Cities* (1904); Zink, *City Bosses*, 69; Myers, *Tammany Hall*, chs. xxiii–xxix; M. R. Werner, *Tammany Hall* (1928), chs. iv–vi; M. D. Hirsch, "More Light on Boss Tweed," *Pol. Sci. Quar.*, LX (1945), 267; S. J. Tilden, *New York City "Ring"* (1873); G. E. Vickers, *Fall of Bossism* (1883); Godkin, *Problems*, 123; W. H. Tolman, *Municipal Reform Movements* (1895). ❡ City Expositions: M. E. Curti, "America at World's Fairs," *Am. Hist. Rev.*, LV (1950), 833; Tallmadge, *Architecture in America*, 162–5, 195–213; J. S. Ingram, *Centennial Exposition* (1876); S. G. W. Benjamin, "American Art since the Centennial," *New Princeton Rev.*, IV (1887), 14; Maurice Neufeld, "White City," Ill. State Hist. Soc., *Jour.*, XXVII (1934–35), 71; B. C. Truman, *et al.*, *World's Fair* (1893). ❡ Biographies: Mackenzie, *Bell*, chs. i–xi; Moore, *Burnham*, I, chs. iv–vi; T. L. Stoddard, *Master of Manhattan* (1931) (Croker), chs. v–xxiv; Dyer, *Edison* (1929), I, chs. ix, xi–xviii; W. A. Simonds, *Edison* (1934), chs. ix–x, xiii–xxiii; John Foord, *A. H. Green* (1913), chs. vii–xvi; C. O. Johnson, *C. H. Harrison* (1928), chs. v, ix–xv; Paine, *Nast*, chs. xviii–xxx; Schuyler, *Roeblings*, chs. vii, xiii; D. B. Steinman, *Builders of the Bridge* (1945) (Roeblings), chs. xvi–xx; Bigelow, *Tilden*, I, chs. viii–x; Flick, *Tilden*, chs. xvi–xviii; D. T. Lynch, *Tweed* (1927), chs. xxv–xxxi; Prout, *Westinghouse*, chs. iv–vi, xiii. ❡ Maps: Paullin, *Atlas*, plates 64–5, 77–9.

Sources — Official: Census publications (§ 7); U.S. Centennial Commission, *International Exhibition, 1876.* ❡ Unofficial Compilations: *American (Appletons') Annual Cyclopædia;* National Municipal League, *Proc.* (from 1895); P. M. Angle, ed., *Great Chicago Fire* (1946); *American Magazine of Civics* (from 1889); *Paving and Municipal Engineering* (from 1890); *Scientific American* (esp. "50th Anniversary Number," July 25, 1896). ❡ Personal: M. P. Breen, *Thirty Years of New York Politics* (1899), chs. iii–lxiv; Clews, *Fifty Years*, ch. xxxii; C. H. Harrison, *Stormy Years* (1935), chs. i–xv; T. L. Johnson, *My Story*, chs. ii–xi; Ward McAllister, *Society as I Have Found It* (1890), chs. vii–xxvii; Tilden, *Writings*, I, chs. xxiv, xxviii–xxx. ❡ Travelers' Descriptions: Pierce, *As Others See Chicago*, 191; [Price Collier], *America and Americans* (1897), chs. ii–iii, ix–x, xix; Faithfull, *Three Visits*, chs. ii–iii, vii–viii, xxii; S. R. Hole, *Tour in America* (1895), chs. iv–v, xviii–xix, xxi–xxii; T. S. Hudson, *Scamper through America* (1882), 29, 54, 218; Muirhead, *Land of Contrasts*, ch. xi; S. C. de Soissons, *Parisian in America* (1896), ch. vii; Steevens, *Land of Dollar*, chs. ii–iii, vi, xi, xiv, xvii.

Bibliography — Burlingame, *Engines of Democracy*, 545; Patton, *Battle for Municipal Reform*, 77; R. C. Brooks, "Bibliography of Municipal Problems," *Municipal Affairs*, V (1901), 1; Munro, *Bibliography of Municipal Government*.

214. URBAN SOCIAL PROBLEMS, 1865–1900

Summary — Rapid growth of cities (§ 213). — Attack on poverty: state boards of charities from 1864; Charity Organization Societies from 1877; social settlements from 1886; professional social workers; philanthropic work of churches (§ 216). — Slums: extent; Jacob A. Riis and other reformers; remedial efforts. — Safeguarding youth: Society for the Prevention of Cruelty to Children, 1874; country vacations for poor children from 1877; summer camps from 1881; playgrounds from 1885; child-labor problem. — Crime and penal reform: lawlessness on the frontier and in the cities; tramp evil; lax law enforcement; agitation for prison reform; Elmira Reformatory (1877) and its influence. — Public health movement: state boards of health from 1867; recurrent epidemics; germ theory of disease; new preventive methods. — Later developments (§ 231).

General — Nevins, *Emergence of Modern America*, 131, 140, 301, 319; Schlesinger, *Rise of City*, 37, 108, 128, 156, 244, 349, 360.

Special — New Trends in Charity: J. S. Lowell, *Public Relief and Private Charity* (1884); A. G. Warner, *American Charities* (1894), chs. vi–xx; Watson, *Charity Organization Movement*, chs. vi–viii; R. A. Woods and A. J. Kennedy, *Settlement Horizon* (1922), chs. iv–v, xvi–xvii, xxi–xxii; Jane Addams, *et al.*, *Philanthropy and Social Progress* (1893); C. R. Henderson, *Social Settlements* (1899); Hull-House, *Maps and Papers* (1895); Woods, *City Wilderness*, and *Americans in Process*. ❬ Slums: James Ford, *et al.*, *Slums and Housing* (1936), I, 140; De Forest and Veiller, *Tenement House*, I, 92, 131, 191, 293, II, 17, 67, 231; M. T. Reynolds, *Housing of Poor* (1893); B. O. Flower, *Civilization's Inferno* (1893); J. A. Riis, *How the Other Half Lives* (1890), and *Children of Poor* (1892), and *Ten Years' War* (1900). ❬ Safeguarding Youth: R. C. McCrea, *Humane Movement* (1910), ch. v; S. H. Coleman, *Humane Society Leaders* (1924), ch. iii; R. A. Woods, *et al.*, *Poor in Great Cities* (1895), 131; W. S. Ufford, *Fresh Air Charity* (1897); Joseph Lee, *Constructive and Preventive Philanthropy* (1902), chs. vii–xiii; C. E. Rainwater, *Play Movement* (1921), 15; A. P. Stevens, *et al.*, "Child Slavery," *Arena*, X (1894), 117. ❬ Frontier Lawlessness: Wayne Gard, *Frontier Justice* (1949); Emerson Hough, *Story of Outlaw* (1907), esp. chs. xi–xxi; W. N. Burns, *Tombstone* (1933); W. M. Raine, *Famous Sheriffs & Western Outlaws* (1929); Langford, *Vigilante Days*; Webb, *Texas Rangers*, chs. xi–xix; C. C. Rister, "Outlaws and Vigilantes of Southern Plains," *Miss. Valley Hist. Rev.*, XIX (1933), 537. ❬ Urban Crime and Vice: C. A. Ellwood, "Has Crime Increased since 1880?" Am. Inst. of Criminal Law, *Jour.*, I (1910), 378; Cesare Lombroso, "Why Homicide Has Increased," *No. Am. Rev.*, CLXV (1897), 641, CLXVI (1898), 1; E. L. Pearson, *Studies in Murder* (1924), 3; Herbert Asbury, *Gangs of New York* (1928), chs. ix–xii; C. L. Brace, *Dangerous Classes of New York* (1872); T. F. Byrnes, *Professional Criminals* (1886); Helen Campbell, *et al.*, *Darkness and Daylight* (1891), chs. ix, xvi–xviii, xxii–xxvi, xxix–xlii; A. E. Costello, *Our Police Protectors* (1884), chs. xi–xxiii; C. H. Parkhurst, *Our Fight with Tammany* (1895); B. P. Eldridge and W. B. Watts, *Our Rival, the Rascal* (1896); W. T. Stead, *If Christ Came to Chicago!* (1894). ❬ Tramps: J. J. McCook, "Tramp Problem," National Conference of Charities and Correction, *Proc.*, 1895, 288, and "Tramps," *Charities Rev.*, III (1893), 57, and "Tramp Census," *Forum*, XV (1893), 753; Jack London, *The Road* (1907); Josiah Flynt (J. F. Willard), *Tramping with Tramps* (1899), and *Notes of Itinerant Policeman* (1900), and *World of Graft* (1901); W. A. Wyckoff, *Workers* (1897–98). ❬ Prisons and Prison Reform: McKelvey, *American Prisons*, chs. iii–ix; C. R. Henderson, ed., *Correction and Prevention* (1910), I–II, IV; E. C. Wines and T. W. Dwight, *Prisons* (1867); E. C. Wines, *State of Prisons* (1880); Cable, *Silent South*, 111; J. C. Powell, *American Siberia* (1891); H. H. Hart, *Reformation of Criminals* (1890); H. M. Boies, *Prisoners and Paupers* (1893); Wines, *Punishment and Reformation*. ❬ Public Health Movement (also § 217): Shryock, *Modern Medicine*, chs. xiv–xvii; M. P. Ravenel, ed., *Half Century* *of Public Health* (1921); Sigerist, *American Medicine,* ch. viii; H. R. M. Landis, "Reception of Koch's Discovery in United States," *Annals Medical Hist.,* IV (1932), 531; H. I. Bowditch, *Public Hygiene* (1877); C. R. Henderson, *Social Spirit in America* (1897), ch. v; S. W. Abbott, *Condition of Public Hygiene* (1900). ❢ Biographies: Linn, *Jane Addams,* chs. vi–x; W. E. Wise, *Jane Addams* (1935), chs. xi–xv; W. N. Burns, *Billy the Kid* (1926); Emma Brace, *C. L. Brace* (1894), 293; Alexander Gardiner, *Canfield* (1930), chs. iii–ix; S. N. Lake, *Wyatt Earp* (1931), chs. viii–xxvii; Wilstach, *Wild Bill Hickok;* Love, *Jesse James;* W. R. Stewart, *Josephine S. Lowell* (1911), chs. iv–xxi; H. E. Wilson, *Mary McDowell* (1928), chs. ii–iv; Louise Ware, *Jacob A. Riis* (1939), chs. iii–xiv; Pringle, *Roosevelt,* ch. xi; Woods, *R. A. Woods,* chs. iv–xiv.

Sources — Official: *Congressional Doc.;* 56 Cong., 1 Sess., *H. Doc.,* Nos. 459, 476, 566; census reports; F. H. Wines, "Report on Crime, Pauperism, and Benevolence," *Eleventh Census,* XXII–XXIII; C. D. Wright, "Slums of Baltimore, Chicago, New York and Philadelphia," Commissioner of Labor, *Special Report,* 1894; E. R. L. Gould, "Housing of Working People," *ibid.,* 1895; N. Y. Senate Comm. to Investigate Police Dept. (Lexow Comm.), *Report and Proceedings* (1895); reports of state boards of Charities and Corrections, and of state and city Boards of Health. ❢ Unofficial Compilations: S. P. Breckinridge, comp., *Public Welfare Administration* (1927), 245, 365, 427, 502, 529, 628; Edith Abbott, ed., *Pioneers in Social Welfare* (1937), 151; *American (Appletons') Annual Cyclopædia;* National Conference of Charities and Correction, *Proc.* (from 1874); National Prison Assoc., *Proc.* (from 1884); Am. Public Health Assoc., *Public Health, Papers and Reports* (1875–95), and *Journal* (from 1891). ❢ Personal: Addams, *Twenty Years at Hull-House,* chs. v–xvi; Z. R. Brockway, *Fifty Years of Prison Service* (1912), pt. 2; T. T. Crittenden, *Memoirs* (1910), 131; Emmett Dalton and Jack Jungmeyer, *When the Daltons Rode* (1931); L. W. Moore, *His Own Story* (1893); C. H. Parkhurst, *Forty Years in New York* (1923), ch. vii; Riis, *Making of an American,* chs. ix–xiii; Roosevelt, *Autobiography,* ch. vi; Lincoln Steffens, *Autobiography* (1931), I, pt. 2, chs. vi–vii, ix–x; Graham Taylor, *Pioneering on Social Frontiers* (1930), chs. viii–x, xxi; L. D. Wald, *House on Henry Street* (1915), chs. i–ii; G. W. Walling, *Recollections of New York Chief of Police* (1887).

Bibliography (also § 213) — W. H. Tolman and W. I. Hull, *Handbook of Sociological Information* (1894); Watson, *Charity Organization Movement,* 543; C. W. Montgomery, *Bibliography of College, Social, University and Church Settlements* (1905 ed.); Ford, *Slums and Housing,* II, 973; Kuhlman, *Guide to Material on Crime;* Shryock, "Public Health Movement," 654.

215. TEMPERANCE AND WOMEN'S RIGHTS, 1865–1900

Summary — Earlier history (§ 152). — Temperance movement: effects of Civil War on liquor business; rural *v.* urban attitudes; Prohibition party from 1869; Women's Temperance Crusade, 1873–74; Women's Christian Temperance Union from 1874; legal restrictions on the liquor traffic; American Anti-Saloon League, 1895. — Changing position of women: causes; increase in industry, business, and the professions; new educational facilities; club movement from 1868; improved civil status of married women; agitation for equal suffrage and results. — The family: declining size; rising divorce rate; servant problem; food. — Later developments (§§ 226, 229).

General — Nevins, *Emergence of Modern America,* 273, 279, 335, 377; Oberholtzer, *History,* IV, 429, 581, V, 752; Schlesinger, *Rise of City,* 121, 136, 154, 204, 353.

Special — Temperance: Herbert Asbury, *Great Illusion* (1950), 68; D. L. Colvin, *Prohibition* (1926), chs. iii–xviii; Cherrington, *Prohibition,* 158; J. G. Woolley and W. E. Johnson, *Temperance Progress* (1903), chs. ix–xii, xviii; A. F. Fehlandt, *Drink Reform* (1904), chs. vii–xii; E. A. Hendricks, "South Carolina Dispensary System," *No. Car. Hist. Rev.,* XXII (1945), 176, 320; Simkins, *Tillman Movement,* ch. viii; A. T. Wittenmyer, *Woman's Temperance Crusade* (1877); Dorchester, *Liquor Problem,* 392;

Strong, *Our Country*, ch. viii; Boies, *Prisoners and Paupers,* ch. xi; E. L. Fanshawe, *Liquor Legislation* (1893), chs. i–xix; F. H. Wines and John Koren, *Liquor Problem in Its Legislative Aspects* (1898); John Koren, *Economic Aspects of Liquor Problem* (1899); Raymond Calkins, *Substitutes for Saloon* (1901); J. S. Billings, ed., *Physiological Aspects of Liquor Problem* (1903). ❡ Advance of Women: H. A. Bruce, *Woman in Making of America* (1928), ch. vii; I. H. Irwin, *Angels and Amazons* (1933), bk. 2; E. R. Groves, *American Woman* (1944), 180, 211; Faithfull, *Three Visits,* chs. iii, v–vi, xvii–xx; A. N. Meyer, ed., *Woman's Work* (1891); W. F. Tillett, "Southern Womanhood," *Century,* XLIII (1891), 9; C. V. C. de Varigny, *La Femme aux États Unis* (1893); Mme. Blanc (Thérèse Bentzon), *Condition of Women* (1895); F. E. Willard and M. A. Livermore, eds., *American Women* (1897); Abbott, *Women in Industry,* chs. viii–xiii; H. S. Campbell, *Prisoners of Poverty* (1887), and *Women Wage-Earners* (1893), chs. iv–vi, ix–xi; Woody, *Women's Education in United States,* II, chs. iv–ix; E. H. Clarke, *Sex in Education* (1873); A. C. Brackett, ed., *Education of American Girls* (1874), chs. vii–xi, and *Woman and Higher Education* (1893); S. A. Burstall, *Education of Girls* (1894); M. R. Smith, "Statistics of College and Non-College Women," Am. Stat. Assoc., *Publ.,* VII (1900), 1; J. C. Croly, *Woman's Club Movement* (1898), 15; M. I. Wood, *General Federation of Women's Clubs* (1912), 31. ❡ Civil and Political Status of Women: Stanton, *Woman Suffrage,* II, chs. xvii–xxvi, III, chs. xxvii–lv, IV, chs. i–lxxii; J. P. Bishop, *Law of Married Women* (1875); James Schouler, *Law of Domestic Relations* (1889); G. J. Bayles, *Woman and the Law* (1901); Porter, *Suffrage in United States,* 228; C. C. Catt and N. R. Shuler, *Woman Suffrage and Politics* (1923), chs. iv–ix; Gail Hamilton (M. A. Dodge), *Woman's Wrongs* (1868); Horace Bushnell, *Women's Suffrage* (1869); L. P. Brockett, *Woman* (1869), chs. xvi–xxi; Francis Parkman, "Woman Question," *No. Am. Rev.,* CXXIX (1879), 303, CXXX (1880), 16; J. W. Howe, *et al.,* "Other Side of Woman Question," *ibid.,* CXXIX, 413; T. W. Higginson, *Common Sense about Women* (1881), chs. lxxii–cv; H. K. Johnson, *Woman and the Republic* (1897). ❡ Family: Calhoun, *American Family,* III, chs. v–xii; G. E. Howard, *Matrimonial Institutions* (1904), II, ch. xvi, III, chs. xvii–xviii; J. S. Billings, "Diminishing Birth-Rate," *Forum,* XV (1893), 467; F. A. Bushee, "Declining Birth-Rate," *Popular Sci. Mo.,* LXIII (1903), 355; J. P. Lichtenberger, *Divorce* (1909); Alfred Cahen, *Statistical Analysis of Divorce* (1932), chs. ii, v, ix; T. D. Woolsey, *Divorce and Divorce Legislation* (1869); C. F. and C. F. B. Thwing, *Family* (1886), chs. ix, xi–xii; Duncan Convers, *Marriage and Divorce* (1889); S. G. Fisher, *Increase of Divorce* (1890); W. F. Willcox, *Divorce Problem* (1897); L. M. Salmon, *Domestic Service* (1901); Cummings, *American and His Food,* chs. iv–ix. ❡ Biographies: R. C. Dorr, *Susan B. Anthony* (1928), chs. xiv–xxiv; Harper, *Susan B. Anthony,* I, chs. xv–xxix, II, III, chs. li–lviii; M. G. Peck, *Carrie C. Catt* (1944), 47–102; Richards and Elliott, *Julia Ward Howe,* I, chs. xiii, xvii; Palmer, *Alice Freeman Palmer,* chs. iv–viii; Lutz, *Created Equal* (Stanton), chs. xiii–xxiii; Blackwell, *Lucy Stone,* 201; R. C. Strachey, *Frances Willard* (1912), chs. vii–x; Mary Earhart, *Frances Willard* (1944), chs. vii–xv; E. L. N. Sachs, *"Terrible Siren"* (1928) (Victoria C. Woodhull), chs. iv–xiv.

Sources — Official: census publications, esp. *Social Statistics of Cities, 1890 (Eleventh Census),* and *Marriage and Divorce, 1867–1906 (Special Report,* 1909), and *Women in Gainful Occupations, 1870 to 1920 (Census Monographs,* IX, 1929); U.S. Commissioner Educ., *Report,* 1889–90, II, 695 (temperance textbooks); F. G. French, "Educational Status of Women in Different Countries," *ibid.,* 1894–95, I, 893; "Working Women in Large Cities," U.S. Commissioner Labor, *Annual Report,* 1888; "Economic Aspects of Liquor Problem," *ibid.,* 1897; C. M. Beyer, "History of Labor Legislation for Women," Women's Bur., *Bull.,* No. 66 (1929); H. G. Wadlin, "Relation of Liquor Traffic to Pauperism," Mass. Bur. Labor Stat., *Annual Report,* 1895, pt. 1. ❡ Unofficial Compilations: *Cyclopædia of Temperance and Prohibition* (1891); National Divorce Reform League (from 1897 National League for Protection of Family), *Annual Reports* (from 1885); *American (Appletons') Annual Cyclopædia.* ❡ Personal: J. B. Gough, *Platform Echoes* (1885); Howe, *Reminiscences,* chs. xvii–xviii; M. A. Livermore, *Story of My Life* (1897), chs. xxix–xxx; Powderly, *Thirty Years,* 580; A. H. Shaw, *Story of a Pioneer,* chs. vii–xi; Stanton and Blatch, *Stanton,* I, chs. xv–xxvi, II, 105; F. E. Willard, *Glimpses of Fifty Years* (1889), 368.

Bibliography — Colvin, *Prohibition*, 120, 199, 237, 261, 303; Calhoun, *American Family*, III, 333; M. L. Franklin, *Woman Suffrage* (1913), 30, 159, 186, 303.

216. REORIENTATION OF RELIGION, 1865–1900

Summary — Attitude of religious bodies toward Southern Reconstruction (§ 189). — Adjustment of church to urban conditions: difficulties; city missions; the social gospel; institutional churches; Christian Socialism; Y. M. C. A. and Y. W. C. A. — The changing Sabbath. — Intellectual challenges to orthodoxy: evolutionary hypothesis (§ 217), higher criticism, and study of comparative religion; heresy trials; World's Parliament of Religions, 1893. — Catholic problems: third plenary council, 1884; Cahensly movement; education; relations to state; "Americanism." — Judaism: I. M. Wise and reform; Pittsburgh Conference, 1885. — New faiths: Christian Science from 1875; Theosophy from 1875; Ethical Culture movement from 1876. — Revival efforts: Moody and Sankey; Salvation Army from 1879. — Agnostic attack on religion. — Foreign missions. — Growth of church membership. — Negro church (§ 212); Mormons (§ 208); Chautauqua movement (§ 217). — Later developments (§§ 229–30).

General — W. E. Garrison, *March of Faith* (1933), chs. i–xiii; Rowe, *History of Religion*, chs. viii–ix, xi–xii; Schlesinger, *Rise of City*, ch. x; Stokes, *Church and State*, II, 255, 392; Sweet, *Story of Religion*, 479, 517.

Special — Alienation of Workingmen: H. F. May, *Protestant Churches and Industrial America* (1949), pts. 2–3; R. H. Johnson, "Baptists in Age of Big Business," *Jour. of Religion*, XI (1931), 63; Washington Gladden, *Applied Christianity* (1886), 1, 146, and *Tools and the Man*, and *Social Facts and Forces* (1897); O. F. Adams, "Aristocratic Drift of Protestantism," *No. Am. Rev.*, CXLII (1886), 194; Loomis, *Modern Cities*, ch. iii; C. M. Morse, "Church and Working Man," *Forum*, VI (1888), 653; R. T. Ely, *Social Aspects of Christianity* (1889), 30; Strong, *New Era*, ch. x; J. R. Commons, *Social Reform and Church* (1894); H. F. Perry, "Workingman's Alienation from the Church," *Am. Jour. Sociol.*, IV (1899), 621. ⟨ Socializing Trends: A. L. Drummond, *American Protestantism* (1949), bk. 5, chs. i–iv; C. H. Hopkins, *Rise of Social Gospel* (1940), chs. i–xi; May, *Protestant Churches and Industrial America*, pt. 4; A. I. Abell, *Urban Impact on American Protestantism* (1943), chs. ii–x; Gabriel, *American Democratic Thought*, ch. xv; James Dombrowski, *Early Days of Christian Socialism* (1936); Farish, *Circuit Rider Dismounts*, chs. ii–iii, vii–ix; Josiah Strong, *Religious Movements for Social Betterment* (1900); G. W. Mead, *Modern Methods in Church Work* (1896); John O'Grady, *Catholic Charities* (1931), chs. vi–xx; Joseph Leiser, *American Judaism* (1925), 151, 206; B. D. Bogen, *Jewish Philanthropy* (1917), chs. iv, vii, ix, xiv, xvi, xviii; J. B. Clark, *Leavening Nation* (1903), ch. xvii; Campbell, *Darkness and Daylight*, chs. i–ii, viii, x–xi, xv; Edward Judson, *Institutional Church* (1899); J. H. W. Stuckenberg, *Christian Sociology* (1880); Gilman, *Socialism and American Spirit*, ch. vii; F. M. Sprague, *Socialism* (1893). ⟨ Sabbath: H. E. Young, "Sunday Laws," Am. Bar Assoc., *Report*, 1880, 109; J. G. Woerner, "Sunday Laws," *Am. Law Rev.*, XVIII (1884), 778; A. E. Waffle, *Lord's Day* (1886); W. F. Crafts, *Sabbath for Man* (1894), 82, 587, 639. ⟨ Intellectual Challenges: A. D. White, *Warfare of Science with Theology* (1896), I, 313; B. J. Loewenberg, "Controversy over Evolution in New England," *N. Eng. Quar.*, VIII (1935), 232; Joseph Le Conte, *Religion and Science* (1873), chs. xiv–xvi; Charles Hodge, *What Is Darwinism?* (1874); M. J. Savage, *Religion of Evolution* (1876); Asa Gray, *Natural Science and Religion* (1880); G. F. Wright, *Science and Religion* (1882); Arnold Guyot, *Creation* (1884); B. F. Tefft, *Evolution and Christianity* (1885); W. W. McLane, *Evolution in Religion* (1892); W. N. Rice, *Twenty-Five Years of Scientific Progress* (1894), ch. iv; George Harris, *Century's Change in Religion* (1914), chs. iii–iv; Orello Cone, *Gospel Criticism* (1891); Washington Gladden, *Who Wrote the Bible?* (1891), and *Seven Puzzling Bible Books* (1897); J. F. Clarke, *Ten Great Religions* (1871); J. H. Barrows, ed., *World's Parliament of Religions* (1893). ⟨ Catholic Problems (§ 211): Theodore Maynard, *American Catholicism* (1941), chs. xix–xxviii; Gerald Shaughnessy, *Has Immigrant Kept Faith?* (1925), 146; J. J. Meng, "Growing Pains in Catholic Church," U. S. Cath. Hist. Soc., *Records and Studies*, XXXVI (1947),

17; H. J. Browne, "Italian Problem," *ibid.*, XXXV (1946), 46, and *Catholic Church and Knights of Labor* (1947); Fergus MacDonald, *Catholic Church and Secret Societies* (1946); A. I. Abell, "Reception of Leo XIII's Labor Encyclical," *Rev. Politics*, VII (1945), 464; T. T. McAvoy, "Americanism and Frontier Catholicism," *ibid.*, V (1943), 275; John Higham, "American Party," *Pacific Hist. Rev.*, XIX (1950), 37; Myers, *History of Bigotry*, chs. xxi–xxii; H. J. Desmond, *A. P. A. Movement* (1912); W. H. J. Traynor, "Policy and Power of A. P. A.," *No. Am. Rev.*, CLXII (1896), 658; T. J. Jenkins, "A. P. A. Conspirators," *Cath. World*, LVII (1893), 685. ⓒ Judaism: David Philipson, *Reform Movement in Judaism* (1931). ⓒ New Faiths: C. S. Braden, *These Also Believe* (1949), 180, 462; A. B. Kuhn, *Theosophy* (1930), chs. ii–xii; Stow Persons, *Free Religion* (1947), chs. iii–viii; H. W. Dresser, *New Thought Movement* (1919), chs. i–ix. ⓒ Revivalism: F. G. Beardsley, *American Revivals* (1912), chs. xiv–xv; G. C. Loud, *Evangelized America* (1928), ch. xvi; H. C. Weber, *Evangelism* (1929), pts. 2–3; F. St. G. de L. Booth-Tucker, *Social Relief Work of Salvation Army* (1900). ⓒ Foreign Missions: D. L. Leonard, *Missionary Annals* (1899), chs. x–xv; J. S. Dennis, *Christian Missions and Social Progress* (1897–1906), II, 103, III; W. E. Strong, *American Board* (1910), chs. ix–xxv. ⓒ Church Growth: Philip Schaff, "Progress of Christianity," *Princeton Rev.*, LV (1879), 209; H. K. Carroll, *Religious Forces* (1893); Daniel Dorchester, *Christianity* (1895), 570, and "Evangelical Churches," *Christian Advocate*, LXXVI (1901), 52. ⓒ Biographies: T. D. Bacon, *Leonard Bacon* (1931), chs. xv–xvii; Abbott, *Beecher*, chs. xii–xvii; Hibben, *Beecher*, chs. xxi–xxx; C. E. Bechofer-Roberts, *Mysterious Madame* (Blavatsky) (1913), chs. v–viii; Allen, *Brooks*, II; Bates and Dittemore, *Eddy*, chs. vii–xviii; Dakin, *Mrs. Eddy*, chs. v–xxiii; Powell, *Eddy*, 98; Ellis, *Cardinal Gibbons*, I, chs. iii–xv, II, ch. xvi; E. G. Smith, *Ingersoll* (1904), chs. iv–v, vii; J. H. Moynihan, *Archbishop Ireland* (1953), chs. i–vii; Stephen Bell, *Rebel, Priest and Prophet* (1937) (McGlynn), 15; Zwierlein, *Bishop McQuaid*, II–III; Bradford, *Moody*, chs. ii–vii; Moody, *Moody*, chs. xiv–lxx; R. M. Offord, *Jerry McAuley* (1907); W. R. Sharpe, *Rauschenbusch* (1942), chs. iii–vii; D. S. Schaff, *Philip Schaff* (1897), chs. x–xviii.

Sources — Official: 50 Cong., 1 Sess., *Misc. Sen. Docs.*, No. 108, and 2 Sess., *ibid.*, No. 43; census publications, esp. *Statistics of Churches* (Eleventh Census), and *Religious Bodies: 1906* (Special Report, 1910); Mass. Bur. of Labor, *Annual Report*, 1885, pt. 2. ⓒ Unofficial: proceedings and other publications of churches and church organizations; W. A. Blakely, *American State Papers Bearing on Sunday Legislation* (1891), 192; *American (Appletons') Cyclopædia.* ⓒ Personal: Abbott, *Reminiscences*, chs. xiii–xix; M. B. Booth, *Beneath Two Flags* (1889), chs. ii–xx; J. F. Clarke, *Autobiography*, chs. xvi–xxi; Mary Baker Eddy, *Retrospection* (1891), and *Miscellaneous Writings* (1896); Gladden, *Recollections*, chs. xii–xxii; G. E. Macdonald, *Fifty Years of Freethought* (1929–31), I, chs. vii–xxiv; W. S. Rainsford, *Story of Varied Life* (1924), chs. xii–xxi; C. M. Sheldon, *Life Story* (1925), chs. iii–vii; W. J. Tucker, *My Generation* (1919), ch. vii; A. D. White, *Autobiography*, I, 422, II, 494, 566; I. M. Wise, *Reminiscences* (1901). ⓒ New Bibles: Mary Baker Eddy, *Science and Health* (1875; many revisions); Felix Adler, *Creed and Deed* (1877); H. P. Blavatsky, *Isis Unveiled* (1877).

Bibliography — S. J. Case, *et al.*, *Bibliographical Guide to History of Christianity* (1931), 170; Mode, *Source Book for American Church History* (1921), 626; Stokes, *Church and State*, III, ch. xxxviii; May, *Protestant Churches and Industrial America*, 267; Crafts, *Sabbath for Man*, 610; E. C. Richardson, comp., *Periodical Articles on Religion, 1890–1899* (1907).

217. INTELLECTUAL ADVANCES, 1865–1900

Summary — Development of public schools in North and West: earlier history (§ 151); compulsory attendance; increase of normal schools; spread of kindergartens from 1873; multiplication of high schools; curricular changes. — Public-school movement in South (§§ 189, 195): difficulties; philanthropic aid; contest over Blair Education bill in Congress, 1884–88. — Adult education: Redpath and other lecture bureaus; Chautauqua movement from 1874. — Higher education: increased financial support, especially from Morrill Acts of 1862 (§ 199) and 1890 and private benefactions; German influences; leadership of new generation of university presidents; elective system; graduate instruction; summer schools; extension courses; higher standards of professional training. — Education of women (§ 215) and of Negroes and Indians (§ 212). — Progress of knowledge: specialization; strife over biological evolution; scientific and learned societies; research work of federal and state governments and of universities; significant additions to knowledge. — Later developments (§ 229).

General — Curti, *Growth of American Thought*, chs. xix–xxv; Nevins, *Emergence of Modern America*, 238, 264, 362; Oberholtzer, *History*, III, 449, IV, 536; Schlesinger, *Rise of City*, 160, 202.

Special — Education: E. G. Dexter, *Education in United States* (1904), chs. xi–xxix; R. G. Boone, *Education in United States* (1894), chs. x–xxi; Butler, *Education in United States*; H. K. Beale, *History of Freedom of Teaching* (1941), 173. ❧ Pre-college Education: Cubberley, *Public Education in United States*, 449, 513, 539, 549, 627, 663; E. W. Knight, *Education in United States* (1929), 461, 499; Curti, *Social Ideas of American Educators*, chs. vi–xiii; E. H. Reisner, *Evolution of Common School* (1930), chs. xx–xxv; N. C. Vandewalker, *Kindergarten* (1908), chs. ii–xi; C. D. Aborn, *et al.*, eds., *Pioneers of Kindergarten* (1924); Charles De Garmo, *Herbart and Herbartians* (1895), pt. 3; J. A. Burns, *et al.*, *History of Catholic Education* (1937), chs. vi–x; B. L. Pierce, *Public Opinion and Teaching of History* (1926), chs. ii, vi. ❧ Public Education in South: Knight, *Public Education in South*, chs. ix–xii; Bruce, *Rise of New South*, chs. xxii–xxviii; C. W. Dabney, *Universal Education in South* (1936), I, chs. vii–xix; W. H. Page, *Rebuilding of Old Commonwealths* (1902). ❧ Adult Education: R. L. Richmond, *Chautauqua* (1943), chs. iii–vii; J. L. Hurlbut, *Chautauqua* (1921), chs. iii–xviii; H. J. Thornton, "Critics and Reformers at Chautauqua," *N. Y. Hist.*, XXVI (1945), 307, and "Chautauqua and Midwest," *Wisc. Mag. Hist.*, XXXIII (1949–50), 152; J. H. Vincent, *Chautauqua Movement* (1886). ❧ Higher Education: W. C. Ryan, *Early Graduate Education* (1939); C. F. Thwing, *Education since Civil War* (1910), chs. v, vii–xii, xiv–xv, and *Higher Education in America*, chs. xvii–xxii, and *American and German University* (1928), chs. iii–vi; James Bryce, *American Commonwealth*, II, ch. cii, and "American College," *Atl. Monthly*, LXXV (1895), 703; J. M. Barker, *Colleges in America* (1894); Gabriel Compayré, *L'Enseignement Supérieur aux États-Unis* (1896); Athanasius Zimmermann, *Die Universitäten in den Vereinigten Staaten* (1896); D. C. Gilman, *University Problems* (1898); D. E. Phillips, "Elective System," *Pedagogical Seminary*, VIII (1901), 206; W. W. Willoughby, "Summer Schools," U. S. Commissioner Educ., *Report*, 1891–92, II, 893; L. R. Klemm, "Legal Education," *ibid.*, 1890–91, I, 376; E. R. Cunningham, "Medical Education," *Annals Medical Hist.*, VII (1935), 228; A. C. True, "Agricultural Education," Dept. of Ag., *Yearbook*, 1899, 157; J. B. Sears, *Philanthropy in Higher Education* (1922), ch. iv; histories of particular colleges and universities. ❧ College Life: H. D. Sheldon, *Student Life and Customs* (1901), ch. v; G. S. Hall, "Student Customs," Am. Antiq. Soc., *Proc.*, XIV (1900–01), 83; "Social Life in Colleges," *Lippincott's*, XXXIX–XL (1887–88); "Undergraduate Life," *Scribner's*, XXI–XXII (1897); A. D. White, "Fraternities," *Forum*, III (1887), 243; E. H. L. Randolph, "Greek-Letter Societies," *N. Eng. Mag.*, XVII (1897), 70. ❧ Scientific Organizations (§§ 4, 50–1): Bates, *Scientific Societies*, ch. iii; Goode, *Smithsonian Institution*, chs. iv–xv; F. B. Sanborn, "Twenty-Five Years," *Jour. Soc. Sci.*, XXVII (1890), pp. xliii–xlix; J. F. Jameson, "American Historical Association," *Am. Hist. Rev.*, XV (1909), 1; R. T. Ely, "American Economic Association," Am. Econ. Assoc., *Publ.*, XI (1910), 47; S. W. Fernberger, "American Psychological Association," *Psych. Bull.*, XXIX (1932), 1; D. S. Martin, "American Association," *Popular Sci. Monthly*, LIII (1898), 822; H. L. Fairchild, *Geological Society of America* (1932), chs. v–xix; Morris Fishbein, *American Medical Association* (1947), 71. ❧ Strife over Evolution: B. J. Loewenberg, "Reaction of American Scientists to Darwinism," *Am. Hist. Rev.*, XXXVIII (1933), 687, and "Darwinism Comes to America," *Miss. Valley Hist. Rev.*, XXVIII (1940), 339; Sidney Ratner, "Evolution and Rise of Scientific Spirit," *Philos. of Science*, III (1936), 104; Richard Hofstadter, *Social Darwinism* (1944); E. D. Cope, *On Hypothesis of Evolution* (1870), and *Origin of Fittest* (1887); John Fiske, "Agassiz and Darwinism," *Popular Sci. Monthly*, III (1873), 692, and *Cosmic Philosophy* (1874), and *Century of Science* (1899), chs. i–iv; Louis

Agassiz, "Evolution and Permanence of Type," *Atl. Monthly*, XXXIII (1874), 92; Asa Gray, *Darwiniana* (1876). ❡ Natural Sciences: Dana, *et al.*, *Century of Science*; W. J. McGee, "Fifty Years of American Science," *Atl. Monthly*, LXXXII (1898), 307; Rice, *Twenty-Five Years*, chs. i–ii; Jordan, *Leading Men of Science*, 211; Jaffe, *Men of Science*, chs. xii–xv; E. B. McKinley, "Theobald Smith," *Science*, LXXXII (1935), 575; Jenks Cameron, *Bureau of Biological Survey* (1929), 12; G. A. Weber, *Bureau of Chemistry and Soils* (1928), 7; Milton Conover, *Office of Experiment Stations* (1924), 16; E. F. Smith, *Chemistry*, ch. xii; R. H. Chittenden, *Physiological Chemistry in United States* (1930), chs. i–iii; Young, *Biology*; L. O. Howard, "Applied Entomology in United States," *Ag. Hist.*, III (1929), 131; Wiest, *Agricultural Organization*, ch. xi; True, *Agricultural Education*, 126; Merrill, *American Geology*, chs. vi–xv; H. N. Smith, "King, Powell, and Establishment of Geological Survey," *Miss. Valley Hist. Rev.*, XXXIV (1947), 37; E. G. Boring, *Experimental Psychology* (1929), ch. xx; E. F. Buchner, "Quarter Century of Psychology," *Am. Jour. Psych.*, XIV (1903), 402; E. S. Holden, "Achievements in Astronomy," *Forum*, XV (1893), 744; Simon Newcomb, "Recent Astronomical Progress," *ibid.*, XXV (1898), 109; T. S. Fiske, "Mathematical Progress," *Science*, XXI (1905), 209. ❡ Medicine (§ 214): Packard, *History of Medicine*, II, chs. xii–xv; Sigerist, *American Medicine*, chs. iv–vii, ix; G. F. Shrady, "Recent Triumphs in Medicine and Surgery," *Forum*, XXIII (1897), 28; Deutsch, *Mentally Ill in America*, 202; Taylor, *Dentistry*, chs. viii–ix, xi–xv. ❡ Social Sciences and Humanities: Trent, *Cambridge History of American Literature*, III, bk. 3, chs. xv, xvii, xxi, xxiii, IV, chs. xxiv–xxv; Odum, *American Masters of Social Science*, chs. ii–iv, vi–ix; Gabriel, *American Democratic Thought*, chs. xix–xxii; Stow Persons, ed., *Evolutionary Thought in America* (1950), chs. iv–viii; H. S. Commager, *American Mind* (1950), chs. iv–v, x; Kraus, *History of American History*, chs. viii–xiii; Dorfman, *Economic Mind*, III, chs. i–xiii; A. W. Small, *Origins of Sociology* (1924), ch. xix; Merriam, *American Political Theories*, ch. viii; Riley, *American Thought*, chs. vii–viii; Townsend, *Philosophical Ideas*, chs. vii–xi; H. W. Schneider, *American Philosophy* (1946), chs. xxx–xxxvii; Cleon Forbes, "St. Louis School of Thought," *Mo. Hist. Rev.*, XXV (1930–31), 83, 289, 461, 609, XXVI (1931), 68; Austin Warren, "Concord School of Philosophy," *N. Eng. Quar.*, II (1929), 199; J. E. Sandys, *Classical Scholarship* (1908), III, ch. xli. ❡ Biographies: Dall, *Baird*, chs. viii–xii; J. W. Caughey, *H. H. Bancroft* (1946), chs. vi–xxi; H. M. Lydenberg, *J. S. Billings* (1924), chs. iii–v; Osborn, *Cope*, chs. iv–viii; J. S. Clark, *Fiske*, I, chs. x–xvi, xviii, II, chs. xx–xxxvi; Gilman, *Dana*, chs. xii, xiv–xvi; Fleming, *Draper*, chs. x–xii; James, *Eliot*, I, chs. vi–x, II, chs. xi–xiii; Muriel Rukeyser, *Willard Gibbs* (1942), chs. viii–xiv; Franklin, *Gilman*, chs. iii–vii; Abraham Flexner, *Gilman* (1946), chs. ii–vi; Lorine Pruette, *G. S. Hall* (1926), chs. v–vii, ix; Goodspeed, *Harper*, chs. ii–v; K. F. Leidecker, *Yankee Teacher* (1946), chs. ix–xxix (W. T. Harris); Perry, *William James*, chs. x–xxiii; Bradley, *Lea*, chs. iv, vii–viii; E. F. Goldman, *McMaster* (1943), chs. ii–vii; Ellwood Hendrick, *Lewis Miller* (1925), chs. xviii–xxv; Stern, *L. H. Morgan*, 22; Cushing, *Osler*, I, chs. xi–xix; Hendrick, *Training of an American*, chs. ii–vi (W. H. Page); H. D. Sedgwick, *Parkman* (1904), ch. xxii; Horner, *Redpath*, chs. viii–xvii; Howe, *Rhodes*, 51; Shaler, *Autobiography*, chs. xviii–xxvi; H. E. Starr, *W. G. Sumner* (1925), chs. vi–xvi, xxii; H. M. Jones, *Tyler*, chs. v–x; L. H. Vincent, *J. H. Vincent* (1925), chs. xi–xxii; Munroe, *Walker*, chs. vi–xxii; Samuel Chugerman, *L. F. Ward* (1939), 31, 82; Baker, *Woodrow Wilson*, I, chs. viii–xi, II, chs. xii–xiv; John Fiske, *E. L. Youmans* (1894), chs. ix–xvii.

Sources — Official: *Statutes at Large*, XXIV, 440, XXVI, 417; U.S. Commissioner Educ., *Reports* (annual, from 1867); U. S. Bur. Educ., *Circulars of Information* (from 1887); reports of state and local educational authorities. ❡ Unofficial: Paul Monroe, *Cyclopedia of Education* (1911–13); W. R. Baird, *College Fraternities* (1879–   ); *Annual Record of Science*; proceedings and journals of learned, scientific, and professional societies; *American (Appletons') Annual Cyclopædia*. ❡ Personal: H. B. Adams, *Historical Scholarship* (1938); Agassiz, *Letters and Recollections*, chs. iv–xvi; Burbank and Hall, *Harvest of Years*, chs. ii–xvii; D. C. Gilman, *Launching of a University* (1906), chs. i–ix; Gray, *Letters*, II, chs. vi–viii; Hall, *Life and Confessions*, chs. v–ix; Newcomb, *Reminiscences*, chs. vi–xiii; A. D. White, *Autobiography*, I, chs. xvii–xxv.

Bibliography — Curti, *Growth of American Thought*, 836; Cubberley, *Public Education* *in United States*; Bates, *Scientific Societies*, 193; Sigerist, *American Medicine*, 289; Trent, *Cambridge History of American Literature*, IV, 728, 782, 794; Hofstadter, *Social Darwinism*, 177.

218. JOURNALISM, LETTERS, AND THE ARTS, 1865–1900

Summary — New trends in journalism: influence of Civil War, of urbanization (§§ 213–4), and of outstanding editors; yellow journalism; growing dominance of profit motive; linotype (1885) and improved presses; coöperative news-gathering. — Magazines: great increase; new types; advent of inexpensive magazines in the 1890's. — New currents in literature: regional fiction; realism; the short story; humor; poetry; the dime novel. — Business aspects of authorship: literature as a career; International Copyright Act, 1891; methods of book distribution. — Public-library movement. — Tendencies in the graphic and plastic arts: French influences; creative work of American artists; spread of art schools and museums. — Advances in architecture: H. H. Richardson; significance of the Chicago World's Fair (§ 213); domestic architecture; the skyscraper. — Music and the drama (§ 219). — Later developments (§ 229).

General — Nevins, *Emergence of Modern America*, 203, 228, 260; Oberholtzer, *History*, III, 443, 455; Schlesinger, *Rise of City*, 175, 247; Sullivan, *Our Times*, I, 183, 271.

Special — Lewis Mumford, *Brown Decades* (1931); Thomas Beer, *Mauve Decade* (1926). — Newspapers: Mott, *American Journalism*, chs. xxiii–xxxiv; Bleyer, *American Journalism*, chs. xi–xv; Rosewater, *Cooperative News-Gathering*, chs. xiii–xxii; Gramling, *AP*, chs. vi–xv; Pollard, *Presidents and Press*, 397; histories of particular newspapers (§ 53); "Man Who Invented Sunday Newspaper" (Morrill Goddard), *Am. Rev. Revs.*, XXII (1900), 619; D. F. Wilcox, "American Newspaper," Am. Ac. of Pol. and Soc. Sci., *Annals*, XVI (1900), 56; Iles, *Leading American Inventors*, 393. ❡ Magazines: Mott, *American Magazines*, III; Presbrey, *Advertising*, 452; H. F. Cline, "B. O. Flower and the Arena," *Journalism Quar.*, XVII (1940), 139, 247; R. P. Fairfield, "Flower," *Am. Lit.*, XXII (1950), 272; M. A. DeW. Howe, *Atlantic Monthly* (1919), chs. i–iv; W. H. Ward, "Fifty Years of *Independent*," *Independent*, L (1898), 1642; Gustav Pollak, *Fifty Years of Idealism* (1920), pt. 1 (the *Nation*). ❡ Literature: Spiller, *Literary History*, II, chs. xlviii–lx, lxii–lxiii; Trent, *Cambridge History of American Literature*, II, bk. 3, chs. i, iv–vii, III, chs. viii–xiv, xix–xx, IV, ch. xxix; F. L. Pattee, *American Literature since 1870* (1915), and *New American Literature* (1930), chs. i–vii, and *Development of Short Story* (1923), chs. viii–xiv; Parrington, *Main Currents*, III, bks. 1, 2; E. C. Wagenknecht, *Cavalcade of American Novel* (1952), chs. vi–xi; Carl Van Doren, *American Novel* (1940), chs. vi–xii; Taylor, *Economic Novel*; Howard Haycraft, *Murder for Pleasure* (1941), ch. v; V. W. Brooks, *New England: Indian Summer* (1940), chs. i–xxiii; Holliday, *Southern Literature*, chs. v–vi; Moses, *Literature of South*, chs. xvii–xviii; Dondore, *Prairie*, chs. vi–vii; L. L. Hazard, *Frontier in American Literature* (1927), chs. v–vii; J. L. and J. B. Gilder, eds., *Authors at Home* (1888); H. C. Vedder, *American Writers* (1894); C. D. Warner, *Relation of Literature to Life* (1896); "Twenty Years' Retrospect," *Dial*, XXVIII (1900), No. 333. ❡ Humor: Rourke, *American Humor*, 204; Tandy, *Crackerbox Philosophers*, chs. v–vi; Robert Ford, *American Humourists* (1897). ❡ Dime Novels: E. L. Pearson, *Dime Novels* (1929); M. E. Curti, "Dime Novels," *Yale Rev.*, XXVI (1937), 761; Albert Johannsen, *House of Beadle and Adams* (1950), I, 47, II; J. L. Cutler, *Patten and His Merriwell Saga* (1934), 11. ❡ Publishing: Hart, *Popular Book*, chs. ix–xi; F. L. Mott, *Golden Multitudes* (1947), chs. xxii–xxxi; R. H. Shove, *Cheap Book Production* (1937); D. M. Dozer, "Tariff on Books," *Miss. Valley Hist. Rev.*, XXXVI (1949), 73; Harper, *House of Harper*, chs. xvii–xli; G. H. Putnam, comp., *Question of Copyright* (1891), 1, 333; R. R. Bowker, *Copyright* (1912), 37, 348. ❡ Public Libraries: Green, *Public Library Movement*; Ditzion, *Democratic Culture*; T. W. Koch, *Carnegie Libraries* (1917); "Public Libraries," U.S. Bur. Educ., *Special Report*, 1876, pt. 1; W. I. Fletcher, *Public Libraries* (1894); C. A. Cutter, "Public Libraries," Commissioner Educ., *Report*, 1900, II, 1352. ❡ Fine Arts: Larkin, *Art and Life in America*, bk. 4; La Follette, *Art in America*, chs. vi–viii; Holger Cahill and A. H. Barr, Jr., *Art in America* (1935), chs. i–iii; Cortissoz, *American Artists*;

Mather, *American Spirit in Art*, chs. vi–xv, xviii–xxii. ⁊ Graphic Arts: Barker, *American Painting*, divisions 6, 7; Isham, *American Painting*, chs. xvi–xxvii; C. H. Caffin, *American Painting* (1907), chs. vii–xvi; Eugen Neuhaus, *American Art* (1931), chs. viii–x, xii–xxi, xxiv, xxvi; Pauline King, *American Mural Painting* (1902); Weitenkampf, *American Graphic Art*; Maurice and Cooper, *Nineteenth Century in Caricature*, chs. xxvi–xxxi; Taft, *Photography*, chs. xv–xxi; pictorial reproductions (§ 18). ⁊ Sculpture: Taft, *American Sculpture*, chs. xiv–xxvii; J. W. McSpadden, *Famous Sculptors of America* (1927), chs. i–vi. ⁊ Architecture: Tallmadge, *American Architecture*, chs. vi–x; Fiske Kimball, *American Architecture* (1928), chs. xi–xiv; Mumford, *Sticks and Stones*, chs. v–vi; Hamlin, *American Spirit in Architecture*, chs. xii–xv; Francisco Mujica, *Skyscraper* (1929), chs. i–ii; W. A. Starrett, *Skyscrapers* (1928), chs. i–iii; Samuel Sloan, *Homestead Architecture* (1866); S. B. Reed, *House-Plans for Everybody* (1878); L. H. Gibson, *Convenient Houses* (1889), and *Beautiful Houses* (1895); Montgomery Schuyler, *American Architecture* (1892). ⁊ Biographies: H. R. Mayes, *Alger* (1928), chs. x–xii; Seitz, *Bennetts*, chs. x–xv, and *Artemus Ward*, chs. vi–ix; Moore, *Burnham*, I, chs. ii–ix; Biklé, *Cable*, chs. iii–xiv; Paine, *Mark Twain*, I, chs. xlix–civ, II; M. M. Brashear, *Mark Twain* (1934), chs. vi–viii; Berryman, *Crane*; Elliott, *Crawford*, chs. iv–xiii; Candace Stone, *Dana and the Sun* (1938); C. J. Rosebault, *When Dana Was the Sun* (1931), chs. xvii–xxx; Genevieve Taggard, *Emily Dickinson* (1930); Heermann, *Duveneck*; C. W. Ackerman, *George Eastman* (1930), chs. ii–v; Lloyd Goodrich, *Eakins* (1933), chs. ii–vi; Randel, *Edward Eggleston*, chs. ix–xvi; Slason Thompson, *Field*, chs. vii–xx; A. V. Adams, *D. C. French* (1932); Ogden, *Godkin*, I, chs. vii–viii, II, chs. ix–xvii; Harris, *Harris*, chs. ix–xxii; Stewart, *Harte*, chs. xvii–xxxvii; J. K. Winkler, *Hearst* (1928), chs. iii–vii; H. H. Peckham, *J. G. Holland* (1940), chs. iv–ix; Cooke, *Howells*, 28; Inness, *Inness*, chs. v–xii; Ruth Odell, *Helen Hunt Jackson* (1939), chs. iv–vi; C. P. Kelley, *Early Development of Henry James* (1930); F. O. Matthiessen, *Henry James, Major Phase* (1946), and *Jewett*; Cecilia Waern, *La Farge* (1896), chs. ii–v; Starke, *Lanier*, chs. iv–xxiii; Greenslet, *Lowell*, 164; Moore, *McKim*, chs. v–xiv; George Britt, *Forty Years — Forty Millions* (1935) (F. A. Munsey), chs. iv–vi; E. W. Parks, *Craddock* (1941) (Mary N. Murfree); Paine, *Nast*, chs. xv–lxiii; Walker, *Norris*, chs. iv–xi; Hendrick, *Training of an American* (W. H. Page), chs. vii–viii; Page, *Page*, chs. ix–xiv; Seitz, *Pulitzer*, chs. iii–x; G. S. Johns, "Pulitzer in St. Louis," *Mo. Hist. Rev.*, XXV–XXVI (1931–32); Abbott, *Pyle*, chs. ii–xi; M. G. Van Rensselaer, *Richardson* (1888), chs. iv–xx; Monroe, *J. W. Root*, chs. iv–viii; F. F. Sherman, *A. P. Ryder* (1920); Downes, *Sargent*, chs. i–iv; M. I. Griffin, *F. R. Stockton* (1939), 25; A. A. Fields, *C. D. Warner* (1904), chs. ii–iv; Pennell, *Whistler*, chs. xii–xlii; Everett Rich, *William Allen White* (1941), chs. v–x; Baldwin, *Stanford White*, chs. v–xxxi; Canby, *Whitman*, chs. xxii–xxxi.

Sources — Official: *Statutes at Large*, XXVI, 1106; *Tenth Census*, VIII; *Twelfth Census*, IX, 1037; U. S. Commissioner Educ., *Reports* (annual, from 1867). ⁊ Unofficial Compilations: G. P. Rowell, *American Newspaper Directory* (annual, from 1869); Ayer, *American Newspaper Annual*; Gregory, *Union List of Serials*, and *American Newspapers* (list); Am. Library Assoc., *Papers and Proc.* (from 1876). ⁊ Personal: Henry Adams, *Education*, chs. xix–xxiv, and *Letters*, chs. iv–xvi; Bok, *Americanization*, chs. iii–xxiii; William Brotherhead, *Forty Years among Old Booksellers* (1891), 17; Dickinson, *Letters*, 205; B. O. Flower, *Progressive Men, Women, and Events* (1914); Ford, *Forty-Odd Years*, chs. iii–v, ix, xiv–xvii; Garland, *Son of Middle Border*, chs. xxvi–xxxii, and *Daughter of Middle Border*, chs. i–vii, and *Roadside Meetings*; R. W. Gilder, *Letters* (1916), chs. ii–ix, xi; Holt, *Octogenarian Editor*, chs. v–xix; W. D. Howells, *Life in Letters*, I, chs. vi–xx, II, chs. xxi–xxvii, and *Literary Passions* (1895), and *Literature and Life* (1902); James, *Letters*, I, 15; R. U. Johnson, *Remembered Yesterdays*, chs. ii–ix; Grace King, *Memories* (1932), chs. iv–xv; J. R. Lowell, *Letters* (1893), I, ch. v, II, chs. vi–xi, and *New Letters* (1932), 116; McClure, *Autobiography*, chs. v–vii; M. A. McRae, *Forty Years in Newspaperdom* (1924), chs. iii–viii; H. L. Mencken, *Happy Days* (1940), and *Heathen Days* (1943), chs. i–v; Mitchell, *Memoirs of Editor*, chs. iii–xiv; G. H. Putnam, *Memories of Publisher* (1915), chs. iv–xiv; Riley, *Letters*, 10; Saint-Gaudens, *Reminiscences*, I, chs. iii–xiv, II, chs. i–vii; M. E. Stone, *Fifty Years a Journalist* (1921), 31; Ticknor, *Glimpses of Authors*, chs. vii–xix; Tooker, *Joys and Tribulations of Editor*, chs. ii–xi, xiii; Wallace, *Autobiography*, II, pt. 2, chs. viii, x–xiv.

Bibliography (§§ 18, 52–3, 64–5) — Schlesinger, *Rise of City*, 437, 443, 464, 469; Ford, *Bibliography on Journalism*; Spiller, *Literary History*, III; H. B. Adams, *Public Libraries and Popular Education* (1900), ch. xviii; Larkin, *Art and Life in America*, 483, 499; G. H. Edgell, *American Architecture of Today* (1928), 379; H. R. Hitchcock, *Architectural Books* (1946); McSpadden, *Famous Sculptors*, 369.

219. RECREATION AND SPORTS, 1865–1900

Summary — Conditions conducive to greater leisure. — Music: conservatories; symphony orchestras; grand opera; creative work in music; the phonograph (1888) and its effects; the craze for popular songs; light opera. — Changes in the theater: leading managers, performers, and playwrights; serious drama; melodrama; burlesque; vaudeville. — Tent shows: the circus; Buffalo Bill's Wild West Show from 1883. — Multiplication of secret fraternal orders. — Society life (§ 213). — Rise of sports: reasons; commercialization; principal games; the bicycle vogue; athletic and country clubs.

General — Dulles, *America Learns to Play*, chs. xi–xvi; Nevins, *Emergence of Modern America*, 89, 216, 258; Schlesinger, *Rise of City*, ch. ix; Sullivan, *Our Times*, I, 219.

Special — Music: Howard, *Our American Music*, chs. x–xiv, xvii; H. C. Lahee, *Annals of Music*, 52, and *Grand Opera in America* (1902), chs. v–ix; E. E. Hipsher, *American Opera and Its Composers* (1934), chs. xiii–xlv; H. E. Krehbiel, *Chapters of Opera* (1911), chs. vii–xix; Irving Kolodin, *Metropolitan Opera* (1936), 1, 515; M. A. DeW. Howe, *Boston Symphony Orchestra* (1931), chs. i–v; Rupert Hughes, *Contemporary American Composers* (1900); Byrn, *Progress of Invention*, ch. xxii; Wittke, *Tambo and Bones*, chs. iii–v; Isaac Goldberg, *Tin Pan Alley* (1930), chs. v–vi; Spaeth, *Read 'Em and Weep*, 61; Paskman and Spaeth, *Gentlemen Be Seated*, chs. viii–x; L. C. Strang, *Celebrated Comedians of Light Opera* (1900), and *Prima Donnas and Soubrettes of Light Opera* (1900). ❡ Theater: Hornblow, *History of Theatre*, II, chs. xxiii–xxix; Coad and Mims, *American Stage*, chs. viii–xi; C. M. Rourke, *Troupers of Gold Coast* (1928); A. H. Quinn, *American Drama from Civil War* (1936), I, chs. i–x; M. J. Moses, *American Dramatist* (1925), chs. ix–xvii; Mayorga, *American Drama*, chs. xii–xiii; Moses and Brown, *American Theatre*, 75; Bernard Sobel, *Burleycue* (1931); Douglas Gilbert, *American Vaudeville* (1940), 10; F. E. McKay and C. E. L. Wingate, eds., *Famous American Actors* (1896); J. B. Clapp and E. F. Edgett, *Players of Present* (1899–1901); Norman Hapgood, *Stage in America* (1901); L. C. Strang, *Players and Plays of Last Quarter Century* (1902), and *Famous Actors of the Day* (1899), and *Famous Actresses of the Day* (1901). ❡ Circus: E. C. May, *Circus from Rome to Ringling* (1932), chs. xi–xxvii; Winifred Johnston, "Passing of the 'Wild West,'" *Southwestern Rev.*, XXI (1935), 33. ❡ Fraternal Orders: C. W. Ferguson, *Fifty Million Brothers* (1937), chs. ii, v–vi, ix, xii, xiv–xxi; Walter Basye, *History and Operation of Fraternal Insurance* (1919), chs. i, iv–v; B. H. Meyer, "Beneficiary Societies," *Am. Jour. Sociol.*, VI (1901), 646; W. B. Hill, "Great American Safety-Valve," *Century*, XLIV (1892), 383; W. S. Harwood, "Secret Societies," *No. Am. Rev.*, CLXIV (1897), 617. ❡ Sport: Krout, *American Sport*, chs. ii–xii; R. B. Weaver, *Amusements and Sports* (1939), chs. vi, viii–xvi; Herbert Manchester, *Four Centuries of Sport* (1931), chs. xi–xvi; F. W. Janssen, comp., *American Amateur Athletic and Aquatic History* (1893); R. M. Smith, *Baseball* (1947), chs. iii–xii; G. L. Moreland, *Balldom* (1914), 11; Weyand, *American Football*, chs. i–ii; Alexander Johnston, *Ten — and Out* (1927), 41; Jeffery Farnol, *Famous Prize Fights* (1928), 165; J. P. Paret, *Lawn Tennis* (1912), pt. 1, chs. ii–vi, pt. 2, ch. vii; R. P. Elmer, *Archery* (1933), ch. iii; W. S. Vosburgh, *Racing* (1922), 69; Samuel Crowther and Arthur Ruhl, *Rowing and Track Athletics* (1905), pt. 1, chs. ii–v, vii–xiv, pt. 2, chs. iii–xiii; R. F. Kelley, *Rowing* (1932), chs. iii–ix; W. P. Stephens, *Yachting* (1904), chs. ix–xxi; Nigel Lindsay, *The America's Cup* (1930), 31; F. E. Leonard, *Physical Education* (1923), chs. xxii–xxviii. ❡ Bicycle: D. B. Landis, "Evolution of Bicycle," Lancaster County Hist. Soc., *Papers*, XXXV (1931), 277; L. H. Porter, *Cycling for Health and Pleasure* (1895); J. B. Bishop, "Influence of Bicycle," *Forum*, XXI (1896), 680; I. B. Potter, *Gospel of Good Roads* (1892); N. S. Shaler, *American Highways* (1896), ch. vi. ❡ Country Clubs: C. W. Whitney, "Evolution of Country Club,"

Harper's Mag., XC (1894), 16; Robert Dunn, "Country Club," *Outing*, XLVII (1905–06), 160. ⟨ Biographies: Werner, *Barnum*, ch. xiii; E. A. Barron, *Lawrence Barrett* (1889), chs. iv–x; William Winter, *Belasco* (1918), I, 22, and *Edwin Booth*, 38; H. W. H. Powel, *Walter Camp* (1926), chs. i–v; Walsh, *Buffalo Bill*, ch. xxvii (W. F. Cody); Daly, *Augustin Daly*, chs. vii–xlix; Theodore Dreiser, *Twelve Men* (1919), ch. iii (Paul Dresser); R. H. Davis, *"Ruby Robert"* (1926), chs. i–vi (Fitzsimmons); I. F. Marcosson and Daniel Frohman, *Charles Frohman* (1916), chs. ii–ix; Joseph Kaye, *Victor Herbert* (1931), chs. iii–xi; Winter, *Joseph Jefferson*, 180; Gilman, *MacDowell*, 4, 97; MacKaye, *Mackaye*, I, chs. vi–xvi, II; Vance Thompson, *Life of Ethelbert Nevin* (1913), chs. ii–xvii; Dibble, *John L. Sullivan*, chs. ii–vii; C. E. Russell, *American Orchestra and Theodore Thomas* (1927), chs. iv–xiii.

Sources — Unofficial: *American (Appletons') Annual Cyclopædia*; A. C. Stevens, *Cyclopædia of Fraternities* (1896); Arthur Preuss, *Dictionary of Secret and Other Societies* (1924); E. J. Lanigan, *Baseball Cyclopedia* (1922); Odell, *Annals of New York Stage*, VIII–XV; *New York Clipper; Folio* (1869–95); *New York Dramatic Mirror* (from 1879); *Musical Year-Book; Musical Courier* (from 1880); *Outing*. ⟨ Personal: Rudolph Aronson, *Theatrical and Musical Memoirs* (1913), chs. i–ix; H. C. Barnabee, *Reminiscences* (1913), chs. xxvii–xxxvii; P. T. Barnum, *Struggles and Triumphs* (1927), II, 589; H. A. Clapp, *Reminiscences of Dramatic Critic* (1902); W. F. Cody, *Life and Adventures* (1917), ch. xxiii; C. R. Cooper, *Under the Big Top* (1923); J. J. Corbett, *Roar of Crowd* (1925), chs. i–xvi; W. C. Coup, *Sawdust & Spangles* (1901); Damrosch, *Musical Life*, chs. ii–xiv; Anna De Koven, *Musician and His Wife* (1926), chs. vi–xiv; Drew, *My Years on Stage*, chs. iv–xxvi; H. T. Finck, *Adventures in Golden Age of Music* (1926), 17; Moses and Gerson, *Clyde Fitch*, 3; Ford, *Forty-Odd Years*, chs. vi–xiii, xvii; Robert Grau, *Forty Years Observation of Music and Drama* (1909); E. B. Grossmann, *Edwin Booth* (1894), 31; C. K. Harris, *After the Ball* (1926), chs. i–vii; Jefferson, *Autobiography*, chs. x–xvii; Leavitt, *Fifty Years*; Theodore Roosevelt, *Big Game Hunting* (1899); Otis Skinner, *Footlights and Spotlights* (1924), chs. ii–xvi; H. B. Smith, *First Nights and First Editions* (1931), chs. v–xxvii; J. P. Sousa, *Marching Along* (1928), chs. ii–xi; Thomas Stevens, *Around World on Bicycle* (1887–88); J. L. Sullivan, *Life and Reminiscences* (1892), 28; Augustus Thomas, *Print of My Remembrance* (1922), chs. v–xx; R. F. Thomas, *Memoirs of Theodore Thomas* (1911), chs. ii–xx; Theodore Thomas, *Musical Autobiography*, I, chs. vi–xi; J. R. Towse, *Sixty Years of Theater* (1916), chs. vi–xxiii; J. D. Travers and J. R. Crowell, *Fifth Estate* (1926), chs. i–v; G. P. Upton, *Musical Memories* (1908); Winter, *Wallet of Time*.

Bibliography (§ 65) — Howard, *Our American Music*, 644; B. M. Baker, *Dramatic Bibliography* (1933), 19, 60, 246; Trent, *Cambridge History of American Literature*, IV, 760; I. T. E. Firkins, *Index to Plays* (1927); C. M. Van Sockum, *Sport* (1914).

Chapter *Twenty-three*

THE CRUMBLING OF NATIONAL ISOLATION
1875–1900

220. RELATIONS WITH LATIN AMERICA, 1875–1899

Summary — Earlier phases (§ 194). — Steps toward inter-American coöperation: the United States as mediator in boundary controversies; Pan American Congress, 1889; Bureau of American Republics (later the Pan American Union, 1890); Blaine, reciprocity, and the McKinley Tariff, 1890 (§ 209). — Chilean crisis, 1890–91: conduct of American minister toward Chilean revolution; other incidents; outcome. — United States and Brazilian revolution, 1889–93. — Venezuela's boundary dispute with British Guiana: Venezuelan appeals to the United States; the Olney Doctrine and Cleveland's intervention, 1895; popular reactions; arbitral settlement, 1899. — Relations with Mexico. — Canal diplomacy (§ 222). — Cuban question (§ 225).

General — Bailey, *Diplomatic History*, 435, 443, 477; Bemis, *Diplomatic History*, 415, 540, 736, 755, and *American Secretaries of State*, VII–IX; C. R. Fish, *Path of Empire* (1919), chs. iv, vi; Oberholtzer, *History*, III, 361, IV, 163, V, 99, 148, 153, 347, 438; Rhodes, *History*, VIII, 152, 374, 443.

Special — A. W. Eister, *United States and A. B. C. Powers* (1950), chs. ii–iii. — Inter-American Coöperation: Robertson, *Hispanic-American Relations*, 388; A. F. Tyler, *Foreign Policy of Blaine* (1927), chs. v, vii; A. C. Wilgus, "Blaine and Pan American Movement," *Hispanic Am. Hist. Rev.*, V (1922), 662; C. B. Casey, "Pan American Union," *ibid.*, XIII (1933), 437. ❡ Chile: Sherman, *United States and Chile*, chs. v–vi; Evans, *Chile and United States*, 97; A. T. Volwiler, "Harrison, Blaine, and Foreign Policy," Am. Philos. Soc., *Proc.*, LXXIX (1938), 637; Osgood Hardy, "Itata Incident," *Hispanic Am. Hist. Rev.*, V (1922), 195, and "Was Egan a 'Blundering Minister'?" *ibid.*, VIII (1928), 65. ❡ Brazil: Hill, *United States and Brazil*, 260; J. F. Rippy, "United States and Establishment of Republic of Brazil," *Southwestern Pol. Sci. Quar.*, III (1922), 39; C. A. Timm, "United States and Brazil during Naval Revolt of 1893," *ibid.*, V (1924), 119. ❡ Venezuela Question: Perkins, *Monroe Doctrine, 1867–1907*, 44, 136, and *Hands Off*, 171; Henderson, *Diplomatic Questions*, 411; A. L. P. Dennis, *Adventures in Diplomacy* (1928), ch. ii; P. R. Fossum, "Anglo-Venezuelan Controversy," *Hispanic Am. Hist. Rev.*, VIII (1928), 299; N. M. Blake, "Background of Cleveland's Venezuelan Policy," *Am. Hist. Rev.*, XLVII (1942), 259; T. C. Clark, "Olney's Real Credit in Venezuela Affair," Mass. Hist. Soc., *Proc.*, LXV (1940), 112; G. B. Young, "Intervention under Monroe Doctrine," *Pol. Sci. Quar.*, LVII (1942), 247; J. F. Rippy, "Mexican Reactions to Cleveland's Message," *ibid.*, XXXIX (1924), 280; C. J. Child, "Venezuela-British Guiana Boundary Arbitration of 1899," *Am. Jour. Int. Law*, XLIV (1950), 682; P. L. Phillips, "Guiana and Venezuela Cartography," Am. Hist. Assoc., *Report*, 1897, 681; G. L. Burr, "Search for Venezuela-Guiana Boundary," *Am. Hist. Rev.*, IV (1899), 470; James Bryce, "British Feeling on Venezuelan Question," *No. Am. Rev.*, CLXII (1896), 145; Andrew Carnegie, "Venezuelan Question," *ibid.*, 129; Marcus Baker, *Geographic Results of*

Venezuela Dispute (1900). ❡ Mexico: Rippy, *United States and Mexico*, chs. xvii–xix; Callahan, *American Foreign Policy in Mexican Relations*, 361; P. S. Relyea, *Relations between United States and Mexico under Diaz* (1924), chs. ii–iv; R. D. Gregg, *Border Troubles* (1937), 17; C. W. Hackett, "Recognition of Diaz by United States," *Southwestern Hist. Quar.*, XXVIII (1924), 34. ❡ Haiti: Logan, *Relations of United States with Haiti*, 365. ❡ Biographies: Muzzey, *Blaine*, 414; Stanwood, *Blaine*, 241, 311; McElroy, *Cleveland*, II, ch. vi; Nevins, *Cleveland*, ch. xxxiv, and *Henry White*, ch. viii; Barrows, *Evarts*, ch. xxiii; James, *Olney*, chs. x–xi.

Sources — General: *Congressional Record*, 44–56 Congs.; *Foreign Relations* (*General Index*, 1861–99); Moore, *Digest of International Law*, I, 160, 296, II, 791, 1107, 1113, VI, 34, 533; Malloy, Redmond, and Treworth, *Treaties, Conventions*; Richardson, *Messages and Papers*, VII–IX; Bartlett, *American Diplomacy*, 341; Gantenbein, *Latin-American Policy*, 49, 340, 447. ❡ Inter-American Coöperation: J. B. Scott, *International Conferences of American States* (1931), 3; Belmont, *American Democrat*, chs. vii–viii. ❡ Chile: Ministerio de Relaciones Exteriores (Chile), *Estados Unidos i Chile* (1891); M. A. Matta, *Cuestiones recientes con la legación i el gobierno de los Estados Unidos* (1892); United States and Chile Claims Commission, *Minutes of Proceedings* (1894); R. D. Evans, *Sailor's Log* (1901), chs. xx–xxiii. ❡ Venezuela: Department of State, *Correspondence in Relation to Boundary Controversy* (1896); U. S. Commission to Investigate True Divisional Line, *Report* (1896–97); *British Guiana Boundary* (London, 1898); Ministerio de Relaciones Interiores, *Venezuela y la Gran Bretaña* (1890); W. L. Scruggs, *Venezuelan Question* (1896); Cleveland, *Presidential Problems*, ch. iv, and *Letters*, ch. xiii; Parker, *Recollections*, 189; A. D. White, *Autobiography*, II, ch. xxxix.

Bibliography — Bemis and Griffin, *Guide to Diplomatic History*, 429, 538, 588, 590.

221. EXPANDING INTERESTS IN THE PACIFIC, 1875–1899

Summary — Earlier phases (§ 194). — International competition in the Pacific. — American relations with Hawaii: reciprocity treaty, 1875; investments; lease of Pearl Harbor, 1884; revolution, and establishment of a republic, 1893; abortive treaty of annexation, 1893; annexation by joint resolution, 1898. — Relations with Samoa: coaling station, 1872; treaty of 1878; rivalry with Germany and Great Britain; tripartite protectorate, 1889–99; partition of the islands, 1899. — Minor acquisitions. — Relations with Japan, 1865–99. — Relations with China: immigration question (§ 211); Anglo-American interest in equal trading rights; Hay's Open Door policy, 1899. — Later developments (§ 225).

General — Bailey, *Diplomatic History*, ch. xxviii; Bemis, *Diplomatic History*, ch. xxv, and *American Secretaries of State*, VII–IX; Dennis, *Adventures in Diplomacy*, chs. iv, viii; F. R. Dulles, *America in Pacific* (1932), 105, 163; Foster, *Diplomacy in Orient*, chs. x–xii; Oberholtzer, *History*, II, 512, V, 162, 327, 473, 547, 618.

Special — Hawaii: J. W. Pratt, *Expansionists of 1898* (1936), 34, 215, 317; Kuykendall and Day, *Hawaii*, chs. xv–xviii; Stevens, *American Expansion in Hawaii*, chs. vii–xi; D. M. Dozer, "Opposition to Hawaiian Reciprocity," *Pacific Hist. Rev.*, XIV (1945), 157; W. A. Russ, Jr., "Role of Sugar in Hawaiian Annexation," *ibid.*, XII (1943), 339; Donald Rowland, "Establishment of Republic of Hawaii," *ibid.*, IV (1935), 201; T. A. Bailey, "United States and Hawaii during Spanish-American War," *Am. Hist. Rev.*, XXXVI (1931), 552, and "Japan's Protest against Annexation," *Jour. Modern Hist.*, III (1931), 46; W. D. Alexander, *Later Years of Hawaiian Monarchy and Revolution of 1893* (1896); J. A. Gillis, *Hawaiian Incident* (1897); L. A. Thurston, *Hand-book on Annexation of Hawaii* (1897); A. T. Mahan, *Interest of America in Sea Power* (1897), ch. ii; Hermann von Holst, *Annexation of Hawaii* (1898); Nevins, *Cleveland*, ch. xxx; Gresham, *Gresham*, II, ch. xlvii; James, *Olney*, ch. ix. ❡ Samoa: G. H. Ryden, *Foreign Policy in Relation to Samoa* (1933), chs. v–xv; Sylvia Masterman, *International Rivalry in Samoa* (1934), chs. vi–viii; Alfred Vagts, *Deutschland und Vereinigten Staaten* (1935), I, ch. x; Otto, graf zu Stolberg-Wernigerode, *Germany and United States* (1937), 196; Keim, *German-*

American Relations, ch. v; C. E. Schieber, *American Sentiment toward Germany* (1923), ch. ii; J. W. Ellison, "Partition of Samoa," *Pacific Hist. Rev.*, VIII (1939), 259; C. C. Tansill, *Foreign Policy of Bayard* (1940), 3; Tyler, *Foreign Policy of Blaine*, ch. ix. ❡ Minor Acquisitions: D. N. Leff, *Uncle Sam's Pacific Islets* (1940), chs. ii–vii. ❡ Japan: Treat, *Diplomatic Relations between United States and Japan*, I, ch. xxii, II; F. C. Jones, *Extraterritoriality in Japan* (1931), chs. iii–ix. ❡ China: Dennett, *Americans in Eastern Asia*, chs. xxiv–xxvii, xxix–xxxii, and *Hay*, ch. xxiv; Griswold, *Far Eastern Policy*, chs. i–ii; Dulles, *China and America*, chs. vii–viii; P. T. Moon, *Imperialism and World Politics* (1926), 320; R. S. McCordock, *British Far Eastern Policy* (1931), 192; F. H. Harrington, *God, Mammon, and Chinese* (1944), chs. i–xvi; H. J. Noble, "United States and Sino-Korean Relations, 1885–87," *Pacific Hist. Rev.*, II (1933), 292.

Sources — General: *Congressional Record*, 44–56 Congs.; *Foreign Relations* (*General Index*, 1861–99); Moore, *Digest of International Law*, I, 162, 494, 536; Malloy, Redmond, and Treworth, *Treaties, Conventions*; Richardson, *Messages and Papers*, VII–IX; Bartlett, *American Diplomacy*, 358, 408. ❡ Hawaii: 52 Cong., 2 Sess., *Sen. Ex. Doc.*, Nos. 76–7; 53 Cong., 2 Sess., *H. Ex. Doc.*, No. 47; 55 Cong., 3 Sess., *Sen. Doc.*, No. 16; Liliuokalani, *Hawaii's Story* (1898); S. B. Dole, *Memoirs of Hawaiian Revolution* (1936); L. A. Thurston, *Memoirs of Hawaiian Revolution* (1936); M. H. Krout, *Hawaii* (1898); Lucien Young, *Real Hawaii* (1899); Pettigrew, *Triumphant Plutocracy*, ch. xxii. ❡ Samoa: *Collection of Congressional Documents Regarding Samoan Affairs* (1874–95); G. H. Bates, "Aspects of Samoan Question," *Century*, XV (1889), 945, XVI (1889), 25; H. C. Ide, "Our Interest in Samoa," *No. Am. Rev.*, CLXV (1897), 155; R. L. Stevenson, *Footnote to History* (1892). ❡ China and the Open Door (§ 237).

Bibliography — Bemis and Griffin, *Guide to Diplomatic History*, 372, 379, 469.

222. CANAL DIPLOMACY, 1866–1899

Summary — Earlier phases (§ 173). — American interest in Nicaraguan route: Darien Canal Commission, 1866; treaty with Nicaragua, 1867; Interoceanic Canal Commission, 1872–76. — De Lesseps's project of a Panama canal: Société Civile, 1876; construction and financial difficulties, 1881–89; formation of the New Panama Company, 1889. — American counterplans: discussions in Congress, 1879–81; efforts of Hayes and later presidents to abrogate the Clayton-Bulwer treaty; Maritime Canal Company, and Nicaraguan waterway, 1889–93; continued interest in Nicaraguan route; effect of Spanish-American War on canal question (§ 225). — Later developments (§ 238).

General — Bemis, *American Secretaries of State*, VII–IX; Dewey, *National Problems*, 117; M. P. DuVal, *Cadiz to Cathay* (1940), chs. iii–v; Mack, *Land Divided* (1944), chs. xviii–xxxiv; D. C. Miner, *Fight for Panama Route* (1940), 17; Oberholtzer, *History*, II, 498, IV, 351, 706, V, 612; Perkins, *Monroe Doctrine, 1867–1907*, 65; Sparks, *National Development*, ch. xiii; Williams, *Anglo-American Isthmian Diplomacy*, ch. ix.

Sources — Official: *Congressional Globe*, and *Congressional Record*, 39–56 Congs.; *Diplomatic Correspondence*, and *Foreign Relations* (*General Index*, 1861–99); Moore, *Digest of International Law*, III, 13, 23, 39, 188, 254; Malloy, Redmond, and Treworth, *Treaties, Conventions*; Richardson, *Messages and Papers*, VI–IX; 39 Cong., 1 Sess., *Sen. Ex. Doc.*, II, No. 62; 42 Cong., 2 Sess., *Sen. Ex. Doc.*, III, No. 6; 46 Cong., 1 Sess., *Sen. Ex. Doc.*, I, No. 15, 2 Sess., *Sen. Ex. Doc.*, IV, No. 112; 47 Cong. (spec. sess.), *Sen. Ex. Doc.*, No. 5, 1 Sess., *Sen. Ex. Doc.*, IV, No. 78, VI, No. 194, *Sen. Reports*, III, No. 368, *H. Reports*, VI, No. 1698, 2 Sess., *Sen. Reports*, I, No. 952, *H. Ex. Doc.*, XXIII, No. 107; 48 Cong., 1 Sess., *Sen. Ex. Doc.*, I, No. 26, VI, No. 123, 2 Sess., *Sen. Misc. Doc.*, I, No. 12; 49 Cong., 2 Sess., *Sen. Ex. Doc.*, I, No. 50; 51 Cong., 2 Sess., *Sen. Ex. Doc.*, No. 5, *Sen. Reports*, I, No. 1944; 52 Cong., 1 Sess., *Sen. Ex. Doc.*, I, No. 4; 53 Cong., 2 Sess., *Sen. Ex. Doc.*, I, No. 5, 3 Sess., *Sen. Ex. Doc.*, I, No. 20; 54 Cong., 1 Sess., *Sen. Doc.*, XIII, No. 315, *Sen. Reports*, VI, No. 1109; 55 Cong., 2 Sess., *Sen. Reports*, VIII, No. 1265. ❡ Unofficial: Interoceanic Canal Congress, *Compte Rendu* (1879); L. N. B. Wyse, *Rapports sur l'exploration de l'isthme américain* (1879); Nicaragua Canal Construction Company, *Interoceanic Canal of Nicaragua* (1891); *American (Appletons') Annual Cyclopædia.* ❧ Contemporary Accounts: Félix Belly, *Ā Travers l'Amérique Centrale* (1867); W. H. Webb, *Monroe Doctrine and Isthmian Canal* (1881); T. J. Lawrence, *Essays on Disputed Questions* (1884), Nos. 2–3; Auguste Garçon, *Histoire du canal de Panama* (1886); L. N. B. Wyse, *Canal de Panama* (1886); Félix Paponot, *Achèvement du Canal de Panama* (1888); Paul Ponsolle, *Le Tombeau des Milliards* (1890); Gustave Rouanet, *Complicités du Panama* (1893); Keasbey, *Nicaragua Canal;* Hector Pétin, *États-Unis et Doctrine de Monroe* (1900); I. D. Travis, *Clayton-Bulwer Treaty* (1900), ch. vi.

Bibliography — Bemis and Griffin, *Guide to Diplomatic History*, 203, 554; Mack, *Land Divided*, 598; Williams, *Anglo-American Isthmian Diplomacy*, 331.

223. PEACE MOVEMENT AND ARBITRATION, 1865–1900

Summary — Earlier phases (§ 152). — American Red Cross: Geneva treaty, 1864; Clara Barton's fight for ratification; Senate approval, 1882; Red Cross in action. — Peace movement: effect of Civil War; campaigns for arbitration and reform of international law and against militarism and navalism. — Official moves: settlement of *Alabama* claims, 1872 (§ 194); Congressional resolutions for arbitration, 1874; Senate action, 1882; Pan American Congress, 1889 (§ 220); Congressional resolutions for permanent treaties of arbitration, 1890; the fur-seals-and-fisheries arbitrations (§ 224); resolutions of House of Commons (1893) and French Chamber of Deputies (1895); the Venezuela boundary arbitration, 1896–99 (§ 220); the abortive Anglo-American general arbitration treaty, 1897; American participation in Hague Conference, 1899. — Later developments (§ 239).

General — Schlesinger, *Rise of City*, 364.

Special — Red Cross: F. R. Dulles, *American Red Cross* (1950), chs. i–iii; Barton, *Barton*, II, chs. vii–xi⸱⸱; B. C. Williams, *Clara Barton* (1941), chs. xi–xix. ❧ Peace Movement: Curti, *Peace or War*, 74; A. C. F. Beales, *History of Peace* (1931), chs. vi–ix; Devere Allen, *Fight for Peace* (1930), 465; Whitney, *American Peace Society*, chs. xv–xxviii. ❧ Arbitration: World Peace Foundation, *Arbitration and United States* (1926), 463, 492; James, *Olney*, ch. xii; N. M. Blake, "Olney-Pauncefote Treaty," *Am. Hist. Rev.*, L (1945), 228; T. K. Ford, "Genesis of First Hague Conference," *Pol. Sci. Quar.*, LI (1936), 354; F. W. Holls, *Peace Conference at Hague* (1900); J. B. Scott, *Hague Peace Conferences* (1909), I, chs. ii, vi; Perkins, *Monroe Doctrine, 1867–1907*, 289; W. D. Puleston, *Mahan* (1939), ch. xxx; A. T. Mahan, *Lessons of War with Spain* (1899), 207.

Sources — Official: *Congressional Globe* and *Congressional Record*, 39–56 Congs.; *Diplomatic Correspondence*, and *Foreign Relations* (*General Index*, 1861–99); Moore, *Arbitrations*, II, 2111, V, 5062; Richardson, *Messages and Papers*, VI–IX. ❧ Unofficial: *American Conference on International Arbitration* (1896); Clara Barton, *Red Cross* (1898); Howe, *Reminiscences*, ch. xv; Seth Low, "International Conference of Peace," *No. Am. Rev.*, CLXIX (1899), 625; Scott, *Hague Peace Conferences*, II, 1; A. D. White, *Autobiography*, II, chs. xlv–xlix, and *First Hague Conference* (1905); *American (Appletons') Annual Cyclopædia.*

Bibliography — Bemis and Griffin, *Guide to Diplomatic History*, 620; Curti, *Peace or War*, 322.

224. MISCELLANEOUS DIPLOMATIC QUESTIONS, 1875–1900

Summary — United States participation in multilateral treaties, beginning with Universal Postal Union, 1864, and including the International Red Cross (§ 223). — Dispute with Germany and other countries from 1879 over meat embargoes. — Controversy with Great Britain over the Newfoundland fisheries, 1883–98. — Bering Sea controversy with Britain over fur sealing, 1868–98. — Difficulties with Italy over New Orleans lynchings, 1891–92. — Policy toward Boer War, 1899. — Relations with Russia. — Later developments (§ 239).

General — Bailey, *Diplomatic History*, 438, 446, 456, 525; Bemis, *American Secretaries of State*, VII–IX; Dewey, *National Problems*, 112, 205; Oberholtzer, *History*, IV, 447, 491, 685, V, 151, 155, 342; Sparks, *National Development*, 147.

Special — Multilateral Treaties: J. C. Faries, *Rise of Internationalism* (1915), ch. iv; Wriston, *Executive Agents*, ch. ix; J. F. Sly, "Genesis of Postal Union," *Int. Conciliation*, No. 233 (1927). ❦ Pork Dispute with Germany: Stolberg-Wernigerode, *Germany and United States*, 150; Tyler, *Foreign Policy of Blaine*, ch. xii; L. L. Snyder, "Pork Dispute," *Jour. Modern Hist.*, XVII (1945), 16. ❦ Fisheries: Henderson, *Diplomatic Questions*, ch. v; Callahan, *American Foreign Policy in Canadian Relations*, 358; C. C. Tansill, *Canadian-American Relations* (1943), chs. i–iv, and *Foreign Policy of Bayard*, chs. vi–x; G. R. Dulebohn, *Foreign Policy under Cleveland Administrations* (1941), 63; C. B. Elliott, *United States and Northeastern Fisheries* (1887), 84; J. I. Doran, *Our Fishery Rights* (1888). ❦ Fur Seals: Tansill, *Canadian-American Relations*, chs. x–xii; Callahan, *American Foreign Policy in Canadian Relations*, 438; Henderson, *Diplomatic Questions*, ch. i; Tyler, *Foreign Policy of Blaine*, ch. xiii; S. B. Stanton, *Behring Sea Controversy* (1892); Joseph Stanley-Brown, "Bering Sea Controversy," *Yale Rev.*, II (1893–94), 194, and "Fur Seals and Bering Sea Arbitration," Am. Geog. Soc., *Jour.*, XXVI (1894), 326; Andrew Wishart, *Behring Sea Question* (1893); Gresham, *Gresham*, II, ch. xlvi. ❦ New Orleans Lynchings: J. E. Coxe, "New Orleans Mafia Incident," *La. Hist. Quar.*, XX (1937), 1067; J. A. Karlin, "New Orleans Lynchings of 1891 and American Press," *ibid.*, XXIV (1941), 187, and "Indemnification of Aliens," *Southwestern Soc. Sci. Quar.*, XXV (1945), 235, and "Some Repercussions of New Orleans Mafia Incident of 1891," Wash. State Coll., *Research Studies*, XI (1943), 267; R. H. Marr, "Mafia Case," *Am. Law Rev.*, XXV (1891), 414. ❦ Boer War: J. H. Ferguson, *American Diplomacy and Boer War* (1939). ❦ Russia: T. A. Bailey, *America Faces Russia* (1950), 117; Cyrus Adler and A. M. Margalith, *With Firmness in Right* (1946), 171.

Sources — *Congressional Record*, 44–56 Congs.; *Foreign Relations* (*General Index*, 1861–99); J. B. Moore, *Digest of International Law*, I, 803, 895, VI, 837, and *Arbitrations*, I, 763, V, 4759; Malloy, Redmond, and Treworth, *Treaties, Conventions;* Richardson, *Messages and Papers*, VII–IX. ❦ Fisheries: 45 Cong., 2 Sess., *H. Ex. Doc.*, No. 89; 51 Cong., 1 Sess., *Sen. Report*, No. 1530; W. H. Trescot, *Letters Reviewing Bayard-Chamberlain Treaty* (1888). ❦ Fur Seals: 50 Cong., 2 Sess., *Sen. Ex. Doc.*, No. 106; 51 Cong., 1 Sess., *Sen. Report*, No. 1530, 1 Sess., *H. Ex. Doc.*, No. 450, 2 Sess., *H. Ex. Doc.*, No. 144; 52 Cong., 1 Sess., *Sen. Ex. Doc.*, No. 55; 53 Cong., 2 Sess., *Sen. Ex. Doc.*, No. 177; 55 Cong., 2 Sess., *Sen. Doc.*, Nos. 59, 164.

Bibliography — Bemis and Griffin, *Guide to Diplomatic History*, 384, 445, 453, 644, 647; McFarland, *New England Fisheries*, ch. xx.

225. CUBA AND THE WAR WITH SPAIN, 1875–1900

Summary — The United States and Cuba's insurrection against Spain, 1868–78 (§ 194). — New Cuban uprising, 1895: efforts of United States to restore peace; De Lôme letter and *Maine* explosion, February, 1898; declaration of war and the Teller resolution, April 19–20. — Spanish-American War: blockade of Cuba; destruction of Cervera's fleet, July 3; capture of Santiago, July 17; army scandals; occupation of Puerto Rico, July 25; battle of Manila Bay, May 1; seizure of Guam, June 21; capture of Manila, August 13; Europe's attitude; financing of the war. — Peace negotiations: protocol, August 12; peace of Paris, December 10. — Issue of imperialism: in Senate; before public; in presidential campaign of 1900; McKinley's reëlection. — Later developments (§ 238).

General — Fish, *Path of Empire*, chs. vii–xii; J. H. Latané, *America as World Power* (1907), 5, 123; Walter Millis, *Martial Spirit* (1931); Oberholtzer, *History*, V, 477, 627; Peck, *Twenty Years*, 531; Rhodes, *History*, IX, 44, 132.

Special — Cuba under Spain: C. E. Chapman, *Cuban Republic* (1927), 69; H. S. Rubens, *Liberty* (1932), chs. i–xix; A. G. Robinson, *Cuba and Intervention* (1905), 27. ❡ Diplomacy: Bemis, *Diplomatic History*, 436, and *American Secretaries of State*, VII–IX; Bailey, *Diplomatic History*, 494; Chadwick, *United States and Spain*, I, chs. xx–xxix, III, chs. xx–xxi; H. E. Flack, *Spanish-American Diplomatic Relations* (1906); E. J. Benton, *International Law and Diplomacy of Spanish-American War* (1908); Orestes Ferrara, *Last Spanish War* (1937); L. H. Jenks, *Our Cuban Colony* (1928), chs. iii–iv; Holt, *Treaties Defeated*, ch. viii; Perkins, *Monroe Doctrine, 1867–1907*, 263; J. V. L. Findlay, *International Aspects of Cuban Question* (1898); E. M. Ríos, *El Tratado de Paris* (1904). ❡ War Sentiment: Pratt, *Expansionists of 1898*, 209, 224, 326; M. M. Wilkerson, *Public Opinion and Spanish-American War* (1932); J. E. Wisan, *Cuban Crisis in New York Press* (1934); S. S. Auxier, "Propaganda Activities of Cuban Junta," *Hispanic Am. Hist. Rev.*, XIX (1939), 286, and "Middle Western Newspapers and Spanish-American War," *Miss. Valley Hist. Rev.*, XXVI (1940), 523. ❡ War: Chadwick, *United States and Spain*, II, III, chs. i–xix; R. H. Titherington, *Spanish-American War* (1900); Maclay, *United States Navy*, III, 39; Sprout, *Rise of American Naval Power*, ch. xiv; R. S. West, Jr., *Admirals of American Empire* (1948), chs. x–xx; J. R. Spears, *Our Navy in War with Spain* (1898); J. D. Long, *New Navy* (1903), I, 12, II, 1; Ganoe, *United States Army*, 370; M. F. Steele, *American Campaigns* (1922), I, ch. xxvii, II, 299; H. H. Sargent, *Campaign of Santiago* (1907); E. J. McClernand, "Santiago Campaign," *Infantry Jour.*, XXI (1922), 280; C. C. Drake, "Santiago Campaign," *Quartermaster Rev.*, XII (1933), No. 5, p. 21; W. T. Sexton, *Soldiers in Sun* (1939); J. A. Le Roy, *Americans in Philippines* (1914), I, chs. iv–xi, II, chs. xii–xx; Dion Williams, "Battle of Manila Bay," U. S. Naval Inst., *Proc.*, LIV (1928), 345; L. W. Walker, "Guam's Seizure," *Pacific Hist. Rev.*, XIV (1945), 1; T. A. Bailey, "Dewey and Germans at Manila," *Am. Hist. Rev.*, XLV (1939), 59; J. B. Moore, "Maritime Law in War with Spain," *Pol. Sci. Quar.*, XV (1900), 399; Ratner, *American Taxation*, 226. ❡ Attitude of Europe: J. F. Rippy, "European Powers and Spanish-American War," *James Sprunt Hist. Studies*, XIX (1927), No. 2, p. 22; B. A. Reuter, *Anglo-American Relations during Spanish-American War* (1924), chs. iv–vii; Keim, *German-American Relations*, ch. vi; Schieber, *American Sentiment toward Germany*, 109; L. B. Shippee, "Germany and Spanish-American War," *Am. Hist. Rev.*, XXX (1925), 754; L. M. Sears, "French Opinion of Spanish-American War," *Hispanic Am. Hist. Rev.*, VII (1927), 25. ❡ Imperialism and Election of 1900: G. H. Knoles, "Cleveland on Imperialism," *Miss. Valley Hist. Rev.*, XXXVII (1950), 303; F. H. Harrington, "Anti-Imperialist Movement," *ibid.*, XXII (1935), 211, and "Literary Aspects of Anti-Imperialism," *N. Eng. Quar.*, X (1937), 650; Robinson, *Cuba and Intervention*, chs. vi–ix; Stanwood, *Presidency*, II, ch. i; T. A. Bailey, "Election of 1900, a Mandate on Imperialism?" *Miss. Valley Hist. Rev.*, XXIV (1937), 43. ❡ Biographies: Acheson, *Bailey*, chs. ix–x; Williams, *Bryan*, 196; Dingley, *Nelson Dingley*, ch. xxiii; E. A. Falk, *Fighting Bob Evans* (1931), 220; C. M. Older, *Hearst* (1936), chs. xxi–xxiii; Gillett, *Hoar*, chs. xx–xxiii; Kohlsaat, *McKinley to Harding*, chs. xiv, xviii; Olcott, *McKinley*, I, ch. xxiii, II, chs. xxiv–xxix; Puleston, *Mahan*, chs. xxvii–xxix; James, *Olney*, ch. xiii; Seitz, *Pulitzer*, 238, 311; Robinson, *Reed*, 354; Pringle, *Roosevelt*, 173; Fuess, *Schurz*, 351; Ellis, *Teller*, ch. xx; Nevins, *Henry White*, ch. ix.

Sources — Official: *Congressional Record*, 44–57 Congs.; *Foreign Relations* (*General Index*, 1861–99); *Spanish Diplomatic Correspondence and Documents, 1896–1900* (transl. by U. S. State Dept., 1905); Moore, *Digest of International Law*, V, 375, 858, VI, 102; Malloy, Redmond, and Treworth, *Treaties, Conventions*; Richardson, *Messages and Papers*, VII–X; 55 Cong., 2 Sess., *Sen. Doc.*, XXI, No. 207; 56 Cong., 1 Sess., *ibid.*, XVII–XXIV, No. 221, XXXIV, No. 388, 2 Sess., *ibid.*, XI, No. 148, XXV, No. 231; 57 Cong., 1 Sess., *H. Doc.*, CIII–CIV, No. 485; "Documentos referentes al período de la guerra en Puerto Rico," *Boletin histórico Puerto Rico*, VI (1919), 40. ❡ Unofficial: Bartlett, *American Diplomacy*, 369; *Appletons' Annual Cyclopædia*; Nathan Sargent, comp., *Dewey and Manila Campaign* (1947). Personal: R. A. Alger, *Spanish-American War* (1901); Stephen Bonsal, *Fight for Santiago* (1899); Cleveland, *Letters*, ch. xv; James Creelman, *On Great Highway* (1901), chs. viii–x; R. H. Davis, *Cuban and Porto Rican Campaigns* (1899), and *Notes of War Correspondent* (1910), 45; Dewey, *Autobiography*, chs. xiii–xix; J. T. Dickman, ed., *Santiago Campaign* (1927); Evans, *Sailor's Log*, chs. xxxiv–xxxix; Funston, *Memories*, pt. 1; W. A. M. Goode, *With Sampson* (1899); F. S. Hastings, *Ranchman's Recollections* (1921), ch. vii; Hoar, *Autobiography*, II, ch. xxxiii; George Kennan, *Campaigning in Cuba* (1899); J. D. Long, *America of Yesterday*, chs. vii–ix, and "Papers," Mass. Hist. Soc., *Coll.*, LXXVIII (1939); Miles, *Serving Republic*, chs. xv–xvii; J. D. Miley, *In Cuba with Shafter* (1899); F. D. Millet, *Expedition to Philippines* (1899); Theodore Roosevelt, *Autobiography*, ch. vii, and *Rough Riders* (1899); Schley, *Forty-five Years*, chs. xxiv–xxxvi; C. D. Sigsbee, *The "Maine"* (1899); Joseph Wheeler, *Santiago Campaign* (1898); A. D. White, *Autobiography*, II, 144, 160.

Bibliography — Bemis and Griffin, *Guide to Diplomatic History*, ch. xviii; C. M. Trelles, *Biblioteca histórica cubana* (1922–24), I, 404, II, 1; Reuter, *Anglo-American Relations*, 191.

PART VI

America in the Twentieth Century

Chapter Twenty-four

SOCIAL AND ECONOMIC CONDITIONS, 1900–1920

226. AMERICAN POPULATION, 1900–1920

Summary — Growth of Population: increase in numbers; fall in death rate; change in birth rate and family size (§ 229); conditions of health; relative decline in rural population; shift to cities; internal migration; regional differences. — Continued Flow of Immigration: (§ 211); British; German; Scandinavian; Jewish; Italian; Slavic; Near Eastern; Oriental; Filipino; economic adjustment; cultural impact; Americanization. — Exclusion of Orientals: (§ 212); 1905, Asiatic Exclusion League; 1906, San Francisco school question; 1907–08, Gentlemen's Agreement; land question. — Immigration Restriction: (§ 212); 1894, Immigration Restriction League; nativism; literacy test vetoes; 1903 law; 1907 law; Dillingham Committee investigation; position of labor, of South, of Wilson; 1917, literacy test; (§ 244). — Negroes: (§ 212); low status; economic disabilities; 1906, Brownsville affair; lynching; exclusion from suffrage; discrimination in education; efforts to enter industry; segregation; B. T. Washington; W. E. DuBois, 1909–11, National Association for Advancement of Colored People; 1910, Urban League. — Indians: Burke Act, 1906. — Development of the Pacific Coast: effect of Panama Canal, of new railroads; development of Alaska; gold, coal discoveries; growth of population and of wealth, of new cities, of industries; development of irrigation, and of agriculture, of Oriental trade; rivalry of ports, improvement of harbors; 1906, San Francisco earthquake. — Urbanization: growth of cities; suburban development; housing; other urban problems; effects on rural life; influence of the auto (§ 227, 229).

General — H. U. Faulkner, *Quest for Social Justice* (1931), ch. i, and *Decline of Laissez-Faire* (1951), ch. v; Commons, *History of Labour*, III, § 1; Stephenson, *American Immigration*, chs. xvii–xix, xxi; Ogg, *National Progress*, ch. vii.

Special — Growth of Population: R. M. La Follette, ed., *Making of America* (1905), I, 1; *Century of Population Growth* (1909); C. W. Thornthwaite, *Internal Migration* (1934); J. M. Gillette and G. R. Davies, "Measure of Rural Migration," Am. Stat. Assoc., *Quar. Publ.*, XIV (1915), 642; C. C. Taylor, "Our Rural Population Debacle," *Am. Econ. Rev.*, XVI (1926), 156; J. D. Hicks, "Western Middle West," *Ag. Hist.*, XX (1946), 65; Vance, *Human Geography of South*; Odum, *Southern Regions*; W. S. Thompson and P. K. Whelpton, *Population Trends*. ❑ Immigration: I. S. Hourwich, *Immigration and Labor* (1912); E. de S. Brunner, *Immigrant Farmers and Children* (1929); R. E. Park, *Immigrant Press and Its Control* (1922); E. L. Anderson, *We Americans* (1937); S. C. Johnson, *History of Emigration from United Kingdom to North America, 1763–1912* (1913), chs. ii–xiv; Faust, *German Element*, II; Foerster, *Italian Immigration*; Balch, *Our Slavic Fellow Citizens*; Samuel Joseph, *History of Baron de Hirsch Fund* (1935). ❑ Oriental Exclusion: H. S. Millis, *Japanese Problem in United States* (1915); S. L. Gulick, *Japanese Problem* (1914); Carey McWilliams, *Prejudice* (1944), ch. ii. ❑ Immigration Restriction: W. S. Bernard, *American Immigration Policy* (1950), ch. i: Garis, *Immigration Restriction*, ch. iv; Myers, *History of Bigotry*, chs.

459

xxiii–xxiv. ❡ Negroes: Franklin, *Slavery to Freedom,* ch. xxiii; Woodward, *Origins of New South,* chs. xii, xiii; T. D. Clark, *Southern Country Editor,* ch. xviii; Rackham Holt, *G. W. Carver* (1943), chs. xiii–xviii; R. B. Vance, "Aycock of North Carolina," *Southwestern Rev.,* XVIII (1933), 288. ❡ Indians: F. E. Leupp, *Indian and His Problem* (1910); G. E. E. Lindquist, ed., *Red Man in United States* (1923); ❡ Pacific Coast: Brigham, *Geographical Influences,* ch. x; Bowman, *Forest Physiography,* chs. ix–xiii; H. H. Bancroft, *New Pacific* (1913); Schafer, *Pacific Northwest,* ch. xix; R. G. Cleland, *California in Our Time* (1947); D. S. Jordan, *California and Californians* (1903). ❡ Urbanization: De Forest and Veiller, *Tenement House;* W. S. Thompson, *Growth of Metropolitan Districts* (1947); Linn, *Jane Addams.* ❡ Maps: Paullin, *Atlas,* plates 36, 70–79.

Sources — Growth of Population: Thirteenth, Fourteenth Censuses. ❡ Immigration: Abbott, *Immigration: Select Documents;* U.S. Immigration Commission, *Report* (41 vols., 1911); President's Commission on Immigration and Naturalization, *Hearings* (1952), 1839; Mass. Commission on Immigration, *Report* (1914); Edward Steiner, *On Trail of Immigrant* (1906); Gompers, *Seventy Years,* II, ch. xxxi; *American Jewish Year Book* (1905–20); Powderly, *Path I Trod,* 301; P. F. Hall, *Immigration* (1906). ❡ Negro: *Negro Year Book* (1912–); National Association for Advancement of Colored People, *Annual Report* (1911–); R. S. Baker, *Following the Color Line* (1908); Washington, *Negro in South;* U.S. Bur. Educ., *Bull.,* Nos. 38, 39 (1916). ❡ Pacific Coast: Greely, *Handbook of Alaska;* J. S. Maclain, *Alaska and Klondike* (1905); W. S. Edward, *In To Yukon* (1909); C. R. Enock, *Great Pacific Coast* (1913); Eugene McElwaine, *Truth About Alaska* (1901); Jeremiah Lynch, *Three Years in Klondike* (1904); W. L. Fisher, "Alaska Coal Problems," Bureau of Mines, *Bull.,* No. 36 (1911). ❡ Urbanization: Charles Stelzle, *Son of Bowery* (1926), chs. i–iv, xix, xxiii; ❡ Other Periodicals: *Collier's; World's Work; Sunset; Overland; Out West; Pacific Monthly.* ❡ Contemporary accounts: E. G. Murphy, *Problems of Present South* (1904); J. M. Moore, *South Today* (1916); Edwin Mims, *Advancing South* (1926), chs. ii, iii, x.

Bibliography — Faulkner, *Quest for Social Justice,* 333, and *Decline of Laissez Faire,* 391; Stephenson, *American Immigration,* 293, 299; C. W. Smith, *Check-List Relating to Pacific Northwest.*

227. ECONOMIC EXPANSION

Summary — Finance: 1907 panic; investment functions of banking; development of insurance; financial coalitions; Morgan; Rockefeller-Harriman-Stillman; also §§ 236–8. — Manufacturing: consolidation and trusts, 1899–1903; United States Steel, 1901; copper; sugar; tobacco; oil; new industries and processes; automobile; Duryea, Ford, Haynes, Selden, 1911, patent decision; electrical equipment; the telephone and wireless; industry in the South. — Transportation: railroads, terminal construction, continued combination, Northern Pacific, Morgan securities, relationships to finance, New Haven, 1898–1901, electrification of urban rapid transit, subways, elevated lines; interurban trolleys; canal revival; 1907, Inland Waterways Commission; 1914, Panama Canal (§§ 222, 238); the automobile; highway expansion; the airplane; 1903 Langley; Wright Brothers. — Extractive industries: agriculture; development of lumbering; oil, Texas, Louisiana, Oklahoma; new coal and mineral resources; dams and hydroelectric power; the fisheries, salmon, use of trawlers. — Commerce: international merchant marine; retailing; expansion of department, chain, mail order stores; also §§ 236–8. — Distribution of wealth: business as a career; scientific management; education, relation to law, advertising, accountancy. — Professions: see also: §§ 209–10, 233, 246.

General — Faulkner, *Quest for Social Justice,* chs. ii, vi, and *Decline of Laissez Faire,* chs. ii–iv, vi–x, xiii, xiv; A. L. Bernheim, ed., *Big Business* (1937); Keir, *March of Commerce,* chs. ix–xvii; F. C. Mills, *Economic Tendencies in United States* (1932), chs. i–iv; W. M. Persons, "Index of General Business Conditions, 1875–1913," *Rev. of Econ. Stat.,* IX (1927), 20; W. C. Schluter, *Pre-War Business Cycle, 1907–1914* (1923); F. L. Allen, *Lords of Creation* (1935), chs. i–vi; Ogg, *National Progress,* ch. v; Sullivan, *Our Times,*

I, chs. xiv, xviii, xxii, II, chs. xv–xviii, xxxviii, IV, chs. ii–iv; La Follette, *Making of America*, III–VII.

Special — Finance: A. A. Young, "Analysis of Bank Statistics," *Rev. of Econ. Stat.*, VI (1924), 284, VII (1925), 19, IX (1927), 121; Hepburn, *History of Currency*, chs. xxi, xxii; A. D. Noyes, *Forty Years*, chs. xi–xv, and *War Period of American Finance, 1908–1925* (1926), ch. i; G. W. Edwards, *Evolution of Finance Capitalism* (1938), chs. x, xi; W. O. Scroggs, *Century of Banking Progress* (1924); Moody, *Masters of Capital;* E. T. B. Perine, *Story of Trust Companies* (1916); B. H. Beckhart, ed., *New York Money Market* (4 vols., 1931–32); Gras, *Massachusetts First National Bank*, chs. x, xi; I. B. Cross, *Financing an Empire: Banking in California* (4 vols., 1927); Am. Ac. of Pol. Soc. Sci., *Lessons of Financial Crisis* (1908); A. H. Hansen, *Cycle of Prosperity and Depression, 1902–1908* (1921); O. M. W. Sprague, "Crisis of 1914," *Am. Econ. Rev.*, V (1915), 499; Cleona Lewis, *America's Stake in International Investments* (1938), chs. ii–iv, ix–xvi. ❡ Industry: V. S. Clark, *History of Manufactures*, III; Malcolm Keir, *Manufacturing* (1928); E. E. Day and Woodlief Thomas, *Growth of Manufactures 1899 to 1923* (1928); Solomon Fabricant, *Output of Manufacturing 1899–1937* (1940); Harry Jerome, *Mechanization in Industry* (1934); Woodward, *Origins of New South*, ch. xi; Mims, *Advancing South*, ch. iv; Burlingame, *Engines of Democracy*, chs. xvii–xxv; Young, *American Cotton Industry;* Copeland, *Cotton Manufacturing;* H. B. Brown, *Cotton* (1917); Cole, *American Wool Manufacture;* J. W. Hammond, *Men and Volts: Story of General Electric* (1941); Howard and Ralph Wolf, *Rubber* (1936); A. D. Flinn and Ruth Cobb, *Research Laboratories in Industrial Establishments* (1921); Allen, *Shoe Industry;* R. G. Blakey, *United States Beet Sugar Industry* (1912); Kuhlmann, *Flour Milling Industry;* Clemen, *American Livestock Industry*, chs. xix–xxxvi; Scott Nearing, *Anthracite* (1915); Eliot Jones, *Anthracite Coal Combination;* H. R. Mussey, *Combination in Mining*, and *What Coal Commission Found* (1925); Epstein, *Automobile Industry;* Rister, *Oil*, chs. v–xii; L. M. Fanning, *American Oil Operations* (1947); Boyce House, *Oil Boom* (1941); Gerald Forbes, *Flush Production* (1942). ❡ Transportation: Moody, *Railway Builders;* A. C. Laut, *Romance of Rails* (2 vols., 1929); Slason Thompson, *American Railways;* Riegel, *Western Railroads;* H. L. Staples and A. T. Mason, *Fall of a Railroad Empire* (1947); Corliss, *Main Line of Mid-America*, chs. xxxi–xxxiv; Montgomery Schuyler, *Westward the Course of Empire* (1906); Walker, *Rapid Transit;* J. A. Miller, *Fares, Please!* (1941); D. F. Wilcox, *Analysis of Electric Railway Problem* (1921); also § 231; G. H. Gilbert, L. I. Wightman, and W. L. Saunders, *Subways and Tunnels of New York* (1912); H. G. Moulton, *Waterways vs. Railways* (1912); Harlow, *Old Towpaths;* Herbert Quick, *American Inland Waterways* (1909); N. E. Whitford, *History of Barge Canal of New York State* (1922); D. H. Smith, *Panama Canal: Its History, Activities and Organization* (1927); H. E. Howe, *New Stone Age* (1921); C. L. Dearing, *American Highway Policy* (1941), ch. ii; F. L. Paxson, "Highway Movement," *Am. Hist. Rev.*, LI (1946), 236; R. S. Holland, *Historic Airships* (1928); Victor Lougheed, *Vehicles of Air* (1919). ❡ Agriculture: Harold Barger and H. H. Landsberg, *American Agriculture, 1899–1939* (1942); Peffer, *Closing of Public Domain;* Frederick Strauss and L. H. Bean, "Gross Farm Income," Dept. of Ag., *Technical Bull.*, No. 703 (1940); Malin, *Winter Wheat;* M. R. Benedict, *Farm Policies of United States* (1953), ch. vii; A. C. True, *History of Agricultural Experimentation* (1937), 165; H. F. Wilson, *Hill Country*, chs. x–xvii; O. M. Kile, *Farm Bureau Movement* (1921); Gladys Baker, *County Agent* (1939), chs. i, ii; Wiest, *Agricultural Organization;* R. H. Elsworth, *Development of Farmers' Cooperative Organizations* (1924); B. H. Hibbard, "Farm Tenancy in 1920," *Jour. of Farm Econ.*, III (1921), 168; Ivan Wright, *Bank Credit and Agriculture* (1922); E. G. Nourse, *American Agriculture and European Market* (1924). ❡ Commerce: Williams, *Economic Foreign Policy;* Ervin Hexner, *International Cartels* (1946); P. M. Zeis, *American Shipping Policy* (1938); Hutchins, *American Maritime Industries;* Allan Nevins and J. A. Krout, *Greater City: New York* (1948), 125; Hower, *Macy's*, chs. xii, xiii. ❡ Firms: Tarbell, *Standard Oil Company;* Montague, *Standard Oil Company;* Bridge, *Carnegie Steel Company;* H. L. Wilgus, *History of United States Steel Corporation* (1901); Arundel Cotter, *Authentic History of United States Steel Corporation* (1916); Abraham Berglund, *United States Steel* (1907); Daggett, *Southern Pacific;* Trottman, *Union Pacific;* Hungerford, *Baltimore and Ohio;* R. T. Swaine, *Cravath Firm* (1946); Albert Boyden, *Ropes-Gray* (1942). ❦ Wealth: W. I. King, *Wealth and Income of People of United States* (1915), and *National Income and Its Purchasing Power* (1930); W. C. Mitchell, *et al., Income in United States, 1909–1919* (2 vols., 1921–22). ❦ Professions: Ivy Lee, "Modern Lawyer," *World's Work,* VIII (1904), 4873; F. R. Aumann, *Changing American Legal System* (1940), chs. iv–viii; H. B. Drury, *Scientific Management* (3 ed., 1922). ❦ Biographies: Hendrick, *Carnegie,* II, ch. v; T. W. Lamont, *Henry P. Davidson* (1933), chs. iv–viii, x, xi; Tarbell, *Gary;* Jenkins, *Duke;* Winkler, *DuPont,* pt. 4; Dyer and Martin, *Edison,* II; Sward, *Ford;* Harvey, *Frick;* Kennan, *Harriman,* I, chs. vii–xvii, II, chs. xviii, xx, xxii, xxix; Pyle, *Hill;* Harvey O'Connor, *Mellon's Millions* (1933), chs. vi, vii; Allen, *Morgan,* chs. ix, xi, xii; Corey, *House of Morgan,* chs. xxii, xxiii, xxvi–xxx; Nicolson, *Morrow,* ch. v; Nevins, *Rockefeller,* II, ch. xli; Burr, *Portrait of Banker* (James Stillman); Copley, *Taylor;* Kelly, *Wright Brothers;* E. E. Freudenthal, *Flight into History* (1949). ❦ Maps: Paullin, *Atlas,* plates 140–1.

Sources — Government Publications and Statistical compilations: (§ 7); *Statistical Abstract;* Dept. Ag., *Bull.,* and *Yearbook; Census of Agriculture* (3 vols., 1925); *Census of Manufactures* (1904, 1914); *Census of Mining* (1902 [1905], 1910, 1920); *Census of Street and Electric Railways* (1902 [1905], 1917 [1920]); Dept. of Commerce, *Commercial Relations,* and *Consular Trade Reports,* and *Foreign Commerce and Navigation of United States;* Commissioner of Corporations, *Report on Steel Industry* (3 vols., 1911–13); Federal Electric Railways Commission, *Proc.* (3 vols., 1920); Federal Trade Commission, *Report on Grain Trade* (7 vols., 1920–26); Geol. Surv., *Mineral Resources of United States* (annual); [U. S.] Industrial Commission, *Reports* (19 vols., 1900–02); Inland Waterways Commission, *Preliminary Report* (1908), and *Final Report* (1912); Interstate Commerce Commission, *Annual Report,* and *Statistics of Railways;* Isthmian Canal Commission, *Annual Reports* (1904–14); National Monetary Commission, *Report* (1912); Pujo Committee, *Investigation of Financial and Monetary Conditions in United States* (3 vols., 1913); Tariff Board, *Pulp and Newsprint* (1911), and *Wool* (4 vols., 1912), and *Cotton* (2 vols., 1912). ❦ Congressional Documents and Hearings: "Commission on Country Life," 60 Cong., 2 Sess., *Sen. Doc.,* No. 705; "Intercoastal Waterways," 62 Cong., 2 Sess., *H. Doc.,* No. 391; Merchant Marine Commission, "Report," 58 Cong., 3 Sess., *Sen. Doc.,* No. 2,755 (3 vols., 1904–05); "Development of American Merchant Marine," 59 Cong., 1 Sess., *Sen. Report,* No. 10; [Stanley] Committee [of H.], *Hearings on Investigation of United States Steel Corporation* (8 vols., 1912); "Taylor System," 62 Cong., 1 Sess., *H. Res.,* No. 90 (1912). ❦ Contemporary Accounts: E. R. A. Seligman, ed., *Currency Problem* (1908); L. D. Brandeis, *Business — a Profession* (1914); O. S. Marden, *Choosing a Career* (1905), and *Exceptional Employee* (1913), and *Selling Things* (1916); F. W. Taylor, *Principles of Scientific Management* (1911), and *Shop Management* (1911); Clews, *Fifty Years;* Noyes, *Market Place,* ch. viii; L. O. Howard, *Fighting the Insects* (1933); D. G. Fairchild, *Exploring for Plants* (1930). ❦ Other Sources: Bailey, *Cyclopedia of American Agriculture;* Poor, *Manual of Railroads;* Slason Thompson, *Railway Library* (1906–16); E. L. Bogart and C. M. Thompson, eds., *Readings on Economic History of United States* (1916); Flügel and Faulkner, *Readings in Economic History;* L. C. Marshall, ed., *Readings in Industrial Society* (1923). ❦ Periodicals: *Wallace's Farmer; Rev. Econ. Stat.; Commercial and Financial Chronicle;* § 7.

Bibliography — Kirkland, *American Economic Life,* 709, 717; H. H. B. Meyer, *List of References on Shipping* (1919); Edwards, *Bibliography of History of Agriculture;* Library of Congress, General Reference and Bibliography Division, *Cartels, Combines, and Trusts* (1944); Larson, *Guide to Business History,* 798; Burlingame, *Engines of Democracy,* 545.

228. PROBLEMS OF LABOR, 1900–1919

Summary — Earlier phases (§§ 183, 205, 210). — Conditions of labor: labor force; wages; hours; unemployment; accidents; labor of women and children; relations to immigration (§ 226). — Labor organization: American Federation of Labor; Gompers;

International Ladies Garment Workers; other unions. — Strikes: 1901, steel strike; 1902, anthracite coal strike: President Roosevelt's interference; 1903, Mar. 18, Commission's report (§ 234); 1903–04, second Cripple Creek strike, dynamite and deportation, 1907, Moyer and Haywood trial; 1909–10, revolt of shirtwaist and cloakmakers; 1909, McKees Rock; 1912–13, Lawrence, Paterson strikes; 1910, *Los Angeles Times* dynamiting, Macnamara case. — Efforts at conciliation: new management policies, company unions, protective associations, labor spies, state police, profit sharing, pension schemes, arbitration; 1902, labor conference of National Civic Federation; 1910, Brandeis and protocol of peace in garment industry. — Radicalism: socialism; anarchism; De Leon; Debs; Social Democratic, Socialist-Labor, parties; impact on labor unions; 1905, I. W. W. — Labor and government: relations to local government, San Francisco labor movement; 1903, Department of Commerce and Labor established; 1913, Department of Labor; state labor bureaus; 1906, American Association for Labor Legislation; 1906, Liability of Common Carriers overturned by Supreme Court; 1907, Hours of Railroad Employees Act; 1908, Roosevelt's message on employers' liability, new act sustained by the Court; 1908, Danbury Hatters' case, injunction issue in presidential campaign; 1908–10, Bucks Stove case; 1913, Seamen's Act; 1914, Clayton Act (§ 235); state legislation on children, women, minimum wages, hours, employers' liability, workingmen's compensation; attitude of courts, 1910, Ritchie (Illinois) woman labor case; 1911, Gompers contempt case. — Relationship to humanitarianism, politics (§§ 229–31, 232–4).

General — Commons, *History of Labour*, III, §§ 2, 3, 399, IV, chs. i–xxiv; Faulkner, *Decline of Laissez Faire*, chs. xi, xii, and *Quest for Social Justice*, ch. iii; Kirkland, *History of American Economic Life*, 515; Selig Perlman, *History of Trade Unionism in United States* (1922); Dulles, *Labor in America*, chs. xi–xii; Orth, *Armies of Labor;* Sullivan, *Our Times*, II, chs. xiv, xxiv; La Follette, *Making of America*, VIII.

Special — Conditions: Solomon Fabricant, *Employment in Manufacturing 1899–1939* (1942); Douglas, *Real Wages;* National Industrial Conference Board, *Wages in United States, 1914–1930* (1931); Bur. Labor Stat., *History of Wages* (*Bull.*, No. 604, 1934); H. N. Hart, *Fluctuations in Unemployment 1902–1917* (1918); Stelzle, *Son of Bowery*, chs. viii–xiv, xx; Robert Hunter, *Poverty* (1904); C. H. Parker, *Casual Laborer* (1920); John Ryan, *Living Wage* (1906); R. C. Chapin, *Standard of Living among Workingmen's Families in New York* (1909); L. B. More, *Wage Earners' Budgets* (1907); J. C. Kennedy, *et al., Wage and Family Budgets in Chicago Stockyards* (1914); F. H. Streightoff, *Standard of Living among Industrial People* (1911); Peter Roberts, *Anthracite Coal Industry* (1901); W. E. Fisher and Anne Bezanson, *Wage Rates in Bituminous Coal* (1932); Abbott, *Women in Industry;* T. S. McMahon, *Women and Economic Revolution* (1912); C. E. Persons, "Women's Work and Wages," *Quar. Jour. Econ.*, XXIX (1915), 201; S. P. Breckinridge, *Women in Twentieth Century* (1933), chs. vii–xiv; E. N. Clopper, *Child Labor in City Streets* (1912); W. J. Lauck and Edgar Sydenstricker, *Conditions of Labor in American Industries* (1917); John Spargo, *Bitter Cry of Children* (1906); "Summary of Report on Conditions of Women and Child Wage Earners," Dept. of Labor, *Bull.*, No. 175 (1915). ❡ Labor Organization: Lorwin, *American Federation Labor*, chs. iii–v; J. M. Budish and George Soule, *New Unionism in Clothing Industry* (1920); Mason, *Brandeis*, ch. xix; Louis Levine, *Women's Garment Workers* (1924), chs. xv–xxviii; Joel Seidman, *Needle Trades* (1942); Benjamin Stolberg, *Tailors Progress* (1944); Hart, *Commonwealth History of Massachusetts*, V, ch. xiv; Roy, *Coal Miners;* Rastall, *Cripple Creek District;* G. P. West, *Report on Colorado Strike* (1915); A. E. Albrecht, *International Seamen's Union* (1923), chs. i–iii; Melech Epstein, *Jewish Labor in U.S.A.* (1950); Alice Henry, *Trade Union Woman* (1915); H. W. Laidler, *Boycotts and Labor Struggle* (1914); Leo Wolman, *Boycott in American Trade Unions* (1916), and *Growth of American Trade Unions.* ❡ Radicalism: C. R. Lewis, *History of American Political Thought* (1937), ch. x; Haynes, *Social Politics*, chs. ix–xi; Egbert and Persons, *Socialism and American Life*, I, ch. vi; Fine, *Labor and Farmer Parties*, chs. viii–ix; Quint, *Forging of American Socialism*, chs. x, xi; Ira Kipnis, *American Socialist Movement* (1952); Hillquit, *History of Socialism;* John Spargo, *Socialism* (1910); Adamic, *Dynamite*, chs. xiv–xvi, xviii–xxiv; D. J. Saposs, *Left Wing Unionism* (1926); *Daniel De Leon;* P. F. Brissenden, *I. W. W.* (1919); J. S. Gambs, *Decline of*

I. W. W. (1932). ❧ Labor and Government: Frankfurter and Greene, *Labor Injunction;* Bruce Smith, *State Police* (1925); E. H. Davidson, *Child Labor Legislation in Southern Textile States* (1939); Bowers, *Beveridge,* bk. 3, chs. v–vi; H. L. Sumner and E. A. Merritt, *Child Labor Legislation in United States* (1915); John Lombardi, *Labor's Voice in Cabinet* (1942), pts. 1, 2; J. A. Tobey, *Children's Bureau* (1925); J. R. Commons and J. B. Andrews, *Principles of Labor Legislation* (1927); Groat, *Courts in Labor Cases;* I. M. Rubinow, *Social Insurance* (1913); C. R. Henderson, *Industrial Insurance in United States* (1904); D. H. Van Doren, *Workmen's Compensation and Insurance* (1918); E. H. Downey, *Workmen's Compensation* (1924); G. F. Michelbacker and T. M. Niel, *Workmen's Compensation Insurance* (1925); Crystal Eastman, *Work Accidents and Law* (1910); W. H. Tolman, *Social Engineering* (1909). ❧ Biographies: Irving Stone, *Clarence Darrow* (1941), chs. vii, viii; Ginger, *Debs,* pts. 3, 4; Harvey, *Gompers,* chs. vii–xii; Croly, *Hanna,* ch. xxv; Rogoff, *Meyer London;* Glück, *Mitchell.*

Sources — Government documents and other statistical material: Loewe *v.* Lawler, 221 U.S., 1; Gompers *v.* Bucks Stove Co., 221 U.S., 418; Department of Labor, *Bull.* (1896–1912); Bur. of Labor Stat., *Bull.* (1913–20); Commissioner of Labor, *Reports* (1900–13); Industrial Commission, *Final Report* (1902); Commission on Industrial Relations, *Final Report* (12 vols., 1915–16); Anthracite Coal Strike Commission, *Report on Strike of 1902* (1903; 1920); C. P. Neill, "Report on Strike in Lawrence, 1912," 62 Cong., 2 Sess., *Sen. Doc.,* No. 870, and "Report on Conditions in Iron and Steel Industry," 4 vols., 62 Cong., 1 Sess., *Sen. Doc.,* No. 110; Mass. Bur. of Stat., *Twenty-third Annual Report: Strikes and Lockouts for 1912* (1913); H. D. Kube and R. H. Danhof, *Changes in Distribution of Manufacturing Wage Earners* (1942); also §§ 7, 45; state publications (§ 46). ❧ Labor Publications: Am. Federation of Labor, *Report of Proceedings* (1900–   ), and *Am. Federationist* (1900–   ), and *Weekly News Service* (1911–   ); *American Labor Year Book* (annual). ❧ Other Sources: George Creel, *Rebel at Large* (1947), ch. xvii; Darrow, *My Life,* chs. xiv–xxiv; Debs, *Writings and Speeches;* Powderly, *Path I Trod;* John Mitchell, *Organized Labor* (1903); Gompers, *Seventy Years,* II; W. D. Haywood, *Bill Haywood's Book* (1929); Felix Frankfurter, *Oregon Minimum Wage Cases: Brief for Defendants* (1916); P. H. Douglas, C. N. Hitchcock, and W. E. Atkins, eds., *Worker in Modern Economic Society* (1923); D. J. Saposs, ed., *Readings in Trade Unionism* (1925).

Bibliography — Commons, *History of Labour;* H. H. B. Meyer, *List of References on Child Labor* (1916); Kirkland, *History of American Economic Life,* 713; Egbert and Persons, *Socialism and American Life,* II.

229. CULTURAL AND SOCIAL TRENDS

Summary — Earlier developments (§§ 213–9). — Changes in family life: effects of urbanization; birth control; divorce; changing position of women (§§ 228, 230); child welfare; changes in housing, apartment house; food habits. — Expositions: 1901, Buffalo; 1904, St. Louis; 1905, Portland; 1909, Seattle; 1915, San Francisco, Panama Pacific. — Education: theories of John Dewey, psychology of G. S. Hall and E. L. Thorndike; adult education; high schools; junior colleges; graduate schools, of business, of journalism; improvement of standards in the South; academic freedom, American Association of University Professors; foundations, 1902, General Education Board; Rockefeller Institute (medicine), 1913, Rockefeller Foundation; museums; libraries. — Philosophy and religion: pragmatism, instrumentalism, and critical realism; rise in church membership; Sunday schools; sectarian developments; revivalism, Billy Sunday; Protestantism; development of liberalism and theology in religion; social gospel; union of sects; interdenominational coöperation; local federations; 1908, Federal Council of Churches of Christ in America; development of Negro churches; Catholic Church, new stocks, cardinals; removed from control of Propaganda; development of Conservative Judaism; growth of Christian Science; New Thought. — Medicine and Science: fight on tuberculosis; Gorgas, Reed, tropical disease, Yellow fever, malaria; treatment of hookworm, anemia; attention to diet; nursing; public health; advances in chemistry; engineering; inventions. — Literature: realism, Jack London, Garland, Dreiser, Norris; Henry James;

short stories; popular fiction, Tarkington; movements in poetry, Moody, Markham, Lindsay, Sandburg, Amy Lowell, Frost. — Music: influence of Negro; jazz; vogue of light opera; rise of symphony orchestra; the phonograph. — Theater: Charles Frohman, Klaw and Erlanger, "the syndicate"; vaudeville; emergence of movies; little theater, 1915 Provincetown players; revues. — Fine Arts: realism in painting, Bellows, Luks; Armory Show; architecture, skyscraper, Sullivan; landscape architecture; city planning. — Journalism: yellow press, comics, the columnists, sport news, syndicates, chains, influence of advertising, tabloid; magazines, muckraking, women's, popular. — Athletics: professionalism; spectator sports; golf; tennis; amusement parks, park movement; Olympic competition. — Later developments (§§ 252, 253).

General — Faulkner, *Quest for Social Justice,* chs. vii–xii; Slosson, *Great Crusade,* ch. xiv; Sullivan, *Our Times,* I, chs. i–iii, xvi, xvii, xix, II, chs. i–xii, xxiv, III, chs. ix–xi, xiii; IV, chs. v–xi; La Follette, *Making of America,* I, 69; Gabriel, *American Democratic Thought,* chs. xxi, xxii; Dulles, *America Learns to Play,* chs. xvii, xviii; Mims, *Advancing South,* chs. v–ix, xi; K. G. Busbey, *Home Life in America* (1910); L. R. Morris, *Not So Long Ago* (1949), and *Postscript to Yesterday* (1947).

Special — Family Life: R. E. Baber and E. A. Ross, *Changes in Size of American Families* (1924); M. W. Dennett, *Birth Control Laws* (1926); W. E. Carson, *Marriage Revolt* (1915); F. S. Hall and E. W. Brooke, *American Marriage Laws* (1919); Breckenridge, *Women,* chs. i–vi; J. B. Mangold, *Problems of Child Welfare* (1914); J. A. Riis, *Battle with Slums* (1902); Homer Folks, *Care of Destitute, Neglected and Delinquent Children* (1902); H. H. Hart, ed., *Preventive Treatment of Neglected Children* (1915); L. H. Gulick and L. P. Ayres, *Medical Inspection of Schools* (1913); H. H. Lou, *Juvenile Courts* (1927); N. P. Gist, *Secret Societies* (1940). ❡ Education: I. L. Kandel, *Twenty-Five Years of American Education* (1924); Mabel Newcomer, *Financial Statistics 1910–1920* (1924); H. A. Yeomans, *Abbott Lawrence Lowell* (1948); C. F. Thwing, *Guides, Philosophers and Friends* (1927); E. E. Slosson, *Great American Universities* (1910); Abraham Flexner, *American College* (1908); Baker, *Woodrow Wilson,* II, chs. xv–xvii; Link, *Wilson,* chs. i–iii; W. F. Russell and E. C. Elliott, eds., *Columbia University* (1937), II; Curti, *Social Ideas of American Educators,* chs. ix–xv; J. M. Pangburn, *Evolution of American Teachers College* (1932); L. V. Koos, *Junior College* (2 vols., 1924); Woody, *Woman's Education in United States;* J. D. Eggleston and R. W. Bruere, *Work of Rural Schools* (1913); Nevins, *Rockefeller,* II, chs. xliii, xlviii; Hendrick, *Carnegie,* II, chs. viii–ix. ❡ Philosophy and Religion: Schneider, *American Philosophy,* ch. viii; Hopkins, *Social Gospel,* chs. xii–xviii; G. B. Smith, ed., *Religious Thought in Last Quarter Century* (1927); E. R. Hooker, *United Churches* (1926); E. B. Sanford, *Origin and History of Federal Council* (1916); C. S. Macfarland, *Churches of Federal Council* (1916); Stelzle, *Son of Bowery,* chs. vi–vii, xv, xviii; E. W. Rice, *Sunday School Movement, 1780–1917* (1917), and *American Sunday School Union, 1817–1917* (1917); W. M. Tippy, *Church a Community Force* (1914); H. F. Ward, *Year Book of Church and Social Service* (1915); Ellis, *Cardinal Gibbons,* II, chs. xvii, xviii; Sibyl Wilbur, *Life of Mary Baker Eddy* (1913); Georgine Milmine, *Mary Baker G. Eddy* (1909); Dakin, *Mrs. Eddy;* Rolvix Harlan, *John Alexander Dowie* (1906); Dresser, *New Thought.* ❡ Science: Paul De Kruif, *Microbe Hunters* (1926), ch. xi; Flexner, *Welch;* Helen Clapesattle, *Doctor Mayo* (1941); S. A. Knopf, *History of National Tuberculosis Association* (1922); Benjamin Harrow, *Vitamines* (1921); L. L. Dock, *History of Nursing* (4 vols., 1912); H. H. Moore, *Public Health in United States* (1923); R. D. Leigh, *Federal Health Administration* (1927); J. A. Tobey, *National Government and Public Health* (1926); Ravenel, *Public Health;* E. E. Slosson, *Creative Chemistry* (1919); E. E. Slosson and O. W. Caldwell, eds., *Science Remaking World* (1924); R. K. Duncan, *Chemistry of Commerce* (1907); Hale Harrison, *American Chemistry* (1921); H. E. Howe, *Chemistry in World's Work* (1926); H. E. Howe, ed., *Chemistry in Industry* (2 vols., 1924); Julius Stieglitz, ed., *Chemistry in Medicine* (1928); F. H. Garrison, *Introduction to History of Medicine* (3 ed., 1924); F. B. Karpf, *American Social Psychology* (1932). ❡ Literature: Hart, *Popular Book,* chs. xii–xiii; Lehmann-Haupt, *Book in America,* 208; Oscar Cargill, *Intellectual America* (1941); Van Wyck Brooks, *New England: Indian Summer* (1940), chs. xxiv, xxv; Pattee, *Short*

Story; Granville Hicks, *Great Tradition* (1935), chs. vi, vii; Alfred Kazin, *On Native Grounds* (1942); Spiller, *Literary History,* II; Horace Gregory and Marya Zaturenska, *History of American Poetry* (1946); Edmund Wilson, *Axel's Castle* (1931); C. A. Smith, *O. Henry;* Elias, *Dreiser;* Cooke, *Howells.* ❦ Music: J. T. Howard, *Our American Music,* chs. xii–xv, and *Our Contemporary Composers* (1941); Dorothy Scarborough, *On Trail of Negro Folk Songs* (1925); H. E. Krehbiel, *Afro-American Folksongs* (1914); J. W. Johnson, *Book of American Negro Spirituals* (1925); R. N. Deft, *Religious Folk Songs of Negro* (1927); Harris, *After the Ball;* Howe, *Boston Symphony Orchestra;* P. A. Otis, *Chicago Symphony Orchestra* (1925); F. A. Wister, *Twenty-Five Years of the Philadelphia Orchestra* (1925); Russell, *American Orchestra and Theodore Thomas;* Hipsher, *American Opera;* De Koven, *Musician and His Wife.* ❦ Theater: Hornblow, *History of Theatre,* II, chs. xxx, xxxi; W. L. Phelps, *Twentieth Century Theatre* (1918); Archibald Henderson, *Changing Drama* (1914); O. M. Sayler, *Our American Theatre* (1913); C. D'A. Mackay, *Little Theatre* (1917); Louise Burleigh, *Community Theatre* (1917); Moses, *American Dramatist;* Caroline Coffin, *Vaudeville* (1914); Paskman and Spaeth, *Gentlemen, Be Seated!;* Robert Withington, *English Pageantry* (1918–20), II, ch. ix; John Drinkwater, *Life of Carl Laemmle* (1931); L. A. Griffith, *When Movies Were Young* (1925); F. A. Talbot, *Moving Pictures* (1912); B. J. Lubschez, *Story of the Moving Picture* (1920). ❦ Fine Arts: Larkin, *Art and Life in America,* pt. 5; Aaron, *America in Crisis,* ch. ix; Allen, *Morgan,* ch. x; Hamlin, *American Spirit in Architecture,* chs. xv–xxiv; Tallmadge, *Architecture in America,* chs. x, xi; Kimball, *Architecture;* Edgell, *Architecture;* Starrett, *Skyscrapers;* Joseph Hudnut, *American Sculpture* (1929); McSpadden, *Famous Sculptors;* Taft, *American Sculpture,* pt. 3; Isham, *American Painting;* Weitenkampf, *American Graphic Art;* Cortissoz, *American Artists.* ❦ Journalism: Mott, *American Journalism,* chs. xxxi–xxxv; Bleyer, *American Journalism,* chs. xiv–xvi; Murrell, *Graphic Humor,* II, chs. vii–x. ❦ Athletics: L. H. Weir, ed., *Parks, a Manual* (2 vols., 1928); Rainwater, *Play Movement;* E. A. Rice, *Brief History of Physical Education* (1924); A. G. Spalding, *America's National Game Baseball* (1911), chs. xxi–xxxii; J. J. McGraw, *My Thirty Years in Baseball* (1923); J. J. Evers and H. S. Fullerton, *Touching Second* (1910); Weyand, *American Football,* chs. iii–vi; Powel, *Walter Camp;* A. A. Stagg and W. W. Stout, *Touchdown* (1927); P. H. Davis, *Football* (1911); Wind, *American Golf,* pts. 1, 2; Travers and Crowell, *Fifth Estate;* Alexander Johnston, *Ten — and Out;* Corbett, *Roar of Crowd;* Jack Johnson, *Jack Johnson in the Ring — and Out* (1927).

Sources — Periodicals: *Atlantic Monthly; Century; Harper's; Scribner's; North American Review; McClure's; Cosmopolitan; Saturday Evening Post; Munseys; Colliers; Theatre* (1901–20); *Am. Architect; Architectural Rev.; Architectural Record; House Beautiful; American; N.Y. Times; N.Y. World* (§§ 52, 53). ❦ Memoirs, Abbott, *Reminiscences;* Henry Adams, *Letters,* II; George Arliss, *Up the Years* (1928); Aronson, *Memoirs;* John Barrymore, *Confessions of an Actor* (1926); Poultney Bigelow, *Seventy Summers* (2 vols., 1925); Bok, *Americanization;* N. M. Butler, *Across Busy Years* (1939–40), I, ch. viii; Carnegie, *Autobiography,* chs. xix, xx; G. M. Cohan, *Twenty Years on Broadway* (1925); Eddie Foy and A. F. Harlow, *Clowning through Life* (1928); Gibbons, *Retrospect;* Gladden, *Recollections;* W. C. Gorgas, *Sanitation in Panama* (1915); G. S. Hall, *Life and Confessions;* W. S. Hart, *My Life* (1929); DeWolfe Hopper, *Once a Clown Always a Clown* (1927); R. U. Johnson, *Remembered Yesterdays;* F. F. Kelly, *Flowing Stream* (1939), §§ 11–14; M. Koenigsberg, *King News* (1941), chs. x–xv; William Lawrence, *Memories of a Happy Life* (1926); McClure, *Autobiography,* ch. viii; McRae, *Forty Years;* Mitchell, *Memoirs of Editor;* Putnam, *Memories;* Skinner, *Footlights;* Sousa, *Marching Along;* Thomas, *Print of My Remembrance;* Tooker, *Joys and Tribulations;* Trudeau, *Autobiography;* Watterson, *"Marse Henry";* W. A. White, *Autobiography,* chs. lii–liv; H. W. Wiley, *Autobiography* (1930); Woodrow Wilson, *Public Papers,* I, II; Winter, *Other Days,* and *Wallet of Time.* ❦ Government Documents: U.S. Commissioner of Education, *Annual Report;* U.S. Bur. of Education, *Biennial Survey,* and *Bull.* ❦ Collections: Handlin, *This Was America,* chs. xxviii–xxxiii; W. D. P. Bliss, *New Encyclopedia of Social Reform* (1907); Moses and Brown, *American Theatre; New International Year Book; Am. Year Book.* ❦ Other Contemporary Works: W. R. Harper, *Trend in Higher Education* (1905); C. W. Eliot, *University Administration* (1908); Thorstein Veblen,

Higher Learning in America (1918); Upton Sinclair, *Goose Step* (1923); Charles Stelzle, *Workingman and Social Problems* (1903); C. B. Thompson, *Churches and Wage Earners* (1909); Walter Rauschenbusch, *Christianity and the Social Crisis* (1907), and *Christianizing the Social Order* (1912); John Dewey, *School and Society* (1899), and *Democracy and Education* (1916).

Bibliography — Mott, *American Journalism*, 610; Theodore Schroeder, ed., *List of References on Birth Control* (1918).

Chapter Twenty-five

THE IMPACT OF REFORM ON POLITICS, 1900–1920

230. SOURCES OF THE PROGRESSIVE MOVEMENT

Summary — Intellectual and cultural background (§ 229); literature and reform; influence of social science, development of academic sociology, economics; conceptions of planning and control; social Darwinism. — Religious aspects: social gospel; Catholic and Jewish conceptions of charity; threat of popular disbelief (§ 229). — Populist antecedents (§ 209). — Relations to labor, to radicalism (§ 228). — Conservative response: doctrines of pessimism; the law and the courts (§ 234); vestiges of states' rights. — Humanitarianism in action: trends in philanthropy; foundations; education (§ 229); urban social work; housing; temperance movement, prohibition (§ 244); prison reform; treatment of insane; public health; protection of labor. — Women's rights movement: (§ 229); new economic situation; social aspects; suffrage movement; 1920, nineteenth amendment; relation to progressivism. — New political devices, initiative, referendum, recall; progressive politics (§§ 231–5). — Peace movement (§ 239). — Later developments (§§ 249, 251–3).

General — Faulkner, *Decline of Laissez Faire*, ch. xv, and *Quest for Social Justice*, ch. iv; P. W. Slosson, *Great Crusade and After* (1930), ch. i; Sullivan, *Our Times*, I, chs. viii–ix; Bowers, *Beveridge*, bk. 3, chs. i–iv; Aaron, *Men of Good Hope*, chs. vii, viii; Lewis, *American Political Thought*, chs. viii, ix, xi, xii; E. F. Goldman, *Rendezvous with Destiny* (1952), chs. v–ix; John Chamberlain, *Farewell to Reform* (1932); Louis Filler, *Crusaders for American Liberalism* (1950); Gabriel, *American Democratic Thought*, chs. xxiii, xxv; Ogg, *National Progress*, chs. ix, x; La Follette, *Making of America*, II, 397; C. C. Regier, *Era of Muckrakers* (1932), chs. i–v; B. P. DeWitt, *Progressive Movement* (1915), chs. i–vi.

Special — Development of Social Science: Dorfman, *Economic Mind*, III, chs. xiv–xxi; Odum, *American Masters of Social Science*; Barnes, *New History*; H. E. Barnes, ed., *History and Prospects of Social Sciences* (1925); Hayes, *Recent Developments in Social Sciences*; A. G. Gruchy, *Modern Economic Thought* (1947); Ogburn and Goldenweiser, *Social Sciences*; Gee, *Research in Social Science*; Hofstadter, *Social Darwinism*, chs. vii, viii, x; M. G. White, *Social Thought*, chs. i–xi. ❡ Humanitarianism in Action: Cherrington, *Prohibition*; P. H. Odegard, *Pressure Politics* (1928); Stelzle, *Son of Bowery*, chs. v, xvii; De Forest and Veiller, *Tenement House*; E. E. Wood, *Housing the Unskilled Wage Earner* (1919); Woods and Kennedy, *Settlement Horizon*; McKelvey, *American Prisons*, ch. x; Deutsch, *Mentally Ill in America*, chs. xiv–xix; C. G. Roe, *Panders and Their White Slaves* (1910); Rubinow, *Social Insurance*; Stanton, *Woman Suffrage*, V, VI; Catt and Shuler, *Woman Suffrage and Politics*; I. H. Irwin, *Story of Woman's Party* (1921); Breckenridge, *Women*, chs. xv–xix; E. A. Hecker, *Short History of Women's Rights* (2 ed., 1914), chs. viii, ix; Wood, *Federation of Women's Clubs*; Hart, *Commonwealth History of Massachusetts*, V, ch. vii. ❡ Political Conceptions: R. C. Brooks, *Corruption in American Politics* (1910); J. R. Commons, *Proportional Representation* (1907); W. B. Munro, *Initiative, Referendum, and Recall* (1912); E. P. Oberholtzer, *Referendum in America*

(1912). ❡ Biographies: Harper, *Susan B. Anthony*, III; Dabney, *Dry Messiah*, chs. iv–ix; Chamberlain, *Osborne*; Pringle, *Roosevelt*, bk. 1; Justin Stewart, *Wayne Wheeler* (1928), chs. i–v; Baker, *Woodrow Wilson*, I, ch. viii.

Sources — Contemporary Writings: H. D. Croly, *Promise of American Life* (1909); W. E. Weyl, *New Democracy* (1912); Walter Lippmann, *Preface to Politics* (1913), and *Drift and Mastery* (1914); R. C. Dorr, *What Eight Million Women Want* (1910); Elizabeth McCracken, *Women of America* (1904); Jessie Taft, *The Woman Movement from Point of View of Social Consciousness* (1915); W. O. Atwood, *et al.*, *Liquor Problem* (1905). ❡ Reports of Organizations: Anti-Saloon League, *Year-book*; Chicago Vice Commission, *Social Evil* (1911); Hartford Vice Commission, *Report* (1913); Minneapolis Vice Commission, *Report* (1911); N.Y. Committee of Fifteen, *Social Evil* (2 ed., 1912); Portland (Ore.) Vice Commission, *Report* (1913); U.S. Brewers' Assoc., *Yearbook*. ❡ Periodicals: newspapers (§ 53); *Nation*; *Independent*; *Outlook*; *Literary Digest*. ❡ Other Collections: Bliss, *Encyclopedia of Social Reform*; Manning, Potter, Davies, *Select Problems*, II, ch. i; C. A. Beard and B. E. Shultz, *Documents on Initiative, Referendum and Recall* (1912). ❡ Personal Material: Henry Adams, *Education*; R. S. Baker, *American Chronicle* (1945), chs. viii–xxvi; H. S. Blatch and Alma Lutz, *Challenging Years* (1940); Bryan, *Memoirs*, pt. 1, ch. xi, pt. 2, chs. vii, xvii; Heaton, *Story of a Page*, chs. xx, xxii; M. D. Howe, ed., *Holmes-Pollock Letters* (2 vols., 1941), I, chs. iii, iv; Lodge and Roosevelt, *Correspondence*, I; Norris, *Fighting Liberal*, chs. i–x; Roosevelt, *Autobiography*, chs. i–vii; Steffens, *Autobiography*, pts. 1–3; O. G. Villard, *Fighting Years* (1939), chs. ix–xii; W. A. White, *Selected Letters* (Walter Johnson, ed., 1947), 34.

Bibliography — Faulkner, *Decline of Laissez Faire*, 410; Goldman, *Rendezvous with Destiny*, 469.

231. STATE AND LOCAL REFORMS

Summary — Earlier developments (§§ 153, 192). — Problems of state government: expanded functions; relation to utilities and "interests"; the governorship; the legislatures; the bureaucracy; relations to party system. — State reform: Wisconsin idea, R. M. La Follette, legislative reference library, use of experts; "Oregon Plan," W. S. U'Ren; Missouri, J. W. Folk; New York, insurance investigation (§ 233), C. E. Hughes, Sulzer impeachment; New Jersey, Woodrow Wilson; other states; civil service; new constitutions; primaries; direct election of senators (§ 235); reorganization of institutions; utility, banking investigations; public utility commissions; labor, reform, workmen's compensaton legislation (§ 228); 1912, minimum wage for women; 1908, ten-hour law; conflicts with courts, 1905, Lockner Case, 1908, Muller *v.* Oregon. — Municipal problems: urbanization; expansion of services and budgets; efficiency; franchises; problems of effective government; the machines, bosses. — Civic reform: home rule; charters; commission (Galveston), manager (Des Moines, Dayton) forms; city planning; municipal research; housing; municipal ownership of utilities; juvenile courts; milk, water supply; Toledo, "Golden Rule" Jones, Brand Whitlock; Cleveland, T. L. Johnson, N. D. Baker; Milwaukee, Seidel; New York, Tammany Hall, Seth Low; 1906–09, San Francisco exposures.

General — Regier, *Muckrakers*, chs. vi, vii; Goldman, *Rendezvous with Destiny*, ch. viii; Filler, *Crusaders*, chs. viii, xv; De Witt, *Progressive Movement*, chs. x–xvi; Haynes, *Social Politics*, ch. viii; D. F. Wilcox, *Analysis of Electric Railway Problem* (1921); Sullivan, *Our Times*, III, chs. iii–iv.

Special — States in General: P. S. Reinsch, *American Legislatures* (1907); Woodward, *Origins of New South*, ch. xiv; Harper, *History of Woman Suffrage*, VI, chs. i–l. ❡ Particular States: G. E. Mowry, *California Progressives* (1951); A. D. Kirwan, *Revolt of Rednecks* (1951), chs. xi–xiii; Haynes, *Third Party Movements* (Iowa), chs. xxviii, xxix; Hart, *Commonwealth History of Massachusetts*, V, chs. vi, xxi; W. A. White, *Coolidge*, chs. viii–xii; Mason, *Brandeis*, chs. vi–xv; A. P. Loring, "Short Account Massachusetts Constitutional Convention," *New Eng. Quar.*, VI (1933), Supplement; M. E. Hennessey, *Four Decades of Massachusetts Politics* (1935); Folwell, *Minnesota*, III, chs.

xiii–xv; W. G. Helmes, *John A. Johnson* (1949); James Kerney, *Political Education of Woodrow Wilson* (1926), chs. i–viii, xii, xiii; R. E. Noble, Jr., *New Jersey Progressivism before Wilson* (1946); Link, *Wilson*, I, chs. iv–ix; Baker, *Woodrow Wilson*, III, chs. i–iii; J. P. Tumulty, *Woodrow Wilson* (1921), chs. i–xiii; Blum, *Tumulty*, chs. i–iii; Flick, *History of New York*, VIII, ch. vii; J. A. Friedman, *Impeachment of Governor William Sulzer* (1939); S. B. Thomas, *Boss or Governor* (1914); J. W. Forrest and James Malcolm, *Tammany's Treason* (1913); Howard Hurwitz, *Theodore Roosevelt and Labor in New York State* (1943); H. F. Gosnell, *Boss Platt* (1924); Myers, *Tammany Hall*, chs. xxx–xxxvii; J. D. Barnett, *Operation of the Initiative, Referendum and Recall in Oregon* (1915); A. H. Eaton, *Oregon System* (1912); Walter Davenport, *Power and Glory: Boies Penrose* (1931); R. D. Bowden, *Boies Penrose* (1937); W. A. Flint, *Progressive Movement in Vermont* (1941); E. A. Fitzpatrick, *McCarthy of Wisconsin* (1944), chs. iii–xi; F. C. Howe, *Wisconsin* (1912); A. O. Barton, *La Follette's Winning of Wisconsin* (2 ed., 1924). ❡ Municipalities in General: Zink, *City Bosses*; D. F. Wilcox, *Great Cities* (1910), and *Municipal Franchises* (2 vols., 1910); J. J. Hamilton, *Dethronement of City Boss* (1910); E. S. Bradford, *Commission Government in American Cities* (1911); Henry Bruere, *New City Government* (1912); F. H. MacGregor, *City Government by Commission* (1911); Tao-Shuen Chang, *History and Analysis of Commission and City Manager Plans* (1918); La Follette, *Making of America*, II, 417; M. R. Beard, *Women's Work in Municipalities* (1915); C. L. King, *Regulation of Municipal Utilities* (1912); C. D. Thompson, *Public Ownership* (1925). ❡ Particular Cities: Marvin Wachman, *History of Social Democratic Party of Milwaukee* (1945); Nevins and Krout, *New York*, 61; Leonora Arent, *Electric Franchise in New York City* (1919); L. H. Pink, *Gaynor* (1931); Mortimer Smith, *William Jay Gaynor* (1950); Walter Bean, *Boss Ruef's San Francisco* (1952).

Sources — State and local records (§ 47); "Campaign Contributions," Testimony, Committee on Privileges and Elections, 62 Cong., 2 Sess., *Sen. Res.* 79; *Report of Joint Committee of Senate and Assembly New York to Investigate Life Insurance Companies* (1907); *Proceedings of Court for Trial of Impeachment of William Sulzer* (2 vols., 1913); magazines (§§ 52, 230); newspapers (§ 53). ❡ Annuals: *New International Year Book* (1907–   ); *American Year Book* (1910–19). ❡ Reports of Organizations: National Civic Federation, Committee on Public Ownership, *Municipal and Private Operation of Public Utilities* (3 vols., 1907); National Municipal League, *Annual Report*. ❡ Contemporary Accounts: Lincoln Steffens, *Shame of Cities*, and *Upbuilders* (1909); Franklin Hichborn, *"The System" as Uncovered by San Francisco Graft Prosecution* (1915); D. W. Bartlett, *Better City* (1907); F. C. Howe, *City the Hope of Democracy* (1905). ❡ Personal material: E. P. Costigan, *Papers Relating to Progressive Movement in Colorado* (C. B. Goodykoontz, ed., 1941); Creel, *Rebel at Large*, chs. vii–ix, xiii–xvi; Heaton, *Story of a Page*, chs. xvi, xvii; F. C. Howe, *Confessions of a Reformer* (1925), chs. xi–xxiv; T. L. Johnson, *My Story*, chs. xii–xxv; R. M. La Follette, *Autobiography* (1913), chs. vi–viii; Lane, *Letters*, ch. iii; Fremont Older, *My Own Story* (1919); Roosevelt, *Autobiography*, ch. viii; C. E. Russell, *Bare Hands and Stone Walls* (1933), chs. ix, xii, xiii; Steffens, *Autobiography*; Whitlock, *Forty Years of It*, chs. xxii–l; Woodrow Wilson, *Public Papers*, II.

Bibliography — Flick, *History of New York*, VIII, 268; Goldman, *Rendezvous with Destiny*, 476; E. W. Stirn, *Annotated Bibliography of Robert M. La Follette* (1937).

232. CONSERVATION

Summary — Termination of free land era; first efforts at conservation (§§ 199, 207–08); economic pressures (§§ 226, 227). — Rushes to newly opened Indian reservations; migration to Canadian Northwest. — Irrigation and reclamation in Utah and the arid Southwest. — Theodore Roosevelt's policy: 1898, Gifford Pinchot, Chief of Division of Forestry; 1901, Dec. 3, message; 1902, Newlands Reclamation Act; 1904, Kinkaid Homestead Act; 1905, American Forestry Congress; Forestry Service. — 1907, extension of forest reserves; public land convention; Inland Waterways Commission. — 1908, Lakes to Gulf Deep Waterways Convention; White House conferences of governors on conservation. — 1909, Jan., report of Conservation Commission presented to Congress; Feb., North American Conservation Conference; Mar. 3, National Waterways Commission act; land frauds; Appalachian Reserve bills. — Taft's policy; 1909, Lakes to Gulf Deep Waterways Convention; National Conservation Congress; Land Classification Board; Pinchot's attack on Secretary of Interior Ballinger (§ 234); Alaska Coal Lands, Cunningham claim, L. R. Glavis; 1910, conservation message, land act providing for entry of surface and reservation of minerals, Reclamation Certificates Act, withdrawal Act; 1911, Conservation of Navigable Waters Act; Grazing Homestead Act.

General — Robbins, *Our Landed Heritage*, chs. xix–xxiv; Loomis Havemeyer, *et al.*, eds., *Conservation of Our Natural Resources* (1936); Stuart Chase, *Tragedy of Waste* (1925), and *Rich Land, Poor Land* (1936); G. E. Mowry, *Theodore Roosevelt and Progressive Movement* (1946), ch. iii; Pringle, *Theodore Roosevelt*, bk. 2; Baker, *Woodrow Wilson*, VI, ch. iv; Gifford Pinchot, "How Conservation Began," *Ag. Hist.*, XI (1937), 255; Ogg, *National Progress*, ch. vi.

Special — Land: Hibbard, *Public Land Policies*, chs. xii, xiii; Peffer, *Closing Public Domain*; Marion Clawson, "Administration of Federal Range Lands," *Quar. Jour. of Econ.*, LIII (1939), 435; J. H. Anderson, "Jurisdiction over Federal Lands within the States," *No. Car. Law Rev.*, VII (1929), 299; F. M. Blackmer, "West, Water, and Grazing Laws," *Survey Graphic*, XXVI (1937), 387. ❡ Forests: Ise, *Forest Policy*, chs. iv–xi; Cameron, *Forest Control*, chs. ix, x; H. A. Smith, "Early Forestry Movement in United States," *Ag. Hist.*, XII (1938), 326. ❡ Oil: Ise, *Oil Policy*. ❡ Reclamation: A. R. Golzé, *Reclamation in United States* (1952), ch. i; G. W. James, *Reclaiming Arid West* (1917); Smythe, *Arid America*; R. P. Teele, "Land Reclamation Policies," Dept. Ag., *Dept. Bull.*, No. 1257 (1924); Dorothy Lampen, *Economic and Social Aspects of Federal Reclamation* (1930); F. W. Blackmar, "Mastery of Desert," *No. Am. Rev.*, CLXXXII (1906), 676; R. M. Boening, "History of Irrigation in Washington," *Wash. Hist. Quar.*, IX (1918), 259, X (1919), 21; J. T. Ganoe, "Desert Act since 1891," *Ag. Hist.*, XI (1937), 266, and "Origin of Reclamation Policy," 34. ❡ Ballinger-Pinchot Controversy: A. T. Mason, *Brandeis*, ch. xvii, and *Bureaucracy Convicts Itself* (1941); H. L. Ickes, "Not Guilty! Richard A. Ballinger," *Sat. Eve. Post*, CCXII (May 25, 1940), No. 48, p. 9; K. W. Hechler, *Insurgency* (1940), ch. vii; Pringle, *Taft*, I, chs. xxv–xxvii; Matthew Josephson, *President Makers* (1940), ch. x; Filler, *Crusaders*, ch. xxvi. ❡ Maps: Paullin, *Atlas*, plates 59, 96.

Sources — Government Documents: Henry Gannett, "Report of National Conservation Commission," 60 Cong., 2 Sess., *Sen. Doc.*, No. 676 (3 vols., 1909); "Hearings before Committee of Investigation of Interior Department and Bureau of Forestry," 61 Cong., 3 Sess., *Sen. Doc.*, No. 719. ❡ Contemporary Works: Am. Forest Congress, *Proc.* (1905); Gifford Pinchot, *Fight for Conservation* (1910), and *Breaking New Ground*, chs. xii–xxxvi, xli–xc. ❡ Personal Accounts: Newlands, *Public Papers*, I, ch. ii–v; Roosevelt, *Autobiography*, ch. xi, and *Works*, XVIII. ❡ Other Collections: Manning, Potter, Davies, *Select Problems*, II, ch. v.

Bibliography — Robbins, *Our Landed Heritage*.

233. REGULATION OF ECONOMIC ACTIVITIES

Summary — Problems of concentration and control: railroad combinations; rise of trusts, Standard Oil, high finance, Wall Street groups; banking alliances (§ 227); Supreme Court limitation of Sherman Act (§ 210); state regulation (§ 231); 1901, United States Steel Corporation. — Regulation of trusts: 1902, Industrial Commission report; Theodore Roosevelt's policy; 1903, Bureau of Corporations; 1904–07, prosecutions; "immunity investigations"; 1907, Act forbidding corporation political contributions; Tennessee Coal and Iron affair; 1909, telephone merger; Sugar trust scandal; 1909–10, Taft prosecutions; 1911, Supreme Court dissolution of American Tobacco and Standard Oil; rule of reason. — Railroad policy: 1902, Interstate Commerce Commission, report on rebates; 1903, Elkins Anti-rebate act; Harriman's railroad purchases; 1904, Mar. 14, dissolution of

Northern Securities; 1906, June 29, Hepburn Railway Rate act, commodities clause; 1910, Mann-Elkins Railway act. — Banking and Currency: panic of 1907 (§ 227); 1908, Aldrich-Vreeland, Emergency Currency Act; National Monetary Commission; other efforts at reform; 1910, Postal Savings Bank Act. — Tariff: demands for revision; 1908, campaign pledges; 1909, Payne-Aldrich Act, special session, bill, presented, limitation of amendments, passage in House, protective amendments in Senate; attacks by Middle Western "Insurgent Republicans"; log-rolling, "jokers," passage in Senate, non-concurrence of House, presidential influence, enactment, provision for Tariff Commission; problems of maximum and minimum clause; Canadian reciprocity; 1911, extra session to consider reciprocity; July 26, reciprocity act; rejected by Canada (§ 239). — Food Inspection: 1906, Meat Inspection Act, Pure Food Act. — Income tax. — Political aspects (§ 234). — Later developments (§ 235).

General — Faulkner, *Quest for Social Justice*, ch. v, and *Decline of Laissez Faire*, chs. viii, ix, xv; E. F. Humphrey, *Economic History* (1931), ch. xli; Dewey, *Financial History*, ch. xxi; Pringle, *Taft*, II, chs. xxxiv, xxxvii, and *Roosevelt*, bk. 2; Mason, *Brandeis*, chs. xx–xxii; Hechler, *Insurgency*, chs. vi, viii; De Witt, *Progressive Movement*, chs. vii–ix; Sullivan, *Our Times*, II, chs. xvii, xix, xxvi, xxvii, III, ch. vii; Ogg, *National Progress*, chs. ii–iv; Filler, *Crusaders*, chs. ix, xiv–xviii.

Special — Trusts in General: Ripley, *Trusts, Pools, and Corporations*; M. N. Nelson, *Open Price Associations* (1922); A. R. Burns, *Decline of Competition* (1932); Knauth, *Policy of United States towards Industrial Monopoly* (1914); Jenks and Clark, *Trust Problem*; Eliot Jones, *Trust Problem* (1921); Seager and Gulick, *Trust and Corporation Problems*; John Moody, *Truth about Trusts* (1904); J. B. and J. M. Clark, *Control of Trusts* (1912); M. W. Watkins, *Industrial Combinations and Public Policy* (1927); E. D. Durand, *Trust Problems* (1915); J. C. Bonbright and G. C. Means, *Holding Company* (1932); A. S. Dewing, *Corporate Promotions*, and *Financial Policy of Corporations* (1934); E. S. Mead, *Trust Finance* (1903); W. H. S. Stevens, *Unfair Competition* (1917); Stephenson, *Aldrich*, ch. xxi; Mowry, *Roosevelt and Progressive Movement*, ch. ii; David Bryn-Jones, *Frank B. Kellogg* (1937), chs. v–vi. ❡ Particular Trusts: Eliot Jones, *Anthracite Coal Combination*; Mussey, *Combination in Mining*; E. H. Davenport and S. R. Cooke, *Oil Trusts* (1924); Nevins, *Rockefeller*, II, chs. xlvi–xlvii. ❡ Railroads: F. H. Dixon, *Railroads and Government* (1922); W. Z. Ripley, *Railroads: Rates and Regulations*, and *Railroads: Finance and Organization* (1915); J. I. Bogen, *Anthracite Railroads* (1927); J. C. Bonbright, *Railroad Capitalization* (1920); Sharfman, *Interstate Commerce Commission*; F. H. Dixon, "Mann-Elkins Act," *Quar. Jour. Econ.*, XXIV (1910), 593; Kennan, *Harriman*, chs. xx, xxii, xxv–xxviii; B. H. Meyer, *History of the Northern Securities Case* (1906). ❡ Banking and Currency: J. L. Laughlin, *Federal Reserve Act* (1933), chs. i–v; E. W. Kemmerer, *Postal Savings* (1917); Lamont, *Davison*, ch. xii. ❡ Tariff: Taussig, *Tariff History*, ch. viii; Bowers, *Beveridge*, bk. 4, ch. iii; U. S. Tariff Commission, *Reciprocity* (1919); S. K. Hornbeck, *Most Favored Nation Clause* (1910). ❡ Maps: Paullin, *Atlas*, plate 120.

Sources — Government Documents: *Congressional Record*; "Shipping Trust," 62 Cong., H. Joint Res., 72, H. Res. 587, *Hearings* (5 vols., 1912–14); "Trust Legislation," 63 Cong., 2 Sess., H. Committee on Judiciary, *Hearings* (4 vols., 1914); Northern Securities Co. *v.* United States, 193 U.S., 197; Swift and Company *v.* United States, 196 U.S., 375; United States *v.* Standard Oil Company, 221 U.S., 1; United States *v.* American Tobacco Company, 221 U.S., 106; Commissioner of Corporations, *Report on Beef Industry* (1905), and *Report on Freight Rates in Oil* (1906), and *Report on Petroleum Industry* (2 vols., 1907), and *Report on Prices of Tobacco* (1909), and *Report on Tobacco Industry* (3 vols., 1911–13), and *Report on Steel Industry* (3 vols., 1911–13), and *Report on International Harvester Corporation* (1913), and *Report on Trust Laws* (1913); Federal Trade Commission, *Reports*; Industrial Commission, *Preliminary Report on Trusts* (2 vols., 1900–01); Interstate Commerce Commission, *Annual Report*, and (Bur. Stat.), *Interstate Commerce Commission Activities* (1937), chs. ii–viii; Merchant Marine Commission, *Report* (1905); U.S. *v.* American Asiatic Steamship Co. (testimony, 3 vols., 1913–14); U.S. *v.* Hamburg-Amerikanische P-A., *et al.* (testimony, 1913). ❡ Contemporary Works: L. D. Brandeis, *Other People's Money* (1913); Bridge, *Trust: Its Book*; W. M. Collier, *Trusts* (1900); R. T. Ely, *Monopolies and Trusts* (1900); Frank Parsons, *Heart of Railroad Problem* (1906); E. A. Ross, *Sin and Society* (1907), chs. v, vi; Upton Sinclair, *Jungle* (1906); C. R. Van Hise, *Concentration and Control* (r. ed., 1914). ❧ Personal Accounts: A. W. Dunn, *From Harrison to Harding* (1922), II, ch. i; Foraker, *Notes*, II, chs. xl, xliv, xlv; Lane, *Letters*, ch. iv; Lodge and Roosevelt, *Correspondence*, II; Newlands, *Public Papers*, I, chs. xi–xiii, II, chs. xv, xvii, xix, xxi; Roosevelt, *Autobiography*, chs. xii, xiii, and *Letters*, III, IV, and *Works*, XVIII; H. W. Wiley, *Autobiography* (1930), chs. xvi–xxi.

Bibliography — H. H. B. Meyer, comp., *List on Federal Control of Commerce and Corporations* (3 ed., 1913), and *List on Federal Control: Special Aspects* (1914); Leisa Bronson, comp., *Cartels and International Patent Agreements* (1943); W. C. Mitchell, "Publications of the National Monetary Commission," *Quar. Jour. Econ.*, XXV (1911), 563.

234. REFORM IN NATIONAL POLITICS

Summary — Election of 1900: Republican convention, McKinley and Roosevelt nominated, "full-dinner pail"; Democratic convention, Bryan nominated; anti-imperialism; Populists; Socialists; Republican success. — 1901, Sept., McKinley assassinated; accession of Roosevelt; traits and prior career. — First administration: labor issues (§ 228); 1901–03, Panama question (§ 238); other diplomatic issues (§§ 236–9). — Campaign of 1904: Roosevelt renominated; Democratic convention, Parker nominated, omission of money and income tax planks, Parker's gold-standard telegram; trust issue; corporation contributions; election of Roosevelt; Democratic governors. — 1905–07, investigations and suits (§§ 231, 233); regulatory legislation (§ 233); postal and land frauds investigations; governmental reorganization; conservation (§ 232); panic of 1907 (§ 227); business reaction against administration. — Campaign of 1908: Republicans nominate Taft, Roosevelt's influence, La Follette's rejected platform; Democrats nominate Bryan; minor parties; election of Taft. — 1909, extra session, income tax amendment submitted, tariff (§ 233); Ballinger-Pinchot dispute (§ 232). — Insurgency: control of Aldrich, Cannon; La Follette's roll call tactics; 1910, March 19, Speaker Cannon overruled by Progressives and Democrats; rules question; program of Progressives; 1910, Mann-Elkins Interstate Commerce act (§ 233), Commerce Court; enabling act for New Mexico and Arizona; Publicity of Campaign Contributions act. — Campaign of 1910: high cost of living (§ 226); Democratic House; Progressives' balance of power in Senate; increased Socialistic vote; state elections Democratic. — 1912, Parcel Post. — Organization of Progressive Party: 1910, "New Nationalism"; Ossawatomie Speech; 1911, National Progressive Republican League. — 1912 election (§ 235).

General — Sullivan, *Our Times*, I, chs. iv–vii, xiii, II, chs. xiii, xx–xxv, III, chs. i–viii, IV, chs. xii–xxi; Josephson, *President Makers*, chs. i–ix; Stanwood, *Presidency*, II, chs. i–iii; Binkley, *American Political Parties*, ch. xiv; Goldman, *Rendezvous with Destiny*, ch. x; Pollard, *Presidents and the Press*, 569, 601; Robinson, *Presidential Vote*; Bowers, *Beveridge*, bks. 3, 4; Hechler, *Insurgency*, chs. iii–xiii; Ogg, *National Progress*, chs. i, viii; Regier, *Muckrakers*, chs. viii–xv; Filler, *Crusaders*, chs. iv, xxiv–xxix.

Special — Theodore Roosevelt: Hofstadter, *American Political Tradition*, ch. ix; Pringle, *Theodore Roosevelt*, bk. 1, ch. xvi, bk. 2, bk. 3, chs. i–v; Shaw, *Cartoon History of Roosevelt's Career*, chs. xvii, xviii; Mowry, *Roosevelt and Progressive Movement*, ch. i. ❧ Constitutional Questions: Kelly and Harbison, *American Constitution*, chs. xx, xxii, xxiii; Boudin, *Government by Judiciary*, II, chs. xxvii–xxxviii; Gustavus Myers, *History of Supreme Court* (1912), chs. xv–xviii; Walker, *Sherman Law*, chs. viii, ix; F. B. Clark, *Constitutional Doctrines of Justice Harlan* (1915), chs. iii–vi. ❧ Other Issues: § 225; Harrington, "Anti-Imperialist Movement," and "Literary Aspects of Anti-Imperialism," 650; T. A. Bailey, "Was the Election of 1900 a Mandate on Imperialism?" *Miss. Valley Hist. Rev.*, XXIV (1937), 43; Ratner, *American Taxation*, chs. xii, xiii; Humphrey, *Economic History*, chs. xlii, xliii. ❧ Biographies: Stephenson, *Aldrich*, chs. xiii–xx; Acheson,

Bailey, chs. xii–xviii; Werner, *Bryan*, ch. iv; Busbey, *Cannon*, chs. x–xii; Croly, *Hanna*, chs. xxi–xxiii, xxvi; Bent, *Holmes*, chs. xiv, xv; Bryn-Jones, *Kellogg*, ch. viii; Alfred Lief, *Democracy's Norris* (1939), chs. iii–v; Jessup, *Root*, I, ch. xii, II, chs. xxxii–xxxix; Pringle, *Taft*, I, chs. xvii–xxix, II, chs. xxx, xxxiv, xxxvii. ❡ Maps: Paullin, *Atlas*, plates 109–110.

Sources — *Congressional Record*; public documents (§ 45). ❡ Personal Materials: Baker, *American Chronicle*, chs. xxi, xxvii, xxviii; Butler, *Across Busy Years*, I, ch. x; Bryan, *Memoirs*, pt. 1, chs. vii, ix; A. W. Butt, *Taft and Roosevelt Intimate Letters* (2 vols., 1930); Champ Clark, *My Quarter Century*, II, chs. xi, xxi, xxii, xxvii; Dunn, *Harrison to Harding*, I, chs. xxi–xxiv, II, chs. iii–vi, ix; Foraker, *Notes*, II, chs. xxxix; Gompers, *Seventy Years*, II, chs. xxxiv–xxxv; Heaton, *Story of a Page*, ch. xv; La Follette, *Autobiography*, chs. ix–x; Lodge and Roosevelt, *Correspondence*, II; Norris, *Fighting Liberal*, chs. x–xviii; Roosevelt, *Autobiography*, ch. x, and *Works*, XVII, XVIII, and *Letters*, III–VI; Straus, *Under Four Administrations*, chs. vi–xii; J. E. Watson, *As I Knew Them* (1936), chs. i–iv; W. A. White, *Autobiography*, chs. xlvi–li. ❡ Newspapers: (§ 53); *Literary Digest*; other magazines (§ 52); *New International Year Book* (1908–12); *American Year Book* (1911–12).

Bibliography — Hofstadter, *American Political Tradition*, 368; Goldman, *Rendezvous with Destiny*, 481; Hechler, *Insurgency*, 227.

235. THE NEW FREEDOM

Summary — Election of 1912: division in Republican Party, Taft nominated; Progressive Party, La Follette, Roosevelt nominated; Baltimore Democratic convention, influence of Bryan, Tammany issue, Wilson nominated; Socialists, E. V. Debs; campaign; Wilson elected. — Organization of the administration: character and ideas of Wilson; cabinet; Colonel E. M. House; role of Bryan; political considerations; Brandeis in Supreme Court. — Finance (§ 233): Pujo Committee revelations; 1913, Federal Reserve Act; 1916, Federal Farm Loan Act; 1909–13, income tax (Sixteenth Amendment); 1914, Underwood Tariff. — Trusts: Clayton Act; Federal Trade Commission; Railroad regulation. — Labor legislation: § 228; Clayton Act provisions; Seamen's Act; Adamson eight-hour railroad act. — 1913, Seventeenth Amendment, popular election of senators. — Conservation measures (§ 232). — Election of 1916 (§ 240).

General — Ogg, *National Progress*, chs. xi–xiii, xix; Sullivan, *Our Times*, IV, chs. xxii–xxix; Binkley, *Powers of President*, ch. xi; Stanwood, *Presidency*, II, ch. iv; Kelly and Harbison, *American Constitution*, ch. xxiv; Pollard, *Presidents and Press*, 630; Josephson, *President Makers*, chs. xi–xv; Paxson, *American Democracy and World War*, I, chs. i–vii; Humphrey, *Economic History*, ch. xliii; Stein, *Third Term Tradition*, ch. viii.

Special — Woodrow Wilson: Link, *Wilson*, chs. x–xv; Baker, *Woodrow Wilson*, I, II, III, chs. iv–vii, IV, chs. i, iii–v, vii, VI, ch. iv; Hofstadter, *American Political Tradition*, ch. x; Bell, *Woodrow Wilson*, chs. vi, vii; William Diamond, *Economic Thought of Woodrow Wilson* (1943); Kerney, *Wilson*, chs. ix–xi, xiv–xxiii; Tumulty, *Wilson*, chs. xiv–xix, xxii–xxiv; Harley Notter, *Origin of Foreign Policy of Woodrow Wilson* (1937), chs. i–v. ❡ Other Biographies: Stephenson, *Aldrich*, chs. xxii–xxiii; Acheson, *Bailey*, chs. xix–xxi; Bowers, *Beveridge*, bk. 4, ch. vii; Mason, *Brandeis*, chs. xxiii–xxvii, xxx–xxxiii; Werner, *Bryan*, chs. v, vi; J. C. Long, *Bryan* (1928), chs. xii–xv; Fitzpatrick, *McCarthy of Wisconsin*, ch. xii; Nicolson, *Morrow*, chs. vii, viii; Lief, *Democracy's Norris*, chs. vi, vii; Hendrick, *Page*, I, chs. iii, iv; Mowry, *Roosevelt and Progressive Movement*, chs. iv–xi; Pringle, *Roosevelt*, bk. 3, ch. v, and *Taft*, I, chs. xxxix–xliv; Blum, *Tumulty*, chs. iv–vi, viii. ❡ Economic Controls: Taus, *Central Banking Functions*, ch. vi; Hepburn, *History of Currency*, chs. xxiii, xxv; P. M. Warburg, *Federal Reserve System* (2 vols., 1930); H. P. Willis, *Federal Reserve System* (1923); Laughlin, *Federal Reserve Act*, ch. viii; S. E. Harris, *Twenty Years of Federal Reserve Policy* (2 vols., 1933), I; Noyes, *War Period of American Finance*, ch. i; Lamont, *Davison*, chs. ix, xii; Corey, *House of Morgan*, chs. xxxi–xxxiii; Benedict, *Farm Policies*, ch. viii; E. S. Sparks, *History and Theory of Agricultural Credit* (1932), ch. vii; Clara Eliot, *Farmer's Campaign for Credit* (1927), chs. i–v; E. R. A. Seligman, *Economics of Farm Relief* (1929); Ivan Wright, *Bank Credit, and Farm Mortgage Financing* (1923), chs. i–v; R. J. Bulkley, "Federal Farm Loan Act," *Jour. Pol. Econ.*, XXV (1917), 129; T. C. Blaisdell, *Federal Trade Commission* (1932); G. C. Henderson, *Federal Trade Commission* (1925). ❡ Taxation: Taussig, *Tariff History*, ch. ix; Seligman, *Income Tax*; Ratner, *American Taxation*, chs. xiv, xv. ❡ Labor: Harvey, *Gompers*, ch. xiii. ❡ Maps: Paullin, *Atlas*, plates 110, 120.

Sources — Government Publications: *Congressional Record*; 38 *Statutes at Large*, 273, 730; 39 *Statutes at Large*, 360, 721; Wilson *v.* New, 243 U.S., 332; H. Committee on Banking and Currency, *Money Trust Investigation* (3 vols., 1913); Federal Trade Commission, *Trust Laws* (1915), and *Pipe Line Transportation of Petroleum* (1916), and *Newsprint Paper Industry* (1917), and *Book Paper Industry* (1917), and *Coal* (1917). ❡ Personal Material: Baker, *American Chronicle*, chs. xxix–xxxi; Belmont, *American Democrat*, ch. xviii; Champ Clark, *My Quarter Century*, ch. xxviii; Josephus Daniels, *Wilson Era* (2 vols., 1944–46), I, chs. i–xiv, xx, xxi, xliv; Dunn, *Harrison to Harding*, II, chs. xii–xvi; E. E. Garrison, *Roosevelt, Wilson and Federal Reserve Law* (1931); Carter Glass, *Adventures in Constructive Finance* (1927); Gompers, *Seventy Years*, II, ch. xxxvi; House, *Intimate Papers*, I, chs. i, ii, iv–vi; D. F. Houston, *Eight Years with Wilson's Cabinet* (2 vols., 1926), I, chs. i–vii, x–xiii; Howe, *Holmes-Pollock Letters*, I, ch. v; H. L. Ickes, "Who Killed the Progressive Party?" *Am. Hist. Rev.*, XLVI (1941), 306, and *Autobiography*; La Follette, *Autobiography*, chs. xi–xiii; McAdoo, *Crowded Years*; Newlands, *Public Papers*, II, chs. xiv, xvi, xviii, xx–xxiv; D. R. Richberg, *Tents of Mighty* (1930), chs. i–ii; Roosevelt, *Letters*, V, VI, and *Works*, XIX; Villard, *Fighting Years*, chs. xiii–xiv; Watson, *As I Knew Them*, chs. v–vi; W. A. White, *Autobiography*, chs. lxi–lxx; Woodrow Wilson, *Public Papers*, I, III, IV, and *Selected Literary and Political Papers*, I–III. ❡ Contemporary Accounts: W. J. Bryan, *Tale of Two Conventions* (1912), and *Memoirs*, pt. 1, ch. x; Butt, *Taft and Roosevelt*, II, chs. liii–lix, xci–xciii; Lane, *Letters*, ch. v, vi; Theodore Roosevelt, *New Nationalism* (1910); Woodrow Wilson, *New Freedom* (1913). ❡ Magazines: §§ 52, 230; *New Republic* (1914–18); *Current History* (1914–18). — *American Year Book* (1912–19).

Bibliography — Hofstadter, *American Political Tradition*, 370; L. S. Turnbull, comp., *Woodrow Wilson, a Selected Bibliography* (1948).

Chapter Twenty-six

THE DIPLOMACY OF EXPANSION, 1900–1917

236. TERRITORIAL RESPONSIBILITIES

Summary — Conceptions of imperialism, manifest destiny (§§ 153, 168, 220, 225); navalism. — Acquisitions (§§ 221, 225). — Constitutional relations to United States: 1900, Puerto Rico Tariff act; 1901, Insular cases; 1902, Philippine Tariff act; question of citizenship. — Cuba (§ 238). — Philippines: revolt of Aguinaldo, 1899; military operations; restoration of order; government by commissions; Taft's role; 1901, Spooner amendment; 1902, Organic Act; 1903, Friar's Lands Agreement; 1907, general election, first assembly; 1916, Jones Act. — Alaska: development (§ 226); boundary dispute (§ 239). — Hawaii: 1900, territorial government. — Puerto Rico: 1900, territorial government (Foraker Act). — Wilson's policy; 1917, acquisition of Virgin Islands. — Guam; Samoa; Canal Zone.

General — J. W. Pratt, *America's Colonial Experiment* (1950), chs. iii, v–vii; W. H. Haas, ed., *American Empire* (1940); Bailey, *Diplomatic History*, chs. xxxiii, xxxv; Bemis, *American Secretaries of State*, IX, 325, and *Diplomatic History*, chs. xxvi, xxvii; Sullivan, *Our Times*, I, chs. xx, xxi; Faulkner, *Quest for Social Justice*, ch. xiii; Kirkland, *American Economic Life*, ch. xvii; B. H. Williams, *Economic Foreign Policy*; D. Y. Thomas, *Military Government*, bk. 3; W. F. Willoughby, *Territories and Dependencies of United States*, (1905), chs. iii–ix; W. W. Willoughby, *Constitutional Law*, I, chs. xxvii–xxxi; Hofstadter, *Social Darwinism*, ch. ix; Westcott, *American Sea Power*, chs. xvi–xix; Sprout, *Rise of American Naval Power*, chs. xv–xvii; Scott Nearing and Joseph Freeman, *Dollar Diplomacy* (1925), chs. i, ii, vii, ix.

Special — Local histories by place (§ 62). ❡ Philippines: J. R. Hayden, *Philippines* (1942); D. C. Worcester, *Philippines* (1914); J. S. Reyes, *Legislative History of American Economic Policy toward Philippines* (1923); W. C. Forbes, *Philippine Islands* (2 vols., 1928); J. H. Blount, *American Occupation* (1912), chs. xii–xxix; Moorfield Storey and M. P. Lichanco, *Conquest of Philippines 1898–1925* (1926); C. B. Elliott, *Philippines* (1916–17), I, chs. xvii–xviii, II; C. H. Forbes-Lindsay, *Philippines under Spanish and American Rules* (1906); H. P. Willis, *Our Philippine Problem* (1905); John Foreman, *Philippine Islands* (1906), chs. xvi–xx, xxiv–xxxi; F. B. Harrison, *Cornerstone of Philippine Independence* (1922). ❡ Alaska: § 226; H. W. Clark, *Alaska*. ❡ Virgin Islands: Tansill, *Purchase of Danish West Indies*. ❡ Puerto Rico: Knowlton Mixer, *Porto Rico* (1926), ch. v; B. W. and J. W. Diffie, *Porto Rico* (1931), chs. iii–viii. ❡ Biographies: Bowers, *Beveridge*, pt. 2; Frederick Palmer, *Bliss Peacemaker* (1934), ch. ix; Kennan, *Harriman*, I, ch. vii; Dennett, *Hay*, ch. xvii; Taylor, *Mahan*; Cortissoz, *Reid*, ch. xiv; Jessup, *Root*, I, chs. xvi–xviii; Morison, *Sims*, chs. vi–xviii; Pringle, *Taft*, I, chs. xi–xiv; Baker, *Woodrow Wilson*, IV, chs. ii, viii. ❡ Maps: Paullin, *Atlas*, plate 96.

Sources — *Congressional Record*; Interior Dept., *Annual Report*; *Philippine Census* (4 vols., 1903; 4 vols., 1918); Philippine Commission, *Report* (4 vols., 1900; 4 vols.,

1905), and *Journal* (6 vols., 1906–13); "Special Report of William H. Taft on Philippines," 60 Cong., 1 Sess., *Sen. Doc.*, VII, No. 200; Secretary of War, *Annual Report*. ❡ Contemporary Tracts: Brooks Adams, *America's Economic Supremacy* (1900; M. W. Childs, ed., 1947), and *New Empire* (1902); Edward Atkinson, *Cost of War* (1902); F. H. Giddings, *Democracy and Empire* (1900), ch. xvii; J. B. Moore, *Collected Papers* (1944), III; A. B. Shaw, *Political Problems of American Development* (1907); Moorfield Storey, *What Shall We Do about Our Dependencies?* (1903); Josiah Strong, *Expansion under New World Conditions* (1900). ❡ Contemporary Accounts: A. C. Harris, *Alaska and Klondike* (1897); D. C. Worcester, *Philippine Islands* (1898); Mrs. Campbell Dauncey, *Englishwoman in Philippines* (1906); L. S. Rowe, *United States and Porto Rico* (1904). ❡ Personal Material: Larz Anderson, *Letters and Journals* (1940), ch. xi; Daniels, *Wilson Era*, I, chs. xv, xvii, xxii–xliii; Foraker, *Notes*, II, chs. xxxiii, xxxviii; Lodge and Roosevelt, *Correspondence*, II; Newlands, *Public Papers*, I, chs. vi, ix; Roosevelt, *Works*, XVIII; Seward, *Reminiscences*, 455; Woodrow Wilson, *Public Papers*, III, IV, 415. ❡ Periodicals: *Current History* (1914–20); *Literary Digest* (1900–20); other magazines (§ 52); newspapers (§ 53).

Bibliography — Pratt, *America's Colonial Experiment*, 391.

237. INTERESTS IN THE ORIENT, 1900–1917

Summary — Earlier relations (§ 221); — China: Chinese boycotts; 1899, Hay, "Open Door" and integrity of China; 1900, Boxer insurrection; indemnity; 1903, Chinese commercial treaty; problems of Chinese loans, concessions, railroads; 1909, Shanghai Opium Conference. — 1904–05, Russo-Japanese War; 1905, Sept. 5, Peace of Portsmouth. — Japanese relations: 1906–07, San Francisco school question; 1907, Gentlemen's Agreement, compromise immigrant act; cruise of the American fleet into Pacific; 1908, Root-Takahira Agreement; 1910, consortium; 1913, California alien land legislation; 1914, Japanese demands on China. — Later developments (§§ 243, 250).

General — Bailey, *Diplomatic History*, chs. xxxiii–xxxv; Bemis, *American Secretaries of State*, IX, 325, and *Diplomatic History*, ch. xxvii; Griswold, *Far Eastern Policy*, chs. ii–iv; Ogg, *National Progress*, chs. xvii; Nearing and Freeman, *Dollar Diplomacy*, ch. iii; Dennis, *Adventures in Diplomacy*, chs. viii–x, xiii, xiv.

Special — China: J. G. Reid, *Manchu Abdication and the Powers* (1935); W. L. Langer, *Diplomacy of Imperialism* (1951), ch. xxi; S. C. Y. Pan, *American Diplomacy Concerning Manchuria* (1938); Shii-lun Pan, *Trade with China* (1924); F. V. Field, *American Participation in China Consortiums* (1931); G. A. Finch, "American Diplomacy and Financing China," *Am. Jour. Int. Law*, XVI (1922), 25; C. F. Remer, *Foreign Investments in China* (1933), and *Foreign Trade of China* (1926); M. C. Hsu, *Railway Problems* (1915). ❡ Russo-Japanese War: Tyler Dennett, *Roosevelt and Russo-Japanese War* (1925); W. B. Thorson, "American Opinion and Portsmouth Conference," *Am. Hist. Rev.*, LIII (1948), 439. ❡ Japan: P. J. Treat, *Japan and United States, 1853–1921* (1921), chs. ix, x, and *Diplomatic Relations between United States and Japan*, chs. vi–xiv; F. R. Dulles, *Forty Years of American-Japanese Relations* (1937), chs. i–vi; O. J. Clinard, *Japan's Influence on American Naval Power* (1947), chs. i–iv; Eleanor Tupper and G. E. McReynolds, *Japan in American Opinion* (1937), chs. i–iii; T. A. Bailey, *Theodore Roosevelt and Japanese-American Crises* (1934), and "Root-Takahira Agreement of 1908," *Pacific Hist. Rev.*, IX (1940), 19. ❡ Biographies: Lamont, *Davison*, ch. xiii; Kennan, *Harriman*, II, ch. xviii; Dennett, *Hay*, chs. xxiii–xxvi; Jessup, *Root*, II, chs. xxvii–xxviii; Pringle, *Roosevelt*, bk. 2, chs. viii–x; H. D. Croly, *Willard Straight* (1924); Pringle, *Taft*, II, ch. xxxvi; Nevins, *Henry White*, ch. xi; Baker, *Woodrow Wilson*, IV, ch. ii; Tien-Yi Li, *Woodrow Wilson's China Policy* (1952). ❡ Other aspects: L. M. Gelber, *Rise of Anglo-American Friendship 1898–1906* (1938), ch. x; Vagts, *Deutschland und Vereinigten Staaten*, II, ch. xi; E. H. Zabriskie, *American-Russian Rivalry in Far East* (1946), chs. iv–vii.

Sources — Government Documents: *Congressional Record; Foreign Relations* (1900–

17); J. V. A. MacMurray, comp., *Treaties and Agreements Concerning China 1894–1919* (2 vols., 1921); Clyde, *United States Policy toward China*, chs. xxiii–xxxviii; Bartlett, *American Diplomacy*, ch. xxv. ❧ Personal Material: Anderson, *Letters and Journals*, chs. xii, xv, xvi; Daniels, *Wilson Era*, I, ch. xvi; Lodge and Roosevelt, *Correspondence*, II; Newlands, *Public Papers*, I, ch. ix; Roosevelt, *Letters*, IV–VI; A. D. White, *Autobiography*, II, ch. xlii. ❧ Periodicals: *Literary Digest* (1900–17); *Current History* (1914–17); §§ 52, 53; *American Year Book* (1910–17); *New International Year Book* (1907–17).

Bibliography — Bemis and Griffin, *Guide to Diplomatic History*, ch. xvii.

238. LATIN AMERICA

Summary — Earlier developments (§§ 220, 222). — Cuba: occupation; Governor Leonard Wood; 1901, Platt Amendment, Cuban Constitution; 1902, withdrawal of United States, reciprocity treaty; 1906, insurrection, intervention, Taft mission; 1912, 1917, incidents. — Canal diplomacy: 1901, Hay-Pauncefote treaty; 1902, Spooner canal act, purchase of French company; 1903, Hay-Herran treaty, rejected by Colombia; 1903, revolution in Panama, Roosevelt's action; relations with England (§ 239); building the canal (§ 226); question of tolls (§ 239). — Caribbean: Theodore Roosevelt, "Big Stick"; corollary to Monroe Doctrine; 1902, Venezuela incident, Drago Doctrine; relations to England, Germany (§ 239); Taft, dollar diplomacy; Wilson policy; 1904, Santo Domingo debt; 1907, Dominican Republic protectorate, 1916, marine intervention; 1910, Haiti, financial reorganization, 1914 marine occupation; 1914, Nicaragua treaty. — Mexico: 1910, revolution; 1912, Madero recognized; Huerta revolt; 1914, landing at Vera Cruz; 1916, Villa expedition; watchful waiting. — South America; 1905, Pan-American arbitration treaty. — Later developments (§ 250).

General — Ogg, *National Progress*, chs. xiv–xvi; Bemis, *Latin-American Policy of United States*, chs. ix–xi, and *American Secretaries of State*, IX, 325, and *Diplomatic History*, chs. xxviii–xxx; Bailey, *Diplomatic History*, chs. xxxii, xxxiii, xxxv, xxxvi; Dennis, *Adventures in Diplomacy*, chs. vii, x–xiii; Nearing and Freeman, *Dollar Diplomacy*, chs. iv–vi; Pratt, *America's Colonial Experiment*, chs. iii–iv; Perkins, *Monroe Doctrine, 1867–1907*, chs. v, vi; Dennett, *Hay*, chs. xxi–xxiii, xxviii, xxx; Hendrick, *Page*, I, chs. vi–viii; Pringle, *Roosevelt*, bk. 2, chs. v, vi; Shaw, *Cartoon History of Roosevelt's Career*, chs. xv, xvi; Jessup, *Root*, I, chs. xiv, xv, xxiii–xxv; Pringle, *Taft*, II, chs. xxxv, xxxvi; Blum, *Tumulty*, ch. vii; Nevins, *Henry White*, chs. x, xiii; Baker, *Woodrow Wilson*, IV, chs. ii, vi, viii, VI, ch. ii; Bell, *Woodrow Wilson*, chs. xx–xxi; Notter, *Foreign Policy of Wilson*, ch. v.

Special — Cuba: Jenks, *Cuban Colony*, chs. v–x; D. A. Lockmiller, *Magoon in Cuba* (1938); H. F. Guggenheim, *United States and Cuba* (1934); Robinson, *Cuba and Intervention*, chs. x–xxi; R. H. Fitzgibbon, *Cuba and United States* (1935), chs. i–vi. ❧ Canal Diplomacy: Mack, *Land Divided*, pt. 4; H. G. Miller, *Isthmian Highway* (1929); Philippe Bunau-Varilla, *Panama* (1914); Croly, *Hanna*, ch. xxiv; M. P. DuVal, *Cadiz to Cathay* (1940), chs. vi–xvii; W. F. Johnson, *Four Centuries of the Canal* (1907), chs. ix–xxi; Miner, *Fight for Panama Route*, chs. iii–xi; W. D. McCain, *United States and Panama* (1937), chs. i–ix; Parks, *Colombia and United States*, chs. xxiv–xxvii; Gorgas and Hendrick, *Gorgas*, chs. iv–viii; Bishop, *Goethals*. ❧ Caribbean: Perkins, *Hands Off*, chs. vi, vii; W. H. Callcott, *Caribbean Policy* (1942), chs. iii–ix; C. L. Jones, *Caribbean since 1900* (1936), chs. i–xvi; D. G. Munro, *United States and Caribbean* (1934); H. C. Hill, *Roosevelt and Caribbean* (1927); S. W. Livermore, "Theodore Roosevelt, Navy, and Venezuela," *Am. Hist. Rev.*, LI (1946), 452; Selig Adler, "Bryan and Wilsonian Caribbean Penetration," *Hispanic-Am. Hist. Rev.*, XX (1940), 198; H. P. Davis, *Black Democracy* (1936), pt. 2, chs. i–v; L. L. Montague, *Haiti and United States* (1940), chs. x–xiii; Welles, *Naboth's Vineyard*, II, chs. ix–xiv; C. D. Kepner and J. H. Soothill, *Banana Empire* (1935), chs. i–iv; Carl Kelsey, "American Intervention in Haiti," *Am. Ac. Pol. Soc. Sci.*, *Annals*, C (1922), 109; I. J. Cox, *Nicaragua and United States* (1927), chs. i, ii; H. N. Denny, *Dollars for Bullets* [Nicaragua] (1929); M. M. Knight, *Americans in Santo Domingo* (1928), ch. viii. ❧ Mexico: Carreño, *Diplomacia*, chs. xiv–xvi; Rippy,

United States and Mexico, chs. xix–xxi; Callahan, *American Foreign Policy in Mexican Relations*, ch. xiv; Edgar Turlington, *Mexico and Her Foreign Creditors* (1930); Gregg, *Border Troubles*; Palmer, *Bliss*, ch. xi; G. M. Stephenson, *John Lind* (1935), chs. xiv–xvii; Hicks, *Reed*, ch. vii. ❡ South America: M. A. Marsh, *Bankers in Bolivia* (1928); J. F. Rippy, *Capitalists and Colombia* (1931), chs. iv–vii; Hendrick, *Carnegie*, II, ch. vii. ❡ Other Aspects: Gelber, *Rise of Anglo-American Friendship*, ch. vi; Vagts, *Deutschland und Vereinigten Staaten*, II, chs. xii–xvi; Schieber, *American Sentiment toward Germany*, ch. iv.

Sources — Government Publications: *Congressional Record; Foreign Relations*; 58 Cong., 1 Sess., *H. Doc.*, I, No. 8, 2 Sess., *Sen. Doc.*, III, No. 95, IV, No. 143, V, No. 166, XV, 316, 3 Sess., *Sen. Doc.*, VII, 119; 59 Cong., 1 Sess., *Sen. Doc.*, XV, No. 231, 2 Sess., *Sen. Doc.*, V, No. 307, 401, XXIX, 533, XXX–XXXIII; 60 Cong., 2 Sess., *Sen. Doc.*, XX, No. 542; 63 Cong., 2 Sess., *Sen. Doc.*, No. 474; *Official Opinions of the Attorneys-General*, XXIV, 144; Isthmian Canal Commission, *Reports*. ❡ Other Collections: Gantenbein, *Latin-American Policy*, 59, 100, 359, 487, 504, 561, 600; Malloy, Redmond, Treworth, *Treaties, Conventions*, I, 782, II, 1349; Moore, *Digest of International Law*, VI, 586, § 962; VII, 140; Bartlett, *American Diplomacy*, ch. xxiv. ❡ Personal Materials: Creel, *Rebel at Large*, ch. xi; Daniels, *Wilson Era*, I, chs. xv, xviii, xix; Dunn, *Harrison to Harding*, chs. xi, xvii; Foraker, *Notes*, II, chs. xxxii, xxxvii, xli–xliii; Heaton, *Story of a Page*, ch. xix; House, *Intimate Papers*, I, chs. vii, viii; Lane, *Letters*, ch. viii; Lodge and Roosevelt, *Correspondence*, II; Moore, *Collected Papers*, III–V; Newlands, *Public Papers*, I, chs. vii, viii; Theodore Roosevelt, "How We Acquired the Panama Canal," *Outlook*, XCIX (1911), 314, and *Autobiography*, chs. xiv, xv, and *Letters*, III–VI; W. F. Sands and J. M. Lalley, *Our Jungle Diplomacy* (1944); Woodrow Wilson, *Public Papers*, III, IV, and *Selected Literary and Political Papers*, II. ❡ Periodicals: *Current History* (1914–20); *Literary Digest* (1900–20); §§ 52, 53; *New International Year Book* (1907–19); *American Year Book* (1910–19).

Bibliography — Bemis and Griffin, *Guide to Diplomatic History*; A. P. C. Griffin, *List on International Arbitration* (1908), 77, 114, 132; Morrison, *List Relating to Inter-oceanic Routes*.

239. EUROPE AND INTERNATIONAL PEACE, 1900–1914

Summary — Earlier developments (§§ 222–4). — Anglo-American relations; Hay-Pauncefote Treaty; American attitude in Boer War; 1909, Bryce-Root treaty on fisheries; 1910, Hague Tribunal decision; Canadian reciprocity; Panama tolls (§ 238); fisheries; economic ties. — Imperialism; navalism; 1903, Navy League (§ 230). — Alaska boundary dispute, fur seal issue; 1903, decision. — Peace movement; 1907–13, congresses; 1910, World Peace Foundation; 1907, Nobel Peace Prize; 1914, Carnegie Endowment; 1906, Algeciras Conference; 1899, 1907, Hague conferences; 1908–10, arbitration treaties. — Venezuela crisis and Drago Doctrine (§ 238). — Intercession on behalf of minorities, Jews in Rumania, Russia.

General — Bemis, *American Secretaries of State*, IX, X, and *Diplomatic History*, ch. xxxi; Paxson, *American Democracy and World War*, I, chs. iii, vii; Dennis, *Adventures in Diplomacy*, chs. v–vi, xv–xx.

Special — R. H. Heindel, *American Impact on Great Britain* (1940), chs. v–xv; Gelber, *Anglo-American Friendship*; Ferguson, *American Diplomacy and Boer War*; Langer, *Diplomacy of Imperialism*, chs. xviii, xx; F. A. Southard, *American Industry in Europe* (1931); Brebner, *North Atlantic Triangle*, chs. xiii, xiv; Keenleyside and Brown, *Canada and United States*; Herbert Marshall, *et al.*, *Canadian American Industry* (1936); W. G. Swartz, "Proposed Canadian-American Reciprocity Agreement of 1911," *Jour. Econ. and Bus. Hist.*, III (1930), 118; L. E. Ellis, *Reciprocity 1911* (1939); Tansill, *Canadian-American Relations*, chs. vi–xiv; Callahan, *American Foreign Policy in Canadian Relations*, chs. xi, xviii–xx; T. A. Bailey, "Theodore Roosevelt and Alaska Boundary Settlement," *Canadian Hist. Rev.*, XVIII (1937), 123, and "North Pacific Sealing Convention 1911,"

Pacific Hist. Rev., IV (1935), 1; Holt, *Treaties Defeated*, ch. ix; Vagts, *Deutschland und Vereinigten Staaten*, I, II, chs. xvii, xviii; Schieber, *American Sentiment toward Germany*, chs. v–vii; Allen, *Fight for Peace*; Merze Tate, *Disarmament Illusion* (1942), chs. xv–xvii; Curti, *Peace or War*, chs. v–vii; Scott, *Hague Peace Conferences*; J. W. Foster, *Arbitration and Hague Court* (1904); Adler and Margalith, *With Firmness in Right*, ch. ix; M. E. Curti, *Bryan and World Peace* (1931), chs. i, ii; Hendrick, *Carnegie*, II, ch. xiv; Dennett, *Hay*, chs. xviii–xxi, xxix–xxxiii; Cortissoz, *Reid*, xv–xxi; Jessup, *Root*, I, ch. xxix, II, chs. xxix–xxxi; Pringle, *Taft*, II, ch. xxxviii; Nevins, *Henry White*, chs. xii, xiv–xvii; Baker, *Woodrow Wilson*, IV, ch. ii; Notter, *Foreign Policy of Wilson*, ch. v.

Sources — Government Documents: *Congressional Record; Foreign Relations*; "North Atlantic Coast Fisheries Arbitration," 61 Cong., 3 Sess., *Sen. Doc.*, No. 870 (8 vols.); Alaskan Boundary Tribunal, *Proc.* (7 vols., 1904); Savage, *Policy of United States toward Maritime Commerce*, I, chs. xiv, xv; J. B. Scott, ed., *Text of Peace Conferences* (1908), and *Hague Conventions and Declarations* (1915), and *Reports to Hague Conferences* (1916; 1917), and *Proceedings of Hague Peace Conferences* (4 vols., 1920–21), and *American Addresses at Peace Conference* (1916).   ❡ Unofficial collections: *Brassey's Naval Annual* (1900–1914); *Jane's Fighting Ships* (1900–14); Bartlett, *American Diplomacy*, ch. xx; *American Year Book* (1910–14); *New International Year Book* (1907–14).   ❡ Personal Material: Carnegie, *Autobiography*, II, ch. xxi; Dunn, *Harrison to Harding*, ch. x; J. J. Jusserand, *What Befell Me* (1933), chs. x–xii; Robert Lansing, "North Atlantic Fisheries Arbitration," *Am. Jour. Int. Law*, V (1911), 1; Lodge and Roosevelt, *Correspondence*, II; Moore, *Collected Papers*, II–IV; Roosevelt, *Letters*, IV–VI; A. D. White, *Autobiography*, II, chs. xl, xliii, xlv–xlix; Woodrow Wilson, *Selected Literary and Political Papers*, I, 366.   ❡ Periodicals: *Literary Digest; Current History*.

Bibliography — Bemis and Griffin, *Guide to Diplomatic History*, chs. xvi, xx.

Chapter Twenty-seven

THE WORLD WAR

240. EUROPE'S WAR AND AMERICAN NEUTRALITY, 1914–1916

Summary — War in Europe; causes; development. — Neutrality: Wilson's attitude; Bryan; pacifists; Ford peace ship; war party, Theodore Roosevelt; ethnic groups, British, Irish, Germans; allied propaganda. — War relief, Belgium. — Preparedness. — Economic involvement; question of loans, Bryan's resignation, Lansing; munitions trade. — Incidents: doctrines of legal blockade; 1909, London Naval Conference; contraband; submarine; 1915, German announcement, Wilson's "strict accountability" note; 1915, *Lusitania, Arabic, Ancona, Persia* incidents; suspension of submarine campaign; 1916, *Sussex* incident; McLemore Resolution defeated. — House mission; House-Grey memorandum. — Election of 1916. — See also: § 241.

General — Slosson, *Great Crusade*, ch. i; Sullivan, *Our Times*, IV, ch. i, V, chs. i–iii, vi–vii, ix–xii; Bailey, *Diplomatic History*, chs. xxxvii–xxxviii; Bemis, *Diplomatic History*, ch. xxxii, and *American Secretaries of State*, X; Ogg, *National Progress*, chs. xviii–xxi; Paxson, *American Democracy and World War*, I, chs. vii–xix; Dexter Perkins, *America and Two Wars* (1944), chs. i, ii; C. H. Grattan, *Why We Fought* (1929), chs. i–xii; Walter Millis, *Road to War* (1935), chs. i–vi; C. C. Tansill, *America Goes To War* (1938), chs. i–xx; Charles Seymour, *American Diplomacy during World War* (1934), and *American Neutrality* (1935).

Special — War in Europe: Quincy Howe, *World History* (1949–53), I; G. W. F. Hallgarten, *Imperialismus vor 1914* (2 vols., 1951); S. B. Fay, *Origins of World War* (1938); Erich Brandenburg, *From Bismarck to World War* (1927). ❧ American Attitudes: H. C. Peterson, *Propaganda for War* (1939); Russell Buchanan, "Theodore Roosevelt and American Neutrality," *Am. Hist. Rev.*, XLIII (1938), 7; Curti, *Peace or War*, ch. viii; G. M. Stephenson, "Attitude of Swedish-Americans toward the World War," Miss. Valley Hist. Assoc., *Proc.*, X, pt. 1 (1918), 79; Carl Wittke, *German-Americans and World War* (1936), chs. i–iv; C. J. Child, *German-Americans in Politics* (1939); Schieber, *American Sentiment toward Germany*, chs. v–vii; M. L. Degen, *History of Woman's Peace Party* (1939), chs. i–v; C. C. Cummins, *Indiana Public Opinion and World War* (1945); Edwin Costrell, *How Maine Viewed War* (1940); J. C. Crichton, *Missouri and World War* (1947); J. D. Squires, *British Propaganda* (1935); J. M. Read, *Atrocity Propaganda* (1941); H. S. Foster, "How America Became Belligerent," *Am. Jour. Sociol.*, XL (1935), 464. ❧ Neutrality Questions: A. M. Morrissey, *American Defense of Neutral Rights* (1939); R. W. Van Alstyne, "Policy of United States Regarding Declaration of London," *Jour. Modern Hist.*, VII (1935), 435; Edwin Borchard, "Neutrality Claims against Great Britain," *Am. Jour. Int. Law*, XXI (1927), 764; E. C. Phillips, "American Participation in Belligerent Commercial Controls," *ibid.*, XXVII (1933), 675; T. A. Bailey, "German Documents Lusitania," *Jour. Modern Hist.*, VIII (1936), 320, and "Sinking of the Lusitania," *Am. Hist. Rev.*, XLI (1935), 54. ❧ Relief Operations: E. E. Hunt, *War Bread* (1916); G. I. Gay, *Statistical Review of Relief Operations* (1925). ❧ Economic

Factors: H. C. Syrett, "Business Press and American Neutrality," *Miss. Valley Hist. Rev.*, XXXII (1945), 215; J. V. Fuller, "Munitions Traffic," *Jour. Modern Hist.*, VI (1934), 280; R. W. Van Alstyne, "Private American Loans to the Allies," *Pacific Hist. Rev.*, II (1933), 180. ❡ Preparedness: Sprout, *Rise of American Naval Power*, ch. xviii; R. B. Perry, *Plattsburg Movement* (1942). ❡ Biographies: Baker, *Woodrow Wilson*, IV, ch. ix, V, chs. i–ii, VI, chs. i, v–vii; Kerney, *Wilson*, chs. xxiv–xxviii; Bell, *Woodrow Wilson*, chs. ix, x; Tumulty, *Wilson*, chs. xxv–xxxii; Notter, *Foreign Policy of Wilson*, chs. vi, vii; Long, *Bryan*, ch. xvi; Curti, *Bryan*, chs. iii, iv; Lamont, *Davison*, chs. xiv–xvii; Mott, *Herrick*, chs. xv–xxx; A. D. H. Smith, *Mr. House* (1940), ch. vi; A. M. Arnett, *Claude Kitchin* (1937); Nicolson, *Morrow*, ch. ix; Hendricks, *Page*, I, chs. v, ix–xi, III, chs. i–vii; Hicks, *Reed*, chs. viii–xi; Pringle, *Roosevelt*, bk. 3, chs. vi, vii; Mowry, *Roosevelt and Progressive Movement*, chs. xii–xv, and *California Progressives*, chs. viii–xi; Pringle, *Taft*, II, ch. xiv; Blum, *Tumulty*, ch. vii; Nevins, *Henry White*, ch. xviii. ❡ Maps: Paullin, *Atlas*, plate 111.

Sources — *Congressional Record; Foreign Relations*, and supplements, *World War*, and *Lansing Papers*; Savage, *Policy of United States Toward Maritime Commerce*, II, chs. i–v; *Documents diplomatiques français*; Gooch and Temperley, *British Documents*; Lepsius, *Die Grosse Politik*; Bartlett, *American Diplomacy*, ch. xxvi; "Special Committee Investigating the Munitions Industry," 73 Cong., 2 Sess., *Sen. Res.*, No. 206 (40 pts. 1934–43). ❡ Personal Material: Johann, graf von Bernstorff, *Memoirs* (1936), 97, and *My Three Years in America* (1920), chs. i–x; Bryan, *Memoirs*, pt. 2, chs. xii–xv; Creel *Rebel at Large*, ch. xx; Daniels, *Wilson Era*, I, chs. xlv–xlvi, l, lx–lxii; Dunn, *Harrison to Harding*, II, chs. xviii–xxi, xxiii–xxiv; House, *Intimate Papers*, I, chs. ix–xiv, II, chs. i–xii; Houston, *Eight Years*, I, chs. viii–ix; Lansing, *War Memoirs*, chs. i–xii; McAdoo, *Crowded Years*; Roosevelt, *Works*, XX; W. G. Sharp, *War Memoirs* (1931), chs. i–viii; Villard, *Fighting Years*, chs. xvi–xvii; W. A. White, *Autobiography*, lxii–lxxv; Brand Whitlock, *Letters and Journal* (Allan Nevins, ed., 1936), I, ch. iii, II, chs. i–vii; Woodrow Wilson, *Public Papers*, III–V, and *Selected Literary and Political Papers*, II. ❡ Periodicals: *American Year Book; New International Year Book; Current History; Life; Literary Digest; Nation; N.Y. Times; N.Y. Evening Post*; (§§ 52, 53).

Bibliography — Bemis and Griffin, *Guide to Diplomatic History*, ch. xxii; § 241; Leopold, "Mississippi Valley and Foreign Policy," 625.

241. AMERICA'S ENTRY INTO THE WAR, 1916–1917

Summary — Neutrality problems (§ 240). — Road to war: failure of Wilson's mediation efforts; Dec., 1916, question of arms; Feb., 1917, resumption of submarine warfare, rupture of diplomatic relations; Mar., 1917, Zimmerman Note revealed; Russian Revolution (§ 243); Apr., 1917, declaration of war. — Interpretations of war causes: neutral rights, Perkins, Seymour; revisionists, Barnes, Beard, Tansill; others.

General — Goldman, *Rendezvous with Destiny*, ch. xi; Sullivan, *Our Times*, V, chs iii–v, viii, xiii–xiv; Paxson, *American Democracy and World War*, I, chs. xix–xxii; Bemis, *American Secretaries of State*, X, and *Diplomatic History*, ch. xxxiii.

Special — Interpretations of the Causes: Scott Nearing, *Great Madness* (1917); C. F. Gauss, *Why We Went to War* (1918); J. K. Turner, *Shall It Be Again?* (1922); H. E Barnes, *Genesis of World War* (1920); Grattan, *Why We Fought*, chs. xiii–xv; Seymour *American Diplomacy*; Millis, *Road to War*, chs. vii–xii; N. D. Baker, *Why We Went to War* (1936); B. E. Schmitt, "American Neutrality," *Jour. Modern Hist.*, VIII (1936), 200; Edwin Borchard and W. P. Lage, *Neutrality for United States* (1940); Tansill *America Goes to War*; Paul Birdsall, "Neutrality and Economic Pressures," *Sci. and Society*, III (1939), 217; D. F. Fleming, "Our Entry into World War," *Jour. of Pol.*, II (1940), 75. ❡ Other Aspects: Russell Buchanan, "American Editors Examine War Aims," *Pacific Hist. Rev.*, IX (1940), 253; Degen, *Woman's Peace Party*, ch. vi; M. B. Guthrie "Anti-War Minority in Congress," *Historian*, II (1940), 85. ❡ Biographies: Bowers *Beveridge*, bk. 5, chs. i, ii; A. D. H. Smith, *Mr. House*, ch. vii; Nicolson, *Morrow*, ch. x;

Hendrick, *Page*, I, chs. xii, xiii, II, chs. xiv–xxi, III, chs. viii–xv; Pringle, *Taft*, II, ch. xlvii; Blum, *Tumulty*, ch. ix; Baker, *Woodrow Wilson*, V, chs. iii–viii, VI, chs. vii–xii; Bell, *Woodrow Wilson*, ch. xi; Notter, *Foreign Policy of Wilson*, ch. viii. ❡ Maps: Paullin, *Atlas*, plate 120.

Sources — § 240; *Congressional Record; Foreign Relations*, including *Lansing Papers*, and *World War*. ❡ Periodicals: *Current History; Literary Digest; American Year Book; New International Year Book*. ❡ Personal Materials: Bernstorff, *Three Years*, chs. xi, xii; Daniels, *Wilson Era*, II, chs. ii–iv; Sharp, *War Memoirs*, chs. ix–xi; House, *Intimate Papers*, II, chs. xii–xv; Houston, *Eight Years*, I, chs. xiv–xvi; Lane, *Letters*, ch. vii; Robert Lansing, *War Memoirs* (1935), chs. i–xviii, and *Papers (Foreign Relations)*; Norris, *Fighting Liberal*, chs. xviii–xx; Whitlock, *Letters and Journal*, II, ch. viii; Woodrow Wilson, *Public Papers*, IV, V.

Bibliography — R. W. Leopold, "Problem of American Intervention, 1917," *World Politics*, II (1950), 405; Bemis and Griffin, *Guide to Diplomatic History*, ch. xxii; Goldman, *Rendezvous with Destiny*, 483.

242. CONDUCT OF THE WAR AT HOME AND ABROAD

Summary — Recruitment; manpower problem; the draft. — Finances; liberty bonds; loans. — Food administration; supplies; mobilization of industry; transport; railroads nationalized; shipping. — Economic repercussions; effects on labor; internal migrations; position of the Negro, other ethnic groups (§§ 226, 240, 244). — Propaganda, Committee on Public Information; war hysteria, censorship, sedition laws. — War at sea. — War in France: A. E. F.; trench warfare; supply; Red Cross; other agencies; Chateau-Thierry, Belleau Woods, Meuse-Argonne offensive. — Far Eastern events (§ 243). — Armistice. — Diplomatic events (§ 243).

General — Slosson, *Great Crusade*, ch. ii; George Soule, *Prosperity Decade* (1947), chs. i–iii; Paxson, *American Democracy and World War*, II; Sullivan, *Our Times*, V, chs. xv–xxvi; Pendleton Herring, *Impact of War* (1941), ch. vii; J. B. McMaster, *United States in World War* (2 vols., 1918–20); W. L. S. Churchill, *World Crisis* (4 vols., 1923–29); B. H. Liddell Hart, *Real War* (1930); C. R. M. F. Cruttwell, *History of Great War* (1934); John Buchan, *History of Great War* (4 vols., 1921–22); Louis Smith, *American Democracy and Military Power*, ch. xii; Josephson, *President Makers*, ch. xvi; Mills, *Economic Tendencies*, ch. v.

Special — Manpower: T. G. Frothingham, *American Reinforcement in World War* (1927); E. H. Crowder, *Spirit of Selective Service* (1920); Norman Thomas, *Conscientious Objector* (1923). ❡ Economic Mobilization: J. M. Clark, *Costs of World War* (1931); G. B. Clarkson, *Industrial America in World War* (1923); Benedict Crowell and R. F. Wilson, *How America Went to War* (6 vols., 1921); Lewis, *America's Stake in International Investments*, ch. vi; B. M. Baruch, *American Industry in War* (R. H. Hippelheuser, ed., 1941); W. F. Willoughby, *Government Organization in War Time* (1919); R. B. Kester, "War Industries Board," *Am. Pol. Sci. Rev.*, XXXIV (1940), 655; C. B. Swisher, "Control of War Preparations," *ibid.*, XXXIV (1940), 1085; Noyes, *War Period of American Finance*, chs. ii–v; W. C. Mitchell, *History of Prices during War* (1919); Dewey, *Financial History*, ch. xxii; Ratner, *American Taxation*, chs. xvi–xviii; Taus, *Central Banking Functions*, ch. vii; W. D. Hines, *War History of American Railroads* (1928); E. R. Johnson and T. W. Van Metre, *Principles of Railroad Transportation*; W. J. Cunningham, "Railroads under Government Operation," *Quar. Jour. Econ.*, XXXV (1921), 288, XXXVI (1921), 30; W. P. Elderton, *Shipping Problems* (1927); J. A. Salter, *Allied Shipping Control* (1921); Herbert Stein, *Government Price Policy during the World War* (1939). ❡ Labor and War: Commons, *History of Labour*, IV, chs. xxv–xxxiii; Beard, *American Labor Movement*, ch. xii; Lombardi, *Labor's Voice in Cabinet*, pt. 3; "National War Labor Board History," *Bur. Labor Stat., Bull.*, No. 287 (1922); Lorwin, *American Federation of Labor*, chs. vi, vii; Albrecht, *International Seamen's Union*, chs. iv–vi; Alexander Bing, *War-Time Strikes* (1921); Fine, *Labor and Farmer Parties*, ch. x;

Franklin, *Slavery to Freedom*, ch. xxiv; R. H. Leavell, *et al.*, *Negro Migration in 1916–1917* (1919); L. V. Kennedy, *Negro Peasant Turns Cityward* (1930); E. J. Scott, *Negro Migration during War* (1920); I. DeA. Reid, *Negro Immigrant* (1939); Wesley, *Negro Labor*, ch. x; V. W. Lanfear, *Business Fluctuations and American Labor Movement* (1924); G. S. Watkins, *Labor Problems and Labor Administration during World War* (2 vols., 1920). ❡ Agriculture: A. B. Genung, "Agriculture in World War Period," *Yearbook of Agriculture*, 1940, 277; F. M. Surface, *American Pork Production in the World War* (1926); F. M. Surface and R. L. Bland, *American Food in World War* (1931); W. C. Mullendore, *History of United States Food Administration* (1941). ❡ Propaganda and Censorship: George Creel, *How We Advertised America* (1920); J. R. Mock and Cedric Larson, *Words That Won the War* (1939); G. G. Bruntz, *Allied Propaganda and Collapse of German Empire* (1938); Weyl, *Treason*, ch. xvi; Henry Landau, *Enemy Within* (1937); R. H. Abrams, *Preachers Present Arms* (1933); Chafee, *Free Speech*, chs. ii, iii; Mott, *American Journalism*, ch. xxxvi; Kelly and Harbison, *American Constitution*, ch. xxv; Park, *Immigrant Press*, ch. xvii; Wittke, *German-Americans and World War*, chs. v–vii; J. A. Gathings, *International Law and American Treatment of Alien Enemy Property* (1940), chs. v–vii; Degen, *Woman's Peace Party*, ch. vii. ❡ Religious and Philanthropic Organizations: Ellis, *Cardinal Gibbons*, II, ch. xix. ❡ Military Events: Benedict Crowell and R. F. Wilson, *Road to France* (2 vols., 1921); John Dickinson, *Building of an Army* (1922); Palmer, *Bliss*, chs. xiii–xxvii, xxxi; E. C. Parsons, *Great Adventure: Lafayette Escadrille* (1937); Sprout, *Rise of American Naval Power*, ch. xix; Westcott, *American Sea Power*, ch. xx; Knox, *Navy*, chs. xxv–xxxvii; Morison, *Sims*, chs. xix–xxiv; H. R. Rudin, *Armistice, 1918* (1944). ❡ Biography: Baker, *Woodrow Wilson*, VII, VIII; Tumulty, *Wilson*, chs. xxxiii–xxxiv; Bell, *Woodrow Wilson*, ch. xii; Frederick Palmer, *Newton D. Baker* (2 vols., 1931); Ginger, *Debs*; Winkler, *DuPont*, pt. 5; Harvey, *Gompers*, chs. xv, xvi; H. S. Gray, *Character "Bad" Story of a Conscientious Objector* (1934); Bent, *Holmes*, ch. xvi; Bryn-Jones, *Kellogg*, chs. ix–x; Lief, *Democracy's Norris*, chs. viii–ix; Nicolson, *Morrow*, ch. xi; Hendrick, *Page*, II, chs. xxii–xxvii; Freidel, *Franklin D. Roosevelt*, I, xiii–xx; Jessup, *Root*, II, chs. xl–xliii; Blum, *Tumulty*, chs. ix, x. ❡ Local Histories: Hart, *Commonwealth History of Massachusetts*, V, ch. xx; Franklin Holbrook and Livia Appel, *Minnesota in the War* (2 vols., 1928–32).

Sources — Government Documents: *Foreign Relations*, including *World War*; Army War College, Historical Section, *Order of Battle of Land Forces in the World War* (1931); *Official Record of United States in Great War* (1923); Federal Trade Commission, *High Cost of Living* (1917); Special Committee to Investigate Munitions Industry, "Hearings" (§ 240). ❡ Periodicals: *N. Y. Times*; *Current History*; *Literary Digest*; *American Year Book* (1917–19). ❡ Personal Materials, Civilian: Robert Alexander, *Memories of World War* (1931); Baker, *American Chronicle*, chs. xxxiii–xl; Belmont, *American Democrat*, ch. xix; R. L. Bullard, *Personalities and Reminiscences* (1925); Creel, *Rebel at Large*, chs. xxi–xxii; Daniels, *Wilson Era*, II, chs. v–xvii; Gompers, *Seventy Years*, II, chs. xxxviii–xliv; Hoover, *Memoirs*, I; House, *Intimate Papers*, III, chs. i–v, IV, chs. iii–v; Houston, *Eight Years*, I, chs. xvii–xix; Lane, *Letters*, chs. ix, x; Lansing, *War Memoirs*, chs. xviii–xxiii; David Lloyd-George, *War Memoirs* (6 vols., 1933–37); McAdoo, *Crowded Years*; Franz von Papen, *Memoirs* (1952); Richberg, *Tents of Mighty*, ch. iii; Franz von Rintelen, *Dark Invader* (1933); Roosevelt, *Works*, XXI; Whitlock, *Letters and Journals*, II, chs. ix–xi; Woodrow Wilson, *Selected Literary and Political Papers*, II, and *Public Papers*, V; Art Young, *His Life and Times* (J. N. Beffel, ed., 1939), chs. xxix–xxxv. ❡ Personal Material, Military: J. J. Pershing, *My Experiences* (2 vols., 1931); J. G. Harbord, *Leaves from a War Diary* (1925). ❡ Other Collections: Manning, Potter, Davies, *Select Problems*, II, ch. vii.

Bibliography — E. R. Drewry, "Historical Units of Agencies of First World War," National Archives, *Bull.*, No. 4 (1942), 1; W. G. Leland and N. D. Mereness, comps., *Introduction to American Official Sources for the Economic and Social History of the World War* (1926); F. F. Holbrook, "Collection of State War Service Records," *Am. Hist. Rev.*, XXV (1919), 72; N. D. Mereness, ed., "American Historical Activities during World War," Am. Hist. Assoc., *Report*, 1919, I, 204; Mott, *American Journalism*, 734; Soule, *Prosperity Decade*, 336; F. A. Ross and L. V. Kennedy, *Bibliography of Negro*

Migration (1934); A. R. Wright, "Food and Society; War-Time Archives," *Am. Scholar,* VII (1938), 243.

243. THE PEACE THAT FAILED

Summary — Statements of war aims; Fourteen Points; Allied secret treaties; conceptions of international organization. — War-Time diplomacy; relations with neutrals. — Election of 1918. — Negotiating the treaties; Wilson's trips to Paris; the peace mission; attitude of Senate; disputes among the Allies. — League of Nations; covenant; attached to Treaty of Versailles. — Divisive issues; Shantung and Far East; Italy, Trieste; Poland; minorities policy; European revolutions; attitudes toward Soviets; Siberian intervention. — Struggle for ratification; composition of Senate; Republican policy; reservations; irreconcilables; attitudes of German-Americans, other ethnic groups. — Postwar aid in Europe. — Election of 1920. — Failure of ratification. — Later developments (§ 250).

General — Bailey, *Diplomatic History,* chs. xxxix–xl; Bemis, *Diplomatic History,* chs. xxxiii, xxxiv, and *American Secretaries of State,* x; Paxson, *American Democracy and World War,* III, chs. i, iv–viii; Holt, *Treaties Defeated,* ch. x; Perkins, *America and Two Wars,* chs. iii, iv; Goldman, *Rendezvous with Destiny,* ch. xii; Josephson, *President Makers,* ch. xvii.

Special — R. J. Bartlett, *League to Enforce Peace* (1944); H. W. V. Temperley, et al., *History of Peace Conference* (6 vols., 1920-24); G. B. Noble, *Policies and Opinions at Paris* (1935); F. S. Marston, *Peace Conference of 1919* (1944); T. A. Bailey, *Woodrow Wilson and Lost Peace* (1944), and *Woodrow Wilson and Great Betrayal* (1945); R. S. Baker, *Woodrow Wilson and World Settlement* (3 vols., 1922); Bell, *Woodrow Wilson,* chs. xiv–xviii; Paul Birdsall, *Versailles Twenty Years After* (1941); Hunter Miller, *Drafting the Covenant* (1928); Tumulty, *Wilson,* chs. xxxv–xlv; Aaron, *America in Crisis,* ch. x; D. F. Fleming, *United States and League of Nations* (1932); C. A. Berdahl, *Policy of United States with Respect to League* (1932); R. W. Logan, *Senate and Versailles Mandate System* (1945); Perkins, *Hands Off,* ch. viii; T. A. Bailey, *Policy of United States toward Neutrals* (1942); Degen, *Woman's Peace Party,* ch. viii; R. H. Fifield, *Woodrow Wilson and Far East* (1952); Clinard, *Japan's Influence on Naval Power,* ch. v; Tupper and McReynolds, *Japan in American Opinion,* chs. iv–v; Griswold, *Far Eastern Policy,* chs. v–vii; Treat, *Japan and United States 1853–1921,* chs. xi, xii; E. A. Falk, *From Perry to Pearl Harbor* (1943), ch. viii; Dulles, *Forty Years of American-Japanese Relations,* chs. vii–ix; Sidney Brooks, *America and Germany, 1918–1925* (1927); W. S. Graves, *America's Siberian Adventure* (1931); D. W. Grantham, "Southern Senators and League," *No. Car. Hist. Rev.,* XXVI (1949), 187; Selig Adler, "Congressional Election of 1918," *So. Atlantic Quar.,* XXXVI (1937), 4; S. W. Livermore, "Sectional Issue in 1918 Elections," *Miss. Valley Hist. Rev.,* XXXV (1948), 29; Stein, *Third Term Tradition,* ch. ix; Bowers, *Beveridge,* pt. 5, chs. iii, iv; Palmer, *Bliss,* chs. xxviii–xxx, xxxii–xxxvii; Ellis, *Cardinal Gibbons,* II, chs. xx–xxii; M. P. Briggs, *Herron and European Settlement* (1932); A. D. H. Smith, *Mr. House,* chs. viii–ix; Karl Schriftgiesser, *Gentleman from Massachusetts* (1944), chs. xvi–xxi (Lodge); Hicks, *Reed,* chs. xiv–xvi; Jessup, *Root,* II, chs. xliv–xlv; Pringle, *Taft,* II, ch. xlix; Blum, *Tumulty,* chs. xi–xiii; Nevins, *Henry White,* chs. xix–xxiii. ❡ Maps: Paullin, *Atlas,* plate 111.

Sources — *Congressional Record; Foreign Relations,* including *World War,* and *Lansing Papers,* and *Paris Peace Conference,* and *Russia;* Savage, *Policy of United States Toward Maritime Commerce,* II, chs. vi–xii. ❡ Personal Material: Wilson, *Selected Literary and Political Papers,* II, and *Public Papers,* IV, V; Baker, *American Chronicle,* chs. xli–lv; B. M. Baruch, *Making of the Reparation and Economic Sections of the Treaty* (1920); W. L. S. Churchill, *Aftermath* (1929); Georges Clemenceau, *Grandeur and Misery of Victory* (1930); Creel, *Rebel at Large,* chs. xxiii, xxvi; H. H. Bandholtz, *Undiplomatic Diary* (1933); Belmont, *American Democrat,* ch. xx; Stephen Bonsal, *Unfinished Business* (1944); Daniels, *Wilson Era,* II, chs. xxviii–xxxix; Gompers, *Seventy*

Years, II, chs. xlv–xlvi; Sharp, *War Memoirs*, chs. xii–xvi; C. H. Haskins and R. H. Lord, *Some Problems of the Peace Conference* (1920); Hoover, *Memoirs*, I; House, *Intimate Papers*, III, chs. vii–xiv, IV, chs. i, ii, vi–xiv; E. M. House and Charles Seymour, eds., *What Really Happened at Paris* (1921); Houston, *Eight Years*, I, ch. xx, II, chs. xxi–xxiii; Hunter Miller, *My Diary at Peace Conference* (21 vols., 1928); J. M. Keynes, *Economic Consequences of Peace* (1919); Lansing, *War Memoirs*, chs. xviii–xxiii; David Lloyd-George, *War Memoirs*, and *Memoirs of Peace Conference* (1939); H. C. Lodge, *Senate and League* (1925); Moore, *Collected Papers*, V; Norris, *Fighting Liberal*, ch. xxi; Harold Nicolson, *Peacemaking, 1919* (1933); Raymond Poincaré, *Memoirs* (1931); J. T. Shotwell, *At Paris Peace Conference* (1937); C. T. Thompson, *Peace Conference Day by Day* (1920); Straus, *Under Four Administrations*, ch. xvi; Villard, *Fighting Years*, chs. xx–xxii; Whitlock, *Letters and Journal*, I, ch. iv, II, ch. xii. ❡ Collections: Bartlett, *American Diplomacy*, ch. xxvii; Clyde, *United States Policy toward China*, ch. xxxix; J. T. Shotwell, ed., *Origins of International Labor Organization* (2 vols., 1934); P. M. Burnett, *Reparation at Paris Peace Conference* (2 vols., 1940). ❡ Periodicals: *N.Y. Times;* (London) *Times; Current History; Literary Digest.*

Bibliography — Bemis and Griffin, *Guide to Diplomatic History*, ch. xxii; Goldman, *Rendezvous with Destiny*, 485; R. C. Binkley, "Ten Years of Peace Conference History," *Jour. Modern Hist.*, I (1929), 607; Paul Birdsall, "Second Decade of Peace Conference History," *ibid.*, XI (1939), 362.

244. DOMESTIC CONSEQUENCES

Summary — Postwar situation; demobilization. — Economy: change, debtor to creditor nation; expanded manufactures; position of farmers. ❡ Labor unrest: strikes; failure of unionization; radical efforts. — Red scare; deportations; Boston police strike; decline of I. W. W., socialists. — Non-Partisan League; other new political activities. — Renewed immigration, internal migration; efforts at restriction, literacy law, quota plan. — Stimulus to nationalisms; American Legion; ethnic groups, Italians, Zionists, Garvey movement. — Prohibition; 1917–19, eighteenth amendment, 1920, Volstead Act. — Nineteenth Amendment (§ 230). — See also: §§ 248, 251, 253.

General — Slosson, *Great Crusade*, chs. iii–v, xi; Soule, *Prosperity Decade*, ch. iv; Paxson, *American Democracy and World War*, III, chs. i–iii, viii, ix.

Special — Benedict Crowell and R. F. Wilson, *Demobilization* (1921); Wecter, *When Johnny Comes Marching Home*, pt. 3; J. R. Mock and Evangeline Thurber, *Report on Demobilization* (1944); Lewis, *America's Stake in International Investments*, ch. xvii; Mills, *Economic Tendencies*, ch. v; P. A. Samuelson and E. E. Hagen, *After the War* (1943); Noyes, *War Period of American Finance*, chs. vi–vii; Blum, *Tumulty*, chs. xi–xiii; Myers, *History of Bigotry*, chs. xxiv–xxvii; Chafee, *Free Speech*, chs. iv–vi; A. G. Hays, *Let Freedom Ring* (1928); Bernard, *American Immigration Policy*, ch. i; Garis, *Immigration Restriction*, ch. v; Mason, *Brandeis*, chs. xxix, xxxv–xxxvi; Fine, *Labor and Farmer Parties*, ch. xi; Haynes, *Social Politics*, chs. xii, xiii; Theodore Saloutos, "Rise of Non-Partisan League in North Dakota," *Ag. Hist.*, XX (1946), 43, and "Expansion and Decline of Non-Partisan League," *ibid.*, XX (1946), 235; S. P. Huntington, "Election Tactics of Non-Partisan League," *Miss. Valley Hist. Rev.*, XXXVI (1950), 613; Arthur Capper, *Agricultural Bloc* (1922); Andrew Bruce, *Non-Partisan League* (1921); H. E. Gaston, *Non-Partisan League* (1920); C. E. Russell, *Non-Partisan League* (1920); A. S. Tostlebe, *Bank of North Dakota* (1924); Dulles, *Labor in America*, ch. xiii; Lombardi, *Labor's Voice in Cabinet*, pt. 4; Lorwin, *American Federation of Labor*, ch. viii; Albrecht, *International Seamen's Union*, ch. vii; Adamic, *Dynamite*, chs. xxv–xxviii; Lanfear, *Business Fluctuations and Labor;* Harvey, *Gompers*, chs. xvii–xix; Interchurch World Movement, Commission of Inquiry, *Report on Steel Strike of 1919* (1920); W. Z. Foster, *Great Steel Strike* (1920); W. A. White, *Coolidge*, ch. xv; Dabney, *Dry Messiah*, ch. x; Stewart, *Wheeler*, chs. vi–viii; Odegard, *Pressure Politics.* ❡ Maps: Paullin, *Atlas*, plate 120.

Sources — Personal Materials: Creel, *Rebel at Large*, ch. xxv; Gompers, *Seventy Years*, II, ch. xlvii; Houston, *Eight Years*, II, chs. xxiv–xxix; Lane, *Letters*, ch. xi; Villard, *Fighting Years*, chs. xviii–xix; Woodrow Wilson, *Public Papers*, V. ¶ Periodicals: *Collier's*; *Current History*; *Nation*; *New Republic*; *World's Work*; *Masses*; *N.Y. Times*.

Bibliography — Soule, *Prosperity Decade*, 336; Ross and Kennedy, *Bibliography of Negro Migration*.

Chapter Twenty-eight

DECADE OF PROSPERITY, 1920–1929

245. RETURN TO NORMALCY: THE HARDING ADMINISTRATION, 1920–1923

Summary — Republican convention of 1920; Harding and the "smoke-filled room." — Democratic convention; James M. Cox. — Third parties, Socialist, Farmer-Labor. — Campaign; issues; "normalcy"; round robin. — Election. — Harding as president: establishment of Bureau of Budget; Ohio Gang and little green house on K Street; Alaska trip; Harding's death (Aug. 2, 1923); Teapot Dome; Veterans' Bureau; other scandals; Walsh investigation.

General — S. H. Adams, *Incredible Era* (1939); F. L. Paxson, *American Democracy and World War*, III; H. U. Faulkner, *From Versailles to New Deal* (1950), chs. i–vii; Slosson, *Great Crusade*, ch. iii; F. L. Allen, *Only Yesterday* (1931), chs. i–vi; Sullivan, *Our Times*, VI; Karl Schriftgiesser, *This Was Normalcy* (1948), chs. i–xvi; F. W. Friendly and E. R. Murrow, eds., "I Can Hear It Now" (recording), III.

Special — Election of 1920: Fine, *Labor and Farmer Parties*, chs. xi–xiii; Haynes, *Social Politics*, 299; Ray Ginger, *Debs*, ch. xx; Gaston, *Nonpartisan League;* Russell, *Nonpartisan League;* Bruce, *Nonpartisan League;* Watson, *As I Knew Them*, 207; J. K. Pollock, *Party Campaign Funds* (1926); Robinson, *Presidential Vote;* S. J. Eldersveld, "Influence of Metropolitan Party Pluralities in Presidential Elections since 1920," *Am. Pol. Sci. Rev.*, XLIII (1949), 1189; A. M. Schlesinger and E. M. Eriksson, "Vanishing Voter," *New Republic*, Oct. 15, 1924. ⦅ Harding: H. S. New, "Senatorial Oligarchy," *Sat. Eve. Post*, May 28, 1932; Pusey, *Hughes*, II, chs. xxxix–lix; W. A. White, *Masks in a Pageant* (1928), 389; E. G. Lowry, *Washington Close-Ups* (1921); C. W. Thompson, *Presidents I've Known* (1929), 325; C. G. Dawes, *First Year of Budget of United States* (1923); B. N. Timmons, *Charles G. Dawes* (1953), ch. xv; F. M. Marx, "Bureau of Budget," *Am. Pol. Sci. Rev.*, XXXIX (1945), 653, 869; D. K. Price, "General Dawes and Executive Staff Work," *Public Administration Rev.*, XI (1951), 167. ⦅ Personal Material: Daniels, *Wilson Era* (1946), II; Cox, *Journey Through Years*, chs. xx–xxv; Hoover, *Memoirs*, II, chs. i–xxvi; W. A. White, *Autobiography*, and *Selected Letters;* I. H. Hoover, *Forty-Two Years in White House* (1934); 231; Butler, *Across Busy Years.* ⦅ Scandals: M. R. Werner, *Privileged Characters* (1935), chs. i–iv; M. E. Ravage, *Story of Teapot Dome* (1924); Ise, *Oil Policy;* H. M. Daugherty and Thomas Dixon, *Inside Story of Harding Tragedy* (1932); Nan Britton, *President's Daughter* (1927).

Sources — Senate Select Committee, "Investigation of Veterans Bureau," 68 Cong., 1 Sess., *Sen. Report*, No. 103, (3 pts., 1924), and "Investigation of Attorney General," 68 Cong., 1 Sess., *Hearings* (11 pts., 1924); Senate Public Lands Committee, "Leases upon Naval Oil Reserves," 67 Cong., 2–4 Sess., 68 Cong., 1 Sess., 70 Cong., 1 Sess., *Hearings* (20 pts., 1923–28); McGrain *v.* Daugherty, 273 U.S. 135; Sinclair *v.* United States, 279 U. S. 263.

246. THE ECONOMICS OF PROSPERITY, 1921–1929

Summary — Demobilization of war controls (§ 244). — Postwar inflation and depression, 1919–22. — Prosperity: rise of automotive industry; increase in labor productivity; advances in "scientific management" and in research and technology; increased use of electric power. — Structure of industry: concentration; rise of holding companies; government support for trade associations. — Advertising and promotion; spread of installment buying; real estate speculation; cult of the saleman. — Role of Wall Street: increase in stock speculation; sales on margin; increase in brokers' loans. — Role of government; Federal Reserve policy; Treasury policy; surtax reduction. — Distribution of prosperity; sick industries. — Foreign economic policy: Fordney-McCumber tariff (Sept. 19, 1922); foreign loan policy.

General — Thomas Wilson, *Fluctuations in Income and Employment* (1948), chs. xi–xvii; Soule, *Prosperity Decade;* Williamson, *Growth of American Economy,* chs. xxxv–xlviii; Allen, *Lords of Creation,* chs. viii–xiv; Slosson, *Great Crusade,* ch. vi; Faulkner, *Versailles to New Deal,* chs. iv, viii; President's Conference on Unemployment, *Recent Economic Changes* (2 vols., 1929); Maurice Leven, *et al., America's Capacity to Consume* (1934); E. G. Nourse, *et al., America's Capacity to Produce* (1934); W. W. Leontief, *Structure of American Economy, 1919–1929* (1941); L. R. Klein, *Economic Fluctuations in United States, 1921–1941* (1950); F. C. Mills, *Economic Tendencies, and Behavior of Prices* (1927); Stuart Chase, *Prosperity* (1929); W. F. Ogburn, ed., *Recent Social Changes* (1929).

Special — National Income and Product: Simon Kuznets, *National Income* (1946), and *National Product* (1946); Harold Barger, *Outlay and Income, 1921–1938* (1942); G. J. Stigler, *Trends in Output and Employment* (1947); Fabricant, *Output of Manufacturing;* A. F. Burns, *Production Trends since 1870* (1934); J. J. Polak, "Fluctuations in Consumption, 1919–1932," *Rev. Econ. Stat.,* XXI (1939), 1. ❡ Distributive Shares: R. C. Epstein, *Industrial Profits* (1934); Douglas, *Real Wages;* National Industrial Conference Board, *Wages in United States, 1914–1930,* and *Cost of Living, 1914–1930* (1931); P. F. Brissenden, *Earnings of Factory Workers, 1899–1927* (1929); M. A. Beney, *Wages, Hours and Employment, 1914–1936* (1936); Simon Kuznets and Elizabeth Jenks, *Shares of Upper Income Groups in Income and Savings* (1953); Evans Clark, ed., *Internal Debt of United States* (1933). ❡ Depression, 1919–22: W. F. Payne, *Business Behavior, 1919–22* (1942); National Housing Agency, *Housing After World War I* (1945); E. J. Howenstine, Jr., "Demobilization," *Quar. Jour. Econ.,* LVIII (1943), 91, and "Public Works after World War I," *Jour. Pol. Econ.,* LI (1943), 523; W. M. Persons, "Crisis of 1920," *Am. Econ. Rev.,* XII (1922), 5; President's Conference on Unemployment, *Report* (1921). ❡ Government and Business: Merle Fainsod and Lincoln Gordon, *Government and American Economy* (1941); L. S. Lyon, M. W. Watkins, and Victor Abramson, *Government and Economic Life* (2 vols., 1939–40); Solomon Fabricant and R. E. Lipsey, *Trend of Government Activity since 1900* (1952); C. H. Wooddy, *Growth of Federal Government, 1915–1932* (1934); D. M. Keezer and Stacy May, *Public Control of Business* (1930); M. W. Watkins, *Public Regulation of Competitive Practices* (1940); Henderson, *Federal Trade Commission;* Blaisdell, *Federal Trade Commission;* Sharfman, *Interstate Commerce Commission;* A. D. Gayer, *Public Works in Prosperity and Depression* (1938), chs. i–iv; E. J. Howenstein, Jr., "Public Works Policy in Twenties," *Social Research,* XIII (1946), 479. ❡ Public Finance: Ratner, *American Taxation,* chs. xix, xx; E. A. Goldenweiser, *American Monetary Policy* (1951), ch. viii; Taus, *Central Banking Functions,* ch. viii; Lauchlin Currie, *Supply and Control of Money* (1934); Noyes, *War Period of American Finance;* H. G. Hendricks, *Federal Debt, 1919–1930* (1933); W. F. Willoughby, *Financial Operations of National Government* (1931); W. W. Riefler, *Money Rates and Money Markets* (1930); Blakey, *Federal Income Tax,* chs. viii–xi. ❡ Banking Policy: J. M. Chapman, *Concentration of Banking* (1934); Horace Secrist, *National Bank Failures and Non-Failures* (1938); H. P. Willis and J. M. Chapman, *Banking Situation* (1934); W. N. Peach, *Security Affiliates of National Banks* (1941). ❡ Federal Reserve Policy: Harris, *Federal Reserve Policy;* C. O. Hardy, *Credit Policies of Federal Reserve System* (1932); Warburg, *Federal Reserve System;* L. E. Clark,

Central Banking Under Federal Reserve System (1935); W. R. Burgess, *Reserve Banks and Money Market* (1927); A. C. Miller, "Responsibility for Federal Reserve Policies," *Am. Econ. Rev.*, XXV (1935), 442. ❧ Economic Concentration: J. K. Galbraith, *American Capitalism* (1952); M. A. Adelman, "Measurement of Economic Concentration," *Rev. Econ. Stat.*, XXXIII (1951), 269; G. W. Nutter, *Extent of Enterprise Monopoly 1899–1931* (1951); A. A. Berle, Jr., and G. C. Means, *Modern Corporation and Private Property* (1932); Burns, *Decline of Competition;* H. W. Laidler, *Concentration of Control in Industry* (1931); Seager and Gulick, *Trust and Corporation Problems;* Bonbright and Means, *Holding Company;* W. J. A. Donald, *Trade Associations* (1933). ❧ Investment Market: Twentieth Century Fund, *Security Markets* (1935); A. R. Koch, *Financing of Large Corporations, 1920–1939* (1943); W. Z. Ripley, *Main Street and Wall Street* (1927); Ferdinand Pecora, *Wall Street Under Oath* (1936); J. T. Flynn, *Security Speculation* (1934); C. C. Abbott, *New York Bond Market, 1920–1930* (1937); Beckhart, *New York Money Market,* II–IV; A. W. Dakin, "Foreign Securities in American Money Market," *Harvard Bus. Rev.*, X (1932), 227; C. R. Noyes, "Gold Inflation, 1921–1929," *Am. Econ. Rev.*, XX (1938), 181; F. R. Macaulay, *Movements of Interest Rates, Bond Yields and Stock Prices* (1938); Corey, *House of Morgan;* Arthur Pound and S. T. Moore, eds., *They Told Barron* (1930), and *More They Told Barron* (1931); Noyes, *Market Place.* ❧ Manufacturing and Technology: C. A. Bliss, *Structure of Manufacturing Production* (1939); Fabricant, *Output of Manufacturing;* Sigfried Giedion, *Mechanization Takes Command* (1948); Burlingame, *Engines of Democracy;* Temporary National Economic Committee, *Technology in Our Economy* (Monograph, No. 22, 1941); H. S. Person, ed., *Scientific Management in American Industry* (1929); R. G. Tugwell, *Industry's Coming of Age* (1927); Jerome, *Mechanization in Industry;* R. A. Brady, *Industrial Standardization* (1929); E. E. Hunt, ed., *Scientific Management since Taylor* (1924); Solomon Fabricant, *Labor Savings in American Industry, 1899–1939* (1945). ❧ Automobile Industry: Kennedy, *Automobile Industry;* Epstein, *Automobile Industry;* L. H. Seltzer, *Financial History of Automobile Industry* (1928); R. M. Cleveland and S. T. Williamson, *Road is Yours* (1951); Paxson, "Highway Movement"; C. L. Dearing, *American Highway Policy* (1941). ❧ Public Utilities: J. M. Gould, *Output and Productivity in Electric and Gas Utilities, 1899–1942* (1946); Twentieth Century Fund, *Power Industry and Public Interest* (1944); John Bauer and Nathaniel Gold, *Electric Power Industry* (1939); N. S. Buchanan, "Origin and Development of Public Utility Holding Company," *Jour. Pol. Econ.*, XLIV (1936), 31; M. H. Waterman, *Financial Policies of Public Utility Holding Companies* (1932); H. S. Raushenbush and H. W. Laidler, *Power Control* (1929); H. S. Raushenbush, *High Power Propaganda* (1928), and *Power Fight* (1932); W. E. Mosher and F. G. Crawford, *Public Utility Regulation* (1933); M. L. Ramsay, *Pyramids of Power* (1937); Ernest Gruening, *Public Pays* (1931); C. D. Thompson, *Confessions of Power Trust* (1932); Samuel Insull, *Public Utilities in Modern Life* (1924). ❧ Transportation: Harold Barger, *Transportation Industries, 1899–1946* (1951); Thor Hultgren, *American Transportation in Prosperity and Depression* (1948); H. G. Moulton, *et al.*, *American Transportation Problem* (1933); D. P. Locklin, *Railroad Regulation since 1920* (1928); W. M. W. Splawn, *Consolidation of Railroads* (1925); W. N. Leonard, *Railroad Consolidation under Transportation Act of 1920* (1946); H. L. Smith, *Airways* (1942); F. A. Magoun and Eric Hodgins, *History of Aircraft* (1931); E. E. Freudenthal, *Aviation Business* (1940). ❧ Mining Industries: Harold Barger and S. H. Schurr, *Mining Industries, 1899–1939* (1944); V. E. Spencer, *Production, Employment and Productivity in the Mineral Extractive Industries* (1940); W. H. Hamilton and H. R. Wright, *Way of Order for Bituminous Coal* (1928), and *Case of Bituminous Coal* (1925); E. E. Hunt, F. G. Tryon and J. H. Willits, *What the Coal Commission Found* (1925); E. T. Devine, *Coal Economic Problems* (1925); J. L. Lewis, *Miners' Fight for American Standards* (1925). ❧ Oil: Ise, *Oil Policy;* G. W. Stocking, *Oil Industry and Competitive System* (1925); Ralph Arnold and W. J. Kemnitzer, *Petroleum in United States and Possessions* (1931); M. W. Watkins, *Oil: Stabilization or Conservation* (1937); W. A. Ver Wiebe, *Oil Fields* (1930); S. W. Tait, Jr., *Wildcatters* (1946). ❧ Real Estate: H. B. Vanderblue, "Florida Land Boom," *Jour. Land and Public Utility Econ.*, III, (1927), 113, 252; Sakolski, *Great American Land Bubble.* ❧ Other Industries: H. T. Warshow, ed., *Representative Industries* (1928); C. R. Daugherty, *et al.*, *Economics of Iron and Steel* (2 vols., 1937); N. R. Danielian, *A.T. & T.* (1939); Reavis Cox, *Competition in Tobacco Industry, 1911–1932* (1933); W. F. Maxwell, "Building Industry since War," *Rev. Econ. Stat.*, XIII (1931), 68; Broadus and G. S. Mitchell, *Industrial Revolution in South* (1930); W. J. Carson, ed., *Coming of Industry to South* (1931). ❡ Distribution: *Recent Economic Changes*, I, 321; M. P. McNair, "Trends in Large-Scale Retailing," *Harvard Bus. Rev.*, X (1931), 6; Ralph Borsodi, *Distribution Age* (1927); G. B. Hotchkiss, *Milestones of Marketing* (1938); Chase, *Tragedy of Waste;* Ralph Cassady, Jr., and W. L. Jones, *Changing Competitive Structure in Wholesale Grocery Trade* (1949); "A. and P. and the Hartfords," *Fortune*, Mar., 1933; "Case History of a Chain Store," *ibid.*, Nov., 1934; "Woolworth's $250,000,000 Trick," *ibid.*, Nov., 1933. ❡ Consumer Credit: C. O. Hardy, ed., *Consumer Credit and Its Uses* (1938); Evans Clark, *Financing the Consumer* (1930); E. R. A. Seligman, *Economics of Installment Selling* (1927). ❡ Advertising: F. A. Burt, *American Advertising Agencies* (1940); James Rorty, *Our Master's Voice* (1934); Stuart Chase and F. J. Schlink, *Your Money's Worth* (1927); C. A. Stocking, "Modern Advertising and Economic Theory," *Am. Econ. Rev.*, XXI (1931), 43; R. S. Durstine, *This Advertising Business* (1929). ❡ Export of Capital: Department of Commerce, *United States in World Economy* (1943); Herbert Feis, *Diplomacy of Dollar 1919–1932* (1950); Lewis, *America's Stake in International Investments;* M. F. Jolliffe, *United States as Financial Centre, 1919–1933* (1935); J. T. Madden, *et al., America's Experience as Creditor* (1937); A. I. Bloomfield, "Mechanism of Adjustment of Balance of Payments: 1919–1929," *Quar. Jour. of Econ.*, LVII (1943), 333; P. M. Mazur, *America Looks Abroad* (1930); W. A. Brown, Jr., *International Gold Standard 1914–1934* (1940); J. W. Angell, *Financial Foreign Policy* (1933); Max Winkler, *Foreign Bonds* (1933); Dept. of Commerce, *Handbook of American Underwriting of Foreign Securities, 1914–1929* (1930); Siegfried Stern, *United States in International Banking* (1951); C. W. Phelps, *Foreign Expansion of American Banks* (1927); South-ard, *American Industry in Europe;* R. R. Kuczynski, *American Loans to Germany* (1927), and *Bankers' Profits from German Loans* (1932); Remer, *Foreign Investments in China;* Marshall, *et al., Canadian-American Industry;* Max Winkler, *Investments of United States Capital in Latin America* (1929); Kepner and Soothill, *Banana Empire;* Rippy, *Capitalists and Colombia;* Marsh, *Bankers in Bolivia.* ❡ Foreign Trade: P. W. Bidwell, *Tariff Policy of United States* (1933); National Industrial Conference Board, *Trends in Foreign Trade of United States* (1930); J. H. Adler, *et al., Pattern of Import Trade since 1923* (1952); Abraham Berglund and P. G. Wright, *Tariff on Iron and Steel* (1929); M. A. Smith, *Tariff on Wool* (1926); P. G. Wright, *Sugar in Relation to the Tariff* (1924), and *Tariff on Animal and Vegetable Oils* (1928), and *American Tariff and Oriental Trade* (1931); L. R. Edminster, *Cattle Industry and Tariff* (1926); F. W. Taussig, "United States Tariff Commission," *Am. Econ. Rev.*, XVI (1926), 171; C. P. Goodykoontz, "Edward P. Costigan and Tariff Commission, 1917–1928," *Pacific Hist. Rev.*, XVI (1947), 410. ❡ Shipping Policy: Zeis, *American Shipping Policy;* H. K. Murphey, *American Merchant Marine Problem* (1929); D. H. Smith and P. V. Betters, *United States Shipping Board* (1931); E. S. Gregg, "Failure of Merchant Marine Act of 1920," *Am. Econ. Rev.*, XI (1921), 601. ❡ Philosophy of Prosperity: C. C. Chapman, *Development of Business and Banking Thought, 1913–1936* (1936); J. W. Prothro, "Business Ideas and the American Tradition," *Jour. of Pol.*, XV (1953), 67; W. T. Foster and Waddill Catchings, *Road to Plenty* (1928); T. N. Carver, *Present Economic Revolution in United States* (1925); Garet Garrett, *American Omen* (1928); P. M. Mazur, *American Prosperity* (1928); E. A. Filene, *Way Out* (1924). ❡ Business Leaders: F. W. Taussig and C. S. Joslyn, *American Business Leaders* (1932); R. W. Babson, *Actions and Reactions* (1935); W. P. Chrysler and Boyden Sparkes, *Life of an American Workman* (1938); Jenkins, *Duke;* Marquis James, *Alfred I. Du Pont* (1941); Winkler, *Du Pont;* Ackerman, *Eastman;* Dyer and Martin, *Edison;* H. S. Firestone and Samuel Crowther, *Men and Rubber* (1926); Alfred Lief, *Harvey Firestone* (1951); Sward, *Ford;* Henry Ford and Samuel Crowther, *My Life and Work* (1922), and *Today and Tomorrow* (1926); Harry Bennett and Paul Marcus, *We Never Called Him Henry* (1951); Tarbell, *Gary;* T. M. Girdler and Boyden Sparkes, *Bent Straps* (1943); J. H. Hammond, *Autobiography* (2 vols., 1935); P. H. Love, *Andrew W. Mellon* (1929); O'Connor, *Mellon's Millions;* Nicolson, *Morrow;* J. C. Penney, *Man with a Thousand Partners* (1931); M. R. Werner, *Julius Rosenwald* (1939); A. P. Sloan, Jr. and Boyden

Sparkes, *Adventures of a White-Collar Man* (1941); Hermann Hagedorn, *The Magnate: William Boyce Thompson* (1935); F. A. Vanderlip and Boyden Sparkes, *From Farm Boy to Financier* (1935); J. K. Winkler, *Five and Ten: Life of F. W. Woolworth* (1940); I. M. Tarbell, *Owen D. Young* (1932).

Sources — Demobilization: H. Commerce Committee, "Return of Railroads to Private Ownership," 66 Cong., 1 Sess., *Hearings* (3 vols., 1919); Cong. Conference Committee, "Federal Control of Railroads," 66 Cong., 2 Sess., *H. Report*, No. 650. ❡ Government and Business: American Column & Lumber Company, *et al. v.* United States, 257 U.S. 377; United States *v.* American Linseed Oil Company, *et al.*, 262 U.S. 371; Massachusetts *v.* Mellon 262 U.S. 447; Wolff Packing Company *v.* Court of Industrial Relations 262 U.S. 522; Cement Manufacturers' Protective Association, *et al. v.* United States, 268 U.S. 588; Maple Flooring Manufacturers Association, *et al. v.* United States, 268 U.S. 563; Tyson & Brothers *v.* Banton, 273 U.S. 418. ❡ Concentration: Federal Trade Commission, "Open-Price Trade Associations," 70 Cong., 2 Sess., *Sen. Doc.*, No. 226, and *Chain Store Inquiry* (7 vols., 1932–35). ❡ Banking: House Banking Committee, "Branch, Chain and Group Banking," 71 Cong., 2 Sess., *Hearings* (15 pts., 1930–1). ❡ Federal Reserve Policy: Federal Reserve Board, *Federal Reserve Bulletin*, and *Annual Report;* Sen. Banking Committee, "Operation of National and Federal Reserve Banking Systems," 71 Cong., 3 Sess., *Hearings* (7 pts., 1931). ❡ Investment Market: Sen. Banking Committee, "Brokers' Loans," 70 Cong., 1 Sess., *Hearings* (1928), and "Stock Exchange Practices," 72 Cong., 1 Sess., 73 Cong., 1, 2, Sess., *Hearings* (26 pts., 1932–34). ❡ Utilities: Federal Trade Commission, *Utility Corporations* (96 vols., 1929–37). ❡ Railroads: Sen. Interstate Commerce Committee, "Investigations of Railroads," 76 Cong., 3 Sess., *Sen. Report*, No. 1182, and 77 Cong., 3 Sess., *Sen. Report*, No. 714. ❡ Coal: U.S. Coal Commission, *Report*, 68 Cong., 2 Sess., *Sen. Doc.*, No. 195; Sen. Interstate Commerce Committee, "Conditions in Coal Fields," 70 Cong., 1 Sess., *Hearings* (10 pts., 1928). ❡ Oil: Federal Trade Commission, "Petroleum Prices, Profits and Competition," 70 Cong., 1 Sess., *Sen. Doc.*, No. 61; Federal Oil Conservation Board, *Reports* (5 vols., 1926–1932). ❡ Foreign Securities: Sen. Finance Committee, "Foreign Bonds," 72 Cong., 1 Sess., *Hearings* (4 pts., 1931). ❡ Tariff: Sen. Finance Committee, "Proposed Tariff Act of 1921," 67 Cong., 2 Sess., *Sen. Doc.*, No. 108, and "Digest of Tariff Hearings on H. R. 7456," 67 Cong., 2 Sess. (1922); H. Ways and Means Committee, "Tariff Readjustment," 70 Cong., 2 Sess., *Hearings* (18 pts., 1929); Sen. Finance Committee, "Tariff Act of 1929," 71 Cong., 1 Sess., *Hearings* (18 pts., 1929).

Bibliography — Soule, *Prosperity Decade*, 336; Library of Congress, *List of References on Trusts in United States* (1931); Special Libraries Assoc., *Trade Associations* (1934); P. M. Day, "Federal Reserve Banking System," N.Y. Public Library, *Bull.*, XXXV (1931), 229, 447; Library of Congress, *List of References on National and State Banks* (1933), and *List of References on Branch, Group, and Chain Banking* (1932), and *Books on Investments 1923–1931* (1932), and *Advertising* (1930); Dept. of Commerce, *Reading List on Installment Buying* (1928), and *Chain Store Bibliography* (1928); Library of Congress, *Public Utilities* (1928; supplements 1931, 1934); Securities and Exchange Commission, *List of References on Public Utilities* (1936); Library of Congress, *List of Recent References on Coal* (1927), and *Petroleum Industry* (1928); W. Z. Ripley, "Railroads," *Quar. Jour. of Econ.*, XL (1925), 152; Bur. of Railway Econ., *Railroad Consolidation* (1930), and *List of References on Railroad Holding Companies* (1931), and *Government Ownership of Railways* (1929); Bur. of Public Roads, *Motor Transport* (1933); Library of Congress, *List of References on Transportation* (1933); National Advisory Committee for Aeronautics, *Bibliography of Aeronautics* (11 vols., 1921–32); Library of Congress, *Selected List of Writings on American Merchant Marine* (1936), and *List of Books on Prominent American Business Men* (1932).

247. AGRICULTURAL POLICY, 1920–1929

Summary — Expansion in farm output; price collapse of 1921. — Attempts to deal with surplus: farm bloc; Federal Intermediate Credit Act (1923); McNary-Haugen bill (1924–28); export debenture plan; Agricultural Marketing Act (June 15, 1929). —

Changes in structure of agriculture: increase in tenancy; increase in indebtedness; decrease in farm population; new life on the farm, mechanization, electrification, telephones, automobiles. — Conservation of natural resources.

General — *Recent Economic Changes*, II, ch. viii; Barger and Landsberg, *American Agriculture;* Benedict, *Farm Policies*, chs. ix–xi; Chester Davis, "Development of Agricultural Policy since the World War," *Yearbook of Agriculture*, 1940, 297; Dept. of Ag., *Net Farm Income and Parity Report, 1943* (1944); Strauss and Bean, *Gross Farm Income;* J. L. Fulmer, *Agricultural Progress in Cotton Belt* (1950); L. J. Ducoff, *Wages of Agricultural Labor* (1944); S. E. Johnson, *Changes in American Farming* (1949); H. C. and A. D. Taylor, *Story of Agricultural Economics* (1952); J. S. Davis, *On Agricultural Policy, 1926–1938* (1939); Wilson Gee, *American Farm Policy* (1934), chs. ii–iii; A. E. Taylor, *Corn and Hog Surplus of Corn Belt* (1932); R. B. Vance, *Human Factors in Cotton Culture* (1929); Dale, *Range Cattle Industry;* Slosson, *Great Crusade*, ch. vii; Faulkner, *Versailles to New Deal*, ch. ix; Theodore Saloutos and J. D. Hicks, *Agricultural Discontent in Middle West* (1951), chs. vi–xiv,

Special — Farm Bloc: Nye, *Midwestern Progressive Politics*, 310; Russell Lord, *Wallaces of Iowa* (1947), chs. vii–ix; A. M. Christensen, "Agricultural Pressure and Governmental Response, 1919–1929," *Ag. Hist.*, XI (1937), 33; Grant McConnell, *Decline of Agrarian Democracy* (1953); O. M. Kile, *Farm Bureau through Three Decades* (1948); Ray Tucker and F. R. Barkley, *Sons of the Wild Jackass* (1932); Capper, *Agricultural Bloc;* J. A. Neprosh, *Brookhart Campaigns in Iowa* (1932). ⁋ Price Collapse of 1921: R. R. Enfield, *Agricultural Crisis: 1920–1923* (1924); C. L. Holmes, "Agricultural Readjustment in the Corn Belt," *Jour. Farm Econ.*, VII (1925), 229; "Agricultural Situation," *Am. Ac. Pol. Soc. Sci., Annals* CXVII (1925); A. S. Link, "Federal Reserve Policy and Agricultural Depression," *Ag. Hist.*, XX (1946), 166. ⁋ Agricultural Credits: Eliot, *Farmer's Campaign for Credit;* J. B. Norman, *Farm Credits* (1924); C. L. Benner, *Federal Intermediate Credit System* (1926); Frieda Baird and C. L. Benner, *Ten Years of Federal Intermediate Credits* (1933). ⁋ Farm Relief: J. D. Black, *Agricultural Reform in United States* (1929); Seligman, *Economics of Farm Relief;* D. C. Blaisdell, *Government and Agriculture* (1940); J. S. Davis, *Farm Export Debenture Plan* (1929); D. N. Kelley, "McNary-Haugen Bills, 1924–1928," *Ag. Hist.*, XIV (1940), 170; G. N. Peek and H. S. Johnson, *Equality for Agriculture* (1922); H. C. Wallace, *Our Debt and Duty to Farmer* (1925); R. G. Tugwell, "Reflections on Farm Relief," *Pol. Sci. Quar.*, XLIII (1928), 481. ⁋ Foreign Trade: E. G. Nourse, *American Agriculture and European Market*, and "Trend of Agricultural Exports," *Jour. Pol. Econ.*, XXXVI (1928), 330; § 246. ⁋ Marketing: F. E. Clark and L. D. H. Weld, *Marketing Agricultural Products* (1932); B. F. Goldstein, *Marketing* (1928); J. B. Baer and G. P. Woodruff, *Commodity Exchanges* (1929); G. W. Hoffman, *Future Trading upon Organized Commodity Markets* (1932); J. P. Warbasse, *Co-operative Democracy* (1927); H. C. Filley, *Cooperation in Agriculture* (1929); N. H. Comish, *Co-operative Marketing of Agricultural Products* (1929); R. F. Bergengren, *Cooperative Banking* (1923); E. G. Nourse and J. G. Knapp, *Co-operative Marketing of Livestock* (1931). ⁋ Processing: Clemen, *American Livestock Industry;* G. M. Weber and C. L. Alsberg, *American Vegetable-Shortening Industry* (1934); W. A. Sherman, *Merchandising Fruits and Vegetables* (1928). ⁋ Scientific Agriculture: Dept. of Ag., *Technology on Farm* (1940); Arthur Williams, *Power on Farm* (1927); C. R. Ball, "History of Wheat Improvement," *Ag. Hist.*, IV (1930), 48; H. W. Peck, "Influence of Agricultural Machinery and the Automobile on Farming," *Quar. Jour. Econ.*, XLI (1927), 534; C. B. Smith and M. C. Wilson, *Agricultural Extension System* (1930). ⁋ Tenancy: E. A. Goldenweiser and L. E. Truesdell, *Farm Tenancy* (1924); L. C. Gray, "Trend in Farm Ownership," *Am. Ac. Pol. Soc. Sci., Annals*, CXLII (1929), 20; L. E. Truesdell, "Farm Tenancy Moves West," *Jour. Farm Econ.*, VIII (1926), 443; H. A. Turner, "Absentee Farm Ownership," *Jour. Land Public Utility Econ.*, III (1927), 48; C. O. Brannen, *Relation of Land Tenure to Plantation Organization* (1924). ⁋ Rural Depopulation: L. E. Truesdell, *Farm Population* (1926); O. E. Baker, "Rural-Urban Migration," *Assoc. Am. Geog., Annals*, XXIII (1933), 59; T. N. Carver, "Rural Depopulation," *Jour. Farm Econ.*, IX (1927), 1; Jacob Perlman, "Recent Recession of Farm Population," *Jour.*

Land Public Utility Econ., IV (1928), 45; Taylor, "Our Rural Population Debacle," 156; Wilson Gee, "Qualitative Study of Rural Depopulation," *Am. Jour. Sociol.*, XXXIX (1933), 210. ◖ Land and Water Policy: Robbins, *Our Landed Heritage*, 398; Peffer, *Closing Public Domain*, chs. ix-x; Dept. of Ag., *Changes in Utilization of Land, 1914–1924* (1926); Ganoe, "Desert Land Act since 1891," 266; J. K. Kerwin, *Federal Water-Power Legislation* (1926); A. D. Frank, *Development of Federal Flood Control on Mississippi* (1930); Lampen, *Federal Reclamation;* P. L. Kleinsorge, *Boulder Canyon Project* (1941). ◖ Farm Life: J. M. Williams, *Expansion of Rural Life* (1926); E. L. Kirkpatrick, *et al.*, *Family Living in Farm Homes* (1924), and (with J. T. Sanders), *Relation between Ability to Pay and Standard of Living among Farmers* (1926), and *Farmer's Standard of Living* (1926); C. B. Sherman, "Development of Rural Fiction," *Ag. Hist.*, XII (1938), 67.

Sources — Price Collapse of 1921: "Agricultural Crisis," 67 Cong., 1 Sess., *H. Report,* No. 408. ◖ Farm Relief: "Agricultural Surplus Control Bill," 70 Cong., 1 Sess., *Sen. Report,* No. 500, *H. Report,* No. 1141; Sen. Ag. Committee, "Farm Relief Legislation," 71 Cong., 1 Sess., *Hearings* (1929); H. Ag. Committee, "Agricultural Relief," 71 Cong., 1 Sess., *Hearings* (9 pts., 1929). ◖ Processing: H. Ag. Committee, "Meat-Packer Legislation," 66 Cong., 3 Sess., *Hearings* (1920); Dept. of Ag., "Merger of Meat-Packing Companies," 67 Cong., 4 Sess., *Sen. Doc.*, No. 283; Federal Trade Commission," "Competition and Profits in Bread and Flour," 70 Cong., 1 Sess., *Sen. Doc.*, No. 98. ◖ Flood Control: H. Flood Control Committee, 70 Cong., 1 Sess., *Hearings* (7 pts., 1927–28); Dept. of Ag., "Relation of Forestry to Control of Floods in Mississippi Valley," 70 Cong., 2 Sess., *H. Doc.*, No. 573.

Bibliography — E. E. Edwards, *Selected References on History of Agriculture in United States* (1939); Shannon, *Farmer's Last Frontier*, ch. xvi; Bur. of Ag. Econ., *American Farm Problem* (1934), and *Agricultural Economics* (1929), and *Agricultural Relief* (1933); J. S. Davis, "Recent Books on Agricultural Situation," *Quar. Jour. Econ.*, XLIII (1929), 532, and "Literature of Agricultural Situation," *ibid.*, XLIV (1929), 138; Bur. of Ag. Econ., *Agricultural Labor 1915–1935* (1935), and *Large Scale and Corporation Farming* (1929), and *Farm Tenancy 1925–1934* (1935), and *Taxation and the Farmer* (1928), and *Wheat* (1931), and *Meat Industry* (1928), and *Rural Standards of Living* (1930); B. Y. Landis, *Guide to Literature of Rural Life* (1932); Dept. of Ag., *List of Publications 1901 to 1925* (1927), and *List of Publications 1926 to 1930* (1932), and *Index to Publications 1901–1925* (1932), and *Index to Publications 1926–1930* (1935), and *Index to Department Bulletins Nos. 1–1500* (1936).

248. LABOR MOVEMENT, 1920–1929

Summary — Postwar strikes: railroad shopmen (July 1, 1922) and Daugherty injunction (Sept. 1); coal strike (Apr. 1); Herrin massacre (June); establishment of Coal Commission (Sept. 22). — Harding and the campaign against the 12-hour day. — American Federation of Labor; decline in militancy and membership. — Disappearance of I.W.W. — Failure of Communist dual unionism. — Role of the courts in limiting picketing (Truax *v.* Corrigan, 1921); in reducing labor's protection under the Clayton Act (Duplex *v.* Deering, 1921); in opposing minimum wage legislation (Adkins case, 1922). — Open shop drive by employers; company unions. — Social legislation; role of National Consumers' League.

General — Commons, *History of Labour*, III, IV, § 4; Dulles, *Labor in America*, ch. iv; "Fifty Years' Progress of American Labor," *Monthly Labor Rev.*, LXXI (1950), 1; J. B. S. Hardman, ed., *American Labor Dynamics* (1928); J. D. Durand, *Labor Force, 1890–1960* (1948), chs. ii-v; Fabricant, *Employment in Manufacturing;* Ogburn, *Recent Social Changes*, 80.

Special — Labor Organization: Leo Wolman, *Ebb and Flow in Trade Unionism* (1936), chs. iii-iv; D. J. Saposs, "American Labor Movement Since War," *Quar. Jour. Econ.*, XLIX (1935), 236; Selig Perlman, *Theory of Labor Movement* (1928); Lorwin,

American Federation of Labor; W. C. Roberts, comp., *American Federation of Labor* (2 vols., 1919–24); Harold Seidman, *Labor Czars* (1938); Lanfear, *Business Fluctuations and Labor;* V. J. Wyckoff, *Wage Policies of Labor Organizations in Depression* (1926). ❧ Coal: A. F. Hinrichs, *United Mine Workers and Non-Union Coal Fields* (1923); Suffern, *Coal Miners' Struggle;* W. J. Walsh, *United Mine Workers* (1931); Lewis, *Miners' Fight for Standards.* ❧ Railroads: H. D. Wolf, *Railway Labor Board* (1927); L. A. Wood, *Union-Management Cooperation on Railroads* (1931); Richberg, *Tents of Mighty.* ❧ Others: William Haber, *Industrial Relations in Building* (1930); T. L. Norton, *Trade-Union Policies in Massachusetts Shoe Industry, 1919–29* (1932); G. S. Mitchell, *Textile Unionism and South* (1931). ❧ Left-Wing Unionism: Saposs, *Left-Wing Unionism;* Gambs, *Decline of I. W. W.;* James Oneal and G. A. Werner, *American Communism* (1947), ch. x; D. M. Schneider, *Workers' (Communist) Party and Unions* (1928); Ralph Chaplin, *Wobbly* (1948). ❧ Labor Leaders: Stolberg, *Tailor's Progress;* W. Z. Foster, *From Bryan to Stalin* (1937), and *Pages from a Worker's Life* (1939); Gompers, *Seventy Years,* II; Reed, *Philosophy of Gompers;* Haywood, *Haywood's Book;* Matthew Josephson, *Sidney Hillman* (1953); J. A. Wechsler, *Labor Baron, John L. Lewis* (1944); S. D. Alinsky, *John L. Lewis* (1949). ❧ Working Conditions: Lazare Teper, *Hours of Labor* (1932); Cahill, *Shorter Hours;* Isador Lubin, *Absorption of Unemployed by Industry* (1929); R. M. Woodbury, *Workers' Health and Safety* (1927); Beyer, *Labor Legislation for Women;* National Consumers' League, *National Consumers' League 1899–1924* (1925); Mary Anderson and M. N. Winslow, *Woman at Work* (1952); Josephine Goldmark, *Impatient Crusader: Florence Kelley* (1953); W. F. Cottrell, *Railroader* (1940); Lois Macdonald, *Southern Mill Hills* (1928); H. J. Lahne, *Cotton Mill Worker* (1944). ❧ Strikes: J. I. Griffin, *Strikes* (1939); H. M. Douty, "Trend of Industrial Disputes, 1922–1930," Am. Stat. Assoc., *Jour.,* XXVII (1932), 168; M. H. Vorse, *Passaic Textile Strike, 1926–1927* (1927); Albert Weisbord, *Passaic* (1926); Liston Pope, *Millhands and Preachers: Gastonia* (1942); F. E. Beal, *Proletarian Journey* (1937), chs. viii–xv; Am. Civil Liberties Union, *Justice — North Carolina Style* (1930). ❧ Employer Attitudes: S. H. Slichter, "Current Labor Policies of American Industries," *Quar. Jour. Econ.,* XLIII (1929), 393; A. G. Taylor, *Labor Policies of National Association of Manufacturers* (1927); Herbert Feis, *Labor Relations in Procter and Gamble* (1928); Savel Zimand, *Open Shop Drive* (1921); Sidney Howard, *Labor Spy* (1924); Clinch Calkins, *Spy Overhead* (1937); Leo Huberman, *Labor Spy Racket* (1937); Edward Levinson, *I Break Strikes* (1935). ❧ Role of Government: C. O. Gregory, *Labor and Law* (1946); W. L. McNaughton, *Development of Labor Relations Law* (1941); E. E. Witte, *Government in Labor Disputes* (1932); Edward Berman, *Labor and Sherman Act,* and "Supreme Court Interprets Railway Labor Act," *Am. Econ. Rev.,* XX (1930), 619; Frankfurter and Greene, *Labor Injunction;* J. I. Seidman, *Yellow Dog Contract* (1932); A. G. Hays, *Trial by Prejudice* (1933); Elias Lieberman, *Unions before the Bar* (1950).

Sources — Cases: Duplex Printing Press Co. *v.* Deering, 254 U.S. 443; American Steel Foundries *v.* Tri-City Central Trades Council, 257 U.S. 184; Truax *v.* Corrigan, 257 U.S. 312; United Mine Workers *v.* Coronado Coal Company, 259 U.S. 344; Adkins *v.* Children's Hospital, 261 U.S. 525; Coronado Coal Company *v.* United Mine Workers, 268 U.S. 295; Texas and N. O. Railroad *v.* Brotherhood of Railway Clerks, 281 U.S. 548.

Bibliography — M. S. Pitzele, ed., "Significant Books on Labor," *Monthly Labor Rev.,* LXXI (1950), 87; L. A. Thompson, "Injunctions in Labor Disputes," *ibid.,* XXVII (1928), 631; P. F. Brissenden, "Labor Turnover," *ibid.,* XXIV (1927), 842; Industrial Relations Counselors, *Unemployment Compensation* (1928), and *Unemployment Insurance* (1932); L. A. Thompson, *Unemployment Insurance and Reserves* (1935), and "Five Day Week," *Monthly Labor Rev.,* XXXII (1931), 501; E. L. Stone, "Public Old-Age Pensions," *ibid.,* XXII (1922), 1414, XXVIII (1929), 1161, XXXIII (1932), 738; National Child Labor Committee, *Child Labor 1920–1927* (1927); J. S. Gummere, "Bibliography of American Workmen's Compensation Commission Reports," *Law Library Jour.,* XXVIII (1935), 42; Dept. of Labor, *List on Minimum Wage for Women* (1925).

249. POLITICS, 1924–1929

Summary — Republican party in 1924; Calvin Coolidge nominated. — Democratic party: A. E. Smith and W. G. McAdoo; nomination of J. W. Davis. — Progressive Party; Socialist and American Federation of Labor endorsement. — Coolidge elected. — Rise of progressive Republicans ("sons of the wild jackass"). — Congressional elections of 1926. — Coolidge, "I do not choose to run" (Aug. 2, 1927); Herbert Hoover nominated. — Democrats nominate Smith. — Campaign; Hoover elected; "solid south" splintered.

General — Faulkner, *Versailles to New Deal*, chs. vii–ix; Allen, *Only Yesterday*, ch. vii; Schriftgiesser, *This Was Normalcy*, chs. xv–xxv; Walter Lippmann, *Men of Destiny* (1927); O. G. Villard, *Prophets True and False* (1928); Kirby, *Highlights;* Murrow and Friendly, "I Can Hear It Now," III.

Special — Calvin Coolidge: W. A. White, *Coolidge;* C. M. Fuess, *Calvin Coolidge* (1940); Coolidge, *Autobiography* (1929). ❡ Other Political Leaders: C. O. Johnson, *Borah of Idaho* (1936); B. N. Timmons, *Dawes*, chs. xvi–xx, and *Garner of Texas* (1948), chs. vi–viii; W. E. Edge, *Jerseyman's Journal* (1948), chs. vi–vii; Hull, *Memoirs*, vol. I, chs. vii–x; B. C. and Fola La Follette, *La Follette* (2 vols., 1953); A. R. Longworth, *Crowded Hours* (1933); C. L. de Chambrun, *Nicholas Longworth* (1933); Love, *Mellon;* O'Connor, *Mellon's Millions;* Norris, *Fighting Liberal;* Lief, *Democracy's Norris;* G. W. Pepper, *Philadelphia Lawyer* (1944); Watson, *As I Knew Them.* ❡ 1924 Election: § 245; T. A. Huntley, *John W. Davis* (1924); K. C. MacKay, *Progressive Movement* (1947); J. H. Shideler, "La Follette Campaign," *Wisc. Mag. Hist.*, XXXIII (1950), 444. ❡ Coolidge Administration: Calvin Coolidge, *Foundations of Republic* (1926); C. B. Slemp, *Mind of President* (1926); C. G. Dawes, *Notes as Vice-President, 1928–1929* (1935); Cyril Clemens and A. P. Daggett, "Coolidge's 'I Do Not Choose to Run,'" *N. Eng. Quar.*, XVIII (1945), 147; C. H. Wooddy, *Case of Frank L. Smith* (1931). ❡ Hoover: Herbert Hoover, *Memoirs*, and *American Individualism* (1922); Hofstadter, *American Political Tradition*, ch. xi; W. H. Irwin, *Herbert Hoover* (1928). ❡ Alfred E. Smith: H. F. Pringle, *Alfred E. Smith* (1937); A. E. Smith, *Up to Now* (1929); Norman Hapgood and Henry Moskowitz, *Up from City Streets* (1927). ❡ 1928 Election: § 245; R. V. Peel and T. C. Donnelly, *Campaign of 1928* (1931); Samuel Lubell, *Future of American Politics* (1952), ch. iii; J. K. Pollock, "Campaign Funds in 1928," *Am. Pol. Sci. Rev.*, XXIX (1929), 59; W. F. Ogburn and N. S. Talbot, "Measurement of Factors in Election of 1928," *Social Forces*, VIII (1929), 175; G. C. Fite, "Agricultural Issue in Campaign of 1928," *Miss. Valley Hist. Rev.*, XXXVII (1951), 653; Michael Williams, *Shadow of Pope* (1932), chs. x–xv; Herbert Hoover, *New Day* (1928); A. E. Smith, *Campaign Speeches* (1929). ❡ Local Politics: Zink, *City Bosses;* Werner, *Tammany Hall*, ch. vii.

Bibliography — Stirn, *Bibliography of LaFollette.*

250. FOREIGN POLICY, 1921–1929

Summary — Resurgence of isolationism; rejection of League of Nations. — Arms limitation; Washington Conference; Five-Power Naval Treaty (Feb. 6, 1922); disarmament negotiations. — Kellogg-Briand Pact (Jan. 15, 1929). — Relations with League and World Court. — Intervention and conciliation in Latin America; Nicaragua, Mexico. — Far Eastern policy; Nine-Power Treaty (Feb. 6, 1922). — Foreign economic policy; reparations and war debts, foreign lending (§ 246), tariff (§ 246). — Immigration policy (§ 251). — Recognition policy. — Popular attitudes, internationalism, isolationism, pacifism.

General — Allan Nevins, *United States in Chaotic World* (1950), chs. i–v; Perkins, *America and Two Wars;* Bemis, *Diplomatic History*, chs. xxxv–xli; Bailey, *Diplomatic History*, chs. xli–xliii; Council on Foreign Relations, *Survey of American Foreign Rela-*

tions: 1928 (1928); R. W. Van Alstyne, *American Crisis Diplomacy* (1952); E. M. Earle, "Half-Century of American Foreign Policy 1898–1948," *Pol. Sci. Quar.*, LXIV (1949), 168; F. H. Simonds, *American Foreign Policy in Post-War Years* (1935); Drew Pearson and Constantine Brown, *American Diplomatic Game* (1935); Theodore Roosevelt, Jr., *Colonial Policies* (1937).

Special — State Department: Bemis, *American Secretaries of State*, X; Pusey, *Hughes*, II, chs. xxxix–lvii; C. E. Hughes, *Pathway of Peace* (1925); Bryn-Jones, *Kellogg*; J. C. Grew, *Turbulent Era* (1952), chs. xvi–xxvii; William Phillips, *Ventures in Diplomacy* (1953); H. R. Wilson, *Diplomat between Wars* (1941); G. H. Stuart, *The Department of State* (1949); "Ten Years under Rogers Act," *Am. Foreign Service Jour.*, XI (1934), 341, 390. ❡ Congress and Foreign Policy: Johnson, *Borah*; G. L. Grassmuck, *Sectional Biases in Congress on Foreign Policy* (1951); Leopold, "Mississippi Valley and Foreign Policy"; E. E. Dennison, *Senate Foreign Relations Committee* (1942); A. C. F. Westphal, *House Committee on Foreign Affairs* (1942). ❡ Arms Limitation: Merze Tate, *United States and Armaments* (1948), chs. v–x; B. H. Williams, *United States and Disarmament* (1931); H. H. and Margaret Sprout, *Toward a New Order of Sea Power* (1940); G. T. Davis, *Navy Second to None* (1940); Roger Burlingame, *General Billy Mitchell* (1952); John Wheeler-Bennett, *Disarmament and Security* (1932); D. P. Myers, *World Disarmament* (1932). ❡ Washington Conference: R. L. Buell, *Washington Conference* (1922); C. L. Hoag, *Preface to Preparedness* (1941); J. C. Vinson, "Drafting of Four-Power Treaty," *Jour. Modern Hist.*, XXV (1953), 40. ❡ Kellogg-Briand Pact: R. H. Ferrell, *Peace in Their Time* (1952); J. E. Stoner, *S. O. Levinson and Pact of Paris* (1943); S. O. Levinson, *Outlawry of War* (1921); D. H. Miller, *Peace Pact of Paris* (1928); D. P. Myers, *Origin of Paris Pact* (1929); J. T. Shotwell, *War as Instrument of Policy* (1929); C. C. Morrison, *Outlawry of War* (1927); H. L. Stimson, *Pact of Paris* (1932). ❡ Pacifism: Allen, *Fight for Peace*; F. B. Boeckel, *Between War and Peace* (1928); Selig Adler, "War-Guilt Question, 1918–1928," *Jour. Modern Hist.*, XXII (1951), 1. ❡ International Coöperation: D. F. Fleming, *United States and World Organization, 1920–1933* (1938), and *United States and World Court* (1945); C. A. Berdahl, "Relations of United States with Assembly of League," *Am. Pol. Sci. Rev.*, XXVI (1932), 99, and "Relations of United States with Council of League," *ibid.*, XXVI (1932), 497; F. R. Coudert, "United States and Court of International Justice," *Am. Bar Assoc. Jour.*, XVIII (1932), 415; H. M. Wriston, "American Participation in International Conferences," *Am. Jour. Int. Law*, XX (1926), 33; James Myers, "American Relations with International Labor Office, 1919–1932," *Am. Ac. Pol. Soc. Sci., Annals*, CXLVI (1933), 135; Keith Clark, *International Communications American Attitude* (1931). ❡ Debts and Reparations: H. G. Moulton and Leo Pasvolsky, *World War Debt Settlements* (1926), and *War Debts and World Prosperity* (1932); Carl Bergmann, *History of Reparations* (1927); C. G. Dawes, *Journal of Reparations* (1939); R. C. Dawes, *Dawes Plan in Making* (1925); G. P. Auld, *Dawes Plan and New Economics* (1927), and "Dawes and Young Loans," *Foreign Affairs*, XIII (1934), 6; D. P. Myers, *Reparation Settlement* (1930); J. W. Wheeler-Bennett, *Wreck of Reparations* (1933). ❡ Relations with American States: Keenleyside and Brown, *Canada and United States*; E. W. McInnis, *Unguarded Frontier* (1942); Bemis, *Latin American Policy of United States*; Perkins, *Hands Off*, ch. viii; Laurence Duggan, *Americas: Search for Hemispheric Security* (1949); C. E. Hughes, *Our Relations to Western Hemisphere* (1928); C. H. Haring, *South America Looks at United States* (1928); Winkler, *Investments in Latin America*; J. O. Murdock, "Arbitration and Conciliation in Pan America," *Am. Jour. Int. Law*, XXIII (1929), 273; Dexter Perkins, *United States and Caribbean* (1947); Fitzgibbon, *Cuba and United States*; H. F. Guggenheim, *United States and Cuba* (1934); Jenks, *Cuban Colony*; P. G. Wright, *Cuban Situation* (1931); Welles, *Naboth's Vineyard*; Knight, *Americans in Santo Domingo*; Montague, *Haiti and United States*; A. C. Millspaugh, *Haiti, 1915–1930* (1931); Howard Cline, *United States and Mexico* (1953); E. H. Gruening, *Mexico and Its Heritage* (1928); F. S. Dunn, *Diplomatic Protection of Americans in Mexico* (1933); Nicolson, *Morrow*; A. H. Feller, *Mexico Claims Commission, 1923–1934* (1935); Cox, *Nicaragua and United States*; H. L. Stimson, *American Policy in Nicaragua* (1927); Denny, *Dollars for Bullets*; McCain, *United States and Panama*; Sands and Lalley, *Our Jungle Diplomacy*; A. P. Whitaker, *United States and South America* (1948); Rippy, *Capitalists and Colom-*

bia; Parks, *Colombia and United States*; Marsh, *Bankers in Bolivia*; Hill, *United States and Brazil*; Evans, *Chile and United States*; C. H. Haring, *Argentina and United States* (1941); O. E. Smith, Jr., *Yankee Diplomacy in Argentina* (1953). ❡ Great Britain: C. C. Brinton, *United States and Britain* (1948); Nicholas Roosevelt, *America and England* (1930); Esme Howard, *Theatre of Life* (2 vols., 1935–36). ❡ Continental Europe: D. C. McKay, *United States and France* (1951); André Tardieu, *France and America* (1927); T. B. Mott, *Myron T. Herrick* (1929); H. H. Fisher and Sidney Brooks, *America and New Poland* (1928); F. D. Scott, *United States and Scandinavia* (1950). ❡ Near East and Africa: L. V. Thomas and R. N. Frye, *United States and Turkey and Iran* (1951); L. J. Gordon, *American Relations with Turkey* (1932); E. A. Speiser, *United States and Near East* (1949); F. E. Manuel, *Realities of American-Palestine Relations* (1949); F. J. Manheim, "United States and Ethiopia," *Jour. Negro Hist.*, XVII (1932), 141. ❡ Far East: Griswold, *Far Eastern Policy*; G. F. Kennan, *American Diplomacy, 1900–1950* (1951), ch. iii; E. M. Patterson, ed., "American Policy in Pacific," Am. Ac. Pol. Soc. Sci., *Annals*, CLXVIII (1933); J. K. Fairbank, *United States and China* (1948); Wên-huan Ma, *American Policy toward China in Debates of Congress* (1934); R. T. Pollard, *China's Foreign Relations, 1917–1931* (1933); A. E. Kane, *China and Washington Conference* (1937); Yamato Ichihashi, *Washington Conference and After* (1928); Dorothy Borg, *American Policy and Chinese Revolution, 1925–1928* (1947); E. O. Reischauer, *United States and Japan* (1950); Tupper and McReynolds, *Japan in American Opinion*; H. C. Bywater, *Sea-Power in Pacific* (1921); Pauline Tompkins, *American-Russian Relations in Far East* (1949); Forbes, *Philippine Islands*; G. L. Kirk, *Philippine Independence* (1936). ❡ Recognition Policy: Taylor Cole, *Recognition Policy since 1901* (1928); Chesney Hill, *Recent Policies of Non-Recognition* (1933); J. L. McMahon, *Recent Changes in Recognition Policy* (1933); L. L. Jaffe, *Judicial Aspects of Foreign Relations* (1933); R. P. Browder, *Origins of Soviet-American Diplomacy* (1953); Bailey, *America Faces Russia*, ch. xxi; W. A. Williams, *American-Russian Relations, 1781–1947* (1952), ch. vii; F. L. Schuman, *American Policy toward Russia since 1917* (1928); Meno Lovenstein, *American Opinion of Soviet Russia* (1941); P. H. Anderson, *Attitude of American Leftist Leaders Toward Russian Revolution* (1942); J. G. Hodgson, comp., *Recognition of Soviet Russia* (1925).

Sources — *Foreign Relations*; P. C. Jessup, comp., *United States and Court of International Justice* (1931); Gantenbein, *Latin-American Policy*; Clyde, *United States Policy toward China*.

Bibliography — W. L. Langer and H. F. Armstrong, eds., *Foreign Affairs Bibliography, 1919–32* (1933); Carnegie Endowment, *Disarmament and Security* (1931); League of Nations, *Annotated Bibliography on Disarmament and Military Questions* (1931); Library of Congress, *List of References on Washington Conference* (1925; supplements, 1927, 1929), and *Disarmament* (1929; supplement, 1934), and *List on Reparations* (1932; supplement, 1933), and *Inter-Allied Debt* (1931; supplements, 1933, 1934, 1936); D. S. Jordan, *For International Peace* (1927); W. H. Kelchner, *Inter-American Conferences, 1926–1933* (1933); Pan-American Union, *Selected List on Inter-American Relations* (1932); Library of Congress, *United States Relations with Mexico and Central America* (1928), and *Selected List on Relations with Union of Soviet Socialist Republics, 1919–1935* (1935); G. W. Cotts, *United States and Haiti* (1931).

251. CIVIL LIBERTIES AND MINORITIES, 1921–1929

Summary — Postwar red scare; Palmer hysteria; Lusk inquiry; Sacco-Vanzetti case. — Radical political parties. — Supreme Court decisions; *Gitlow* case (1925), *Whitney* case (1927). — Revival of Ku Klux Klan. — Immigration Act of 1924, establishment of quotas, and Oriental exclusion. — Status of foreign nationality groups in United States. — Status of Negroes. — Censorship in literature; attacks on textbooks.

General — Chafee, *Free Speech*, chs. vii–x; Slosson, *Great Crusade*, ch. xi; Hays, *Let Freedom Ring*; J. M. Mecklin, *Ku Klux Klan* (1924); Norman Hapgood, *Professional Patriots* (1928); E. F. A. Dowell, *History of Criminal Syndicalism Legislation* (1937).

Special — Postwar Red Scare: J. P. Clark, *Deportations of Aliens* (1931); L. F. Post, *Deportations Delirium* (1923); R. D. Warth, "Palmer Raids," *So. Atl. Quar.*, XLVIII (1949), 1; W. S. Bernard, "Arms and the Alien: Post-war Hysteria," *Rocky Mountain Law Rev.*, XI (1939), 243; Lombardi, *Labor's Voice in Cabinet*, ch. xiv; Felix Frankfurter, *Case of Sacco and Vanzetti* (1927); G. L. Joughin and E. M. Morgan, *Legacy of Sacco and Vanzetti* (1948). ¶ Radical Political Parties: Egbert and Persons, *Socialism and American Life*, I, 302; Morris Hillquit, *Loose Leaves from Busy Life* (1934); Russell, *Bare Hands*; Oscar Ameringer, *If You Don't Weaken* (1940); Arnold Petersen, *Revolutionary Milestones* (1931); Henry Kuhn and O. M. Johnson, *Socialist Labor Party* (1931); Oneal and Werner, *American Communism*, chs. iii–xiii; Benjamin Gitlow, *I Confess* (1940); W. Z. Foster, *History of Communist Party of United States* (1952); C. E. Ruthenberg, *Speeches and Writings* (Jay Lovestone, ed., 1928); Jay Lovestone, *Pages from Party History* (1929); J. P. Cannon, *History of American Trotskyism* (1944); Alexander Bittelman, *Fifteen Years of Communist Party* (1934). ¶ Supreme Court: Max Lerner, ed., *Mind and Faith of Justice Holmes* (1943), 289; Frankfurter, *Holmes*; Francis Biddle, *Mr. Justice Holmes* (1942); Holmes, *Dissenting Opinions*, 39, 229; Mason, *Brandeis*, chs. xxxv–xxxvi; Alfred Lief, ed., *Social and Economic Views of Mr. Justice Brandeis* (1930), 209. ¶ Immigration: Wittke, *We Who Built America*, pt. 3; Donald Young, *American Minority Peoples* (1932); Sidney Kansas, *United States Immigration, Exclusion and Deportation* (1940); Handlin, *Uprooted*; D. H. Smith and H. G. Herring, *Bureau of Immigration* (1924). ¶ Immigration Act of 1924: Garis, *Immigration Restriction*; R. W. Paul, *Abrogation of Gentlemen's Agreement* (1936). ¶ Negro: Franklin, *Slavery to Freedom*, chs. xxv–xxvi; Myrdal, *American Dilemma*; E. L. Tatum, *Changed Political Thought of Negro, 1915–1940* (1951); W. D. Weatherford and C. S. Johnson, *Race Relations* (1934); W. E. B. Du Bois, *Black Folks, Then and Now* (1939); Alain Locke, *New Negro* (1925); M. J. Herskovits, *American Negro* (1928); B. H. Nelson, *Fourteenth Amendment and Negro since 1920* (1946); A. F. Raper, *Tragedy of Lynching* (1933); Walter White, *Rope and Faggot* (1929); R. L. Jack, *History of National Association for Advancement Colored People* (1943); J. H. Harmon, A. G. Lindsay, and C. G. Woodson, *Negro as Businessman* (1929); L. J. Green and C. G. Woodson, *Negro Wage Earner* (1930); S. D. Spero and A. L. Harris, *Black Worker* (1931); Wesley, *Negro Labor*; National Urban League, *Negro Membership in Unions* (1930); E. E. Lewis, *Mobility of Negro* (1931), and "Southern Negro and Labor Supply," *Pol. Sci. Quar.*, XLVIII (1933), 172; Kennedy, *Negro Peasant Turns Cityward*; B. E. Mays and J. W. Nicholson, *Negro's Church* (1932); Loggins, *Negro Author*; Reid, *Negro Immigrant*; G. F. Robinson, Jr., "Negro in Politics in Chicago," *Jour. Negro Hist.*, XVII (1932), 180. ¶ Negro Leaders: H. F. Gosnell, *Negro Politicians* (1935); C. O. Peare, *Mary McLeod Bethune* (1951); W. E. B. Du Bois, *Dusk of Dawn* (1940); A. J. Garvey, *Philosophy and Opinions of Marcus Garvey* (1923); M. A. Garvey, *Aims and Objects* (1924); R. G. Brisbane, Jr., "Some New Light on Garvey," *Jour. Negro Hist.*, XXXVI (1951), 53; J. W. Holley, *You Can't Build a Chimney from Top* (1948); J. W. Johnson, *Along This Way* (1933); Walter White, *Man Called White*. ¶ Censorship: M. L. Ernst and Alexander Lindsey, *Censor Marches On* (1940); M. L. Ernst and William Seagle, *To the Pure* (1928); M. W. Dennett, *Who's Obscene?* (1930); C. R. Gillett, *Burned Books* (1932); Walter Lippmann, *American Inquisitors* (1928); L. H. Allen, *Bryan and Darrow at Dayton* (1925); Maynard Shipley, *War on Modern Science* (1927); Stone, *Darrow*; Pierce, *Public Opinion and Teaching History*; C. G. Miller, *Poisoned Loving-Cup* (1928); American Civil Liberties Union, *Gag on Teaching* (1931).

Sources — Deportations: Dept. Justice, "Report on Persons Advising Overthrow of Government," 66 Cong., 1 Sess., *Sen. Doc.*, No. 153; H. Immigration Committee, "Communist and Anarchist Deportation Cases," 66 Cong., 2 Sess., *Hearings* (1920), and "I. W. W. Deportation Cases," *ibid.*, and "Communist Deportation Cases," *ibid.*; H. Rules Committee, "Investigation of Louis F. Post," 66 Cong., 2 Sess., *Hearings* (1920). — ¶ Bolshevism: Sen. Foreign Relations Committee, "Russian Propaganda," 66 Cong., 2 Sess., *Hearings* (13 pts., 1920), and *Sen. Report*, No. 526; Dept. Justice, *Red Radicalism Described Its Leaders* (1920); [Lusk Committee], *Revolutionary Radicalism* (1920). ¶ Civil Liberties Cases: Gitlow *v.* New York, 268 U.S. 652; Whitney *v.* California, 274 U.S. 357; Stromberg *v.* California, 283 U.S. 359; Near *v.* Minnesota, 283 U.S. 697;

Powell *v.* Alabama, 287 U.S. 45. ❡ Immigration: H. Immigration Committee, "Restriction of Immigration," 67 Cong., 1 Sess., *H. Report*, No. 4, and "Immigration," 67 Cong., 2 Sess., *Hearings* (1922–23), and "Restriction of Immigration," 68 Cong., 1 Sess., *H. Report*, No. 350; Sen. Immigration Committee, "Selective Immigration Legislation," 68 Cong., 1 Sess., *Hearings* (1924).

Bibliography — Schroeder, *Free Speech Bibliography*; Work, *Bibliography of Negro*; Egbert and Persons, *Socialism and American Life*, II; W. R. Janeway, *Bibliography of Immigration 1900–1930* (1934); Library of Congress, *Deportation of Aliens* (1931), and *Immigration* (1930), and *List on the "National Origins" Provision* (1926), and *Select List on Chinese Immigration* (1929); A. E. MacGeorge, "Restriction of Immigration, 1920 to 1925," *Monthly Labor Rev.*, XXII (1926), 510; E. S. Bogardus, *Mexican Immigrant* (1929).

252. INTELLECTUAL LIFE, 1921–1929

Summary — Reëxamination of America: in criticism (Mencken, Brooks); in fiction (Lewis, Dreiser, Fitzgerald, Dos Passos); in philosophy (Dewey); in economics (Veblen, Mitchell); in history and biography ("New History"; debunkers); expatriates (Eliot, Pound, Hemingway). — Defense of existing order: New Humanism (Babbitt, More); literature of acceptance (Tarkington, Guest). — New developments in theater (O'Neill); in films (Griffiths, Chaplin). — Democratization of culture; book clubs; "lively arts." — Progressivism and conservatism in education. — New tendencies in theology (fundamentalism and modernism). — Architecture and the arts. — Music.

General — Commager, *American Mind*, chs. xiv–xx; Spiller, *Literary History*, II, chs. lxx–lxxx; Slosson, *Great Crusade*, chs. xii–xv; Allen, *Only Yesterday*, chs. viii–ix; M. G. White, *Social Thought*; Morris, *Postscript to Yesterday*; Cargill, *Intellectual America*; Gilbert Seldes, *Seven Lively Arts* (1924); Larkin, *Art and Life in America*, chs. xxix–xxx; Gabriel, *American Democratic Thought*, chs. xxviii–xxx; Curti, *Growth of American Thought*, ch. xxvii; J. W. Krutch, *Modern Temper* (1929); J. K. Hutchens, ed., *American Twenties* (1952); William Hodapp, ed., *Pleasures of Jazz Age* (1948).

Special — Literary Life: Edmund Wilson, *Shores of Light* (1952); Kazin, *On Native Grounds*; Malcolm Cowley, ed., *After the Genteel Tradition* (1937); Irene and Allen Cleaton, *Books and Battles* (1937); F. J. Hoffman, *et al.*, *Little Magazine* (1946), and *Freudianism and Literary Mind* (1945); Albert Parry, *Garrets and Pretenders* (1933); Margaret Anderson, *My Thirty Years' War* (1930); Malcolm Cowley, *Exile's Return* (1934); O. H. Dunbar, *House in Chicago* (1947); Burton Rascoe, *Before I Forget* (1937); Carl Van Doren, *Three Worlds* (1936); Caresse Crosby, *Passionate Years* (1953); Margaret Anderson, ed., *Little Review Anthology* (1952); Burton Rascoe and Groff Conklin, eds., *Smart Set Anthology* (1934); Hart, *Popular Book*; A. P. Hackett, *Fifty Years of Best Sellers: 1895–1945* (1945); Haycroft, *Murder for Pleasure*; Douglas Waples and R. W. Tyler, *What People Want to Read About* (1931); O. H. Cheney, *Economic Survey of Book Industry, 1930–1931* (1931); Roger Burlingame, *Of Making Many Books* (1946); G. H. Doran, *Chronicles of Barabbas* (1935); Ferris Greenslet, *Under the Bridge* (1943); G. P. Putnam, *Wide Margins* (1942); F. A. Stokes, *Publisher's Random Notes* (1935). ❡ Novel: J. W. Beach, *American Fiction, 1920–1940* (1941), and *Twentieth Century Novel* (1932); Maxwell Geismar, *Writers in Crisis* (1942), and *Last of Provincials* (1947); Van Doren, *American Novel*; W. M. Frohock, *Novel of Violence, 1920–1950* (1950); I. H. Herron, *Small Town in Literature* (1939); Irving Howe, *Sherwood Anderson* (1951); E. K. Brown and Leon Edel, *Willa Cather* (1953); Edith Lewis, *Willa Cather Living* (1953); F. O. Matthiessen, *Theodore Dreiser* (1951); Elias, *Dreiser*; Helen Dreiser, *My Life with Dreiser* (1951); Dorothy Dudley, *Forgotten Frontiers: Dreiser* (1932); Irving Howe, *William Faulkner* (1952); F. J. Hoffman and O. W. Vickery, eds., *William Faulkner* (1951); Mizener, *F. Scott Fitzgerald*; J. K. McCaffery, *Ernest Hemingway* (1950); C. H. Baker, *Hemingway* (1952); Philip Young, *Ernest Hemingway* (1952); Sinclair Lewis, *From Main Street to Stockholm, Letters, 1919–1930* (Harrison Smith, ed., 1952); Floyd Dell, *Upton Sinclair* (1927); Richard Walser, ed., *Enigma of*

Thomas Wolfe (1953). ❧ Poets: Gregory and Zaturenska, *History of American Poetry*; Cleanth Brooks, *Modern Poetry* (1939); F. O. Matthiessen, "American Poetry, 1920–1940," *Sewanee Review* (1947); René Tanpin, *L'Influence du symbolisme français sur la poésie américaine* (1929); Horton, *Hart Crane*; Brom Weber, *Hart Crane* (1948); F. O. Matthiessen, *Achievement of T. S. Eliot* (2 ed., 1947); J. G. Fletcher, *Life Is My Song* (1937); Lawrence Thompson, *Fire and Ice: Robert Frost* (1942); L. C. Powell, *Robinson Jeffers* (1934); Alfred Kreymborg, *Troubadour* (1925); E. L. Masters, *Vachel Lindsay* (1935), and *Across Spoon River* (1936); Edna St. Vincent Millay, *Letters* (A. R. MacDougall, ed., 1952); Harriet Monroe, *Poet's Life* (1938); A. S. Amdur, *Poetry of Ezra Pound* (1936); Emery Neff, *Edwin Arlington Robinson* (1948); E. A. Robinson, *Selected Letters* (Ridgely Torrence, ed., 1940); K. W. Detzer, *Carl Sandburg* (1941); Louis Untermeyer, *From Another World* (1939). ❧ Critics: W. V. O'Connor, *Age of Criticism, 1900–1950* (1952); Bernard Smith, *Forces in American Criticism* (1939); C. H. Grattan, ed., *Critique of Humanism* (1930); Norman Foerster, ed., *Humanism and America* (1930), and *Toward Standards* (1930); L. J. A. Mercier, *Le Mouvement humaniste aux États-Unis* (1928); Frederick Manchester and Odell Shepard, *Irving Babbitt* (1941); Lewisohn, *Upstream*; William Manchester, *Disturber of Peace: H. L. Mencken* (1951); Edgar Kemler, *Irreverent Mencken* (1950); H. L. Mencken, *Days of H. L. Mencken* (1947); Robert Shafer, *Paul Elmer More and American Criticism* (1935); Zeitlin and Woodbridge, *Stuart P. Sherman.* ❧ Social Scientists: Herman Ausubel, *Historians and Their Craft* (1950); Gruchy, *Modern Economic Thought*; C. E. Ayres, *et al.,* "Institutional Economics," *Am. Econ. Rev.*, XLI (1951), 47; G. A. Lundberg, *et al., Trends in American Sociology* (1929); J. R. Commons, *Myself* (1934); R. T. Ely, *Ground under Our Feet* (1938); Alvin Johnson, *Pioneer's Progress* (1952); Herbert Heaton, *Scholar in Action: Edwin F. Gay* (1952); A. F. Burns, *Wesley Clair Mitchell* (1952); L. S. Mitchell, *Two Lives* (1953); L. V. Hendricks, *James Harvey Robinson* (1946); E. A. Ross, *Seventy Years of It* (1936); Dorfman, *Veblen*; David Riesman, *Thorstein Veblen* (1953). ❧ Lawyers: § 251; Samuel Williston, *Some Modern Tendencies in Law* (1929); Cohen, "Legal Philosophy in America"; Jerome Frank, *Law and Modern Mind* (1930); Roscoe Pound, "Call for Realist Jurisprudence," *Harvard Law Rev.*, XLIV (1931), 697; K. N. Llewellyn, *Bramble Bush* (1930), and "Realistic Jurisprudence," *Columbia Law Rev.*, XXX (1930), 431, and "Some Realism about Realism," *Harvard Law Rev.*, XLIV (1931), 1222; Learned Hand, "Justice Louis D. Brandeis," *Jour. Soc. Philos.*, IV (1939), 144; Stone, *Darrow*; A. G. Hays, *City Lawyer* (1942); M. D. Howe, ed., *Holmes-Laski Letters* (2 vols., 1953), and *Holmes-Pollock Letters.* ❧ Philosophers: M. R. Cohen, *Dreamer's Journey* (1949); Sidney Hook, *John Dewey* (1939), and *John Dewey: Philosopher of Science* (1950); P. A. Schilpp, ed., *Philosophy of John Dewey* (1939); Palmer, *Autobiography.* ❧ Educators: Abraham Flexner, *I Remember* (1940), and *Funds and Foundations* (1952), and *Universities: American, English, German* (1930), and *Do Americans Really Value Education?* (1927); J. H. Newlon, "John Dewey's Influence," *School and Society*, XXX (1929), 691; E. C. Moore, "John Dewey's Contribution," *ibid.*, XXXI (1930), 37; Samuel Tenenbaum, *William Heard Kilpatrick* (1951); Yeomans, *Lowell*; E. C. Lindeman, *Wealth and Culture* (1936); E. V. Hollis, *Philanthropic Foundations and Higher Education* (1938); R. B. Fosdick, *Story of Rockefeller Foundation* (1952). ❧ Theologians: S. G. Cole, *History of Fundamentalism* (1931); H. E. Fosdick, *Christianity and Progress* (1922); R. M. Jones, *New Studies in Mystical Religion* (1927); Stephen Wise, *Challenging Years* (1949); Bruce Barton, *Man Nobody Knows* (1925). ❧ Press: Mott, *American Journalism*, chs. xxxvii–xliii; Lee, *Daily Newspaper*; O. G. Villard, *Some Newspapers and Newspaper Men* (1926), and *Disappearing Daily* (1944); Kent Cooper, *Barriers Down* (1942); Gramling, *AP*; Rosewater, *Cooperative News-Gathering*; Silas Bent, *Ballyhoo* (1927); S. M. Bessie, *Jazz Journalism* (1938); Oliver Carlson, *Brisbane* (1937); Creel, *Rebel at Large*; E. D. Coblentz, ed., *William Randolph Hearst* (1952); W. R. Hearst, *Selections from Writings and Speeches* (1948); Carlson and Bates, *Hearst*; Ferdinand Lundberg, *Imperial Hearst* (1936); D. E. Weingast, *Walter Lippmann* (1949); John Tebbel, *American Dynasty: McCormicks, Medills, and Pattersons* (1947); Mary MacFadden and Émile Gauvreau, *Dumbbells and Carrot Strips: Bernarr MacFadden* (1953); C. B. Driscoll, *Life of O. O. McIntyre* (1938); C. R. McCabe, ed., *Damned Old Crank* (1951) (E. W. Scripps); Johnson, *William Allen White's America.* ❧ Theater: J. W. Krutch, *American Drama Since 1918*

(1939); A. S. Downer, *Fifty Years of American Drama, 1900–1950* (1951); Eleanor Flexner, *American Playwrights: 1918–1938* (1938); Gilbert, *Vaudeville*; Moses and Brown, *American Theatre*; G. J. Nathan, *World of George Jean Nathan* (Charles Angoff, ed., 1952); Burns Mantle, ed., *Best Plays and Yearbook of Drama* (1919–1950); B. H. Clark, *Eugene O'Neill* (1947); Tallulah Bankhead, *Tallulah* (1952); Gene Fowler, *Good Night, Sweet Prince* (1944) (John Barrymore); Norman Katkov, *Fabulous Fanny* (1953) (Fanny Brice); Ward Morehouse, *George M. Cohan* (1943); Katharine Cornell, *I Wanted to Be an Actress* (1939); R. L. Taylor, *W. C. Fields* (1949); Eddie Cantor and David Freedman, *Ziegfeld* (1934); K. S. Crichton, *Marx Brothers* (1950). ⁌ Films: Jacobs, *Rise of Film*; Paul Rotha, *Film till Now* (1930); Terry Ramsaye, *Million and One Nights* (2 vols., 1926); B. B. Hampton, *History of Movies* (1931); Arthur Mayer, *Merely Colossal* (1953); Raymond Moley, *Hays Office* (1945); Upton Sinclair, *Upton Sinclair Presents William Fox* (1933); Drinkwater, *Laemmle*; Theodore Huff, *Charlie Chaplin* (1951); Ralph Hancock and Letitia Fairbanks, *Douglas Fairbanks* (1953). ⁌ Arts: Cahill and Barr, *Art in America*; F. P. Keppel and R. L. Duffus, *Arts in American Life* (1933); J. I. H. Baur, *Revolution and Tradition in Modern American Art* (1951); Peyton Boswell, Jr., *Modern American Painting* (1940); Martha Cheney, *Modern Art* (1939); T. H. Benton, *Artist in America* (1937); George Biddle, *American Artist's Story* (1939); L. E. Schmeckebier, *John Steuart Curry's Pageant* (1943); Rockwell Kent, *This Is My Own* (1940); Elisabeth Carey, *George Luks* (1931); C. M. Rourke, *Charles Sheeler* (1938); Art Young, *Life and Times*; Kimball, *Architecture*; Hamlin, *American Spirit in Architecture*; F. L. Wright, *Autobiography*, and *Modern Architecture* (1931); R. A. Cram, *My Life in Architecture* (1936); C. W. Condit, *Rise of Skyscraper* (1952); H. R. Hitchcock, *In Nature of Materials: Buildings of Frank Lloyd Wright* (1942); Howard, *Our American Music*, and *Our Contemporary Composers*; A. V. Adams, *French*; Aaron Copland, *Our New Music* (1941); Paul Rosenfeld, *Hour with American Music* (1929); Henry Cowell, ed., *American Composers on American Music* (1933); Irving Kolodin, *Story of Metropolitan* (1953).

Bibliography — Spiller, *Literary History*, III; Coan and Lillard, *America in Fiction*; F. B. Millett, *Contemporary American Authors* (1940); Nathan Van Patten, *Index to Work of American and British Authors, 1923–1932* (1934); Allen Tate, *Recent American Poetry and Criticism* (1943); W. A. Hammond, *Bibliography of Philosophy of Fine Arts 1900 to 1932* (1934); M. H. Thomas and H. W. Schneider, *Bibliography of John Dewey* (1939); W. W. Brickman, *Guide to Research in Educational History* (1949); Office of Education, *Education of Native and Minority Groups 1923–1932* (1933); Harold Leonard, ed., *Film as Art* (1941); Library of Congress, *List on Moving Picture Industry* (1922; supplement, 1936), and *Journalism* (1931); Cannon, *Journalism*; M. E. Disbrow, *Criticism of Newspaper Advertising since 1915* (1931).

253. SOCIAL CURRENTS, 1921–1929

Summary — Jazz age; manners and morals. — Prohibition: failure of enforcement; bootlegging and speakeasies; prohibition and crime; pressure groups, dry and wet. — The techniques of ballyhoo; press sensationalism; sports; heroism (Lindbergh). — Changes in social structure: continued urbanization; social mobility; demographic changes. — Social welfare movements: medicine, social work, humanitarian reform. — Religion. — Recreation. — Crime.

General — Slosson, *Great Crusade*; President's Research Committee on Social Trends, *Recent Social Trends* (2 vols., 1933); Allen, *Only Yesterday*; Morris, *Not So Long Ago*; Sullivan, *Our Times*, VI; H. E. Stearns, ed., *Civilization in United States* (1922); E. H. Gruening, *These United States* (2 vols., 1923–24); Kirby Page, ed., *Recent Gains in American Civilization* (1928); Ogburn, *Recent Social Changes*, 107; Walter Lippmann, *Preface to Morals* (1929); J. T. Adams, *Our Business Civilization* (1929); Charles Merz, *Great American Bandwagon* (1928); Laurence Greene, *Era of Wonderful Nonsense* (1939).

Special — Foreign Reactions: Handlin, *This Was America*, 464; H. S. Commager, ed., *America in Perspective* (1947), 286; Nevins, *America through British Eyes*, 401; D. W.

Brogan, *Government of the People* (1933); J. A. Spender, *Through English Eyes* (1928); C. E. M. Joad, *Babbitt Warren* (1927); Sisley Huddleston, *What's Right with America* (1930); Muir, *America the Golden*; André Siegfried, *America Comes of Age* (1927); Georges Duhamel, *Scènes*; Count Hermann Keyserling, *America Set Free* (1929). ❡ Folkways: Lynd, *Middletown*; Ruth Lindquist, *Family in Present Social Order* (1931); Alfred Cohen, *Statistical Analysis of American Divorce* (1932); D. L. Cohn, *Combustion on Wheels, an Informal History of Automobile Age* (1944); Sanford Winston, *Illiteracy in United States* (1930); Gist, *Secret Societies*; Ferguson, *Fifty Million Brothers*; B. B. Lindsey, *Revolt of Modern Youth* (1925); P. H. Nystrom, *Economics of Fashion* (1928); Cleveland Amory, *Last Resorts* (1952); G. J. Stigler, *Domestic Servants in United States, 1900–1940* (1946); Willcox, *Demography*. ❡ Prohibition: Asbury, *Great Illusion*; Charles Merz, *Dry Decade* (1931); J. H. S. Bossard and Thorstein Sellin, eds., "Prohibition: a National Experiment," Am. Ac. Pol. Soc. Sci., *Annals*, CLXIII (1932); L. F. Schmeckebier, *Bureau of Prohibition* (1929); M. E. Stone, *American Liquor Control* (1943); Odegard, *Pressure Politics*; Dabney, *Dry Messiah: Cannon*; G. C. Root, *Women and Repeal* (1934); M. H. Tillitt, *Price of Prohibition* (1932); Clark Warburton, *Economic Results of Prohibition* (1932); F. R. Black, *Ill Starred Prohibition Cases* (1931); H. E. Barnes, *Prohibition Versus Civilization* (1932); R. L. Jones, *Eighteenth Amendment and Foreign Relations* (1933). ❡ Religion: H. W. Schneider, *Religion in 20th Century America* (1952); H. P. Douglass and E. deS. Brunner, *Protestant Church as Social Institution* (1935); T. T. McAvoy, "Catholic Church between Two Wars," *Rev. of Politics*, IV (1942), 409; C. S. MacFarland, *Across the Years* (1936); O'Connell, *Recollections*; H. H. Stroup, *Jehovah's Witnesses* (1945); Sinclair Lewis, *Elmer Gantry* (1927). ❡ Social Work: A. G. Warner, *et al.*, *American Charities and Social Work* (1930), pt. 3; Taylor, *Pioneering on Social Frontiers*; I. M. Cannon, *On Social Frontier of Medicine* (1952); Edith Abbott, *Tenements of Chicago, 1908–1935* (1936); Addams, *Second Twenty Years at Hull-House*; J. W. Linn, *Jane Addams* (1935); L. D. Wald, *Windows on Henry Street* (1934); Mary Simkhovitch, *Neighborhood* (1938). ❡ Medicine: R. H. Shryock, *Development of Modern Medicine*, and *American Medical Research Past and Present* (1947); C. P. Oberndorf, *History of Psychoanalysis* (1953); R. T. Legge, "Progress of American Industrial Medicine," *Am. Jour. Public Health*, Aug., 1952; B. J. Stern, *American Medical Practice* (1945); Fishbein, *American Medical Association*; W. B. Cannon, *Way of an Investigator* (1945); G. W. Crile, *Autobiography* (2 vols., 1947); J. F. Fulton, *Harvey Cushing* (1946); E. H. Thomson, *Harvey Cushing* (1950); Clapesattle, *Doctors Mayo*; W. Alanson White, *Autobiography of a Purpose* (1938); Hans Zinsser, *As I Remember Him* (1940). ❡ Humanitarian Reform: § 230; Bur. Labor Stat., *Care of Aged Persons* (1930); Frank Tannenbaum, *Osborne of Sing Sing* (1933). ❡ Recreation: J. F. Steiner, *Americans at Play* (1933); Dulles, *America Learns to Play*, chs. xvii–xix; John Durant and Otto Bettman, *Pictorial History of American Sport* (1952); Robert Smith, *Baseball*; Tom Meany, *Babe Ruth* (1947); G. H. Ruth, *Babe Ruth Story* (1948); Wind, *American Golf*; Gene Sarazen and H. W. Wind, *Thirty Years of Golf* (1950); W. T. Tilden, *My Story* (1948); Paul Gallico, *Farewell to Sport* (1938); Allison Danzig and Peter Brandwein, *Sport's Golden Age* (1948); John Harvey, *Racing in America: 1922–1936* (1937). ❡ Popular Music: Douglas Gilbert, *Lost Chords* (1942); E. B. Marks and A. J. Liebling, *They All Sang* (1934); Rudi Blesh and Harriet Janis, *They All Played Ragtime* (1950); Rudi Blesh, *Shining Trumpets* (1946); Eddie Condon, *We Called It Music* (1947); Robert Goffin, *Jazz* (1946); Benny Goodman and Irving Kolodin, *Kingdom of Swing* (1939); W. C. Handy, *Father of the Blues* (1941); Wilder Hobson, *American Jazz* (1939); Winthrop Sargeant, *Jazz* (1946); Barry Ulanov, *Duke Ellington* (1946). ❡ Radio: G. L. Archer, *Big Business and Radio* (1939); K. S. Tyler, *Modern Radio* (1944); L. F. Schmeckebier, *Federal Radio Commission* (1932); Martin Codel, ed., *Radio and Its Future* (1930); H. L. Jome, *Economics of Radio Industry* (1925). ❡ Heroes in the Air: John Lardner, "Lindbergh Legends," Isabel Leighton, ed., *Aspirin Age* (1949); C. A. Lindbergh, *Spirit of St. Louis* (1953); C. J. V. Murphy, *Struggle: Life of Richard E. Byrd* (1928); R. E. Byrd, *Skyward* (1928). ❡ Crime: Daniel Bell, "Crime as an American Way of Life," *Antioch Rev.*, XIII (1953), 131; Craig Thompson and Allen Raymond, *Gang Rule in New York* (1940); Herbert Asbury, *Gangs of New York*, and *Barbary Coast* (1933); Lloyd Lewis and H. J. Smith, *Chicago*; E. D. Sullivan, *Rattling the Cup on Chicago Crime* (1929); G. L. Hostetter and T. Q. Beesley,

It's a Racket (1929); F. D. Pasley, *Al Capone* (1930); D. H. Clarke, *In Reign of Rothstein* (1929); John Boettiger, *Jake Lingle* (1931); Raymond Moley, *Tribunes of People* (1932); L. E. Lawes, *Twenty Thousand Years in Sing Sing* (1932).

Sources — H. Alcoholic Liquor Traffic Committee, "Survey of Alcoholic Liquor Traffic," 68 Cong., 2 Sess., *Hearings* (1925); H. Judiciary Committee, "Prohibition Amendments," 71 Cong., 2 Sess., *Hearings* (4 pts., 1930); Treasury Dept., *Digest of Supreme Court Decisions Interpreting Prohibition Act* (1929); National [Wickersham] Commission on Law Observance and Enforcement, "Enforcement of Prohibition Laws," 71 Cong., 3 Sess., *Sen. Doc.*, No. 307; Federal Trade Commission, "Report on Radio Industry," 67 Cong., 4 Sess., *H. Res.*, No. 548.

Bibliography — Slosson, *Great Crusade*, 439; J. E. Johnsen, *Problem of Liquor Control* (1934), 27; D. C. Nicholson and R. P. Graves, *Selective Bibliography on Eighteenth Amendment* (1931); Library of Congress, *Selected List on Liquor Traffic* (1932); A. F. Kuhlman, *Guide to Material on Crime and Criminal Justice* (1929); D. C. Culver, *Bibliography of Crime and Criminal Justice, 1927–1931* (1934); K. O'S. McCarthy, "Racketeering," *Jour. Criminal Law and Criminology*, XXII (1931), 578; Esther Connor, "Crime Commissions since 1920," *ibid.*, XXI (1930), 129; Library of Congress, *Crime and Criminal Justice* (1930; supplement, 1935).

Chapter Twenty-nine

GREAT DEPRESSION, 1930–1941

254. ONSET OF DEPRESSION, 1929–1933

Summary — Crash, October 1929; analysis of causes. — Course of depression: 1929–32, effects on production, employment, national income; in finance; in industry; in agriculture. — Problem of unemployed: attempts at local relief; at federal coördination of local efforts. — Social impact of depression; spread of misery and despair. — Federal policies, 1929–30, appeals for confidence. — Increasing discontent; congressional elections of 1930. — Demand for national action: by business (Chamber of Commerce); by Congress (Wagner, Costigan, LaFollette); by labor; radicalism. — Federal policies, 1930–33: Hoover vetoes; Reconstruction Finance Corporation (Jan. 22, 1932). — Crises of 1932: agrarian violence; Bonus Army; banking crisis. — Politics: Democratic revival; conventions of 1932; campaign; election. — Interregnum.

General — Broadus Mitchell, *Depression Decade* (1947); Dixon Wecter, *Age of Great Depression* (1948); F. L. Allen, *Since Yesterday* (1940); Faulkner, *Versailles to New Deal*, chs. viii–xi; C. A. Beard and G. H. E. Smith, *The Old Deal and The New* (1940); Hoover, *Memoirs*, II, III.

Special — Causes of Depression: Thomas Wilson, *Fluctuations in Income and Employment*, chs. xiii–xvii; A. H. Hansen, *Business Cycles and National Income* (1951), chs. iii–v, xxv–xxvi, and *Full Recovery or Stagnation?* (1938), chs. xvi–xix, and *Fiscal Policy and Business Cycles* (1941), chs. i–iii; J. A. Schumpeter, *Business Cycles* (1939), chs. xiv, xv, and "Decade of Twenties," *Am. Econ. Rev.*, XXXVI (suppl., 1946), 1; Temporary National Economic Committee, "Investigation of Concentration of Economic Power," 75 Cong., 3 Sess., *Hearings* (1941), pt. 9, pp. 3495, 3538, 3837; Nourse, *America's Capacity to Produce*; Leven, *America's Capacity to Consume*; Irving Fisher, *Stock Market Crash — And After* (1930); Pecora, *Wall Street under Oath*; Max Lowenthal, *Investor Pays* (1936). ⁅ Social Impact of Depression: Gilbert Seldes, *Years of Locust* (1933); Edmund Wilson, *American Jitters* (1932), M. A. Hallgren, *Seeds of Revolt* (1933); Saloutos and Hicks, *Agricultural Discontent*, chs. xiv, xv; J. N. Leonard, *Three Years Down* (1939); C. J. Enzler, *Some Social Aspects of Depression* (1939); Edward Angly, comp., *Oh Yeah?* (1931); W. W. Waters and W. C. White, *B. E. F.* (1933). ⁅ Hoover's Policies: Hoover, *State Papers*; W. S. Myers and W. H. Newton, *Hoover Administration* (1936); R. L. Wilbur and A. M. Hyde, *Hoover Policies* (1937); R. G. Tugwell, *Mr. Hoover's Economic Policy* (1932); Ratner, *American Taxation*, ch. xxi; J. T. Flynn, "Inside R.F.C.," *Harper's*, CLXVI (1933), 161; T. G. Joslin, *Hoover Off the Record* (1934); E. A. Stokdyk and C. H. West, *Farm Board* (1930); Forrest Crissey, *Alexander Legge* (1936). ⁅ Relief Policies: J. C. Brown, *Public Relief, 1929–1939* (1940); R. M. Kellogg, *United States Employment Service* (1933); J. C. Colcord, *et al.*, *Emergency Work Relief* (1932). ⁅ Demand for Planning: C. A. Beard, ed., *America Faces Future* (1932); Gerard Swope, *Swope Plan* (1931); P. H. Douglas, *Coming of a New Party* (1932); George Soule, *Planned Society* (1932); H. W. Laidler, *Socialist*

Planning and a Socialist Program (1932); Norman Thomas, *America's Way Out* (1931); Howard Scott, *et al.*, *Introduction to Technocracy* (1933). ❡ Politics and Interregnum: R. V. Peel and T. C. Donnelly, *1932 Campaign* (1935); E. E. Robinson, *They Voted For Roosevelt* (1947); Louise Overacker, "Campaign Funds in Depression," *Am. Pol. Sci. Rev.*, XXVII (1933), 769; Hull, *Memoirs*; Timmons, *Garner*; Farley, *Behind the Ballots*, ch. ii; Flynn, *You're the Boss*, chs. viii–x; Moley, *After Seven Years*, chs. i–v; Rosenman, *Working With Roosevelt*, chs. iii–vi; E. K. Lindley, *Roosevelt Revolution* (1933), chs. i–iii, H. L. Mencken, *Making a President* (1932); Myers and Newton, *Hoover Administration*, ch. xix; J. T. Flynn, "Hoover's Apologia," *Southern Rev.*, I (1936), 721; Jesse H. Jones and Edward Angly, *Fifty Billion Dollars* (1951), chs. ii–v.

Sources — Sen. Manufactures Committee, "Unemployment Relief," 72 Cong., 1 Sess., *Hearings* (1932), and "Federal Aid for Unemployment Relief," 72 Cong., 2 Sess., *Hearings* (1933); Sen. Banking Committee, "Unemployment Relief," 72 Cong., 1 Sess., *Hearings* (1932), and "Creation of Reconstruction Finance Corporation," *ibid.*; H. Banking Committee, "Reconstruction Finance Corporation," *ibid.*; Sen. Banking Committee, "Further Unemployment Relief," 72 Cong., 2 Sess., *Hearings* (1933); Sen. Manufactures Committee, "Establishment of National Economic Council," 72 Cong., 1 Sess., *Hearings* (1932); Sen. Finance Committee, "Investigation of Economic Problems," 72 Cong., 2 Sess., *Hearings* (1933); H. Labor Committee, "Six-Hour Day, Five-Day Week," *ibid.*; H. Committee to Investigate Communist Activities, "Investigation," 71 Cong., 2 Sess., *Hearings* (1930–31), and "Report," 71 Cong., 3 Sess., *H. Report*, No. 2290.

Bibliography — W. W. Shirley, "World Depression," *N.Y. Public Library Bull.*, XXXVII (1933), 970, 1040; L. A. Thompson, "National Economic Councils," *Monthly Labor Rev.*, XXXII (1931), 1249; E. C. and L. M. Brooks, "Decade of 'Planning' Literature," *Social Forces*, XII (1934), 427; Library of Congress, *Economic Councils and Economic Planning* (1932), and *List on Economic Planning* (1933), and *List on Technocracy* (1933), and *Federal Farm Board* (1931); Bur. Ag. Econ., *Farmers' Response to Price* (1932), and *Farmers' Strikes 1932–1933* (1933), and *State Measures for Relief of Agricultural Indebtedness* (1933).

255. FOREIGN POLICY, 1929–1932

Summary — Economic nationalism, Smoot-Hawley tariff (June 17, 1930). — Debt and reparations moratorium (proposed June 20, 1931). — London Naval Conference and continuing disarmament efforts. — Retreat from Latin America; Havana Conference (1928), Clark Memorandum on Monroe Doctrine (1929). — Japanese aggression in Manchuria, Stimson Doctrine (January 7, 1932).

General — Bailey, *Diplomatic History*, ch. lxiii; Nevins, *United States in a Chaotic World*, chs. v–viii; W. S. Myers, *Foreign Policies of Herbert Hoover* (1940); Stimson and Bundy, *On Active Service*, chs. vii–xi; H. L. Stimson, "Bases of American Foreign Policy," *Foreign Affairs*, XI (1933), 383; Council on Foreign Relations, *Survey of American Foreign Relations* (1929–31), and *United States in World Affairs*; § 250.

Special — Foreign Economic Policy: §§ 246, 250; Bidwell, *Tariff Policy*; J. M. Jones, Jr., *Tariff Retaliation* (1934); F. W. Taussig, "Tariff, 1929–30," *Quar. Jour. Econ.*, XLIV (1930), 175; Abraham Berglund, "Tariff Act of 1930," *Amer. Econ. Rev.*, XX (1930), 467; E. E. Schattschneider, *Politics, Pressures and Tariff* (1935). ❡ Coöperation with International Organizations: § 250; R. M. Cooper, *American Consultation in World Affairs* (1934); U. P. Hubbard, *Cooperation with League of Nations, 1931–1936* (1937). ❡ Western Hemisphere: § 250; Alexander de Conde, *Herbert Hoover's Latin-American Policy* (1951); H. L. Stimson, *United States and Other American Republics* (1931). ❡ Far East: § 250; H. L. Stimson, *Far Eastern Crisis* (1936); Hoover, *Memoirs*, II, ch. xlviii; S. R. Smith, *Manchurian Crisis, 1931–1932* (1948); Robert Langer, *Seizure of Territory: Stimson Doctrine* (1947); Reginald Bassett, *Democracy and Foreign Policy, Sino-Japanese Dispute, 1931–33* (1952); P. H. Clyde, "Diplomacy of Secretary Stimson and Manchuria, 1931," *Miss. Valley Hist. Rev.*, XXXV (1948), 187; E. R. Perkins, "Non-application of Sanctions Against Japan, 1931–1932," D. E. Lee and G. E. McReynolds, eds., *Essays in History and International Relations in Honor of George Hubbard Blakeslee* (1949), 215; B. J. Wallace, "How the United States 'Led the League' in 1931," *Am. Pol. Sci. Rev.*, XXXIX (1945), 101.

Sources — *Foreign Relations of the United States, 1929–32* (14 vols., 1943–48); State Department, *Peace and War: United States Foreign Policy, 1931–41* (1943), and *Foreign Relations of United States: Japan, 1931–41* (2 vols., 1943); Gantenbein, *Latin-American Policy;* H. Insular Affairs Committee, "Independence for Philippine Islands," 72 Cong., 1 Sess., *Hearings* (1932); Sen. Territories Committee, "Independence for Philippine Islands," 72 Cong., 1 Sess., *Hearings* (1932).

Bibliography — Council on Foreign Relations, *United States in World Affairs; Foreign Affairs;* Library of Congress, *London Naval Conference* (1930); Carnegie Endowment for International Peace, *Hoover-Stimson Doctrine* (1934).

256. FRANKLIN D. ROOSEVELT AND NEW DEAL

Summary — Ancestry and early years. — As New York state senator, 1910–13. — As Assistant Secretary of the Navy, 1913–20. — As vice-presidential candidate, 1920. — Illness and retirement, 1921–28. — As Governor of New York, 1929–32. — Political philosophy and methods; brain trust. — Character and personality. — Roosevelt as president; purpose and techniques of New Deal.

General — Lindley, *Franklin D. Roosevelt;* Hofstadter, *American Political Tradition,* ch. xii; John Gunther, *Roosevelt in Perspective* (1950); Emil Ludwig, *Roosevelt* (1938); Earle Looker, *This Man Roosevelt* (1932); D. P. Geddes, ed., *Franklin Delano Roosevelt* (1945); J. T. Flynn, *Roosevelt Myth* (1948); J. N. Rosenau, ed., *Roosevelt Treasury* (1951); F. D. Roosevelt, *F.D.R. Personal Letters,* and "Rendezvous with Destiny" (radio addresses, recording, ed., by César Saerchinger); James Fleming, "Mr. President from FDR to Eisenhower" (recording); Murrow and Friendly, "I Can Hear It Now," I; F. D. Roosevelt, *Public Papers; Franklin D. Roosevelt Collector* (1948–   ).

Special — Ancestry and Early Years: Freidel, *Franklin D. Roosevelt,* I; Karl Schrift-giesser, *Amazing Roosevelt Family* (1942); D. W. Delano, Jr., *Franklin Roosevelt and the Delano Influence* (1946); S. D. Roosevelt, *My Boy Franklin* (1933); Eleanor Roosevelt, *This is My Story* (1937); Ruby Black, *Eleanor Roosevelt* (1940). ❰ As Governor: F. D. Roosevelt, *Public Papers [as] Governor of New York* (4 vols., 1930–39). ❰ Recollections of Roosevelt: Eccles, *Beckoning Frontiers;* Farley, *Behind the Ballots,* and *Jim Farley's Story;* Flynn, *You're the Boss;* Hull, *Memoirs;* H. L. Ickes, "My Twelve Years with F.D.R.," *Sat. Eve. Post* (June 5–July 24, 1948); Jesse Jones, *Fifty Billion Dollars;* R. W. McIntire, *White House Physician* (1946); Charles Michelsen, *Ghost Talks* (1941); Moley, *After Seven Years;* Henry Morgenthau, Jr., "Morgenthau Diaries," *Collier's,* Sept. 27–Nov. 1, 1947; Arthur Mullen, *Western Democrat* (1940); Henrietta Nesbitt, *White House Diary* (1948); Frances Perkins, *Roosevelt I Knew* (1946); M. F. Reilly and W. J. Slocum, *Reilly of White House* (1947); D. C. Roper and F. H. Lovette, *Fifty Years of Public Life* (1941); Rosenman, *Working With Roosevelt;* Sherwood, *Roosevelt and Hopkins;* E. W. Starling and Thomas Sugrue, *Starling of White House* (1946); Stimson and Bundy, *On Active Service;* R. G. Tugwell, "Experimental Roosevelt," *Pol. Quar.,* July–Sept. 1950; Grace Tully, *F.D.R., My Boss* (1949). ❰ Philosophy of New Deal: A. A. Berle, Jr., *New Directions in New World* (1940); D. C. Coyle, *Roads to a New America* (1938); M. S. Eccles, *Economic Balance and a Balanced Budget* (1940); Mordecai Ezekiel, *$2,500 a Year* (1936), and *Jobs for All* (1939); H. L. Ickes, *New Democracy* (1934); F. D. Roosevelt, *Looking Forward* (1933), and *On Our Way* (1934); R. G. Tugwell, *Battle for Democracy* (1935), and *Industrial Discipline and Governmental Arts* (1933); H. A. Wallace, *New Frontiers* (1934), and *Democracy Reborn* (1945). ❰ History of New Deal: D. W. Brogan, *Era of Franklin D. Roosevelt* (1950); Basil Rauch, *History of New Deal* (1944); Mitchell, *Depression Decade;* Wecter, *Age of Great Depression;* Beard and Smith, *Old Deal and New;* T. R. Amlie, *Let's Look at the Record* (1950); Marquis Childs, *I Write from Washington* (1942).

Bibliography — Mitchell, *Depression Decade*, 408; Wecter, *Age of Great Depression*, 317; R. L. Jacoby, *Calendar of Speeches and Statements of Franklin D. Roosevelt, 1910–1920* (1952); Library of Congress, *Selected List on New Deal* (1940).

257. NEW DEAL AND INDUSTRIAL RECOVERY, 1933–1940

Summary — Banking crisis, emergency legislation (1933); Banking Act (1935). — National Recovery Administration (1933–35), origins, performance, termination. — Early monetary policy (1933–35): end of gold standard; managed currency experiments; Silver Purchase Act (1934). — Securities legislation: Securities Act (1933); Securities Exchange Act (1934); Public Utilities Holding Company Act (1935). — Shift in New Deal philosophy: 1934–35, from national planning to reinvigoration of market; attacks on price inflexibility; anti-monopoly campaign, 1937–38; Temporary National Economic Committee. — Tax policy; undistributed profits tax. — Compensatory fiscal policy (Keynes, Eccles, Henderson, Hansen). — Recession of 1937; budget fight of 1937–38 (Morgenthau against "the spenders"). — Trends in national income, employment, production.

General — Thomas Wilson, *Fluctuations in Income and Employment*, chs. xvii–xviii; Mitchell, *Depression Decade*, chs. iv, v, vii; Rauch, *History of New Deal*, chs. ii–viii; Brogan, *Era of Roosevelt*, chs. iii–iv; Moley, *After Seven Years*, chs. v–viii; E. K. Lindley, *Roosevelt Revolution*, chs. iii–viii, and *Halfway with Roosevelt* (1936); A. A. Berle, *et al.*, *America's Recovery Program* (1934); § 246.

Special — Banking Crisis: J. F. T. O'Connor, *Banking Crisis* (1938); C. D. Bremer, *American Bank Failures* (1935); C. B. Upham and Edwin Lamke, *Closed and Distressed Banks* (1934); A. A. Ballantine, "When All Banks Closed," *Harvard Bus. Rev.*, XXVI (1948), 129; J. I. Bogen and Marcus Nadler, *Banking Crisis* (1933); Guy Emerson, "Guaranty of Deposits," *Quar. Jour. Econ.*, XLVIII (1934), 229. ❧ NRA and Fair Trade Policy: L. S. Lyon, *et al.*, *National Recovery Administration* (1935); J. M. Clark, *et al.*, "National Recovery Administration; Report of President's Committee of Analysis," 75 Cong., 1 Sess., *H. Doc.*, No. 158; C. F. Roos, *NRA Economic Planning* (1937); H. S. Johnson, *Blue Eagle* (1935); D. R. Richberg, *Rainbow* (1936); C. A. Pearce, *NRA Trade Practice Programs* (1939); E. G. Nourse, *Marketing Agreements under NRA* (1935); R. H. Connery, *Administration of an NRA Code* (1938); P. C. Campbell, *Consumer Representation in New Deal* (1940); Benjamin Werne, ed., *Business and Robinson-Patman Law* (1938); Wright Patman, *Robinson-Patman Act* (1938). ❧ Monetary Policy: § 246; G. G. Johnson, Jr., *Treasury and Monetary Policy, 1933–1938* (1939); A. W. Crawford, *Monetary Management under New Deal* (1940); J. D. Paris, *Monetary Policies, 1932–1938* (1938); J. R. Reeve, *Monetary Reform Movements* (1943); Leo Pasvolsky, *Current Monetary Issues* (1933); A. S. Everest, *Morgenthau, New Deal and Silver* (1950); C. O. Hardy, *Warren-Pearson Price Theory* (1935). ❧ Securities Regulation: W. E. Atkins, *et al.*, *Regulation of Security Markets* (1946); Twentieth Century Fund, *Security Markets*; W. O. Douglas, *Democracy and Finance* (1940); Raymond Vernon, *Regulation of Stock Exchange Members* (1941); R. L. Weissman, *New Wall Street* (1939); H. V. Cherrington, *Investor and Securities Act* (1942); T. K. Haven, *Investment Banking under Securities and Exchange Commission* (1940); E. D. Kennedy, *Dividends to Pay* (1939); Emanuel Stein, *Government and Investor* (1941); Flynn, *Security Speculation*. ❧ Public Utilities: § 246; J. C. Bonbright, *Public Utilities and National Power Policies* (1940); R. D. Baum, *Federal Power Commission and State Regulation* (1942). ❧ Lending Agencies: Jesse Jones, *Fifty Billion Dollars*; Herbert Spero, *Reconstruction Finance Corporation Loans to Railroads, 1932–1937* (1939); J. D. Glover, "Industrial Loan Policy of RFC," *Harvard Bus. Rev.*, XVII (1939), 465. ❧ Banking Act of 1935: Eccles, *Beckoning Frontiers*, 182, and *Economic Balance*; A. D. Gayer, "Banking Act of 1935," *Quar. Jour. Econ.*, L (1935), 97; Jacob Viner, "Recent Legislation and Banking Situation," *Am. Econ. Rev.*, XXVI (1936, supp.), 96; Rixey Smith and Norman Beasley, *Carter Glass* (1939); F. A. Bradford, "Banking Act of 1935," *Am. Econ. Rev.*, XXV (1935), 661. ❧ Tax Policy: Ratner, *American Taxation*, chs. xxii–xxiii; Blakey, *Federal Income Tax*; Roy Blough, *Federal Taxing Process* (1952); Gerhard Colm and Fritz

Lehman, *Economic Consequences of Recent Tax Policy* (1938); M. S. Kendrick, *Undistributed Profits Tax* (1937); G. E. Lent, *Impact of Undistributed Profits Tax, 1936–37* (1948). ❡ Compensatory Fiscal Policy: S. E. Harris, ed., *New Economics* (1947); L. R. Klein, *Keynesian Revolution* (1947); Keynes, *General Theory of Employment*; R. F. Harrod, *John Maynard Keynes* (1951); A. H. Hansen, *Guide to Keynes* (1953), and *Business Cycles and National Income*, and *Full Recovery or Stagnation*; H. H. Villard, *Deficit Spending and National Income* (1941); J. K. Galbraith and G. G. Johnson, Jr., *Economic Effects of Federal Works Expenditures, 1933–1938* (1940); R. V. Gilbert, et al., *Economic Program for American Democracy* (1938); A. E. Burns and D. S. Watson, *Government Spending and Economic Expansion* (1941); R. W. Lindholm, *Public Finance and Fiscal Policy* (1950); George Terborgh, *Bogey of Economic Maturity* (1945); K. D. Roose, "Recession of 1937–1938," *Jour. Pol. Econ.*, LVI (1948), 239; Henry Morgenthau, Jr., "Struggle for a Program," *Colliers*, Oct. 4, 1947; Joseph Alsop and Robert Kintner, *Men Around President* (1939). ❡ Price Rigidity and Anti-monopoly: § 246; G. C. Means, "Industrial Prices, Relative Inflexibility," 74 Cong., 1 Sess., Sen. Doc. No. 13; T. W. Arnold, *Bottlenecks of Business* (1940), and *Democracy and Free Enterprise* (1942); W. H. Hamilton, *Antitrust in Action* (1940); C. D. Edwards, "Thurman Arnold and Antitrust Laws," *Pol. Sci. Quar.*, LVIII (1943), 338. ❡ TNEC: David Lynch, *Concentration of Economic Power* (1946); "Papers Relating to Temporary National Economic Committee," *Am. Econ. Rev.*, XXXII (1942), supplement; "Publications of the Temporary National Economic Committee," *Am. Econ. Rev.*, XXXI (1941), 347; TNEC, "Investigation of Concentration of Economic Power; Description of Hearings and Monographs," 76 Cong., 3 Sess., *Sen. Committee Print* (1941), and *Hearings* (31 parts, 6 supplements, 1939–41), and *Monographs* (Nos. 1–43, 1940–41), and "Final Report and Recommendations," 77 Cong., 1 Sess., *Sen. Doc.*, No. 35, and "Final Report of Executive Secretary," 77 Cong., 1 Sess., *Sen. Committee Print* (1941). ❡ Housing: L. W. Post, *Challenge of Housing* (1938); M. W. Straus and Talbot Wegg, *Housing Comes of Age* (1938); Nathan Straus, *Four Years Of Public Housing* (1941), and *Seven Myths of Housing* (1944); National Resources Planning Board, *Housing: Continuing Problem* (1940); M. H. Schoenfeld, "Progress of Public Housing," *Monthly Labor Rev.*, LI (1940), 267; C. L. Harriss, *History and Policies of Home Owners' Loan Corporation* (1952). ❡ Special Industries: Moulton, *American Transportation Problem*; National Resources Planning Board, *Transportation and National Policy* (1942); C. M. Fuess, *Joseph B. Eastman* (1952); Watkins, *Oil*; E. V. Rostow, *National Policy for Oil* (1948); R. H. Baker, *National Bituminous Coal Commission* (1941); Freudenthal, *Aviation Business*; D. H. Wallace, *Market Control in Aluminum* (1937); C. R. Daugherty, et al., *Economics of Iron and Steel*. ❡ Economic Trends: § 246; L. R. Klein, "National Income and Product, 1929–50," *Am. Econ. Rev.*, XLIII (1953), 117; Arthur Smithies, "American Economy in Thirties," *ibid.*, XXXVI (1946, supplement), 11; National Resources Committee, *Structure of American Economy* (2 vols., 1939–40); Spurgeon Bell, *Productivity, Wages, and National Income* (1940); Epstein, *Industrial Profits*; Horst Mendershausen, *Changes in Income Distribution during Great Depression* (1946); G. J. Stigler, *Trends in Output and Employment* (1947).

Sources — NRA: Sen. Finance Committee, "National Industrial Recovery," 73 Cong., 1 Sess., *Hearings* (1933); H. Ways and Means Committee, "National Industrial Recovery," 73 Cong., 1 Sess., *Hearings* (1933); Sen. Finance Committee, "Investigation of National Recovery Administration," 74 Cong., 1 Sess., *Hearings* (4 vols.). ❡ R.F.C.: Sen. Banking Committee, "To Extend Functions of Reconstruction Finance Corporation," 74 Cong., 1 Sess., *Hearings* (1935); H. Banking Committee, "To Extend Functions of Reconstruction Finance Corporation," 74 Cong., 1 Sess., *Hearings* (1935); Reconstruction Finance Corporation, *Seven-Year Report* (1939). ❡ Securities Regulation: H. Commerce Committee, "Federal Securities Act," 73 Cong., 1 Sess., *Hearings* (1933), and "Stock Exchange Regulation," 73 Cong., 2 Sess., *Hearings* (1934), and "Public Utility Holding Companies," 74 Cong., 1 Sess., *Hearings* (3 pts., 1935); Sen. Commerce Committee, "Public Utility Holding Company Act of 1935," 74 Cong., 1 Sess., *Hearings* (2 pts., 1935); Federal Trade Commission, *Utility Corporations*; Sen. Committee to Investigate Lobbying, "Investigation," 74 Cong., 1 and 2 Sess., 75 Cong., 3 Sess., *Hearings* (8 pts., 1935–38). ❡ Banking: Sen. Banking Committee, "Banking Act of

1935," 74 Cong., 1 Sess., *Hearings* (1935); H. Banking Committee, "Banking Act of 1935," *ibid.;* and "Monetary Policy of Plenty Instead of Scarcity," 75 Cong., 1 and 3 Sess., *Hearings* (1938). ⟨ Chain Stores: Federal Trade Commission, "Chain Stores," and "Final Report" (1935). ⟨ Housing: Sen. Banking Committee, "National Housing Act," 73 Cong., 2 Sess., *Hearings* (1934); H. Banking Committee, "National Housing Act," *ibid.;* Sen. Banking Committee, "Home Owners' Loan and National Housing Act," 74 Cong., 1 Sess., *Hearings* (1935); Sen. Education and Labor Committee, "Slum and Low-Rent Public Housing," 74 Cong., 1 Sess., *Hearings* (1935), and "United States Housing Act of 1936," 74 Cong., 2 Sess., *Hearings* (1936). ⟨ Transport: Federal Coordinator of Transportation, "Regulation of Transportation Agencies," 73 Cong., 2 Sess., *Sen. Doc.,* No. 152; Sen. Commerce Committee, "Investigation of Railroads," 74 Cong., 2 Sess., 75 Cong., 1, 2, and 3 Sess., 77 Cong., 2 Sess., *Hearings* (29 pts., 1937–42), and *Reports* (1937–42).

Bibliography — Mitchell, *Depression Decade,* 408; Library of Congress, *List on Securities Act of 1933* (1935), and *List on Securities and Exchange Act of 1934* (1935); G. C. Leininger, "Bibliography on Utility Holding Companies," *Jour. Land and Public Utility Econ.,* XI (1935), 419; Library of Congress, *References on Housing* (1934; supplement, 1935).

258. NEW DEAL PUBLIC WORKS, RELIEF, AND SOCIAL SECURITY, 1933–1940

Summary — Number and condition of unemployed. — Public works programs; Ickes and Public Works Administration. — Emergency work relief programs: Hopkins and Civil Works Administration (1933); Federal Emergency Relief Administration (1934); Works Progress Administration (1935); character of WPA programs. — Policy conflicts, Ickes and Hopkins. — Civilian Conservation Corps and National Youth Administration. — Social Security Act (1935); Federal Security Administration and welfare programs.

General — Mitchell, *Depression Decade,* chs. iii, ix; Rauch, *History of New Deal,* chs. iv, vi–viii, x; Wecter, *Age of Great Depression,* chs. iv–x; National Resources Planning Board, *Security, Work, and Relief Policies* (1942); Grace Abbott, *From Relief to Social Security* (1941); Lewis Meriam, *Relief and Social Security* (1946); T. E. Whiting and T. J. Woofter, Jr., *Summary of Relief and Federal Work Program Statistics* (1941).

Special — Unemployed: Paul Webbink, "Unemployment, 1930–40," *Am. Econ. Rev.,* XXX (1941), 248; Census of Employment (1937), *Final Report* (4 vols., 1938); E. W. Bakke, *Unemployed Worker* (1940), and *Citizens Without Work* (1940); Eli Ginzberg, *et al., Unemployed* (1943); R. C. Atkinson, *et al., Public Employment Service* (1938); F. S. Chapin and S. A. Queen, *Social Work in Depression* (1937); S. A. Stouffer, *et al., Family in Depression* (1937); Ruth Cavan and K. H. Ranck, *Family and Depression* (1938); W. L. Morgan, *Family Meets Depression* (1939); Mirra Komarovsky, *Unemployed Man and His Family* (1940); L. V. Armstrong, *We Too Are People* (1938). ⟨ Relief: Brown, *Public Relief;* Edith Abbott, *Public Assistance* (1940); E. A. Williams, *Federal Aid for Relief* (1939); M. D. Lane and Francis Steegmuller, *America on Relief* (1938); Grace Adams, *Workers on Relief* (1939); G. L. Palmer and K. D. Wood, *Urban Workers on Relief* (1936); C. C. Zimmerman and N. L. Whetten, *Rural Families on Relief* (1938); J. C. Colcord, *Cash Relief* (1936); A. L. Radowski, *Work Relief in New York State, 1931–1935* (1947); Enid Baird and H. B. Brinton, *Average General Relief Benefits, 1933–1938* (1940); Maxine Davis, *They Shall Not Want* (1937); J. D. Coppock, *Food Stamp Plan* (1947); R. C. White and M. K. White, *Social Aspects of Relief Policies in the Depression* (1937). ⟨ Federal Work Relief: D. G. Howard, *WPA and Federal Relief Policy* (1943); A. W. Macmahon, *et al., Administration of Federal Work Relief* (1941); H. L. Hopkins, *Spending to Save* (1936); Sherwood, *Roosevelt and Hopkins,* ch. iii; Corrington Gill, *Wasted Manpower* (1939); E. W. Gilboy, *Applicants for Work Relief* (1940); D. S. Campbell, *et al., Educational Activities of Works Progress Administration* (1939); A. E. Burns and Peyton Kerr, "Survey of Work-Relief Wage Policies," *Am. Econ. Rev.,* XXVII (1937), 711, and "Recent Changes in Work-Relief Wage Policy," *ibid.,* XXXI (1941), 56; WPA, *Inventory: Appraisal of Results* (1938);

Alsberg, *America Fights Depression;* § 267. ❰ Public Works: Gayer, *Public Works;* J. F. Isakoff, *Public Works Administration* (1938); J. K. Williams, *Grants in Aid under Public Works Administration* (1939); Galbraith and Johnson, *Economic Effects of Works Expenditures;* H. L. Ickes, *Secret Diary* (1953), I, and *Back to Work* (1935), and *Accomplishments of Federal Emergency Administration* (1936); Public Works Administration, *America Builds* (1939). ❰ CCC and NYA: Betty and E. K. Lindley, *New Deal For Youth* (1938); L. L. Lorwin, *Youth Work Programs* (1941); Kenneth Holland and F. E. Hill, *Youth in CCC* (1942); Civilian Conservation Corps, *CCC At Work* (1941); P. O. Johnson and O. L. Harvey, *National Youth Administration* (1938). ❰ Social Security: P. H. Douglas, *Social Security* (1939); Abraham Epstein, *Insecurity* (1938); E. M. Burns, *American Social Security* (1949); Perkins, *Roosevelt I Knew*, ch. xxiii; Abbott, *Relief to Social Security;* S. E. Harris, *Economics of Social Security* (1941); President's Committee on Economic Security, *Report* (1935). ❰ Health and Welfare: S. D. Collins and Clark Tibbitts, *Social Aspects of Health in Depression* (1937); Hugh Cabot, *Doctor's Bill* (1935); J. P. Warbasse, *Cooperative Medicine* (1936); I. S. Falk, *et al.*, *Costs of Medical Care* (1933); James Rorty, *American Medicine Mobilizes* (1939); I. S. Falk, *Security Against Sickness* (1936); Oliver Garceau, *Political Life of American Medical Association* (1941); "American Medical Association," *Fortune*, Nov. 1938.

Sources — Relief and Public Works: H. and Sen. Labor Committees, "Unemployment Relief," 73 Cong., 1 Sess., *Joint Hearings* (1933); Sen. Labor Committee, "Additional Public Works Appropriations," 73 Cong., 2 Sess., *Hearings* (1934); Sen. Appropriations Committee, "First Deficiency Appropriation Bill, 74 Cong., 2 Sess., *Hearings* (1936), and "Emergency Relief Appropriations, 75 Cong., 1 Sess., *Hearings* (1937); H. Appropriations Committee, "Extension of Public Works Administration," 75 Cong., 1 Sess., *Hearings* (1937); Sen. Committee to Investigate Unemployment and Relief, "Department of Public Works," 76 Cong., 1 Sess., *Hearings* (1939); Sen. Banking Committee, "Works Financing Act of 1939, 76 Cong., 1 Sess., *Hearings* (1939); H. Appropriations Committee, "Investigation of Works Progress Administration," 76 Cong., 1 and 3 Sess., *Hearings* (4 pts., 1939–40). ❰ Youth: Sen. Labor Committee, "American Youth Act," 74 Cong., 2 Sess., and 75 Cong., 3 Sess., *Hearings* (1936–38), and "Termination of CCC and NYA," 77 Cong., 2 Sess., *Hearings* (1942). ❰ Social Security: Sen. Finance Committee, "Economic Security Act," 74 Cong., 1 Sess., *Hearings* (1935); H. Ways and Means Committee, "Economic Security Act," *ibid.;* H. Labor Committee, "Unemployment, Old Age, and Social Insurance," 74 Cong., 1 Sess., *Hearings* (1935); Sen. Labor Committee, "Social Insurance," 74 Cong., 2 Sess., *Hearings* (1936), and "National Health Program," 76 Cong., 1 Sess., *Hearings* (3 pts., 1939); William Haber and W. J. Cohen, *Readings in Social Security* (1948).

Bibliography — J. K. Wilcox, *Unemployment Relief Documents* (1936); Chicago University Library, *Unemployment and Relief Documents* (1934); *Subject Index of Research Bulletins Issued by FERA and WPA, Division of Social Research* (1937); WPA, *Industrial Change and Employment Opportunity — A Selected Bibliography* (1939); L. A. Menefee and M. M. Chambers, comps., *American Youth* (1938); Civilian Conservation Corps, *Civilian Conservation Corps Bibliography* (1939); Helen Baker, *Social Security* (1939); Social Security Board, *Brief Reading List on Social Security Act* (1941); Library of Congress, *Health Insurance* (1938).

259. NEW DEAL AGRICULTURAL POLICY, 1933–1940

Summary — Agricultural unrest, 1933; farm holiday movement. — Agricultural Adjustment Administration. — Farm Credit Administration and mortgage refinancing. — Tenancy problems: Resettlement Administration (1935); Farm Security Administration (1937); Bankhead-Jones Farm Tenancy Act (1937). — Migratory farm workers. — Droughts of 1934, 1936. — AAA declared unconstitutional (Jan. 6, 1936); Soil Conservation and Domestic Allotment Act (Feb. 29, 1936). — Agricultural Adjustment Act of 1938; "ever normal granary." — Rural Electrification Administration. — Farm organization; Farm Bureau Federation; Farmer's Union; Grange. — Changes in agricultural production, technology, rural living.

General — § 247; Benedict, *Farm Policies,* chs. xii–xv; Saloutos and Hicks, *Agricultural Discontent,* chs. xv–xix; Nye, *Midwestern Progressive Politics,* 350; Lord, *Wallaces,* chs. x, xi; O. V. Wells, "Agriculture Today," *Yearbook of Agriculture,* 1940, 385; Blaisdell, *Government and Agriculture;* J. D. Black, *Parity, Parity, Parity* (1942); O. E. Baker, *et al., Agriculture in Modern Life* (1939); E. G. Nourse, *Government in Relation to Agriculture* (1940); Dept. Ag., *Net Farm Income;* J. M. Gaus and L. O. Wolcott, *Public Administration and Department of Agriculture* (1940).

Special — E. G. Nourse, *et al., Three Years of Agricultural Adjustment Administration* (1937); Wallace, *New Frontiers;* M. L. Wilson, *Farm Relief and Domestic Allotment Plan* (1933); Mordecai Ezekiel and L. H. Bean, *Economic Bases for Agricultural Adjustment Act* (1933); E. G. Nourse, *Marketing under AAA* (1935); H. I. Richards, *Cotton and AAA* (1936); J. D. Black, *Dairy Industry and AAA* (1935); D. A. Fitzgerald, *Livestock under AAA* (1935); J. E. Dalton, *Sugar* (1937); H. B. Rowe, *Tobacco under AAA* (1935); J. S. Davis, *Wheat and AAA* (1935); R. E. Martin, "Referendum Process in Agricultural Adjustment Programs," *Ag. Hist.,* XXV (1951), 34. ❡ Rural Poverty: M. L. Wilson, "Problem of Poverty in Agriculture," *Jour. of Farm Econ.,* XXII (1940), 10; C. C. Taylor, *et al., Disadvantaged Classes in Agriculture* (1938); C. M. Wilson, *Landscape of Rural Poverty* (1940); Waller Wynne, Jr., *Five Years of Rural Relief* (1938); Zimmerman and Whetten, *Rural Families on Relief.* ❡ Tenancy: P. V. Maris, *Land Is Mine* (1950); A. F. Raper and I. DeA. Reid, *Sharecroppers All* (1941); J. D. Black and R. H. Allen, "Growth of Farm Tenancy," *Quar. Jour. Econ.,* LI (1937), 393; National Resources Committee, *Farm Tenancy* (1937); C. S. Johnson, *et al., Collapse of Cotton Tenancy* (1935); A. F. Raper, *Preface to Peasantry* (1936); F. C. Frey and T. L. Smith, "Influence of AAA Cotton Program upon Tenant, Cropper and Laborer," *Rural Sociology,* I (1936), 483; Harold Hoffsommer, "AAA and Cropper," *Social Forces,* XIII (1935), 494; Southern Tenant Farmers' Union, *Disinherited Speak* (1936); Erskine Caldwell and Margaret Bourke-White, *You Have Seen Their Faces* (1937); Norman Thomas, *Plight of Sharecropper* (1934); Howard Kester, *Revolt Among Sharecroppers* (1936); H. H. Kroll, *I Was a Sharecropper* (1937). ❡ Migratory Labor: Carey McWilliams, *Factories in Field* (1939), and *Ill Fares the Land* (1942); J. N. Webb, *Migratory-Casual Worker* (1937); J. N. Webb and Malcolm Brown, *Migrant Families* (1939); W. S. Thompson, *Internal Migration in Depression* (1937); Dept. of Labor, *Migration of Workers* (2 vols., 1938); C. E. Lively and Conrad Taeuber, *Rural Migration* (1939); John Steinbeck, *Grapes of Wrath* (1939). ❡ Erosion and Conservation: § 260. ❡ Rural Electrification: Marquis Childs, *Farmer Takes a Hand* (1952); F. W. Muller, *Public Rural Electrification* (1944); H. S. Person, "Rural Electrification Administration," *Ag. Hist.,* XXIV (1950), 70; M. L. Cooke, "Early Days of Rural Electrification," *Am. Pol. Sci. Rev.,* XLII (1948), 431. ❡ Farm Organizations: Wesley McCune, *Farm Bloc* (1943); Kile, *Farm Bureau;* McConnell, *Decline of Agrarian Democracy;* W. P. Tucker, "Populism Up-to-date," *Ag. Hist.,* XXI (1947), 198; S. C. Sufrin, "Labor Organization in Agricultural America, 1930–1935," *Am. Jour. Sociol.,* XLIII (1938), 544. ❡ Changes in Rural Living: Dept. of Ag., *Technology on Farm;* E. deS. Brunner and Irving Lorge, *Rural Trends in Depression* (1937); Dwight Sanderson, *Rural Life in Depression* (1937); B. L. Melvin and E. N. Smith, *Rural Youth* (1938); E. deS. Brunner and J. H. Kolb, *Rural Social Trends* (1933).

Sources — Sen. Ag. Committee, "Agricultural Adjustment Act of 1937," 75 Cong., 1 Sess., *Hearings* (1937); H. Ag. Committee, "General Farm Legislation," 75 Cong., 1 Sess., *Hearings* (1937); Sen. Ag. Committee, "Agricultural Equality Act of 1937," 75 Cong., 1 Sess., *Hearings* (1937), and *General Farm Legislation* (75 Cong., 2 Sess., 20 pts., 1937); Sen. Banking Committee, "Farm Credit Act of 1935," 74 Cong., 1 Sess., *Hearings* (1935); H. Ag. Committee, "Refinancing Farm Mortgages," 74 Cong., 1 Sess., *Hearings* (1935), and "Farm Tenancy," 75 Cong., 1 Sess., *Hearings* (1937), and "Farm Security Act 1937," 75 Cong., 1 Sess., *H. Reports,* Nos. 586, 1065; H. Committee to Investigate Interstate Migration, "Interstate Migration," 76 Cong., 3 Sess., *Hearings* (10 pts., 1940–41), and "Report," 77 Cong., 1 Sess., *H. Report,* No. 369.

Bibliography — Bur. Ag. Econ., *Domestic Allotment Plans* (1933), and *Incidence of Processing Taxes* (1937), and *Government Control of Cotton* (1936), and *Large Scale Farming* (1937); Dept. Ag., *Bibliography on Land Settlement* (1934); L. O. Bercaw, *Southern Sharecropper* (1935).

260. NEW DEAL CONSERVATION AND REGIONALISM, 1933–1940

Summary — Tennessee Valley Authority (May 18, 1933). — National Resources Planning Board. — Soil conservation. — Flood control. — Reforestation. — Power development; Federal Power Commission; National Power Policy Commission. — Role of Interior Department (Ickes), Army Engineers. — Concept of "regionalism" and regional development. — Economic problems of South. — Economic problems of West.

General — National Resources Planning Board, *National Resources Development* (1943); A. F. Gustafson, *et al.*, *Conservation* (1939); A. E. Parkins and J. R. Whitaker, eds., *Our National Resources* (1936); National Resources Committee, *Patterns of Resource Use* (1939); National Resources Board, *Report on National Planning and Public Works in Relation to Natural Resources* (1934); Peffer, *Closing Public Domain*.

Special — Conservation Programs: L. H. Gulick, *American Forest Policy* (1951); R. G. Lillard, *Great Forest* (1947); Arthur Maass, *Muddy Waters* (1951); H. S. Person, *et al.*, *Little Waters* (1936); John Bauer and Peter Costello, *Public Organization of Electric Power* (1949); Bauer, *Electric Power Industry;* Twentieth Century Fund, *Power Industry and Public Interest;* Baum, *Federal Power Commission and State Regulation.* ❧ Soil Erosion and Conservation: P. B. Sears, *Deserts on March* (1935); H. H. Bennett, *Conservation Practices and Flood Control* (1936); W. E. Leuchtenberg, *Flood Control Politics* (1953); Russell Lord, *Behold Our Land* (1938); Chase, *Rich Land, Poor Land;* Marion Clawson, *Uncle Sam's Acres* (1951); C. M. Hardin, *Politics of Agriculture* (1952); Wellington Brink, *Big Hugh* [Bennett] (1951). ❧ TVA: D. E. Lilienthal, *TVA* (r. ed., 1953); C. H. Pritchett, *TVA* (1943); Herman Finer, *TVA* (1944); Philip Selznick, *TVA and Grass Roots* (1949); J. S. Ransmeier, *Tennessee Valley Authority* (1942); N. I. Wengert, *Valley of Tomorrow TVA and Agriculture* (1952); Willson Whitman, *God's Valley* (1939); D. E. Lilienthal and R. H. Marquis, "Conduct of Business by Federal Government," *Harvard Law Rev.*, LIV (1941), 545; Willson Whitman, *David Lilienthal* (1948); Barnes, *Willkie*, chs. iv–ix. ❧ Regionalism: National Resources Committee, *Regional Factors in National Planning* (1935); "Symposium on Regional Planning," *Iowa Law Rev.*, XXXII (1947), 193; National Resources Committee, *Thirteen Regional Planning Reports* (1936–43), and *Twenty-Two Drainage Basin Committee Reports* (1937); W. E. Leuchtenberg, "Roosevelt, Norris and the 'Seven Little TVAs'," *Jour. of Pol.*, XIV (1952), 418; H. W. Odum and Katharine Jocher, eds., *In Search of Regional Balance* (1945); H. W. Odum and H. E. Moore, *American Regionalism* (1938); K. B. Lohmann, *Regional Planning* (1936); A. R. Mangus, *Rural Regions* (1940). ❧ National Resources Planning Board: John Millett, *Process of Government Planning* (1947); R. G. Tugwell, "Utility of the Future in the Present," *Public Administration Rev.*, VIII (1947), 49; National Resources Committee, *City and County Planning* (1937); A. G. Gruchy, "Economics of National Resources Committee," *Am. Econ. Rev.*, XXIX (1939), 60; C. E. Merriam, "National Resources Planning Board," *Am. Pol. Sci. Rev.*, XXXVIII (1944), 1075. ❧ South: National Emergency Council, *Report on Economic Conditions of South* (1938); J. V. Van Sickle, *Planning for South* (1943); H. W. Odum, *Southern Regions*, and *Way of South* (1947); Vance, *Human Geography of South;* R. B. Vance and Nadia Danilevsky, *All These People* (1945); Cash, *Mind of South;* Key, *Southern Politics;* H. L. Herring, *Southern Industry and Regional Development* (1940); R. A. Livesey, *South in Action* (1949); Wendell Berge, "Monopoly and South," *So. Econ. Jour.*, XIII (1947), 360; Daniels, *Southerner Discovers South;* W. P. Webb, *Divided We Stand* (1937); Federal Writers Project, *These Are Our Lives* (1939). ❧ West: Bernard De Voto, "West: Plundered Province," *Harper's*, CLXIX (1934), 355; Rufus Terral, *Missouri Valley* (1947); R. G. Baumhoff, *Damned Missouri Valley* (1951); Lillard, *Nevada;* Charles McKinley, *Uncle Sam in Pacific Northwest* (1952); R. L. Neuberger, *Our Promised Land* (1938); Howard, *Montana;* Forest Service, *Western Range* (1936).

Sources — Joint Committee on Investigation of TVA, "Investigation," 75 Cong., 3 Sess., *Hearings* (7 vols., 1939), and "Report," 76 Cong., 1 Sess., *Sen. Doc.*, No. 56; Sen. Ag. Committee, "Creation of Conservation Authorities," 75 Cong., 1 Sess., *Hearings* (1937); Board of Investigation and Research, "Report on Interterritorial Freight Rates," 78 Cong., 1 Sess., *H. Doc.*, Nos. 145, 303.

Bibliography — Bur. Ag. Econ., *Soil Erosion* (1935); Soil Conservation Service, *Bibliography on Soil Conservation* (1936); California University, Bur. of Public Administration, *Land Utilization* (1935); Bur. Ag. Econ., *Land Utilization* (1936); Hardin, *Politics of Agriculture*; Lilienthal, *TVA*, 227; B. L. Foy, comp., *Bibliography of Tennessee Valley Authority* (1949); A. M. Norwood, comp., *Congressional Hearings, Reports and Documents Relating to TVA, 1933–1946* (1946); Katherine McNamara, *Bibliography of City Planning, 1928–1935* (1936); J. M. Agnew, *Southern Bibliography: Fiction, 1929–1938* (1939).

261. LABOR MOVEMENT, 1933–1940

Summary — Labor under NRA; Section 7-A; Wagner Board. — Fight for Wagner-Connery Labor Relations Act (1935); National Labor Relations Board. — Labor unrest, 1934–35; San Francisco general strike. — Industrial Unionism: formation of Committee for Industrial Organization (1935); John L. Lewis; Sidney Hillman; David Dubinsky. — Congress of Industrial Organizations (1937). — Organizing campaigns of 1937, steel, auto, rubber, textiles. — LaFollette Civil Liberties investigation and industrial warfare. — Wages and working conditions; under NRA; child labor; Fair Labor Standards Act (1938). — Housecleaning in NLRB; Smith Committee, 1939–40. — Labor and politics; Labor's Non-Partisan League; American Labor Party; Lewis in 1940. — Communism and the unions. — Labor racketeering.

General — § 248; Selig Perlman, *Labor in New Deal Decade* (1945); Harris, *American Labor*; R. R. R. Brooks, *When Labor Organizes* (1937), and *Unions of Their Own Choosing* (1939); S. T. Williamson and Herbert Harris, *Trends in Collective Bargaining* (1945); G. G. Higgins, *Voluntarism in Organized Labor, 1930–1940* (1944); Clinton Golden and H. J. Ruttenberg, *Dynamics of Industrial Democracy* (1942); Bell, *Productivity, Wages and National Income*; J. B. Parrish, "Changes in Labor Supply, 1930–1937," *Am. Econ. Rev.*, XXIX (1939), 325; Bur. of Labor Stat., *Handbook of Labor Statistics* (1941).

Special — Labor Under NRA: L. L. Lorwin and Arthur Wubnig, *Labor Relations Boards* (1935); C. R. Daugherty, *Labor Under NRA* (1934); Lois MacDonald, *et al.*, *Labor and NRA* (1934); L. C. Marshall, *Hours and Wages in NRA Codes* (1935); M. H. Schoenfeld, "Analysis of Labor Provisions of NRA Codes," *Mo. Labor Rev.*, XL (1935), 574; D. A. McCabe, "Effects of Recovery Act upon Labor Organizations," *Quar. Jour. Econ.*, XLIX (1934), 52. ❡ Industrial Unionism: Herbert Harris, *Labor's Civil War* (1940); Walter Galenson, *Rival Unionism* (1940); Edward Levinson, *Labor on March* (1938); R. R. R. Brooks, *As Steel Goes* (1940). ❡ Wagner Act and N.L.R.B.: Irving Bernstein, *New Deal Collective Bargaining Policy* (1950); L. G. Silverberg, *Wagner Act* (1945); Joseph Rosenfarb, *National Labor Policy* (1946); S. M. Salny, *Independent Unions under Wagner Act* (1944); C. O. Gregory and H. A. Katz, *Policy Development under National Labor Relations Act* (1947); H. O. Eby, *Labor Relations Act in Courts* (1943); M. C. Doan, "State Labor Relations Acts," *Quar. Jour. Econ.*, LVI (1942), 507. ❡ Wages and Hours Law: O. W. Phelps, *Legislative Background of Fair Labor Standards Act* (1939); P. H. Douglas and Joseph Hackman, "Fair Labor Standards Act of 1938," *Pol. Sci. Quar.*, LIII (1938), 491, LIV (1939), 29; Irving Richter, "Four Years of Fair Labor Standards Act," *Jour. Pol. Econ.*, LI (1943), 95; Tell Ertl and T. T. Read, *Labor Standards and Metal Mining* (1947). ❡ Unions and Leaders: Irving Howe and B. J. Widick, *UAW and Walter Reuther* (1949); Seidman, *Needle Trades*; B. R. Brazeal, *Brotherhood of Sleeping Car Porters* (1946); H. S. Roberts, *Rubber Workers* (1944); Lahne, *Cotton Mill Worker*; C. H. Green, *Headwear Workers* (1944); Jacob Loft, *Printing Trades* (1944); § 248. ❡ Miscellaneous: Louise Overacker, "Labor's Political Contribution," *Pol. Sci. Quar.*, LIV (1939), 56; Seidman, *Labor Czars*.

Sources — Sen. Labor Committee, "To Create a National Labor Board," 73 Cong., 2 Sess., *Hearings* (3 pts., 1934), and "National Labor Relations Board," 74 Cong., 1 Sess., *Hearings* (3 pts., 1935); H. Labor Committee, "Labor Disputes Act," 74 Cong., 1 Sess., *Hearings* (1935); Sen. Judiciary Committee, "Investigation of National Labor Relations Board, 75 Cong., 3 Sess., *Hearings* (1938); Sen. Labor Committee, "National Labor Relations Act Proposed Amendments," 76 Cong., 1 and 3 Sess., *Hearings* (24 pts., 1939–40); H. Labor Committee, "Proposed Amendments to National Labor Relations Act," 76 Cong., 1 and 3 Sess., *Hearings* (9 vols., 1939–40); H. Committee to Investigate National Labor Relations Board, "National Labor Relations Act," 76 Cong., 1, 2, and 3 Sess., *Hearings* (30 vols., 1940); Sen. Labor Committee, "Fair Labor Standards Act of 1937," 75 Cong., 1 Sess., *Joint Hearings* (3 pts., 1937); Conference Committee, "Fair Labor Standards Act of 1938, Conference Report to Sen. 2475," 75 Cong., 3 Sess., *H. Report*, No. 2738; Sen. Labor Committee, "Violations of Free Speech and Rights of Labor," 74 Cong., 2 Sess., 75 Cong., 1 and 2 Sess., 76 Cong., 1–3 Sess., *Hearings* (75 pts., 1936–41); C. O. Gregory and H. A. Katz, *Labor Law* (1948); J. M. Landis and Marcus Manoff, eds., *Cases on Labor Law* (1942); Charles Aikin, ed., *National Labor Relations Board Cases* (1939); NLRB *v.* Jones and Laughlin Steel Corp., 301 U.S. 1; Senn *v.* Tile Layers' Protective Union, 301 U.S. 468; Apex Hosiery Co. *v.* Leader, 310 U.S. 469; Thornhill *v.* Alabama, 310 U.S. 88; United States *v.* Darby, 312 U.S. 100; United States *v* Hutcheson, 312 U.S. 219; Milk Wagon Drivers' Union *v.* Meadowmoor Dairies, 312 U.S. 287; American Federation of Labor *v.* Swing, 312 U.S. 321; Carpenters & Joiners Union *v.* Ritter's Cage, 315 U.S. 722.

Bibliography — § 248.

262. POLITICS, 1933–1940

Summary — Politics of New Deal: Roosevelt; Farley; New Dealers, Corcoran, Hopkins. — Revival of Opposition: 1934–36, Republican activity; conservative Democrats; American Liberty League; thunder on left, Huey Long, Father Coughlin, Townsend movement. — Liberalism in States: Floyd Olson and Farmer-Labor party; La Guardia; the La Follettes; Upton Sinclair and EPIC. — Campaign of 1936; Roosevelt and Garner; Landon and Knox. — Court fight (§ 263). — Divisions in Democratic Party: Garner, Farley, and Southern Democrats; "purge" and congressional elections, 1938. — Third term movement. — New Republican leaders, Taft, Dewey, rise of Willkie. — Campaign of 1940; Roosevelt and Wallace; Willkie and McNary. — Left-wing parties, Socialists. — Communist Party: from revolutionary militancy to popular front (1935); front organizations; infiltration into labor and government; Communist underground and espionage. — Anti-Communism; Dies Committee.

General — § 256; Lubell, *Future of American Politics*; Eleanor Roosevelt, *This I Remember* (1949); Alsop and Kintner, *Men Around the President*; Stanley High, *Roosevelt — And Then?* (1937); Louise Overacker, *Presidential Campaign Funds* (1946), ch. ii; W. C. Clark, *Economic Aspects of President's Popularity* (1943); Pendleton Herring, *Politics of Democracy* (1940); A. N. Holcombe, *Middle Classes in American Politics* (1940); J. T. Salter, ed., *Public Men In and Out of Office* (1946); Robinson, *They Voted for Roosevelt*.

Special — Conservative Opposition: Frederick Rudolph, "American Liberty League," *Am. Hist. Rev.*, LVI (1950), 19; Herbert Hoover, *Challenge to Liberty* (1934), and *Addresses upon the American Road* (1938); O. L. Mills, *What of Tomorrow?* (1935); L. W. Douglas, *Liberal Tradition* (1935); J. P. Warburg, *Money Muddle* (1934); A. S. Cleveland, "NAM: Spokesman for Industry?" *Harvard Bus. Rev.*, XXVI (1948), 353. ❡ Thunder on the Left: A. M. Bingham and Selden Rodman, eds., *Challenge to New Deal* (1934); R. G. Swing, *Forerunners of American Fascism* (1935); A. M. Bingham, *Insurgent America* (1935); [J. F. Carter], *American Messiahs* (1935); G. H. Mayer, *Political Career of Floyd B. Olson* (1951); J. F. Carter, *La Guardia* (1937); Huey Long, *Every Man a King* (1933), and *My First Days in White House* (1935); H. T. Kane, *Louisiana Hayride* (1941); Upton Sinclair, *I, Governor of California* (1933), and *I, Can-*

didate for Governor (1935); F. E. Townsend, *New Horizons* (1943), and *Ready Reference Book* (1941); Twentieth Century Fund, *Townsend Crusade* (1936); C. E. Coughlin, *Lectures on Social Justice* (1935); W. C. Kernan, *Ghost of Royal Oak* (1940). ❡ Campaign of 1936: W. F. Ogburn and L. C. Coombs, "Economic Factor in Roosevelt Elections," *Am. Pol. Sci. Rev.*, XXXIV (1940), 719; A. M. Landon, *America at Crossroads* (1936); Frederick Palmer, *This Man Landon* (1936); Frank Knox, *"We Planned It That Way"* (1938); J. P. Kennedy, *I'm for Roosevelt* (1936). ❡ Campaign of 1940: P. H. Appleby, "Roosevelt's Third-Term Decision," *Am. Pol. Sci. Rev.*, XLVI (1952), 754; Barnes, *Willkie*, chs. xi–xiii; Stanley Walker, ed., *This Is Wendell Willkie* (1940); M. E. Dillon, *Wendell L. Willkie* (1952); H. O. Evjen, "Willkie Campaign," *Jour. of Pol.*, XIV (1952), 241; "This Man Willkie," *New Republic*, Sept. 2, 1940; Fred Rodell, *Democracy and Third Term* (1940). ❡ Machine Politics: C. W. Van Devander, *Big Bosses* (1944); D. D. McKean, *Boss: Hague Machine* (1940); W. M. Reddig, *Tom's Town, Kansas City* (1947); J. F. Dinneen, *Purple Shamrock, Curley of Boston* (1949). ❡ Lobbies: K. G. Crawford, *Pressure Boys* (1939); V. O. Key, *Politics Parties and Pressure Groups* (1948); Schattschneider, *Politics, Pressures and Tariff*; Karl Schriftgiesser, *Lobbyists* (1951). ❡ Socialist Party: Egbert and Persons, *Socialism and American Life*, I, 369; Norman Thomas, *America's Way Out*, and *After the New Deal What?* (1936); H. W. Laidler, *American Socialism* (1937). ❡ Communist Party: Egbert and Persons, *Socialism and American Life*, I, 346; Oneal and Werner, *American Communism*; Eugene Lyons, *Red Decade* (1941); Granville Hicks, "How Red Was the Red Decade?" *Harper's*, July, 1953; Richard Crossman, ed., *God That Failed* (1949); H. D. Lasswell and Dorothy Blumenstock, *World Revolutionary Propaganda* (1939); Wilson Record, *Negro and Communist Party* (1951); W. A. Nolan, *Communism Versus Negro* (1951); Whittaker Chambers, *Witness* (1952); H. J. Wadleigh, "Why I Spied for Communists," *New York Post*, July 11–24, 1949; Gitlow, *I Confess*; Beal, *Proletarian Journey*; Hede Massing, *This Deception* (1951); Alistair Cooke, *Generation on Trial* (1950); Ralph de Toledano and Victor Lasky, *Seeds of Treason* (1952); H. Committee on Un-American Activities, "Shameful Years," 82 Cong., 2 Sess., *H. Report*, No. 1229; Cannon, *History of American Trotskyism*; W. Z. Foster, *Toward Soviet America* (1932); Earl Browder, *Communism in United States* (1935), and *People's Front* (1938), and *Second Imperialist War* (1940); A. R. Ogden, *Dies Committee* (1943); William Gellerman, *Martin Dies* (1944); J. A. Wechsler, *Age of Suspicion* (1953).

Sources — H. Special Committee to Investigate Campaign Expenditures, "Report," 75 Cong., 1 Sess., *H. Report*, No. 151; Sen. Special Committee to Investigate Campaign Expenditures, "Report," 77 Cong., 1 Sess., *Sen. Report*, No. 47; H. Committee to Investigate Old Age Pension Plans, "Old-Age Pension Plans," 74 Cong., 2 Sess., *Hearings* (2 vols., 1936–37), and "Report," 74 Cong., 2 Sess., *H. Report*, No. 2857; H. Committee on Un-American Activities, "Investigation," 75 Cong., 3 Sess. — 78 Cong., 2 Sess., *Hearings* (17 vols., 1938–44), and *Index* (1942); Sen. Judiciary Committee, *Institute of Pacific Relations* (15 pts., 82 Cong., 1 and 2 Sess., 1952); Institute of Pacific Relations, *Commentary on McCarran Report on IPR* (1953); H. Un-American Activities Committee, "Communist Espionage," 80 Cong., 2 Sess., *Hearings* (1948).

Bibliography — Egbert and Persons, *Socialism and American Life*, II; Library of Congress, *List Relating to Huey Long* (1935).

263. NEW DEAL AND COURTS, 1933–1940

Summary — The old Court; nature and record. — Courts and New Deal: Schechter Case (May 27, 1935); Butler Case (Jan. 5, 1936); Carter Case (May 18, 1936); Tipaldo Case (June 1, 1936); proposals for court reform by constitutional amendment; Roosevelt's court plan, 1937; court fight. — Court reverses itself: Parrish Case (Mar. 29, 1937); Jones and Laughlin Case (Apr. 12, 1937); Black appointment (Aug. 12, 1937); Roosevelt court. — Development of administrative law. — Attack on formalism in law.

General — Swisher, *American Constitutional Development*, chs. xxxiv–xxxviii; R. H. Jackson, *Struggle for Judicial Supremacy* (1941); E. S. Corwin, *Twilight of Supreme*

Court, and *Court Over Constitution* (1938), and *Constitutional Revolution, Ltd.* (r. ed., 1946); C. P. Curtis, Jr., *Lions Under Throne* (1947); Paul Freund, *On Understanding Supreme Court* (1951); C. E. Hughes, *Supreme Court* (1936); Carr, *Supreme Court and Judicial Review*; F. V. Cahill, Jr., *Judicial Legislation* (1952); Virginia Wood, *Due Process of Law, 1932–1949* (1951).

Special — Old Court: Pusey, *Hughes,* chs. lxiii–lxxii; Samuel Hendel, *Charles Evans Hughes and Supreme Court* (1951); Mason, *Brandeis,* ch. xxix; "Mr. Justice Cardozo," *Columbia Law Rev.,* XXXIX (1939), 1, and *Harvard Law Rev.,* LII (1939), 353, and *Yale Law Jour.,* XLVIII (1939), 371; J. F. Paschal, *Mr. Justice Sutherland* (1951); E. McK. Eriksson, *Supreme Court and New Deal* (1941); Drew Pearson and Robert Allen, *Nine Old Men* (1936). ❡ Court Fight: Joseph Alsop and Turner Catledge, *168 Days* (1938); W. R. Barnes and A. W. Littlefield, eds., *Supreme Court Issue and Constitution* (1937); I. F. Stone, *Court Disposes* (1937); M. J. Pusey, *Supreme Court Crisis* (1937); Max Lerner, "Great Constitutional War," *Va. Quar. Rev.,* XVIII (1942), 530. ❡ Roosevelt Court: C. H. Pritchett, *Roosevelt Court* (1948); Wesley McCune, *Nine Young Men* (1947); A. M. Schlesinger, Jr., "Supreme Court; 1947," *Fortune,* Jan., 1947; Wallace Mendelson, "Justices Black and Frankfurter: Supreme Court Majority and Minority Trends," *Jour. of Pol.,* XII (1950), 66; C. H. Pritchett, "Libertarian Motivations on Vinson Court," *Am. Pol. Sci. Rev.,* XLVII (1953), 321; R. E. Cushman, ed., "Ten Years of Supreme Court," *ibid.,* XLI (1947), 1142, XLII (1948), 32; S. J. Konefsky, *Chief Justice Stone* (1945), and *Constitutional World of Frankfurter* (1949); J. P. Frank, *Mr. Justice Black* (1949); Charlotte Williams, *Hugo L. Black* (1950); V. M. Barnett, Jr., "Mr. Justice Jackson and Supreme Court," *Western Pol. Quar.,* I (1948), 223. ❡ Administrative Law: J. M. Landis, *Administrative Process* (1938); Roscoe Pound, *Administrative Law* (1942); R. E. Cushman, *Independent Regulatory Commissions* (1941); E. P. Herring, *Public Administration and Public Interest* (1936), and *Federal Commissioners* (1936); Jerome Frank, *If Men Were Angels* (1942); Harold Stein, ed., *Public Administration and Policy Development* (1952); Walter Gellhorn, *Federal Administrative Proceedings* (1941); Avery Leiserson, *Administrative Regulation* (1942); W. H. Nicholls, "Federal Regulatory Agencies and Courts," *Am. Econ. Rev.,* XXXIV (1944), 56; C. G. Haines, "Adaptation of Administrative Law to Constitutional Theories," *Am. Pol. Sci. Rev.,* XXXIV (1940), 1; J. P. Chamberlain, *et al., Judicial Function in Federal Administrative Agencies* (1942); President's Committee on Administrative Management, *Administrative Management* (1937); J. P. Clark, *Rise of New Federalism* (1938); Herbert Emmerich, *Essays on Federal Reorganization* (1950); P. H. Appleby, *Big Democracy* (1945).

Sources — New Deal Cases: Schechter *v.* United States, 295 U.S. 495; Railroad Retirement Board *v.* Alton R.R. Co., 295 U.S. 330; United States *v.* Butler, 297 U.S. 1; Ashwander *v.* TVA, 297 U.S. 288; Morehead *v.* New York, ex rel. Tipaldo, 298 U.S. 587; Carter *v.* Carter Coal Co., 298 U.S. 238; West Coast Hotel *v.* Parrish, 300 U.S. 379; NLRB *v.* Jones and Laughlin Steel Corp., 301 U.S. 1; Helvering *v.* Davis, 301 U.S. 619; United States *v.* Darby, 312 U.S. 100; Sen. Judiciary Committee, "Reorganization of Federal Judiciary," 75 Cong., 1 Sess., *Hearings* (6 pts., 1937), and "Report," 75 Cong., 1 Sess., *Sen. Report,* No. 711.

Bibliography — Library of Congress, *Supreme Court Issue* (1938).

264. MINORITIES UNDER NEW DEAL, 1933–1940

Summary — Negroes under the New Deal; change in political allegiance. — Beginnings of the civil rights movement; anti-lynching and anti-polltax bills. — Scottsboro case and its aftermath. — Indians. — Jews; problems of anti-Semitism. — Refugees. — Other foreign nationality groups; political influence; process of assimilation.

General — D. R. Young, *Minority Peoples in Depression* (1937); Carey McWilliams, *Brothers Under Skin* (1943); Louis Adamic, *Nation of Nations* (1945), and *From Many Lands* (1940); L. G. Brown, *Immigration* (1933); Handlin, *Uprooted*; W. L. Warner and Leo Srole, *Social Systems of American Ethnic Groups* (1945); Rose, *Race Prejudice*; Bruno Bettelheim and Morris Janowitz, *Dynamics of Prejudice* (1950).

Special — Negroes: § 251; C. S. Johnson, *Patterns of Negro Segregation* (1943); Weatherford and C. S. Johnson, *Race Relations*; R. M. E. Sterner, *et al.*, *Negro's Share* (1945); C. S. Mangum, Jr., *Legal Status of Negro* (1940); H. L. Moon, *Balance of Power* (1948); C. G. Woodson, *Negro Professional Man* (1934); C. S. Johnson, *Negro College Graduate* (1938); A. L. Harris, *Negro Capitalist* (1936); H. R. Cayton and G. S. Mitchell, *Black Workers and New Unions* (1939); H. R. Northrup, *Organized Labor and Negro* (1944); C. L. Franklin, *Negro Unionist* (1936); E. F. Frazier, *Negro Youth* (1940), and *Negro Family* (1939); W. L. Warner, *et al.*, *Color and Human Nature* (1941); Allison Davis and John Dollard, *Children of Bondage* (1940); Roi Ottley, *New World A-Coming* (1943); Drake and Cayton, *Black Metropolis*; Claude McKay, *Harlem* (1940); E. R. Embree, *Brown Americans* (1943); Langston Hughes, *Big Sea* (1940); Richard Wright, *Black Boy* (1945), and *Native Son* (1940); Haywood Patterson and Earl Conrad, *Scottsboro Boy* (1950). ❡ Indians: G. E. E. Lindquist, *et al.*, *Indian in American Life* (1944); Debo, *And Still the Waters Run*, and *Road to Disappearance*; Dale, *Indians of Southwest*, Laura Thompson, *Culture in Crisis: A Study of the Hopi* (1950). ❡ Jews: A. L. Lebeson, *Pilgrim People* (1950); A. I. Gordon, *Jews in Transition* (1949); M. J. Karpf, *Jewish Community Organization* (1938); D. S. Strong, *Organized Anti-Semitism in America 1930–40* (1941); Henry Cohen, "Crisis and Reaction," *Am. Jewish Archives*, V (1953), 71. ❡ Refugees: M. R. Davie, *Refugees in America* (1947); D. P. Kent, *Refugee Intellectual* (1953); Jane Carey, "Admission and Integration of Refugees," *Jour. of Int. Affairs*, VII (1953), 66.

Sources — Sen. Judiciary Committee, "Punishment for Lynching," 73 Cong., 2 Sess., 74 Cong., 1 Sess., *Hearings* (1934–35), and "Report," 73 Cong., 2 Sess., *Sen. Report*, No. 710, 74 Cong., 1 Sess., *ibid.*, No. 34, and "Investigation of Lynchings," 74 Cong., 2 Sess., *Sen. Report*, No. 1561, and *Anti-lynching*, 75 Cong., 1 Sess., *Sen. Report*, No. 793; Sen. Indian Affairs Committee, "Survey of Conditions," 70–73 Cong., *Hearings* (33 pts., 1929–35), and 77 Cong., 1 Sess. — 78 Cong., 1 Sess., *Hearings* (1942–4).

Bibliography — Library of Congress, *Immigration* (1943), and *List on Lynching* (1940); Ross and Kennedy, *Bibliography of Negro Migration*; E. E. Edwards and W. D. Rasmussen, *Bibliography on Agriculture of Indians* (1942).

265. FOREIGN POLICY, 1933–1936

Summary — Good Neighbor policy in Latin America: Marines withdrawn from Haiti (1934); cancellation of Platt Amendment (1934); Buenos Aires conference (1936); activities of Export-Import Bank. — Foreign economic policy: Cordell Hull; London Economic Conference; multilateralism and the reciprocal trade agreements program; Tripartite Agreement (1936). — European policy: collaboration with League; World Court fight (1935). — Far Eastern policy: Roosevelt and Stimson Doctrine; Tydings-McDuffie Act (1935). — Isolationism and pacifism: Johnson Act (1934); Nye Committee (1935); neutrality legislation (1935–37).

General — Bailey, *Diplomatic History*, ch. xliv; Allan Nevins, *New Deal and World Affairs* (1950), chs. i–v; Bemis, *Diplomatic History*, chs. xxxviii–xli; Council on Foreign Relations, *United States in World Affairs*; Hull, *Memoirs*; Sumner Welles, *Time for Decision* (1944); H. B. Hinton, *Cordell Hull* (1942); C. A. Beard, *American Foreign Policy 1932–40* (1946); R. A. Dahl, *Congress and Foreign Policy* (1950); § 250.

Special — International Organization: Hubbard, *Cooperation of United States with League*; L. F. Schmeckebier, *International Organizations in which United States Participates* (1935). ❡ Neutrality: Borchard and Lage, *Neutrality for United States*; J. M. Seavey, *Neutrality Legislation* (1939); M. S. Stedman, *Exporting Arms 1935–1945* (1947); Elton Atwater, *American Regulation of Arms Exports* (1941); W. T. Stone, *International Traffic in Arms* (1933); H. C. Engelbrecht and F. C. Hanighen, *Merchants of Death* (1934); "Arms and Men," *Fortune*, Mar., 1934; E. W. Crecraft, *Freedom of Seas* (1935);

P. C. Jessup, *International Security* (1935); A. W. Dulles and H. F. Armstrong, *Can We Be Neutral?* (1936); Quincy Wright, *Neutrality and Collective Security* (1936). ❡ Foreign Economic Policy: A. D. Gayer and C. T. Schmidt, *American Economic Foreign Policy* (1939); Herbert Feis, *Changing Pattern of International Economic Affairs* (1940); Madden, *America's Experience as Creditor*; Lewis, *America's Stake in International Investments*; H. J. Tasca, *Reciprocal Trade Policy* (1938); W. R. Allen, "International Trade Philosophy of Cordell Hull," *Am. Econ. Rev.*, XLIII (1953), 101; R. L. Buell, *Hull Trade Program* (1939); J. D. Larkin, *Trade Agreements* (1940); J. M. Letiche, *Reciprocal Trade Agreements in World Economy* (1948); Carl Kreider, *Anglo-American Trade Agreement* (1943); Adler, *Pattern of Import Trade*; R. C. Snyder, "Commercial Policy in Treaties 1931 to 1939," *Am. Econ. Rev.*, XXX (1940), 787; Carl Kreider, "Effect of American Trade Agreements on Third Countries," *ibid.*, XXXI (1941), 780; A. E. Taylor, *New Deal and Foreign Trade* (1935); H. A. Wallace, *America Must Choose* (1934); G. N. Peek and Samuel Crowther, *Why Quit Our Own?* (1936); C. A. Beard and G. H. Smith, *Open Door at Home* (1934); Peter Molyneux, *Cotton South and American Trade Policy* (1936); E. L. Dulles, *Export-Import Bank* (1944); Pasvolsky, *Current Monetary Issues*; World Peace Foundation, *Monetary and Economic Conference Documents* (1933); Moley, *After Seven Years*, ch. vii; Cox, *Journey Through Years*, chs. xxxi–xxxii; J. P. Nichols, "Roosevelt's Monetary Diplomacy in 1933," *Am. Hist. Rev.*, LVI (1951), 295; Warburg, *Money Muddle*; S. E. Harris, *Exchange Depreciation* (1936); Dept. of Commerce, *United States in World Economy*, and *Foreign Trade, 1936–1949* (1950). ❡ Soviet Union: Browder, *Origins of Soviet-American Diplomacy*. ❡ Good Neighbor Policy: E. O. Guerrant, *Roosevelt's Good Neighbor Policy* (1950); Bemis, *Latin American Policy of United States*; Duggan, *Americas*; Perkins, *Hands Off*, chs. ix–x; Josephus Daniels, *Shirt-Sleeve Diplomat* (1947); W. C. Gordon, *Expropriation of Foreign-Owned Property in Mexico* (1941); C. G. Fenwick, *Inter-American Regional System* (1949); Cline, *United States and Mexico*; Perkins, *United States and Caribbean*; O. F. Smith, *Yankee Diplomacy*. ❡ Far East: Griswold, *Far Eastern Policy*; S. K. Hornbeck, *United States and Far East* (1942); Grew, *Turbulent Era*, and *Ten Years in Japan*; T. A. Bisson, *American Policy in Far East, 1931–1941* (1941); R. P. Browder, "Soviet Far Eastern Policy and American Recognition, 1932–1934," *Pacific Hist. Rev.*, XXI (1952), 263. ❡ Dependencies: G. A. Grunder and W. E. Livezey, *Philippines and United States* (1951); G. I. Kirk, *Philippine Independence, 1936*; David Bernstein, *Philippine Story* (1947); R. G. Tugwell, *Stricken Land Puerto Rico* (1947); A. D. Gayer, et al., *Sugar Economy of Puerto Rico* (1938); L. H. Evans, *Virgin Islands* (1945); E. S. Pomeroy, "American Policy Respecting the Marshalls, Carolines, and Marianas, 1898–1941," *Pacific Hist. Rev.*, XVII (1948), 43, and *Pacific Outpost: American Strategy in Guam and Micronesia* (1953).

Sources — S. S. Jones, *Documents on American Foreign Relations*, VI; Dept. of State, *Peace and War*; *Foreign Relations*, including *Japan 1931–1941* (2 vols., 1943), and *Soviet Union, 1933–1939* (1952); Dept. of State, *Peace in Americas* (1950); H. Foreign Affairs Committee, "Exportation of Arms," 72 Cong., 2 Sess., 73 Cong., 1 Sess., *Hearings* (1933); Sen. Committee Investigating Munitions Industry, "Munitions Industry," 73 and 74 Cong., *Hearings* (39 pts., 1934–36), and "Reports," 74 Cong., 1 Sess., *Sen. Report*, No. 944, and *Index* (1943); Sen. Finance Committee, "To Prevent Profiteering in War," 74 Cong., 2 Sess., *Hearings* (1936); Sen. Foreign Relations Committee, "Neutrality," 74 Cong., 2 Sess., *Hearings* (1936); H. Foreign Affairs Committee, "American Neutrality Policy," (74–75 Cong., *Hearings*, 1935–37); H. Ways and Means Committee, "Reciprocal Trade Agreements," 73 Cong., 2 Sess., *Hearings* (1934); Sen. Finance Committee, "Reciprocal Trade Agreements," 73 Cong., 2 Sess., *Hearings* (1934); H. Ways and Means Committee, "Extending Reciprocal Trade Agreement Act," 75 Cong., 1 Sess., *Hearings* (1937); Sen. Finance Committee, "Extending Reciprocal Trade Agreement Act," 75 Cong., 1 Sess., *Hearings* (1937); H. Insular Affairs Committee, "Independence for Philippine Islands"; Sen. Territories Committee, "Independence for Philippine Islands"; H. Insular Affairs Committee, "Philippine Independence," 73 Cong., 2 Sess., *H. Report*, No. 968; Sen. Territories Committee, "Philippine Independence," 73 Cong., 2 Sess., *Sen. Report*, No. 494; Joint Preparatory Committee on Philippine Affairs, *Report of May 20, 1938* (3 vols., 1938).

Bibliography — R. G. Woolbert, *Foreign Affairs Bibliography 1932–42* (1945); Council on Foreign Relations, *United States in World Affairs; Foreign Affairs*; Carnegie Endowment for International Peace, *Peace Movement* (1940), and *Neutrality* (1938), and *Traffic in Arms* (1933), and *Philippine Independence* (1939), and *Intellectual Relations United States and Latin America* (1935); Library of Congress, *References on American National Defense* (1936), and *Recent References on Neutrality* (1941), and *References on Traffic in Arms* (1934), and *Nationalism* (1934); G. A. Cam, "United States Neutrality Resolutions," N. Y. Public Library, *Bull.*, XLI (1937), 417; Tariff Commission, *Reciprocal Trade* (1936).

266. COMING OF WAR, 1937–1941

Summary — Roosevelt and the threat of fascism: Spanish Civil War; "quarantine" speech (Oct. 5, 1937); acceleration of rearmament; national defense message (Jan. 28, 1938); Munich Agreement (Sept. 30, 1938) and its repercussions. — "Great Debate": isolation and intervention; Stalin-Hitler Pact and American Communism; outbreak of war in Europe (Sept. 1, 1939). — Defense mobilization: "business as usual" against expansion; destroyer deal (Sept. 2, 1940); Selective Service Act (Sept. 16, 1940). — Consolidation of inter-American front; Panama, 1939; Havana, 1940. — Lend-Lease Act (March 11, 1941). — Proclamation of "an unlimited national emergency" (May 27, 1941). — Freezing of German and Italian assets (June 14) and Japanese assets (July 25, 1941). — Atlantic Charter (Aug. 14, 1941). — Mounting tension in Far East: final negotiations with Japan; Pearl Harbor (Dec. 7, 1941).

General — W. L. Langer and S. E. Gleason, *Challenge to Isolation, 1937–1940* (1952), and *Undeclared War* (1953); Basil Rauch, *Roosevelt from Munich to Pearl Harbor* (1950); Bailey, *Diplomatic History*, chs. xlv–xlvi; Bemis, *Diplomatic History*, chs. xlii–xliv; Nevins, *New Deal and World Affairs*, chs. vi–vii; Council on Foreign Relations, *United States in World Affairs;* Hull, *Memoirs*, chs. xxix–lxv; Welles, *Time for Decision*, chs. ii–vii; Sherwood, *Roosevelt and Hopkins*, chs. v–xix; Rosenman, *Working with Roosevelt*, chs. x–xvi, Stimson, *On Active Service*, chs. xii–xv; Joseph Alsop and Robert Kintner, *American White Paper* (1940); Forrest Davis and E. K. Lindley, *How War Came* (1942); C. C. Tansill, *Back Door to War* (1952); Beard, *American Foreign Policy.*

Special — American Defense Planning: M. S. Watson, *Chief of Staff* (1950); Elias Huzar, *Purse and Sword* (1950); E. J. King and W. M. Whitehill, *Fleet Admiral King* (1952), chs. xxv–xxviii; R. S. Cline, *Washington Command Post* (1951); W. F. Craven and J. L. Cate, eds., *Army Air Forces in World War II* (5 vols., 1948–53), I; F. C. Waldrop, ed., *MacArthur on War* (1942). ❡ Threat of Nazism: A. L. C. Bullock, *Hitler* (1952); Konrad Heiden, *Der Fuehrer* (1944); W. L. S. Churchill, *Gathering Storm* (1948); J. W. Wheeler-Bennett, *Munich* (1948); H. L. Trefousse, *Germany and American Neutrality* (1951); W. E. Dodd, *Ambassador Dodd's Diary, 1933–1938* (1941); Phillips, *Ventures;* W. W. Kaufmann, "Two American Ambassadors," Gordon Craig and Felix Gilbert, eds., *Diplomats, 1919–1939* (1953); J. E. Davies, *Mission to Moscow* (1941); Williams, *American-Russian Relations*, ch. viii; F. J. Harriman, *Mission to North* (1941). ❡ Spanish Civil War: Gerald Brenan, *Spanish Labyrinth* (2 ed., 1950); Herbert Feis, *Spanish Story* (1948); H. L. Matthews, *Two Wars and More to Come* (1938). ❡ Far East: Herbert Feis, *Road to Pearl Harbor* (1950); Grew, *Turbulent Era*, and *Ten Years in Japan;* Nathaniel Peffer, *Prerequisites to Peace in Far East* (1940); H. S. Quigley, *Far Eastern War*, (1942); W. C. Johnstone, *United States and Japan's New Order* (r. ed., 1941); Walter Millis, *This is Pearl!* (1947); C. A. Beard, *President Roosevelt and Coming of War* (1948); I. C. Y. Hsu, "Kurusu's Mission," *Jour. Modern Hist.*, XXIV (1952), 301. ❡ Hemisphere Policy: A. P. Whitaker, ed., *Inter-American Affairs* (annual; 1942–　), I; C. G. Fenwick, "Inter-American Neutrality Committee," *Amer. Jour. Int. Law*, XXXV (1941), 12; E. C. Stowell, "Habana Conference," *ibid.*, XXXV (1941), 123; J. F. Rippy, *Caribbean Danger Zone* (1940). ❡ Great Debate: Walter Johnson, *Battle Against Isolationism* (1944); W. S. Cole, *America First* (1953); R. H. Smuckler, "Region of Isolationism," *Am. Pol. Sci. Rev.*, XLVII (1953), 386; J. C. Donovan, "Congressional Isolationists and the Roosevelt Foreign Policy," *World Politics*, II

(1951), 299; R. N. Stromberg, "American Business and Approach to War," *Jour. Econ. Hist.*, XIII (1953), 58; Borchard and Lage, *Neutrality for United States;* Harold Lavine and James Wechsler, *War Propaganda* (1940); N. J. Spykman, *American's Strategy* (1942); R. L. Buell, *Isolated America* (1940); A. W. Dulles and H. F. Armstrong, *Can America Stay Neutral?* (1939); Herbert Hoover, *Shall We Send Our Youth to War* (1939); H. S. Johnson, *Hell-bent for War* (1941); A. M. Lindbergh, *Wave of Future* (1940); J. F. Dulles, *War, Peace and Change* (1939); C. H. Grattan, *Deadly Parallel* (1939); Norman Thomas and B. D. Wolfe, *Keep America Out of War* (1939); Browder, *Second Imperialist War.* ❡ Pro-Fascist Activities: L. G. Turrou, *Nazi Spies* (1939); Harold Lavine, *Fifth Column* (1940); Eleanor Bontecou, *Federal Loyalty-Security* (1953), ch. i; Max Lowenthal, *Federal Bureau of Investigation* (1950); J. R. Carlson, *Undercover* (1943); Martin Dies, *Trojan Horse in America* (1940); John Norman, "Influence of Pro-Fascist Propaganda on Neutrality," Lee and McReynolds, *Essays in Honor of Blakeslee*, 193; Lawrence Dennis, *Dynamics of War and Revolution* (1940); "Fascism in United States," *Fortune*, Nov. 1940. ❡ Defense Mobilization: § 270; Eliot Janeway, *Struggle for Survival* (1951); Civilian Production Administration, *Industrial Mobilization for War* (1947), I; D. M. Nelson, *Arsenal of Democracy* (1946); Aubrey Toulmin, Jr., *Diary of Democracy: Senate War Investigating Committee* (1947); Stein, *Public Administration*, 285; F. C. Lane, *et al.*, *Ships for Victory* (1951); E. P. Allen, *Policies Governing Private Financing of Emergency Facilities* (1946); S. E. Harris, *Economics of Defense* (1941); C. T. Schmidt, *American Farmers in World Crisis* (1941); Norman Beasley, *Knudsen* (1947). ❡ Aid to Allies: W. L. S. Churchill, *Their Finest Hour* (1949), and *Grand Alliance* (1950); E. R. Stettinius, Jr., *Lend-Lease* (1944); Henry Morgenthau, Jr., "Story Behind Lend-Lease," *Colliers*, Oct. 18, 1947; Herbert Feis, *Seen from E.A.* (1947); H. V. Morton, *Atlantic Meeting* (1943); L. W. Holborn, ed., *War and Peace Aims of the United Nations* (1943).

Sources — J. W. Gantenbein, ed., *Documentary Background of World War II, 1931–41* (1948); S. S. Jones, *Documents on American Foreign Relations, 1938–41*, I–III; Kathleen Freeman, ed., *What They Said at the Time* (1945); Rex Stout, ed., *Illustrious Dunderheads* (1942); Dept. of State, *Peace and War; Foreign Relations;* Dept. of State, *United States and Italy, 1936–1946* (1946); Sen. Foreign Relations Committee, "Neutrality," 76 Cong., 1 Sess., *Hearings* (20 pts., 1939); H. Foreign Affairs Committee, "American Neutrality Policy," 76 Cong., 1 Sess., *Hearings* (1939); Conference Committee, "Neutrality Act of 1939," 76 Cong., 2 Sess., *H. Report*, No. 1475; Sen. Military Affairs Committee, "Compulsory Military Training," 76 Cong., 3 Sess., *Hearings* (1940); H. Military Affairs Committee, "Selective Compulsory Military Training," 76 Cong., 3 Sess., *Hearings* (1940); Sen. Foreign Relations Committee, "To Promote Defense," 77 Cong., 1 Sess., *Hearings* (3 pts., 1941); H. Foreign Affairs Committee, "Lend-Lease Bill," 77 Cong., 1 Sess., *Hearings* (1941); Sen. Committee Investigating National Defense, "Defense," 77 Cong., 1 Sess., *Hearings* (1941); Joint Committee on Pearl Harbor Attack, "Pearl Harbor Attack," 79 Cong., 1 Sess., *Hearings* (38 pts., 1946), and "Report," 79 Cong., 2 Sess., *Sen. Doc.*, No. 244.

267. INTELLECTUAL LIFE, 1933–1940

Summary — Impact of depression on intellectual life. — Drift to the left; social novel; "proletarian literature." — Renewal of faith in American traditions; rediscovery in literature, art, history, and biography. — WPA and intellectual life; guides; arts projects. — Social realism and the stage. — Film and radio. — New Deal and economic, political, thought. — Theology of crisis; Reinhold Niebuhr. — Debate in education.

General — § 252; Wecter, *Age of Great Depression*, chs. xii, xiii; Allen, *Since Yesterday;* Leo Gurko, *Angry Decade* (1947); Douglas Waples, *Reading Habits in Depression* (1937); R. L. Duffus, *Our Starving Libraries* (1933); Chafee, *Free Speech*, chs. xi, xii, xv; Milton Crane, ed., *Roosevelt Era* (1947).

Special — Drift to Left: Egbert and Persons, eds., *Socialism and American Life*, I, 599; Lyons, *Red Decade;* J. T. Farrell, *Note On Literary Criticism* (1936); I. deW.

Talmadge, ed., *Whose Revolution?* (1941); Granville Hicks, *et al.*, eds., *Proletarian Literature* (1935); Hicks, *Great Tradition;* Henry Hart, ed., *American Writers' Congress* (1935), and *Writer in a Changing World* (1937); William Phillips and Philip Rahv, eds., *Partisan Reader, 1934–44* (1946). ⟨ WPA and Cultural Life: Grace Overmyer, *Government and Arts* (1939); Jacob Baker, *Government Aid to Professional Service Workers* (1936); Campbell, *Educational Activities of WPA;* H. F. Davis, *Arena Story of Federal Theater* (1940); Willson Whitman, *Bread and Circuses* (1937); WPA, Federal Writers' Project, *American Guide Series* (1937–52); H. G. Alsberg, ed., *American Guide* (1949); "Work of the Federal Writers' Project of WPA," *Publishers' Weekly,* CXXXV (1939), 1130; Katharine Kellock, "WPA Writers," *Am. Scholar,* IX (1940), 473; R. C. Binkley, "Cultural Program of WPA," *Harvard Educ. Rev.,* IX (1939), 156; Federal Theatre Project, *Federal Theatre Plays* (2 vols., 1938). ⟨ Arts: § 252; Monroe Wheeler, ed., *Painters and Sculptors of Modern America* (1942); Darrell Garwood, *Artist in Iowa: Grant Wood* (1944); Suzanne La Follette, "American Art: Economic Aspects," *Am. Mag. Art,* XXVIII (1935), 337; Elizabeth Mock, ed., *Built in USA, 1932–1944* (1944); James and K. M. Ford, *Modern House in America* (1940). ⟨ Theater: § 252; E. M. Gagey, *Revolution in American Drama* (1947); Harold Clurman, *Fervent Years: Group Theatre* (1945); Norris Houghton, *Advance from Broadway* (1941). ⟨ Films: § 252; L. C. Rosten, *Hollywood* (1941); Margaret Thorp, *America at the Movies* (1939); Parker Tyler, *Magic and Myth of Movies* (1947); M. D. Haettig, *Economic Control of Motion Picture Industry* (1944). ⟨ Radio: Hadley Cantril and G. W. Allport, *Psychology of Radio* (1935); Hadley Cantril, *Invasion from Mars* (1940); P. F. Lazarsfeld, *Radio and Printed Page* (1940); P. F. Lazarsfeld and F. N. Stanton, eds., *Radio Research* (1941); Tyler, *Modern Radio.* ⟨ Political and Economic Thought: §§ 256–7, 262; T. W. Arnold, *Symbols of Government* (1935), and *Folklore of Capitalism* (1937); James Burnham, *Managerial Revolution* (1941); John Chamberlain, *American Stakes* (1940); E. H. Chamberlin, *Theory of Monopolistic Competition* (6 ed., 1948); Edgar Kemler, *Deflation of American Ideals* (1941); Max Lerner, *Ideas Are Weapons* (1939); Walter Lippmann, *Good Society* (1937), and *Method of Freedom* (1934); David Spitz, *Patterns of Anti-Democratic Thought* (1949); A. F. Burns, "Brookings Inquiry," *Quar. Jour. of Econ.,* L (1936), 476; H. H. Villard, "Moulton's Theoretical Analysis," *Pol. Sci. Quar.* LIII (1938), 387. ⟨ Depression and Religion: S. C. Kincheloe, *Religion in Depression* (1937); J. A. Hutchison, ed., *Christian Faith and Social Action* (1953); M. F. Thelen, *Man as Sinner in Contemporary Theology* (1946); W. M. Horton, *Realistic Theology* (1934); George Hammar, *Christian Realism* (1940); J. C. Bennett, "Contribution of Reinhold Niebuhr," *Religion in Life,* VI (1937), 268; Reinhold Niebuhr, *Nature and Destiny of Man* (2 vols., 1941–43), and *Moral Man and Immoral Society* (1932); C. W. Kegley and R. W. Bretall, eds., *Theology of Paul Tillich* (1953); J. C. Bennett, *Social Salvation* (1935); F. E. Johnson, *Social Gospel Re-examined* (1940); D. C. Macintosh, *Social Religion* (1939); Sidney Hook, *et al.,* "New Failure of Nerve," *Partisan Rev.,* X (1943), 2; H. N. Wieman, *et al., Religious Liberals Reply* (1947); J. A. Ryan, *Seven Troubled Years, 1930–1936* (1937). ⟨ Education: National Education Association, *Education in Depression* (1937), and *Education and Economic Well-Being* (1940); O. W. Caldwell, *et al., Depression, Recovery and Higher Education* (1937); I. L. Kandel, *End of An Era* (1941); R. F. Butts, *College Charts Its Course* (1939); R. L. Duffus, *Democracy Enters College* (1936); R. M. Hutchins, *Higher Learning in America* (1936); R. S. Lynd, *Knowledge for What?* (1939); Alexander Meiklejohn, *Education between Two Worlds* (1942); Mark Van Doren, *Liberal Education* (1943); H. K. Beale, *Are American Teachers Free?* (1936); Calvin Grieder, "Principal Emergency Federal Educational Projects, 1933–1944," *Educ. Forum,* May, 1945; Newton Edwards and H. G. Richey, *Extent of Equalization through State School Funds* (1938).

Sources — § 258; Sen. Educ. Committee, "Bureau of Fine Arts," 75 Cong., 3 Sess., *Hearings* (1938); H. Commerce Committee, "Motion-Picture Films," 74 Cong., 2 Sess., *Hearings* (1936); Sen. Educ. Committee, "Assistance to States in Public Education," 75 Cong., 1 Sess., *Hearings* (1937); H. Educ. Committee, "Federal Aid to States for Support of Public Schools," 75 Cong., 1 Sess., *Hearings* (1937). ⟨ Civil Liberties cases: deJonge *v.* Oregon, 299 U.S. 253; Herndon *v.* Lowry, 301 U.S. 242; Minersville

School District *v.* Gobitis, 310 U.S. 586; Hague *v.* C.I.O., 307 U.S. 496; W. Va. State Board of Education *v.* Barnette, 319 U.S. 624.

Bibliography — § 252; Kirkir Quinn, *et al.*, "American Poetry, 1930–1940," *Accent*, I (1941), 213; Library of Congress, *Moving Pictures* (1936), and *Recent References on Communication* (1935), and *Radio* (1941); E. E. Buehler, *Federal Aid for Education* (1934); R. A. Beals and Leon Brody, comps., *Literature of Adult Education* (1941).

268. SOCIAL CURRENTS, 1933–1940

Summary — Impact of the depression. — Effect on living standards, on family life, on social mobility. — Folkways of employment and relief. — Manners and morals. — Crime and the depression. — Special sociological studies (§ 8).

General — Wecter, *Age of Great Depression;* Allen, *Since Yesterday;* H. E. Stearns, ed., *America Now* (1938); Margaret Mead, *And Keep Your Powder Dry* (1942); Willcox, *Demography.*

Special — Foreign Comment: D. W. Brogan, *American Character* (1944); H. G. Wells, *New America — New World* (1935); H. J. Laski, *American Democracy* (1948); André Maurois, *En Amérique* (1933), and *États-Unis 39.* ❡ Impact of Depression: §§ 254, 258; Soc. Sci. Res. Counc., *Research Bulletins on Social Aspects of Depression* (1937); Enzler, *Social Aspects of Depression;* E. C. Ridley and O. F. Nolting, eds., *What Depression Has Done to Cities* (1935); W. F. Ogburn, ed., *Social Change and New Deal* (1934), and *Social Changes during Depression and Recovery* (1935); R. S. Vaile, *Social Aspects of Consumption in Depression* (1937); National Resources Committee, *Consumer Incomes 1935–36* (1938); Dept. Ag., *Family Income and Expenditures* (7 pts., 1939–40), and *Family Housing and Facilities* (1940), and *Family Food Consumption* (1941), and *Family Expenditures for Medical Care* (1941); Bur. Labor Stat., "Differences in Living Costs in Northern and Southern Cities," *Mo. Labor Rev.*, XLIX (1939), 22; Evans, *American Photographs.* ❡ Youth: American Youth Commission, *Youth and Future* (1942); White House Conference on Children, *Children in a Democracy* (1940); Thacher Winslow and F. P. Davidson, eds., *American Youth* (1940); Maxine Davis, *Lost Generation* (1936); Howard Bell, *Youth Tell Their Story* (1938); D. D. Bromley and F. H. Britten, *Youth and Sex* (1938); Office of Educ., *Youth* (6 pts., 1936); Census Bureau, *Facts About Youth in 1940 Census* (1941). ❡ Recreation: J. F. Steiner, *Recreation in Depression* (1937); Julius Weinberger, "Economic Aspects of Recreation," *Harv. Bus. Rev.*, XV (1937), 448; J. R. Tunis, *Democracy in Sport* (1941); Gallico, *Farewell to Sport;* Joe Louis, "My Story," *Life* (Nov. 8, 15, 1948); § 253. ❡ Crime: Bell, "Crime as an American Way of Life"; Thorsten Sellin, *Crime in Depression* (1937); A. C. Millspaugh, *Crime Control by National Government* (1937); Judicial Conference of Senior Circuit Judges, *Report of Committee on Punishment for Crime* (1942); H. E. Barnes and N. K. Teeters, *New Horizons in Criminology* (1947); Bruce Smith, *Police Systems* (1940); E. L. Irey and W. J. Slocum, *Tax Dodgers* (1948); J. E. Hoover, *Persons in Hiding* (1938); L. V. Harrison and Elizabeth Laine, *After Repeal* (1936); Charles Hamilton, ed., *Men of the Underworld* (1952); Craig Thompson and Allen Raymond, *Gang Rule in New York;* M. H. Purvis, *American Agent* (1936); S. B. Whipple, *Lindbergh Crime* (1935); C. R. Cooper, *Ten Thousand Public Enemies* (1935); V. W. Peterson, *Barbarians in Our Midst* (1952). ❡ Special Studies: H. D. Anderson and P. E. Davidson, *Occupational Mobility in an American Community* (1937), and *Occupational Trends* (1940), and *Occupational Trends in American Labor* (1945); Hadley Cantril, "Identification with Social and Economic Class," *Jour. of Abnormal and Soc. Psychology*, XXXVIII (1943), 78; G. R. Leighton, *Five Cities* (1939); Lynd, *Middletown in Transition;* West, *Plainville;* W. L. Warner and P. S. Lunt, *Social Life of Modern Community* (1941), and *Status System of a Modern Community* (1942); Whyte, *Street Corner;* Anderson, *We Americans;* Dollard, *Caste and Class in a Southern Town;* Davis, Gardner, and Gardner, *Deep South;* Hortense Powdermaker, *After Freedom* (1939); W. C. Holley, *et al., Plantation South, 1934–1937*

(1940); E. O. Moe and C. C. Taylor, *Culture of a Contemporary Rural Community, Irwin, Iowa* (1942); MacLeish and Young, *Landoff*; E. H. Bell, *Culture of a Contemporary Rural Community; Sublette, Kansas* (1942); P. G. Cressey, *Taxi-Dance Hall* (1932); William Gellermann, *American Legion as Educator* (1938); John Bainbridge, *Little Wonder; Reader's Digest* (1946); St. Clair McKelway, *Gossip Walter Winchell* (1940).

Sources — Sen. Commerce Committee, "Investigation: So-called Rackets" 73 Cong., 2 Sess., *Hearings* (7 pts., 1933–34); Sen. Judiciary Committee, "Equal Rights for Men and Women," 75 Cong., 3 Sess., *Hearings* (2 pts., 1938).

Bibliography — Wecter, *Age of Great Depression*, 317; Attorney General's Advisory Committee on Crime, *Bibliography on Recreation and Delinquency* (1936), and *Bibliography on Juvenile Delinquency* (1936), and *Bibliography on Housing and Crime* (1936), and *Bibliography on Jails* (1937).

Chapter Thirty

WAR AND ITS AFTERMATH, 1941–1952

269. SECOND WORLD WAR: MILITARY ASPECTS, 1941–1945

Summary — Initial Japanese success: the Philippines, Malaya, Burma, Dutch East Indies. — Pacific turning points: Battle of Coral Sea (May, 1942); Battle of Midway (June, 1942). — Planning European operations; "Hitler First" decision. — Central strategic issue, cross-channel attack (Marshall) or "soft underbelly" (Churchill). — European Theater: securing sea routes; North African invasion (Nov. 7, 1942); invasion of Sicily (July 1943); Italian surrender (Sept. 8, 1943); strategic bombing of Germany, 1942–44. — Establishment of initiative in Pacific: Guadalcanal campaign (Aug. 7, 1942); Battle of Bismarck Sea (Mar., 1943); New Guinea campaign (1943–44); central strategic issue, campaign through South Pacific (MacArthur) or Central Pacific (Nimitz); Tarawa (Nov., 1943); Leyte Gulf (Oct., 1944); economic pressure on Japan; submarine blockade; strategic bombing. — Second front in France (June 6, 1944): Allied break-through; capture of Paris (Aug. 25); entry into Belgium, Holland; German counteroffensive in Ardennes (Dec. 16); 9th Army reaches Rhine (Mar. 2, 1945); American and Russian units meet (Apr. 25); German surrender (May 7). — Reduction of Japan: Iwo Jima (Feb.–Mar., 1945); Okinawa (Apr.–June); first atomic bomb dropped on Hiroshima (Aug. 6); Japanese surrender (Aug. 14). — The American as soldier and sailor; story of G. I. Joe.

General — W. L. S. Churchill, *Second World War* (6 vols., 1948–   ); J. F. C. Fuller, *Second World War, 1939–45* (1948); W. P. Hall, *Iron Out of Calvary* (1946); Walter Millis, ed., *War Reports of Marshall Arnold King* (1947); *United States Army in World War II* (91 vols., 1947–   ); S. E. Morison, *History of United States Naval Operations in World War II* (14 vols., 1947–   ); Craven and Cate, *Army Air Force in World War II*; *Operational Narratives of the Marine Corps in World War II* (1947–   ); A. H. Brune, *Strategy in World War II* (1947); Bernard Brodie, *Guide to Naval Strategy* (1944); W. D. Puleston, *Influence of Sea Power in World War II* (1947); D. S. Ballantine, *U.S. Naval Logistics in Second World War* (1947); R. J. Casey, *Battle Below: War of Submarines* (1945); Walter Karig, *et al., Battle Reports* (6 vols., 1944–52); Cline, *Washington Command Post*; Maurice Matloff and E. M. Snell, *Strategic Planning for Coalition Warfare, 1941–42* (1953); M. H. Gillie, *Forging the Thunderbolt: Development of Armored Force* (1947); Chester Wardlow, *Transportation Corps* (1951); Oliver LaFarge, *Eagle in Egg: Military Air Transport* (1949); Alfred Vagts, *Landing Operations* (1946); Wallace Carroll, *Persuade or Perish* (1948); Stewart Alsop and Thomas Braden, *Sub Rosa; O.S.S. and American Espionage* (1946); J. P. Baxter, *Scientists Against Time* (1946); L. R. Thiesmeyer and J. E. Burchard, *Combat Scientists* (1947); J. C. Boyce, ed., *New Weapons for Air Warfare* (1947); J. E. Buchard, ed., *Rockets, Guns and Targets* (1948); G. M. Barnes, *Weapons of World War II* (1947); E. C. Andrus, *et al.,* eds., *Advances in Military Medicine* (2 vols., 1948); Van Rensselaer Sill, *American Miracle War Construction* (1947); S. McK. Rosen, *Combined Boards of Second World War* (1951); R. M. Leighton, "Allied Unity of Command," *Pol. Sci. Quar.,* LXVII (1952), 399; Roosevelt,

Public Papers and Addresses, and *Personal Letters,* IV; Sherwood, *Roosevelt and Hopkins;* Stimson, *On Active Service;* Leahy, *I Was There;* King and Whitehill, *Fleet Admiral King;* Hull, *Memoirs;* Forrestal, *Forrestal Diaries;* Robert Payne, *Marshall Story* (1951); H. H. Arnold, *Global Mission* (1949); L. H. Brereton, *Brereton Diaries* (1946).

Special — War in Europe: D. D. Eisenhower, *Crusade in Europe,* and *Report on Operations in Europe* (1946); Chester Wilmot, *Struggle for Europe* (1952); A. M. Schlesinger, Jr., "Wilmot's War," *Reporter,* Apr. 29, 1952; U.S. Strategic Bombing Survey, *Summary Report (European War)* (1945), and *Effects of Strategic Bombing on German Economy* (1945), and *Effects of Strategic Bombing on German Morale* (1946); W. B. Smith, "Eisenhower's Decisions," *Sat. Eve. Post,* June–July, 1946; Bradley, *Soldier's Story;* G. S. Patton, *War As I Knew It* (1947); A. T. Harris, *Bomber Offensive* (1947); Daniel Lerner, *Sykewar* (1949); H. C. Butcher, *Three Years with Eisenhower* (1946); A. J. Liebling, *Road Back to Paris* (1944); Kathleen Summersby, *Eisenhower* (1948). ⊄ Italian Campaign: M. W. Clark, *Calculated Risk* (1950); C. G. Starr, ed., *Salerno to the Alps* (1948); Christopher Buckley, *Road to Rome* (1945); Alan Moorehead, *Eclipse* (1945); Benito Mussolini, *Memoirs, 1942–1943,* and *Fall of Mussolini* (1948); Pietro Badoglio, *Italy in Second World War* (1948); Galeazzo Ciano, *Ciano Diaries, 1939–1943* (1946). ⊄ Second Front and After: Frederick Morgan, *Overture to Overlord* (1950); Albert Norman, *Operation Overlord* (1952); F. W. DeGuingaud, *Operation Victory* (1947); Alfred Stanford, *Force Mulberry* (1951); War Department Historical Division, *Omaha Beachhead* (1946); R. S. Allen, *Lucky Forward Patton's Third Army* (1947); Ralph Ingersoll, *Top Secret* (1946); Hans Speidel, *Invasion 1944* (1950); R. E. Merriam, *Dark December: Battle of Bulge* (1947); S. L. A. Marshall, *et al., Bastogne* (1946); H. M. Cole, *Lorraine Campaign* (1950). ⊄ Nazis: Elizabeth Wiskemann, *Rome-Berlin Axis* (1949); Felix Gilbert, ed., *Hitler Directs His War* (1950); Adolf Hitler, *Hitler's Secret Conversations* (1953); Paul Schmidt, *Hitler's Interpreter* (1951); F. H. Hinsley, *Hitler's Strategy* (1951); A. K. Martjenssen, *Hitler and His Admirals* (1949); Milton Shulman, *Defeat in West* (1947); B. H. Liddell Hart, *German Generals Talk* (1948); Joseph Goebbels, *Goebbels Diaries, 1942–1943* (1948); Ulrich von Hassell, *Von Hassell Diaries* (1947); Heinz Guderian, *Panzer Leader* (1952); A. W. Dulles, *Germany's Underground* (1947); H. B. Gisevius, *To Bitter End* (1948); Hans Rothfels, *German Opposition to Hitler* (1948); H. R. Trevor-Roper, *Last Days of Hitler* (1947). ⊄ Pacific War: Gilbert Cant, *Great Pacific Victory* (1946). ⊄ Philippines: W. D. Edmonds, *They Fought With What They Had* (1951); J. M. Wainwright, *General Wainwright's Story* (1946); Allison Ind, *Bataan* (1944); M. L. Quezon, *The Good Fight* (1946); C. P. Romulo, *I Saw the Fall of Philippines* (1942); W. L. White, *They Were Expendable* (1942). ⊄ Navy's War: R. L. Sherrod, *History of Marine Corps Aviation* (1952); J. A. Isely and P. A. Crowl, *U.S. Marines and Amphibious War* (1951); W. F. Halsey and J. Bryan, *Admiral Halsey's Story* (1947); H. M. Smith and Percy Finch, *Coral and Brass* (1949); J. L. Zimmerman, *Guadalcanal* (1949); John Miller, Jr., *Guadalcanal* (1949); J. N. Rentz, *Bougainville and Northern Solomons* (1948); Ira Wolfert, *Battle for Solomons* (1943); F. O. Hough and J. A. Crown, *Campaign on New Britain* (1952); J. R. Stockman, *Battle for Tarawa* (1947); R. L. Sherrod, *Tarawa* (1944); J. A. Field, Jr., *Japanese at Leyte Gulf* (1947); C. V. Woodward, *Battle for Leyte Gulf* (1947); C. W. Boggs, Jr., *Marine Aviation in Philippines* (1951); C. W. Hoffman, *Saipan* (1950); Joseph Bryan and Philip Reed, *Mission Beyond Darkness* (1945); R. J. Casey, *Torpedo Junction* (1942); Stanley Johnston, *Queen of Flat-Tops* (1942). ⊄ MacArthur's War: R. L. Eichelberger and Milton Mackaye, *Our Jungle Road to Tokyo* (1950); Walter Krueger, *From Down Under to Nippon* (1953); R. R. Smith, *Approach to Philippines* (1953); J. K. Eyre, *Roosevelt-MacArthur Conflict* (1950); G. C. Kenney, *General Kenney Reports* (1949); R. H. Rovere and A. M. Schlesinger, Jr., *General and President* (1951), ch. ii; Clark Lee and Richard Henschel, *Douglas MacArthur* (1952), chs. xiii–xv. ⊄ China: C. F. Romanus and Riley Sunderland, *Stilwell's Mission to China* (1953); J. W. Stilwell, *Stilwell Papers* (1948); C. L. Chennault, *Way of a Fighter* (1949); T. H. White and Annalee Jacoby, *Thunder Out of China* (1946); Jack Belden, *Retreat With Stilwell* (1943). ⊄ Japan: U.S. Strategic Bombing Survey, *Summary Report (Pacific War)* (1946), and *Effects of Strategic Bombing on Japan's War Economy* (1946), and *Effects of Atomic Bombs on Hiroshima and Nagasaki* (1946), and *Effects of Strategic Bombing on Japanese Morale* (1946), and *Interrogation of Japanese Officials* (2 vols., 1946); R. E. Appleman, *et al., Okinawa* (1948); E. M. Zacharias, *Secret Missions* (1946); Toshidazu Kase, *Journey to the Missouri* (1950); H. L. Stimson, "Decision to Use Atomic Bomb," *Harper's,* CXCIV (1947), 97; J. R. Hersey, *Hiroshima* (1946). ❡ The American in War: Stouffer, *American Soldier;* Ernie Pyle, *Here is Your War* (1943), and *G.I. Joe* (1944), and *Brave Men* (1945); Bill Mauldin, *Up Front,* and *Bill Mauldin's Army* (1951); *Best from Yank* (1945); Debs Myers, *et al., Yank; G.I. Story of War* (1947); *New Yorker Book of War Pieces* (1947); P. C. Davis, "Negro in Armed Services," *Va. Quar. Rev.,* XXIV (1948), 499; D. D. Nelson, *Integration of Negro into the Navy* (1951); George Biddle, *Artist at War* (1944). ❡ Novels: J. G. Cozzens, *Guard of Honor* (1948); Thomas Heggen, *Mister Roberts* (1946); Norman Mailer, *Naked and Dead* (1949); J. A. Michener, *Tales of South Pacific* (1947); Irwin Shaw, *Young Lions* (1948); Herman Wouk, *Caine Mutiny* (1951).

Bibliography — National Archives, *Federal Records of World War II* (1951), II; C. E. Dornbusch, ed., *Unit Histories of World War II* (1950; supplement, 1952), and "Checklists of *Yank* and *Stars and Stripes*" (n.d.); G. H. Knoles, "Pacific War," *Pacific Hist. Rev.,* XVI (1947), 420.

270. HOME FRONT, 1941–1945

Summary — War production organization; War Production Board (Jan. 16, 1942). — Materials control; "czars" (rubber, petroleum, solid fuels, food, shipbuilding, transportation); Controlled Materials Plan (Nov. 2, 1942); direct scheduling (1943–44). — Relations with military; Munitions Board. — Production of food and fiber; new farm policies. — Scientific advance; Office of Scientific Research and Development; Manhattan Project. — Relations with Congress; Truman Committee. — Mobilization of labor: War Manpower Commission (Apr. 18, 1942); campaign for national service law (1943–44); adjustment of industrial disputes; labor's no-strike pledge; War Labor Board (Jan. 12, 1942); wage stabilization policy (Little Steel formula, July 16, 1942); wage control in Stabilization Act of 1942. — Economic stabilization: Office of Price Administration (Apr. 11, 1941) and selective price controls; struggle to control agricultural prices; seven point stabilization program (Apr. 27, 1942); Stabilization Act of 1942; Office of Economic Stabilization (Oct. 3, 1942); civilian rationing; resignation of Leon Henderson. — Financing the war; tax policies; Ruml Plan; bond drives. — War Information; Office of Censorship; Office of Facts and Figures; Office of War Information. — Coördination of war agencies; role of Bureau of Budget; Office of War Mobilization (May 27, 1943). — Politics: Democratic setbacks in 1942 congressional elections; New Deal on defensive; 1944 election (Roosevelt and Truman; Dewey and Bricker); death of Roosevelt and accession of Truman (Apr. 12, 1945). — Civil liberties during war. — Minorities: Negroes (Fair Employment Practices Commission, June 25, 1941); Detroit race riots, July, 1943; struggle against segregation in armed services; relocation of Japanese-Americans. — Social history of home front.

General — Bur. of Budget, *United States at War* (1946); Janeway, *Struggle for Survival;* Brogan, *Era of F. D. Roosevelt,* chs. xv–xvii, J. R. Craf, *Survey of American Economy, 1940–1946* (1947); Simon Kuznets, *National Product in Wartime* (1945); Cantril, *Public Opinion, 1935–46;* L. H. Gulick, *Administrative Reflections from World War II* (1948); L. D. White, ed., *Civil Service in Wartime* (1945).

Special — Industrial Mobilization: Civilian Production Administration, *Industrial Mobilization for War;* R. H. Connery, *Navy and Industrial Mobilization in World War II* (1951); H. M. Somers, *Presidential Agency, OWMR* (1950); Nelson, *Arsenal of Democracy;* Toulmin, *Diary of Democracy;* Bruce Catton, *War Lords of Washington* (1948); David Novik, *et al., Wartime Production Controls* (1949); J. L. O'Brian and Manly Fleischmann, "War Production Board Administrative Policies," *George Wash. Law Rev.* XIII (1944), 1; David Novik and G. A. Steiner, *Wartime Industrial Statistics* (1949); Committee on Public Administration Cases, *Feasibility Dispute* (1950);

Tom Lilley, *et al.*, *Problems of Accelerating Aircraft Production* (1947); J. D. Morgan, *Domestic Mining Industry* (1949); Bradley Stoughton, *History of Tools Division, War Production Board* (1949); Drummond Jones, *Role of Office of Civilian Requirements* (1946); J. W. Frey and H. C. Ide, eds., *History of Petroleum Administration* (1946); H. L. Ickes, *Fightin' Oil* (1943); F. A. Howard, *Buna Rubber* (1947); J. B. Eastman, *Selected Papers and Addresses 1942–44* (1948); Office of Defense Transportation, *Civilian War Transport* (1948); Lane, *Ships for Victory;* G. H. Moore, *Production of Industrial Materials* (1944); G. M. Kammerer, *Impact of War on Federal Personnel Administration* (1951). ❡ Scientific Mobilization: Irvin Stewart, *Organizing Scientific Research for War* (1948); Baxter, *Scientists Against Time;* C. G. Suits, *et al.*, *Applied Physics* (1948); W. A. Noyes, Jr., ed., *Chemistry* (1948); H. D. Smyth, *Atomic Energy for Military Purposes* (1945); C. W. Bray, *Psychology and Military Proficiency* (1948). ❡ Economic Stabilization: L. V. Chandler, *Inflation, 1940–1948* (1951); H. C. Mansfield, *et al.*, *Short History of OPA* (1949); W. J. Wilson, *et al.*, *Beginnings of OPA* (1947); T. B. Worsley, *Wartime Economic Stabilization and Government Procurement* (1949); J. K. Galbraith, *Theory of Price Control* (1952); S. E. Harris, *Inflation and American Economy* (1945); P. G. Pranck, ed., *Problems in Price Control* (1948); V. B. Zimmerman, *Problems in Price Control* (1947); D. F. Cavers, *et al.*, *Problems in Price Control* (1947); R. J. Benes, *et al.*, *Problems in Price Control* (1947), and *Studies in Industrial Price Control* (1947); N. L. Nathanson and Harold Leventhal, *Problems in Price Control* (1947); R. I. Campbell, *History of Basic Metals Price Control* (1948); Wilfred Carsel, *Wartime Apparel Price Control* (1947); R. B. Armstrong, *et al.*, *Problems in Price Control* (1947); J. A. Bliss, *OPA and Public Utility Commissions* (1947); I. H. Putnam, *Volunteers in OPA* (1947); J. L. Afros, "Labor Participation in Office of Price Administration," *Am. Pol. Sci. Rev.*, XL (1946), 458; V. A. Thompson, *Regulatory Process in OPA Rationing* (1950); J. A. Kershaw, *History of Ration Banking* (1947); E. S. Redford, *Field Administration of Wartime Rationing* (1947); W. A. Nielander, *Wartime Food Rationing in United States* (1947); Judith Russell and Renee Fantin, *Studies in Food Rationing* (1947); J. A. Maxwell, "Gasoline Rationing, United States," *Quar. Jour. Econ.*, LX (1946), 561, LXI (1946), 125; P. M. O'Leary, "Wartime Rationing," *Am. Pol. Sci. Rev.*, XXXIX (1945), 1089. ❡ Farm Policy: W. W. Willcox, *Farmer in Second World War* (1947); Bela Gold, *Wartime Economic Planning in Agriculture* (1949); Benedict, *Farm Policies*, chs. xvi–xvii; Benjamin Baker, *Wartime Food Procurement and Production* (1951); J. D. Black and C. A. Gibbons, "War and American Agriculture," *Rev. of Econ. Stat.*, XXVI (1944), 1; G. S. Shepherd, *Agricultural Price Control* (1945); A. S. Tostlebe, *Impact of War on Financial Structure of Agriculture* (1945); E. L. Butz, *Production Credit System* (1944); W. D. Arant, "Wartime Meat Policies," *Jour. Farm Econ.*, XXVIII (1946), 903. ❡ Mobilization of Labor: Dept. Labor, *Problems and Policies of Dispute Settlement* (1950); Fred Witney, *Wartime Experiences of National Labor Relations Board* (1949); National War Labor Board, *Termination Report* (3 vols., 1947–49); D. M. Keezer, "Observations on War Labor Board," *Am. Econ. Rev.*, XXXVI (1946), 233; Wayne Morse, "National War Labor Board," *Ore. Law Rev.*, XXII (1942), 1; H. S. Kaltenborn, *Governmental Adjustment of Labor Disputes* (1943); Doris Duffy, *Role of Government in Labor-Management Production Committees* (1947); International Labour Office, *Labour Management Co-operation in United States War Production* (1948); Joseph Shister, "National War Labor Board," *Jour. Pol. Econ.*, LIII (1945), 37; H. R. Northrup, "Railway Labor Act and Railway Labor Disputes," *Am. Econ. Rev.*, XXXVI (1946), 324; R. J. Purcell, *Labor Policies of National Defense Advisory Commission and Office of Production Management, May 1940–April 1942* (1946); Herman Feldman, ed., "Labor Relations and War," An. Ac. Pol. Soc. Sci., *Annals*, CCXXIV (1942); Williamson and Harris, *Collective Bargaining;* L. P. Adams, *Wartime Manpower Mobilization* (1951). ❡ Financing the War: R. G. Blakey and G. C. Blakey, "Federal Revenue Act of 1942," *Am. Pol. Sci. Rev.*, XXXVI (1942), 1069; E. D. Allen, "Treasury Tax Policies in 1943," *Am. Econ. Rev.*, XXXIV (1944), 707; Mabel Newcomer, "Congressional Tax Policies in 1943," *ibid.*, XXXIV (1944), 734; G. E. Lent, "Excess-Profits Taxation," *Jour. Pol. Econ.*, LIX (1951), 481; Ratner, *American Taxation*, ch. xxiv; R. K. Merton, *Mass Persuasion of a War Bond Drive* (1946). ❡ Politics: Childs, *I Write From Washington;* Jonathan Daniels, *Frontier on the Potomac* (1946), and *Man of Independence* (1950); John Harding, "The 1942

Congressional Elections," *Am. Pol. Sci. Rev.*, XXXVIII (1944), 41; Louise Overacker, "Presidential Campaign Funds, 1944," *ibid.*, XXXIX (1945), 899; Joseph Gaer, *First Round: CIO Political Action Committee* (1944); G. E. Allen, *Presidents Who Have Known Me* (1950). ❡ Communism: Earl Browder, *Victory — and After* (1942), and *Teheran* (1944); W. Z. Foster, *et al.*, *Marxism–Leninism vs. Revisionism* (1946); O. R. Pilat, *Atom Spies* (1952); Joint Committee on Atomic Energy, *Soviet Atomic Espionage* (82 Cong., 1 Sess., 1951). ❡ Civil Liberties and Minorities: E. S. Corwin, *Total War and Constitution* (1947); Francis Biddle, *Democratic Thinking and War* (1944); Byron Price, "Governmental Censorship in Wartime," *Am. Pol. Sci. Rev.*, XXXVI (1942), 837; T. F. Koop, *Weapons of Silence* (1946); M. Q. Sibley and P. E. Jacob, *Conscription of Conscience: Conscientious Objector, 1940–1947* (1952). ❡ Negroes: Malcolm Ross, *All Manner of Man* (1948); E. L. Brown, *Why Race Riots?* (1944); H. R. Northrup, "Organized Labor and Negro Workers," *Jour. Pol. Econ.*, LI (1943), 206; Ottley, *New World A-Coming;* Richard Wright, *Twelve Million Black Voices* (1943). ❡ Japanese-Americans: Morton Grodzins, *Americans Betrayed* (1949); D. S. Thomas, *et al.*, *Salvage: Japanese American Evacuation and Resettlement* (1952); A. H. Leighton, *Governing of Men* (1945); McWilliams, *Prejudice;* War Relocation Authority, *WRA* (1946); E. V. Rostow, "Japanese-American Cases — Disaster," *Yale Law Jour.*, LIV (1945), 489; U.S. Army, Western Defense Command and Fourth Army, *Final Report, Japanese Evacuation* (1943). ❡ Social History: Jack Goodman, ed., *While You Were Gone* (1946); W. F. Ogburn, *American Society in Wartime* (1943); J. S. Bruner, *Mandate from People* (1944); G. B. Watson, ed., *Civilian Morale* (1942); John Dos Passos, *State of the Nation* (1944); Samuel Grafton, *American Diary* (1943); Max Lerner, *Public Journal* (1945); Selden Menefee, *Assignment: U.S.A.* (1943); R. J. Havighurst and H. G. Morgan, *Social History of a War Boom Community* (1951); L. J. Carr and J. E. Stermer, *Willow Run: Industrialization and Cultural Inadequacy* (1952); Reuben Hill, *Families Under Stress* (1949); M. B. Clinard, *Black Market* (1952); Harry Lever and Joseph Young, *Wartime Racketeers* (1945).

Sources — Production: Civilian Production Administration, *Minutes of War Production Board* (1946), and *Minutes of Planning Committee* (1946); Sen. Committee Investigating National Defense Program, "Investigation of National Defense Program," (77 Cong., 1 Sess. — 80 Cong., 1 Sess., *Hearings and Reports* (1941–48); H. Military Affairs Committee, "Investigation of National Defense Program," 77 Cong., 2 Sess., *H. Reports*, Nos. 1767, 1873, 2081, 2148, 2246, 2272, 2588, and "Investigation of National War Effort," 78 Cong., 2 Sess., *H. Report*, No. 1903; H. Naval Affairs Committee, "Investigation of Naval Defense Program, 77 Cong., 2 Sess., *Hearings* (7 vols., 1942), and "Investigation of Progress of War Effort," 78 Cong., 1 and 2 Sess., *Hearings* (5 vols., 1943–44), and "Report," 78 Cong., 2 Sess., *H. Report*, No. 2056; Sen. Committee to Study Small Business, "Small Business and War Program," 77 Cong., 1 Sess., *Hearings* (1942), and "Problems of American Small Business," 77 Cong., 2 Sess. — 79 Cong., 2 Sess., *Hearings* (97 pts., 1942–46); H. Ways and Means Committee, "Renegotiation of War Contracts," 78 Cong., 1 Sess., *Hearings* (1943); H. Merchant Marine Committee, "Production in Shipbuilding Plants," 78 Cong., 1 and 2 Sess., *Executive Hearings* (4 pts., 1943–44), and "Investigation of Shipyard Profits," 79 Cong., 2 Sess., *Hearings* (1946); H. Commerce Committee, "Petroleum Investigation," 77 Cong., 2 Sess., 79 Cong., 2 Sess., *Hearings* (1942–46); Sen. Committee Investigating Petroleum Resources, *Wartime Petroleum Policy* (79 Cong., 1 Sess., 1946); Sen. Military Affairs Committee, "Technological Mobilization," 78 Cong., 2 Sess., *Hearings* (3 vols., 1942–43), and "Scientific and Technical Mobilization," 78 Cong., 1 and 2 Sess., *Hearings* (16 pts., 1943–44). ❡ Stabilization: Sen. Banking Committee, "Emergency Price Control Act," 77 Cong., 1 Sess., *Hearings* (1941); H. Banking Committee, "Price Control Bill," 77 Cong., 1 Sess., *Hearings* (2 pts., 1941); Sen. Banking Committee, "Extension of Emergency Price Control Act of 1942," 78 Cong., 2 Sess., *Hearings* (1944); H. Banking Committee, "Extension of Emergency Price Control Act," 78 Cong., 2 Sess., *Hearings* (2 vols., 1944); Sen. Banking Committee, "Extending the Emergency Price Control Acts of 1942, as Amended," 79 Cong., 1 Sess., *Hearings* (1945). ❡ Manpower: Sen. Labor Committee, "Investigation of Manpower Resources," 77 Cong., 2 Sess., *Hearings* (2 pts., 1942–43); Sen. Military Affairs Committee, "Manpower," 77 Cong., 2 Sess., *Hearings* (1942), and

"Manpower (National War Service Bill)," 78 Cong., 1 Sess., *Hearings* (22 pts., 1943); H. Military Affairs Committee, "Full Utilization of Manpower," 78 Cong., 1 Sess., *Hearings* (1943); Sen. Military Affairs Committee, "National War Service Bill," 78 Cong., 2 Sess., *Hearings* (3 pts., 1944). ❡ Elections: H. Special Committee to Investigate Campaign Expenditures, *Hearings* (78 Cong., 2 Sess., 1944), and "Report," 78 Cong., 2 Sess., *H. Report,* No. 2093; Sen. Special Committee to Investigate Campaign Expenditures, "Report," 79 Cong., 1 Sess., *Sen. Report,* No. 101. ❡ Living Conditions: H. Committee Investigating National Defense Migration, *Hearings* (77 Cong., 1 and 2 Sess., 1941–42), and "Reports," 77 Cong., 1 Sess., *H. Reports,* Nos. 1286, 1553, and 77 Cong., 2 Sess., *ibid.,* Nos. 2396, 2589; H. Public Buildings Committee, "Housing National Defense," 77 Cong., 2 Sess., *Hearings* (1942); H. Naval Affairs Committee, "Investigation of Congested Areas," 78 Cong., 1 Sess., *Hearings* (8 pts., 1943–44); Sen. Labor Committee, "Wartime Health and Education," 78 Cong., 1, 2 Sess., *Hearings* (7 pts., 1944–45). ❡ Civil Liberties: Taylor *v.* Mississippi, 319 U.S. 583; Hartzel *v.* United States, 322 U.S. 680; Keegan *v.* United States, 325 U.S. 478. ❡ Japanese-Americans: H. Committee Investigating National Defense Migration, "Reports," 77 Cong., 2 Sess., *H. Reports,* Nos. 1911, 2124; Hirabayashi *v.* United States, 320 U.S. 81; Korematsu *v.* United States, 323 U.S. 214; *Ex Parte Endo,* 323 U.S. 283.

Bibliography — National Archives, *Federal Records of World War II,* (1950), I, and *Materials Relating to the Historical Programs of Civilian Agencies during World War II* (1952); National Historical Publications Commission, *List of World War II Historical Studies by Civilian Agencies* (1951); L. J. Cappon, "War Records Projects in States," Am. Assoc. for State and Local Hist., *Bull.,* I (1944), 189; J. H. Rodabaugh, "War Records Projects in States," *ibid.,* II (1947), 1; W. J. Wilson, *et al., OPA Bibliography* (1948).

271. FOREIGN POLICY, 1941–1945

Summary — Organization: role of Roosevelt, of H. L. Hopkins; limitations of State Department (Sumner Welles resignation, 1943); role of military, and doctrine of "military expediency"; new operating agencies, lend-lease, economic warfare, political warfare, inter-American relations. — Foreign policy within the coalition: declaration by United Nations (Jan. 1, 1942); Great Power conferences (Casablanca, Jan., 1943; First Quebec, Aug., 1943; Moscow, Oct., 1943; Cairo, Nov., 1943; Teheran, Dec., 1943; Second Quebec, Sept., 1944; Yalta, Feb., 1945). — Relations with Great Britain: Roosevelt-Churchill liaison; establishment of Combined Chiefs of Staff (Jan. 27, 1942) and Combined Boards. — Relations with Soviet Union: lend-lease arrangements; dissolution of Comintern (May 23, 1943); dissolution of American Communist Party (1944). — Relations with China: attempts to aid Chiang Kai-shek; conflicts in American policy (Chennault, Stilwell); growing irritation with Chungking. — Relations with France: Vichy policy; North Africa; attitude toward De Gaulle and French Committee of National Liberation. — Relations with governments-in-exile, Poland, Yugoslavia, Czechoslovakia, other groups. — Relations with American republics; Rio de Janeiro conference (Jan., 1942); Argentina; Chapultepec conference (Mar., 1945). — War aims: one world (Willkie); century of the common man (Wallace); American century (Luce); great-power world (Lippmann).

General — Bailey, *Diplomatic History,* chs. xlvi–xlvii, Bemis, *Diplomatic History,* chs. xliv–xlv; Nevins, *New Deal and World Affairs,* chs. vii–x; Sherwood, *Roosevelt and Hopkins;* Hull, *Memoirs;* Leahy, *I Was There;* Sumner Welles, *Time for Decision,* and *Seven Decisions That Shaped History* (1950); Roosevelt, *Public Papers,* and *Personal Letters;* W. A. Brown, Jr. and Redvers Opie, *American Foreign Assistance* (1953), chs. ii–iii; E. F. Penrose, *Economic Planning for Peace* (1953); D. L. Gordon and Royden Dangerfield, *Hidden Weapon; Economic Warfare* (1947); Rosen, *Combined Boards;* Herbert Feis, *Seen from E.A.,* and *Petroleum and American Foreign Policy* (1944); Elliott Roosevelt, *As He Saw It* (1946).

Special — Great Britain: J. G. Winant, *Letter from Grosvenor Square* (1947); D. W. Brogan, "America and Britain, 1939–1946," *Yale Rev.,* XXXV (1946) 193. ❡ Soviet

Union: E. R. Stettinius, Jr., *Roosevelt and Russians* (1949); W. A. Harriman, "Statement Regarding Wartime Relations with Soviet Union," Sen. Armed Services and Foreign Relations Committees, "Military Situation in Far East," 82 Cong., 1 Sess., *Hearings* (1951), 3328; J. R. Deane, *Strange Alliance* (1947); T. H. V. Motter, *Persian Corridor and Aid to Russia* (1952); George Fischer, "Genesis of Soviet Relations in World War II." *Rev. Politics*, XII (1950), 363; Raymond Dennett and J. E. Johnson, eds., *Negotiating With Russians* (1951); Byrnes, *Speaking Frankly;* A. H. Z. Carr, *Truman, Stalin and Peace* (1950); Tompkins, *American-Russian Relations;* D. J. Dallin, *Big Three* (1945); Stanislaw Mikolajczyk, *Rape of Poland* (1948); Jan Ciechanowski, *Defeat in Victory* (1947); Constantin Fotitch, *War We Lost* (1948). ❡ China: § 269; Herbert Feis, *China Tangle* (1953); Fairbank, *United States and China.* ❡ France: W. L. Langer, *Our Vichy Gamble* (1947); McKay, *United States and France;* R. R. Pierre-Gosset, *Conspiracy in Algiers* (1945); Kenneth Pendar, *Adventure in Diplomacy* (1945); H. F. d'Ornano, *L'Action gaulliste aux États-Unis, 1940–1945* (1948); Jacques Soustelle, *Envers et contre tout* (2 vols., 1947–50); Maxime Weygand, *Recalled to Service* (1952). ❡ European Neutrals: M. C. Taylor, ed., *Wartime Correspondence between Roosevelt and Pope Pius XII* (1947); C. J. H. Hayes, *Wartime Mission in Spain* (1945); W. L. Beaulac, *Career Ambassador* (1951); E. J. Hughes, *Report from Spain* (1947). ❡ American Republics: Guerrant, *Roosevelt's Good Neighbor Policy*, ch. vii; E. S. Furniss, Jr., "American Wartime Objectives in Latin America," *World Politics*, II (1950), 373; Whitaker, *Inter-American Affairs, 1941–45;* Duggan, *Americas;* Perkins, *United States and Caribbean;* A. M. Schlesinger, Jr., "Good Fences Make Good Neighbors," *Fortune*, Aug., 1946; *History of Office of Coordinator of Inter-American Affairs* (1947). ❡ War Aims Discussion: Herbert Hoover and Hugh Gibson, *Problems of Lasting Peace* (1942); Walter Lippmann, *U.S. Foreign Policy* (1943), and *U.S. War Aims* (1944); H. R. Luce, *American Century* (1941); Spykman, *America's Strategy;* H. A. Wallace, *Century of Common Man* (1943); Welles, *Time for Decision;* W. L. Willkie, *One World* (1943).

Sources — S. S. Jones, *Documents on American Foreign Relations*, IV–VI; Sen. Foreign Relations Committee, "Decade of American Foreign Policy: Basic Documents," 81 Cong., 1 Sess., *Sen. Doc.*, No. 123; Dept. of State, *In Quest of Peace and Security: Selected Documents* (1951); Commerce Dept., *International Transactions 1940–45* (1948), and *Foreign Aid by United States 1940–1951* (1952); Dept. State, *Bull.*, 1941–45, and *Participation in International Conferences, 1941–1945* (1947), and *United States Relations with China;* Holborn, *War and Peace Aims;* L. L. Lorwin, *Postwar Plans of United Nations* (1943); H. Committee to Investigate Katyn Massacre, *Hearings* (82 Cong., 2 Sess., 1952); Sen. Foreign Relations Committee, "Nomination of Charles E. Bohlen," 83 Cong., 1 Sess., *Hearings* (1953).

272. MAKING PEACE, 1941–1947

Summary — Planning Postwar World: State Department's Advisory Committee on Post-War Foreign Policy (1942–43); United Nations Relief and Rehabilitation Administration (Nov. 9, 1943); Bretton Woods conference (July, 1944); Dumbarton Oaks conference (Aug.–Oct., 1944); San Francisco conference; United Nations Charter (Apr.–June, 1945); UN specialized agencies. — Policy toward Germany: "unconditional surrender" (Jan. 24, 1943); dismemberment proposal (Teheran); European Advisory Commission (1944–45); Morgenthau Plan (Sept. 15, 1944), ensuing debate; Potsdam conference (July–Aug., 1945); occupation policies. — Policy toward Japan: initial post-surrender policy, retention of emperor; establishment of Far Eastern Commission (1946); MacArthur and occupation; Japanese peace treaty (Sept. 8, 1951). — Policy toward lesser Axis states: peace treaties with Italy, Bulgaria, Hungary, Rumania, and Finland (Feb. 10, 1947). — Colonial Questions: Roosevelt and Churchill on problems of empire; UN and non-self-governing territories. — Economic Reconstruction: termination of lend-lease (Aug. 21, 1945); British loan (1946), and Export-Import Bank loans; movement toward multilateral trade (International Trade Organization, 1948).

General — Dept. of State, *Making Peace Treaties, 1941–1947* (1947), and *Postwar Foreign Policy Preparation, 1939–45* (1950); Bailey, *Diplomatic History*, chs. xlviii–xlix;

Bemis, *Diplomatic History*, chs. xlv, xlvi; § 271; Council on Foreign Relations, *United States in World Affairs*, 1945–47; W. L. Neumann, *Making the Peace, 1941–1945* (1950); Vandenberg, *Private Papers*; Carr, *Truman, Stalin and Peace*.

Special — Occupation Policy: Hajo Holborn, *American Military Government* (1947); C. J. Friedrich, *et al.*, *American Experiences in Military Government in World War II* (1948); Dept. of State, *Cartels and Combines in Occupied Areas* (1947). ❧ Economic Reconstruction: Penrose, *Economic Planning for Peace*; A. H. Hansen, *America's Role in World Economy* (1945); George Woodbridge, comp., *UNRRA* (3 vols., 1950); Marvin Klemmé, *Inside Story of UNRRA* (1949); Henry Morgenthau, Jr., "Bretton Woods," *Foreign Affairs*, XXIII (1945), 82; J. H. Ferguson, "Anglo-American Financial Agreement," *Yale Law Jour.*, LV (1946), 1140. ❧ Germany: Dept. of State, *Occupation of Germany* (1947), and *United States Economic Policy toward Germany* (1946); P. E. Mosely, "Dismemberment of Germany," *Foreign Affairs*, XXVIII (1950), 487, and "Occupation of Germany," *ibid.*, 580; Hull, *Memoirs*; Stimson and Bundy, *On Active Service*, ch. xxii; Henry Morgenthau, Jr., *Germany Is Our Business* (1945); L. D. Clay, *Decision in Germany* (1950), and *Germany* (1950); F. L. Howley, *Berlin Command* (1950); C. J. Friedrich, "Rebuilding German Constitution," *Am. Pol. Sci. Rev.*, XLIII (1949), 461, 704; Harold Zink, *American Military Government in Germany* (1947); Elmer Plischke, *History of Allied High Commission for Germany* (1951); B. U. Ratchford and W. D. Ross, *Berlin Reparations Assignment* (1947); J. K. Pollock and J. H. Meisel, *Germany under Occupation* (1947); M. M. Knappen, *And Call It Peace* (1947); Wolfgang Friedmann, *Allied Military Government of Germany* (1947); Russell Hill, *Struggle for Germany* (1947); Drew Middleton, *Struggle for Germany* (1949); S. K. Padover, *Experiment in Germany* (1946); Julian Bach, Jr., *America's Germany* (1946); J. S. Martin, *All Honorable Men* (1950); J. E. DuBois, Jr., *Devil's Chemists* (1952); R. H. Jackson, *Case Against Nazi War Criminals* (1946), and *Nurnberg Case* (1947); Sheldon Glueck, *Nuremberg Trial and Aggressive War* (1946). ❧ Lesser Axis States: Byrnes, *Speaking Frankly*; Sumner Welles, *Where Are We Heading?* (1946), chs. ii–iii; P. E. Mosely, "Peace-Making, 1946," *Int. Organization*, I (1947), 22; R. G. Neumann, "United States and Soviet Satellites," *Rev. Politics*, XI (1949), 220. ❧ Japan: Reischauer, *United States and Japan*; Dept. of State, *Occupation of Japan* (1946); SCAP, *Political Reorientation of Japan, 1945 to 1948* (2 vols., 1949), and *Japanese Land Reform Program* (1950); John Gunther, *Riddle of MacArthur* (1951); E. M. Martin, *Allied Occupation of Japan* (1948); Russell Brines, *MacArthur's Japan* (1948); W. R. Fishel, "Japan under MacArthur," *Western Pol. Quar.*, IV (1951), 210; R. A. Fearey, *Occupation of Japan* (1950); W. M. Ball, *Japan* (r. ed., 1949); C. D. Edwards, "Dissolution of Japanese Combines," *Pacific Affairs*, XIX (1946), 227; J. B. Keenan and B. F. Brown, *Crimes Against International Law* (1950); A. F. Reel, *Case of General Yamashita* (1949). ❧ Colonial Questions: Dept. State, *United States and Non-Self-Governing Territories* (1947); Rupert Emerson, *et al.*, *America's Pacific Dependencies* (1949).

Sources — S. S. Jones, *Documents on American Foreign Relations*, VIII, IX; Sen. Foreign Relations Committee, *Decade of American Foreign Policy*; Dept. State, *Bull.*, 1941–47, and *Participation of United States in International Conferences, 1945 to 1947* (2 vols., 1948), and *Axis in Defeat: Documents* (1945), and *Germany 1947–1949* (1950), and *United States and Italy*; H. R. Isaacs, ed., *New Cycle in Asia: Selected Documents* (1947); H. Foreign Affairs Committee, "To Enable United States to Participate in United Nations Relief and Rehabilitation Administration," 78 Cong., 1 and 2 Sess., *Hearings* (1944), and "Reconstruction Fund," 78 Cong., 2 Sess., *Hearings* (1944), and "Further Participation in Work of UNRRA," 79 Cong., 1 Sess., *Hearings* (1945); Sen. Banking Committee, "Bretton Woods Agreement Act," 79 Cong., 1 Sess., *Hearings* (1945); H. Banking Committee, "Bretton Woods Agreements Act," 79 Cong., 1 Sess., *Hearings* (2 vols., 1945); International Military Tribunal, *Trial of Major War Criminals 1945–1946* (42 vols., 1947–49), and *Trials of War Criminals 1946–1949* (15 vols., 1949–53); U.S. Chief Counsel, *Nazi Conspiracy and Aggression* (10 vols., 1946–48).

Bibliography — *Foreign Affairs*; Council on Foreign Relations, *United States in World Affairs*.

273. POSTWAR FOREIGN POLICY, 1947–1953

Summary — Break-up of wartime coalition: Soviet violations of Yalta agreements; end of collaboration by Communists. — Mounting tensions: reparations; atomic energy control; Iran; Greece; Germany (Byrnes's Stuttgart speech, Sept. 6, 1946). — Reorientation of policy: Truman Doctrine (Mar. 12, 1947); Marshall Plan (June 5, 1947); interim aid to Western Europe (1947); Economic Cooperation Administration (Apr. 3, 1948); Voice of America (1947); Berlin airlift (June 25, 1948); Point Four program (Jan. 20, 1949); North Atlantic Pact (Apr. 4, 1949); support for European unification. — Changes in military policy: postwar demobilization; rejection of universal military training; establishment of unified military establishment (National Security Act of 1947); National Security Council; rearmament (1950–53). — Far East: attempts to resolve Chinese Civil War, Marshall mission, 1945–46, Wedemeyer Report, 1947; debate over aid to Nationalist government; defeat of Chiang Kai-shek and retirement to Formosa; post mortems; China Lobby. — War in Korea (June 25, 1950); UN assistance; proclamation of national emergency (Dec. 16, 1950); policy differences between Washington and MacArthur; recall of MacArthur (Apr. 11, 1951); truce negotiations (1951–53). — Latin America: Argentina and the problem of intervention (U.S. Blue Book, Feb. 11, 1946); change of policy (1947); Rio de Janeiro conference and Inter-American Treaty (Aug.–Sept., 1947); Bogotá conference (Apr., 1948). — Middle East: Palestine controversy and Republic of Israel (recognized, 1948); attempted mediation Iran oil dispute (1951–52). — Republican policy changes: relations with Allies; military cutbacks.

General — Bailey, *Diplomatic History*, chs. xlix–li; Bemis, *Diplomatic History*, ch. xlvi; Council on Foreign Relations, *United States in World Affairs*, 1947–51; William Hillman, ed., *Mr. President* (1952); Byrnes, *Speaking Frankly*; J. F. Byrnes, "Byrnes Answers Truman," *Collier's*, Apr. 26, 1952; H. S. Truman, *New Era in World Affairs* (1949); D. G. Acheson, *Strengthening Forces of Freedom* (2 vols., 1950); McGeorge Bundy, ed., *Pattern of Responsibility* (1952); Forrestal, *Diaries*; Vandenberg, *Private Papers*; W. L. S. Churchill, *Sinews of Peace* (1949); Brookings Institution, *Major Problems of United States Foreign Policy, 1947–52* (annually, 1947–).

Special — Organization of Foreign Policy: W. Y. Elliott, *et al.*, *United States Foreign Policy* (1952); D. S. Cheever and H. F. Haviland, Jr., *American Foreign Policy and Separation of Powers* (1952); J. L. McCamy, *Administration of Foreign Affairs* (1950); W. J. Parks, *United States Administration of International Economic Affairs* (1951); E. W. Barrett, *Truth Is Our Weapon* (1953); C. A. H. Thomson, *Overseas Information Service* (1948); Sherman Kent, *Strategic Intelligence* (1949); J. R. Childs, *American Foreign Service* (1948); Stein, *Public Administration and Policy Development*, 661; G. A. Almond, *American People and Foreign Policy* (1950). ❰ United Nations: A. H. Feller, *United Nations and World Community* (1952); L. M. Goodrich and Edvard Hambro, *Charter of United Nations* (1949); Grayson Kirk and L. H. Chamberlain, "Organization of San Francisco Conference," *Pol. Sci. Quar.*, LX (1945), 321; Werner Levi, *Fundamentals of World Organization* (1950); H. F. Haviland, Jr., *Political Role of General Assembly* (1951); S. M. Schwebel, *Secretary-General* (1952); F. S. Dunn, *War and Minds of Men* (1950); E. P. Chase, *United Nations in Action* (1950); Clyde Eagleton, ed., *Annual Review of United Nations Affairs* (1950–). ❰ Atomic Energy Control: Bernard Brodie, ed., *Absolute Weapon* (1946); J. R. Newman and B. S. Miller, *Control of Atomic Energy* (1948); Dept. of State, *International Control of Atomic Energy* (3 vols., 1946–49), and *Report on International Control of Atomic Energy* (1946); Frederick Osborn, *Atomic Impasse, 1948* (1948); Joint Committee on Atomic Energy, *Hydrogen Bomb and International Control* (81 Cong., 2 Sess., 1950). ❰ Breakup of Coalition: Kennan, *American Diplomacy*, 107; W. B. Smith, *My Three Years in Moscow* (1950); F. C. Barghoorn, *Soviet Image of United States* (1950); Isaac Deutscher, *Stalin* (1949), chs. xii–xiv; Dennett and Johnson, *Negotiating With Russians*; [Canada], *Royal Commission Report on Information Leakage on Atomic Research to Soviet Agents* (1946); A. B. Lane, *I Saw Poland Betrayed* (1948); Martin Ebon, *World Communism Today* (1948); Foster, *Marxism-Leninism vs. Revisionism*. ❰ Economic Policy: Brown and Opie, *American Foreign Assistance*, chs. iv–xxii; R. F. Mikesell, *United States Economic*

Policy and International Relations (1952); S. E. Harris, ed., *Foreign Economic Policy* (1948); J. N. Behrman, "Political Factors in International Financial Cooperation, 1945–50," *Am. Pol. Sci. Rev.*, XLVII (1953), 431; Council of Economic Advisers, *Impact of Foreign Aid upon Domestic Economy* (1948); J. A. Krug, *Report on National Resources and Foreign Aid* (1947); Clair Wilcox, *Charter for World Trade* (1949); E. S. Mason, *Controlling World Trade* (1946); Letiche, *Reciprocal Trade Agreements in World Economy*; Brian Tew, *International Monetary Cooperation 1945–52* (1952); C. P. Kindleberger, *Dollar Shortage* (1950); Adler, *Pattern of Import Trade*; Wendell Berge, *Cartels: Challenge to a Free World* (1944); Dept. of State, *Point Four* (1950), and *Technical Assistance in Action* (1951), and *Point Four Pioneers* (1951), and *Land Reform* (1952); Public Affairs Institute, *Bold New Program Series* (8 vols., 1950); H. L. Hoskins, ed., "Aiding Underdeveloped Areas Abroad," Am. Ac. Pol. Soc. Sci., *Annals*, CCLXVIII (1950); Ernest Bloch, "United States Foreign Investment and Dollar Shortage," *Rev. of Ec. Stat.*, XXXV (1953), 154; [Gray Committee], *Report on Foreign Economic Policies* (1950); [Rockefeller Committee], *Partners in Progress* (1951); [Bell Committee], *Trade and Tariff Policy* (1953); J. E. Meade, *Theory of International Economic Policy* (1951). ❮ Military Policy: Vannevar Bush, *Modern Arms and Free Men* (1949); Atomic Energy Commission, *Effects of Atomic Weapons* (1950); D. V. Bradley, *No Place to Hide* (1948); R. E. Lapp, *Must We Hide?* (1949), and *New Force* (1953); B. H. Williams, ed., "Search for National Security," Am. Ac. Pol. Soc. Sci., *Annals*, CCLXXVIII (1951); President's Air Policy Commission, *Survival in Air Age* (1948); President's Advisory Commission on Universal Training, *Program for National Security* (1947). ❮ Europe: Lewis Galantière, *America and Mind of Europe* (1952); H. S. Ellis, *Economics of Freedom* (1950); S. E. Harris, *European Recovery Program* (1948); [Harriman Committee], *European Recovery and American Aid* (1948); W. L. Hickman, *Genesis of European Recovery Program* (1949); Lincoln Gordon, "ERP in Operation," *Harvard Bus. Rev.*, XXVII (1949), 129. ❮ North Atlantic Pact: Drew Middleton, *Defense of Western Europe* (1952); H. L. Hoskins, *Atlantic Pact* (1949); Theodore Geiger and H. van B. Cleveland, *Making Western Europe Defensible* (1951); R. H. Heindel, *et al.*, "North Atlantic Treaty in Senate," *Am. Jour. Int. Law*, XLIII (1949), 633. ❮ Far East: Feis, *China Tangle*; K. S. Latourette, *American Record in Far East* (1952); H. M. Vinacke, *United States and Far East* (1952); J. C. Vincent, *et al.*, *America's Future in Pacific* (1947); J. K. Fairbank, *et al.*, *Next Step in Asia* (1949); Carsun Chang, *Third Force in China* (1952); Tompkins, *American-Russian Relations*; Charles Wertenbaker, *et al.*, "China Lobby," *Reporter*, Apr. 15, 29, 1952; H. R. Isaacs, *No Peace for Asia* (1947); T. E. Dewey, *Journey to Far Pacific* (1952); Arthur Goodfriend, *Only War We Seek* (1951). ❮ Korean War: G. M. McCune and A. L. Grey, Jr., *Korea Today* (1950); A. L. Grey, Jr., "Thirty-Eighth Parallel," *Foreign Affairs*, Apr., 1951; E. G. Meade, *American Military Government in Korea* (1951); C. C. Mitchell, Jr., *Korea, Second Failure in Asia* (1951); Rovere and Schlesinger, *General and President*; Dept. of State, *Korea, 1945 to 1948* (1948), and *U. S. Policy in Korean Crisis* (1950), and *Conflict in Korea* (1951); L. M. Goodrich, "United Nations and Korea," *Jour. of Int. Affairs*, Spring, 1952; P. E. Mosely, "Soviet Policy and War," *ibid.*, Spring, 1952; N. J. Padelford, "United Nations and Korea," *Int. Organization*, Nov., 1951; A. E. Stevenson, "Korea in Perspective," *Foreign Affairs*, Apr., 1952; Douglas MacArthur, *Revitalizing a Nation* (1952); J. W. Ballantine, *Formosa* (1952); Dept. of Army, *Korea — 1950* (1952); Karig, *Battle Report*, VI; Beverly Smith, "Why We Went to War in Korea," *Sat. Eve. Post*, Nov. 10, 1951; W. L. White, *Back Down the Ridge* (1953); S. L. A. Marshall, *River and Gauntlet* (1953); M. B. Voorhees, *Korean Tales* (1952). ❮ Middle East: Speiser, *United States and Near East*; Thomas and Frye, *United States and Turkey and Iran*; W. N. Brown, *United States and India and Pakistan* (1953); Manuel, *American-Palestine Relations*; B. C. Crum, *Behind the Silken Curtain* (1947); Richard Crossman, *Palestine Mission* (1947); J. G. McDonald, *My Mission in Israel, 1948–1951* (1951); R. F. Mikesell and H. B. Chenery, *Arabian Oil* (1949); H. L. Hoskins, *Middle East Oil* (1950); Kermit Roosevelt, *Arabs, Oil and History* (1949); A. C. Millspaugh, *Americans in Persia* (1946). ❮ Western Hemisphere: Keenleyside and Brown, *Canada and United States*; F. H. Soward, "Changing Relations of Canada and United States," *Pacific Hist. Rev.*, XXII (1953), 155; Whitaker, *Inter-American Affairs*; A. B. Fox, *Freedom and Welfare in Caribbean* (1949); Whitaker, *United States and South America*; Perkins, *United States and Caribbean*; Cline, *United*

States and Mexico; Dept. of State, *Blue Book on Argentina* (1946); H. Foreign Affairs Committee, "Inter-American Study Mission, Report," 82 Cong., 2 Sess., *H. Report*, No. 1454. ❮ Foreign Policy Discussion: J. F. Dulles, *War or Peace* (1950); Herman Finer, *America's Destiny* (1947); P. G. Hoffman, *Peace Can Be Won* (1951); Kennan, *American Diplomacy*; Walter Lippmann, *Cold War* (1947); Hans J. Morgenthau, *In Defense of National Interest* (1951); R. A. Taft, *Foreign Policy for Americans* (1951); Welles, *Where Are We Heading?*

Sources — S. S. Jones, *Documents on American Foreign Relations*, 1948; Sen. Foreign Relations Committee, *Decade of American Foreign Policy*; Dept. State, *Bull.*, 1947– ; "Review of Bipartisan Foreign Policy Consultations since World War II," 82 Cong., 1 Sess., *Sen. Doc.*, No. 87; Dept. of Commerce, *Foreign Aid*; Dept. of State, *Participation in International Conferences, July 1, 1947 . . . June 30, 1950* (3 vols., 1949–51). ❮ National Security: H. Committee on Post-War Military Policy, "Proposal to Establish Department of Armed Forces," 78 Cong., 2 Sess., *Hearings* (1944), and "Universal Military Training," 79 Cong., 1 Sess., *Hearings* (2 pts., 1945); Sen. Military Affairs Committee, "Department of Armed Forces, Military Security," 79 Cong., 1 Sess., *Hearings* (1945), and "Demobilization," 79 Cong., 1 Sess., *Hearings* (3 pts., 1945–46); Sen. Armed Services Committee, "National Defense Establishment," 80 Cong., 1 Sess., *Hearings* (3 pts., 1947), and "Report," 80 Cong., 1 Sess., *Sen. Report*, No. 239, "Universal Military Training," 81 Cong., 2 Sess., *Hearings* (1948). ❮ Aid to Greece and Turkey: *Dept. State, Aid to Greece and Turkey State Papers* (1947); Sen. Foreign Relations Committee, "Assistance to Greece and Turkey," 80 Cong., 1 Sess., *Hearings* (1947); H. Foreign Affairs Committee, "Assistance to Greece and Turkey," 80 Cong., 1 Sess., *Hearings* (1947). ❮ European Aid: Sen. Banking and Currency Committee, "Anglo-American Financial Agreement," 79 Cong., 2 Sess., *Hearings* (1946); Sen. Foreign Relations and H. Foreign Affairs Committee, "European Recovery Program: Basic Documents," 80 Cong., 1 Sess., *Sen. Doc.*, No. 111; H. Foreign Affairs Committee, "United States Foreign Policy for Post-War Recovery," 80 Cong., 1 and 2 Sess., *Hearings* (2 pts., 1948); Sen. Foreign Relations Committee, "European Recovery Program," 80 Cong., 2 Sess., *Hearings* (3 pts., 1948); H. Select Committee on Foreign Aid, "Final Report," 80 Cong., 2 Sess., *H. Report*, No. 1845; Sen. Foreign Relations Committee, "Extension of European Recovery," 81 Cong., 1 Sess., *Hearings* (1949); H. Foreign Affairs Committee, "Extension of European Recovery Program," 81 Cong., 1 Sess., *Hearings* (2 pts., 1949); Sen. Foreign Relations Committee, "North Atlantic Treaty," 81 Cong., 1 Sess., *Hearings* (3 pts., 1949), and "Military Assistance Program," 81 Cong., 1 Sess., *Joint Hearings* (1949); H. Foreign Affairs Committee, "Mutual Defense Assistance Act of 1949," 81 Cong., 1 Sess., *Hearings* (1949); Sen. Foreign Relations Committee, "Extension of European Recovery — 1950," 81 Cong., 2 Sess., *Hearings* (1950); and "Mutual Security Act of 1951," 82 Cong., 1 Sess., *Hearings* (1951). ❮ Far East: Dept. State, *United States Relations with China*; H. Foreign Affairs Committee, "Korean Aid," 81 Cong., 1 Sess., *Hearings* (1949); Sen. Armed Services and Foreign Relations Committees, "Military Situation in Far East," 82 Cong., 1 Sess., *Hearings* (5 pts., 1951); Sen. Foreign Relations Committee, "Japanese Peace Treaty," 82 Cong., 2 Sess., *Hearings* (1952). ❮ Trade Policy: Sen. Finance Committee, "1945 Extension of Reciprocal Trade Agreements," 79 Cong., 1 Sess., *Hearings* (1945), and "International Trade Organization," 80 Cong., 1 Sess., *Hearings* (2 pts., 1947); H. Ways and Means Committee, "Reciprocal Trade Agreements Program," 80 Cong., 1 Sess., *Hearings* (2 pts., 1947); Sen. Finance Committee, "Extension of Reciprocal Trade Agreements Act," 81 Cong., 1 Sess., *Hearings* (2 pts., 1949); H. Ways and Means Committee, "1949 Extension of Reciprocal Trade Agreements Act," 81 Cong., 1 Sess., *Hearings* (1949); H. Foreign Affairs Committee, "Membership and Participation in International Trade Organization," 81 Cong., 2 Sess., *Hearings* (1950). ❮ United Nations: H. Foreign Affairs Committee, "Structure of United Nations," 80 Cong., 2 Sess., *Hearings* (1948); Sen. Foreign Relations Committee, "Revision of United Nations Charter," 81 Cong., 2 Sess., *Hearings* (1950).

Bibliography — *Foreign Affairs*; Council on Foreign Relations, *United States in World Affairs*; R. K. Turner, "Bibliography on World Organization," *Int. Organization*, Aug., 1950; *United Nations Documents Index* (monthly); Moor and Chamberlin, *How to Use*

United Nations Documents; "Unit Histories of Korean War," *Publisher's Weekly,* Mar. 7, 1953; Library of Congress, *United States and Postwar Europe* (1948), and *Cartels and International Patent Agreements* (1943).

274. POSTWAR ECONOMIC PROBLEMS, 1945–1953

Summary — Demobilization and reconversion: Baruch report (1944); fight in WPB (1944); contract termination; surplus property disposal; lifting of manpower and priority controls (1944–45); inflation (general price controls ended, Nov. 9, 1946). — Full employment policy: Employment Act of 1946; Council of Economic Advisers; postwar economic problems. — Atomic energy and McMahon Act (Aug. 1, 1946). — Labor: Taft-Hartley Act (June 23, 1947); expulsion of Communists from CIO; federal government and strikes in essential industries; steel case. — Fair Deal and debate over "welfare state" (1949–50). — Agricultural policy; Brannan Plan. — Health and welfare: social security amendments; housing and rent control; compulsory health insurance. — Natural resources policy; offshore oil. — Remobilization: Defense Production Act, Sept. 8, 1950; "broad mobilization base" policy. — Republican changes in resources, power, and regulatory policy.

General — W. S. Woytinsky, *et al., Employment and Wages in United States* (1953); Klein, "National Income and Product"; *Economic Reports of the President* (1947–   ); Council of Economic Advisers, *Reports and Reviews* (1947–   ); J. F. Dewhurst, *et al., America's Needs and Resource* (1947); Chandler, *Inflation 1940–1948*; Galbraith, *American Capitalism*; Joint Committee on Economic Report, "Low-Income Families and Economic Stability," 81 Cong., 2 Sess., *Sen. Reports,* Nos. 146, 231; H. S. Ellis, ed., *Survey of Contemporary Economics* (1948); Federal Reserve System, *Postwar Economic Studies* (8 vols., 1945–47).

Special — Demobilization and Reconversion: Stein, *Public Administration,* 215, 313; J. D. Small, *From War to Peace* (1946); Office of Contract Settlement, *History of War Contract Terminations* (1947); J. C. Sitterson, *Development of Reconversion Policies* (1946); National Resources Planning Board, *Report* (1943); B. M. Baruch and J. M. Hancock, *Report on War and Post-War Adjustment* (1944); Sen. Military Affairs Committee, "War Mobilization and Post-War Adjustment," 78 Cong., 2 Sess., *Sen. Report,* No. 1036. ❡ Full Employment Policy: *Economic Reports of the President;* S. K. Bailey, *Congress Makes a Law Employment Act of 1946* (1950); S. E. Harris, ed., "How to Manage National Debt," *Rev. of Econ. Stat.,* XXXI (1949), 15; James Tobin, "Monetary Policy and Management of Public Debt," *ibid.,* XXXV (1953), 118; H. C. Murphy, *National Debt* (1950); Daniel Hamberg, "Recession of 1948–49," *Econ. Jour.,* LXII (1952), 1; E. G. Nourse, *Economics in Public Service* (1953); R. A. Musgrave, *et al., Public Finance and Full Employment* (1945). ❡ Economic Concentration: Galbraith, *American Capitalism;* Clair Wilcox, "Concentration of Power in American Economy," *Harvard Bus. Rev.,* Nov., 1950; Adelman, "Measurement of Concentration," 269; Smaller War Plants Corporation, "Economic Concentration," 79 Cong., 2 Sess., *Sen. Doc.,* No. 206; Federal Trade Commission, *Merger Movement* (1948); John Lintner and J. K. Butters, "Effect of Mergers," *Rev. of Ec. Stat.,* XXXII (1950), 30; Solomon Fabricant, "Is Monopoly Increasing?" *Jour. of Econ. Hist.,* XIII (1953), 89; G. W. Stocking and M. W. Watkins, *Monopoly and Free Enterprise* (1951); E. S. Mason, "Current Status of Monopoly," *Harvard Law Rev.,* LXII (1949), 1265; M. A. Adelman, "Effective Competition and Anti-Trust Laws," *ibid.,* LXI (1948), 1289; C. D. Edwards, *Maintaining Competition* (1949), and "Public Policy and Business Size," *Jour. Bus. University Chi.,* Oct., 1951; M. A. Adelman, "Business Size and Public Policy," *ibid.;* D. E. Lilienthal, *Big Business* (1953); P. F. Drucker, *Concept of Corporation* (1946); W. W. Leontief, *et al., Studies in Structure of American Economy* (1953). ❡ Debate on Economic Policy: [H. S. Truman], *Truman Program* (1949); S. E. Harris, ed., *Saving American Capitalism* (1948); S. H. Slichter, *American Economy* (1948); E. G. Nourse, *The 1950's Come First* (1951); D. M. Wright, *Capitalism* (1951); Chester Bowles, *Tomorrow Without Fear* (1946); H. A. Wallace, *Sixty Million Jobs* (1945); R. R. Nathan, *Mobilizing for Abundance* (1944); Irwin Ross, *Strategy for Liberals* (1949); Jules Abels, *Welfare State* (1951);

Sheldon Glueck, ed., *Welfare State* (1952). ❢ Labor: H. A. Millis and E. C. Brown, *From the Wagner Act to Taft-Hartley* (1950); C. O. Gregory, *Labor and Law* (1949 ed.), ch. xiv; J. T. Dunlop, *Collective Bargaining* (1949); O. W. Phelps, "Public Policy in Labor Disputes," *Jour. Pol. Econ.*, LV (1947), 189; Daniel Bell, "Taft-Hartley, Five Years Old," *Fortune*, July, 1952; E. C. Brown, *National Labor Policy* (1950); Sen. Labor Committee, *Factors in Successful Collective Bargaining* (1951), and *Labor-Management Relations in the Southern Textile Industry* (1952); S. H. Slichter, "Taft-Hartley Act," *Quar. Jour. Econ.*, LXIII (1949), 1, and "Revision of Taft-Hartley Act," *ibid.*, LXVII (1953), 149; B. H. Levy, "Collective Bargaining," *Harvard Bus. Rev.*, XXVI (1948), 468; Joel Seidman, "Democracy in Labor Unions," *Jour. Pol. Econ.*, LXI (1953), 221; C. C. Killingsworth, *State Labor Relations Acts* (1948); Sen. Labor Committee, "Use of State Court Injunctions in Labor Disputes," 81 Cong., 2 Sess., *Sen. Doc.*, No. 7; C. W. Mills, *New Men of Power* (1948); Eli Ginzberg, *Labor Leader* (1948); Jack Barbash, *Unions and Telephones* (1952); Howe and Widick, *UAW*; Fay Calkins, *CIO and Democratic Party* (1952); M. M. Johnson, *Crime on Labor Front* (1950); C. E. Lindblom, *Unions and Capitalism* (1949). ❢ Agricultural Policy: Benedict, *Farm Policies*, chs. xviii–xx; W. E. Hendrix, "Brannan Plan in Cotton South," *Jour. Farm Econ.*, XXXI (1949), 487; H. G. Halcrow and R. E. Huffman, "Great Plains Agriculture and Brannan's Farm Program," *ibid.*, XXXI (1949), 497; C. C. Taylor, *et al.*, *Rural Life in the United States* (1949); President's Commission on Migratory Labor, *Migratory Labor in American Agriculture* (1951); I. W. Duggan and R. U. Battles, *Financing Farm Business* (1950). ❢ Regional Problems: R. L. Mighell and J. D. Black, *Interregional Competition in Agriculture* (1951); S. E. Harris, *Economics of New England* (1952); Council of Economic Advisers, *New England Economy* (1951); J. D. Black, *Rural Economy of New England* (1950); A. G. Mezerik, *Revolt of South and West* (1946); M. E. Garnsey, *America's New Frontier* (1950); Wendell Berge, *Economic Freedom for West* (1946); C. B. Hoover and B. U. Ratchford, *Economic Resources and Policies of South* (1951), and *Impact of Federal Policies on Economy of South* (1949); Albert Lepawsky, *State Planning and Economic Development in South* (1949); G. E. McLaughlin and Stefan Robock, *Why Industry Moves South* (1949); Lively, *South in Action*; Fritz Machlup, *Basing-Point System* (1949); G. H. Sage, *Basing-Point Pricing Systems* (1951); Earl Latham, *Group Basis of Politics* (1952). ❢ Atomic Energy: Newman and Miller, *Control of Atomic Energy*; S. H. Schurr and Jacob Marschak, *Economic Aspects of Atomic Power* (1950); R. A. Dahl and R. S. Brown, *Domestic Control of Atomic Energy* (1951); J. R. Newman, "Atomic Energy Industry," *Yale Law Jour.*, LX (1951), 1263; Walter Isard, "Some Economic Implications of Atomic Energy," *Quar. Jour. Econ.*, LXII (1948), 202; *Bulletin of the Atomic Scientists* (1945–   ). ❢ Health and Welfare: President's Commission on Health Needs of Nation, *Building America's Health* (5 vols., 1952–53); R. E. Rothenberg and Karl Pickard, *Group Medicine in Action* (1949); E. H. Huntington, *Cost of Medical Care* (1951); O. R. Ewing, *Nation's Health* (1948); S. E. Harris, *National Health Insurance* (1953); G. W. Bachman and Lewis Meriam, *Issue of Compulsory Health Insurance* (1948); T. J. Horder, ed., *Health and Social Welfare, 1945–1946* (1946). ❢ Natural Resources: President's Materials Policy Commission, *Resources for Freedom* (5 vols., 1952); Interior Dept., *Years of Progress, 1945–52* (1953); Lillard, *Great Forest*; Maass, *Muddy Waters*; President's Water Resources Policy Commission, *Report* (3 vols., 1950); J. W. Fesler, ed., "Government and Water Resources," *Am. Pol. Sci. Rev.*, XLIV (1950), 575; R. W. DeRoos, *Thirsty Land*; *Central Valley Project* (1948); L. L. Durisch and H. L. Macon, *Upon Its Own Resources; Conservation and State Administration* (1951). ❢ Remobilization: B. H. Williams, "Search for National Security," 110; Eliot Janeway, "Drive and Direction of Mobilization," *Harvard Bus. Rev.*, XXIX (1951), 99, and "Balancing America's Metal Requirements," *ibid.*, XXIX (1951), 92; S. E. Harris, *Economics of Mobilization and Inflation* (1951); L. V. Chandler and D. H. Wallace, eds., *Economic Mobilization and Stabilization* (1951); Aaron Director, ed., *Defense, Controls, and Inflation* (1952).

Sources — Economic Demobilization: Sen. Committee on Post-War Economic Policy and Planning, 78 Cong., 1 and 2 Sess., 79 Cong., 1 Sess., *Hearings* (15 pts., 1943–45); H. Committee on Post-War Economic Policy and Planning, 78 Cong., 2 Sess., 79 Cong., 1 and 2 Sess., *Hearings* (9 pts., 1944–47); Sen. Military Affairs Committee, "Problems of

Contract Termination," 78 Cong., 1 and 2 Sess., *Hearings* (16 pts., 1943–44), and "Mobilization and Demobilization Problems," 78 Cong., 2 Sess., *Hearings* (16 pts., 1944); H. Committee to Investigate Disposition of Surplus Property, 79 Cong., 2 Sess., *Hearings* (15 pts., 1946–7). ❡ Postwar Stabilization: H. Banking Committee, "1945 Stabilization Act," 79 Cong., 1 Sess., *Hearings* (1945); Sen. Banking Committee, "1946 Extension of Emergency Price Control and Stabilization Acts," 79 Cong., 2 Sess., *Hearings* (2 vols., 1946); Jt. Committee on Economic Report, "Current Price Developments," 80 Cong., 1 Sess., *Hearings* (1947); Sen. Banking Committee, "National Stabilization," 80 Cong., 2 Sess., *Hearings* (2 pts., 1948), and "Inflation Control," 80 Cong., 2 Sess., *Hearings* (1948). ❡ Full Employment: Sen. Banking Committee, "Full Employment Act of 1945," 79 Cong., 1 Sess., *Hearings* (1945); Joint Committee on Economic Report, 80 Cong., 2 Sess. — 82 Cong., 2 Sess., *Hearings* (1948–52); "Compendium of Materials on Monetary, Credit and Fiscal Policies," 81 Cong., 2 Sess., *Sen. Doc.*, No. 132 (1950). ❡ Monopoly and Small Business: Sen. Committee to Study Problems of American Small Business, 80 Cong., 1 and 2 Sess., *Hearings* (44 pts., 1947–48); H. Judiciary Committee, "Study of Monopoly Power," 81 Cong., 1 and 2 Sess., 82 Cong., 1 Sess., *Hearings* (1949–51). ❡ Labor: H. Labor Committee, "Amendments to National Labor Relations Act," 80 Cong., 1 Sess., *Hearings* (6 vols., 1947); Sen. Labor Committee, "Labor Relations Program," 80 Cong., 1 Sess., *Hearings* (5 pts., 1947); Joint Committee on Labor-Management Relations, 80 Cong., 2 Sess., *Hearings* (2 pts., 1948); Sen. Labor Committee, "Labor Relations," 81 Cong., 1 Sess., *Hearings* (6 pts., 1949); H. Labor Committee, "National Labor Relations Act of 1949," 81 Cong., 1 Sess., *Hearings* (1949); Sen. Banking Committee, "Economic Power of Labor Organizations," 81 Cong., 1 Sess., *Hearings* (2 pts., 1949); United States v. United Mine Workers, 330 U.S. 258; Youngstown Sheet and Tube Co. v. Sawyer, 343 U.S. 579. ❡ Farm Policy: Sen. Ag. Committee, "Agriculture Adjustment Act of 1949," 81 Cong., 1 Sess., *Hearings* (1949), and "Farm Price-Support Program," 81 Cong., 1 Sess., *Hearings* (1949). ❡ Regional Problems: Sen. Committee to Investigate Centralization of Heavy Industry," 78 Cong., 2 Sess., *Hearings* (5 pts., 1945); H. Ag. Committee, "Agricultural and Economic Problems of Cotton Belt," 80 Cong., 1 Sess., *Hearings* (2 vols., 1947). ❡ Housing and Rent Control: Sen. Banking Committee, "General Housing Act of 1945," 79 Cong., 1 Sess., *Hearings* (2 pts., 1946); Joint Committee on Housing, "Study and Investigation," 80 Cong., 1 Sess., *Hearings* (4 pts., 1948); Sen. Banking Committee, "General Housing Legislation," 81 Cong., 1 Sess., *Hearings* (1949); H. Banking Committee, "Housing Act of 1949," 81 Cong., 1 Sess., *Hearings* (1949); Sen. Banking Committee, "Extension of Rent Control," 80 Cong., 2 Sess., 81 Cong., 2 Sess., *Hearings* (3 pts., 1948). ❡ Atomic Energy: Sen. Atomic Energy Committee, 79 Cong., 1 and 2 Sess., *Hearings* (5 pts., 1945–46), and "Atomic Energy Act of 1946," 79 Cong., 2 Sess., *Hearings* (5 pts., 1946), and "Confirmation of Commission and Manager," 80 Cong., 1 Sess., *Hearings* (1947). ❡ Health: Sen. Labor Committee, "National Health Program," 79 Cong., 2 Sess. — 81 Cong., 1 Sess., *Hearings* (12 pts., 1946–49); H. Commerce Committee, "National Health Plan," 81 Cong., 1 Sess., *Hearings* (1949). ❡ Social Security: H. Ways and Means Committee, "Amendments to Social Security Act," 79 Cong., 2 Sess., *Hearings* (10 pts., 1946), and "Social Security Act Amendments of 1949," 81 Cong., 1 Sess., *Hearings* (2 pts., 1949); Sen. Finance Committee, "Social Security Revision," 81 Cong., 2 Sess., *Hearings* (3 pts., 1940). ❡ Minimum Wage: H. Labor Committee, "Minimum Wage Standards," 80 Cong., 1 Sess., *Hearings* (4 vols., 1948); Sen. Labor Committee, "Fair Labor Standards Act Amendments," 80 Cong., 2 Sess. — 81 Cong., 1 Sess., *Hearings* (3 pts., 1948–49); H. Labor Committee, "Amendments to Fair Labor Standards Act of 1948," 81 Cong., 1 Sess., *Hearings* (2 vols., 1949). ❡ Natural Resources: Sen. Interior Affairs Committee, "National Resources Policy," 81 Cong., 1 Sess., *Hearings* (1949); Sen. Judiciary Committee, "Title to Submerged Lands," 80 Cong., 1 Sess., *Hearings* (1948); Joint Committees on Judiciary, "Title to Submerged Lands," 80 Cong., 2 Sess., *Joint Hearings* (1948); Sen. Interior Affairs Committee, "Submerged Lands," 81 Cong., 1, 2 Sess., *Hearings* (1950); United States v. Louisiana, 339 U.S. 699; United States v. Texas, 339 U.S. 707; Sen. Irrigation Committee, "To Establish a Missouri Valley Authority," 79 Cong., 1 Sess., *Hearings* (1945); Sen. Public Works Committee, "Columbia Valley Administration," 81 Cong., 1 Sess., *Hearings* (1949); H. Public Works Committee, "Columbia Valley Administration," 81 Cong., 1 Sess., *Hearings* (1949). ❡ Remobilization: Director of Defense Mobilization, *Quarterly Reports to the President* (1951–); Sen. Banking Committee, "Defense Production Act of 1950," 81 Cong., 2 Sess., *Hearings* (1950), and "Defense Production Act Amendments," 82 Cong., 1 Sess., *Hearings* (1951); H. Banking Committee, "Defense Production Act Amendments," 82 Cong., 1 Sess., *Hearings* (1951); Joint Committee on Defense Production, *Progress Reports* (1951–); H. Judiciary Committee, *Mobilization Program*, 82 Cong., 1 Sess., *H. Report*, No. 1217.

Bibliography — S. P. Kessler, comp., *Industry-wide Collective Bargaining* (1948); United Nations, *International Bibliography on Atomic Energy* (1949–); L. C. Longarzo, *Selective Bibliography of Atomic Energy* (1951).

275. POLITICS, 1945–1953

Summary — Truman moves right (1945–46); elimination of New Dealers; effect of congressional elections of 1946. — Split in liberal and labor forces, formation of anti-Communist Americans for Democratic Action (1947) and pro-Communist group leading to Progressive Party (1948). — Truman moves left (1947–48); fight with 80 Congress. — Election of 1948: Democratic convention, civil rights fight, Dixiecrat bolt, Truman's whistlestop campaign; Republican convention and campaign; Truman reëlected. — Promulgation of Fair Deal (Jan. 5, 1949). — Congressional elections of 1950. — Corruption in government (1951–52). — 1952 elections. — Adlai Stevenson. — Eisenhower as President.

General — Lubell, *Future of American Politics*; Daniels, *Man of Independence*; Hillman, *Mr. President*; Forrestal, *Diaries*; Gunther, *Inside USA*; Salter, ed., *Public Men*; Key, *Southern Politics*; Herbert Block, *Herblock Book* (1952).

Special — Harry S. Truman: Truman, *Truman Program*; Frank McNaughton and Walter Hehmeyer, *Harry Truman: President* (1948); F. M. Riddick, "Eighty-First Congress," *Western Pol. Quar.*, IV (1951), 48, and "Eighty-Second Congress," *ibid.*, V (1952), 94. ❧ Republicans: Vandenberg, *Private Papers*; R. A. Taft, "Republican Party," *Fortune*, May, 1949; R. N. Stromberg, *Republicanism Reappraised* (1952). ❧ Election of 1948: Mosteller, *Pre-election Polls*; B. A. Martin and J. E. Holmes, "1948 Elections in Eleven Western States," *Western Pol. Quar.*, II (1949), 89; Morton Leeds, "AFL in 1948 Elections," *Social Research*, XVII (1950), 207; Calkins, *CIO and Democratic Party*; Cecilia Van Auken, "Negro Press in 1948 Presidential Election," *Journalism Quar.*, Dec., 1949; J. A. Wechsler, "My Ten Months With Wallace," *Progressive*, Nov., 1948; Americans for Democratic Action, *Henry Wallace, the First Three Months* (1948), and *Henry A. Wallace, the Last Seven Months of His Presidential Campaign* (1948); H. A. Wallace, "Where I Was Wrong," *This Week*, Sept. 7, 1952; W. G. Carleton, "Fate of Dixiecrat Movement," *Yale Rev.*, XXXVII (1949), 449; S. M. Lemmon, "Ideology of 'Dixiecrat' Movement," *Social Forces*, Dec., 1951. ❧ Election of 1952: Kevin McCann, *Man From Abilene* (1952); A. E. Stevenson, *Major Campaign Speeches* (1953); J. B. Martin, *Adlai Stevenson* (1952); N. F. Busch, *Adlai E. Stevenson* (1952); James Fleming, ed., *Adlai Stevenson Speaks* (recording); V. P. DeSantis, "Presidential Election of 1952," *Rev. of Pol.*, XV (1953), 131; Samuel Lubell, "Who Elected Eisenhower?" *Sat. Eve. Post.*, Jan. 10, 1953; Oscar Handlin, "Payroll Prosperity," *Atlantic Monthly*, Feb., 1953; A. M. Schlesinger, Jr., "Which Road for Democrats?" *Reporter*, Jan. 20, 1953; Angus Campbell, *et al.*, "Political Issues and the Vote: November, 1952," *Am. Pol. Sci. Rev.*, XLVII (1953), 359. ❧ Ideological Debate: Editors of Fortune and R. W. Davenport, *U.S.A. Permanent Revolution* (1951); A. M. Schlesinger, Jr., *Vital Center* (1949); Raymond Moley, *How to Keep Our Liberty* (1952). ❧ Government Reorganization: J. McG. Burns, *Congress on Trial* (1949); B. M. Gross, *Legislative Struggle* (1953); E. S. Griffith, *Congress* (1951); P. H. Douglas, *Economy in National Government* (1952); Herman Finer, "Hoover Commission Reports," *Pol. Sci. Quar.*, LXIV (1949), 404, 579; Bradley Nash and Cornelius Lynde, *Hook in Leviathan* (1950); F. H. Gervasi, *Big Government* (1949); L. W. Koenig, ed., "Hoover Commission," *Am. Pol. Sci. Rev.*, XLIII (1949), 933; W. S. Carpenter, *Unfinished Business of Civil Service Reform* (1952); Commission on Organization of Executive Branch of Government, *Reports, Task Reports, Digests, Indexes*

(1949). ❡ Corruption: P. H. Douglas, *Ethics in Government* (1952); Blair Bolles, *How to Get Rich in Washington* (1952); H. H. Wilson, *Congress: Corruption and Compromise* (1951); Senate Labor Committee, "Ethical Standards in Government," 82 Cong., 1 Sess., *Report* (1951); Schriftgiesser, *Lobbyists*.

Sources — Joint Committee on Organization of Congress, 79 Cong., 1 Sess., *Hearings* (4 pts., 1945), and *Summary of Hearings* (1945); H. Committee to Investigate Commodity Transactions, 80 Cong., 2 Sess., *Hearings* (1949); Sen. Commerce Committee, "Air-Line Industry Investigation," 81 Cong., 1, 2 Sess., *Hearings* (5 pts., 1949–50); H. Committee on Lobbying Activities, *Lobbying* (10 pts., 81 Cong., 2 Sess., 1950); Sen. Banking Committee, "Study of Reconstruction Finance Corporation," 81 Cong., 2 Sess., 82 Cong., 1 Sess., *Hearings* (1950–51); Sen. Committee on Expenditures in Executive Departments, "Influence in Government Procurement," 82 Cong., 1 Sess., *Hearings* (1951); H. Committee on Expenditures in Executive Departments, "Federal Supply Management," 82 Cong., 1 Sess., *Hearings* (1952); H. Ways and Means Committee, "Internal Revenue Investigation," 82 Cong., 1, 2 Sess., *Hearings* (4 pts., 1952); H. Judiciary Committee, "Investigation of Department of Justice," 82 Cong., 2 Sess., 83 Cong., 1 Sess., *Hearings* (1952).

276. INDIVIDUAL RIGHTS IN COLD WAR, 1947–1953

Summary — Civil Liberties and National Security: revelations of Communist espionage and subversion; federal loyalty program (Mar. 21, 1947); conviction of Communist leaders (1949), of Alger Hiss (1950); atomic espionage cases. — Exploitation of fear: anti-Communist demagoguery: Un-American Activities Committee; Senator Joseph R. McCarthy (1950); other congressional investigations; curtailment of academic freedom; employment blacklisting; passport and visa denials. — Civil rights: Report of the President's Committee (1947); Truman's civil rights message (Feb. 2, 1948); Supreme Court decisions against restrictive covenants (Shelley *v.* Kraemer, 1948), against educational discrimination (Sweatt *v.* Painter, 1950); improved opportunities for Negroes. — Immigration policy: McCarran Act (1952). — Religious freedom; church and state.

General — American Civil Liberties Union, *Annual Reports*; Zechariah Chafee, Jr., *Government and Mass Communications* (1947); Arnold Forster, *Measure of Freedom* (1950).

Special — Civil Liberties and Courts: J. L. O'Brian, "New Encroachments on Individual Freedom," *Harvard Law Rev.*, LXVI (1952), 1, and "Changing Attitudes Toward Freedom," *Washington and Lee Law Rev.*, IX (1952), 157; O. K. Fraenkel, *Supreme Court and Civil Liberties* (r. ed., 1952); Pritchett, "Libertarian Motivations on Vinson Court"; Learned Hand, *Spirit of Liberty* (1952); W. O. Douglas, *Being an American* (1948). ❡ Civil Liberties and National Security: Francis Biddle, *Fear of Freedom* (1951); R. K. Carr, *House Committee on Un-American Activities* (1952); Bontecou, *Federal Loyalty-Security*; Alan Barth, *Loyalty of Free Men* (1951); Clair Wilcox, ed., *Civil Liberties under Attack* (1951); H. D. Lasswell, *National Security and Individual Freedom* (1950); Walter Gellhorn, *Security, Loyalty and Science* (1950), and *States and Subversion* (1952); Weyl, *Battle Against Disloyalty*. ❡ Communist Activity: Pilat, *Atom Spies*; Joint Committee on Atomic Energy, *Soviet Atomic Espionage*; H. A. Philbrick, *I Led Three Lives* (1952); Angela Calomiris, *Red Masquerade* (1950); M. L. Ernst and David Loth, *Report on American Communist* (1952); E. E. Palmer, ed., *Communist Problem* (1951); Cooke, *Generation on Trial*; Victor Lasky and Ralph de Toledano, *Seeds of Treason* (1950). ❡ McCarthyism: Jack Anderson and R. W. May, *McCarthy* (1952); J. R. McCarthy, *McCarthyism* (1952); Wisconsin Citizens' Committee, *McCarthy Record* (1952); Sen. Rules Committee, *Investigation of Senators Joseph R. McCarthy and William Benton* (82 Cong., 2 Sess., 1952); G. R. Stewart, *Year of Oath* (1950); R. B. Allen, *et al.*, "Communism and Academic Freedom," *American Scholar*, XVIII (1949), 323; Owen Lattimore, *Ordeal by Slander* (1950). ❡ Minority Tensions: Arnold and Caroline Rose, *America Divided* (1948); T. W. Adorno, *et al.*, *Authoritarian Personality* (1950); Bettelheim and Janowitz, *Dynamics of Prejudice*; Leo Lowenthal and Norbert Guterman, *Prophets of Deceit* (1949); A. M. Rose, *Race Prejudice and Discrimination* (1951). ❰ Civil Rights: President's Committee on Civil Rights, *To Secure These Rights* (1947); Carr, *Federal Protection of Civil Rights*; Konvitz, *Constitution and Civil Rights*; Alison Reppy, *Civil Rights* (1951); Morroe Berger, *Equality by Statute* (1952); Sen. Labor Committee, "Federal Equality of Opportunity in Employment Act," 82 Cong., 2 Sess., *Sen. Report*, No. 2080. ❰ Negroes: A. M. Rose, *Negro in Postwar America* (1950); Bur. Labor Stat., *Negroes in United States* (1952); J. A. Davis, "Negro Employment," *Fortune*, July, 1952; Bucklin Moon, *High Cost of Prejudice* (1947); H. L. Moon, *Balance of Power*; R. C. Weaver, *Negro Labor* (1946); J. W. Dees, Jr., and J. S. Hadley, *Jim Crow* (1951); F. S. Loescher, *Protestant Church and Negro* (1948); D. W. Culver, *Negro Segregation in Methodist Church* (1953); Morton Deutsch and M. E. Collins, *Interracial Housing* (1951); Lillian Smith, *Killers of Dream* (1949); Walter White, *Man Called White*; Ray Sprigle, *In Land of Jim Crow* (1949); Roi Ottley, *No Green Pastures* (1951); Jackie Robinson, *My Own Story* (1948); J. S. Redding, *On Being Negro in America* (1951); C. T. Rowan, *South of Freedom* (1952); Hodding Carter, *Southern Legacy* (1950). ❰ Immigration Policy: President's Commission on Immigration and Naturalization, *Whom We Shall Welcome* (1953); Bernard, *American Immigration Policy*; Davie, *Refugees in America*; F. W. Riggs, *Pressures on Congress: Repeal of Chinese Exclusion* (1950); C. W. Mills, *et al.*, *Puerto Rican Journey* (1950); E. R. Knauff, *Ellen Knauff Story* (1952); "Passport Refusals for Political Reasons: Constitutional Issues," *Yale Law Journal*, LXI (1952), 171. ❰ Church and State: A. W. Johnson and F. H. Yost, *Separation of Church and State in U.S.* (1948); C. H. Moehlman, *Wall of Separation* (1951); V. T. Thayer, *Attack upon American Secular School* (1951); V. C. McCollum, *One Woman's Fight* (1952); Paul Blanshard, *American Freedom and Catholic Power* (1949); J. M. O'Neill, *Catholicism and American Freedom* (1952); R. L. Roy, *Apostles of Discord* (1953).

Sources — Civil Liberties: Bridges *v.* California, 314 U.S. 52; Pennekamp *v.* Florida, 328 U.S. 331; Harris *v.* United States, 331 U.S. 145; Craig *v.* Harney, 331 U.S. 367; Fisher *v.* Adams, 336 U.S. 155; Terminiello *v.* Chicago, 337 U.S. 1; United States *v.* Rabinowitz, 339 U.S. 56; Adler *v.* Board of Education, 342 U.S. 485; Beauharnais *v.* Illinois, 343 U.S. 250. ❰ Loyalty and Subversion: Friedman v. Schwellenbach, 330 U.S. 838; American Communications Association *v.* Douds, 339 U.S. 382; Dennis, *et al.* *v.* United States, 341 U.S. 494; Sen. Judiciary Committee, "Control of Subversive Activities," 80 Cong., 1 Sess. — 81 Cong., 1 Sess., *Hearings* (1948–49), and "Communist Activities among Aliens," 81 Cong., 1 Sess., *Hearings* (3 pts., 1950); Sen. Foreign Relations Committee, "State Department Employee Loyalty Investigation," 81 Cong., 2 Sess., *Hearings: Report* (1950); Sen. Labor Committee, "Communist Domination of Certain Unions," 82 Cong., 1 Sess., *Report* (1951); Sen. Judiciary Committee, "Communist Propaganda Activities," 82 Cong., 1 Sess., *Hearings* (1952), and "Subversive Infiltration of Entertainment Industry," 82 Cong., 1, 2 Sess., *Hearings* (2 pts., 1952), and "Subversive Influence in Educational Process," 82 Cong., 2 Sess., *Hearings* (1952), and "Activities of Citizens Employed by United Nations," 82 Cong., 2 Sess., *Hearings* (1952), and "Communist Domination of Union Officials," 82 Cong., 2 Sess., *Hearings* (1952); H. Un-American Activities Committee, *Index, 1942–47* (1948). ❰ Civil Rights: *Civil Rights Cases*; Smith *v.* Allwright, 321 U.S. 649; Morgan *v.* Virginia, 328 U.S. 373; Sipuel *v.* University of Oklahoma, 332 U.S. 631; Shelley *v.* Kraemer, 334 U.S. 1; Sweatt *v.* Painter, 339 U.S. 629; McLaurin *v.* Oklahoma State Regents, 339 U.S. 637; H. Rules Committee, "To Prohibit Discrimination in Employment," 79 Cong., 1 Sess., *Hearings* (1946); Sen. Labor Committee, "Antidiscrimination in Employment," 80 Cong., 1 Sess., *Hearings* (1947); Sen. Judiciary Committee, "Crime of Lynching," 80 Cong., 2 Sess., *Hearings* (1948); Sen. Rules Committee, "Poll Tax," 80 Cong., 2 Sess., *Hearings* (1948); H. Labor Committee, "Federal Fair Employment Practice Act," 81 Cong., 1 Sess., *Hearings* (1949); Pauli Murray, *States' Laws on Race and Class* (1951). ❰ Immigration: H. Judiciary Committee, "Amending Displaced Persons Act of 1948," 81 Cong., 1 Sess., *Hearings* (1949); Sen. Judiciary Committee, "Displaced Persons," 81 Cong., 1, 2 Sess., *Hearings* (1950); Joint Judiciary Committee, "Revision of Immigration, Naturalization, and Nationality Laws," 82 Cong., 1 Sess., *Joint Hearings* (1951); H. Judiciary Committee, "President's Commission on Immigration and Naturalization,"

82 Cong., 2 Sess., *Hearings* (1952). ❡ Church and State: M. D. Howe, *Cases on Church and State* (1952); Jones *v.* Opelika, 316 U.S. 584, 319 U.S. 103; Marsh *v.* Alabama, 326 U.S. 501; Everson *v.* Board of Education, 330 U.S. 1; Illinois ex rel. McCollum *v.* Board of Education, 333 U.S. 203.

Bibliography — Library of Jewish Information, *Church, State and Education* (1949).

277. SOCIAL AND INTELLECTUAL HISTORY, 1945–1953

Summary — Postwar scene; manners and morals. — Postwar literary tendencies. — Developments in popular arts; mass media; rise of television; movies in travail. — Education; G.I. bill and other government aid; "general education. — Crime; Kefauver Committee (1950–51). — Demographic changes.

General — F. L. Allen, *Big Change* (1952); J. W. Chase, ed., *Years of the Modern* (1949); Gunther, *Inside USA*; Lewis Galantière, *America Today* (1950); Dixon Wecter, *et al.*, *Changing Patterns in American Civilization* (1949); J. S. Davis, "Our Changed Population Outlook," *Am. Econ. Rev.* XLII (1952), 304; J. Walter Thompson Co., *Population and Its Distribution* (1951); *Public Opinion Quarterly*, 1946– .

Special — Travelers' Accounts: H. J. Duteil, *Great American Parade* (1953); Graham Hutton, *Midwest at Noon* (1946); Henry Miller, *Air-Conditioned Nightmare* (1945); F. M. Stern, *Capitalism in America* (1951). ❡ Postwar Scene: Ernie Pyle, *Home Country* (1947); Bill Mauldin, *Back Home* (1947); R. G. Martin, *Best is None too Good* (1948). ❡ Human Relations: National Conference on Family Life, *American Family* (1949); E. A. Strecker, *Their Mothers' Sons* (1951); Philip Wylie, *Generation of Vipers* (1942); A. C. Kinsey, *et al.*, *Sexual Behavior in Human Male* (1948), and *Sexual Behavior in Human Female* (1953); Ferdinand Lundberg and M. F. Farnham, *Modern Woman* (1947); S. M. Gruenberg and H. S. Krech, *Many Lives of Modern Woman* (1952). ❡ Social Relations: David Riesman, *Lonely Crowd*, and *Faces in Crowd* (1952); W. L. Warner, *et al.*, *Social Class in America* (1949), and *Democracy in Jonesville* (1949); C. W. Mills, *White Collar* (1951); Richard Centers, *Psychology of Social Classes* (1949); Gideon Sjoberg, "Are Social Classes in America Becoming More Rigid?" *Am. Sociol. Rev.*, XVI (1951), 775; Walter Goldschmidt, "Social Class in America," *Am. Anthropologist*, LII (1950), 483; M. E. Deeg and D. G. Paterson, "Changes in Social Status of Occupations," *Occupations*, XXV (1947), 205; Maryon Welch, "Ranking of Occupations on the Basis of Social Status," *ibid.*, XXVII (1949), 237; C. R. Walker, *Steeltown* (1950), and *Man on the Assembly Line* (1952); A. deB. Hollingshead, *Elmtown's Youth* (1949); C. B. Stendler, *Children of Brasstown* (1949); Morton Rubin, *Plantation County* (1951); J. H. Fichter, *Southern Parish Church* (1951); A. W. Gouldner, ed., *Studies in Leadership* (1950); W. F. Ogburn, *et al.*, *Social Effects of Aviation* (1946). ❡ Literary Life: Edmund Wilson, *Classics and Commercials* (1950); Lionel Trilling, *Liberal Imagination* (1950); J. W. Aldridge, *After Lost Generation* (1951); J. T. Farrell, *Literature and Morality* (1947); R. P. Blackmur, "Economy of American Writer," *Sewanee Rev.*, LV (1945), 175; Randall Jarrell, *Poetry and Age* (1953); *Partisan Rev.*, *America and the Intellectuals* (1953); J. C. Ransom, ed., *Kenyon Critics* (1951); J. C. Ransom, *New Criticism* (1941); §§ 252, 267. ❡ Mass Communications: Gilbert Seldes, *Great Audience* (1950); W. H. Whyte, Jr., *Is Anybody Listening?* (1952); Chafee, *Government and Mass Communications*; Gershon Legman, *Love & Death, a Study In Censorship* (1949); H. M. McLuhan, *Mechanical Bride: Folklore of Industrial Man* (1951); William Miller, *Book Industry* (1949); Freeman Lewis, *Paper-Bound Books in America* (1952); Bernard Berelson, *The Library's Public* (1949); R. D. Leigh, *Public Library* (1950). ❡ Press: Commission on Freedom of Press, *Free and Responsible Press* (1947); A. J. Liebling, *Wayward Pressman* (1947); M. L. Ernst, *First Freedom* (1946). ❡ Radio: Llewellyn White, *American Radio* (1947); C. A. Siepmann, *Radio, Television, and Society* (1950); Federal Communications Commission, *Public Service Responsibility of Broadcast Licensees* (1946); P. F. Lazarsfeld, *People Look at Radio* (1946); E. J. Kahn, Jr., *The Voice* (1947). ❡ Films: R. A. Inglis, *Freedom of Movies* (1947); Martha Wolfenstein and Nathan Leites, *Movies* (1950); Hortense Powdermaker, *Hollywood Dream Fac-*

tory (1950). ❡ Education: President's Commission on Higher Education, *Higher Education for American Democracy* (6 vols., 1947–48); J. B. Conant, *Education in a Divided World* (1948), and *Education and Liberty* (1953); Commission on Financing Higher Education, *Nature and Needs of Higher Education* (1952); S. E. Harris, *How Shall We Pay for Education?* (1948), and *Market for College Graduates* (1949), and "Economics of Higher Education," *Am. Econ. Rev.*, XLII (1953), 344; W. L. Warner, *et al.*, *Who Shall Be Educated?* (1944); G. J. Stigler, *Employment and Compensation in Education* (1950); Robert Ulich, *Crisis in American Education* (1951); *General Education in a Free Society* (1945); Jacques Barzun, *Teacher in America* (1945); Benjamin Fine, *Our Children Are Cheated* (1947); E. O. Melby, *American Education Under Fire* (1951); David Hulburd, *This Happened In Pasadena* (1951); Ernest Havemann and P. S. West, *They Went to College* (1952); Eli Ginzberg and D. W. Bray, *Uneducated* (1953); F. J. Brown, ed., *National Defense and Higher Education* (1951); Flexner, *Funds and Foundations.* ❡ Science: President's Scientific Research Board, *Science and Public Policy* (5 vols., 1947); H. M. Don, ed., "Social Implications of Modern Science," *Am. Ac. Pol. Soc. Sci., Annals*, CCXLIX (1947); Harold Ward, ed., *New Worlds in Medicine* (1946); L. K. Barnett, *Universe and Dr. Einstein* (1948); G. P. Bush and L. H. Hattery, eds., *Scientific Research* (1950); R. H. Knapp and H. B. Goodrich, *Origins of American Scientists* (1952). ❡ Crime: Estes Kefauver, *Crime in America* (1951); B. B. Turkus and Sid Feder, *Murder, Inc.* (1951); Sheldon and Eleanor Glueck, *Unraveling Juvenile Delinquency* (1950); Albert Deutsch, *Our Rejected Children* (1950); K. J. Scudder, *Prisoners Are People* (1952); J. B. Martin, *Why Did They Kill?* (1953), and *Butcher's Dozen* (1950), and *My Life in Crime* (1952).

Sources — Sen. Labor Committee, "Federal Aid to Education," 80 Cong., 1 Sess., *Hearings* (1947); H. Educ. Committee, "Federal Aid to Education," 80 Cong., 1 Sess., *Hearings* (1947); Sen. Labor Committee, "Education and On-the-Job Training," 80 Cong., 1 Sess., *Hearings* (1947), Sen. Military Affairs Committee, *Hearings on Science Legislation* (5 pts., 79 Cong., 1 Sess., 1945–46); Sen. Committee to Investigate Organized Crime, *Hearings and Report* (81 Cong., 2 Sess., 82 Cong., 1 Sess., 1950–51).

Bibliography — B. L. Smith, *Propaganda*.

REFERENCES ADDED
IN THE SECOND PRINTING

For additional material and the correction of errors the editors are indebted to many historians and state librarians for their helpful advice and suggestions. (The following material is not included in the index.)

46. COLONIAL, STATE, AND LOCAL PUBLIC RECORDS

Georgia

A. B. Saye, *Records of the Commission of 1943–44 to Revise the Constitution of Georgia.* 2 vols. Atlanta, 1946.

Indiana

Executive Journal of Indiana Territory, 1800–1816. W. W. Woollen, *et al.*, eds. Indianapolis, 1900.
Executive Proceedings of the State of Indiana, 1816–1836. Dorothy Riker, ed. Indianapolis, 1947.
L. B. Ewbank and D. L. Riker, *The Laws of Indiana Territory, 1809–1816.* Indianapolis, 1934.
F. S. Philbrick, *Laws of Indiana Territory, 1801–1809.* Springfield, 1930.

Michigan

Laws of the Territory of Michigan, 1805–1835. 4 vols. Lansing, 1871–1884.
Index to the Local and Special Acts of the State of Michigan, 1803 to 1927. Lansing, 1928.

New Hampshire

A. S. Batchellor, ed., *Laws of New Hampshire.* 10 vols. Manchester, 1904–1922.

New York

E. B. O'Callaghan, ed., *Calendar of Historical Manuscripts in the Office of the Secretary of State, Albany, N.Y.* Albany, 1865–66. — Dutch manuscripts 1630–64; English manuscripts 1630–76.
V. H. Paltsits, ed., *Minutes of the Commissioners for Detecting and Defeating Conspiracies in the State of New York. Albany County Sessions, 1778–1781.* 2 vols. Albany, 1909–10.
A. J. F. Van Laer, tr. and ed., *Minutes of the Court of Fort Orange and Beverwyck, 1652–1656, 1657–1660.* 2 vols. Albany, 1920, 1923.
A. J. F. Van Laer, tr. and ed., *Minutes of the Court of Rensselaerswyck, 1648–62.* Albany, 1922.

Oregon

C. H. Carey, ed., *The Oregon Constitution and Proceedings and Debates of the Constitutional Convention of 1857.* Salem, 1926.
E. R. Rockwood, *Oregon State Documents, A Checklist, 1843–1925.* Portland, 1947.

Vermont

State Papers of Vermont. F. H. Dewart *et al.*, eds. 8 vols. Montpelier, 1918– . Published under the auspices of the Secretary of State.

62. STATE AND LOCAL HISTORY

California

R. G. Cleland, *California in our Time (1900–1940)*. N.Y., 1947.
R. G. Cleland, *From Wilderness to Empire; a History of California, 1542–1900*. N.Y., 1944.
T. H. Hittell, *History of California*. 4 vols. San Francisco, 1885–1897.
I. B. Richman, *California under Spain and Mexico, 1535–1847* . . . Boston and N.Y., 1911.

Georgia

I. W. Avery, *The History of the State of Georgia from 1850 to 1881*. N.Y., 1881.
Hugh McCall, *The History of Georgia*. 2 vols. Atlanta, 1909.
A. B. Saye, *A Constitutional History of Georgia*. Atlanta, 1948.
W. B. Stevens, *A History of Georgia*. 2 vols. N.Y., 1847.

Illinois

Theodore Pease, *The Story of Illinois*. Chi. [1951].

Indiana

R. B. Sealock, "A List of References on Indiana History, 1949," *Ind. Hist. Bull.*, V (1949), 26.
J. D. Barnhart and Donald Carmony, *Indiana: From Frontier to Industrial Commonwealth*. Lewis, 1954.

Kansas

Annals of Kansas, 1886–1925. Vol. 1, 1886–1910. Topeka [1954].
F. W. Blackmar, ed., *Kansas, a Cyclopedia of State History* . . . 2 vols. Chi., 1912.
W. E. Connelley, *History of Kansas* . . . 5 vols., Chi., 1928.
Everett Dick, *The Sod House Frontier, 1854–1890*. N.Y., 1937 — New ed. Lincoln, Neb. [1954].

Maryland

J. Van L. McMahon, *Historical View of the Government of Maryland*. Balt., 1831.

Michigan

F. C. Bald, *Michigan in Four Centuries*. N.Y., 1954.
G. N. Fuller, *Michigan: A Centennial History of the State and Its People*. 2 vols. Chi., 1939.

Montana

M. G. Burlingame, *The Montana Frontier*. Helena, 1942.
M. A. Leeson, *History of Montana, 1739–1885*. Chi., 1885.
R. G. Raymer, *Montana, the Land of the People*. 3 vols. Chi., 1930.
H. F. Sanders, *A History of Montana*. 3 vols. Chi., 1913.

Nebraska

J. C. Olson, *History of Nebraska*. Lincoln, 1955.

New Hampshire

Philip Guyol, *Democracy Fights*. Hanover, 1951.
W. G. Saltonstall, *Ports of Piscataqua*. Cambridge, 1941.
F. B. Sanborn, *The History of New Hampshire*. Boston, 1904.

New Jersey

H. F. Wilson, *The Jersey Shore*. 3 vols. N.Y., 1953.

New York

Julius Goebel, Jr. and T. R. Naughton, *Law Enforcement in Colonial New York: a Study in Criminal Procedure (1664–1776)*. N.Y., 1944.

F. B. Hough, *A History of Lewis County in the State of New York* . . . Albany, 1860.

G. R. Howell and Jonathan Tenney, eds., *Bicentennial History of Albany. History of the County of Albany, N.Y. from 1609 to 1886* . . . N.Y., 1886.

W. A. Knittle, *Early Eighteenth Century Palatine Emigration. A British Government Redemptioner Project to Manufacture Naval Stores*. Phila., 1937.

Oklahoma

John Ally, *City Beginning in Oklahoma Territory*. Norman, 1939.

E. E. Dale and J. L. Rader, *Readings in Oklahoma History*. N.Y., 1930.

Roy Gittinger, *Formation of the State of Oklahoma, 1803–1906*. Norman, 1939.

E. C. McReynolds, *Oklahoma, a History of the Sooner State*. Norman, 1954.

D. A. Stewart, *Government and Development of Oklahoma Territory*. Oklahoma City, 1933.

M. H. Wright, *A Guide to the Indian Tribes of Oklahoma*. Norman, 1951.

M. H. Wright, *Story of Oklahoma*. Guthrie, 1949.

Oregon

G. N. Belknap, *McMurtrie's Oregon Imprints, A Supplement*. Portland, 1950.

G. N. Belknap, *McMurtrie's Oregon Imprints: Second Supplement*. Portland, 1954.

C. H. Carey, *History of Oregon*. Chi., 1922.

R. C. Clark, *History of the Willamette Valley, Oregon*. Chi., 1927.

L. A. McArthur, *Oregon Geographic Names*, 3 ed. Portland, 1952.

D. C. McMurtrie, *Oregon Imprints, 1847–1870*. Eugene, 1950.

Tennessee

Gilbert Govan, *Chattanooga Country, 1540–1951*. N.Y., 1952.

J. G. M. Ramsey, *Annals of Tennessee History*. Charleston, 1853.

Vermont

A. M. Hemenway, *Vermont Historical Gazetteer*. 5 vols. Burlington, 1867–91.

H. F. Wilson, *The Hill Country of Northern New England*. Montpelier, 1947.

Virginia

William Couper, *History of the Shenandoah Valley*. 3 vols. N.Y. [1952].

F. B. Kegley, *Kegley's Virginia Frontier: The Beginnings of the Southwest*. Roanoke, 1938.

R. T. Whitaker, *Virginia's Eastern Shore*, 2 vols. Richmond, 1951.

Washington

H. H. Bancroft, *History of Washington, Idaho, and Montana. 1845–1889. (History of the Pacific States*, Vol. XXXI) San Francisco, 1890.

E. S. Meany, *History of the State of Washington*. N.Y., 1929.

Lancaster Pollard, *History of the State of Washington*. 4 vols. N.Y., 1937.

Washington State Historical Society, *Building a State, 1889–1939*. Tacoma, 1940.

O. O. Winther, *The Great Northwest, a History*. N.Y., 1950.

INDEX

So that this index might be as full as possible, every effort was made to economize space. Abbreviations were used more frequently than in the text, and considerations of consistency, though not of clarity, were often sacrificed to bring in the maximum number of entries. Every book and article cited in the *Guide* is listed by author, editor, or title. Within each entry, titles are given first alphabetically, then by analytic subjects in the order of appearance. General items precede the specific ones which follow chronologically.